DATE DUE

DEMCO 38-296

HANDBOOK of HYDRAULIC RESISTANCE

3rd Edition

I.E. Idelchik
Research Institute for Gas Purification
Moscow

Editor
M. O. Steinberg
Research Institute for Gas Purification
Moscow

Translated by
Greta R. Malyavskaya
A. V. Luikov Heat and Mass Transfer Institute
Minsk

Translation Editor
Oleg G. Martynenko
A. V. Luikov Heat and Mass Transfer Institute
Minsk

begell
house

Library of Congress Cataloging-in-Publication Data

Idel'chik, I. E.
      [Spravochnik po gidravlicheskim soprotivleniiam. English]
      Handbook of hydraulic resistance /I.E. Idelchik ; translated by
Great R. Malyaskaya ; translation editor, Oleg G. Martynenko ;
editor, M.O. Shteinberg. --- 3rd ed., rev. and augm.
        p.   cm.
      Includes bibliographical references and index.
      ISBN 1-56700-074-6
      1. Fluid dynamics. 2. Frictional resistance (Hydrodynamics)
I. Shteinberg, M. O.   II. Title.
TA357.I3413 1993
620.1'064---dc20

                         92-27383
                         CIP

TABLE OF CONTENTS

EDITOR'S PREFACE

The first edition of the *Handbook of Hydraulic Resistance* has been used by knowledgeable engineers in English-speaking countries since 1966, when an English translation sponsored by the U.S. Atomic Energy Commission became available. Although the book was not readily available or publicized, its extensive coverage and usefulness became known through citation, reference, and personal recommendations to a limited body of engineering prac titioners in the Western world.

Because there exists no English-language counterpart to Professor Idelchik's book, the translation and publication of the revised and augmented second edition of the Handbook of Hydraulic Resistance has been undertaken. The extensive coverage provided by this book becomes self-evident when one reviews the hundreds of illustrations of flow passages contained herein. Most of these are sufficiently basic to allow application to nearly any shape of flow passage encountered in engineering practice.

The editor of this translation has had extensive experience in using the first edition and has learned to appreciate not only the extent of coverage of this book but also its limitations. Based on this experience, the editor has tried to utilize American terminology whenever necessary for clarity while trying to preserve the original manuscript as faithfully as possible. Sometimes this resulted in overly detailed description, and the temptation always existed to rewrite or condense some of the explanatory chapters and sections. However, since this is a translation, the original was followed as faithfully as possible in order to maintain the author's style and approach. In the text the flow passages of interest are variously described as pipelines, ducts, conduits, or channels—all denoting an internal flow passage or pipe. Similarly, there are references to gas, air, steam, and water, when the term *fluid* would have been quite adequate in most cases. Since retaining the original translated terms did not affect the technical correctness of the text, changes were made only in isolated cases.

Section 1-1 provides general directions for using the book, allowing readers to make their own interpretation. The majority of readers may wish to use this handbook primarily as a source book for pressure loss or hydraulic resistance coefficients, applying these coefficients in their own accustomed way. The editor believes that these users may benefit from the few observations that follow.

The many sketches, diagrams, and graphs are self-explanatory, with flow directions and areas indicated. The values of pressure loss coefficients may be used over the limits indicated for the particular graph. The nondimensionality of the parameters of most graphs allows them to be used in the English system as well as the metric system. This permits interchangeable use of this book with other sources of pressure loss coefficients.

It should be noted that, unless otherwise stated, the data apply to Newtonian fluids considered as incompressible. It is also assumed, unless otherwise stated, that the inlet conditions and exit conditions are ideal; that is, there are no distortions. Very few experimental data exist on the effect of inlet flow distortion on the pressure loss coefficient for most flow devices.

Where friction factors are required to find the overall pressure loss coefficient of a component, the values obtained by the favored sources most familiar to the reader may be used in place of the data shown herein. Particular attention should be paid to the limits of applicability of the data provided as well as to the reference flow area used, when there is a flow area change. Much of the data are shown in tabular as well as graphical form. The former allows use of computers in the interpolation of intermediate values.

In any compilation of empirical data, the accuracy decreases with increasing complexity of the component, due to analytical and experimental uncertainties. This book is no exception. A good rule to follow is to check more than one source, if possible.

Although there will be many flow configurations for which no explicit resistance values are given in this book, it is entirely possible to make up combinations of simple shapes to simulate a complex component, provided suitable engineering judgment is applied. The latter, of course, requires familiarity with the way the data are presented and with the effect of exit conditions from one component on the inlet conditions of the adjacent component.

The editor of this translation would be remiss if he did not acknowledge that differences in engineering practice, nomenclature, engineering standards, and training may have an effect on the ability to fully utilize all that is presented in this work. One example is the difficulty in understanding the descriptive terms for some flow system components. However, the graphical presentations of much of the material in this book will help the reader overcome most such difficulties.

In a work of this nature, it is very probable that errors of translation or data reporting have occurred. The editor and the publisher would be most grateful to the readers and users of this handbook for information on such items.

Erwin Fried

PREFACE TO THE ENGLISH EDITION

The present edition of the *Handbook of Hydraulic Resistance,* translated into English from the second Russian edition of the book (Mashinostroenie Publishing House, Moscow, 1975), differs markedly from its first edition (Gosenergoizdat, Moscow, 1960), translated into English in 1966 (*Handbook of Hydraulic Resistance,* Israel Program for Scientific Translations, Jerusalem, 1966) and into French in 1969 (*Memento des pertes de charge,* Eyrolles Editeur, Paris, 1969).

The second edition of the book has been substantially augmented by incorporating a considerable body of totally new data on hydraulic resistances obtained as a result of research work in recent years. By and large, as compared with the first, the second edition contains more than 40% new and revised data.

When this edition was prepared, all of the misprints and errors discovered in the Russian edition were corrected, and some more precise definitions and changes were made.

The book is based on the utilization, systematization, and classification of the results of a large number of studies carried out and published at different times in different countries. A large portion of the data was obtained by the author as a result of investigations carried out by him.

It is quite clear that the methods of investigation, the models used, and, consequently, the accuracy of the results obtained and reported by various authors differ markedly in many cases. Such differences in the results could also be due to the fact that the majority of local hydraulic resistance coefficients are greatly influenced not only by the regime of flow but also by the prehistory of the flow, that is, conditions of supply to the section considered, nature of the velocity profiles, and degree of turbulence at the inlet and in some cases by the subsequent history of the flow as well; that is, flow removal from the test section.

Many complex elements of pipelines exhibit great instability of flow due to periodic fluid separation from the walls, periodic changes of place and magnitude of separation, and eddy formation resulting in large oscillations of hydraulic resistance.

The author was faced with an enormously difficult task: to discover and, where necessary, discard experimental results of questionable validity in that diverse body of data compiled on the hydraulic resistance coefficients; to clear up cases where large variations in the resistance coefficients of the sections are regular and correspond to the essence of the hydrodynamic pattern and those cases where they are due to the experimental uncertainty; and to select the most reliable data and find a successful format for presenting the material so that it is accessible and understandable to nonspecialists in aerodynamics and hydraulics. It had to be taken into account that, in practice, the configurations of sections of and impedances in pipelines, their geometric parameters, the conditions of entry and exit of the flow, and its regimes are so diverse that it is not always possible to find the required reported experimental data necessary to calculate the hydraulic resistances. The author has therefore incorporated in this handbook not only results that have been thoroughly verified in laboratories but also those provided by less rigorous experimental investigations and those predicted or obtained by approximate calculations based on separate experimental studies. In some cases, tentative data are shown and are so noted in the text. We think this approach is justified because the facilities used under industrial conditions, and consequently the conditions of flow passages in them, can greatly differ among themselves and differ from laboratory conditions, under which the majority of hydraulic resistance coefficients have been obtained. In many complex elements of pipelines, these coefficients, as shown above, cannot be constant due to the nature of the phenomena occurring in them; thus, they can vary over wide ranges.

The author hopes that the present edition will not only be useful for the further development of engineering science and technology in the English-speaking countries but will also aid in fostering friendly relations between the peoples of these countries and the Soviet people.

I. E. Idelchik

PREFACE TO THE 2nd RUSSIAN EDITION

There does not seem to be any branch of engineering that is not somehow involved with the necessity for moving liquids or gases through pipes, channels, or various types of apparatus. The degrees of complexity of hydraulic or fluid systems can therefore be widely different.

In some cases these are systems that for the most part are composed of very long straight pipes, such as oil pipelines, gas lines, water conduits, steam pipes, and air ducts of ventilation plants in industrial use. In other cases they are pipelines that are relatively short but that abound in fittings and branches, various impedances in the form of valves, orifices, and adjusting devices, grids, tees, etc. as found in air ducts of complex ventilation systems; gas flues of metallurgical works, chemical and other factories, boiler furnaces, nuclear reactors, and dryers; fuel and oil pipes and various manifolds of aircraft and rockets.

Most frequently the system through which a liquid or gas moves constitutes a large single unit (e.g., boilers, furnaces, heat exchangers, engines, air- and gas-cleaning equipment, and chemical, petrochemical, metallurgical, food, textile, and other manufacturing equipment).

In all cases, it is essential that the fluid resistance of these systems be properly calculated. Furthermore, the adequate design of sophisticated present-day installations consisting of complex-shaped parts of hydraulic and fluid lines is impossible without insight into the principal physicomechanical processes occurring in them and consideration of suggestions for the improvement of flow conditions and reduction in the local fluid resistance of these elements. The requisite information is given in this handbook.

A great body of new data on resistance coefficients accumulated since the first edition of this book has required an extensive revision of the text to account for the results of recent studies. But since it was not practically possible to incorporate all the newly published data on such flow resistance, this gap has been supplemented by an extensive listing of pertinent references.

The handbook consists of 12 chapters. Each chapter, except for the first one, contains data on a definite group of fittings or other parts of pipelines and fluid network elements having similar conditions of liquid or gas motion through them. The first chapter is a synopsis of general information on hydraulics of pressure systems and aerodynamics needed for design calculation of the elements of air-gas pipelines and hydraulic networks. All of the subsequent chapters contain:

- An explanatory part giving, as a rule, a brief account of the subject matter of the section, an outline of the main physicochemical processes occurring in complex elements of pipelines, additional clarifying remarks and practical recommendations for the calculation and choice of separate network elements, and recommendations on ways to reduce their hydraulic resistance.

- A computational part giving the coefficients or, in some instances, the absolute values of the fluid resistances of straight sections and of a wide range of complex-shaped parts of pipelines, fittings, various impedances, and other elements of the fluid networks. In each chapter the data are represented by special diagrams that contain a schematic of the element considered, calculation formulas, graphs, and tables of the numerical values of the resistance coefficients.

It is essential for the present-day design analysis of hydraulic (fluid) networks with the use of electronic computers that the resistance coefficients be given in the form of convenient design formulas. Moreover, it is often practical to represent in a concise form the functional dependence of the resistance coefficient on the main governing parameters.

Graphical representation of this dependence is advantageous because, on the one hand, it furnishes a rather vivid illustration of the nature of this dependence and, on the other hand, it makes it possible to obtain intermediate values of the resistance coefficients not listed in tables. The resistance coefficients given in tabular form are the principal values, which can be conveniently used in calculations.

The measurement units are given in the SI system. In selected cases, for convenience of usage, some quantities are also given in the meter-kilogram (force)-second system.

I. E. Idelchik

PREFACE TO THE 3rd EDITION

The 3rd edition of this Handbook is augmented with the most important results of investigations carried out in recent years. Some of the sections in the book have been refined and changed.

The Handbook has been composed on the basis of processing, systematization, and classification of the results of a great number of investigations published at different times. The essential part of the book is the outcome of investigations carried out by the author.

The results of investigations (the accuracy with which the models and fittings of pipelines were created, the accuracy of measurements, etc.) carried out by different specialists could differ among themselves. This might also be possible because the majority of local fluid resistances experience the influence of not only the mode of flow, but also the flow "prehistory" (the conditions of its supply to the given section, the velocity profile, and the degree of flow agitation at the inlet, etc.) and in some cases also the subsequent "history" of a flow (flow discharge from the section). All these conditions could be different in the studies undertaken by various authors.

In many complex elements of pipeline systems, a great instability of flow is observed due to the periodicity of flow separation from the walls, periodic variation of the place, and magnitude of the zone of flow separation and eddy formation. This results in different values of hydraulic resistances.

The author was faced with a difficult problem: when selecting most variegated information on hydraulic resistances, it was necessary to reveal and discard the questionable results of experiments to get a deeper understanding in which cases the great difference between the resistance coefficients of sections is regular, corresponding to the essence of the phenomena that occur during the motion of streams through them, and in which they are not regular; to select the most reliable data and find the most pertinent form of the presentation of information to make it accessible and understandable for engineers and technicians.

The configuration of sections and obstacles in pipeline systems, their geometric parameters, conditions of supply and removal, and of the modes of flow are so diverse that one often fails to find out from literature the necessary experimental data for the calculation of their hydraulic resistances. Therefore, the author incorporated not only the data thoroughly verified by laboratory investigations, but also those which were obtained theoretically or by approximate calculations based on separate experimental studies, and in some cases tentative data (specified in the text). This is permissible because the accuracy of fabrication and mounting of the systems of pipes and equipments in industrial conditions and, consequently, the conditions for the flow of streams may greatly differ between separate installations and differ from laboratory conditions at which the majority of fluid resistance coefficients were obtained, and also because of the fact that for many complex elements these coefficients cannot be constant quantities.

The present edition of this Handbook should assist in increasing the quality and efficiency of the design and usage of industrial power engineering and other constructions and also of the devices and apparatus through which liquids and gases move.

NOMENCLATURE

Symbol	Name of quantity	Abridged notation in SI units
a_1	speed of sound	m/s
a_{cr}	critical speed of sound	m/s
$a*$	speed of sound in frozen flow	m/s
a, b	sides of a rectangle	m
c_p and c_v	specific heats of gases at constant pressure and constant volume, respectively	J/kg°C
c_x	coefficient of drag	–
D, d	cross-section diameters	m
$D_h = 4F/\Pi; d_h = 4f/\Pi$	hydraulic or equivalent diameter (4 × hydraulic radius)	m
F, f	cross-sectional areas	m²
$\bar{f} = F_{or}/F_{gr}$	area ratio of a grid, orifice, perforated plate, etc.	–
G	mass flow rate of liquid (gas)	kg/s
g	gravitational acceleration	m/s²
h	height	m
$k = c_p/c_v$	specific heat ratio	–
l	length of flow segment, depth of channel, or thickness of orifice	m
$\mathrm{Ma} = w/a_1$	Mach number	–
$M = 1/F \int_F (w/w_0)^2 \, dF$	coefficient of momentum (Boussinesq coefficient)	–
m_0	wetting intensity	m³/m³
m	exponent	–
$N = 1/F \int_F (w/w_0)^3 \, dF$	coefficient of kinematic energy (Coriolis coefficient)	–
N_m	power	W
n	polytropic exponent	–
n_{ar}	area ratio (degree of enlargement or reduction of cross section); polytropic exponent; number of elements	–
n_{el}	number of elements	–
$p_\bullet$	static pressure	Pa
p_f	total pressure or flow stagnation pressure	Pa
p_{ex}	excess pressure	Pa
Δp	overall pressure difference	Pa
P_{dr}	drag force	N
Q	volumetric flow rate	m³/s
R	gas constant	J/kg K
R_h	hydraulic radius ($\frac{1}{4} D_h$)	m
R_0, r	radii of cross sections of a circular pipe or curved pipe length	m

Symbol	Name of quantity	Abridged notation in SI units
$\mathrm{Re} = wD_h/\nu$	Reynolds number	–
S, s	spacing (distance between rods in a bundle of pipes, between grid holes, etc.)	m
S_{fr}	length of a free jet	m
S_0	surface area	m²
S_m	frontal area of a body in a flow	m²
$T(t)$	thermodynamic temperature	K (°C)
T^*	thermodynamic flow stagnation temperature	K
ν_{sp}	specific volume	m³/kg; m/s
v	side discharge (inflow) velocity	m/s
w	stream velocity	m/s
w'	longitudinally fluctuating stream velocity	m/s
z	dust content	g/m³
z_d	dust capacity	kg/m²
α	central angle of divergence or convergence; angle of a wye or tee branching; angle of stream incidence	degrees
δ	angle of turning (of a branch, elbow); angle of valve opening	
δ_t	thickness of a wall, boundary layer, or wall layer	m
δ_j	height of joint	m
Δ	equivalent uniform roughness of walls	m
Δ_0	mean height of wall roughness protuberances (absolute roughness)	m
$\overline{\Delta}_0 = \Delta_0/D_h;\ \overline{\Delta} = \Delta/D_h$	relative roughness of walls	–
$\varepsilon = F_{con}/F_0$	coefficient of jet contraction	–
ε'	porosity (void fraction)	–
$\varepsilon_t = \sqrt{\overline{w'^2}}/w_0$	degree of turbulence	–
$\zeta \equiv \Delta p/(\rho w^2/2)$	coefficient of fluid resistance (pressure loss coefficient)	–
ζ_{loc}	coefficient of local fluid resistance	–
ζ_{fr}	coefficient of friction resistance of the segment of length l	–
η	dynamic viscosity	Pa s
η_Π	cleaning coefficient	–
$\lambda = \zeta_{fr}/(l/D_h)$	friction coefficient [friction resistance of the segment of relative unit length ($l/D_h = 1$)]	–
$\lambda_c = w/a_{cr}$	relative (reduced) stream velocity	–
μ	discharge coefficient	–
μ_{con}	mass concentration of suspended particles in flow	–
ν	kinematic viscosity	m²/s
ρ	density of liquid (gas)	kg/m²
ρ^*	density of frozen gas flow	kg/m³
ρ_{cr}	density of gas at critical velocity	kg/m³
Π	cross-sectional (wetted) perimeter	m
ϕ	velocity coefficient	–

SUBSCRIPTS

Subscripts listed for the quantities F, f, D, d, Π, a, b, w, ρ, Q, and p refer to the following cross sections or pipe segments:

0	governing cross section or minimum area
1	larger cross section in the case of expansion or contraction of the flow segment

2	larger cross section after equalization of the stream velocity
k	intermediate cross section of curved channel (elbow, branch) or the working chamber of the apparatus
con	contracted jet section at the discharge from an orifice (nozzle)
or	orifice or a single hole in the perforated plate or screen
gr	front of the perforated plate, screen, orifice
br, st, ch	side branch, straight passage, and common channel of a wye or tee, respectively
out	outlet
∞	velocity at infinity

Subscripts 0, 1, 2, k, and d at l refer, respectively, to the straight inlet, straight outlet, intermediate (for a curved channel), and diffuser pipe lengths.

Subscripts at Δp and ζ refer to the following forms of the fluid resistances:

loc	local
fr	friction
ov	overall
d	total resistance of a diffuser in the network
out	total resistance of a diffuser or a branch at the outlet from the network
int	internal resistance of a diffuser
exp	resistance to flow expansion in a diffuser
sh	shock resistance at sudden enlargement of the cross section
br and st	resistance of a branch and straight passage of a wye or tee (for the resistance coefficients reduced to the velocity in respective branch pipes)
r.br., r.st.	resistance coefficients of the side branch and of the straight passage of a wye or tee reduced to the velocity in a common channel of a wye or tee

USEFUL CONVERSIONS OF UNITS

Physical quantity	Given in → Gives ←	Multiplied by → Divided by ←	Gives Given in	Approximate or useful relationship
Length	ft	0.3048	m	$3\frac{1}{4}$ ft $\simeq$ 1 m
	in	25.4 (exact)	mm	1 in $\simeq$ 25 mm
	mil	0.0254	mm	
	yard	0.9144	m	
	mile (mi)	1609.3	m	1 mi $\simeq$ 1.6 km
	km	0.621388	mi	
Area	ft^2	0.092903	m^2	100 ft^2 $\simeq$ 9 m^2
	in^2	645.16	mm^2	1 in^2 $\simeq$ 650 mm^2
	acre	4047.0	m^2	
Volume	ft^3	0.028317	m^3	35 ft^3 $\simeq$ 1 m^3
	U.S. gal	0.003785	m^3	260 gal $\simeq$ 1 m^3
	U.S. gal	3.785	liter (L)	1 gal $\simeq$ $3\frac{3}{4}$ L
	L (liter)	0.2642	U.S. gal	1 L $\simeq$ 0.26 gal
	Brit. gal	0.004546	m^3	
	U.S. gal	0.13368	ft^3	
	barrel (U.S. pet.)	0.15898	m^3	
	barrel (U.S. pet.)	42	U.S. gal	
Velocity	ft/s[a]	0.3048	m/s	10 ft/s $\simeq$ 3 m/s
	m/s	3.2808	ft/s	
	ft/min	0.00508	m/s	100 ft/min $\simeq$ 0.5 m/s
	mi/h	1.6093	km/h	30 mi/h $\simeq$ 48 km/h
	km/h	0.6214	mi/h	50 km/h $\simeq$ 31 mi/h
	knots	1.852	km/h	
Mass	lb_m	0.45359	kg	1 lb_m $\simeq$ .45 kg
	kg	2.2046	lb_m	1 kg $\simeq$ 2.2 lb_m
	metric ton	2204.6	lb_m	metric ton = 10^3 kg
	ton (2000 lb_m)	907.18	kg	
Force	lb_f	4.44822	N = kg m/s^2	
	lb_f	0.45359	kg_f	1 N $\simeq$ 0.1 kg_f
	kg_f	2.2046	lb_f	$\simeq$ 0.22 lb_f
	kg_f	9.80665	N	
	dyne	0.00001 (exact)	N	
Amount of substance	lb_m-mol	453.6	kmol	
	g-mol	1.000	mol	
	kg-mol	1.000	kmol	
	mol	1000	kmol	
Mass flow rate	lb_m/h	0.0001260	kg/s	10^3 lb/h $\simeq$ .13 kg/s
	kg/s	7936.51	lb_m/h	
	lb_m/s	0.4536	kg/s	
	lb_m/min	0.00756	kg/s	

Reprinted from International System of Units (SI), J. Taborek, in *Heat Exchanger Design Handbook*, pp. xxvii-xxix, Hemisphere, Washington, D.C., 1984.

Physical quantity	Given in Gives ⟶ ⟵	Multiplied by ⟶ Divided by ⟵	Gives Given in	Approximate or useful relationship
Volume flow rate	U.S. gal/min	6.309×10^{-5}	m^3/s	
	U.S. bbl/day	0.15899	m^3/day	
	U.S. bbl/day	1.84×10^{-6}	m^3/s	
	ft^3/s	0.02832	m^3/s	
	ft^3/min	0.000472	m^3/s	
Mass velocity	$lb_m/h\ ft^2$	1.356×10^{-3}	$kg/s\ m^2$	
(mass flux)	$kg/s\ m^2$	737.5	$lb_m/h\ ft^2$	
Energy (work)	Btu^b	1055.056	$J = N\ m =$ $W\ s$	1 Btu ≃ 1000 J
(heat)	Btu	0.2520	kcal	1 kcal ≃ 4 Btu
	Btu	778.28	ft lb_f	
	kcal	4186.8	J	1 kcal ≃ 4000 J
	ft lb_f	1.3558	J	
	W h	3600	J	
Power	Btu/h	0.2931	$W = J/s$	10^6 Btu/h ≃ 300 kW
	W	3.4118	Btu/h	
	kcal/h	1.163	W	
	ft lb_f/s	1.3558	W	1000 kW ≃ 3.5×10^6 Btu/h
	hp (metric)	735.5	W	
	Btu/h	0.2520	kcal/h	
	tons refrig.	3516.9	W	
Heat flux	$Btu/h\ ft^2\ °F$	3.1546	W/m^2	$1000\ Btu/h\ ft^2$ ≃ 3.2
	W/m^2	0.317	$Btu/h\ ft^2$	kW/m^2
	$kcal/cm^2\ s\ °C$	41.868	W/m^2	
Heat transfer coefficient	$Btu/h\ ft^2\ °F$	5.6784	$W/m^2\ K$	$1000\ Btu/h\ ft^2\ °F$ ≃
	$W/m^2\ K$	0.1761	$Btu/h\ ft^2\ °F$	$5600\ W/m^2\ K$
	$kcal/cm^2\ s°C$	41.868	$W/m^2\ K$	
Heat transfer resistance	$(Btu/h\ ft^2\ °F)^{-1}$	0.1761	$(W/m^2\ K)^{-1}$	$0.001\ (Btu/h\ ft^2\ °F)^{-1}$ ≃
	$(W/m^2\ K)^{-1}$	5.6784	$(Btu/h\ ft^2\ °F)^{-1}$	$0.000\ 18\ (W/m^2\ K)^{-1}$
Pressure	lb_f/in^2 (psi)	6.8948	$kN/m^2 = kPa$	1 psi ≃ 7 kPa
	kPa	0.1450	psi	14.5 psi ≃ 100 kPa
	bar	100	kPa	
	lb_f/ft^2	0.0479	kPa	
	mm Hg (torr)	0.1333	kPa	1000 kPa = 1 MPa ≃
	in Hg	3.3866	kPa	150 psi
	$mm\ H_2O$	9.8067	Pa	
	$in\ H_2O$	249.09	Pa	1 in H_2O ≃ .25 kPa
	at (kg_f/cm^2)	98.0665	kPa	
	atm (normal)	101.325	kPa	atm = 760 mmHg
Mass flux	$lb_m/ft^2\ s$	4.8824	$kg/m^2\ s$	
	$lb_m/ft^2\ h$	0.001356	$kg/m^2\ s$	

Physical and Transport Properties				
Thermal conductivity	Btu/ft h°F	1.7308	W/m K	steel ≃ 50 W/m K
	W/m K	0.5778	Btu/ft h°F	water (20°C) ≃ 0.6 W/m K
	kcal/m h°C	1.163	W/m K	air (STP) ≃ 24 mW/m K
Density	lb_m/ft^3	16.0185	kg/m^3	$62.4\ lb_m/ft^3$ ≃ $1000\ kg/m^3$
	kg/m^3	0.06243	lb_m/ft^3	
	lb_m/U.S. gal	119.7	kg/m^3	
Specific heat capacity	$Btu/lb_m\ °F$	4186.8	J/kg K	1 $Btu/lb_m\ °F$ ≃ 4.2
	kcal/kg°C	4186.8	J/kg K	kJ/kg K
Enthalpy	Btu/lb_m	2326	J/kg	
	$kcal/kg_m$	4186.8	J/kg	
Dynamic (absolute)	centipoise (cP)	0.001	kg/m s	$kg/m\ s = N\ s/m^2 = Pa\ s$
viscosity	poise (P)	0.1	Pa s	
	cP	1.000	mPa s	
	cP	1000	μPa s	water (100°C), 0.31 cP

Physical quantity	Given in Gives	Multiplied by / Divided by	Gives Given in	Approximate or useful relationship
	lb_m/ft h	0.0004134	Pa s	
	lb_m/ft h	0.4134	cP	
	cP	2.4189	lb_m/ft h	air (100°C), 0.021 cP
	lb_m/ft s	1.4482	Pa s	
Kinematic viscosity	stoke (St), cm^2 s	0.0001	m^2/s	
	centistoke (cSt)	10^{-6}	m^2/s	
	ft^2/s	0.092903	m^2/s	
Diffusivity	ft^2/s	0.092903	m^2/s	
Thermal diffusivity	m^2/h	0.0002778	m^2/s	
	ft^2/s	0.092903	m^2/s	
	ft^2/h	25.81×10^{-6}	m^2/s	
Surface tension	dyne/cm	0.001	N/m	
	dyne/cm	6.852×10^{-5}	lb_f/ft	
	lb_f/ft	14.954	N/m	

Temperature relations: $\quad °C = \frac{5}{9}[°F - 32] \quad °C = (°F + 40)\frac{5}{9} - 40 \quad \Delta T(°C) = \frac{9}{5}\Delta T(°F) \quad mK = °C + 273.15$

$°F = \frac{9}{5}(°C) + 32 \quad °F = (°C + 40)\frac{9}{5} - 40 \quad \Delta T(°F) = \frac{5}{9}\Delta t(°C) \quad R = °F + 459.67$

Miscellaneous: Acceleration of gravity (standard): $\quad g = 9.806\ 65$ m/s^2

Gas constant: $\quad R = 8314.3$ m N/K kmol

Stefan-Boltzmann constant: $\quad 5.669\ 7 \times 10^{-8}$ W/m^2 K^4

1.714×10^{-9} Btu/ft^2 h R^4

---

[a] Even though the abbreviations s and h were introduced only with the SI, they are used here throughout for consistency.

[b] The calorie and Btu are based on the International Standard Table values. The thermochemical calorie equals 4.184 J (exact) and is used in some older texts.

READER'S GUIDE AND INTRODUCTION

Resistance to flow is an important engineering subject; it is applicable to every branch of engineering where flows of liquids and gases take place. A few areas where the knowledge of the resistance to flow is a normal requirement in the design and operation of fluid loops, circuits, and systems are air conditioning and ventilation, aeronautical engineering, biochemical and pharmaceutical engineering, chemical engineering, civil engineering, mechanical engineering, nuclear engineering, petroleum engineering, power engineering, as well as all hydraulic, agricultural and space engineering plants, systems, and equipment. The importance of exact and true values of flow resistance is, primarily, a question of determining the pumping — or energy — requirements for any apparatus or, eventually, for the entire plant involved in the motion of fluid. Needless to say, energy requirements are equivalent to funding, capital, or operational costs, and are therefore of prime importance to the practice of engineering.

Professor Idelchik's *Handbook of Hydraulic Resistance* has gained worldwide recognition and reputation among engineers through usage over the last 35 years when the first edition was published in Moscow. This latest, posthumous, third edition contains approximately 30% more data than the previous one; it was completed and delivered to the publishers literally a few months before the author's death in 1990.

The use of this Handbook can easily be likened to the use of an illustrated catalog. Various pieces of equipment and flow components, including fittings and even entire systems, have been assembled in separate chapters and catalogued, using illustrations, graphs, and tabular data. It is essential to note that the users, both old and new, should acquaint themselves with Chapter 1 before succumbing to the appeal of simply looking up specific values of resistance coefficients, drag values, friction factors, or other data directly in the appropriate chapters. The reading of Chapter 1 will — in the final tally — save a tremendous amount of time in the subsequent use of this Handbook.

CHAPTER 1
GENERAL INFORMATION AND ELEMENTS OF AERODYNAMICS AND HYDRAULICS OF PRESSURE SYSTEMS

At the outset, it should be noted that most of the values listed in the Handbook are dimensionless; however, the text is written using SI Units.

In the simplest of terms, flowing systems are set in motion by a difference in pressure, and the resistance to flow is offered by friction and other mechanical flow-hindering aspects of the materials of construction of the conduits and equipment. The dependencies of the hydraulic resistance on the dimensions, configuration, shape, surface roughness, and other features and properties of the material of construction, the relationships between the hydraulic resistance and properties of the flowing medium such as density and viscosity (in turn, these depend on temperature), and the correlation between the fluid-flow regimes, turbulent, laminar, velocity, and boundary layer considerations are all lucidly explained in this chapter.

The salient features and descriptions in Chapter 1 are:

- Pressure Drop
- Velocity Distribution
- Resistance Coefficient
- Tables of Hydraulic Resistance in Systems
- Tables of Units of Physical Quantities
- Tables of Properties of
    Liquids and Gases
    Density and Viscosity for
    Pure and Multicomponent Fluids
- Fluid Flow Regimes, Boundary Layers
- Equilibria of Liquids and Gases
- Equations of Fluid Motion

- Buoyancy (net Driving Head)
- Hydraulic Resistance of Networks
- Distribution of Static Pressure
- Flows Through Orifices
    Discharge Coefficients
- Pressurizers (Superchargers)
- Methods of Calculating Fluid
    Resistance of Systems
- Forced Ventilation
- Scrubbing of Gases
- Wind Tunnel

Of worthy note and special reading recommendation are the sections in Chapter 1 that offer step-by-step examples of calculation flow resistances.

Each of the subsequent chapters in this Handbook is divided into two parts: EXPLANATIONS AND PRACTICAL RECOMMENDATIONS and DIAGRAMS OF FRICTION OR RESISTANCE COEFFICIENTS. Again, it is strongly suggested that the reader, who should by now be generally well versed in the concepts and procedures in Chapter 1, peruse the first part of the chapter that is being consulted, before getting into the second part with its detailed catalog of tables, graphs, equations, and illustrations.

The first part of each chapter — from Chapter 2 through Chapter 12 — will provide the readers with the engineering and mathematical apparatus and background of the given problem, configuration, flow regime, fluid properties and fluid velocity, materials of construction, roughness, and other specifics within the chapter title topic.

The Handbook has well over 1000 illustrations and almost triple the number of tables. The illustrations in the second part of each chapter, or the Diagram Sections, are intended as the catalog of various pieces of equipment, configurations, shapes, spacings, forms, and sequences. After a few perusals, the readers will easily become acquainted with the Handbook and will find an efficient way to go through the presented material.

The following Guide to Chapters 2 through 12 offers a non-alphabetized and not necessarily sequential listing of the topics covered. This guide should be consulted when seeking a specific item, or configuration, for which resistance information is needed.

CHAPTER 2
RESISTANCE TO FLOW IN STRAIGHT TUBES AND CONDUITS: FRICTION COEFFICIENTS AND ROUGHNESS

- Exponents in Equations
- Roughness of Materials
    Metals
    Cement
    Glass and Plastics
- Growth of Asperities with Time (Fouling)
- Flow Regimes

- Channel Shapes
    Circular
    Triangular
    Square
    Starlike
    Annular (Concentric and Eccentric)

- Tube Bundles
  - Arrays
- Materials
- Joints
  - Welded
  - Recessed
- Flexible Tubes
  - Rubber Hoses
  - Plywood Channels
  - Plastic Hoses

CHAPTER 3
RESISTANCE TO FLOW AT THE ENTRANCE IN TUBES AND CONDUITS: RESISTANCE COEFFICIENTS OF INLET SECTIONS

In using this chapter, the reader should be aware of the fact that the entry into a vessel or channel is usually an exit from another vessel or channel. Thus, other chapters should be consulted to determine whether other resistance coefficients apply. For example, the entry into a vessel may be an elbow with an orifice or a screen. Data for these may also be found in other appropriate chapters.

- Entrance Losses
- Sharp Edges
- Wall Effects
- Conical Sections
- Angular Entries
- Mountings
- Sudden Contractions
- Side Orifices
- Annular Inlets
- Circular Orifices
- Square Orifices
- Inlets, Flush Mounted
  - Bellmouth
  - Baffled
  - Unbaffled
  - Bevelled Edge
- Perforated Plates
- Shafts, Intake
  - With Louvers
  - Without Louvers
- Fans
- Turbines

CHAPTER 4
RESISTANCE TO FLOW THROUGH ORIFICES WITH SUDDEN CHANGES IN VELOCITY AND FLOW AREA: RESISTANCE COEFFICIENTS OF SECTIONS WITH SUDDEN EXPANSION, SUDDEN CONTRACTION, ORIFICES, DIAPHRAGMS, AND APERTURES

- Perforated Plates
- Diffusers
  - Straight
  - Angular
- Ejectors
- Mixing Chambers
- Channels
  - Stepwise
  - Thick-edged
  - Sharp-edged
- Regimes
  - Turbulent
  - Laminar
  - Subsonic
- Velocity Distribution
- Elbows
  - With Guide Vanes
- Tubes, Circular
- Channels, Plane
- Jets

- Effect of Location
- Shapes
- Configurations

- Flaps, hinged
- Exhausts
  Gratings, Elliptical

CHAPTER 5
RESISTANCE TO FLOW WITH A SMOOTH CHANGE IN VELOCITY: RESISTANCE COEFFICIENTS OF DIFFUSERS AND CONVERGING AND OTHER TRANSITION SECTIONS

- Diffusers
- Inlet Nozzles, Smooth
- Elbows
- Throttling Devices
- Fittings
  With Grids
  Without Grids
  Short
  Long
  Curved Axis
- Guide Vanes
  Annular

- Baffles
- Inserts
- Screens
- Perforated Plates
- Pumps
- Fans
- Turbines
- Nozzles
  Converging
- Transition Sections
- Branching Pipes

CHAPTER 6
RESISTANCE TO FLOW WITH CHANGES OF THE STREAM DIRECTION: RESISTANCE COEFFICIENTS OF CURVED SEGMENTS — ELBOWS, BENDS, ETC.

- Bypasses
- Tubes, Helical
- Flow Regimes
- Roughness
- Velocity Distribution
- Welded Bends
- Joints, Threaded
- Goosenecks
- Elbows
  180°
  U-Shaped
  Sharp Corners
- Elbows and Turns
  In Space
  Round and Square
  With and Without Vanes
  Steps

- Bends, circular
  Z-Shaped
  Square
  Downstream of Pumps
  Multi-element
  90°
  S-Shaped
  Same and Different Planes
  Cylindrical
- Guide Vanes
- Turns, Annular
- Pump Outlets
- Pulverized Materials
- Dust
- Bypasses, at different angles
- Bends, Wire
  Tape Covered
- Vanes, Profiled
  Different Spacings
  Different Corners

CHAPTER 7
RESISTANCE IN THE CASES OF MERGING OF FLOW STREAMS AND DIVISION INTO FLOW STREAMS: RESISTANCE COEFFICIENTS OF WYES, TEES, AND MANIFOLDS

- Wyes
  - Converging
  - Diverging
  - Different Velocities
  - Different Angles
  - Different Materials
  - 4-Way
- Fittings
  - Welded
  - Threaded
  - Seams
  - Butt-Joint
  - Square
  - Non-symmetric
  - With Partitions
  - Without Partitions
- Straight Passages
- Partitions
- Flow Regimes
- Headers
  - Inlet
  - Outlet
  - Different Angles
  - Z-Shaped
  - ⊓-Shaped
- Crosses, Diverging

CHAPTER 8
RESISTANCE TO FLOW THROUGH BARRIERS UNIFORMLY DISTRIBUTED OVER THE CHANNEL CROSS SECTION: RESISTANCE COEFFICIENTS OF GRIDS, SCREENS, POROUS LAYERS, AND PACKINGS

- Grids
  - Tray
  - Fouling
  - Grating
- Perforated Plates
  - Patterns
  - Edges
  - Materials: Ceramics, Plastics
- Screens
  - Circular Wire
  - Silk Threads
  - Two-Plane
  - Other Materials
- Filters
- Porous Media
  - Powders
- Packed Beds
  - Configurations
  - Raschig Rings
  - Packings
  - Jets, in
  - Lumped, irregular
- Flow Regimes
- Pressure Levels

CHAPTER 9
RESISTANCE TO FLOW THROUGH PIPE FITTINGS AND LABYRINTH SEALS: RESISTANCE COEFFICIENTS OF THROTTLING DEVICES, VALVES, PLUGS, LABYRINTH SEALS, AND COMPENSATORS

- Devices
  - Flow Stopping
  - Throttling
  - Control
- Valves
  - Globe
  - Gate
  - Disk
  - Butterfly
  - Tray, with and without bottom guides
  - Conical
  - Spherical
  - Effects of Location
  - Effects of Sequence
  - Throttling
  - Disk Throttling
  - Check
  - Suction
  - Ball
- Faucets
- Taps
- Plugs
  - Conical
  - Spherical
  - Segmented
  - Rollerlike
- Plungers
- Labyrinth Seals
  - Angle-Globe
  - Dividing Walls
  - Gate, Plane-Parallel
- Positions of Fittings
- Transitions, Asymmetric
- Seals
  - Gate
  - Revolving
  - Spherical
  - Disks
  - Seats
- Valves in Pipes
  - Cylindrical
  - Rectangular
- Stuffing Boxes
  - Lyre-Shaped
- Coils

CHAPTER 10
RESISTANCE TO FLOW PAST OBSTRUCTIONS IN A TUBE: RESISTANCE COEFFICIENTS OF SECTIONS WITH PROTURBERANCES, TRUSSES, GIRDERS, AND OTHER SHAPES

- Beams, Square
- Spheres
- Cylinders
  - Multiple
- Wires
- Ellipses
- Triangles
- Cones
- Roughness
- Flow Regimes
- Fins
- Laths
- Spacers, bracers
- Fairings
- Wedges
- Profiles, Shaped
  - Drop-Shaped
- Angles
- Octahedrons
- Tetrahedrons
- Trusses

CHAPTER 11
RESISTANCE TO FLOW AT THE EXIT FROM TUBES AND CHANNELS: RESISTANCE COEFFICIENTS OF EXIT SECTIONS

- Discharge into a Larger Vessel
- Free Discharge into a Larger Vessel
- Diffusers, Straight
    Conical
    Annular
- Velocity Distribution
- Impingement Upon a Baffle
- Exit Edges
- Fans, Diffusers at Outlets
- Orifices
    Circular
    Rectangular

- Gratings
- Louvers
- Compressors
    Operating
    Idling
- Perforated Plates
- Diffusers, Multiple
- Exhaust Fans
- Gratings
- Screens

CHAPTER 12
RESISTANCE TO FLOW THROUGH VARIOUS TYPES OF APPARATUS:* RESISTANCE COEFFICIENTS OF APPARATUS AND OTHER EQUIPMENT

Gas and Air Scrubbers

- Dust Separators and Traps
- Cyclones
- Wet Scrubbers
- Venturi Scrubbers
- Perforated Plates
- Scrubbers with Wood Packing
- Scrubbers, Centrifugal

Heat Exchangers

- Honeycomb Radiators
- Finned Tube
- Tubular Plate
- Cross-Flow
- Tube Bundles
    Staggered
    Variable Pitch
    In-line
    Oval
    Transverse

- Plate
- Two-pass
- Shell-and-Tube
- Finned (Ribbed) Tube
- Notched Tube
- Air Heaters
- Electric Heaters
- Heating Furnace
- Wire Fins

Filters

- Roll Filters
- Bag
- Frame Filters
- Laboratory Filters
- Ventilation Filters
- Oil Filters
- Electrostatic Filters

Combined Effects of Bends-Wyes, Cross Section and Their Orientation

William Begell

*Most of the equipment described in this chapter is of Soviet design and manufacture. However, the illustrations are clear and explicit enough so that the reader can identify configurations that are similar to equipment used in the West.

ONE

GENERAL INFORMATION AND ELEMENTS OF AERODYNAMICS AND HYDRAULICS OF PRESSURE SYSTEMS

1-1 GENERAL DIRECTIONS

1. A portion of the total energy that is expended to overcome the resistance forces arising from the flow of real (viscous) fluids through pipes and channels is irretrievably lost for a given system or network. This loss of energy is due to irreversible conversion of mechanical energy (the work of resistance forces) into heat. Therefore, the term fluid resistance, or hydraulic loss, represents the irreversible loss of total energy over a given system length. The ratio of the total stream energy (power) loss to the kinetic energy (power) or of the total pressure loss, averaged over the mass flow rate, to the velocity (dynamic) pressure over an arbitrary flow section is called the coefficient of hydraulic resistance.*

2. The total energy (pressure) loss is a substantially positive quantity. However, the difference in total energies (total pressures) over a given segment and, correspondingly, the coefficient of hydraulic resistance governed by this difference may sometimes take on negative values as well. This occurs when external forces with respect to the given flow appear in the channel. For example, when the fluid flow is aspirated through a side channel flush-mounted into the pipe wall at an angle exceeding 90° (see Chapter 3) and external flow (with respect to the side channel) takes place, the latter becomes the source of additional pressure. As a result, the flow in the side channel acquires additional energy, which, at some values of the ratio w_∞/w_0, can exceed the amount of energy expended for the mechanical work of the channel resistance forces.

Another example is provided by a converging wye (see Chapter 7), where at some values of the ratio Q_{br}/Q_{ch} a portion of the flow energy in the channel is expended for aspiration of the fluid through a branch (ejector effect); that is, the flow in the branch acquires additional energy at the expense of the energy of the external (with respect to it) flow in the wye passage.

The negative values of the resistance in the above examples indicate that there is an increase, rather than a decrease, of the energy.

---

*In what follows, the words "hydraulic" and "full" will often be omitted for briefness; more simple expressions "resistance of the section", "coefficient of section resistance", "pressure losses," or simply "loss" will mean hydraulic resistance and full pressure losses, respectively.

3. The basic reference data given in this book are the friction coefficients ζ_{fr} of straight pipe (channel) segments of length l, the friction coefficients per unit length ($l/D = 1$) of the segment,* and the local fluid resistances for pipe fittings, flow impedances, valves, and other elements of pipelines, as well as of some industrial equipment and devices.

4. When using this handbook and the well-known formula [Equation (1-65)] for evaluation of the resistance

$$\Delta p_{ov} = \zeta_{ov} \frac{\rho w^2}{2} = \zeta_{ov} \frac{\rho}{2} \left(\frac{Q}{F}\right)^2 \tag{1-1}$$

it is assumed that all quantities in this equation are given, including all geometric parameters of the system component being calculated, except for the overall coefficient of fluid resistance $\zeta_{ov} = \zeta_{loc} + \zeta_{fr}$ (see Section 1-6). The unknown values are only those of ζ_{ov} and, correspondingly, of ζ_{loc} and ζ_{fr}.

5. In plots that refer to short pipes and channels whose ζ_{fr} is negligible compared with ζ_{loc}, the local resistance coefficient can be treated as the overall coefficient ζ.**

In graphs that refer to relatively long pipes and channels (diffusers, converging sections, smooth outlet pipes, and other components), the values of both the local resistance coefficients ζ_{loc} and the friction coefficients ζ_{fr} are generally given.

The resistance coefficients, plotted on graphs containing tentative data, are to be considered as overall coefficients ζ. In adding the pressure drops for the network considered, the frictional losses in the fittings are not to be taken into account again.

6. The values of ζ_{loc} given in this handbook include not only the local pressure drops (local resistance***) over a short segment adjacent to a pipe element of variable area configuration, but also the pressure drop downstream of this element. This is done to equalize the velocities over the straight exit section of the pipe. Inasmuch as the local losses are arbitrarily determined as the difference between the total losses and frictional losses in the straight exit section, the latter should also be taken into account.

7. In the case of a stream discharged from a fitting or some other element into a large plenum or into the atmosphere, the given coefficients of local resistance also take into account the velocity (dynamic) pressure losses $\rho w_{ex}^2/2$ at the exit.****

8. The values of the local resistance coefficients given in this handbook assume, except for special cases, uniform velocity distribution in the inlet section of the component. Such conditions are usually observed following a smooth inlet nozzle and for steady-state flows.

---

*The friction coefficient ζ_{fr} is sometimes called the coefficient of linear frictional resistance. Henceforth the term "friction coefficient" will be used in a more general sense and will be understood to represent both ζ_{fr} and sometimes λ.

**Henceforth, for simplicity the subscript "ov" to the resistance coefficient ζ and to the total resistance Δp will be omitted.

***Local resistance here and further on refers to local losses of total pressure and not only to the fitting in which these losses occur.

****The special literature often uses the expression "pressure losses for creation of velocity". Actually, the nonrecoverable pressure is not spent at all to create "velocity" in the system; there occurs a transition of static pressure into a dynamic one (the transformation of the pressure energy into kinetic energy). Dynamic pressure is, for the given system, lost only in the case if the flow leaves the given system (enters into the surrounding medium). In this case the dynamic pressure is determined by flow velocity in the exit section of the system. For example, with the aid of a diffuser this velocity can be brought to a minimum and, consequently, the loss of dynamic pressure will be minimum.

In the case of unsteady-state motion of liquid, the local resistance leads to the loss of flow stability, causing in it the formation of the unsteady-state eddies for the creation of which a certain energy is spent.[24,26]

9. The mutual effect of local hydraulic resistances in some cases leads to an increase in the values of ζ_{loc} of the considered shaped portions of pipelines, and in other cases to their decrease. In separate sections, for certain shaped portions the values of the coefficients of local resistances are given with the mutual effect taken into account. In particular, the values of ζ_d and ζ for diffusers (Sections 5 and 11) are given as functions of the length of the preceding straight (inlet) section, and also of some previous shaped portions; for some elbows and branches (Section 6) the values of ζ_{loc} are given for the interacting separate elements (separate bends), etc. The mutual effect of local resistances is considered (in the scope of the data available) in Section 12.

10. In the general case, the pressure drop can be expressed as the sum of two terms, which are proportional to the first and second powers of the velocity, respectively:[28]

$$\Delta p = k_1 w + k_2 w^2 \tag{1-2}$$

Correspondingly, the resistance coefficient is

$$\zeta \equiv \frac{\Delta p}{\rho w^2/2} = \frac{2k_1}{\rho w} + \frac{2k_2}{\rho} = \frac{A}{\mathrm{Re}} + B = \frac{A}{\mathrm{Re}} + k_3 \zeta_{qu} \tag{1-3}$$

where A is a constant; ζ_{qu} is taken as ζ for the region of the square law of resistance (similarity region $\mathrm{Re} \gtrsim 10^4$). At very low Reynolds number ($\mathrm{Re} \lesssim 25$), the second term of Equation (1-2) can be neglected, while at very large Re one can neglect the first term of this expression and assume that $k_3 = 1\,l$, Equation (1-3). Within $25 \lesssim \mathrm{Re} \lesssim 10^5$, the proportionality factor k_3 can be equal to, higher than, or less than unity.

11. The dependence of the local resistance coefficients on Reynolds number is given only in those cases when its effect is known or can be evaluated approximately.

12. In practice, the effect of Re on the local resistance is mainly evident at its small values ($\mathrm{Re} < 10^5$). Therefore, when $\mathrm{Re} \geq 10^5 - 2 \times 10^5$, the local resistance coefficients may be assumed independent of the value of Re. At smaller values of Re, its effect should be taken into account.

13. When there is no indication of the Reynolds number at which the values of ζ were obtained, it may be assumed that the given resistance coefficient for turbulent flow ($\mathrm{Re} \geq 2 \times 10^3$) is practically independent of Re even when it is small. In the case of a laminar flow ($\mathrm{Re} < 2 \times 10^3$), these data can be used only for a very rough estimate of the resistance and only when $\mathrm{Re} \gtrsim 10^2$.

14. Most values of the resistance coefficients given in this handbook, except when specified otherwise, were obtained at Mach numbers $\mathrm{Ma} \leq 0.3$. However, nearly all of the values of ζ, ζ_{loc}, and ζ_{fr} may also be used at higher subsonic velocities up to about $\mathrm{Ma} = 0.8$. In some cases the dependence of ζ on Ma or λ_c is given.

15. Most of the values of the local resistance coefficients were obtained for commercial smooth pipe or channel walls. Because the effect of roughness on the local resistance has not been studied extensively, the walls of fittings and of other flow components considered in the handbook should be assumed smooth unless otherwise specified. The effect of roughness, which begins to manifest itself only at $\mathrm{Re} > 4 \times 10^4$, may be approximated by multiplying ζ by a factor of 1.1–1.2 (higher for large roughness).

16. The shape of the cross section of fittings and other parts is shown in cases where it affects the resistance coefficient or where the values of this coefficient were obtained for

specific cross sections. When the shape of the cross section is not indicated or no additional data on the resistance of noncircular components are given, the resistance coefficient for a polygonal or rectangular cross section having an aspect ratio of $a_0/b_0 = 0.5-2.0$ should be assumed to have the same value as for a circular cross section.

17. The graphs and tables of resistance coefficients given in this handbook are based on either theoretical formulas or experimental data. In the latter case the values of ζ obtained from approximate formulas can differ somewhat from those given by the curves and in the tables. In such cases the formulas can be used only for tentative calculations.

18. The hydraulic resistance coefficients are independent of the kind of fluid* flowing through a pipeline system and are mainly governed by the geometry of the network element considered and, in some cases, by the flow regime (Reynolds or Mach number). The data given in the handbook apply equally well for the calculation of the resistance of purely hydraulic lines and for the calculation of gas, air, in various networks and equipment installations.

19. The hydraulic resistance of a network may be calculated by using tables such as Tables 1-14 to 1-16.

20. The values of the resistance coefficients given in the handbook are for components of pipes and channels of different shapes and parameters. However, in the design of new systems one should choose optimum shapes and parameters that would yield minimum values of the resistance coefficients.

The minimum values of ζ can be determined from the curves or tables of resistance plotted in the graphs or from the guidelines given in the explanatory part of each section of the handbook.

21. Table 1-1 shows the units of the most important physical quantities and their relation of SI units.

1-2 PROPERTIES OF LIQUIDS AND GASES

Density of Flowing Medium

1. Values for the density of water and of some other commercial liquids at different temperatures are given in Table 1-2 and 1-3, respectively.

Values for the density of some commerical gases under normal physical conditions ($t = 0°C$; $p = 101.325$ kPa; dry gas and for their relative density with respect to air, the density of which is taken to be unity, are given in Table 1-4.

2. For multicomponent gases (blast furnace gas, coke gas, and others) the density of the mixture is determined by the formula:

$$\rho_{mix} = \frac{\rho_1 v_1 + \rho_2 v_2 + \dots + \rho_n v_n}{100}$$

where $\rho_1, \rho_2, \dots, \rho_n$ are the densities of the components of the mixture at 0°C and 101.325 kPa (Table 1-4), in kg/m³; $v_1, v_2, \dots, v_n$ are the volume fractions of the components according to the data given by a gas analysis, in percent.

*If it is homogeneous and incompressible.

Table 1-1 Units of the most important physical quantities and their relation of SI units*

Name and dimension of quantity	Name and designation of unit	Relationship to SI units
Length (L)	meter (m)	–
	centimeter (cm)	$1 \text{ cm} = 10^{-2} \text{ m}$
	millimeter (mm)	$1 \text{ mm} = 10^{-3} \text{ m}$
	micrometer (μ)	$1 \text{ } \mu\text{m} = 10^{-6} \text{ m}$
	nanometer (nm)	$1 \text{ nm} = 10^{-9} \text{ m}$
	angström (Å)	$1 \text{ A} = 10^{-10} \text{ m} = 0.1 \text{ nm}$
Volume (L^3)	cubic meter (m³)	–
	cubic centimeter (cm³)	$1 \text{ cm}^3 = 10^{-6} \text{ m}^3$
	liter (l)	$1 \text{ l} = 10^{-3} \text{ m}^3$
Velocity (LT^{-1})	meter per second (m/s)	–
	kilometer per hour (km/h)	$1 \text{ km/h} = 0.277788 \text{ m/s}$
	centimeter per second (cm/s)	$1 \text{ cm/s} = 10^{-2} \text{ m/s}$
	meter per hour (m/h)	$1 \text{ m/h} = 277.788 \times 10^{-6} \text{ m/s}$
	meter per minute (m/min)	$1 \text{ m/min} = 16.667 \times 10^{-3} \text{ m/s}$
Acceleration (LT^{-2})	meter per second squared (m/s²)	–
	centimeter per second squared (cm/s²)	$1 \text{ cm/s}^2 = 10^{-2} \text{ m/s}^2$
Angular velocity (T^{-1})	radian per second (rad/s)	–
Rotation frequent (T^{-1})	reciprocal seconds (s⁻¹)	–
	rotations per minute (ppm)	$1 \text{ rpm} = \dfrac{1}{60} \text{ s}^{-1}$
	rotations per second (rps)	$1 \text{ rps} = 1 \text{ s}^{-1}$
Mass (M)	kilogram (kg)	–
	gram (g)	$1 \text{ g} = 10^{-3} \text{ kg}$
	ton (t)	$1 \text{ t} = 10^3 \text{ kg}$
	kilogram-force seconds squared per meter (kg-force s²/m)	$1 \text{ kg-force s}^2/\text{m} = 9.80665 \text{ kg}$
Density ($L^{-3}M$)	kilogram per cubic meter (kg/m³)	–
	kilogram per liter (kg/l)	
	kilogram per cubic decimeter (kg/dm³)	$1 \text{ kg/l} = 1 \text{ g/ml} = 1 \text{ kg/dm}^3$
	gram per milliliter (g/m)	$1 \text{ g/cm}^3 = 1 \text{ t/m}^3 = 10^3 \text{ kg/m}^3$
	gram per cubic centimeter (g/cm³)	
	ton per cubic meter (t/m³)	
	kilogram-force seconds squared per meter to fourth power (kg-force s²/m⁴)	$1 \text{ kg-force s}^2/\text{m}^4 = 9.80665 \text{ kg/m}^3$
Specific volume (L^3M^{-1})	cubic meter per kilogram (m³/kg)	–
	cubic centimeter per gram (cm³/g)	$1 \text{ cm}^3/\text{g} = 10^{-3} \text{ m}^3/\text{kg}$
	cubic meter per ton (m³/t)	$1 \text{ m}^3/\text{t} = 10^{-3} \text{ m}^3/\text{kg}$
Momentum (impulse) (LMT^{-1})	kilogram meter per second (kg m/s)	–
	kilogram-force second (kg-force s)	$1 \text{ kg-force s} = 9.80665 \text{ kg m/s}$
Momentum of momentum (moment of impulse) (L^2MT^{-1})	kilogram meter squared per second (kg m²/s)	–
	kilogram-force meter second (kg ms)	$1 \text{ kg-force m/s} = 9.80665 \text{ kg m}^2/\text{s}$
Force (gravity force, lift force); weight (LMT^{-2})	newton (N or m kg s⁻²)	–
	dyne (dyn)	$1 \text{ dyn} = 10^{-5} \text{ N} = 10 \text{ } \mu\text{N}$
	kilogram-force (kg-force)	$1 \text{ kg-force} = 9.80665 \text{ N}$
	gram-force (g-force)	$1 \text{ g-force} = 9.80665 \times 10^{-3} \text{ N} = 9.80665 \text{ mN}$
	ton-force (t-force)	$1 \text{ t-force} = 9.80665 \times 10^3 \text{ N} = 9.80665 \text{ kN}$

*Table compiled in collaboration with L. P. Stotsky.

Table 1-1 Units of the most important physical quantities and their relation of SI units* (continued)

Name and dimension of quantity	Name and designation of unit	Relationship to SI units
Specific weight $(L^{-2}MT^{-2})$	newton per cubic meter (N/m³)	–
	dyne per cubic centimeter (dyn/cm³)	1 dyn/cm³ = 10 N/m³
	kilogram-force per cubic meter (kg-force/m³)	1 kg-force/m³ = 980,665 N/m³
Force moment; moment of a couple; torque (L^2MT^{-2})	newton meter (N m)	–
	dyne centimeter (dyn cm)	1 dyn cm = 10^{-7} N m
	kilogram-force meter (kg-force m)	1 kg-force m = 9.80665 N m
Power impulse (LMT^{-1})	newton-second (N s)	–
	dyne-second (dyn s)	1 dyn s = 10^{-5} N s
	kilogram-force second (kg-force s)	1 kg-force s = 9.80665 N s
Pressure; mechanical stress; moduli of elasticity, shear, rigidity; bulk modulus $(L^{-1}MT^{-2})$	pascal (Pa or N/m² or m⁻¹ kg s⁻²)	–
	kilopascal (kPa)	1 kPa = 10^3 Pa
	megapascal (MPa)	1 MPa = 10^6 Pa
	gigapascal (GPa)	1 GPa = 10^9 Pa
	dyne per square centimeter (dyn/cm²)	1 dyn/cm² = 10^{-1} Pa
	kilogram-force per square centimeter or atmosphere (kg-force/cm² or atm)	1 kg-force/cm² = 98.0665 kPa = 0.0980665 MPa
	standard atmosphere (atm)	1 atm = 101.325 kPa = 0.101325 MPa
	bar (bar)	1 bar = 10^5 Pa = 10^{-1} MPa
	kilogram-force per square meter (kg-force/m²)	1 kg-force/m² = 1 mm H₂O = 9.80665 Pa
	millimeter of water column (mm H₂O)	
	kilogram-force per square millimeter (kg-force/mm²)	1 kg-force/mm² = 9.80665 × 10^6 Pa = 9.80665 MPa
	millimeter of mercury column (mm Hg)	1 mm Hg = 1 torr = 133.332 Pa
Pressure gradient $(L^{-2}MT^{-2})$	pascal per meter (Pa/m)	–
Work, energy (L^2MT^{-2})	joule (J or m² kg s⁻²)	–
	kilowatt hour (kW h)	1 kW h = 3.6 × 10^6 J
	erg (erg)	1 erg = 10^{-7} J
	kilogram-force meter (kg-force m)	1 kg-force m = 9.80665 J
	horsepower hour (hp h)	1 hp h = 2.648 MJ
	liter atmosphere (1 atm)	1 atm = 101.328 J
Specific work; specific energy (L^2T^{-2})	joule per kilogram (J/kg)	–
	erg per gram (erg/g)	1 erg/g = 10^{-4} J/kg
	kilogram-force meter per kilogram (kg-force m/kg)	1 kg-force m/kg = 9.80665 J
Power (L^2MT^{-3})	watt (W or m² kg s⁻³)	–
	kilowatt (kW)	1 kW = 10^3 W
	megawatt (MW)	1 MW = 10^6 W
	erg per second (erg/s)	1 erg/s = 10^{-7} W
	kilogram-force meter per second (kg-force m/s)	1 kg-force m/s = 9.80665 W
Mass rate of flow (MT^{-1})	kilogram per second (kg/s)	–
	gram per second (g/s)	1 g/s = 10^{-3} kg/s
	kilogram per hour (kg/h)	1 kg/h = 277.778 × 10^{-6} kg/s
	kilogram per minute (kg/min)	1 kg/min = 16.667 × 10^{-3} kg/s
	ton per hour (t/h)	1 t/h = 0.277778 kg/s

*Table compiled in collaboration with L. P. Stotsky.

Table 1-1 **Units of the most important physical quantities and their relation of SI units* (continued)**

Name and dimension of quantity	Name and designation of unit	Relationship to SI units
Volume rate of flow (L^3T^{-1})	cubic meter per second (m³/s)	–
	cubic meter per hour (m³/h)	1 m³/h = 277.778 $\times$ 10^{-6} m³/s
	liter per second (l/s)	1 l/s = 10^{-3} m³/s
	liter per minute (l/min)	1 l/min = 16.667 $\times$ 10^{-6} m³/s
	liter per hour (l/h)	1 l/h = 277.778 $\times$ 10^{-9} m³/s
Dynamic viscosity ($L^{-1}MT^{-1}$)	pascal second (Pa s)	–
	millipascal second (mPa s)	1 mPa s = 10^{-3} Pa s
	poise (ps)	1 ps = 10^{-1} Pa s
	centipoise (cps)	1 cps = 10^{-3} Pa s = 1 mPa s
	kilogram-force second per meter squared (kg-force s/m²)	1 kg-force s/m² = 9.8066 Pa s
Kinematic viscosity (L^2T^{-1})	meter squared per second (m²/s)	–
	centimeter squared per second (cm²/s)	1 cm²/s = 1 st = 10^{-4} m²/s
	stokes (st)	
	millimeter squared per second (mm²/s)	1 mm²/s = 10^{-6} m²/s
	centistokes (cst)	1 cst = 1 mm²/s = 10^{-6} m²/s
	meter squared per hour (m²/h)	1 m²/h = 277.778 $\times$ 10^{-6} m²/s
Surface tension (MT^{-2})	newton per meter (N/m)	–
	dyne per centimeter (dyn/cm)	1 dyn/cm = 10^{-3} N/m = 1 mN/m
	kilogram-force per meter (kg-force/m)	1 kg-force/m = 9.80665 N/m
Thermodynamic temperature (θ)	Kelvin (°K)	–
Centigrade temperature (θ)	centigrade degree (°C)	$t_c = T_K - 273.15$; 1°C = 1 K
Quantity of heat; enthalpy (L^2MT^{-2})	joule (j)	–
	kilojoule (kJ)	1 kJ = 10^3 J
	megajoule (MJ)	1 MJ = 10^6 J
	gigajoule (GJ)	1 GJ = 10^9 J
	calorie (cal)	1 cal = 4.1868 J
	kilocalorie (kcal)	1 kcal = 4.1868 kJ
	megacalorie (Mcal)	1 Mcal = 4.1868 MJ
	gigacalorie (Gcal)	1 Gcal = 4.1868 GJ
Specific quantity of heat; specific enthalpy (L^2T^{-2})	joule per kilogram (J/kg)	–
	kilojoule per kilogram (kJ/kg)	1 kJ/kg = 10^3 J/kg
	calorie per gram (cal/g)	
	kilocalorie per kilogram (kcal/kg)	1 cal/g = 1 kcal/kg = 4.1868 kJ/kg
Heat capacity of the system ($L^2MT^{-2}\theta^{-1}$)	joule per kelvin (J/K)	–
	joule per centigrade degree (J/°C)	1 J/°C = 1 J/K
	calorie per centigrade degree (cal/°C)	1 cal/°C = 4.1868 J/K
	kilocalorie per centigrade degree (kcal/°C)	1 kcal/°C = 4.1868 kJ/K
Specific heat of the system ($L^2T^{-2}\theta^{-1}$)	joule per kilogram kelvin (J/kg K)	–
	kilojoule per kilogram kelvin (kJ/kg K)	1 kJ/kg K = 10^3 J/kg K
	calorie per gram centigrade degree (cal/g °C)	1 cal/g °C = 1 kcal/kg °C = 4.1868 $\times$ 10^3 J/kg K
Volumetric specific heat ($L^{-1}MT^{-2}\theta^{-1}$)	joule per cubic meter kelvin (j/m³ K)	–
	kilocalorie per cubic meter centigrade degree (kcal/m³ °C)	1 kcal/m³ °C = 4.1868 $\times$ 10^3 J/m³ K

*Table compiled in collaboration with L. P. Stotsky.

Table 1-1 Units of the most important physical quantities and their relation of SI units* (continued)

Name and dimension of quantity	Name and designation of unit	Relationship to SI units
Entropy of the system $(L^2MT^{-2}\theta^{-1})$	joule per kelvin	–
	kilocalorie per kelvin (kcal/K)	1 kcal/K = 4.1868 kJ/kg
Specific entropy $(L^2T^{-2}\theta^{-1})$	joule per kilogram kelvin (J/kg K)	–
	kilojoule per kilogram kelvin (kJ/kg K)	1 kJ/kg K = 10^3 J/kg K
	calorie per gram kelvin (cal/g K)	1 cal/g K = 1 kcal/kg K = 4.1868 kJ/kg K
Specific gas constant $(L^3T^{-2}\theta^{-1})$	joule per kilogram kelvin (J/kg K)	–
	joule per kilogram centigrade degree (J/kg °C)	1 J/kg °C = 1 J/kg K
	kilogram-force meter per kilogram centigrade degree (kg-force m/kg °C)	1 kg-force m/kg °C = 9.80665 kg K
Molar gas constant $(L^2MT^{-2}\theta^{-1}N^{-1})$	joule per mole kelvin (J/mol K)	–
	joule per mole centigrade degree (J/mol °C)	1 J/mol °C = 1 J/mol K
	kilogram-force meter per mole centigrade degree (kg-force m/mol °C)	1 kg-force m/mol °C = 9.80665 J/mol K
Heat flux; heat power (L^2MT^{-3})	watt (W)	–
	kilowatt (kW)	1 kW = 10^3 W
	megawatt (MW)	1 MW = 10^6 W
	calorie per second (cal/s)	1 cal/s = 4.1868 W
	kilocalorie per hour (kcal·ih)	1 kcal/h = 1.163 W
	megacalorie per hour (Mcal/h)	1 Mcal/h = 1.63 kW
	gigacalorie per hour (Gcal/h)	1 Gcal/h = 1.163 MW
Thermal conductivity $(LMT^{-3}\theta^{-1})$	watt per meter kelvin (W/m K)	–
	watt per meter centigrade degree (W/m °C)	1W/m °C = 1 W/m K)
	calorie per second per centimeter centigrade degree (cal/s cm °C)	1 cal/s cm °C = 418.68 W/m K
	kilocalorie per hour per meter centigrade degree (kcal/h m °C)	1 kcal/h m °C = 1.163 W/m K
Heat transfer coefficient $(MT^{-3}\theta^{-1})$	watt per square meter kelvin (W/m² K)	–
	watt per square meter centigrade degree (W/m² °C)	1 W/m² °C = 1 W/m² K
	kilocalorie per hour per square meter centigrade degree (kcal/h m² °C)	1 kcal/h m² °C = 1.1163 W/m² K
	calorie per second per square centimeter centigrade degree (cal/s cm² °C)	1 cal/s cm² °C = 418.68 W/m² K

*Table compiled in collaboration with L. P. Stotsky.

Table 1-2 Density of water

t, °C	0	10	20	30	40	50	60
ρ, kg/m³	999.87	999.73	998.23	995.67	992.24	988.07	983.24

t, °C	70	80	90	100	120	140	160
ρ, kg/m³	977.81	971.83	965.34	958.38	943.40	926.40	907.50

Table 1-3 Densities of various liquids[35,36]

Type of liquid	t, °C	ρ, kg/m³	Type of liquid	t, °C	ρ, kg/m³
Ammonia	−34	684	Medium machine oil	10	898
Aniline	15	1,026		20	892
Acetone	15	796		50	876
Gasoline	15	680–755	Mineral lubrication oil	15	890–960
Benzene	15	884	Olive oil	15	920
	60	836	Paraffin oil	18	925
Bromine	15	3,190	Turpentine oil	15	870
Butane (normal)	−0.5	606	Cottonseed oil	15	930
Water	(see Table 1-2)	–	Natural mineral oil	15	700–900
Seawater	15	1,020–1,030	Liquefied ozone	−5	537
Glycerin (anhydrous)	10	1,264	Carbon bisulfide	15	1,270
	20	1,260	Sulfuric acid (87%)	15	1,800
	40	1,250	Sulfuric acid (fuming)	15	1,890
Coal tar	15	1,200	Turpentine	18	870
Dichloroethane	15	1,175–1,200	Mercury	20	13,550
Nitrogen dioxide	3.2	1,484	Methyl alcohol (methanol)	15	810
Sulfur dioxide	−10	1,472	Ethyl alcohol (ethanol)	15–18	790
Kerosene	15	790–820	Tetrabromoethane	15	2,964
Lignite oil	20	970	Chlorine	0	1,469
Wood oil	15	920	Methyl chloride	0	954
Castor oil	15	970	Ethyl chloride	0	919
Coconut oil	15	930	Chloroform	15–18	1,480
Linseed oil (boiled)	15	940	Hydrogen cyanide	0	715
Light machine oil	10	899	Ethyl ether	15–18	740
	20	898			
	50	895			

Viscosity

1. Viscosity is a characteristic of all real liquids and gases and is manifested in motion through internal friction. First, one can identify the dynamic viscosity η, which is the ratio of the shear stress to the velocity gradient (velocity variation per unit length of the normal to the direction of fluid motion), that is,

$$\eta = \frac{\tau}{dw/dy}$$

where τ is the shear stress; dw/dy is the velocity gradient in the direction of the normal y. Second, one can identify the kinematic viscosity ν, which is the ratio of the dynamic viscosity of the fluid to its density; $\nu = \eta/\rho$.

2. Tables 1-5 and 1-6 contain conversion factors for the dynamic viscosity η and the kinematic viscosity ν.

3. The dynamic and kinematic viscosities depend on the physical state parametrs of the fluid medium. The dynamic viscosity of fluids is dependent only on temperature and independent of the pressure (for perfect gases).

With an increase of temperature, the viscosity of gases and vapors increases, while that of liquids decreases. For water vapor, an increase in the dynamic viscosity is observed with an increase in pressure.

The kinematic viscosity of liquids and gases is a function of both temperature and pressure.

Table 1-4 Density of dry gas at 0°C and 101.325 kPa and specific heats of 1 kg at 20°C[36]

Type of gas	Chemical formula	Density ρ, kg/m³	Relative density in reference to air	c_p		c_v		$k = \dfrac{c_p}{c_v}$
				kJ/kg °C	kcal/kg °C	kJ/kg °C	kcal/kg °C	
Nitrogen	N_2	1.2507	0.9673	1.043	0.249	0.745	0.178	1.40
Ammonia	NH_3	0.7676	0.5937	2.161	0.515	1.649	0.394	1.31
Argon	Ar	1.7820	1.3782	0.523	0.125	0.315	0.075	1.66
Acetylene	C_2H_2	1.1733	0.9074	1.672	0.399	1.357	0.324	1.23
Butane (normal)	C_4H_{10}	2.6730	2.0673	1.918	0.458	1.733	0.414	1.11
Isobutane	C_4H_{10}	2.6680	2.0634	1.633	0.390	–	–	–
Air	–	1.2930	1.0000	1.005	0.240	0.716	0.171	1.40
Hydrogen	H_2	0.0899	0.0695	14.286	3.410	10.132	2.420	1.11
Water vapor at 100°C	H_2O	0.8598	0.6462	2.135	0.510	–	–	–
Helium	He	0.1785	0.1380	5.192	1.240	3.113	0.744	1.67
Nitrous oxide	N_2O	1.9780	1.5298	0.879	0.210	0.687	0.164	1.28
Oxygen	O_2	1.4290	1.1052	0.914	0.219	0.653	0.156	1.40
Krypton	Kr	3.7080	2.8677	0.251	0.060	0.152	0.036	1.67
Xenon	Xe	5.8510	4.5251	0.159	0.038	0.096	0.023	1.66
Methane	CH_4	0.7170	0.5545	2.228	0.532	1.710	0.408	1.30
Neon	Ne	0.9300	0.7192	1.030	0.246	0.618	0.148	1.67
Ozone	O_3	2.2200	1.7169	–	–	–	–	1.29
Nitric oxide	NO	1.3400	1.0363	0.976	0.233	0.695	0.166	1.40
Carbon monoxide	CO	1.2500	0.9667	1.043	0.249	0.745	0.178	1.40
Propane	C_3H_8	2.0200	1.5622	1.633	0.390	1.432	0.342	1.22
Propylene	C_3H_6	1.9140	1.4802	1.549	0.370	1.336	0.319	1.16
Hydrogen sulfide	H_2S	1.5390	1.1903	1.059	0.253	0.804	0.192	1.32
Carbon oxysulfide	COS	2.7210	2.1044	–	–	–	–	–
Sulfur dioxide	SO_2	2.9270	2.2637	0.632	0.151	0.502	0.120	1.26
Carbon dioxide	CO_2	1.9760	1.5282	0.846	0.202	0.656	0.157	1.29
Chlorine	Cl_2	3.2170	2.4880	0.481	0.115	0.356	0.085	1.35
Methyl chloride	CH_3Cl	2.3080	1.7850	0.804	0.192	0.639	0.153	1.26
Ethane	C_2H_6	1.3570	1.0495	1.752	0.418	1.476	0.353	1.19
Ethylene	C_2H_4	1.2610	0.9752	1.554	0.371	1.258	0.300	1.24

Table 1-5 Relationship between units of dynamic vicosity η

Unit of measurement	μps (micropoise)	cps (centipoise)	ps (poise)	Pa s kg/ms	kg/m h	kg-force s/m²	lb/ft s	lb/ft h
1 μps (micropoise)	1	10^{-4}	10^{-6}	10^{-7}	3.6×10^{-4}	1.02×10^{-8}	6.72×10^{-8}	2.42×10^{-4}
1 cps (centipoise)	10^4	1	10^{-2}	10^{-3}	3.6	1.02×10^{-4}	6.72×10^{-4}	2.42
1 ps (poise)	10^6	10^2	1	10^{-1}	3.6×10^2	1.02×10^{-2}	6.72×10^{-2}	2.42×10^2
1 Pa s (kg/m s)	10^7	10^3	10	1	3.6×10^3	1.02×10^{-1}	6.72×10^{-1}	2.42×10^3
1 kg/m h	2.78×10^3	2.78×10^{-1}	2.78×10^{-3}	$.78 \times 10^{-4}$	1	2.83×10^{-5}	1.867×10^{-4}	6.72×10^{-1}
1 kg-force s/m²	9.81×10^7	9.81×10^3	9.81×10	9.81	3.53×10^4	1	6.592	2.373×10^4
1 lb/ft s	1.488×10^7	1.488×10^3	1.488×10	1.488	5.36×10^3	1.52×10^{-1}	1	3.6×10^3
1 lb/ft h	4.13×10^3	4.13×10^{-1}	4.13×10^{-3}	4.13×10^{-4}	1.488	4.22×10^{-5}	2.78×10^{-4}	1

Table 1-6 Relationship between units of kinematic viscosity ν

Unit of measurement	mm²/s, cst	cm²/s, st	m²/s	m²/h	ft²/s	ft²/h
1 mm²/s = 1 cst (centistokes)	1	10^{-2}	10^{-6}	3.60×10^{-3}	1.07×10^{-5}	3.87×10^{-2}
1 cm²/s = 1 st (stokes)	10^2	1	10^{-4}	3.60×10^{-1}	1.07×10^{-3}	3.87
1 m²/s	10^6	10^4	1	3.60×10^3	1.07×10	3.87×10^4
1 m²/h	2.78×10^2	2.78	2.78×10^{-4}	1	2.99×10^{-3}	1.07×10
1 ft²/s	9.30×10^4	9.30×10^2	9.30×10^{-2}	3.35×10^2	1	3.60×10^3
1 ft²/h	2.58×10	2.58×10^{-1}	2.58×10^{-5}	9.30×10^{-2}	2.78×10^{-4}	1

4. The temperature dependence of the viscosity of gases can be approximated by Sutherland's formula:

$$\eta = \eta_0 \frac{273 + C}{T + C} \left(\frac{T}{273}\right)^{3/2}$$

where η_0 is the dynamic viscosity of the gas at 0°C and C is a constant that depends on the type of gas.

Values of the dynamic viscosity η for various gases as a function of the temperature, the constant C, and the temperature range over which the value of this constant has been experimentally verified are given in Table 1-7.

The values of the kinematic viscosity ν for the same gases as a function of the temperature at a pressure of 101.325 kPa are given in Table 1-8.

The values of ν for air are also presented in Figure 1-1.

5. The kinematic viscosity of a gas mixture can be determined by Mann's approximate formula:

$$\nu_{mix} = \frac{100}{v_1/\nu_1 + v_2/\nu_2 + \ldots + v_n/\nu_n}$$

where $\nu_1, \nu_2, \ldots, \nu_n$ are the kinematic viscosities of the components and $v_1, v_2, \ldots, v_n$ are the volume fractions of the mixture components (in percent).

The dynamic viscosity of the mixture can be determined by the approximate formula

$$\eta_{mix} = \frac{100}{G_1/\eta_1 + G_2/\eta_2 + \ldots + G_n/\eta_n}$$

where $\eta_1, \eta_2, \ldots, \eta_n$ are the dynamic viscosities of the components and $G_1, G_2, \ldots, G_n$ are the mass fractions of the mixture components (in percent).

6. The dependence of the dynamic, η, and kinematic, ν, viscosities of water on temperature and pressure is given in Table 1-9. Moreover, the temperature dependence of ν for water at $p_a = 101.325$ kPa is presented in Figure 1-2.

1-3 FLUID FLOW REGIMES

1. The flow regimes of a liquid or gas can be laminar or turbulent. Within the laminar regime, the flow is stable, the stream layers move without mixing with each other and flow smoothly past any obstacles encountered in their way.

The turbulent regime is characterized by a random displacement of finite masses of liquid or gas which mix strongly with each other.

2. The flow regime of a liquid or gas depends on the relationship between the inertia and viscosity forces (internal friction) in the stream, which can be expressed by a dimensionless group, the Reynolds number:

$$\text{Re} = \frac{\rho w D_h}{\eta} = \frac{w D_h}{\nu}$$

3. For each practical installation there is a certain range of "critical" Reynolds numbers at which the flow passes from one regime into the other (transition region). The lower limit

Table 1-7 Dynamic viscosity of gases $\eta \times 10^6$, Pa s, at a pressure of 101.325 kPa as a function of temperature and of the constant B in Sutherland's formula[35,36,52,53]

Gas	Formula	Temperature t, °C													C	Temperature range, °C
		−20	0	20	40	60	80	100	150	200	300	400	600	800		
Nitrogen	N_2	15.75	16.60	17.48	18.35	19.25	20.00	20.82	22.90	24.60	28.10	31.10	36.60	41.30	104	25–280
Ammonia	NH_3	8.60	9.30	10.05	10.78	11.45	12.15	12.80	14.60	–	–	–	–	–	503	20–300
Argon	Ar	–	21.20	22.20	–	–	–	27.10	–	32.10	36.70	41.00	48.70	55.40	142	20–827
Acetylene	C_2H_2	9.02	9.60	10.21	10.82	11.45	12.02	12.60	–	–	–	–	–	–	215	–
Butane	C_4H_{10}	–	6.90	7.40	–	–	–	9.50	–	–	–	–	–	–	358	–
Hydrogen	H_2	8.04	8.40	8.80	9.18	9.59	9.96	10.30	11.30	12.10	13.90	15.40	18.30	21.00	71	20–100
Water vapor	H_2O	8.20	8.93	9.67	10.40	11.13	11.87	12.60	–	16.04	20.00	23.90	31.45	38.65	961	20–406
Air	–	16.20	17.12	18.09	19.04	19.98	20.89	21.90	–	26.02	29.72	33.01	39.06	44.30	111	16–825
Helium	He	17.50	18.60	19.55	20.40	21.35	22.05	22.90	–	27.00	30.70	34.20	40.70	46.50	0	21–100
Sulfur dioxide	SO_2	–	11.60	12.60	–	–	–	16.30	–	20.70	24.60	–	–	–	306	300–825
Nitrous oxide	N_2O	–	13.70	14.60	–	–	–	18.30	–	22.50	26.50	–	–	–	260	25–280
Oxygen	O_2	18.15	19.20	20.25	21.30	22.35	23.40	24.40	–	29.00	33.10	36.90	43.50	49.30	125	20–280
Krypton	Kr	–	23.30	24.60	–	–	–	30.60	–	–	–	–	–	–	188	–
Xenon	Xe	–	21.10	22.60	–	–	–	28.70	–	–	–	–	–	–	252	–
Methane	CH_4	9.55	10.20	10.80	11.50	12.14	12.70	13.30	14.70	16.10	18.60	–	–	–	164	20–250
Nitric oxide	NO	–	17.90	18.80	–	–	–	22.70	–	26.80	–	–	–	–	128	20–250
Carbon monoxide	CO	15.95	16.80	17.68	18.55	19.15	20.24	21.02	22.90	24.70	27.90	–	–	–	100	up to 130
Pentane (p)	C_5H_{12}	–	6.20	–	–	–	–	–	10.00	10.30	–	–	–	–	383	–
Propane	C_3H_8	7.00	7.50	8.00	8.54	9.05	9.58	10.01	11.30	12.50	14.40	–	–	–	278	20–250
Propylene	C_3H_6	–	7.80	8.35	–	–	–	10.70	14.10	–	–	–	–	–	487	–
Hydrogen sulfide	H_2S	–	11.60	12.40	–	–	–	15.90	–	–	–	–	–	–	331	–
Carbon dioxide	CO_2	12.80	13.80	14.70	15.70	16.70	17.55	18.45	–	22.60	26.40	29.90	36.20	41.35	254	20–250
Chlorine	Cl_2	11.45	12.30	13.20	14.10	15.00	15.90	16.80	18.90	21.00	25.00	–	–	–	350	100–250
Methyl chloride	CH_3Cl	–	9.80	10.60	–	–	–	13.60	–	17.50	–	–	–	–	454	–
Ethyl chloride	C_2H_5Cl	–	9.40	10.50	–	–	–	–	14.30	–	–	–	–	–	411	–
Hydrogen cyanide	HCN	–	–	7.40	–	–	–	–	–	–	–	–	–	–	901	–
Ethane	C_2H_6	–	8.60	9.20	–	–	–	11.50	12.80	14.20	–	–	–	–	252	20–250
Ethylene	C_2H_4	8.85	9.45	10.10	10.70	11.20	11.85	12.40	14.00	15.40	–	–	–	–	225	20–250

Table 1-8 Kinematic viscosity of gases $\nu \times 10^6$, m²/s, at a pressure of 101.325 kPa as a function of temperature[35,36,52,53]

Gas	Formula	Temperature t, °C												
		−20	0	20	40	60	80	100	150	200	300	400	600	800
Nitrogen	N_2	11.67	13.30	15.00	16.85	18.80	20.65	22.30	28.30	34.10	47.20	61.40	93.50	130.00
Ammonia	NH_3	6.81	12.00	14.00	16.00	18.10	20.35	22.70	29.30	36.00	–	–	–	–
Argon	Ar	–	11.90	13.30	–	–	–	20.70	–	31.20	43.30	56.50	87.50	123.00
Acetylene	C_2H_2 4.73	8.20	9.35	10.60	11.94	13.25	14.70	–	–	–	–	–	–	–
Butane	C_4H_{10}	–	25.80	29.70	–	–	–	48.50	–	–	–	–	–	–
Hydrogen	H_2	84.00	93.50	105.00	117.30	130.00	143.00	156.60	195.00	233.00	324.00	423.00	651.00	918.00
Water vapor	H_2O 9.50	11.12	12.90	14.84	16.90	18.66	21.50	–	–	–	–	–	–	–
Air	–	11.66	13.20	15.00	16.98	18.85	20.89	23.00	30.00	34.90	48.20	63.20	96.50	134.00
Helium	He	9.12	10.40	11.74	13.12	14.55	15.97	17.50	–	26.20	36.10	47.30	72.80	102.50
Sulfur dioxide	SO_2	–	4.00	4.60	–	–	–	7.60	–	12.20	17.60	–	–	–
Nitrous oxide	N_2O	–	6.82	7.93	–	–	–	12.70	–	19.70	28.20	–	–	–
Oxygen	O_2	11.04	13.40	15.36	17.13	19.05	21.16	23.40	–	35.20	48.70	63.80	97.50	135.70
Krypton	Kr	–	6.26	7.13	–	–	–	13.70	–	–	–	–	–	–
Xenon	Xe	–	3.59	4.15	–	–	–	6.70	–	–	–	–	–	–
Methane	CH_4	12.57	14.20	16.50	18.44	20.07	22.90	25.40	31.8	39.00	54.50	–	–	–
Nitric oxide	NO	–	13.30	15.10	–	–	–	23.20	–	30.50	–	–	–	–
Carbon monoxide	CO	11.86	13.50	15.16	17.00	18.96	21.00	22.70	28.4	34.30	46.85	–	–	–
Propane	C_3H_8	3.04	3.70	4.26	4.90	5.52	6.18	6.76	8.70	10.84	15.10	–	–	–
Propylene	C_3H_6	–	4.08	4.70	–	–	–	7.70	11.4	–	–	–	–	–
Hydrogen sulfide	H_2S	–	7.62	8.70	–	–	–	14.10	–	19.80	28.00	37.30	65.20	82.00
Carbon dioxide	CO_2	5.62	7.00	8.02	9.05	10.30	12.10	12.80	–	–	–	–	–	–
Chlorine	Cl_2	3.09	3.80	4.36	5.02	5.66	6.36	7.15	9.10	11.50	16.25	–	–	–
Methyl chloride	CH_3Cl	–	4.28	4.90	–	–	–	8.05	–	13.10	–	–	–	–
Ethane	C_2H_6	–	6.35	7.28	–	–	–	11.60	14.70	18.10	–	–	–	–
Ethylene	C_2H_4	6.80	7.50	8.66	9.73	10.85	12.15	13.40	17.30	21.20	–	–	–	–

$\nu \times 10^6$ m²/s

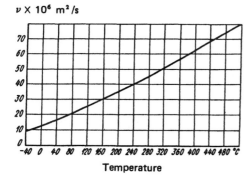

Temperature

Figure 1-1 Kinematic viscosity of air as a function of its temperature at a pressure of 101.325 kPa.

of the critical Reynolds number for a circular pipe is about 2300. The upper limit of Re depends on the inlet conditions, the condition of the wall surface, and other parameters.

4. In the flow of a real (viscous) fluid past a surface, the layer that is in immediate contact with the solid surface adheres to it. As a consequence, a velocity profile is established transverse to the flow, varying from zero at this surface to the velocity *w* of the undisturbed stream (Figure 1-3). This region in which the velocity variation occurs is called the boundary or wall layer.

5. In the case of flow in straight pipes (channels), two regions are distinguished: the starting length region of the flow and the region of stabilized flow (Figure 1-3*a*).

By the starting length we mean the length of the pipe over which the uniform velocity profile, corresponding to the cross section at the inlet of the fluid through a smooth entry or collector, passes gradually into the normal profile corresponding to stabilized flow.

6. For the laminar flow regime, the stabilized velocity profile is established following a parabolic law (Figure 1-3*b*, 1), while for the turbulent flow regime, it follows approximately logarithmic or exponential laws (Figure 1-3*b*, 2).

7. For laminar flow, the starting length (i.e., the distance from the inlet section just behind a smooth entry, to the section where the axial velocity profile differs by about 1% from the velocity profile of a fully stabilized flow) of a circular pipe or of a rectangular tube with an aspect ratio $a/b = 0.7$ to 1.5 can be determined from the formular

$$\frac{L_{st}}{D_h} = B \text{ Re} \tag{1-4}$$

where $B = L_{st}/D_h$ Re is the reduced length of the starting section (according to Boussinesq[71] $B \approx 0.065$, according to Shiller[63] $B \approx 0.029$) and L_{st} is the length of the starting section of the pipe.

The length L_{st} can be quite large; for example, at Re = 2000, $L_{st} = 130D_h$.

8. In the case of turbulent flow the starting length of an annular pipe with smooth walls can be determined from the formula of Solodkin and Guinevsky:[50]

$$\frac{L_{st}}{D_h} = b\, '\text{lg Re} + (a' - 4.3b') \tag{1-5}$$

where $a' = f_1(D_{in}/D_{ex})$ and $b' = f_2(D_{in}/D_{ex})$ are determined from the corresponding curves of Figure 1-4, where D_{in} and D_{ex} are the diameters of the internal and external pipes, respectively.

Table 1-9 Dynamic and kinematic viscosities of water as functions of temperature and pressure[53]

t, °C	0	10	20	30	40	50	60	70	80	90	100	110	120
p, MPa	0.0981	0.0981	0.0981	0.0981	0.0981	0.0981	0.0981	0.0981	0.0981	0.0981	0.101	0.143	0.198
η, MPa s	1.790	1.300	1.010	0.802	0.654	0.549	0.470	0.406	0.355	0.315	0.282	0.259	0.238
$\nu \times 10^6$, m²/s	1.792	1.306	1.006	0.805	0.659	0.556	0.478	0.415	0.365	0.326	0.295	0.272	0.250

t, °C	130	140	150	160	170	180	190	200	210	220	230	240	250
p, MPa	0.270	0.360	0.476	0.618	0.798	1.003	1.255	1.565	1.910	2.300	2.800	3.350	3.980
η, MPa s	0.221	0.201	0.186	0.174	0.163	0.153	0.144	0.136	0.135	0.125	0.120	0.115	0.111
$\nu \times 10^6$, m²/s	0.233	0.217	0.203	0.191	0.181	0.173	0.165	0.158	0.153	0.148	0.145	0.141	0.137

t, °C	260	270	280	290	300	310	320	330	340	350	360	370
p, MPa	4.690	5.500	6.400	7.440	8.600	9.870	11.30	12.85	14.70	16.50	18.70	21.10
η, MPa s	0.107	0.102	0.098	0.094	0.091	0.088	0.085	0.081	0.078	0.073	0.067	0.057
$\nu \times 10^6$ m²/s	0.135	0.133	0.131	0.129	0.128	0.128	0.127	0.127	0.127	0.126	0.126	0.126

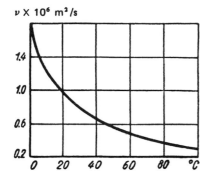

Figure 1-2 Kinematic viscosity of water as a function of its temperature at 101.325 kPa.

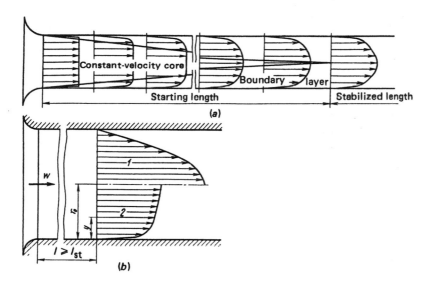

Figure 1-3 Velocity distribution over the pipe cross section : (*a*) stream deformation over the starting length; (*b*) velocity profile over the stabilized length; (1) laminar flow; (2) turbulent flow.

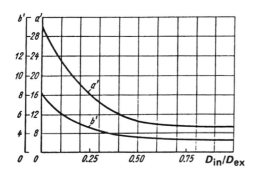

Figure 1-4 Coefficients a' and b' plotted against the ratio of annular pipe diameters D_{in}/D_{ex}.

When $D_{in}/D_{ex} \to 0$ ($D_{in} \to 0$), the annular pipe transforms into the pipe of circular section, for which Equation (1-5) takes the form

$$\frac{L_{st}}{D_0} = 7.88 \lg \mathrm{Re} - 4.35 \tag{1-6}$$

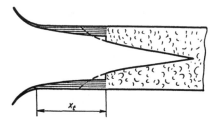

Figure 1-5 Mixed inlet section of the pipe.

When $D_{in}/D_{ex} \rightarrow 1.0$, the annular pipe is transformed into a flat plate, for which Equation (1-4) becomes

$$\frac{L_{st}}{D_h} = 3.28 \lg \text{Re} - 4.95 \tag{1-7}$$

It follows from Equations (1-4)–(1-7) that for a turbulent mode of flow the starting length L_{st} is considerably shorter than for laminar flow; for example, at $\text{Re} = 5 \times 10^5$, $L_{st} \approx 35D_h$. According to Kirsten's experimental data, the values of L_{st} exceed those obtained from the above formulas by 40–50%.

9. When the fluid upstream of the entrance is undisturbed and the inlet of the fluid occurs completely smoothly through an entry nozzle with very smooth walls, the flow pattern in the inlet section of the starting length is mixed ("mixed inlet section"). It is characterized by formation of a laminar boundary layer at the walls even at large Reynolds numbers greatly exceeding the critical Reynolds number. This boundary layer downstream of the inlet becomes thicker and at some distance from it x_t (at the "transition" point) becomes turbulent (Figure 1-5). Farther along, this turbulent layer fills up the whole cross section of the pipe, with the transverse velocity distribution asymptotically approaching that for a stabilized turbulent flow.

10. The relative distance $\bar{x}_t$ from the transition point to the inlet depends on the Reynolds number and can be approximated from a formula suggested by Filippov:[59]

$$\bar{x}_t = \frac{x_t}{D_0} = \frac{3.04 \times 10^5}{\text{Re} (1 + \eta_t)}$$

where $\eta_t = (w_{cot} - w_0)/w_0$ is found from Shiller's[63] data and w_0 and w_{cor} are the axial mean velocity and the velocity in the core of the flow. At larger Re, $\eta_t \rightarrow 0$ and $\bar{x}_t = 3.04 \times 10^5/\text{Re}$. The dependence of x_t on Re is given in Figure 1-6.

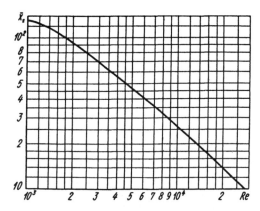

Figure 1-6 Dependence of $\bar{x}_t$ on Re.

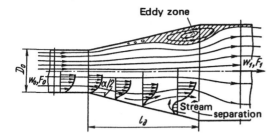

Figure 1-7 Flow separation and formation of eddies in a diffuser.

11. The thickness of the boundary layer at a given distance from the initial section of a straight pipe (channel) can increase or decrease, depending on whether the flow of the medium is decelerated (on enlargement of the flow area) or accelerated (on contraction of the flow area).

A too sudden expansion of flow area can initiate flow separation from the wall, which is accompanied by formation of vortices (Figure 1-7).

1-4 EQUILIBRIUM OF LIQUIDS AND GASES

1. A liquid or gas is in equilibrium if, for each arbitrarily isolated portion of it, the result of all the forces acting on this portion is equal to zero.

2. The equation of equilibrium of the same volume of a fluid at constant density has the form

$$gz_0 + \frac{p_0}{\rho} = gz_1 + \frac{p_1}{\rho} \tag{1-8}$$

where z_0 and z_1 are the coordinates of two fluid particles in the given volume relative to the reference plane (the corresponding geometric heights, Figure 1-8), in m, and p_0 and p_1 are the static pressures (absolute) at the levels of the particles chosen, in Pa.

3. The pressure at any arbitrary point in the liquid or gas volume can be determined if the pressure at some other point of the same volume is known, as well as the difference between the depth of immersion of one point relative to the other, $h = z_1 - z_0$ (see Figure 1-8):

$$\left.\begin{aligned} p_1 &= p_0 - g\rho\,(z_1 - z_0) = p_0 - g\rho h \\ p_0 &= p_1 + g\rho\,(z_1 - z_0) = p_1 - g\rho h \end{aligned}\right\} \tag{1-9}$$

It is for this reason that, for example, the pressure exerted on the walls of a vessel filled with a stationary hot gas ($\rho_g < \rho_a$) at a level $h = z_g - z_a$, located above the surface that

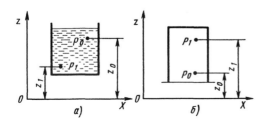

Figure 1-8 Determination of the pressure at an arbitrary point in the liquid (gas) volume from the pressure at a given point: (a) $\rho > \rho_a$; (b) $\rho_g < \rho_a$.

separates the gas and air (Figure 1-9), is lower, on both the gas side (p_g) as well as the air side (p_h), than the pressure p_a at the surface of separation:

$$p_g = p_a - g\rho_g h \tag{1-10}$$

and

$$p_h = p_a - g\rho_a h \tag{1-11}$$

where ρ_g and ρ_a are the densities of the gas and the air (averaged over the height h), in kg/m³.

4. The pressure of a stationary hot gas in a vessel at a level $h = z_g - z_a$ above that of the atmospheric pressure of air at the same level h can be obtained by virtue of Equations (1-10) and (1-11) from:

$$p_g - p_h = gh(\rho_a - \rho_g)$$

1-5 EQUATIONS OF FLUID MOTION

Flow Rate Equation and Mean Flow Velocity

1. The flow rate of a fluid (liquid or gas) is defined as the mass or volume of fluid passing a given cross section of the pipe (channel) per unit of time.

Two types of flow rates are distinguished: the mass flow rate (for example, G kg/s) and the volumetric flow rate (for example, Q m³/s).

2. In a generalized form, at any transverse distribution of the flow velocities, the volumetric flow rate is expressed by the formula

$$Q = \int_F dQ = \int_F w \, dF \tag{1-12}$$

where w is the flow velocity at the given point across the pipe (channel) in m/s.

The mass flow rate is

$$G = \rho Q = \int_F \rho w \, dF \tag{1-13}$$

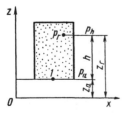

Figure 1-9 Determination of the pressure of a hot gas in a vessel at an arbitrary height in excess of atmospheric pressure at the same level.

3. The transverse distribution of the velocities in the pipe is hardly ever uniform. To simplify the solution of practical problems use is made of a fictitious mean velocity of the flow:

$$w_m = \frac{\int_F w \, dF}{F} = \frac{Q}{F} \tag{1-14}$$

from which

$$Q = w_m F \tag{1-15}$$

4. The volumetric flow rate and, consequently, the velocity of the gas flow depend on the fluid temperature, pressure, and humidity.*

If under normal conditions (0°C, 101.325 kPa, dry gas) the volumetric flow rate of the gas is Q_{nc} m³/s and the mean velocity is w_{nc} m/s, then under the operating conditions

$$Q_{op} = Q_{nc} \frac{T}{273} \frac{p_{nc}}{p_{op}} \left(1 + \frac{m}{0.804}\right) \tag{1-16}$$

and, correspondingly,

$$w_{op} = w_{nc} \frac{T}{273} \frac{p_{nc}}{p_{op}} \left(1 + \frac{m}{0.804}\right) \tag{1-17}$$

where m is the content of water vapor in the gas, in kg/m³; p_{op} is the operating gas pressure at the given location F, in Pa, and p_{nc} is the pressure of the gas under normal conditions, in Pa.

In the case of a dry gas at a pressure of 101.325 kPa ($p = p_{nc}$), the volumetric flow rate and, accordingly, the gas flow velocity under operating conditions are determined from the relations:

$$Q_{op} = Q_{nc} \frac{T}{273} \qquad w_{op} = w_{nc} \frac{T}{273}$$

The density of the gas at operating conditions is

$$\rho_{op} = (\rho_{nc} + m) \frac{273}{T} \frac{1}{1 + m/0.804} \frac{p_{op}}{p_{nc}} \tag{1-18}$$

where ρ_{nc} is the density of the dry gas at normal conditions, in kg/m³.

For a dry gas at a pressure of 101.325 kPa

$$\rho_{op} = \rho_{nc} \frac{273}{T}$$

*A perfect gas is considered, which obeys the equation $pv = RT$ and for which the internal energy is a function of the temperature alone.

Equation of Continuity of a Stream

1. The continuity equation is the result of application of the law of the conservation of mass to a moving medium (liquid, gas).

In the general case, the continuity equation can be written for any distribution of velocities in two pipe sections 0-0 and 1-1 (Figure 1-10) as

$$\int_{F_0} \rho_0 w \, dF = \int_{F_1} \rho_1 w \, dF \tag{1-19}$$

where subscripts 0 and 1 refer to the appropriate cross section.

In the case of an incompressible homogeneous medium the density across the pipe is always constant, and therefore

$$\rho_0 \int_{F_0} w \, dF = \rho_1 \int_{F_1} w \, dF$$

2. On the basis of Equations (1-13)–(1-15), the equation of continuity (the flow rate equation) for a uniform compressible flow and for any incompressible flow can be written as:

$$\left.\begin{array}{l} \rho_0 w_0 F_0 = \rho_1 w_1 F_1 = \rho w F = G \\ \rho_0 Q_0 = \rho_1 Q_1 = \rho Q = G \end{array}\right\} \tag{1-20}$$

where w_0 and w_1 are the mean velocities at sections 0-0 and 1-1, respectively, in m/s.

If the density of the moving medium does not vary long the flow, that is, $\rho_0 = \rho_1 = \rho$, the equation of continuity (flow rate) is of the form

$$w_0 F_0 = w_1 F_1 = w F \quad \text{or} \quad Q_0 = Q_1 = Q = \frac{G}{\rho}$$

Energy Equation (Bernoulli Equation) for Compressible and Incompressible Fluids

1. According to the law of conservation of energy for the medium moving through a pipe (channel), the energy of the liquid (gas) flow passing through section 0-0 per unit time (see Figure 1-10) is equal to the sum of energies of the liquid (gas) flow passing through section 1-1 per unit time plus the internal (thermal) and mechanical energies dissipated along the segment between these sections.

2. In the general case of an inelastic (liquid) and elastic (gas) flow with nonuniform transverse velocity and pressure distribution,* the corresponding energy equation will have the form

$$\int_{F_0} \left(p + \frac{\rho w^2}{2} + g\rho z + \rho U \right) w \, dF =$$

$$\int_{F_1} \left(p + \frac{\rho w^2}{2} + g\rho z + \rho U \right) w \, dF + \Delta N_{tot} \tag{1-21}$$

*Assuming no heat transfer and shaft work over the given segment.

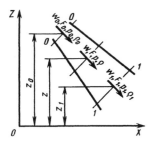

Figure 1-10 Scheme of the flow and its basic parameters for two sections of a channel.

where z is the geometric height of the centroid of the corresponding section, in m; p is the static pressure (absolute) at the point of the corresponding section, in Pa, U is the internal specific heat energy of the gas flow (which a frictionless flow would have had), in J/kg; and ΔN_{tot} is the total power lost over the segment between sections 0-0 and 1-1, which characterizes the value of the mechanical energy dissipated into heat, in W.

3. By relating the energy of the flow to the mass flow rate ($G = \int_F \rho w \, dF$), then, on the basis of Equation (1-21) we obtain

$$\Delta e_{tot} = \frac{\Delta N_{tot}}{G} = \frac{1}{G} \int_{F_0} \left(\frac{p}{\rho} + \frac{w^2}{2} + gz + U \right) \rho w \, dF$$

$$- \frac{1}{G} \int_{F_1} \left(\frac{p}{\rho} + \frac{w^2}{2} + gz + U \right) \rho w \, dF = e_0 - e_1 \qquad (1\text{-}22)$$

where

$$e_0 = \frac{1}{G} \int_{F_0} \left(\frac{p}{\rho} + \frac{w^2}{2} + gz + U \right) \rho w \, dF$$

and

$$e_1 = \frac{1}{G} \int_{F_1} \left(\frac{p}{\rho} + \frac{w^2}{2} + gz + U \right) \rho w \, dF$$

are the specific energies averaged over the mass flow rate through sections 0-0 and 1-1, respectively, in J/kg; $\Delta e_{tot} = \Delta N_{tot}/G$ is the total loss of the specific energy over the segment between sections 0-0 and 1-1, in J/kg.

Having divided Equation (1-22) by g, we obtain

$$\Delta H_{tot} = \frac{\Delta e_{tot}}{g}$$

$$= \frac{1}{G} \int_{F_0} \left(\frac{p}{g\rho} + \frac{w^2}{2g} + z + \frac{U}{g} \right) \rho w \, dF - \frac{1}{G} \int_{F_1} \left(\frac{p}{g\rho} + \frac{w^2}{2g} + z + \frac{U}{g} \right) \rho w \, dF$$

$$= H_0 - H_1$$

where

$$H_0 = \frac{1}{G} \int_{F_0} \left(\frac{p}{g\rho} + \frac{w^2}{2g} + z + \frac{U}{g} \right) \rho w \, dF$$

and

$$H_1 = \frac{1}{G} \int_{F_1} \left(\frac{p}{g\rho} + \frac{w^2}{2g} + z + \frac{U}{g} \right) \rho w \, dF$$

are the pressure heads averaged over the mass flow rate in sections 0-0 and 1-1, respectively, in *m*.

4. By relating the energy of the flow to the volumetric flow rate in a certain section, for instance, 0-0 ($Q_0 = \int_{F_0} w \, dF$), then

$$\Delta p_{tot} \equiv \frac{\Delta N_{tot}}{Q_0} = \frac{1}{Q_0} \int_{F_0} \left(p + \frac{\rho w^2}{2} + g\rho z + \rho U \right) w \, dF - \frac{1}{Q_0} \int_{F_1} \left(p + \frac{\rho w^2}{2} + g\rho z + \rho U \right) w \, dF$$

or

$$\Delta p_{tot} = \frac{1}{Q_0} \int_{F_0} \left(p + \frac{\rho w^2}{2} + g\rho z + \rho U \right) w \, dF - \frac{Q_1}{Q_0} \cdot \frac{1}{Q_1} \int_{F_1} \left(p + \frac{\rho w^2}{2} + g\rho z + \rho U \right) w \, dF$$

However,

$$\frac{Q_1}{Q_0} = \frac{\int_{F_0} \rho \, dF}{\int_{F_1} \rho \, dF} = \frac{\rho_0}{\rho_1}$$

and

$$\rho_0 Q_0 = \rho_1 Q_1 = G$$

therefore it is possible to write

$$\Delta p_{tot} \equiv \frac{\Delta N_{tot}}{Q_0} = \frac{1}{G} \int_{F_0} \left(p + \frac{\rho w^2}{2} + g\rho z + \rho U \right) w \, dF$$

$$- \frac{\rho_0}{\rho_1} \frac{1}{G} \int_{F_1} \left(p + \frac{\rho w^2}{2} + g\rho z + \rho U \right) \rho w \, dF = p_0^* - p_1^* \qquad (1\text{-}23)$$

where

$$p_0^* = \frac{1}{G} \int_{F_0} \left(p + \frac{\rho w^2}{2} + g\rho z + \rho U \right) w \, dF$$

is the total pressure averaged over the mass flow rate in section 0-0*

$$p_1^* = \frac{p_0}{p_1} \cdot \frac{1}{G} \int_{F_1} \left(p + \frac{\rho w^2}{2} + g\rho z + \rho U \right) \rho w \, dF$$

is the total pressure averaged over the mass flow rate in section 1-1 and reduced to the volumetric flow rate in section 0-0, that is, to Q_0; $\Delta p_{tot} = \Delta N_{tot}/Q_0$ are the total losses of the total pressure over the segment between sections 0-0 and 1-1 reduced to the volumetric flow rate Q_0.

5. In most practical cases, the static pressure p in straight-line flow is constant across the flow, even when the velocity distribution is greatly nonuniform. The variation of the gas density over the cross section due to varying velocities can then be neglected (with Ma $= w/a_1 < 1.0$). Therefore, in place of Equation (1-21) we can write

$$(p_0 + g\rho_0 z_0 + \rho_0 U)w_0 F_0 + \int_{F_0} \frac{\rho w^2}{2} \, dF =$$

$$(p_1 + g\rho_1 z_1 + \rho_1 U)w_1 F_1 + \int_{F_1} \frac{\rho w^2}{2} \, dF + \Delta N_{tot}$$

or, solving in ΔN_{tot} and taking into account Equation (1-20), we obtain

$$\Delta N_{tot} = (p_0 + N_0 \frac{\rho_0 w_0^2}{2} + g\rho_0 z_0 + \rho_0 U_0)Q_0 -$$

$$(p_1 + N_1 \frac{\rho_1 w_1^2}{2} + g\rho_1 z_1 + \rho_1 U_1)Q_1 \qquad (1\text{-}24)$$

where

$$N_0 = \frac{1}{F_0} \int_{F_0} \left(\frac{w}{w_0} \right)^3 dF$$

and

$$N_1 = \frac{1}{F_1} \int_{F_1} \left(\frac{w}{w1} \right)^3 dF$$

are the kinetic energy coefficients (the Coriolis coefficients) for sections 0-0 and 1-1, respectively; they characterize the degree of the nonuniformity of kinetic energy and velocity distributions over these sections.

*In the case of segments with nonuniform flow distribution over the cross section (when the stagnation temperature remains constant along the flow and when the energy losses are calculated from the total pressure measured at different points of the cross section) the total pressure logarithms should be averaged rather than the total pressure itself:

$$\ln p_m^* = \frac{1}{G} \int_G \ln p^* \, dG$$

However, for moderate nonuniformity of flow and at Ma < 1, the deviation from this rule does not cause appreciable error.[41]

6. By relating the energy of the flow to the mass flow rate, we obtain the generalized Bernoulli equation, which is written for a real fluid accoounting for the specific loss of energy (internal and external, that is, mechanical) over the segment considered,

$$\frac{p_0}{\rho_0} + N_0 \frac{w_0^2}{2} + gz_0 + U_0 = \frac{p_1}{\rho_1} + N_1 \frac{w_1^2}{2} + gz_1 + U_1 + \Delta e_{tot} \tag{1-25}$$

and correspondingly

$$\frac{p_0}{g\rho_0} + N_0 \frac{w_0^2}{2g} + z_0 + \frac{U_0}{g} = \frac{p_1}{g\rho_1} + N_1 \frac{w_1^2}{2g} + z_1 + \frac{U_1}{g} + \Delta H_{tot} \tag{1-26}$$

or

$$\Delta e_{tot} \equiv \frac{\Delta N_{tot}}{G} = \left(\frac{p_0}{\rho_0} + N_0 \frac{w_0^2}{2} + gz_0 + U_0 \right) - \left(\frac{p_1}{\rho_1} + N_1 \frac{w_1^2}{2} + gz_1 + U_1 \right)$$

$$= e_0 - e_1 \tag{1-27}$$

and

$$\Delta H_{tot} \equiv \frac{\Delta N_{tot}}{gG} = \left(\frac{p_0}{g\rho_0} + N_0 \frac{w_0^2}{2g} + z_0 + \frac{U_0}{g} \right) - \left(\frac{p_1}{g\rho_1} + N_1 \frac{w_1^2}{2g} + z_1 + \frac{U_1}{g} \right)$$

$$= H_0 - H_1$$

7. By relating the energy of the flow to the volumetric flow rate (for example, to Q_0) we obtain the Bernoulli generalized equation in the form

$$p_0 + N_0 \frac{\rho_0 w_0^2}{2} + g\rho_0 z_0 + \rho_0 U_0 = p_1 + N_1 \frac{\rho_1 w_1^2}{2} g\rho_1 z_1 + \rho_1 U_1 + \frac{\Delta N_{tot}}{Q_0}$$

$$= \left(p_1 + N_1 \frac{\rho_1 w_1^2}{2} + g\rho_1 z_1 + \rho_1 U_1 \right) \frac{p_0}{\rho_1} + \Delta p_{tot} \tag{1-28}$$

or

$$\Delta p_{tot} \equiv \frac{\Delta N_{tot}}{Q_0} = \left(p_0 + N_0 \frac{\rho_0 w_0^2}{2} + g\rho_0 z_0 + \rho_0 U_0 \right) - \left(p_1 + N_1 \frac{\rho_1 w_1^2}{2} + g\rho_1 z_1 + \rho_1 U_1 \right) \frac{p_0}{\rho_1}$$

$$= p_0'^* - p_1'^* \tag{1-29}$$

where

$$p_0'^* = p_0 + N_0 \frac{\rho_0 w_0^2}{2} + g\rho_0 z_0 + \rho_0 U_0$$

is the total pressure in section 0-0;

$$p_1'^* = p_1 + N_1 \frac{\rho_1 w_1^2}{2} + g\rho_1 z_1 + \rho_1 U_1$$

is the total pressure in section 1-1 reduced to the volumetric flow rate in section 0-0.

All the terms of Equation (1-28) are given in pressure units, that is, in Pa and are $g\rho_0 z_0$, $g\rho_1 z_1$, elevation pressure; p_0, p_1, static pressure; $N_0(\rho_0 w_0^2/2)$, $N_1(\rho_1 w_1^2/2)$, dynamic pressure; $\Delta p_{tot} \equiv \Delta N_{tot}/Q_0$, total losses of the total pressure (total hydraulic resistance) resulting from the overcoming of the hydraulic resistance of the segment between sections 1-1 and 2-2.

8. A change in the internal energy, $U_0 - U_1$, depends on the thermodynamic process that the gas undergoes on its way from sections 0-0 and 1-1. In the case of a polytropic process, the gas parameters change according to

$$\frac{p_0}{\rho_0^n} = \frac{p_1}{\rho_1^n} = \frac{p}{\rho^n} \tag{1-30}$$

where n is the polytropic exponent, which in many cases can be considered to be approximately constant for the short local resistance segment in view of the limitation of the section and to be lying within the limits $1 < n < k$ ($k = c_p/c_v$ is the isentropic exponent, cf. Table 1-4).

9. Based on the laws of thermodynamics,[68] with no heat addition from the outside

$$U_1 - U_0 = \int_{p_1}^{p_0} p \, dv = \frac{p_0}{\rho_0} - \frac{p_1}{\rho_1} - \int_{p_1}^{p_0} \frac{dp}{\rho}$$

$$= \frac{p_0}{\rho_0} - \frac{p_1}{\rho_1} - \frac{n}{n-1}\left(\frac{p_0}{\rho_0} - \frac{p_1}{\rho_1}\right) \tag{1-31}$$

where $v = 1/\rho$ is the specific volume of the gas, in m³/kg.

On the basis of Equations (1-27), (1-30), and (1-31) we obtain

$$\Delta e_{tot} = g(z_0 - z_1) + N_0 \frac{w_0^2}{2} - N_1 \frac{w_1^2}{2} + \frac{n}{n-1}\left(\frac{p_0}{\rho_0} - \frac{p_1}{\rho_1}\right)$$

or

$$\Delta e_{tot} = g(z_0 - z_1) + N_0 \frac{w_0^2}{2} - N_1 \frac{w_1^2}{2} - \frac{n}{n-1}\frac{p_0}{\rho_0}\left[\left(\frac{p_1}{p_0}\right)^{(n-1/n)} - 1\right] \tag{1-32}$$

10. In a number of cases, when performing approximate calculations, the process can be considered isentropic. For this process the polytropic exponent n in Equations (1-31) and (1-32) will be replaced by the isentropic exponent k.

11. In some cases the state of the flow is changed, following an isotherm (constant temperature). There the pressure is proportional to the gas density

$$\frac{p_0}{\rho_0} = \frac{p_1}{\rho_0} = \frac{p}{\rho} \tag{1-33}$$

$$\int_{p_1}^{p_0} \frac{dp}{\rho} = \frac{p_0}{\rho_0} \ln \frac{p_0}{p_1} \tag{1-34}$$

Then, on the basis of Equations (1-27) and (1-34), we obtain in the final form

$$\Delta e_{tot} = g(z_0 - z_1) + N_0 \frac{w_0^2}{2} - N_1 \frac{w_1^2}{2} - \frac{p_0}{\rho_0} \ln \frac{p_0}{p_1} \tag{1-35}$$

12. Gubarev[20] in his experiments demonstrated that in parts of the system such as fittings and converging wyes, the state of the gas follows a polytropic relation that is similar to an isotherm. Then, the polytropic exponent for air passing through a converging wye becomes $n \approx 1.0$ and for air passing through impedances, $n \approx 1.15$.

13. Formulas (1-32) and (1-35) can be used not only in the case of high gas flow velocities, but also in the case of low velocities when they are accompanied by large pressure drops over the segments of local resistance.

14. The basic similarity groups of gas flows are the Mach number or the reduced velocity $\lambda_c \equiv w/a_{cr}$

The Mach number is

$$\text{Ma} \equiv \frac{w}{a_1} \tag{1-36}$$

where a_1 is the speed of sound;

$$a_1 = \sqrt{k\frac{p}{\rho}} = \sqrt{kRT} \tag{1-37}$$

For air

$$a_1 \approx 20.1\sqrt{T}$$

15. The flow velocity equal to the local speed of sound and called the critical velocity is

$$a_{cr} = \sqrt{\frac{2k}{k+1}\frac{p^*}{\rho^*}} = \sqrt{\frac{2k}{k+1}RT^*} \tag{1-38}$$

where p^* is the pressure of the stagnated gas flow (total pressure); ρ^* is the density of the stagnated gas flow; T^* is the stagnated gas flow temperature (stagnation temperature).

The speed of sound in a stagnated medium is

$$a^* = \sqrt{k\frac{p^*}{\rho^*}} = \sqrt{kRT^*} \tag{1-39}$$

so that

$$a_{cr} = a^*\sqrt{\frac{2}{k+1}}$$

For air

$$a^* = 20.1\sqrt{T^*}$$
$$a_{cr} = 18.3\sqrt{T^*} \tag{1-40}$$

The reduced velocity is

$$\lambda_c \equiv \frac{w}{a_{cr}} = w \Big/ \sqrt{\frac{2k}{k+1}\frac{p^*}{\rho^*}} = w \Big/ \sqrt{\frac{2k}{k+1}RT^*} \tag{1-41}$$

16. Should an ideal gas jet with velocity $w_0 = w$ and having no energy losses ($\Delta e_{tot} = 0$) and no effect of heat be retarded isentropically (at $n = k$; $p_0 = p$; $\rho_0 = \rho$; $z_0 = z_1 = 0$; $N_0 = N_1 = 1$; $ap_1 = p^*$ is the total or stagnation pressure) up to velocity $w_2 = 0$, then Equation (1-32) will take the form

$$\frac{w^2}{2} = \frac{k}{k-1}\frac{p}{\rho}\left[\left(\frac{p^*}{p}\right)^{(k-1)/k} - 1\right]$$

whence

$$\frac{p^*}{p} = \left(1 + \frac{k-1}{k}\frac{w^2}{kp/\rho}\right)^{k/(k-1)}$$

or, taking into account equations (1-36) and (1-37)

$$\frac{p^*}{p} = \left(1 + \frac{k-1}{k}Ma^2\right)^{k/(k-1)} \tag{1-42}$$

17. There is the following relationship between the numbers Ma and λ_c

$$Ma = \sqrt{\frac{2}{k+1}}\frac{\lambda_c}{\sqrt{1 - \frac{k-1}{k+1}\lambda^2}} \tag{1-43}$$

or

$$\lambda_c = \frac{\sqrt{\frac{k+1}{2}}Ma}{\sqrt{1 + \frac{k-1}{2}Ma^2}}$$

On the basis of Equations (1-42) and (1-43) the following equation is obtained

$$\pi(\lambda_c) \equiv \frac{p}{p^*} = \left(1 - \frac{k-1}{k+1}\lambda_c^2\right)^{k/(k-1)} \tag{1-44}$$

Taking into account the relation analogous to relation (1-29), i.e.,

$$\frac{p^*}{p} = \left(\frac{\rho^*}{\rho}\right)^k \tag{1-45}$$

the density of a perfectly stagnated gas will be given by

$$\varepsilon(\lambda_c) \equiv \frac{\rho^*}{\rho} = \left(1 - \frac{k-1}{k+1}\lambda_c^2\right)^{1/(k-1)} \tag{1-46}$$

Correspondingly, the stagnation temperature is

$$\tau(\lambda_c) \equiv \frac{T^*}{T} = \left(\frac{\rho^*}{\rho}\right)^{k-1} = 1 - \frac{k-1}{k+1}\lambda_c^2 \tag{1-47}$$

The gas dynamic functions (1-44), (1-46), and (1-47) are presented in Table 1-10. This table also contains the functions that characterize the mass flux

$$q(\lambda_c) \equiv \frac{\rho w}{\rho_{cr} a_{cr}} = \left(\frac{k+1}{2}\right)^{1/(k-1)} \lambda_c \left(1 - \frac{k-1}{k+1}\lambda_c^2\right)^{1/(k-1)}$$

(this function is called the reduced density of mass flux) and

$$y(\lambda_c) \equiv \frac{F_{cr}p^*}{Fp} = \frac{q(\lambda_c)}{\pi(\lambda_c)} = \left(\frac{k+1}{2}\right)^{1/(k-1)} \frac{\lambda_c}{1 - \dfrac{k-1}{k+1}\lambda_c^2}$$

The quantity reciprocal to $y(\lambda_c)$ characterizes the change in the static momentum in the isentropic flow section depending on velocity.

Moreover, Table 1-10 contains also the function

$$\chi(\lambda_c) = \frac{k+1}{2k}\left(\frac{1}{\lambda_c^2} + 2\ln\lambda_c\right)$$

which makes it possible to calculate friction losses over the segment 0-1 (over the length $\bar{l} = l/D_h$):

$$\chi(\lambda_{c0}) - \chi(\lambda_{c1}) = \int_0^{\bar{l}} \lambda_{fr}\, d\bar{x}$$

18. The rate of mass flow is expressed in terms of the functions $q(\chi_c)$ and $y(\lambda_c)$:

$$G = m\frac{p^*Fq(\lambda_c)}{g\sqrt{T^*}} = m\frac{pFq(\lambda_c)}{\pi(\lambda)g\sqrt{T^*}} = m\frac{pFy(\lambda_c)}{g\sqrt{T^*}}$$

where m is the coefficient equal for air to $0.3965\ K^{0.5}\ s^{-1}$.

19. Expanding Equation (1-42) in a series by Newton's binomial rule, the following expression can be obtained for the total pressure

$$p^* = p + \frac{\rho w^2}{2}\left[1 + \frac{1}{4}\mathrm{Ma}^2 + \frac{(2-k)}{24}\mathrm{Ma}^4 + \cdots\right] =$$

$$p + \frac{\rho w^2}{2}(1 + \delta_{com}) \tag{1-48}$$

Table 1-10 Gasdynamic functions for a subsonic flow and the function $\chi(\lambda_v)$ at $k = 1.4$

λ_v	τ	π	ε	V	y	Ma	χ
0.01	0.99998	0.99994	0.99996	0.01577	0.01577	0.00913	8563.5
0.02	0.99993	0.99977	0.99983	0.03154	0.03155	0.01836	2136.14
0.03	0.99985	0.99948	0.99963	0.04731	0.04733	0.02739	946.367
0.04	0.99973	0.99907	0.99933	0.06306	0.06311	0.03652	530.195
0.05	0.99958	0.99854	0.99896	0.07879	0.07890	0.04565	337.720
0.06	0.99940	0.99790	0.99850	0.09450	0.09470	0.05479	233.271
0.07	0.99918	0.99714	0.99796	0.11020	0.11051	0.06393	170.368
0.08	0.99893	0.99627	0.99734	0.12586	0.12633	0.07307	129.599
0.09	0.99865	0.99528	0.99663	0.14149	0.14216	0.08221	101.692
0.10	0.99833	0.99418	0.99584	0.15709	0.15801	0.09136	81.7669
0.11	0.99798	0.99296	0.99497	0.17265	0.17387	0.10052	67.0543
0.12	0.99760	0.99163	0.99401	0.18816	0.18975	0.10968	55.8890
0.13	0.99718	0.99018	0.99297	0.20363	0.20565	0.11884	47.2209
0.14	0.99673	0.98861	0.99185	0.21904	0.22157	0.12801	40.3612
0.15	0.99625	0.98694	0.99065	0.23440	0.23751	0.13719	34.8430
0.16	0.99573	0.98515	0.98937	0.24971	0.25347	0.14637	30.3405
0.17	0.99518	0.98324	0.98300	0.26495	0.26946	0.15556	26.6212
0.18	0.99460	0.98123	0.98655	0.28012	0.28548	0.16476	23.5153
0.19	0.99398	0.97910	0.98503	0.29523	0.30153	0.17397	20.8966
0.20	0.99333	0.97686	0.98342	0.31026	0.31761	0.18319	18.6695
0.21	0.99265	0.97451	0.98173	0.32521	0.33372	0.19241	16.7609
0.22	0.99193	0.97205	0.97996	0.34008	0.34986	0.20165	15.1139
0.23	0.99118	0.96948	0.97810	0.35487	0.36604	0.21089	13.6836
0.24	0.99040	0.99680	0.97617	0.36957	0.38226	0.22015	12.4345
0.25	0.98958	0.96401	0.97416	0.38417	0.39851	0.22942	11.3378
0.26	0.98873	0.96112	0.97207	0.39868	0.41481	0.23869	10.3704
0.27	0.98785	0.95812	0.96990	0.41309	0.43115	0.24799	9.51321
0.28	0.98693	0.95501	0.96765	0.42740	0.44753	0.25729	8.75071
0.29	0.98598	0.95180	0.96533	0.44160	0.46396	0.26661	8.06987
0.30	0.98500	0.94848	0.96292	0.45569	0.48044	0.27594	7.45985
0.31	0.98398	0.94506	0.96044	0.46966	0.49697	0.28528	6.91153
0.32	0.98293	0.94153	0.95788	0.48352	0.51355	0.29464	6.41722
0.33	0.98185	0.93790	0.95524	0.49726	0.53018	0.30402	5.97035
0.34	0.97958	0.93418	0.95253	0.51087	0.54687	0.31341	5.56534
0.35	0.97958	0.93035	0.94974	0.52435	0.56361	0.32282	5.19738
0.36	0.97840	0.92642	0.94687	0.53771	0.58042	0.33224	4.86235
0.37	0.97718	0.92239	0.94393	0.55093	0.59728	0.34168	4.55665
0.38	0.97593	0.91827	0.94091	0.56401	0.61421	0.35114	4.27717
0.39	0.97465	0.91405	0.93782	0.57695	0.63120	0.36062	4.02120
0.40	0.97333	0.90974	0.93466	0.58975	0.64826	0.37012	3.78635
0.41	0.97198	0.90533	0.93142	0.60240	0.66539	0.37963	3.57055
0.42	0.97060	0.90083	0.92811	0.61490	0.68259	0.39917	3.37194
0.43	0.96918	0.89623	0.92473	0.62724	0.69987	0.39873	3.18890
0.44	0.96773	0.89155	0.92127	0.63943	0.71722	0.40830	3.01999
0.45	0.96625	0.88677	0.91775	0.65146	0.73464	0.41790	2.86393
0.46	0.96473	0.88191	0.91415	0.66333	0.75215	0.42753	2.71957
0.47	0.96318	0.87696	0.91048	0.67503	0.76974	0.43717	2.58590
0.48	0.96160	0.87193	0.90675	0.68656	0.78741	0.44684	2.46200
0.49	0.95998	0.86681	0.90294	0.69792	0.80517	0.45653	2.34705
0.50	0.95833	0.86160	0.89907	0.70911	0.82301	0.46625	2.24032
0.51	0.95665	0.85632	0.89512	0.72012	0.84095	0.47600	2.14113
0.52	0.95493	0.85095	0.89111	0.73095	0.85898	0.48576	2.04889
0.53	0.95318	0.84551	0.88704	0.74160	0.87711	0.49556	1.96305
0.54	0.95140	0.83998	0.88289	0.75206	0.89533	0.50538	1.88313
0.55	0.94958	0.83438	0.87868	0.76234	0.91366	0.51524	1.80866

Table 1-10 Gasdynamic functions for a subsonic flow and the function $\chi(\lambda_v)$ at $k = 1.4$ (continued)

λ_v	τ	π	ε	V	y	Ma	χ
0.56	0.94773	0.82871	0.87441	0.77243	0.93208	0.52511	1.73926
0.57	0.94583	0.82296	0.87007	0.78232	0.95062	0.53502	1.67454
0.58	0.94393	0.81714	0.86567	0.79202	0.96926	0.54496	1.61417
0.59	0.94198	0.81124	0.86121	0.80152	0.98801	0.55493	1.55783
0.60	0.94000	0.80528	0.85668	0.81082	1.00688	0.56493	1.50525
0.61	0.93798	0.79925	0.85209	0.81992	1.02586	0.57497	1.45676
0.62	0.93593	0.79315	0.84745	0.82881	1.04496	0.58503	1.41033
0.63	0.93385	0.78699	0.84274	0.83750	1.06418	0.59513	1.36753
0.64	0.93173	0.78077	0.83797	0.84598	1.08353	0.60526	1.32757
0.65	0.92958	0.77448	0.83315	0.85425	1.10301	0.61543	1.29025
0.66	0.92740	0.76813	0.82826	0.86231	1.12261	0.62563	1.25541
0.67	0.92518	0.76172	0.82332	0.87016	1.14235	0.63537	1.22289
0.68	0.92293	0.75526	0.81833	0.87778	1.16223	0.64615	1.19254
0.69	0.92065	0.74874	0.81327	0.88519	1.18225	0.65646	1.16423
0.70	0.91833	0.74217	0.80817	0.89238	1.20241	0.66682	1.13783
0.71	0.91598	0.73554	0.80301	0.89935	1.22271	0.67721	1.11321
0.72	0.91360	0.72886	0.79779	0.90610	1.24317	0.68764	1.09029
0.73	0.91113	0.72214	0.79253	0.91262	1.26378	0.69812	1.06894
0.74	0.90873	0.71536	0.78721	0.91892	1.28454	0.70864	1.04909
0.75	0.90625	0.70855	0.78184	0.92498	1.30574	0.71919	1.03064
0.76	0.90373	0.70168	0.77643	0.93082	1.32656	0.72980	1.01351
0.77	0.90118	0.69478	0.77096	0.93643	1.34782	0.74045	0.99762
0.78	0.89860	0.68783	0.76545	0.94181	1.36925	0.75114	0.98291
0.79	0.89598	0.68085	0.75989	0.94696	1.39085	0.76188	0.96931
0.80	0.89333	0.67383	0.75428	0.95187	1.41263	0.77267	0.95675
0.81	0.89065	0.66677	0.74863	0.95655	1.43460	0.78350	0.94518
0.82	0.88793	0.65968	0.74294	0.96099	1.45676	0.79439	0.93455
0.83	0.88518	0.65255	0.73720	0.96519	1.47910	0.80532	0.92479
0.84	0.88240	0.64540	0.73141	0.96916	1.50164	0.81631	0.91588
0.85	0.87958	0.63822	0.72559	0.97289	1.52439	0.82735	0.90775
0.86	0.87673	0.63101	0.71973	0.97638	1.54733	0.83844	0.90037
0.87	0.87385	0.62378	0.71383	0.97964	1.57049	0.84959	0.89370
0.88	0.87093	0.61652	0.70788	0.98265	1.59386	0.86079	0.88770
0.89	0.86798	0.60924	0.70191	0.98542	1.61745	0.87205	0.88234
0.90	0.86500	0.60194	0.69589	0.98795	1.64127	0.88337	0.87758
0.91	0.86198	0.59463	0.68984	0.99024	1.66531	0.89475	0.87339
0.92	0.85893	0.58730	0.68375	0.99229	1.88959	0.90619	0.86975
0.93	0.85585	0.57995	0.67763	0.99410	1.71411	0.91768	0.86662
0.94	0.85273	0.57259	0.67148	0.99567	1.73887	0.92925	0.86398
0.95	0.84958	0.56522	0.66530	0.99699	1.76389	0.94087	0.86381
0.96	0.84640	0.55785	0.65908	0.99808	1.76389	0.94087	0.86008
0.97	0.84318	0.55046	0.65284	0.99892	1.81469	0.96432	0.85876
0.98	0.83993	0.54307	0.64456	0.99952	1.84049	0.97614	0.85785
0.99	0.83665	0.53568	0.64026	0.99988	1.86657	0.98804	0.85731
1.00	0.83333	0.52828	0.63394	1.00000	1.89293	1.00000	0.85714

The correction for the effect of gas compressibility is

$$\delta_{\text{com}} = \frac{1}{4}\text{Ma}^2 + \frac{2-k}{24}\text{Ma}^4 \approx \frac{1}{4}\text{Ma}^2$$

For a jet of an incompressible fluid the total pressure is

$$p^* = p + \frac{\rho w^2}{2} \tag{1-49}$$

If the number $Ma \equiv w/a_1$ is very small, then Relation (1-48) is expressed in the form of Relation (1-49).

20. Table 1-11 presents the values of δ_{com}, δ_ρ, and ΔT_1 as functions of the number Ma_0 and of the air flow velocity w_0 ($k = 1.41$) at 0°C and 101.325 kPa.[68]

The correction for density is given by

$$\delta_\rho = \frac{\rho_0 - \rho_0}{\rho_0} = \left(\frac{p_1}{p_0}\right)^{1/k} - 1 \cong \frac{Ma_0^2}{2}\left(1 + \frac{Ma_0}{7} + \cdots\right)$$

and the correction for temperature is

$$\Delta T_1 = T_1 - T_0 = T_0\left[\left(\frac{p_1}{p_0}\right)^{k-1/k} - 1\right] = T_0\frac{k-1}{2} Ma_0^2 = 59.2\ Ma_0^2 \qquad (1\text{-}50)$$

The subscripts 0 and 1 relate to sections 0-0 and 1-1 of the given flow, respectively.

21. For an incompressible liquid, to which a gas at small flow velocities (practically up to $w \approx 150$ m/s) can also be referred, $U_0 \approx U_1$. Then, on the basis of Equation (1-27) we obtain

$$g\rho_0 z_0 + p_0 + N_0 \frac{\rho_0 w_0^2}{2} = \left(g\rho_1 z_1 + p_1 + N_1 \frac{\rho_1 w_1^2}{2}\right)\frac{\rho_0}{\rho_1} + \Delta p_{tot} \qquad (1\text{-}51)$$

or

$$\Delta p_{tot} = \left(g\rho_0 z_0 + p_0 + N_0 \frac{\rho_0 w_0^2}{2}\right) - \left(g\rho_1 z_1 + p_1 + N_1 \frac{\rho_1 w_1^2}{2}\right)\frac{\rho_0}{\rho_1} \qquad (1\text{-}52)$$

22. In the case of a small pressure drop (practically equal to about 10,000 Pa), $\rho_0 = \rho_1 = \rho$; then instead of Equation (1-51) we have

$$g\rho_0 z_0 + p_0 + N_0 \frac{\rho w_0^2}{2} = g\rho z_1 + p_1 + N_1 \frac{\rho w_1^2}{2}\bigg) + \Delta p_{tot} \qquad (1\text{-}53)$$

and with uniform flow velocity, when $N_0 = N_1 = 1$,

$$g\rho z_0 + p_0 + \frac{\rho w_0^2}{2} = g\rho z_1 + \frac{\rho w_1^2}{2}\bigg) + \Delta p_{tot}$$

or

$$\Delta p_{tot} = \left(g\rho z_0 + p_0 + \frac{\rho w_0^2}{2}\right) - \left(g\rho z_1 + p_1 + \frac{\rho w_1^2}{2}\right) \qquad (1\text{-}54)$$

Table 1-11 Dependence of δ_{com}, δ_ρ, and ΔT_1 on w_0 and Ma_0

w_0, m/s	34	68	102	136	170	203	238	272	306	340
Ma_0	0.1	0.2	0.3	0.4	0.5	0.6	0.7	0.8	0.9	1.0
δ_{com}, %	0.25	1.0	2.25	4.0	6.2	9.0	12.8	17.3	21.9	27.5
δ_ρ, %	0.50	2.0	4.5	8.0	12.9	18.9	26.8	35.0	45.3	57.2
ΔT_1, °C	0.59	2.4	5.4	9.5	14.8	21.3	29.0	37.8	48.0	59.2

Buoyancy or Net Driving Head (Self-Draught)

1. If we add to, and subtract the quantities p_{z_0} and p_{z_1} from each side of Equation (1-51), respectively, we obtain

$$g\rho z_0 + p_0 + p_{z_0} - p_{z_0} + N_0 \frac{\rho w_0^2}{2} = g\rho z_1 + p_1 + p_{z_1} + N_1 \frac{\rho w_1^2}{2} + \Delta p_{\text{tot}} \qquad (1\text{-}55)$$

where p_{z_0} and p_{z_1} are the values of the atmospheric pressure at heights z_0 and z_1, in Pa.
On the basis of Equation (1-11), we get

$$p_{z_0} = p_a - g\rho_a z_0; \quad p_{z_1} = p_a - g\rho_a z_1 \qquad (1\text{-}56)$$

where p_a is the atmospheric pressure in the reference plane (Figure 1-11), in Pa, and ρ_a is the average density of atmospheric air over the height z, in kg/m³. In the present case, the density is considered to be practically equal at the two-heights, z_0 and z_1, in kg/m³.
After performing suitable manipulation on Equation (1-55), we obtain

$$(\rho - \rho_a)g z_0 + (p_0 - p_{z_0}) + N_0 \frac{\rho w_0^2}{2}$$

$$= (\rho - \rho_a)g z_1 + (p_1 - p_{z_1}) + N_1 \frac{\rho w_1^2}{2} + \Delta p_{\text{tot}} \qquad (1\text{-}57)$$

2. On the basis of Equation (1-57), the loss of total pressure over the segment between sections 0-0 and 1-1 is

$$\Delta p_{\text{tot}} = (p_0 - p_{z_0}) - (p_1 - p_{z_1}) + N_0 \frac{\rho w_0^2}{2} - N_1 \frac{\rho w_1^2}{2} + g(\rho_a - \rho)(z_1 - z_0)$$

or in a simplified form

$$\Delta p_{\text{tot}} = (p_{0,\text{st}} - p_{1,\text{st}}) + (p_{0d} - p_{1d}) + p_s = p_{0,\text{tot}} - p_{1,\text{tot}} + p_s \qquad (1\text{-}58)$$

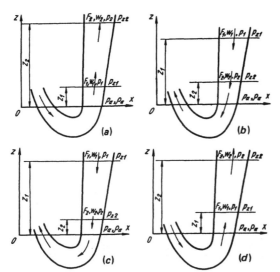

Figure 1-11 Choice of the ''self-draught'' (driving head, buoyancy) sign; (a) $\rho > \rho_a$; (b) $\rho < \rho_a$; (c) ρ_a; (d) $\rho < \rho_a$.

where $p_d = N(\rho w^2/2)$ is the dynamic pressure in the given section of the stream (always a positive value), in Pa; $p_{st} = p - p_z$ is the excess static pressure, that is, the difference between the absolute pressure p in the section of the stream at height z and the atmoshperic pressure p_z at the same height, in Pa; this pressure can be either positive or negative; and $p_{tot} = p_d + p_{st}$ is the total pressure in the given section of the stream, in Pa.

The excess elevation pressure (net driving head for gases) is

$$p_s = g(z_2 - z_1)(\rho_a - \rho) \tag{1-59}$$

3. The excess elevation pressure (net driving head) is produced by the fluid, which tends to descend or rise depending on the medium (lighter or heavier) in which the fluid is located. This pressure can be positive or negative depending upon whether it promotes or hinders the fluid flow.

If at $\rho > \rho_a$ the flow is directed upward (Figure 1-11a), and at $\rho < \rho_a$ downward (Figure 1-11b), the excess pressure p_s will be negative and will hinder the flow. If, on the other hand, at $\rho > \rho_a$ the flow is directed downward (Figure 1-11c), and at $\rho < \rho_a$ it is upward (Figure 1-11d), the excess pressure p_s will be positive and will enhance the flow.

4. By solving Equation (1-58) in the drop of total pressures $\Delta p_{tot} = p_{0,tot} - p_{1,tot}$ which determines the pressure developed by a supercharger, then

$$p_{sup} = \Delta p_{tot} = \Delta p_{tot} - g(z_1 - z_0)(\rho_a - \rho) = \Delta p_{tot} - p_s$$

When $\rho > \rho_a$ and the flow is directed upward or $\rho < \rho_a$ and the flow is directed downward, there is a negative driving head (elevation pressure). Then

$$p_{sup} = \Delta p_{tot} + p_s$$

Otherwise

$$p_{sup} = \Delta p_{tot} - p_s$$

In the general case

$$p_{sup} = \Delta p_{tot} \pm p_s$$

5. When the densities of the flowing medium, ρ, and of the surrounding atmoshpere, ρ_a, are equal and the pipes (flow channels) are horizontal, then the elevation pressure (net driving head) is zero. Then Equation (1-58) simplifies to:

$$\Delta p_{tot} = p_{0,tot} - p_{1,tot}$$

6. In cases when both the static pressure and the velocity are nonuniform over the cross section and this nonuniformity cannot be neglected, the total hydraulic resistance of the segment should be determined as the difference between the total pressures plus (or minus) the net driving head (if it is not zero):

$$\Delta p_{tot} = \frac{1}{Q} \int_{F_0} (p_{st} + p_d) w \, dF - \frac{1}{Q} \int_{F_1} (p_{st} + p_d) w \, dF + p_s$$

where $(1/Q)\int_{F_0}(p_{st} + p_d)w\,dF$ is the excess total pressure of the liquid (gas) stream passing through a given cross section F, in Pa, and $p_{st} + p_d$ is the excess total pressure in the given cross section, in Pa.

1-6 HYDRAULIC RESISTANCE OF NETWORKS

1. In each flow system, as well as in its separate segments, that portion of the total pressure which is spent in overcoming the forces of hydraulic resistance is irreversibly lost. The molecular and turbulent viscosity of the moving medium irreversibly converts the mechanical work of the resistance forces into heat. Therefore, the total energy (thermal energy inclusive) of the flow over the given segment of the pipe remains constant in the absence of heat conduction through the walls. However, in this case the state of the flow undergoes a change because of the pressure drop. The temperature, on the other hand, does not change at constant velocity. This can be attributed to the fact that the work of expansion due to a pressure drop is entirely converted into the work of overcoming the resistance forces and the heat generated by this mechanical work compensates for the expansion-induced cooling.

At the same time, the energy acquired by the flow resulting from the work of a compressor, fan, etc., in the form of kinetic or thermal energy, is lost for the given system during the discharge of the fluid into the atmosphere or into another reservoir.

2. Two types of the total pressure (hydraulic resistance) losses in the pipeline are considered:

- Pressure losses resulting from friction (frictional drag), Δp_{fr}
- Local pressure losses (local resistance), Δp_{loc}

The fluid friction loss is due to the viscosity (both molecular and turbulent) of real liquids and gases in motion, and results from momentum transfer between the molecules (in laminar flow) and between the individual particles (in turbulent flow) of adjacent fluid layers moving at different velocites.

3. The local losses of total pressure are caused by the following: local disturbances of the flow; separation of flow from the walls; and formation of vortices and strong turbulent agitation of the flow at places where the configuration of the pipeline changes or fluid streams meet or flow past obstructions (entrance of a fluid into the pipeline, expansion, contraction, bending and branching of the flow, flow through orifices, grids, or valves, filtration through porous bodies, flow past different protuberances, etc.). All of these phenomena contribute to the exchange of momentum between the moving fluid particles (i.e., friction), thus enhancing energy dissipation.

The local pressure losses also include the dynamic pressure losses occuring during liquid (gas) discharge from the system or network into another reservoir or into the atmosphere.

4. The phenomenon of flow separation and eddy formation is associated with the difference of velocities over the cross section of the flow and with a positive pressure gradient along the flow. The latter develops when the flow velocity is retarded (for example, in an expanding channel, downstream of a sharp bend, when passing a body) in accordance with the Bernoulli equation. The difference in velocities over the cross section of a negative pressure gradient (e.g., accelerated motion in a contracted channel) does not lead to flow separation. The flow in smoothly contracting segments is even more stable than over segments of constant cross section.

5. The total pressure losses in any complex element of the pipeline are inseparable. However, for ease of calculation they are arbitrarily subdivided, in each element of the

pipeline, into local losses (Δp_{loc}) and frictional losses (Δp_{fr}). It is also assumed that the local losses (local resistance) are concentrated in one section, although they can occur virtually throughout the entire length, except, of course, for the case of flow leaving the system, when its dynamic pressure becomes immediately lost.

6. The two kinds of losses are summed according to the principle of superposition of losses and consist of the arithmetic sum of the frictional and local losses:

$$\Delta p_{ov} = \Delta p_{fr} + \Delta p_{loc}$$

In fact, the value of Δp_{fr} should be taken into account only for relatively long fittings or only for elements (branch pipes, diffusers with small divergence angles, etc.), or when this value is commensurable with Δp_{loc}.

7. Present-day hydraulic calculations use the dimensionless coefficient of fluid resistance, which conveniently has the same value in dynamically similar flows, that is, flows over geometrically similar regions and with equal Reynolds numbers or other pertinent similarity criteria, irrespective of the kind of fluid or of the flow velocity (at least up to Ma $= 0.8$–0.9) and transverse dimensions of the segments being calculated.

8. The fluid resistance coefficient is defined as the ratio of the total energy (power) lost over the given segment $(0\text{-}0)$–$(1\text{-}1)$ to the kinetic energy (power) in the section taken (for example, $0\text{-}0$) or (which is the same) the ratio of the total pressure lost over the same segment to the dynamic pressure in the section taken, so that on the basis of Equations $(1\text{-}21)$ and $(1\text{-}23)$ for the general case, that is, for the case of nonuniform distribution of all the flow parameters over the section and of variable density along the flow, it is possible to write

$$\zeta \equiv \frac{\Delta N_{tot}}{\rho_0 F_0 w_0^3/2} = \frac{\Delta N_{tot}}{Q_0 \rho_0 F_0 w_0^2/2} = \frac{\Delta p_{tot}}{\rho_0 w_0^2/2} = \frac{p_0^* - p_1^*}{\rho_0 w_0^2/2}$$

$$= \frac{2}{\rho_0 w_0^2} \left[\frac{1}{G} \int_{F_0} \left(p + \frac{\rho w^2}{2} + g\rho z + \rho U \right) \rho w \, dF \right.$$

$$\left. - \frac{\rho_0}{\rho_i} \frac{1}{G} \int_{F_1} \left(p + \frac{\rho w^2}{2} + g\rho z + \rho U \right) \rho w \, dF \right] \qquad (1\text{-}60)$$

For the case of uniform distribution of static pressure and density over the section, but which are variable along the flow, the resistance coefficient based on Equation $(1\text{-}29)$ will acquire the form

$$\zeta \equiv \frac{\Delta N_{tot}}{\rho_0 F_0 w^3/2} = \frac{\Delta N_{tot}}{Q_0 \rho_0 F_0 w_0^2/2} = \frac{\Delta p_{tot}}{\rho_0 w_0^2/2} = \frac{p_0'^* - p_1'^*}{\rho_0 w_0^2/2}$$

$$= \frac{2}{\rho_0 w_0^2} \left[\left(p_0 + N_0 \frac{\rho_0 w_0^2}{2} + g\rho_0 z_0 + \rho_0 U_0 \right) \right.$$

$$\left. - \left(p_1 + N_1 \frac{\rho_1 w_1^2}{2} + g\rho_1 z_1 + \rho_1 U_1 \right) \right] \qquad (1\text{-}61)$$

If the density is invariable along the flow ($\rho_0 = \rho_1 = \rho = $ const.)

$$\zeta \equiv \frac{\Delta p_{tot}}{\rho w_0^2/2}$$

9. The value of ζ depends on the velocity, and consequently on the flow cross section. In a general case (ρ_i is variable along the flow) the resistance coefficient $\zeta_i \equiv (\Delta p_{tot})/(\rho_i w_i^2/2)$ based on the flow velocity w_i in the ith section (F_i) is calculated for another section (for example, F_0) using the formula

$$\zeta_0 \equiv \frac{\Delta p_{tot}}{\rho_0 w_0^2/2} = \zeta_i \frac{\rho_i}{\rho_0} \left(\frac{w_i}{w_0}\right)^2 \tag{1-62}$$

since

$$\Delta p_{tot} = \zeta_0 \frac{\rho_0 w_0^2}{2} = \zeta_i \frac{\rho_i w_i^2}{2}$$

Taking into account the flow rate equation $\rho_0 w_0 F_0 = \rho_i w_i F_i$, we obtain

$$\zeta_0 = \zeta_i \frac{\rho_0}{\rho_i} \left(\frac{F_0}{F_i}\right)^2 \tag{1-63}$$

When $\rho_0 = \rho_i = \rho$

$$\zeta_0 = \zeta_i \left(\frac{F_0}{F_i}\right)^2 \tag{1-64}$$

10. The overall fluid resistance of any network element is

$$\Delta p_{ov} = \Delta p_{loc} + \Delta p_{fr} = (\zeta_{loc} + \zeta_{fr}) \frac{\rho w^2}{2} = \zeta_{ov} \frac{\rho w^2}{2}$$

or

$$\Delta p_{ov} = \zeta_{ov} \frac{\rho_{op} w_{op}^2}{2} = \zeta_{ov} \frac{\rho_{op}}{2} \left(\frac{Q_{op}}{F}\right)^2 \tag{1-65}$$

In accordance with the arbitrarily accepted principle of superposition of losses we have

$$\zeta_{ov} = \zeta_{loc} + \zeta_{fr}$$

Here, $\zeta_{fr} \equiv \Delta p_{fr}/(\rho_{op} w_{op}^2/2)$ is the friction loss coefficient in the given element of pipe (channel); $\zeta_{loc} = \Delta p_{loc}/(\rho_{op} w_{op}^2/2)$ is the coefficient of local resistance of the given element of pipe (channel); w_{op} is the mean flow velocity at section F under the operating conditions, in m/s [see Equation (1-17)]; Q_{op} is the volumetric flow rate of a liquid or a working gas, m³/s [see Equation (1-16)]; ρ_{op} is the density of a liquid or a working gas, in kg/m³ [see Equation (1-18)]; and F is the cross-sectional area of the pipe (channel) element being calculated, in m².

11. The friction loss coefficient of the element considered is defined through the friction factor of hydraulics λ as:

$$\zeta_{fr} = \frac{\lambda \cdot l}{D_h}$$

The coefficients λ and, hence, ζ_{fr} at the constant value of l/D_h and incompressible flow, is a function of Re and of the roughness of the channel walls, $\overline{\Delta}_0 = \Delta_0/D_h$ or $\overline{\Delta} = \Delta/D_h$.

12. The local resistance coefficient ζ_{loc} is mainly a function of the geometric parameters of the pipe (channel) element considered and also of some general factors of motion, which include:

- The velocity distribution and the degree of turbulence at the entrance of the pipe element considered; this velocity profile, in turn, depends on the flow regime, the shape of the inlet, the shape of varous fittings and obstacles, and their distance upstream from the element considered, as well as the length of the preceding straight pipe;
- The Reynolds number; and
- The Mach number, $Ma \equiv w/a_1$.

13. The principle of superposition of losses is used not only for calculation of a separate element of the pipe (channel), but also in the hydraulic calculation of the entire network. This means that the sum of the losses in separate elements of the pipe (channel) yields the total resistance of the system. Here it is understood, of course, that the mutual enhancement or interference effect of the adjacent elements is taken into account.

14. The principle of superposition of losses can be realized by two methods: (1) by summing the total pressure losses in separate sections (elements) of the system; or (2) by summing the resistance coefficients of separate sections (elements), which were first normalized to a certain velocity and then expressing the total resistance of the system through its total coefficient of resistance.

In the first method, it should be taken into account that in the case of a great difference between the densitites of liquid (gas) over different sections (elements), the values of the total pressure losses, taken as the losses of energy (power) which are related to the volumetric flow rate $\Delta N_{tot}/Q = \Delta p_{tot}$ through a formula analogous to Equation (1-23), depend on the fact to which section of the channel this volumetric flow rate is related. Therefore, the losses in different sections should be summed only after their normalization to the same volumetric flow rate. Thus, when these losses are normalized to the flow rate Q_0 in section 0-0, then the total losses of the total pressure in the entire system will be

$$\Delta p_{sys} = \sum_{i=1}^{n} \frac{\Delta N_i}{Q_0} = \sum_{i=1}^{n} \frac{\Delta N_i}{Q_i} \frac{Q_i}{Q_0}$$

$$= \sum_{i=1}^{n} \Delta p_i \frac{\rho_0}{\rho_i} = \sum_{i=1}^{n} \zeta_i \frac{\rho_i w_i^2}{2} \frac{\rho_0}{\rho_i} = \sum_{i=1}^{n} \frac{\rho_0 w_i^2}{2} \tag{1-66}$$

where i is the number of the network section (element) being calculated; n is the total number of such sections (elements); $\Delta p_i = \Delta N_i/Q_i$ are the total (overall) losses of total pressure (resistance) in the ith section (element) of the system,* normalized to the volumetric flow rate of the medium Q_i through this section (element); $\zeta_i \equiv 2\Delta p_i/((\rho_i w_i^2)$ is the resistance coefficient of the given section (element) of the network normalized to the velocity w_i.

In the second method, the general resistance coefficient of the network is

$$\zeta_{0,sys} \equiv \frac{\Delta p_{sys}}{\rho_0 w_0^2/2} = \sum_{i=1}^{n} \zeta_{\phi i} = \sum_{i=1}^{n} \zeta_i \frac{\rho_0}{\rho_i} \left(\frac{F_0}{F_1}\right)^2 \tag{1-67}$$

---

*Here, the subscripts "tot" or "ov" at Δp and ζ for individual sections (elements) of the network are omitted.

where

$$\zeta_{\phi i} \equiv \frac{\Delta p_i}{\rho_0 w_0^2 / 2}$$

is the resistance coefficient of the given (ith) element of the network normalized to the velocity w_0 in the adopted section of the network F_0 [see Equation (1-63)]; ζ_i is the resistance coefficient of the given (ith) section (element) of the network normalized to the velocity w_i in the section F_i of the same section (element). Generally, the coefficient ζ_i includes also the correction for the mutual effect of adjacent elements of the network.

The total losses of the total pressure over the entire network are given by

$$\Delta p_{\text{sys}} = \zeta_{0,\text{sys}} \frac{\rho_0 w_0^2}{2} = \sum_{i=1}^{n} \zeta_{\phi i} \frac{\rho_0 w_0^2}{2} = \sum_{i=1}^{n} \zeta_i \frac{\rho_0}{\rho_i} \left(\frac{F_0}{F_1}\right)^2 \frac{\rho_0 w_0^2}{2}$$

$$= \sum_{i=1}^{n} \zeta_i \frac{\rho_0}{\rho_i} \left(\frac{F_0}{F_1}\right)^2 \frac{\rho_0}{2} \left(\frac{Q_0}{F_1}\right)^2$$

or

$$\Delta p_{\text{sys}} = \sum_{i=1}^{n} \zeta_i \frac{\rho_{\text{op}}}{\rho_{\text{ip}}} \left(\frac{F_0}{F_1}\right)^2 \frac{\rho_{\text{op}}}{2} \left(\frac{Q_{\text{op}}}{F_0}\right)^2 \tag{1-68}$$

and at $\rho_i = \rho_0 = \rho$

$$\Delta p_{\text{sys}} = \sum_{i=1}^{n} \zeta_i \left(\frac{F_0}{F_1}\right)^2 \frac{\rho_p}{2} \left(\frac{Q_0}{F_0}\right)^2 \tag{1-69}$$

1-7 DISTRIBUTION OF STATIC PRESSURE OVER THE SECTIONS OF A NETWORK OF RATHER HIGH RESISTANCE

1. The loss of specific energy over any (ith) segment in a network can be defined through the resistance coefficient of the given segment:

$$\Delta e_{i,\text{tot}} \equiv \frac{\Delta N_{i,\text{tot}}}{G} = \frac{\Delta N_{i,\text{tot}}}{G w_i^2 / 2} \frac{w_i^2}{2} = \zeta_i \frac{w_i^2}{2}$$

where $i = 1, 2, 3, \ldots$.
From this, the equation analogous to Equation (1-23) for two sections (i-I)–(i-I) and i-i takes the form

$$g z_{i-1} + \frac{p_{i-1}}{\rho_{i-1}} + N_{i-1} \frac{w_{i-1}^2}{2} + U_{i-1} = g z_i + \frac{p_i}{\rho_i} + U_i + (N_i + \zeta_i) \frac{w_i^2}{2}$$

The latter equation, together with Equations (1-30), (1-31), and (1-32) for the ith and (i-1)th sections, leads to the following relation allowing the calculation of the static pressure in section i-i if it is known for section (i-1)–(i-1):

$$\frac{p_i}{p_a} = \left\{ \left(\frac{p_{i-1}}{p_a} \right)^{(n-1)/n} + \frac{n-1}{n} \left[g\rho_{i-1}(z_{i-1} - z_i) \right. \right.$$

$$\left. \left. + N_{i-1} \frac{\rho_{i-1}w_{i-1}^2}{2} - (N_i + \zeta_i) \frac{\rho_{i-1}w_i^2}{2} \right] \left(\frac{p_{i-1}}{p_a} \right)^{-1/n} \frac{1}{p_a} \right\}^{n/(n-1)} \qquad (1\text{-}70)$$

In this case, all of the quantities with the subscript i-1 as well as ζ_i, N_i, z_i, and w_i are known (assigned or calculated). Only the quantity p_i/p_a is unknown.

2. In the majority of cases the process can be regarded to be isentropic. Then, the exponent n in Equation (1-70) can be replaced by k. For locking devices $n \approx 1.15$,[20] and Equation (1-70) acquires the form

$$\frac{p_i}{p_a} = \left\{ \left(\frac{p_{i-1}}{p_a} \right)^{0.13} + 0.13 \left[g\rho_{i-1}(z_{i-1} - z_i) + N_{i-1} \frac{\rho_{i-1}w_{i-1}^2}{2} \right. \right.$$

$$\left. \left. - (N_i + \zeta_i) \frac{\rho_{i-1}w_i^2}{2} \right] \left(\frac{p_{i-1}}{p_a} \right)^{-0.87} \frac{1}{p_a} \right\}^{7.67} \qquad (1\text{-}71)$$

For T-joints and other analogous shaped elements, when $n \approx 1$ and the pressure is proportional to the gas tensity [see Equation (1-33) in which, in a general case, the subscript will be i-1 and i, respectively],

$$\ln \frac{p_i}{p_{i-1}} = \frac{1}{p_{i-1}} \left\{ g\rho_{i-1}(z_{i-1} - z_i) + N_{i-1} \frac{\rho_{i-1}w_{i-1}^2}{2} \right.$$

$$\left. - (N_i + \zeta_i) \frac{\rho_{i-1}w_i^2}{2} \right] = A \qquad (1\text{-}72)$$

Then

$$\frac{p_i}{p_{i-1}} = e^A \quad \text{and} \quad p_i = p_{i-1}e^A$$

or

$$\frac{p_i}{p_a} = \frac{p_{i-1}}{p_a} e^A \qquad (1\text{-}73)$$

3. Pressure distribution along the network is calculated in the following order: using the quantitites which are given for initial section 0-0 ($i = 1$) and which enter, in the case of $n > 1$, into the right-hand side of Equation (1-70), the value of pressure p_1/p_a in section 1-1 is calculated. On the basis of Equations (1-20) and (1-30) the values of w_1 and ρ_1 are calculated and, correspondingly, the pressure p_2/p_a from Equation (1-71) for the sections 2-2 and so [Equations (1-20) and (1-30) are used with subscripts i-1 and i].

Analogously, calculations are also made for the case $n = 1$, using Equations (1-20), (1-33), and (1-73).

1-8 GENERALIZED FORMULAE OF RESISTANCE FOR HOMOGENEOUS AND HETEROGENEOUS SYSTEMS[9,10]

1. The total resistance to the motion of a Newtonian fluid can be considered as a sum of resistance forces:

1. Viscous forces that hinder the irrotational (laminar) motion of fluid;
2. Those opposing the change in the momentum of the system when secondary fluid flows originate in it under the influence of some external forces;
3. A group of driving forces that involve the projections of external forces onto the axis of motion, so that it is possible to write that the resistance force per unit volume of the system is

$$\frac{\Delta p}{L} = \frac{k_1 \eta w_0}{l^2} + \frac{n \rho w_0^2}{l} + \Sigma F_1 \pm \Sigma F_2$$

where $k_1 \eta w_0 / l^2$ is the viscous resistance force per unit volume of the system; w_0 is the flow velocity averaged over the channel section; $n \rho w_0^2 / l$ are the additional resistance forces per unit volume of the system that oppose the motion of fluid in the case of turbulent mode of flow and also during the flow through individual obstacles (local resistances); $\Sigma F_1 = \Sigma m_i w_i / V$ is the resistance force which is numerically equal to the sum of external forces per unit volume of the system that develop and suppress internal flows in it; this force follows from the momentum conservation law of the system (m_i and w_i are the mass and velocity of the volume element inside of which no internal motions originate any longer; V is the volume of region B [Figure 1-12]; ΣF_2 is the sum of the projections, onto the pipe axis, of the potential part of external forces which act on the fluid and which are related to the unit volume of the system; this sum of forces can be either a driving force (minus sign) or the resistance force (plus sign); k_1 is the coefficient of the shape (for a pipe of circular cross section $k_1 = 32$); l is the characteristic dimension (it is the diameter for a pipe and $l = D_h = 4F/\Pi$ for a channel), L is the length of the system segment considered; n is the proportionality factor; when the fluid flows through obstacles, it is equal to the coefficient of local resistances ζ_{loc}.

2. The internal flows can be induced by the influence of Archimedian forces on a fluid under the condition of heat ($\rho g \beta_t \Delta T$) or mass ($\Delta \rho g$) transfer (where β_t and ΔT are the termal coefficient of fluid expansion and the temperature head, respectively; $\Delta \rho$ is the difference of densities).

In electromagnetic fields, the internal flows in a system can originate under the action of a group of forces; these are induction electromagnetic forces that suppress the internal flows; conduction electromagnetic forces that result from the interaction of electric current with a current-conducting fluid and from the interaction of the magnetic field of the current with the external magnetic field; electromagnetic forces that originate during the interaction of an electric layer at the phase interfaces with the external electric and magnetic fields.[16,57] Internal forces can also originate, for example, during the flow of a fluid in a straight pipe rotating around its axis.[66]

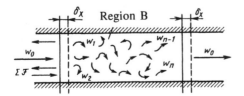

Figure 1-12 Scheme of internal eddy motion of fluid and of the effect of external forces on it.

3. In heterogeneous (nonuniform) systems, the phases of which have substantially different densities, the internal flows originate due to a relative motion of phases. In this case, the force per unit volume of the system that drives individual local particles is defined as

$$F = (\rho_p - \rho)g$$

where ρ_p is the density of a particle, in kg/m^3.

This motion is hindered by the viscous forces $k_1 \eta w_0 / l^2$ and by the forces ΣF_1 that follow from the momentum conservation law. Therefore, for one local particle these forces are

$$\Sigma F_1 = (\rho_p - \rho)g - k_1 \eta w_0 / l^2$$

In the case of the volumetric concentration of the dispersed phase μ_{con}, the forces that induce the internal flows in a unit volume of the system are

$$\Sigma F_1 = \left[(\rho_p - \rho)g - \frac{k_1 \eta w_0}{l^2} \right] \mu_{con}$$

4. Simple transformations of the expression $\Delta p / L$ make it possible to obtain the friction coefficient

$$\lambda = \frac{\Delta p}{L} \frac{2l}{\rho w_0^2} = \frac{2k_1}{B} \tag{1-74}$$

where

$$B = \frac{Re}{1 + \dfrac{n}{k_1} Re + \dfrac{\Sigma F_1 l^2}{k_1 \eta w_0} \pm \dfrac{\Sigma F_2 l^2}{k_1 \eta w_0}} \tag{1-75}$$

Equation (1-75) is a generalized criterion of hydrodynamic similarity. It follows from Equation (1-74) that the relationship between the resistance coefficient and the above-indicated criterion should be linear under any conditions of fluid motion in the system.

In particular, for a turbulent flow in straight circular pipes ($\Sigma F_1 = 0$ and $\Sigma F_2 = 0$) Equation (1-74) takes the form

$$\lambda = \frac{64}{Re} \left(1 + \frac{n}{32} Re \right) = \frac{64}{Re} + 2n$$

where n can be found by equating the values of λ from the latter relation to its values from Diagram 2-1. The function $n = f(Re)$ is presented in Table 1-12.

Table 1-12 The function $n = f(Re)$

Re	n	Re	n
0–2 × 10^3	0	10^5	0.0087
2.5 × 10^3	0.0042	10^6	0.006
4 × 10^3	0.0120	10^7	0.004
10^4	0.0128	10^8	0.003
2 × 10^4	0.0098		

5. When, during the fluid flow through pipes and channels, the external forces simultaneously contribute to and hinder the development of internal flows in the system (for example, during the motion of fluids having appreciable electrical conductivity, in a longitudinal magnetic field,[5,11,14,32,61] the generalized criterion of hydrodynamic similarity is

$$B = \frac{\mathrm{Re}}{1 + \frac{n}{32}\mathrm{Re} - \sqrt{\frac{n}{32}}\,\mathrm{Ha}}$$

where $\mathrm{Ha} = B_0 l \sqrt{\sigma/\eta}$ is the Hartman number (B_0 is the magnetic field induction; σ is the electrical conductivity of the fluid; $l = D_h$ is the hydraulic diameter).

In this case the resistance coefficient is

$$\lambda = \frac{64}{B} \tag{1-76}$$

6. During the flow of conducting fluids in pipes or channels in the transverse magnetic field, two cases are considered: (a) a plane-parallel flow in a channel when the magnetic field induction vector is normal to the large side of the magneto-hydrodynamic (MHD) channel;[11,14,37,61] for this case

$$B = \frac{\mathrm{Re}}{1 + \frac{n}{k_1}\mathrm{Re} - \left(\frac{n}{k_1}\right)^{0.5}\beta^{0.25}\mathrm{Ha} + \frac{\mathrm{Ha}}{\beta^{0.25}k_1^{0.5}}}$$

$$\lambda = \frac{2k_1}{B} \tag{1-77}$$

where $\beta = a/b$ is the aspect ratio of the channel; when $\beta = 1:15$ and $\beta = 1:17$, it was obtained that $k_1 = 44$ and for $\beta = 1:25$ that $k_1 = 32.7$; (b) the flow in the φ-field, when the magnetic induction vector is parallel to the large side of the MHD channel;[5,64] for this case

$$B = \frac{\mathrm{Re}}{1 + \frac{n}{k_1}\mathrm{Re} - \left(\frac{n}{k_1}\right)^{0.5}\beta^{0.25}\mathrm{Ha} + \frac{\mathrm{Ha}}{\beta k_1^{0.5}}}$$

whereas λ can be found from Equation (1-77); when $\beta = 14.5$, $k_1 = 44$; when $\beta = 32$, $k_1 = 48$.

The intermediate case is the MHD flow in a channel at $\beta = 1$ or in a circular pipe when λ is determined from Equation (1-76).

7. When a fluid flows in a bent pipe, the system experiences the centrifugal inertia forces. These forces bring about the redistribution of pressures over the section due to which transverse (secondary) flows originate. In this case λ is found from Equation (1-77) and

$$B = \frac{\mathrm{Re}}{1 + \frac{n}{k_1}\mathrm{Re} + \frac{m}{32}\sqrt{\frac{D}{2R}}\,\mathrm{Re}}$$

where D is the diameter of the pipe cross section; R is the mean radius of the pipe bent rounding; $m = 1.76 \times 10^{-1}$ for the laminar regime of flow; $m = 1.57 \times 10^{-2}$ for the turbulent regime of flow.

In coiled pipes the fluid flow varies simultaneously in two directions with the rounding radii R_1 and R_2. For this case the values of λ are found from Equation (1-77) and

$$B = \frac{\mathrm{Re}}{1 + \dfrac{n}{32}\,\mathrm{Re} + \dfrac{m}{32}\left[\left(\sqrt{\dfrac{D}{2R_1}}\,\mathrm{Re}\right)^2 + \left(\sqrt{\dfrac{D}{2R_2}}\,\mathrm{Re}\right)^2\right]^{0.5}}$$

For a fluid moving in a pipe the axis of which is normal to the rotation axis of this pipe, the fluid experiences the action of the Coriolis inertia forces that redistribute the pressure in the fluid and induce internal flows.[66] For this case, the values of λ are determined from Equation (1-77) and

$$B = \frac{\mathrm{Re}}{1 + \dfrac{n}{32}\,\mathrm{Re} + \dfrac{m}{16}\,\mathrm{Re}\,\dfrac{\omega D}{w_0} \pm \dfrac{R}{32D}\,\mathrm{Re}\,\dfrac{\omega^2 D^2}{w_0^2}}$$

where R is the mean radius of pipe rotation and ω is the angular speed of pipe rotation.

8. In the case of nonisothermal flow in pipes and channels, in the flow core and near the wall, the viscosities and densities of the fluid in the flow core and near the wall can be substantially different due to the difference of temperatures of the fluid in these zones, and this leads to the origination of internal flows (heat convection).

For this case

$$B = \frac{\mathrm{Re}}{1 + \dfrac{n}{k_1}\,\mathrm{Re} + \dfrac{2\delta}{k_1 l}\,\dfrac{\rho g \beta_t \Delta T l^2}{\eta w_0}}$$

where

$$l = D_h$$

$$\delta \approx 3 \times 10^{-4} - 5 \times 10^{-4}\ \mathrm{m}$$

During the pipe flow of different oils the coefficient λ is found from Equation (1-77) and for the channel flow $\lambda = 77.4/B$.

In the case of nonisothermal flow of low-viscous fluids (for example, water) the thermal convection even at small temperature differences can substantially influence the resistance, and in this case

$$B = \frac{\mathrm{Re}}{1 + \dfrac{n}{32}\,\mathrm{Re} \pm \dfrac{\rho g \beta_t \Delta T D^2}{32 \eta w_0}}$$

9. The forces that induce internal flows in a heterogenous system due to the relative motion of phases depend on both the difference of the densities of the fluid and dispersed

particles and the characteristic dimension and shape of these particles and the velocity of their motion in the fluid.

In the case of the flow of suspensions in straight hydraulically smooth pipes, the generalized hydrodynamic criterion is defined as

$$B = \frac{\text{Re}}{1 + \dfrac{n}{32}\,\text{Re} + \dfrac{[(\rho_p - \rho)g - k_2\eta w_2/l_2^2]\mu D^2}{32\eta w_0}}$$

where w_2 is the velocity of the relative motion of a disperse particle in the fluid; k_2 is the coefficient of the shape of the disperse particle (for a sphere, $k_2 = 12$); l_2 is the characteristic dimension of the particle (for a sphere, $l_2 = d_{\text{loc}}$).

For the pipe flow of dusted streams, when the density of solid particles ρ_p is much smaller than the gas density ρ, the latter quantity can be neglected. Then

$$B = \frac{\text{Re}}{1 + \dfrac{n}{32}\,\text{Re} + \dfrac{[\rho_p g - k_2\eta w_2/l_2^2]\mu D^2}{32\eta w_0}}$$

For the pipe of gas-liquid mixtures, $\rho \gg \rho_2$ (where ρ_2 is the density of gas bubbles); therefore

$$B = \frac{\text{Re}}{1 + \dfrac{n}{32}\,\text{Re} + \dfrac{[\rho g - k_2\eta w_2/l_2^2]\mu D^2}{32\eta w_0}}$$

In all three cases the resistance coefficient λ can be taken according to Equation (1-77).

1-9 LIQUID AND GAS FLOW THROUGH AN ORIFICE

Flow of an Incompressible Fluid

1. The velocity w_{con} of jet discharge for an incompressible fluid passing from the exit section of a submerged nozzle or orifice in the wall of vessel A into vessel B (Figure 1-13), is expressed, based on the Bernoulli and continuity equations, by the following formula:*

$$w_{\text{con}} = \varphi \sqrt{\frac{2}{\rho}} \sqrt{g\rho(z_1 - z_2) + (p_1 - p_2)}$$

where the velocity coefficient φ has the form:

$$\varphi = \frac{1}{\sqrt{\zeta_{\text{con}}(1 - 2) + \varepsilon^2[N_2(F_0/F_2)^2 - N_1(F_0/F_1)^2]}} \tag{1-78}$$

*In the case of a gas flow, the quantities z and l are neglected.

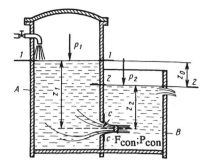

Figure 1-13 Discharge from a submerged orifice.

Here, z_1 and z_2 are the depths to which the center of gravity of the orifice (nozzle) is submerged relative to the free liquid level in vessels A and B, respectively, in m; p_1 and p_2 are the pressures on the free surface in respective vessels (sections 1-1 and 2-2), in Pa; N_1 and N_2 are the kinetic energy coefficients in sections 1-1 and 2-2; F_1 and F_2 are the areas of these cross sections, in m²; $\epsilon = F_{\mathrm{con}}/F_0$ is the coefficient of contraction of the nozzle exit section (for an orifice in a thin wall it is the coefficient of jet contraction in the narrowest cross section of the jet); F_{con} is the area of the jet (not of the nozzle) cross section at the exit from the nozzle; in the case of an orifice in a thin wall (Figure 1-14), F_{con} is the area of the contracted cross section of the jet, in m²; F_0 is the area of the exit cross section of the nozzle (orifice), in m²; and $\zeta_{(1-2)} = \Delta p_{(1\text{-}2)}/(\rho w_{\mathrm{con}}^2/2)$ is the resistance coefficient of the entire flow path from section 1-1 to section 2-2 reduced to the velocity w_{con}.

2. In the general case of the flow from vessel A into vessel B (see Figure 1-13), the pressure losses consist of the losses over the stretch from section 1-1 to the exit from the nozzle or orifice (section c-c) and shock losses at the jet expansion from the narrow section c-c at the exit from the nozzle (orifice) to section 2-2, that is,

$$\zeta_{\mathrm{con}(1-2)} = \zeta_{\mathrm{con,noz}} - 1 + \zeta_{\mathrm{sh}} = \zeta_{\mathrm{con,noz}} - 1 + \left(1 - \varepsilon\frac{F_0}{F_2}\right)^2$$

$$= \zeta_{\mathrm{con,noz}} - 2\varepsilon\frac{F_0}{F_2} + \left(\frac{F_0}{F_2}\right)^2$$

where $\zeta_{\mathrm{con,noz}}$ is the total resistance coefficient of the nozzle or orifice, which also includes the dynamic pressure losses at the exit, reduced to the velocity w_{con}.

The resistance coefficient $\zeta_{\mathrm{con}(1-2)}$ can be expressed in terms of the resistance coefficient $\zeta_{0(1-2)} = \Delta p_{1-2}/(\rho w_0^2/2)$, reduced to the mean velocity w_0 at the exit from the nozzle (orifice):

$$\zeta_{\mathrm{con}(1-2)} = \zeta_{0(1-2)}\left(\frac{w_0}{w_{\mathrm{con}}}\right)^2 = \zeta_{0(1-2)}\varepsilon^2 = \left[\zeta_{0,\mathrm{noz}} - 2\varepsilon\frac{F_0}{F_2} + \left(\frac{F_0}{F_2}\right)^2\right]\varepsilon^2$$

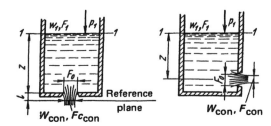

Figure 1-14 Discharge from a vessel through an orifice in the bottom or wall.

whence, having substituted into Equation (1-78), we obtain

$$\phi = \frac{1}{\varepsilon\sqrt{\zeta_{0,noz} - 2\varepsilon^{F_0/F_2} + (F_0/F_2)^2 + N_2(F_0/F_2)^2 - N_1(F_0/F_1)^2}}$$

3. In the case of the liquid flow from vessel A into vessel B of large volume, that is, at $F_0 \ll F_2$

$$\phi = \frac{1}{\varepsilon\sqrt{\zeta_{0,noz} - N_1(F_0/F_1)^2}}$$

while at $F_0 \ll F_1$

$$\phi = \frac{1}{\varepsilon\sqrt{\zeta_{0,noz}}}$$

When the flow discharges from vessel A through a nozzle in the bottom of the vessel its velocity is

$$w_{con} = \phi\sqrt{\frac{2}{\rho}}\sqrt{g\rho(z + l) + (p_1 - p_{con})}$$

where l is the distance from the exit orifice to the reference plane (Figure 1-14), in m, and p_{con} is the static pressure at the exit from the nozzle (or in a contracted jet section behind the orifice in a thin wall), in Pa.

4. The volumetric flow rate of an incompressible fluid through a nozzle (orifice) in the side wall of the vessel is

$$Q = w_{con}\varepsilon F_0 = \phi\varepsilon F_0\sqrt{2/\rho[g\rho(z_1 - z_2) + (p_1 - p_2)]}$$

$$= \mu F_0\sqrt{2/\rho[g\rho(z_1 - z_2) + (p_1 - p_2)]} \qquad (1\text{-}50)$$

and through the bottom of the vessel

$$Q = \mu F_0\sqrt{2/\rho[g\rho(z_1 + l) + (p_1 - p_{con})]}$$

When p_1, p_2, and p_{con} are equal to atmospheric pressure, the fluid flow rate through the nozzle in the side wall of the vessel is

$$Q = \mu F_0\sqrt{2g(z_1 - z_2)}$$

through the vessel bottom is

$$Q = \mu F_0\sqrt{2g(z_1 + l)}$$

5. The coefficient of discharge, μ, through an orifice in a thin wall depends on the shape of its inlet edge, on the area ration F_0/F_1, and on the Reynolds number (because ε, φ, and ζ depend on these parameters).

6. The coefficient of discharge, μ, through nozzle in the bottom or in the wall of a vessel can vary over wide ranges (from zero to values above unity, since the shape and

other parameters of the nozzles can vary significantly). The coefficient of discharge is also a function of the Reynolds number Re_T, Froude number $Fr = 2P_{dis}/gD_0$, and of the Weber number $We = 2p_{dis}\rho D_0/\sigma$, where σ is the coefficient of surface tension of the liquid. At $Fr \geq 10$ and $We \geq 200$, the influence of gravitational and surface forces on the discharge coefficient can be neglected.

7. The dependence of the coefficients ε, φ, and μ for an orifice in a thin wall on Re_T = $w_T D_0/\nu$, where $w_T = \sqrt{2/\rho[g\rho z + p_1 - p_{con}]}$ is the theoretical velocity of discharge through an orifice in the contracted jet section at $w_1 = 0$ and D_0 is the orifice diameter, can be determined at $F_0/F_1 = 0$ from the curves of Figure 1-15. The function $\mu = f(Re_0)$ at small Re_0 ($Re_0 = w_0 D_0/\nu = \mu Re_T$) is given in Figure 1-16.

8. The values of μ for orifices and nozzles of certain shapes (Figure 1-17) can be determined from Table 1-13 and from Figure 1-18 and 1-19.

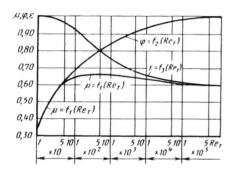

Figure 1-15 Velocity coefficient φ, coefficient of filling the section (jet contraction) ε, and coefficient of discharge μ through an orifice in a thin wall plotted against Reynolds number Re.[2]

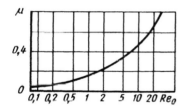

Figure 1-16 Dependence of the discharge coefficient on Re number (small Re's) for discharge from orifices.[2]

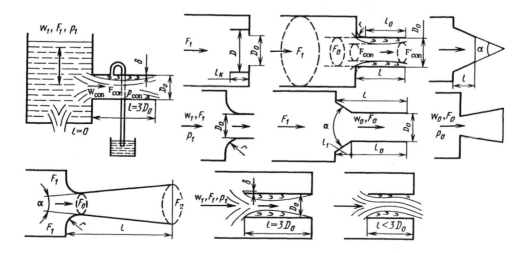

Figure 1-17 Discharge from a vessel through various nozzles.

Table 1-13 Values of the Discharge Coefficients μ

Shape of the orifice, nozzle	Formulae for calculation of μ	
	At different F_0/F_1	At $F_0/F_1 \to 0$
Orifice in a thin ($l/D_0 \leqslant 0.1$) wall (bottom) of a vessel[2,27] (Figure 1-17,a)		
$Re_0 = \dfrac{w_0 D_0}{\nu} \geqslant 10^5$	$\mu = \dfrac{1}{1 + 0.707\sqrt{1 - F_0/F_1}}$	$\mu \approx 0.59$
$Re_0 \leqslant 10$	—	$\mu \approx \sqrt{\dfrac{Re_0}{25.2 + Re_0}}$
$10 < Re_0 \leqslant 40$	—	$\mu \approx \dfrac{Re_r}{10 + 1.5 Re_r}$
$40 < Re_r \leqslant 300$	—	$\mu \approx \dfrac{Re_r}{5 + 1.5 Re_r}$
$300 < Re_r \leqslant 10^4$	—	$\mu \approx 0.59 + \dfrac{0.27}{Re_r^{1/6}}$
$10^4 < Re_r < 10^5$	—	$\mu \approx 0.59 + \dfrac{B_1}{\sqrt{Re_r}}$
		$B_1 = 5.5$ for a circular section;[2] $B_1 = 8.9$ for a rectangular section[60]
Orifice in a thin wall with a thickened inlet edge (Figure 1-17,b) at $\dfrac{D - D_0}{D_0} = 0.11$ and $l_{ch}/D_0 = 0.5$ (optimal parameters); $F_0/F_1 > 4$–5 $Re = 2.6 \times 10^4 \div 4 \times 10^{413}$	—	0.925
Orifice with a rounded inlet ($r/D_0 > 0$) (canoidal nozzle, Figure 1-17,c) $Re \geqslant 10^{5,27}$	$\mu = \dfrac{1}{\sqrt{1.07 - 0.07 F_0/F_1}}$	0.97
External cylindrical nozzle:[31] sharp inlet edge (Figure 1-17,a,d); $F_0/F_1 > 4$–5; $l/D_0 = 1$–7	$\mu = \sqrt{a_0^2 + 0.463} - a_0$ $a_0 = \dfrac{14.8}{l/D_0} + \dfrac{5.8}{Re_r}$	—
$Re_r < 10^2\, l/D_0$		
$10^2\, l/D_0 < Re_r < 3 \times 10^{-3}\, l/D_0$	$\mu = \sqrt{b_0^2 + 0.588} - b_0$ $b_0 = \dfrac{25}{l/D_0} + \dfrac{7.4}{Re_r}$	

0.82

—

$3 \times 10^{-3} \, l/D_0 < Re_r < 10^5$

$$\mu = \cfrac{1}{\sqrt{1.5 + \cfrac{0.336}{Re_r^{0.25}} \, l/D_0}}$$

$Re \geq 10^{5}$[27]

Rounded inlet edge ($r/D_0 > 0$; Figure 1-17,d):

$F_0/F_1 > 4\text{-}5$
$Re_r < 10 \, l/D_0$

$$\mu = \cfrac{1}{\sqrt{1.5 - 0.5F_0/F_1}}$$

$\mu = \sqrt{a_2^2 + 0.5} - a_2$ (a)

$a_2 = \cfrac{16}{Re_r}(0.25r/D_0 + l_0/D_0) + \cfrac{6.3}{Re_r}$

for $l_0/D_0 < 0.5$

$\mu = \sqrt{b_2^2 + 0.714} - b_2$ (b)

$b_2 = \cfrac{30.4}{Re_r}(0.25r/D_0 + l_0/D_0) + \cfrac{90}{Re_r}$

$10 \, l/D_0 < Re_r < 10^2 \, l/D_0$

at $l_0/D_0 > 0.5$
μ by formula (a)
μ by formula (b)

$10^2 \, l/D_0 < Re_r < 10^3 \, l/D_0$
$Re_r > 10^3 \, l/D_0$

$$\mu = \cfrac{1}{\sqrt{N_0 + \zeta_r + \cfrac{0.33}{Re_r^{0.25}}(0.25r/D_0 + l_0/D_0)}}$$

N_0 from Diagrams 4-2 and 4-3:
ζ_r from Diagram 3-4

Outer cylindrical nozzle, conical inlet
(Figure 1-17,e):
$F_0/F_1 > 4\text{-}5$[31]

$\mu = \sqrt{a_3^2 + 0.476} - a_3$
$a_3 = \cfrac{15.2}{Re_r}(nl_1/D_0 + l_c/D_0) + \cfrac{6.0}{Re_r}$ (a)

$Re_r \leq 10 \, l/D_0$

n — from the table

α°...0	10	20	40	60	80	100	120
n	0.63	0.46	0.26	0.13	0.04	0.02	0.01
	At $l_0/D_0 < 0.05$						
c...1.70	1.41	1.40	1.42	1.45	1.48	1.53	1.56
	At $l_0/D_0 > 0.05$						
c...1.70	1.56	1.48	1.41	1.43	1.45	1.50	1.54

Table 1-13 Values of the Discharge Coefficients μ (continued)

Shape of the orifice, nozzle	Formulae for calculation of μ	
	At different F_0/F_1	At $F_0/F_1 \to 0$
At $l_0/D_0 \leq 0.5 l/D_0$ $10l/D_0 < Re_t < 60l/D_0$ $$\mu = \sqrt{b_3^2 + \frac{25.2}{2cRe_t}} - b_3 \text{ (b)}$$ $$b_3 = \frac{85}{2cRe_t}\left(nl_1/D_0 + l_0/D_0 + \frac{25.2}{2cRe_t}\right)$$ n and c — from the table At $l_0/D_0 > 0.5 l/D_0$: μ — from formula (a) μ — from formula (b) $60l/D_0 < Re_t, 10^3 l/D_0$ $Re_t > 2 \times 10^3$ $$\mu = \frac{1}{\sqrt{N_0 + \zeta_k + \frac{0.33}{Re_t^{0.25}}(nl_1/D_0 + l_0/D_0)}}$$ N_0 — from Diagrams 4-2 and 4-3 ζ_k — from Diagram 3-7 $$\mu = \frac{1}{\sqrt{1.2 - 0.2F_0/F_1}}$$		
External conical converging nozzle ($\alpha = 13°$; Figure 1-17,e) $Re_t \geq 10^5$		0.92
External conical diverging nozzle; sharp inlet edge $F_2/F_0 = 2$; $\alpha = 15°$ (Figure 1-17,i) $Re_t \geq 10^5$		0.65–0.7
External smoothly converging-diverging nozzle (Venturi tube) ($\alpha = 6$–$8°$; $F_2/F_0 = 4$–5 (Figure 1-17, k)[27]		–

$Re \times 10^{-5}$	1	2	3	4	≥ 6
μ	2.15	2.32	2.43	2.50	2.52

Internal cylindrical nozzle:
inlet edge of different thicknesses ($\delta/D_0 > 0$);
$F_0/F_1 > 4$–5; $l/D_0 = 3$ (Figure 1-17, *l*)
$Re_f < 2 \times 10^4$[48]

At any δ/D_0

Re_f	...	5	10	20	50	100	200
μ	...	0.03	0.05	0.11	0.21	0.34	0.46

At certain values of δ/D_0

Re_f	...	500	10^3	2×10^3	10^4
At $\delta/D_0 = 0.004$–0.006					
μ	...	0.57	0.64	0.69	0.70
At $\delta/D_0 = 0.02$–0.03					
μ	...	0.59	0.66	0.72	0.75
At $\delta/D_0 = 0.04$					
μ	...	0.62	0.70	0.75	0.80

Sharp inlet edge ($\delta/D_0 \cong 0$); $l/D_0 = 3$
(Figure 1-17,*l*)
$Re > 10^5$[27]

$$\mu = \frac{1}{\sqrt{2 - F_0/F_1}}$$ ... 0.7

Internal cylindrical nozzle. Inlet edge is
of different thicknesses ($\delta/D_0 > 0$); $l/D_0 < 3$;
$F_0/F_1 > 4$-5
Stalling flow (Figure 1-17.*m*)[48]

$$\mu = 0.495 + 4\delta/D_0$$ ... —

For a compressible fluid[45]

$$\mu_{comp} \cong \mu + \frac{Ma^2_{comp}}{8} + \frac{Ma^4}{80}$$ ... —

$Ma_{comp} = \dfrac{w_{comp}}{a}$ — is the Mach number

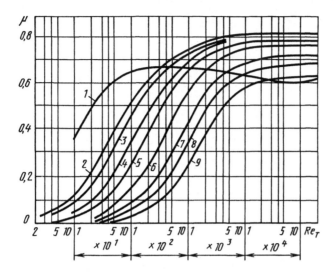

Figure 1-18 Dependence of the discharge coefficient on the Reynolds number Re for discharge from outer cylindrical nozzles:[55] (1) discharge coefficient for orifices in a thin wall; the length of the nozzle; (2) 1d; (3) 1.5d; (4) 3d; (5) 5d; (6) 10d; (7) 20d; (8) 30d; (9) 50d.

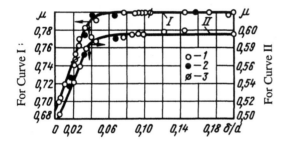

Figure 1-19 Dependence of the discharge coefficient on the relative thickness of the wall for the inner cylindrical nozzle:[48] (1) d = 10 mm; (2) d = 15 mm; (3) d = 30 mm.

Discharge of a Compressible Gas

1. When a gas (vapor, air) issues at high pressure into the atmoshpere, a significant change occurs in its volume. Therefore, it is necessary to take into account the compressibility of the gas. Neglecting the nozzle losses for an ideal gas and the effect of its mass, the velocity of the adiabatic discharge can be determined from the Saint-Wantzel formula as:

$$w_0 = \sqrt{2 \frac{k}{k-1} \frac{p_1}{\rho_1} \left[1 - \left(\frac{p_0}{p_1}\right)^{(k-1)/k} \right]} \qquad (1\text{-}79)$$

and the mass discharge G, with allowance for losses in the nozzle ($\mu = 1/\sqrt{\zeta}$):

$$G = \mu F_0 \sqrt{\frac{2k}{k-1} \rho_1 p_1 \left[\left(\frac{p_0}{p_1}\right)^{2/k} - \left(\frac{p_0}{p_1}\right)^{(k+1)/k} \right]} \qquad (1\text{-}80)$$

where the subscript 1 indicates that the respective quantities refer to the section of the pipe (vessel) upstream of the constricted nozzle section, and 0, to the smallest section of the nozzle or to the medium into which the gas issues.

2. At the given pressure p_1 and density ρ_1 in the vessel, the discharge velocity and the mass discharge at the given F_0 depend on the pressure of the medium into which the gas issues, i.e., on the ratio p_0/p_1.

With decrease in p_0/p_1, the discharge velocity w_0 increases until this ratio becomes equal to the critical pressure ratio:

$$\frac{p_0}{p_1} = \left(\frac{p_0}{p_1}\right)_{cr} = \left(\frac{2}{k+1}\right)^{k/(k+1)}$$

When $p_0/p_1 = (p_0/p_1)_{cr}$, the velocity in the nozzle throat F_0 is equal to the speed of sound in the given medium.

With a further decrease in p_0/p_1, the velocity in the smallest cross section remains equal to the local speed of sound

$$w_{cr} = a_{cr} = \sqrt{\frac{2k}{k+1} RT_1} = \sqrt{\frac{2k}{k+1} \frac{p_1}{\rho_1}}$$

Thus, with decrease of the pressure ratio below the critical value the mass flow rate of the gas does not increase at constant values of p_1, ρ_1, and F_0:

$$G = \mu F_0 \rho_0 w_0 = \mu F_0 \left(\frac{2}{k+1}\right)^{1/(k-1)} \sqrt{\frac{2k}{k+1} \rho_1 p_1} \tag{1-81}$$

Equations (1-79) and (1-80) can therefore be used for the calculation of the velocity and, correspondingly, of the flow rate only when $p_0/p_1 \geqslant (p_0/p_1)_{cr}$. When $p_0/p_1 < (p_0/p_1)_{cr}$, Equation (1-81) should be used. In this case the mass discharge is independent of the external pressure p_0 and is controlled by the pressure p_1 in the vessel, increasing with its rise.

1-10 WORK OF THE SUPERCHARGER* IN A SYSTEM**

1. To set a liquid or gas medium at the ends of a given piping system in motion, it is necessary to create a difference of the total pressures by means of a pressure-boosting device (pump, fan, flue-gas fan, compressor).

2. In the most general case, the total pressure developed in the supercharger is spent: (1) to overcome the difference of pressures in the intake and discharge volumes; (2) to overcome excessive elevation pressure (negative buoyancy) that is, to raise a liquid or gas, heavier than the atmoshperic air, a height z from the initial to the final section of the system (in the case of positive buoyancy [self-draught***] the height z is subtracted from the supercharger pressure); and (3) to create a dynamic pressure at the exit of the liquid (gas) (Figure 1-20) from the system (not from a supercharger); that is, the total pressure p_{tot} (Pa),**** developed in the supercharger is comprised of

---

*Supercharger refers to a pressure enhancement device such as a booster pump; supercharge refers to pressurization.

**The case of incompressible fluid is considered.

***The term "self-draught" can be considered as the net driving head or buoyancy.

****In what follows, the quantity p_{tot} will be called simply pressure instead of total pressure.

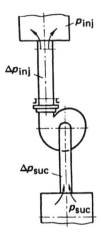

Figure 1-20 A supercharger in the system.

$$P_{tot} = (p_{inj} - p_{suc}) \pm p_s + (\Delta p_{suc} + \Delta p_{inj}) + \frac{\rho w_{ex}^2}{2} \tag{1-82}$$

where p_{suc} is the excess pressure in the suction volume, p_{inj} the excess pressure in the injection volume, p_s the excess elevation pressure (buoyancy), Δp_{suc} the pressure losses (resistance) over the suction stretch of the system, Δp_{inj} the pressure losses (resistance) over the injection stretch, and w_{ex} the flow velocity at the exit from the system, in m/s.

3. In the case when the pressures of the suction and injection volumes are equal ($p_{suc} = p_{inj}$), we have

$$P_{tot} = \Delta p_{suc} + \Delta p_{inj} + \frac{\rho w_{ex}^2}{2} \pm p_s = \Delta p_{sys} \tag{1-83}$$

where Δp_{sys} is calculated from Equation (1-66) or (1-68) [or (1-69)] for the entire system as a sum of the losses over the suction and injection stretches of the system (including the dynamic pressure losses at the exit from the system), while the buoyancy p_s is calculated from Equation (1-59).

4. Since at $p_s = 0$ the sum of all the losses in the system is equal to the difference between the total pressures upstream and downstream of the supercharger, then

$$P_{tot} = \left(p_{st,inj} + \frac{\rho w_{inj}^2}{2} \right) - \left(p_{st,suc} + \frac{\rho w_{suc}^2}{2} \right)$$

$$= p_{inj}^* - p_{suc}^* \tag{1-84}$$

where $p_{suc}^* - p_{inj}^*$ are the excess total pressures respectively upstream and downstream of the supercharger, in Pa; $p_{st,suc}$ and $p_{st,inj}$ are the excess static pressures respectively upstream and downstream of the supercharger, in Pa; and w_{suc} and w_{inj} are the mean stream velocities upstream and downstream of the supercharger, respectively, in m/s.

5. Under normal operating conditions of the supercharger, p_{tot}, is positive, that is,

$$p_{tot,inj} > p_{tot,suc}$$

At the same time both the static and the dynamic pressure can be smaller downstream of the supercharger than upstream of it.

6. In a specific case of equal cross-sectional areas of the suction and injection orifices

$$\frac{\rho w_{suc}^2}{2} = \frac{\rho w_{inj}^2}{2}$$

and therefore the pressure created by the supercharger will be

$$p_{tot} = p_{st,inj} - p_{st,suc} \qquad (1\text{-}85)$$

that is, the pressure created by the supercharger is equal to the difference between the static pressures immediately downstream and upstream of the supercharger.

7. The power on the supercharger shaft is determined from

$$N_{sup} = \frac{Q_{op}p_{tot,op}}{\eta_{tot}} = \frac{Q_{op}\Delta p_{sys}}{\eta_{tot}} \qquad (1\text{-}86)$$

where Q_{op} is the volumetric flow rate of the medium being displaced under operating conditions, in m^3/s, taken for that section to which all the pressure losses are reduced by a formula similar to Equations (1-66)-(1-69); $p_{tot,op}$ is the pressure created by a supercharger under operating conditions, in Pa, equal to the total pressure losses Δp_{sys} reduced to the same volumetric flow rate.

8. Usually the volumetric flow rate of the medium displaced is a specified quantity, while the pressure created by a supercharger is calculated from Equations (1-82)-(1-85) for the prescribed conditions in the system, that is, for given difference of pressures in the suction and injection volumes ($p_{inj} - p_{suc}$), excess elevation pressure ($\pm p_{el}$). The resistance coefficients ζ_{fr} and ζ_{loc}, the flow velocity in each element, and, consequently, the value of Δp_{tot} depend on the shapes and dimensions of the system.

9. To determine whether a given supercharger meets the required predictions of Q_{op} and $p_{tot,op}$, it is necessary first to reduce these quantities to those conditions (density) of the medium for which the supercharger performance is given. Then if the flow rate of the medium being displaced is given in m^3/s for normal conditions, it is recalculated for the operating conditions from Equation (1-16).

10. The reduced pressure of the supercharger is

$$p_{red} = p_{cal}\frac{\rho_{per}}{\rho_{nc}}\frac{T_w}{T_{per}}\frac{p_{per}}{p_{sup}} \qquad (1\text{-}87)$$

where p_{cal} is the calculated pressure of the supercharger, in Pa; ρ_{per} is the density of the medium at which the performance of the supercharger is determined under normal conditions ($t = 0°C$; $B = 101.325$ kPa), in kg/m^3; $\rho_{n.c.}$ is the density of the medium for which the supercharger is chosen at normal conditions, in kg/m^3; T_w is the working temperature of the displaced medium in the supercharger, in K; P_{in} is the working pressure (absolute) of the displaced medium in the supercharger, in Pa; T_{per}, p_{per} are the temperature (K) and pressure (Pa) of the medium at which the supercharger performance was determined; in the case of fans $p_{per} = 101.325$ kPa.

11. In the case of high-head superchargers the density of the medium being displaced is related to the mean pressure on the rotor. Then p_{sup} in Equation (1-87) is replaced by the mean absolute pressure on the rotor:

$$p_m = p_{sup} + (\Delta p_{inj} - 0.5\Delta p_{sys})$$

where Δp_{inj} are the pressure losses in the injection section of the system, in Pa, and Δp_{sys} are the total pressure losses in the whole system, in Pa.

12. The rated power on the supercharger shaft is

$$N_{sup} = \frac{Q_{op}p_{cal}}{\eta_{tot}} = \frac{Q_{op}p_{tot,per}\rho_{nc}T_{per}p_{inj}}{\eta_{tot}\rho_{per}T_w p_{per}}$$

$$= N_{per}\frac{\rho_{nc}}{\rho_{per}}\frac{T_{per}}{T_w}\frac{p_{inj}}{p_{per}}$$

where $p_{tot,per}$ is the pressure created by the supercharger according to specification, in Pa, and N_{per} is the power on the supercharger shaft according to specification, in W.

1-11. EXAMPLES OF THE METHOD OF CALCULATION OF THE FLUID RESISTANCE OF SYSTEMS

Example 1-1. Forced Ventilation System

A schematic diagram for the calculation of the ventilation system network is presented in Figure 1-21.

Given the:

1. Total quantity of the air sucked from the atmosphere, $Q = 0.89$ m³/s, under normal conditions;
2. Flow rate through lateral branches, $Q = 0.22$ m³/s, under normal conditions;
3. Temperature of the external (atmospheric) air, $t = -20°C$;
4. Air temperature downstream of the heater, $t = 20°C$, and
5. Material from which the ducts are made: sheet steel (oil-coated), roughness $\Delta \approx 0.15$ mm (see Table 2-5)

Since the gas temperature in the system varies (due to a heater), we shall use the first method of the superposition of losses, that is, summation of the absolute losses in the separate elements of the network, reduced in this case to the volumetric flow rate of air through the entry section of the fan (Figure 1-20, 7):

$$\Delta p_{sys} = \sum_i \Delta p_i = \sum_i \frac{\Delta N_i}{Q_7} = \sum_i \zeta_i \frac{\rho_7 w_i^2}{2}$$

where $\rho_7 = 1.4$ kg/m³.

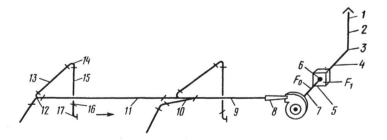

Figure 1-21 Scheme of calculation of the ventilation system network.

The calculation of the resistance is given in Table 1-14. According to this table, for the fan to be selected, we have

$$Q_{opi} = 0.955 \text{ m}^3/\text{s} \quad \text{and} \quad \Delta p_{sys} = \Delta p_{tot} = 225 \text{ Pa}$$

The power on the fan rotor at a fan efficient of $\eta_{tot} = 0.6$ is

$$N_{sup} = \frac{Q_{op}P_{tot}}{\eta_{tot}} = \frac{Q_7 \Delta p_{sus}}{\eta_{tot}} = \frac{0.955 \cdot 225}{0.6} \text{ W} = 0.36 \text{ kW}$$

Example 1-2. Installation for the Scrubbing of Sintering Gases

The schematic of the installation is shown in Figure 1-22
Given the:

1. Total volumetric flow rate of the gas (at $t = 20°C$ and $p = 101.325$ kPa), $Q = 278 \text{ m}^3/\text{s}$;
2. Density of the gas at normal conditions, $\rho = 1.3 \text{ kg/m}^3$;
3. Kinematic viscosity of the gas at normal conditions, $\nu - 1.32 \times 10^{-5} \text{ m}^2/\text{s}$;
4. Internal coating of the gas mains (comparatively long): sheet steel, roughness taken to be the same as for seamless corroded steel pipes (after several years of service), $\Delta \approx 1.0$ mm (see Table 2-5);
5. Gas cleaning, done in a wet scrubber, rate of spraying $A \approx 0.014 \text{ m}^3/\text{m}^2$ s (see Diagram 12-11).

In the present case the gas temperature in the system varies due to cooling; therefore, as done in Example 1-1, we use the first method of superposition of losses: summation of the absolute losses in the separate elements of the network, reduced to the volumetric flow rate, for example through section 0-0, that is, through the section of entry into an elbow 1(Figure 1-21), where $\rho = 0.18 \text{ kg/m}^3$.

The calculation of the resistance is given in Table 1-15.
The self-draught created by the exhaust flue is equal to:

$$p_s = H_n(\rho_a - \rho_g)g$$

where $H_n = 62$ m is the height of the flue; ρ_a is the density of the atmoshperic air, in kg/m³; ρ_g is the density of the gas the inlet to the exhaust flue, in kg/m³; g is the gravitational acceleration, assumed to be 9.8 m/s².

At the temperature of atmoshperic air $t_{air} = 0°C$ we have

$$\rho_a = 1.29 \text{ kg/m}^3$$

At the temperature $t_g = 40°C$, the mean density of the gas is

$$\rho_g = 1.13 \text{ kg/m}^3$$

whence

$$p_s = 62(1.29 - 1.13) \times 9.81 \approx 98 \text{ Pa}$$

This positive self-draught (buoyancy) favors the motion of the stream, therefore it should be subtracted from the total losses (see Table 1-15). The power on the shaft of the flue blower intended only for this installation at $\eta_{tot} = 0.6$ is $N_{sup} = Q_{op}P_{tot}/\eta_{tot} = Q_1 \Delta p_{sys}/0.6 = 430.13 \cdot 200.6$ W ≈ 946 kW.

Table 1-14 Calculation of the resistance in the forced ventilation system (see Figure 1-20)

Element of the system	Diagram and basic dimensions of the element	Parameters	$Q_{op,i}$, m³/s	t_i, °C	ρ_i, kg/m³	$v_i \times 10^5$, m²/s	w_i, m/s	$\frac{\rho_i w_i^2}{2}$, Pa	$Re = \frac{w_i D_{hi}}{v} \times 10^{-5}$	$\zeta_{loc,i}$	λ_i	$\zeta_{fr,i} = \lambda_i \frac{l_i}{D_{hi}}$	$\zeta_i = \zeta_{loc,i} + \zeta_{fr,i}$	$\Delta p_i = \zeta_i \frac{\rho_i w_i^2}{2}$, Pa	Basis for determination of ζ_i (reference to figure)
1 Supply vent	$h = 300\,MM$; $D_0 = 495\,MM$; $F_0 = 0.193\,M^2$; $7.5°$	$\dfrac{h}{D_0} = 0.6$	0.825	−20	1.40	1.17	4.27	$\frac{1.2(4.27)^2}{2}$ = 10.94	1.80	0.30	—	—	0.30	3.28	3-1
2 Straight stretch (vertical)	$D_0 = 495\,MM$; $l = 4000\,MM$	$\dfrac{l}{D_0} = 8.0$; $\bar{\Delta} = \dfrac{\Delta}{D_0} = 0.0003$	0.825	−20	1.40	1.17	4.27	10.94	1.80	—	0.018	0.144	0.144	1.58	2-5
3 Elbow bend	$D_0 = 495\,MM$; $r = 100\,MM$	$\delta = 90°$; $\dfrac{r}{Dp} = 0.2$; $\bar{\Delta} = 0.0003$	0.825	−20	1.40	1.17	4.27	10.94	1.80	0.44	0.018	0.024	0.464	5.08	6-9

No.	Description	Diagram	Parameters													
4	Straight stretch (horizontal)	$D_0 = 495\,MM$, $L = 1000\,MM$	$\dfrac{l}{D_0} = 2.0$; $\Delta = 0.0003$	0.825	−20	1.40	1.17	4.27	10.94	1.80	−	0.018	0.036	0.036	0.40	2–5
5	Air heater with three rows of smooth pipes		$\rho_m w_0 = 3.86\ kg/m^2\,s$	−	−	−	−	−	−	−	−	−	−	−	9.90	12–26
6	Sudden sharp contraction	$D_0 = 495\,MM$, $F_0 = 0.193\,M^2$, $F_1 = 0.386\,M^2$	$\dfrac{F_0}{F_1} = 0.5$	0.955	+20	1.20	1.5	4.95	14.70	1.64	0.25	−	−	0.25	3.68	4–9
7	Straight stretch (horizontal)	$D_0 = 495\,MM$, $L = 1000\,MM$	$\dfrac{l}{D_0} = 2.0$; $\Delta = 0.0003$	0.955	+20	1.20	1.5	4.95	14.7	1.64	−	0.0185	0.037	0.037	0.55	2–5

Table 1-14 Calculation of the resistance in the forced ventilation system (see Figure 1-20) (continued)

Element of the system	Diagram and basic dimensions of the element	Parameters	$Q_{op,i}$, m³/s	t_i, °C	ρ_i, kg/m³	$v_i \times 10^3$, m²/s	w_i, m/s	$\frac{\rho_i w_i^2}{2}$, Pa	$Re = \frac{w_i D_{hi}}{v} \times 10^{-5}$	$\zeta_{loc,i}$	λ_i	$\zeta_{fr,i} = \lambda_i \frac{l_i}{D_{hi}}$	$\zeta_i = \zeta_{loc,i} + \zeta_{fr,i}$	$\Delta p_i = \zeta_i \frac{\rho_i w_i^2}{2}$, Pa	Basis for determination of ζ_i (reference to figure)
8 Pyramidal diffuser (rectangular cross section)	$D_0 = 250\,mm$; $D_f = 375\,mm$; $F_0 = 0.049\,m^2$; $F_1 = 0.111\,m^2$	$n = \frac{F_1}{F_0} = 2.25$; $\alpha = 10°$	0.955	+20	1.20	1.5	19.5	228	3.25	0.19	–	–	0.19	43.0	5-77
9 Straight stretch (horizontal)	$D_0 = 375\,mm$; $F_0 = 0.111\,m^2$; $l = 4000\,mm$	$\frac{l}{D_0} = 10.7$; $\bar{\Delta} = 0.0004$	0.955	+20	1.20	1.5	8.6	44.5	2.15	–	0.018	0.193	0.193	8.57	2-5
10 Flow divider (Passage with division of flow)	$D_c = 375\,mm$; $D_n = 265\,mm$; $F_c = 0.111\,m^2$; $F_n = 0.056\,m^2$	$\frac{F_n}{F_c} = 0.5$; $\frac{Q_n}{Q_c} = 0.5$; $\frac{w_n}{w_c} = 1.0$; $\alpha = 15°$	0.478	+20	1.20	1.5	8.6	44.5	1.5	0	–	–	–	0	7-2 As in an inlet wye
11 Straight stretch (horizontal)	$D_0 = 265\,mm$; $l = 5000\,mm$	$\frac{l}{D_0} = 18.8$; $\bar{\Delta} = 0.00056$	0.478	+20	1.20	1.5	8.6	44.5	1.5	–	0.019	0.36	0.36	16.0	2-5
12 Symmetrical smooth wye (dovetail) in discharge region (division of flow)	$D_\delta = 195\,mm$; $D_c = 265\,mm$; $F_\delta = 0.03\,m^2$; $F_c = 0.056\,m^2$	$\frac{Q_\delta}{Q_c} = 0.5$; $\frac{F_\delta}{F_c} = 0.50$; $\frac{R}{D_c} = 1.5$	0.239	+20	1.20	1.5	8.0	38.4	1.04	0.25	0.019	0.05	0.30	11.5	7-30

No.	Component	Diagram	Parameters													Ref.
13	Straight stretch (horizontal)	$D_0=195MM$, $l=4000MM$	$\frac{l}{D_0}=20.5$; $\Delta=0.00077$; $\delta=90°$	0.239	+20	1.20	1.5	8.0	38.4	1.04	–	0.02	0.41	0.41	15.7	2–5
14	90° bend	$D_0=195MM$, $F_0=0.03M^2$, $R=400MM$	$\frac{R_0}{D_0}=2.0$; $\Delta=0.00077$	0.239	+20	1.20	1.5	8.0	38.4	1.04	0.24	0.02	0.065	0.305	11.7	6–1
15	Straight stretch (horizontal)	$D_0=195MM$, $l=4000MM$	$\frac{l}{D_0}=20.5$; $\Delta=0.00077$	0.239	+20	1.20	1.5	8.0	38.4	1.04	–	0.02	0.41	0.41	15.7	2–5
16	Butterfly valve	$D_0=195MM$	$\delta=5°$	0.239	+20	1.20	1.5	3.0	38.4	1.04	0.25	–	–	0.28	10.8	9–17
17	Intake nozzle at the exit from the bend	$D_0=195MM$, $l=4000MM$, $r=40MM$	$\frac{l}{D_0}=2.0$; $\frac{r}{D_0}=0.20$; $\Delta=0.00077$	0.239	+20	1.20	1.5	3.0	38.4	1.04	1.70	0.02	0.06	1.76	67.6	11–18

$$\sum_{i=1}^{17}\Delta p_i=\Delta p_{sus}\approx225\ Pa$$

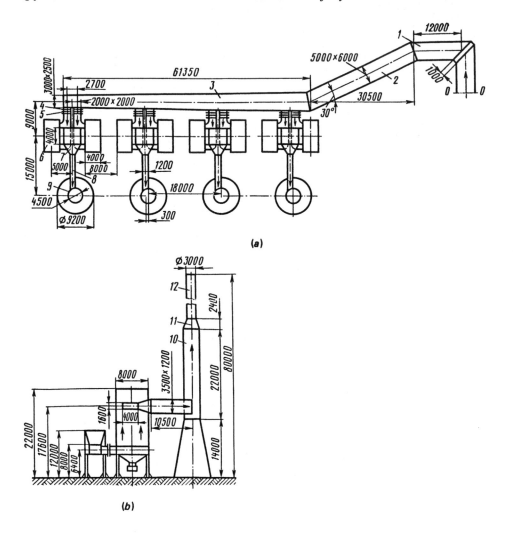

Figure 1-22 Scheme of calculation of the installation for scrubbing sintering gases: (*a*) plan of an installation; (*b*) side view.

Example 1-3. Low-Velocity, Closed-Circuit, Open-Throat Wind Tunnel

A layout of the wind tunnel (aerodynamic circuit) is shown in Figure 1-23.
Given the:

1. Diameter of the working section (nozzle exit section), $D_0 = 5000$ mm;
2. Length of the working section, $l_{ws} = 8000$ mm;
3. Flow velocity in the working section (at the exit from the nozzle), $w_0 = 60$ m/s;
4. Air temperature, $t \approx 20°C$; $\rho = 1.22$ kg/m³;
5. Kinematic viscosity, $\nu = 1.5$ mm²/s; and
6. Material from which the tunnel is made: concrete with roughness of the internal surface, $\Delta = 2.5$ mm (see Table 2-5).

At low velocities, changes in the pressure and temperature along the tunnel can be neglected in hydraulic calculations. Therefore, it is convenient here to use the second method of superposition of losses: summation of the reduced resistance coefficients of the separate elements of the system (see Section 1-6).

Table 1-15 Calculation of the resistance of the system of installation for wet scrubbing of sintering gases (Figure 1-21)

Type of element	Diagram and basic dimensions of element	Parameters	$Q_{op,i}$, m³/s	t_i, °C	ρ_i, kg/m³	$\nu \times 10^5$ m²/s
1 Right angle elbow	$F_0 = 30 M^2$; $F_1 = 30 M^2$; $b_0 = 5000 \times 6000 MM$; $t_1 = 2500 M$; $D_r = \frac{4F_0}{\Pi_0} = \frac{4 \cdot 30}{22}$ $= 5450 = 5.45 M$	$\frac{F_1}{F_0} = 1.0$; $\frac{t_1}{b_0} = \frac{2500}{5000} = 0.5$; $\bar{\Delta} = \frac{\Delta}{b_0} = 0.0002$	430	150	0.84	3
2 Compound bend	$l_1 = 28500 MM$; $b_0 = 5000 \times 6000 MM$; $D_r = 5.5 M$	$\frac{l_0}{b_0} = 5.6$; $\frac{\Delta}{b_0} = 0.0002$ $\alpha = 30°$	430	150	0.84	3
3 Distributing header	$b_0 = 6000 \times 5000 MM$; $b_1 = 3000 \times 2500 MM$; $b_0 = 2000 \times 2000 MM$; $l_0 = 6000 MM$: $D_r = \frac{4F_s}{\Pi_1} = \frac{4 \cdot 7.5}{2(3+2.5)} = 2.72 M$; $D_{cp} = \frac{D_0 + D_L}{2} = \frac{5.5 + 2.75}{2} = 4.11M$	$\frac{w_{1n}}{w_0} = \frac{w_{2n}}{w_0} = \frac{w_{3n}}{w_0} = \frac{w_{4n}}{w_0} = \frac{w_n}{w_0} = 1.0$; $\frac{l_0}{D_{hav}} = \frac{6,000}{410} = 14.5$; $\bar{\Delta} = \frac{\Delta}{D_{hav}} = \frac{1.0}{41.00} = 0.00024$ $k = 1 - \frac{F_k}{F_{sup}} = 1 - \frac{F_{n4}}{F_0}$ $= 1 - \frac{7.5}{30} = 0.75$ $\bar{f} = \frac{\Sigma F_s}{F_0} = \frac{\Sigma F_s}{F_{st}} = \frac{4 \times 2 \times 4}{30} = 1.07$; $\alpha = 90°$	430	150	0.84	3.0
4 Lateral branch of the distributing header	$F_{n4} = 7.5 M^2$ $F_{\delta 4} = 4.0 M^2$ $w_n = w_c$	$\frac{F_s}{F_c} = \frac{2 \times 4}{7.5} \cong 1.0$; $\frac{Q_s}{Q_c} = \frac{Q_s}{Q_{n4}} = 1.0$; $\frac{w_s}{w_c} = 1.0$	$\frac{430}{4} \frac{273 + 120}{273 + 150}$ $= 100$	120	0.90	2.7

and

Table 1-15 Calculation of the resistance of the system of installation for wet scrubbing of sintering gases (Figure 1-21) (continued)

Type of element	Diagram and basic dimensions of element	Parameters	$Q_{op,i}$, m³/s	t_i, °C	ρ_i, kg/m³	$\nu \times 10^5$ m²/s
5 Butterfly valve (at 10% closing, $\delta = 5°$)	$F_0 = 4 M^2$	$\frac{F_h}{F_0} = 0.9 \ (\delta = 5°)$	$\frac{100}{2} = 50$	120	0.90	2.7
6 Wet scrubber	(see Diagram 12-11); $F = 32$ m²	At the entrance $t = 120°C$; at the exit $t = 50°C$; rate of liquid spraying $A = 0.014$ m³/m² s	$50 \cdot \frac{273+85}{273+120}$ $= 50 \times 0.91$ $= 45.5$	$\frac{120+50}{2} = 85$	1.0	–
7 Exit stretch of the scrubber-symmetric tee	$W_{1b}\ F_{1b}$ $W_{2b}\ F_{2b}$ W_a, F_c $F_b = 4000 \times 1600 = 6.4 M^2$ $F_c = 3500 \times 1200 = 4.2 M^2$	$\frac{F_c}{2F_s} = \frac{4.2}{2 \times 6.4} = 0.33;$ $\frac{Q_s}{Q_c} = 0.5$	$45.5 \cdot \frac{273+50}{273+85}$ $= 45.5 \times 0.9$ $= 41$	50	1.0	
8 Straight horizontal stretch	3500 1200 W_0, F_0 l_0 $l_0 = 10500\ MM$ $F_0 = 3500 \times 1200 = 4.2 M^2$ $D_r = \frac{4 \cdot 4.2}{2(3.5+1.2)} \approx 1.8 M^2$	$\frac{l_0}{D_h} = \frac{10.5}{1,800} = 5.8$ $\overline{\Delta} = \frac{1.0}{1,800} = 0.0006$	$2 \times 40 = 80$	50	1.10	1.8
9 Inlet to the flue	Ø 4500 v_0, F_0 $F_0 = 4.2 M^2$ $F_1 = 15.8 M^2$	$\frac{F_0}{F_1} = \frac{4.2}{15.8} \approx 0.27$	$2 \times 40 = 80$	50	1.10	1.8

	Sketch / parameters	Calculation				
10 First straight stretch of the flue	$D_0 = 4500\,MM$ $F_0 = 15.8\,M^2$ $l_0 = 22000\,MM$	$\dfrac{l_0}{D_0} = \dfrac{22.0}{4.5} = 4.9;$ $\bar{\Delta} = \dfrac{1.0}{4500} = 0.00022$	$80\dfrac{313}{323} = 77.5$	40	1.13	1.7
11 Transition passage-converging section	$D_1 = 4500\,MM$ $D_0 = 3000\,MM$ $F_1 = 15.8\,M^2$ $F_0 = 7.05\,M^2$ $l_1 = 2400\,MM$ $\alpha = 34°$	$\dfrac{F_0}{F_1} = \dfrac{7.05}{15.8} = 0.45;$ $\dfrac{l_0}{D_0} = \dfrac{2400}{3000} = 0.8;$ $\alpha = 34°;$ $\bar{\Delta} = \dfrac{1.0}{3000} = 0.00033$	$80\dfrac{313}{323} = 77.5$	40	1.13	1.7
12 Second straight stretch of the flue	$D_0 = 3000\,MM$ $F_0 = 7.05\,M^2$ $L_0 = 41500\,MM$	$\dfrac{l_0}{D_0} = \dfrac{41,500}{3000} \approx 14;$ $\bar{\Delta} = \dfrac{1.0}{3000} = 0.00033$	$80\dfrac{313}{323} = 77.5$	40	1.13	1.7
Exit from the flue		–	$80\dfrac{313}{323} = 77.5$	40	1.13	1.7
Driving head in the entire flue		–	–	–	1.13	–

Table 1-15 Calculation of the resistance of the system of installation for wet scrubbing of sintering gases (Figure 1-21) (continued)

Type of element	Type of element	Diagram and basic dimensions of element w_i, m/s	$\frac{\rho_i w_i^2}{2}$, Pa	$Re = \frac{w_i D_{Hi}}{\nu_i} \times 10^{-6}$	$\zeta_{loc,i}$	Parameters λ_i	$\zeta_{fr,i} = \lambda_i \frac{l_i}{D_{Hi}}$	$\zeta_i = \zeta_{loc,i} + \zeta_{fr,i}$	$\Delta p_i = \zeta_i \frac{\rho_i w_i^2}{2}$, Pa	Basis for determination of ζ_i (reference to diagram)	$Q_{op,i}$, m³/s	t_i, °C	ρ_i, kg/m³	$\nu \times 10^5$ m²/s
1	Right angle elbow	14.3	86	2.6	0.72	–	–	0.72	62.0	6–10				
2	Compound bend	14.3	86	2.6	0.20	0.014	0.079	0.28	24.0	6–13				
3	Distributing header	14.3	86	~2.0	2.6	–	–	2.6	224	7–40				
and 4	Lateral branch	$w_n \approx w_c = 13.3$	80	–	–	–	–	–	–					
5	Butterfly valve (at 10% closing, δ = 5°)	12.5	65.6	–	0.28	–	–	0.28	18.4	9–17				
6	Wet scrubber	1.42	0.85	–	960	–	–	960	816	12–11 Tentatively as in Diagram 4-9 (sudden contraction) and a symmetric tee 90° (Diagram 7-29)				
7	Exit stretch of the scrubber-symmetric wye	9.8	40.4	–	≈2.0	–	–	2.0	80.8					
8	Straight horizontal stretch	19.0	152	1.9	–	0.018	0.10	0.10	16.0	2–5				
9	Inlet to the flue	19.0	152	1.9	0.53	–	–	0.53	80	4–1 (sudden expansion)				
10	First straight stretch of the flue	4.9	10.1	1.3	–	0.015	0.074	0.074	0.75	2–5				
11	Transition passage–converging section	11.0	51.0	~2.0	0.05	0.014	0.01	0.06	3.24	5–23				
12	Second straight stretch of the flue	11.0	540	2.15	–	0.014	0.20	0.2	10.2	2–5				
	Exit from the flue	11.0	51.0	2.15	1.0	–	–	1.0	51.0	11–1				
	Driving head in the entire flue	–	–	–	–	–	–	–	–72.3					

Equation (1-59): $p_c = z(\rho_a - \rho_g)g$, where

$\rho_a = 1.29$ at $t = 0°C$

$p_{st,1} = \frac{p_1}{p_{12}} p_{st} = \frac{0.84}{1.13} p_{st} = 72.3$ (reduced to Q_1)

$\sum_{i=1}^{12} \Delta p_i = \Delta p_{sys} \approx 1320$ Pa

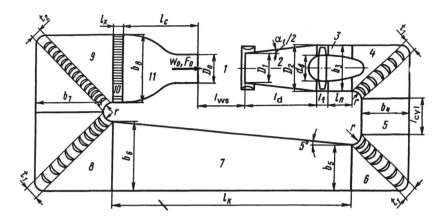

Figure 1-23 Schematic diagram of a closed-circuit, open-throat wind tunnel (dimensions in m): $D_0 = 5$; $D_1 = 5.35$; $D_2 = 8$; $d_{in} = 4$; $b_3 = 8$; $b_4 = 8$; $b_5 = 8$; $b_6 = 12$; $b_7 = 12$; $b_8 = 12$; $t_1 = 2.2$; $t_2 = 1.5$; $l^{work,sect} = 8$; $l_d = 13.5$; $l_{fan} = 2$; $l_{tr} = 5$; $l_{cyl} = 6$; $l_{el} = 43.5$; $l_h = 1.5$; $l_{ch} = 13.5$; $r = 1.6$; $\alpha_1 = 7°$.

The calculation of the tunnel resistance is given in Table 1-16. According to this table the total resistance of the tunnel is

$$\Delta p_{sys} = \sum_i^{11} \zeta_{0i} \frac{\rho w_0^2}{2} = 0.30\left(\frac{1.22}{2}\right)60^2 \approx 660 \text{ Pa}$$

The volumetric air flow rate through the working section (nozzle) is

$$Q = w_0 F_0 = 60(19.6) = 1175 \text{ m}^3/\text{s}$$

The power on the fan shaft at a fan efficiency $\eta_{tot} \approx 0.7$ is:

$$N_{sup} = \frac{Q \Delta p_{sys}}{\eta_{tot}} = \frac{1175(660)}{0.7} \text{ W} \approx 1100 \text{ kW}$$

The aerodynamic calculations use the concept of the "quality" of a wind tunnel K, which is defined as the ratio of the velocity pressure in the working section of the tunnel to its total resistance.

For the present case

$$K = \frac{0.5 \rho w_0^2}{0.5 \rho w_0^2 \sum_i^{11} \zeta_{0i}} = \frac{1}{0.30} \approx 3.3$$

Table 1-16 Calculation of resistance of the wind tunnel (Figure 1-22)

Type of element	Diagram and basic dimensions of the element	Parameters
1 Circular open throat	$D_0 = 5000 мм; l = 8000 мм$	$\dfrac{l_{ws}}{D_0} = \dfrac{8.0}{5.0} = 1.6$
2 First diffuser	$D_1 = 5350 мм$ $D_2 = 8000 мм$ $l_a = 13500 мм$ $F_0 = \dfrac{\pi}{4}\,5000^2 = 19$	$\alpha = 7°;\ n = \dfrac{F_2}{F_1} = \left(\dfrac{8.0}{5.35}\right)^2 = 2.24$ $\dfrac{w_{max}}{w_0} > 1.12;\ k_d \approx 1.8;$ $\overline{\Delta} = \dfrac{\Delta}{D} \approx 0.0004$
3 Adapter (from an annular section to a square)	$l_b = 2000\ MM \quad d_f = 4000\ MM$ $l_n = 5000\ MM \quad D_2 = 8000\ MM$ $b_3 = 8000\ MM$	$\overline{d}_{fan} = \dfrac{d_{fan}}{D_2} = 0.5;\ n = \dfrac{F_3}{F_{fan}}$ $\overline{d}_{fan} = \dfrac{F_3}{(1 - \overline{d}_{fan}^2)F_{fan}}$ $\overline{d}_{fan} = \dfrac{8.0^2}{1 - 0.25(\pi/4)8.0^2} = 1.7;$ $\alpha_3 \approx 15°;\ \overline{\Delta} \approx 0.0004$ $\dfrac{w_{max}}{w_0} > 1.2;\ k_1 \approx 1.8$
4 Elbow 1 with reduced number of guide vanes	$b_3 = b_4 = 8000\ MM$ $t_I = 2000\ MM$ $r = 1600\ MM$	$\dfrac{b_4}{b_3} = 1.0;$ $\dfrac{r}{b_3} = 0.2;\ \overline{\Delta} = 0.0003$
5 Cylindrical stretch	$b_4 = 8000\ MM$ $l_4 = 6000 MM$	$\dfrac{l_4}{b_4} = \dfrac{6.0}{8.0} = 0.75;\ \overline{\Delta} = 0.0003$
6 Elbow 2; guide vanes as for elbow	$b_4 = b_5 = 8000\ MM$ $r = 1600 MM$ $t_I = 2200 MM$	$\dfrac{b_5}{b_4} = 1.0;$ $\dfrac{r}{D_5} = 0.2$

Table 1-16 Calculation of resistance of the wind tunnel (Figure 1-22) (continued)

Type of element	Diagram and basic dimensions of the element	Parameters
7 Reverse channel (second diffuser)	 $b_5 = 8000 \text{ мм}$ $b_6 = 12000 \text{ мм}$ $l_\kappa = 43500 \text{ мм}$	$\alpha_2 = 5.5°;$ $n = \dfrac{F_6}{F_5} = \left(\dfrac{12,0}{8.0}\right)^2 = 2.25$ $\dfrac{w_{max}}{w_0} \approx 1.1; \; k_1 \approx 1.8;$
8 Elbow 3; same conditions as for elbow 1	 $b_6 = b_7 = 12000 \text{ мм}$ $r = 1600 \text{ мм}$ $t_1 = 1500 \text{ мм}$	$\dfrac{b_7}{b_6} = 1.0;$ $\dfrac{r}{D_6} = 0.13$
9 Elbow 4; same conditions as for elbow 3, but number of guide vanes is normal	 $b_7 = b_8 = 12000 \text{ мм}$ $r = 1600 \text{ мм}$ $t_2 = 1500 \text{ мм}$	$\dfrac{b_8}{b_7} = 1.0;$ $\dfrac{r}{D_8} = 0.13$
10 Honeycomb (coated sheet iron lacquered)	$l_x = 1500 \text{ мм}; \; d_x = 200 \text{ мм}$ 	$\dfrac{l_x}{d_x} = 7.5; \; \bar{f} = \dfrac{F_x}{F_8} = 0.9;$ $\bar{\Delta} = \dfrac{0.2}{200} = 0.001$
11 Nozzle (curvilinear linear converging section)		$\alpha \approx 35°;$ $n = \dfrac{12,0}{(\pi/4)5.0^2} = 7.35$

Table 1-16 Calculation of resistance of the wind tunnel (Figure 1-22) (continued)

Type of element — Area ratio $\dfrac{F_0}{F_i}$	$\left(\dfrac{F_0}{F_i}\right)^2$	w_i, m/s	$Re = \dfrac{w_i D_{hi}}{v} \times 10^{-6}$	$\zeta_{loc.i}$	λ_i	$\zeta_{fr.i} = \lambda_i \dfrac{l_i}{D_{hi}}$	$\zeta_i = \zeta_{loc.i} + \zeta_{fr.i}$	$\zeta_{0i} = \zeta_i \left(\dfrac{F_0}{F_i}\right)^2$	Basis for determination of ζ_i (reference to figure)
1.0	1.0	60	20	0.13	–	–	0.13	0.13	4–25
$\left(\dfrac{5.0}{5.35}\right)^2 = 0.875$	0.77	52.5	19	0.05	0.01	0.16	0.066	0.051	5–2
$\dfrac{F_0}{F_{fan}} = \dfrac{5.0^2}{0.75 \times 8.0^2}$	0.27	31	18	0.19	0.011	0.01	0.20	0.054	5–22
$\dfrac{F_0}{F_{fan}} = 0.52$									
$\dfrac{(\pi/4)5.0^2}{8.0^2} = 0.306$	0.096	18	10	0.155	0.011	0.015	0.17	0.016	6–21; increased by 1.2 in order to allow for influence of diffuser placed before it
0.306	0.096	18	10	–	0.011	0.008	0.008	0.001	2–5
0.306	0.096	18	10	0.12	0.011	0.015	0.135	0.015	6–21
0.306	0.096	18	10	0.046	0.011	0.011	0.057	0.006	5–4
$\dfrac{\pi}{4}\dfrac{5.0^2}{120^2} = 0.137$	0.0181	8.2	6.5	0.15	0.011	0.015	0.165	0.003	6–21
0.137	0.0181	8.2	6.5	0.17	0.011	0.015	0.185	~0.004	6–21
$\dfrac{0.137}{0.9} = 0.152$	0.0232	9.1	$\dfrac{w_i d_x}{v} = 0.12$	0.11	0.060	0.45	0.565	0.013	$\zeta_i = \zeta_{in} + \zeta_{ex} + \zeta_{fr}$, where $\zeta_{in} \approx 1 - \bar{f}$ (see Diagram 3-1); $\zeta_{ex} = (1 - \bar{f})^2$ (see Diagram 4-1) $\zeta_{fr} = \lambda(l_x/d_x)$
7.35	54	60	20	–	0.008	0.003	0.003	0.003	5–23

$$\sum_{osys} = \sum_{i=1}^{11} \zeta_{0i} \approx 0.30$$

REFERENCES

1. Abramovich, G. N., *Applied Gas Dynamics*, Nauka Press, Moscow, 1969, 824 p.
2. Altshul, A. D., *Hydraulic Resistance*, Nauka Press, Moscow, 1982, 224 p.
3. Altshul, A. D. and Kiselyov, P. G., *Hydraulics and Aerodynamics*, Moscow, 1975, 327 p.
4. Mochan, S. I. (Ed.), *Aerodynamic Calculation of Boiler Equipment*, Energiya Press, Leningrad, 1977, 255 p.
5. Branover, G. G., Gelfgat, Yu. M., and Vasiliyev, A. S., Turbulent flow in a plane perpendicular to the magnetic field, *Izv. Akad. Nauk Latv. SSR, Ser. Fiz.-Tekh. Nauk*, no. 4, 78–84, 1966.
6. Burdukov, A. P., Valukina, N. V., and Narkoryakov, V. E., Specific features of gas-liquid bubble mixture flow at small Reynolds numbers, *Zh. Prikl. Mekh. Tekh. Fiz.*, no. 4, 137–139, 1975.
7. Burdum, G. D., *Handbook of the International System of Units*, Iz. Standartov, Moscow, 1971, 231 p.
8. Vakina, V. V., Discharge of viscous liquids at high pressure drops through throttling washers, *Vestn. Mashinostr.*, no. 8, 93–101, 1965.
9. Vitkov, G. A. and Orlov, I. I., Hydraulic calculations of systems from their overall characteristics (heterogeneous systems). Deposited at VINITI 28.01.1980 under No. 337–80, Moscow, 1980, 16 p.
10. Vitkov, G. A. and Orlov, I. I., Hydraulic calculations of systems from their overall characteristics (homogeneous systems). Deposited at VINITI 28.01.1980 under No. 338–80, Moscow, 1980, 30 p.
11. Vulis, L. A., Paramonova, T. A., and Fomenko, B. A., Concerning the resistance to liquid metal flow in magnetic field, *Magnitn. Gidrodin.*, no. 1, 68–74, 1968.
12. Hartman, U. and Lazarus, F., Experimental study of mercury flow in a homogenous magnetic field, in *MHD-Flows in Channels*, Garris, L. (Ed.), Moscow, 1963, 262 p.
13. Geller, Z. I., Skobeltsyn, Yu. A., and Mezhdivo, V. Kh., Influence of rings on flow discharge from nozzles and orifices, *Izv. VUZov, Neft Gaz*, no. 5, 65–67, 1969.
14. Genin, L. G. and Zhilin, V. G., Influence of the longitudinal magnetic field on the coefficient of resistance to mercury flow in a round tube, *Teplofiz. Vysok. Temp.*, vol. 4, no. 2, 233–237, 1966.
15. Guizha, E. A., Stabilization of Forced Turbulent Flows Downstream of Local Resistances, Thesis (Cand. of Techn. Sciences), Kiev, 1986, 186 p.
16. Gil, B. B., An approximate method for calculating the velocity field in the MDH-separation problems, in *New Physical Methods for the Separation of Mineral Raw Material*, Moscow, pp. 59–68, 1969.

17. Guinevsky, A. S. and Solodkin, E. E., Hydarulic resistance of annular channels, in *Industrial Aerodynamics*, pp. 202–215 no. 20, Oborongiz, Moscow, 1961.
18. Guinevsky, A. S. and Solodkin, E. E., Aerodynamic characteristics of the starting length of a circular tube with a turbulent boundary layer flow, in *Industrial Aerodynamics*, pp. 155–168, no. 12, Oborongiz, Moscow, 1959.
19. Grabovsky, A. M. and Kostenko, G. N., Bases of the Use of SI Units in *Thermal and Hydraulic Calculations*, Tekhnika Press, Kiev, 1965, 106 p.
20. Gubarev, N. S. Local resistance of the high-pressure air-pipeline fittings, *Sudostroenie*, no. 3, 41–46, 1957.
21. Gukhman, A. A., *Introduction to the Similarity Theory*, Moscow, 1963, 254 p.
22. Deich, M. E. and Zaryankin, A. E., *Hydrogasdynamics*, Moscow, 1984, 284 p.
23. Elovskikh, Yu. P., Concerning the calculation of the parameters of gas in a pipeline, in *Pneumatics and Hydraulics*, no. 6, pp. 132–141, Moscow, 1979.
24. Zelkin, G. G., Hydraulic induction in discharging incompressible fluid into a full and empty pipeline with local resistances, *J. Eng. Phys. (U.S.S.R.)*, vol. 47, no. 5, 856–857, 1984.
25. Zelkin, G. G., *Unsteady-State Flows in Local Resistances*, Minsk, 1981, 141 p.
26. Zelkin, G. G., The phenomenon of hydraulic induction in unsteady-state motion of incompressible viscous fluid, *J. Eng. Phys. (U.S.S.R.)*, vol. 21, no. 6, 1127–1130, 1971.
27. Idelchik, I. E., Nozzles, *Large Soviet Encyclopedia*, vol. 29, 184–185, 1953.
28. Idelchik, I. E., *Fluid Resistances (Physical and Mechanical Fundamentals)*, Gosenergeizdat, Moscow, 1954, 316 p.
29. Idelchik, I. E., Some notes concerning hydraulic losses in motion of a real fluid in forced systems, *Izv. VUZov, Energetika*, no. 9, 99–104, 1975.
30. Kiselyov, P. G., *Hydraulics, Fundamentals of the Mechanics of Liquid*, Moscow, 1980, 360 p.
31. Komlev, A. F., Skobeltsyn, Yu. A., and Geller, Z. I., Influence of the shape and dimensions of the entrance on the discharge coefficient of outer cylindrical nozzles, *Izv. VUZov, Neft:Gas*, no. 11, 59–61, 1968.
32. Levin, V. B. and Chenenkov, A. I., Experimental investigation of the turbulent flow of an electrically conducting liquid in a tube in the longitudinal magnetic field, *Magnitn. Gidrodin.*, no. 4, 147–150, 1966.
33. Loitsyanskiy, L. G., *Mechanics of Liquids and Gases*, 5th ed. revised, Moscow, 1978, 736, p.
34. Lyatkher, V. M. and Prudovskiy, A. M., *Hydrodynamic Modelling*, Moscow, 1984, 392 p.
35. Makarov, A. N. and Sherman, M. Ya., *Calculation of Throttling Devices*, Metalloizdat, Moscow, 1953, 283 p.
36. Malkov, M. P. and Pavlov, K. F., *Handbook of Deep Cooling*, Gostekhizdat, Moscow, 1947, 411 p.
37. Mergertroid, V., Experimental MHD-flows in channels, in *MHD-Flows in Channels*, Moscow, 1963, pp. 196–201.
38. Mikheev, M. A., Filimonov, S. S., and Khrustalyov, B. A., *Convective and Radiative Heat Transfer*, Moscow, 1960.
39. Monin, A. S. and Yaglom, A. M., *Statistical Hydromechanics*, Part 1, Fizmatizdat, 1965, 640 p.; Part II Nauka Press, Moscow, 1967, 720 p.
40. Nevelson, M. I., *Centrifugal Ventilators*, Gosenergoizdat, 1954, 335 p.
41. Petukhov, B. S. and Krasnoshchyokov, E. A., Hydarulic resistance in viscous nonisothermal motion of fluid in tubes, *Zh. Tekh. Fiz.*, vol. 28, no. 6, 1207–1209, 1958.
42. Petukhov, B. S., *Heat Transfer and Resitance in Laminar Liquid Flow in Tubes*, Moscow, 1967, 412 p.
43. Pisarevskiy, V. M. and Ponomarenko, Yu. B., Concerning variations in the gas density and pressure in local resistances of pipelines, *Izv. VUZov, Mashinostr.*, 66–70, 1979.
44. Prandtl, L., *Fundamentals of Hydro- and Aerodynamics*, McGraw-Hill, 1934, Russian translocation — GIIL, 1953, 520 p.
45. *Industrial Aerodynamics (Trudy TsAGI)*, no. 7 (air conduits), Moscow, 1954, 154 p.
46. Rikhter, G., *Hydraulics of Pipe Lines*, ONTI Press, 1936, 340 p.
47. Sedov, L. I., *Self-Similar and Dimensional Methods in Mechanics*, Nauka Press, Moscow, 1967, 428 p.
48. Skobeltsyn, Yu, A., Mezhidov, V. Kh., and Geller, Z. I., Flow discharge from inner cylindrical nozzles with incomplete contraction due to a baffle or tapering, *Izv. VUZov, Neft Gas*, no. 9, 71–74, 1967.
49. Skobeltsyn, Yu. A., Bashilov, E. B., and Geller, Z. I., Flow discharge from external cylindrical capillary nozzles, *Izv. VUZov, Neft Gaz*, no. 10, 80–84, 1971.
50. Solodkin, E. E. and Guinevsky, A. S., *Turbulent Flow of Viscous Fluid Over the Starting Lengths of Axisymmetric and Plane Channels*, Oborongiz, Moscow, 1957 (Trudy TsAGI No. 701).
51. Kiselyov, P. G. (Ed.), *Handbook of Hydraulic Calculations*, 4th ed., Moscow, 1972, 312 p.
52. *Handbook of Chemistry*, Vol. 1, Goskhimizdat, Moscow, 1951, 1072 p.
53. Vargaftik, N. B. (Ed.), *Handbook of the Thermal Properties of Liquids and Gases*, Nauka Press, Moscow, 1972, 720 p.
54. Stepanov, P. M., Ovcharenko, I. Kh., and Skobeltsyn, Yu. A., *Handbook of Hydraulics for Land Reclaimants*, Moscow, 1984, 207 p.

55. Stochek, N. P. and Shapiro, A. S., *The Hydraulics of Liquid-Propellant Rocket Engines*, Moscow, 1978, 127 p.

56. Tananyev, A. V., *The Flow in the MHD-Equipment Channels*, Moscow, 1979, 364 p.

57. Blum, E. Ya., Zaks, M. V., Ivanov, U. I., and Mikhailov, Yu. A., *Heat and Mass Transfer in the Electromagnetic Field*, Riga, 1967, 223 p.

58. Fabrikant, N. Ya., *Aerodynamics*, Gostekhizdat, Moscow, 1964, 814 p.

59. Filippov, G. V., On turbulent flow over starting lengths of straight circular tubes, *Zh. Tekh. Fiz.*, vol. 28, no. 8, 1823–1828, 1958.

60. Frenkel, V. Z., *Hydraulics*, Gosenergoizdat, Moscow, 1956, 456 p.

61. Khozhainov, A. I., Turbulent liquid metal flow in the MHD-channels of round cross section, *Zh. Tekh. Fiz.*, vol. 36, no. 1, 147–150, 1966.

62. Jen, P., *Stalling Flows*, Vol. 1, 298 p.; Vol. 2, 280 p.; Vol. 3, 3p., Mir Press, Moscow, 1972.

63. Shiller, L., *Flow of Liquids in Pipes*, Tekhizdat, Moscow, 1936, 230 p.

64. Schlichting, G., *Boundary Layer Theory*, Nauka Press, Moscow, 1974, 711 p.

65. Shcherbinin, E. V., An electrically conducting liquid in the intrinsic magnetic field of the electric current, *Magnitn. Gidrodin.*, no. 1, 68–74, 1975.

66. Shchukin, V. K., *Heat Transfer and Hydrodynamics of Internal Flows in the Fields of Body Forces*, Moscow, 1970, 331 p.

67. Elterman, V. M., *Air Screens*, Mashinostroenie Press, Moscow, 1966, 164 p.

68. Yuriev, B. N., *Experimental Aerodynamics*, ONTI, 1936, 315 p.

69. Barach, A. L., The flow of heavy gases through small orifices, including comparison between oxygen and perfluoropropane, C_3F_8, and perfluorobutane, C_4F_{10}, *Am. I. Med. Sci.*, Vol. 243, no. 1, 30–34, 1962.

70. Benedict, P. and Carlucci, A., *Handbook of Specific Losses in Flow Systems*, Plenum Press, Data Division; New York, 1970, 30 p.

71. Boussinesq, I., Memoir sur l'influence des frottements dans les mouvements reguliers des fluides, *J. Math. Pur Appl.*, no. 13, 377, 1868.

72. Forst, T. H., The compressible discharge coefficient of a Borda pipe and other nozzles, *J. R. Aeronaut. Soc.*, no. 641, 346–349, 1964.

73. Iversen, H. W., Orifice coefficients for Reynolds numbers from 4 to 50000, *Trans. ASME*, vol. 78, no. 2, 359–364, 1956.

74. Jackson, R. A., The compressible discharge of air through small thick plate orifices, *Appl. Sci. Res.*, vol. A13, nos. 4–5, 241–248, 1964.

75. Kolodzie, P. A., Jr. and Van Winkle, M., Discharge coefficients through perforated plates, *AIChE J.*, vol. 3, 305–312, 1959.

76. Maa Yer., Ru., Gas flow through an annular gap, *J. Vac. Sci. Technol.*, vol. 5, 153–154, 1968.

77. Murakami, M. and Katayama, K., Discharge coefficients of fire nozzles, *Trans. ASME*, vol. D88, no. 4, 706–716, 1966.

78. Wielogorski, J. W., Flow through narrow rectangular notches, *Engineer*, vol. 221, 963–965, 1966.

RESISTANCE TO FLOW IN STRAIGHT TUBES AND CONDUITS FRICTION COEFFICIENTS AND ROUGHNESS

2-1 EXPLANATIONS AND PRACTICAL RECOMMENDATIONS

1. The pressure losses along a straight tube (conduit) of constant cross section (linear or friction losses) are calculated from the Darcy-Weisbach equation:

$$\Delta p_{fr} = \frac{\lambda}{4} \frac{s_0}{F_0} \frac{\rho w_0^2}{2} = \lambda \frac{\Pi_0}{4 F_0} l \frac{\rho w_0^2}{2} = \frac{\lambda}{4} \frac{l}{R_h} \frac{\rho w_0^2}{2} \tag{2-1}$$

or

$$\Delta p_{fr} = \lambda \frac{l}{D_h} \frac{\rho w_0^2}{2} = \zeta \frac{\rho w_0^2}{2} \tag{2-2}$$

where Π_0 is the perimeter; R_h is the hydraulic radius; s_0 is the area of the friction surface.

2. The use of the hydraulic (equivalent) diameter D_h as the characteristic length in resistance Equations (2-1) and (2-2) is permissible only in cases when the thickness δ_0 of the boundary layer (within which the velocity changes from zero to nearly a maximum value) is very small over the entire or almost the entire perimeter of the cross section compared with the dimensions of the channel cross section ($\delta_0 \ll D_h$).[38]

3. In the case of a turbulent flow at large Reynolds numbers, $Re = w_0 D_0/\nu$, the velocity, for the most part, changes within a thin boundary layer. Therefore, when D_h is used as a characteristic dimension, the resistance law for tubes of different cross sections remains about the same. However, even in turbulent flow individual geometries have different friction resistance coefficients.

4. The hydraulic resistance of a tube (channel) with a stabilized laminar flow cannot be calculated through the use of D_h. For these flow conditions its use is permissible only for the inlet portion of the starting length of the tube when the thickness δ_0 is still very small.[42] Appropriate corrections should be made for the effect of the cross-sectional shape of tubes (channels) to allow the resistance to be calculated from Equations (2-1) and (2-2).

5. The resistance to the motion of a liquid or a gas under conditions of laminar flow is due to the force of internal friction (viscosity), which manifests itself when one layer of the liquid (gas) moves relative to the other. Viscosity forces are proportional to the first power of the flow velocity.

6. Due to the overriding effects of the viscosity forces in laminar flow, even flow past surface asperities appears to be smooth. Therefore the roughness of the walls, unless it is very significant, does not affect the flow resistance. Under these conditions of flow the friction coefficient is always a function of the Reynolds number alone.

7. As the Reynolds number increases, the inertia forces, which are proportional to the velocity squared, begin to dominate. Turbulent motion is then initiated, which is characterized by the development of transverse velocity components giving rise to agitation of the fluid throughout the entire stream and to momentum exchange between randomly moving masses of fluid. All this causes a significant increase in the resistance to motion in turbulent flow as compared with the case for laminar flow.*

When the surface of the walls is rough, separation occurs in the flow past roughness asperities and the resistance coefficient becomes a function not only of the Reynolds number but also of the relative roughness

$$\overline{\Delta}_0 = \frac{\Delta_0}{D_h} \left(\overline{\Delta} = \frac{\Delta}{D_h} \right)$$

8. Pipes and channels can be either smooth or rough, with the roughness being either uniform or nonuniform. These two types of roughness differ according to the shape of such protuberances, their dimensions, the spaces between them, etc. The majority of commerical pipes and tubes have nonuniform roughness.

9. The averaged height Δ_0 of asperities, in terms of the absolute length units, is called the absolute geometric roughness. The ratio of the average height of asperities to the tube diameter, that is, $\overline{\Delta}_0 = \Delta_0/D_0$ or $\overline{\Delta}_0/D_h$ ($\overline{\Delta} = \Delta/D_h$), is called the relative roughness. In view of the fact that the geometric characteristics of the absolute roughness cannot adequately determine the flow resistance of the tube, the concept of the hydraulically equivalent uniform-grain roughness Δ is introduced, which is determined by measuring the resistance.

10. Although the resistance coefficient for smooth tubes should decrease with increasing Re, rough tubes show an increase in the coefficient λ with increase of this number with constant geometric roughness. This is explained by the effect of a viscous sublayer. When the thickness of the viscous sublayer is larger than roughness protuberances ($\delta_t > \Delta$, Figure 2-1a), the latter are entirely covered with this layer. At low velocities, typical of a laminar sublayer, the fluid moves smoothly past surface irregularities and they have no effect on the character of the flow. In this case λ decreases with a rise in Re.

11. With an increase in the Reynolds number, the laminar sublayer becomes thinner and, at Re attaining a certain value, it can become smaller than the height of the asperities ($\delta_t > \Delta$, Figure 2-1b). The asperities enhance the formation of vortices and hence increase the pressure losses, which result in the rise of λ with increasing Re.

---

*Nevertheless, since the resistance coefficient λ is determined as the ratio of the overall pressure losses to the velocity pressure

$$\lambda = \frac{\Delta p_{fr}}{(l/D_h)(\rho w_0^2/2)}$$

it always increases with a decrease in Re.

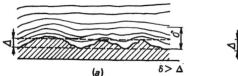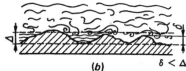

Figure 2-1 Flow past roughness asperities for different modes of flow: (a) $\delta_t > \Delta$; (b) $\delta_t < \Delta$.

Thus, tubes can be considered smooth as long as the height of asperities is smaller than the thickness of the laminar sublayer.

12. The equivalent roughness Δ depends on:

• The material of tubular products and the method by which they were manufactured. For example, iron pipes manufactured by centrifugal casting are smoother than welded tubes. Tubes manufactured by the same method have, as a rule, the same equivalent roughness irrespective of their diameter.
• The properties of the fluid flowing in a tube; liquids may cause corrosion on the inner surface of the tube, resulting in formation of protuberances and deposition of scale.
• The service life and history of the tubes.

13. The dependence of the frictional resistance coefficient λ on Re and $\overline{\Delta}_0$, as determined by the experiments of Nikuradse[87] for a stabilized flow (see Section 1-3) in tubes with uniform grain roughness* (Figure 2-2), suggests the existence of three principal regimes of flow.

14. The first regime, called the laminar regime, involves small values of the Reynolds number (up to Re ≈ 2000) and is characterized by λ being independent of roughness. From the Hagen-Poiseuille law[172]

$$\lambda = \frac{64}{\text{Re}} \tag{2-3}$$

15. The second regime, called the transition regime, consists of three segments of the resistance curves for uniform roughness:

• The segment related to the transition (critical) region between laminar and turbulent flow (approximately with Re = 2000–4000). The resistance coefficient λ in this region increases with Re. However, this coefficient remains independent of the value of relative roughness.
• The segment for which the resistance curves of tubes with different roughness coincide with the Blasius curve for smooth tubes

$$\lambda = \frac{0.3164}{\text{Re}^{0.25}}$$

According to this equation, the resistance law is valid within the range of Re numbers which is the smaller, the greater the relative roughness.

---

*A form of artificial sand uniform grain roughness is meant here, as obtained by Nikuradse. The curves for other forms of artificial roughness can differ somewhat.[152]

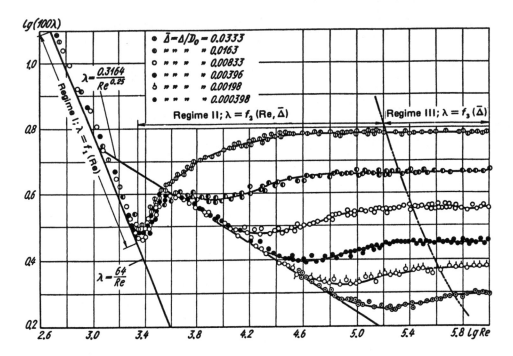

Figure 2-2 Dependence of the resistance coefficient λ on Re for tubes with uniform grain roughness.[190]

- The segment for which the resistance curves of tubes with different roughness diverge from each other, departing from the straight line obtained from Equation (2-4). Here, the resistance coefficients for certain ranges of Re* increase with increasing relative roughness.

16. The third regime is called the quadratic or square-law regime, the regime of rough walls, and sometimes the regime of turbulent self-similarity. It is characterized by the resistance coefficients for each value of the relative roughness becoming constant, independent of Re.

17. It follows from Nikuradse's[87] resistance equations for rough tubes [see Equation (2-5)] and Filonenko[171] and Altshul's[6] resistance equation for smooth tubes [see Equation (2-8)] that tubes with uniform grain roughness can be considered hydraulically smooth provided that

$$\overline{\Delta} \le \overline{\Delta}_{\text{lim}}$$

where

$$\overline{\Delta}_{\text{lim}} = \frac{\Delta}{D_h} \quad \overline{\Delta}_{\text{lim}} = \frac{181 \lg \text{Re} - 16.4}{\text{Re}}$$

For the range of Reynolds numbers up to Re $= 10^5$, the Blasius formula gives

$$\overline{\Delta}_{\text{lim}} \approx 17.85 \, \text{Re}^{-0.875}$$

*Within these ranges of Re, λ ceases to increase.

From this, the boundary (limiting) values of the Reynolds number, at which roughness begins to be important, can be defined as

$$Re'_{lim} = \frac{26.9}{\overline{\Delta}^{1.143}}$$

18. For tubes with uniform grain roughness the limiting value of the Reynolds number, for which the quadratic law of resistance will hold, is determined from

$$Re''_{lim} = \frac{217 - 382 \lg \overline{\Delta}}{\overline{\Delta}}$$

which follows from Nikuradze's[87] formula for a stabilized flow in the transitional and quadratic regions, i.e., within the limits

$$\frac{26.9}{\overline{\Delta}^{1.143}} \leq Re \leq \frac{217 - 382 \lg \overline{\Delta}}{\overline{\Delta}}$$

This formula has the following form:

$$\lambda = \frac{1}{[a_1 + b_1 \lg(Re\sqrt{\lambda} + c_1 \lg \overline{\Delta})]^2} \tag{2-5}$$

where at $3.6 \leq \overline{\Delta} \, Re \, \sqrt{\lambda} \leq 10$
$a_1 = -0.8 \quad b = +2.0 \quad c_1 = 0$ (smooth walls)
at $10 \leq \overline{\Delta} \, Re \, \sqrt{\lambda} \leq 20$
$a_1 = +0.068 \quad b = 1.13 \quad c_1 = -0.87$
at $20 \leq \overline{\Delta} \, Re \, \sqrt{\lambda} \leq 40$
$a_1 = +1.538 \quad b_1 = 0 \quad c_1 = -2.0$
at $40 \leq \overline{\Delta} \, Re \, \sqrt{\lambda} \leq 191.2$
$a_1 = +2.471 \quad b_1 = -0.588 \quad c_1 = -2.588$
at $\overline{\Delta} \, Re \, \sqrt{\lambda} > 191.2$
$a_1 = +1.138 \quad b_1 = 0 \quad c_1 = -2.0$

which*

*Teplov,[128] having made a more rigorous treatment of Nikuradze's[87] experiments, has shown that for the quadratic region the following formula is more appropriate:

$$\lambda = \frac{1}{\left(1.8 \lg \dfrac{8.3}{\overline{\Delta}}\right)^2}$$

Closely coinciding with this is the formula suggested by Altshul:[6]

$$\lambda = \frac{1}{(1.8 \lg 10/\overline{\Delta})^2}$$

However, taking into account that Equation (2-6) deviates from the experiment data by not more than 5%, but to the side of adding to the safety margin, it can be used in practical calculations of pipelines including the nonlined power conduits.[7]

$$\lambda = \frac{1}{\left(2 \lg \dfrac{3.7}{\bar{\Delta}}\right)^2} \tag{2-6}$$

19. Proceeding from the assumption that laminar and turbulent flows occur simultaneously and applying the normal law of distribution to determine the probability of occurrence of rerespective regimes, Kerensky[50] suggested a single formula for the friction resistance of tubes with uniform grain roughness for the zone of the replacement of regimes*

$$\lambda = \lambda_{\text{lam}} p_{\text{lam}} + \lambda_{\text{sm}} p_{\text{sm}} + \lambda_r p_r \tag{2-7}$$

where λ_{lam}, λ_{sm}, and λ_r are the friction resistance coefficients in laminar (2-3) and turbulent flow in smooth (2-4) and rough tubes (2-6);

$$p_{\text{lam}} = 1 - p_t$$
$$p_{\text{sm}} = (1 - p_{r\text{-}t})p_t$$
$$p_r = p_{r\text{-}t}p_t$$

are the probabilities for the appearance of laminar and turbulent regimes of flow in smooth and rough tubes at the given Reynolds number; in this case

$$p_{r\text{-}t} = 2\phi(U)$$

where

$$U = \frac{\text{Re}}{\sigma_r}, \qquad \sigma_r = \frac{275}{\bar{\Delta}}, \qquad p_t = \frac{1}{2} + \phi(U)$$

where

$$U = \frac{\text{Re} - \text{Re}_r}{\sigma_t} = \frac{\text{Re} - 2850}{600}; \qquad \phi(U) = \frac{1}{\sqrt{2\pi}} \int_0^U \exp(-t^2/2)\, dt$$

is the normalized Laplace function (the integral of probabilitites; see Reference Table 18.8-9).

20. The resistance curves $\lambda - f(\text{Re},\bar{\Delta})$ for a stabilized flow in tubes with nonuniform roughness (commercial tubes) show that for this case there also exist three main flow regimes: laminar, transition, and quadratic (Figure 2-3). However, unlike the case of flow in tubes with uniform grain roughness, here one should take into account the following two specific features:

● For different degrees of roughness the resistance coefficient is not the same over the section related to the transition region between the laminar and turbulent flows (critical

---

*Treatment of turbulent flows in a boundary layer and tubes utilizing the principle of superposition of molecular and turbulent viscosities allowed Millionshchikov[77,78] to find a general formula for the friction resistance which is applicable for all flow regimes. About the same approach was used in the work of Svirsky and Platon[107] and also in the work of Adamov.[4]

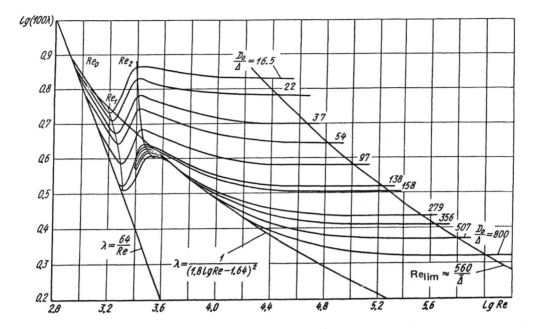

Figure 2-3 Dependence of the resistance coefficient λ on the Reynolds number Re and the relative roughness $\overline{\Delta}$ for nonuniform roughness.[100,106]

zone or zone of change of regime) the resistance coefficient depends on the relative roughness and on the Reynolds number; pressure losses in this zone are proportional to the velocity raised to a power greater than two.[100]

● The transition segment of a purely turbulent regime is free of a deflection typical of the curves of λ in tubes with uniform grain roughness (see Figure 2-2). In this case, there is a progressive and smooth decrease in the resistance curves with increase in Re, with the lowest position being attained in the quadratic regime.[82,171]

21. The curves of the friction coefficients for commercial tubes with relative equivalent roughness $\overline{\Delta} > 0.007$ will, at some value of Re, depart from the Hagen-Poiseuille law to the side of higher λ's, and the greater the relative roughness, the earlier this departure will occur (see Figure 2-3). The Reynolds number corresponding to the onset of this departure can be determined from the equation suggested by Samoilenko:[106]

$$Re_0 = 754 \exp\left(\frac{0.0065}{\overline{\Delta}}\right)$$

22. There is a transition curve with boundaries Re_1 and Re_2 which corresponds to each value of $\overline{\Delta}$ in the region where a change in flow regime occurs in the range Re_1 and Re_2 (see Figure 2-3). For tubes with $\overline{\Delta} > 0.007$ the following equation is obtained, based on the data of Samoilenko:[106]

$$Re_1 = 1160\left(\frac{1}{\overline{\Delta}}\right)^{0.11}$$

that is, Re_1 decreases with an increase in the relative roughness $\overline{\Delta}$.

The Reynolds number that determines the Re_2 boundary for tubes with any roughness is

$$Re_2 = 2090\left(\frac{1}{\overline{\Delta}}\right)^{0.0635}$$

23. At $Re_1 > Re_2$, tubes with nonuniform roughness (commercial tubes) can be considered hydraulically smooth (with an accuracy up to 3–4%) provided that

$$\overline{\Delta} < \overline{\Delta}_{lim} \approx \frac{15}{Re}$$

From this, the limiting Reynolds number at which commercial tubes cease to be hydraulically smooth is

$$Re'_{lim} \approx \frac{15}{\overline{\Delta}}$$

24. In the case of nonuniform roughness the limiting Reynolds number at which the quadratic law of resistance will hold can, within 3–4% accuracy, be written as (see Diagram 2-4):

$$Re''_{lim} \approx \frac{560}{\overline{\Delta}}$$

25. For a stabilized laminar flow (up to $Re \approx 2000$) the resistance coefficient λ for circular tubes, which is independent of the relative roughness of walls, is determined from Equation (2-3) or from curve a of Diagram 2-1.
26. For the critical region of a stabilized flow ($Re = 2000$–4000), the friction coefficient λ of a circular tube with hydraulically (commercially) smooth walls is determined from curve b of Diagram 2-1.
27. For the region of purely turbulent stabilized flow ($Re > 4000$) the friction coefficient λ of circular tubes with hydraulically (commercially) smooth walls is determined from curve c of Diagram 2-1 or is calculated from Filonenko[141] and Altshul's[6] formula*

$$\lambda = \frac{1}{(1.8 \ln Re - 1.64)^2}$$

28. The friction coefficient λ for stabilized flow in the transition region where there occurs a change of flow regime is determined from curve $\lambda = f(Re,\overline{\Delta})$ of Diagram 2-3 or from formulas suggested by Samoilenko:[106]

At $Re_0 < Re < Re_1$ and $\overline{\Delta} \geqslant 0.007$

$$\lambda = 4.4\,Re^{-0.595} \exp\left(-\frac{0.00275}{\overline{\Delta}}\right)$$

---

*This formula is very similar to the formulas of Konakov,[54] Murin,[82] and Yakimov.

At $Re_1 < Re < Re_2$

$$\lambda = (\lambda_2 - \lambda^*) \exp\{-[0.0017(Re_2 - Re)]^2\} + \lambda^*$$

where at $\overline{\Delta} \leqslant 0.007$, $\lambda^* = \lambda_1$, and at $\overline{\Delta} = 0.0007$, $\lambda^* = \lambda_1 - 0.0017$.
The coefficients λ_1 and λ_2, which correspond to Re_1 and Re_2, are

at $\overline{\Delta} \leqslant 0.007$ $\lambda_2 \approx 0.032$

at $\overline{\Delta} > 0.007$ $\lambda_1 = 0.0775 - \dfrac{0.0109}{\overline{\Delta}^{0.286}}$

at $\overline{\Delta} \leqslant 0.007$ $\lambda_2 = 7.244(Re_2)^{-0.643}$

at $\overline{\Delta} > 0.007$ $\lambda_2 = \dfrac{0.145}{\overline{\Delta}^{-0.244}}$

$$Re_0 = 754 \exp\left(\frac{0.0065}{\overline{\Delta}}\right)$$

$$Re_1 = 1160\left(\frac{1}{\overline{\Delta}}\right)^{0.11}$$

$$Re_2 = 2090\left(\frac{1}{\overline{\Delta}}\right)^{0.0635}$$

29. For a stabilized flow and the region of purely turbulent flow ($Re > Re_2$), the friction coefficient λ of all commercial circular tubes* (with nonuniform roughness of walls), except for special cases for which the values of λ are given separately, can be determined from the curves of Diagram 2-4 plotted on the basis of the Colebrook-White** formula:[171]

$$\lambda = \frac{1}{[2 \lg (2.51/Re\sqrt{\lambda}) + \overline{\Delta}/3.7]^2} \tag{2-9}$$

or for engineering calculations, from Altshul's[6] approximate formula***

$$\lambda = 0.11\left(\overline{\Delta} + \frac{68}{Re}\right)^{0.25} \tag{2-10}$$

---

*Including steel, concrete, and iron-concrete pressure tunnels.[7]

**The Colebrook-White curves lie somewhat above (by 2–4%) similar curves of Murin[82] and hence provide some safety margin for the calculations. Analogous formulas were obtained by Adamov,[3] Filonenko,[141] and Frenkel[144]. The interpolation formula of Colebrook has now been theoretically substantiated[6].

***The formula close to Equation (2–10) was also obtained by Adamov;[4] at $68/Re < \overline{\Delta}$ it coincides with the formula of Shifrinson: $\lambda = 0.11(\overline{\Delta})^{0.25}$. There is another simple formula convenient for application in the transient region (within $\lambda = 0.0001$–0.01) which was suggested by Lobaev: $\lambda = 1.42/(\lg Re/\overline{\Delta})^2$.

30. For the region with a change of regime of a stabilized flow in commercial tubes, a single formula can also be used to calculate the friction coefficient (as suggested by Adamovich), viz.

$$\lambda = \lambda_{lam}(1 - p) + \lambda_t p$$

where λ_{lam} is determined from Equation (2-3), λ_t from Equation (2-9) or (2-10), and

$$p = \frac{1}{2}\left[\text{erf}\left(\frac{\text{Re} - \text{Re}_0}{\sqrt{2}\,\sigma}\right) + \text{erf}\left(\frac{\text{Re}_0}{\sqrt{2}\,\sigma}\right)\right]$$

in which $\text{Re}_0 = 1530(\overline{\Delta})^{-0.08}$ and $\sigma = 540$. Here the tabulated function of errors is used in the form

$$\text{erf}(z) = \frac{2}{\sqrt{\pi}}\int_0^z \exp(-t^2)\,dt$$

(see Reference 56 Table 18.8-10).

31. A single formula for calculating the friction coefficient in the zone with the change of regimes was also suggested by Slisskiy[110]

$$\lambda = \lambda_{lam}(1 - \gamma) + \lambda_t \gamma$$

where γ is the intermittency factor;

$$\gamma = \sin^{3/2}\left(\pi/2\,\frac{\text{Re} - \text{Re}_{low}}{\text{Re}_{up} - \text{Re}_{low}}\right)$$

$$\text{Re}_{low} = 1000\,\exp\left(\frac{0.00465}{\overline{\Delta}}\right)$$

$$\text{Re}_{up} = 1600(\overline{\Delta})^{-0.16}$$

where Re_{low} and Re_{up} are the lower and upper boundaries of the transition zone.

The coefficients λ_{lam} and λ_t are calculated respectively from Equation (2-3) and from Teplov's[128] formula

$$\lambda_t = \left(1.8\,\lg\frac{8.25}{56/\text{Re} + \overline{\Delta}}\right)^{-2}$$

32. The friction coefficients λ for circular tubes, except in special cases for which the values of λ are given separately with any kind of roughness (both uniform and nonuniform) for stabilized flow in the quadratic region, i.e., virtually when $\text{Re} > 560/\overline{\Delta}$, are determined from the graphs of Diagram 2-5 plotted on the basis of Equation (2-6).

The specific feature of flow in channels with the complex geometry of cross sections is the presence of convective transfer across the flow due to the motion of large-scale vortices and secondary flows (Figure 2-4)*. This fact and also the variable roughness of the channel walls are responsible for the nonuniform distribution of shear on the flow boundaries.

*It is imperative to distinguish between the secondary flows observed in straight channels of complex cross section and those originating for other reasons in curvilinear channels.

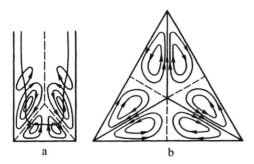

a   b

Figure 2-4 Schemes of secondary flows: (*a*) in a rectangular tube; (*b*) in an equilateral triangular tube.

Therefore, the friction coefficients can be calculated most accurately when replacing the flow characteristics averaged over the channel cross section (mean velocity, Reynolds number, mean relative roughness, mean shear stress) by the local characteristics (local relative roughness, local Reynolds number, local friction factors of hydraulics, local shear stresses).[133] As the local governing flow parameters, it is recommended to use the local characteristic dimension of flow, the flow velocity averaged over this dimension, and the local roughness of walls. The other local characteristics of the flow are expressed in terms of these determining quantities.

33. The local shear stress τ_w at the point of the wetted perimeter is expressed in terms of the local velocity w_w averaged over the normal to the wall:

$$\tau_w = \lambda_{\text{loc}} \frac{\rho w_w^2}{2}$$

where λ_{loc} is the local friction coefficient, being a function of the local Reynolds number and local relative roughness

$$\lambda_{\text{loc}} = f\left(\frac{w_w l}{\nu}, \frac{\Delta}{l}\right)$$

l is the characeristic local dimension of the flow, depending on the shape of the channel cross section (for example, for a square channel l is the distance from the wall to the corner bisector).

34. In the specific case of a rectangular channel, for which it is assumed that the shear stresses on the long and short sides of it differ, but their distribution over the walls is uniform, Skrebkov[112,113] and Skrebkov and Lozhkiu[114] suggested a formula which relates the friction coefficient of the channel with its shape and roughness:

$$\lambda = 4 \frac{b/h}{1 + b/h} \left(1 + \frac{\lambda_{\text{sh}}}{\lambda_{\text{long}}} \frac{h}{b}\right) \lambda_{\text{long}}$$

where λ_{sh} and λ_{long} are the friction coefficients respectively on the short and long walls of the channel; b and h are the halves of the width and of the height of the channel, respectively.

The coefficients λ_{sh} and λ_{long} are calculated by the laws of resistance of a plane wall (λ_{pl}) depending on the characteristic Reynolds number and wall roughness:[112-114]

$$(\lambda_{\text{pl}})_{\text{sh}} = f[(\text{Re}_{\text{pl}})_b, \overline{\Delta}_{\text{sh}}]$$

$$(\lambda_{\text{pl}})_{\text{long}} = f[(\text{Re}_{\text{pl}})_h, \overline{\Delta}_{\text{long}}]$$

where

$$(\text{Re}_{\text{pl}})_b = \frac{\text{Re}}{4}(1 + b/h), \quad (\text{Re}_{\text{pl}})_b = \frac{\text{Re}}{4}\left(\frac{1 + b/h}{b/h}\right)$$

$$\text{Re} = \frac{w_0 D_h}{\nu}$$

For smooth walls

$$\lambda_{\text{pl}} = \frac{1}{(3.6 \lg \text{Re}_{\text{pl}} - 2)^2}$$

for commercial walls

$$\lambda_{\text{pl}} = 0.024\left(\frac{54}{\text{Re}_{\text{pl}}} + \frac{\Delta}{l}\right)^{0.25}$$

for rough walls

$$\lambda_{\text{pl}} = \frac{1}{(4 \lg l/\Delta + 3.48)^2}$$

35. In many cases it is easier to determine the resistance coefficient of noncircular tubes by the introduction into the formulas for circular tubes the corresponding correction factors $\lambda_{\text{non-c}} = k_{\text{non-c}}\lambda$, where λ is the friction coefficient of circular tubes at the same Reynolds number, $\text{Re} = w_0 D_h/\nu = w_0 D_0/\nu$; $\lambda_{\text{non-c}}$ is λ for noncircular tubes; $k_{\text{non-c}}$ is the correction factor allowing for the effect of tube cross-sectional shape.*

36. For tubes with nearly circular cross sections (for example, a circle with one or two notches, starlike shapes, see Diagram 2-6), it can be assumed, according to the data of Nikuradse[87] and Shiller,[158] that $k_{\text{non-c}} \approx 1.0$ for all flow regimes.

For rectangular tubes for laminar flow ($\text{Re} \leqslant 2000$), the correction factor, which depends on the aspect ratio a_0/b_0, lies in the range $k_{\text{non-c}} = k_{\text{rec}} = 0.89\text{--}1.50$. When $a_0/b_0 = 1.0$ (square), $k_{\text{rec}} = k_{\text{quad}} = 0.89$ or

$$\lambda_{\text{quad}} = \frac{57}{\text{Re}}$$

and when $a_0/b_0 \to 0$ (plane slot), $k_{\text{rec}} = k_{\text{pl}} = 1.50$ or

$$\lambda_{\text{pl}} = \frac{96}{\text{Re}}$$

For turbulent flow ($\text{Re} > 2000$), $k_{\text{rec}} = 1.0\text{--}1.1$. When $a_0/b_0 = 1.0$, $k_{\text{quad}} \approx 1.0$, and when $a_0/b_0 \to 0$, $k_{\text{pl}} \approx 1.1$.[40,180]

---

*A. G. Temkin[125,126] suggests calling the correction factor $k_{\text{non-c}}$ the criterion of Leibenson (Le), who made an important contribution to the hydraulics of pipelines. In the works cited, Temkin gives corresponding formulas to calculate the number Le.

37. For elliptical tubes in laminar flow (Re $\leqslant$ 2000) the correction factor, which depends on the ratio of the ellipse axes (see Petukhov),[95] is determined as

$$k_{\text{non-c}} \equiv k_{\text{ell}} = \frac{1}{8}\left(\frac{D_h}{b_0}\right)^2\left[1 + \left(\frac{b_0}{a_0}\right)^2\right]$$

where a_0 and b_0 are the major and minor semiaxes of the ellipse.

For turbulent flow this factor can be approximated as $k_{\text{ell}} \approx 1.0$.

38. For a round annular tube (a tube within a tube) the correction factor, which is a function of the diameter ratio d/D_0 (see Leibenson[68] and Petukhov),[95] can be found for laminar flow (Re $\leqslant$ 2000) from

$$k_{\text{non-c}} = k_{\text{ann}} = \frac{(1 - d/D_0)^2}{1 + (d/D_0)^2 + [1 - (d/D_0)^2]/\ln d/D_0}$$

where d and D_0 are the diameters of the inner and outer cylinders of the annular tube.

In the case of turbulent flow k_{ann} depends only slightly on d/D_0 and lies in the range 1.0–1.07.[29] The resistance coefficient λ_{ann} of such a tube can also be calculated from the following formula[39]

$$\lambda_{\text{ann}} = \left(\frac{0.02d}{D_0 + 0.98}\right)\left(\frac{1}{\lambda} - 0.27\frac{d}{D_0} + 0.01\right)$$

39. The inner cylinder of a circular annular tube is centered by means of longitudinal or spiral fins (see Diagram 2-7). A narrow annular tube ($d/D_0 \approx 0.9$) with three longitudinal fins is approximately equivalent to a rectangular channel with aspect ratio $a_0/b_0 \approx 0.06$, for which, in the case of laminar flow, the correction factor (based on the experiments of Subbotin et al.),[120] is $k'_{\text{ann}} = k_{\text{rec}} \approx 1.36$

For turbulent flow, the correction factor can be taken the same as that for an annular tube with no fins (according to paragraph 38).

40. For an annular tube with spiral fins, the correction factor, which depends on the relative pitch of the winding of fins, T/d (see Diagram 2-7), can approximately be determined for all the flow regime from the following formula:[120]

$$k''_{\text{ann}} = 1 + \frac{20}{(T/d)^2}k'_{\text{ann}}$$

where k'_{ann} is the correction factor for an annular tube with longitudinal fins.

41. The friction coefficient of an eccentric annular tube (see Diagram 2-7) for both laminar and turbulent flows depends on the eccentricity and the relative width of the annular channel.

42. The correction factor for laminar flow is calculated from the approximate formula of Gostev and Riman[30]

$$k_{\text{non-c}} = k_{\text{ell}} = \frac{1}{(1 + B_1\bar{e})^2}k_{\text{ann}}$$

where $\bar{e} = 2e/D_0 - d$ is the eccentricity (e is the distance between the centers of the inner and outer cylinders); B_1 is a coefficient that depends on the ratio d/D_0, obtained on the basis of the data of Johnston and Sparrow[178] (see Diagram 2-7, graph c); and k_{ann} is the correction factor for a concentric ring.

43. The correction factor for turbulent flow is

$$k_{ell} = k'_{ell} k_{ann}$$

where $k'_{ell} = \lambda/\lambda_{ann}$ is the ratio of the resistance coefficient of an eccentric annular tube to the resistance coefficient of a concentric annular tube.

The coefficient k'_{ell} for narrow annular channels ($d/D_0 \geqslant 0.7$) is nearly independent of d/D_0 and is a function only of eccentricity (see graph d of Diagram 2-7 for $d/D_0 = 0.5$ and $d/D_0 \geqslant 0.7$).

When $d/D_0 \geqslant 0.7$, the correction factor can be determined from the formula of Kolesnikov:[21]

$$k'_{ell} = 1 - 0.9(1 - 2/3\bar{e})\bar{e}^2$$

44. The correction factor k_{non-c} for laminar flow of tubes with a cross section in the form of an isosceles triangle (see Migai)[76] is

$$k_{non-c} = k_{tr} = \frac{3}{4} \frac{(1 - \text{tg}^2 \beta)(B + 2)}{(B - 2)(\text{tg} \beta + \sqrt{1 + \text{tg}^2 \beta})^2}$$

where

$$B = \sqrt{4 + \frac{5}{2} \frac{1}{\text{tg}^2 \beta}} - 1$$

is a parameter, and β is half the apex angle of the isosceles triangle, in degrees.

For an equilateral triangle ($\beta = 30°$)

$$k'_{tr} = 0.833$$

For a right triangle

$$k''_{tr} = \frac{3}{2} \cdot \frac{(1 - 3 \text{tg}^2 \beta)(B + 2)}{(3/B - 4)(\text{tg} \beta + \sqrt{1 + \text{tg}^2 \beta})^2}$$

and for an equilateral rectangular triangle ($\beta = 45°$)

$$k''_{tr} = 0.825$$

45. In the case of turbulent flow, the correction factor k_{non-c} for an equilateral triangle varies in the range $k_{non-c} = 0.75$–1.0 depending on the angle β: the larger the angle, the higher is k_{tr}.[170] For an equilateral traingle we may assume $k_{tr} = 0.95$.[158]

46. The correction factor for laminar flow for a tube with a cross section in the form of a circular sector is $k_{non-c} = k_{sec} = 0.75$–$1.0$, depending on the angle β;[5] for turbulent flow k_{sec} can be assumed the same as for an equilateral triangle (paragraph 45).

47. The resistance of the starting length of tubes (immediately downstream of a smooth inlet) which are characterized by a nonstabilized flow (see Section 1-3), is higher than in the sections with stabilized flow. The closer to the inlet, the higher is the friction coefficient

$\lambda_{\text{non-st}}$ of the section of a nonstabilized flow. This is due to the fact that with a smooth entrance the boundary layer in the initial sections is much thinner than in subsequent ones, and consequently the shear forces at the walls in these sections are higher. This refers to both nonstabilized laminar and nonstabilized turbulent flow if it is already entirely agitated at the inlet to the tube.

48. In the case of a very smooth entrance, when at Re > Re_{cr} a "mixed" flow regime sets in, the coefficient $k_{\text{non-st}}$ of short tubes (whose length is much shorter than the starting length) is, within certain ranges of the Reynolds number, much smaller for a stabilized turbulent flow which is due to the laminar behavior of the boundary layer in the inlet section of the tube (see Section 1-3). At Re = 2×10^5, the average friction coefficient for a short tube of length $l/D_0 = 2.0$ is seven- to eightfold lower than λ for a stabilized flow (Figure 2-5, see also Filippov).[138]

49. Creation of conditions under which the flow becomes turbulent in the boundary layer at the inlet into the tube leads to an increase in the coefficient $\lambda_{\text{non-st}}$ for short lengths as well (see Figure 2-5). Therefore, for short tubes in real devices (in which the flow at the inlet is very much perturbed as a rule), the local value of the friction coefficient $\lambda'_{\text{non-st}}$ should be determined, for example, from the formula of Sukomel et al.[122] for the conditions of turbulent boundary layer flow

$$\lambda'_{\text{non-st}} \equiv \frac{\Delta p}{\rho w_0^2/2 \times \Delta x/D_0} = \frac{0.344}{(\text{Re} \times x/D_0)^{0.2}} = k'_{\text{non-st}}\lambda \qquad (2\text{-}11)$$

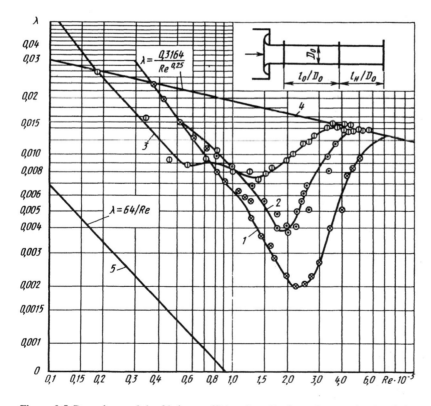

Figure 2-5 Dependence of the friction coefficient λ on Re for a short starting length($l_{st}/D_0 = 2$) with smooth walls: (1) test section is installed immediately downstream of a smooth inlet ($l_0/D_0 = 0$); (2) upstream straight section of length $l_0/D_0 = 0.4$ is installed between the smooth inlet and the test section; (3) relative length of the upstream section is $l_0/D_0 = 4.3$; (4) the resistance curve is according to Blasius; (5) Hagen-Poiseuille curve.

where

$$k'_{\text{non-st}} \approx 1.09 \frac{\text{Re}^{0.05}}{(x/D_0)^{0.2}} \tag{2-12}$$

λ is the friction coefficient of a stabilized flow; $\Delta x = x_1 - x_2$ is a small portion of the tube length from x_1 to x_2.

The average value of the friction coefficient $\lambda''_{\text{non-st}}$ over the entire given length l of the starting section can be calculated for the conditions of a turbulent boundary layer flow from another equation of the same authors

$$\lambda''_{\text{non-st}} \equiv \frac{\Delta p}{\rho w_0^2/2 \times \Delta x/D_0} = \frac{0.43}{(\text{Re} \times x/D_0)^{0.2}} = k''_{\text{non-st}}\lambda \tag{2-13}$$

where

$$k''_{\text{non-st}} \approx 1.36 \frac{\text{Re}^{0.05}}{(x/D_0)^{0.2}} \tag{2-14}$$

Equations (2-11) to (2-14) are correct at least within the range $1.7 \times 10^4 \leqslant \text{Re} \leqslant 10^6$. For practical calculations these equations can also be used in the case of noncircular channels; moreover, the upper limit of Re can be raised. The values of $\lambda'_{\text{non-st}}$ and $\lambda''_{\text{non-st}}$ are listed in Table 1 of Diagram 2-21.

50. In the case of high sub- and supersonic velocities of a gas flow, that is, in the case of a compressible gas, both under the conditions of cooling and in an adiabatic flow, the friction coefficient for the conditions of a turbulent boundary layer flow is[122]

$$\lambda_{\text{com}} = \lambda'_{\text{non-st}}[\tau(\tilde{\lambda})]^{0.4}$$

and accordingly

$$\lambda''_{\text{com}} = \lambda''_{\text{non-st}}[\tau(\tilde{\lambda})]^{0.4}$$

where $\tau(\tilde{\lambda})$ is the gas dynamic function determined from Equation (1-47); $\lambda'_{\text{non-st}}$ and $\lambda''_{\text{non-st}}$ are found from Equations (2-11) and (2-13), respectively.

51. The friction coefficient of the starting length for nonstabilized laminar flow is calculated from the equation similar to Equation (2-13) in which $k_{\text{non-st}}$ is a function of the parameter $x/(D_h\text{Re})$. It is determined from Table 2 of Diagram 2-21 obtained on the basis of Frenkel's[44] data.

52. Flow channels made of bundles of circular cylinders (tubes or rods), such as are widely used in many heat-exchanging systems (e.g., fuel elements of atomic reactors or tubes in conventional heat exchangers), have flow cross sections of shapes other than circular. Usually, the cylinders (rods) in a bundle are placed either in an equilateral triangle or a rectangular pattern (Figure 2-6). The correction factor for the cross-sectional shape of a longitudinal tube bundle depends on both the relative pitch of the cylinders s/d (s is the distance between the axes of the cylinders) and the shape of the tube array and number of cylinders.

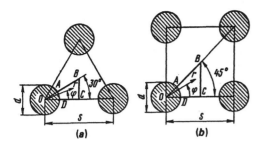

Figure 2-6 Arrangement of cylinders or tubes in the array of (*a*) an equilateral triangle and (*b*) a square.

53. For laminar liquid flow along the bundle without support plates (i.e., an infinite space) the correction factor $k_{\text{non-st}}$[68] is:

$$k_{\text{non-st}} = k_{\text{bund}} = \frac{(\bar{d}^2 - 1)^3}{4\bar{d}^4 \ln \bar{d} - 3\bar{d}^4 + \bar{d}^2 - 1}$$

where $\bar{d} = d_*/d$;

- With cylinders located in the corners of the equilateral triangle (triangular array)

$$d_* = \left(\frac{2\sqrt{3}}{\pi}\right)^{1/2} s$$

$$D_h = d\left[\frac{6}{\pi\sqrt{3}} \left(\frac{s}{d}\right)^2 - 1\right]$$

In this case the correction factor can be determined with the limits $1.0 \leqslant s/d \leqslant 1.5$ from an approximate formula $k_{\text{bund}} \approx 0.89 s/d + 0.63$.
- With cylinders located in the corners of a square with side s

$$d_* = 2s/\sqrt{\pi}$$

$$D_h = 4s^2/(\pi d) - d$$

and

$$k_{\text{bund}} \approx 0.96 \frac{s}{d} + 0.64$$

54. In the case of turbulent liquid flow through a bundle of loosely arranged cylinders (without baffle plates) in a triangular or square array with $s/d = 1.0$, the correction factor $k_{\text{bund}} = 0.64$ (see Ibraguimov et al.).[40]

For an array with a small number of cylinders held by a baffle plate the correction factor increases and can exceed unity.

A relative spacing s/d between the cylinders has different effects on the resistance coefficient, depending on the form of the array (see Diagram 2-9).

For a baffled bundle of finned cylinders at $s/d = 1.05$ the correction factor may be taken the same as the for annular finned tubes (see paragraphs 39 and 40).

55. The shape (bulging) of the cross section of flat-rolled tubes (made from metallic strips) depends on the extent to which they expand under internal pressure and is characterized by the ratio of the cross-sectional semiaxes a_0/b_0.

The friction coefficient of flat-rolled aluminum and steel tubes (see Maron and Roev)[74] is:

At $4 \times 10^3 < \text{Re} < 4 \times 10^4$.

$$\lambda = \frac{A_1}{\text{Re}^{0.25}}$$

and at $4 \times 10^4 < \text{Re} < 2 \times 10^5$:

$$\lambda = \frac{A_2}{\text{Re}^{0.12}}$$

where the coefficients A_1 and A_2 depend on the ratio of the tube semiaxes a_0/b_0 and are determined from the graphs of Diagram 2-10.

56. The resistance of steel tubes with welded joints on which there are metal upsets or burrs is higher than the resistances of seamless tubes. When the weld joints are separated by a relative distance $\bar{l} = l_j/\delta_j \geqslant 50$, the additional resistance of welded tubes may be assumed constant and independent of $\bar{l}$.

Within the limits $\bar{l} \leqslant 50$, the effect of a single joint decreases with decreasing distance between them, so that

$$\zeta_j = k_4 \zeta_j^0$$

where ζ_j and ζ_j^0 are the coefficients of resistance of one joint at a distance $\bar{l}$ and at a distance $\bar{l} \geqslant 50$, respectively; k_4 is the correction factor for the interaction effect of joints. This correction factor can be determined approximately from the dependence of the resistance coefficient for a longitudinal row of cylinders placed in a tube on the relative distance $\bar{l} = l_{\text{cyl}}/d_{\text{loc}} = l_j/d_{\text{loc}}$ between the cylinders in the form[18]

$$\zeta_{\text{cyl}} = n_j[2 \lg \bar{l} + 1] (d_{\text{loc}}/D_0)^{1.4} \tag{2-15}$$

where n_j is the number of cylinders or, in the given case, the number of joints over the tube segment of given length.

57. The interaction effect of cylinders in a longitudinal row manifests itself up to about $\bar{l} = 50$. The interaction effect of the joints is analogous to the same effect of the cylinders in a longitudinal row. Therefore, the correction factor k_4 can be approximately determined as the ratio $\zeta_{\text{cyl}}/(\zeta_{\text{cyl}})\bar{l} = 50$. This means that after corresponding cancellations Equation (2-15) will yield

$$k_4 = 0.23[2 \lg \bar{l} + 1]$$

The coefficient ζ_j^0 is determined depending on δ_j/D_0 from the plot a of Diagram 2-1 or from the formula:[6]

$$\zeta_j^0 = 13.8(\delta_j/D_0)^{3/2} = k_5(\delta_j/D_0)^{3/2*}$$

---

*According to the experiments of Altshul.[6] the coefficient $k_5 = 8.26$ for rectangular joints and $k_5 = 4.14$ for rounded joints.

The overall resistance of the segment of tubes with joints is

$$\zeta = n_j\left(\lambda \frac{l_j}{D_0} + \zeta_j\right)$$

where λ is determined as a function of Re and $\overline{\Delta}$ from the graphs of Diagram 2-1 through 2-5.

58. Arc and resistance welded joints have less effect on the flow resistance than joints with backing rings, since the height of the joint is then smaller. On the average, it is possible to take the "equivalent height of the electrical arc and resistance welded joints"* to be δ_{eq} = 3 mm, while the height of a joint with a backing ring is δ = 5 mm.

59. In practice, the resistance of steel tubes with coupled joints can be considered equal to the resistance of welded tubes.

In calculations of cast-iron piping, one may neglect the additional resistance caused by the presence of bell and spigot joints.

60. Annular grooves on the inner surface of a tube also increase its resistance. The overall resistance of the segment with grooves is

$$\zeta \equiv \frac{\Delta p}{\rho w_0^2/2} = n_{gr}\left(\lambda \frac{l_{gr}}{D_0} + \zeta_{gr}\right)$$

where n_{gr} is the number of grooves over the considered segment of the tube; l_{gr} is the distance between the grooves; ζ_{gr} is the resistance coefficient of one groove; when $l_{gr}/D_0 \geqslant 4$[133]

$$\zeta_{gr} = 0.046b/D_0$$

where b is the width of the groove; at $l_{gr}/D_0 = 2$

$$\zeta_{gr} = 0.059b/D_0$$

at $l_{gr}/D_0 < 4$

$$\zeta_{gr} = f(b/D_0, l_{gr}/D_0)$$

is determined from the graph of Diagram 2-12.

61. The water conduits withdrawn from operation at State Electric Stations have the roughness of walls which varies substantially. To take into account this factor[7] it is recommended to introduce into Equation (2-10) the additional parameter α_r (correction for the local roughness), so that the indicated formula takes the form

$$\lambda = 0.11\left(\overline{\Delta} + \alpha_r \frac{68}{Re}\right)^{0.25} \tag{2-16}$$

The parameter α_r can vary within wide ranges (see Table 1-5).

62. The surfaces of concrete pipelines differ from the surfaces of other tubes by the presence of longitudinal and transverse seams, shuttering marks, cavities, and other irregularities. The state of the concrete surfaces of pipelines varies in the process of service, that is, their roughness increases. In calculations of the resistance of such pipelines the effect of

---

*This expression is understood to refer to the height of a joint with a backing ring, the flow resistance of which is equivalent to the arc (and contact) welded joints.

the joints, local resistances, blockings, and other complicating factors can also be taken into account by Equation (2-16), which involves the correction factor α_r, the values of which are listed in Table 2-5.

63. Formation of deposits in pipelines is a complex process which depends on the physicochemical properties of the liquid transported (with regard to the method and the scale of its cleaning), the pipeline material, and the coating characteristics, as well as on hydraulic parameters such as mean flow velocity, liquid pressure, and tube diameter.

64. Taking into account the tendency of water to form deposits in pipelines, Kamershtein suggests that for water-supplying pipelines the natural waters be divided into the following groups, each determining the character and intensity of the reduction in the transporting capacity of pipelines:

- Group I. Weakly saline, noncorrosive water with a stability index from -0.2 to 0.2; water with a moderate content of organic substances and free iron.
- Group II. Weakly saline, corrosive water with a stability index up to -1.0; water containing organic substances and free iron in quantities below 3 g/m^3.
- Group III. Very corrosive water with a stability index from -1.0 to 2.5, but with a small content of chlorides and sulfates (les than 100–150 g/m^3); water with an iron content above 3 g/m^3.
- Group IV. Corrosive water with a negative stability index, but with a high content of sulfates and chlorides (above 500–700 g/m^3); nontreated water with a high content of organic substances.
- Group V. Water distinguished by appreciable carbonate and low constant density with a stability index above 0.8; heavily saline and corrosive water.

65. The dependence of the roughness asperity height Δ_t (mm) on number of years of service is determined from a formula derived by Mostkov on the basis of Kamershtein's experiments:

$$\Delta_t = \Delta + \alpha_1 t \tag{2-17}$$

where Δ is the initial height of the roughness asperities (see Table 2-5); α_y is the rate of increase in the number of asperities (millimeters per year), which is dependent on the physicochemical properties of water (see Table 2-1).

66. The dependence of the fluid transport capacity of water-supplying pipelines on the time of their service, properties of the transported water, and pipeline diameter is expressed as

$$Q_t = Q(1 - 0.01 n t_y^m)$$

where Q is the predicted transporting capacityof a pipeline, t_y is the duration of service (years), and n and m are parameters that depend on physicochemical properties of the transported water (see Table 2-1).*

67. Because they have higher flow rates, gas pipelines are less subjected to mechanical contamination than water pipelines. Dry gases that do not cause corrosion of the inner surface of the tube may even somewhat reduce the roughness as the tubes are slightly abraded by the dry gas.

68. Moisture and hydrogen sulfide, carbonic acid, and oxygen, which are contained in gases, cause corrosion of the metal of tubes, which is accompanied by changes in the size,

---

*The increase in the resistance of water-supplying pipelines in the process of service has been refined in Reference 128.

Table 2-1 Values of the parameters α_y, n, m[a]

Water quality group	Pipeline diameter D_0, mm	α_y, mm/year	n	m
I	150–300	0.005–0.055	4.4	0.5
	400–600	0.025	2.3	0.5
II	150–300	0.055–0.18	6.4	0.5
	400–600	0.07	2.3	0.5
III	150–300	0.18–0.40	11.6	0.4
	400–600	0.20	6.4	0.5
IV	150–300	0.40–0.60	18.0	0.35
	400–600	0.51	11.6	0.40
V	150–300	0.60–3.0	32.0	0.25
			18.0	0.35

[a] The value of the parameter α_y increases with a decrease in the pipeline diameter. The numerator contains the limits of variation of α_y and the denominator the most probably average value.

shape, and distribution of asperities on the inner surface of the duct. The transporting capacity of gas conduits is sometimes reduced with time by 15% or more due to corrosion and contamination.

69. Growth of asperities on the inner surface of ventilation air ducts during service may be taken into account through a formula similar to Equation (2-17):[62]

$$\Delta_t = \Delta + \alpha_m t_m$$

where α_m is the rate of growth of asperities, in millimeters per month (see Table 2-2) and t_m is the duration of service, in months.

70. According to Datochnyi,[31] motion of gas in low-pressure gas pipelines is possible in all flow regimes, except the quadratic one, while in gas pipelines with moderate and high pressures it occurs under transition and quadratic conditions. All gas pipelines operate principally under transition conditions. For refined formulas for calculating gas pipelines of low and high pressure, see Altshul.[6]

71. The resistance of flexible tubes made of metallic strips (metallic hoses; see Diagram 2-12) substantially (by a factor of 2-2.5) exceeds that of smooth tubes. At Re $= 5 \times 10^6$ to 4×10^5, the friction coefficient of such tubes changes only slightly ($\lambda = 0.025$–0.0285). It depends on the direction of the flow along the hose; at places where the flow runs off the edges of the inner strip it is somewhat smaller than at places where the flow impinges on the edges.[146]

Table 2-2 Growth of surface asperities in air pipelines during service[62]

Region of use of air pipelines or ducts	Kind of local suction	Limits of variation of α_m mm/mon
Conveyor soldering of small ratio components with application of the KST flux	Aspirating (sucking) funnel or hood	2.3–4.4
Impregnation of abrasive disks with bakelite	Bakelitization chamber	0.92–1.36
Cooking on a kitchen range	Circumferential suction	0.34–0.49
Chrome-plating of articles in a galvanic bath	Suction from two sides of the bath	0.49–0.80
Exhaust section of air pipeline installed outside a building	–	0.03

72. High hydraulic resistance is also exhibited by a flexible air conduit made by winding a glass fabric strip round a steel-wire framework. The resistance of such air conduits is primarily determined by the crimpness of their surfaces (rather than conventional roughness). The friction coefficient of glass-fabric air conduits with regular crimpy surface can be determined from an approximate formula of Klyachko and Makarenkova,[53] which reflects the structural dependence of λ on the air conduit diameter and the strip width b:

$$\lambda \approx \lambda_0 (D_0/D_0')^{D_0'/D_0} (b/b_0)^m$$

where λ_0, D_0', and b_0 are the friction coefficient, diameter, and width of the strip of an air conduit; $\lambda_0 = 0.052$; $D_0' = 0.1$ m; $b_0 = 0.02$; m is the coefficient which takes into account the change in the winding pitch; for the construction considered $m = 1/5$. Air conduits of diameters $D_0 \leqslant 0.2$ m have glass-fabric strip width $b = 0.02$ m and those with the diameters $D_0 > 0.2$, $b = 0.03$ m.

More accurate values of λ obtained experimentally for glass-fabric air conduits[53] are presented as a function of the diameter D_0 and Reynolds number in the respective table of Diagram 2-13.

73. The resistance of flexible corrugated tubes to turbulent flow depends on the ratio of the height of the crimp crest h to its length l_{cr} and depends only slightly on the Reynolds number.

74. The friction coefficient λ of reinforced rubber hoses, whose characteristics are given in Diagram 2-14, does not depend on the Reynolds number in the range $\geqslant 4000$, owing to the appreciable roughness of such hoses. The value of λ increases with increasing diameter of hoses since the height of the inner seams is then also increased.[131,132]

When determining pressure losses from Equation (2-2) it is necessary that the nominal hose diameter d_{nom} be replaced by d_{cal} determined from curve b of Diagram 2-14, depending on the mean inner pressure.

75. The friction coefficient λ of smooth rubber hoses, whose characteristics are given in Diagram 2-15, can be determined from the Toltsman-Shevele[132] formula:

$$\lambda = \frac{A}{Re^{0.265}}$$

where, at Reynolds numbers (Re $= w_0 d_{nom}/\nu$) from 5,000 to 120,000, the value of $A = 0.38$ to 0.52 (depending on the quality of the hoses).

If pressure losses are determined from Equation (2-2), the diameter should be calculated based on the mean internal pressure (according to curve b of Diagram 2-14).

76. The friction coefficient λ of smooth reinforced rubber hoses is determined from the curves of Diagram 2-16, depending on the average internal pressure and d_{nom}.

In determining pressure losses from Equation (2-2) it is necessary that the calculated rather than a nominal diameter of the hose be multiplied by the correction factor k, which is found from curves c and d of Diagram 2-17, depending on the average internal pressure.

77. For large-diameter (300–500 mm) tubes made from rubberized material, such as may be used for ventilation of shafts, and the connections made with wire rings closed at the ends by pipe sockets (see Diagram 2-17), the total resistance is composed (according to Adamov) of the friction resistance and the resistance of joints

$$\zeta = \frac{\Delta p}{\rho w_0^2/2} = n_c \left(\lambda \frac{l_j}{D_0} + \zeta_c \right)$$

where n_c is the number of connections; λ (see Diagram 2-17) is determined for different degrees of tension: small (with extensive crimping and fractures), medium (with minor crimping), and large (without crimping); l_j is the distance between the joints, in m; and ζ_c is the resistance coefficient of one connection (see Diagram 2-16).

78. The friction coefficients λ of plywood tubes (made from birch plywood with fibers running lengthwise) are determined according to the data of Adamov and Idelchik[1] given in Diagram 2-18.

79. The friction coefficients of tubes made from polymers (plastic) can be determined from formulas of Offengenden,[91,92] which are given in Diagram 2-19. Indicated there also are the regions of the applicability of these formulas. As a rule, plastic tubes relate to tubes with slight roughness ($\Delta \leqslant 30$ μm). Tubes made from fluoroplastic have the smallest absolute roughness and those made from glass-reinforced plastic, and from phaolete the greatest roughness. The plastic tubes also have micro- and macrowaviness.[92] When $5 \times 10^4 \leqslant$ Re $\leqslant 3 \times 10^5$, to make hydraulic calculation of plastic tubes, it is possible to use in the first approximation (with an error up to 25% and above) the formula of Colebrook-White (2-9) or similar formulas (see above) with the substitution of the values of Δ given in Table 2-4. For polyethylene (nonstabilized), fluoroplastic, and polypropylene tubes the value of Δ is not determined, as the coefficient λ for them can be determined from formulas for smooth tubes.[92]

80. The local resistance coefficients for different types of joints of plastic tubes can be determined from corresponding formulas[92] given in Diagram 2-20.

81. All the values of λ recommended above refer to an incompressible fluid. In order to approximate the effect of gas compressibility for a section of very large length, one may use the formula derived by Voronin:[22]

$$\lambda_{com} = \lambda\left(1 + \frac{k-1}{2}M^2\right)^{-0.47}$$

where λ and λ_{com} are the friction coefficients, respectively, for incompressible and compressible liquid (gas).

The formula shows that up to Ma $= 0.6$, the effect of compressibility may be neglected within 3% or less error. An appreciable decrease in the coefficient λ_{com} is observed only in a narrow transonic region and also at supersonic flow velocities by about 15%).[121,122]

82. When a liquid (gas) moves in a pipeline (conduit) of constant cross section and there is an outflow or inflow through porous side walls, slots, or side branches (Figure 2-7), the resistance coefficient λ varies along this path due to a change of the average flow velocity (Re) along the flow path.

83. The local resistance coefficient λ_{loc} of a cylindrical tube with porous walls and uniform and circular (over the whole perimeter) outflow, that is, when

$$\bar{v} \equiv v/v_s = 1 \quad \text{and} \quad \bar{w} \equiv w/w_0 = 1 - \alpha_0\bar{x}$$

in the case of laminar flow is calculated from the formula of Bystrov and Mikhailov.*[18]

$$\lambda_{loc} = 32(3 + \bar{a}_0/[\text{Re}_0(1 - \alpha_0\bar{x})]$$

$$\lambda_{loc} = \lambda + 5.54\varepsilon'v/w \tag{2-18}$$

---

*The coefficient α_0 introduced by the author into this formula extends it also to the case of transit flow rate ($\alpha_0 < 1$).

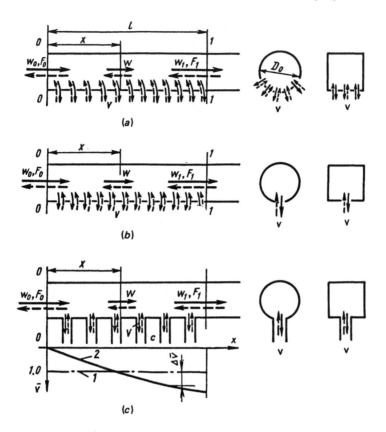

Figure 2-7 Diagram of flow with a change in the flow rate along the path: (*a*) collector with perforated walls; (*b*) collector with a longitudinal slot; (*c*) collector with side branches. (1) $\bar{v} = 1.0 = $ const.; (2) $\bar{v}$ with variable discharge.

when $\varepsilon' > 0.2$

$$\lambda_{\text{loc}} = \lambda + 5.54\varepsilon'v/w + \frac{N_v}{\varepsilon' \cdot v/w}\left(1 - \frac{v/w_0}{v/w}\right) \tag{2-19}$$

Here λ is the friction coefficient of a smooth tube determined from the graphs of Diagram 2-1:

$$N_v = 0.0256B(\varepsilon' \cdot v/w)^{0.435}$$

$$B = \frac{\lambda_\varepsilon - \lambda}{0.2 - \lambda}$$

λ_ε is determined from the expression

$$\lg \lambda_\varepsilon = \lg \lambda \exp(-6.63\varepsilon'^3)$$

where ε' is the porosity factor of the tube walls.

Within the range $20 \leqslant l/D \leqslant 125$, the resistance coefficient of the porous segment of the tube of length l is

at $\varepsilon' \leqslant 0.2$

$$\zeta \equiv \frac{\Delta p}{\rho w_0^2/2} = \frac{l}{D_0}\left[\lambda\left(1 - \alpha_0 + \frac{\lambda_0^2}{3}\right) + 5.54\varepsilon \cdot \alpha_0/\overline{f}\cdot(1 - 0.5\alpha)\right]$$

Here $v_s = w_0/\overline{f}$ is the average velocity of outflow (inflow) through side orifices; $\overline{f} = \Sigma f/F_0$ is the ratio of the overall area of the side surfaces (branches) of the porous segment of the tube; $\alpha_0 = 1 - w_1/w_0$; $\overline{x} = x/l$; $\text{Re}_0 = w_0 D_0/v$; $\tilde{a}_0$ is determined by the velocity profile at the inlet to the discharge collector (for the parabolic profile $\tilde{a}_0 \approx -0.17$; for the cosinusoid profile $\tilde{a}_0 \approx -0.33$); w_0 and w_1 are the average velocity in the initial ($x = 0$) and final ($x = l$) sections of the porous segment of the tube.

The resistance coefficient of the porous tube segment of length l[44] is

$$\zeta \equiv \frac{\Delta p}{\rho w_0^2/2} - l/D_0\left[\frac{32(3 + \tilde{a})}{\text{Re}_0}(1 - 0.5\alpha_0)\right]$$

84. The local friction coefficient λ_{loc} under the same conditions as those in paragraph 83 is calculated in the case of turbulent flow and $20 \leqslant L/D \leqslant 125$ from the formula:[18]

at $\varepsilon' \leqslant 0.2$

$$\zeta = \frac{\Delta p}{\rho w_0^2/2} = \frac{l}{D_0}\left\{\lambda\left(1 - \alpha_0 + \frac{\lambda_0^2}{3}\right) + 5.54\varepsilon' \cdot \alpha_0/\overline{f}\cdot(1 - 0.5\alpha_0)\right.$$

$$+ \frac{0.00157\alpha_0^{0.435}\overline{f}^{0.565}}{(\varepsilon')^{0.565}}[1 - 4.565(1 - \alpha_0)^{3.5}$$

$$+ \left.3.565(1 - \alpha_0)^{4.565}]\right\}$$

85. The local friction coefficient λ_{loc} of a discharging collector with one-sided and uniform outflow and with turbulent flow[18] is

$$\lambda_{\text{loc}} = \lambda + 8\varepsilon'v/w$$

whereas the resistance coefficient of the entire section of the collector of length l[44] is

$$\zeta \equiv \frac{\Delta p}{\rho w_0^2/2} = \frac{l}{D_0}\left[\lambda\left(1 - \alpha_0 + \frac{\alpha_0^2}{3}\right) + 8\varepsilon' \cdot \alpha_0/\overline{f}\cdot(1 - 0.5\alpha)\right]$$

86. With a circular and uniformly variable outflow from a cylindrical tube, when the relative velocity of the outflow $\overline{v}$ varies linearly from $\overline{v}_0 = 1 - \Delta\overline{v}$ to $\overline{v}_1 = 1 + \Delta\overline{v}$ and accordingly $\overline{w} \equiv w/w_0 = 1 - \alpha_0(1 - \Delta\overline{v})\overline{x} - \alpha_0\Delta\overline{v}x^{-2}$,

$$\overline{v} \equiv v/v_s = \alpha_0(1 - \Delta\overline{v} + 2\Delta\overline{v}\overline{x})$$

where $\Delta\bar{v} \equiv v/v_s$ is the departure of the relative velocity from its average value (from unity, see Figure 2-7).

The local resistance coefficient in the case of laminar flow is

$$\lambda_{lam} = \frac{32(3 + \tilde{a}_0)}{Re_0[1 - \alpha_0(1 - \Delta\bar{v})\bar{x} - \alpha_0\Delta\bar{v}\bar{x}^2]}$$

The resistance coefficient of a porous segment of length l^{44} is

$$\zeta \equiv \frac{\Delta p}{\rho w_0^2/2} = \frac{32(3 + \tilde{a}_0)}{Re_0} \cdot l/D_0[1 - 0.5\alpha_0 + 1/6\alpha_0\Delta\bar{v}]$$

87. In the case of turbulent flow under identical conditions as those in paragraph 86, the local friction coefficient λ_{loc} is determined approximately from Equation (2-18) and (2-19). The resistance coefficient of the porous segment of length l^{44} is

at $\varepsilon \leq 0.2$

$$\zeta \equiv \frac{\Delta p}{\rho w_0^2/2} = l/D_0\left\{\lambda\left[1 - \alpha_0 + \frac{\alpha_0}{3}(\Delta\bar{v} + \alpha_0\right.\right.$$

$$\left.\left. - 0.5\alpha_0\Delta\bar{v} + 0.1\alpha_0\Delta\bar{v}^2)\right] + 5.54\varepsilon'\cdot\alpha_0/\bar{f}\cdot(1 - 0.5\alpha_0)\right\}$$

at $\varepsilon > 0.2$

$$\zeta \equiv \frac{\Delta p}{\rho w_0^2/2} = l/D_0\left\{\lambda\left[1 - \alpha_0 + \frac{\alpha_0}{3}(\Delta\bar{v} + \alpha_0\right.\right.$$

$$\left.\left. - 0.5\alpha_0\Delta\bar{v} + 0.1\alpha_0\Delta\bar{v}^2)\right] + 5.54\varepsilon'\cdot\alpha_0/\bar{f}\cdot(1 - 0.5\alpha_0) + \Delta\lambda\right\}$$

where

$$\Delta\lambda = \frac{0.0256B}{(\varepsilon\cdot\alpha/\bar{f})^{0.565}} \cdot \left\{\int_0^1 \frac{[1 - \alpha_0(1 - \Delta\bar{v})\bar{x} - \alpha_0\Delta\bar{v}\bar{x}^2]^{2.565}}{(1 - \Delta\bar{v} + 2\Delta\bar{v}\bar{x})^{0.565}} d\bar{x}\right.$$

$$- \int_0^1 \frac{[1 - \alpha_0(1 - \Delta\bar{v})\bar{x} - \alpha_0\Delta\bar{v}\bar{x}^2]^{3.565}}{(1 - \Delta\bar{v} + 2\Delta\bar{v}\bar{x})^{0.565}} d\bar{x}$$

$$= \left.\frac{0.0256B}{(\varepsilon\cdot\alpha_0/\bar{f})^{0.565}}(J_1 - J_2)\right\}$$

J_1 and J_2 are the first and second integrals in the expression for $\Delta\lambda$.

The value of $\Delta\lambda$ can be determined numerically on a computer. The calculated values of the difference $J_1 - J_2$ are presented in Table 2-3.

Table 2-3 The values of J_1–J_2

o_0	\multicolumn{8}{c}{v}							
	0	0.1	0.2	0.3	0.4	0.6	0.8	1.0
0.1	0.042	0.040	0.038	0.036	0.035	0.031	0.028	0.024
0.2	0.070	0.067	0.064	0.061	0.059	0.053	0.048	0.042
0.3	0.086	0.083	0.080	0.077	0.074	0.068	0.061	0.054
0.4	0.093	0.091	0.088	0.085	0.083	0.077	0.070	0.061
0.5	0.094	0.092	0.090	0.088	0.086	0.081	0.074	0.065
0.6	0.090	0.089	0.088	0.087	0.086	0.082	0.076	0.067
0.7	0.084	0.084	0.084	0.084	0.083	0.080	0.075	0.067
0.8	0.076	0.077	0.078	0.079	0.079	0.078	0.074	0.066
0.9	0.068	0.070	0.072	0.073	0.074	0.074	0.072	0.065
1.0	0.061	0.064	0.066	0.068	0.070	0.071	0.070	0.063

88. In the case of turbulent flow and one-sided nonuniform outflow (see Figure 2-7), the local friction coefficient is determined according to Reference 18 as:

at $\varepsilon' \leq 0.2$

$$\lambda_{loc} = 6.5\varepsilon' v/w$$

at $\varepsilon' > 0.2$

$$\lambda_{loc} = \lambda + N_{dis\text{-}c}\varepsilon' v/w$$

where

$$N_{dis\text{-}c} \approx 7.4\varepsilon'(l/D_0)^{0.5}[1 - \exp(-0.016l/D_0 \cdot \zeta_{br}/\overline{f}^{\,2})^{0.6}]$$

($\zeta_{br} \equiv \Delta p/(\rho v_s^2/2)$ is the overall resistance coefficient of the side branch of the collector reduced to the velocity v_s).

The resistance coefficient of the porous segment of length l^{AA} is

at $\varepsilon' \leq 0.2$

$$\zeta \equiv \frac{\Delta p}{\rho w_0^2/2} = l/D_0 \left\{ \lambda[1 - \alpha_0 + \alpha_0/3(\Delta\overline{v} + \alpha_0 - 0.5\alpha_0\Delta\overline{v} \right.$$

$$\left. + 0.1\alpha_0\Delta\overline{v}^2)] + 6.5\varepsilon' \cdot \alpha_0/\overline{f} \cdot (1 - 0.5\alpha_0) \right\}$$

at $\varepsilon' > 0.2$

$$\zeta \equiv \frac{\Delta p}{\rho w_0^2/2} = l/D_0 \left\{ \lambda[1 - \alpha_0 + \alpha_0/3(\Delta\overline{v} + \alpha_0 - 0.5\alpha_0\Delta\overline{v} \right.$$

$$\left. + 0.1\alpha_0\Delta\overline{v}^2)] + N_{dis\text{-}c}\varepsilon' \cdot \alpha_0/\overline{f} \cdot (1 - 0.5\alpha_0) \right\}$$

102   *Handbook of Hydraulic Resistance, 3rd Edition*

89. In the case of a turbulent flow and uniform inflow (injection) the local friction coefficient is

$$\lambda_{loc} = 1.5\varepsilon' v/w \tag{2-20}$$

Then the resistance coefficient of the porous segment of length l^{44} is

$$\zeta \equiv \frac{\Delta p}{\rho w_0^2/2} = 1.5\varepsilon' \cdot \alpha_0 \overline{f} \cdot l/D_0 \cdot (1 - 0.5\alpha_0)$$

90. For a turbulent flow and uniformly variable inflow (injection), when the relative velocity of inflow varies according to the linear law from $\overline{v}_0 = 1 + \Delta\overline{v}$ to $\overline{v}_1 = 1 - \Delta\overline{v}$ and accordingly $\overline{w} = 1 - \alpha_0(1 + \Delta\overline{v})\overline{x} + \alpha_0\Delta\overline{v}\overline{x}^{-2}$,

$$\overline{v} = \alpha_0(1 + \Delta\overline{v} - 2\Delta\overline{v}\cdot\overline{x})$$

The local friction coefficient is determined approximately from Equation (2-20), whereas the resistance coefficient of the porous segment of length l is

$$\zeta \equiv \frac{\Delta p}{\rho w_0^2/2} = 1.5\varepsilon' \cdot \alpha_0 \overline{f} \cdot l/D_0 (1 - 0.5\alpha_0 - 0.17\alpha_0\cdot\Delta\overline{v})$$

91. The resistance coefficient of the side branching of collectors[15,16] is

in the case of outflow (discharging collector)

$$\zeta_{br} \equiv \frac{\Delta p}{\rho v_s^2/2} = 0.25\overline{f}^2 + (f_s/f_a)^2 + \zeta_{ap} + \zeta_{seg}$$

in the case of injection (intake collector)

$$\zeta_{br} = 1.5\overline{f}^2\left(\frac{1}{n_s} - \frac{1}{n_s^2} - 0.125\right) + 0.75 + (f_s/f_a)^2 + \zeta_{ap} + \zeta_{seg}$$

for paired collectors (Π-like or Z-like)

$$\zeta_{br} = 0.2\overline{f}^2 + 1.75 + \zeta_{ap} + \zeta_{seg}$$

Here f_s and f_a are the areas of the side orifice and of the final cross section of the entire branching (exit into an infinite space); ζ_{ap} is the resistance coefficient of any apparatus involved in the system of the side branching and reduced to the velocity v_s; ζ_{seg} is the resistance coefficient of all the segments of the side branching upstream and downstream of the apparatus reduced to the velocity v_s; n_s is the number of side branchings.

92. The introduction of macroscopic particles into the flow of a liquid or gas, or the addition of polymer molecules with a very large molecular mass relative to the liquid, substantially reduces the friction coefficient in tubes (Thomas effect).[264]

Addition of polymers to a liquid or solid particles to a gas leads to a notable decrease of the transverse velocity pulsations and of the turbulent friction expressed in terms of the Reynolds stresses, and as a result the resistance coefficient decreases. These additives do

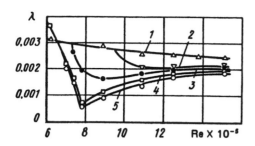

Figure 2-8 Friction coefficient of a smooth plate in a dust-laden air flow ($G_m = 3.7$ g/s):[214] (1) pure air; (2) 1680 μm; (3) 840 μm; (4) 200 μm; (5) 100 μm.

not decrease the resistance coefficient of laminar flow and do not contribute to its preservation.

The maximum decline in the resistance coefficient is observed in the region of low Reynolds numbers of a fully developed turbulent flow (Figure 2-8).

93. The friction coefficient also varies depending on the concentration and kind of polymer (in water) and, correspondingly, on the size of suspended solid particles (in an air flow). The higher the concentration of the polymer (polyacrilamide, PAA) in water at the given Reynolds number (Figure 2-9), the more appreciable is the decrease in the coefficient λ (similar results can be observed also from the data of other works (see References 11, 12, 97, 98, 111).

The coefficient λ is determined[210] from the formula

$$\frac{1}{\sqrt{\lambda}} = -2 \lg\left[\left(\frac{\mathrm{Re}_{*\mathrm{thr}}}{\mathrm{Re}_*}\right)^{\alpha_{\mathrm{pol}}/5.75}\left(\frac{2.51}{\mathrm{Re}\sqrt{\lambda}} + \frac{\overline{\Delta}}{3.7}\right)\right]$$

where $\mathrm{Re}_* = (w_*/D_0)/\nu$ is the dynamic Reynolds number; $\mathrm{Re}_{*\mathrm{thr}} = (w_{*\mathrm{thr}}D_0)/\nu$ is the threshold Reynolds number corresponding to the start of the decrease in hydraulic resistance; [$w_* = \sqrt{\tau_0/\rho}$ is the dynamic velocity (τ_0 is the shear stress on the wall); $w_{*\mathrm{thr}}$ is the threshold dynamic velocity]; α_{pol} is the parameter, depending on the kind and concentration of polymer (it can be determined from experimental data).

94. With the rise of concentration of solid particles μ (Figure 2-10) the friction coefficient λ first falls very sharply or, which is the same, the ratio $(\lambda_0 - \lambda)/\lambda_0$ reaches a maximum, after which it begins to decrease until at $\mu = 2$–3 it becomes equal to zero. The smaller the fraction of suspended particles, the larger is the maximum of $(\lambda_0 - \lambda)/\lambda_0$ and the earlier this maximum occurs, but at the smaller values of μ the friction coefficient starts to decrease.

95. In the case of pneumatic transport, when density and dimensions of solid particles suspended in the flow are nearly always substantial, the effect of the cross-current velocities

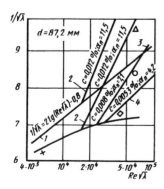

Figure 2-9 Function $1/\sqrt{\lambda} = f(\mathrm{Re}\sqrt{\lambda})$ for water with surfactants of different concentrations:[210] (1) for smooth tubes; (2), (3), (4) by formula of paragraph 93 at different concentrations of surfactants: + = tap water; □ = water + PAA (c = 0.0053%); ○ = water + PAA (c = 0.008%); △ = water + PAA (c = 0.012%).

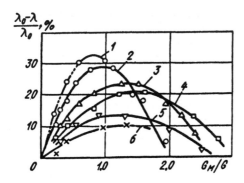

Figure 2-10 Friction resistance on the surface of a circular tube at different ratios of the mass flow rates:[214] (1) 60 μm; (2) 15 μm; (3) 100 μm; (4) 200 μm; (5) 840 μm; (6) 1680 μm; λ_0 is the value of λ at $\mu = 0$.

of turbulent flow on the mechanism of particle suspension and the friction drag becomes negligible. In this case, such additional factors as the drag of particles, the lift exerted on them, and the gravitational force and other factors, which increase resistance to the transporting flow motion, are of prime importance (see the list of references to Chapter 2).

96. When the flow in a horizontal tube is steady (far from the inlet, absence of transported material effects), the difference between the densities of suspended particles and air is substantial and the dimensions of particles are such that individual particles periodically strike the tube wall and bounce off it, thus executing a continuous bouncing motion.

97. The loss of energy during impact on the wall is responsible for a decrease in the translational velocity of particles, which subsequently recovers again due to interaction of particles with the flow. This causes an additional expenditure of energy by a transporting flow.

98. In the presence of heat transfer through the tube walls the liquid (gas) temperature varies over both its length and cross section; the latter leads to a change in the fluid density and viscosity and as a result, in the velocity profile and fluid resistance.[51]

99. The friction coefficient of a nonisothermal flow of a liquid is calculated from the equation

$$\frac{\lambda_{\text{non}}}{\lambda_{\text{is}}} = \left(\frac{\eta_w}{\eta_{\text{fl}}}\right)^n \tag{2-21}$$

where λ_{non} and λ_{is} are the friction coefficients in the case on nonisothermal and isothermal motion, respectively (in calculations of λ_{is} the density and viscosity are taken for the average fluid temperature); η_w and η_{fl} are the dynamic viscosities, respectively, at the temperature of the tube wall T_w and average fluid temperature T_{fl}; $n = f(\eta_w/\eta_{\text{fl}}, \text{Pe·}d/l)$, see Table 2-4; $\text{Pe} = wl/a_t$ is the Peclet number; a_t is the thermal diffusivity, m^2/s.

When the fluid is cooled, $\eta_w/\eta_{\text{fl}} > 1$; it follows from Equation (2-21) that the friction coefficient increases. When the fluid is heated, $\eta_w/\eta_{\text{fl}} < 1$; λ_{non} becomes smaller than λ_{is}.

Table 2-4 The values of *n* in Equation 21

Pe·d/l	η_w/η_{fl}					Pe·d/l	η_w/η_{fl}				
	0.1	1.0	10	100	1000		0.1	1.0	10	100	1000
60	0.78	0.67	0.58	0.51	0.44	1,000	0.33	0.29	0.25	0.22	0.19
100	0.67	0.58	0.50	0.44	0.38	1,500	0.36	0.26	0.22	0.19	0.17
150	0.59	0.51	0.45	0.39	0.33	2,500	0.28	0.25	0.21	0.18	0.16
200	0.54	0.47	0.41	0.35	0.31	5,000	0.26	0.23	0.20	0.17	0.15
400	0.44	0.38	0.33	0.29	0.25	10,000	0.25	0.21	0.19	0.16	0.14
600	0.39	0.34	0.29	0.25	0.22	30,000	0.22	0.19	0.17	0.14	0.13

100. To determine the friction coefficient of hydraulically smooth tubes with turbulent fluid flow the following formula can be used:[75]

$$\lambda_{non} = \frac{1}{[1.82\,\lg(\mathrm{Re}\sqrt{\eta_w/\eta_{fl}}) - 1.64]^2}$$

101. The friction coefficient for a nonisothermal turbulent flow of a heated gas can be calculated from the approximate formula of Kutateladze-Leontiyev which is valid within the ranges Re $= 10^5 - 6 \times 10^6$ and $T_w/T_g = 1$–3:

$$\lambda_{non}/\lambda_{is} = \frac{4}{\sqrt{T_w/T_g} + 1)^2}$$

where T_g is the mean-mass gas temperature.

102. In determining the equivalent roughness of the walls of the calculated segment of the tubes (channel), one may use the data given in Table 2-5.

Table 2-5 Equivalent roughness of the surfaces of tubes and channels

Group	Type of tubes, material	State of tube surface and conditions of use	Δ, mm	Ref.
		A. Metal tubes		
I	Seamless tubes made from brass, copper, lead	Commercially smooth	0.0015–0.0100	
	Aluminum tubes		0.015–0.06	187
II	Seamless steel tubes (commercial)	New, unused	0.02–0.10[a]	42, 152, 185, 197
		Cleaned after many years of use	Up to 0.04	187
		Bituminized	Up to 0.04	187
		Superheated steam pipes of heating systems and water pipes of heating systems with deaeration and chemical treatment of running water	0.10	82
		After one year of use in gas pipelines	0.12	42
		After several years of use as tubing in gas wells under various conditions	0.04–0.20	7
		After several years of use as casings in gas wells under different conditions	0.06–0.22	7
		Saturated steam ducts and water pipes of heating systems with minor water leakage (up to 0.5%) and deaeration of water supplied to balance leakage	0.20	82
		Pipelines of water heating systems independent of the source of supply	0.20	
		Oil pipelines for intermediate operating conditions	0.20	82
		Moderately corroded	~0.4	197
		Small depositions of scale	~0.4	197
		Steam pipelines operating periodically and condensate pipes with the open system of condensate	0.5	82
		Compressed air pipes from piston- and turbocompressors	0.8	82

Table 2-5 (continued) Equivalent roughness of the surfaces of tubes and channels

Group	Type of tubes, material	State of tube surface and conditions of use	Δ, mm	Ref.
		A. Metal tubes		
		After several years of operation under different conditions (corroded or with small amount of scale)	0.15–1.0	7
		Condensate pipelines operating periodically and water heating pipes with no deaeration and chemical treatment of water and with substantial leakage from the system (up to 1.5–3%)	1.0	32
		Water pipelines previously used	1.2–1.5	
		Poor condition	≥5.0	
III	Welded steel tubes	New or old, but in good condition	0.04–0.10	179, 187
		New, bituminized	~0.05	186
		Used previously, corroded, bitumen partially dissolved	~0.10	197
		Used previously, uniformly corroded	~0.15	197
		Without noticeable unevenness at joints; lacquered on the inside layer (10 mm thick); adequate state of surface	0.3–0.4	182
		Gas mains after many years of use	~0.5	197
		With simple or double transverse riveted joints; lacquered 10 mm thick on the inside or with no lacquer, but no corroded	0.6–0.7	179
		Lacquered on the inside, but rusted; soiled when transporting water, but not corroded	0.95–1.0	179
		Layered deposits; gas mains after 20 years of use	1.1	197
		With double transverse riveted joints, not corroded soiled during transport of water	1.2–1.5	152, 197
		Small deposits	1.5	197
		With double transverse riveted joints, heavily corroded	2.0	179
		Appreciable deposits	2.0–4.0	197
		Used for 25 years in municipal gas mains, nonuniform deposits of resin and naphthalene	2.4	197
		Poor condition of the surface	≥5.0	179
IV	Riveted steel tubes	Lateral and longitudinal riveting with one line of rivets; 10 mm thick lacquered on the inside; adequate state of the surface	0.3–0.4	179
		With double longitudinal riveting and simple lateral riveting; 10 mm thick lacquered on the inside, or without lacquer, but not corroded	0.6–0.7	179
		With simple lateral and double longitudinal riveting; from 10 to 20 mm thick lacquered or torred on the inside	1.2–1.3	179
		With four to six longitudinal rows of rivets; long period of use	2.0	179
		With four lateral and six longitudinal rows of rivets; joints overlapped on the inside	4.0	179
		Very poor condition of the surface; uneven overlapping of joints	≥5.0	179
V	Roofing steel sheets	Oiled	1.10–0.15	
		Not oiled	0.02–0.04	

Table 2-5 (continued) Equivalent roughness of the surfaces of tubes and channels

Group	Type of tubes, material	State of tube surface and conditions of use	Δ, mm	Ref.
		A. Metal tubes		
VI	Galvanized steel tubes	Bright galvanization; new	0.07–0.10	197
		Ordinary galvanization	0.1–0.15	197
VII	Galvanized sheet steel	New	0.15	185
		Used previously for water	0.18	171
VIII	Steel tubes	Coated with glass enamel on both sides	0.001–0.01	
	Cast-iron tubes	New	0.25–1.0	171
IX		New, bituminized	0.10–0.15	197
		Asphalt-coated	0.12–0.30	185
		Water pipelines, used previously	1.4	152
		Used previously, corroded	1.0–1.5	197
		With deposits	1.0–1.5	185, 197
		Appreciable deposits	2.0–4.0	197
		Cleaned after use for many years	0.3–1.5	171
		Heavily corroded	Up to 3.0	179
X	Water conduits of electric power stations, steel	New, clean		
		Seamless (withoug joints), well fitted	0.015–0.04	7, 26
		Welded lengthwise, well fitted	0.03–0.012	
		Same, with transverse welded joints	0.08–0.17	
		New, clean, coated on the inside		
		Bituminized when manufactured	0.014–0.018	
		Same, with transverse welded joints	0.20–0.60	
		Galvanized	0.10–0.20	
		Roughly galvanized	0.40–0.70	
		Bituminized, curvilinear in plan	0.10–1.4	
		Used, clean		
		Slightly corroded or with incrustation	0.10–0.30	
		Moderately corroded or with slight deposits	0.30–0.70	
		Heavily corroded	0.80–1.5	
		Cleaned of deposits or rust	0.15–0.20	
		Formerly used (mounting in industrial conditions)		
		All welded, up to 2 years of service, without deposits	0.12–0.24	
		Same, up to 20 years of service, without deposits	0.6–5.0	
		With iron-bacterial corrosion (heavily rusted)	3.0–4.0	
		Heavily corroded, with incurstation (deposits from 1.5 to 9 mm thick)	3.0–5.0	
		Same, with deposits from 3 to 25 mm thick	6.0–6.5	
		Used, coated on the inside		
		Bituminized (coal-tar varnish, coal tar), up to 2 years of service	0.1–0.35	

Note: For new water conduits $\alpha_r = 1.3$–1.5
For new bituminized water conduits $\alpha_r = 1.3$
For used water conduits the value of α_r may vary within wide limits (up to 85), depending on the time of service, properties of water, kind of deposits, etc.

Table 2-5 (continued) Equivalent roughness of the surfaces of tubes and channels

Group	Type of tubes, material	State of tube surface and conditions of use	Δ, mm	Ref.
		B. Concrete, Cement, and Other Tubes and Conduits		
I	Concrete tubes	Water conduits without surface finish		7, 26
		New, plaster finish, manufactured with the aid of steel formwork with excellent quality (sections are mated thoroughly, joints are prime coated and smoothed) ($\alpha_r = 1$)	0.05–0.15	
		Used, with corroded and wavy surface; wood framework ($\alpha_r > 3.0$)	1.0–4.0	
		Old, poorly manufactured, poorly fitted; the surface is overgrown and has the deposits of sand, gravel, clay particles ($\alpha_r > 3$)	3.0–6.0	
		Very old with the surface heavily damaged and overgrown for years of service ($\alpha_r > 3$)	5.0 and above	
		Water conduits with subsequent finish of the surface (plastered, smoothed)		
		New, with a very smooth surface, manufactured with the aid of steel or oiled steel casing with excellent quality of work; hand-smoothing with trowels; joints are prime coated and smoothed (without asperities) ($\alpha_r = 1$)	0.10–0.20	
		New or previously used, smooth; also monolithic (steel casing) or sectional tubes with sections up to 4 m long of good quality; cement finish hand-smoothed; joints are smoothed ($\alpha_r > 1$, but < 1.5)	0.15–0.35	
		Previously used, without deposits, with moderately smooth surface; monolithic (steel or wooden casing), asperities removed, joints are prime coated, but not smooth ($\alpha_r > 1.5$, but ≤ 2.5)	0.30–0.60	
		Prefabricated and monolithic (fabricated on site), previously used, with cement plaster wood floated, joints are rough ($\alpha_r > 2.5$, but ≤ 3.0)	0.50–1.0	
		Water conduits with concrete sprayed surface or of sprayed concrete		
		Carefully smoothed air-placed concrete or sprayed concrete on concrete surface ($\alpha_r \approx 2.5$)	0.50	
		Brushed air-placed concrete or sprayed concrete on concrete surface ($\alpha_r > 3.0$)	2.30	
		Nonsmoothed air-placed concrete or sprayed concrete on concrete surface ($\alpha_r > 3.0$)	3.0–6.0	
		Smoothed air-placed concrete or sprayed concrete on concrete surface ($\alpha_r > 3.0$)	6.0–17.0	

Table 2-5 (continued) Equivalent roughness of the surfaces of tubes and channels

Group	Type of tubes, material	State of tube surface and conditions of use	Δ, mm	Ref.
		B. Concrete, Cement, and Other Tubes and Conduits		
II	Reinforced concrete tubes	New	0.25–0.34	26
		Nonprocessed	2.5	187
III	Asbestos-cement tubes	New	0.05–0.10	
		Average	0.60	
IV	Cement tubes	Smoothed	0.3–0.8	
		Nonprocessed	1.0–2.0	187
		Joints not smoothed	1.9–6.4	179
V	Conduit with a cement-mortar plaster	Good plaster made of pure cement with smoothed joints; all asperities removed; metal casing	0.05–0.22	179
		Steel-troweled	0.5	
VI	Plaster over a metallic screen	–	10–15	
VII	Ceramic salt-glazed conduits	–	1.4	
VIII	Slag-concrete slabs	–	1.5	
IX	Slag and alabaster-filling slabs	Carefully made slabs	1.0–1.5	171
		C. Wood, Plywood, and Glass Tubes		
I	Wood tubes	Boards very thoroughly dressed	0.15	
		Boards well dressed	0.30	
		Boards undressed, but well fitted	0.70	
		Boards undressed	1.0	197
		Staved	0.6	
II	Plywood tubes	Of good-quality birch plywood with transverse grain	0.12	1
		Of good-quality birch plywood with longitudinal grain	0.03–0.05	1
III	Glass tubes	Pure glass	0.0015–0.010	185
		D. Tunnels		
I		Tunnels in Rocks (Rough)		
		Blast-hewed in rock mass with little jointing	100–140	
		Blast-hewed in roch mass with appreciable jointing	130–500	
		Roughly cut with highly uneven surfaces	500–1500	
II		Tunnels Unlined		
		Rocks:		
		gneiss (D = 3–13.5 m)	300–700	
		granite (D = 3–9 m)	200–700	
		Shale (D = 9–12 m)	250–650	
		quartz, quartzite (D = 7–10 m)	200–600	
		sedimentary rocks (D = 4–7 m)	400	
		nephrite-bearing (D = 3–8 m)	200	

2.2 DIAGRAMS OF FRICTION COEFFICIENTS

Circular tube with smooth walls; stabilized flow[6,175,193]

Diagram
2-1

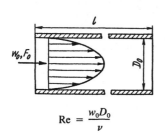

$$\mathrm{Re} = \frac{w_0 D_0}{\nu}$$

1. Laminar regime (Re ≤ 2000):

$$\lambda = \frac{\Delta p}{[(\rho w_0^2/2)(l/D_0)]} = \frac{64}{\mathrm{Re}} = f(\mathrm{Re}) \quad \text{see graph a.}$$

2. Transition regime (200 ≤ Re ≤ 400):

$$\lambda = f(\mathrm{Re}) \quad \text{see graph b.}$$

3. Turbulent regime ($4000 < \mathrm{Re} < 10^5$):

$$\lambda = \frac{0.3164}{\mathrm{Re}^{0.25}} \quad \text{see graph c.}$$

4. Turbulent regime (Re > 4000):

$$\lambda = \frac{1}{(1.8\ \lg\ \mathrm{Re}\ -\ 1.64)^2} \quad \text{see graph c.}$$

Re	100	200	300	400	500	600	700	800	900	1000
λ	0.640	0.320	0.213	0.160	0.128	0.107	0.092	0.080	0.071	0.064

Re	1100	1200	1300	1400	1500	1600	1700	1800	1900	2000
λ	0.058	0.053	0.049	0.046	0.043	0.040	0.038	0.036	0.034	0.032

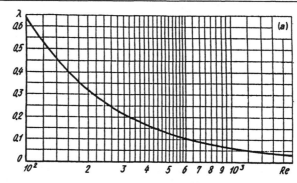

Re	$2\cdot10^3$	$2.5\cdot10^3$	$3\cdot10^3$	$4\cdot10^3$	$5\cdot10^3$	$6\cdot10^3$	$8''10^3$	10^4	$1.5\cdot10^4$	
λ	0.032	0.034	0.040	0.040	0.038	0.036	0.033	0.032	0.028	

Re	$2\cdot10^4$	$3\cdot10^4$	$4\cdot10^4$	$5\cdot10^4$	$6''10^4$	$8\cdot10^4$	10^5	$1.5\cdot10^5$	$2\cdot10^5$	$3\cdot10^5$
λ	0.026	0.024	0.022	0.021	0.020	0.019	0.018	0.017	0.016	0.015

Re	$4\cdot10^5$	$5\cdot10^5$	$6\cdot10^5$	$8\cdot10^5$	10^6	$1.5\cdot10^6$	$2\cdot10^6$	$3\cdot10^6$	$4\cdot10^6$	
λ	0.014	0.013	0.013	0.012	0.012	0.011	0.011	0.010	0.010	

Re	$5\cdot10^6$	$8\cdot10^6$	10^7	$1.5\cdot10^7$	$2\cdot10^7$	$3\cdot10^7$	$6\cdot10^7$	$8\cdot10^7$	10^8	
λ	0.009	0.009	0.008	0.008	0.008	0.007	0.007	0.006	0.006	

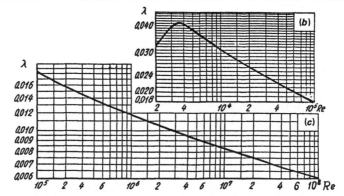

Circular tube with walls of uniform roughness; stabilized flow; Re > 2000[87,190]	Diagram 2-2

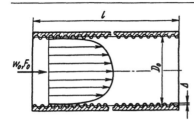

$$\zeta \equiv \frac{\Delta p}{\rho w_0^2/2} = \lambda \frac{l}{D_0}$$

$$\lambda \equiv \frac{\Delta p}{(\rho w_0^2/2)(l/D_0)} = \frac{1}{[a_1 + b_1 \lg (Re\sqrt{\lambda}) + c_1 \lg \overline{\Delta}]^2}$$

$\lambda \equiv f(Re)$ see graph; the values of a_1, b_1, and c_1 are given below:

For the single formula for calculating λ, see paragraph 19 of Section 2-1.

$\overline{\Delta}Re\sqrt{\lambda}$	a_1	b_1	c_1
3.6–10	−0.800	2.000	0
10–20	0.068	1.130	−0.870
20–40	1.538	0.000	−2.000
40–20	2.471	−0.588	−2.588
>191.2	1.138	0	−2.000

$$\overline{\Delta} = \frac{\Delta}{D_0}$$

for Δ see Table 2-5 (Section 2-1); for ν, see Section 1-2. At $\Delta < \overline{\Delta}_{lim}D_0$, for the values of λ, see Diagram 2-1, where $\overline{\Delta}_{lim} \approx 17.85\ Re^{-0.875}$.

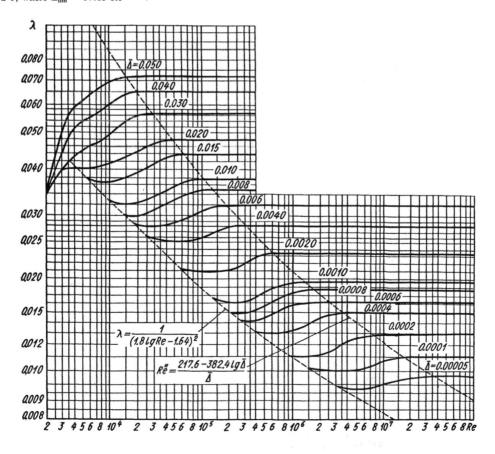

$$\lambda = \frac{1}{(1.8\,LgRe - 1.64)^2}$$

$$Re'' = \frac{217.6 - 382.4\,lg\,\overline{\Delta}}{\overline{\Delta}}$$

Diagram
2-2

Values of λ

$\bar{\Delta} = \dfrac{\Delta}{D}$	Re									
	2×10^3	3×10^3	4×10^3	6×10^3	10^4	2×10^4	4×10^4	6×10^4	10^5	2×10^5
0.05	0.032	0.052	0.060	0.063	0.069	0.072	0.072	0.072	0.072	0.072
0.04	0.032	0.044	0.052	0.055	0.060	0.065	0.065	0.065	0.065	0.065
0.03	0.032	0.040	0.044	0.046	0.050	0.056	0.057	0.057	0.057	0.057
0.02	0.032	0.040	0.040	0.041	0.042	0.044	0.048	0.049	0.049	0.049
0.015	0.032	0.040	0.040	0.038	0.037	0.039	0.042	0.044	0.044	0.044
0.010	0.032	0.040	0.040	0.038	0.033	0.032	0.035	0.036	0.038	0.038
0.008	0.032	0.040	0.040	0.038	0.033	0.030	0.032	0.033	0.035	0.035
0.006	0.032	0.040	0.040	0.038	0.033	0.028	0.028	0.029	0.030	0.032
0.004	0.032	0.040	0.040	0.038	0.033	0.027	0.025	0.025	0.026	0.028
0.002	0.032	0.040	0.040	0.038	0.033	0.027	0.023	0.021	0.021	0.021
0.001	0.032	0.040	0.040	0.038	0.033	0.027	0.023	0.021	0.018	0.017
0.0008	0.032	0.040	0.040	0.038	0.033	0.027	0.023	0.021	0.018	0.016
0.0006	0.032	0.040	0.040	0.038	0.033	0.027	0.023	0.021	0.018	0.016
0.0004	0.032	0.040	0.040	0.038	0.033	0.027	0.023	0.021	0.018	0.016
0.0002	0.032	0.040	0.040	0.038	0.033	0.027	0.023	0.021	0.018	0.016
0.0001	0.032	0.040	0.040	0.038	0.033	0.027	0.023	0.021	0.018	0.016
0.00005	0.032	0.040	0.040	0.038	0.033	0.027	0.023	0.021	0.018	0.016

Values of λ

$\bar{\Delta} = \dfrac{\Delta}{D}$	Re								
	4×10^5	6×10^5	10^6	2×10^6	4×10^6	6×10^6	10^7	2×10^7	$>10^8$
0.05	0.072	0.072	0.072	0.072	0.072	0.072	0.072	0.072	0.072
0.04	0.065	0.065	0.065	0.065	0.065	0.065	0.065	0.065	0.065
0.03	0.057	0.057	0.057	0.057	0.057	0.057	0.057	0.057	0.057
0.02	0.049	0.049	0.049	0.049	0.049	0.049	0.049	0.049	0.049
0.015	0.044	0.044	0.044	0.044	0.044	0.044	0.044	0.044	0.044
0.010	0.038	0.038	0.038	0.038	0.038	0.038	0.038	0.038	0.038
0.008	0.035	0.035	0.035	0.035	0.035	0.035	0.035	0.035	0.035
0.006	0.032	0.032	0.032	0.032	0.032	0.032	0.032	0.032	0.032
0.004	0.028	0.028	0.028	0.028	0.028	0.028	0.028	0.028	0.028
0.002	0.022	0.023	0.023	0.023	0.023	0.023	0.023	0.023	0.023
0.001	0.018	0.018	0.020	0.020	0.020	0.020	0.020	0.020	0.020
0.0008	0.016	0.017	0.018	0.019	0.019	0.019	0.019	0.019	0.019
0.0006	0.015	0.016	0.017	0.017	0.017	0.017	0.017	0.017	0.017
0.0004	0.014	0.014	0.014	0.015	0.016	0.016	0.016	0.016	0.016
0.0002	0.014	0.013	0.012	0.012	0.013	0.014	0.014	0.014	0.014
0.0001	0.014	0.013	0.012	0.011	0.011	0.011	0.012	0.012	0.012
0.00005	0.014	0.013	0.012	0.011	0.010	0.010	0.010	0.010	0.011

Circular tube with walls of uniform roughness; stabilized flow;
critical zone $(\mathrm{Re}_0 < \mathrm{Re} < \mathrm{Re}_2)$[100,106]

Diagram
2-3

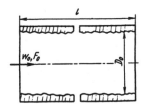

$$\zeta \equiv \frac{\Delta p}{\rho w_0^2/2} = \lambda \frac{l}{D_0}$$

$$\lambda \equiv \frac{\Delta p}{(\rho w_0^2/2)(l/D_0)}$$

	Diagram 2-3

1. $Re_0 < Re < Re_1; \overline{\Delta} \geqslant 0.007$

$$\lambda = 4.4\, Re^{-0.595} \exp\left(-\frac{0.00275}{\overline{\Delta}}\right) = f(Re,\, \overline{\Delta})$$

2. $Re_1 < Re < Re_2$

$$\lambda = (\lambda_2 - \lambda^*) \exp\{-[0.0017\,(Re_2 - Re)]^2\} + \lambda^* = f(Re,\, \overline{\Delta})$$

at $\overline{\Delta} \leqslant 0.007$, $\lambda^* = \lambda_1 \approx 0.032$, and $\lambda_2 = \lambda_2' = 7.244\, Re_2^{-0.643}$

at $\overline{\Delta} > 0.007$, $\lambda^* = \lambda_1 - 0.0017 = 0.0758 - \dfrac{0.0109}{\overline{\Delta}^{0.286}}$,

and $\lambda_2 = \lambda_2'' = \dfrac{0.145}{\overline{\Delta}^{0.244}}$

at $\overline{\Delta} > 0.007$:

$$Re_0 = 754 \exp\left(\frac{0.0065}{\overline{\Delta}}\right) \qquad Re_1 = 1160\left(\frac{1}{\overline{\Delta}}\right)^{0.11}$$

at any $\overline{\Delta}$:

$$Re_2 = 2090\left(\frac{1}{\overline{\Delta}}\right)^{0.0635}$$

For the values of Re_0, Re_1, Re_2, λ_1, λ_2', and λ_2'', see the table;

$$Re = \frac{w_0 D_0}{\nu} \qquad \overline{\Delta} = \frac{\Delta}{D_0}$$

where for Δ, see Table 2-5, Section 2-1; for ν, see Section 1-2.

3. For the single formula to calculate λ, see paragraph 30 of Section 2-1.

Values of λ

$\overline{\Delta}$	$Re \times 10^{-3}$							
	1	1.1	1.2	1.3	1.4	1.5	1.6	1.8
0.025	0.065	0.061	0.058	0.056	0.053	0.051	0.049	0.046
0.017	0.064	0.068	0.055	0.053	0.050	0.048	0.046	0.043
0.0125	–	–	0.053	0.050	0.048	0.046	0.044	0.040
0.0100	–	–	–	0.049	0.046	0.044	0.042	0.039
0.0080	–	–	–	–	–	0.043	0.040	0.037
0.0070	–	–	–	–	–	–	–	0.036
0.0060	–	–	–	–	–	–	–	–
0.0050	–	–	–	–	–	–	–	–
0.0040	–	–	–	–	–	–	–	–
0.0030	–	–	–	–	–	–	–	–
0.0024	–	–	–	–	–	–	–	–
0.0020	–	–	–	–	–	–	–	–

Diagram
2-3

Values of λ

$\overline{\Delta}$	Re $\times 10^{-3}$										
	2	2.2	2.4	2.6	2.8	3	3.2	3.4	3.6	3.8	4
0.025	0.049	0.053	0.057	0.059	0.059	0.059	0.059	0.059	0.060	0.060	0.060
0.017	0.044	0.047	0.051	0.053	0.054	0.054	0.054	0.054	0.054	0.054	0.054
0.0125	0.040	0.043	0.046	0.049	0.050	0.050	0.050	0.051	0.051	0.051	0.051
0.0100	0.037	0.039	0.043	0.046	0.047	0.048	0.048	0.049	0.048	0.050	0.050
0.0080	0.035	0.037	0.040	0.043	0.045	0.046	0.046	0.047	0.047	0.048	0.048
0.0070	0.033	0.035	0.038	0.041	0.044	0.045	0.045	0.045	0.046	0.046	0.046
0.0060	0.033	0.035	0.038	0.041	0.043	0.044	0.044	0.044	0.045	0.045	0.045
0.0050	0.033	0.035	0.037	0.039	0.042	0.043	0.043	0.043	0.044	0.044	0.044
0.0040	0.032	0.034	0.036	0.039	0.041	0.042	0.043	0.043	0.044	0.044	0.044
0.0030	0.032	0.033	0.035	0.038	0.040	0.041	0.042	0.043	0.043	0.044	0.044
0.0024	0.032	0.033	0.035	0.037	0.039	0.040	0.041	0.042	0.043	0.043	0.043
0.0020	0.032	0.033	0.034	0.036	0.037	0.038	0.040	0.041	0.042	0.042	0.042

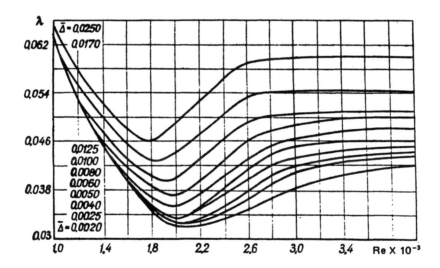

Intermediate values of Re and λ

$\overline{\Delta}$	Re_0	Re_1	Re_2	λ_1	λ_1'	λ_2''
0.00125	2000	2000	3190	0.032	0.0406	–
0.00197	2000	2000	3100	0.032	0.0412	–
0.0028	2000	2000	3029	0.032	0.0417	–
0.0036	2000	2000	2987	0.032	0.0420	–
0.0063	2000	2000	2880	0.032	0.0431	–
0.0072	1850	1995	2860	0.0329	–	0.0436
0.0185	1070	1799	2690	0.0437	–	0.0547
0.0270	960	1725	2630	0.0469	–	0.0600
0.0450	870	1633	2548	0.0510	–	0.0673
0.0600	830	1575	2500	0.0532	–	0.0730

Circular tube with walls of nonuniform roughness; stabilized flow; Re > Re[10,171]	Diagram 2-4

$$\mathrm{Re} = \frac{w_0 D_0}{\nu}$$

For Re$_2$, see Diagram 2-3

$$\zeta \equiv \frac{\Delta p}{\rho w_0^2/2} = \lambda \frac{l_0}{D_0}$$

$$\lambda \equiv \frac{\Delta p}{(\rho w_0^2/2)(l/D_h)} = \frac{1}{[2 \lg (2.51/\mathrm{Re} \sqrt{\lambda} + \overline{\Delta}/3.7)]^2}$$

or within the limits of $\overline{\Delta} = 0.00008$–$0.0125$:

$$\lambda \approx 0.11\left(\overline{\Delta} + \frac{68}{\mathrm{Re}}\right)^{0.25} \qquad \text{see graph a}$$

$$\overline{\Delta} = \frac{\Delta}{D_0}$$

for Δ, see Table 2-5, Section 2-1; for ν, see Section 1-2.

At $\Delta < \overline{\Delta}_{\mathrm{lim}} D_0$, for λ see Diagram 2-1; for $\overline{\Delta}_{\mathrm{lim}}$ see graph b as a function of Re. The manner in which the roughness of the tube walls during their use is taken into account is considered under paragraphs 63–69 of Section 2-1.

For Re$_2$, see Diagram 2-3.

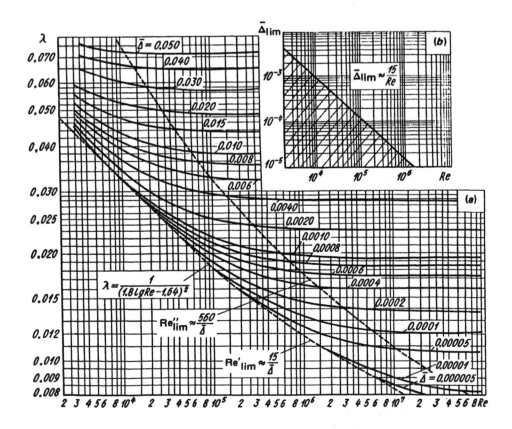

Diagram
2-4

Values of λ

$\bar{\Delta} = \dfrac{\Delta}{D_h}$	Re								
	3×10^3	4×10^3	6×10^3	10^4	2×10^4	4×10^4	6×10^4	10^5	2×10^5
0.05	0.077	0.076	0.074	0.073	0.072	0.072	0.072	0.072	0.072
0.04	0.072	0.071	0.068	0.067	0.065	0.065	0.065	0.065	0.065
0.03	0.065	0.064	0.062	0.061	0.059	0.057	0.057	0.057	0.057
0.02	0.059	0.057	0.054	0.052	0.051	0.050	0.049	0.049	0.049
0.015	0.055	0.053	0.050	0.048	0.046	0.045	0.044	0.044	0.044
0.010	0.052	0.049	0.046	0.043	0.041	0.040	0.039	0.038	0.038
0.008	0.050	0.047	0.044	0.041	0.038	0.037	0.036	0.035	0.035
0.006	0.049	0.046	0.042	0.039	0.036	0.034	0.033	0.033	0.032
0.004	0.048	0.044	0.040	0.036	0.033	0.031	0.030	0.030	0.028
0.002	0.045	0.042	0.038	0.034	0.030	0.027	0.026	0.026	0.024
0.001	0.044	0.042	0.037	0.032	0.028	0.025	0.024	0.023	0.021
0.0008	0.043	0.040	0.036	0.032	0.027	0.024	0.023	0.022	0.020
0.0006	0.040	0.040	0.036	0.032	0.027	0.023	0.022	0.021	0.018
0.0004	0.036	0.040	0.036	0.032	0.027	0.023	0.022	0.020	0.018
0.0002	0.036	0.040	0.036	0.032	0.027	0.022	0.021	0.019	0.017
0.0001	0.036	0.040	0.036	0.032	0.027	0.022	0.021	0.019	0.017
0.00005	0.036	0.040	0.036	0.032	0.027	0.022	0.021	0.019	0.016
0.00001	0.036	0.040	0.036	0.032	0.027	0.022	0.021	0.019	0.016
0.000005	0.036	0.040	0.036	0.032	0.027	0.022	0.021	0.019	0.016

Values of λ

$\bar{\Delta} = \dfrac{\Delta}{D_h}$	Re								
	4×10^5	6×10^5	10^6	2×10^6	4×10^6	6×10^6	10^7	2×10^7	$> 10^8$
0.05	0.072	0.072	0.072	0.072	0.072	0.072	0.072	0.072	0.072
0.04	0.065	0.065	0.065	0.065	0.065	0.065	0.065	0.065	0.065
0.03	0.057	0.057	0.057	0.057	0.057	0.057	0.057	0.057	0.057
0.02	0.049	0.049	0.049	0.049	0.049	0.049	0.049	0.049	0.049
0.015	0.044	0.044	0.044	0.044	0.044	0.044	0.044	0.044	0.044
0.010	0.038	0.038	0.038	0.038	0.038	0.038	0.038	0.038	0.038
0.008	0.035	0.035	0.035	0.035	0.035	0.035	0.035	0.035	0.035
0.006	0.032	0.032	0.032	0.032	0.032	0.032	0.032	0.032	0.032
0.004	0.028	0.028	0.028	0.028	0.028	0.028	0.028	0.028	0.028
0.002	0.024	0.023	0.023	0.023	0.023	0.023	0.023	0.023	0.023
0.001	0.021	0.020	0.020	0.020	0.020	0.020	0.020	0.020	0.020
0.0008	0.020	0.019	0.019	0.019	0.019	0.019	0.019	0.019	0.019
0.0006	0.018	0.018	0.017	0.017	0.017	0.017	0.017	0.017	0.017
0.0004	0.017	0.017	0.016	0.016	0.016	0.016	0.016	0.016	0.016
0.0002	0.016	0.015	0.015	0.014	0.014	0.014	0.014	0.014	0.014
0.0001	0.015	0.014	0.013	0.013	0.012	0.012	0.012	0.012	0.012
0.00005	0.014	0.013	0.013	0.012	0.011	0.011	0.011	0.011	0.011
0.00001	0.014	0.013	0.012	0.011	0.010	0.009	0.009	0.009	0.009
0.000005	0.014	0.013	0.012	0.011	0.009	0.009	0.009	0.008	0.008

Circular tube with rough walls; stabilized flow; regime of quadratic resistance law ($Re_{lim} > 560/\overline{\Delta}$).[99,190]	Diagram 2-5

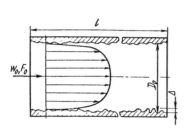

$$\zeta \equiv \frac{\Delta p}{\rho w_0^2/2} = \lambda \frac{l}{D_0}$$

$$\lambda \equiv \frac{\Delta p}{(\rho w_0^2/2)(l/D_0)} = \frac{1}{[2 \lg (3.7/\overline{\Delta})]^2} = f(\overline{\Delta})$$

$$\overline{\Delta} = \frac{\Delta}{D_0}$$

for Δ, see Table 2-5 of Section 2-1; for ν, see Section 1-2.

The manner in which increase in the asperities on tube walls during use is taken into account is considered under paragraphs 63–69.

$\overline{\Delta} = \dfrac{\Delta}{D_0}$	0.00005	0.0001	0.0002	0.0003	0.0004	0.0005	0.0006	0.0007	0.0008
λ	0.010	0.012	0.013	0.014	0.015	0.016	0.017	0.018	0.018
$\overline{\Delta} = \dfrac{\Delta}{D_0}$	0.0009	0.001	0.002	0.003	0.004	0.005	0.006	0.008	0.010
λ	0.019	0.020	0.023	0.026	0.028	0.031	0.032	0.035	0.038
$\overline{\Delta} = \dfrac{\Delta}{D_0}$	0.015	0.020	0.025	0.030	0.035	0.040	0.045	0.050	
λ	0.044	0.049	0.053	0.057	0.061	0.065	0.068	0.072	

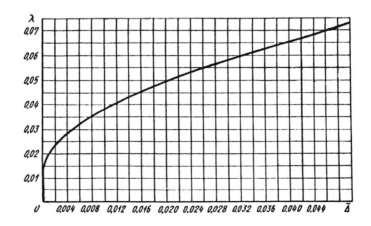

Tubes of rectangular, elliptical, and other types of cross section; stabilized flow.[87,158]	Diagram 2-6

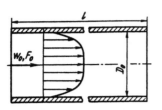

$$\zeta \equiv \frac{\Delta p}{\rho w_0^2/2} = \lambda_{\text{non-}c} \frac{1}{D_h}$$

$$D_h = \frac{4F_0}{\Pi_0} \quad \text{Re} = \frac{w_0 D_h}{\nu} \quad \lambda_{\text{non-}c} \equiv \frac{\Delta p}{(\rho w_0^2/2)(l/D_h)} = k_{\text{non-}c}\lambda$$

where λ is determined as for circular tubes from Diagrams 2-1 through 2-5

Shape of tube (conduit) cross section and schematic	Correction factor $k_{\text{non-}c}$

Correction factor $k_{\text{non-}c}$

Laminar regime (Re < 2000, curve 1)

$\dfrac{b_0}{a_0}$	0	0.1	0.2	0.4	0.6	0.8	1.0
$k_{\text{non-}c} = k_{\text{rec}}$	1.50	1.34	1.20	1.02	0.94	0.90	0.89

Turbulent regime (Re > 2000, curve 2)

$k_{\text{non-}c} = k_{\text{rec}}$	1.10	1.08	1.06	1.04	1.02	1.01	1.0

Rectangle:

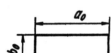

$$D_h = \frac{2a_0 b_0}{a_0 + b_0}$$

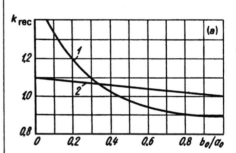

Trapezoid:

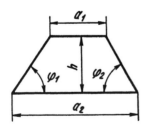

$k_{\text{non-}c}$ is determined in approximately the same way as for a rectangle

$$D_h = 2h \bigg/ \left[1 + \frac{h}{\beta_1 + \beta_2}\left(\frac{1}{\sin \varphi_1} + \frac{1}{\sin \varphi_2}\right)\right]$$

Diagram
2-6

Shape of tube (conduit) cross section and schematic	Correction factor k_{non-c}

Circle with one or two recesses. Star-shaped circle

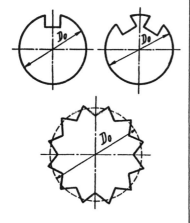

$$k_{non-c} = k_{rec} = k_{st} \approx 1.0$$

Ellipse

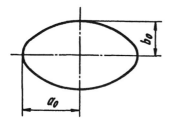

$$D_h \approx \frac{4a_0 b_0}{1.5(a_0 + b_0) - \sqrt{a_0 b_0}}$$

More precisely:

$$D_h \approx \frac{\pi a_0 b_0}{0.983 a_0 + 0.311 b_0 + 0.287 b_0^2/a_0}$$

Laminar regime (Re $\leqslant$ 2000):

$$k_{non-c} = k_{ell} = \frac{1}{8}\left(\frac{D_h}{b_0}\right)^2\left[1 + \left(\frac{b_0}{a_0}\right)^2\right] \text{ see graph b}$$

$\dfrac{b_0}{a_0}$	0.1	0.2	0.3	0.4	0.5	0.6	0.7	0.8	0.9	1.0
k_{ell}	1.21	1.16	1.11	1.08	1.05	1.03	1.02	1.01	1.01	1.0

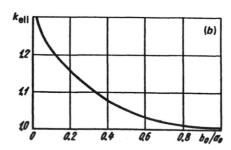

Turbulent regime (Re $>$ 2000); $k_{ell} \approx 1.0$

Circular tubes; stabilized flow[29,30,39,65,95,120,205]

Diagram 2-7

$$D_h = D_0 - d$$

$$D_h = \frac{4F_0}{\Pi_0} \qquad Re = \frac{w_0 D_h}{\nu} \qquad \zeta \equiv \frac{\Delta p}{\rho w_0^2/2} = \lambda_{non-c} = \lambda_{non-c}\frac{1}{D_h} \qquad \lambda_{non-c} \equiv \frac{\Delta p}{(\rho w_0^2/2)(l/D_h)} = k_{non-c}\lambda$$

where λ is determined in the same way as for circular tubes from Diagram 2-1 through 2-5

Shape of tube (conduit) cross section	Schematic	Correction factor, k_{non-c}

Laminar regime (Re < 2000): $k_{non-c} = k_{1r} = \dfrac{1 - (d/D_0)^2}{1 + (d/D_0)^2 + [1 - (d/D_0)^2]/(\ln d/D_0)}$,

see curve k_{1r} of graph a.

d/D_0	0	0.1	0.2	0.3	0.4	0.5	0.6	≥0.7
k_{1r}	1.0	1.40	1.44	1.47	1.48	1.49	1.49	1.50

Turbulent regime (Re > 2000): $\lambda_{non-c} \equiv \lambda_r = \left(\dfrac{0.02d}{D_0} + 0.98\right)\left(\dfrac{1}{\lambda} - 0.27\dfrac{d}{D_0} + 0.1\right)$

$k_{non-c} = k_{2r}$, see curves of graph a

Values of k_{2r}

Re	d/D_0									
	0	0.1	0.2	0.3	0.4	0.5	0.6	0.7	0.8	1.0
10^4	1.0	1.03	1.04	1.05	1.05	1.06	1.06	1.07	1.07	1.07
10^5	1.0	1.02	1.03	1.04	1.05	1.05	1.06	1.06	1.06	1.06
10^6	1.0	1.02	1.03	1.04	1.04	1.05	1.05	1.05	1.05	1.06
10^7	1.0	1.01	1.02	1.03	1.03	1.04	1.04	1.04	1.05	1.05

Concentric annulus:
$$D_h = D_0 - d$$

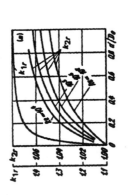

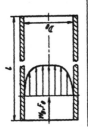

Longitudinal fins ($d/D_0 \approx 0.9$)

Laminar regime at Re ≤ 3×10^3

$k_{non-c} = k_r'' = 1.36$

Turbulent regime at Re > 3×10^5;

for k_r'', see k_{2r} or a concentric annulus without fins

Concentric narrow annulus ($d/D_0 \approx 0.9$) with longitudinal fins

$$D_h = D_0 \frac{(1 - d/D_0)(1 + d/D_0 - 6b/\pi D_0)}{(1 + d/D_0) + (3/\pi)(1 - d/D_0) - 6b/\pi D_0}$$

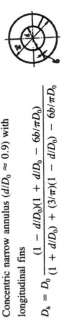

	Diagram 2-7

Shape of the tube (channel) cross section	Schematic

Spiral fins

$$D_h = D_0 \left\{ \left(1 - \frac{d}{D_0} \right) \left[\frac{2(T/\pi d)(d/D_0)}{1 - d/D_0} (A - B) - \frac{6b}{\pi D_0} \right] \right/$$

$$\frac{d}{D_0} \frac{T}{\pi d} \left(\frac{1}{A} + \frac{d/D_0}{B} \right) + \frac{3}{\pi} \left(1 - \frac{d}{D_0} \right) - \frac{6b}{\pi D_0} \right\}$$

$$A = \sqrt{1 + \left(\frac{d}{D_0} \frac{T}{\pi d} \right)^2}$$

$$B = \frac{d}{D_0} \sqrt{1 + \left(\frac{T}{\pi d} \right)^2}$$

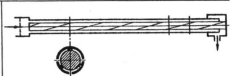

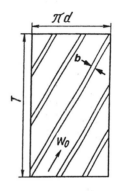

Eccentric annulus
$$D_h = D_0 - d$$
$$\bar{e} = \frac{2e}{D_0 - d}$$

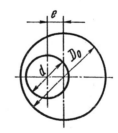

Correction factor $k_{\text{non-c}}$

Spiral fins for all values of Re

$$k_r'' \approx k_{\text{non-c}} = \left(1 + \frac{20}{(T/d)^2} \right) k_r' = A_1 k'r$$

for A_1 see graph b; for k_r' see concentric annulus with fins

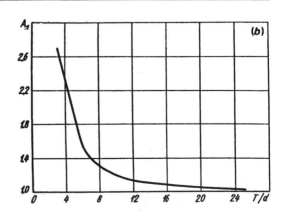

T/d	3.5	4.5	6.0	8.0	10	25
A_1	2.63	1.98	1.56	1.31	1.20	1.03

	Diagram 2-7

Correction factor $k_{\text{non-}c}$

Laminar regime (Re $\leqslant$ 2000):

$$k_{\text{non-}c} = k_{\text{ell}} = \frac{1}{(1 + B_1 \bar{e})^2} \, k_{1r}$$

where for $B_1 = f(d/D_0)$, see graph c; for k_{1r}, see concentric annulus without fins

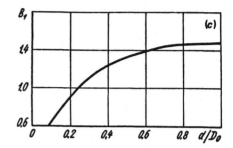

d/D_0	0	0.1	0.2	0.3	0.4	0.5	0.6	0.8	1.0
B_1	0	0.65	0.90	1.10	1.22	1.30	1.39	1.45	1.48

Turbulent regime (Re $>$ 2000):
$k''_{\text{ell}} = k'_{\text{ell}} k_{2r}$; for k'_{ell} at $d/D_0 = 0.5$,
see curve 1 of graph 2; at $d/D_0 \geqslant 0.7$,
see curve 2 of graph 2
or $k'_{\text{ell}} = 1 - 0.9(1 - 2/3\bar{e})\bar{e}^2$

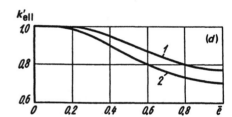

Values of k'_{ell}

d/D_0	$\bar{e}$					
	0	0.2	0.4	0.6	0.8	1.0
0.5 (curve 1)	1.0	1.0	0.95	0.87	0.80	0.77
$\geqslant$0.7 (curve 2)	1.0	0.98	0.90	0.80	0.73	0.70

Tubes of triangular (and similar) cross section; stabilized flow[76,95,158]	Diagram 2-8

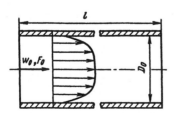

$$D_h = \frac{4F_0}{\Pi_0} \quad \text{Re} = \frac{w_0 D_h}{\nu}$$

where λ s determined in the same

	Diagram 2-8

Shape of the tube (channel) cross section	Schematic
Isosceles triangle: $B = \sqrt{4 + \dfrac{5}{2}\left(\dfrac{1}{\tan^2\beta} - 1\right)}$ $D_h = \dfrac{2h}{1 + \sqrt{1/\tan^2\beta + 1}}$	
Right triangle: for D_h see isosceles triangle	
Equilateral triangle $(\beta = 30°)$: for D_h see isosceles triangle	
Sector of a circle: $D_h = \dfrac{2\pi D_0 \beta/180°}{1 + \pi\beta/180°}$ $(\beta - 6°)$	

$$\zeta \equiv \frac{\Delta p}{\rho w_0^2/2} = \lambda_{\text{non-c}}\frac{1}{D_h} \quad \lambda_{\text{non-c}} \equiv \frac{\Delta p}{(\rho w_0^2/2)(l/D_h)} = k_{\text{non-c}}\lambda$$

way as for circular tubes from Diagram 2-1 through 2-5.

							Diagram 2-8

Correction factor $k_{\text{non-c}}$

Laminar regime (Re $\leqslant$ 2000):

$$k_{\text{non-c}} = k'_{\text{tr}} = \frac{3}{4} \frac{1 - \text{tg}^2\,\beta\,(B + 2)}{(B - 2)(\text{tg}\,\beta + \sqrt{1 + \text{tg}^2\,\beta})^2} \quad \text{see curve 1.}$$

β, deg	0	10	20	30	40	60	80	90
k'_{tr}	0.75	0.81	0.82	0.83	0.82	0.80	0.75	0.78

Turbulent regime (Re > 2000), see curve 2

k'_{tr}	0.75	0.84	0.89	0.93	0.96	0.98	0.90	1.0

Laminar regime:

$$k_{\text{non-c}} = k'_{\text{tr}} = \frac{3}{4} \frac{(1 - 3\,\text{tg}^2\,\beta)\,(B + 2)}{\{(3\,\text{tg}\,\beta)/[2\sqrt{4\,\text{tg}^2\,\beta + 5/2(1 - \text{tg}^2\,\beta)}] - 2\}\,(\text{tg}\,\beta + \sqrt{1 + \text{tg}^2\,\beta})^2} \quad \text{see curve 4.}$$

β, deg	0	10	20	30	40	60	80	90
k'_{tr}	0.75	0.78	0.80	0.81	0.82	0.81	0.77	0.75

Turbulent regime: for k''_{tr} see k'_{tr} of isosceles triangle (curve 2)

Laminar regime: $k_{\text{non-c}} \equiv k''_{\text{tr}} = 0.835$
Turbulent regime: $k_{\text{non-c}} \equiv k''_{\text{tr}} = 0.95$

Laminar regime: $k_{\text{sec}} = k_{\text{tr}}$; see curve 3

β, deg	0	10	20	30	40	60	80	90
$k_{\text{non-c}} = k_{\text{sec}}$	0.75	0.82	0.86	0.89	0.92	0.95	0.98	1.0

Turbulent regime: for k_{sec}, see k'_{tr} of isosceles triangle (curve 2)

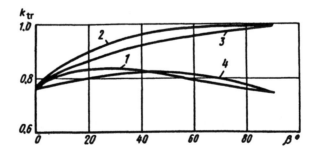

Bundles of tubes, rods; parallel interstitial flow[40,41,68,119,120,157]

	Diagram 2-9

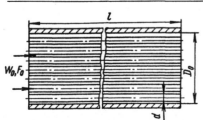

$$D_h = \frac{4F_0}{\Pi_0} \quad \text{Re} = \frac{w_0 D_h}{\nu} \quad \zeta \equiv \frac{\Delta p}{\rho w_0^2/2} = \lambda_{\text{non-c}}\,\frac{l}{D_h}$$

$$\lambda_{\text{bun}} \equiv \frac{\Delta p}{(\rho w_0^2/2)(l/D_h)} = k_{\text{bun}}\lambda$$

where λ is determined in the same way as for circular tubes from Diagrams 2-1 through 2-5.

	Diagram 2-9

Shape of channel cross section and schematic	Correction factor k_{bun}

Triangular, loose array (without shroud, equilateral triangle)

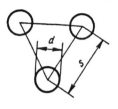

$$D_h = d\left[\frac{6}{\sqrt{3\pi}}\left(\frac{s}{d}\right)^2 - 1\right]$$

Laminar regime (Re ⩽ 2000); $1.0 \leqslant s/d \leqslant 1.5$;
$k_{bun} \approx 0.89 s/d + 0.63$ or see curve 1 of graph a (Table 1).

s/d	1.0	1.05	1.10	1.20	1.30	1.40	1.50
k_{bun}	1.52	1.56	1.61	1.70	1.79	1.88	1.97

Turbulent regime at $s/d = 1.0$: $k_{bun} = 0.64$

Rectangular loose array (without shroud)

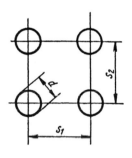

$$D_h = d\left(\frac{4}{\pi}\frac{s_1 s_2}{d^2} - 1\right)$$

Laminar regime; at $1.0 \leqslant s/d \leqslant 1.5$;
$k_{bun} \approx 0.96 s/d + 0.63$ or see curve 1 of graph a (Table 2).

s/d	1.0	1.05	1.10	1.20	1.30	1.40	1.50
k_{bun}	1.59	1.64	1.68	1.78	1.88	1.98	2.07

Turbulent regime; $s/d = 1.0$: $k_{bun} = 0.64$

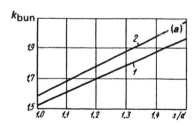

Turbulent regime (Re > 2000)
a) Array without fins: $k_{bun} = f(s/d)$, see graph b.

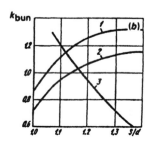

	Diagram 2-9

Shape of channel cross section and schematic	Correction factor k_{bun}

Triangular array with shroud; z is the number of rods (cylinders) in a bundle; for D_h, see triangular loose array

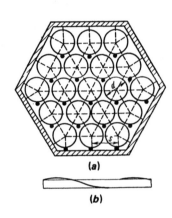

(a)

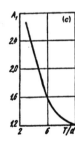

(b)

Values of k_{bun}

Curve	1.0	1.05	1.10	1.20	1.30	1.40
			s/d			
	Shaped shroud, $z = 19$ and 37					
1	0.85	1.0	1.12	1.25	1.29	1.30
	Hexahedral shroud, $z = 37$					
2	0.70	0.84	0.95	1.06	1.13	1.15
	Triangular $z = 3$					
3	–	1.30	1.25	0.95	0.72	0.57

b) Array with helical fins: $k'_{bun} = \left[1 + \dfrac{20}{(T/d)^2}\right] k_{bun} = A_1 k_{bun}$

where for k_{bun} see graph b; for A_1 see graph c; for T see Diagram 2-7

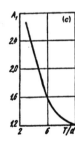

T/d	3.5	4.5	6.0	10
A_1	2.63	1.98	1.56	1.20

Rectangular four-tube array; for D_h see rectangular loose array	

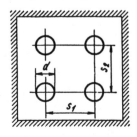

Turbulent regime;
a) Array without fins:
  1) At $s/d = 1.45$, $k_{bun} = 0.97$
  2) When a rod is in contact with walls, $k_{bun} = 0.71$;
  3) When rods and walls are in contact, $k_{bun} = 0.68$.
b) Array with helical fins: for k_{bun} see triangular array with shroud.

Tubes made from aluminum or steel strips (plane-welded); Stabilized flow[74]	Diagram 2-10

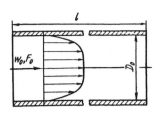

$$\zeta \equiv \frac{\Delta p}{\rho w_0^2/2} = \lambda \frac{l}{D_h}$$

a) $4 \times 10^3 < \mathrm{Re} < 4 \times 10^4$

$$\lambda \equiv \frac{\Delta p}{(\rho w_0^2/2)(l/D_h)} = \frac{A_1}{\mathrm{Re}^{0.25}}$$

where $A_1 = f(a_0/b_0)$, see graph a;

b) $4 \times 10^4 < \mathrm{Re} < 2 \times 10^5$

$$\lambda = \frac{A_2}{\mathrm{Re}^{0.12}}$$

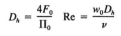

$$D_h = \frac{4F_0}{\Pi_0} \quad \mathrm{Re} = \frac{w_0 D_h}{\nu}$$

D_h is determined in the same way as for an ellipse (see Diagram 2-6)

where $A_2 = f(a_0/b_0)$, see graph a. $\mathrm{Re}^{0.25}$ and $\mathrm{Re}^{0.12}$, see graph b.

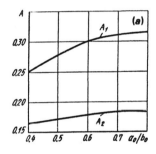

$\dfrac{a_0}{b_0}$	0.4	0.5	0.6	0.7	0.8
A_1	0.250	0.275	0.300	0.310	0.316
A_2	0.165	0.17	0.18	0.185	0.185

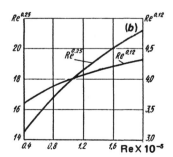

$\mathrm{Re} \times 10^{-5}$	0.4	0.6	0.8	1	1.2	1.4	1.6	1.8	2
$\mathrm{Re}^{0.25}$	14.1	15.7	16.8	17.8	18.6	19.3	20.0	2.06	21.1
$\mathrm{Re}^{0.12}$	3.57	3.75	3.88	3.98	4.07	4.15	4.21	4.27	4.33

Welded tube with joints; stabilized flow[6.194]	Diagram 2-11

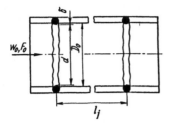

$$\zeta \equiv \frac{\Delta p}{\rho w_0^2/2} = n_0 \left(\lambda \frac{l_j}{D_0} + \zeta_j \right)$$

where n_0 is the number of joints over the section; for λ see Diagrams 2-2 through 2-6; ζ_j is the resistance coefficient of one joint:

1) At $\frac{l_j}{\delta_d} < 50$

$$\zeta_j \equiv \frac{\Delta p}{\rho w_0^2/2} = k_4 \zeta_j^0 \text{ where } \zeta_j^0 = 13.8 \left(\frac{\delta_j}{D_0} \right)^{3/2}$$

see graph a; $k_4 = 0.23\,(2\,\lg l_j/\delta_j + 1)$, see graph b;

2) At $\frac{l_j}{\delta_d} \geqslant 50$

$$\zeta_j \equiv \frac{\Delta p}{\rho w_0^2/2}, \quad \text{see Table 3.}$$

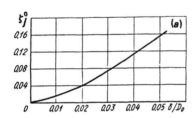

Table 1

$\dfrac{\delta_j}{D_0}$	0.01	0.02	0.03	0.04	0.05	0.06
ζ_j^0	0.017	0.039	0.075	0.115	0.15	0.20

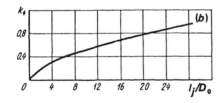

Table 2

$\dfrac{l_j}{\delta_j}$	4	8	12	16	20	24	30	50
k_4	0.51	0.65	0.73	0.78	0.83	0.86	0.91	1.0

Values of ζ_j for welded joints of different types   **Table 3**

Type of joint	Tube diameter D_0, mm							
	200	300	400	500	600	700	800	900
With backing rings ($\delta_j = 5$ mm)	0.06	0.03	0.018	0.013	0.009	0.007	0.006	0.005
Made by electro-arc and contact (resistance) welding ($\delta_j = 3$ mm)	0.026	0.0135	0.009	0.006	0.004	0.0028	0.0023	0.002

Tubes with rectangular annular recesses; stabilized flow; Re $\geq 10^{5.133}$

Diagram 2-12

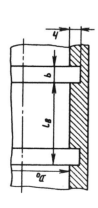

$$\zeta \equiv \frac{p}{\rho w_0^2/2} = n_r(\lambda l_r/D_0 + \zeta_r),$$

where n_r is the number of recesses over the section; for λ see Diagrams 2-2 through 2-6; ζ_r is the resistance coefficient of a recess:

at $l_r/D_0 \geq 4$: $\zeta_r \approx 0.046\ b/D_0$;

at $l_r/D_0 = 2$: $\zeta_r = \zeta_{max} \approx 0.059\ b/D_0$;

at $l_r/D_0 < 4$: $\zeta_r = f(b/D_0,\ l_r/D_0)$; see the curves.

l_r/D_0	Values of λ							
	0.06	0.10	0.14	0.18	0.22	0.26	0.28
0.35	0.0019	0.0033	0.0048	0.0065	0.0075	0.0090	0.0097
1.0	0.0027	0.0043	0.0062	0.0081	0.0105	0.0127	0.0137
2.0	0.0028	0.0047	0.0073	0.0094	0.0120	0.0142	0.0156
3.0	0.0020	0.0039	0.0064	0.0084	0.0113	0.0133	0.0148
4.0	0.0017	0.0033	0.0052	0.0070	0.0089	0.0110	0.0120

Flexible circular tubes; stabilized turbulent flow[53,146,194]	Diagram 2-13

$$\zeta \equiv \lambda \frac{l}{D_0}$$

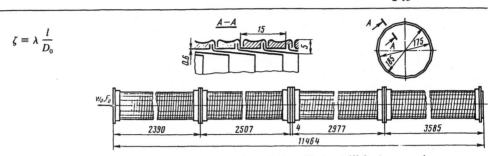

1. Tube made of metallic strip (metallic hose);[146] for λ see graph a.

Values of λ

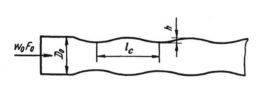

(a)

		Re $\times$ 10^{-4}			
Curve	5	8	1.2	1.6	4
a) Flow running over the edges					
1	0.0250	0.0254	0.0256	0.0257	0.0257
b) Flow entering the edges					
2	0.0250	0.0262	0.0275	0.0284	0.0285

2. Corrugated tube;[194] for λ see graph b.

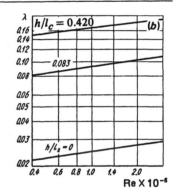

c = corrugation.

Values of λ

$\dfrac{h}{l_h}$	Re $\times$ 10^{-5}							
	0.4	0.6	0.8	1	1.4	2	2.5	3
0.421	0.150	0.155	0.162	0.168	0.175	0.180	0.185	0.190
0.083	0.082	0.088	0.090	0.092	0.098	0.103	0.105	0.110
0	0.022	0.023	0.024	0.025	0.026	0.027	0.028	0.029

3. Tube made from glass cloth[53] (see paragraph 72 of Section 2-1) $\lambda \approx 0.052 \, (10D_0)^{0.1/D_0} (50b)^{0.2}$, see the Table b is the width of the band wound around the wire tramwork of the tube made from glass cloth (when $D_0 \leq 0.2$ m, $b = 0.02$ m; when $D_0 > 0.2$ m, $b \geq 0.03$ m).

Values of λ

D_0, m	1.0	1.1	1.4	1.6–1.7	1.8	1.9	2.3	2.6–2.7	2.8	2.9	3.3
0.100	–	0.053	0.53	0.051	0.05	–	–	–	–	–	–
0.155	–	0.063	–	–	–	0.063	0.064	0.064	–	–	–
0.193	0.070	–	–	–	–	0.072	0.072	0.073	–	–	–
0.250	–	–	–	–	–	–	–	–	0.085	0.077	0.82

Steel reinforced rubber hoses; stabilized flow[132]

$$Re = \frac{w_0 d_{nom}}{\nu} > 4 \times 10^4$$

Diagram
2-14

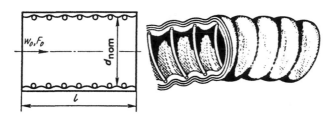

$$\zeta \equiv \frac{\Delta p}{\rho w_0^2/2} = \lambda \frac{l}{d_{cal}}$$

where λ is determined from graph a as a function of the nominal diameter d_{nom}; d_{cal} is the calculated diameter determined as a function of the internal excessive pressure p_{ex} at different d_{nom}; see graph b: for ν see 1-2.

Characteristics of the hose

Internal nominal diameter d_{nom}, mm	25	32	38	50	65
Diameter of the helix wire, mm	2.8	2.8	2.8	3.0	3.4
Pitch, mm	15.6	15.6	17.6	20.0	20.8
Cloth insert 1.1 mm thick, nos. 1	1	1	1	1	
Rubber layer, mm	1.5	1.5	2.0	2.0	2.0
Diameter of cotton helix, mm	1.8	1.8	1.8	1.8	1.8
Rubber layer, mm	1.5	1.5	1.5	1.5	1.5
Cloth inset 1.1 mm thick, nos. 2	2	2	2	2	3

d_{nom}, mm	25	32	38	50	65
λ	0.051–0.057	0.053–0.066	0.072–0.090	0.083–0.094	0.085–0.100

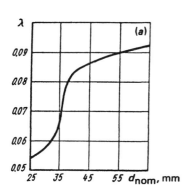

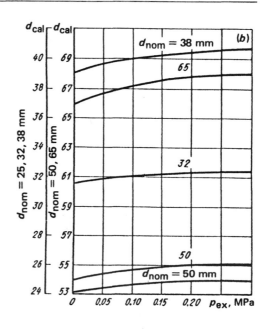

Smooth-rubber hoses; stabilized flow[132]	Diagram 2-15

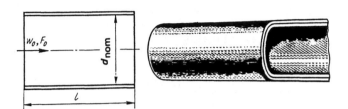

$$\zeta \equiv \frac{\Delta p}{\rho w_0^2/2} = \lambda \frac{l}{d_{cal}}$$

where $\lambda = A/Re^{0.265}$, see curves $\lambda = f(Re)$ of graph a: $A = 0.38-0.52$ within the limits of $Re = w_0 d_{cal}/\nu = 5,000-120,000$ and depending on the hose quality; d_{cal} is the calculated diameter determined as a function of the internal excessive pressure p_{ex}, see graph b; for ν see Section 1-2.

Characteristics of the hose

Internal nominal diameter d_{nom}, mm	25	32	38	50	65
Rubber layer (internal), mm	2	2	2	2.2	2.2
Cloth insert 1.1 mm thick, nos.	2	2	2	3	3
Rubber layer (external), mm	0.9	0.9	0.9	1.2	1.2

Values of λ

	Re × 10^{-4}							
A	0.4	0.6	1	2.0	4.0	6.0	10	20
0.52	0.057	0.052	0.046	0.038	0.031	0.028	0.025	0.020
0.38	0.042	0.038	0.033	0.028	0.023	0.020	0.018	0.015

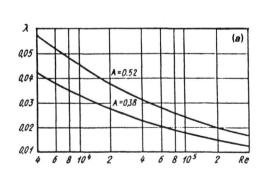

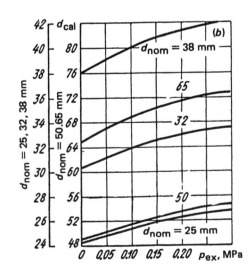

Steel reinforce smooth-rubber hoses; stabilized flow[132]

Diagram
2-16

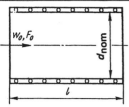

$$\delta \equiv \frac{\Delta p}{\rho w_0^2/2} = \lambda \frac{l_{out}}{d_{cal}}$$

where $\lambda = f(Re, d_{nom}, p_{ex})$, see graph a and b, d_{cal} is the calculated diameter, which is determined as a function of the average internal pressure p_{ex}, see graph c; $l_{out} = kl$; k is determined as a function of the average internal excess pressure p_{ex}, see graph d; $Re = w_0/d_{nom}/\nu$; for ν see Section 1-2.

Values of λ at $d_{nom} = 65$ mm

p_{ex}, MPa	$Re \times 10^{-5}$							
	0.4	0.6	0.8	1	1.4	2	2.5	4
0.025	0.03	0.03	0.03	0.03	0.03	0.03	–	–
0.05	0.04	0.03	0.03	0.03	0.03	0.03	0.03	0.03
0.10	0.05	0.05	0.05	0.04	0.04	0.04	0.04	0.03
0.15	0.07	0.07	0.07	0.07	0.07	0.06	0.06	0.05
0.20	0.09	0.09	0.09	0.09	0.09	0.08	0.08	0.07
0.25	0.11	0.11	0.11	0.11	0.11	0.11	0.11	–

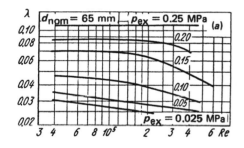
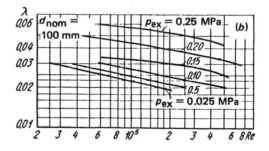

Values of λ at $d_{nom} = 100$ mm

p_{ex}, MPa	$Re \times 10^{-5}$									
	0.25	0.4	0.6	0.8	1	1.4	2	2.5	4	6
0.025	0.03	0.03	0.03	0.02	0.02	0.02	–	–	–	–
0.05	–	0.03	0.03	0.03	0.02	0.02	0.02	0.02	–	–
0.10	–	–	0.03	0.03	0.03	0.03	0.02	0.02	0.02	–
0.15	–	–	0.03	0.03	0.03	0.03	0.03	0.03	0.03	0.02
0.20	–	–	0.05	0.05	0.04	0.04	0.04	0.04	0.04	0.03
0.25	–	–	–	0.06	0.06	0.06	0.05	0.05	0.05	–

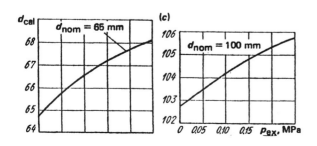
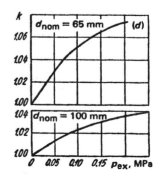

| Tube made from tarpaulin-type rubberized material; stabilized flow [according to Adamov] | Diagram 2-17 |

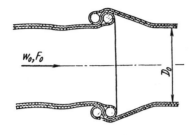

$\zeta \equiv \dfrac{\Delta p}{\rho w_0^2/2} = n_j \left(\lambda \dfrac{l_j}{D_0} + \zeta_j \right)$, where n_j is the number of pipes (joints); l_j is the distance between joints;

$\lambda \equiv \dfrac{\Delta p}{(\rho w_0^2/2)(l_j/D_0)} = f_1(\text{Re})$, see graph a for different degrees of the tube tension; $\zeta_j = f_2(\text{Re})$, see graph b;

$\text{Re} = \dfrac{w_0 D_0}{\nu}$; for ν see Section 1-2.

Values of λ

Degree of tube tension	Re $\times 10^{-5}$								
	1	2	3	4	5	6	7	8	9
Good	0.024	0.020	0.018	0.016	0.014	0.013	0.012	0.011	0.011
Moderate	0.064	0.042	0.034	0.028	0.025	0.023	0.021	0.020	0.019
Poor	0.273	0.195	0.139	0.110	0.091	0.074	0.063	0.054	0.048

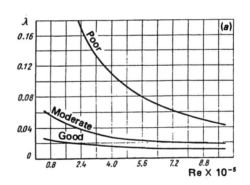

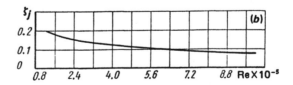

Re $\times 10^{-5}$	1	2	3	4	5	6	7	8	10
ζ_j	0.20	0.17	0.14	0.12	0.11	0.10	0.09	0.08	0.08

Tube made from birch plywood with longitudinal grain; stabilized flow[1]	Diagram 2-18

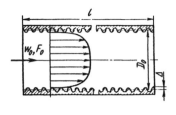

$$\lambda \equiv \frac{\Delta p}{(\rho w_0^2/2)(l/D_h)}, \text{ see curves } \lambda = f(\text{Re}) \text{ for different } \overline{\Delta};$$

$\overline{\Delta} = \dfrac{\Delta}{D_h}$; for Δ see Table 2-3; Re $= \dfrac{w_0 D_h}{\nu}$, for ν

see Section 1-2.

$$D_h = \frac{4F_0}{\Pi_0}$$

Values of ζ

	Re $\times 10^{-5}$						
$\overline{\Delta}$	0.2	0.3	0.4	0.6	0.8	1	1.5
0.00140	0.030	0.028	0.027	0.025	0.024	0.023	–
0.00055	–	–	–	0.021	0.21	0.019	0.018
0.00030	–	–	–	–	–	0.018	0.017
0.00015	–	–	–	–	–	0.018	0.017
0.00009	–	–	–	–	–	0.018	0.017

continued

	Re $\times 10^{-5}$						
$\overline{\Delta}$	2	3	4	6	8	10	20
0.00140	–	–	–	–	–	–	–
0.00055	0.017	0.018	0.018	–	–	–	–
0.00030	0.017	0.016	0.016	0.016	–	–	–
0.00015	0.016	0.015	0.014	0.014	0.014	0.013	–
0.00009	0.016	0.014	0.014	0.013	0.012	0.012	0.011

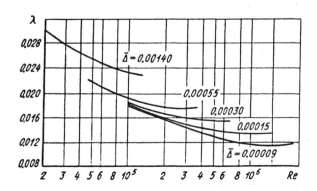

Plastic tubes; stabilized flow[91,92]   Diagram 2-19

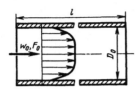

$$\zeta \equiv \frac{\Delta p}{\rho w_0^2/2} = \lambda l/D_0$$

1. Polyethylene (stabilized), rigid-vinyl plastic
   at $40\ \text{mm} \leq D_0 \leq 300\ \text{mm}$ and

$$8 \times 10^3 \leq \text{Re} = \frac{w_0 D_0}{\nu} \leq 7.5 \times 10^5:$$

$$\lambda = \frac{0.29 - 0.00023 D_0}{\text{Re}^{0.22}}, \quad \text{see Table 1}$$

(D_0, in mm; the coefficient at D_0, in mm^{-1})

2. Glass cloth
   at $100\ \text{mm} \leq D_0 \leq 150\ \text{mm}$ and $10^4 \leq \text{Re} \leq 3 \times 10^5:$

$$\lambda = \frac{0.282 - 0.000544 D_0}{\text{Re}^{0.19}}, \quad \text{see Table 2}$$

3. Faolite
   at $70\ \text{mm} \leq D_0 \leq 150\ \text{mm}$ and $10^4 \leq \text{Re} \leq 2 \times 10^5:$

$$\lambda = \frac{0.274 - 0.000662 D_0}{\text{Re}^{0.2}}, \quad \text{see Table 2}$$

Table 1 Values of λ for polyethylene and rigid-vinyl plastic

Re $\times 10^{-4}$	D_0, mm					
	40	100	160	200	250	300
0.8	0.039	0.037	0.035	0.034	0.032	0.031
2	0.031	0.030	0.029	0.028	0.026	0.025
5	0.026	0.025	0.024	0.023	0.022	0.021
10	0.022	0.021	0.020	0.020	0.019	0.018
50	0.016	0.015	0.014	0.014	0.013	0.012
80	0.014	0.013	0.013	0.012	0.012	0.011

Table 2 Values of λ for glass closs and Faolite

Re $\times 10^{-4}$	D_0, mm					
	60	80	100	120	140	160
			Glass cloth			
1	0.043	0.041	0.040	0.038	0.036	0.034
5	0.032	0.031	0.030	0.028	0.026	0.025
10	0.028	0.027	0.026	0.024	0.023	0.022
30	0.023	0.022	0.021	0.020	0.019	0.018
			Faolite			
1	0.037	0.035	0.033	0.031	0.029	0.027
5	0.027	0.025	0.024	0.022	0.021	0.019
10	0.023	0.022	0.021	0.019	0.018	0.017
20	0.020	0.019	0.018	0.017	0.016	0.015

Tables made from plastics (polythene or rigid vinyl) with joints; stabilized flow[91,92]	Diagram 2-20

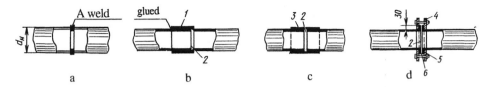

No	Joint	Material
a	Welded	Polyethylene
b	Funneled	Vinyl plastic
c	Coupled	"_"
d	Flanged	Polyethylene

1, funnel; 2, circular recess; 3, coupling; 4, flange; 5, flanged end of the tube; 6, gasket (rubber ring) 15 × 4 mm

$$\zeta \equiv \frac{\Delta p}{\rho w_0^2/2} = n_j(\lambda l_j/D_0 + \zeta_j)$$

where n_j is the number of joints over the section; for λ, see Diagrams 2-1 through 2-5; ζ_j is the resistance coefficient of one joint; at $50 \leq D_0 \leq 300$ mm:

a) welded joint
   at $1.8 \times 10^5 = \text{Re} \leq 5 \times 10^5$

$$\zeta_j = \frac{0.0046}{D_0^{1.75}}; \quad \text{see the Table}$$

   (D_0 is in m; the coefficient at D_0 is in m^{-1}).

b) Joint with the help of a funnel
   at $2.4 \times 10^5 \leq \text{Re} \leq 5.6 \times 10^5$

$$\zeta_j = (0.113–0.225)D_0 \quad \text{(see the Table)};$$

c) Joint with the help of coupling
   at $1.8 \times 10^5 \leq \text{Re} \leq 6 \times 10^5$
   $$\zeta_j = 0.045 - 0.156D_0 \quad \text{(see the Table)};$$

d) Joint with the help of flanges
   at $2.8 \times 10^5 \leq \text{Re} \leq 5 \times 10^5$
   $$\zeta_j = 0.148 - 0.344D_0 \quad \text{(see the Table)};$$

Values of ζ_j for different types of joints and D_0

Joint	D_0, m						
	0.05	0.075	0.10	0.15	0.20	0.25	0.30
Welded	0.411	0.224	0.146	0.079	0.057	0.037	0.028
Funneled	0.102	0.096	0.091	0.079	0.068	0.570	0.046
Coupled	0.044	0.033	0.029	0.022	0.014	0.006	0.002
Flanged	0.131	0.130	0.114	0.096	0.079	0.062	0.045

Tube of any cross section behind a smooth inlet
(starting length); nonstabilized flow[22.2-144]

Diagram
2-21

$$D_h = \frac{4F_0}{\Pi_0}$$

$$\zeta \equiv \frac{\Delta p}{\rho w_0^2 / 2} = \lambda \frac{l}{D_h}$$

Turbulent flow:

$$\lambda_{\text{non-st}} = \frac{\Delta p}{(\rho w_0^2/2)(x/D_h)} = \frac{0.43}{(\text{Re} \cdot x/D_h)^{0.2}} = \kappa_{\text{non-st}} \lambda$$

where for λ see Diagrams 2-1 through 2-17.

$$k''_{\text{non-st}} \approx 1.36 \frac{\text{Re}^{0.05}}{(x/D_h)^{0.2}}, \quad \text{see Table 1;}$$

see Diagrams 2-1 to 2-20

$$\lambda'_{\text{non-st}} \equiv \frac{\Delta p}{(\rho w_0^2/2)(\Delta x/D_h)} = \frac{0.344}{(\text{Re} \cdot x/D_h)^{0.2}} = \kappa'_{\text{non-st}}$$

$$\text{where } k'_{\text{non-st}} \approx 1.09 \frac{\text{Re}^{0.05}}{(x/D_h)^{0.2}}, \quad \text{see Table 1;}$$

Parameter	x/D_h											
	1	2	4	6	8	10	14	20	30	40	50	70
	Re = 10^4											
$k''_{\text{non-st}}$	2.15	1.88	1.64	1.51	1.43	1.36	1.27	1.18	1.09	1.03	1.0	1.0
$k'_{\text{non-st}}$	1.73	1.50	1.31	1.21	1.14	1.09	1.02	1.0	1.0	1.0	1.0	1.0
	Re = $5 \cdot 10^4$											
$k''_{\text{non-st}}$	2.34	2.04	1.78	1.63	1.54	1.47	1.38	1.28	1.18	1.12	1.07	1.0
$k'_{\text{non-st}}$	1.87	1.63	1.42	1.31	1.23	1.18	1.10	1.03	1.0	1.0	1.0	1.0

Re = 10^5

$k''_{\text{non-st}}$	2.43	2.11	1.84	1.70	1.60	1.52	1.43	1.32	1.23	1.16	1.11	1.03
$k'_{\text{non-st}}$	1.94	1.69	1.47	1.36	1.28	1.22	1.14	1.06	1.0	1.0	1.0	1.0

Re = $5 \cdot 10^5$

$k''_{\text{non-st}}$	2.62	2.28	1.99	1.84	1.74	1.65	1.55	1.44	1.33	1.25	2.00	1.12
$k'_{\text{non-st}}$	2.10	1.83	1.59	1.47	1.39	1.32	1.24	1.15	1.06	1.0	1.0	1.0

Re = 10^6

$k''_{\text{non-st}}$	2.71	2.36	2.05	1.90	1.78	1.71	1.60	1.49	1.37	1.30	1.24	1.16
$k'_{\text{non-st}}$	2.17	1.89	1.64	1.52	1.43	1.37	1.28	1.19	1.10	1.04	1.04	

Re = $5 \cdot 10^6$

$k''_{\text{non-st}}$	2.94	2.56	2.23	2.05	1.94	1.65	1.74	1.61	1.49	1.40	1.35	1.26
$k'_{\text{non-st}}$	2.35	2.05	1.78	1.64	1.55	1.48	1.39	1.29	1.19	1.12	1.08	1.0

Re = 10^7

$k''_{\text{non-st}}$	3.05	2.65	2.31	2.12	2.02	1.94	1.80	1.68	1.55	1.47	1.39	1.30
$k'_{\text{non-st}}$	2.44	2.12	1.85	1.70	1.61	1.54	1.44	1.34	1.24	1.17	1.11	1.04

Laminar flow (Re $\leq$ 2000):

$$k_{\text{non-st}} = f\left(\frac{x}{D_h} \cdot \frac{1}{Re}\right) \quad \text{see Table 2}$$

$\frac{x}{D_h} \cdot \frac{1}{Re} \times 10^3$	2	5	10	15	20	25	30	40
$k_{\text{non-st}}$	1.95	1.64	1.37	1.25	1.17	1.12	1.08	1.0

REFERENCES

Single-Phase Flow

1. Adamov, G. A. and Idelchik, I. E., Experimental Study of the Resistance of Plywood Pipes of Circular and Square Cross Sections in a Fully Developed Turbulent Flow, *Trudy No. 670*, BNT MAP, Moscow, 1948, 27 p.
2. Adamov, G. A. and Idelchik, I. E., Experimental study of turbulent flow over the starting lengths of straight tubes of circular and square cross sections, *Tekh. Otchyoty*, no. 124, BNT MAP, Moscow, 1948, 14 p.
3. Adamov, G. A., General equation for the law of resistance in turbulent flow, and new formulae for the resistance coefficient of rough tubes, *Vestn. Inzh. Tekh.*, no. 1, 15–21, 1952.
4. Adamov, G. A., Approximate calculation of fluid resistance and of motion of gases and liquids in pipelines, in *Problems of Prospecting and Utilization of Gas Deposits*, pp. 231–264, Gostopizdat, Moscow, 1953.
5. Altshul, A. D., *Hydraulic Friction Losses in Pipelines*, Gosenergoizdat, Moscow, 1963, 256 p.
6. Altshul, A. D., *Hydraulic Resistance*, Nedra Press, Moscow, 1982, 224 p.
7. Altshul, A. D. and Polyakova, E. N., Concerning the problem of frictional pressure losses in concrete pressure water tunnels, *Vopr. Gidravliki Vodosnabzhen.*, no. 174, 25–30, 1980.
8. Ainola, L. Ya. and Liyv, U. R., Friction coefficient for accelerated tube flows, in *Unsteady-State Processes in the Systems of Water Supply and Water Removing*, Collected Papers of the Tomsk Polytechnic Institute, no. 569, 21–31, 1984.
9. Aronov, I. Z., Gomon, V. I., and Dreitser, G. A., Investigation of heat transfer and hydraulic resistance in water flow in tubes with circular vortex generators, in *Hydraulics, Present-Day Problems of the Hydrodynamics and Heat Transfer in the Elements of Power and Cryogenic Engineering Equipment*, pp. 101–109, no. 7, Moscow, 1978.
10. Baibakov, B. S., Oreshkin, O. F., and Prudovskiy, A. M., Friction resistance to an accelerated flow in a tube, *Izv. Akad. Nauk SSSR, Mekh. Zhidk. Gaza*, no. 5, 137–139, 1981.
11. Barenblatt, G. I., Gorodtsov, V. A., and Kalashnikov, V. N., Turbulence of anomalous fluids, in *Heat- and Mass Transfer*, vol. 3, pp. 3–23, Minsk, 1968.
12. Barenblatt, G. I. and Kalashnikov, V. N., Concerning the effect of supermolecular formations, *Izv. Akad. Nauk SSSR, Mekh. Zhidk. Gaza*, no. 3, 68–73, 1968.
13. Bogdanov, F. F., Study of hydraulic resistance in smooth tube bundles in a longitudinal flow, *At. Energ.*, vol. 23, no. 1, 15–21, 1967.
14. Bogomolov, N. A., Improved method of aerodynamic calculation of new flexible ventilation air ducts, *Izv. VUZov, Gorn. Zh.*, no. 4, 22–25, 1963.
15. Brodov, Yu. M., Plotnikov, P. N., and Ryabchikov, A. Yu., Determination of the surface of shaped helical tubes, *Izv. VUZov, Energ.*, no. 12, 103–104, 1981.
16. Bronshtein, I. N. and Semendyayev, K. A., *Handbook of Mathematics for Engineers and Students of Higher Engineering Colleges*, Moscow, 1980, 974 p.
17. Buleev, N. I., Polusukhina, K. N., and Pyshin, V. G., Hydraulic resistance and heat transfer in a turbulent flow of liquid through a grid of rods, *Teplofiz. Vysok. Temp.*, vol. 2, no. 5, 74–753, 1964.
18. Bystrov, P. I. and Mikhailov, V. S., *Hydrodynamics of Collector Heat Exchanging Apparatus*, Moscow, 1982, 223 p.
19. Varfolomeyeva, A. P., *The Hydraulics of Pipelines of Water Heating Systems (A Review)*, oddset printing by the Central Scientific-Technical Institute for Civil Engineering and Architecture, Moscow, 1976, 66 p.
20. Vasilchenko, A. Y. and Barbaritskaya, M. S., Resistance in a non-isothermal fluid motion in longitudinally finned tubes, *Teploenergetika*, no. 7, 17–22, 1969.
21. Guinevskiy, A. S., Ed., *Introduction into the Aerohydrodynamics of Container Transport*, Moscow, 1986, 232 p.
22. Voronin, F. S., Effect of contraction on the friction coefficient in a turbulent gas flow, *Inzh. Fiz. Zh.*, vol. 2, no. 11, 81–85, 1959.
23. Galimzyatov, F. G., *Near-Wall Turbulent Motion*, Ufa, 1979, 119 p.
24. Gandelsman, A. F., Gukhman, A. A., and Iliyukhin, I. V., Study of the change in the friction coefficient in a supersonic gas flow, *Teploenergetika*, no. 1, 17–23, 1955.
25. Gerashchenko, L. S., Concerning the determination of pressure losses in iron-concrete pressure tunnels with thin-walled cores, in *Land Reclamation and Water Handling Facilities*, no. 49, pp. 61–65, Kiev, 1980.
26. Altshul, A. D., Voitinskaya, Yu. A., Kazenov, V. V., and Polyakova, E. N., *Hydraulic Friction Losses in the Water Pipelines of Electric Power Stations*, Moscow, 1985, 104 p.
27. Mukurdimov, R. M., Resh, Yu. A., Gusanova, A. M., et al., Hydraulic Resistances of the Butt Joints of Polyethylene Pipelines, Collected Papers of the Tashkent Institute for the Railway Transport Engineers, no. 72, pp. 27–37, 1970.

28. Subbotin, V. I., Ibragimov, M. Kh., Ushakov, P. A., Bobkov, V. P., et al., *Hydrodynamics and Heat Transfer in Atomic Power Equipment (Fundamentals of Calculation)*, Moscow, 1975, 350 p.

29. Guinevsky, A. S. and Solodkin, E. E., Hydraulic resistance of annular channels, in *Industrial Aerodynamics*, pp. 202–215, no. 20, Oborongiz, Moscow, 1961.

30. Gostev, E. A. and Riman, I. S., Fluid flow in an annular channel having an eccentricity, in *Industrial Aerodynamics*, pp. 58–64, no. 30, Mashinostroenic Press, Moscow, 1973.

31. Datochnyi, V. V., Hydraulic calculation of municipal gas mains, *Gazov. Promst.*, no. 12, 12–13, 1961.

32. Dzyubenko, B. V. and Dreitser, G. A., Investigation of heat transfer and hydraulic resistance in a heat exchanging apparatus with flow swirling, *Izv. Akad. Nauk SSSR, Energ. Transp.*, no. 5, 163–171, 1979.

33. Dzyubenko, B. V. and Iyevlev, V. M., Heat transfer and hydraulic resistance in the intertube space of a heat exchanger with flow swirling, *Izv. Akad. Nauk SSSR, Energ. Transp.*, no. 5, 117–125, 1980.

34. Dmitriyev, A. F., Hydraulic Resistance and Kinematics of Flow in Drainage Pipeline Drainage Systems, Thesis (Dr. of Technical Sciences), Leningrad, 1985, 250 p.

35. Dreitser, G. A. and Paramonov, N. V., Hydraulic resistance and heat transfer in helical tubes of small relative diameter and large pitch, in *Hydraulics, Present-Day Problems of the Hydraulics and Heat Transfer in the Elements of Power and Cryogenic Engineering Equipment*, pp. 10–20, no. 7, Moscow, 1978.

36. Egorov, A. I., *Hydraulic Calculation of Tubular Systems for Water Distribution in Water-Supply Treating Structures*, Stroiizdat, Moscow, 1960, 123 p.

37. Eroshenko, V. M., Ershov, A. V., and Zaichik, L. I., Calculation of the developed turbulent tube flow with injection and suction, *Teplofiz. Vys. Temp.*, vol. 19, no. 1, 102–108, 1981.

38. Zegzhada, A. P., *Frictional Hydraulic Losses in Channels and Pipelines*, Gosenergoizdat, Moscow, 1957, 27 p.

39. Zolotov, S. S., Hydraulic resistance of channels of annular cross section, *Proc. Leningrad Ship-building Inst.*, no. 74, 41–49, 1971.

40. Ibraguimov, M. Kh., et al., Calculation of hydraulic resistance coefficients for fluid flow in channels on non-circular cross section, *At. Energ.*, vol. 23, no. 4, 300–305, 1967.

41. Ibraguimov, M. Kh., Isupov, I. A., and Subbotin, V. I., Calculation and experimental investigation of velocity fields in channels of complex shape, in *Liquid Metals*, pp. 234–250, Atomizdet, Moscow, 1967.

42. Idelchik, E. E., *Hydraulic Resistances (Physical and Mechanical Fundamentals)*, Gosenergoizdat, Moscow, 1954, 316 p.

43. Idelchik, I. E., Determination of the friction coefficient of the steel pipes of the Saratov-Moscow gas main, Tech. Rept. No. 59, 1945, 7 p.

44. Idelchik, I. E. and Shteinberg, M. O., Concerning the total pressure losses in porous cylindrical tubes with discharges in passage at different laws of the longitudinal velocity distribution, *Teploenergetika*, no. 1, 70–72, 1988.

45. Kagan, L. I., A new formula for the hydraulic resistance coefficient, in *Heating and Ventilation and Constructional Thermophysics (Collected Papers)*, no. 1, 119–125, 1971.

46. Kadaner, Ya. S. and Rassadkin, Yu. P., Laminar vapor flow in a heat pipe, *Inzh. Fiz. Zh.*, vol. 28, no. 2, 208–216, 1975.

47. Kazennov, V. V. and Mityureva, N. E., About the frictional pressure losses in the pressure tunnels of electrical power stations, in *The Problems of Hydraulics and Water Supply*, pp. 31–37, no. 174, Moscow, 1980.

48. Kalinin, E. K. and Yarkho, S. A., On the effect of non-isothermicity on the hydraulic resistance coefficient for a turbulent flow of water in tubes with artificial flow agitation, *Teplofiz, Vys. Temp.*, vol. 4, no. 5, 736–738, 1966.

49. Karman, T., Some problems of the theory of turbulence, in *Problems of Turbulence*, M. A. Velikanov and N. G. Shveikovsky, Eds., pp. 35–74, ONTI, 1936.

50. Kerensky, A. M., On the relationship between the friction coefficient and the Reynolds number and relative roughness, *Teploenergetika*, no. 10, 78–79, 1972.

51. Kirillov, P. L., Yuriyev, Yu. S., and Bobkov, V. P., *Handbook of Thermohydraulic Calculations (Nuclear Reactors, Heat Exchangers, Steam Generators)*, Moscow, 1984, 296 p.

52. Klyachko, L. S., Concerning the theoretical determination of the frictional resistance coefficient of smooth pipelines in the mode of developed turbulence, in *The Problems of Design and Mounting of Sanitary-Enginnering Systems*, pp. 32–33, no. 46, Leningrad, 1978.

53. Klyachko, L. S. and Makarenkova, T. G., Generalized hydraulic characteristics of flexible glass cloth air conduits, in *Industrial, Heating-Ventilation and Sanitary-Engineering Systems and the Technology of Their Mounting*, pp. 72–76, Leningrad, 1984.

54. Konakov, V. K., New formula for the friction coefficient of smooth tubes, *Dokl. Akad. Nauk SSSR*, vol. 25, no. 5, 14–24, 1950.

55. Konobeyev, V. I. and Zhavoronkov, N. M., Hydraulic resistance in tubes with wavy roughness, *Khim. Mashinostr.*, no. 1, 17–24, 1962.

56. Korn, G. and Korn, T., *Handbook of Mathematics*, Moscow, 1974, 831 p.

57. Kochenov, I. S. and Novoselsky, O. Yu., Hydraulic resistance of channels with permeable walls, *J. Eng. Phys.*, vol. 16, no. 3, 405–412, 1969.

58. Kochenov, I. S. and Romadona, V. L., Resistance coefficient in fluid flow with outflow through a porous wall, *J. Eng. Phys.*, vol. 2, no. 11, 78–80, 1959.

59. Kravchuk, A. I., Determination of the hydraulic friction coefficient in perforated prefabricated pipelines, in *Hydraulics and Hydroengineering*, pp. 32–36, no. 38, Kiev, 1984.

60. Campbell, D. and Slattern, C., Flow over the tube starting length, *Tekh. Mekh.*, vol. 85, no. 1, 51–57, 1963 (Russian translation from *Trans. ASME, Ser. D*).

61. Krivoshein, B. V., et al., Numerical solution of equations describing a non-isothermal flow of the real gas in pipelines, *J. Eng. Phys.*, vol. 13, no. 4, 542–548, 1967.

62. Krupkin, G. Ya., Study of a change of the friction resistance in metallic air ducts depending on the conditions of service, Thesis (Cand. Sci.), Leningrad Engineering Building Inst., 1970, 146 p.

63. Kudryashev, L. I. and Filippov, G. V., On the mixed boundary layer over the starting length of a circular tube, *Collected Papers of the Kuibyshev Industrial Inst.*, no. 8, 7–12, 1959.

64. Kuliev, S. M., Esman, B. I., and Akhundov, U. Kh., Experimental determination of hydraulic losses in the concentric annular space, *Neft. Khoz.*, no. 12, 12–15, 1967.

65. Latyshenkov, A. M., Results of the full-scale hydraulic investigations of water-supplying channel, *Proc. Hydraulic Laboratory of the All-Union Scientific Research Inst.*, "VODGEO", vol. 10, 247–254, 1963.

66. Levkoyeva, N. V., Investigation of the Effect of Liquid Viscosity on Local Resistances, Thesis (Cond. of Technical Sciences), Moscow, 1959, 186 p.

67. Levchenko, Yu. D., et al., Hydrodynamics in an annular gap with logitudinal fins, in *Liquid Metals*, pp. 102–110, Atomizdat, Moscow, 1967.

68. Leibenson, L. S., *Collected Works* vol. 3, 3–13, Akad. Nauk SSSR, 1955.

69. Lelchuk, V. L. and Elfimov, G. I., Hydraulic resistance in adiabatic subsonic turbulent flow of a compressible gas in a cylindrical tube, in *Heat and Mass Transfer*, vol. 1, pp. 479–488, Energiya Press, Moscow, 1968.

70. Lobaev, B. N., New formulae for calculation of tubes in the transient region, *Nov. Stroit. Tekh.*, pp. 24–31, Kiev, 1954.

71. Lukash, A. Yu., Investigation of the Resistances of Water Heating Pipeline Systems, Thesis (Cand. of Technical Sciences), Kiev, 1967, 172 p.

72. Lyatkher, V. M., Analysis and selection of calculation formulae for the friction coefficient in tubes, *Sb. Statei Stud. Nauchno. Obschch.*, pp. 78–85, MEI, 1954.

73. Lyakhov, V. K. and Kugai, V. I., Experimental investigation of the effect of the temperature factor on heat transfer and hydraulic resistance in turbulent air flow in the self-similar region of rough tubes, in *Teplo i Massoobmen*, vol. 1, 534–538, Energiya Press, Moscow, 1968.

74. Maron, V. I. and Roev, G. A., Hydraulic resistance coefficient of a plane-rolled tube, *Tr. Mosk. Inst. Neftekhim. Gazov, Prom.*, no. 101, 108–113, 1972.

75. Mayatskiy, G. A. and Novichkova, O. G., A formula for calculating the resistance coefficient in nonisothermal liquid motion, *Izv. VUZov. Energ.*, no. 10, 95–97, 1959.

76. Migai, V. K., Hydraulic resistance of triangular channels in laminar flow, *Izv. VUZov, Energ.*, no. 5, 122–124, 1963.

77. Millionshchikov, M. D., *Turbulent Flows in a Boundary Layer and in Tubes*, Nauka Press, Moscow, 1969, 28 p.

78. Millionshchikov, M. D., Turbulent flows in the wall layer and in tubes, *At. Energ.*, vol. 28, no. 3, 207–219, 1970.

79. Millionshchikov, M. D., Turbulent flows in tubes of non-circular cross section, *At. Energ.*, vol. 29, no. .1, 16–18, 1970.

80. Mitrokhovich, A. I., Resistance and throughput capacity of smooth-wall polyethylene drain pipes which have been in use, *Gidrotekh. Melior. Torf. Pochv.*, vol. 4, no.2, 83–89, 1969.

81. Mikheyev, M. A. and Mikheyeva, I. M., *Fundamentals of Heat Transfer*, Moscow, 1977, 344 p.

82. Murin, G. A., Hydraulic resistance of steel tubes, *Izv. VTI*, no. 10, 21–27, 1948.

83. Murin, G. A., Hydraulic resistance of steel oil pipe-lines, *Neft. Khoz.*, no. 4, 15–19, 1951.

84. Nazarchuk, M. M. and Panchenko, V. N., Surface friction during adiabatic flow of a compressible gas in tubes, *J. Eng. Phys.*, vol. 16, no. 5, 835–842, 1969.

85. Revunov, O. K., Buturlin, V. F., Dmitriyenko, N. A., and Rubashkin, I. F., Some results of the study of hydraulic resistances of tubes glass-enamel coated on the both sides, in *The Technique of Irrigation and the Regime of Watering Crops*, pp. 55–61, Novocherkassk, 1982.

86. Nikitin, I. K., Extension of the semi-empirical theory of turbulence to the flow over rough surfaces with different properties of roughness, in *Turbulentnye Techeniya*, pp. 62–69, Nauka Press, Moscow, 1970.

87. Nikuradse, I., Laws governing turbulent flow in smooth tubes, in *Probl. Turbulentnosti*, M. A. Velikanov and N. G. Shveikovsky, Eds., pp. 75–150, ONTI Press, 1936.

88. Novikov, I. I. and Voskresensky, K. D., *Applied Thermodynamics and Heat Transfer,* Atomizdat, Moscow, 1961, 760 p.

89. Bogolyubov, Yu. N., Brodov, Yu. M., Buglayev, V. T., et al., Correlation of the data on the hydraulic resistance in helically shaped tubes, *Izv. VUZov. Energ.,* no. 4, 71–73, 1980.

90. Odelsky, E. Kh., On wave resistance in distant gas pipelines, *Izv. VUZov, Energ.,* no. 4, 81–83, 1958.

91. Offengenden, Yu. S., Absolute and equivalent roughness of tubes made from plastic materials, in *Vopr. Gidravliki,* pp. 102–125, Trudy MGMI, Moscow, 1969.

92. Offengenden, Yu. S., Hydraulic calculation of plastic pipelines, *Gidrotekh. Melior.,* no. 1, 24–28, 1972.

93. Pavlov, O. V., Experimental investigation of hydraulic resistances in plastic tubes, in *Dvizheniye Gidro-i Aerosmesei Gorn Porod v Trubakh,* pp. 108–110, Nauka Press, Moscow, 1966.

94. Petrukhno, A. I., Overall resistance coefficient of flexible pipelines with portions of pulsation of walls, in *Vopr. Gidrotekh. Gidravliki,* pp. 35–41, Urozhai Press, Kiev, 1969.

95. Petukhov, B. S., *Heat Transfer and Resistance During Laminar Fluid Flow in Tubes,* Energiya Press, Moscow, 1967, 412 p.

96. Platon, V. P., Effect of roughness on liquid resistance during its motion in tubes, in *Nauch. Progress Vopr. Melior.,* pp. 53–58, Shtintsa Press, Kishinyov, 1972.

97. Povkh, I. L., Pogrebnyak, V. G., and Toryanik, A. I., Resistance to the turbulent flow of the solutions of polymers and micella-forming surfactants, *J. Eng. Phys.,* vol. 37, no. 5, 793–797, 1979.

98. Povkh, I. L. and Stupin, A. B., Experimental investigation of turbulent tube flow of water polymer solutions, *J. Eng. Phys.,* vol. 22, no. 1, 59–65, 1972.

99. Prandtl, L., Results of recent studies of turbulence (Russian translation), in *Probl. Turbulentnosti,* M. A. Velikanov and N. G. Shveikovsky, Eds., pp. 9–34, ONTI Press, 1936.

100. Preger, E. A. and Samoilenko, L. A., Investigation of hydraulic resistance of pipelines in the transient mode of flow of liquids and gases, in *Issled. Vodosnabzhen. Kanalizatsii (Trudy LISI),* no. 50, 27–39, Leningrad, 1966.

101. Riman, I. S., The longitudinal flow of a hydraulically nonstabilized stream past a bundle of rods, in *Industrial Aerodynamics,* pp. 171–180, no. 1 (33), Moscow, 1986.

102. Riman, I. S., Concerning the frictional resistance in liquid flow through noncircular tubes, in *Industrial Aerodynamics,* pp. 190–195, no. 1(33), Moscow, 1986.

103. Richter, H., *Hydraulics of Pipelines,* ONTI Press, 1936, 230 p.

104. Rozovsky, I. L. and Zalutsky, E. V., On the energy balance in a uniform turbulent flow, in *Gidravlika i Gidrotekh. (Resp. Mezhved. Nauch.-Tekhn. Sbornik),* no. 8, 16–23, 1969.

105. Saveliyev, P. A. and Voskresenskiy, Yu. S., Investigation of the hydraulic resistance of helically shaped tubes at high Reynolds numbers, *Izv. VUZov. Energ.,* no. 5, 73–77, 1981.

106. Samoilenko, L. A., Investigation of the Hydraulic Resistances of Pipelines in the Zone of Transition from Laminar into Turbulent Motion, Thesis (Cand. of Technical Science), Leningrad, 1968, 172 p.

107. Svirskiy, G. E. and Platon, V. P., Resistance in liquid flow through smooth cylindrical tubes, in *Scientific Progress in the Problems of Melioration,* pp. 58–63, Kishinev, 1972.

108. Sinelshchikov, V. S. and Smirnova, G. N., Calculation of the resistance coefficient for an artificially twisted flow in rough tubes, in *Hydraulics and Hydraulic Engineering,* pp. 65–70, no. 30, Kiev, 1980.

109. Slezkin, N. A., *Dynamics of Viscous Fluid,* GHTL Press, 1955, 519 p.

110. Slisskiy, P. M., Methodological recommendations on the computer calculations of pipelines and the coefficient of hydraulic friction in the transition zone, in *Collected Papers on Hydraulics,* pp. 31–44, Moscow, 1983.

111. Dobrychenko, V. M., Lobachev, V. G., Povkh, I. L., and Eidelman, A. Ye., Reduction of hydraulic losses by the muffling additions of surfactants, *J. Eng. Phys.,* vol. 30, no. 2, 240–245, 1976.

112. Skrebkov, G. P., Hydraulic resistance of rectangular canal beds with the walls of different roughnesses, *Izv. VUZov. Energ.,* no. 12, 110–115, 1978.

113. Skrebkov, G. P., Canals and beds with variable friction around the perimeter and their hydraulic calculation, in *Hydraulics and Heat Transfer During Uniform Motion of Liquid in Channels,* pp. 3–28, Cheboksary, 1980.

114. Skrebkov, G. P. and Lozhkin, S. N., Application of the LeShatelier principle to the calculation of a uniform flow in packed rods channels, *Teplofiz. Vys. Temp.,* vol. 23, no. 4, 748–753, 1985.

115. Golshtein, S., Ed., *State-of-the-Art in Hydroaerodynamics of Viscous Fluid,* vol. 1, 1948, 320 p.

116. Solodkin, E. E. and Guinevsky, A. S., Turbulent viscous fluid flow over starting lengths of axisymmetric and plane channels, *Trudy TsAGI,* vyp. 701, Oborongiz, Moscow, 1957, 55 p.

117. Stepanov, P. M., Ovcharenko, I. Kh., and Skobeltsyn, Yu. A., *Handbook of Hydraulics for Land Reclaimers,* Moscow, 1984, 207 p.

118. Subbotin, V. I., Gabrianovich, B. N., and Sheinina, A. V., Hydraulic resistance in longitudinal flow past bundles of smooth and finned rods, *At. Energ.,* vol. 33, no. 5, 889–892, 1972.

119. Subbotin, V. I., Ushakov, P. A., and Gabrianovich, B. N., Hydraulic resistance in longitudinal fluid flow past rod bundles, *At. Energ.,* vol. 9, no. 4, 308–310, 1960.

120. Subbotin, V. I., Ushakov, P. A., and Sheinina, A. V., Hydraulic resistance of narrow annular channels with spiral fins, *At. Energ.*, vol. 21, no. 1, 13–16, 1966.

121. Sukomel, A. S., Investigation of the Friction Resistance and of the Reduction Coefficient in High-Velocity Gas Motion in Tubes, Thesis (Cand. of Technical Sciences), Moscow, 1955, 184 p.

122. Sukomel, A. S., Velichko, V. I., and Abrosimov, Yu. G., *Heat Transfer and Friction in Turbulent Gas Flow in Short Channels*, Moscow, 1979, 216 p.

123. Supolkin, G. A ., Equivalent roughness of steel and iron pipelines, *Dokl. Akad. Nauk Tadzh. SSR*, vol. 1, no. 4, 23–26, 1958.

124. Targ, S. M., *Basic Problems of the Theory of Laminar Flows*, Gosteortekhizdat, Moscow, 1951, 150 p.

125. Temkin, A. G., Investigation of the hydrodynamics of liquid flow in the channels of complex geometry, in *Heat and Mass Transfer in Capillary-Porous Bodies*, pp. 156–159, no. 8, Moscow, 1957.

126. Temkin, A. G., Frictional properties of channels of complex geometry with turbulent flow, *J. Eng. Phys.*, vol. 1, no. 5, 23–29, 1958.

127. Tepaks, L. A., *Uniform Turbulent Flow in Tubes and Channels*, Tallinn, 1975, 283 p.

128. Teplov, A. V., On the laws governing pressure fluid motion in tubes, in *Teoriya Podobiya i Ego Primen. v Teplotekhn. (Trudy Moskov. Inst. Inzh. Zheleznod. Transp.)*, pp. 72–78, 1961.

129. Tkachuk, A. Ya. and Teslo, A. P., The characteristics of flow in paper rolled pipelines, in *Hydraulics and Hydraulic Engineering*, pp. 91–94, no. 36, Kiev, 1983.

130. Todorov, P. and Shibanski, I., Results of experimental verification of the roughness factor of some hydraulic channels and tunnels, *Izv. Gidravlich. Labor.*, vol. 4, 201–229, 1962.

131. Toltsman, V. F., On the hydraulic calculation of asbestos-cement tubes, *Vodosnabzh. Sanit. Tekh.*, no. 1, 13–16, 1955.

132. Toltsman, V. F. and Shevelev, F. A., Hydraulic resistance of rubber hoses, in *Issled. Gidravlike Truboprovodov*, 1952, 190 p.

133. Trubenok, V. D., Determination of the coefficient of local resistances in tubes with rectangular annular recesses, in *Applied Aerodynamics*, pp. 3–6, Kiev, 1980.

134. Urbonas, P. A., Experimental investigation of the hydraulic resistance coefficient in a bundle of oiled tubes, in *Hydraulics, Present-Day Problems of the Hydrodynamics and Heat Transfer in the Elements of Power and Cryogenic Engineering Equipment*, pp. 78–82, Moscow, 1982.

135. Ushakov, P. A., et al., Heat transfer and hydraulic resistance in dense in-line rod bundles, *At. Energ.*, vol. 13, no. 2, 162–169, 1962.

136. Favorin, M. V., *Inertia Moments of Bodies, Handbook*, Moscow, 1977, 511 p.

137. Filimonov, S. S. and Khrustalyov, B. A., Investigation of heat transfer and hydraulic resistance in turbulent motion of water through tubes with different inlet conditions, in *Heat- and Mass Transfer*, pp. 414–418, vol. 3, Moscow, 1963.

138. Filippov, G. V., Some experimental investigations of the speeding-up effect, *Sb. Tr. Kuibysh. Aviats. Inst.*, vyp. 5, 57–61, 1955.

139. Filippov, G. V., On a turbulent flow in the inlet sections of straight circular tubes, *Zh. Tekh. Fiz.*, vol. 28, no. 8, 1823–1828, 1958.

140. Filippov, G. V., Concerning the influence of roughness on the speeding-up effect, *Sb. Nauch. Tr. Kuibyshev. Ind. Inst.*, vyp. 8, 25–32, 1959.

141. Filonenko, G. K., Formula for the resistance coefficient of smooth tubes, *Izv. VTI*, no. 10(162), 17–23, 1948.

142. Filonenko, G. K., Hydraulic resistance of pipelines, *Teploenergetika*, no. 4, 15–21, 1954.

143. Flyatau, R. S., *Hydrotechnical Calculations of Pipelines*, Gostopizdat, Moscow, 1949, 210 p.

144. Frenkel, N. Z., *Hydraulics*, Gosenergoizdat, Moscow, 1956, 456 p.

145. Khodanovich, I. E. and Odishariya, G. E., Generalizing relation for the resistance coefficient, *Tr. Vses. Nauchno-Issled. Inst. Prir. Gazov*, vyp. 29/37, 3–9, 1967.

146. Khanzhonkov, V. I. and Tarasov, N. F., Aerodynamic resistance of straight and curved flexible tubes made of metallic strip, in *Promaerodinamika*, vyp. 29, 75–81, Mashinostroenic Press, Moscow, 1973.

147. Khomutov, P. V. and Skobeltsyn, Yu. A., Determination of hydraulic resistances of welded joints of pipelines, *Transp. Khranenie Neft. Nefteprod.*, no. 6, 11–13, 1972.

148. Tseitlin, A. S., *Hydraulic Calculation of Ceramic Pipelines*, Gosstroiizdat, Kiev, 1964, 47 p.

149. Tseitlin, A. S., Gritsenko, I. A., and Zorchenko, A. I., Formula for hydraulic calculation of glass pipelines, *Vodosnabzh. Sanit. Tekh.*, no. 8, 29, 1962.

150. Tseitlin, A. S. and Toryanik, E. S., Determination of pressure head in plywood pipes, *Tr. Obedin. Semin. Gidrotekh. Vodokhoz. Stroit.*, vyp. 3, 31–35, Kharkov, 1961.

151. Tsochev, Ts. and Tsachev, Ts., Study of friction resistance for a uniform turbulent flow in ceramic pipelines, *Gidrotekh. Melior.*, vol. 12, no. 8, 228–232, 1967.

152. Shevelev, F. A., Hydraulic resistance of metallic tubes of large diameters, *Gidrotekh. Stroit.*, no. 1, 11–18, 1950.

153. Shevelev, F. A., Study of basic hydraulic laws governing turbulent flow in tubes, *Inzh. Gidravlika*, VNII Vodgeo, Stroizdat, 1953, 220 p.

154. Shevelev, F. A., *Hydraulic Calculation of Asbestos-Cement Pipes*, VNII Vodgeo, 1954, 180 p.

155. Shevelev, F. A., *Tables for Hydraulic Calculation of Steel, Iron and Asbestos-Cement Water Supplying Tubes*, Gosstroiizdat, Moscow, 1962, 138 p.

156. Shevelev, F. A., Lobachev, P. V., and Rudin, M. Ya., Investigation of hydraulic resistances for water flow in plastic tubes, *Sb. Tr. Nauchno-Issled. Inst. Sanit. Tekh., Akad. Stroit. Arkhit. SSSR*, no. 5, 43–59, 1960.

157. Sheinina, A. V., Hydraulic resistance of rod bundles in an axial fluid flow, in *Zhidkiye Metally*, pp. 210–223, Atomizdat, 1967.

158. Shiller, L., *Fluid Flow in Tubes*, ONTI Press, Moscow-Leningrad, 1936, 230 p.

159. Shifrinson, B. L., Hydrodynamic calculation of heating mains, *Teplo i Sila*, no. 1, 23–29, 1935.

160. Shchukin, V. K., Hydraulic resistance of rotating tubes, *J. Eng. Phys.*, vol. 12, no. 6, 782–787, 1967.

161. Timoshenko, V. I., Logachev, P. P., Knyshko, Yu. V., et al., Experimental investigation of the hydraulic resistance of tubes with welded seams, *Izv. VUZov. Neft Gaz*, no. 1, 56–59, 1985.

162. Yakovlev, N. A., Pressure head drops along the length of tubes of star-like cross section with fluid flow in them, *Tr. Leningr. Politekh. Inst.*, no. 274, 127–135, 1966.

163. Ackers, P., Grickmore, M. J., and Holmes, D. W., Effects of use on the hydraulic resistance of drainage conduits, *Proc. Inst. Civ. Eng.*, vol. 28, 339–360, July 1964.

164. Ayukawa, K., Pressure drop in the hydraulic conveyance of solid materials through a bend in a vertical plane, *Bull. JSME*, vol. 12, no. 54, 1388–1396, 1969.

165. Ayukawa, K., The hydraulic transport of solid materials through a horizontal straight pipe, *Bull. JSME*, vol. 11, no. 45, 579–586, 1968.

166. Biswas, I. K., Mechanics of flow through perforated pipes, *Consult. Eng.* (Engl.), vol. 25, no. 5, 491–493, 1964.

167. Boussinesq, J., Memoire sur l'influence des frottements dans les mouvement reguliers des fluides, *J. Math. Pur Appl.*, vol. 13, no. 2, 1868, 377 p.

168. Busse, C. A., Pressure drop of the vapor phase of long heat pipes, Proc. 1st Int. Thermionic Conversion Conf. of Specialists, Palo Alto, CA, 1967, pp. 391–401.

169. Buyuktur, A., Amortissement des perturbations dan les canalisations cylindriques longues, *Publ. Sci. Tech. Minist. Air (Fr.)*, no. 378, 1961, 48 p.

170. Carlson, L. W. and Irvine, T. F., Fully developed pressure drop in triangular spard ducts, *Trans. ASME, Ser. C*, vol. 83, no. 4, 441–444, 1961.

171. Colebrook, F., Turbulent flow in pipes with particular reference to the transition region between the smooth and rough pipe laws, *J. Inst. Civ. Eng.* no. 4, 14–25, 1939.

172. Eifler, W. and Nifsing, R., Experimental investigation of velocity distribution and flow resistance in a triangular array of parallel rods, *Mech. Eng. Des.*, vol. 5, no. 1, 22–42, 1967.

173. Fonck, R. and Hardenne, H., Essais de determination des pertes de charge dans un tube de chargement pour reacteur nucleaire, *Mem. Cent. Etudes Rech. Essais Sci. Genie Civil*, no. 25, 27–41, 1968.

174. Hagen, G., Uber den Einfluss der Temperatur auf die Bewegung des Wassers in Rohren, *Abh. Math. Dtsch. Akad. Wiss. Berlin*, 854, 17–98.

175. Han, L. S., Hydrodynamic entrance lengths for incompressible laminar flow in rectangular ducts, *J. Appl. Mech. Trans. ASME, Ser. E*, E-27, 403–409, 1960.

176. Hering, F., Die Rohrreibungszahl, *Brennst. Waerme-Kraft*, bd. 4, 23–26, 1952.

177. Horton, T. E. and Juan, S. W., Laminar flow in the entrance region of a porous-wall channel, *Appl. Sci. Res.*, vol. A14, no. 4, 233–249, 1964–1965.

178. Johnston, Z. and Sparrow, E. M., Results of laminar flow analysis and turbulent flow experiments for eccentric annular ducts, *AIChE J.*, vol. 11, no. 1143–1145, 1965.

179. Kirschmer, O., Der gegenwärtige Stand unserer Erkenntnisse über die Rohrreibung, *G. W. F. Ausgabe Wasser*, H. 16, 30–40, 1953.

180. Leutheusser, H. J., Turbulent flow in rectangular ducts, *J. Hydraul. Div., Proc. Am. Soc. Civ. Eng.*, vol. 89, HY3, 1–19, May 1963.

181. Malenak, J., Skalicka, J., and Pejchal, V., Urceni velikosti ztraty trenim pri proudeni vzduchu potrubim kruhoveho prucrezu z pozin kovaneho plechu, *Zdrav. Tech. Vzduchotech.*, vol. 9, no. 1, 20–23, 1966.

182. Marechel, H., Pertes de charge continues en conduite forcee de section circulaire, *Ann. Trav. Publics Belg.*, no. 6, 1955.

183. McComas, S. T., Hydrodynamic entrance lengths for ducts of arbitrary cross section, *J. Basic Eng., Trans. ASME, Ser. D*, vol. 89, no. 1–4(9), 1967.

184. Mohandes, A. and Knudsen, J. G., Friction factors in noncircular ducts with sharp corners, *Can. J. Chem. Eng.*, vol. 57, 109–111, February 1979.

185. Moody, L. F., Friction factor for pipe flow, *Trans. ASME*, vol. 66, 97–107, November 1944.

186. Morris, M., A new concept of flow in rough conduits, *Proc. Am. Soc. Civ. Eng.*, no. 390, 109–118, 1954.

187. Müller, W., Druckverlust in Rohrleitungen, *Energietechnik.*, H. 7, 28–35, 1953.

188. Nicol, A. A., Medwell, J. O., and Goel, R. K., Settling length for turbulent flow of air in an annulus, *Can. J. Chem. Eng.*, Vol. 45, no. 2, 97–99, 1967.

189. Novendstern, E. H., Turbulent flow pressure drop model for fuel rod assemblies utilising a helical wire-wrap spacer system, *Nucl. Eng. Des.*, vol. 22, no. 1, 19–29, 1972.

190. Nikuradse, J., Strömungsgesetze in rauhen Rohren, *VDI*, no. 361, 16–53, 1933.

191. Olson, R. M. and Eckert, E. R., Experimental studies of turbulent flow in a porous circular tube with uniform fluid injection through the tube wall, *Pap. Am. Soc. Mech. Eng.*, APM-29, 1965, 11 p.

192. Oosthuizen, P. H., Compressibility effects on low-speed gas flows through pipes, *S. Afr. Mech. Eng.*, vol. 15, no. 7, 165–168, 1966.

193. Poiseuille, J. L. M., Recherrches expermentales sur le mouvement des liquides dans les tubes du tre's petites diame'tres, *Comptes Rendus*, vol. 11, 961–1041, 1841.

194. Rapp, R. and Alperi, R. W., Pressure loss in convoluted pipes, *Building Systems Design*, 26–28, April 1970.

195. Reiner, M. and Scott, B. G. W., The flow of blood through narrow tubes, *Nature (London)*, vol. 184, suppl. 6, 1959.

196. Rehnue, K., Druckverlust in Stabbundeln mit Spiraldraht-Abstandshaltern, *Forsch. Ingenieurwes*, vol. 35, no. 4, 107–112, 1969.

197. Richter, H., *Rohrhydraulik*, Berlin, 1954, 328 s.

198. Rothfus, R. R., Sartory, W. K., and Kermode, R. J., Flow in concentric annuli at high Reynolds numbers, *AJE J.*, vol. 12, no. 6, 1086–1091, 1966.

199. Rubatta, A., Numeri di resistenza per fortissime scabrezze relative, *Energ. Elletr.*, vol. 45, no. 3, 188–193, 1968.

200. Schmidt, D., Die Druckabfallberechnung für, Kompressible Medien. Rohre, Rohrleitungsbau und Rohrleitungstransport, vol. 5, no. 2, 84–86, 1966.

201. Scholz, N., Berechung des laminaren und turbulenten Druckanfalles im Rohreinlauf. *Chem. Ing. Techn.*, vol. 32, no. 6, 404–409, 1960.

202. Siwon, Z., Wsterne badania wspotczynnica tarcia prostoosiowych rur perforowanych przy przeplywie pod cisnieniem, *Pr. Nauk Inst. Inz. Sanit. Wodnef PWr Ser. Stud. i Mater.*, vol. 11, no. 12, 53–67, 1971.

203. Song, C., Charm, S., and Kurland, G., Energy losses for blood flowing through tapered tubes and curved tubes, abstract, part 4, Interscience, New York, 1965.

204. Steele, J. L. and Shove, G. C., Design charts for flow and pressure distribution in perforated air ducts, *Trans. ASAE*, vol. 12, no. 2, 220–224, 1969.

205. Sparrow, E. M. and Lin, S. H., The developing laminar flow and pressure drop in the entrance region of annular ducts, *J. Basic Eng., Trans. ASME*, vol. 86, no. 4, 1964.

206. Tied, W., Berechnung des laminaren und turbulenten Reibungswiderstandes konzentrischer und exzententrischer Ringspalte, *Chem. Ztg. Chem. Appar.*, vol. 90–91, 1966–1967.

207. Wilkins, J. E., Frictional pressure drop in triangular ducts, *Trans. ASME*, vol. C87, no. 3, 427–428, 1965.

208. White, G. L., Friction pressure reducers in well stimulation, *J. Pet. Technol.*, vol. 16, no. 8, 865–868, 1964.

Two-Phase Flow: Pneumatic Transport

209. Avlanov, V. A., Norkin, P. K., and Akimova, S. E., Concerning the reduction of hydraulic losses in pipelines, *Izv. Akad. Nauk Uz SSR, Ser. Tekh. Nauk*, no. 2, 53–54, 1968.

210. Altshul, Yu. A., Reduction of the hydraulic resistance of water supplying pipes, *Vodosnabzh. Sanit. Tekh.*, no. 5, 5–8, 1973.

211. Babukha, G. L., Sergeyev, G. Z., and Shraiber, O. L., On determination of the hydraulic resistance of two-phase flows with dispersed solid substances, *Dopov. Akad. Nauk Ukr. SSR*, no. 7, 25–31, 1969.

212. Bazilevich, V. A., Reduction in resistance to fluid flow by means of polymer additions, *Gidromekhanika*, vyp. 21, pp. 37–41, Naukova Dumka Press, Kiev, 1972.

213. Basilevich, V. A. and Shadrin, A. N., Reduction of hydraulic resistances in pipelines by means of polymer additions, *Gidromekhanika (Resp. Mezhvedomstv. Sb.)*, vyp. 17, 105–113, 1971.

214. Bois, B., Hydrodynamic phenomena in a dust-laden flow, *Teor. Osn. Inzh. Raschyot*, no. 3, 91–99, 1970 (Russian translation from *Trans. ASME*, no. 3, 1969).

215. Branover, G. G. and Tsinover, A. B., *Magnetic Hydrodynamics of Noncompressible Media*, Nauka Press, Moscow, 1970, 379 p.

216. Vasetskaya, N. G. and Iosilevich, V. A., On the construction of the semi-empirical theory of turbulence for weak polymer solutions, *Izv. Akad. Nauk SSSR, Mekh. Zhidk. Gaza*, no. 2, 136–146, 1970.

217. Gazuko, I. V. and Gorodtsov, V. A., On the effect of resistance reduction in rough tubes by means of water-solvable polymer additions, *Izv. Akad. Nauk. SSSR, Mekh. Zhidk. Gaza*, no. 6, 163–166, 1968.

218. Gallyamov, A. K., On hydraulic resistances during simultaneous flow of liquid and gas in a non-horizontal pipeline, *Tr. Mosk. Inst. Neftekhim. Gazov. Prom.*, vyp. 57, 197–200, 1965 (1966).

219. Garmash, N. G., Calculation formulae for determination of flow pressure losses during transportion grain and dust-like materials, *Izv. VUZov, Mashinostr.*, no. 4, 107–123, 1964.

220. Deich, M. E. and Filippov, G. A., *Hydrodynamics of Two-Phase Media*, Energiya Press, Moscow, 1968, 423 p.

221. Dzyadzio, A. M., *Penumatic transport in Grain-Processing Factories*, Zagotizdat, Moscow, 1961, 237 p.

222. Doguin, M. E., A critical equation for calculating the hydraulic resistance of pneumatic transport pipelines, *Tr. Mosk. Inst. Inzh. Zheleznodorozhn. Transp.*, vyp. 139, 66–72, 1961.

223. Doguin, M. E. and Karpov, A. I., Calculation of the resistance of the starting length during pneumatic transport, *J. Eng. Phys.*, no. 7, 631–639, 1961.

224. Doguin, M. E. and Lebedev, V. P., Study of resistances during pneumatic transport in a horizontal pipeline, *Sb. Nauchn. Tr. Tomsk. Elektromekh. Inst. Inzh. Zheleznod. Transp.*, vol. 29, 164–175, 1960.

225. Doguin, M. E. and Lebedev, V. P., Roughness of tubes under the conditions of pneumatic transport, *Izv. VUZov, Energ.*, no. 7, 113–115, 1962.

226. Donat, E. V., Hydraulic resistance of vertical pipelines with smooth walls during pneumatic transport of solid particles, *Khim. Neft. Mashinostr.*, no. 7, 15–17, 1965.

227. Zhivaikin, L. Ya. and Volguin, B. P., Hydraulic resistance in a descending two-phase flow in film apparatus, *Khim. Prom.*, no. 6, 19–25, 1963.

228. Zorina, E. F. and Styrikov, A. S., Effect of local resistances on the laws governing hydraulic transport, *Tr. Leningr. Inst. Vodn. Transp.*, vyp. 119, 77–95, 1968.

229. Zuyev, F. G., Methods for calculating pressure losses in side branches during pneumatic transport, *Tr. Mosk. Tekhnol. Inst. Pishch. Prom.*, vyp. 14, 108–122, 1960.

230. Kapitonov, E. N. and Lebedev, K. I., Study of the hydraulic resistance of the heat transfer during motion of boiling solutions in a horizontal tube, *Khim. Prom.*, no. 7, 18–25, 1965.

231. Karpov, A. I., The Borda problem under the conditions of pneumatic transport for tubes arranged horizontally, *Sb. Nauchn. Tr. Tomsk. Elektromekh. Inst. Inzh. Zhel.-Dor. Transp.*, vol. 29, 159–167, 1960.

232. Karpov, A. I., On the hydraulic resistance of the starting length during motion of a gas mixture, *Izv. VUZov, Energ.*, no. 9, 103–105, 1964.

233. Klimentov, A. N., The Bernoulli equation for a pulp flow, *Gidrotekh. Stroit.*, no. 4, 28–32, 1954.

234. Klyachko, L. S., An analytical method to allow for pressure losses in pipelines with flows carrying a solid dispersed medium, *Vopr. Proektir. Montazha Sanitarno-Tekhn. Sistem*, pp. 125–127, Stroiizdat, 1970 (*Trudy Inst. VNIIGS*, vyp. 28).

235. Koptev, D. V., On the coefficient of resistance to the motion of aeromixture during pneumatic transport (review), *Sb. Nauchn. Rabot Inst. Okhr. Tr. VTsSPS*, vyp. 1(27), 21–36, 1964.

236. Kostyuk, G. F., Hydraulic resistance of the solid phase in a fluidized state, *Izv. VUZov, Neft Gaz*, no. 11, 16–21, 1966.

237. Kornilov, G. G. and Chernikin, V. I., Procedure of the hydraulic calculation of pipelines during motion of gas-liquid mixtures, Collected Papers, Transport i Khraneniye Neft i Nefteproduktov, no. 3, 3–6, 1966.

238. Kudryavtseva, Z. M., Investigation of dust-gas mixture motion in a tube, *J. Eng. Phys.*, vol. 10, no. 1, 78–85, 1966.

239. Laats, M. K., Experimental investigation of the dynamics of an air-dust jet, *J. Eng. Phys.*, vol. 10, no. 1, 11–15, 1966.

240. Maltsev, M. V., Hydraulic losses during motion of multiphase mixtures in vertical tubes, *Sb. Tr. Mosk. Inzh. Stroit. Inst.*, vyp. 45, 31–53, 1963.

241. Markov, Yu. A. and Smoldyrev, A. E., On the hydraulic resistances in ascending flows of a hydro-mixture in tubes, *Izv. Akad. Nauk SSSR, Mekh.*, no. 5, 182–184, 1965.

242. Mochan, S. I., Local resistances in motion of two-phase mixtures, *Vopr. Teplootdachi Gidravliki Dvukhfazn. Sred*, pp. 1–38, Gosenergoizdat, Moscow-Leningrad, 1961.

243. Permyakov, B. A. and Ryndin, G. N., Determination of the resistance coefficients of a helical pipeline during pneumatic transport of dust, *Dokl. Konf. Nauchno-Tekh. Obshch. Energ. Elektr. Prom. pri VTI*, pp. 37–43, BM, 1969.

244. Rassokhin, N. G., Shvetsov, R. S., and Melnikov, V. N., Experimental investigation of the hydraulic resistance in water-vapor mixture flow in annular channels with an internal heat releasing surface, *Tr. Mosk. Energ. Inst.*, vyp. 73, 73–78, 1965.

245. Rakhmatulin, Kh. A., et al., Towards the theory of pneumatic transport in a horizontal tube, *Dokl. Akad. Nauk UzSSR*, no. 4, 6–9, 1967.

246. Saks, S. E., Hydraulic resistances in turbulent flow of multidispersed aerosols, *J. Eng. Phys.*, vol. 14, no. 4, 327–333, 1968.

247. Sochilov, V. V., Study of the pressure head losses in local resistances during transportation of a hydromixture, *Sb. Tr. Mosk. Inzh. Stroit. Inst.*, vyp, 45, 43–48, 1963.

248. Tarasov, V. K., Raikhman, E. S., and Evstafiev, V. P., Experimental deinvestigation of the hydraulic characteristics of inclined pipelines transporting gas-saturated mineral water, *Sb. Tr. Mosk. Inzh. Stroit. Inst.*, no. 89, 97–102, 1972.

249. Teletov, S. G., Resistance coefficients of two-phase mixtures, *Dokl. Akad. Nauk SSSR*, vol. 8, no. 51, 41–48, 1946.

250. Uspensky, V. A., *Pneumatic Transport*, Metallurgizdat, 1959, 152 p.

251. Fadeyev, I. G., The friction coefficient during continuous-flow pneumatic transport, *Khim. Tekhnol. Topl. Masel*, no. 8, 17–22, 1969.

252. Khabakhpasheva, E. and Perepelitsa, B. V., Fields of velocities and turbulent pulsations with small additions of high-molecular weight substances to water, *J. Eng. Phys.*, vol. 14, 598, 1968.

253. Khodanovich, I. E. and Mamaev, V. A., Evaluation of the throughput capacity of gas pipelines during transportation of two-phase systems, *Tr. Vses. Nauchno.-Issled. Inst. Prirodn. Gazov*, vyp. 13(2), 13–31, 1961.

254. Shvab, V. A., On the basic laws governing resistance in horizontal tubes during pneumatic transport, *Vopr. Gidravliki Zapylen. Potoka*, vol. 29, 1–20, Tomsk. Elektromekh. Inst. Inzh. Zhel.-Dor. Transp., 1960.

255. Elperin, I. T., Smolsky, B. M., and Levental, L. I., Concerning reduction of the hydraulic resistance of pipelines, *J. Eng. Phys.*, vol. 10, no. 2, 236–239, 1966.

256. Anderson, G. H. and Mantzouranis, B. G., Two-phase (gas-liquid) flow phenomena. 1. Pressure drop and hold up for two-phase flow in vertical tubes, *Chem. Eng. Sci.*, vol. 12, no. 2, 109–126, 1960.

257. Aoki, S., Schiki, T., and Takahashi, T., Pressure drop for two-phase flow in the pipe. 1. The theory of pressure drop, *Bull. Tokyo Inst. Technol.*, no. 49, 127–139, 1962.

258. Cermak, J. O., Jicha, J. J., and Lightner, R. G., Two-phase pressure drop across vertically mounted thick plate restrictions, *Trans. ASME, Ser. C.*, vol. 86, no. 2, 227–239, 1964.

259. Doig, J. D. and Poper, C. H., Energy requirements in pneumatic conveying *Aust. Chem. Eng.*, vol. 4, no. 2, 9–23, 1963.

260. Kikkawa, Sh., Utsumi, R., Sakai, K., and Nutaba, T., On the pressure drop and clogging limit in the horizontal pneumatic conveyance pipe, *Bull. JSME*, vol. 8, no. 32, 1965.

261. Lottes, P. A., Expansion losses in two-phase flow, *Nucl. Sci. Eng.*, vol. 9, no. 1, 26–31, 1961.

262. Peters, L. K. and Klinzing, G. E., Friction in turbulent flow of solids-gas system, *Can. J. Chem. Eng.*, vol. 50, no. 4, 441–444, 1972.

263. Toms, B. A., Some observations on the flow of linear polymer solutions through straight tubes at large Reynolds numbers, *Proc. Int. Rheol. Congr.*, pp. 135–141, Schveningen, Holland, 1948.

264. Turnblade, B. C., The molecular transit time and its correlation with the stability of externally pressurized gas-lubricated bearings, *Trans. ASME*, vol D85, no. 2, 297–304, 1963.

265. Schlag, A., Les pertes de charge en conduites transportant des materiaux solides, *Bull. Mens Cent. Belg. Eutde Docume. Eaux*, no. 111, 70–76, 1960.

266. Uematsu, T. and Morikawa, Y., Druckverluste im krummer einer wagerechten Forderung von kornigen Gutern, *Bull. JSME*, vol. 4, no. 15, 531–538, 1961.

267. Uematsu, T., Pneumatische Forderung in Lotrechter Rohrleitung, *Bull. JSME*, vol. 8, no. 31, 367–375, 1965.

THREE

RESISTANCE TO FLOW AT THE ENTRANCE INTO TUBES AND CONDUITS
Resistance Coefficients of Inlet Sections

3-1 EXPLANATIONS AND PRACTICAL RECOMMENDATIONS

1. Resistance of the flow at the entrance into a straight tube or conduit of constant cross section (Figure 3-1) is governed by two parameters: the relative thickness δ_1/D_h of the inlet tube wall edge, and the relative distance b/D_h from the tube edge to the wall in which the tube is installed.

2. The resistance coefficient ζ of the straight inlet section is a maximum when the edge is very sharp ($\delta_1/D_h = 0$) and when the tube edge is at an infinite distance from the wall in which the tube is mounted ($b/D_h = \infty$). In this case, $\zeta = 1.0$.

3. The minimum value of the resistance coefficient ζ is 0.5, and can be attained by thickening the inlet edge. The coefficient ζ has this same value when the tube is mounted flush with the wall ($b/D_h = 0$).

4. The effect of the wall on the inlet resistance coefficient virtually ceases at $b/D_h \geq 0.5$. This case corresponds to the condition where the tube entrance inlet edge is at an infinite distance from the wall.

5. When the flow enters a straight tube or conduit it separates by inertia from the inner surface close behind the entrance if the inlet orifice edge is insufficiently rounded. This separation of the flow and the induced formation of eddies constitute the major sources of the inlet pressure losses. Flow separation from the tube walls leads to a decrease in the jet cross section (jet contraction). For a straight inlet orifice with a sharp edge, the jet contraction coefficient $\varepsilon = F_{con}/F_0$ is equal to 0.5 for turbulent flow.

6. When the inlet wall is thickened, beveled, or rounded or when the edge of the tube or conduit is adjacent to the wall into which the tube is mounted, the flow passes the inlet edge more smoothly and the flow separation zone becomes shorter, thus decreasing the inlet resistance.

7. A substantial decrease in the resistance occurs when the flow enters the tube through a smooth inlet, the cross section of which forms an arc of a circle, etc.; Figure 3-2a). Thus, for example, for a circular nozzle or collector having a relative value of the radius of curvature

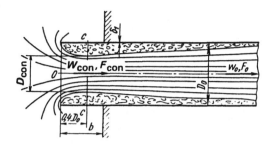

Figure 3-1 Flow pattern at the inlet into a straight tube from an infinite space.

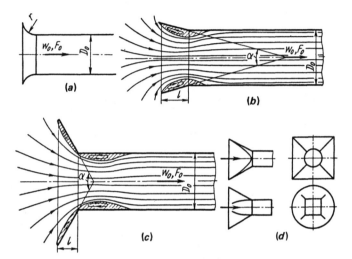

Figure 3-2 Schematic diagrams of smooth inlet sections.

of $r/D_h = 0.2$, the resistance coefficient ζ decreases to 0.04–0.05 as compared to a value of $\zeta = 1.0$ at $r/D_h = \delta_1/D_h = 0$, a sharp edge.*

8. A relatively low resistance is also observed when the flow enters the tubes through inlets with straight boundaries shaped like a truncated cone (Figure 3-2b and c) or in the form of contracting sections with a transition from rectangular to circular, or from circular to rectangular (Figure 3-2d). The resistance coefficient of such inlets depends both on the contraction angle α and on the relative length l/D_h of the contracting section. For each length of the conical inlet there exists an optimum value of α at which the resistance coefficient ζ is a minimum. Practically, the optimum value of α for a fairly wide range of l/D_h (of order 0.1 to 1.0) lies within the limits of 40–60°. For such angles and, for example, the relative length $l/D_h = 0.2$, the resistance coefficient is equal to 0.2.

9. Pressure losses in a conical inlet are mainly associated with flow separation in two locations: directly downstream of the inlet section and over the straight section following

---

*When the tube inlet is smooth, the only losses are those of the total pressure in the boundary layer. These are not observed in the core of the flow. Therefore, the resistance coefficient of a favorable or smooth inlet (collector) can be determined most accurately by experiment, through measurement of the total pressure distribution and the velocity in the outlet section of the inlet collector. The measurements in the boundary layer should then be made with the use of a microprobe. In this case the resistance coefficient is

$$\zeta \equiv \frac{\Delta p}{\rho w_0^2/2} = \frac{1/F_0 \int_{F_0} (p_0 - p_0') w \, dF}{(\rho w_0^3/2) F_0}$$

where w is the velocity in the outlet section of the collector; p_0, p_0' is the total pressure upstream of the collector entrance and at its outlet.

Editor's note: The term ''collector'' is used to denote an entry to a pipe or conduit, such as a nozzle.

this entry (Figure 3-2*b* and *c*). The losses in the first location dominate when the contraction angle α of the conical entry is relatively small (Figure 3-2*b*). The losses in the second location start to dominate at large values of α and increase with increases in this angle (Figure 3-2*c*). For $\alpha = 0°$, this reverts to the conventional case of a straight inlet for which $\zeta = 1$. For $\alpha = 180°$, the inlet channel is flush mounted into the wall and $\zeta = 0.5$.

10. When the inlet section is mounted into the end-face wall at an angle (see Diagrams 3-2 and 3-3), the inlet resistance increases. The resistance coefficient in the case of circular or square cross sections and $w_\infty = 0$ can be calculated from Weisbach's formula[49]

$$\zeta \equiv \frac{\Delta p}{\rho w_0^2/2} \approx 0.5 + 0.3 \cos \delta + 0.2 \cos^2 \delta$$

For other shapes of the channel cross sections the resistance coefficients are given on Diagram 3-2 (rounded off to 10%)[20].

11. When a flow with velocity w_∞ passes the wall into which a tube is mounted (see scheme on Diagram 3-3), the behavior is, in most respects, similar to that occurring when the flow discharges through an orifice in the wall under the same conditions (see Chapter 4, paragraphs 40–47). However, there are some differences. Thus, when the flow is sucked into a straight channel, there are no velocity pressure losses in the aspirated jet, with the result that the resistance coefficient is much lower than in the case of discharge from an orifice. Moreover, when the angles of inclination δ of straight sections are greater than $90°$, the coefficient ζ takes on negative values, owing to an increase in the ram effect at certain velocity ratios $w_\infty/w_0 > 0$ (see Diagram 3-3).

12. A baffle or wall (Figure 3-3) placed in front of the inlet section at a relative distance $h/D_h < 0.8$–1.0 will increase the inlet resistance. This increase becomes greater the closer the baffle is to the inlet orifice of the tube, that is, the smaller h/D_h is.

13. The resistance coefficient of inlet sections, which are not flush mounted with the wall and which have different thicknesses of the rounded or beveled entrances with a baffle placed before the entrance, is determined from the author's approximate formula[12,13]

$$\zeta \equiv \frac{\Delta p}{\rho w_0^2/2} \approx \zeta' + \frac{\sigma_1}{n^2}$$

where ζ' is the coefficient which accounts for the effect of the inlet edge shape and which is determined in the same way as ζ in Diagrams 3-1, 3-4, and 3-6; σ_1 is the coefficient accounting for the effect of the baffle or screen; where $\sigma_1 = f(h/D_h)$, shown in the curve of Diagram 3-8.

The resistance coefficient of smooth collectors mounted flush with the wall, with a baffle placed before the entrance, is determined from the curves $\zeta = f(h/D_h, r/D_h)$ of Diagram 3-5.

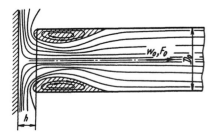

Figure 3-3 Inlet section with a baffle in front of the entrance.

14. In inlet sections with a sudden transition from a larger cross section of area F_1 to a smaller one of area F_0 (Borda mouthpiece, Figure 3-4), the resistance coefficient at large Reynolds numbers (Re $= w_0 D_h/\nu > 10^4$ depends on the area ratio F_0/F_1 and can be calculated from the formula

$$\zeta \equiv \frac{\Delta p}{\rho w_0^2/2} = \zeta'\left(1 - \frac{F_0}{F_1}\right)^m \tag{3-1}$$

where ζ' is a coefficient which depends on the inlet edge shape of the smaller channel (see Diagram 3-9) and which is determined in the same way as ζ from Diagrams 3-1, 3-2, and 3-6; m is an exponent depending on the inlet conditions; for values of $b/D_h = 0$–0.01 it varies from 0.75 to 1.0, while for $b/D_h > 0.01$ it can be assumed equal to 1.0.[12,13]

When the inlet edge of a narrow channel is mounted flush with the end-face wall of a wider channel ($b/D_h = 0$), this represents a typical case of sudden contraction, which is considered in Chapter 4, paragraphs 22–24.

15. The resistance coefficient of inlet sections depends also on the location and the manner in which they were mounted into the wall. Thus, a lowered resistance coefficient can be attained by installing an annular lip or an annular step ahead of the inlet section enclosing the orifice (Figure 3-5). If the edge of the lip or of the step is sharp, the flow, upon entering this section, separates from its surface. The resulting recirculation favors smooth inflow of the fluid into the main inlet section of the tube without separation. As a result, the inlet resistance decreases considerably.

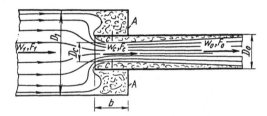

Figure 3-4 Schematic diagram of flow with a sudden contraction.

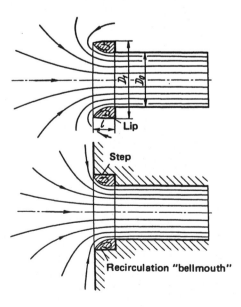

Figure 3-5 Entrance through a circular bellmouth.

16. The optimum dimensions of the enlarged section, over which the recirculation bellmouth is formed, must correspond to the vertical dimensions of the region adjacent to the contracted cross section of the stream at the straight tube with sharp edges and, similarly, in a tube mounted flush with the wall. In fact, Khanzhonkov[30] has shown experimentally that the lowest resistance coefficient $\zeta = 0.10$–0.12 is obtained with the use of a lip of $l/D_0 \approx 0.25$ and $D_1/D_0 \approx 1.2$ and with the use of a step of $l/D_0 \approx 0.2$ and $D_1/D_0 \approx 1.3$.

With a rounded inlet edge, the lowest resistance coefficient in these cases would be 0.07–0.08.

17. The values of ζ in the case of other modes of mounting the inlet sections (in the end-face wall or between the walls) are given in Diagrams 3-10 and 3-11.

18. The resistance coefficient for the flow entering into a straight section through a single orifice or an orifice grid (entry with sudden expansion, $F_1 = \infty$; see Diagram 3-12) at $\text{Re} = w_{or}d_h/\nu > 10$ for the general case (inlet edges of any shape and of any thickness) is calculated from the author's approximate formula[13,14]

$$\zeta \equiv \frac{\Delta p}{\rho w_0^2/2} = \left[\zeta' + (1 - \overline{f})^2 + \tau(1 - \overline{f}) + \lambda \frac{l}{d_h} \right] \frac{1}{\overline{f}^2} \qquad (3\text{-}2)$$

where ζ' is the coefficient which accounts for the shape of the inlet and which is determined in the same way as ζ for inlet sections with the end-face wall from Diagrams 3-1, 3-2, 3-4, and 3-7; τ is the coefficient accounting for the effect of the grid (orifice) wall thickness, inlet edge shape, and conditions of flow passage through the orifice; λ is the friction coefficient over the length (depth) of the grid orifices, determined as a function of Re and $\overline{\Delta} = \Delta/d_h$ from Diagrams 2-2 through 2-6; $\overline{f} = F_{or}/F_0 = F_{or}/F_{gr}$ is the area ratio.

19. The general case of the flow entry through an orifice or an orifice grid consists of a number of particular cases:

● Sharp edges of orifices ($\overline{l} = l/d_h \approx 0$), for which $\zeta' = 0.5$ and $\tau = 1.41$; in this case Equation (3-2) is reduced to the following formula derived by the author.[12,13]

$$\zeta \equiv \frac{\Delta p}{\rho w_0^2/2} = (1.707 - \overline{f})^2 \frac{1}{\overline{f}^2} = \left(\frac{1.707}{\overline{f}} - 1 \right)^2 \qquad (3\text{-}3)$$

● Thickened edges of orifices for which the coefficient $\zeta' = 0.5$ and

$$\tau = (2.4 - \overline{l}) \times 10^{-\varphi(\overline{l})}, \qquad (\overline{l} = l/D_h) \qquad (3\text{-}4)$$

where

$$\varphi(\overline{l}) = 0.25 + 0.535\overline{l}^8/(0.05 + \overline{l}^7) \qquad (3\text{-}5)$$

● Beveled or rounded (in the flow direction) edges of orifices for which it is assumed that $\lambda l/D_h = 0$ and $\tau \approx 2\sqrt{\zeta'}$; the case

$$\zeta \equiv \frac{\Delta p}{\rho w_0^2/2} = (1 - \sqrt{\zeta'} - \overline{f})^2 \frac{1}{\overline{f}^2} \qquad (3\text{-}6)$$

In the case where the edges of orifices are beveled in the flow direction, ζ' is determined similarly to ζ for a conical collector with an end-face wall from Diagram 3-7 as a function of the contraction angle α and the relative length $\bar{l} = l/D_h$. For the values of $\alpha = 40$–$60°$, it is determined from the formula

$$\zeta' = 0.13 + 0.34 \times 10^{-(3.45\bar{l} + 88.4\bar{l}^{2.3})} \tag{3-7}$$

In the case of orifices with rounded edges, the coefficient ζ' is determined in the same way as ζ for a circular collector with the end-face wall as a function of $\bar{r} = r/D_h$ from Diagram 3-4 or from the formula

$$\zeta = 0.03 + 0.47 \times 10^{-7.7\bar{r}} \tag{3-8}*$$

20. For transition and laminar flow regions (Re $= w_0 D_h/\nu < 10^4$–10^5) and conventional entrance of flow (without orifices or grids), the resistance coefficient can be determined from the formula analogous to Equation (1-3):

$$\zeta \equiv \frac{\Delta p}{\rho w_0^2/2} \approx \frac{A}{Re} + \zeta_{qu}$$

where ζ_{qu} is taken as ζ for the quadratic region (Re $> 10^4$–10^5), $A = 30.^2$

21. For transition and laminar regions with entrance of flow through an orifice or a grid, the resistance coefficient can be calculated from the following approximate formulas (according to paragraphs 30–36 of Chapter 4):

At $30 < Re < 10^4$–10^5:

$$\zeta \equiv \frac{\Delta p}{\rho w_0^2/2} = \frac{\zeta_\phi}{\bar{f}^2} + \bar{\varepsilon}_{0Re}\zeta_{qu}$$

At $10 < Re < 30$:

$$\zeta \equiv \frac{33}{Re}\frac{1}{\bar{f}^2} + \bar{\varepsilon}_{0Re}\zeta_{qu}$$

At $Re < 10$:

$$\zeta = \frac{33}{Re}\frac{1}{\bar{f}^2}$$

where $\zeta_\phi = f_1(Re\ F_0/F_1)$, as shown in the graph of Diagram 4-19 (it is postulated that $\bar{f} = F_{or}/F_0$ corresponds to the ratio F_0/F_1); $\bar{\varepsilon}_{0Re} = f_2(Re)$, in Diagram 4-19. ζ_{qu} is the resistance coefficient of the inlet section with an orifice (grid) of the given shape which is determined similarly to ζ from Equations (3-2)–(3-8).

22. With lateral (transverse) entrance into the end section of the tube (Figure 3-6) the resistance is much higher than that with straight entrance and sudden expansion (through an orifice, grid), particularly at $\bar{f} > 0.2$, since more complicated conditions for the flow of liquid (air) are observed in the case of lateral entrance.

---

*Calculations according to paragraphs b and c can be performed virtually starting from the values Re $= 10^4$ and higher.[5]

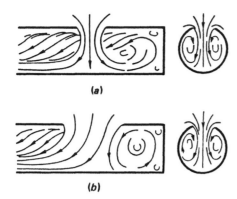

(a)

(b)

Figure 3-6 Schematic diagrams of flow entering into a side orifice in the end section of a tube: (a) at small values of $\bar{f}$, and (b) at large values of $\bar{f}$.

23. On the basis of visual observations, Khanzhonkov and Davydenko[31] showed that at small $\bar{f}$ the jet, which enters through an orifice into the tube, moves to the opposite wall, over which it spreads in all directions. Part of the jet moves toward the closed end of the tube, rotates through 180°, and flows into the other end of the tube in the form of two rotating streams (Figure 3-6a).

At some ("critical") values of $\bar{f}$ air inflow into the closed space of the tube nearly ceases, while the jet in the form of two rotating streams flows completely into the opposite end of the tube (Figure 3-6b).

24. This type of a flow is not only responsible for the increased resistance of the side inlet, but is the reason for the complex dependence of the resistance coefficient ζ on the area ratio $\bar{f}$. (Figure 3-7). A sharp decrease in ζ corresponds to the "critical" value of $\bar{f}$ at which the above rearrangement of the flow occurs after entrance into the tube.

25. According to the author's data, flow entrance into the tube through two side orifices, located one opposite the other, increases the inlet resistance, which becomes greater the higher the value of $\bar{f}$.

26. Entrance through side orifices is often utilized in ventilating shafts of rectangular cross section. Such orifices are furnished with louvers to prevent the entry of particulate matter. The resistance coefficient of such shafts also depends not only on the relative area of the orifices, but on their relative arrangement. Diagram 3-17 presents the resistance coefficients of intake shafts with differently positioned side orifices. The values of ζ are given here for orifices with and without fixed louvers.

27. The resistance of intake shafts with straight entrances, but provided with canopies (see Diagram 3-18), is similar to the resistance of conventional inlet sections with baffles. For ventilating shafts of circular cross section, for which the relative thickness δ_1 of the inlet edges lies within 0.01–0.002, the effect of this parameter may be neglected and the resistance coefficient ζ assumed to have values similar to those for shafts with sharp inlet edges.

The relative distance h/D_h between the canopy hood and the inlet edge of the shaft can be assumed equal to 0.4. Larger distances would require extremely large canopy hoods, otherwise atmospheric contaminants might enter the shaft.

Of all the available constructions of intake shafts one should recommend the one with a conical entry section at the inlet. This shaft has the minimum resistance coefficient, $\zeta = 0.48$.[28]

28. When the flow enters the tube through a screen, the total resistance coefficient can be approximated as the sum of the separate resistance coefficients of the screen and of the inlet, that is,

$$\zeta \equiv \frac{\Delta p}{\rho w_0^2/2} \approx \zeta' + \frac{\zeta_{sc}}{n^2}$$

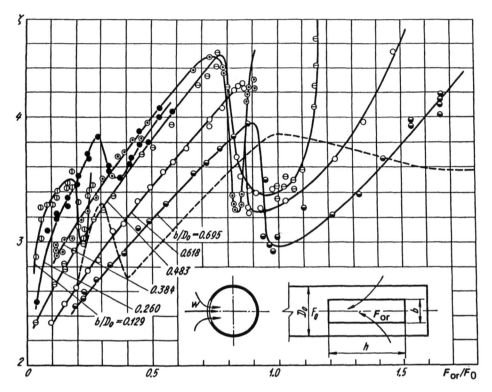

Figure 3-7 Dependence of the inlet resistance coefficient of a side orifice in the end section of the tube on the relative area $\bar{f}$: solid lines, experiments of Khanzhonkov and Davydauko[31] with one orifice; dashed lines, experiments of the author[15] with two side orifices opposite each other: $\zeta \leq \dfrac{\Delta p}{\rho w_0^2/2}$

where ζ' is the resistance coefficient of the inlet, without a screen, determined as ζ for the given shape of the inlet edge from the corresponding graphs of Diagrams 3-1 and 3-4 through 3-8; ζ_{sc} is the resistance coefficient of the screen, determined as ζ from the corresponding graphs of Diagram 8-6; $n = F_1/F_0$ is the area ratio of the cross section in the place where the screen is mounted to the minimum cross section of the inlet length.

29. The resistance coefficient of a fixed louver grating depends both on its open area coefficient $\bar{f} = F_{or}/F_{gr}$ and on the relative depth of the channels l/b_1'. For each open area coefficient of the grating there is an optimum value of the relative depth $(l/b_1')_{opt}$ at which the resistance coefficient is minimal. It is therefore recommended that, as a rule, gratings be used which have the optimal values of l/b': $(l/b_1')_{opt} \approx 11(1 - \bar{f})$.*

30. In the case of standard gratings with fixed louvers, the inlet edges of the fins are cut along the vertical (see scheme of a Diagram 3-19). However, it is more beneficial that the inlet edges be cut along the horizontal (see scheme b). This provides a 40% decrease in the resistance.

31. The resistance coefficient of gratings with fixed louvers at the entrance to the channel** is determined as:

At $l/b_1' \geq (l/b_1')_{opt}$

$$\zeta \equiv \frac{\Delta p}{\rho w_0^2/2} = k\left[0.85 + \left(1 - \bar{f}\,\frac{F_{gr}}{F_0}\right)^2 + \zeta_{fr}\right]\frac{1}{\bar{f}^2}\left(\frac{F_0}{F_{gr}}\right)^2$$

---

*This formula was obtained by the author on the basis of Bevier's[37] data.

**The formulas agree satisfactorily with the experimental data of Bevier[37] and Cobb.[40]

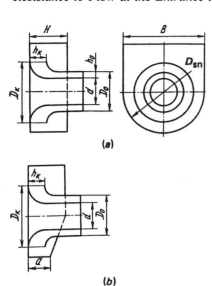

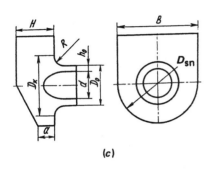

Figure 3-8 Inlet pipes of axial stationary turbo machines; (*a*) circular annular entry (collector) formed by two curviliner surfaces; (*b*) the same with a sloping bottom of the annular entry; (*c*) circular collector formed by a curvilinear outer surface and a center body.

At $l/b_1' < (l/b_1')_{opt}$

$$\zeta = \frac{\Delta p}{\rho w_0^2/2} = k\left[0.85 + \left(1 - \overline{f}\,\frac{F_{gr}}{F_0}\right)^2 + \zeta_{fr}\right]\frac{1}{\overline{f}^2}\left(\frac{F_0}{F_{gr}}\right)^2 + \Delta\zeta$$

where $\Delta\zeta = 0.5[11(1 - \overline{f}) - l/b_1']$; $\zeta_{fr} = \lambda l/b_1'$; $\overline{f} = F_{or}/F_0$, see Diagram 3-19; $k = 1.0$ for a standard grating (inlet edges cut vertically); $k = 0.6$ for an improved grating (inlet edges cut horizontally); and λ is the coefficient of hydraulic friction along the length (depth) of the louver channels, determined depending on Re $= w_{or}b_1'/\nu$ from Diagrams 2-1 through 2-5.

32. The primary requirement for inlet pipes to axial flow turbo machines (Figure 3-8) is that the total pressure losses should be minimal and the velocity profile in the outlet section of the inlet collector, which supplies air directly to the blade rims of the machines, should be almost undistorted.

33. As demonstrated by the experiments of Dovzhik and Kartavensky,[10] for inlet pipes designed on the basis of the use of a collector with two curvilinear surfaces (Figure 3-8*a*), these conditions are best fulfilled for a high degree of pipe constriction ($n_p \geq 3.5$, where $n_p = F_{in}/F_0$, $F_{in} = $ HB is the area of entrance into a scroll or volute). In this case, the degree of collector constriction should be close to the degree of pipe constriction ($n_{col} = n_p$, where $n_{col} = F_{col}/F_0 = 2h_{col}/h_0[D_{col}/D_0(1 + \overline{d})]$ and $\overline{d} = d/D_0$), while the radial dimension of the pipe should be large ($D_{scr} = D_{scr}/D_0 > 1.3$). Sloping of the back wall in the bottom of the scroll (Figure 3-8*b*) insignificantly, within certain limits, decreases the pressure losses

in the pipe. With the above optimization parameters, the resistance coefficient of the pipe is $\zeta \equiv \Delta p/(\rho_0 w_0^2/2) = 0.12\text{–}0.15$ (where $w_0 = c_a$ is the average axial velocity in the outlet section of the circular collector [in section F_0] and ρ_0 is the gas density in the same cross section).

34. It is advisable to use the above collector (Figure 3-8a) in cases where the pipe has a large degree of contraction (axial compressors, turbines). When the degree of contraction need not be large (fans) and the available radial dimensions of the pipe are substantially limited, it is advisable to use a pipe in which the circular collector is formed by the one curvilinear surface (Figure 3-8c). In this case, the pipe will have the minimum resistance coefficient at $n_p \geq 3.5$, $H/D_0 \geq 0.95$ and $\overline{D}_{yn} = 1.15\text{–}1.25$. At larger values of $\overline{D}_{yn}(>1.0)$ it is advisable that the front wall of the scroll be inclined up to $a/H \approx 0.4$. This inclination of the wall provides additional reduction in the resistance coefficient.

35. Nonuniform velocity distribution both in the radial direction and circumferentially about the outlet section of the collector, obtained at the above optimum parameters of the pipes (departure from the average velocity c_a of the order of 15–20%), does not influence the characteristics of the compressor stages. However, velocity nonuniformity leads to a periodic change in the aerodynamic forces acting on the blades of the rotor, which adversely affects the fatigue strength of the machine.[19]

36. In the engines of aircraft, ships, and also of subway cars, air intakes are installed (intake pipes, Figure 3-9). The aerodynamic characteristics of these devices depend on the operational and constructional parameters.

Detailed investigations of the aerodynamic characteristics of intake pipes of aircraft engines are described in Reference 11. The results of the investigations of the aerodynamics of air intakes of gas-turbine ships are given in Reference 6.

37. The inlet conditions into an intake pipe, the inlet section of which is arranged on a solid surface (wing of an aircraft, hood of an aircraft engine, fuselage of a helicopter, body of a ship, top of a car, etc.), depend on the velocity ratio w_{in} at the entrance to the pipe or, which is the same, on the velocity w_0 at the exit from the pipe to the velocity w_∞ of the free stream (flight velocity, ship motion velocity, car velocity). When the inlet area is selected so that at the given flow rate through the pipe the ratio w_{in}/w_∞ is smaller than unity, one observes retardation (expansion) of the jet accompanied by an increase in the static pressure. The formation of the positive pressure gradient along the jet in the presence of a relatively thick boundary layer on the solid surface leads (as in a conventional thick-walled diffuser) to flow separation from this surface (Figure 3-9a). With an increase in the pressure gradient and, consequently, with a decrease of the ratio w_{in}/w_∞, the separation becomes more intensive and the inlet pressure losses increase.

38. The pipe can have such an area of the inlet orifice at which the velocity ratio w_{in}/w_∞ for the given flow rate will be equal to, or higher than, unity. When $w_{in}/w_\infty = 1$, the cross-sectional area and correspondingly the velocity, and consequently the static pressure

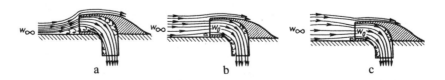

Figure 3-9 Different cases of flow inlet into the pipe:[11] a, at small discharge coefficients (W_{in}/W_x is much smaller than unity); b, at large discharge coefficients; c, at $W_{in}/W_x \geq 1$.

along the jet remain virtually constant up to the entrance into the pipe. In this case, no flow separation from the surface can occur (Figure 3-9*b*) and air enters the pipe virtually without loss.

39. At $w_{in}/w_\infty > 1$ the flow enters a pipe with acceleration (the jet is contracted) and, consequently, this is accompanied by a fall in the pressure. Therefore, flow separation from the solid surface is even more impossible. However, in the case of a very appreciable jet contraction, such inflow may lead to flow separation from the inner edge of the pipe (Figure 3-9*c*). This separation can be eliminated by using rather a smooth (thick) inlet edge.

40. The values of the resistance coefficients of the entrances to the intake pipes ($\zeta_{in} \equiv \Delta p/\rho w_0^2/2$) with different versions of the location of inlet sections with respect to the solid surface (in the given case the surface of the aircraft engine hood) and at different velocity ratios w_0/w_∞ are given in Diagram 3-22. This diagram also contains the schemes of the versions of testing of pipes. The pressure losses associated with the entrance of flow into an intake pipe are smallest when the pipe is located directly near the front edge of the hood (version 1). In this case, there is no flow separation before the entrance, whereas the substantial increase in loss with a decreasing velocity ratio at $w_0/w_\infty < 0.3$ is due to the flow separation after its entrance to the pipe (see paragraph 39).

41. The influence of the flow separation from the solid surface before the entrance to the pipe on the inlet resistance can be considerably decreased or entirely eliminated by increasing the distance h of the protruding portion of the pipe from the solid surface, especially if the neck of the pipe could be streamlined for the overflow of the boundary layer (see version 6 on Diagram 3-22). However, it is necessary here to take into account the increase in the drag of the pipe with an increase in the indicated distance from the solid surface.

42. The total energy losses in the intake pipe (air-intake device) are composed of the inlet pipe energy losses and internal losses over the entire pipe from the entrance to exit of flow from it. The general (total) resistance coefficient of the intake pipe is

$$\zeta_p \equiv \frac{\Delta p}{\rho w_0^2/2} = \zeta_{in} + \zeta_{ex}$$

where $\zeta_{in} \equiv \Delta p/\rho w_0^2/2$ is the resistance coefficient of the entrance depending on the velocity ratio w_0/w_∞ and on the location of the pipe (air-intake device) on the given object; $\zeta_{ex} \equiv \Delta p/\rho w_0^2/2$ is the coefficient of internal resistance of the entire section of the air-intake device from the entrance to the exit of flow from it.

43. The drag of the pipe is composed of two values: the "hydraulic" c_{xh} and external frontal resistance c_{xo}. The hydraulic frontal resistance originates due to the loss of momentum by the flow entering the pipe. The external frontal resistance is induced by the external flow past the pipe and its interference onto the adjacent part of the aircraft (helicopter, ship, car).

44. Diagram 3-23 depicts some schemes of the inlet elements of industrial axial fans. This diagram also gives the resistance coefficients of the inlet elements calculated according to the recommendations of Bychkova[3,4] for different inlet and operational conditions of the fans.

45. Diagram 3-24 presents the schemes of the inlet elements of radial (centrifugal) fans and the values of the resistance coefficients of these elements according to the same recommendations as given in paragraph 44.

3-2 DIAGRAMS OF RESISTANCE COEFFICIENTS

Entrance into a straight tube of constant cross section; $Re = w_0 D_h / \nu > 10^4$ [12,13]	Diagram 3-1

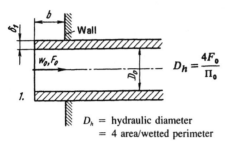

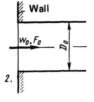

$$D_h = \frac{4F_0}{\Pi_0}$$

D_h = hydraulic diameter
= 4 area/wetted perimeter

1) Entrance into a tube at a distance ($b/D_h < 0.5$) from wall in which it is mounted.

2) Entrance into tube mounted flush with the wall ($b/D_h = 0$).

3) Entrance into tube at a distance from the wall ($b/D_h < 0.5$) in which it is mounted.

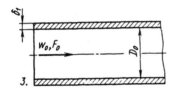

1) and 2) $\zeta \equiv \dfrac{\Delta p}{\rho w_0^2/2}$, see curve $\zeta = f\left(\dfrac{\delta_1}{D_h}\right)$ at the given $\dfrac{b}{D_h}$.

3) $\zeta \equiv \dfrac{\Delta p}{\rho w_0^2/2}$, see curve $\zeta = f\left(\dfrac{\delta_1}{D_h}\right)$ at $\dfrac{b}{D_h} \geq 0.5$.

For computer calculations at $\delta/D_h < 0.05$ and $0.01 < b/D_h < 0.05$:

$$\zeta \equiv \frac{\Delta p}{\rho w_0^2/2} \sum_{i=0}^{3} \left\{ \sum_{j=0}^{4} [a_{i,j}(b/D_h)^j] \right\} (\delta/D_h)$$

where for $a_{i,j}$, see the Table

Values of $a_{i,j}$

i	0	1	2	3	4
			j		
0	0.549356	9.22856	−79.0065	258.742	−268.925
1	−4.93702	−681.756	7,189.72	−24,896.6	26,416.2
2	160.273	17,313.6	−212,416.0	766,932	−827,816
3	1,650.38	−139,018	1,930,080	−7,239,530	795,042

Values of ζ

ζ_1/D_h	0	0.002	0.005	0.010	0.020	0.050	0.100	0.200	0.300	0.500	∞
						b/D_h					
0	0.50	0.57	0.63	0.68	0.73	0.80	0.86	0.92	0.97	1.00	1.00
0.004	0.50	0.54	0.58	0.63	0.67	0.74	0.80	0.86	0.90	0.94	0.94
0.008	0.50	0.53	0.55	0.58	0.62	0.68	0.74	0.81	0.85	0.88	0.88
0.012	0.50	0.52	0.53	0.55	0.58	0.63	0.68	0.75	0.79	0.83	0.83
0.016	0.50	0.51	0.51	0.53	0.55	0.58	0.64	0.70	0.74	0.77	0.77
0.020	0.50	0.51	0.51	0.52	0.53	0.55	0.60	0.66	0.69	0.72	0.72
0.024	0.50	0.50	0.50	0.51	0.52	0.53	0.58	0.62	0.65	0.68	0.68
0.030	0.50	0.50	0.50	0.51	0.52	0.52	0.54	0.57	0.59	0.61	0.61
0.040	0.50	0.50	0.50	0.51	0.51	0.51	0.51	0.52	0.52	0.54	0.54
0.050	0.50	0.50	0.50	0.50	0.50	0.50	0.50	0.50	0.50	0.50	0.50

Diagram
3-1

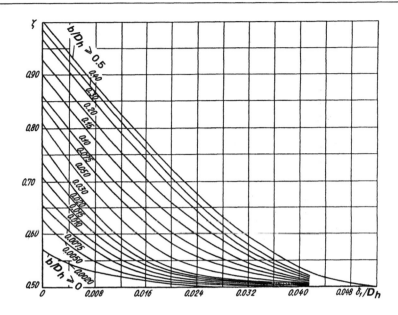

Entrance from an infinite space ($w_\infty = 0$) into a tube mounted flush into a wall at any angle δ; Re $= w_0 D_h/\nu \geqslant 10^4$ [20,49]

Diagram
3-2

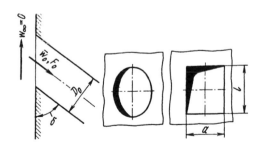

$$D_h = \frac{4F_0}{\Pi_0}$$

For circular and square orifices

$$\zeta \equiv \frac{\Delta p}{\rho w_0^2/2} = 0.5 + 0.3 \cos \delta + 0.2 \cos^2 \delta$$

For orifices of any shapes

$$\zeta \equiv \frac{\Delta p}{\rho w_0^2/2} = f(\delta)$$

Values of ζ (rounded up to 10%)

$\dfrac{l}{a}$	δ, degrees						
	20	30	45	60	70	80	90
1.0	0.96	0.90	0.80	0.70	0.63	0.56	0.50
0.2–0.5	0.85	0.80	0.70	0.62	0.56	0.50	0.45
2.0	1.04	1.00	0.90	0.80	0.70	0.58	0.45
5.0	1.58	1.45	1.20	0.95	0.78	0.60	0.45

Diagram
3-2

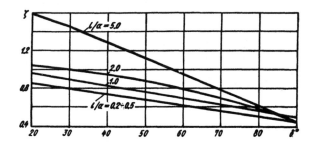

Entrance into a tube mounted flush into a wall in the presence
of a passing flow ($w_\infty > 0$); Re $= w_0 D_h/\nu \geqslant 10^{4}$ [20]

Diagram
3-3

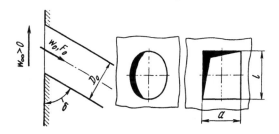

$$\zeta \equiv \frac{\Delta p}{\rho w_0^2/2} \text{, see curves } \zeta = f\left(\frac{w_\infty}{w_0}\right)$$

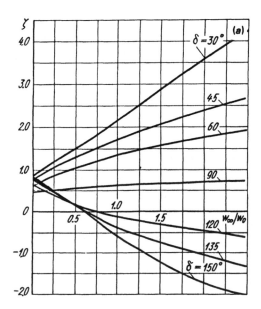

**Values of ζ (rounded up to 10%) for
circular and square cross sections,
i.e., at $l/a = 1.0$ (see graph a)**

	$\dfrac{w_\infty}{w_0}$					
δ, deg	0	0.5	1.0	1.5	2.0	2.5
30	0.90	1.55	2.18	2.85	3.50	4.00
45	0.80	1.30	1.72	2.08	2.30	2.60
60	0.65	1.04	1.35	1.58	1.70	1.86
90	0.50	0.56	1.62	0.66	0.70	0.70
120	0.65	0.15	−0.15	−0.30	−0.50	−0.60
150	0.85	0.15	−0.60	−1.22	−1.70	−2.0

Diagram
3-3

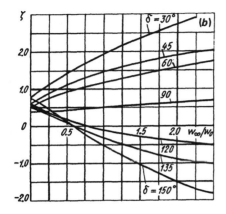

**Values of ζ (rounded up to 10%)
at $l/a = 0.2-0.5$ (see graph b)**

δ, deg	$\dfrac{w_\infty}{w_0}$					
	0	0.5	1.0	1.5	2.0	2.5
30	0.80	1.30	1.85	2.20	2.50	2.75
45	0.67	1.10	1.43	1.65	1.83	2.0
60	0.58	0.92	1.25	1.45	1.60	1.75
90	0.45	0.45	0.60	0.67	0.75	0.85
120	0.53	0.15	−0.10	−0.30	−0.40	−0.50
150	0.80	0.13	−0.50	−1.00	−1.35	−1.70

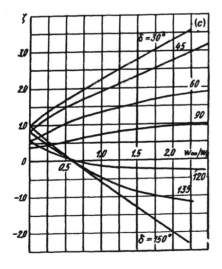

**Values of ζ at $l/a = 2.0$
(see graph c)**

δ, deg	$\dfrac{w_\infty}{w_0}$					
	0	0.5	1.0	1.5	2.0	2.5
30	1.00	1.68	2.22	2.78	3.32	3.80
45	0.88	1.46	1.90	2.30	2.77	3.20
60	0.60	1.02	1.35	1.60	1.75	1.87
90	0.45	0.55	0.75	0.87	0.95	0.95
120	0.60	0.10	−0.13	−0.20	−0.23	−0.30
150	1.00	0.15	−0.60	−1.30	−2.00	−2.5

Diagram
3-3

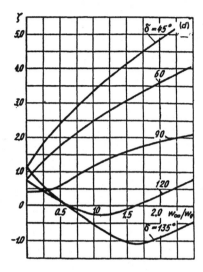

Values of ζ at $l/a = 5.0$
(see graph d)

δ, deg	$\dfrac{w_\infty}{w_0}$					
	0	0.5	1.0	1.5	2.0	2.5
45	1.20	2.40	3.30	4.12	4.85	5.50
60	0.90	1.72	2.47	3.08	3.60	4.10
90	0.45	0.60	1.18	1.78	1.88	2.10
120	0.80	0.12	-0.23	-0.10	-0.35	-0.80
135	1.20	0.12	-0.53	-1.05	-0.88	-0.45

Circular bellmouth inlet (collector) without baffle;   Diagram
$\mathrm{Re} = w_0 D_h/\nu > 10^{4}$ [12,13]   3-4

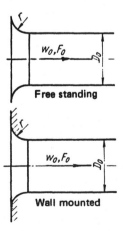

Free standing

Wall mounted

$$D_h = \frac{4F_0}{\Pi_0}$$

$\zeta \equiv \dfrac{\Delta p}{\rho w_0^2/2}$, see curves a and b as a function of $\dfrac{r}{D_h}$

For case 'c': $\zeta = 0.03 + 0.47 \times 10^{-7.7\bar{r}}$; $\quad \bar{r} = r/D_h$

	Diagram 3-4

Values of ζ

Bellmouth (collector) characteristics	$\dfrac{r}{D_h}$										
	0	0.01	0.02	0.03	0.04	0.05	0.06	0.08	0.12	0.16	≥ 0.20
a) Free standing	1.0	0.87	0.74	0.61	0.51	0.40	0.32	0.20	0.10	0.06	0.03
b) Wall mounted	0.5	0.44	0.37	0.31	0.26	0.22	0.20	0.15	0.09	0.06	0.03

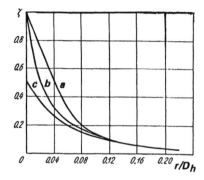

Circular bellmouth, wall mounted (collector) with a facing baffle; $\mathrm{Re} = w_0 D_h / \nu > 10^{4\,18}$	Diagram 3-5

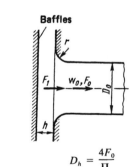

$$\zeta \equiv \frac{\Delta p}{\rho w_0^2 / 2}, \text{ see curves } \zeta = f\left(\frac{h}{D_h}, \frac{r}{D_h}\right)$$

$$D_h = \frac{4F_0}{\Pi_0}$$

Values of ζ

$\dfrac{r}{D_h}$	$\dfrac{h}{D_h}$									
	0.10	0.125	0.15	0.20	0.25	0.30	0.40	0.50	0.60	0.80
0.2	–	0.80	0.45	0.19	0.12	0.09	0.07	0.06	0.05	0.05
0.3	–	0.50	0.34	0.17	0.10	0.07	0.06	0.05	0.04	0.04
0.5	0.65	0.36	0.25	0.10	0.07	0.05	0.04	0.04	0.03	0.03

Diagram
3-5

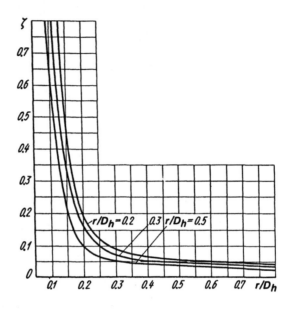

Converging conical nozzle (collector) without wall mounting:
$Re = w_0 D_h/\nu > 10^4$ [12,13]

Diagram
3-6

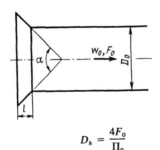

$$\zeta \equiv \frac{\Delta p}{\rho w_0^2/2} \text{ , see curves } \zeta = f(\alpha) \text{ for different } \frac{l}{D_h}$$

$$D_h = \frac{4F_0}{\Pi_0}$$

Values of ζ (approximate)

$\frac{l}{D_h}$	α, degrees								
	0	10	20	30	40	60	100	140	180
0.025	1.0	0.96	0.93	0.90	0.86	0.80	0.69	0.59	0.50
0.050	1.0	0.93	0.86	0.80	0.75	0.67	0.58	0.53	0.50
0.075	1.0	0.87	0.75	0.65	0.58	0.50	0.48	0.49	0.50
0.10	1.0	0.80	0.67	0.55	0.48	0.41	0.41	0.44	0.50
0.15	1.0	0.76	0.58	0.43	0.33	0.25	0.27	0.38	0.50
0.25	1.0	0.68	0.45	0.30	0.22	0.17	0.22	0.34	0.50
0.60	1.0	0.46	0.27	0.18	0.14	0.13	0.21	0.33	0.50
1.0	1.0	0.32	0.20	0.14	0.11	0.10	0.18	0.30	0.50

Diagram
3-6

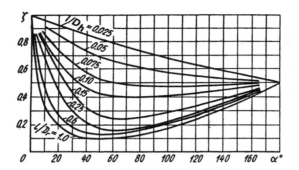

Converging conical nozzle (collector) wall mounted;
$\mathrm{Re} = w_0 D_h/\nu > 10^{4}$ [12,13]

Diagram
3-7

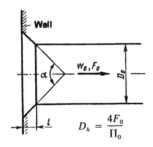

$$\zeta = \frac{\Delta p}{\rho w_0^2/2} ,\ \text{see curves } \zeta = f(\alpha) \text{ for different } \frac{l}{D_h}$$

$$D_h = \frac{4F_0}{\Pi_0}$$

Values of ζ (approximate)

$\dfrac{l}{D_h}$	α, degrees								
	0	10	20	30	40	60	100	140	180
0.025	0.50	0.47	0.45	0.43	0.41	0.40	0.42	0.45	0.50
0.050	0.50	0.45	0.41	0.36	0.33	0.30	0.35	0.42	0.50
0.075	0.50	0.42	0.35	0.30	0.26	0.23	0.30	0.40	0.50
0.10	0.50	0.39	0.32	0.25	0.22	0.18	0.27	0.38	0.50
0.15	0.50	0.37	0.27	0.20	0.16	0.15	0.25	0.37	0.50
0.60	0.50	0.27	0.18	0.13	0.11	0.12	0.23	0.36	0.50

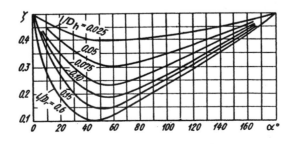

Various inlets with facing baffle;	Diagram
$\text{Re} = w_0 D_h/\nu > 10^4$ [12,13]	3-8

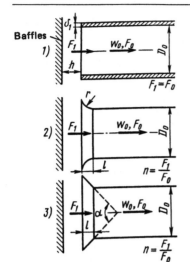

$$D_h = \frac{4F_0}{\Pi_0}$$

$$\zeta \equiv \frac{\Delta p}{\rho w_0^2/2} \approx \zeta' + \frac{\sigma_1}{n^2}$$

where 1) for ζ', see curve $\zeta = f(\delta_1/D_h)$ at $b/D_h \geq 0.50$ on Diagram 3-1; 2) for ζ', see curves $\zeta = f(r/D_h)$ on Diagram 3-4; 3) for ζ', see curve $\zeta = f(\alpha, l/D_h)$ on Diagram 3-6; for σ_1, see curve $\sigma_1 = f(h/D_h)$

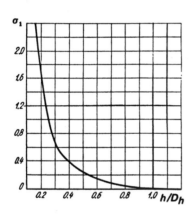

$\dfrac{h}{D_h}$	0.20	0.30	0.40	0.50	0.60	0.70	0.80	1.0	∞
σ_1	1.60	0.65	0.37	0.25	0.15	0.07	0.04	0	0

Entry from a limited volume ($F_0/F_1 > 0$) at $b/D_h > 0$;	Diagram
$\text{Re} = w_0 D_h/\nu > 10^4$ [12,13]	3-9

$$D_h = \frac{4F_0}{\Pi_0} \qquad \zeta \equiv \frac{\Delta p}{\rho w_0^2/2} = \zeta'\left(1 - \frac{F_0}{F_1}\right)$$

Inlet edge	Scheme	Coefficient ζ'
Sharp of thick	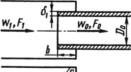	From curves $\zeta = f\left(\dfrac{\delta_1}{D_h}, \dfrac{b}{D_h}\right)$ of Diagram 3-1
Rounded (bellmouth)		From curves $\zeta = f\left(\dfrac{r}{D_h}\right)$ of Diagram 3-4 (graphs a and c)
Beveled (conical)	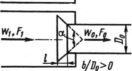	From curves $\zeta = f\left(\alpha, \dfrac{l}{D_h}\right)$ of Diagram 3-6

Inlets with different type mountings of a straight tube to an end wall; inlet thickness $\delta_1 = 0.03$–$0.04\ a_0$; Re $= w_0 a_0/\nu > 10^4$ [12,13]		Diagram 3-10
Inlet conditions	Configuration	Resistance coefficient $\zeta \equiv \dfrac{\Delta p}{\rho w_0^2/2}$
Entrance with the end wall on one side of the tube (conduit)		0.58
Entrance with end walls on two opposite sides of the tube (conduit)		0.55
Entrance with end walls on two adjacent sides of the tube (conduit)		0.55
Entrance with end walls on three sides of the tube (conduit)		0.52
Entrance with end walls on four sides of the tube (conduit)		0.50

Inlets with different mounting of the straight conduit between the walls; inlet edge thickness $\delta_1 = 0.03$–$0.04\ a_0$; $Re = w_0 a_0/\nu > 10^{4}$ [12,13]		Diagram 3-11

Inlet conditions	Configuration	Resistance coefficient $\zeta \equiv \dfrac{\Delta p}{\rho w_0^2/2}$

Entrance into a tube (channel) with a visor projection on one side at $l/a_0 = 0.5$

$\dfrac{l}{a_0}$	0	0.10	0.20	0.30	0.40	0.50
ζ	0.60	0.63	0.65	0.67	0.68	0.68

Entrance into a tube (channel) with visor projections on two sides at $l/a_0 = 0.5$ — 0.82

Entrance into a tube (channel) mounted on top of a wall — 0.63

Entrance into a tube (channel) mounted between two walls — 0.71

Entrance into a tube (channel) mounted in an L-shaped angle (between two walls) — 0.77

Entrance into a tube (channel) clamped between three walls making a U-shape — 0.92

Entrance into a straight tube through an orifice or a perforated plate (grid) with sharp-edged orifices ($l/d_h = 0–0.015$); Re $= w_{or}d_h/\nu \geqslant 10^5$ [12,13]	Diagram 3-12

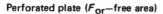

Perforated plate (F_{or}—free area)

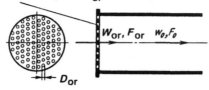

Orifice plate (F_{or}—free area)

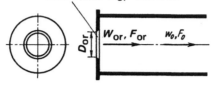

$$d_h = \frac{4f_{or}}{\Pi_{or}} \quad \bar{f} = \frac{F_{or}}{F_{gr}} = \frac{F_{or}}{F_0} = \frac{\Sigma f_{or}}{F_0}$$

$$\zeta \equiv \frac{\Delta p}{\rho w_0^2/2} \approx (1.707 - \bar{f})^2 \frac{1}{\bar{f}^2}, \text{ see curve } \zeta = f(\bar{f}).$$

$\bar{f}$	0.05	0.10	0.15	0.20	0.25	0.30	0.35	0.40	0.45
ζ	1100	258	98	57	38	24	15	11	7.8

$\bar{f}$	0.50	0.55	0.60	0.65	0.70	0.75	0.80	0.90	1.0
ζ	5.8	4.4	3.5	2.6	2.0	1.7	1.3	0.8	0.5

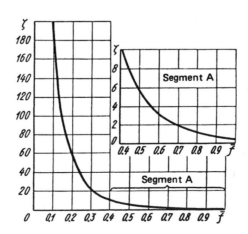

Entrance into a straight tube through an orifice plate or a perforated plate (grid) with differently shaped orifice edges: Re = $w_{or}d_h/\nu \geq 10^4$ [12,13]	Diagram 3-13

$$d_h = \frac{4f_{or}}{\Pi_{or}} \qquad \overline{f} = \frac{F_{or}}{F_0} = \frac{\Sigma f_{or}}{F_0}$$

Characteristics of plate, grid, or orifice edge	Configuration	Resistance coefficient [$\zeta \equiv \Delta p/(\rho w_0^2/2)$]

Thick orifices

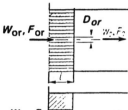

$$\zeta \approx \left[0.5 + (1 - \overline{f})^2 \right.$$

$$\left. + \tau(1 - \overline{f}) + \lambda \frac{l}{d_h} \right] \times \frac{1}{\overline{f}^2}$$

where for τ see graph a
$\varphi(\overline{l}) = 0.25 + 0.535\overline{l}^8/(0.05 + \overline{l}^7)$; or $\tau = 2.4 - \overline{l}) \times 10^{-\varphi(\overline{l})}$ for see Diagrams 2-2 through 2-6;
$\zeta_0 = 0.5 + (1 - \overline{f})^2 + \tau(1 - \overline{f})$

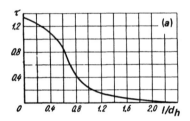

$\overline{l} \equiv l/d_h$	0	0.2	0.4	0.6	0.8
τ	1.35	1.22	1.10	0.84	0.42

$\overline{l} \equiv l/d_h$	1.0	1.2	1.6	2.0	2.4
τ	0.24	0.16	0.07	0.02	0

Orifices with beveled edges

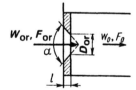

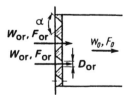

$\zeta = (1 + \sqrt{\zeta'} - \overline{f})^2 \dfrac{1}{\overline{f}^2}$, where at $\alpha = 40$–60° for ζ' see graph b or $\zeta' = 0.13 + 0.34 \times 10^{-(3.45\overline{l} + 88.4\overline{l})^{-2.3}}$, at other d's, ζ' is determined as ζ from Diagram 3-7

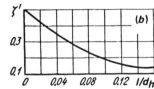

$\overline{l} \equiv l/d_h$	0.01	0.02	0.03	0.04
ζ'	0.46	0.42	0.38	0.35

$\overline{l} \equiv l/d_h$	0.06	0.08	0.12	0.16
ζ'	0.29	0.23	0.16	0.13

	Diagram
	3-13

Orifices with rounded edges

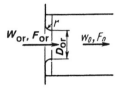

$$\zeta = (1 + \sqrt{\zeta'} - \bar{f})^2 \frac{1}{\bar{f}^2} \,, \text{ where for } \zeta' \text{ see}$$

graph c or $\zeta' = 0.03 + 0.47 \times 10^{-7.7\bar{r}}$

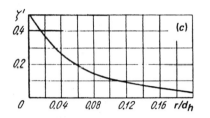

$\bar{r} \equiv r/d_h$	0	0.01	0.02	0.03	0.04	0.05
ζ'	0.50	0.44	0.37	0.31	0.26	0.22
$\bar{r} \equiv r/d_h$	0.06	0.08	0.12	0.16	0.20	
ζ'	0.20	0.15	0.09	0.06	0.02	

Entrance into a straight tube (conduit) through an orifice plate	Diagram
or a perforated plate (grid) with differently shaped orifice edges;	3-14
transition and laminar flow regions (Re $= w_{or}D_h/\nu < 10^4 - 10^5$)[16]	

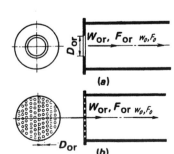

(a)

(b)

1) $30 < \text{Re} < 10^4 - 10^5$: $\zeta \equiv \dfrac{\Delta p}{\rho w_0^2/2} = \zeta_\phi \dfrac{1}{\bar{f}^2} + \bar{\varepsilon}_0 \, \text{Re} \, \zeta_{qu}$

2) $10 < \text{Re} < 30$: $\zeta = \dfrac{33}{\text{Re}} \dfrac{1}{\bar{f}^2} + \bar{\varepsilon}_0 \, \text{Re} \, \zeta_{qu}$

3) $\text{Re} < 10$: $\zeta = \dfrac{33}{\text{Re}} \dfrac{1}{\bar{f}^2}$

where $\zeta_\phi = f_1(\text{Re}, F_0/F_1)$, see Diagram 4-19 (it should be kept in mind that $\bar{f} = F_{or}/F_0$ corresponds to F_0/F_1; $\bar{\varepsilon}_0 \, \text{Re} = f_2$ (Re), see the same graph; ζ_{qu} is determined as ζ at $\text{Re} > 10^4 - 10^5$, see Diagrams 3-12 and 3-13

Entrances into a tube with a screen at the inlet		Diagram 3-15
Entrance characteristics	Configuration	Resistance coefficient $\zeta \equiv \dfrac{\Delta p}{\rho w_0^2/2}$
Entrance with sharp inlet edge ($\delta_1/D_h = 0$)	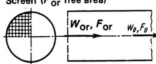	$\zeta \approx 1 + \zeta_{sc}$ where ζ_{sc} is determined as ζ for a screen from Diagram 3-6
Entrance with thickened inlet edge ($\delta_1/D_h > 0$)	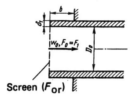	$\zeta = \zeta' + \zeta_{sc}$ where for ζ', see curves $\zeta = f(\delta_1/D_h, b/D_h)$ of Diagram 3-1; for ζ_{sc}, see above
Bellmouth (collector) entry	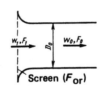	$\zeta = \zeta' + \dfrac{\zeta_{sc}}{n^2}$ where for ζ', see curves $\zeta = f(r/D_h)$ of Diagram 3-4; for ζ_{sc}, see above
Conical nozzle (collector)	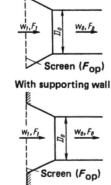	$\zeta = \zeta' + \dfrac{\zeta_{sc}}{n^2}$ where for ζ', see curves $\zeta = f(\alpha, l/D_h)$ on Diagrams 3-6 and 3-7, respectively; for ζ'_{sc}, see above

Entrance into a straight circular tube through the first side orifice; $Re = w_{or}b/\nu > 10^{4}$ [15]	Diagram 3-16

$$\zeta \equiv \frac{\Delta p}{\rho w_0^2/2} , \text{ see curves } \zeta = f(\overline{f})$$

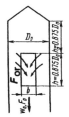

1. Single orifice

$$\overline{f} = \frac{bh}{\frac{\pi D_0^2}{4}}$$

2. Two orifices on opposite sides

$$\overline{f} = \frac{2bh}{\frac{\pi D_0^2}{4}}$$

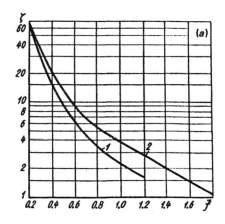

Values of ζ (graph a)

Number of orifices	$\overline{f}$						
	0.2	0.3	0.4	0.5	0.6	0.7	0.8
One (curve 1)	64.5	30.0	14.9	9.0	6.27	4.54	3.54
Two (curve 2)	65.5	36.5	17.0	12.0	8.75	6.85	5.50

Number of orifices	$\overline{f}$					
	0.9	1.0	1.2	1.4	1.6	1.8
One (curve 1)	2.70	2.28	1.60			
Two (curve 2)	4.54	3.84	2.76	2.01	1.40	1.10

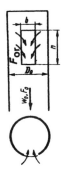

Entrance into a straight circular tube through the first side orifice; $\mathrm{Re} = w_{oc}b/\nu > 10^{4}$ [15]		Diagram 3-16

Values of ζ (graph b)

Curve	$\dfrac{b}{D_0}$	$\overline{f}$							
		0.1	0.2	0.3	0.4	0.5	0.6	0.7	0.8
1	0.13	335	850.	–	–	–	–	–	–
2	0.26	305	85.0	42.2	22.5	15.6	11.6	–	–
3	0.38	280	79.0	38.3	23.2	16.0	11.7	9.30	6.40
4	0.48	260	75.0	36.3	22.0	15.2	11.3	8.80	6.85
5	0.62	235	61.0	32.5	20.0	13.8	10.2	8.00	6.50
6	0.7	230	63.0	30.2	18.4	12.8	9.40	7.35	5.95

Curve	$\dfrac{b}{D_0}$	$\overline{f}$							
		0.9	1.0	1.1	1.2	1.3	1.4	1.5	1.6
1	0.13	–	–	–	–	–	–	–	–
2	0.26	–	–	–	–	–	–	–	–
3	0.38	5.40	–	–	–	–	–	–	–
4	0.48	4.20	3.40	3.80	–	–	–	–	–
5	0.62	4.00	3.30	2.82	2.50	2.30	2.15	2.05	–
6	0.7	4.85	2.95	2.50	2.22	2.02	1.83	1.70	1.56

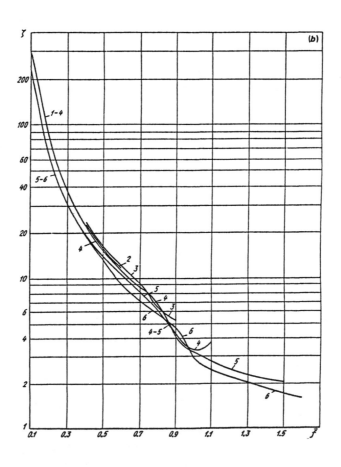

Intake shafts of rectangular cross section; side orifices with and without fixed louver grating[19]	Diagram 3-17

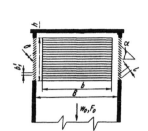
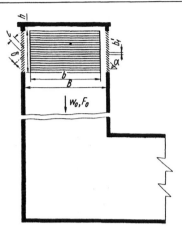

$$\frac{h}{B} = 0.5 \quad \overline{f}' = \frac{nbh}{F_0} = \frac{F_{gr}}{F_0}$$

Straight shafts

						Resistance coefficient $\zeta \equiv \dfrac{\Delta p}{\rho w_0^2/2}$	
No. of orifices	Layout of orifices Without louvers	With louvers	$\overline{f}'$	$\dfrac{b}{h}$	Without louvers	$\alpha = 30°$; $b_1'/h = 0.029$; $l/b_1' = 1.6$; $\delta/l_1' = 0.058$	$\alpha = 45°$; $b_1'/h = 0.024$; $l/b_1' = 1.4$; $\delta/b_1' = 0.07$
1			0.44	1.5	12.6	17.5	–
2			0.88	1.5	3.60	5.40	–
2			0.88	1.5	4.20	6.30	–
3			1.30	1.5	1.80	3.20	–
4			1.74	1.5	1.20	2.50	3.80
4			1.16	1.0	2.00	3.60	6.00
4			0.58	0.5	8.00	13.7	21.5

Intake shafts of rectangular cross section; side orifices with and without fixed louver grating[19]	Diagram 3-17

Shafts with bends

No. of orifices	Layout of orifices Without louvers	Layout of orifices With louvers	$\overline{f}'$	$\dfrac{b}{h}$	Resistance coefficient $\zeta \equiv \dfrac{\Delta p}{\rho w_0^2/2}$ Without louvers	$\alpha = 30°$; $b_1'/h = 0.029$; $l/b_1' = 1.6$; $\delta/b_1' = 0.058$	$\alpha = 45°$; $b_1'/h = 0.024$; $l/b_1' = 1.4$; $\delta/b_1' = 0.07$
1			0.44	1.5	14.0	18.6	–
1			0.44	1.5	16.0	19.0	–
1			0.44	1.5	16.7	20.0	–
2			0.88	1.5	4.50	6.50	–
2			0.88	1.5	5.20	7.00	–
2			0.88	1.5	5.30	7.20	–
3			0.88	1.5	5.30	7.50	–
3			1.30	1.5	2.60	3.90	–
3			1.30	1.5	3.00	4.50	–
3			1.30	1.5	3.40	5.10	–
4			1.74	1.5	2.70	4.00	5.60
4			1.16	1.0	3.10	4.70	6.90
4			0.58	0.5	9.00	14.4	22.0

Straight intake circular shafts; $Re = w_0 D_0/\nu > 10^{4}$ [28]		Diagram 3-18
Shaft characteristic	Schematic	Resistance coefficient

1. With a plane top	$2D_0$ δ_1, h D_0 w_0, F_0 **(a)**	
2. With a cone top	$2D_0$, $0.3D_0$ δ_1, h w_0, F_0 D_0 **(b)**	$\zeta \equiv \dfrac{\Delta p}{\rho w_0^2/2}$, see curves $\zeta = f\left(\dfrac{h}{D_0}\right)$
3. With a canopy top and sharp inlet edge	$2D_0$, $0.3D_0$ δ_1, h w_0, F_0 D_0 **(c)**	
4. With a canopy top and thickened inlet edge	$2D_0$, $0.3D_0$ δ_1, h w_0, F_0 D_0 **(d)**	
5. With a canopy top and a cone	$2D_0$, $0.3D_0$ δ_1, h w_0, F_0 D_0 **(e)**	
6. With a convergent entry and a canopy top	$2D_0$, $0.3D_0$ δ_1, $1.26D_0$ $15°$, D_0 w_0, F_0 D_0 **(f)**	

Values of ζ

Scheme	h/D_0										
	0.1	0.2	0.3	0.4	0.5	0.6	0.7	0.8	0.9	1.0	∞
1	–	4.40	2.15	1.78	1.58	1.35	1.23	1.13	1.10	1.06	1.06
2	–	48.0	6.40	2.72	1.73	1.47	1.26	1.16	1.07	1.06	1.06
3	2.63	1.83	1.53	1.39	1.31	1.19	1.15	1.08	1.07	1.06	1.06
4	2.13	1.30	0.95	0.84	0.75	0.70	0.65	0.63	0.60	0.60	0.60
5	2.90	1.90	1.59	1.41	1.33	1.25	1.15	1.10	1.07	1.06	1.06
6	1.32	0.77	0.60	0.48	0.41	0.30	0.29	0.28	0.25	0.25	0.25

Entrance into a straight channel through a fixed louver grating at $\bar{f} = F_{or}/F_{gr} = 0.1-0.9$	Diagram 3-19

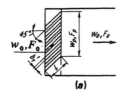

(a)

Inlet edges of fins cut vertically

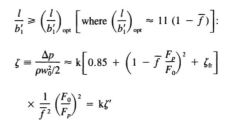

$$\frac{l}{b'_1} \geqslant \left(\frac{l}{b'_1}\right)_{opt} \left[\text{where } \left(\frac{l}{b'_1}\right)_{opt} \approx 11\,(1 - \bar{f})\right]:$$

$$\zeta \equiv \frac{\Delta p}{\rho w_0^2/2} \approx k\left[0.85 + \left(1 - \bar{f}\,\frac{F_p}{F_0}\right)^2 + \zeta_{fr}\right]$$

$$\times \frac{1}{\bar{f}^2}\left(\frac{F_0}{F_p}\right)^2 = k\zeta'$$

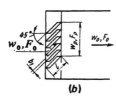

(b)

Inlet edges of fins cut horizontally

$$\frac{l}{b'} < \left(\frac{l}{b'_1}\right)_{opt}: \zeta \equiv \frac{\Delta p}{\rho w_0^2/2} \approx k\zeta' + \Delta\zeta$$

where $k = 1.0$ for scheme a: $k = 0.6$ for scheme b;

$$\Delta\zeta \approx 0.5\left[11\,(1 - f) - \frac{l}{b'_1}\right]; \zeta_{fr} = \lambda\frac{l}{b'_1};$$

for λ see Diagrams 2-1 through 2-6.

At $\dfrac{l}{b'_1} = \left(\dfrac{l}{b'_1}\right)_{opt}, \dfrac{F_{or}}{F_{gr}} = \dfrac{F_{or}}{F_0}$ and $\lambda = 0.064$

(at Re $= w_{or}b'_1/\nu \approx 10^3$); for values of ζ', see curve $\zeta' = f(\bar{f})$.

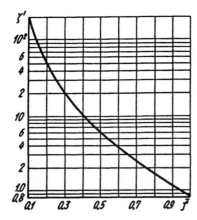

$\bar{f}$	0.1	0.2	0.3	0.4	0.5	0.6	0.7	0.8	0.9	1.0
ζ'	235	52.5	20.5	10.5	6.00	3.60	2.35	1.56	1.18	0.85

Entrance into a straight channel through stamped or cast and shaped perforated plates	Diagram 3-20

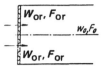

$$w_{or} = \frac{Q}{F_{or}}; \; F_{or} \text{ — clear area of the grid } \zeta \equiv \frac{\Delta p}{\rho w_0^2/2},$$

see curve $\zeta = f(\overline{f})$ of Diagram 3-12 (approximately)

Inlet pipes of axial stationary turbo-machines[10]	Diagram 3-21

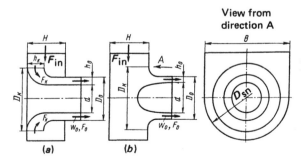

View from direction A

Converging annular collector (scheme a) formed by two curvilinear surfaces at $n_{ar} \geqslant 3.5$; $n_{col} \approx n_{ar}$; $\overline{D}_{sn} \geqslant 1.3$ (optimal parameters)

$$\zeta \equiv \frac{\Delta p}{\rho w_0^2/2} \approx 0.07$$

Annular collector (scheme b) formed by one curvilinear surface at $n_{ar} \geqslant 3.5$; $\overline{H} \geqslant 0.95$; $\overline{D}_{sn} \geqslant 1.15\text{--}1.25$ (optimal parameters)

$$\zeta \equiv \frac{\Delta p}{\rho w_0^2/2} \approx 0.08$$

$$n_{ar} = \frac{F_{in}}{F_0} \quad n_{col} = \frac{F_{col}}{F_0} = 2\frac{h_{col}}{h_0}\frac{D_{col}}{D_0(1+\overline{d})}$$

$$\overline{d} = \frac{d}{D_0} \quad \overline{D}_{sn} = \frac{D_{sn}}{D_0} \quad \overline{H} = \frac{H}{D_0}$$

Air-intake devices (intake pipes) (at velocities much below sonic ones)[11]

Diagram 3-22

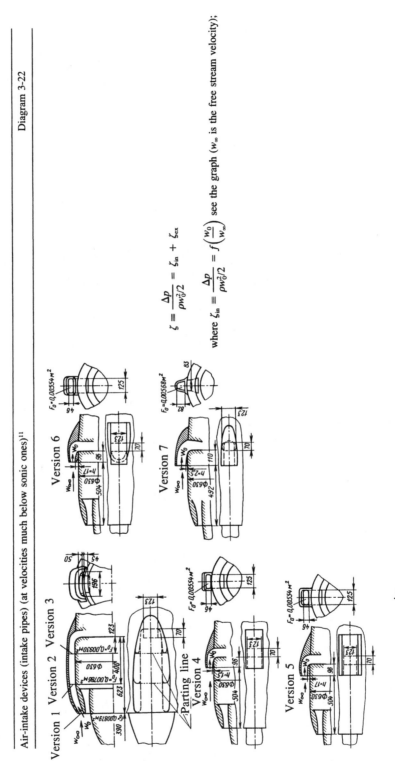

$$\zeta \equiv \frac{\Delta p}{\rho w_0^2/2} = \zeta_{in} + \zeta_{ex}$$

where $\zeta_{in} \equiv \frac{\Delta p}{\rho w_0^2/2} = f\left(\frac{w_0}{w_\infty}\right)$ see the graph (w_∞ is the free stream velocity);

$\zeta_{ex} \equiv \frac{\Delta p}{\rho w_0^2/2}$ is determined depending on the shape and geometric parameters of the entire air-intake device from the data of the Handbook.

Values of ζ_{in}

Version	w_0/w_∞									
	0.1	0.2	0.25	0.3	0.4	0.5	0.6	0.7	0.8	0.9
1	5.0	1.5	1.0	0.7	0.4	0.35	0.25	0.15	0.03	0.3
2	–	–	6.0	5.0	2.5	1.5	0.8	0.45	0.25	0.10
3	–	–	6.0	5.0	2.5	1.5	0.8	0.45	0.25	0.10
4	–	–	5.4	3.2	1.5	0.70	0.45	0.25	0.20	0.05
5	–	5.3	3.2	2.3	1.2	0.70	0.40	0.20	0.10	0.05
6	–	4.3	2.8	1.9	0.9	0.5	0.25	0.20	0.10	0.05
7	–	3.5	2.6	1.9	1.2	0.9	0.7	0.5	0.4	0.15

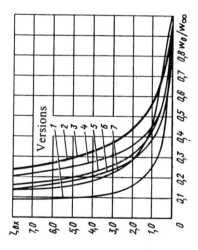

Inlet elements of axial fans[3,4,26]	Diagram 3-23

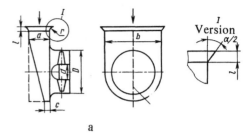

$$\zeta \equiv \frac{\Delta p}{\rho w_0^2/2}$$

z_{bl} is the number of blades of the fan wheel;

a

$$F_0 = \frac{\pi}{4}(D^2 - d^2); \quad w_0 = Q/F_0; \quad \bar{l} = l/D; \quad \bar{d} = d/D$$

Values of ζ of the elements
($d = 0.3–0.45$; $z_{bl} = 3–4$)

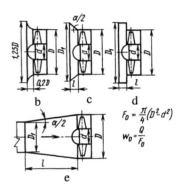

$$F_0 = \frac{\pi}{4}(D^2 - d^2)$$
$$w_0 = \frac{Q}{F_0}$$

	Operational conditions of the fan	
	Maximum full pressure	Maximum flow rate
Inlet element	P_{max}	Q_{max}
Inlet box (a):		
a = 0.75D; b = 2D;	0.15	0.07
$\bar{c} = 0.2D; l = 0$		
c = a	0.34	0.2
c = 0.2D; $\bar{l} = l/D = 0.1$	0.03	0.08
c = 0.DD; $0.1 < l \leq 0.3$	0.03	0.06
$\alpha = 40°$		
Confuser, cone (b, c):		
$\bar{l} = 0.1$	0.07	0.09
$\bar{l} = 0.2$	0	0.02
$\bar{l} = 0.3; \alpha = 60°$	0.03	0
$\bar{l} = 0.1; \alpha = 80°$	0.07	0.06
$l = 0.2; \alpha = 80°$	0.03	0.05
Step (d)		
$D_1/D = 1; \bar{l} = 0$	Flow separation	0.35
$D_1/D = 1.25; \bar{l} = 0.1$	0.07	0.15
$0.1 < \bar{l} \leq 0.3$	0.03	0.10
Diffuser (e):		
$\alpha = 8–12°; n_{ar} = 2$	0.12	0.15

Note: The fan is of type K-121.

Inlet elements of centrifugal fans[3,4,25,33]	Diagram 3-24

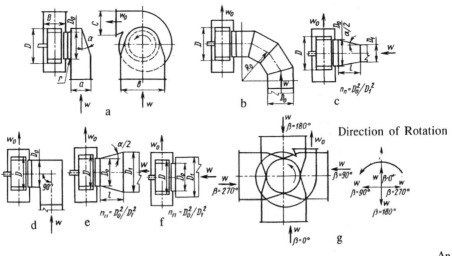

η^f is the fan efficiency

$F_0' = B \cdot C$

$w_0 = Q/F_0'$

$F_k = ab; \quad F_0 = \dfrac{\pi}{4} D_0^2$

$\bar{l} = l/D_0$

$$\zeta \equiv \frac{\Delta p}{\rho w_0^2/2}$$

Values of ζ of the elements (the blades of the fan are bent backward)

Inlet element	Angle of element installation β^0	$\eta^f \geq \eta^f_{max}$	$Q = Q_n$ $\eta^f = \eta^f_{max}$	$\eta^f \geq 0.9\, \eta^f_{max}$	Type of fan
Inlet box (a):					
$F_k/F_0 = 1.7$	0	0.3	0.3	0.3	Ts4-76
$b/a = 2.3; \alpha = 12°$					
$F_k/F_0 = 1.2$	90	0.5	0.5	0.5	
$b/a = 2.3; \alpha = 12°$	180	0.6	0.6	0.7	
	270	0.5	0.5	0.3	
$F_k/F_0 = 1-1.5$	0–270	0.07	0.7	0.7	
$b/a = 2.3; \alpha = 0°$					
Composed elbow (b):	0–270	0.15	0.15	0.15	Ts4-70
$R/D_0 = 1.5$					
Diffuser (c):					
$\bar{l} = 0.8; n_{ar} = 1.5$	–	0.5	0.5	0.5	Ts4-76
$\bar{l} = 0.8; n_{ar} = 2$	–	0.5	0.8	0.8	
$\bar{l} = 1.4; n_{ar} = 1.5$	–	0.2	0.3	0.3	
$\bar{l} = 1.4; n_{ar} = 2$	–	0.2	0.3	0.65	
Simple elbow (d):	0–270	1.0	1.0	1.0	Ts4-70
Conical confuser (e):					
$\bar{l} = 1; n_{ar} = 0.67$	–	0.7	0.3	0.2	Ts4-76
$\bar{l} = 1.2; n_{ar} = 0.5$	–	0.8	0.4	0.3	
$\bar{l} = 1.4; n_{ar} = 0.4$	–	0.5	0.1	0.1	

Operational conditions*
$Q < Q_n$ nominal $Q > Q_n$

Inlet elements of centrifugal fans[3,4,25,33]	Diagram 3-24

Values of ζ of the elements (the blades of the fan are bent forward)

Inlet element	Angle of element installation β^0	$Q < Q_n$ nominal $Q > Q_n$ $\eta^f \geqslant 0.9\ \eta^f_{max}$	$Q = Q_n$ $\eta^f = \eta^f_{max}$	$\eta^f > 0.9\ \eta^f_{max}$	Type of fan
Inlet box (a):					
$F_k/F_0 = 1.3$	0	0.3	0.3	0.35	Ts9-55
$b/a = 2.4;\ \alpha = 12°$	180	0.45	0.45	0.5	
	270	0.2	0.2	0.3	
$F_k/F_0 = 1.1;$					
$b/a = 2.3;\ \alpha = 12°$	0	0.5	0.5	0.5	Ts9-55
$F_k/F_0 = 1.2{-}1.8$	0–270	0.85	0.85	0.85	
$b/a = 2.3;\ \alpha = 0°$					
Composed elbow (b):					
$R \geqslant 1.5\ D_0$	0	0.3	0.3	0.4	
	90	0.4	0.4	0.4	
	180	0.5	0.5	0.4	
	270	0.3	0.3	0.35	
Diffusor (c):					
$\bar{l} = 0.5;\ n_{ar} = 1.5$	–	0	0.2	0.2	
$\bar{l} = 0.5;\ n_{ar} = 2.0$	–	0.5	0.8	0.7	
$\bar{l} = 0.8;\ n_{ar} = 1.5$	–	0.1	0.15	0.1	
$\bar{l} = 0.8;\ n_{ar} = 2.0$	–	0.3	0.3	0.2	Ts14-46
$\bar{l} = 0.4;\ n_{ar} = 1.5$	–	0.2	0.2	0.15	
$\bar{l} = 0.4;\ n_{ar} = 2.0$	–	0.4	0.5	0.4	
Simple elbow (d):	0–270	2.0	2.0	2.0	Ts9-55
Conical confuser (e)					
$\bar{l} = 1.5$	–	0	0	0	
$n_{ar} = 0.4{-}0.7$					
Step (eddy collector) (f)					
$n_{ar} \geqslant 0.7$	–	0	0	0	Ts14-16

*The operational conditions of the fan that correspond to the maximum efficiency η^f_{max} are called nominal, with the flow rate Q_n. The working region of the fan characteristic is that for which $\eta^f \geqslant 0.9\ \eta^f_{max}$.

REFERENCES

1. Averiyanov, A. G., et al., *Ventilation of Shops of Shipbuilding Works,* Sudostrosnic Press, Moscow, 1969, 268 p.
2. Altshul, A. D., *Hydraulic Resistances,* Nedra Press, Moscow, 1970, 216 p.
3. Bychokova, L. A., Entrance elements of installations with axial fans, *Vodosnabzh. Sanit. Tekh.,* no. 5, 29–31, 1977.
4. Bychkova, L. A., *Recommendations for Calculating the Hydraulic Resistances of the Complicated Elements of Ventilation Systems,* Moscow, 1981, 32 p.
5. Ginevskiy, A. S., Eds., *Introduction into the Aerohydrodynamics of the Container Pipe-line Transport,* Moscow, 1986, 232 p.
6. Zakharov, A. M., Bulygin, P. A., Raikin, L. I., et al., *Air-Intakes and Gas-Dischargers of Fast-Gas-Turbine Ships,* Leningrad, 1977, 207. p.
7. Gretsov, N. A., Hydraylic resistances and a rational shape of rectiaxial converging tubes with a baffle before the inlet, *Tr. Mosk. Skh. Akad.,* vyp. 87, 37–42, 1963.
8. Davydov, A. P., Investigation of the operation of the suction orifice with an inner screen, in *Investigations in the Fields of Heating, Ventilation and Air Conditioning* (Sb. Tr. LISI), no. 110, 27–34, 1975.
9. Dzyadzio, A. M., *Pneumatic Transport in Grain-Processing Factories,* Zagotizdat, Moscow, 1961, 250 p.
10. Dovzhik, S. A. and Kartavenko, V. M., Experimental investigation of inlet nozzles of axial stationary turbomachines, *Prom. Aerodin.,* vyp. 29, 56–73, Mashinostr. Press, 1973.
11. Idelchik, I. E., The aerodynamics of the intake branch pipes of aircraft engines, *Tekhn. Vozdush. Flota,* nos. 5–6, 1–10, 28, 1944.
12. Idelchik, I., E., Hydraulic resistance during flow entrance in channels and passage through orifices, *Prom. Aerodin.,* no. 2, 27–57, BNT, NKAP, 1944.
13. Idelchik, I. E., *Hydraulic Resistances (Physical and Mechanical Fundamentals),* Gosenergoizdat, Moscow, 1954, 316 p.
14. Idelchik, I. E., Determination of the resistance coefficients in discharge through orifices, *Gidrotekh. Stroit.,* no. 5, 31–36, 1953.
15. Idelchik, I. E., *Handbook of Hydraulic Resistances (Local Resistance Coefficients and Friction Resistances),* Gosenergoizdat, Moscow, 1960, 464 p.
16. Idelchik, I. E., Account for the effect of viscosity on the hydraulic resistance of diaphragms and grids, *Teploenergetika,* no. 9, 75–80, 1960.
17. Levin, B. M., Local inlet losses during ground suction under water, *Tr. Mosk. Inst. Inzh. Zheleznodorozhn. Transp.,* vyp. 122, 281–312, 1959.
18. Nosova, M. M., Resistance of inlet and exit bellmouths with baffles, *Prom. Aerodin.,* no. 7, 95–100, Oborongiz, Moscow, 1956.
19. Nosova, M. M. and Tarasov, N. F., Resistance of intake ventilating shafts, *Prom. Aerodin.,* no. 12, 197–215, Oboronogiz, Moscow, 1959.
20. Nosova, M. M. and Barnakova, T. S., Resistance of inlet and exit orifices in the presence of the passing stream, *Prom. Aerodin.,* no. 15, 20–37, Oborongiz, Moscow, 1959.
21. Oslyansky, Ya. L., Pressure head losses in the intake pipe of a dredger during suction of a water-ground mixture, *Tr. Leningr. Inst. Vodn. Transp.,* vyp. 119, 135–142, 1968.
22. Staroverov, I. G., Ed., *Handbook for a Designer of Industrial, Living and Communal Buildings and Structures,* Stroiizdat, Moscow, 1969, 536 p.
23. Stemenko, V. A., Study of the resistance coefficients of inlet boxes of fans of the kinematics of air flow in them, *Sb. Tr. Inst. Gorn. Mekh. Tekhn. Kibern. M.M. Fyodorova,* no. 17, 32–43, 1967.
24. Stepanov, P. M., Ovcharenko, I. Kh., and Skobeltsyn, Yu. A., *Handbook of Hydraulics for Land Reclaimers,* Moscow, 1984, 207 p.
25. Steshenko, V. A. and Pak, V. V., Shaping of the inlet boxes of centrifugal double — suction gans, *Vopr. Gorn. Mekh.,* no. 17, 43–47, 1967.
26. Surnov, N. V., Inlet devices of axial fans, *Prom. Aerodinam.,* vyp. 9, 28–34, 1957.
27. Temnov, V. K., Coefficient of the hydraulic resistance of a smooth entrance during turbulent fluid flow, *Izv. VUZov, Energ.,* no. 4, 89–93, 1963.
28. Khanzhonkov, V. I., Resistance of inflow and outflow shafts, *Prom. Aerodin.,* no. 3, 210–214, 1947.
29. Khanzhonkov, V. I., Aerodynamic characteristics of collectors, *Prom. Aerodin.,* no. 4, 45–62, 1953.
30. Khanzhonkov, V. I., Reduction of the aerodynamic resistance of orifices by means of annular fins and recesses, *Prom. Aerodin.,* no. 4, 45–62, 1953.
31. Khanzhonkov, V. I. and Davydenko, N. I., Resistance of side orifices of the terminal section of a pipeline, *Prom. Aerodin.,* no. 15, 38–46, Oborongiz, Moscow, 1959.

32. Shepelev, I. A. and Tyaglo, I. G., Suction patterns in the vicinity of outflow orifices (based on reported data), in *Mestnaya Vytyazhn. Ventilyatsiya*, pp. 81–90, 1969.

33. Bruk, A. D., Matikashvili, T. I., Nevelson, M. I., et al., *Centrifugal Fans*, Moscow, 1975, 415 p.

34. Ashino, I., On the theory of the additional loss at the pipe entrance in viscous fluid. 1st rept. On the influence of rounded entrance, *Bull. JSME*, vol. 14, no. 45, 463–468, 1969.

35. Ashino, J., On the theory of the additional loss at the pipe entrance in viscous fluid. 2nd rept. When an entrance is tapered type, *Bull. JSME*, vol. 12, no. 51, 522–529, 1969.

36. Basavarajaiah, B. S., Exit loss in a sharp edged pipe, *J. Inst. Eng. (India) Civ. Eng.*, Vol. 43, no. 11, part 6, 549–563, 1963.

37. Bevier, C. W., Resistance of wooden louvers to fluid flow, *Heating, Piping and Air Conditioning*, pp. 35–43, May 1955.

38. Bossel, H. H., Computation of axisymmetric contractions, *AIAA J.*, vol. 7. no. 10, 2017–2020, 1969.

39. Campbell, W. D. and Slattery, I. C., Flow in the entrance of a tube, *Trans. ASME*, vol. D85, no. 1, 41–45, Discuss. pp. 45–46, 1963.

40. Cobb, P. R., Pressure loss of air flowing through 45-degree wooden louvers, *Heating, Piping and Air Conditioning*, pp. 35–43, December 1953.

41. Kubiček, L., Ssaci nástavce, *Strojirehstvi*, no. 4, 427–433, 1954.

42. Gibbings, J. C., The throat profile for contracting ducts containing incompressible irrotational flows, *Int. J. Mech. Sci.*, vol. 11, no. 3, 29–301, 1969.

43. Hebans, G. G., Crest losses for two-way drop inlet, *J. Hydraul. Div. Proc. Am. Soc. Civ. Eng.*, vol. 95, no. 3, 919–940, 1969.

44. Lundgren, T. S., Sparrow, E. N., and Starr, J., Pressure drop due to the entrance region in ducts of arbitrary cross section, *Trans. ASME*, vol. D86, no. 3, 620–626, 1964.

45. Oosthuizen, P. H., On the loss coefficient for a sharp-edged pipe entrance, *Bull. Mech. Eng. Educ.*, vol. 7, no. 2, 157–159, 1968.

46. Rimberg, D., Pressure drop across sharp-end capillary tubes, *Ind. Eng. Chem. Fundam.*, vol. 6, no. 4, 599–603, 1967.

47. Unger, J., Strömung in zylindrischen Komälen mit Versperrungen bei holen Reynolds-zahlen, *Forsch. Ingenieurwes.*, Bd. 45, N 3, S. 69–100, 1979.

48. Webb, A., Head loss of a sudden expansion, *Int. J. Mech. Eng.*, vol. 8, no. 4, 173–176, 1980.

49. Weisbach, G., *Lehrbuch der Ingenieur und Maschinenmechanik*, 11 Aufl., 1850, 320 p.

RESISTANCE TO FLOW THROUGH ORIFICES WITH SUDDEN CHANGE IN VELOCITY AND FLOW AREA
Resistance Coefficients of Sections with Sudden Expansion, Sudden Contraction, Orifices, Diaphragms, and Apertures

4-1 EXPLANATIONS AND PRACTICAL RECOMMENDATIONS

1. An abrupt enlargement of a tube (channel) cross-sectional area gives rise to so-called shock losses. In the case of uniform velocity distribution over the cross section of the smaller upstream channel in turbulent flow ($\mathrm{Re} = w_0 D_h/\nu > 10^4$), the local resistance coefficient of the "shock" depends only on the cross-sectional area ratio F_0/F_2 (measure of expansion $n = F_2/F_0$) and is calculated from the Borda-Carnot formula as

$$\zeta_{\text{loc}} \equiv \frac{\Delta p}{\rho w_0^2/2} = \left(1 - \frac{F_0}{F_2}\right)^2 \tag{4-1}$$

The total resistance coefficient of the section with an abrupt expansion* is

$$\zeta \equiv \frac{\Delta p}{\rho w_0^2/2} = \zeta_{\text{loc}} + \zeta_{\text{fr}} = \zeta_{\text{loc}} + \frac{\zeta_{\text{fr}}'}{n_{\text{ar}}^2} \tag{4-2}$$

where

$$\zeta_{\text{fr}}' \equiv \frac{\Delta p_{\text{fr}}}{\rho w_2^2/2} = \lambda \frac{l_2}{D_{2h}}$$

2. In an abruptly expanded section a jet is formed which is separated from the remaining medium by a bounding surface that disintegrates into strong vortices (Figure 4-1). The length

---

*The additional coefficient ζ_{fr} is incorporated if it was disregarded when friction losses throughout the piping system were determined.

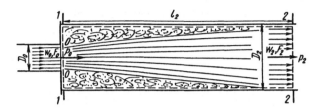

Figure 4-1 Schematic diagram of flow at an abrupt expansion.

l_2 of the section over which the vortices develop and gradually disappear while the flow completely speads over the cross section ranges from 8 to $12D_{2h}$ (D_{2h} is the hydraulic diameter of the larger section). The shock losses at abrupt expansion are associated with this formation of vortices over the length l_2.

3. When an abrupt expansion of the tube cross section occurs only in one plane (Figure 4-2), the shock losses decrease with an increase in the aspect ratio B/H (B is the width of the larger cross section; H is the constant height of the channel); in this case the local resistance coefficient is

$$\zeta_{loc} = k_1 \left(1 - \frac{F_0}{F_2} \right)^2$$

where $k_1 \leq 1$ is the correction factor which depends on the aspect ratio B/H.

4. For practical conditions, the velocity distribution over the conduit length upstream of an abrupt expansion is, as a rule, never uniform. This substantially contributes to the losses as compared with those predicted by Equation (4-1).

In order to calculate the local resistance coefficient of a shock for a flow with nonuniform velocity distribution at large Re, it is necessary to use a generalized formula that allows for this nonuniformity, provided the velocity distribution over the channel cross section[13,15]

$$\zeta_{loc} = \frac{\Delta p}{\rho w_0^2/2} = \frac{1}{n_{ar}^2} + N - 2\frac{M}{n_{ar}} \qquad (4\text{-}3)$$

The total resistance coefficient is calculated from a formula similar to Equation (4-2).

In Equation (4-3) $M = (1/F_0)\int_{F_0}(/w_0)^2 \, dF$ is the flow momentum coefficient (the Boussinesq coefficient) at the exit from the smaller channel into the larger one; $N = (1/F_0)\int_{F_0}(w/w_0)^3 \, dF$ is the coefficient of the kinetic energy of the flow (the Coriolis coefficient) in the same section.

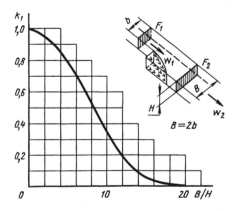

Figure 4-2 Dependence of k_1 on B/H.

An approximation can be made that $N \approx 3M - 2$. The approximation is more correct the nearer M and N are to unity.

The last expression leads to the following approximate formula for determining the local resistance coefficient

$$\zeta_{loc} = \frac{\Delta p}{\rho w_0^2/2} \approx N\left(1 - \frac{2}{3n_{ar}}\right) + \frac{1}{n_{ar}^2} - \frac{4}{3n_{ar}}$$

5. If the velocity distribution over the cross section is known, the coefficients M and N can be easily calculated. However, if this distribution is unknown, it must be determined experimentally. Then the coefficients M and N can be determined by graphic integration from the curves obtained for the velocity distribution.

6. In diffusers with divergence angles up to $\alpha = 8$–$10°$ and over long straight sections of constant cross section with a developed turbulent velocity profile (see Section 1-3) the distribution of velocities over the cross section is close to the power function law

$$\frac{w}{w_{max}} = \left(1 - \frac{y}{R_0}\right)^{1/m}$$

where w and w_{max} are the velocity at the given point and the maximum velocity over the cross section, respectively, m/s; R_0 is the section radius, m; y is the distance from the tube axis to the given point, m; and m is an exponent which can vary from 1 to ∞.

7. At $m = 1$, the velocity profile acquires the shape of a triangle (Figure 4-3). At $m = 8$, it takes on the shape of a rectangle, that is, the velocity distribution over the section is completely uniform. The velocity profile is already amost rectangular at $m = 8$–10. This value of m can be used for long straight sections with turbulent flow. The values $m = 2$–6 can be used for long diffusers ($n_1 = F_1/F_0 > 2$):

at $\alpha = 2°$ $m \approx 6$ at $\alpha = 6°$ $m \approx 3$
at $\alpha = 4°$ $m \approx 4$ at $\alpha = 8°$ $m \approx 2$

8. With the power-law distribution, the values of M and N in Equation (4-3) can be calculated from the author's formulas[12,13]

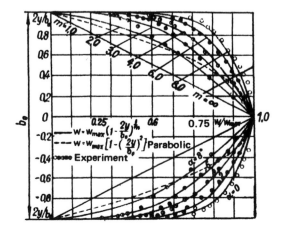

Figure 4-3 Velocity distribution in plane diffusers with divergence angles up to 8° and comparison with the power law.

For circular and square tubes:

$$M = \frac{(2m + 1)^2 (m + 1)}{4m^2 (m + 2)}$$

$$N = \frac{(2m + 1)^3 (m + 1)^3}{4m^4 (2m + 3)(m + 3)}$$

for a rectangular tube or diffuser (with the aspect ratio of the rectangular cross section $a_0/b_0 = 0.3$–3.0)

$$M = \frac{(m + 1)^2}{m(m + 2)}$$

$$N = \frac{(m + 1)^3}{m^2(m + 3)}$$

9. Over long straight sections of tubes and channels (usually at a distance over $10D_h$ from the inlet) for laminar flow, a parabolic velocity profile is developed

$$\frac{w}{w_{max}} = 1 - \left(\frac{y}{R_0}\right)^2$$

In this case, for a circular or square tube $M = 1.33$ and $N = 2$, and for a plane (rectangular) tube $M = 1.2$ and $N = 1.55$.

10. In tubes and channels directly downstream of perforated plates, in elbows behind guide vanes, and in other similar cases, the velocity profile resembles a trigonometric function (Figure 4-4), which for a plane channel is calculated from the author's formula[13,15]

$$\frac{w}{w_{max}} = 1 + \frac{\Delta w}{w_0} \sin 2k_1 \pi \frac{2y}{b_0}$$

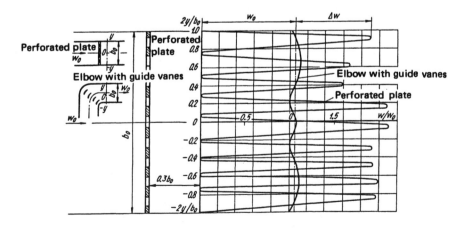

Figure 4-4 Velocity distribution resembling a sinusoidal function (downstream of perforated plates and guide vanes).[15]

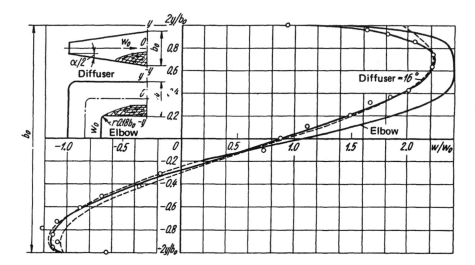

Figure 4-5 Asymmetric velocity distribution downstream of an elbow and in a diffuser with the divergence angle at which flow separation takes place.[15]

where b_0 is the width of the plane channel, m; Δw is the departure of velocity at the given point of the narrow channel cross section from the section-average velocity w_0, m/s; and k is an integer.

In this case

$$M = 1 + \frac{1}{2}\left(\frac{\Delta w}{w_0}\right)^2 \quad N = 1 + \frac{3}{2}\left(\frac{\Delta w}{w_0}\right)^2$$

11. A nonsymmetrical velocity field (Figure 4-5) is established downstream of diffusers with divergence angles at which flow separation occurs ($\alpha \geq 14°$), elbows, branches, and so on. In particular, in plane diffusers with divergence angles $\alpha = 15$–$20°$ and in straight elbows ($\delta = 90°$), the velocity distribution is governed by:[13,15]

$$\frac{w}{w_0} = 0.585 + 1.64 \sin\left(0.2 + 1.95\frac{2y}{b_0}\right)$$

In this case $M = 1.87$ and $N = 3.7$

12. When a nonuniform velocity field develops in a tube (channel) of constant cross section ($n = 1$), subsequent equalization of the flow is also accompanied by irreversible pressure losses (losses for flow deformation), which are calculated by a formula obtainable from Equations (4-2) and (4-3):

$$\zeta \equiv \frac{\Delta p}{\rho w_0^2/2} = 1 + N - 2M + \zeta_{fr} \tag{4-4}$$

or accordingly from

$$\zeta \equiv \frac{\Delta p}{\rho w_0^2/2} \approx \frac{1}{3}(N - 1) + \zeta_{fr}$$

where M and N are determined in accordance with the nonuniformity pattern obtained. These losses are taken into account only in the case when they were disregarded during determination of the local resistance of fittings and obstructions which resulted in a nonuniform velocity distribution over the straight section.

13. The coefficients M and N for the inlet section of the ejector mixing chamber, when the "main"* portion of the free jet enters it, (Figure 4-6) are calculated from the author's formulas[13,15]

$$ M = \frac{1}{\bar{q}^2} \frac{F_2}{F_0} \qquad N = \frac{1}{\bar{q}^3} \left(\frac{F_2}{F_0}\right)^2 \bar{e} $$

where F_2/F_0 is the area ratio of the given free jet (mixing chamber) section to the inlet jet (inlet nozzle) section; $\bar{q} = Q/Q_0$ is the dimensionless flow rate through the given section, that is, the ratio between the flow rate of the medium passing through the tube (mixing chamber) and the initital flow rate of the jet (at the exit from the inlet nozzle); $\bar{e} = E/E_0$ is the dimensionless kinetic energy of the jet at the given cross section, that is, the ratio between the energy of the jet at the entrance to the tube (mixing chamber) and the initial energy of the jet.

The values of F_2/F_0, F_j/F_0, $\bar{q}$, and $\bar{e}$ depend on the relative length of the free jet s/D_h and are determined from the corresponding curves of Diagrams 11-24 and 11-25

14. The resistance of the section with an abrupt expansion can be substantially reduced by installing baffles (Figure 4-7a). When the baffles are correctly installed,** the losses are reduced by 35–40%, so that the local resistance coefficient of such a section can be approximated from

$$ \zeta_{loc} \equiv \frac{\Delta p_{loc}}{\rho w_0^2/2} \approx 0.6 \, \zeta'_{loc} $$

where ζ'_{loc} is the resistance coefficient of the section with an abrupt expansion without baffles, which is determined as ζ from the data given in Diagram 4-1.

15. A substantial decrease in the resistance of the section with an abrupt expansion is also attainable by arranging "pockets" immediately downstream of the narrow cross section (Figure 4-7b) which favor the formation of a steady recirculation ring (for circular tubes) or two steady vortices (for a plane channel) which act like pumps.[44]

16. Pressure losses over the section with an abrupt expansion can be reduced substantially also by disintegration of vortices by means of transverse partitions (Figure 4-8).[21] The upper edges of these partitions should be located at the level of the upper boundary of the recirculation zone and must not extend into the active flow. Obviously, lateral fins also decrease the intensity of the reverse flow in the channel and replace the unsteady vortices with steady ones.[21]

17. When the gas flow velocity in the section b-b (Figure 4-9) is close to the speed of sound and remains subsonic over the jet section between cross sections c-c and n-n, then[7] the shock losses can be determined with a sufficient accuracy from the above-given formulas for an incompressible fluid (in the case of the relative (reduced) velocity $\lambda_{ex} = w/a_{cr} \leqslant$ 0.75 the error is practically equal to zero; at $\lambda_{ex} = 1$, the error is 8%).

18. In the general case, a stepwise channel with a flow can have a supersonic nozzle at the inlet and then the geometric shape of the channel will be characterized by the dimensions of three sections: by the area of the critical section F_{cr}, by the area of nozzle cross section

---

*The "main" portion of a free jet is defined in Chapter 11.

**The general rules to be followed when installing the baffles are given in Chapter 5 (paragraph 65).

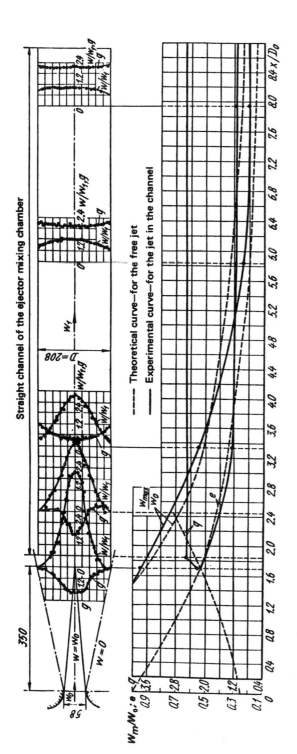

Figure 4-6 Velocity distribution over the main section of the free jet and after its entrance into the mixing chamber of the ejector: (dashed lines) a theoretical curve for the free jet; (solid lines) experimental curve for the jet in the channel.[12] $g = (p - p_a)/(\rho w_1^2/2)$

Figure 4-7 Sections with abrupt expansions: (a) with baffles; (b) with "pockets".

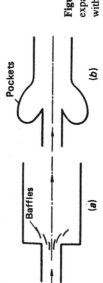

Figure 4-8 Schematic of the section with abrupt expansion and transverse barriers.

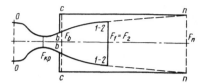

Figure 4-9 Schematic diagram of a step diffuser (with an abrupt expansion of the cross-sectional area).

at the exit F_{ex}, and by the area of the cross section of a cylindrical channel F_{tot}. In the specific case, $F_{cr} = F_{ex}$ and the supersonic nozzle is absent.

19. If in any cross section of the jet over the section c-n the jet velocity is higher than the speed of sound, then in this case compression shock losses should be taken into account. Thus, the total pressure losses are composed of the straight compression shock losses and shock losses (according to Borda-Carnot) originating when a subsonic jet expands from section 2-2 to section n-n.[7]

20. The relative losses of total pressure in a stepwise channel can be determined as

$$\frac{\Delta p_{tot}}{p^*} = 1 - \sigma$$

where σ is the ratio of total pressures in cross sections n-n and 0-0:

$$\sigma = \frac{p^*_{tot}}{p^*_0} \approx \frac{p_{tot}}{p^*_0} + \frac{\rho_{tot} w^2_{tot}}{2p^*_0}$$

or after corresponding transformations

$$\sigma = \frac{p_{tot}}{p^*_0} + \frac{k}{2}\left(\frac{2}{k+1}\right)^{(k+1)/k}\left(\frac{F_{cr}}{F_{tot}}\right)^2 \times \frac{1}{\lambda_1^2}\left(1 - \frac{k-1}{k+1}\lambda_1^2\right)^{1/(k-1)} \tag{4-5}$$

where $\lambda_1 = w_1/a_{cr}$ is the reduced velocity in section 1-1; it is determined from the relation

$$\frac{p_{tot}}{p^*_0} = \left(\lambda_1^2 - \frac{k-1}{k+1}\right)\left(1 - \frac{k-1}{k+1}\lambda_1^2\right)^{1/(k-1)} + \frac{km}{\lambda_1}\left(\frac{k+1}{2}\right)^{k/(k-1)}$$

$$\times \left[1 - \frac{m}{\lambda_1}\left(\frac{k+1}{2}\right)^{1/(k-1)}\left(1 - \frac{k-1}{k+1}\lambda_1^2\right)^{1/(1-k)}\right] \tag{4-6}$$

where $m = F_{cr}/F_{tot}$.

For air ($k = 1.41$)

$$\sigma = \frac{p_{tot}}{p^*_0} + 0.2344\frac{m^2}{\lambda_1^2\left(1 - \frac{1}{6}\lambda_1^2\right)^{2.5}}$$

and Equation (4-6) acquires the form

$$\frac{p_{tot}}{p^*_0} = \left(\lambda_1^2 - \frac{1}{6}\right)\left(1 - \frac{\lambda_1^2}{6}\right)^{2.5} + 0.7396\frac{m}{\lambda_1}\times\left[1 - \frac{m}{1.5774\left(1 - \frac{1}{6}\lambda_1^2\right)^{2.5}\lambda_1}\right]$$

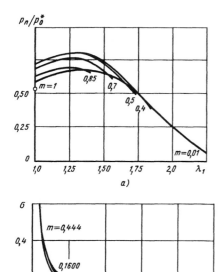

Figure 4-10 Dependence of the pressure ratios p_{tot}/p_0^* on $\lambda_1(a)$ and of the pressure recovery coefficient σ on p_0^*/p_{tot} (b).[7]

21. The dependence of p_{tot}/p_0^* on λ_1 and m at $k = 1.41$ is presented in Figure 4-10a and the relation $\sigma = f(p_0^*/p_{tot}, m)$ in Figure 4-10b.

(At small values of λ_1 for the given values of p_{tot}/p_0^* and m, two values of λ_1 are obtained. However, as σ weakly depends on λ_1 at small values of λ_1, the choice of λ_1 virtually does not influence the value of σ.[7]

The above-given formulas apply for the values $1 \leqslant \lambda_1 \leqslant \lambda_{lim}$, where λ_{lim} corresponds to the full expansion of the supersonic jet up to $F_1 = F_{tot}$.

22. When the cross section abruptly contracts, the phenomenon is basically similar to that observed when shock losses occur during an abrupt expansion. But now such losses occur mainly when the jet, compressed during the entry from a broad channel into a narrow one (section c-c, Figure 4-11), expands until it fills the entire section of the narrow channel (section 0-0).

23. The coefficient of local resistance to an abrupt contraction at large Reynolds numbers ($Re > 10^4$) can be approximately determined from the author's formula[12,13]

$$\zeta_{loc} = \frac{\Delta p_{loc}}{(\rho w_0^2/2)} = 0.5\left(1 - \frac{F_0}{F_1}\right)$$

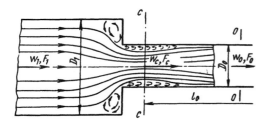

Figure 4-11 Schematic diagram of flow with an abrupt contraction of the cross-sectional area.

or, more exactly, from the formula which the author derived by processing the experimental results obtained by other research workers

$$\zeta_{loc} = \frac{\Delta p_{loc}}{(\rho w_0^2/2)} = 0.5\left(1 - \frac{F_0}{F_1}\right)^{3/4}$$

In this case, the total resistance coefficient is

$$\zeta \equiv \frac{\Delta p}{\rho w_0^2/2} = \zeta_{loc} + \zeta'_{fr}$$

where

$$\zeta'_{fr} \equiv \frac{\Delta p_{fr}}{\rho w_0^2/2} = \lambda \frac{l_0}{D_{0h}}$$

(l_0 is the length of the straight section downstream of the contraction).

24. The resistance of the contracting section can be substantially reduced by arranging a smooth transition from a wide section to the narrow one with the aid of a nozzle (collector) with curvilinear or rectilinear boundaries (see Diagram 4-9). The author recommends determining the local resistance coefficient of such a contracting section at Re $> 10^4$ from the formula*:

$$\zeta_{loc} \equiv \frac{\Delta p_{loc}}{(\rho w_0^2/2)} = \zeta'\left(1 - \frac{F_0}{F_1}\right)^{3/4}$$

where ζ' is the coefficient which depends on the shape of the inlet edge of the narrow channel mounted flush with the wall (see Diagrams 3-1, 3-4, and 3-7).

25. In the general case of the flow passing from one volume into another through an opening in the wall, the following phenomena are observed and are illustrated in Figure 4-12. The flow passes from channel 1, located before the partition A with an opening of diameter D_0, into channel 2, located behind the partition. The cross sections of both channels may be larger than, or equal to, the cross section of the opening. Flow passage through the opening is accompanied by distortion of the trajectories of particles with the result that they continue their motion by inertia toward the axis of the opening. This reduces the initial area of the jet cross section F_1 until the area F_c (section c-c) is smaller than the area of the cross section of the opening F_0. Starting with section c-c, the trajectories of the moving particles are straightened and thereafter an abrupt jet expansion takes place.

26. In the general case the resistance coefficient of the flow passage through an opening with sharp edges in the wall ($l/D_h = 0$, Figure 4-12a) is calculated for the self-similar (quadratic) flow region (Re $= w_0 D_0/\nu \geq 10^5$) by the author's refined formula:

$$\zeta \equiv \frac{\Delta p}{\rho w_0^2/2} = \left[1 + 0.707\sqrt{\left(1 - \frac{F_0}{F_1}\right)^{3/4}} - \frac{F_0}{F_2}\right]^2$$

$$= \left[0.707\left(1 - \frac{F_0}{F_1}\right)^{0.375} + \left(1 - \frac{F_0}{F_2}\right)\right]^2 \tag{4-7}$$

*Equation (7-25) recommended in Reference 3 gives close agreement with experiment at large values of F_0/F_1 and considerable discrepancy (up to 20%) at low values of F_0/F_1.

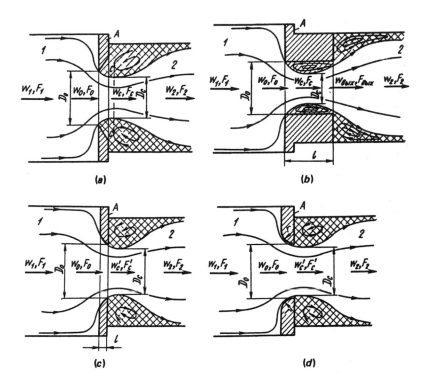

Figure 4-12 Flow passage through an orifice in the wall from one volume into another: (*a*) sharp-edged orifice ($l/D_h \approx 0$); (*b*) orifice with thick edges ($l/D_h > 0$); (*c*) orifice with edges beveled in the flow direction; (*d*) orifice with edges rounded in the flow direction.

27. Thickening (Figure 4-12*b*), beveling (Figure 4-12*c*), or rounding (Figure 4-12*d*) of the orifice edges reduces the effect of the jet contraction in the opening (increases the jet contraction coefficient ε), that is, decreases the jet velocity in its smallest section ($F'_c \geqslant F_c$ and $w'_c < w_c$). And since it is this velocity which determines the shock losses at discharge from the orifice, the total resistance of the passage throught it is decreased.

28. The resistance coefficient of the flow passing through orifices in the wall, with edges of any shape and of any thickness, is calculated at great Reynolds number (virtually for Re $\geqslant 10^5$) (in the general case considered under paragraph 25) from the author's generalized and refined formula:

$$
\zeta \equiv \frac{\Delta p}{\rho w_0^2/2} = \zeta'\left(1 - \frac{F_0}{F_1}\right)^{3/4} + \left(1 - \frac{F_0}{F_2}\right)^2
$$

$$
+ \tau\sqrt{\left(1 - \frac{F_0}{F_1}\right)^{3/4}}\left(1 - \frac{F_0}{F_2}\right) + \zeta_{\text{fr}}
$$

$$
= \zeta'\left(1 - \frac{F_0}{F_1}\right)^{0.75} + \tau\left(1 - \frac{F_0}{F_1}\right)^{0.375}\left(1 - \frac{F_0}{F_2}\right) \qquad (4\text{-}8)
$$

$$
+ \left(1 - \frac{F_0}{F_2}\right)^2 + \zeta_{\text{fr}}
$$

where ζ' is a coefficient which depends on the shape of the orifice inlet edge and is determined as ζ from Diagrams 3-1 through 3-4 and 3-7; τ is the coefficient representing the effect of the wall thickness, the inlet edge shape of the opening, and conditions of flow passage through the opening, in the case of thick edges it is determined from the formulas similar to Equations (3-4) and (3-5) or from the curve $\tau = f(l/D_h)$ in Diagram 4-12, while for beveled or rounded edges, it is approximated by $\tau \approx 2\sqrt{\zeta'}$, where ζ' is determined from formulas similar to Equations (3-7) and (3-8) or from Diagram 4-13; $\zeta_{fr} = \lambda(l/D_h)$ is the friction coefficient over the entire depth of the orifice opening; and λ is the hydraulic friction factor of the opening depth determined from diagrams in Chapter 2. In the case of beveled or rounded edges, ζ_{fr} is assumed to be zero.

29. The general case of flow passage through an opening in the wall can be divided into a number of particular cases:

- $F_1 = F_0$, a sudden expansion of the cross section (see Figure 4-1); for this Equation (4-8) reduces to Equation (4-1).
- $F_2 = F_0$, a sudden contraction of the cross section (see Figure 4-11); Equation (4-8) is then reduced to the form of Equation (3-1) at $m = 3/4$.
- $F_1 = \infty$, entrance with a sudden expansion (entrance through an orifice plate or a perforated plate at the entrance of a tube); in this case Equation (4-8) has the following form (if ζ is expressed in terms of the velocity w_2 downstream of the entrance)*:

$$\zeta \equiv \frac{\Delta p}{\rho w_0^2/2} = \left[\zeta' + \left(1 - \frac{F_0}{F_2}\right)^2 + \tau\left(1 - \frac{F_0}{F_2}\right) + \zeta_{fr} \right]\left(\frac{F_2}{F_0}\right)^2 \tag{4-9}$$

- $F_2 = \infty$, discharge from an opening into an infinite space (flow discharge through an orifice or a perforated plate at the end of the tube, see Diagram 11-22); in this case Equation (4-8) has the form (if ζ is expressed in terms of the velocity w_1 upstream of the opening)**

$$\zeta \equiv \frac{\Delta p}{\rho w_0^2/2} = \left[1 + \zeta'\left(1 - \frac{F_0}{F_1}\right)^{3/4} + \tau\sqrt{\left(1 - \frac{F_0}{F_1}\right)^{3/4}} + \zeta_{fr} \right]\left(\frac{F_1}{F_0}\right)^2$$

$$= \left[1 + \zeta'\left(1 - \frac{F_0}{F_1}\right)^{0.75} + \tau\left(1 - \frac{F_0}{F_1}\right)^{0.375} + \zeta_{fr} \right]\left(\frac{F_1}{F_0}\right)^2 \tag{4-10}$$

- $F_1 = F_2$, restriction orifice, perforated plate, see Diagrams 4-14 to 4-17); in this case Equation (4-8) reduces to the following form (if ζ is expressed in terms of the velocity w_1 before the opening):

$$\zeta \equiv \frac{\Delta p}{\rho w_1^2/2} = \left[\zeta'\left(1 - \frac{F_0}{F_1}\right)^{3/4} + \tau\sqrt{\left(1 - \frac{F_0}{F_1}\right)^{3/4}} \right.$$

$$\times \left(1 - \frac{F_0}{F_1}\right) + \left(1 - \frac{F_0}{F_1}\right)^2 + \zeta_{fr} \left]\left(\frac{F_1}{F_0}\right)^2\right.$$

$$= \left[\zeta'\left(1 - \frac{F_0}{F_1}\right)^{0.75} + \tau\left(1 - \frac{F_0}{F_1}\right)^{1.375} \right. \tag{4-11}$$

$$\left. + \left(1 - \frac{F_0}{F_1}\right)^2 + \zeta_{fr} \right]\left(\frac{F_1}{F_0}\right)^2$$

*Subscript 0 corresponds to subscript or and subscript 2 to subscript 0 in Chapter 3.
**Subscript 0 corresponds to subscript or and subscript 1 to subscript 0 in Chapter 11.

- $F_1 = F_2 = \infty$, an opening in the wall between infinite flow areas (passage through an opening from one large volume into another, see Diagram 4-18); in this case Equation (4-8) reduces to the form

$$\zeta \equiv \frac{\Delta p}{\rho w_0^2/2} = \zeta' + \tau + 1 + \zeta_{fr} \tag{4-12}$$

30. The resistance coefficient of a restriction having orifice edges of different shapes and at $Re \geq 10^5$ is expressed as follows:

- With sharp-edged orifices, $\zeta' = 0.5$; $\tau = 1.41$, and $\zeta_{fr} = 0$, so that Equation (4-8) is reduced to the author's formula of the form

$$\zeta \equiv \frac{\Delta p}{\rho w_1^2/2} = \left[0.707 \sqrt{\left(1 - \frac{F_0}{F_1}\right)^{3/4}} + 1 - \frac{F_0}{F_1} \right]^2 \left(\frac{F_1}{F_0}\right)^2$$

$$= \left[0.707 \left(1 - \frac{F_0}{F_1}\right)^{0.37} + 1 - \frac{F_0}{F_1} \right]^2 \left(\frac{F_1}{F_0}\right)^2 \tag{4-13}$$

- With thick-edged orifices $\zeta' = 0.5$; resulting in

$$\zeta \equiv \frac{\Delta p}{\rho w_1^2/2} = \left[0.5\left(1 - \frac{F_0}{F_1}\right)^{3/4} + \tau \sqrt{\left(1 - \frac{F_0}{F_1}\right)^{3/4} \left(1 - \frac{F_0}{F_1}\right)} \right.$$

$$\left. + \left(1 - \frac{F_0}{F_1}\right)^2 + \zeta_{fr} \right] \left(\frac{F_1}{F_0}\right)^2$$

$$= \left[0.5\left(1 - \frac{F_0}{F_1}\right)^{0.75} + \tau \left(1 - \frac{F_0}{F_1}\right)^{1.375} \right. \tag{4-14}$$

$$\left. + \left(1 - \frac{F_0}{F_1}\right)^2 + \zeta_{fr} \right] \left(\frac{F_1}{F_0}\right)^2$$

where

$$\tau = (2.4 - \bar{l}) \times 10^{-\varphi/\bar{l}} \tag{4-15}$$

$$\varphi(\bar{l}) = 0.25 + 0.535 \, \bar{l}^{\,8}/(0.05 + \bar{l}^{\,7}), \quad (\bar{l} = l/D_h) \tag{4-16}$$

- With beveled or round-edged orifices $\tau \approx 2\sqrt{\zeta'}$ and $\zeta_{fr} = 0$, then

$$\zeta \equiv \frac{\Delta p}{\rho w_1^2/2} = \left[1 + \sqrt{\zeta'\left(1 - \frac{F_0}{F_1}\right)^{3/4}} - \frac{F_0}{F_2} \right]^2 \left(\frac{F_1}{F_0}\right)^2$$

$$= \left[1 - \frac{F_0}{F_1} + \sqrt{\zeta'} \left(1 - \frac{F_0}{F_2}\right)^{0.375} \right]^2 \left(\frac{F_1}{F_0}\right)^2 \tag{4-17}$$

In the case of orifices with beveled edges at $\alpha = 40$–$60°$

$$\zeta' = 0.13 + 0.34 \times 10^{-(3.45\bar{l} + 88.4\bar{l}^{2.3})} \tag{4-18}$$

or see Diagram 4-13; at other values of α, ζ' is determined as ζ from Diagram 3-7.

For round-edged orifices ζ' is determined as ζ for a circular nozzle with an end face wall, i.e.,

$$\zeta' = 0.03 + 0.47 \times 10^{-7.7\bar{r}}, \quad (\bar{r} = r/D_h) \tag{4-19}$$

or from the curve of Diagram 4-13.

31. The resistance coefficient of an aperture in the wall of an infinite area having opening edges of different shapes and at $Re \geq 10^5$ is expressed as follows:

- With sharp-edged orifices, $\zeta' = 0.5$, $\tau = 1.41$, and $\zeta_{fr} = 0$, so that, on the basis of Equation (4-12),

$$\zeta \equiv \frac{\Delta p}{\rho w_0^2/2} \approx 2.9$$

and, according to the author's experiments,[12]

$$\zeta = 2.7\text{--}2.8$$

- With thick-edged orifices $\zeta' = 0.5$ and Equation (4-8) takes on the form

$$\zeta \equiv \frac{\Delta p}{\rho w_0^2/2} = 1.5 + \tau + \zeta_{fr} = \zeta_0 + \zeta_{fr} \tag{4-20}$$

where $\zeta_0 = 1.5 + \tau$ was obtained experimentally by the author and presented in the form $\zeta_0 = f(l/D_h)$ (curve a) in Diagram 4-18.

$$\zeta_0 = 1.5 + (2.4 - \bar{l}) \times 10^{-\varphi(\bar{l})} \tag{4-21}$$

where $\varphi(\bar{l})$ is determined from Equation (4-16).
- With beveled or rounded (in the flow direction) edges of the opening it is assumed that $\zeta_{fr} = 0$ and $\tau \approx 2\sqrt{\zeta'}$; then

$$\zeta \equiv \frac{\Delta p}{\rho w_0^2/2} = (1 + \sqrt{\zeta'})^2 \tag{4-22}$$

where ζ' is determined in the manner described in paragraph 30, part 3.

32. The resistance coefficient of a flow with an abrupt change in the cross section depends (Figure 4-13) not only on the geometric parameters of the section, but also on the flow regime (a function of the Reynolds number $Re = w_0 D_h/\nu$).[20] In the case considered, as in the case of friction, three specific flow regions can be distinguished:

- The laminar regime, in which ζ depends linearly on Re (in logarithmic coordinates);
- The transition regime, in which the linear dependence $\zeta = f(Re)$ is violated; and
- The self-similar turbulent regime (the region of the quadratic resistance law), in which an effect of the Reynolds number on the resistance coefficient is virtually absent.

The limiting values of Re beyond which the laminar pattern of the flow ceases, as well as the limiting values of Re at which the transition regime terminates, depend on the geometry of the section.

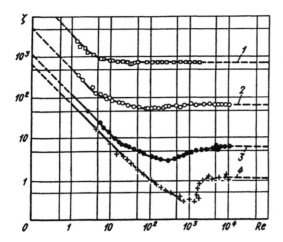

Figure 4-13 Dependence of the resistance coefficient of orifices on the Reynolds number for different values of F_0/F_1.[20] (1) 0.05; (2) 0.16; (3) 0.43; (4) 0.64.

33. The resistance coefficient with an abrupt change in the cross section can be expressed in a general form for all the flow regions from Equation (1-3) at $k_3 = 1$

$$\zeta = \frac{A}{\text{Re}} + \zeta_{\text{quad}} \tag{4-23}$$

where A is a coefficient depending on the geometry of the section considered.

34. For the case of an abrupt expansion of the flow area, the resistance coefficient for the transition region ($10 < \text{Re} < 10^4$) can be determined from the experimental curves $\zeta = f(\text{Re}, F_0/F_1)$ obtained by Altshul,[3] Karev,[17] and Veziryan.[6] (see Diagram 4-1).

For the laminar region ($\text{Re} < 10$) the resistance coefficient is

$$\zeta \equiv \frac{\Delta p}{\rho w_0^2/2} \approx \frac{30}{\text{Re}} \tag{4-24}$$

35. For the case of an abrupt contraction of the flow area, the resistance coefficient in the transition region ($10 < \text{Re} < 10^4$) can be determined (see Reference 18) from the curves $\zeta = f(\text{Re}, F_0/F_1)$ of Diagram 4-10 and in the laminar region ($\text{Re} < 6$–7) from Equation (4-24) applies.

36. For the case of flow passage through openings in a wall (the general case of passage is shown in Figure 4-12; restriction, aperture) the resistance coefficient in the transition and laminar regions can be found:

- Within $30 < \text{Re} < 10^4$–10^5* from the author's formula[16]

$$\zeta \equiv \frac{\Delta p}{\rho w_0^2/2} \approx \left(\frac{1}{\varphi^2} - 1\right) + \frac{0.342}{\varepsilon_0^2 \text{Re}}$$

$$\times \left[1 + 0.707\sqrt{\left(1 - \frac{F_0}{F_1}\right)^{3/4}} - \frac{F_0}{F_2}\right]^2 \tag{4-25}$$

$$= \zeta_\varphi + \overline{\varepsilon}_{0\,\text{Re}} \zeta_{0\text{quad}}$$

*For sharp-edged orifices the upper limit of Re is taken as 10^5, while for other shapes it is of the order of 10^4.

where ϕ is the velocity coefficient of discharge from the sharp-edged orifice, which depends on Re and the area ratio F_0/F_1; $\varepsilon_{0\mathrm{Re}} = F_{\mathrm{con}}/F_0$ is the fluid jet area ratio of the sharp-edged orifice section at $F_0/F_1 = 0$ ($F_1 = \infty$), which depends on the Reynolds number; $\zeta_\phi = (1/\phi^2 - 1)$ is determined from the curves $\zeta_\phi = f_1(\mathrm{Re}, F_0/F_1)$ of Diagram 4-19; $\varepsilon_{0\mathrm{Re}} = 0.342/\varepsilon_{0\mathrm{Re}}^2$ is determined from the curve $\bar{\varepsilon}_{0\mathrm{Re}} = f(\mathrm{Re})$ of the same diagram; $\zeta_{0\mathrm{quad}}$ is the resistance coefficient of the given type of flow restriction for the self-similar (quadratic) region, which is determined as ζ from Equations (4-7)–(4-22), where $\zeta_0 = \Delta p/\rho w_0^2$.

- Within $10 < \mathrm{Re} < 30$ from the approximation suggested by the author

$$\zeta \equiv \frac{\Delta p}{\rho w_0^2/2} = \frac{A}{\mathrm{Re}} + \bar{\varepsilon}_{0\mathrm{Re}}\zeta_{\mathrm{quad}} \tag{4-26}$$

while at $\mathrm{Re} < 10$

$$\zeta \equiv \frac{\Delta p}{\rho w_0^2/2} = \frac{A}{\mathrm{Re}} \tag{4-27}$$

where $A = 33$.[3]

37. If the resistance coefficient is expressed in terms of the velocity w_1 in section F_1 upstream of the orifice (and not w_0 in the orifice itself), then Equations (4-25)–(4-27) are replaced by

$$\zeta_1 \equiv \frac{\Delta p}{\rho w_1^2/2} = (\zeta_\phi + \bar{\varepsilon}_{0\mathrm{Re}}\zeta_{\mathrm{quad}})\left(\frac{F_1}{F_0}\right)^2$$

$$\zeta_1 \equiv \frac{\Delta p}{\rho w_1^2/2} = \frac{33}{\mathrm{Re}}\bar{\varepsilon}_{0\mathrm{Re}}\zeta_{\mathrm{quad}}\left(\frac{F_1}{F_0}\right)^2$$

$$\zeta_1 \equiv \frac{\Delta p}{\rho w_1^2/2} = \frac{33}{\mathrm{Re}}\left(\frac{F_1}{F_0}\right)^2$$

38. At low values of the area coefficients F_0/F_1 of the restriction, the flow through the orifice attains high velocities (high Mach numbers), even at relatively low velocity in the pipeline upstream of the restriction. Here, the compressibility effect, which sharply increases the resistance coefficient of the restriction, becomes noticeable.

$$\zeta_{\mathrm{M}} \equiv \frac{\Delta p}{\rho_1 w_1^2/2} = k_{\mathrm{M}}\zeta$$

where ζ_{M} is the resistance coefficient of the restriction at small Mach numbers determined as given under 25–31; k_{M} is the coefficient which considers the effect of compressibility in the contracted section of the jet during its passage through the orifice (see Diagram 4-20); and $\mathrm{Ma}_1 = w_1/a_1$ is the Mach number upstream of the restriction.

39. A significant decrease in the resistance of the orifice can be attained by installing an annular rib at the inlet into the straight channel or a ledge at the inlet into the orifice (Figure 4-14). Thus, for example, according to Khanzhonkov's[27] experiments, the installation of an annular rib with $D_1/D_0 \approx 1.22$ and $l/D_0 \approx 0.25$ reduces the resistance coefficient of

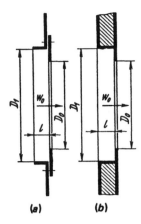

(a)   (b)

Figure 4-14 Entrance into the orifice: (*a*) through an annular rib; (*b*) through a ledge.

the orifice in the wall of an infinite upstream area from $\zeta \approx 2.7$–2.8 (obtained without a rib) to $\zeta = 1.15$.

40. When the flow enters through a smooth inlet nozzle (collector) installed in the wall of an infinite surface area (see Diagram 4-21), the flow resistance is made up of the resistance of entrance into the nozzle, the frictional resistance over the straight section, and the exit resistance. The resistance coefficient of such a section is determined from

$$\zeta \equiv \frac{\Delta p}{\rho w_0^2/2} = \zeta' + \zeta_{\text{fr}}$$

where ζ' is the coefficient representing the inlet and outlet losses, which is determined from the curves $\zeta = f(l/D_h, r/D_h)$ of Diagram 4-21, and $\zeta_{\text{fr}} = \lambda l/D_h$ is the friction coefficient over the straight section of the nozzle.

41. When the flow discharges through an orifice in the wall in the presence of the passing stream* (see Diagram 4-22), the resistance coefficient in the case of both entrance from the stream (suction, aspiration) and discharge into the stream (influx) is a function of the velocity ratio w_∞/w_0, as shown in Reference 27.

42. In the absence of the passing stream ($w_\infty = 0$), the fluid approaches the orifice from all sides, while the flow discharges symmetrically into the stream, with the smallest contraction of the jet section.

In the presence of the passing stream, the fluid approaches the orifice from one side, while the flow discharges at an angle with a more contracted section of the jet downstream of the orifice. The jet contraction causes an increase of the velocity pressure, which is lost at the exit for the given system.

43. At small velocities of the passing stream ($w_\infty \ll w_0$), the above increase in the velocity pressure is smaller than the increase in the difference of pressures upstream and downstream of the orifice causing the jet discharge, which is due to the blowing effect produced by the velocity pressure of the incoming flow. This blowing effect enhances escape through the orifice, which is equivalent to a decrease in the flow resistance coefficient ζ.

At large velocities w_∞, the increase in the velocity pressure of the jet, owing to its large contraction downstream of the orifice, becomes more appreciable than the blowing effect, and the coefficient ζ increases as a result.

---

*The passing stream (w_∞) moves independently of the flow discharging through the orifice under the influence of its own driving force—for example, wind, opposing stream on an airplane, etc.

44. In the case of influx into the stream, an increase in the velocity of the passing stream within $w_\infty/w_0 = 1$–2 also decreases the coefficient ζ. This is due to the fact that the incident flow around the jet issuing from the orifice produces a region with elevated pressure on its upstream side and a large recirculating zone on its downstream side in which rare faction is created. At small velocities w_∞ the dimensions of the recirculation zone are appreciable and the actual pressure difference, which affects the flow discharge through the orifice, exceeds the pressure difference obtained at $w_\infty = 0$.

At more substantial velocities of the passing stream the latter exerts a strong throttling effect on the jet escaping from the orifice, forcing it against the wall (see Figure 4-11*b*, 2 at $w_\infty > w_0$) and reducing the dimensions of the recirculation zone, and the coefficient ζ increases.

45. In the cases of both suction and discharge, the resistance coefficients ζ remain practically the same for square and circular apertures, as well as for orifices with rounded edges. At the same time, their values depend substantially on the orientation of orifices of elongated (rectangular) shape. The largest values of ζ are obtained for the orifices with their longer sides placed perpendicular to the flow.

46. In the case of suction, the larger resistance coefficients ζ for elongated orifices with their larger side perpendicular to the flow are due to a major portion of the flow entering these apertures from the wall region. The flow entering the orifice therefore has a small amount of kinetic energy, and the additional blowing (diffusion) effect is small.

When the elongated orifices are arranged with their larger side parallel to the flow, the portion of the perimeter facing the flow is small and the prevailing portion of the flow enters the orifice from its upper layers, which have a higher velocity. This increases the blowing effect and correspondingly decreases the resistance coefficient.

47. In the case of discharging flow (influx), for elongated orifices placed with their longer side normal to the flow, an increase in ζ is explained by the fact that the throttling effect exerted by the passing stream on the jet escaping from the orifice is more pronounced than with the larger side placed parallel to the flow, since the front surface of the jet in the former case is larger than in the latter.

48. Baffles installed at the edges of orifices (see schemes of Diagram 4-22) have a substantial effect on the values of ζ in the case of suction as well as discharge. An inclined baffle increases and a straight one decreases the value of the resistance coefficient. In the first case, the baffle compresses the flow passing through the orifice; consequently, the velocity pressure, lost on escape from the orifice, increases. In the second case the baffle weakens the effect of flow contraction, which correspondingly decreases the velocity pressure losses at the exit from the orifice.

49. When the fluid passes through the apertures in a wall, fitted with various flaps (projections), the resistance is higher than in the absence of flaps, since they complicate the flow trajectory. In this case, the resistance coefficient becomes a function of the angle of opening of the flaps, α, and of the relative length of the flaps l_{fl}/b_{fl}.

50. The open working section of a wind tunnel (see Diagram 4-25) can also regarded as a section with abrupt expansion.

The main source of losses in this section is ejection dissipation of energy. The second source of losses is cutting off of the "added masses" from the surrounding medium by the wind tunnel diffuser.

The kinetic energy of the portion of the jet that was cut off turns to be lost for the wind tunnel and, therefore, constitutes a part of the resistance of the open working section.

The coefficient of total resistance of the open working section (w.s.) is calculated from Abramovich's[1] formula.

For a circular (or rectangular) cross section:

$$\zeta \equiv \frac{\Delta p}{\rho w_0^2/2} = 0.1 \frac{l_{\text{w.s.}}}{D_h} - 0.008 \left(\frac{l_{\text{w.s.}}}{D_h}\right)^2$$

where $D_h = 4F_0/\Pi_0$ is the hydraulic diameter of the exit section of the tunnel nozzle, m.

For an elliptical cross section:

$$\zeta \equiv \frac{\Delta p}{\rho w_0^2/2} = 0.145 \frac{l_{\text{w.s.}}}{D_h} - 0.0017 \frac{l_{\text{w.s.}}}{a_0 b_0}$$

where

$$D_h \approx \frac{4a_0 b_0}{1.5(a_0 + b_0) - \sqrt{a_0 b_0}}$$

$l_{\text{w.s.}}$ is the length of the open working section of the wind tunnel, m; and a_0 and b_0 are the ellipse semiaxes, m.

4-2 DIAGRAMS OF RESISTANCE COEFFICIENTS

Sudden expansion of a flow having a uniform velocity distribution[13,15,17]	Diagram 4-1

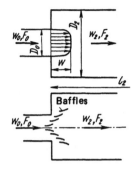

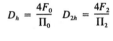

$$D_h = \frac{4F_0}{\Pi_0} \quad D_{2h} = \frac{4F_2}{\Pi_2}$$

$n_{ar} = \dfrac{F_2}{F_0} \Pi$ is the perimeter

1. At $\mathrm{Re} = \dfrac{w_0 D_h}{\nu} \geq 3.3 \times 10^3$:

a) Without baffles

$$\zeta \equiv \frac{\Delta p}{\rho w_0^2/2} = \left(1 - \frac{F_0}{F_2}\right)^2 + \frac{\zeta_{fr}}{n_{ar}^2} = \zeta_{loc} + \frac{\zeta_{fr}}{n_{ar}^2}$$

where $\zeta_{loc} = f(F_0/F_2)$, see graph a; $\zeta_{fr} = \lambda(l_2/D_{2h})$; for λ see Chapter 2.

b) With baffles

$$\zeta \equiv \frac{\Delta p}{\rho w_0^2/2} \approx 0.6 \left(1 - \frac{F_0}{F_2}\right)^2 + \frac{\zeta_{fr}}{n_{ar}^2}$$

Relative losses with a sudden expansion at supersonic velocities are considered in paragraphs 20 and 21 of Section 4-1

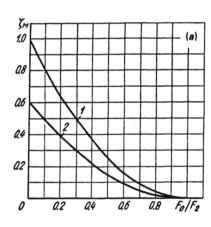

Values of ζ'

$$F_0/F_2 = \frac{1}{n_{ar}}$$

0	0.1	0.2	0.3	0.4	0.5	0.6	0.7	0.8	1.0
Without baffles (curve 1)									
1.00	0.81	0.64	0.50	0.36	0.25	0.16	0.09	0.04	0
With baffles (curve 2)									
0.60	0.49	0.39	0.30	0.21	0.15	0.10	0.05	0.02	0

2. When $500 \leq \mathrm{Re} < 3.3 \times 10^3$, for ζ_{loc} see graph b or ζ_{loc} is determined from the formula

$$\zeta_{loc} = -8.44556 - 26.163(1 - F_0/F_2)^2 - 5.38086(1 - F_0/F_2)^4$$
$$+ \lg \mathrm{Re}\,[6.007 + 18.5372(1 - F_0/F_2)^2 + 3.9978\,(1 - F_0/F_2)^4]$$
$$+ (\lg \mathrm{Re})^2\,[-1.02318 - 3.0916(1 - F_0/F_2)^2 - 0.680943(1 - F_0/F_2)^4]$$

Values of ζ

$\dfrac{F_0}{F_2} = \dfrac{1}{N_{ar}}$	Re											
	10	15	20	30	40	50	10^2	2×10^2	5×10^2	10^3	2×10^3	3×10^3	$\geq 3 \times 10^3$
0.1	3.10	3.20	3.00	2.40	2.15	1.95	1.70	1.65	1.70	2.00	1.60	1.00	0.81
0.2	3.10	3.20	2.80	2.20	1.85	1.65	1.40	1.30	1.30	1.60	1.25	0.70	0.64
0.3	3.10	3.10	2.60	2.00	1.60	1.40	1.20	1.10	1.10	1.30	0.95	0.60	0.50
0.4	3.10	3.00	2.40	1.80	1.50	1.30	1.10	1.00	0.85	1.05	0.80	0.40	0.36
0.5	3.10	2.80	2.30	1.65	1.35	1.15	0.90	0.75	0.65	0.90	0.65	0.30	0.25
0.6	3.10	2.70	2.15	1.55	1.25	1.05	0.80	0.60	0.40	0.60	0.50	0.20	0.16

Sudden expansion of a flow having a uniform velocity distribution[13,15,17]	Diagram 4-1

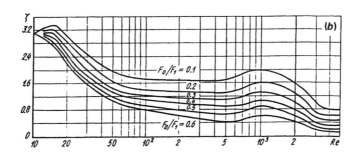

3. At $10 < \text{Re} < 500$, ζ_{loc} is determined from graph b or from the formula:

$$\zeta_{loc} = 3.62536 + 10.744(1 - F_0/F_2)^2 - 4.41041(1 - F_0/F_2)^4$$

$$+ \frac{1}{\lg \text{Re}}\left[-18.13 - 56.77855(1 - F_0/F_2)^2 + 33.40344(1 - F_0/F_2)^4 \right]$$

$$+ \frac{1}{(\lg \text{Re})^2}\left[30.8558 + 99.9542(1 - F_0/F_2)^2 - 62.78(1 - F_0/F_2)^4 \right]$$

$$+ \frac{1}{(\lg \text{Re})^3}\left[-13.217 - 53.9555(1 - F_0/F_2)^2 + 33.8053(1 - F_0/F_2)^4 \right]$$

4. At $\text{Re} < 10$

$$\zeta_{loc} \approx \frac{30}{\text{Re}}$$

Sudden expansion downstream of a long straight section, diffusers, and so on, with exponential velocity distribution; circular or rectangular cross section; $\text{Re} = w_0 D_h/\nu > 3.5 \times 10^3$ [13,15]	Diagram 4-2

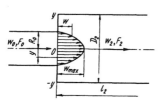

$$\zeta \equiv \frac{\Delta p}{\rho w_0^2/2} = \frac{1}{n_{ar}^2} + N - \frac{2M}{n_{ar}} + \frac{\zeta_{fr}}{n_{ar}^2} = \zeta_{loc} + \frac{\zeta_{fr}}{n_{ar}^2}$$

$$M = \frac{(2m + 1)^2(m + 1)}{4m^2 (m + 2)}$$

where

$$N = \frac{(2m + 1)^3(m + 1)^3}{4m^4(2m + 3)(m + 3)}$$

$\left.\right\}$ see graph b

$\zeta_{loc} = f(m, F_0/F_2)$, see graph a, $\zeta_{fr} = \lambda l_2/D_{2h}$; for λ see Chapter 2

$$D_h = \frac{4F_0}{\Pi_0}; \quad D_{2h} = \frac{4F_2}{\Pi_2};$$

Π is the perimeter

$$n_{ar} = \frac{F_2}{F_0}; \quad \frac{w}{w_{max}} = \left(1 - \frac{y}{R_0}\right)^{1/m}$$

$m \geqslant 1$

Sudden expansion downstream of a long straight section, diffusers, and so on, with exponential velocity distribution; circular or rectangular cross section; Re $= w_0 D_h/\nu > 3.5 \times 10^3$ [13,15]	Diagram 4-2

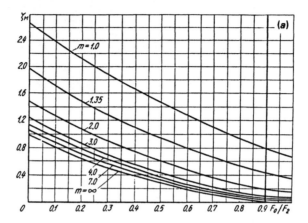

Values of ζ

| m | \multicolumn{10}{c}{$\dfrac{F_0}{F_2} = 1/n_{ar}$} |

m	0	0.1	0.2	0.3	0.4	0.5	0.6	0.7	0.8	1.0
1.0	2.70	2.42	2.14	1.90	1.66	1.45	1.26	1.09	0.94	0.70
1.35	2.00	1.74	1.51	1.29	1.00	0.93	0.77	0.65	0.53	0.36
2.0	1.50	1.28	1.08	0.89	0.72	0.59	0.46	0.35	0.27	0.16
3.0	1.25	1.04	0.84	0.68	0.53	0.41	0.30	0.20	0.14	0.07
4.0	1.15	0.95	0.77	0.62	0.47	0.35	0.25	0.17	0.11	0.05
7.0	1.06	0.86	0.69	0.53	0.41	0.29	0.19	0.12	0.06	0.02
∞	1.00	0.82	0.64	0.48	0.36	0.25	0.16	0.09	0.04	0

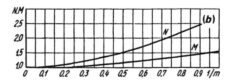

m	1.0	1.35	2.0	3.0	4.0	7.0	∞
N	2.70	2.00	1.50	1.25	1.15	1.06	1.0
M	1.50	1.32	1.17	1.09	1.05	1.02	1.0

Sudden expansion downstream of long plane and straight sections, plane diffusers, and so on, with exponential velocity distribution; $Re = w_0 D_h / \nu > 3.5 \times 10^3$ [13,15]	Diagram 4-3

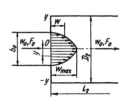

$$\zeta \equiv \frac{\Delta p}{\rho w_0^2 / 2} = \frac{1}{n_{ar}^2} + N - \frac{2M}{n_{ar}} + \frac{\zeta_{fr}}{n_{ar}^2} = \zeta_{loc} + \frac{\zeta_{fr}}{n_{ar}^2}$$

where $\left.\begin{array}{l} M = \dfrac{(m+1)^2}{m(m+2)} \\[3mm] N = \dfrac{(m+1)^3}{m^2(m+3)} \end{array}\right\}$ see graph b;

$\zeta_{loc} = f(m, F_0/F_2)$, see graph a, $\zeta_{fr} = \lambda l_2/D_{2h}$; for λ see Chapter 2.

$$D_h = \frac{4F_0}{\Pi_0}; \quad D_{2h} = \frac{4F_2}{\Pi_2};$$

Π is the perimeter

$$n_{ar} = \frac{F_2}{F_0}; \quad \frac{w}{w_{max}} = \left(1 - \frac{2y}{b_0}\right)^{1/m}$$

$$m \geqslant 1$$

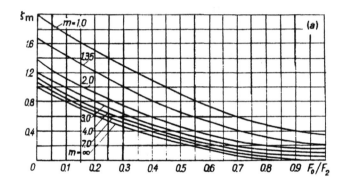

Values of ζ_{loc}

$$\frac{F_0}{F_2} = 1/n_{ar}$$

m	0	0.1	0.2	0.3	0.4	0.5	0.6	0.7	0.8	1.0
1.0	2.00	1.74	1.51	1.28	1.19	0.92	0.77	0.64	0.51	0.34
1.35	1.65	1.40	1.20	1.00	0.83	0.67	0.53	0.41	0.32	0.20
2.0	1.35	1.14	0.94	0.77	0.62	0.48	0.36	0.26	0.19	0.10
3.0	1.19	0.98	0.80	0.64	0.49	0.37	0.24	0.18	0.12	0.05
4.0	1.12	0.92	0.74	0.60	0.46	0.33	0.23	0.14	0.09	0.04
7.0	1.04	0.85	0.64	0.54	0.41	0.28	0.18	0.08	0.05	0.02
∞	1.00	0.81	0.64	0.49	0.36	0.25	0.15	0.08	0.04	0

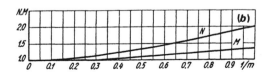

m	1.0	1.35	2.0	3.0	4.0	7.0	∞
N	2.00	1.64	1.35	1.18	1.12	1.04	1.0
M	1.33	1.22	1.13	1.07	1.04	1.02	1.0

Sudden expansion of a plane channel downstream of perforated
plates, guide vanes in elbows, and so on, with sinusoidal velocity
distribution; $Re = w_0 D_h/\nu > 3.5 \times 10^{3}$ [13,15]

Diagram
4-4

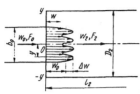

$$D_h = \frac{4F_0}{\Pi_0} ; \quad D_{2h} = \frac{4F_2}{\Pi_2} ; \quad n_{ar} = \frac{F_2}{F_0} ; \quad \frac{w}{w_0} = 1 + \frac{\Delta w}{w_0} \sin 2k_1\pi \frac{2y}{b_0} ;$$

k_1 is an integer; Π is the perimeter;

$$\zeta \equiv \frac{\Delta p}{\rho w_0^2/2} = \frac{1}{n_{ar}^2} + N - \frac{2M}{n_{ar}} + \frac{\zeta_{fr}}{n_{ar}^2} = \zeta_{loc} + \frac{\zeta_{fr}}{n_{ar}^2}$$

where $M = 1 + \frac{1}{2}\left(\frac{\Delta w}{w_0}\right)^2$; $N = 1 + \frac{3}{2}\left(\frac{\Delta w}{w_0}\right)^2$, see graph b; $\zeta_{loc} = +\left(m, \frac{F_0}{F_2}\right)$,

see graph a; $\zeta_{fr} = \frac{\lambda l_2}{D_{2h}}$; for λ see Chapter 2.

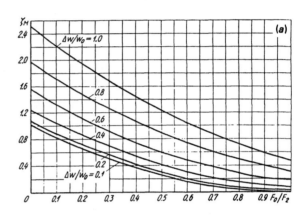

Values of ζ_{loc}

$\dfrac{\Delta w}{w_0}$	$\dfrac{F_0}{F_2} = 1/n_{ar}$									
	0	0.1	0.2	0.3	0.4	0.5	0.6	0.7	0.8	1.0
0.1	1.01	0.83	0.66	0.50	0.38	0.26	0.17	0.10	0.06	0.01
0.2	1.06	0.88	0.70	0.54	0.40	0.29	0.20	0.13	0.07	0.02
0.4	1.24	1.04	0.84	0.68	0.54	0.41	0.30	0.22	0.16	0.08
0.6	1.54	1.31	1.18	0.92	0.75	0.61	0.48	0.39	0.29	0.18
0.8	1.96	1.70	1.47	1.27	1.07	0.89	0.75	0.60	0.49	0.32
1.0	2.50	2.21	1.95	1.70	1.46	1.25	1.05	0.88	0.74	0.50

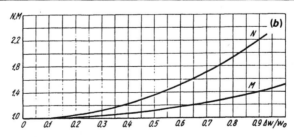

$\dfrac{\Delta w}{w_0}$	0.1	0.2	0.3	0.4	0.5	0.6	0.7	0.8	0.9	1.0
N	1.0	1.06	1.13	1.24	1.37	1.54	1.73	1.96	2.22	2.50
M	1.00	1.02	1.04	1.08	1.12	1.18	1.24	1.32	1.40	1.50

Sudden expansion downstream of a plane diffuser with $\alpha > 10°$, elbows, and so on, with asymmetrical velocity distribution; Re $= w_0 D_h/\nu > 3.5 \times 10^3$ [13, 15]	Diagram 4-5

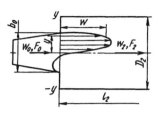

$$D_h = \frac{4F_0}{\Pi_0} \; ; \quad D_{2h} = \frac{4F_2}{\Pi_2} \; ; \quad n_{ar} = \frac{F_2}{F_0} \; ; \quad \Pi \text{ is the perimeter;}$$

$$\frac{w}{w_0} = 0.585 + 1.64 \sin\left(0.2 + 1.95 \frac{2y}{b_0}\right)$$

$$\zeta \equiv \frac{\Delta p}{\rho w_0^2/2} = \frac{1}{n_{ar}^2} + 3.7 - \frac{3.74}{n_{ar}} + \frac{\zeta_{fr}}{n_{ar}^2} = \zeta_{loc} + \frac{\zeta_{fr}}{n_{ar}^2}$$

where $\zeta_{loc} = f(F_0/F_2)$, see graph; $\zeta_{fr} = \lambda l_2/D_{2h}$, for λ see Chapter 2.

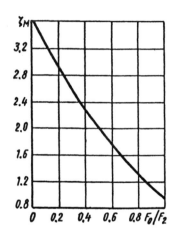

$\dfrac{F_0}{F_2} = 1/n_{ar}$	0	0.1	0.2	0.3	0.4	0.5	0.6	0.7	0.8	1.0
ζ		3.70	3.34	2.99	2.66	2.36	2.09	1.82	1.58	1.35	0.96

Sudden expansion downstream of sections with parabolic velocity distribution; Re $= w_0 D_h/\nu > 3.5 \times 10^3$ [13, 15]	Diagram 4-6

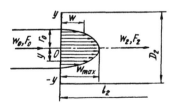

$$\frac{w}{w_{max}} = 1 - \left(\frac{y}{R_0}\right)^2$$

$$D_h = \frac{4F_0}{\Pi_0} \; ; \quad D_{2h} = \frac{4F_2}{\Pi_2} \; ; \quad n_{ar} = \frac{F_2}{F_0} \; ; \quad \Pi \text{ is the perimeter;}$$

1. Circular tube:

$$\zeta \equiv \frac{\Delta p}{\rho w_0^2/2} = \frac{1}{n_{ar}^2} + 2 - \frac{2.66}{n_{ar}} + \frac{\zeta_{fr}}{n_{ar}^2} = \zeta_{loc} + \frac{\zeta_{fr}}{n_{ar}^2}$$

2. Plane channel:

$$\zeta \equiv \frac{\Delta p}{\rho w_0^2/2} = \frac{1}{n_{ar}^2} + 1.55 - \frac{2.4}{n_{ar}} + \frac{\zeta_{fr}}{n_{ar}^2} = \zeta_{loc} + \frac{\zeta_{fr}}{n_{ar}^2}$$

where $\zeta_{loc} = f(F_0/F_2)$; $\zeta_{fr} = \lambda l_2/D_{2h}$, for λ see Chapter 2.

Sudden expansion downstream of sections with parabolic velocity distribution; Re = $w_0 D_h/\nu > 3.5 \times 10^3$ [13,15]										Diagram 4-6	

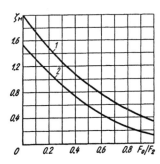

$\dfrac{F_0}{F_2} = 1/n_{ar}$	0	0.1	0.2	0.3	0.4	0.5	0.6	0.7	0.8	1.0
1. Circular tube										
ζ_{loc}	2.00	1.75	1.51	1.30	1.10	0.92	0.78	0.63	0.51	0.34
2. Plane channel										
ζ_{loc}	1.55	1.32	1.11	0.92	0.75	0.60	0.47	0.36	0.27	0.15

Flow deformation in a straight tube (channel); $n_{ar} = 1$; Re = $w_0 D_h/\nu > 3.5 \times 10^3$ [13,15]	Diagram 4-7

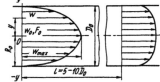

$$D_h = \frac{4F_0}{\Pi_0}$$

Π is the perimeter

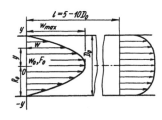

Exponential law of velocity distribution:

$$\frac{w}{w_{max}} = \left(1 - \frac{y}{R_0}\right)^{1/m} \quad m \geq 1$$

$$\zeta \equiv \frac{\Delta p}{\rho w_0^2/2} = 1 + N - 2M + \zeta_{fr} = \zeta_{loc} + \zeta_{fr}$$

$\zeta_{loc} = f(1/m)$; for M and N, see graph b of Diagrams 4-2 and 4-3; $\zeta_{fr} = \lambda l_0/D_0$, for λ see Chapter 2.

Parabolic velocity distribution:

$$\frac{w}{w_{max}} = 1 - \left(\frac{u}{R_0}\right)^2$$

1. Circular tube

$$\zeta_{loc} \equiv \frac{\Delta p}{\rho w_0^2/2} = 0.34$$

2. Plane channel

$$\zeta_{loc} \equiv \frac{\Delta p}{\rho w_0^2/2} = 0.15$$

Flow deformation in a straight tube (channel); $n_{ar} = 1$; $\mathrm{Re} = w_0 D_h/\nu > 3.5 \times 10^{3\ 13,15}$	Diagram 4-7

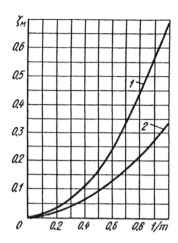

m	1.0	1.35	2.0	4.0	7.0	∞
1. Circular tube						
ζ_{loc}	0.7	0.36	0.16	0.05	0.02	0
2. Plane channel						
ζ_{loc}	0.31	0.19	0.10	0.04	0.02	0

Flow deformation in a straight circular tube with a free jet entering it (ejector); $n_{ar} = 1$; $\mathrm{Re} = w_0 D_h/\nu > 3.5 \times 10^{3\ 13,15}$	Diagram 4-8

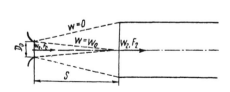

$$D_h = \frac{4F_0}{n_0}\,; \quad D_{2h} = \frac{4F_2}{n_2}\,;$$

$$\zeta \equiv \frac{\Delta p}{\rho w_2^2/2} = 1 + N - 2M + \zeta_{fr} = \zeta_{loc} + \zeta_{fr};$$

$$M = \frac{1}{\bar{q}^2}\left(\frac{F_2}{F_0}\right)\,; \quad N = \frac{1}{\bar{q}^3}\left(\frac{F_2}{F_0}\right)^2 \bar{e}$$

The values of ζ_{loc}, M, and N are determined from the graph as a function of the free jet length S/D_h; $\bar{F} = F_2/F_0 = F_j/F_0$, $\bar{q}$, and $\bar{e}$ are determined as functions of the free jet length S/D_h from Diagrams 11-28 and 11-29; $\zeta_{fr} = \lambda l_2/D_{2h}$; for λ see Chapter 2.

Flow deformation in a straight circular tube with a free jet entering it (ejector); $n_{ar} = 1$; Re $= w_0 D_h/\nu > 3.5 \times 10^3$ [13,15]	Diagram 4-8

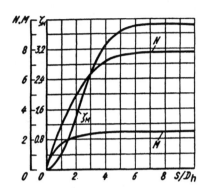

$\dfrac{S}{D_h}$	0.5	1.0	1.5	2.0	2.5	3.0
ζ_{loc}	0.16	0.46	0.84	1.43	2.02	2.54
N	1.65	2.89	3.90	4.85	5.65	6.35
M	1.25	1.71	2.00	2.20	2.30	2.40

$\dfrac{S}{D_h}$	4.0	5.0	6.0	8.0	10	
ζ_{loc}	3.26	3.65	3.80	3.81	3.81	
N	7.20	7.55	7.68	7.70	7.70	
M	2.45	2.45	2.45	2.45	2.45	

Sudden contraction at $b/D_h = 0$; Re $= w_0 D_h/\nu > 10^4$ [12,13]	Diagram 4-9

N	Kind of inlet edge	Configuration	Resistance coefficient
			$\zeta \equiv \dfrac{\Delta p}{\rho w_0^2/2}$

$$\zeta = 0.5\left(1 - \frac{F_0}{F_1}\right)^{3/4} + \zeta_{fr} = 0.5a + \zeta_{fr},$$

where for a see curve $a = f(F_0/F_1)$; $\zeta_{fr} = \lambda \dfrac{l_0}{D_h}$; for λ see Chapter 2

Sudden contraction at $b/D_h = 0$;   Diagram
$\mathrm{Re} = w_0 D_h/\nu > 10^{4}$ [12,13]   4-9

1   Sharp

$\dfrac{F_0}{F_1}$	0	0.2	0.4	0.6	0.8	0.9	1.0
a	1.0	0.850	0.680	0.503	0.300	0.178	0

$$D_h = \frac{4F_0}{\Pi_0}$$

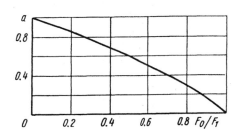

2   Rounded

$$\zeta = \zeta'\left(1 - \frac{F_0}{F_1}\right)^{3/4} + \zeta_{fr} = f'a + \zeta_{fr} \text{, where for } \zeta'$$

see curve $\zeta = f(b/D_h)$ of Diagram 3-4 (curve c);
for a see curve $a = f(F_0/F_1)$ (para. 1); $\zeta_{fr} = \lambda l_0/D_h$;
for λ see Chapter 2.

3   Beveled

$$\zeta = \zeta''\left(1 - \frac{F_0}{F_1}\right)^{3/4} + \zeta_{fr} = \zeta''a + \zeta_{fr} \text{, where for } \zeta''$$

see curve $\zeta = f(\alpha, l/D_h)$ of Diagram 3-7;
for a see curve $a = f(F_0/F_1)$ (para. 1); $\zeta_{fr} = \lambda l_0/D_h$;
for λ see Chapter 2.

Sudden contraction in transition and laminar regions;   Diagram
$\mathrm{Re} = w_0 D_h/\nu < 10^{4}$ [3,18]   4-10

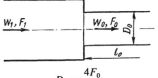

$$\zeta \equiv \frac{\Delta p}{\rho w_0^2/2} = \zeta_{loc} + \zeta_{fr}$$

1. At $10 \leq \mathrm{Re} < 10^4$ ζ_{loc} is determined from curves $\zeta_{loc} = f(\mathrm{Re}, F_0/F_1)$ or from the formula

$$D_h = \frac{4F_0}{\Pi_0}$$

$$\zeta_{loc} = A \cdot B(1 - F_0/F_1),$$

where $A = \sum_{i=0}^{7} a_i (\lg \mathrm{Re})^i$;

$a_0 = -25.12458$; $a_1 = 118.5076$; $a_2 = -170.4147$; $a_3 = 118.1949$;
$a_4 = -44.42141$; $a_5 = 9.09524$; $a_6 = -0.9244027$; $a_7 = 0.03408265$

$$B = \sum_{i=0}^{2} \left\{ \left[\sum_{j=0}^{2} a_{ij}(F_0/F_1)^j \right] (\lg \mathrm{Re})^i \right\};$$

the values of a_{ij} are given below

2. At $\mathrm{Re} < 10$, $\zeta_{loc} \approx \dfrac{30}{\mathrm{Re}}$

Sudden contraction in transition and laminar regions; $\mathrm{Re} = w_0 D_h/\nu < 10^4$ [3,18]	Diagram 4-10

Values of a_{ij}

	$10 \leqslant \mathrm{Re} \leqslant 2 \times 10^3$			$2 \times 10^3 < \mathrm{Re} < 4 \times 10^3$		
i/j	0	1	2	0	1	2
0	1.07	1.22	2.9333	0.5443	-17.298	-40.715
1	0.05	-0.51668	0.8333	-0.06518	8.7616	22.782
2	0	0	0	0.05239	-1.1093	-3.1509

Values of ζ_{loc}

$\dfrac{F_0}{F_1}$	Re													
	10	20	30	40	50	10^2	2×10^2	5×10^2	10^3	2×10^3	4×10^3	5×10^3	10^4	$>10^4$
0.1	5.00	3.20	2.40	2.00	1.80	1.30	1.04	0.82	0.64	0.50	0.80	0.75	0.50	0.45
0.2	5.00	3.10	2.30	1.84	1.62	1.20	0.95	0.70	0.50	0.40	0.60	0.60	0.40	0.40
0.3	5.00	2.95	2.15	1.70	1.50	1.10	0.85	0.60	0.44	0.30	0.55	0.55	0.35	0.35
0.4	5.00	2.80	2.00	1.60	1.40	1.00	0.78	0.50	0.35	0.25	0.45	0.50	0.30	0.30
0.5	5.00	2.70	1.80	1.46	1.30	0.90	0.65	0.42	0.30	0.20	0.40	0.42	0.25	0.25
0.6	5.00	2.60	1.70	1.35	1.20	0.80	0.56	0.35	0.24	0.15	0.35	0.35	0.20	0.20

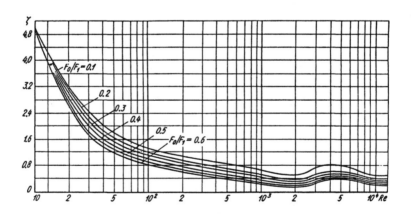

Sharp-edged orifice ($l/D_h = 0-0.015$) installed in a transition section; $\mathrm{Re} = w_0 D_h/\nu \geqslant 10^4$ [13,14]	Diagram 4-11

$$\zeta \equiv \frac{\Delta p}{\rho w_0^2/2} = \left[0.707 \left(1 - \frac{F_0}{F_1} \right)^{0.375} + \left(1 - \frac{F_0}{F_2} \right) \right]^2$$

$$= f\left(\frac{F_0}{F_1} ; \frac{F_0}{F_2} \right)$$

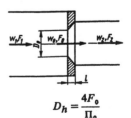

$$D_h = \frac{4F_0}{\Pi_0}$$

Sharp-edged orifice ($l/D_h = 0-0.015$) installed in a transition section; Re $= w_0 D_h/\nu \geqslant 10^{4}$ [13,14]	Diagram 4-11

Values of ζ

F_0/F_2	F_0/F_1										
	0	0.1	0.2	0.3	0.4	0.5	0.6	0.7	0.8	0.9	1.0
0	2.91	2.82	2.72	2.61	2.51	2.39	2.25	2.10	1.92	1.68	1.00
0.2	2.27	2.19	2.10	2.01	1.91	1.81	1.69	1.56	1.41	1.20	0.64
0.4	1.71	1.64	1.56	1.48	1.40	1.31	1.21	1.10	0.97	0.80	0.36
0.6	1.23	1.17	1.10	1.03	0.97	0.89	0.81	0.72	0.62	0.48	0.16
0.8	0.82	0.77	0.72	0.67	0.61	0.56	0.49	0.42	0.34	0.25	0.04
1.0	0.50	0.46	0.42	0.38	0.34	0.30	0.25	0.20	0.15	0.09	0

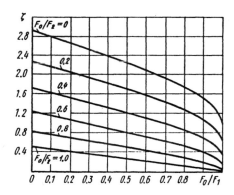

Thick-edged orifice ($l/D_h > 0.015$) installed in a transition section; Re $= w_0 D_h/\nu > 10^{5}$ [13,14]	Diagram 4-12

$$D_h = \frac{4F_0}{\Pi_0}$$

$$\zeta \equiv \frac{\Delta p}{\rho w_0^2/2} \approx 0.5\left(1 - \frac{F_0}{F_1}\right)^{0.75} + \left(1 - \frac{F_0}{F_2}\right)^2 + \tau\left(1 - \frac{F_0}{F_1}\right)^{0.375}$$

$$\times \left(1 - \frac{F_0}{F_2}\right) + \lambda\frac{l}{D_h} \qquad \text{where } \tau = f(l/D_h);$$
$$\text{for } \lambda \text{ see Chapter 2}$$

$$\tau = (2.4 - \bar{l}) \times 10^{-\varphi(\bar{l})}$$

$$\varphi(\bar{l}) = 0.25 + 0.535\bar{l}^8/(0.05 + \bar{l}^8)$$

$\bar{l} \equiv \dfrac{l}{D_h}$	0	0.2	0.4	0.6	0.8
τ	1.35	1.22	1.10	0.84	0.42
$\bar{l} \equiv \dfrac{l}{D_h}$	1.0	1.2	1.6	2.0	2.4
τ	0.24	0.16	0.07	0.02	0

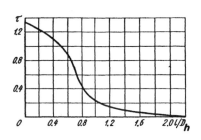

Orifice with beveled and rounded (in flow direction) edges installed in a transition section; $Re = w_0 D_h / \nu \geqslant 10^4$ [13,14]	Diagram 4-13

Orifice	Configuration	Resistance coefficient

With beveled edges

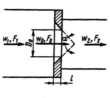

$$D_h = \frac{4F_0}{\Pi_0}$$

$$\zeta \equiv \frac{\Delta p}{\rho w_0^2 / 2} \approx \zeta' \left(1 - \frac{F_0}{F_1} \right)^{0.75}$$

$$+ \left(1 - \frac{F_0}{F_2} \right)^2 + 2 \sqrt{\zeta' \left(1 - \frac{F_0}{F_1} \right)^{0.375}} + \left(1 - \frac{F_0}{F_2} \right)$$

where ζ' at $\alpha = 40\text{--}60°$, see graph a, or $\zeta' = 0.13 + 0.34 \times 10^{-(34\bar{l} + 88.4\bar{l}^{2.3})}$. At other values of α, ζ' is determined as ζ from Diagram 3-7

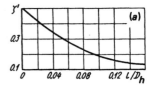

l/D_h	0.01	0.02	0.03	0.04	0.06	0.08	0.12	$\geqslant 0.16$
ζ'	0.46	0.42	0.38	0.35	0.29	0.23	0.16	0.13

With rounded edges

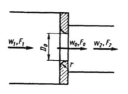

$$\zeta \equiv \frac{\Delta p}{\rho w_0^2 / 2} = \zeta' \left(1 - \frac{F_0}{F_1} \right)^{0.75}$$

$$+ \left(1 - \frac{F_0}{F_2} \right)^2 + 2 \sqrt{\zeta' \left(1 - \frac{F_0}{F_1} \right)^{0.375}} \times \left(1 - \frac{F_0}{F_2} \right)$$

where $\zeta' = f\left(\frac{r}{D_h} \right)$, see graph be or
$$\zeta' = 0.03 + 0.47 \times 10^{-7.7\bar{r}}$$

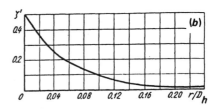

r/D_h	0	0.01	0.02	0.03	0.04	0.05	0.06	0.08	0.12	0.16	$\geqslant 0.2$
ζ'	0.50	0.44	0.37	0.31	0.26	0.22	0.19	0.15	0.09	0.06	0.03

Sharp-edged orifice ($l/D_h = 0$–0.015) in a straight tube; Re $= w_0 D_h/\nu \geqslant 10^5$ [13,14]	Diagram 4-14

$$\zeta_1 \equiv \frac{\Delta p}{\rho w_0^2/2} = \left[\left(1 - \frac{F_0}{F_1}\right) + 0.707\left(1 - \frac{F_0}{F_1}\right)^{0.375}\right]^2 \left(\frac{F_1}{F_0}\right)^2$$

see curve $\zeta_1 = \overline{f}\left(\dfrac{F_0}{F_1}\right)$

$$D_h = \frac{4F_0}{\Pi_0}$$

$\frac{F_0}{F_1}$	0.02	0.03	0.04	0.05	0.06	0.08	0.10	0.12	0.14
ζ_1	7000	3100	1670	1050	730	400	245	165	117
$\frac{F_0}{F_1}$	0.16	0.18	0.20	0.22	0.24	0.26	0.28	0.30	0.32
ζ_1	86.0	65.6	51.5	40.6	32.0	26.8	22.3	18.2	15.6
$\frac{F_0}{F_1}$	0.34	0.36	0.38	0.40	0.43	0.47	0.50	0.52	0.55
ζ_1	13.1	11.6	9.55	8.25	6.62	4.95	4.00	3.48	2.85
$\frac{F_0}{F_1}$	0.60	0.65	0.70	0.75	0.80	0.85	0.90	0.95	1.00
ζ_1	2.00	1.41	0.97	0.65	0.42	0.25	0.13	0.05	0

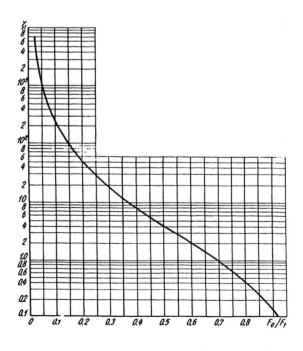

Thick-edged orifice ($l/D_h > 0.015$) in a straight tube (channel);   Diagram
$Re = w_0 D_h / \nu > 10^{3\ 13,14}$ 4-15

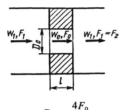

$$D_h = \frac{4F_0}{\Pi_0}$$

$$\bar{l} = l/D_h$$

$$\zeta_1 \equiv \frac{\Delta p}{\rho w_1^2/2} = \left[0.5\left(1 - \frac{F_0}{F_1}\right)^{0.75} + \tau\left(1 - \frac{F_0}{F_1}\right)^{1.375}\right.$$

$$\left. + \left(1 - \frac{F_0}{F_1}\right)^2 + \lambda\frac{l}{D_h}\right]\left(\frac{F_1}{F_0}\right)^2,$$

where τ see the table below or graph a of Diagram 4-12 or

$$\tau = (2.4 - l) \times 10^{-\varphi(\bar{l})};$$

$$\varphi(\bar{l}) = 0.25 + 0.535 l^{-8}/(0.05 + l^{-8}), \quad \text{see Chapter 2.}$$

$$\zeta_0 = 0.5\left(1 - \frac{F_0}{F_1}\right) + \left(1 - \frac{F_0}{F_2}\right)^2 + \tau\sqrt{1 - \frac{F_0}{F_1}}\left(1 - \frac{F_0}{F_2}\right); \quad \text{for } \lambda$$

Values of ζ_1 at $\lambda = 0.02$ At $\lambda = 0.02$ for the values of $\zeta_1 = f(l/D_h, F_0/F_1)$ see the graph

$\bar{l} = l/D_h$	τ	F_0/F_1															
		0.02	0.04	0.06	0.08	0.10	0.15	0.20	0.25	0.30	0.40	0.50	0.60	0.70	0.80	0.90	1.00
0	1.35	6915	1676	716	394	244	99.5	51.4	30.0	18.8	8.56	4.27	2.19	1.11	0.53	0.19	0
0.2	1.22	6613	1602	684	376	233	95.0	49.0	28.6	18.0	8.17	4.08	2.09	1.07	0.51	0.19	0
0.4	1.10	6227	1533	655	360	223	91.0	47.0	27.4	17.2	7.83	3.92	2.01	1.03	0.50	0.19	0.01
0.6	0.84	5708	1382	591	324	201	81.9	42.3	24.6	15.5	7.04	3.53	1.82	0.94	0.46	0.18	0.01
0.8	0.42	4695	1137	485	266	165	67.2	34.6	20.2	12.7	5.77	2.90	1.50	0.78	0.39	0.16	0.02
1.0	0.24	4268	1033	441	242	150	61.0	31.4	18.3	11.5	5.24	2.64	1.37	0.72	0.37	0.16	0.02
1.4	0.10	3948	956	408	224	139	56.4	29.1	17.0	10.7	4.86	2.45	1.29	0.68	0.36	0.16	0.03
2.0	0.02	3783	916	391	215	133	54.1	27.9	16.3	10.2	4.68	2.38	1.26	0.68	0.36	0.17	0.04
3.0	0	3783	916	391	215	133	54.3	28.0	16.4	10.3	4.75	2.43	1.30	0.71	0.39	0.20	0.06
4.0	0	3833	929	397	218	135	55.2	28.6	16.7	10.6	4.82	2.51	1.35	0.75	0.42	0.22	0.08
5.0	0	3883	941	402	221	137	56.0	29.0	17.0	10.8	5.00	2.59	1.41	0.79	0.45	0.24	0.10
6.0	0	3933	954	408	224	139	56.9	29.6	17.4	11.0	5.12	2.67	1.46	0.83	0.48	0.27	0.12
7.0	0	3983	966	413	227	141	57.8	30.0	17.7	11.2	5.25	2.75	1.52	0.87	0.51	0.29	0.14
8.0	0	4033	979	419	231	143	58.7	30.6	18.0	11.4	5.38	2.83	1.57	0.91	0.54	0.32	0.16
9.0	0	4083	991	424	234	145	59.6	31.0	18.3	11.6	6.50	2.91	1.63	0.95	0.58	0.34	0.18
10.0	0	4133	1004	430	237	147	60.5	31.6	18.6	11.9	5.62	3.00	1.68	0.99	0.61	0.37	0.20

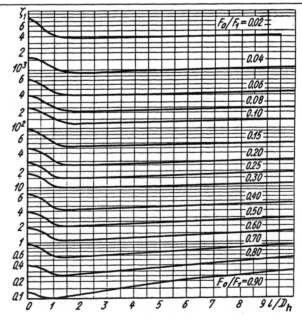

Orifice with beveled edges facing the flow ($\alpha = 40-60°$) in a straight tube; $Re = w_0 D_h / \nu > 10^4$ [13,14]	Diagram 4-16

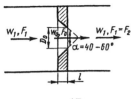

$$\zeta_1 \equiv \frac{\Delta p}{\rho w_1^2/2}\left[1 - \frac{F_0}{F_1} + \sqrt{\zeta'}\left(1 - \frac{F_0}{F_1}\right)^{0.375}\right]^2\left(\frac{F_1}{F_0}\right)^2, \text{ see the graph;}$$

$\zeta' = f(l/D_h)$, see the table below or graph a of Diagram 4-13;

or

$$D_h = \frac{4F_0}{\Pi_0}$$

$$\zeta' = 0.13 + 0.34 \times 10^{-(3.4\bar{l} + 88.4\bar{l}^{2.3})};$$

$$\bar{l} = l/D_h$$

Values or ζ_1

$\bar{l} = l/D_h$	ζ'	F_0/F_1															
		0.02	0.04	0.06	0.08	0.10	0.15	0.20	0.25	0.30	0.40	0.50	0.60	0.70	0.80	0.90	1.0
0.01	0.46	6840	1656	708	388	241	98.2	50.7	29.5	18.5	8.39	4.18	2.13	1.08	0.51	0.18	0
0.02	0.42	6592	1598	682	374	232	94.5	48.7	28.4	17.8	8.05	4.00	2.03	1.02	0.48	0.17	0
0.03	0.38	6335	1535	655	360	223	90.6	46.7	27.2	17.0	7.69	3.80	1.93	0.97	0.45	0.16	0
0.04	0.35	6140	1488	635	348	216	87.7	45.2	26.2	16.4	7.40	3.66	1.84	0.92	0.43	0.15	0
0.06	0.29	5737	1387	592	325	201	81.5	41.9	24.4	15.2	6.83	3.35	1.68	0.83	0.38	0.13	0
0.08	0.23	5297	1281	546	300	185	75.0	38.5	22.3	13.9	6.20	3.02	1.51	0.74	0.33	0.11	0
0.12	0.16	4748	1147	488	267	165	66.7	34.1	19.7	12.2	5.40	2.61	1.29	0.62	0.27	0.09	0
0.16	0.13	4477	1.81	460	251	155	62.7	32.0	18.4	11.4	5.02	2.42	1.18	0.56	0.24	0.08	0

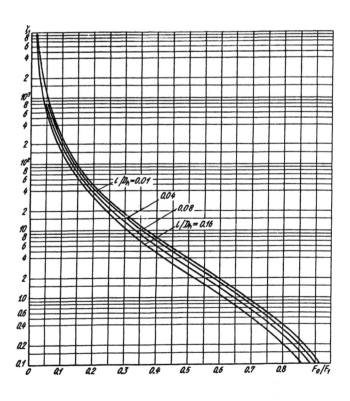

Orifice with rounded inlet edges in a straight tube;   Diagram 4-17
$Re = w_0 D_h / \nu > 10^4$ [13,14]

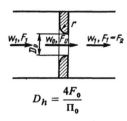

$$\zeta_1 \equiv \frac{\Delta p}{\rho w_1^2 / 2} = \left[1 - \frac{F_0}{F_1} + \sqrt{\zeta'} \left(1 - \frac{F_0}{F_1} \right)^{0.75} \right]^2 \left(\frac{F_1}{F_0} \right)^2, \text{ see the graph.}$$

$\zeta' = f_1\left(\dfrac{r}{D_h}\right)$, see the table below, graph b of Diagram 4-13 or

$\zeta' = 0.03 + 0.47 \times 10^{-7.7\bar{r}}; \quad \bar{r} = r/D_h$

$$D_h = \frac{4F_0}{\Pi_0}$$

Values of ζ_1

r/D_h	ζ'	0.02	0.04	0.06	0.08	0.10	0.15	0.20	0.25	0.30	0.35	0.40	0.45	0.50	0.55	0.60	0.65	0.70	0.75	0.80	0.90	1.0
												F_0/F_1										
0.01	0.44	6717	1628	695	382	236	96.4	49.7	29.0	18.2	12.0	8.24	5.75	4.10	2.91	2.08	1.49	1.05	0.73	0.49	0.18	0
0.02	0.37	6273	1520	648	356	221	89.7	46.2	26.9	16.8	11.1	7.59	5.29	3.75	2.65	1.90	1.35	0.95	0.66	0.44	0.15	0
0.03	0.31	5875	1421	607	332	206	83.6	43.0	25.0	15.6	10.3	7.01	4.87	3.45	2.43	1.74	1.23	0.86	0.59	0.40	0.14	0
0.04	0.26	5520	1336	570	312	193	78.3	40.2	23.4	14.6	9.54	6.51	4.51	3.19	2.24	1.60	1.13	0.79	0.54	0.36	0.12	0
0.06	0.19	4982	1206	513	281	174	70.3	36.0	20.8	12.9	8.46	5.76	3.97	2.79	1.96	1.38	0.97	0.67	0.46	0.30	0.10	0
0.08	0.15	4657	1125	479	262	162	65.3	33.4	19.3	12.0	7.80	5.29	3.63	2.55	1.78	1.25	0.88	0.60	0.41	0.26	0.08	0
0.12	0.09	4085	986	420	229	141	56.8	29.0	16.6	10.2	6.65	4.48	3.06	2.14	1.48	1.03	0.71	0.48	0.33	0.21	0.06	0
0.16	0.06	3745	902	384	210	129	51.8	26.3	15.0	9.26	5.99	4.02	2.73	1.90	1.31	0.91	0.62	0.42	0.28	0.17	0.05	0

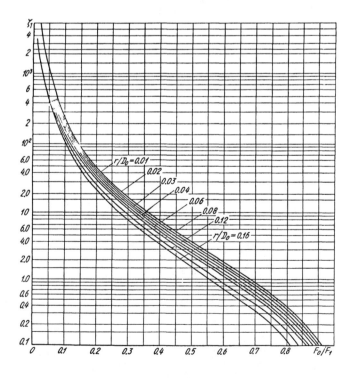

Orifices with various edges in a wall with infinite surface area[13,14]	Diagram 4-18

Orifice edges	Configuration	Resistance coefficient
Sharp ($l/D_h = 0 \to 0.015$)	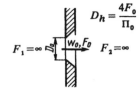 $D_h = \dfrac{4F_0}{\Pi_0}$ $F_1 = \infty$ w_0, F_0 $F_2 = \infty$	$Re = \dfrac{w_0 D_h}{\nu} \geq 10^4$ $\zeta = 2.7\text{–}2.8$
Thick-walled (deep orifice) ($l/D_h > 0.015$)	$F_1 = \infty$ w_0, F_0 $F_2 = \infty$ l	$Re \geq 10^4 \quad \zeta = \zeta_0 + \lambda(l/D_h),$ where $\zeta_0 = f(\bar{l})$ or $\zeta = 1.5 + (2.4 - \bar{l}) \times 10^{-\varphi(\bar{l})} + \lambda l/D_h,$ $\varphi(\bar{l}) = 0.25 + 0.535\bar{l}^8/(0.05 + \bar{l}^7)$ for λ see Chapter 2

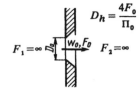

Graph (a):

$\bar{l} \equiv l/D_h$	0	0.2	0.4	0.6	0.8	1.0
ζ_0	2.85	2.72	2.60	2.34	1.95	1.76

$\bar{l} \equiv l/D_h$	1.2	1.4	1.6	1.8	2.0	4.0
ζ_0	1.67	1.62	1.60	1.58	1.55	1.55

Orifice edges	Configuration	Resistance coefficient
Beveled facing flow direction	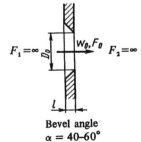 $F_1 = \infty$ w_0, F_0 $F_2 = \infty$ l Bevel angle $\alpha = 40\text{–}60°$	$Re \geq 10^4$ $\zeta = f(\bar{l})$, see graph b or $\zeta = (1 + \sqrt{\zeta'})^2$ where $\zeta' = 0.13 + 0.34 \times 10$ 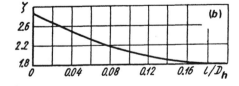

$\bar{l} \equiv l/D_h$	0	0.01	0.02	0.03	0.04	0.05
ζ	2.85	2.80	2.70	2.60	2.50	2.41

$\bar{l} \equiv l/D_h$	0.06	0.08	0.10	0.12	0.16	0.20
ζ	2.33	2.18	2.08	1.98	1.84	1.80

Orifices with various edges in a wall with infinite surface area[13,14]		Diagram 4-18

Orifice edges	Configuration	Resistance coefficient
Rounded facing flow direction	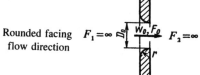	$\mathrm{Re} \geqslant 10^4$ $\zeta = f(\bar{r})$, see graph c or $\zeta = (1 + \sqrt{\zeta'})^2$ where $\zeta' = 0.03 + 0.47 \times 10^{-7.7\bar{r}}$

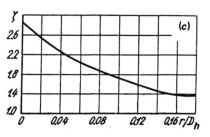

$\bar{r} = r/D_h$	0.01	0.02	0.03	0.04	0.06	0.08	0.12	0.16	0.20
ζ	2.72	2.56	2.40	2.27	2.06	1.88	1.60	1.38	1.37

Orifice with any edges for different conditions of flow in the transient and laminar regions ($\mathrm{Re} = w_0 D_h/\nu < 10^4 - 10^5$)[16]	Diagram 4-19

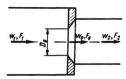

1. At $30 < \mathrm{Re} < 10^4 - 10^5$: $\zeta \equiv \dfrac{\Delta p}{\rho w_0^2/2} = \zeta_\phi + \bar{\varepsilon}_{0\mathrm{Re}} \zeta_{0\mathrm{quad}}$

   and correspondingly $\zeta_1 \equiv \dfrac{\Delta p}{\rho w_1^2/2} = \zeta_\phi \left(\dfrac{F_1}{F_0}\right)^2 + \bar{\varepsilon}_{0\mathrm{Re}} \zeta_{1\mathrm{quad}}$

2. At $10 < \mathrm{Re} < 30$: $\zeta \equiv \dfrac{\Delta p}{\rho w_0^2/2} = \zeta_\phi \left(\dfrac{F_1}{F_0}\right)^2 = \dfrac{33}{\mathrm{Re}} + \bar{\varepsilon}_{0\mathrm{Re}} \zeta_{0\mathrm{quad}}$

   and $\zeta_1 \equiv \dfrac{\Delta p}{\rho w_1^2/2} = \dfrac{33}{\mathrm{Re}} \left(\dfrac{F_1}{F_0}\right)^2 + \bar{\varepsilon}_{0\mathrm{Re}} \zeta_{1\mathrm{quad}}$,

   where for $\bar{\varepsilon}_{0\mathrm{Re}}$ see below.

3. At $\mathrm{Re} < 10$: $\zeta \equiv \dfrac{\Delta p}{\rho w_0^2/2} = \dfrac{33}{\mathrm{Re}}$ and $\zeta_1 \equiv \dfrac{\Delta p}{\rho w_1^2/2} = \dfrac{33}{\mathrm{Re}} \left(\dfrac{F_1}{F_0}\right)^2$,

$\zeta_{0\mathrm{quad}} \equiv \Delta p/(\rho w_0^2/2)$, $\zeta_{1\mathrm{quad}} \equiv \Delta p/(\rho w_0^2/2)$ are determined as ζ at $\mathrm{Re} > 10^4$ from the corresponding Diagrams 4-11 to 4-18.

ζ_ϕ is determined from Table 1 or from the formula

$\zeta_\phi = [18.78 - 7.768 F_1/F_0 + 6.337(F_1/F_0)^2] \exp\{[-0.942 - 7.246 F_0/F_1 - 3.878(F_0/F_1)^2] \lg \mathrm{Re}\}$;

Orifice with any edges for different conditions of flow in the transient and laminar regions (Re $= w_0 D_h/\nu < 10^4 - 10^5$)[16]	Diagram 4-19

$\bar{\varepsilon}_{0\,Re}$ is determined from Table 2 or from the formula $\bar{\varepsilon}_{0\,Re} = \sum\limits_{i=0}^{5} a_i (\lg Re)^i$, where

$a_0 = 0.461465$; $a_1 = -0.2648592$; $a_2 = 0.2030479$;
$a_3 = -0.06602521$; $a_4 = 0.01325519$; $a_5 = -0.001058041$

Values of ζ_ϕ

$\dfrac{F_0}{F_1}$	Re														
	30	40	60	10^2	2×10^2	4×10^2	10^3	2×10^3	4×10^3	10^4	2×10^4	10^5	2×10^5	10^6
0	1.94	1.38	1.14	0.89	0.69	0.64	0.39	0.30	0.22	0.15	0.11	0.04	0.01	0
0.2	1.78	1.36	1.05	0.85	0.67	0.57	0.36	0.26	0.20	0.13	0.09	0.03	0.01	0
0.3	1.57	1.16	0.88	0.75	0.57	0.43	0.30	0.22	0.17	0.10	0.07	0.02	0.01	0
0.4	1.35	0.99	0.79	0.57	0.40	0.28	0.19	0.14	0.10	0.06	0.04	0.02	0.01	0
0.5	1.10	0.75	0.55	0.34	0.19	0.12	0.07	0.05	0.03	0.02	0.01	0.01	0.01	0
0.6	0.85	0.56	0.30	0.19	0.10	0.06	0.03	0.02	0.01	0.01	0	0	0	0
0.7	0.58	0.37	0.23	0.11	0.06	0.03	0.02	0.01	0	0	0	0	0	0
0.8	0.40	0.24	0.13	0.06	0.03	0.02	0.01	0	0	0	0	0	0	0
0.9	0.20	0.13	0.08	0.03	0.01	0	0	0	0	0	0	0	0	0
0.95	0.03	0.03	0.02	0	0	0	0	0	0	0	0	0	0	0

2. Values of $\bar{\varepsilon}_{0\,Re}$

Re	$\bar{\varepsilon}_{0\,Re}$	Re	$\bar{\varepsilon}_{0\,Re}$
		2×10^3	0.69
10	0.34	4×10^3	0.74
20	0.35	6×10^3	0.76
30	0.36	10^4	
40	0.37		0.80
60	0.40	2×10^4	0.82
80	0.43	4×10^4	0.85
10^2	0.45	6×10^4	0.87
2×10^2	0.52	10^5	0.90
4×10^2	0.58	2×10^5	0.95
6×10^2	0.62	3×10^5	0.98
10^3	0.65	4×10^5	1.0

Perforated plates or orifice in tubes at large subsonic velocities (high Mach numbers)[34]	Diagram 4-20

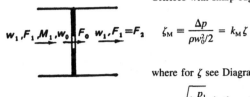

Orifices with sharp edges:

$$\zeta_M \equiv \frac{\Delta p}{\rho w_0^2/2} = k_M \zeta$$

where for ζ see Diagrams 4-11 and 4-12; $k_M = f(\mathrm{Ma}_1)$; $\mathrm{Ma}_1 = \dfrac{w_1}{a}$;

$a_1 = \sqrt{k \dfrac{p_1}{\rho_1}}$ is the velocity of sound; for k see Table 1-4.

For beveled or rounded edges of orifices, see Diagram 8-7.

Values of k_M

$\bar{f}$	\multicolumn{14}{c}{Ma_1}
	0	0.05	0.10	0.15	0.20	0.25	0.30	0.35	0.40	0.45	0.50	0.55	0.60	0.65
0.2	1.00	1.09	1.30	–	–	–	–	–	–	–	–	–	–	–
0.3	1.00	1.03	1.13	1.51	–	–	–	–	–	–	–	–	–	–
0.4	1.00	0.00	1.03	1.14	1.41	–	–	–	–	–	–	–	–	–
0.5	1.00	1.00	1.00	1.03	1.10	1.27	1.85	–	–	–	–	–	–	–
0.6	1.00	0.00	1.00	1.00	1.12	1.30	1.30	1.77	–	–	–	–	–	–
0.7	1.00	1.00	1.00	1.00	1.03	1.08	1.18	1.35	1.68	–	–	–	–	–
0.8	1.00	1.00	1.00	1.00	1.01	1.03	1.07	1.12	1.20	1.37	1.63	2.01	–	–
0.9	1.00	1.00	1.00	1.00	1.00	1.00	1.02	1.04	1.07	1.13	1.21	1.33	1.50	1.75

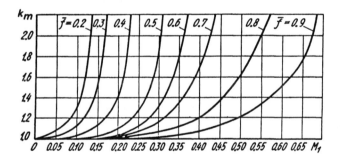

Bellmouth nozzle installed in a wall of infinite surface area, $\mathrm{Re} = w_0 D_h/\nu > 10^{4}$ [27]	Diagram 4-21

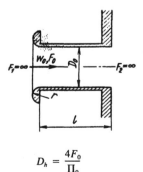

$$\zeta \equiv \frac{\Delta p}{\rho w_0^2/2} = \zeta' + \zeta_{\mathrm{fr}} \,,$$

where $\zeta_{\mathrm{fr}} = \lambda \dfrac{l}{D_h}$; $\zeta' = f\left(\dfrac{l}{D_h}, \dfrac{r}{D_h}\right)$; for λ see Chapter 2.

$$D_h = \frac{4F_0}{\Pi_0}$$

Bellmouth nozzle installed in a wall of infinite surface area, Re $= w_0 D_h/\nu > 10^{4\,27}$	Diagram 4-21

Values ζ'

$\dfrac{r}{D_h}$	$\dfrac{l}{D_h}$											
	0.25	0.50	0.75	1.00	1.25	1.50	1.75	2.0	2.5	3.0	3.5	4.0
0.02	2.64	2.25	1.89	1.68	1.60	1.56	1.54	1.53	1.51	1.50	1.49	1.48
0.04	2.20	1.70	1.42	1.37	1.34	1.33	1.33	1.32	1.32	1.32	1.31	1.30
0.06	1.90	1.30	1.23	1.22	1.22	1.21	1.21	1.21	1.21	1.21	1.20	1.20
0.08	1.44	1.19	1.16	1.15	1.15	1.15	1.15	1.15	1.15	1.15	1.15	1.15
0.10	1.12	1.10	1.10	1.10	1.10	1.10	1.10	1.10	1.10	1.10	1.10	1.10
0.12	1.08	1.08	1.08	1.07	1.07	1.07	1.07	1.07	1.07	1.08	1.08	1.08
0.20	1.04	1.04	1.04	1.04	1.04	1.04	1.04	1.04	1.04	1.05	1.05	1.05
0.50	1.03	1.03	1.03	1.03	1.03	1.03	1.03	1.03	1.03	1.03	1.03	1.03

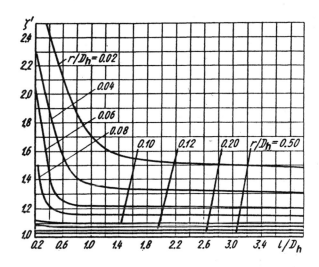

Orifices in a thin wall in the presence of a passing flow $(w_\infty > 0)$; Re $= w_0 D_h/\nu \geq 10^{4\,28}$	Diagram 4-22

Scheme 1

Scheme 2

Arrangement of orifices

Scheme 3

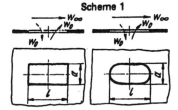

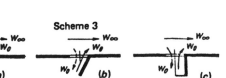

A. Suction orifices (intake; w_0, dashed arrows)

Without baffles (schemes 1 and 2):

$\zeta \equiv \dfrac{\Delta p}{\rho w_0^2/2}$, see graphs a–c. With baffles at a circular orifice (scheme 3): $\zeta \equiv \dfrac{\Delta p}{\rho w_0^2/2}$, see graphs b and d.

Orifices in a thin wall in the presence of a passing flow ($w_\infty > 0$); Re $= w_0 D_h/\nu \geq 10^{4\,28}$	Diagram 4-22

Values of ζ for scheme 1 (graph a)

$\dfrac{l}{a}$	w_∞/w_0							
	0	0.5	1.0	2.0	3.0	4.0	5.0	6.0
0.17	2.70–2.80	2.75–2.85	2.95	4.00	5.20	6.65	8.05	9.50
0.5	2.70–2.80	2.65–2.75	2.85	3.35	4.15	5.00	6.00	7.00
1.0	2.70–2.80	2.65–2.75	2.85	3.35	4.15	5.00	6.00	7.00
2.0	2.70–2.80	2.65–2.75	2.85	3.20	3.80	4.50	5.20	5.95
6.0	2.70–2.80	2.55–2.65	2.65–2.75	3.15	3.55	4.15	4.75	5.45

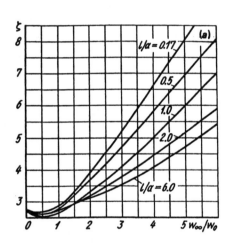 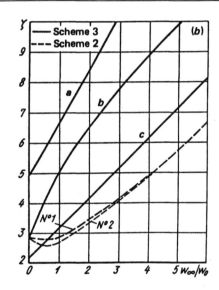

Values of ζ for scheme 2 (graph b)

Arrangement of orifices	w_∞/w_0							
	0	0.5	1.0	2.0	3.0	4.0	5.0	6.0
No. 1	2.70–2.80	2.70–2.80	2.80–2.90	3.50	4.10	4.95	5.75	6.70
No. 2	2.70–2.80	2.55–2.65	2.60–2.70	3.40	4.05	4.95	5.75	6.70

	Diagram 4-22

Values of ζ for scheme 3 (graph b)

Curve	$\dfrac{w_\infty}{w_0}$							
	0	0.5	1.0	2.0	3.0	4.0	5.0	6.0
a	4.95	5.75	6.60	8.45	10.0	–	–	–
b	2.73–2.85	4.00	5.00	6.50	7.80	8.95	10.0	–
c	2.16–2.20	2.60–2.70	3.20	4.20	5.20	6.20	7.20	8.20

	Diagram 4-22

B. Discharge orifices (exit; w_0, solid arrows)

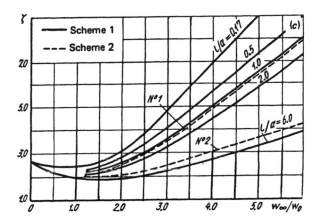

Values of ζ for scheme 1 (graph c)

$\dfrac{l}{a}$	$\dfrac{w_\infty}{w_0}$								
	0	0.5	1.0	1.5	2.0	3.0	4.0	5.0	6.0
0.17	2.70–2.80	2.50–2.60	2.45–2.55	2.55–2.65	3.05	4.75	7.0	9.00	–
0.5	2.70–2.80	2.40–2.50	2.25–2.35	2.45–2.55	2.80–2.90	4.10	5.70	7.30	9.00
1.0	2.70–2.80	2.25–2.35	2.20–2.30	2.25–2.35	2.60–2.70	3.65	5.00	6.50	8.00
2.0	2.70–2.80	2.25–2.35	2.05–2.15	2.05–2.10	2.40–2.50	3.35	4.50	5.80	7.25
6.0	2.70–2.80	2.25–2.35	2.00–2.10	1.90–2.00	1.90–2.00	2.25–2.35	2.75–2.85	3.30	3.90

Orifices in a thin wall in the presence of a passing flow, $w_\infty(w_\infty > 0)$; $\mathrm{Re} = w_0 D_h/\nu \geqslant 10^4$ [28]	Diagram 4-22

Values of ζ for scheme 2 (graph c)

Arrangement of orifices	$\dfrac{w_\infty}{w_0}$								
	0	0.5	1.0	1.5	2.0	3.0	4.0	5.0	6.0
No. 1	2.70–2.80	2.25–2.35	2.00–2.10	2.05–2.15	2.50–2.60	3.50	4.95	6.45	7.90
No. 2	2.70–2.80	2.40–2.50	2.10–2.20	2.05–2.15	2.10–2.20	2.50–2.60	3.00	3.60	4.20

Orifices in a thin wall in the presence of a passing flow,   Diagram
$w_\infty(w_\infty > 0)$; Re $= w_0 D_h/\nu \geqslant 10^{4}$ [28]   4-22

Values of ζ for scheme 3 (graph d)

| | $\dfrac{w_\infty}{w_0}$ | | | | | | | | |
Curve	0	0.5	1.0	1.5	2.0	3.0	4.0	5.0	6.0
1	4.75	4.40	4.05	3.85	3.85	4.40	5.35	6.55	7.75
2	3.00	3.00	3.00	3.00	3.15	4.00	5.65	6.45	7.70
3	2.16–2.20	2.05–2.10	2.10–2.20	2.35–2.45	2.65–2.75	3.50	4.75	6.20	7.55

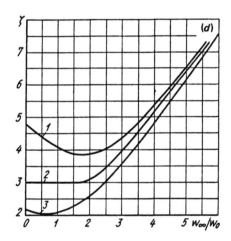

Movable flaps[5]   Diagram
       4-23

Exhaust, single top-hinged flap

 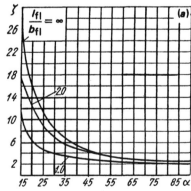

Values of ζ (graph a)

$\dfrac{l_n}{b_n}$	α, degrees						
	15	20	25	30	45	60	90
1.0	11	6.3	4.5	4.0	3.0	2.5	2.0
2.0	17	12	8.5	6.9	4.0	3.1	2.5
∞	30	16	11	8.6	4.7	3.3	2.5

l_n is the flap length;

$$w_0 = \frac{Q}{F_0}; \quad \zeta \equiv \frac{\Delta p}{\rho w_0^2/2}$$

Movable flaps[5]	Diagram 4-23

Intake, single top-hinged flap

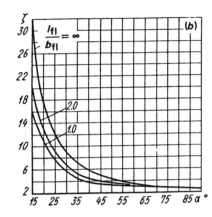

Values of ζ (graph b)

$\dfrac{l_n}{b_n}$	α, degrees						
	15	20	25	30	45	60	90
1.0	16	11	8.0	5.7	3.7	3.1	2.6
2.0	21	13	9.3	6.9	4.0	3.2	2.6
∞	31	18	12.5	9.2	5.2	3.5	2.6

Single center-hinged flap

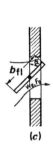

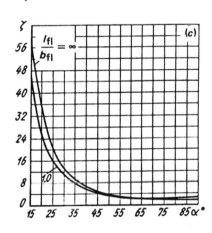

Values of ζ (graph c)

$\dfrac{l_n}{b_n}$	α, degrees						
	15	20	25	30	45	60	90
1.0	46	26	16	11	5.0	3.0	2.0
∞	59	35	21	14	5.0	3.0	2.4

Double, top-hinged flaps

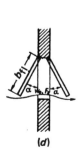

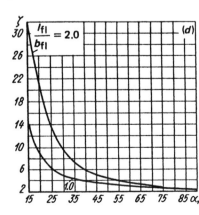

Values of ζ (graph d)

$\dfrac{l_n}{b_n}$	α, degrees						
	15	20	25	30	45	60	90
1.0	14	9.0	6.0	4.9	3.8	3.0	2.4
2.0	31	21	14	9.8	5.2	3.5	2.4

Movable flaps[5]	Diagram 4-23

Double flaps (one top- and the other bottom-hinged)

 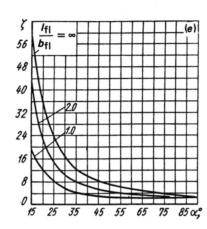

Values of ζ (graph e)

$\dfrac{l_n}{b_n}$	α, degrees						
	15	20	25	30	45	60	90
1.0	19	13	8.5	6.3	3.8	3.0	2.4
2.0	44	24	15	11	6.0	4.0	2.8
∞	59	36	24	17	8.6	5.7	2.8

Grating with adjustable louvers in a wall of infinite surface area ($\bar{f} \approx 0.8$ for completely open louvers)	Diagram 4-24

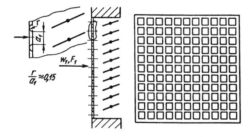

$\zeta \equiv \dfrac{\Delta p}{\rho w_1^2/2} \approx 1.6$, where w_1 is the mean velocity over the total area of the grating in the wall

$\bar{f} = \dfrac{F_0}{F_1}$; F_0 is the open flow area of the grating

Working section (open) of a wind tunnel[1]	Diagram 4-25

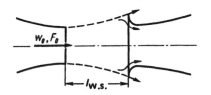

For a rectangular section

$$D_h = \frac{2a_0 b_0}{a_0 + b_0}$$

for an elliptical section

$$D_h = \frac{4a_0 b_0}{1.5(a_0 + b_0) - \sqrt{a_0 b_0}}$$

where a_0 and b_0 are the sides of the rectangle or semiaxes of the ellipse. Circular (or rectangular) cross section:

$$\zeta \equiv \frac{\Delta p}{\rho w_0^2/2} = 0.1 \frac{l_{w.s.}}{D_h} - 0.008 \left(\frac{l_{w.s.}}{D_h}\right)^2 , \text{ see curve } \zeta = f\left(\frac{l_{w.s.}}{D_h}\right)$$

$\dfrac{l_{w.s.}}{D_h}$	0	0.5	1.0	1.5	2.0	2.5	3.0	3.5	4.0	4.5	5.0
ζ	0	0.04	0.08	0.12	0.15	0.18	0.21	0.23	0.25	0.27	0.29

Elliptical cross section:

$$\zeta \equiv \frac{\Delta p}{\rho w_0^2/2} = 0.145 \frac{l_{w.s.}}{D_h} - 0.0017 \frac{l_{w.s.}}{a_0 b_0}$$

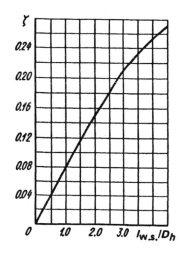

REFERENCES

1. Abramovich, G. N., *Theory of Turbulent Jets*, Fizmatgiz, Moscow, 1960, 715 p.
2. Altshul, A. D., Arzumanov, E. S., and Veziryan, R. E., Experimental study of the dependence of the resistance coefficient in the course of sudden expansion of flow on the Reynolds number, *Neft. Khoz.*, no. 4, 64–70, 1967.
3. Altshul, A. D., *Hydraulic Resistances*, Moscow, 1982, 224 p.
4. Balanin, V. V. and Vasilevskiy, V. P., Determination of the flow resistance coefficient by the method of the theory of turbulent jets, *Tr. Leningr. Inst. Vodn. Transp.*, vyp. 158, 10–16, 1977; vyp. 162, 5–10, 1978.
5. Bromblei, M. F., Discharge coefficients of orifices covered by flaps, in *Sovrem. Vopr. Ventilyats*, pp. 40–65, Stroiizdat, Moscow, 1941.
6. Veziryan, R. E., Investigation of the mutual effect of locking and regulating devices on the hydraulic resistance, *Tr. NIIAvtomat.*, vyp. 2, 25–29, 1974.
7. Volkova, L. P. and Yudelovich, M. Ya., Sock losses in stepwise tubes at supersonic pressure ratios, *Izv. Akad. Nauk SSSR, Otd. Tekh. Nauk*, no. 4, 68–72, 1958.
8. Garkusha, A. V. and Kucherrenko, S. I., Specific features of flow through an annular channel with a step at n = 1.7, *Energ. Mashinostr.*, vyp. 31, 13–18, 1981.
9. Glotov, G. F. and Moroz, E. K., Investigation of the flow of gas in a cylindrical channel with an abrupt expansion of the sonic flow, *Uch. Zap. TsAGI*, vol. 1, no. 2, 53–59, 1970.
10. Dudintsev, L. M., Discharge coefficient of an orifice in the wall with a parallel directed flow, *Izv. VUZov Stroit. Arkhit.*, no. 5, 97–103, 1969.
11. Zhukovsky, I. E., Variation of the Kirchhoff method to determine liquid flow in two dimensions at constant velocity prescribed at the unknown streamline, *Collected Works*, vol. 2, pp. 130–240, Gosizdat, Moscow, 1949.
12. Idelchik, I. E., Hydraulic resistances during entry of flow in channels and passage through orifices, *Prom. Aerodin.*, no. 2, 27–57, 1944.
13. Idelchik, I. E., *Hydraulic Resistances (Physical and Mechanical Fundamentals)*, Gosenergoizdat, 1954, 316 p.
14. Idelchik, I. E., Determination of the resistance coefficients during discharge through orifices, *Gidrotekh. Stroit.*, no. 5, 31–36, 1953.
15. Idelchik, I. E., Shock losses in a flow with a nonuniform velocity distribution, *Tr. TsAGI*, vyp. 662, 2–24, MAP, 1948.
16. Idelchik, I. E., Account for the viscosity effect on the hydraulic resistance of diaphragms and grids, *Teploenergetika*, no. 9, 75–80, 1960.
17. Karev, V. N., Pressure head losses with an abrupt expansion of the pipeline, *Neft. Khoz.*, no. 11/12, 13–16, 1952.
18. Karev, V. N., Pressure head losses with an abrupt contraction of the pipeline, and the effect of local resistances on flow disturbances, *Neft. Khoz.*, no. 8, 3–7, 1953.
19. Levin, A. M. and Malaya, E. M., Investigation of the hydrodynamics of flow with an abrupt expansion, *Tr. Gos. Proektno-Issled. Inst. Vostokgiprogaz*, vyp. 1, 41–47, 1969.
20. Levkoyeva, N. V., Investigation of the Effect of Fluid Viscosity of Local Resistances, Thesis (Cand. of Techn. Sciences), Moscow, 1959, 186 p.
21. Migai, V. K. and Nosova, I. S., Reduction of eddy losses in channels, *Teploenergetika*, no. 7, 49–51, 1977.
22. Morozov, D. I., The optimum degree of a sudden enlargement of the channel, *Tr. Khark. Univ.*, vyp. 4, 53–55, Gidromekhanika, 1966.
23. Panchurin, N. A., Extension of the Borda-Carnot theorem on the pressure head loss during an abrupt expansion to the case of unsteady-state flow, *Tr. Leningr. Inst. Vodn. Transp.*, vyp. 51, 34–39, 1964.
24. Fedotkin, I. M., Hydraulic resistance of throttling diaphragms to a two-phase flow, *Izv. VUZov Energ.*, no. 4, 37–43, 1969.
25. Frenkel, N. A., *Hydraulics*, Gosenergoizdat, 1956, 456 p.
26. Khanzhonkov, V. I., Aerodynamic characteristics of the collectors, *Prom. Aerodin.*, no. 4, 45–64, 1953.
27. Khanzhonkov, V. I., Reduction of the aerodynamic resistance of orifices by means of annular fins and recesses, *Prom. Aerodin.*, no. 12, 181–196, Oborengiz, Moscow, 1959.
28. Khanzhonkov, V. I., Resistance to discharge through an orifice in the wall in the presence of passing stream, *Prom. Aerodin.*, no. 15, 5–19, Oborengiz, Moscow, 1959.
29. Chjen, P., *Separation Flows*, Moscow, 1972, pt 1–300; pt 2–280 p.
30. Shvets, I. T., Repukhov, V. M., and Bogachuk-Kozachuk, K. A., Full pressure losses during air injection into a stalling air flow through orifices in the wall, *Teploenergetika*, 1976.
31. Alvi, Sh. H., Contraction coefficient of pipe orifices, Flow Meas., Proc. FLUMEX 83 I MeCO Conf., Budapest, nos. 20–22, 213–218, 1983.

32. Astarita, G. and Greco, G., Excess pressure drop in laminar flow through sudden contraction, *Ind. Eng. Chem. Fundam.*, vol. 7, no. 1, 27–31, 1968.

33. Ball, J. W., Sudden enlargements in pipelines, *J. Power Div., Proc. Am. Soc. Civil Eng.*, vol. 88, no. 4, 15–27, 1962.

34. Cornell, W. G., Losses in flow normal to plane screens, *Trans. ASME*, no. 4, 145–153, 1958.

35. Dewey, P. E. and Vick, A. R., An investigation of the discharge and drag characteristics of auxiliary — air outlets discharging into a transonic stream, *NACA Tech. Note*, no. 3466, 1955, 38 p.

36. Dickerson, P. and Rice, W., An investigation of very small diameter laminar flow orifices, *Trans. ASME*, vol. D91, no. 3, 546–548, 1969.

37. Forst, T. H., The compressible discharge coefficient of a Borda pipe and other nozzles, *J.R. Aeronaut. Soc.*, no. 641, 346–349, 1964.

38. Geiger, G. E. and Rohrer, W. M., Sudden contraction losses in two-phase flow, *Trans. ASME Ser. C*, vol. 88, no. 1, p. 1–9, 1966.

39. Hebrard, P. and Sananes, F., Calcul de l'ecoulement turbulent decolle en aval de l'elargissement brusque dans une veine de section circulaire, *C.R. Acad. Sci.*, vol. 268, no. 26, A1638–A1641, 1969.

40. Iversen, H. W., Orifice coefficients for Reynolds numbers from 4 to 50,000, *Trans. ASME*, vol. 78, no. 2, 125–133, 1956.

41. Johansen, F., Flow through pipe orifices of low Reynolds numbers, *Proc. R. Soc. London Ser. A.*, vol. 126, no. 801, 125–131, 1930.

42. Kolodzie, P. A. and Van Winkle, M., Discharge coefficients through perforated plates, *AIChE J.*, vol. 3, no. 9, 23–30, 1959.

43. Reichert, V., Theoretische-experimentelle Untersuchungen zur Widerstanscharakteristik von Hydraulikventilen, Wassenschaffliche Zeitschrift der Technischen Universität, Dresden, Bd. 3, Heft 2, S. 149–155, 1982.

44. Ringleb, T., Two-dimensional flow with standing vortexes in diffusers, *Trans. ASME Ser. D*, no. 4, 130–135, 1960.

45. Pearson, H. and Heurteux, B. M., Losses at sudden expansions and contractions in ducts, *Aeronaut. Q.*, bd. 14, no. 1, S., 63–74, 1963.

RESISTANCE TO FLOW WITH A SMOOTH CHANGE IN VELOCITY
Resistance Coefficients of Diffusers and Converging and other Transition Sections

5-1 EXPLANATIONS AND PRACTICAL RECOMMENDATIONS; DIFFUSERS IN A NETWORK

1. A smoothly expanding tubular section, a diffuser, is used in order to make the transition from a tube (channel) of smaller cross section to a larger one (to convert the kinetic energy of flow into the potential energy or of velocity pressure into static pressure) with minimum total pressure losses (Figure 5-1).* Due to the fact that an increase in the cross-sectional area of the diffuser causes a drop in the average flow velocity with an increase in the divergence angle α the total resistance coefficient of the diffuser expressed in terms of the velocity in the smaller (initial) section, becomes smaller up to certain limits of α, than for the equivalent segment of a tube of a tube of constant cross section, the area of which is equal to the initial area of the diffuser.

Starting from this limiting divergence angle of the diffuser, a further increase in this angle considerably increases the resistance coefficient, so that it becomes much larger than that for a straight tube of equivalent length.

2. The increase of the resistance coefficient of a diffuser of a given length with further increases in the divergence angle is caused by enhanced turbulence of the flow, separation of the boundary layer from the diffuser wall, and resultant violent vortex formation.

The boundary layer separates from the walls (see Figure 5-1) due to the adverse pressure gradient along the diffuser walls, resulting from the velocity drop as the cross-sectional area increases (according to the Bernoulli equation).

3. Under constant flow conditions at the entrance and for constant relative length l_d, or at the area ratio $n_{ar} = F_1/F_0$, an increase in the divergence angle α, starting from $\alpha = 0°$, will result in a successive achievement of the four main flow regimes:

---

*The main geometric characteristics of diffusers with straight walls are the divergence angle α, the area ratio $n_{ar1} = F_1/F_0$, and the relative length l_d. These quantities are connected by the following relationships: for a conical diffuser $l_0/D_0 = (\sqrt{n_{ar1}} - 1)/(2 \tan \alpha/2)$, for a plane diffuser $l_d/a_0 = (n_{ar1} - 1)/(2 \tan \alpha/2)$.

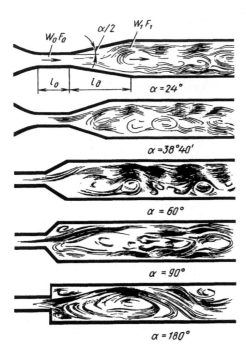

Figure 5-1 Flow patterns in diffusers with different divergence angles at $n_{ar1} = F_1/F_0 = 3.3$.[48]

- Stable regime, nonseparating flow ("separation-free" diffusers);
- Regime with a large nondeveloped flow separation, where the size and intensity of separation change with time (regime of strongly oscillating flows, diffusers with local flow separation);
- Regime of fully developed flow separation, where the major portion of the diffuser is occupied by an extensive zone of reverse circulation (diffusers with substantial flow separation):
- Regime of jet flow, where the main flow is separated from the diffuser walls over the whole perimeter (diffusers with complete flow separation).

4. The inception of flow separation in a diffuser is a function of both its geometric parameters and the flow regime at its inlet (Reynolds numbers $Re = w_0 D_h/\nu$ and Mach numbers $Ma_0 = w_0/a_1$), as well as of the condition of the flow at the inlet (displacement thickness δ^{*1} of the boundary layer or the "momentum loss" thickness δ^{*2}, the level of turbulence, etc.*) Experiments carried out by Idelchik and Ginzburg[54] show that for a conical diffuser ($\alpha = 4°$) installed both immediately behind the smooth inlet (collector) without an insert ($l_0/D_0 = 0$ and the boundary-layer displacement thickness at the inlet $\delta_0^{*1} \approx 0$) and far behind it with a straight insert ($l_0/D_0 \neq 0$ and $\delta_0^{*1} \neq 0$), there is no flow separation along the entire length of the diffuser even when the length corresponds to the section with area ratio $n_x = F_x/F_0 = 16$ (Figure 5-2). "Blurring" of the potential core (the core of constant velocities), the presence of which determines the "starting length" of the diffuser, that is, the section with a nonstabilized flow and a corresponding "extension" of the whole velocity profile at $l_0/D_0 = 0$, terminates at about $n_x = 6$–8. Downstream of this section, that is,

$$*\delta^{*1} = \int_0^\delta \left(1 - \frac{w}{w_c}\right) dy \qquad \delta^{*2} = \int_0^\delta \frac{w}{w_c}\left(1 - \frac{w}{w_c}\right) dy$$

where w_c is the velocity in the potential core along the flow axis.

over the length of stabilized flow (where the boundary layer fills the whole section), a noticeable equalization of the elongated velocity profile is observed.

5. If there is a straight insert ($l_0/D_0 \neq 0$) the starting length of the diffuser (with the core of constant velocities) becomes shorter. For example, at $l_0/D_0 = 20$ and $\alpha = 4°$, the core is retained only up to $n_x = 4$ (see Figure 5-2). As a result, the velocity profiles in the first sections of the starting length are much more extended than at $l_0/D_0 = 0$. In subsequent sections downstream of the starting length ($n_x \geq 6$) the velocity profiles at $l_0/D_0 \neq 0$ become more equalized than at $l_0/D_0 = 0$ and this can be attributed to intensification of flow turbulence.

6. According to the experiments mentioned above, with an increase of α up to 10–14°, the value of n_x at which the core of constant velocities is still preserved increases (since the length of the diffuser at the same n_x is reduced). At the same time, at the divergence angles cited and at certain ratios l_0/D_0 the flow starts to separate despite the presence of the core of constant velocities (Figures 5-3 to 5-5).

7. For practical purposes the regions without separation both in spatial and plane diffusers can, with limited accuracy, be determined with the help of Figure 5-6. Curves 1 and 2 in Figure 5-6 are the result of generalization of numerous experimental data.[36,54,129] The curves separate the whole region of $\alpha = f(n_x)$ into two parts: separation-free diffusers (region I) and separation-prone diffusers (region II). Curve 1 is related to more favorable inlet conditions ($l_0/D_0 \approx 0$, $\delta_0^* \approx 0$). Curve 2 is related to the case where the diffuser is installed downstream of the long inlet section at which $\delta_0^*/D_0 \gg 0$.

8. As a rule, flow starts to separate from the walls of diffusers with divergence angles up to about $\alpha = 40°$, not over the whole perimeter of the section, but in the region where, because of asymmetry of the diffuser, asymmetric velocity profile at the entrance, and so on, the flow velocity in the wall layer is lower than in other regions of the section. As soon

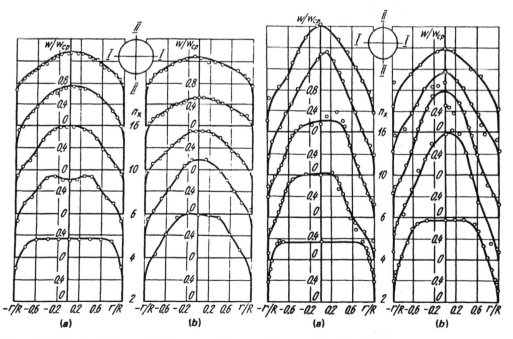

Figure 5-2 Velocity fields over the diamter II–II of different sections (different n_x) of a conical diffuser at $\alpha = 4°$ and Re $= (4–5) \times 10^5$:[54] (a) $l_0/D_0 = 0$; (b) $l_0/D_0 = 20$.

Figure 5-3 Velocity fields over the diamter I–I of different sections (different n_x) of a conical diffuser at $\alpha = 8°$ and Re $= (4–5) \times 10^5$:[54] (a) $l_0/D_0 = 0$; (b) $l_0/D_0 = 10$.

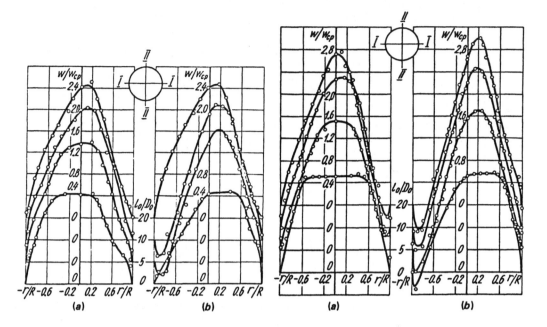

Figure 5-4 Velocity fields in a conical diffuser at α = 10° over the section n_x = 4 at Re = (4–5) × 10^5 and different l_0/D_0:[54] (a) diameter I–I; (b) diameter II–II.

Figure 5-5 Velocity fields in a conical diffuser at α = 10° over the section n_x = 4 at Re = (4–5) × 10^5 and different l_0/D_0:[54] (a) diameter I–I; (b) diameter II–II.

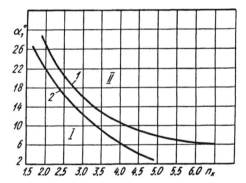

Figure 5-6 Regions of flow separation in diffusers: 1, $l_0/D_0 \approx 0$; 2, $l_0/D_0 \geq 0$.[54,129]

as the flow has separated from one side of the diffuser, the static pressure along the diffuser does ot increase further or event becomes weaker, with the result that the flow does not separate from the opposite side of the diffuser. This phenomenon is responsible for asymmetric velocity distributions over the sections of diffusers (see Figures 5-1 and 5-5).

9. In a symmetrical diffuser with a symmetrical velocity profile at the entrance, the separation of flow from the wall occurs alternately on one side of the diffuser and on the other (Figure 5-7) which leads to substantial oscillations of the whole flow.

10. The profiles of reduced velocities $\lambda_{ci} = w_i/a_{cr}$ at the exit from plane diffusers with divergence angles α equal to 4, 6, and 8° and with $l_0/D_0 = 5.8$ are given in Figure 5-8 for both sonic and supersonic flows over the starting length of diffusers (according to experimental data of Bedrzhitskiy).[6] Up to a certain value of p_{ch}^* in the blowing chamber (upstream of the inlet into a straight entrance section), which corresponds to the formation of the local supersonic zone in the initial section of the diffuser, no flow separation from the diffuser

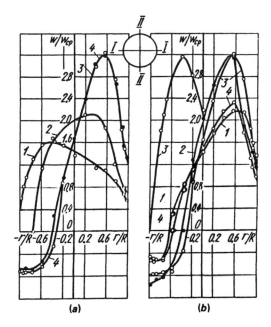

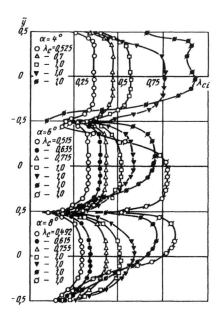

Figure 5-7 Velocity fields in a conical diffuser at α = 20° over the section n_x = 4 at Re = (4–5) × 10⁵ and different l_0/D_0:[54] (a) diameter I–I; (b) diameter II–II; 1, l_0/D_0 = 0; 2, l_0/D_0 = 5; 3, l_0/D_0 = 10; 4, l_0/D_0 = 20.

Figure 5-8 Fields of reduced velocity in the exit sections of plane diffusers at β = 0 and α = 4, 6, and 8°; λ_c is the reduced velocity at the exit from the diffuser.

walls is observed (separation "from under the shock"), and the velocity field at the exit from the diffuser remains uniform. However, starting from a certain position of the compression shock that brings up the rear of the local supersonic zone, separation occurs, as well as a steep increase in the velocity field nonuniformity in the exit section of the diffuser.

11. The resistance coefficients of the diffusers $\zeta_d = \Delta p/(\rho w_0^2/2)$, as well as the flow structure in them and the separation phenomena, depend on many parameters, such as the divergence angle α (for diffusers with rectilinear walls); the area ratio $n_{ar1} = F_1/F_0$; the shape of the cross section; the shape of the boundaries; the boundary-layer thickness (momentum loss thickness) at the entrance; the shape of the velocity profile at the entrance; the degree of flow turbulence at the entrance; the flow regime (Reynolds number Re) both in the boundary layer and in the main flow; and the flow compressibility (Mach number Ma₀).

12. The effect of the Reynolds number on the resistance coefficients of the diffusers is different for different divergence angles. In the case of separation-free diffusers, the character of the relationship $\zeta_d = f(\text{Re})$ is close to the character of the relationship $\lambda = f(\text{Re})$ for straight tubes; the values of ζ_d decrease monotonically with increases in Re (Figure 5-9).

With increases in the divergence angle of the diffusers the character of the dependence of ζ_d on Re becomes complicated (see Figure 5-9), since flow separation from the channel wall becomes important.

13. When the diffusers (not only with small, but also with sufficiently large angles α) are installed directly after a smooth inlet nozzle (collector) (l_0/D_0 = 0), the flow in the boundary layer of the diffuser remains laminar over some distance downstream from the inlet even though the Reynolds numbers of the main flow substantially exceed the critical value Re_{cr}. Just as for λ of straight tubes, this causes a sharper decrease (with increase of Re) in the resistance coefficient of separation-free diffusers and of diffusers with local separation of the flow ($\alpha < 14°$), than might have occurred, had there been a fully developed turbulent flow in the boundary layer over the whole length of the diffuser.

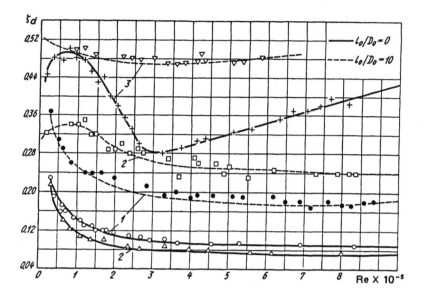

Figure 5-9 Dependence of the resistance coefficient ζ_d of a conical diffuser on Re at $n_{ar1} = 4$ and different values of α and l_0/D_0:[54] 1, $\alpha = 4°$; 2, $\alpha = 10°$; 3, $\alpha = 30°$.

14. In the presence of a straight, sufficiently long insert between a smooth inlet nozzle (collector) and a diffuser: (1) the boundary layer in the beginning of the diffuser is additionally agitated (Figure 5-10) and (2) the boundary layer thickness increases (and, accordingly, the velocity profiles "extend") as early as the entrance into the diffuser (see graph b of Diagram 5-1).

These factors exert directly opposite effects on the diffuser resistance.

15. When the straight insert has a length up to about $l_0/D_0 \approx 10$, the first factor is predominant. At larger values of l_0/D_0, the influence of the first factor is stabilized, while the influence of the second factor continues to increase to some extent. As a result, with further increases in l_0/D_0, the constant influence of this parameter is established (the constant ratio $k_d = \zeta_{dl_0>0}/\zeta_{dl_0=0}$, which takes into account the effect of straight or curved sections upstream of the diffuser) or even some decrease in its effect on the resistance of separation-free diffusers.

16. A thicker boundary layer at the entrance to the diffuser causes somewhat earlier appearance of the wall layer instability and occasional stalling of vortices. The larger the divergence angle of the diffuser, the stronger this phenomenon becomes, until the flow completely separates from the walls at certain values of α. These combined effects increase the total resistance of the diffuser.

17. For diffusers with large divergence angles, at which the flow completely separates from the walls ($\alpha > 14°$), the effect of the Reynolds number and the inlet conditions on

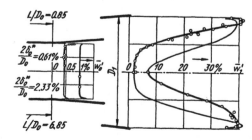

Figure 5-10 Variation of the longitudinal fluctuation of velocity $\overline{w}' = w'/w_0$ in the inlet section of the diffuser with a change in the relative length of the straight starting section l_0/D_0.[172,173]

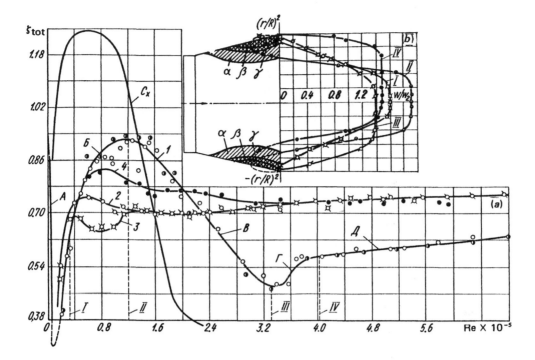

Figure 5-11 The functions $\zeta_{tot} = f_1(Re)$ and $c_x = f_2(Re)$ (a) and the velocity field over the section $n_x = 2$ in a conical diffuser at $\alpha = 30°$, $n_{ar1} = 2$, and $l_1/D_1 = 0$ (b):[54] I, Re = 0.3 × 10⁵; II (α), Re = 1.2 × 10⁵; III (β), Re = 3.3 × 10⁵; IV (γ), Re = 4 × 10⁵; 1, $l_0/D_0 = 0$; 2, $l_0/D_0 = 2$; 3, $l_0/D_0 = 3$ with a turbulizer; 4, $l_0/D_0 = 20$.

the change in the resistance coefficient is due to slightly different factors, namely to the displacement of the separation point along the walls of the diffuser and to a change in the stalling zone thickness together with a change in the mode of the boundary-layer flow.

18. These factors are responsible for the complex character of the resistance curve of separation-prone diffusers installed directly downstream of the smooth collector, that is, at $l_0/D_0 = 0$. As is evident from Figure 5-11, at very small Re an increase in this number first leads to a sharp dropo of the coefficient ζ_{tot}^* until it reaches a certain minimum (segment A, Figure 5-11a), and then ζ_{tot} starts to increase sharply up to its maximum value at Re = 0.8–1.4 × 10⁵ (segment B). This maximum is followed by a new sharp decrease in ζ_{tot} (the crisis of the resistance) until the second minimum of the values of ζ_{tot} (segment C) is attained at Re = 3.3 × 10⁵. Following this minimum, the coefficient ζ_{tot} increases again, first rather sharply (segment D) and then slightly (segment E) with increases in Re.

19. Segment A of curve 1 (see Figure 5-11a) corresponds to a nonseparating laminar flow, where the resistance coefficient is inversely proportional to the Reynolds number, and segment B corresponds to the development of separation of the laminar boundary layer. The maximum of ζ_{tot} corresponds to complete laminar separation occurring close to the inlet section of the diffuser. This is due to the separation zone in laminar flow being most extensive both in its lateral dimensions and its extent (Figure 5-11b, region α) with the clear area of the main flow being the lowest one—whence the maximum of the pressure losses.

---

*Here a diffuser is considered, for example, which is installed at the exit from the network and for which ζ_{tot} is the coefficient of total resistance of the diffuser (which also accounts for the exit velocity pressure losses). A similar phenomenon is also observed in diffusers installed in the network, that is, for the coefficient ζ_d.

20. A sharp drop in ζ_{tot} over segment B of curve 1 (see Figure 5-11a) corresponds to the onset of the crisis when the separated laminar layer becomes turbulent. The layer becomes thinner and, as a result of vigorous turbulent agitation, the flow attaches to the wall again. The separation point (now of the turbulent flow) is thus displaced downstream. In this case, the separation zone greatly diminishes while the clear area of the flow correspondingly increases (see Figure 5-11b, region β), which leads to a sharp drop in the diffuser resistance coefficient.

21. Further increase in the resistance coefficient ζ_{tot} in the postcritical region (segments D and E, Figure 5-11a) is explained by some reverse displacement of the turbulent separation point upstream of the flow (Figure 5-11b, region γ). Such a displacement in the diffuser may occur under the action of the inertia forces that increase with the Reynolds number.

22. The character of the curves $\zeta_{tot} = f(\mathrm{Re})$ for separation-prone diffusers changes, depending on the inlet conditions. In particular, even a short, straight insert ($l_0/D_0 = 2$) installed upstream of the diffuser agitates the flow and simultaneously thickens the boundary layer at the entrance into the diffuser even at relatively small Reynolds numbers. Under these conditions, the maximum of ζ_{tot} decreases within $0.4 \times 10^5 < \mathrm{Re} < 2.3 \times 10^5$, while at $\mathrm{Re} > 2.3 \times 10^5$ the values of ζ_{tot}, as a whole, turn out to be higher (see curves 2, 3, and 4 in Figure 5-11a). The latter is attributed to some displacement of the turbulent separation point upstream of the flow (in the direction of the diffuser inlet) due to the thickening of the boundary layer. The same effect can be achieved by artificial flow turbulence creation upstream of the diffuser inlet.

23. When the divergence angle of the diffuser $\alpha > 30°$, the effect of a straight insert installed upstream of the diffuser decreases sharply and, at $\alpha \geq 60°$, becomes practically negligible. The explanation is that at very large values of α the flow separates so close to the diffuser inlet section that any further backward displacement of the separation point is, naturally, impossible.

24. A straight insert ahead of the diffuser produces a symmetrical velocity profile at the diffuser inlet with the maximum velocity at the center and reduced velocities at the walls ("convex" shape).

When the diffuser is preceded by a curved part of the pipeline or any barrier producing a nonuniform velocity profile at its inlet with reduced velocities at the center and elevated velocities at the walls ("concave" shape), the effect of such a profile on the diffuser resistance will be opposite to the effect of the convex profile; that is, at small angles α the diffuser resistance will increase, while at large angles α it will probably decrease somewhat compared with the resistance when there is a uniform velocity distribution at the inlet.

25. As the experiments and predictions carried out by Voytovich and Emeliyanova[14] show, the roughness of the internal surface of the diffusers increases their resistance at certain limits of the angles and area ratios. The largest roughness-induced increase in resistance occurs at small divergence angles (Figure 5-12).

26. The resistance of the diffusers is affected by the inlet conditions. As the boundary layer thickness ahead of the diffusers (for example, due to the increase in the length of straight insert l_0/D_0), the relative increase in the resistance coefficient ($\zeta_{rough} - \zeta_{smooth})/\zeta_{smooth}$ due to roughness decreases sharply (see Figure 5-12). This shows up mainly with an increase in the divergence angle and area ratio of the diffuser, that is, in the case of a separating flow.

27. In all of the cases, roughness exerts a substantial influence only over the starting length of the diffuser corresponding to the area ratios $n_x \leq 1.5$, that is, in the place where the boundary layer is still thin so that the height of asperities exceeds the thickness of the viscous sublayer. With increases in the viscous sublayer thickness along the flow, the influence of roughness decreases.

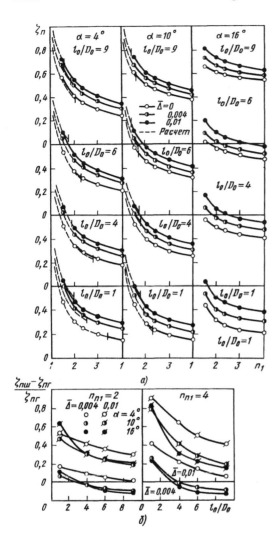

Figure 5-12 Dependence of the diffuser resistance on roughness $\overline{\Delta}$:[14] a, $\zeta_{tot} = f(n_{ar1}, \alpha, l_0/D_0, \overline{\Delta})$; b, $(\zeta_{tot\,rough} - \zeta_{tot\,smooth})/\zeta_{tot\,smooth} = f(l_0/D_0, n_{ar1}, \overline{\Delta})$.

28. The structure of the flow in rectangular diffusers and the character of the resistance curves are basically the same as for conical diffusers. However, the flow conditions in rectangular diffusers are additionally influenced by the corners due to the cross sections, which are conducive to earlier flow separation from the wall. As a result, the resistance in such diffusers in always higher than in conical diffusers. On the other hand, the effect of the upstream straight section insert somewhat decreases, so that a relative rise in the resistance coefficient with l_0/D_0 turns out to be lower in such diffusers than in conical ones.

29. The resistance of plane diffusers (section expansion in one plane only) at the same divergence angles and area ratios is noticeably lower than in diffusers with the section expansion in two-dimensional planes and in many cases is even smaller than in conical diffusers. This is attributed to the fact that at the same divergence angles and area ratios the plane diffusers are correspondingly larger than the conical or rectangular diffusers, with expansion occurring in two planes. Thus, with a smoother change in the cross section, a lower pressure gradient along the flow and a weaker flow separation from the wall result.

30. When there is a nonseparating flow in diffusers, then all of its characteristics, including the resistance coefficient, can be calculated with the help of boundary-layer theory. With the use of these methods, the most extensive results were obtained by Ginevsky et

al.,[5,19-25] Solodkin and Guinevsky,[77-81] Voitovich and Emeliyanova,[14] Deich and Zaryankin,[36] and Emeliyanova.[43]

31. The resistance formula obtained by the boundary-layer theory method for the starting length (for the section with the constant velocity core) of the diffusers installed in the network (taking into account the losses for flow equalization in the straight exit section — on the basis of formula (4-3′), but without friction), has the form[20]

$$\zeta_d \equiv \frac{\Delta p}{\rho w_0^2/2} = \frac{1}{n_{ar1}^2} + \frac{1}{n_{ar1}^2(1 - \Delta_1^*)^3} - \frac{2(1 - \Delta_1^* - \Delta_1^{**})}{n_{ar1}^2(1 - \Delta_1^*)^2} - \frac{\Delta_0^{***}}{(1 - \Delta_0^*)^3}$$

where for a conical diffuser

$$\Delta^* = 2\frac{\delta^*}{R_x} - \left(\frac{\delta^*}{R_x}\right)^2$$

$$\Delta^{**} = 2\frac{\delta^{**}}{R_x} - \left(\frac{\delta^{**}}{R_x}\right)^2$$

$$\Delta^{***} = 2\frac{\delta^{***}}{R_x} - \left(\frac{\delta^{***}}{R_x}\right)^2$$

for δ^* and δ^{**} see the footnote on page 240; $\delta^{***} = \int_0^{\delta_t} w/w_c [1 - (w/w_c)^2] \, r dr$ is the energy loss thickness; R_x is the radius of section (x-x) of the diffuser; δ_t is the boundary layer thickness; subscript 0 refers to the initial section of the diffuser, and subscript 1 to its final section.

The dependence of δ^*/R_x, δ^{**}/R_x, and δ^{***}/R_x on the relative length of the conical diffuser l_d/R_x and divergence angles α is shown in Figure 5-13. Similar relationships were obtained in Reference 5 for plane diffusers.

32. Diagrams 5-1 through 5-5 contain the total resistance coefficients ζ based on the experiments of Idelchik and Ginzburg[51-55] with diffusers installed in a system or network that had a variety of cross-sectional shapes (conical, square, plane), which in turn depend on the basic geometric parameters (α, n_1), inlet conditions ($l_0/D_0 \geq 0$), and flow regime (Re).

33. The total resistance coefficient of a diffuser installed in the network is in the general case (under any inlet conditions)

$$\zeta_{l_0>0} \equiv \frac{\Delta p}{\rho w_0^2/2} = k_d \zeta_{dl_0=0} \tag{5-1}$$

where $\zeta_{dl_0=0}$ is the total resistance coefficient of a diffuser at $l_0/D_0 = 0$ (see Diagram 5-1); $\zeta_{dl_0>0}$ is the resistance coefficient of a diffuser with a straight section or a curved part installed upstream.

34. In the case of an asymmetrical velocity distribution downstream of elbows, throttling devices, and other fittings, it is possible for practical applications to utilize the values of k_d given in Diagrams 5-1 (para. 3) and 5-19) (para. 2). The data shown under para. 3 of Diagram 5-1 were obtained using the results of investigations of a conical diffuser installed downstream of branches with different geometric parameters.[180] Those under para. 2 of Diagram 5-19 have been obtained on the basis of studies of circular diffusers upstream of which different velocity distributions were produced with the aid of special screens.[127]

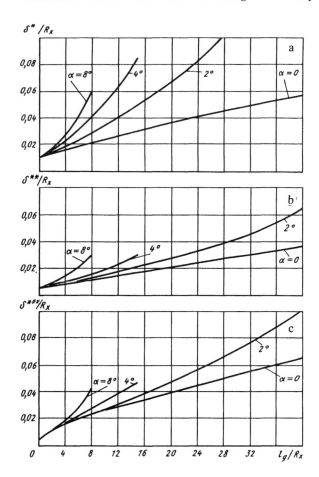

Figure 5-13 Dependence of the boundary layer thickness in preseparation conical diffusers on their relative length at various divergence angles, Re $= 5 \times 10^4$ and $\Delta_0^* = 0.02$:[14] a, $\delta^*/R_x = f(l_d/R_x, \alpha)$; b, $\delta^{**}/R_x = f(l_d/R_x, \alpha)$; c, $\delta^{***}/R_x = f(l_d/R_x, \alpha)$.

35. The data of Diagrams 5-1 through 5-5 consider the simultaneous effect of the parameters Re and $\lambda_0 = w_0/a_{cz}$. In general, these parameters exert a combined effect on the characteristics of the diffusers.[36] However, in the absence of separation and large Reynolds numbers this combined effect is of no importance. Flow compressibility exhibits itself most strongly at small Reynolds numbers in the region of a critical drop in the resistance.

Since there is a lack of data to evaluate the combined influence of the above parameters, this effect can be neglected in practical application calculations, particualrly since in many practical cases Re and λ_0 vary simultaneously.

36. It is sometimes convenient in engineering calculations to resort to a conventional method of dividing the total losses in a diffuser Δp into two parts. Δp_{fr}, the friction losses along the length of the diffuser, and Δp_{exp}, the local losses associated with expansion of the cross section. The total resistance coefficient of the diffuser ζ_d is accordingly composed of the friction resistance coefficient ζ_{fr} and the expansion resistance coefficient ζ_{exp}:

$$\zeta_d = \frac{\Delta p}{\rho w_0^2/2} = \zeta_{fr} + \zeta_{exp} \tag{5-2}$$

37. It is convenient that the "expansion" losses be expressed in terms of the shock coefficient,[47,49] which is the ratio of the actual expansion losses in the diffuser to the theoretical shock losses due to a sudden expansion of the cross section ($\alpha = 180°$), that is,

$$\phi_{\exp} = \frac{\Delta p_{\exp}}{(\rho/2)(w_0^2 - w_1^2)} \tag{5-3}$$

For a uniform velocity profile at the inlet section ($k_d = 1.0$) and large Reynolds numbers (Re $\geq 2 \times 10^5$), the shock coefficient of diffusers with divergence angles $0 < \alpha < 40°$ can be calculated from the author's formula[47,49]

$$\varphi_{\exp} = 32k \cdot \text{tg}^{1.25} \alpha/2 \tag{5-4}$$

where, based on the experiments,[26,52,54] for conical diffusers $k \approx 1$; for pyramidal diffusers with expansion in two planes:

$$k = 0.66 + 0.12 \, \alpha, \quad 4° < \alpha < 12°;$$
$$k = 3.3 - 0.03 \, \alpha, \quad 12° < \alpha < 30°;$$

for plane diffusers

$$k = 2.0 - 0.03 \, \alpha, \quad 4° < \alpha < 12°;$$
$$k = 2.0 - 0.04 \, \alpha, \quad 12° < \alpha < 20°;$$

where α is given in degrees.

The expansion resistance coefficient is expressed in terms of the shock coefficient as

$$\zeta_{\exp} \equiv \frac{\Delta p}{\rho w_0^2/2} = \varphi_{\exp}\left(1 - \frac{1}{n_{ar1}}\right) = 3.2 \, k \cdot \text{tg}^{1.25} \frac{\alpha}{2} \left(1 - \frac{1}{n_{ar1}}\right)^2 \tag{5-5}$$

38. In a more generalized form, the resistance coefficient of a diffuser can be calculated from the interpolation formula of Chernyavskiy and Gordeyev[97,98] using the resistance coefficients given in Diagrams 5-2, 5-4, and 5-5:

$$\zeta \equiv \frac{\Delta p}{\rho w_0^2/2} = \zeta_{fr}' + \zeta_{un} + \zeta_{non}$$

where

$$\zeta_{tr}' = \left(1 + \frac{0.5}{1.5^{\bar{x}}}\right) \zeta_{tr}$$

ζ_{un} is the coefficient which characterizes the expansion losses which could have occurred in the diffuser with a uniform velocity profile in its initial section, that is, at $\bar{l}_0 = l_0/D_{h0} = 0$; ζ_{non} is the coefficient which takes into account additional expansion losses due to the nonuniform velocity profile in the initital section of the diffuser, that is, when there is a straight insert of length l_0 installed upstream.

39. The resistance coefficient for conical diffusers[47,49] is

$$\zeta_{tr} \equiv \frac{\Delta p_{tr}}{\rho w_0^2/2} = \frac{\lambda}{8 \sin \dfrac{\alpha}{2}} \left(1 - \frac{1}{n_{ar1}^2}\right) \tag{5-6}$$

where λ is determined depending on Re and $\overline{\Delta}$ (see Diagrams 2-2 to 2-6);

$$\bar{x} = \int_0^x \frac{dx}{D_0} = \int_0^{\bar{x}} \frac{d(x/D_0)}{1 + 2x/D_0 \cdot \text{tg} \frac{\alpha}{2}} = \frac{\ln\left(1 + 2\bar{x} \cdot \text{tg} \frac{\alpha}{2}\right)}{2 \text{ tg} \frac{\alpha}{2}}$$

where $\bar{x} = x/D_0$;

$$\zeta_{un} = \phi\left(1 - \frac{1}{n_{ar1}}\right)^m \tag{5-7}$$

where $\phi = f(\alpha, \text{Re})$ is the analog of the shock coefficient given on graph d of Diagram 5-2; $m = 1.92$; $\zeta_{non} = 0.044(0.345\alpha)^a[1 - (0.2n_{ar1} + 0.8)^{-3.82}] \cdot (0.154 \bar{l}_0)^b[2.31 \cdot 10^{-6} \text{Re}_0 + 0.2 + 2.54(1 + 0.081\alpha)^{-1.51}]$,

where $a = 0.924/(1 + 1.3 \cdot 10^{-5} \alpha^{3.14})$
   $b = (0.3 + 1.55 \cdot 1.1^{-\alpha})/(1 + 1.03 \cdot 10^{-8} \bar{l}_0^{7.5})$
   $c = 1.05/(1 + 2.3 \cdot 10^{-62} \text{Re}_0^{11})$
   $\text{Re}_0 = w_0 D_0/\nu; \alpha^\circ$

40. For pyramidal diffusers with the sides of the inlet section a_0 and b_0 and with identical divergence angles in both planes the friction coefficient ζ_{tr} is calculated from Equation (5-6).

For a pyramidal diffuser with different divergence angles ($\alpha \neq \beta$) in both planes[47,49]

$$\zeta_u \equiv \frac{\Delta p}{\rho w_0^2/2} = \frac{\lambda}{16}\left(1 - \frac{1}{n_{ar1}^2}\right)\left(\frac{1}{\sin \frac{\alpha}{2}} + \frac{1}{\sin \frac{\beta}{2}}\right) \tag{5-8}$$

The coefficient ζ_{un} is determined from Equation (5-7) where for ϕ see graph c of Diagram 5-4; $m = 1.76$, whereas the coefficient which takes into account the nonuniformity of the velocity profile, that is, at $\bar{l}_0 > 0$[97,98] is

$$\zeta_{non} = 0.024(0.625 \alpha)^s[1 - (2.81n_{ar1} - 1.81)^{-1.04}]$$

$$\times (0.303 \bar{l}_0)^t(4.8 \times 10^{-7} \text{Re}_0 + 1.8)^s$$

where $s = 1.06/(1 + 2.82 \times 10^{-3} \alpha^{2.24}); t = 0.73/(1 + 4.31 \times 10^{-6} \bar{l}_0^{7.31}; u = 1.0/(1 + 1.1 \times 10^{-30} \text{Re}_0^{5.62})$.

The dimensionless hydraulic diameter of the diffuser at $a_0 \neq b_0$ ($a_x \neq b_x$) and $\alpha \neq \beta$, and, consequently, at $a_x = a_0 + 2x \text{ tg}(\alpha/2)$ and $b_x = b_0 + 2x \text{ tg}(\beta/2)$ is equal to

$$\overline{D}_{hx} = \frac{D_{hx}}{D_{ho}} = \frac{2\bar{a}_x\bar{b}_x}{\bar{a}_x + \bar{b}_x}$$

$$= \frac{2\bar{a}_0\bar{b}_0 + 4\bar{x}\left(\bar{a}_0 \text{ tg} \frac{\beta}{2} + \bar{b}_0 \text{ tg} \frac{\alpha}{2}\right) + 8\bar{x}^2 \text{ tg} \frac{\alpha}{2} \text{ tg} \frac{\beta}{2}}{\bar{a}_0 + \bar{b}_0 + 2\bar{x}\left(\text{tg} \frac{\alpha}{2} + \text{tg} \frac{\beta}{2}\right)}$$

where

$$\bar{a}_x \equiv \frac{a_x}{D_{ho}}$$

$$\bar{b}_x = \frac{b_x}{D_{ho}}$$

In this case, after the integration the relative length of the diffuser is

$$\bar{x} = \int_0^{\bar{x}} \frac{d\bar{x}}{\bar{D}_{hx}} = \left[\frac{\bar{a}_0 + \bar{b}_0}{4\,\bar{a}_0\,\mathrm{tg}\,\frac{\beta}{2} - \bar{b}_0\,\mathrm{tg}\,\frac{\alpha}{2}} - \frac{\left(\bar{a}_0\,\mathrm{tg}\,\frac{\beta}{2} + \bar{b}_0\,\mathrm{tg}\,\frac{\alpha}{2}\right)\left(\mathrm{tg}\,\frac{\alpha}{2} + \mathrm{tg}\,\frac{\beta}{2}\right)}{2\,\mathrm{tg}\,\frac{\alpha}{2}\,\mathrm{tg}\,\frac{\beta}{2}} \right]$$

$$\times \ln \frac{2\,\bar{a}_0\bar{x}\,\mathrm{tg}\,\frac{\alpha}{2}\,\mathrm{tg}^2\,\frac{\beta}{2} + \bar{a}_0\bar{b}_0\,\mathrm{tg}\,\frac{\alpha}{2}\,\mathrm{tg}\,\frac{\beta}{2}}{2\,\bar{b}_0\bar{x}\,\mathrm{tg}^2\,\frac{\alpha}{2}\,\mathrm{tg}\,\frac{\beta}{2} + \bar{a}_0\bar{b}_0\,\mathrm{tg}\,\frac{\alpha}{2}\,\mathrm{tg}\,\frac{\beta}{2}} + \frac{\mathrm{tg}\,\frac{\alpha}{2} + \mathrm{tg}\,\frac{\beta}{2}}{8\,\mathrm{tg}\,\frac{\alpha}{2}\,\mathrm{tg}\,\frac{\beta}{2}}$$

$$\times \ln \frac{4\,\bar{x}^2\,\mathrm{tg}\,\frac{\alpha}{2} + \mathrm{tg}\,\frac{\beta}{2} + 2\,\bar{x}\left(\bar{a}_0\,\mathrm{tg}\,\frac{\beta}{2} + \bar{b}_0\,\mathrm{tg}\,\frac{\alpha}{2}\right) + \bar{a}_0\bar{b}_0}{\bar{a}_0\bar{b}_0}$$

At $\alpha = \beta$

$$\bar{x} = \frac{1}{4\,\mathrm{tg}\,\frac{\alpha}{2}}\,\ln \frac{4\,\bar{x}^2\,\mathrm{tg}^2\,\frac{\alpha}{2} + 2\,\bar{x}(\bar{a}_0 + \bar{b}_0)\,\mathrm{tg}\,\frac{\alpha}{2} + \bar{a}_0\bar{b}_0}{\bar{a}_0\bar{b}_0}$$

At $a_0 = b_0$ and $\alpha = \beta$, we have $\bar{a}_0 = \bar{b}_0 = 1$ and

$$\bar{x} = \frac{1}{4\,\mathrm{tg}\,\frac{\alpha}{2}}\,\ln\left(4\,\bar{x}^2\,\mathrm{tg}^2\,\frac{\alpha}{2} + 4\,\bar{x}\,\mathrm{tg}\,\frac{\alpha}{2} + 1\right)$$

41. For a plane diffuser with the sides a_0 and b_0 (where b_0 is constant in length)[47,49]

$$\zeta_{fr} \equiv \frac{\Delta p_{fr}}{\rho w_0^2/2} = \frac{\lambda}{4}\left[\frac{a_0}{b_0}\frac{1}{\mathrm{tg}\,\frac{\alpha}{2}}\left(1 - \frac{1}{n_{ar1}}\right) + \frac{1}{2\sin\frac{\alpha}{2}}\left(1 - \frac{1}{n_{ar1}^2}\right)\right] \qquad (5\text{-}9)$$

Practically, it is possible to assume that

$$\zeta_{fr} = \frac{\lambda}{4\sin\frac{\alpha}{2}}\left[\frac{a_0}{b_0}\left(1 - \frac{1}{n_{ar1}}\right) + 0.5\left(1 - \frac{1}{n_{ar1}^2}\right)\right] \qquad (5\text{-}10)$$

The coefficient ζ_{un} is determined from Equation (5-7), where for ϕ see graph c of Diagram 5-5, $m = 1.64$, whereas the coefficient which takes into account the nonuniformity of the velocity profile, that is, at $\bar{l}_0 > 0$[97,98] is

$$\zeta_{non} = 0.0106(0.625\alpha)^{1.0/(1 + 4.31 \times 10^{-8}\alpha^{4.62})}$$

$$\times \{1 - [0.658(n_{ar1} - 1) + 1]^{-1.79}\}(0.303\bar{l}_0)^{0.75/(1 + 6.32 \times 10^{-6}\bar{l}_0^{7.11})}$$

$$\times (1.65 \times 10^{-5} \, Re_0 + 1.4)^{1.0/(1 + 6.4 \times 10^{-12.9} Re_0^{2.37})}$$

The dimensionless hydraulic diameter of the diffuser at $a_0 = a_x + 2 \, x \, tg(\alpha/2)$ and $b_x = b_0$ is

$$\bar{D}_{hx} = \frac{2 \, \bar{a}_x \bar{b}_x}{\bar{a}_x + \bar{b}_x} = \frac{2\left(\bar{a}_0 + 2 \, \bar{x} \, tg \, \dfrac{\alpha}{2}\right)\bar{b}_0}{\bar{a}_0 + \bar{b}_0 + 2 \, \bar{x} \, tg \, \dfrac{\alpha}{2}}$$

and the relative length of the diffuser is

$$\bar{x} = \int_0^{\bar{x}} \frac{d\bar{x}}{\bar{D}_{hx}} = \frac{\bar{a}_0 + \bar{b}_0}{2 \, \bar{b}_0} \int_0^{\bar{x}} \frac{d\bar{x}}{\bar{a}_0 + 2 \, \bar{x} \, tg \, \dfrac{\alpha}{2}} + \frac{tg \, \dfrac{\alpha}{2}}{\bar{b}_0} \int_0^{\bar{x}} \frac{d\bar{x}}{\bar{a}_0 + 2 \, \bar{x} \, tg \, \dfrac{\alpha}{2}}$$

$$= \frac{\bar{a}_0\left(1 - tg \, \dfrac{\alpha}{2}\right) + \bar{b}_0}{4 \, \bar{b}_0 \, tg \, \dfrac{\alpha}{2}} \, \ln \frac{\bar{a}_0 + 2 \, \bar{x} \, tg \, \dfrac{\alpha}{2}}{\bar{a}_0} + \frac{\bar{x} \, tg \, \dfrac{\alpha}{2}}{\bar{b}_0}$$

At $a_0 = b_0$

$$\bar{x} = \frac{2 - tg \, \dfrac{\alpha}{2}}{4 \, tg \, \dfrac{\alpha}{2}} \, \ln\left(1 + 2 \, \bar{x} \, tg \, \dfrac{\alpha}{2}\right) + \bar{x} \, tg \, \dfrac{\alpha}{2}$$

42. When $\alpha \leqslant 40-50°$, the shock coefficient ϕ_{exp} is smaller than unity (see Figure 5-12). This indicates that the losses in a diffuser are lower than the shock losses at a sudden expansion ($\alpha = 180°$). For angles $\alpha = 50-90°$ the value of ϕ_{exp} becomes somewhat larger than unity, that is, the losses in a diffuser increase compared with the shock losses. Starting from $\alpha = 90°$ and up to $\alpha = 180°$, the value of ϕ_{exp} decreases and approaches unity; this means that the losses in the diffuser become close to the sudden expansion losses and therefore, unless a uniform velocity is expected downstream of the diffuser, it is not advisable to use diffusers with the divergence angles $\alpha > 40-50°$.

When a very short transition piece is needed because of the requirement of limited overall size, then, from the point of view of the resistance, this piece may have divergence angle $\alpha = 180°$.

43. When a uniform velocity profile is required downstream of the transition piece and guide vanes, dividing walls, or perforated plates (screens, nozzles) are to be installed for this purpose, then any diffuser, even one with a very large divergence angle ($\alpha > 50°$), should be preferred to a sudden expansion ($\alpha = 180°$).

44. Since a smooth expansion of the cross section of a tube with rectilinear walls at small divergence angles (a diffuser) leads first to a decrease in the pressure losses compared with the losses in a tube of the same length, but of constant cross section, while larger divergence angles lead again to an increase in these losses, then there probably exists an optimum divergence angle at which the losses are reduced to minimum (see curves $\zeta_d = f(\alpha)$ of Diagrams 5-2, 5-4, and 5-5).

45. The minimum value of the resistance coefficient ζ_{min} of conical diffusers exists within the region $\alpha_{opt} = 4-12°$ and depends mainly on the area ratio n_{ar1} and the relative length l_0/D_0: the smaller n_1 is, the larger is α_{opt} at which this minimum is attained (see graph α of Diagram 5-2); conversely, the parameter l_0/D_0 decreases the value of α_{opt}.

For rectangular (square) diffusers, the upper limit of α_{opt} is much smaller ($7°$). The effect of l_0/D_0 on decrease of α_{opt} is more substantial in this case (see Diagram 5-4).

For plane diffusers, the optimum divergence angle, at which the minimum of the pressure losses is attained, exists within the range $\alpha_{opt} = 6-12°$ (see Diagram 5-5).

46. It is very important for many practical applications to recover the maximum possible static pressure in the minimum length of the diffuser even at the cost of greater energy losses in it.

Theoretically, the larger the area ratio n_{ar1} or the relative length l_d/D_0 at the given divergence angle, the larger is the coefficient of the static pressure recovery η_d of the diffuser:

$$\eta_d = \frac{p_1 - p_0}{\rho w_0^2/2} \tag{5-11}$$

47. Based on the Bernoulli and continuity equations and Equation (5-11), the following relationship exists between the pressure recovery coefficient and the resistance coefficient of the diffuser installed in the network

$$\eta_d = N_0 - N_1\left(\frac{F_0}{F_1}\right)^2 - \zeta_d \tag{5-12}$$

where

$$N_0 = \frac{1}{F_0}\int_{F_0}\left(\frac{w}{w_0}\right)^3 dF \qquad N_1 = \frac{1}{F_1}\int_{F_1}\left(\frac{w}{w_1}\right)^3 dF$$

If nonuniformity in the velocity distribution at the inlet and outlet sections of the diffuser is neglected, that is, if it is assumed that $N_0 = N_1 = 1.0$ (which is often admissible for practical calculations), then

$$\eta_d = 1 - \frac{1}{n_{ar1}^2} - \zeta_d \tag{5-13}$$

An analogous relation is obtained for the total resistance coefficient of the diffuser installed at the outlet from the network:

$$\eta_{tot} = 1 - \zeta_{tot}$$

48. The efficiency of the diffuser is sometimes characterized by the efficiency coefficient, which is the ratio of the actual to the ideal (without losses) increment in the static pressure:

$$\eta_{1d} = \frac{p_1 - p_0}{(p_1 - p_0)_{id}} = \frac{p_1 - p_0}{N_0(\rho w_0^2/2) - N_1(\rho w_1^2/2)} \tag{5-14}$$

where $(p_1 - p_0)_{id}$ is the difference between the static pressures in sections 1-1 and 0-0 for an ideal diffuser (without losses).

The coupling between the efficiency coefficient and the resistance coefficient of a diffuser, installed in the network, is expressed by

$$\eta_{1d} = 1 - \frac{\zeta_d}{N_0 - (N_1/n_{ar1}^2)}$$

at $N_0 = N_1 = 1$

$$\eta_{1d} = 1 - \frac{\zeta_d}{1 - (1/n_{ar1}^2)}$$

A similar relationship is obtained for the total resistance coefficient of the diffuser installed at the exit from the network:

$$\eta_{1tot} = \frac{1 - \zeta_{tot}}{1 - (1/n_{ar1}^2)}$$

49. Owing to flow separation from the diffuser walls with a large area ratio and with a substantial nonuniformity of the velocity distribution over the section, the effective area ratio n_{ar1} at which the maximum possible static pressure recovery is attainable (due to a decrease in the flow velocity) is considerably lower than it might have been in an ideal diffuser (without separation and losses and with uniform velocity distribution over the cross section). In cases where the geometric dimensions of the diffuser (area ratio n_{ar1} and length l_d) are not limited by any requirement (not prescribed), the low values of n_{ar1} allow the use of diffusers with the optimum area ratio [$(n_{ar})_{opt}$ and $(l_d/D_0)_{opt}$] at which η_d attains the absolute maximum* possible for the given inlet conditions (boundary-layer thickness or length l_0/D_0).

50. The values of $\eta_{d\,max}$, ζ_d, $(n_{ar})_{opt}$, and $(l_0/D_0)_{opt}$ for circular and rectangular diffusers, as well as for plane diffusers, obtained from Equation (5-13) and from Diagrams 5-1 through 5-5 are listed in Table 5-1. The limits of the geometric parameters of the diffusers are listed in the same sequence as $\eta_{d\,max}$ and ζ_d.

51. The static pressure recovery coefficients in diffusers with the prescribed geometric parameters can be determined from the curves of η_d vs. n_1 for different divergence angles α and inlet conditions (l_0/D_0) given in Figures 5-14 through 5-16 (the curves are based on the data of Diagrams 5-1 through 5-5 for $Re > 4 \times 10^5$).

---

*Since the finite equalization of velocities and pressures over the section of interest occurs not directly downstream of the diffuser, but at some distance along the straight section behind it, the maximum of the static pressure recovery is attained at the distance downstream of the diffuser (for practical purposes at the distance up to $2D_1$, where D_1 is the diameter of the exit section; for a plane diffuser D_1 is replaced by the larger side of the exit section, i.e., $2a_1$).

Table 5-1 Optimum characteristics of the diffusers

$\dfrac{l_0}{D_0}$	$\eta_{1\max}$	ζ_d	$(\eta_{ar})_{opt}$	$\dfrac{l_0}{D_0}$ opt
		Conical diffusers ($\alpha = 14-10°$)		
0	0.84–0.91	0.13–0.08	6–10	5.8–12.3
2	0.69–0.82	0.29–0.17	6–10	5.8–12.3
5	0.64–0.77	0.30–0.20	4–6	4.1–8.2
10	0.58–0.71	0.17–0.27	2–6	1.7–8.2
20	0.57–0.70	0.19–0.27	2–6	1.7–8.2
		Rectangular diffusers (of square cross section at $\alpha = 10-6°$)		
0	0.74–0.84	0.18–0.13	6	8.2–13.5
10	0.66–0.76	0.28–0.18	4	5.7–9.40
		Plane diffusers ($\alpha = 14-10°$)		
0	0.78–0.80	0.16–0.14	4	12.2–17.0
10	0.71–0.75	0.23–0.17	4–2	12.0–5.70

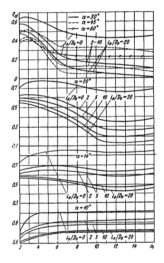

Figure 5-14 Dependence of η_d on n_{ar1} for a conical diffuser.

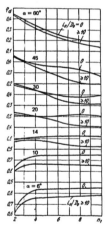

Figure 5-15 Dependence of η_d on n_{ar1} for a rectangular (square) diffuser.

52. Figures 5-17 and 5-18 give the data[144] for conical diffusers with the divergence angle $\alpha = 10°$ in the form of the η'_{1d} vs. the diffuser efficiency calculated from the formula similar to Equation (5-14) and, correspondingly, of the resistance coefficient ζ'_d calculated as the ratio of the difference of total pressures in sections 0-0 and 1-1 to the difference of velocity pressures in the same sections, that is

$$\zeta'_d \equiv \frac{p_0^* - p_1^*}{N_0' \dfrac{\rho_0 w_0^2}{2} - N_1' \dfrac{\rho_1 w_1^2}{2}}$$

vs. the parameters n_{ar1}, δ^*/D_0 and Ma_0.

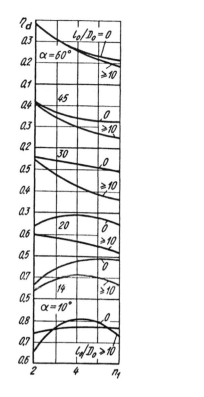

Figure 5-16 Dependence of η_d on n_{ar1} for a plane diffuser.

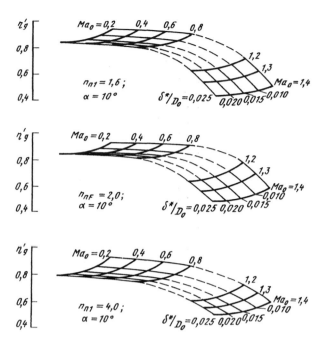

Figure 5-17 Dependence of the efficiency η_{ld} of the diffuser with $\alpha = 10°$ on the Mach number (Ma_0), inlet conditions (δ^*/D_0) and divergence ratio (a_{ar}).[144]

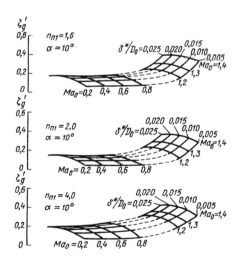

Figure 5-18 Dependence of the resistance coefficient ζ'_d of the diffuser with $\alpha = 10°$ on the Mach number (Ma_0), inlet conditions (δ^*/D_0), and divergence ratio (n_{ar1}).[144]

Here, N'_0 and N'_1 are the coefficients of the nonuniformity in the distributions of flow parameters over the cross sections 0-0 and 1-1; Ma_0 is the Mach number in section 0-0. The coupling between the Mach number and the reduced velocity λ_0 is given by Equation (1-41).

53. The data on the coefficients η'_{1d} and ζ'_d were obtained at the Reynolds number $Re = 2 \times 10^5 - 1.7 \times 10^6$, Mach number at subsonic velocities from $Ma_0 = 0.2$ till the regime of flow choking and at supersonic velocities within the range $Ma_0 = 1.2–1.4$.

There is the following relationship between the quantities ζ'_d and η'_{1d}: $\zeta'_d = 1 - \eta'_{1d}$.

54. The most detailed data in the form of the relationship $\bar{p}_0 = p_1^*/p_0^*$ of the coefficient p_1^* of the total pressure recovery at the exit from conical diffusers in terms of the total pressure (stagnation pressure) p_0^* in the smallest cross section (0-0) on the numbers λ_0 and Re are given in Diagram 5-3. The relationships $\bar{p}_0 = f(\lambda_0, \text{Re})$ (according to the experiments of Idelchik and Ginzburg[27,51-54] are given for the divergence angles $\alpha = 4\text{--}14°$, area ratios $n_{ar1} = 2\text{--}16$, and relative lengths $l_0/D_0 = 0\text{--}10$.

At velocities close to the sonic one, the dependence of $\bar{p}_0$ on λ_0 degenerates into vertical straight lines (see Diagram 5-3). This is explained by the onset of flow choking regime in the diffuser when a compression shock occurs. The larger the relative length of the straight inlet section, the earlier, that is, at the smaller values of λ_0, the choking regime occurs.

55. The relationship between the resistance coefficient of the diffuser and the total pressure coefficient may be obtained on the basis of the following formula:[19]

$$\zeta_d \equiv \frac{\Delta p}{\rho_0^* w_0^2/2} = \frac{k+1}{k}\frac{1}{\lambda_0^2}\ln\frac{1}{\bar{p}_0}$$

where ρ_0^* is the density of the stagnated flow in the inlet section of the diffuser.

For diffusers with small divergence angles at which the pressure losses are small,[2]

$$\zeta_d \equiv \frac{\Delta p}{\rho_0^* w_0^2/2} = \frac{k+1}{k}\frac{1}{\lambda_0^2}(1 - \bar{p}_0)$$

whence

$$\bar{p}_0 = 1 - \frac{k}{k+1}\lambda_0^2\zeta_d$$

where

$$\lambda_0 \equiv \frac{w_0}{a_{cr}}$$

$$a_{cr} = \sqrt{\frac{2k}{k+1}RT_0^*}$$

ρ_0^* is the density of the stagnated flow in the inlet section of the diffuser; T_0^* is the stagnated flow temperature in the same section.

56. In Diagram 5-6 the total pressure recovery coefficients $\bar{p}_0$ and the hydraulic resistance coefficient ζ_d of a plane five-channel subsonic diffuser are given for the following geometric parameters: at α' equal to 8, 12, and 16°; at $\bar{l}_0$ equal to 3.23, 6.45, and 9.68; $n_{ar1} = 6.45$; Re $= (0.6\text{--}4) \times 10^5$.

57. At very low Reynolds numbers (at least within $1 < \text{Re} < 30\text{--}50$) the resistance coefficient of the diffusers is described by the same equation as in the case of a sudden expansion:[4]

$$\zeta \equiv \frac{\Delta p}{\rho w_0^2/2} = \frac{A}{\text{Re}}$$

Here, the quantity A is a function of both the angle and the area ratio

$$A = f(\alpha, n_{ar1})$$

At $\alpha \leq 40°$

$$A = \frac{20\, n_{ar1}^{0.33}}{(\tan \alpha)^{0.75}}$$

58. At high gas flow velocities it is more convenient to operate not on the resistance coefficient, but on the total pressure recovery coefficient at the end of the diffuser p_{01}, expressed in terms of the total pressure (stagnation pressure) p_{00} in its smallest cross section (0-0):

$$\bar{p}_0 = \frac{p_1^*}{p_0^*}$$

59. A resistance located downstream of the diffuser and uniformly distributed over the cross section (provided by a screen, perforated plate or grid, nozzle, air heater, etc.) regulates the flow in both the diffuser and the channel following it. The losses in the diffuser decrease somewhat. However, the total losses in the diffuser and in the grid (screen, etc.) vary only slightly.

For rectilinear diffusers with divergence angles α up to 40–60°, and especially for curvilinear diffusers, these losses remain equal to the sum of losses separately in a diffuser and in a perforated plate or grid,[47-49] that is,

$$\zeta \equiv \frac{\Delta p}{\rho w_0^2/2} = \zeta_{w.gr.} + \frac{\zeta_{gr}}{n_{ar1}^2}$$

where $\zeta_{w.gr.} = \Delta p_{w.gr.}/(\rho w_0^2/2)$ is the resistance coefficient of the diffuser without a grid, determined as ζ from corresponding diagrams of Chapter 5; $\zeta_{gr} = \Delta p_{gr}/(\rho w_{gr}^2/2)$ is the resistance coefficient of the grid (screen, nozzle, etc.), based on the flow velocity at its face, determined as ζ from corresponding diagrams of Chapter 8.

60. The flow conditions in short diffusers (with larger divergence angles) can be greatly improved, and the resistance lowered, by preventing flow separation with them or by attenuating vortex formation.

The main measures that improve flow conditions in the diffusers (Figure 5-19) include boundary-layer suction (Figure 5-19a) and blowing (renewal) (Figure 5-19b); installation of guide vanes (baffles, Figure 5-19c) and dividing walls or splitters (over the whole length of the diffusers, Figure 5-19d, or over part of it, Figure 5-19e); use of curvilinear walls (Figure 5-19f, g, h), stepped walls (stepped diffusers, Figure 5-19 i), and preseparation diffusers (Figure 5-19j); and transverse ribs or fins (Figure 5-19k).

61. With the use of boundary-layer suction (Figure 5-19a), the portion of the flow that separated from the wall reattaches to the surface with the result that the separation zone displaces downstream, the flow becomes smoother, and the resistance diminishes.

Blowing (renewal) of the boundary layer (Figure 5-19b) increases the flow velocity at the walls. In this case the separation zone is also displaced downstream.

62. The efficiency of boundary-layer suction depends on the ratio of the flow rate q of the medium aspirated through the slots in the side walls of the diffuser to the total flow rate Q of this medium through the diffuser (depends on the discharge coefficient $\bar{q} = q/Q$) and

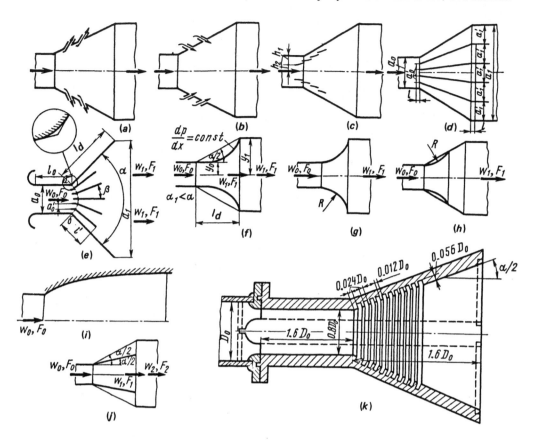

Figure 5-19 Different means of improving operation of short diffusers.

the relative distance between the slot and the inlet section of the diffuser. At $\bar{q} = 0.02$–0.03 the diffuser resistance decreases by 30–40%. In this case the losses in the suction system for the above values of $\bar{q}$ are relatively small.[91,93]

63. Figure 5-20 presents the experimental results obtained by Frankfurt[93] for ζ_{tot} of conical exhaust diffusers with divergence angles $\alpha = 30°$ and $60°$ and area ratio $n_{ar1} = 2$–8, depending on the degree of aspiration $\bar{q} = q_{asp}$ and location of the suction slot $\bar{x}_i = x_i/D_0$ at Re $= (3.7$–4.8$) \times 10^5$. Here, ζ_{tot} takes into account also the losses in the aspiration system. At $\alpha = 30°$, the optimum degree of aspiration lies within $\bar{q} = 0.02$–0.03. In this case, the smallest losses are observed when combined aspiration through slots is used: at the distances $\bar{x}_0 = 0$ and $\bar{x}_1 = x_i/D_0 = 0.78D_0$. For $\alpha = 60°$ the optimum degree of aspiration is observed at $\bar{q} = 0.04$. The losses are smallest when the suction slot is located in the initial section of the diffuser ($\bar{x}_0 = 0$).

64. If there is blowing of the boundary layer in conical diffusers with large divergence angles ($\alpha = 30°$ and $60°$), the zero location ($\bar{x} = 0$) of the blowing slot is optimal.[95] The efficiency of the diffuser with blowing depends on the relative cross-sectional area of the slot $\bar{f}_3 = (f_s/n_s)F_0$ ($n_s = F_s/F_0$). The dependence of the coefficient ζ_{tot} (which also takes into account the energy spent on blowing) on the relative discharge for blowing at different values of $\bar{f}_s$ and area ratio of the diffuser n_{ar1} for $\alpha = 30°$ and $60°$ is given in Figure 5-21. The optimum degree of blowing lies with $\bar{q} = 0.04$–0.12; it is independent of the value of n_{ar1}. The value of ζ_{tot} can be reduced 2–3 times by blowing the boundary layer, or at the same values of ζ_{tot} it is possible to shorten the length of the diffuser by the same number of times. This is confirmed by Figure 5-22 in which the dependence of the minimum coefficient ζ_{totmin} on $\bar{f}_s$ is given at different values of α.

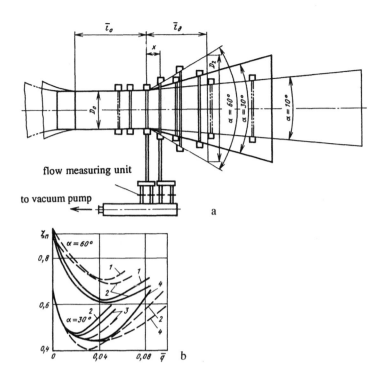

Figure 5-20 Schematic of boundary layer suction (a) and the dependence of ζ_{tot} on the relative discharge $\bar{q}$ (b):[93] solid line, flow suction through a slit in the initial section of a diffuser ($\bar{x}_1 = 0$); dashed line, simultaneous suction through two slits in sections $\bar{x} = 0$ and $\bar{x} = 0.78D_0$ at $\alpha = 30°$; $\bar{x} = 0$ and $\bar{x}_1 = 0.35D_0$ at $\alpha = 60°$; 1, $n_{ar1} = 8$; 2, $n_{ar1} = 4$; 3, $n_{ar1} = 3$; 4, $n_{ar1} = 2$.

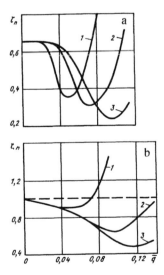

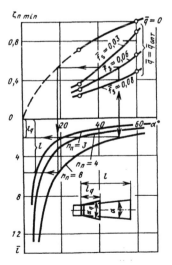

Figure 5-21 Dependence of ζ_{tot} on $\bar{q}$ for boundary layer blowing-off:[95] a, $\alpha = 30°$, $n_{ar1} = 3–8$: 1, $\bar{f}_s = 0.03$; 2, $\bar{f}_s = 0.06$; 3, $\bar{f}_s = 0.08$; b, $\alpha = 60°$; $n_{ar} = 4$ and 8: 1, $\bar{f}_s = 0.03$; 2, $\bar{f}_s = 0.06$; 3, $\bar{f}_s = 0.08$.

Figure 5-22 Overall dependence of the minimal total pressure losses on the slit area at various divergence angles of the diffuser and boundary layer blowing-off.[95]

65. Guide vanes (baffles) deflect a portion of the flow with higher velocities from the central region of the diffuser to its walls into the separation zone (Figure 5-19c); as a result, the separation zone diminishes or vanishes completely. The baffles produce their greatest effect at large divergence angles. Thus, at $\alpha_1 = 90–180°$ the resistance coefficient decreases by almost a factor of 2.

Several general rules can be given when installing baffles (guide vanes) in a diffuser:

- The vanes should be placed ahead of the entrance angle to the diffuser and behind it (Figure 5-19c); the number of vanes should be increased with an increase of the divergence angle.
- The channels between the vanes and the walls should, as a rule, contract; however, at large divergence angles satisfactory results can also be obtained with expanding channels. It is necessary to allow the flow to expand in the peripheral channels just as in the central channel.
- For divergence angle $\alpha = 90°$, the relative distance $h_1/h_2 = 0.95$; for $\alpha = 180°$, $h_1/h_2 = 1.4$ (Figure 5-19c).
- The vanes should have a small curvature and can be made of sheet metal having constant curvature and chord.
- The chord of the vanes can constitute 20–25% of the diameter or the height of the diffuser section.
- The most advantageous angle of inclination of the vanes can be selected by first placing them close behind one another and then rotating each vane through some angle until the minimum resistance of the diffuser is attained.

66. Splitters divide the diffuser with large divergence angles into several diffusers with smaller angles (Figure 5-19d). This provides both a decrease in the resistance and a more uniform velocity distribution over the section.[50]

The efficiency of splitters is greater, the larger the total divergence angle of the diffuser.

The dividing walls or splitters are selected and installed along the whole length of the diffuser with large divergence angles in the following way:

- The number z of splitters is chosen depending on the divergence angle α:

α, degrees	30	45	60	90	120
z		2	4	4	6	8

- The splitters are placed so that the distances a_0' between them at the inlet to the diffuser are strictly equal while the distances a_1' at the exit from it are approximately the same.
- The splitters protrude before and after the diffuser parallel to the diffuser axis. The length l of the protruding parts should not be smaller than $0.1a_0$ and $0.1a_1$, respectively.

67. The rules of arranging the diffusers with shortened walls (guide vanes) following the scheme of Figure 5-19e[96] are

- From Figure 5-23, one finds $\Delta\theta_{opt}$ (the angle between the extension of the line of the outer wall of the diffuser and the line of the displacement of the "source" M^*, that is, the point at which the prolongations of the lines of all the vanes are crossed, Figure 5-24).
- A fictitious divergence angle of the diffuser is calculated as

$$\alpha^* = \alpha + 2\Delta\theta_{opt}$$

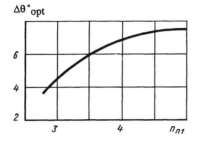

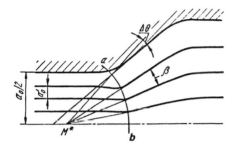

Figure 5-23 Dependence of the angle $\Delta\theta^{\circ}_{opt}$ on the divergence ratio n_{ar1}.[96]

Figure 5-24 Arrangement of guide vanes in a diffuser.[96]

and the arc a–δ of the circle is drawn which connects the angles of the bends of the diffuser walls (the line of transition of the flow in the throat to the flow that ''radially'' escapes from the source M^*) over the radius

$$r = \frac{3a_0}{2\alpha^*_{div}}$$

where a_0 is the diffuser throat width and $\alpha^*_{div} = 0.01745\alpha^*$ is the fictitious divergence angle of the diffuser, in radians.

- The number of vanes is determined so that the divergence angle of the channels between them is approximately

$$\beta = \frac{\alpha^*}{z + 1} \approx 7\text{--}10°$$

whence

$$z = \frac{\alpha^*}{7\text{--}10} - 1$$

- The relative length l'/a'_0 of the vanes is determined as a function of β (Figure 5-19e):

β, degrees	7	8	9	10	12
l'/a'_0	20	16	12	10	9

- The width of the entrance into the diffuser is divided into $z + 1$ equal parts and the vanes are placed radially beginning from the points of intersection of the dividing lines with the transition line a–δ; the length of the vanes is laid off from the transition line (Figure 5-19e).

- The vanes in the zone of the forward edges are curved to provide a smooth transition from the throat into the expanding part of the channel.
- If the diffusers are relatively short and the length of the vanes exceeds the length of the diffuser, the vanes can be shortened to have $l'/l_d = 0.6$.
- When it is necessary to reduce the number of vanes—for example, when the width of the inlet section is small and there is the possibility of a compressibility effect, the vane should be made shorter, since in this case the divergence angle β increases.

68. The variation of the pressure gradient is smoother in a diffuser with curved walls (Figure 5-19f), in which the rate of increase of the cross-sectional area is lower in the initial section than in the end section. This reduces the main cause of flow separation and, consequently, diminishes the main source of losses. A most advantageous diffuser, from this point of view, is one in which the pressure gradient remains constant ($dp/dx = $ const) along the channel in potential flow.

For divergence angles $\alpha = 25$–$90°$, the losses in such diffusers can be reduced to 40% as compared with rectilinear diffusers, the reduction increasing with an increase of the divergence angle within the limits mentioned.[47]

When the divergence angles are small ($\alpha < 15$–$20°$), the losses in curved diffusers become even larger than in rectilinear diffusers. Therefore, the use of curved diffusers is advisable only when the divergence angles are large.

The equation of the boundary of a curved wall diffuser of a circular (or square) cross section for $dp/dx = $ const (Figure 5-19f) has the form

$$y = \frac{y_1}{4\sqrt{1 + [(y_1/y_0)^4 - 1]x/l_d}}$$

The equation of the bounding wall for a plane diffuser is

$$y = \frac{y_1}{\sqrt{1 + [(y_1/y_0)^2 - 1]x/l_d}}$$

The resistance coefficient of a curved wall diffuser at $dp/dx = $ const within the limits $0.1 < F_0/F_1 < 0.9$ can be calculated from an approximate formula based on data from the author's experiments:[47]

$$\zeta \equiv \frac{\Delta p}{\rho w_0^2/2} = \phi_0\left(1.43 - \frac{1.3}{n_{ar1}}\right)\left(1 - \frac{1}{n_{ar1}}\right)^2$$

where ϕ_0 is a coefficient that depends on the relative length of the curved diffuser (see Diagram 5-8).

69. A marked reduction in the resistance is also attained in "radius" diffusers, where the bounding walls completely[100] or partially[55] follow the shape of a circular arc (Figure 5-19g, h).

The resistance coefficients of diffusers with partially circular walls and equivalent angles $\alpha = 45$ and $60°$ are similar to ζ for a longer diffuser with $\alpha = 30°$ without rounding. This means that it is expedient to replace the rectilinear diffuser with $\alpha = 30°$ by a shorter diffuser with the equivalent angles $\alpha = 45$–$60°$, but having circular arc walls. The length of these diffusers is smaller than of a diffuser with $\alpha = 30°$ by ≈ 60–100%.

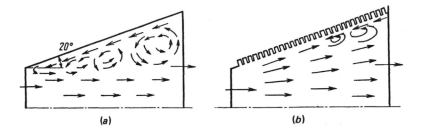

Figure 5-25 Schematic diagram of flow in a diffuser[61,62] (*a*) without fans, (*b*) with fins.

70. Diffusers with a preseparated turbulent boundary layer ("preseparation" diffusers) are also very efficient. An approximate calculation method has been developed by Bychkova[10] and Ginevsky and Bychkova.[21] Initially (just behind the entrance) they are of a bell shape, which transforms into a segment with straight walls (Figure 5-19i). Diffusers of circular cross section have a total divergence angle over this segment equal to $\alpha = 4°$, while in plane diffusers this angle is $\alpha = 6°$. A preseparation diffuser is a diffuser with a nonseparating flow of the minimum length.

71. The combination of blowing with a profiled preseparation section (the Griffith diffuser, (Figure 5-19i) further decreases pressure losses and the length of the diffuser.

72. A considerable reduction in the resistance (by a factor of 2 or more) is attained by arranging transverse ribs or fins in the diffuser (Figure 5-19k).[61,62] The reduction of the resistance is accompanied by equalization of the velocity profile over the diffuser section. All this is due to the fact that macroseparation of the flow from the walls is replaced by a system of minor separations (Figure 5-25), with the largest effect for circular diffusers being attained at $\alpha = 40$–$45°$. The optimum parameters of finning are given in Figure 5-25.

The lateral fins can be made flexible. The resulting vorticity and recirculation due to separation of the boundary layer rotate these fins through an angle, thus varying the efficient cross section of the diffuser and preventing the distribution of reverse stream to the diffuser mouth.[32]

73. In a stepped diffuser (Figure 5-19j), in which a smooth change in the cross-sectional area is followed by a sudden expansion, the main losses (shock losses) occur even at relatively low velocities.

As a result, the losses in the diffuser are greatly reduced (by a factor of 2–3). The coefficient of total resistance of a stepped diffuser of circular or rectangular cross section can be approximated [47] from:

$$\zeta \equiv \frac{\Delta p}{\rho w_0^2/2} = \left(\frac{\lambda}{8 \sin \dfrac{\alpha}{2}} \frac{q^2 + 1}{q^2 - 1} + k_1 \, tg^{1.25} \frac{\alpha}{2}\right) \times (1 - 1/q^2)^2 + (1/q^2 - 1/n_{ar})^2$$

where $q = 1 + 2(l/D_h)tg \; \alpha/2$; $k_1 = 3.2$ for circular diffusers; $k_1 \approx 4$–6 for rectangular diffusers;* $n_{ar} = F_2/F_0$ is the total area ratio of the stepped diffuser (the ratio of the widest part of the diffuser to its smallest part, see Figure 5-19j).

74. The coefficient of the total resistance coefficient of a plane stepped diffuser can be calculated approximately:[47]

---

*The curves in Diagram 5-10 were calculated for $k_1 = 6.0$ which gives a certain safety factor in the calculation.

$$\zeta \equiv \frac{\Delta p}{\rho w_0^2/2} = \left[\frac{\lambda}{8(l_g/a_0)\,\text{tg}\,\dfrac{\alpha}{2}} \left(\frac{a_0}{b_0}\,\frac{q_1}{\text{tg}\,\dfrac{\alpha}{2}} + \frac{q_2}{\sin\dfrac{\alpha}{2}} \right) \right.$$

$$\left. + 3.2\,\text{tg}^{1.25}\,\frac{\alpha}{2} \right] (1 - 1/q_1)^2 + (1/q_1 - 1/n_{\text{ar}})^2$$

where

$$q_1 = 1 + 2(l_g/a_0)\,\text{tg}\,\frac{\alpha}{2}$$

$$q_2 = 1 + (l_g/a_0)\,\text{tg}\,\frac{\alpha}{2}$$

(b_0 is constant along the diffuser length).

75. For each area ratio n and each relative length l_d/D_h (or l_d/a_0) of the stepped diffuser there is an optimum divergence angle α_{opt} at which the total resistance coefficient is minimum (see Diagrams 5-9 through 5-11). It is recommended that stepped diffusers be used with the optimum divergence angles.

The resistance coefficient of such diffusers is

$$\zeta \equiv \frac{\Delta p}{\rho w_0^2/2} = \zeta_{\text{min}}$$

where ζ_{min} is the minimum resistance, which depends on the relative length of the smooth part of the diffuser l_d/D_h (or l_d/a_0) and the total area ratio n of the stepped diffuser (see Diagrams 5-9 through 5-11).

76. The limiting divergence angle α_{min} of the smooth part of the stepped diffuser, that is, the angle at which the steps cease to have influence at the given overall area ratio n_{ar} and relative length l_d/D_h (or l_d/a_0) of the smooth part, is given by

$$\tan\frac{\alpha_{\text{lim}}}{2} = \frac{\sqrt{n_{\text{ar 1}}} - 1}{2l_d/D_h}$$

and correspondingly

$$\tan-\frac{\alpha_{\text{lim}}}{2} = \frac{n_{\text{ar 1}} - 1}{2l_d/a_0}$$

When the relative length l_d/D_h (l_d/a_0) of the stepped diffuser is selected in practice, it is advisable to use not the minimum value ζ_{min}, but a value about 10% higher, which allows a considerable reduction in the length of the diffuser without noticeably inceasing the losses in it. The optimum values of l_d/D_h (l_d/a_0) are given in graphs a of Diagrams 5-9 through 5-11 as a dashed line.

77. When a diffuser is installed behind a fan, one should take into account that there is a great difference between the flow patterns at the fan exit and at the entrance into an isolated diffuser preceded by a straight segment of constant cross section.

As a rule, the velocity profile downstream of a centrifugal fan is asymmetric due to a certain deflection of the flow in the direction of fan rotation. The velocity profile depends both on the type of the fan and on the mode of its operation characterized by the relative flow rate Q/Q_{opt}, where Q_{opt} is the flow rate at maximum efficiency of the fan.

78. The flow deflection to the periphery of fan rotation allows the use of diffusers with larger divergence angles than conventionally used behind centrifugal fans. In this case it is advisable that the plane diffusers with divergence angles $\alpha > 25°$ be made asymmetric so that the outer wall either would be a continuation of the housing or would deviate no more than 10° to the side of the housing, while the inner wall follows along the side of the impeller.

Displacement of the diffuser axis toward the side of the fan housing is not expedient, since the resistance of such diffusers at $\alpha > 15°$ is 2–2.5 times higher than that of symmetrical diffusers whose axis is displaced toward the impeller axis.[58]

79. The resistance coefficient of plane diffusers with divergence angles $\alpha < 15°$ and of pyramidal diffusers with $\alpha < 10°$, installed downstream of centrifugal fans of any type under any working conditions, can be calculated approximately from the data given above for isolated diffusers with the following velocity ratio taken for their inlet section:

$$\frac{w_{max}}{w_0} \approx 1.1$$

When the divergence angles of the diffusers are larger than 10–15°, the values of ζ obtained for isolated diffusers should not be used; the values of ζ should be determined from Diagrams 5-13 through 5-18.

These data are applicable in practice for $Q = Q_{opt}$ and $Q \lessgtr Q_{opt}$.

80. When there is a lack of space following a centrifugal fan, a stepped diffuser can be installed which is much shorter than a straight diffuser for the same resistance. The optimum divergence angle of the diffuser at which the minimum resistance coefficient is obtained can be determined from the corresponding curves of Diagram 5-18.

81. To convert the velocity pressure downstream of the outlet vane ring of axial turbomachines (fans, compressors, turbines), wide use is made of annular diffusers, which are made with rectilinear boundaries (axial-annular diffuser, Figure 5-26), with curvilinear boundaries (radial-annular diffuser, Diagram 5-20), or combined (axial-radial annular diffuser, Diagram 5-20.)

The area ratio of the axial-annular diffuser is determined from the formula given in Diagram 5-19, and that of the radial-circular diffuser is determined from the formulas of Diagram 5-20.

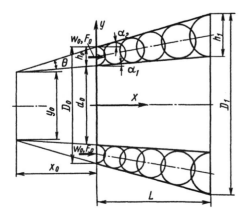

Figure 5-26 Axial-annular diffuser.

82. The internal resistance coefficients* $\zeta_{in} \equiv \Delta p/(\rho w_0^2/2) = \Delta p(\rho c_a/2)$ of the axial-annular diffuser with positive angles α_1, depend on the area ratio n_{ar1} at the given d_0, and have in practice only one curve for each value of $\bar{l}_d = L/D_0$. This kind of dependence of ζ_{in} on n_{ar1} at $\bar{d}_0 = 0.650\text{--}0.688$ and $\bar{l}_d = 0.5\text{--}2.0$ is shown in graph a of Diagram 5-19. The curves $\zeta_{in}' = f(n_{ar1})$ for $\bar{l}_d = 0.5$ and 1.0 were constructed from the experimental data of Dovzhik and Morozov,[40] while the remaining values were constructed to approximately account for both the experimental data of Dovzhik and Morozov[40] and the experimental data of Bushel.[9]

Within the limits $2 < n_{ar1} < 4$ and $0.5 < \bar{L} < 2.0$ the following interpolation formula can be used:

$$\zeta_{in}' \approx \frac{0.25 n_{ar1}^2}{\bar{l}_d^{0.5}}$$

When the velocity field at the inlet to the axial-annular diffuser is nonuniform or when the diffuser is installed downstream of the operating axial machine, the internal resistance coefficient is determined as

$$\zeta_{in} \equiv \frac{\Delta p}{\rho w_0^2/2} \approx k_d \zeta_{in}'$$

where k_d is the correction factor (see Diagram 5-1 or 5-19).

83. The resistance coefficient of an axial-annular diffuser with a converging back fairing (see Diagram 5-19) can be determined from

$$\zeta \equiv \frac{\Delta p}{\rho w_0^2/2} = k_d \phi_d \left(1 - \frac{F_0}{F_1}\right)^2$$

where ϕ_d is the total** shock coefficient determined, depending on the divergence angle α, from graph b of Diagram 5-19.

84. The present chapter considers one type of radial-annular diffuser with the outline of the curvilinear part constructed following a circular arc with $R_1/h_0 = 1.5$ and $R_0/h_0 = 2.0$ (see Diagram 5-20) and one type of axial-radial-annular diffuser with the outline of the curvilinear part constructed following an elliptical arc (see Diagram 5-20 and Figure 5-27) having semiaxes:

$$a = L_s - (L_{in} - b \sin \alpha)$$

and

$$b = \frac{D_1}{2} - r_0 - L_{in} \tan \alpha$$

where $\alpha = (\alpha_1 + \alpha_2)/2$.

---

*By the internal resistance coefficients ζ_{in} and ζ_{in}', here and later, we mean the ratio of the difference of total pressures at the entrance and directly at the exit from the diffuser to the inlet velocity pressure, regardless of the additional losses that might have occurred in the straight exit section behind the diffuser due to equalization of the velocity profile distorted during the passage throught the diffuser.

**The total shock coefficient takes into account the total losses in a diffuser.[47,49]

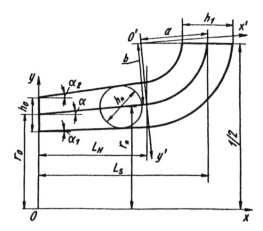

Figure 5-27 Schematic diagrams of construction of an axial-radial-annular diffuser.

The axial line was assumed to be the locus of centers of the circles inscribed in the diffuser outline while the diameters of these circles varied along the axial line from the initial diameter h_0 to the final diameter h_1, linearly. The relative diameter of the hub at the entrance to diffusers of both types is $d_0 = 0.688$.

85. The internal resistance coefficients ζ_{in} of the above types of diffusers* are given in Diagram 5-20 as functions of the area ratio n_1 at different values of "radiality" $\overline{D} = D_1/D_0$ for two cases: with an operating compressor at $\overline{c}_a = 0.5$ (where $\overline{c}_a = c_{a0}/u = \overline{w}_0 = 4Q/[\pi(D_0^2 - d_0^2)u]$; u is the circumferential velocity of the compressor blades at the external radius, m/s; and Q is the flow rate, m³/s) and with an idle compressor.

The value of ζ_{in} for an operating compressor exceeds the corresponding value of ζ_{in} for an idle compressor (turbomachine) by 15–20%. The resistance coefficient of the diffusers under consideration depends on the mode of compressor operation, that is, on the discharge coefficient $\overline{c}_{a0}$ (see Dovzhik and Ginevsky).[39]

86. A combined diffuser—that is, an axial-radial-annular diffuser—in which a radial bend follows a short annular diffuser is somewhat better. In this diffuser, the radial turn is achieved at lower stream velocities, and therefore the pressure losses are somewhat lower. At the same time, the axial dimensions of such a diffuser are much larger than those of a radial-annular diffuser.

87. The resistance of an annular diffuser, like that of the conventional ones, can be noticeably reduced by installing one or several splitters or guiding surfaces, which would divide the diffuser with large α into several diffusers with smaller values of α and would generally regulate the flow in the diffuser. Just as with conventional diffusers, these guiding surfaces are efficient only at large divergence angles and at definite combinations of the angles α_1 and α_2, that is, combinations at which the resistance coefficients of the diffusers without these surfaces are largest.[36,39,40]

88. Different mechanical systems involving such machines as pumps, turbines, and compressors require, besides velocity retardation and turning of the flow, that the supplying channels be of small overall size. This is achieved in diffuser elbows or (which is the same) in curved axis diffusers (Diagram 5-21). The flow in such diffusers is much more complex than in straight axis diffusers and is composed of (1) the flow in a straight axis diffuser and (2) the flow in a curved channel of constant cross section. The latter is accompanied by secondary currents due to nonuniformity of the velocity and pressure field in the direction normal to the plane of the turn and to the existence of boundary layers at the channel walls

*For the values of the total resistance coefficients ζ_{fr}, see Chapter 11.

(see Chapter 6). These factors contribute to an earlier flow separation and cause pressure losses different from those in straight diffusers. Besides the parameters mentioned in paragraph 11, the resistance of the curved axis diffuser is also affected by the angle of curvature of the axis β and the relative curvature radius of the axis R/D_0 (r/b_0).

89. The internal resistance coefficients ζ'_{in} of plane curved axis diffusers of constant length ($l_d/b_0 = 8.3$), most often encountered in multistage pumps, are given in Diagram 5-21 as a function of the divergence angle α* for four values of the relative curvature radius of the inner side wall of the diffuser: $r/b_0 = \infty$, 22.5, 11.6, and 7.5. These data were obtained by Polotsky[69,70] for diffusers installed directly behind a smooth inlet collector, that is, at $l_0/b_0 = 0$.

90. The internal resistance coefficients of spatial curved axis diffusers with exit sections of different shapes (circle, ellipse with a larger axis in the curvature plane, ellipse with a smaller axis in the curvature plane; see Diagram 5-29) at constant length ($l_d/D_0 = 7.15$) and area ratio ($n_{ar1} = 4$)** and different bending angles ($\beta = 0$, 15, and 30°; $R/D_0 = \infty$, 27.30, and 13.65 are given in Diagram 5-22.*** Some data are given for constant values of the Reynolds number (Re $= 5.2 \times 10^5$), and some as a function of Reynolds number. In all the cases the diffusers were tested when they were installed downstream of a smooth inlet collector with a small straight section ($l_0/D_0 = 0.35$).

91. In some types of curved-axis diffusers secondary currents can also exert a positive effect as they transport a portion of the moving medium from the region with larger kinetic energy to the boundary layers which are affected by separation. In this case the resistance coefficient of a curved diffuser becomes noticeably smaller than that of a straight diffuser with the same parameters [compare the curves $\zeta = f(\text{Re})$ for diffusers 9 and 10 of Diagram 5-22]

92. In some cases a curved axis diffuser can be replaced by a straight diffuser with an elbow having guide vanes. The effect on the resistance is evident from the data given in Figure 5-28.

Converging Nozzles in the System

1. Transition from a larger section to a smaller one through a smoothly converging section—converging nozzles—is also accompanied by comparatively large irreversible losses of total pressure. The resistance coefficient of a converging nozzle with rectilinear boundaries (Diagram 5-23) depends on the convergence angle α and the area ratio $n_0 = F_0/F_1$ (and correspondingly on the relative length l_{con}/D_0), while at small Reynolds numbers it also depends on Re.

2. At sufficiently large angles ($\alpha > 10°$) and area ratios ($n_0 < 0.3$), the flow, after passing from the contracting section of a rectilinear converging nozzle to the straight part of the tube, separates from the walls, which is the main source of the local losses of total pressure. The larger α and the lower n_0, the stronger is the flow separation and the greater the resistance of the converging nozzle. The resistance is naturally highest at $\alpha = 180°$, that is, when there is a sudden contraction in the cross section (see Figure 4-12).

The friction losses occur along the length of the contracting section.

---

*For a circular diffuser the divergence angle $\alpha = 8°$.

**By the divergence angle of a curved-axis diffuser we mean an angle made by the side walls of a straight diffuser obtained by "unbending" a curved axial diffuser.

***These data were obtained on the basis of an approximate recalculation of the values of the efficiency taken from Shiringer's experimental work.[173]

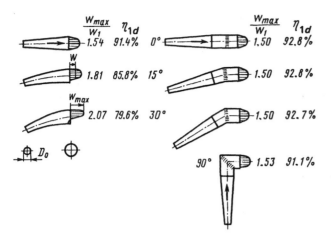

Figure 5-28 The values of η_{1d} and w_{max}/w_1 for curved-axis diffusers at $n_{ar1} = 4$; $l_d/D_0 = 7.15$ ($\alpha = 8°$); $\beta = 15$ and $30°$; $l_0/D_0 = 0.35$; $2\delta_0^*/D = 0.51\%$; Re = 5.2×10^5 and for straight-axis diffusers with flow-straightening elbows.[172,173]

3. For engineering calculations it is convenient to represent the general resistance coefficient of converging nozzles as

$$\zeta \equiv \frac{\Delta p}{\rho w_0^2/2} = \zeta_{loc} + \zeta_{fr}$$

The local resistance coefficient of a converging nozzle[136] is

$$\zeta_{loc} \equiv \frac{\Delta p}{\rho w_0^2/2} = (-0.0125n_0^4 + 0.0224n_0^3 - 0.00723n_0^2 + 0.00444n_0 - 0.00745)$$

$$\times (\alpha_p^3 - 2\pi\alpha_p^2 - 10\alpha_p)$$

where $\alpha_p = 0.01745\alpha$ rad (α in degrees).

The friction resistance coefficient ζ_{fr} of a contracting section is determined from Equations (5-6) and (5-8)–(5-10), where λ is assumed to be approximately constant along the entire section, but dependent on Re at the entrance and on the relative roughness of the walls $\overline{\Delta}$.

Diagram 5-23 also contains the values of the total resistance coefficient ζ obtained experimentally by Yanshin[100] at Re = 5×10^5.

4. Within the limits $10 < \alpha < 40°$, the general resistance coefficient of the converging nozzle with rectilinear boundaries has a minimum which, at least at Re $\geqslant 10^5$, remains practically constant and is equal to $\zeta \approx 0.05$.

5. The resistance of converging nozzles can be greatly diminished by providing a smooth transition from a larger section to a smaller one with the help of curvilinear boundary walls (following the arc of a circle or any other curve; see Diagram 5-23), as well as by bending rectilinear walls of the converging nozzles at the exit into the straight section (thin lines in scheme *a* of Diagram 5-23).

With smooth contraction of the cross section, when the contraction angle is very small ($\alpha < 10°$) or when the contracting section has very smooth curvilinear walls (see scheme *b* of Diagram 5-23), the flow does not separate from the walls at the place of transition into a straight section, and the pressure losses reduce to only friction losses in the contracting portion:

$$\zeta \equiv \frac{\Delta p}{\rho w_0^2/2} \approx \zeta_{fr}$$

6. At very small Reynolds numbers ($1 < \text{Re} < 50$) the resistance coefficient of converging nozzles, like that of diffusers,[4] is

$$\zeta \equiv \frac{\Delta p}{\rho w_0^2/2} = \frac{A}{\text{Re}}$$

Within the limits $5 \leqslant \alpha \leqslant 40°$.

$$A = 20.5 n_0^{-0.5} \tan^{-0.75}$$

Transition Sections

1. There are two kinds of transition sections: (1) those with a variable cross section along the flow, with the shape of the cross section kept constant and (2) those in which both the cross section and its shape vary.

2. The first type includes, in particular, converging-diverging transition pieces (Diagram 5-25). According to experiments carried out by Yanshin[100] the optimal parameters of transition pieces in the form of a converging nozzle with rectilinear walls are as follows:

$$\alpha_{\text{con}} = 30\text{--}40° \quad \text{and} \quad \alpha_d = 7\text{--}10°$$

For a converging nozzle with curvilinear walls the optimal bending radius is $R_{\text{con}} = 0.5\text{--}1.0 D_0$.

3. The resistance coefficient of converging-diverging transition pieces of annular cross section, like that of conventional diffusers, depends on the relative length of the intermediate straight section l_0/D_0 and on the area ratio F_1/F_0 and can be determined from

$$\zeta \equiv \frac{\Delta p}{\rho w_0^2/2} = A(k_1 k_2 \zeta_1 + \Delta \zeta) \tag{5-15)}$$

where ζ_1 is the resistance coefficient of the transition piece with a smooth (curvilinear) converging section at $l_0/D_0 = 1.0$, which is determined at $\text{Re} = w_0 D_0/\nu \geqslant 2 \times 10^5$ from curves $\zeta_1 = f_1(\alpha_d)$ of Diagram 5-25 plotted on the basis of Yanshin's data.[100] At $\text{Re} = 2 \times 10^5$, for coefficient ζ_1 of an annular diffuser, see ζ in Diagram 5-2; $k_1 = \zeta_{1n}/\zeta_{1n\geqslant4}$ is the ratio of the coefficient ζ_1 at $n_1 = F_1/F_0 < 4$ to its value at $n_1 \geqslant 4$, see curves $k_1 = f_2(\alpha_d, F_1/F_0)$ of Diagram 5-5.25; k_2 is the correction for the effect of the relative length l_0/D_0; within the limits $0.25 \leqslant l_0/D_0 \leqslant 5.0$

$$k_2 \approx 0.66 + 0.35 \frac{l_0}{D_0} \tag{5-16}$$

$\Delta \zeta$ is an additional term which considers the effect of l_0/D_0; $A = 1.0$ is for transition with a smooth converging diffuser; $A = f(\alpha_d)$ for transition with a converging diffuser having rectilinear generatrices (see Diagram 5-25).

4. For transition pieces of rectangular (square) cross section and plane transition pieces (for which both contraction and divergence of the cross section occur in one plane), the resistance coefficient can be roughly determined from Equations (5-15) and (5-16), but with ζ_1 replaced by ζ_d of the diffuser at $l_0/D_0 = 0$ from Diagrams 5-4 and 5-5, respectively.

5. In transition pieces that connect tubes of circular and rectangular cross sections (see Diagram 5-27), conversion of an axisymmetric flow into a plane one (and vice versa) is

accompanied by its deformation in two mutually perpendicular planes—by expansion in one plane and contraction in the other.[84] Such a complex flow can simultaneously exhibit the characteristic effects of the diffusers and converging sections. If a longer side of the rectangular section exceeds the diameter of a circular tube ($b_1 > D_0$), stalling phenomena can occur, leading to large pressure losses. Therefore, the transition piece of the type considered should have such a length and a shape as to prevent the possibility of flow separation or to displace it into the region having lower flow velocities. This can be achieved by proper selection of the geometric shape and overall dimensions.

6. As to the shape of the walls forming the transition pieces, the latter can be divided into three characteristic types (Figure 5-29). Type A is obtained when the truncated circular cone (with rectilinear boundaries) is intersected by planes.

Type B is constructed on the basis of a linear change of the cross-sectional areas along the length of the transition pieces; in this case in the plane of symmetry, parallel to the longer side of the rectangle, the boundaries of the transition pieces are rectilinear.

Type C, like type B, retains a linear change of variation of areas over the greater part of the length of the transition pieces, but at the same time provides a more uniform distribution of the average velocity at each location. All the boundary walls in these transition pieces are curvilinear.

7. In the transition pieces of type A, provided $b_1 > D_0$, a nonseparating flow can be produced near the diverging walls at $\alpha = 20$–$30°$. In this case the length of the converging transition segment should be asssumed to be equal to: at $b_1 > 1.5D_0$, $l_{con} \approx 1.8(b_1 > D_0)$, and at $b_1 \leq 1.5D_0$, $l_{con} \approx 1.5b_1$.

The length of the converging transition pieces of types B and C can be reduced by a factor of 1.5–2 as compared with the length of the transition piece of type A. Tentatively, the length of these transition pieces is

$$l_{con} \approx (1\text{–}1.5)b_1$$

In cases where b_1/D_0, the walls of the converging transition pieces taper and then their length should correspond to the optimum angle of convergence, as in annular converging nozzles, that is, $\alpha = 40$–$50°$. In this case

$$l_{con} \approx 1.1(D_0 - a_1) \approx D_0$$

8. An increase in the length of converging transition pieces leads to an increase in friction losses, while a decrease in their length causes an increase in the resistance due to flow separation from diverging walls.

9. Diverging transition pieces, like plane or conical diffusers, also have an optimal length for which there is a minimum hydraulic resistance. It is most important here to prevent separation at the inlet portion of the unit. To achieve this, the complete angle between the diverging walls at the beginning of the transition piece should not exceed 8–10°. Compliance with this condition in transition pieces of type A leads to their comparatively large length, corresponding at $\alpha = 10°$ to

$$l_d \approx 5.7(D_0 - a_1) \approx 6D_0$$

Therefore, to make the length of the diverging transition pieces shorter, type B or C should be used, and their length should be equal to

$$l_d \approx (3\text{–}4)D_0$$

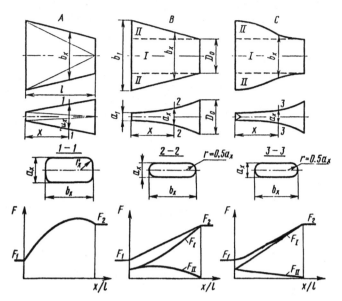

Figure 5-29 Transition pieces having different shapes of the boundary walls.[84]

10. When the relative width of the rectangular cross section is small ($b_1/D_0 < 2$), transition pieces of type B should be used. The walls adjacent to the longer side of the rectangular section should in this case be made curvilinear, while the walls adjacent to a shorter side should be left rectilinear. At $b_1/D_0 > 2$, diverging transition pieces of type C should be used.

11. Dimensions of any cross section along the length of the transition piece of type B can be determined analytically from

$$F_x = F_1 - (F_1 - F_2)\frac{x}{l}$$

$$F_x = 4a_xb_x - (4 - \pi)a_x^2 \qquad (5\text{-}17)$$

$$b_x = D_0 + (b - D_0)\frac{x}{l}$$

where F_x is the cross-sectional area at a distance x from the entrance.

12. The cross-sectional dimensions of transition pieces of type C can be determined from Equation (5-17), using them separately for each of the three characteristic parts of the transition piece shown in Figure 5-29.* For example, when the middle part I is calculated (see Figure 5-29), the width $b_{xI} = D_0$ is known, while the size a_{xI} is determined from the relation $F = f(x/l)$. When parts II are calculated, the size $a_{xII} = a_{xI}$ is known, while the size b_{xII} is determined from the relation $F = f(x/l)$.

The total width of any cross section should be equal to

$$b_x = b_{xI} + b_{xII}$$

13. As for conventional (plane and axisymmetric) diffusers and converging nozzles, the hydraulic resistance of the transition pieces considered depends on the geometric parameters (area ratio n_{ar} and relative lengths of the transition pieces l_d/D_0 and l_{con}/D_0), on the flow

*In important cases, specification and final selection of the optimal shapes and dimensions should be made on the basis of experiments.

pattern (Reynolds number) and inlet conditions. Moreover, the ratio of the sides of the rectangular cross section b_1/a_1, the shape of the walls of the transition pieces, and the method of variation of the cross-sectional areas over the length are important parameters for the above transition pieces.

14. The resistance coefficient of the transition pieces considered can be determined from the interpolation formula of Tanaev:[84]

$$\zeta \equiv \frac{\Delta p}{\rho w_0^2/2} = \zeta_{sim} + A \exp\left(-k_2 \frac{\mathrm{Re}}{\mathrm{Re}_{sim}}\right) \tag{5-18}$$

where the numerical coefficients A and k_2 depend on the method of variation of the values and shape of cross-sectional areas over the length of the transition piece and on the ratio b_1/a_1; ζ_{sim} is the resistance coefficient of the similar flow regime ($\mathrm{Re} \geqslant \mathrm{Re}_{sim} \approx 5 \times 10^5$); w_0 is the average flow velocity in a circular cross section of the transition piece; $A = A_d \approx 0.5$ and $k_2 = k_d = 5.0$ for a diverging transition piece; $A = A_{con} \approx 0.3$ and $k_2 = k_{con} \approx 5.0$ for the converging transition piece.

The first term on the right-hand side of Equation (5-18) is

$$\zeta_{sim} = \left(c_0 + c_1 \frac{b_1}{a_1}\right) n_0^2$$

where c_1 depends on the length and shape of the transition piece. For transition pieces with a linear method of variation of the areas, values of c_1 are given in graph b of Diagram 5-27.

The coefficient c_0 is the resistance of the tube portion of constant cross section, the length of which is equal to the length of the transition piece. Its value is

$$c_0 = \frac{\lambda l}{D_h}$$

where D_h is the average value (over the length of the transition piece) of the hydraulic diameter. At the length of the transition pieces $l/D_0 \approx 3.5$, it can be tentatively assumed that $c_0 \approx 0.06$, $c_{1d} \approx 0.01$—for the diverging transition piece, and $c_{1con} \approx 0.002$—for the converging transition piece. The quantity $n_0 = F_0/F_1$, where F_0 is the area of the circular cross section of the transition piece and $F_1 = a_1/b_1$ is the area of the rectangular cross section.

15. The resistance coefficients of transition pieces in which a rectangular cross section with small aspect ratio ($a_1/b_1 \leqslant 2.0$) changes into an annular cross section, or vice versa (see scheme of Diagram 5-28), can be determined from the data for diffusers of rectangular cross section with equivalent divergence angles. The equivalent angle α_e is determined from the following expressions:

For transition of a circle into a rectangle:

$$\tan \frac{\alpha_e}{2} = \frac{2\sqrt{a_1 b_1/\pi} - D_0}{2l_d}$$

For transition of a rectangle into a circle:

$$\tan \frac{\alpha_e}{2} = \frac{D_1 - 2\sqrt{a_0 b_0/\pi}}{2l_d}$$

5-2 DIAGRAMS OF THE RESISTANCE COEFFICIENTS

Diffusers. Determination of the inlet conditions (k_d)[51-55,127]	Diagram 5-1

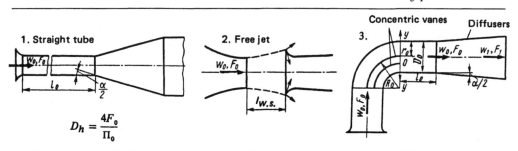

$$D_h = \frac{4F_0}{\Pi_0}$$

1. When w_{max}/w or $2\delta_0^*/D_h$ is known in the symmetrical velocity field upstream of a diffuser (scheme 1), the relative length l_0/D_h is determined from the curves $w_{max}/w_0 = f_1(l_0/D_h)$ (graph a) or alternatively from the curves $2\delta_0^*/D_h = f_2(l_0/D_h)$ (graph b); then, from these values of l_0/D_h, the value of k_d is determined from the appropriate diagrams.

2. For a free jet (working section of a wind tunnel (scheme 2), $w_{max}/w_0 = f_3(l_{w.s.}/D_h)$ (graph c) is determined using the known length $l_{w.s.}/D_h$, then l_0/D_h is determined from graph a, and finally $k_d = f(l_0/D_h)$ is determined from the appropriate diagrams.

3. When diffusers (of any shape) with $\alpha = 6\text{–}14°$ are installed downstream of a branch pipe (scheme 3) or any other curved parts with similar velocity profiles upstream of the diffuser (graph d) $k_d = f(w/w_0, R_0/D_h, l_0/D_h, z)$ is taken from the table below.

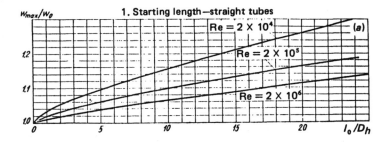

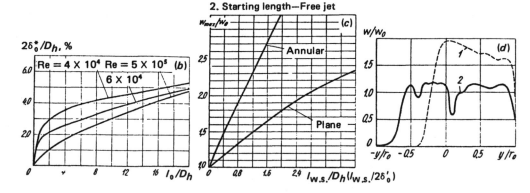

Shape of velocity profiles (graph d)	Parameters of the branching pipe			k_d
	R_0/D_h	l_0/D_h	Number of concentric splitters z	
1	0.8–1.0	0	0	6.8
2	0.8–1.0	0	2	2.1
–	0.8–1.0	0	3	1.9
–	2.0	0	0	2.6
–	2.0	1.0	0	1.0
–	≥3.0	0	0	1.0

Conical diffuser (in the system with $l_1/D_1 > 0$) at $\alpha = 3–180°$[51-55]   Diagram 5-2

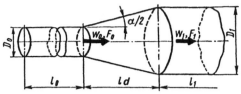

$$n_{ar1} = \frac{F_1}{F_0}, \quad Re = \frac{w_0 D_0}{\nu}$$

1. Uniform velocity field at the entrance into the diffuser ($w_{max}/w_0 = 1.0$ or $l_0/D_0 \approx 9$)*:

$$\zeta \equiv \frac{\Delta p}{\rho w_0^2/2} = \zeta_d = f(\alpha, n_{ar1}, Re)$$

see the table and the curves of graph a; (for approximating formulas see para. 38, 39 of Section 5-1. Calculation of the preseparation diffusers is considered in para. 31 of Sec. 5.1).

2. Nonuniform velocity field at the entrance into the diffuser ($w_{max}/w_0 > 1.0$, $2\delta_0^*/D_0 > 0$ or $l_0/D_h > 0$):

$\zeta \equiv \dfrac{\Delta p}{\rho w_0^2/2} = k_d \zeta_d$; for diffuser downstream of a straight section: $k_d = f\left(\alpha, \dfrac{2\delta_0^*}{D_0}, \dfrac{l_0}{D_0}, n_{ar1}, Re\right)$, see the tables and graphs b and c; for diffusers behind a free jet (working section of a wind tunnel):

$k_d = f\left(\alpha, \dfrac{w_{max}}{w_0}, n_{ar1}, Re\right)$, see the tables and graphs b and c, where $\dfrac{w_{max}}{w_0} = f_1\left(\dfrac{l_0}{D_0}\right)$ or $\dfrac{2\delta_0^*}{D_0} = f_1\left(\dfrac{l_0}{D_0}\right)$,

see Diagram 5-1; for diffusers with $\alpha = 6–14°$ downstream of a shaped (curved) piece $k_d = f(w/w_0)$, see the table of Diagram 5-1.

*Here and later on $l_0/D_0 = 0$ means that the diffuser is installed directly following a smooth collector (inlet nozzle).

ζ_d at $l_0/D_0 = 0$

Re × 10^{-5}	α, degrees						
	3	4	6	8	10	12	14
				$n_{ar1} = 2$			
0.5	0.148	0.135	0.121	0.112	0.107	0.109	0.120
1.0	0.120	0.106	0.090	0.083	0.080	0.088	0.102
2	0.093	0.082	0.070	0.068	0.062	0.062	0.063
≥4	0.079	0.068	0.056	0.048	0.048	0.048	0.051

Re × 10^{-5}	α, degrees						
	16	20	30	45	60	90	120	180
				$n_{ar1} = 2$			
0.5	0.141	0.191	0.315	0.331	0.326	0.315	0.308	0.298
1.0	0.122	0.196	0.298	0.297	0.286	0.283	0.279	0.276
2	0.073	0.120	0.229	0.279	0.268	0.268	0.265	0.263
≥4	0.051	0.068	0.120	0.271	0.272	0.272	0.268	0.268

							Diagram 5-2

| | α, degrees | | | | | | |
| $Re \times 10^{-5}$ | 3 | 4 | 6 | 8 | 10 | 12 | 14 |

$n_{ar1} = 4$

0.5	0.197	0.180	0.165	0.151	0.157	0.174	0.197
1.0	0.154	0.141	0.126	0.119	0.120	0.131	0.155
2	0.120	0.112	0.101	0.096	0.096	0.107	0.120
4	0.101	0.091	0.085	0.079	0.082	0.090	0.107
$\geqslant 6$	0.101	0.091	0.085	0.089	0.080	0.107	0.135

| | α, degrees | | | | | | |
| $Re \times 10^{-5}$ | 16 | 20 | 30 | 45 | 60 | 90 | 120 | 180 |

$n_{ar1} = 4$

0.5	0.225	0.298	0.461	0.606	0.680	0.643	0.630	0.615
1.0	0.183	0.262	0.479	0.680	0.628	0.600	0.593	0.585
2	0.146	0.180	0.360	0.548	0.586	0.585	0.580	0.567
4	0.124	0.172	0.292	0.462	0.562	0.582	0.577	0.567
$\geqslant 6$	0.169	0.240	0.382	0.506	0.560	0.582	0.577	0.567

| | α, degrees | | | | | | |
| $Re \times 10^{-5}$ | 3 | 4 | 6 | 8 | 10 | 12 | 14 |

$n_{ar1} = 6$

0.5	0.182	0.170	0.168	0.168	0.179	0.200	0.240
1.0	0.153	0.144	0.131	0.126	0.132	0.159	0.193
2	0.129	0.118	0.109	0.101	0.101	0.118	0.151
4	0.106	0.095	0.090	0.084	0.087	0.104	0.151
$\geqslant 6$	0.092	0.090	0.080	0.079	0.080	0.098	0.137

| | α, degrees | | | | | | |
| $Re \times 10^{-5}$ | 16 | 20 | 30 | 45 | 60 | 90 | 120 | 180 |

$n_{ar1} = 6$

0.5	0.268	0.330	0.482	0.640	0.766	0.742	0.730	0.722
1.0	0.218	0.286	0.488	0.680	0.755	0.731	0.720	0.707
2	0.185	0.280	0.440	0.640	0.700	0.710	0.708	0.690
4	0.160	0.224	0.360	0.510	0.660	0.696	0.695	0.680
$\geqslant 6$	0.160	0.286	0.456	0.600	0.690	0.707	0.700	0.695

	Diagram 5-2

	α, degrees						
$Re \times 10^{-5}$	3	4	6	8	10	12	14

$$n_{ar1} = 10$$

0.5	0.195	0.181	0.184	0.190	0.200	0.227	0.256
1.0	0.160	0.156	0.155	0.156	0.162	0.184	0.212
2	0.123	0.120	0.120	0.123	0.134	0.151	0.167
4	0.100	0.097	0.097	0.100	0.106	0.128	0.160
$\geqslant 6$	0.085	0.084	0.084	0.085	0.086	0.114	0.160

	α, degrees						
$Re \times 10^5$	16	20	30	45	60	90	120	180

$$n_{ar1} = 10$$

0.5	0.290	0.380	0.585	0.760	0.800	0.834	0.840	0.827
1.0	0.240	0.332	0.572	0.812	0.800	0.820	0.820	0.815
2	0.195	0.240	0.426	0.760	0.800	0.806	0.807	0.808
4	0.195	0.254	0.407	0.605	0.735	0.804	0.805	0.809
$\geqslant 6$	0.212	0.332	0.520	0.600	0.760	0.825	0.840	0.825

	α, degrees						
$Re \times 10^{-5}$	3	4	6	8	10	12	14

$$n_{ar1} \geqslant 16$$

0.5	0.179	0.174	0.176	0.185	0.196	0.224	0.270
1.0	0.148	0.146	0.147	0.147	0.151	0.179	0.233
2	0.118	0.120	0.120	0.120	0.120	0.140	0.176
4	0.120	0.098	0.095	0.094	0.095	0.118	0.160
$\geqslant 6$	0.094	0.085	0.084	0.085	0.094	0.118	0.160

	α, degrees						
$Re \times 10^{-5}$	16	20	30	45	60	90	120	180

$$n_{ar1} \geqslant 16$$

0.5	0.306	0.378	0.600	0.840	0.880	0.880	0.880	0.880
1.0	0.275	0.340	0.600	0.840	0.905	0.877	0.876	0.876
2	0.208	0.280	0.520	0.760	0.868	0.868	0.868	0.868
4	0.191	0.264	0.480	0.700	0.778	0.847	0.868	0.869
$\geqslant 6$	0.212	0.342	0.560	0.720	0.790	0.853	0.874	0.886

Diagram
5-2

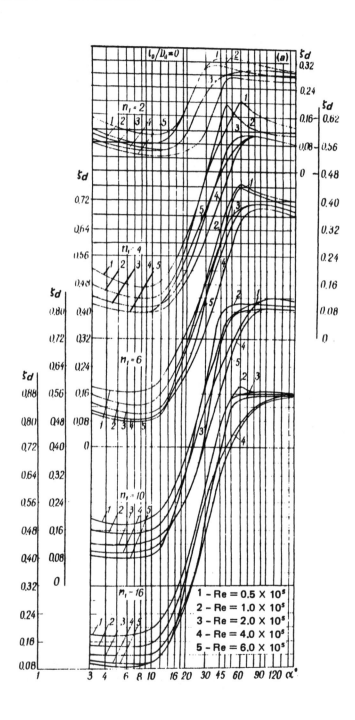

						Diagram 5-2

Values of k_d at $n_1 = 2$

$\dfrac{l_0}{D_0}$	α, degrees												
	3	4	6	8	10	12	14	16	20	30	45	60	>90

$Re = 0.5 \times 10^5$

	3	4	6	8	10	12	14	16	20	30	45	60	>90
2	1.00	1.10	1.20	1.25	1.26	1.26	1.23	1.16	1.05	1.00	1.01	0.01	1.01
5	1.45	1.62	1.75	1.83	1.86	1.80	1.70	1.53	1.10	1.02	1.02	1.02	1.02
10	1.88	1.96	2.05	2.07	2.07	2.05	2.00	1.93	1.60	1.12	1.11	1.10	1.10
≥20	1.68	1.83	1.96	2.00	1.99	1.93	1.85	1.74	1.45	1.03	1.01	1.01	1.01

$Re = 1 \times 10^5$

	3	4	6	8	10	12	14	16	20	30	45	60	>90
2	1.00	1.10	1.20	1.27	1.43	1.60	1.67	1.60	1.10	0.85	0.96	1.11	1.13
5	1.63	1.83	2.00	2.11	2.20	2.19	2.11	1.88	1.20	1.00	1.13	1.15	1.15
10	1.93	2.13	2.41	2.75	2.93	3.00	3.05	2.99	1.40	1.00	1.13	1.15	1.15
≥20	1.86	2.07	2.31	2.60	2.68	2.60	2.45	2.13	1.45	1.00	1.13	1.13	1.15

$Re = 3–4 \times 10^5$

	3	4	6	8	10	12	14	16	20	30	45	60	>90
2	1.31	1.45	1.60	1.80	2.05	2.33	2.40	2.40	2.20	1.56	1.20	1.15	1.13
5	1.53	1.70	1.90	2.14	2.54	2.90	3.02	3.00	2.60	1.56	1.20	1.15	1.13
10	2.20	2.33	2.55	3.00	3.80	4.00	4.07	4.00	3.30	2.00	1.33	1.20	1.25
≥20	1.91	2.07	2.25	2.46	3.20	3.70	3.83	3.73	3.03	1.56	1.20	1.15	1.13

$Re = 2–5 \times 10^5$

	3	4	6	8	10	12	14	16	20	30	45	60	>90
2	1.18	1.33	1.50	1.67	1.95	2.20	2.31	2.13	1.60	1.27	1.14	1.13	1.11
5	1.15	1.75	2.05	2.30	2.60	2.70	2.80	3.58	1.85	1.33	1.15	1.14	1.11
10	2.06	2.25	2.54	2.91	3.40	3.70	3.82	3.73	2.27	1.50	1.26	1.20	1.12
≥20	1.75	1.93	2.28	2.60	3.00	3.22	3.36	3.20	2.10	1.43	1.20	1.16	1.11

$Re > 6 \times 10^5$

	3	4	6	8	10	12	14	16	20	30	45	60	>90
2	1.00	1.14	1.33	1.65	1.90	2.00	2.06	1.90	1.53	1.26	1.10	1.07	1.10
5	1.15	1.33	1.60	1.90	2.06	2.10	1.20	1.90	2.20	1.62	1.30	1.23	1.10
10	1.73	1.90	2.15	2.45	2.93	3.13	3.25	3.15	2.20	1.62	1.30	1.23	1.10
≥20	1.46	1.65	1.95	2.86	2.54	2.65	2.70	2.60	1.70	1.33	1.13	1.12	1.10

Diagram
5-2

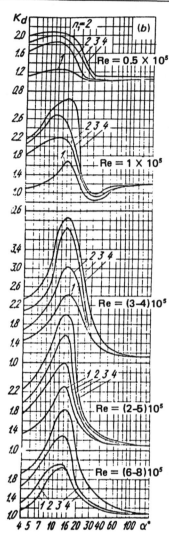

1−l_0/D_0 = 2
2−l_0/D_0 = 5
3−l_0/D_0 = 10
4−l_0/D_0 = 20

Values of k_d at $4 \leqslant n_{ar\,1} \leqslant 16$

$\dfrac{l_0}{D_0}$	α, degrees												
	3	4	6	8	10	12	14	16	20	30	45	60	$\geqslant$90
	Re = 0.5 × 10⁵												
2	1.00	1.04	1.07	1.20	1.33	1.28	1.05	1.14	1.07	1.05	1.05	1.06	1.05
5	1.00	1.25	1.47	1.60	1.66	1.65	1.60	1.58	1.43	1.23	1.08	1.06	1.05
10	1.50	1.65	1.85	1.90	2.10	2.10	2.05	1.93	1.70	1.38	1.26	1.20	1.05
$\geqslant$20	1.30	1.43	1.65	1.85	1.98	1.74	1.75	1.66	1.48	1.23	1.10	1.06	1.05
	Re = 1 × 10⁵												
2	1.05	1.10	1.14	1.26	1.47	1.40	1.28	1.18	1.06	0.95	0.95	0.95	1.02
5	1.30	1.46	1.68	1.93	2.15	2.15	2.05	1.90	1.60	1.07	1.00	1.00	1.02
10	1.67	1.83	2.08	2.28	2.60	2.50	2.43	2.20	1.83	1.30	1.10	1.03	1.02
$\geqslant$20	1.50	1.63	1.93	2.15	2.60	2.50	2.27	2.07	1.73	1.20	1.05	1.07	1.02

													Diagram 5-2

$\frac{l_0}{D_0}$	α, degrees												
	3	4	6	8	10	12	14	16	20	30	45	60	>90
	Re = 3–4 × 10⁵												
2	1.07	1.25	1.40	1.60	2.14	2.25	2.20	2.12	1.90	1.53	1.25	1.10	1.05
5	1.30	1.47	1.67	2.00	2.45	2.53	2.47	2.40	2.20	1.60	1.26	1.15	1.06
10	1.90	2.05	2.30	2.70	3.38	3.30	3.13	3.00	2.65	1.80	1.30	1.15	1.06
≥20	1.52	1.73	2.13	2.50	3.27	3.13	2.93	2.75	2.40	1.67	1.30	1.15	1.06
	Re = 2–5 × 10⁵												
2	1.00	1.20	1.40	1.63	2.05	2.13	2.07	1.95	1.68	1.32	1.15	1.13	1.07
5	1.30	1.47	1.69	2.00	2.27	2.35	2.37	2.27	1.95	1.40	1.19	1.13	1.07
10	1.80	2.00	2.25	2.60	3.30	3.20	3.00	2.80	2.40	1.53	1.26	1.20	1.07
≥20	1.54	1.73	2.12	2.43	3.20	3.00	2.75	2.50	2.10	1.50	1.23	1.15	1.07
	Re ≥ 6 × 10⁵												
2	1.00	1.13	1.42	1.73	1.98	1.93	1.83	1.70	1.50	1.23	1.13	1.10	1.07
5	1.05	1.23	1.60	1.95	2.25	2.20	2.08	1.90	1.55	1.25	1.15	1.10	1.07
10	1.60	1.82	2.15	2.55	3.20	3.02	2.53	2.20	1.83	1.33	1.22	1.18	1.07
≥20	1.35	1.63	2.10	2.43	3.05	2.70	2.23	1.98	1.60	1.30	1.20	1.15	1.07

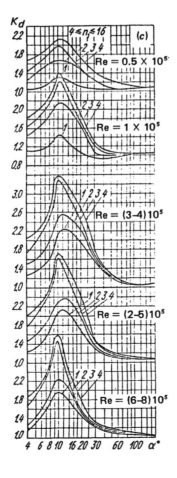

$1 - l_0/D_0 = 2$
$2 - l_0/D_0 = 5$
$3 - l_0/D_0 = 10$
$4 - l_0/D_0 \geq 20$

| | | | | | | | | | | | | | | Diagram 5-2 |

Values of ϕ at different Re numbers

$\alpha°$

0	5	10	15	20	25	30	40	45	50	60	80	140	180

Re = 0.5 × 10⁵

0	0.12	0.26	0.35	0.45	0.58	0.75	0.90	0.95	0.98	1.0	1.02	1.0	1.0

Re = 2 × 10⁵

0	0.08	0.15	0.24	0.32	0.43	0.60	0.82	0.88	0.93	0.95	0.95	0.97	0.99

Re > 6 × 10⁵

0	0.04	0.09	0.18	0.25	0.37	0.52	0.77	0.82	0.88	0.91	0.95	0.97	0.98

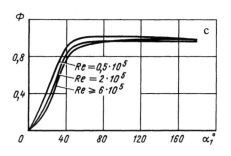

Conical diffusers at large subsonic velocities (in the system with $l_1/D_1 > 0$)   Diagram
(coefficients of total pressure recovery)[27]   5-3

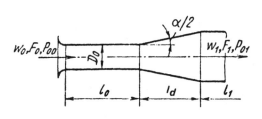

$$\bar{p}_0 \equiv \frac{p_1^{\cdot}}{p_0^{\cdot}} = f\left(\lambda_0, \, \alpha, \, n_1, \, \frac{l_0}{D_0}\right)$$

is determined from the curves of graphs a-e

$$\zeta_d \equiv \frac{\Delta p}{\rho_{00} w_0^2/2} = \frac{k+1}{k} \frac{1}{\lambda_0^2} \ln \frac{1}{\bar{p}_0} \, ;$$

$$k = \frac{c_p}{c_v}, \quad \text{see Table 1-4;}$$

$$\lambda_0 = \frac{w_0}{a_*}, \quad a_{cr} = \sqrt{\frac{2k}{k+1} RT_0^{\cdot}}$$

Diagram
5-3

$\bar{p}_0$ at $\alpha = 4°$ (graph a)

n_{ar1}	λ_0										
	0.1	0.2	0.3	0.4	0.5	0.6	0.7	0.8	0.9	0.94	0.95
	Re $\times 10^{-5}$										
	1.7	3.2	4.6	6.0	7.3	8.6	9.7	10.8	11.7	11.9	12.0

$$\frac{l_0}{D_0} = 0$$

2–6	0.999	0.998	0.995	9.991	9.987	9.983	0.975	0.971	0.964	0.961	0.930
10–16	0.999	0.997	0.994	0.990	0.985	0.980	0.973	0.968	0.961	0.958	0.920

$$\frac{l_0}{D_0} = 2$$

2–6	0.999	0.998	0.995	0.991	0.986	0.981	0.975	0.969	0.962	0.960	–
10–16	0.999	0.007	0.993	0.989	0.984	0.978	0.973	0.967	0.961	0.958	–

$$\frac{l_0}{D_0} = 5$$

2	0.999	0.998	0.995	0.991	0.986	0.980	0.974	0.965	–	–	–
4–6	0.999	0.997	0.994	0.990	0.985	0.978	0.971	0.930	–	–	–
10–16	0.998	0.996	0.993	0.988	0.983	0.977	0.970	0.960	–	–	–

$$\frac{l_0}{D_0} \geqslant 10$$

2–4	0.999	0.997	0.992	0.985	0.978	0.969	0.959	–	–	–	–
6–16	0.999	0.995	0.990	0.983	0.975	0.966	0.955	–	–	–	–

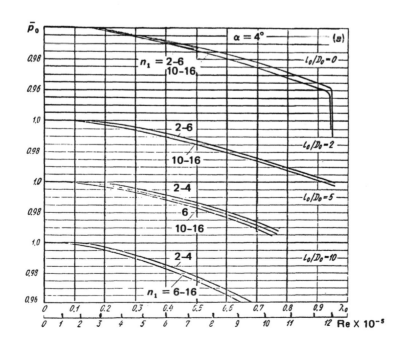

						Diagram 5-3

$\bar{p}_0$ at $\alpha = 6°$ (graph b)

	λ_0										
	0.1	0.2	0.3	0.4	0.5	0.6	0.7	0.8	0.9	0.94	0.95
	Re $\times$ 10^{-5}										
n_{ar1}	1.7	3.2	4.6	6.0	7.3	8.6	9.7	10.8	11.7	11.9	12.0
	$\dfrac{l_0}{D_0} = 0$										
2–4	0.999	0.999	0.996	0.993	0.989	0.984	0.980	0.975	0.970	0.960	0.930
6–16	0.999	0.998	0.995	0.991	0.987	0.983	0.977	0.973	0.966	0.958	0.930
	$\dfrac{l_0}{D_0} = 2$										
2	0.999	0.998	0.995	0.992	0.988	0.983	0.975	0.965	–	–	–
4	0.999	0.997	0.993	0.989	0.984	0.977	0.970	0.960	–	–	–
10–16	0.999	0.996	0.992	0.987	0.982	0.975	0.967	0.958	0.946	–	–
	$\dfrac{l_0}{D_0} = 5$										
2	0.999	0.998	0.995	0.990	0.985	0.977	0.968	0.958	–	–	–
4	0.999	0.996	0.992	0.987	0.981	0.975	0.966	0.955	–	–	–
10–16	0.999	0.995	0.991	0.986	0.980	0.972	0.962	0.950	–	–	–
	$\dfrac{l_0}{D_0} \geqslant 10$										
2	0.999	0.995	0.993	0.987	0.980	0.970	0.958	–	–	–	–
4	0.999	0.996	0.991	0.985	0.977	0.967	0.956	–	–	–	–
10–16	0.998	0.995	0.989	0.982	0.974	0.964	0.952	–	–	–	–

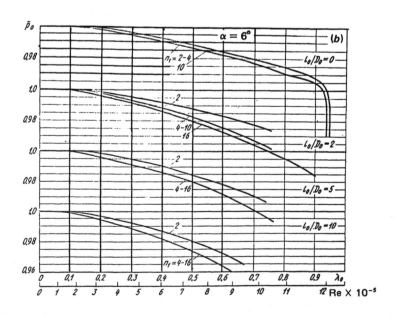

Diagram
5-3

$\bar{p}_0$ at $\alpha = 8°$ (graph c)

n_{ar1}	λ_0									
	0.1	0.2	0.3	0.4	0.5	0.6	0.7	0.8	0.9	0.95
	Re $\times$ 10^{-5}									
	1.7	3.2	4.6	6.0	7.3	8.6	9.7	10.8	11.7	12.0
$\frac{l_0}{D_0} = 0$										
2–16	0.999	0.998	0.995	0.992	0.987	0.982	0.976	0.970	0.962	0.930
$\frac{l_0}{D_0} = 2$										
2	0.999	0.997	0.995	0.992	0.987	0.982	0.975	–	–	–
4	0.999	0.997	0.993	0.989	0.984	0.978	0.971	–	–	–
6–16	0.999	0.996	0.992	0.985	0.979	0.970	0.960	0.950	0.948	–
$\frac{l_0}{D_0} = 5$										
2	0.999	0.997	0.995	0.991	0.987	0.980	0.970	–	–	–
4	0.999	0.996	0.992	0.986	0.979	0.971	0.961	0.948	–	–
6–16	0.999	0.995	0.989	0.983	0.975	0.966	0.955	0.942	–	–
$\frac{l_0}{D_0} \geqslant 10$										
2	0.999	0.996	0.993	0.989	0.984	0.972	–	–	–	–
4	0.999	0.995	0.990	0.984	0.974	0.962	–	–	–	–
6–16	0.999	0.993	0.987	0.980	0.970	0.959	–	–	–	–

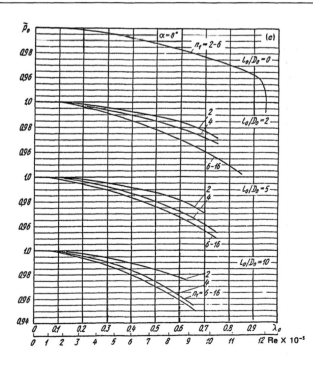

Diagram
5-3

$\bar{p}$ at $\alpha = 10°$ (graph d)

n_{ar1}	λ_0										
	0.1	0.2	0.3	0.4	0.5	0.6	0.7	0.8	0.9	0.95	0.96
	Re $\times 10^{-5}$										
	1.7	3.2	4.6	6.0	7.3	8.6	9.7	10.8	11.7	12.0	12.2
$\dfrac{l_0}{D_0} = 0$											
2	0.999	0.998	0.997	0.995	0.991	0.987	0.984	0.981	–	–	–
4	0.999	0.998	0.997	0.994	0.990	0.985	0.980	0.975	0.971	0.960	0.950
6–16	0.999	0.998	0.996	0.992	0.987	0.982	0.975	0.970	0.963	0.959	0.940
$\dfrac{l_0}{D_0} = 2$											
2	0.999	0.998	0.995	0.991	0.986	0.978	0.968	–	–	–	–
4	0.999	0.997	0.993	0.988	0.981	0.972	0.963	0.950	–	–	–
6	0.999	0.996	0.991	0.984	0.977	0.968	0.958	0.947	–	–	–
10–16	0.999	0.995	0.989	0.981	0.972	0.963	0.953	0.940	–	–	–

n_{ar1}	λ_0										
	0.1	0.2	0.3	0.4	0.5	0.6	0.7	0.8	0.9	0.95	0.96
	Re $\times 10^{-5}$										
	1.7	3.2	4.6	6.0	7.3	8.6	9.7	10.8	11.7	12.0	12.2
$l_0/D_0 = 5$											
2	0.999	0.998	0.995	0.990	0.985	0.978	–	–	–	–	–
4	0.999	0.996	0.992	0.985	0.978	0.967	0.955	–	–	–	–
6–16	0.999	0.996	0.989	0.981	0.973	0.962	0.950	–	–	–	–
$l_0/D_0 \geq 10$											
2	0.999	0.996	0.992	0.988	0.982	0.975	–	–	–	–	–
4–6	0.998	0.995	0.989	0.982	0.971	0.959	–	–	–	–	–
10–16	0.998	0.993	0.985	0.976	0.965	0.954	–	–	–	–	–

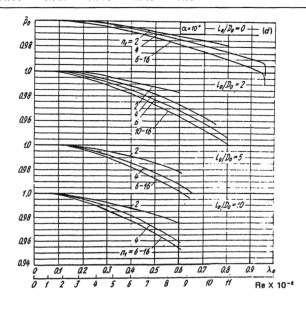

Diagram
5-3

$\bar{p}$ at $\alpha = 14°$ (graph e)

n_{ar1}	λ_0									
	0.1	0.2	0.3	0.4	0.5	0.6	0.7	0.8	0.9	0.95
	Re $\times$ 10^{-5}									
	1.7	3.2	4.6	6.0	7.3	8.6	9.7	10.8	11.7	12.0
	$l_0/D_0 = 0$									
2	0.999	0.998	0.996	0.993	0.990	0.986	0.982	0.976	–	–
4	0.999	0.997	0.994	0.990	0.982	0.974	0.965	0.957	0.948	0.945
6–16	0.999	0.996	0.990	0.984	0.974	0.966	0.956	0.945	0.934	0.924

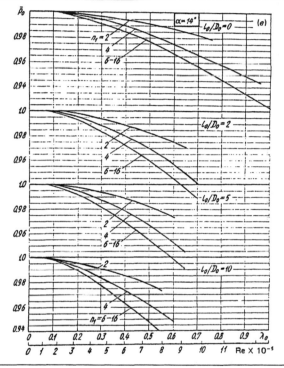

n_{ar1}	λ_0									
	0.1	0.2	0.3	0.4	0.5	0.6	0.7	0.8	0.9	0.95
	Re $\times$ 10^{-5}									
	1.7	3.2	4.6	6.0	7.3	8.6	9.7	10.8	11.7	12.0
	$l_0/D_0 = 2$									
2	0.999	0.997	0.993	0.988	0.982	0.975	0.966	–	–	–
4	0.999	0.995	0.988	0.979	0.970	0.957	0.941	–	–	–
6–16	0.998	0.992	0.983	0.972	0.960	0.945	0.930	–	–	–
	$l_0/D_0 = 5$									
2	0.999	0.997	0.993	0.988	0.982	0.974	–	–	–	–
4	0.998	0.994	0.987	0.978	0.966	0.952	0.938	–	–	–
6–16	0.998	0.991	0.981	0.968	0.953	0.938	0.920	–	–	–
	$l_0/D_0 = 10$									
2	0.999	0.995	0.991	0.985	0.978	0.969	–	–	–	–
4	0.998	0.992	0.984	0.974	0.961	0.948	–	–	–	–
6–16	0.997	0.990	0.972	0.963	0.933	0.922	–	–	–	–

Diffuser of rectangular cross section (in the system with $l_1/D_{1h} > 0$)[26]

Diagram 5-4

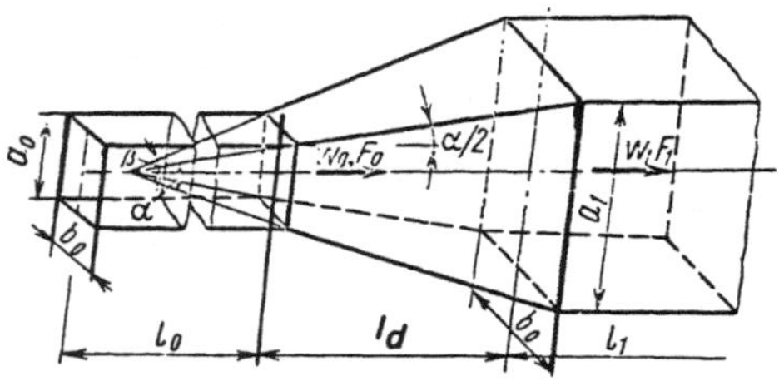

1. Uniform velocity field at the entrance into the diffuser ($w_{max}/w_0 \approx 1.0$ or $l_0/D_h \approx 0$): $\zeta \equiv \Delta p/(\rho w_0^2/2) = \zeta_d = f(\alpha, n_{ar1}, Re)$, see the table and graph a. Approximate formulas are given in para. 40 of Section 5-1).

2. Nonuniform velocity field at the entrance into the diffuser ($w_{max}/w_0 > 1.0$, $2\delta_0^*/D_h > 1.0\%$ or $l_0/D_h \geq 10$): $\zeta \equiv \Delta p/(\rho w_0^2/2) = \zeta_d = f(\alpha, n_{ar1}, Re)$, see table and graph b.

3. For diffusers with $\alpha = 6-14°$ downstream of the shaped piece (elbow) $\zeta \equiv \Delta p/(\rho w_0^2/2) = k_d \zeta_d$, where for ζ_d, see the table and graph a of Diagram 5-4, for $k_d = f(w/w_0)$, see the table of Diagram 5-1; for $w_{max}/w_0 = f(l_0/D_h)$, see Diagram 5-1; $\alpha \geq \beta$.

ζ_d at $l_0/D_h = 0$

Re × 10⁻⁵	α, degrees													
---	4	6	8	10	12	14	16	20	30	45	60	90	120	180
	$n_{ar1} = 2$													
0.5	0.140	0.136	0.135	0.152	0.175	0.200	0.235	0.250	0.300	0.325	0.326	0.325	0.320	0.300
1	0.110	0.110	0.105	0.130	0.160	0.185	0.200	0.230	0.270	0.300	0.315	0.310	0.310	0.300
2	0.095	0.090	0.095	0.116	0.150	0.175	0.180	0.216	0.250	0.285	0.310	0.315	0.325	0.300
≥4	0.085	0.085	0.090	0.112	0.145	0.175	0.185	0.220	0.250	0.285	0.310	0.315	0.325	0.310
	$n_{ar1} = 4$													
0.5	0.170	0.185	0.200	0.245	0.300	0.335	0.380	0.450	0.520	0.580	0.620	0.640	0.640	0.640
1	0.145	0.155	0.180	0.225	0.280	0.335	0.360	0.430	0.500	0.560	0.605	0.630	0.630	0.625
2	0.115	0.135	0.150	0.200	0.260	0.335	0.360	0.420	0.500	0.560	0.605	0.630	0.630	0.625
≥4	0.106	0.118	0.130	0.195	0.260	0.335	0.360	0.430	0.500	0.560	0.605	0.630	0.630	0.625
	$n_{ar1} = 6$													
0.5	0.185	0.190	0.205	0.295	0.370	0.420	0.460	0.525	0.625	0.715	0.775	0.790	0.790	0.785
1	0.155	0.165	0.185	0.250	0.320	0.380	0.420	0.485	0.600	0.695	0.750	0.775	0.770	0.760
2	0.130	0.140	0.165	0.235	0.320	0.360	0.420	0.465	0.580	0.675	0.720	0.760	0.760	0.750
≥4	0.120	0.125	0.145	0.230	0.300	0.360	0.400	0.465	0.580	0.675	0.720	0.760	0.760	0.750
	$n_{ar1} \geq 10$													
0.5	0.180	0.195	0.240	0.300	0.375	0.430	0.470	0.530	0.635	0.750	0.840	0.890	0.890	0.880
1	0.160	0.175	0.205	0.265	0.340	0.400	0.440	0.550	0.615	0.725	0.815	0.880	0.880	0.865
2	0.130	0.155	0.180	0.240	0.320	0.370	0.420	0.490	0.590	0.700	0.795	0.870	0.850	0.860
≥4	0.120	0.135	0.160	0.235	0.320	0.370	0.420	0.490	0.590	0.700	0.795	0.870	0.850	0.860

Diagram 5-4

ζ_d at $l_0/D_h \geqslant 10$

$Re \times 10^{-5}$	α, degrees													
	4	6	8	10	12	14	16	20	30	45	60	90	120	180
$n_{ar1} = 2$														
0.5	0.200	0.240	0.280	0.280	0.298	0.305	0.315	0.325	0.340	0.355	0.355	0.350	0.340	0.310
1	0.175	0.200	0.215	0.235	0.250	0.260	0.275	0.290	0.310	0.330	0.340	0.340	0.320	0.310
2	0.140	0.160	0.180	0.195	0.210	0.225	0.240	0.260	0.280	0.310	0.320	0.335	0.320	0.310
$\geqslant 4$	0.150	0.125	0.140	0.160	0.200	0.195	0.210	0.235	0.265	0.300	0.320	0.335	0.320	0.310
$n_{ar1} = 4$														
0.5	0.260	0.320	0.360	0.400	0.430	0.455	0.480	0.510	0.565	0.610	0.635	0.655	0.650	0.640
1	0.220	0.270	0.320	0.365	0.400	0.435	0.460	0.495	0.550	0.600	0.630	0.650	0.650	0.640
2	0.180	0.230	0.275	0.320	0.365	0.400	0.430	0.470	0.530	0.590	0.620	0.650	0.650	0.640
$\geqslant 4$	0.130	0.180	0.220	0.270	0.320	0.350	0.380	0.430	0.500	0.580	0.620	0.650	0.650	0.640
$n_{ar1} = 6$														
0.5	0.310	0.360	0.400	0.450	0.490	0.530	0.560	0.615	0.685	0.750	0.775	0.795	0.785	0.760
1	0.250	0.305	0.375	0.405	0.455	0.500	0.530	0.580	0.650	0.720	0.775	0.780	0.775	0.760
2	0.190	0.255	0.305	0.370	0.420	0.460	0.495	0.545	0.635	0.710	0.745	0.775	0.775	0.760
$\geqslant 4$	0.140	0.205	0.255	0.320	0.380	0.425	0.460	0.520	0.615	0.695	0.740	0.770	0.775	0.760
$n_{ar1} = 10$														
0.5	0.300	0.360	0.415	0.470	0.520	0.570	0.600	0.670	0.760	0.850	0.900	0.960	0.920	0.880
1	0.240	0.315	0.370	0.455	0.490	0.540	0.580	0.640	0.730	0.830	0.880	0.940	0.910	0.880
2	0.185	0.265	0.325	0.400	0.460	0.515	0.550	0.610	0.715	0.810	0.860	0.930	0.910	0.880
$\geqslant 4$	0.130	0.200	0.270	0.345	0.400	0.460	0.500	0.570	0.680	0.790	0.855	0.930	0.910	0.880

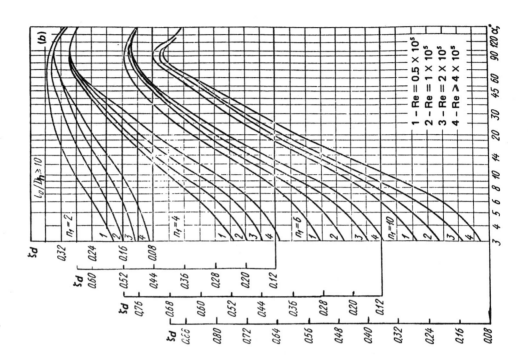

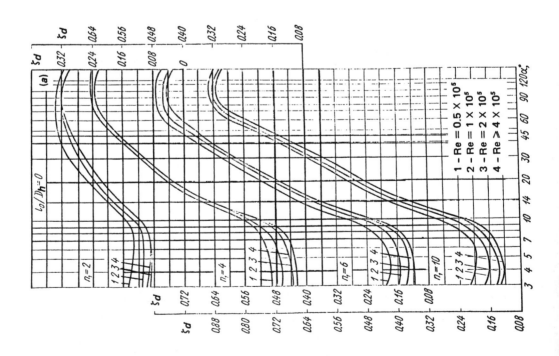

Diagram 5-4

Values of ϕ at various Re numbers

	α_i°																	
0	5	10	15	20	25	30	40	45	50	60	80	140	180				
							Re $= 0.5 \times 10^5$										
0	0.10	0.20	0.28	0.36	0.48	0.60	0.84	0.89	0.97	1.04	1.10	1.09	1.06				
							Re $= 2 \times 10^5$										
0	0.05	0.12	0.23	0.30	0.45	0.60	0.84	0.89	0.97	1.04	1.10	1.09	1.06				

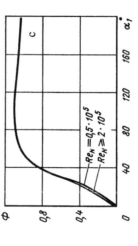

Diffuser with expansion in one plane (in the system with $l_1/D_{1h} > 0$)[26]	Diagram 5-5

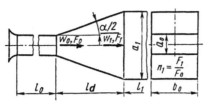

$$D_h = \frac{4F_0}{\Pi_0} ; \quad n_1 = \frac{F_1}{F_0} ; \quad Re = \frac{w_0 D_h}{\nu}$$

1. Uniform velocity field at the entrance into the diffuser ($w_{max}/w_0 \approx 1.0$ or $l_0/D_h \approx 0$):

$$\zeta \equiv \frac{\Delta p}{\rho w_0^2/2} = \zeta_d = f(\alpha, n_{ar1}, Re)$$

see the table and graph a. Approximate formulas are given in paragraph 41 of Section 5-1. Calculation of preseparation diffusers is made in paragraph 31 of Section 5-1.

2. Nonuniform velocity field at the entrance into the diffuser ($w_{max}/w_0 > 1.0$, $2\delta_0^*/D_h > 1.0\%$ or $l_0/D_h \geq 10$):

$$\zeta \equiv \frac{\Delta p}{\rho w_0^2/2} = \zeta_d = f(\alpha, n_{ar1}, Re)$$

see the table and graph b of Diagram 5-5.

3. For diffusers with $\alpha = 6$–$20°$ downstream of a shaped (curved) piece

$$\zeta \equiv \frac{\Delta p}{\rho w_0^2/2} = k_d \zeta_d$$

where for ζ_d see the table and graph a; for $k_d = f(w/w_0)$ and for $w_{max}/w_0 = f(l_0/D_h)$, see Diagram 5-1.

ζ_d at $l_0/D_h = 0$

Re × 10⁻⁵	\$\alpha\$, degrees											
	4	6	8	10	14	20	30	45	60	90	120	180
						$n_{ar1} = 2$						
0.5	0.200	0.165	0.142	0.135	0.125	0.154	0.235	0.350	0.370	0.380	0.370	0.350
1	0.180	0.145	0.125	0.115	0.105	0.120	0.200	0.335	0.370	0.380	0.370	0.350
2	0.163	0.125	0.110	0.100	0.093	0.115	0.200	0.335	0.370	0.380	0.370	0.350
≥4	0.150	0.115	0.100	0.096	0.083	0.115	0.200	0.335	0.370	0.380	0.370	0.350
						$n_{ar1} = 4$						
0.5	0.275	0.225	0.185	0.170	0.182	0.250	0.420	0.600	0.680	0.700	0.700	0.660
1	0.230	0.182	0.160	0.163	0.180	0.250	0.420	0.600	0.680	0.700	0.700	0.660
2	0.210	0.162	0.142	0.140	0.162	0.250	0.420	0.600	0.680	0.700	0.700	0.660
≥4	0.195	0.150	0.133	0.135	0.162	0.250	0.420	0.600	0.680	0.700	0.700	0.660
						$n_{ar1} = 6$						
0.5	0.310	0.250	0.215	0.205	0.210	0.300	0.480	0.650	0.760	0.830	0.830	0.800
1	0.250	0.205	0.175	0.170	0.190	0.300	0.480	0.650	0.760	0.830	0.830	0.800
2	0.235	0.190	0.160	0.158	0.190	0.300	0.480	0.650	0.760	0.830	0.830	0.800
4	0.215	0.165	0.143	0.143	0.190	0.300	0.480	0.650	0.760	0.830	0.830	0.800
≥6	0.200	0.150	0.130	0.130	0.190	0.300	0.480	0.650	0.760	0.830	0.830	0.800

Diagram
5-5

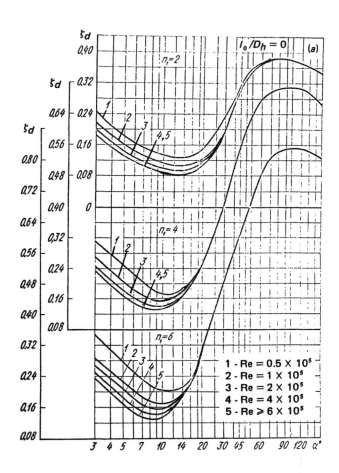

Values of ζ_d at $l_0/D_h \geqslant 10$

Re $\times 10^{-5}$	α, degrees											
	4	6	8	10	14	20	30	45	60	90	120	180
						$n_{\mathrm{ar\,1}} = 2$						
0.5	0.260	0.225	0.210	0.210	0.220	0.240	0.300	0.360	0.370	0.380	0.370	0.350
1	0.225	0.200	0.190	0.190	0.200	0.220	0.270	0.340	0.370	0.380	0.370	0.350
2	0.150	0.130	0.125	0.125	0.150	0.185	0.245	0.340	0.370	0.380	0.370	0.350
4	0.125	0.110	0.100	0.105	0.120	0.155	0.250	0.340	0.370	0.380	0.370	0.350
$\geqslant 6$	0.125	0.110	0.100	0.105	0.120	0.155	0.205	0.340	0.370	0.380	0.370	0.350

Diagram
5-5

Re × 10⁻⁵	α, degrees											
	4	6	8	10	14	20	30	45	60	90	120	180

$n_{ar1} = 4$

0.5	0.300	0.280	0.270	0.275	0.320	0.420	0.570	0.660	0.690	0.700	0.700	0.660
1	0.280	0.250	0.240	0.240	0.295	0.400	0.560	0.650	0.690	0.700	0.700	0.660
2	0.210	0.190	0.195	0.200	0.260	0.380	0.520	0.640	0.680	0.700	0.700	0.660
4	0.185	0.160	0.160	0.170	0.230	0.375	0.520	0.640	0.680	0.700	0.700	0.660
>6	0.170	0.155	0.150	0.160	0.210	0.360	0.520	0.640	0.680	0.700	0.700	0.660

$n_{ar1} = 6$

0.5	0.335	0.310	0.300	0.305	0.360	0.500	0.650	0.760	0.810	0.830	0.830	0.800
1	0.280	0.260	0.255	0.270	0.350	0.490	0.640	0.750	0.800	0.830	0.830	0.800
2	0.215	0.200	0.205	0.220	0.320	0.475	0.610	0.730	0.790	0.830	0.830	0.800
4	0.190	0.180	0.185	0.210	0.300	0.460	0.610	0.730	0.790	0.830	0.830	0.800
⩾6	0.180	0.165	0.165	0.180	0.280	0.440	0.590	0.710	0.780	0.830	0.830	0.800

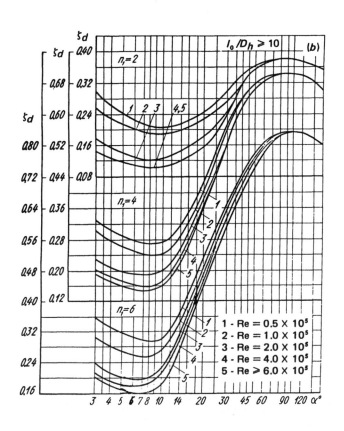

| | | | | | | | | | | | | Diagram 5-5 | |

Values of ϕ at various Re numbers

							α_1°						
0	5	10	15	20	25	30	40	45	50	60	80	140	160
					$Re = 0.5 \times 10^5$								
0	0.10	0.40	0.60	0.69	0.76	0.84	0.92	0.95	0.98	1.02	1.05	1.05	1.03
					$Re = 1 \times 10^5$								
0	0.10	0.30	0.50	0.60	0.68	0.78	0.88	0.90	0.93	0.97	1.00	1.02	1.00

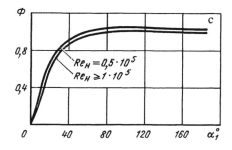

Plane five-channel subsonic diffusers in the system;[55]
$n_{ar1} = 6.45$; Re $(0.6-4) \times 10^5$

Diagram
5-6

$\bar{p}_0 = \dfrac{p_1^*}{p_0^*}$, see graph a;

$\zeta_d = \dfrac{\Delta p}{\rho_0^* w^2/2} - 0.024 - \zeta_{tot}' - 0.024$; for ζ_{tot}' see graph b

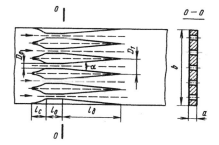

Values of $\bar{p}_0$ at various $\bar{l}_d$

α°					λ_0					
	0.1	0.2	0.3	0.4	0.5	0.6	0.7	0.8	0.9	0.95
					$\bar{l}_d = l_d/D_0 = 3.23$					
8	0.999	0.995	0.990	0.988	0.981	0.975	0.967	0.960	0.950	0.900
12	0.999	0.995	0.990	0.989	0.975	0.963	0.950	0.938	0.870	–
16	0.999	0.996	0.987	0.979	0.968	0.934	0.938	0.920	0.870	–
					$\bar{l}_d = l_d/D_0 = 6.45$					
8	0.999	0.992	0.988	0.979	0.969	0.956	0.945	0.926	0.907	0.88
12	0.998	0.991	0.984	0.976	0.965	0.950	0.930	0.904	0.850	–
16	0.997	0.991	0.983	0.959	0.954	0.954	0.913	0.887	0.82	–
					$\bar{l}_d = l_d/D_0 = 9.68$					
8	0.998	0.990	0.983	0.975	0.963	0.950	0.931	0.913	0.84	–
12	0.996	0.990	0.982	0.970	0.957	0.940	0.917	0.888	0.83	–
16	0.995	0.988	0.978	0.963	0.948	0.927	0.900	0.868	–	–

Diagram
5-6

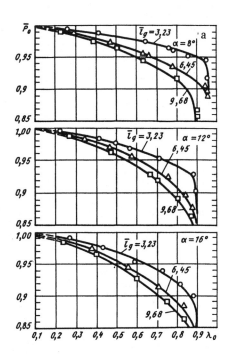

Values of ζ_d at various $\bar{l}_d$

α	\multicolumn{10}{c}{λ_0}
	0.1	0.2	0.3	0.4	0.5	0.6	0.7	0.8	0.9	0.95
\multicolumn{11}{c}{$\bar{l}_d = l_d/D_0 = 3.23$}
8	0.10	0.10	0.11	0.12	0.13	0.12	0.11	0.10	0.10	0.18
12	0.20	0.20	0.21	0.22	0.22	0.21	0.20	0.18	0.18	0.28
16	0.23	0.23	0.23	0.24	0.24	0.24	0.23	0.23	0.33	–
\multicolumn{11}{c}{$\bar{l}_d = l_d/D_0 = 6.45$}
8	0.16	0.16	0.17	0.17	0.18	0.17	0.16	0.15	0.20	–
12	0.23	0.23	0.23	0.24	0.24	0.24	0.24	0.24	0.31	–
16	0.28	0.28	0.28	0.29	0.30	0.30	0.29	0.28	0.38	–
\multicolumn{11}{c}{$\bar{l}_d = l_d/D_0 = 9.68$}
8	0.22	0.22	0.23	0.23	0.23	0.22	0.21	0.20	0.29	–
12	0.30	0.30	0.30	0.30	0.31	0.31	0.30	0.29	0.38	–
16	0.36	0.36	0.37	0.37	0.37	0.36	0.35	0.35	0.43	–

Diagram
5-6

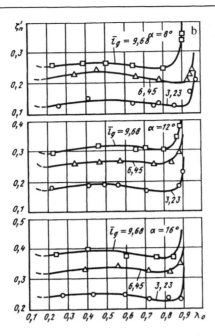

Diffusers of circular cross section (in the system with $l_1/D_1 > 0$);[4]
laminar flow (Re $= w_0 D_h/\nu \geqslant 50$)

Diagram
5-7

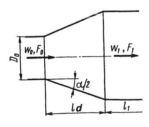

$$\zeta \equiv \frac{\Delta p}{\rho w_0^2/2} = \frac{A}{Re}$$

where at $\alpha \leqslant 40°$

$$A = \frac{20 n_{ar1}^{0.33}}{(\tan \alpha)^{0.75}} \quad \text{see the curves } A = f(\alpha, n_{ar1})$$

$$D_h = \frac{4F_0}{\Pi_0} ; \quad n_{ar1} = \frac{F_1}{F_0}$$

Values of A

n_{ar1}	α, degrees									
	4	6	8	10	14	20	25	30	35	40
1.5	178	130	104	87.5	67.2	50.1	41.4	35.1	30.3	26.3
2	197	144	115	96.8	74.4	55.4	45.8	38.8	33.5	29.1
3	227	166	133	112	85.7	63.8	52.8	44.7	38.6	33.5
4	251	184	147	123	94.8	70.6	58.4	49.5	42.7	37.1
6	290	212	169	142	109	81.4	67.3	57.0	49.2	42.7

Diffusers of circular cross section (in the system with $l_1/D_1 > 0$);[4] laminar flow (Re $= w_0 D_h/\nu \geq 50$)	Diagram 5-7

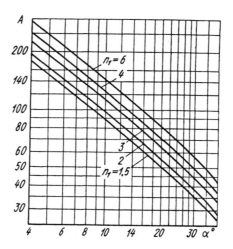

Diffusers with curvilinear boundaries (in the system with $l_1/D_1 > 0$);[47-49] Re $= w_0 D_h/\nu \geq 10^5$	Diagram 5-8

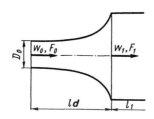

Diffuser of annular or
rectangular cross section

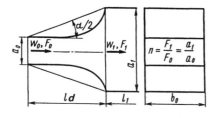

Plane diffuser

$$D_h = \frac{4F_0}{\Pi_0}$$

$\zeta \equiv \dfrac{\Delta p}{\rho w_0^2/2} \approx \phi_0 \sigma_0 d^*$ (the formula is applicable within

$0.1 \leq \dfrac{F_0}{F_1} \leq 0.9$), where $\sigma_0 = 1.43 - \dfrac{1.3 F_0}{F_1} = f\left(\dfrac{F_0}{F_1}\right)$

and $d^* = \left(1 - \dfrac{F_0}{F_1}\right)^2 = f_2\left(\dfrac{F_0}{F_1}\right)$, see graph a;

$\phi_0 = f\left(\dfrac{l_d}{D_h}\right)$ or $\phi_0 = f\left(\dfrac{l_d}{a_0}\right)$, see graph b.

							Diagram 5-8	

Values of σ_0 and d^*

$\dfrac{F_0}{F_1}$	0.1	0.2	0.3	0.4	0.5	0.6	0.7	0.8	0.9
σ_0	1.30	1.17	1.04	0.91	0.78	0.65	0.52	0.39	0.26
d	0.81	0.64	0.49	0.36	0.25	0.16	0.09	0.04	0.01

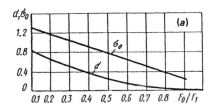

Values of ϕ_0

$\dfrac{l_d}{D_h}\dfrac{l_d}{a_0}$	0	0.5	1.0	1.5	2.0	2.5	3.0	3.5	4.0	4.5	5.0	6.0
1. Diffuser of annular or rectangular cross section												
	1.01	0.75	0.62	0.53	0.47	0.43	0.40	0.38	0.37	–	–	–
2. Plane diffuser												
	1.02	0.83	0.72	0.64	0.57	0.52	0.48	0.45	0.43	0.41	0.39	0.37

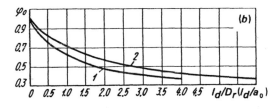

Diffuser of circular cross section with stepped walls (in the system with $l_1/D_1 > 0$);[47-49] Re $= w_0 D_0/\nu > 10^5$	Diagram 5-9

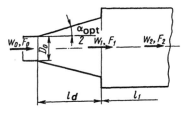

$$\zeta \equiv \frac{\Delta p}{\rho w_0^2/2} \approx \zeta_{min}$$

This formula can be applied for the selection of the optimal angle α_{opt} from graph b; for ζ_{min}, see graph a as a function of l_d/D_0 and n_{ar}

$$n_{ar1} = \frac{F_1}{F_0} = \left(1 + 2\frac{l_d}{D_0}\tan\frac{\alpha}{2}\right)^2 ;$$

$$n_{ar2} = \frac{F_2}{F_1}, \quad n_{ar2} = \frac{F_2}{F_0}$$

Diagram
5-9

Values of ζ_{min}

n_{ar}	$\dfrac{l_d}{D_0}$										
	0.5	1.0	2.0	3.0	4.0	5.0	6.0	8.0	10	12	14
1.5	0.03	0.02	0.03	0.03	0.04	0.05	0.06	0.08	0.10	0.11	0.13
2.0	0.08	0.06	0.04	0.04	0.04	0.05	0.05	0.06	0.08	0.09	0.10
2.5	0.13	0.09	0.06	0.06	0.06	0.06	0.06	0.06	0.07	0.08	0.09
3.0	0.17	0.12	0.09	0.07	0.07	0.06	0.06	0.07	0.07	0.08	0.08
4.0	0.23	0.17	0.12	0.10	0.09	0.08	0.08	0.08	0.08	0.08	0.08
6.0	0.30	0.22	0.16	0.13	0.12	0.10	0.10	0.09	0.09	0.09	0.08
0.8	0.34	0.26	0.18	0.15	0.13	0.12	0.11	0.10	0.09	0.09	0.09
10	0.36	0.28	0.20	0.16	0.14	0.13	0.12	0.11	0.10	0.09	0.09
14	0.39	0.30	0.22	0.18	0.16	0.14	0.13	0.12	0.10	0.10	0.10
20	0.41	0.32	0.24	0.20	0.17	0.15	0.14	0.12	0.11	0.11	0.11

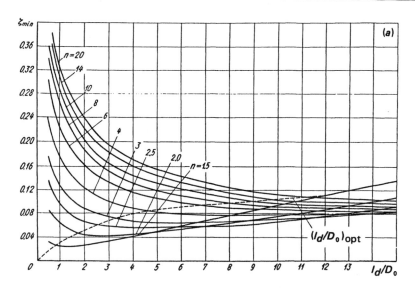

Values of α_{opt}, degrees

n_{ar}	$\dfrac{l_d}{D_0}$										
	0.5	1.0	2.0	3.0	4.0	5.0	6.0	8.0	10	12	14
1.5	17	10	6.5	4.5	3.5	2.8	2.2	1.7	1.2	1.0	0.8
2.0	21	14	8.5	6.2	5.0	4.3	3.8	3.0	2.3	2.0	1.6
2.5	25	16	10	7.4	6.0	5.4	4.8	4.0	3.5	3.0	2.5
3.0	27	17	11	8.5	7.0	6.1	5.6	4.8	4.2	3.8	3.2
4.0	29	20	13	9.8	8.0	7.2	6.6	5.8	5.2	4.8	4.4
6.0	31	21	14	11	9.4	8.2	7.4	6.2	5.6	5.2	4.7
8.0	32	22	15	12	10	8.8	8.0	6.6	5.8	5.4	5.0
10	33	23	15	12	11	9.4	8.4	7.0	6.2	5.5	5.2
14	33	23	16	13	11	9.6	8.7	7.3	6.3	5.6	5.4
20	34	24	16	13	11	9.8	9.0	7.5	6.5	6.0	5.6

Diagram
5-9

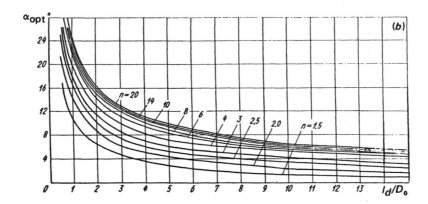

Diffuser of rectangular cross section with stepped walls
(in the system with $l_1/D_{1h} > 0$);[47-49] $Re = w_0 D_h/\nu > 10^5$

Diagram
5-10

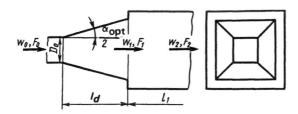

$$\zeta \equiv \frac{\Delta p}{\rho w_0^2/2} \approx \zeta_{min}$$

This formula can be applied for the selection of
the optimal angle α_{opt} from graph b; for ζ_{min}, is
determined from graph a as a function of l_d/D_h
and n_{ar} (with ample safety margin).

$$D_h = \frac{4F_0}{\Pi_0}$$

$$n_{ar1} = \frac{F_1}{F_0} = \left(1 + 2\frac{l_d}{D_h}\tan\frac{\alpha}{2}\right)^2$$

$$n_{ar2} = \frac{F_2}{F_1} \qquad n_{ar} = \frac{F_2}{F_0}$$

Values of ζ_{min}

	l_d/D_h										
n_{ar}	0.5	1.0	2.0	3.0	4.0	5.0	6.0	8.0	10	12	14
1.5	0.04	0.03	0.03	0.04	0.05	0.05	0.06	0.08	0.10	0.11	0.13
2.0	0.11	0.08	0.06	0.06	0.06	0.06	0.07	0.07	0.08	0.09	0.10
2.5	0.16	0.13	0.09	0.08	0.08	0.07	0.08	0.07	0.08	0.08	0.09
3.0	0.21	0.17	0.12	0.10	0.09	0.09	0.09	0.09	0.09	0.09	0.09
4.0	0.27	0.22	0.17	0.14	0.12	0.11	0.11	0.11	0.11	0.10	0.10
6.0	0.36	0.28	0.21	0.18	0.16	0.15	0.14	0.13	0.12	0.12	0.11
8.0	0.41	0.32	0.24	0.21	0.18	0.17	0.16	0.14	0.13	0.12	0.12
10	0.44	0.35	0.26	0.22	0.20	0.18	0.17	0.15	0.14	0.13	0.13
14	0.47	0.37	0.28	0.24	0.21	0.20	0.18	0.16	0.15	0.14	0.14
20	0.49	0.40	0.30	0.26	0.23	0.21	0.19	0.17	0.16	0.15	0.14

Diffuser of rectangular cross section with stepped walls (in the system with $l_1/D_{1h} > 0$);[47-49] Re $= w_0 D_h/\nu > 10^5$	Diagram 5-10

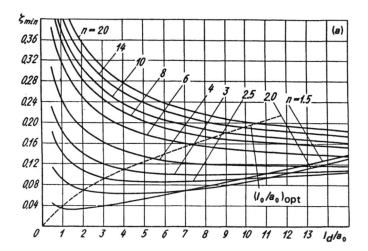

Values of α_{opt}, degrees

n_{ar}	l_d/D_h										
	0.5	1.0	2.0	3.0	4.0	5.0	6.0	8.0	10	12	14
1.5	14	9.0	5.3	4.0	3.3	2.7	2.2	1.7	1.2	1.0	1.0
2.0	18	12	8.0	6.3	5.2	4.5	3.8	3.0	2.3	2.0	1.8
2.5	20	14	9.0	7.2	6.1	5.4	4.8	4.0	3.2	2.9	2.4
3.0	21	15	10	7.8	6.5	5.8	5.2	4.4	3.6	3.3	2.9
4.0	22	16	11	8.5	7.1	6.2	5.5	4.8	4.0	3.8	3.5
6.0	24	17	12	9.4	8.0	6.9	6.2	5.2	4.5	4.3	4.0
8.0	25	17	12	9.7	8.3	7.3	6.5	5.5	4.8	4.6	4.2
10	25	18	12	10	8.7	7.6	6.9	5.8	5.0	4.8	4.5
14	26	18	13	10	9.0	7.8	7.1	6.1	5.2	5.0	4.7
20	26	19	13	11	9.2	8.1	7.3	6.4	5.5	5.2	4.9

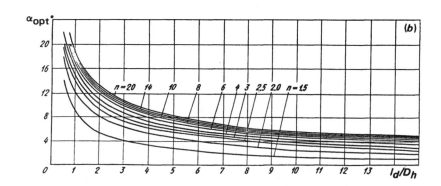

Diffuser with expansion in one plane with stepped walls (in the system with $l_1/D_{1h} > 0$);[47-49] $Re = w_0 D_h/\nu \geqslant 10^5$	Diagram 5-11

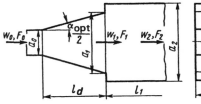

$$\zeta \equiv \frac{\Delta p}{\rho w_0^2/2} \approx \zeta_{min}$$

$$D_h = \frac{4F_0}{\Pi_0}$$

This formula can be applied for the selection of the optimal angle α_{opt} from graph b; for ζ_{min} is determined from graph a as a function of l_d/a_0 and n_{ar}

$$n_{ar1} = \frac{a_1}{a_0} = 1 + 2\frac{l_d}{a_0}\tan\frac{\alpha}{2}$$

$$n_{ar2} = \frac{a_2}{n_{ar1}} \quad n_{ar} = \frac{F_2}{F_0} = \frac{a_2}{a_0}$$

Values of ζ_{min}

n_{ar}	\multicolumn{11}{c}{$\frac{l_d}{a_0}$}

n_{ar}	0.5	1.0	2.0	3.0	4.0	5.0	6.0	8.0	10	12	14
1.5	0.04	0.04	0.04	0.04	0.05	0.06	0.06	0.08	0.10	0.11	0.13
2.0	0.12	0.09	0.07	0.07	0.06	0.07	0.07	0.07	0.08	0.10	0.12
2.5	0.18	0.14	0.11	0.10	0.09	0.09	0.09	0.09	0.09	0.10	0.10
3.0	0.23	0.18	0.14	0.12	0.11	0.11	0.11	0.10	0.10	0.10	0.11
4.0	0.30	0.24	0.19	0.16	0.15	0.15	0.14	0.13	0.12	0.12	0.12
6.0	0.38	0.31	0.25	0.21	0.19	0.18	0.17	0.16	0.15	0.14	0.14
0.8	0.43	0.36	0.28	0.25	0.22	0.20	0.19	0.17	0.16	0.16	0.15
10	0.46	0.38	0.30	0.26	0.24	0.22	0.21	0.19	0.18	0.17	0.16
14	0.50	0.41	0.33	0.29	0.26	0.24	0.22	0.20	0.19	0.18	0.18
20	0.53	0.44	0.35	0.31	0.28	0.25	0.24	0.22	0.20	0.19	0.19

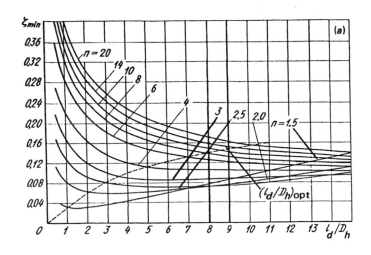

Diagram
5-11

Values of α_{opt}, degrees

n_{ar}	\multicolumn{11}{c}{$\dfrac{l_d}{a_0}$}
	0.5	1.0	2.0	3.0	4.0	5.0	6.0	8.0	10	12	14
1.5	25	18	11	8.0	6.4	5.4	4.7	3.5	2.8	2.4	2.0
2.0	33	23	15	12	9.7	8.4	7.5	6.0	5.2	4.7	4.3
2.5	37	26	18	14	12	10	9.4	8.0	7.0	6.3	5.6
3.0	39	27	20	16	13	12	11	9.1	8.0	7.2	6.4
4.0	42	30	21	17	15	13	12	10	9.0	8.2	7.4
6.0	45	31	23	18	16	14	13	11	10	9.4	8.5
8.0	47	32	23	19	17	15	14	12	11	10	9.1
10	48	33	24	20	17	15	14	12	11	10	9.5
14	49	34	25	20	17	16	14	13	12	11	9.9
20	50	35	25	21	18	16	15	13	12	11	10

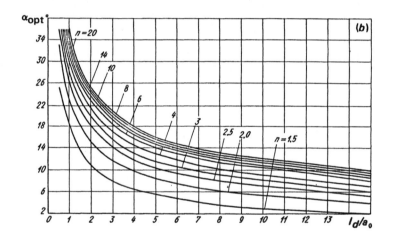

Diffusers of reduced resistance, with a screen	Diagram
(in the system with $l_1/D_1 > 0$);[50,55] $\mathrm{Re} = w_0 D_h/\nu \geqslant 10^5$	5-12

Internal arrangement of diffuser	Scheme	Resistance coefficient
		$$\zeta \equiv \frac{\Delta p}{\rho w_0^2/2}$$

Dividing splitters, number of splitters, z_1		$\zeta \approx 0.65\zeta_d$
	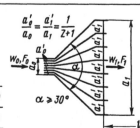	where ζ_d is determined as ζ from Diagrams 5-2, 5-4, and 5-5

α, degrees	30	45	60	90	120
z_1		2	4	6	6	6–8

Diagram
5-12

Baffles

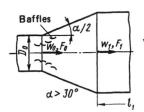

$\zeta \approx 0.65\zeta_d$

where ζ_d is determined as ζ from Diagrams 5-2, 5-4, and 5-5

Rounded insert R in the inlet section; $n_{ar1} = F_1/F_2 = 2\text{–}4$

$$l'/D_0 = \frac{R}{D_0}\sin\alpha$$

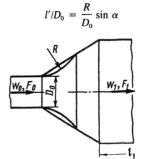

$\zeta = k\zeta_d$

where for ζ_d see Diagrams 5-1 through 5-5:

(a) at $l'/D_0 \approx 0.5$ and $\alpha = 45$ and $60°$, $k \approx 0.72$;

(b) at $l'/D_0 \approx 0.8$ and $\alpha = 60°$, $k \approx 0.67$

Screen or grid (perforated plate) at the exit of diffuser

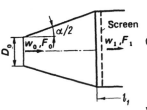

(a) at $\alpha = 0\text{–}60°$

$$\zeta = \zeta_0 + \frac{\zeta_{gr}}{n_{ar1}^2}$$

(b) at $\alpha > 60°$

$$\zeta = (1.2\text{–}1.3)\left(\zeta_0 + \frac{\zeta_{gr}}{n_{ar1}^2}\right)$$

where ζ_0 is determined as ζ from Diagrams 5-2, 5-4 and 5-5, and ζ_{gr} is determined as ζ of the screen or grid from Diagrams 8-1 to 8-7; $n_{ar1} = F_1/F_0$

Diffuser with symmetric expansion in one plane, installed downstream of a centrifugal fan operating in a system with $l_1/D_{1h} > 0^{58}$	Diagram 5-13

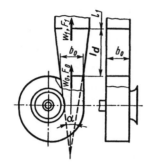

$$\zeta \equiv \frac{\Delta p}{\rho w_0^2/2} = f\left(\frac{F_1}{F_0}\right)$$

see the curves at different α values

Values of ζ

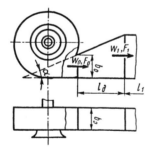

α, degrees	$\dfrac{F_1}{F_0}$					
	1.4	2.0	2.5	3.0	3.5	4.0
10	0.05	0.07	0.09	0.10	0.11	0.11
15	0.06	0.09	0.11	0.13	0.13	0.14
20	0.07	0.10	0.13	0.15	0.16	0.16
25	0.08	0.13	0.16	0.19	0.21	0.23
30	0.16	0.24	0.29	0.32	0.34	0.35
35	0.24	0.34	0.39	0.44	0.48	0.50

Diffuser with asymmetric expansion (at $\alpha_1 = 0$) in one plane, installed downstream of a centrifugal fan operating in a system with $l_1/D_{1h} > 0^{58}$	Diagram 5-14

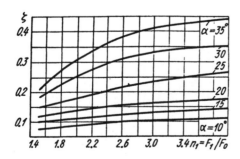

$$\zeta \equiv \frac{\Delta p}{\rho w_0^2/2} = f\left(\frac{F_1}{F_0}\right)$$

see the curves at different α values

Values of ζ

α, degrees	$\dfrac{F_1}{F_0}$					
	1.4	2.0	2.5	3.0	3.5	4.0
10	0.08	0.09	0.10	0.10	0.11	0.11
15	0.10	0.11	0.12	0.13	0.14	0.15
20	0.12	0.14	0.15	0.16	0.17	0.18
25	0.15	0.18	0.21	0.23	0.25	0.26
30	0.18	0.25	0.30	0.33	0.35	0.35
35	0.21	0.31	0.38	0.41	0.43	0.44

Diffuser with asymmetric expansion (at $\alpha_1 = 10°$) in one plane, installed downstream of a centrifugal fan operating in a system with $l_1/D_{1h} > 0$[58]

Diagram
5-15

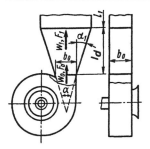

$$\zeta \equiv \frac{\Delta p}{\rho w_0^2/2} = f\left(\frac{F_1}{F_0}\right)$$

see the curves at different α values

Values of ζ

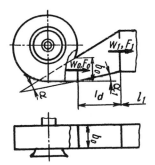

α, degrees	$\frac{F_1}{F_0}$					
	1.4	2.0	2.5	3.0	3.5	4.0
10	0.05	0.08	0.11	0.13	0.13	0.14
15	0.06	0.10	0.12	0.14	0.15	0.15
20	0.07	0.11	0.14	0.15	0.16	0.16
25	0.09	0.14	0.18	0.20	0.21	0.22
30	0.13	0.18	0.23	0.26	0.28	0.29
35	0.15	0.23	0.28	0.33	0.35	0.36

Diffuser with asymmetric expansion (at $\alpha_1 = -10°$) in one plane, installed downstream of a centrifugal fan operating in a system with $l_1/D_{1h} > 0$[58]

Diagram
5-16

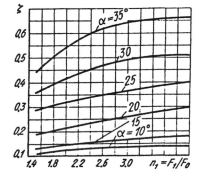

$$\zeta = \frac{\Delta p}{\rho w_0^2/2} - f\left(\frac{F_1}{F_0}\right)$$

see the curves at different α values

Values of ζ

α, degrees	$\frac{F_1}{F_0}$					
	1.5	2.0	2.5	3.0	3.5	4.0
10	0.11	0.13	0.14	0.14	0.14	0.14
15	0.13	0.15	0.16	0.17	0.18	0.18
20	0.19	0.22	0.24	0.26	0.28	0.30
25	0.29	0.32	0.35	0.37	0.39	0.40
30	0.36	0.42	0.46	0.49	0.51	0.51
35	0.44	0.54	0.61	0.64	0.66	0.66

Diffuser of rectangular cross section installed downstream of a centrifugal fan operating in a system with $l_1/D_{1h} > 0^{58}$	Diagram 5-17

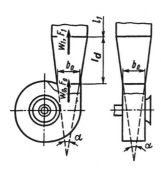

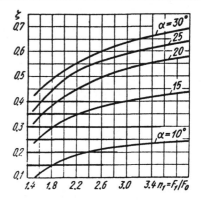

$$\zeta \equiv \frac{\Delta p}{\rho w_0^2/2} = f\left(\frac{F_1}{F_0}\right)$$

see the curves at different α values

Values of ζ

α, degrees	F_1/F_0					
	1.5	2.0	2.5	3.0	3.5	4.0
10	0.10	0.18	0.12	0.23	0.24	0.25
15	0.23	0.33	0.38	0.40	0.42	0.44
20	0.31	0.43	0.48	0.53	0.56	0.58
25	0.36	0.49	0.55	0.58	0.62	0.64
30	0.42	0.53	0.59	0.64	0.67	0.69

Diffuser with stepped walls, installed downstream of a centrifugal fan operating in a system with $l_1/D_{1h} > 0^{58}$	Diagram 5-18

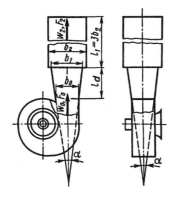

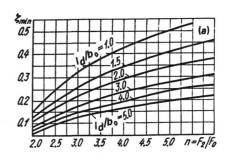

$$\zeta \equiv \frac{\Delta p}{\rho w_0^2/2}, \quad \zeta_{min} = f\left(\frac{F_2}{F_0}\right),$$

see the curves at different l_d/b_0 in graph a;
$\alpha_{opt} = f(F_2/F_0)$, see the curves in graph b
at different l_d/b_0

Values of ζ_{min}

$\dfrac{l_d}{b_0}$	F_2/F_0							
	2.0	2.5	3.0	3.5	4.0	4.5	5.0	6.0
1.0	0.16	0.25	0.33	0.38	0.43	0.47	0.50	0.56
1.5	0.13	0.20	0.26	0.31	0.34	0.38	0.41	0.46
2.0	0.12	0.17	0.22	0.26	0.29	0.33	0.35	0.38
3.0	0.09	0.13	0.18	0.21	0.24	0.26	0.28	0.31
4.0	0.08	0.12	0.15	0.18	0.20	0.22	0.24	0.26
5.0	0.06	0.10	0.13	0.15	0.17	0.18	0.20	0.22

Diagram
5-18

Values of α_{opt}, degrees

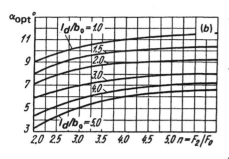

$\dfrac{l_d}{b_0}$	F_2/F_0							
	2.0	2.5	3.0	3.5	4.0	4.5	5.0	6.0
1.0	9	10	10	11	11	11	11	12
1.5	8	9	9	10	10	10	10	10
2.0	7	8	8	9	9	9	9	9
3.0	6	7	7	7	7	8	8	8
4.0	4	5	6	6	7	7	7	8
5.0	3	4	5	6	6	6	6	7

Annular diffusers with inner fairing, in a system
with $l_1/D_1 > 0$; $\bar{d}_0 = 0.688$[40,128]

Diagram
5-19

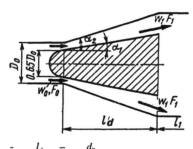

$$\bar{l}_d = \frac{l_d}{D_0} \; ; \quad \bar{d}_0 = \frac{d_0}{D_0}$$

$$n_{ar1} = 1 + \frac{4\bar{l}}{1 - \bar{d}_0^2}\,(\tan^2 \alpha_2 - \tan^2 \alpha_1)$$

$$+ \frac{4\bar{l}}{1 - \bar{d}_0^2}\,(\tan \alpha_2 - \bar{d}_0 \tan \alpha_1)$$

1. Inner diverging fairing ($\alpha_1 = 8–16°$):

$$\zeta_{in} \equiv \frac{\Delta p}{\rho w_0^2/2} = k_d \zeta'_{in}$$

where for ζ'_{in} see graph a, or within $2 < n_{ar1} < 4$ and at
$\bar{l}_d = 0.5–1.0$ determine from the formula

$$\zeta'_{in} \approx \frac{0.25 n_{ar1}^2}{\bar{l}_d^{1.5}}$$

for k_d, see Diagram 5-1 or graph b (when installed downstream of an operating axial flow machine).

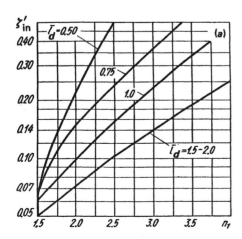

Values of ζ'_m

$\bar{l}_d$	n_{ar1}					
	1.5	2.0	2.5	3.0	3.5	4.0
0.5	0.06	0.22	0.50	–	–	–
0.75	0.06	0.15	0.24	0.35	–	–
1.0	0.06	0.10	0.15	0.23	0.35	0.46
1.5–2.0	0.05	0.07	0.10	0.15	0.18	0.25

Diagram
5-19

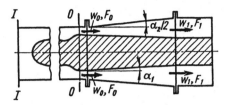

2. Inner converging fairing ($\alpha_1 < 0$):

$$\zeta \equiv \frac{\Delta p}{\rho w_0^2/2} = k_d \phi_d \left(1 - \frac{F_0}{F_1}\right)^2$$

where for ϕ_d see graph c as a function of the divergence
angle α; for k_d see graph b as a function of the divergence
angle α_2 for different velocity profiles shown in graph d.

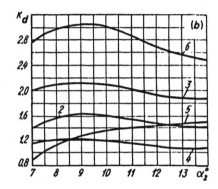

Values of k_d

α_2, degrees	Velocity profile (graphs b and d)					
	1	2	3	4	5	6
7	1.0	1.40	2.00	1.16	0.90	2.74
8	1.0	1.60	2.10	1.21	1.15	2.98
10	1.0	1.60	2.10	1.20	1.36	3.02
12	1.0	1.45	2.00	1.10	1.42	2.70
14	1.0	1.40	1.86	1.08	1.50	2.48

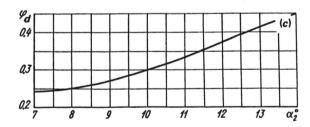

Section I-I

α_2, degrees	ϕ_d
7	0.25
8	0.25
10	0.30
12	0.37
14	0.44

Turbomachinery diffusers (radial-axial and axial-radial-annular) in the system with $l_1/D_1 > 0$; $\bar{d}_0 = 0.688$[39]	Diagram 5-20

1. Radial-annular

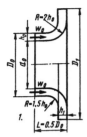

$$\zeta_{in} \equiv \frac{\Delta p}{\rho w_0^2/2} = f(n_{ar}, \alpha_1),$$

where $\zeta_{in} = f_1(n_{ar}, D_1)$; $\zeta_{in} = f(n_{ar}, \alpha_1)$, see graphs a–c.

2. Axial-radial-annular

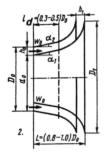

$\bar{D}_1 = 2.06$ $\alpha_2 = 8°$ $\bar{c}_{a0} = 0.5$

$$n_{ar} = 2\frac{h_1}{h_0}\bar{D}_1\frac{1}{1 + \bar{d}_0}$$

$$\bar{D}_1 = \frac{D_1}{D_0}\quad \bar{d}_0 = \frac{d_0}{D_0}$$

$$\bar{c}_{a0} = w_0 = \frac{Q}{\pi(D_0^2 - d_0^2)/4}$$

$$\bar{c}_{a0} = \frac{c_{a0}}{u},$$

where Q is the fluid discharge, m³/s; u is the circumferential velocity on the outer radius, m/s

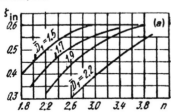

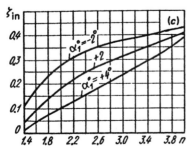

1. Values of ζ_{in}

	n_{ar}							
$\bar{D}_1$	1.4	1.8	2.2	2.6	3.0	3.4	3.8	4.2

(a) Diffuser downstream of operating compressor at $\bar{c}_{a0} = 0.5$

1.5	–	0.45	0.55	0.62	0.65	–	–	–
1.7	–	0.34	0.48	0.56	0.61	0.64	–	–
1.9	–	–	0.37	0.49	0.56	0.62	0.65	–
2.2	–	–	–	0.35	0.45	0.52	0.60	0.65

(b) Diffuser downstream of idle compressor

1.4	0.31	0.41	0.48	0.55	0.60	–	–	–
1.6	0.25	0.33	0.40	0.46	0.52	0.55	–	–
1.8	0.19	0.26	0.33	0.39	0.44	0.48	0.51	–
2.0	–	0.20	0.25	0.30	0.35	0.40	0.43	–

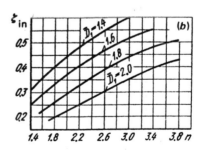

2. Values of ζ_{in}

	n_{ar}						
α_1, degrees	1.8	2.2	2.6	3.0	3.4	3.6	4.0
−2	0.28	0.31	0.35	0.38	0.40	0.41	0.43
+2	0.14	0.22	0.27	0.31	0.35	0.37	0.41
+4	0.08	0.13	0.18	0.24	0.29	0.32	0.39

Diffusers with curved axis (and with expansion in one plane, in the system with $l_d/b_0 = 8.3$; $l_0/b_0 = 0$[69,70]	Diagram 5-21

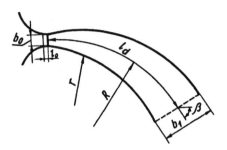

$$\zeta_{in} \equiv \frac{\Delta p}{\rho w_0^2/2} = k_0 \zeta'_{in}; \quad \zeta'_{in} = f\left(\alpha, \frac{r}{b_0}\right); \quad \text{for } k_d, \text{ see Diagram 5-1}$$

Values of ζ'_{in}

$\dfrac{r}{b_0}$	α, degrees							
	2	4	6	8	10	12	14	16
∞ (straight, $\beta = 0$)	0.037	0.068	0.088	0.106	0.123	0.138	0.150	0.160
22.5 ($\beta = 21°\ 15'$)	0.042	0.072	0.097	0.113	0.130	0.144	0.155	0.163
11.6 ($\beta = 40°\ 5'$)	0.043	0.077	0.103	0.124	0.140	0.154	0.163	0.168
7.5 ($\beta = 63°\ 42'$)	0.043	0.081	0.113	0.136	0.153	0.163	0.170	0.175

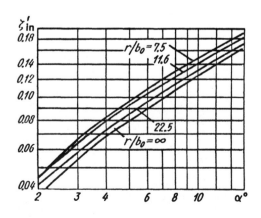

Diffusers of circular cross section with a curved axis in the system with $n_{ar1} = 4$; $l_d/D_0 = 7.15$; $\alpha = 8°$; $l_0/D_0 = 0.35$[172,173]	Diagram 5-22

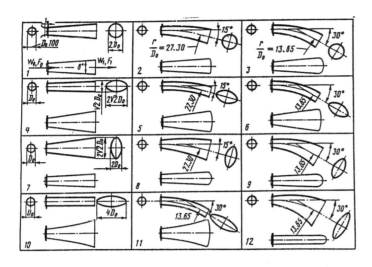

$$\zeta_{in} \equiv \frac{\Delta p}{\rho w_0^2/2}$$

$$= k_d \zeta'_{in}$$

for ζ'_{in}, see the table at Re $\geqslant 5 \times 10^5$ and the curves $\zeta'_{in} = f(\text{Re})$ in the graph; for k_d, see Diagram 5-1

$$n_{ar1} = \frac{F_1}{F_0}$$

$$\text{Re} = \frac{w_0 D_0}{\nu}$$

Diffuser no.	1	2	3	4	5	6	7	8	9	10	11	12
β, degress	0	15	30	0	15	30	15	30	0	30	30	30
R/D_0	∞	27.30	13.65	∞	27.30	13.65	27.30	13.65	∞	13.65	13.65	13.65
ζ'_{in} at Re $\geqslant 5 \times 10^5$	0.081	0.131	0.092	0.087	0.108	0.145	0.154	0.220	0.131	0.115	0.265	0.118

Values of ζ'_{in}

	Re $\times 10^{-5}$									
Diffuser no.	0.10	0.2	0.4	0.6	0.8	1.0	1.2	1.4	1.6	1.8
1. ($\beta = 0$; $Z/D_0 = \infty$)	0.244	0.216	0.178	0.160	0.150	0.140	0.120	0.100	0.088	0.075
2. ($\beta = 15°$; $Z/D_0 = 27,30$)	0.410	0.366	0.290	0.240	0.200	0.180	0.160	0.150	0.132	0.127
3. ($\beta = 30°$; $Z/D_0 = 13,65$)	–	0.385	0.338	0.250	0.230	0.216	0.210	0.200	0.198	0.184
9. ($\beta = 0$; $Z/D_0 = \infty$)	–	–	–	0.340	0.280	0.240	0.180	0.136	0.132	0.132
10. ($\beta = 15°$; $Z/D_0 = 27,30$)	–	0.375	0.265	0.220	0.185	0.175	0.140	0.122	0.113	0.103
11. ($\beta = 30°$; $Z/D_0 = 13,65$)	–	–	–	–	–	0.375	0.300	0.275	0.253	0.244

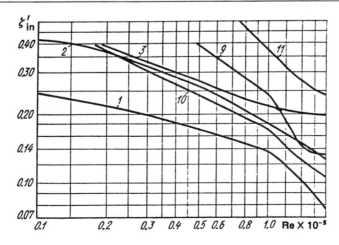

Converging nozzles of circular cross section in the system with $l_0/D_0 > 0$)[47,49,100,136]	Diagram 5-23

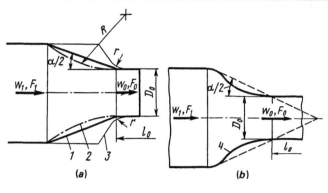

(a)   (b)

1. Rectilinear boundary walls (scheme a, 1):

$$\zeta \equiv \frac{\Delta p}{\rho w_0^2/2} \quad \text{see graph a}$$

(Re $= w_0 D_0/\nu \geq 10^5$) or use the approximate formula

$$\zeta = (-0.0125 n_0^4 + 0.0224 n_0^3 \\ -0.00723 n_0^2 + 0.00444 n_0 \\ -0.00745)(\alpha_r^3 - 2\pi\sigma_r^2 \\ -10\alpha_r) + \zeta_{fr}$$

where $n_0 = F_0/F_1 \leq 1.0$:

$\alpha_r = 0.01745\alpha.$

2. Curvilinear boundary walls — completely over the radius R of the circle (scheme a, 2):

$$\zeta \equiv \frac{\Delta p}{\rho w_0^2/2} \quad \text{see graph b (Re} \geq 10^5)$$

3. Rectilinear boundary walls with rounding at the exit over the radius r (scheme a, 3) at $\alpha = 90°$:

$$\zeta \equiv \frac{\Delta p}{\rho w_0^2/2} \quad \text{see graphs c and d (Re} \geq 10^5)$$

4. Curvilinear boundary walls of double curvature (nozzle, scheme b):

$$\zeta \equiv \frac{\Delta p}{\rho w_0^2/2} = \zeta_{fr}$$

where for ζ_{fr}, see Equations (5-6)–(5-10).

Values of ζ

n_0	α, degrees										
	3	5	10	15–40	50–60	76	90	105	120	150	180
0.64	0.072	0.067	0.054	0.040	0.058	0.076	0.094	0.112	0.131	0.167	0.190
0.45	0.076	0.064	0.052	0.050	0.072	0.104	0.138	0.170	0.202	0.246	0.255
0.39	0.098	0.070	0.051	0.046	0.064	0.110	0.162	0.210	0.250	0.319	0.364
0.25	0.100	0.071	0.047	0.044	0.068	0.127	0.174	0.220	0.268	0.352	0.408
0.16	0.108	0.084	0.048	0.044	0.074	0.136	0.184	0.232	0.278	0.362	0.420
0.10	0.118	0.093	0.053	0.050	0.079	0.142	0.190	0.237	0.285	0.367	0.427

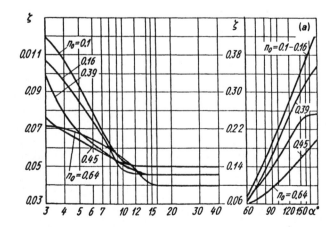

Diagram
5-23

Values of ζ

n_0	R_0/D_0							
	0	0.1	0.2	0.3	0.5	1.0	1.5	2.0
0.64	0.190	0.055	0.046	0.044	0.044	0.044	0.044	0.045
0.45	0.255	0.076	0.065	0.060	0.054	0.052	0.049	0.047
0.33	0.364	0.062	0.056	0.054	0.052	0.048	0.045	0.048
0.25	0.408	0.070	0.068	0.066	0.062	0.053	0.052	0.052

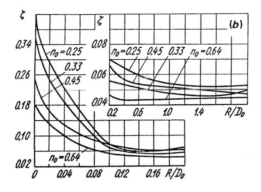

Values of ζ

n_0	r/D_0							
	0	0.02	0.04	0.06	0.08	0.10	0.15	0.20
$\alpha = 90°$								
0.64	0.097	0.063	0.061	0.060	0.059	0.058	0.055	0.052
0.45	0.138	0.074	0.064	0.060	0.058	0.057	0.057	0.057
0.33	0.150	0.113	0.092	0.077	0.066	0.059	0.058	0.057
0.25	0.160	0.108	0.071	0.056	0.053	0.052	0.049	0.045
$\alpha = 120°$								
0.64	0.130	0.087	0.064	0.062	0.060	0.059	0.057	0.054
0.45	0.196	0.138	0.090	0.067	0.065	0.064	0.062	0.060
0.33	0.237	0.165	0.115	0.085	0.072	0.065	0.055	0.053
0.25	0.250	0.170	0.120	0.083	0.063	0.055	0.054	0.053

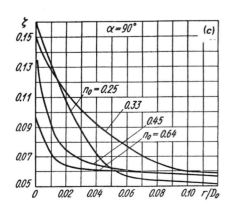

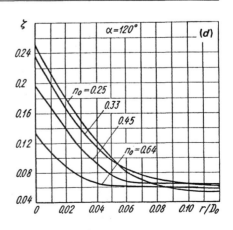

Converging nozzles of circular cross section in the system with $l_0/D_0 > 0$; laminar flow $Re = w_0 D_h/\nu \leqslant 50^4$	Diagram 5-24

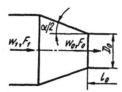

$$\zeta \equiv \frac{\Delta p}{\rho w_0^2/2} = \frac{A}{Re}$$

where at $5° \leqslant \alpha \leqslant 40°$

$$A = \frac{20.5}{n_0^{0.5}(\tan \alpha)^{0.75}}$$

$$D_h = \frac{4F_0}{\Pi_0} ; \quad n_0 = \frac{F_0}{F_1}$$

see curves $\zeta = f(\alpha, n_0)$

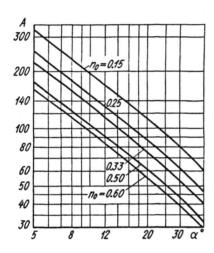

Values of A

n_0	α, degrees							
	5	10	15	20	25	30	35	40
0.15	333	197	144	114	95.0	80.8	69.9	61.0
0.25	255	151	110	87.6	72.8	61.9	53.6	46.8
0.33	221	131	95.5	75.8	63.0	53.6	46.4	40.5
0.5	178	105	77.0	61.1	50.8	43.2	37.4	32.6
0.6	162	95.7	70.0	55.5	46.2	39.3	34.0	29.7

Converging-diverging transition pieces in the system with $l_1/D_h > 0^{100}$	Diagram 5-25

1. Circular cross section
   (a) Curvilinear converging section (scheme a):

$$\zeta \equiv \frac{\Delta p}{\rho w_0^2/2} = k_1 k_2 \zeta_1 + \Delta\zeta$$

where at $Re = w_0 D_h/\nu \geqslant 2 \times 10^5$, $\zeta_1 = f_1(\alpha_d)$, see the graph; at $Re < 2 \times 10^5$, ζ_1 is determined as ζ_d from Diagram 5-2; $k_1 = f_2(\alpha_d, F_1/F_0)$ see the graph; $k_2 \approx 0.66 + 0.35 l_0/D_0$ at $0.25 \leqslant l_0/D_0 \leqslant 5$; for $\Delta\zeta$, see the table.

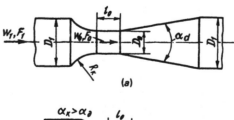

(a)

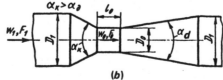

(b)

Converging-diverging transition pieces in the system with $l_1/D_h > 0$[100]	Diagram 5-25

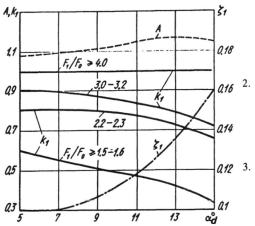

(b) Rectilinear converging section (scheme b):

$$\zeta_{rec} \equiv \frac{\Delta p}{\rho w_0^2/2} = A\zeta_{cur}$$

where ζ_{cur} is determined as ζ for a curvilinear converging section; $A = f(\alpha_d)$, see the graph.

2. Square cross section (tentatively):

$$\zeta \equiv \frac{\Delta p}{\rho w_0^2/2} \quad \text{see paragraph 1, but } \zeta_1 \text{ is}$$

determined as ζ_d at l_0/D_0 from Diagram 5-4;

3. Rectangular cross section with expansion in one plane (tentatively):

$$\zeta \equiv \frac{\Delta p}{\rho w_0^2/2}, \quad \text{see paragraph 1, but } \zeta_1 \text{ is}$$

determined as ζ_d at $l_0/D_0 = 0$ from Diagram 5-5.

Value	α_d, degrees				
	5	7	10	12.5	15
ζ_1	0.10	0.10	0.11	0.13	0.16
A	1.08	1.09	1.13	1.16	1.15

Values of k_1

F_1/F_0	D_1/D_0	α_d, degrees				
		5	7	10	12.5	15
1.5–1.6	≈1.25	0.59	0.55	0.48	0.40	0.33
2.2–2.3	≈1.50	0.81	0.81	0.78	0.77	0.66
3.0–3.2	≈1.75	0.90	0.89	0.85	0.81	0.77
≥4.0	≥2.0	1.0	1.0	1.0	1.0	1.0

Values of $\Delta\zeta$

F_1/F_0	D_1/D_0	l_0/D_0					
		0.25	0.50	0.75	1.00	1.25	1.50
1.5–1.6	≈1.25	−0.012	−0.08	−0.004	0	0.004	0.008
2.2–2.3	≈1.5	−0.020	−0.014	0	0	0	0.014
3.0–3.2	≈1.75	−0.022	−0.016	−0.010	0	0.010	0.014
≥4.0	≥2.0	−0.028	−0.020	−0.010	0	0.010	0.016
F_1/F_0	D_1/D_0	l_0/D_0					
		1.75	2.0	2.5	3.0	3.5	4.0
1.5–1.6	≈1.25	0.012	0.016	–	–	–	–
2.2–2.3	≈1.5	0.020	0.026	0.038	0.048	0.06	0.072
3.0–3.2	≈1.75	0.022	0.027	0.038	0.050	0.062	0.073
≥4.0	≥2.0	0.028	0.030	–	–	–	–

Transition pieces with sharply changing cross sections in the system with $l_1/D_1 > 0$	Diagram 5-26

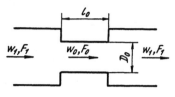

$$\zeta \equiv \frac{\Delta p}{\rho w_0^2/2} = k_1 \zeta_1$$

where at Re $= w_0 D_h/\nu > 10^4$

$$\zeta_1 \equiv 0.5\left(1 - \frac{F_0}{F_1}\right)^{3/4} + \left(1 - \frac{F_0}{F_1}\right)^2 + \lambda \frac{l_0}{D_0}$$

$$= \zeta_{sc} + \zeta_{gr} + \lambda \frac{l_0}{D_0}$$

$\zeta_{sc} \equiv 0.5(1 - F_0/F_1)^{3/4}$, see Diagram 4-9, paragraph 1;
$\zeta_{gr} = (1 - F_0/F_1)$; at Re $< 10^4$, ζ_{sc} is determined as ζ from Diagram 4-10 and ζ_{gr} is determined as ζ from Diagram 4-1; at all the Re numbers $k_1 = f(l_0/D_0, F_1/F_0)$ see the graph. For λ, see Diagrams 2-1 through 2-6.

Values of k_1

$\dfrac{F_1}{F_0} \dfrac{D_1}{D_0}$	$\dfrac{l_0}{D_0}$						
	0.5	0.6	0.7	0.8	1.0	1.4	$\geqslant 2.0$
1.5–1.6 (≈ 1.25)	1.02	1.01	1.0	1.0	1.0	1.0	1.0
2.2–2.3 (≈ 1.5)	1.06	1.03	1.02	1.01	1.0	1.0	1.0
3.0–3.2 (≈ 1.75)	–	1.10	1.06	1.04	1.01	1.0	1.0
$\geqslant 4.0$ ($\geqslant 2$)	–	1.15	1.10	1.08	1.04	1.03	1.0

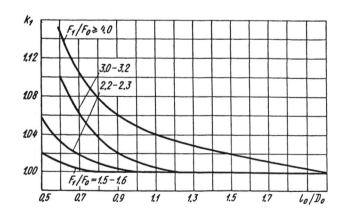

Transitions from rectangular to circular cross sections in the system with $l_0/D_0 > 0;$[7,84] Re $= w_0 D_0/\nu > 10^4$	Diagram 5-27

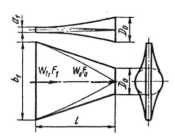

1. Diverging transition piece ($F_0 > F_1$):

$$\zeta_d \equiv \frac{\Delta p}{\rho w_0^2/2} = \zeta_{sim} + 0.5 \exp(-\text{Re} \times 10^{-5})$$

$$= \zeta_{sim} + \Delta\zeta_d$$

$$\Delta\zeta_d = 0.5 \exp(-\text{Re} \times 10^{-5}) \text{ see graph a.}$$

2. Converging transition piece ($F_0 < F_1$):

$$\zeta_{con} \equiv \frac{\Delta p}{\rho w_0^2/2} = \zeta_{sim} + 0.3 \exp(-\text{Re} \times 10^{-5})$$

$$= \zeta_{sim} + \Delta\zeta_{con}$$

$\Delta\zeta_{con} = 0.3 \exp(-\text{Re} \times 10^{-5})$, see graph a; $\zeta_{sim} = \left(c_0 + c_1 \dfrac{b_1}{a_1}\right)\left(\dfrac{F_0}{F_1}\right)^2$; $c_1 = f\left(\dfrac{l}{D_0}\right)$, see graph b ($c_{1d}$, for the diverging transition piece; c_{1con}, for the converging transition piece); $c_0 = \lambda(l/D_h)$; $D_h = D_{1h} + D_0/2 = [2a_1b_1/(a_1 + b_1) + 0.5D_0]$; for λ, see Diagrams 2-1 through 2-6. The choice of the shape and optimal dimensions of the transition pieces is described under paragraphs 101 to 108 (transition pieces).

Re $\times 10^{-4}$	1	2	4	6	8	10	20	40	50
$\Delta\zeta_{con}$	0.272	0.245	0.201	0.165	0.135	0.111	0.041	0.005	0.002
$\Delta\zeta_d$	0.453	0.409	0.335	0.275	0.225	0.185	0.068	0.009	0.003

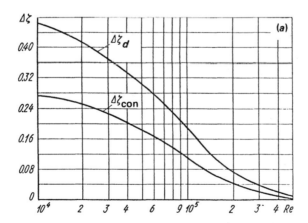

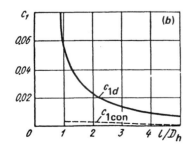

$\dfrac{l}{D_0}$	1.0	1.5	2.0	2.5	3.0	4.0	5.0
C_{1d}	0.055	0.030	0.023	0.018	0.015	0.008	0.006
c_{1con}	0.002	0.002	0.002	0.002	0.0015	0.0010	0

Diffuser with transition from a circle into a rectangle or from a rectangle to a circle, in the system with $l_1/D_1 > 0$	Diagram 5-28

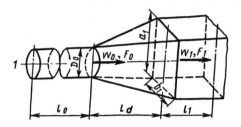

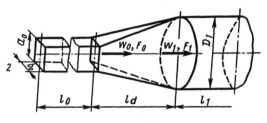

$$\zeta \equiv \frac{\Delta p}{\rho w_0^2/2}$$

see Diagram 5-4 for a pyramidal diffuser of rectangular cross section with an equivalent divergence angle which is determined from the relations:

for transition from a circle into a rectangle

$$\tan \frac{\alpha}{2} = \frac{2\sqrt{a_1 b_1/\pi} - D_0}{2l_d}$$

for transition from a square into a circle

$$\tan \frac{\alpha}{2} = \frac{D_1 - 2\sqrt{a_0 b_0/\pi}}{2l_d}$$

REFERENCES

1. Abramovich, G. N., Aerodynamics of local resistances, *Prom. Aerodin.*, vyp. 211, 65–150, 1935.
2. Abramovich, G. N., *Applied Gas Dynamics*, Nauka Press, 1969, 715 p.
3. Altshul, A. D. and Kalitsun, V. M., On the resistance coefficient of converning diffusers, *Izv. VUZov. Energ.*, no. 7, 130–136, 1960.
4. Artyushkina, G. K., On the hydraulic resistance during laminar fluid flow in conical diffusers, *Tr. LPI*, no. 333, 104–106, 1973.
5. Ginevskiy, A. S., Kolesnikov, A. V., Podolynyi, I. N., and Smoliyanikova, A. N., The aerodynamic characteristics of plane separation-free diffusers, *Prom. Aerodin.*, Vyp. 30, 5–25, 1973.
6. Bedrzhitskiy, E. L., Study of subsonic diffusers, *Prom. Aerodin.*, vyp. 1(33), 123–158, 1986.
7. Bogdanov, Yu. V. and Tananaev, A. V., On the hydraulic resistances of transitions from circles into rectangular slots, *Tr. LPI*, no. 289, 104–109, 1968.
8. Brusilovskiy, I. V., Determination of the optimal parameters of the diffusers of axial fans and of their energy characteristics from the experimental data, *Prom. Aerodin.*, vyp. 2(34), 118–133, 1987.
9. Bushel, A. R., Investigation of short radial and combined diffusers, in *Prom. Aerodin.*, vyp. 28, 121–138, Mashinostroenie Press, 1966.
10. Bychkova, L. A., Aerodynamice characteristics of plane and radial diffusers with a preseparating turbulent boundary layer, in *Prom. Aerodin.*, vyp. 30, 26–33, Mashinostroenie Press, 1973.
11. Vasiliev, Yu. N., Towards the theory of a stepped diffuser, in *Blade Machines and Jet Apparatus*, vyp. 4, 31–35, Mashinostroenie Press, Moscow, 1969.
12. Verigin, I. S., Concerning the effect of the hydrodynamic regime of flow entrance into a conical diffuser on the efficiency of energy conversion when operating in the system 'nozzle - tube - diffuser - tube', Yaroslavl Polytechnic Inst., 1981 (The paper is deposited of VINITI 17.12.1981 under no. 5738-81).
13. Virigin, I. S., Experimental investigation of the resistance of the separated conical diffuser operating in the system 'nozzle - diffuser - straight tube section', Yaroslavl. Polytechnic Inst., 1978 (The paper is deposited at VINITI 15.11.1979 under no. 3879-79).
14. Voitovich, L. N. and Emeliyanova, G. N., Experimental and theoretical investigation of the hydraulic resistance of conical diffusers having a rough surface, *Uch. Zap. TsAGI*, vol. 16, no. 4, 105–110, 1985.
15. Garkusha, A. V., Grincheko, N. Ya., and Kucherenko, S. I., Investigation of flow in an annular conical diffuser, in *Power Engineering Machine Building, Collected Papers of the Kharkov Polytechnic Inst.*, vyp. 31, pp, 21–25, 1981.
16. Garkusha, A. V. and Kucherenko, S. I., Investigation of the characteristics of a swirled flow in an annular stepwise diffuser with resistance at the exit, in *Power Engineering Machine Building, Collected Papers of the Kharkov Polytechnic Inst.*, vyp. 38, 3–10, 1984.
17. German, R., *Supersonic Inlet Diffusers and Introduction to the Inner Aerodynamices*, Fizmatizdat, 1960, 378 p.
18. Gibson, A., *Hydraulics and Its Application*, ONTI Press, 1935, 611 p.
19. Guinevsky, A. S., Energetic characteristics of the subsonic diffuser channels, *Izv. Akad. Nauk SSSR*, OTNI no. 3, 152–154, 1956.
20. Ginevsky, A. S., Calculation of losses in diverging and converging channels, in *Prom. Aerodin.*, no. 7, 5–16, 1956.
21. Ginevsky, A. S. and Bychkova, L. A., Aerodynamic characteristics of plane and axisymmetrical diffusers with a preseparating turbulent boundary layer, in *Teplo i Massoperenos*, vol. 1, pp. 100–115, Energiya Press, Moscow, 1968.
22. Ginevsky, A. S., Emeliyanova, G. N., and Kolesnikov, A. V., The direct and inverse problems in calculation of diffuser channels, *Tr. TsIAM*, no. 1093, 51–60, 1984.
23. Ginevsky, A. S. and Kolesnikov, A. V., Calculation of the starting length and stabilized flow section in plane separation-free diffusers, *Izv. Akad. Nauk SSSR Mekh. Zhidk. Gaza*, no. 6, 31–38, 1969.
24. Ginevsky, A. S. and Solodkin, E. E., Aerodynamic characteristics of the starting length of an annular tube with turbulent boundary layer flow, in *Prom. Aerodin.*, vyp. 12, 155–167, Oborongiz, 1959.
25. Ginevsky, A. S. and Solodkin, E. E., Hydraulic resistance of annular channels, in *Prom. Aerodin.*, vyp. 20, 202–215, Oborongiz, 1961.
26. Ginsburg, Ya. L. and Idelchik, I. E., Main results of the study of diffusers of square and rectangular cross section, in *Industrial Cleaning of Gases and the Aerodynamics of Dust-Capturing Apparatus*, pp. 57–63, Yaroslavl, 1975.
27. Ginzburg, Ya. L. and Idelchik, I. E., Experimental determination of the coefficients of pressure reduction in conical diffusers at large subsonic velocities, *Uch. Zap. TsAGI*, vol. 4, no. 3, 23–31, 1973.

28. Gordeyev, N. N., Seleznyov, K. P., and Chernyavskiy, L. K., An approximate method for calculating the losses in straight and bent diffusers with an arbitrarily varying cross-sectional area and its use for optimizing the elements of turbine machines, in *Thermal Power Engineering*, Trudy LPI, no. 358, 47–53, Leningrad, 1947.

29. Grishanin, K. V., Developed turbulent fluid flow in a conical diffuser with a small divergence angle, *Tr. LIIVT*, vyp. 22, 47–53, 1955.

30. Gubin, M. F., Kazennov, V. V., and Volshanik, V. V., An optimal shape of a rectiaxial diffuser for a swirled liquid flow, *Tr. Mosk. Inzh. Stroit. Inst.*, no. 89, 38–44, 1972.

31. Gurzhienko, G. A., On the developed turbulent flow in conical diffusers with small divergence angles, *Tr. TsAGI*, vyp. 462, 80, 1939.

32. Danilichev, V. N. and Vasiliev, B. V., Investigation of diffusers with flexible transverse fins, *Gidroaeromekhanika*, vyp. 3, 25–30, 1966.

33. Dantsyg, A. Ya., Petrov, N. M., and Ponomaryov, N. N., Concerning the problem of determining the losses in a suddenly diverging channel located downstream of the diffuser, *Izv. VUZov, Aviats. Tekh.*, no. 3, 86–89, 1981.

34. Dantsyg, A. Ya. and Petrov, N. M., Determination of the total pressure losses in stepwise annular diffusers with rectilinear outer walls and uniform velocity field at the entrance, *Izv. VUZov, Aviats. Tekh.*, no. 1, 24–28, 1983.

35. Dantsyg, A. Ya. and Petrov, N. M., Determination of the total pressure losses in stepwise annular diffusers with rectilinear outer walls and uniform velocity field at the entrance, *Izv. VUZov, Aviats. Tekh.*, no. 3, 63–66, 1983.

36. Deich, M. E. and Zaryankin, A. E., *Gas Dynamics of Diffusers and Exit Nozzles of Turbines*, Energiya Press, Moscow, 1970, 384 p.

37. Didenko, O. I., et al., Effect of the divergence angle on the efficiency of annular curvilinear diffusers, *Izv. VUZov*, no. 8, 108–112, 1967.

38. Demidov, S., Investigation of flow and determination of the total pressure losses in circular, plane and annular diffusers, *Tr. TsIAM*, no. 116, 1960.

39. Dovzhik, S. A. and Ginevsky, A. S., Experimental investigation of pressure nozzles of stationary axial machines, *Tekh. Otchyoty.*, no. 130, 15, 1955.

40. Dovzhik, S. A. and Morozov, A. I., Experimental investigation of annular diffusers of axial turbines, in *Prom. Aerodin.*, vyp. 20, 168–201, Oborongiz, 1961.

41. Dorfman, A. Sh., Concerning calculation of the total pressure losses in diffuser channels, *Energomashinostroenie*, no. 8, 5–10, 1966.

42. Dorfman, A. Sh. and Saikovsky, M. I., An approximate method for calculating losses in curvilinear diffusers with separating flows, in *Prom. Aerodin.*, vyp. 28, 98–120, Mashinostroenie Press, Moscow, 1966.

43. Emeliyanova, G. N., Numerical calculation of the aerodynamic characteristics of axisymmetric channels, *Prom. Aerodin.*, vyp. 1 (33), 106–122, Moscow, 1986.

44. Zaryankin, A. F., Golovina, L. G., and Ett, V. V., Effect of the operational parameters on the characteristics of conical diffusers, *Teploenergetika*, no. 4, 27–34, 1967.

45. Zaryankin, A. E. and Kasimov, V. F., About the study of diffusers with a separating flow, in *The Problems of Turbines*, Trudy MEI, vyp. 385, 14–19, 1978.

46. Idelchik, I. E., Aerodynamics of intake nozzles, *TVF*, no. 5, 1–10; no. 6, 28, 1944.

47. Idelchik, I. E., Aerodynamics of the flow and pressure head losses in diffusers, in *Prom. Aerodin.*, no. 3, 132–209, 1947.

48. Idelchik, I. E., Equalizing action of the resistance placed behind a diffuser, *Tr. TsAGI*, vyp. 662, 25–52, 1948.

49. Idelchik, I. E., *Hydraulic Resistances (Physical and Mechanical Fundamentals)*, Gosenergoizdat, 1954, 316 p.

50. Idelchik, I. E., Investigation of short diffusers with dividing walls, *Teploenergetika*, no. 8, 21–26, 1958.

51. Idelchik, I. E. and Ginzburg, Ya. L., Concerning the magnetic field effect on the flow in diffusers, *Magn. Gidrodin. Akad. Nauk LatvSSR*, no. 1, 148–151, 1970.

52. Idelchik, I. E. and Ginzburg, Ya. L., On investigation of the effect of the Reynolds number and the inlet conditions on the laws governing flow motion in diffusers, in *Probl. Ventilyatsii i Konditsion. Vozdukha*, pp. 224–231, Vyssh. Shkola Press, Minsk, 1969.

53. Idelchik, I. E. and Ginzburg, Ya. L., On the mechanism of the effect of inlet conditions on the resistance of diffusers, *J. Eng. Phys.*, vol. 16, no. 3, 413–416, 1969.

54. Idelchik, I. E. and Ginzburg, Ya. L., Basic results of new experimental investigations of conical diffusers, in *Mekh. Ochistka Prom. Gazov*, pp. 178–210, NIIOGAZ, 1974.

55. Idelchik, I. E. and Ginzburg, Ya. L., Simple means of reducing the resistance of short diffusers with large divergence angles, *Vodosnabzh. Sanit. Tekh.*, no. 10, 27–30, 1971.

56. Carlson, J. J., Johnson, J. P., and Sage, C. J., Effect of the form of the wall on flow patterns and characteristics of plane diffusers with a rectilinear axis, in *Teor. Osn. Inzh. Rschyot.*, vol. 89, no.1, 173–185, Ser. D, Mir Press, 1967 (Russian translation from *Trans. ASME*).

57. Kirilenko, D. A. and Pankov, O. M., Aerodynamic investigation of a plane multichannel subsonic diffuser, *Izv. VUZov, Mashinostr.*, no. 3, 54–57, 1979.

58. Lokshin, I. L. and Gazirbekova, A. Kh., Operation of the diffusers installed behind a centrifugal fan, in *Prom. Aerodin.*, no. 6, 127–152, BNI MAP, 1955.

59. Mazo, A. S., The aerodynamic characteristics of annular conical diffusers, Deposited at NII Avtoprom, no. 496, Moscow, 1980.

60. Mazo, A. S., Experimental investigation of the structure of flow in an annular curvilinear diffuser with flow turning, *Trudy NAMI*, vyp. 176, 151–160, 1979.

61. Migai, V. K., Towards investigation of finned diffusers, *Teploenergetika*, no. 10, 33–39, 1962.

62. Migai, V. K., About the effect of the initial turbulence on the efficiency of diffuser flows, *Izv. VUZov Energ.*, no. 2, 131–136, 1966.

63. Migai, V. K., Concerning the calculation of losses in diffusers with flow separation, *Teploenergetika*, no. 9, 38–40, 1983.

64. Migai, V. K., Reduction of vortical losses in channels, *Teploenergetika*, no. 7, 49–51, 1979.

65. Migai, V. K. and Gudkov, E. I., *Design and Calculation of the Exit Diffusers of Turbines*, Leningrad, 1981, 272 p.

66. Mikheyev, V. P. and Goman, V. G., Nonisothermal gas flow in the channel of variable cross section, *Izv. VUZov Energ.*, no.7, 89–95, 1969.

67. Nelson, Young, and Hadson, Calculation of an axisymmetric shaped diffuser with boundary layer suction, *Power Engineering Machines and Installations, Trans. ASME* (Russian translation), no. 1, 137–144, Moscow, 1975.

68. Ovchinnikov, O. N., Effect of the inlet velocity profile on operation of diffusers, *Tr. Leningr. Politekh. Inst.*, no. 176, 45–53, 1955.

69. Polotsky, N. D., The results of investigation of a flow in plane curvilinear diffusers, *Tr. Vses. Inst. Gidromashinostr.*, vyp. 31, 3–17, 1962.

70. Polotsky, N. D., Energetic characteristics of curvilinear diffusers, *Energomashinostroenie*, no. 3, 12–16, 1964.

71. Reno, –, Johnson, J. P., and Kline, S. J., Characteristics and calculation of plane diffusers with a straight axis, *Teor. Osn. Inzh. Raschyot.*, no. 3, 160–172, Mir Press, 1967 (translated into Russian from *Trans. ASME, Ser. D*).

72. Rozovsky, I. L. and Levin, A. M., On the straight compressible gas flow in a diffuser at subsonic velocities, *Dopov. Akad. Nauk UkrSSR Ser. Tekh. Navul*, no. 4, 50–55, 1948.

73. Romanenko, P. N., Leontiev, A. I., and Oblivin, A. N., Study of the resistance and heat transfer during air motion in diffusers and converging diffusers, in *Teplo-i Massoperenos*, vol. 3, pp. 349–360, Gosenergoizdat, Moscow-Leningrad, 1963.

74. Savin, N. M., Experimental investigation of the dependence of the limiting plane diffuser divergence angle on the relative length and the numbers Re and λ, in *Lopatochyne Mashiny i Struinye Apparaty*, vyp. 4, 10–16, Masinostroenie Press, Moscow, 1970.

75. Sedach, V. S., Muslin, B. K., and Kovalenko, A. A., Hydraulic losses in pulsating flow of a gas through a snail-shaped diffuser, *Izv. VUZov Energ.*, no. 1, 128–132, 1969.

76. Simuni, L. I., Effect of nonisothermicity on separation phenomenon in a plane diffuser, *Tr. Leningr. Politekh. Inst.*, no. 265, 21–23, 1966.

77. Solodkin, E. E. and Guinevsky, A. S., Turbulent flow of a viscous liquid over the starting lengths of axisymmetric and plane channels, *Tr. TsAGI*, vyp. 701, 56, Oborongiz, 1957.

78. Solodkin, E. E. and Guinevsky, A. S., Stabilized turbulent flow of viscous fluid in a plane diffuser channel at small divergence angles, *Tr. BNI MAP*, vyp. 728, 26–39, 1958.

79. Solodkin, E. E. and Ginevsky, A. S., Turbulent flow in the initial section of a diffuser channel, *Tr. BNI MAP*, vyp. 728, 1–25, 1958.

80. Solodkin, E. E. and Guinevsky, A. S., Concerning the problem of the effect of the initial nonuniformity on the characteristics of the diffuser channels, in *Prom. Aerodin.*, no. 12, 1959.

81. Solodkin, E. E. and Guinevsky, A. S., Turbulent nonisothermal flow of a viscous compressible gas in the initial sections of axisymmetric and plane diverging channels with zero pressure gradient, in *Teplo-i Massoperenos*, vol. 1, pp. 189–202, Nauka i Tekhnika Press, Minsk, 1965.

82. Stsilard, K. S., Investigation of diffusers of aerodynamic high velocity tubes, *Tekh. Zametki*, no. 160, 35, TsAGI, 1938.

83. Sadgy, – and Johnson, J. P., Construction and characteristic of two-dimensional curvilinear diffusers, *Teor. Osn. Inzh. Rasch.*, no. 4, 23–44, Mir Press, 1967 (translated into Russian from *Trans. ASME Ser. D*).

84. Tananaev, A. V., Hydraulics of the MHD-Machines, *Atomizdat*, 1970, 209 p.

85. Targ, S. M., Basic Problems of the Theory of Laminar Flows, *Gostekhteorizdat*, 1951, 150 p.

86. Tarshish, M. S., Concerning the coupling between unsteady-state fluid flow losses and the Coriolis and Boussinesq coefficients, in *Methods of the Investigation and Hydraulic Calculation of Water Spilling Hydraulic Engineering Constructions* (Collected papers of the conferences and meetings on hydraulic engineering), pp. 61–64, Leningrad, 1985.

87. Whitemen, –, Reno, –, and Kline, S. J., Effect of the inlet conditions on the characteristics of two-dimensional subsonic diffusers, in *Tekh. Mekhan,* no. 3, 44–58, 1961 (translated into Russian from *Trans. ASME Ser. E*).

88. Fedyaevsky, K. K., Critical review of works on retarded and accelerated turbulent boundary layers, *Tkh. Zametki,* no. 158, 45, TsAGI, 1937.

89. Fendrikov, I. A., Fridlyand, V. Ya., and Yanko, A. K., Study of the change in the charcteristics of a conical diffuser on the flow inlet conditions, *Gidromekhanika (Respubl. Mezhved. Sborn. Akad. Nauk UkrSSR),* pp. 113–117, 1971.

90. Fox, – and Kline, S. J., Flow patterns in curvilinear subsonic diffusers, *Tekh. Mekhan.,* no. 3, 3–19, 1962 (translated into Russian from *Trans. ASME Ser. E*).

91. Frankfurt, M. O., Towards determination of losses in a diffuser with thinner boundary layer by slot suction, in *Prom. Aerodin.,* vyp. 30, 34–40, Mashinostroenie Press, 1973.

92. Frankfurt, M. O., Towards the estimation of losses in a conical diffuser with a large divergence angle, *Prom. Aerodin.,* vyp. 1(33), 168–170, Moscow, 1986.

93. Frankfurt, M. O., Experimental investigation of diffusers with air slot suction from a boundary layer, in *Prom. Aerodin.,* vyp. 30, 41–49, Mashinostroenie Press, 1973.

94. Frankfurt, M. O., Experimental investigation of jet diffusers, *Uch. Zap. TsAGI,* vol. 13, no. 2, 78–86, 1982.

95. Frankfurt, M. O., Experimental investigation of the characteristics of conical diffusers with a tangential blowing, *Prom. Aerodin.,* vyp. 1(33), 158–168, Moscow, 1986.

96. Feil, –, A system of vanes for subsonic diffusers with very large divergence angles, *Teor. Osn. Inzh. Raschyot.,* no. 4, 151–158, Mir Press, 1964 (translated into Russian from *Trans. ASME Ser. D*).

97. Chernyavskiy, L. K. and Gordeyev, N. N., Generalization of experimental data on the losses in straight diffusers with a constant divergence angle, *Teploenergetika,* no. 6, 75–77, 1985.

98. Chernyavskiy, L. K. and Gordeyev, N. N., Generalization of experimental coefficients for the losses of diffusers installed in the system, *Teploenergetika,* no. 10, 72–74, 1986.

99. Sherstyuk, A. N., Investigation of plane diffusers with closed boundary layers at the inlet, *Turbines, Trudy MEI,* vyp. 504, 52–60, 1980.

100. Yanshin, B. I., *Hydraulic Characteristics of Breechblocks and Elements of Pipelines,* Mashinostroenie Press, 1965, 260 p.

101. Ackeret, J., Grenzschichten in geraden und gekrummten Dissusoren, *Int. Union Theor. Angew. Mech. symp.,* Freiburg (Br. 1957), 1958, 130 p.

102. Blau, F., Die Verbesserung des hydraulischen Wirkungrades von Diffusoren mit Rechtekprofile und grossen Öffnungswinkel durch Einbau von Leitblechen oder von Kurzdiffusoren, *Mitt Forschungsanst. Schiffahrt. Wasser und Grundbau,* Berlin, no.9, 5–48, 1963.

103. Bouthier, M. and Cavaille, G., Etude des ecoulements gazeux dans les gaines fortement divergentes, *Bull. Centre Rech. Essais Chatou,* no. 4, 83–93, 1963.

104. Bradshow, P., Performance of a diffuser with fully developed pipe flow at entry, *J. R. Aeronaut. Sco.,* vol. 67, no. 635, 1963, 733 p.

105. Carlson, J. J., Johnson, J. P., and Sagi, C. J., Effects of wall shape on flow regimes and performance in straight two-dimensional diffusers, *Trans. ASME,* vol. D89, no. 1, 151–159, 1967.

106. Cerny, L. C. and Walawender, W. P., The flow of a viscous liquid in a converging tube, *Bull. Math. Biophys.,* vol. 28, no. 1, 11–24, 1966.

107. Cerny, L. C. and Walawender, W. P., Blood flow in rigid tapered tubes, *Am. J. Physiol.,* vol. 210, no. 2, 341–346, 1966.

108. Chaturwedi, M. C., Flow characteristics of axisymmetric expansion, *J. Hydraul. Div. Proc. Am. Soc. Civil. Eng.,* vol. 89, no. 3, part 1, 61–92, 1964.

109. Cocanover, A. B., A Method for Predicting the Performance of Subsonic Diffusers of Several Geometries, Ph.D. thesis, Stanford University, 107 pp.; *Diss. Abstr.,* vol. 26, no. 7, 3831, 1966.

110. Cockrell, D. J., Diamond, M. J., and Jones, C. D., The diffuser inlet flow parameter, *J. R. Aeronaut. Soc.,* vol. 69, no. 652, 275–278, 1965.

111. Cockrell, D. J. and Markland, E., The effects of inlet conditions on incompressible fluid flow through conical diffusers, *J. R. Aeronaut. Soc.,* vol. 66, no. 613, 51–52, 1962.

112. Cockrell, D. J. and Markland, E., A review of incompressible diffuser flow, *Aircraft Eng.,* vol. 35, no. 10, 286–292, 1963.

113. Dönch, T., Divergente und konvergente turbulente Strömungen mit kleinen Öffnungswinkeln, *VDI Forschungsarb.*, no. 282, 1929, 70 p.

114. Eiffel, G., Souffleries aerodynamiques, Resume des principaux travaux executes pendant la guerre au laboratorie aerodynamique, 135–175, 1918.

115. Fernholz, H., Eine grenzschichttheoretische Untersuchung optimalen Unterschalldiffusoren, *Ing. Arch.*, vol. 35, no. 3, 192–201, 1966.

116. Furuya, Y. and Sato, T., Pressure recovery efficiency of short conical diffusers and fevreghened diffusers, *Bull. ISME,* vol. 3, XI, no. 12, 437–443, 1960.

117. Gardel, A., Perte de charge dans un etranglement conique, *Bull. Tech. Suisse Romande,* vol. 88, no. 21, 313–320, 1962.

118. Gibbings, I. C., Flow in contracting ducts, *AIAA J.*, vol. 2, no. 1, 191–192, 1964.

119. Gibson, A., On the flow of water through pipes and passages having converging or diverging boundaries, *Proc. R. Soc.,* vol. 83, 27–37, 1910.

120. Gibson, A., On the resistance to flow of water through pipes or passages having diverging boundaries, *Trans. R. Soc.,* vol. 48, 123–131, 1911.

121. Chose, S. and Kline, S. J., The computation of optimum pressure recovery in two-dimensional diffusers, *J. Fluids Eng.,* vol. 100, 419–426, 1978.

122. Goldsmith, E. L., The effect of internal contraction, initial rate of subsonic diffuser and coil and center body shape on the pressure recovery of a conical center body intake of supersonic speed, *Aeronaut. Res. Counc. Rep. Mem.,* no. 3204, 131–140, 1962.

123. Hackeschmidt, M. and Vogelsang, E., Versuche an Austrittsgehäuse mit neuartigen Diffusoren, *Maschinenbautechnik,* vol. 15, no. 5, 251–257, 1966.

124. Hofmann, A., *Die Energieumsetzung in saugrohrähnlicherweiterten Düsen,Mitteilungen,* no. 4, 75–95, 1931.

125. Imbach, H. E., Beitrag zur Berechnung von rotationssymetrischen turbulenten Diffusorströmungen, Brown Boveri Mitt., vol. 51, no. 12, 784–802, 1964.

126. Jahn, K., Ein Beitrag zum Problem der Siebdiffusoren, *Maschinenbautechnik,* vol. 19, no. 2, 35–45, 1970.

127. Jezowiecka-Kabsch, K., Wplyw ksztaltow dyfuzorow na wysokosc stratthydraulicznych, *Pr. Nauk Inst. Tech. Cieplnej i Aparatury Przen. PW,* sv. 3, 51 s., 1971.

128. Johnston, J. H., The effect of inlet conditions on the flow in annular diffusers, C.O.N. 178, Memo. M 167, no. 1, 21–30, 1953.

129. Johnston, J. P. and Powers, C. A., Some effects of inlet blockage and aspect ratio on diffuser performance, *Trans. ASME,* vol. D91, no.3, 551–553, 1969.

130. Kline, S. J., On the nature of stall, *Trans. ASME Ser. D,* vol. 81, no. 3, 305–320, 1969.

131. Kline, S. J., Moore, C. A., and Cochran, D. L., Wide-angle, diffusers of high performance and diffuser flow mechanisms, *J. Aeronaut. Sci.,* vol. 24, no. 6, 469–470, 1957.

132. Kline, S. J., Abbott, D. E., and Fox, R. W., Optimum design of straight-walled diffusers, *Trans. ASME Ser. D.,* vol. 81, no. 3, 321–331, 1959.

133. Kmonicek, V., Scurgerea subsonica in difusoare conice, *Stud. Cercet. Mec. Apl. Acad. RPP,* Sv. 12, No. 2, S. 383–390, 1961.

134. Kmonicek, V., Ovlivenini cinnosti prostych kuzelovyck difusori vlozenymi telesy, *Strojnicky casop,* sv. 14, no. 5, 484–498, 1963.

135. Kmonicek, V. and Hibs, M., Vysledki experimentalniho a teoretickeho vyzkumu mezikruhovych difusorovych kanalu, Lake, probl. ve stavbe spalov turbin, Praha, SCAU, 371–397, 1962.

136. Toshisuke, K. and Tatsuhiro, U., On the characteristics of divided flow and confluent flow in headers, *Bull. JSME,* no. 52, 138 143, 1969.

137. Levin, L. and Clermont, F., Etude des pertes de charge singulieres dans les convergents coniques, *Le Genie Civil,* vol. 147, no. 10, 11–20, 1970.

138. Liepe, F., Experimentale untersuchungen über den Einfluss des Dralles auf die Stromung in Schlanken Kegeldiffusoren, *Wiss. Z. TH, Dresden,* vol. 8, no. 2, 330–335, 1962.

139. Liepe, F. and Jahn, K., Untere Wirkungsgrade von Kegel diffusoren, *Maschinenbautechnik,* no. 11, 41–52, 1962.

140. Limberg, H., Scurgerea de intrare laminara intr-un canal convergent, *Stud. Cercet. Mec. Apl. Acad. RPR,* vol. 12, no. 1, 3–10, 1961.

141. Linneken, H., Betrachtungen uber Wirkungsgrade gasdurchstromter Diffusoren, *Konstruktion,* vol. 15, no. 7, 10–17,1963.

142. Livesey, J. L. and Turner, J. T., The dependence of diffuser performance upon inlet flow conditions, *J. R. Aeronaut. Sco.,* vol. 69, no. 6159, 794–795, 1965.

143. Livesey, J. L. and Hugh, T., Some preliminary results for conical diffusers with high subsonic entry Mach numbers, *J. Mech. Eng. Soc.,* vol. 8, no. 4, 384–391, 1966.

144. Lau, W. T. F., An analytical method for the design of two-dimensional contractions, *J. R. Aeronaut. Soc.,* vol. 68, no. 637, 59–62, 1964.

145. Markland, E. and North, F., *Performance of Conical Diffusers Up the Choking Condition,* Proc. 6th Conf. Fluid Machinery, Budapest, Vol. 2, 703–713, 1979.

146. Mathieson, R. and Lee, R. A., Diffusers with boundary layer suction, *Int. Assoc. Hydraul. Res. 10th Congr., London,* vol. 4, no. 249, 81–88, 1964.

147. McDonald, A. T. and Fox, R. W., An experimental investigation of incompressible flow in conical diffusers, *Pap. Am. Soc. Mech. Eng.,* no. FE-25, 9 p. 1966.

148. McDonald, A. T., Fox, R. W., and Dewoestine, R. V., Effects of swirling inlet flow on pressure recovery in conical diffusers, *AIAA J.,* vol. 9, no. 10, 2014–2018, 1971.

149. Naumann, Efficiency of diffusers on high subsonic speeds, Reports and Transactions, no. 11, A, 1–20, June 1964.

150. Nikuradse, I., Untersuchungen uber die Stromungen des Wassers in konvergenten und divergenten Kanalen, *VDI Forschungsarb.,* no. 289, 1929, 60 p.

151. Patterson, G., Modern diffuser design, *Aircraft Eng.,* 1–15, 1938.

152. Peryez, S., Der Einfluss des Diffusorwirkungsgarde auf den Austrittverlust im Dampfturbinen, *Brennst. Waerme Kraft,* Vol. 13, no. 9, 9–15, 1961.

153. Peters, H., Energieumsetzung in Querscnittserweiterung bei verschiedenen Zulaufbedingungen, *Ing. Arch.,* no. 1, 7–29, 1931.

154. Pohl, K., Strömungverhaltnisse in einen Diffusor mit vorgeschalteten Krummer, *Ing. Arch.,* no. 29, 21–28, 1960.

155. Polzin, J., Strömungsuntersuchungen an einem ebenen Diffusor, *Ing. Arch.,* no. 5, 30–49, 1950.

156. Prechter, H. P., Gesichtspunkte sur Auslegung von Diffusoren unter Berúcksichtigung neuerer Forschungsergebnisse, *Der. Maschinenmarkt,* vol. 13, no. 82, 31–39, 1961.

157. Raghunathan, S. and Kar, S., Theory and performance of conical diffuser exit duct combinations, *Pap. Am. Soc. Mech. Eng.,* vol. NWA/FE-45, 1968, 8 p.

158. Rao, D. M., A method of flow stabilization with high pressure recovery in short conical diffusers, *Aeronaut. J.,* vol. 75, no. 725, 336–339, 1971.

159. Rao, P. V. and Dass, H. S., Design and testing of streamline shapes for axisymmetric diffuser, *J. Inst. Eng. India,* Vol. 62, pt. ME 2, 39–46, 1981.

160. Rao, D. M. and Raju, K. N., The use of splitters for flow control in wide angle conical diffusers, *Tech. Note. Nat. Aeronaut. Lab. Bangalore,* no. AE-26, 1964, 19 p.

161. Rao, D. H. and Raju, K. N., Experiments on the use of screens and splitters in a wide-angle conical diffuser, *Tech. Note Nat. Aeronaut. Lab. Bangalore,* no. AE-24, 1964, 23 p.

162. Rao, P., Samba, S., Vyas, B. D., and Raghunathan, S., Effect of inlet circulation on the performance of subsonic straight conical diffusers, *Ind. J. Technol.,* vol. 9, no. 4, 135–137, 1971.

163. Ringleb, F. O., Two-dimensional flow with standing vortexes in ducts and diffusers, *Trans. ASME Ser. D.* vol. 82, no. 4, 921–927, 1960.

164. Robertson, J. M. and Fraser, N. R., Separation prediction for conical diffusers, *Trans. ASME Ser. D.,* vol. 82, no. 1, 135–145, 1960.

165. Robertson, J. M. and Fraser, H. R., Investigation of the boundary layer stall in a conical diffuser, *Trans. ASME,* vol. 81, no. 1, 35–43, 1961.

166. Runstadler, P. W. and Dean, R. C., Straight channel diffusor performance at high inlet Mach nubmers, *Pap, Am. Soc. Mech. Eng.,* NWA/FE-19, 1968, 16 p.

167. Sagi, J., The design and performance of two-dimensional curved subsonic diffusers, *Diss. Abstr.,* vol. B.28, no. 7, 1968.

168. Schlichting, H. and Gersten, K., Berechnung der Strömung in rotationssymmetrischen Diffusoren mit Hilfe der Grenzschichttheorie, *Z. Flugwiss.,* vol. 9, no. 4, 5, 18–27, 1961.

169. Sharan, W. Kr., Improving diffuser performance by artificial means, *AIAA J.,* vol. 10, no. 8, 1105–1106, 1972.

170. Siedschlag, H. J., Die Strömung in Diffusoren Verschiedener Querschnittsformen, *Wiss. Z. Tech. Univ. Dresden,* vol. 12, no. 1, 85–96, 1963.

171. Sisojev, V., O stepenu korisnog dejstva nadzvue difozora aerotunela, *Tehnika,* sv. 16, no. 3, 100–104, 1961.

172. Sokwan, L., Vortex phenomena in a conical diffuser, *AIAA J.,* vol. 5, no. 6, 1072–1078, 1967.

173. Sprenger, H., Messungen an Diffusoren, *Z. Angew. Math. Phys.,* vol.7, no. 4, 372–374, 1957.

174. Sprenger, H., Experimentelle Untersuchungen an geraden und gekrummten Diffusoren, *Mitt. Inst. Aerodyn (ETH Zurich),* vol. 84, no. 27, 1959.

175. Stock, H. W., Compressible turbulent flows in long circular cross-section diffusers of large area ratio, *Z. Flugwiss. Weltraumforsch,* Bd. 9, Heft 3, S. 143–155, 1985.

176. Stull, F. D. and Velkoff, H. R., Effects of transverse ribs on pressure recovery in two-dimensional subsonic diffusers, *AIAA Pap.,* no. 1141, 1972, 11 p.

177. Squire, H. B., Experiments on conical diffuser, Reports and Memoranda, no. 2751, 41–60, November 1950.

178. Stevens, S. G. and Markland, E., The effect of inlet conditions on the performance of two annular diffusers, *Pap. Am. Soc. Mech. Eng.,* NWA/FE-38, 1968, 15 p.

179. Stratford, B. S. and Tubbs, H., The maximum pressure rise attainable in subsonic diffusers, *J. R. Aeronaut. Soc.,* vol. 69, no. 652, 275–278, 1965.

180. Szablewski, W., Turbulente Strömungen in divergenten Kanalen mittlerer und starker Druckanstieg, *Ing. Arch.,* vol. 22, no. 4, 268–281, 1954.

181. Winter, H., Strömungsverhältnisse in einem Diffusor mit vorgeschalteten Krummer, *Maschinenbau Warmenwirtschaft,* no. 2, 38–49, 1953.

182. Winternitz, F. A. L. and Ramsay, W. J., Effect of inlet boundary layer on pressure recovery, energy conversion and losses in conical diffusers, *J. R. Aeronaut. Soc.,* vol. 61, no. 554, 15–23, 1957.

183. Wolf, S. and Johnson, J. P., Effects of nonuniform inlet velocity profiles on flow regimes and performance in two-dimensional diffusers, *Pap. Am. Soc. Mech. Eng.,* no. WA/FE-25, 1969, 13 p.

184. Wu, J. H. T., On a two-dimensional perforated intake diffuser, *Aerosp. Eng.,* vol. 21, VII, no. 7, 13–19, 1962.

185. Van Dewoestine, R. V. and Fox, R. W., An experimental investigation of the effect of subsonic inlet Mach number on the performance of conical diffusers, *Int. J. Mech. Sci.,* vol. 8, no. 12, 759–769, 1966.

186. Villeneuve, F., Contribution a l'etunde de l'ecoulement dans on diffuseur a six degres, *Publ. Sci. Tehc. Minist. Air,* no. 397, 1963, 69 p.

RESISTANCE TO FLOW WITH CHANGES OF THE STREAM DIRECTION
Resistance Coefficients of Curved Segments— Elbows, Bends, etc.

6-1 EXPLANATIONS AND PRACTICAL RECOMMENDATIONS

1. Bending of a flow in curved tubes and channels (elbows, bends, and bypasses*) results in the appearance of centrifugal forces directed from the center of curvature to the outer wall of the tube. This causes an increase of the pressure at the outer wall and its decrease at the inner wall, when the flow passes from the straight to the curved section of the pipe (until it is completely turned). Therefore, the flow velocity will correspondingly be lower at the outer wall and larger at the inner wall (Figure 6-1). Thus, in this bend a diffuser effect occurs near the outer wall and a bellmouth effect occurs near the inner wall. The passage of flow from the curved into the straight section, after turning, is accompanied by these effects in the reverse order: by a diffuser effect near the inner wall and by a bellmouth effect near the outer wall.

2. The diffuser phenomena lead to corresponding flow separation from both walls. In this case, separation from the inner wall is intensified by inertial forces acting in the curved zone in the direction toward the outer wall. An eddy zone, formed as a result of flow separation from the inner wall, propagates far ahead and across, greatly reducing the cross section of the main stream.

3. The appearance of centrifugal forces and the presence of boundary layers at the walls explain the occurrence of a secondary (transverse) flow in a curved tube, i.e., the formation

---

*Bypasses are meant to be curved sections in which the inner and outer walls represent arcs of concentric circles with inlet and outlet cross sections being equal:

$$r_0 \geq 0 \quad \text{and} \quad r_1 = r_0 + b_0$$

where r_0 is the radius of curvature of the inner walls and r_1 is the radius of curvature of the outer wall. Since the two walls have the same center of curvature, the bend is characterized by the radius of curvature R_0 of its axis when $R_0/b_0 \geq 0.5$.

Elbows are meant to be curved sections, the curvatures of the inner and outer walls of which are not arcs of concentric circles.

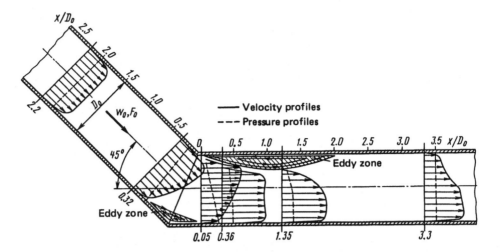

Figure 6-1 Variation of velocity and pressure profiles in an elbow and a straight section downstream.

of the so-called vortex pair, which is superimposed on the main stream parallel to the channel axis and imparts a helical shape to the streamlines (Figure 6-2).

4. The main portion of pressure losses in curved tubes is due to formation of eddies at the inner wall, and this, together with the secondary flows, determines the nature of the velocity distribution downstream of the bend.

The magnitude of the resistance coefficient of curved tubes and the flow structure within them vary under the influence of both the factors governing the degree of flow turbulence and the inlet velocity profile shape. These factors and the Reynolds number Re = $w_0 D_h / \nu$; relative roughness of walls $\bar{\Delta} = \Delta / D_h$; inlet conditions: relative length of the straight starting section l_0 / D_0,* relative distance from the preceding shaped piece, etc.; and geometric parameters of the tube, i.e., the angle of the bend δ, the relative radius of curvature r/D_0 or R_0/D_0 (R_0/b_0) (Figure 6-3), the aspect ratio (relative elongation) a_0/b_0, the ratio of the inlet area to the exit area F_1/F_0, etc.

5. Other conditions being equal, the curved tube offers the largest resistance in the case when the curvature at the inner wall is a sharp corner; the flow separates from this wall most vigorously. At the angle of bend $\delta = 90°$, the region of flow separation at the inner wall downstream of the bend amounts to 0.5 of the tube width. Hence, the intensity of eddy (vortex) formation and the resistance of the curved tube (channel) increase, with an increase in the angle of the bend. Rounding of the elbow corners (especially of the inner corner) makes the flow separation much smoother and, consequently, lowers the resistance.

*Here l_0/D_0 is the length of the straight section downstream of a smooth inlet (collector).

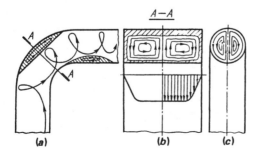

A–A

(a)   (b)   (c)

Figure 6-2 Vortex pair in an elbow: (*a*) longitudinal section; (*b*) cross section (rectangular channel); (*c*) cross section (of a circular tube).

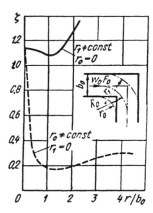

Figure 6-3 Scheme of rounding of an elbow and the dependence of the resistance coefficient of an elbow on the curvature radius r/b_0.

6. If the outer of the elbow is left sharp (radius of the outer curvature $r_1 = 0$)and only the inner corner is rounded, an increase in the radius of inner curvature r_0, then the minimal resistance of the elbow with a 90° bend will be attained at $r_0/b_0 = 1.2$–1.5. With a further increase in r_0/b_0, the resistance will grow noticeably. Such an increase in the resistance is due to the fact that if the inner corner is rounded, the cross-sectional area at the place of bending increases considerably, and hence the velocity decreases. This intensifies the diffuser separation of flow, originating at the place of transition from the starting length into the elbow.

7. Rounding the outer corner and keeping the inner corner sharp ($r_0 = 0$) does not lead to a noticeable decrease in the elbow resistance. A significant increase in the radius of curvature of the outer wall even causes an increase in the elbow resistance. This indicates that it is undesirable to round the outer wall alone (with the inner corner kept sharp), since then the cross-sectional area of the flow decreases at the place of flow turning and increases the diffuser losses, which originate during flow passage from the elbow to the exit section of the pipe.

The minimum resistance is achieved by an elbow for which $r_1/b_0 = r_0/b_0 + 0.6$ (an elbow of the optimum shape), while the resistance close to the minimum is offered by a bend or by a "normal" elbow for which $r_1/b_0 = r_0/b_0 + 1.0$. Since a bend is technically more easily achieved, it can supplant an optimal elbow in the majority of cases.

8. The resistance of right-angle elbows can be greatly reduced by installing a fairing on the inner corner (see Diagram 6-10). The optimum value of the relative curvature radii of the fairing amounts to $r_0/b_0 = 0.45$. If such a fairing is installed, the resistance coefficient of the elbow bend ($\delta = 90°$) diminishes from $\zeta = 1.15$ to $\zeta = 0.55$.[30]

Rounding of the outer corner of the elbow with the radius $r_1/b_0 = 0.45$ additionally reduces the losses by 5%, i.e., up to $\zeta = 0.49$.

Reduction in the elbow resistance can also be attained by beveling (along the chord) sharp corners of the bend (especially the inner corner; see Diagram 6-10).

9. A change in the ratio of the areas F_1/F_0 of the entrance to and exit from the elbow changes its resistance. With an increase in the cross-sectional area downstream of the bend, the diffuser effect increases, which intensifies the flow separation and the formation of vortices (increases the eddy zone). At the same time, when the discharge is constant, the flow velocity in the exit section decreases. The effect of the velocity decrease, expressed as a decrease in the pressure losses, is greater (with the increase in the ratio F_1/F_0 up to certain limits) than the effect of the increasing eddy zone, which leads to higher losses. As a result, the total losses in the elbow of enlarged cross section decrease within certain limits.

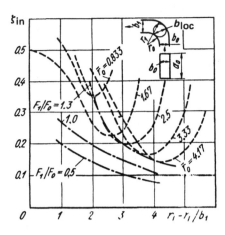

Figure 6-4 Dependence of ζ_{in} of elbows with $\delta = 90°$ on r_1/b_0 at different values of r_0/b_0.[77]

10. The resistance of straight elbows ($\delta = 90°$) with sharp corners is minimum for the ratio F_1/F_0 lying within 1.2–2.0. In elbows and bends with smooth turns the optimal ratio F_1/F_0 is closer to unity; in some cases it is even less than unity, which is clearly seen in Figure 6-4. The internal resistance coefficient* ζ_{in} of plane bends with $\delta = 90°$ and height-to-width ratio $a_0/b_0 = 2.4$ depends on the relative curvature radius of the outer wall r_1/b_0 at different values of the relative curvature radius of the inner wall r_0/b_0. The envelope of the curves $\zeta = f(r_0/b_0, r_1/b_0)$, over the whole range of values of r_0/b_0 and r_1/b_0, is higher for the diffuser channel when $F_1/F_0 = 1.3$ and lower when $F_1/F_0 = 0.5$. The intermediate position is occupied by a channel of constant cross section ($F_1/F_0 = 1.0$).

Figure 6-4 can provide guidelines for the choice of optimal relationships between r_0/b_0 and r_1/b_0 of plane branches with $\delta = 90°$.

In the absence of data on the resistance of elbows and expanding bends, it is possible to neglect a decrease in the pressure losses within the above limits of F_1/F_0 and to assume that the resistance coefficient is the same as for $F_1/F_0 = 1$. An increase in the resistance at values of F_1/F_0 differing substantially from the optimal values should not be neglected.

11. The resistance of curved tubes (channels) decreases with an increase in the relative elongation of the cross-sectional area of the elbow a_0/b_0 and increases when a_0/b_0 decreases within the limits of less than unity.

12. In the majority of cases, for the convenience of engineering calculations, the total resistance coefficient of elbows and bends is determined as the sum of the coefficient of local resistance of the bend ζ_{loc} and the friction coefficient ζ_{fr}:

$$\zeta = \zeta_{loc} + \zeta_{fr}$$

where $\zeta_{fr} = \lambda(l/D_h)$ is calculated as ζ for straight sections with λ taken from Diagrams 2-1 through 2-6 as a function of the Reynolds number and of the relative roughness $\overline{\Delta} = \Delta/D_h$; l is the length of the elbow or bend measured along the axis.

The ratio

$$\frac{l}{D_h} = \pi \frac{\delta°}{180°} \frac{R_0}{D_h} = 0.0175 \frac{R_0}{D_h} \delta°$$

*The internal resistance coefficient ζ_{in} is determined as the ratio of the difference of total pressures at the entrance and exit from the bend to the velocity pressure at the entrance. It does not consider the additional losses that would have occurred in a straight exit section downstream of the bend due to further equalization of the velocity profile distorted when the flow turns in the branch.

Then

$$\zeta_{fr} = 0.0175 \frac{R_0}{D_h} \delta\lambda$$

13. The coefficient of local resistance of branches is calculated from the formula suggested by Abramovich:[1]*

$$\zeta_{loc} \equiv \frac{\Delta p}{\rho w_0^2/2} - A_1 B_1 C_1 \qquad (6\text{-}1)$$

where A_1 is the coefficient that allows for the effect of the angle of the bend δ; B_1 is the coefficient that allows for the effect of the relative curvature radius of the bend R_0/D_0 (R_0/b_0); and C_1 is the coefficient that allows for the effect of the relative elongation of the bend cross section a_0/b_0.

The value of A_1 can be determined from the data of Nekrasov:[31]

at $\delta = 90°$ $A_1 = 1.0$

at $\delta < 70°$ $A_1 = 0.9 \sin \delta$

at $\delta > 100°$ $A_1 = 0.7 + 0.35 \dfrac{\delta}{90}$

or from graph a of Diagram 6-1.

The value of B_1 can be calculated from the approximate formulas:**

at $\dfrac{R_0}{D_0} \left(\dfrac{R_0}{b_0}\right) < 1.0$ $B_1 = \dfrac{0.21}{(R_0/D_0)^{0.25}}$

at $\dfrac{R_0}{D_0} \left(\dfrac{R_0}{b_0}\right) \geq 1.0$ $B_1 = \dfrac{0.21}{\sqrt{R_0/D_0}}$

or from graphs b and c of Diagram 6-1. The value of C_1 is determined from graph d of Diagram 6-1.

14. The total resistance of very smooth curvilinear tubes and channels (bends, coils) ($R_0/D_0 \geq 3.0$) can be considered as an increased friction coefficient at which the resistance coeffficient is dependent not only on the Reynolds number and roughness, but also on the relative curvature radius R_0/D_0 (R_0/b_0) or on the parameter $\text{Re}\sqrt{2R_0/D_0}$:

$$\zeta = f\left(\text{Re}, \overline{\Delta}, \frac{R_0}{D_0}, \text{Re}\sqrt{\frac{2R_0}{D_0}}\right)$$

Here $\zeta = \lambda_{cur}(l/D_h) = 0.0175(R_0/D_0)\delta\lambda_{cur}$, where λ_{cur} is the coefficient of hydraulic friction of a curved channel (bend).

---

*Abramovich's formula contains a numerical factor 0.73, which is included here in the quantity B_1.

**For a rectangular cross section R_0/D_0 should be replaced by R_0/b_0.

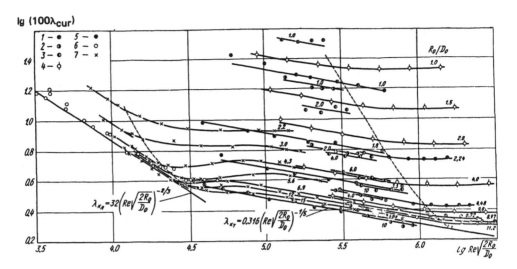

Figure 6-5 Resistance coefficient λ_{el} of smooth 90° bends as a function of the dimensionless parameter $\mathrm{Re}\sqrt{2R_0/D_0}$:[56] 1, Ito, $D_0 = 35$ mm, brass; 2, Goffman, $D_0 = 43$ mm, brass; 3, Goffman, $D_0 = 43$ mm, rough brass; 4, Tsimerman, $D_0 = 50$ mm, steel; 5, Gregorik, $D_0 = 89.3$ mm, steel; 6, Idelchik, smooth; 7, Lee, $D_0 = 26$ mm, steel.

15. The dependence of the hydraulic friction coefficient of smoothly curved tubes (bends), λ_{cur}, on $\mathrm{Re}\sqrt{2R_0/D_0}$, R_0/D_0, and $\bar{\Delta}$, established by various authors (Figure 6-5), points to the existence of a close analogy for such tubes with straight tubes (see Chapter 2). In this case, four flow regimes are possible.

The first regime, within the limits up to $\mathrm{Re} = 6.5 \times 10^3$, is laminar. It is characterized by the condition where the straight lines of resistance for different R_0/D_0 and $\bar{\Delta}$ are parallel to each other and form a sharp angle with the abscissa $\ln \mathrm{Re}\sqrt{2R_0/D_0}$.

The second regime, with $6.5 \times 10^3 < \mathrm{Re} < 4 \times 10^4$, is a transition regime. The coefficient λ_{cur} under these conditions is practically independent of the Reynolds number.

The third regime is turbulent, which corresponds to $4 \times 10^4 < \mathrm{Re} < 3 \times 10^5$. The resistance curves of smooth bends exhibit behavior similar to that of the resistance curves of straight commercial pipes (with nonuniform roughness) in the transition region (see Diagram 2-4): they decline smoothly with an increase in the parameter $\mathrm{Re}\sqrt{2R_0/D_0}$. Besides, for different R_0/D_0 and $\bar{\Delta}$ these curves are also parallel to each other.

The fourth regime is observed at $\mathrm{Re} > 3 \times 10^5$; the curves $\lambda_{cur} = f(\mathrm{Re}\sqrt{2R_0/D_0})$ are parallel to the abscissa so that λ_{cur} practically ceases to depend on Re and remains a function of R_0/D_0 and $\bar{\Delta}$ alone.

16. For smooth curved tubes (made of glass, brass, lead, rubber, steel at $\bar{\Delta} < 0.0002$, etc.) at any δ, including spirals (coils), the value of λ_{cur} up to $\mathrm{Re} \approx 10^5$ can be calculated from the following equation* (see also Diagram 6-2):

$$\lambda_{cur} = \frac{a}{\mathrm{Re}^n(2R_0/D_0)^m} \tag{6-2}$$

*Equation (6-2) was derived by Aronov[3,4] on the basis of his experiments and those of Adler[51] and White.[95] Data close to the values of λ_{cur} obtained by Aronov are given in the works of Kvitkovsky,[24] Koshelev et al.,[27] Mazurov and Zakharov,[28] and Shchukin[48] et al.

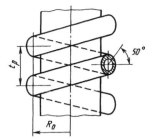

Figure 6-6 Schematic representation of the winding of a helical tube.

17. Analogous formulas have been obtained for curvilinear channels of square cross section[84] (see Diagram 6-2). Formulas for the rectangular cross section of different orientation differ somewhat: the value of λ_{cur} can be calculated from the formulas suggested by Dementiyev and Aronov[12] (see also Diagram 6-2):

at $Re = (0.5–7) \times 10^3$

$$\lambda_{cur} = [1.97 + 49.1(D_h/2R_0)^{1.32}(b/h)^{0.37}]Re^{-0.46} = A_{lam}Re^{-0.46}$$

or

$$\lambda_{cur}/A_{lam} = Re^{-0.46}$$

at $Re = (7–38) \times 10^3$

$$\lambda_{cur} = [0.316 + 8.65(D_h/2R_0)^{1.32}(b/h)^{0.34}]Re^{-0.25} = A_{tur}Re^{-0.25}$$

or

$$\lambda_{cur}/A_{tur} = Re^{-0.25}$$

18. Within the limits of the suberitical Dean number which is determined approximately from the formula[89]

$$(De)_{cr} = 2 \times 10^4(D_h/2R_0)^{0.82}$$

{where $R_0' = R_0[1 + t_p/(2\pi R_0)^2]$; t_p is the spiral pitch (Figure 6-6)}, it is possible to use the following single formula for calculating the hydraulic friction coefficient λ_{cur} which will be valid for any cross-sectional shape of a curvilinear channel (circular, rectangular, quadratic, and elliptical):[89]

$$\lambda_{cur} = 0.1008f(\gamma)(Re\sqrt{D_h/2R_0})^{0.5}[1 + 3.945f(\gamma)(Re\sqrt{D_h/2R_0})^{-0.5}$$

$$+ 7.782f(\gamma)(Re\sqrt{D_h/2R_0})^{-1} + 9.097f(\gamma)(Re\sqrt{D_h/2R_0})^{-1.5}$$

$$+ 5.608f(\gamma)(Re\sqrt{D_h/2R_0})^{-2}]$$

where $\lambda = f(\mathrm{Re})$ is the hydraulic friction coefficient determined for the given cross-sectional shape of the channel from the corresponding diagrams of Chapter 2; $\gamma = b_0/a_0$ is the ratio of the channel cross section axes;

for the rectangular cross section

$$f(\gamma) = D_h/2 \quad \text{at} \quad \gamma < 1$$

$$f(\gamma) = 2/D_h \quad \text{at} \quad \gamma > 1$$

for the elliptical cross section

$$f(\gamma) = 2\gamma/(\gamma + 1) \quad \text{at} \quad \gamma < 1$$

$$f(\gamma) = (\gamma + 1)/(2\gamma) \quad \text{at} \quad \gamma > 1$$

19. The coefficient of local resistance of elbows with sharp corners can be calculated for the entire range of angles $0 \leq \delta \leq 180°$ from the equation

$$\zeta_{\mathrm{loc}} \equiv \frac{\Delta p}{\rho w_0^2/2} = C_1 A \zeta'$$

where ζ' is determined by Weisbach's equation:[92]

$$\zeta' = 0.95 \sin^2 \frac{\delta}{2} + 2.05 \sin^4 \frac{\delta}{2}$$

A is the correction factor, which is obtained from the experimental data of Richter[79] and Schubart[81] and is determined from the curve $A = f(\delta)$ of Diagram 6-5.

20. The local resistance coefficients of any elbows and bends can be considered constant and independent of the Reynolds number only when $\mathrm{Re} > 2 \times 10^5$–$3 \times 10^5$. At lower values of this number, it influences the resistance value and this influence increases with decreasing values of Re. This is particularly true of bends, as well as of elbows with smooth inner curvature.

21. The dependence $\zeta = f(\mathrm{Re})$ is complex and, according to the author's data,[16,17] its character is mainly determined by a change in the flow regime in the boundary layer. In particular, in bends with $R_0/b_0 = 0.55$–1.5, especially when the bends are installed close to the smooth entrance, the phenomenon is similar to that observed for a flow around a cylinder or a sphere.

22. Starting with very small values of the Reynolds number, the coefficient of total resistance* ζ_{tot} of the bend drops at $R_0/b_0 \approx 0.5$–1.5, reaching the first minimum at about $\mathrm{Re} = 5 \times 10^4$ (Figure 6-7). Following this, there is a slight increase in ζ_{tot} until it reaches the value corresponding to $\mathrm{Re}_{\mathrm{cr}}$ (in this case at about 10^5), at which there occurs a sharp drop in the resistance coefficient (the resistance crisis in the transition regime) until the second minimum at $\mathrm{Re} = 0.2$–2.5×10^5 (developed or postcritical regime), whereupon there follows a slight increase in the resistance coefficient.

23. At relatively small Reynolds numbers (approximately up to $\mathrm{Re} = 10^5$), the boundary layer is laminar in a bend installed close to a smooth entrance; therefore at moderately large

---

*The coefficient ζ_{tot} also includes the velocity pressure losses at the exit from the bend into the atmosphere.

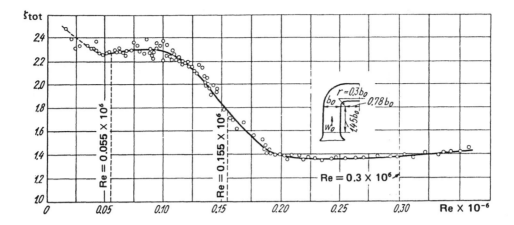

Figure 6-7 Dependence of the total resistance coefficient ζ_{tot} on the Reynolds number for a bend with $\delta = 90°$ and smooth walls ($\overline{\Delta} = 0.00003$).[17]

R_0/b_0 the separation of the flow from the walls of the inner curvature is laminar. The critical Reynolds number, at which ζ_{tot} starts to decrease, is characterized by transition from laminar to turbulent flow. Turbulization of the separated boundary layer, which leads to an intensified momentum exchange between separate fluid particles, causes the jet expansion in this layer resulting in the contraction of the inner eddy zone (Figure 6-8).

24. As the Reynolds number increases, the transition point moves progressively upstream, while the separated boundary layer expands until it again clings to the inner wall of the bend. However, the centrifugal forces in the turning region prevent the layer from adhering to the entire curvature of the bend, causing the flow to separate again from the wall, but this time it is the separation of a turbulent layer at a larger distance from the inner curvature (see Figure 6-8).

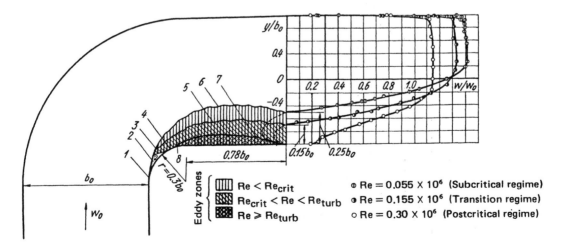

Figure 6-8 Regions of flow separation from the inner wall and distribution of velocities over the mean line of the cross section of a bend with smooth walls at different flow regimes:[17] 1, point of laminar separation; 2, "dead" zone; 3, transition point; 4, point of reattachment of the separated layer; 5, turbulent expansion of the separated layer; 6 and 7, lower boundary of the separated laminar and turbulent layers, respectively; 8, point of turbulent separation.

25. In the first instant after the reattachment of the layer, a closed eddy zone is formed between the point of laminar separation and the point of flow attachment. With further increase in Re, this zone disappears completely, when the transition point coincides with the point of laminar separation. This moment corresponds to completion of the transition flow regime, subsequent to which the resistance coefficient does not decrease any further and takes on almost a constant value. In the case considered, it occurs at Re = 2–2.5 × 10^5.

26. Separation of the laminar layer at the point closest to the beginning of the curvature of the bend naturally produces the most extensive eddy zone at the inner wall (see Figure 6-8). As the transition point approaches the point of laminar separation, this zone compresses. The zone has the smallest dimensions during turbulent separation at the point furthest removed from the beginning of the curvature.

27. The effect of the Reynolds number on the local resistance coefficient of bends and elbows at Re $\geqslant 10^4$ is accounted for by the coefficients k_{Re} in the expressions for the local resistance coefficients ζ_{loc} on respective diagrams. The values of k_{Re} are represented by the curves of k_{Re} vs. Re,[17,88] which, pending further refinement, are taken tentatively for all angles δ.

28. The resistance coefficient ζ_{loc} at Re < 2 × 10^3 can be determined from the formula suggested by Zubov:[13]

$$\zeta_{loc} = (k_1 + 1)\zeta_{sim.loc} + A/Re$$

where $\zeta_{sim.loc}$ is the value of ζ_{loc} at Re > 2 × 10^5 (similarity region); k_1 is the correction factor; for an elbow with a recess

$\delta°$ ...	30	45	75	90
k_1	6.0	3.6	1.5	1.3

A is a coefficient that depends on the geometric parameters of the elbow (bend), on R_0/D_0 in particular; according to some data (see e.g., Reference 2), for an elbow of 90° $A \approx 400$; for a 135° elbow, $A \approx 600$; at Re $\leqslant 10^3$ for a 90° elbow, $r/D_0 = 2.6$, $A \approx 1300$; for a 180° elbow, $r/D_0 = 1.5–2.0$, $A \approx 1200$.

29. The influence of fluid compressibility at large subsonic flow velocities on the resistance of curved channels can be taken into account by the coefficient k_λ, which can be determined from the following empirical formula obtained[74] by processing the results of experimental investigations of some types of elbows and bends:

$$k_\lambda \equiv \zeta_\lambda/\zeta = 1 + \alpha_1\lambda_c$$

where $\lambda_c \equiv w_{av}/a_{cr}$ is the reduced flow velocity at the entrance into a curved channel; $w_{av} = (1/2)(w_0 + w_1)$; k_λ and ζ are the resistance coefficients of the curved channel, respectively, at the given subsonic value of λ_c and at its small value determined from the graphs in the corresponding diagrams of the present chapter; α_1 and β are constants the values of which are given in Diagram 6-4. It is evident that $\zeta_\lambda \equiv k_\lambda\zeta$.

30. The condition of the inner surface (uniform or local roughness, roughness over the whole surface or over a part of it) of elbows and bends, just before the curvature at large Reynolds numbers,[17] has a greater effect on the local resistance coefficient than on the friction coefficient. At small Re the resistance coefficient of a bend, the inner wall of which has a different degree of roughness, barely differs from ζ_{tot} of a bend with a smooth inner

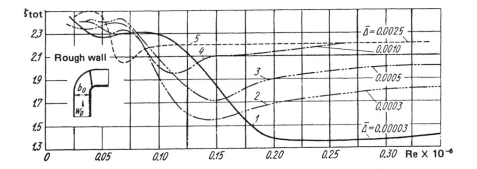

Figure 6-9 Resistance curves $\zeta_{tot} = f(\mathrm{Re})$ of the bend with different relative roughness of the surface of the entire inner wall:[17] 1, smooth walls; 2, rolling paper; 3, poster stamped paper; 4, emery paper no. 140; 5, emery paper no. 60.

wall (Figure 6-9). As Re increases, the resistance coefficient decreases sharply; at some value of this number, ζ_{tot} attains the minimum and then increases again.

31. The critical Reynolds number, at which the minimum value of ζ_{tot} is achieved, and the Reynolds number at which ζ_{tot} starts to increase again depend on the relative roughness $\overline{\Delta} = \Delta/D_h$. The larger $\overline{\Delta}$, the smaller are the above values of Re and the larger are the corresponding minimum values of ζ_{tot} and of ζ_{tot}, which are achieved at large Re (under selfsimilar conditions).

32. As long as the Reynolds number is small, the laminar boundary layer is so thick that it almost completely covers the asperities of roughness (Figure 6-10*a*) and they negligibly influence the state of the flow. As a result, the boundary layer, which has separated from the inner curvature of the bend, remains laminar, while the value of the resistance of the bend with rough walls virtually resembles the value of ζ_{tot} of the bend with smooth walls.

33. As the value of Re increases, the boundary layer becomes thinner and the asperities of roughness partially start to protrude (Figure 6-10*b*) and agitate the flow. When compared with a smooth wall, the point of laminar-to-turbulent boundary-layer flow transition is displaced closer to the beginning of the bend curvature and turbulent separation occurs earlier; i.e., both the critical Reynolds number, at which the resistance coefficient starts to decrease, and the value of Re at which the minimum value of ζ_{tot} is attained, decrease.

34. As the Reynolds number increases further, the thickness of the boundary layer progressively diminishes and the asperities protrude even more from the layer, causing local stalls of the flow (Figure 6-10*c*), owing to which the turbulent point of separation from the inner wall moves upstream. This displacement of the separation point naturally leads to expansion of the eddy region and again to an increase in the resistance coefficient of the bend. The greater the relative roughness, the earlier and more vigorous is its effect. Consequently, the earlier the minimum of resistance is reached, the larger is the value of this minimum and the value of ζ_{tot} at large Reynolds numbers.

35. The resistance coefficient of the bend is affected primarily by the state of the surface of the inner wall. The roughness of the remaining three walls has virtually no influence on the value of ζ_{tot} (Figure 6-11).

36. In case of partial (local) roughness or local asperities on the inner wall of the bend, the curves of the resistance coefficient of bends are smoother (without a marked minimum). The value of ζ_{tot} at large Reynolds numbers is larger, the closer the asperity is to the start of the curvature of the bend and the larger its dimensions are (Figure 6-12).

37. When elbows and bends are not smoothly rounded, i.e., when there are very small relative radii of internal rounding within the limits $0 < r/D_0 < 0.05$ ($0.5 < R_0/D_0 < 0.55$),

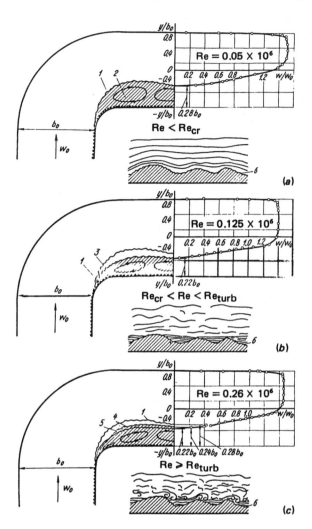

Figure 6-10 Regions of flow sepration and velocity distributions over the mean line of the cross section of a bend with rough wall ($\overline{\Delta} = 0.001$) under different flow conditions:[17] (*a* and *c*) laminar and turbulent flow, respectively, over asperities of roughness; (*b*) transition regime: 1, lower boundary of the separated laminar layer at $\mathrm{Re} < \mathrm{Re}_{cr}$; 2, laminar separation; 3, turbulent expansion of the separated layer at $\mathrm{Re}_{cr} < \mathrm{Re} < \mathrm{Re}_{dev}$, 4, turbulent separation at $\mathrm{Re} \geqslant \mathrm{Re}_{dev}$, 5, lower boundary of the separated turbulent layer at $\mathrm{Re}_{cr} < \mathrm{Re} < \mathrm{Re}_{dev}$, 6, roughness asperities.

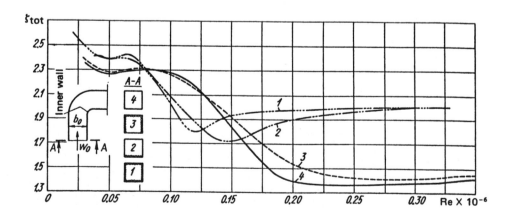

Figure 6-11 Resistance curves $\zeta_{out} = f(\mathrm{Re})$ for different walls (sides) of a bend covered with rough paper:[17] 1, all four walls are rough (stamped paper, $\overline{\Delta} = 0.0005$); 2, inner wall is rough, the remaining walls smooth; 3, inner wall is smooth, the remaining three walls rough; 4, all the walls are smooth ($\overline{\Delta} = 0.00003$).

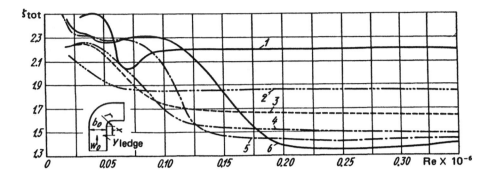

Figure 6-12 Resistance curves $\zeta_{\text{out}} = f(\text{Re})$ of a bend with local roughness and different asperities on the inner wall.[17] 1, the whole inner surface of the wall is rough ($\overline{\Delta} = 0.002$); 2, wire step at a distance from the curvature $x/b_0 = 0.13$; 3 and 4, rough pasted strip ($\overline{\Delta} = 0.002$) at distances $x/b_0 = 0.13$ and 0.63, respectively; 5, flute layer at a distance $x/b_0 = 1.45$; 6, smooth walls ($\overline{\Delta} = 0.00003$).

then the effect of the general roughness Δ (and not of local asperities) is considerably weaker than for smoothly curved elbows and bends. In this case the place of flow separation is fixed near the corner of the bend. The effect of the general roughness in such elbows and bends can tentatively be calculated by the following equation (until refined experimentally):

$$\zeta \equiv \frac{\Delta p}{\rho w_0^2/2} = k_\Delta \zeta_{\text{sm}} \qquad (6\text{-}3)$$

where at $\text{Re} > 4 \times 10^4$ and $\overline{\Delta} < 0.001$

$$k_\Delta \approx (1 + 0.5 \times 10^3 \,\overline{\Delta})$$

while at $\text{Re} > 4 \times 10^4$ and $\overline{\Delta} > 0.001$

$$k_\Delta \approx 1.5$$

ζ_{sm} is determined as ζ_{loc} for smooth walls ($\overline{\Delta} \approx 0$).

38. The effect of general roughness in elbows and bends with relative radii of inner curvature within $0.05 < r/D_0 < 1.0$ ($0.55 < R_0/D_0 < 1.5$) can be accounted for by the coefficient k_Δ in Equation (6-3), which at $4 \times 10^4 \times \text{Re} < 2 \times 10^5$ and $\overline{\Delta} < 0.001$ is given tentatively, until refined experimentally, by the equation of Abramovich[1]

$$k_\Delta = \frac{\lambda_\Delta}{\lambda_{\text{sm}}}$$

and at $\text{Re} > 2 \times 10^5$ and $\overline{\Delta} < 0.001$ is given tentatively by the equation[17]

$$k_\Delta \approx 1 + \overline{\Delta} \times 10^3$$

and at $\text{Re} > 4 \times 10^4$ and $\overline{\Delta} > 0.001$, tentatively by

$$k_\Delta \approx 2$$

Here λ_{sm} is the coefficient of hydraulic friction of a smooth tube determined as λ at the given $Re > 4 \times 10^4$ from Diagrams 2-1 and 2-6; λ_Δ is the coefficient of hydraulic friction of a rough tube, determined as λ, at the given $Re > 4 \times 10^4$ and $\overline{\Delta} = 0{-}0.001$, from Diagrams 2-2 through 2-6.

39. The effect of the general roughness on bends with $R_0/D_0 > 1.5$ can be accounted for approximately by the following equations based on the author's data[17] and those of Reference 64 in Chapter 4: at $Re > 4 \times 10^4$ and $\overline{\Delta} < 0.001$

$$k_\Delta \approx 1 + \overline{\Delta}^2 \times 10^6$$

and at $Re > 4 \times 10^4$ and $\overline{\Delta} > 0.001$

$$k_\Delta \approx 2.0$$

40. At $Re < 4 \times 10^4$, the resistance coefficient of all the elbows and bends can be considered practically independent of the degree of general roughness, being a function of the Reynolds number alone. It is therefore calculated according to paragraph 28 of this chapter.

41. The resistance coefficients of elbows with rounded corners of the bend and with diverging or converging exit cross section ($n_{ar1}^2 = F_1/F_0 = b_1/b_0 \neq 1.0$) can be approximated from the following equation:[37]

$$\zeta \equiv \frac{\Delta p}{\rho w_{con}^2/2} = A_1 C_1 \exp(-k_1/n_{ar})$$

where $A_1 = f(\delta)$ and $C_1 = f(a_0/b_{con})$ are determined in the same way as above; $k_1 = -2.3$ lg ζ_0; ζ_0 is the resistance coefficient of the elbow at $n_{ar} = F_1/F_0 = 1.0$ and $\delta = 90°$; w_{con} is the mean velocity in the contracted section of the elbow; b_{con} is the width of the contracted section of the elbow.

42. All other conditions being equal, the coefficients of local resistances of welded bends are higher than those of smooth bends, since welding seams on their inner surfaces increase the local roughness. With increase in the diameter of the bend, the relative value of the local roughness (seams) decreases, and the resistance coefficient decreases accordingly.

All other conditions being equal, the coefficient of local resistance of corrugated elbows is higher than for bent and welded elbows. Since the absolute dimensions of the corrugations increase with the bend diameter, the resistance coefficient also increases.

Elbows made of sheet material, fabricated from several interlocked links or corrugated, also result in curved sections with an increased resistance coefficient.

43. In the case of cast iron (steel) branches with threaded joints, a projection is formed at the junction between the straight and curved sections, which sharply changes the cross section (Figure 6-13), creating additional pressure losses. The smaller dimensions of such bends, the larger is the relative magnitude of the projection. Therefore, the resistance coefficient of standard gas fittings, which usually have small dimensions, is much higher than ζ of ordinary turns with a flanged joint.

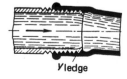

Γ ledge   **Figure 6-13** Threaded cast-iron elbows.

The values of the resistance coefficients of gas pipe fittings given in Diagram 6-3 can be extended to standard bends and fittings with dimensions which are close to those given in these diagrams.

44. The resistance of combined (joint) bends and elbows depends greatly on the relative distance l_{el}/D_0 between the two elbows; the total resistance coefficient ζ for sharply bent channels can be larger or smaller than the sum of the resistance coefficients of two separate bends, while for smoothly bent channels it can be smaller than the resistance coefficient of even one isolated (single) bend.

45. The difference between the local resistance coefficients of smoothly connecting bends is mainly determined by the position of the maximum velocities (the "core" of the flow) before the entrance into the second bend and by the direction of inertia forces in it.

46. According to Goldenberg[8,10] and Goldenberg and Umbrasas,[9] different situations are possible. Thus, for the "gooseneck"-type branch with $\delta = 30°$ and $R_0/b_0 = 1.0$, these are (Figure 6-14):

- The insert between the bends is small (in the present case $l_{el}/D_0 < 2.5$); the inertia forces in the second bend hinder the development of the transverse (secondary) flow caused by the first bend. The net velocity of the transverse flow is smaller than it would have been downstream of a separate bend and the resistance coefficient ζ_{loc} of the gooseneck-type channel is smaller than the resistance coefficient (ζ_{is}) of a separate (isolated) branch with the same geometric parameters (δ and R_0/b_0), i.e., $\zeta_{loc} < \zeta_{is}$.
- The insert increase up to the value $l_{el}/D_0 = 5.0$. In this case the inertia forces in the second bend, acting on the core, increase the intensity of the transverse circulation. Thus the losses increase and attain the maximum when the core of the flow at the entrance into the second bend occupies a postion which corresponds to positions I and II on the scheme of Figure 6-14. Hence, $\zeta_{is} < \zeta_{loc} < 2\zeta_{is}$.
- The insert is increased up to $l_{el}/D_0 = 11.0$. The inertia forces have a lesser effect on the flow (this is also favored by a simultaneous transverse equalization of the flow). The point (minimum) of the curve ζ_{loc} has a corresponding position in the second bend, where the magnitude of transverse circulation is not appreciably affected. The resistance coefficient of the gooseneck-type channel is approximately equal to the resistance coefficient of one isolated bend: $\zeta_{loc} = \zeta_{is}$.

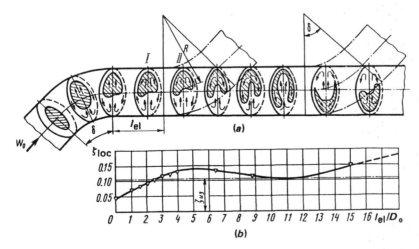

Figure 6-14 Characteristics of a turn of the "gooseneck" type at $\delta = 30°$, $R_0/D_0 = 1.0$, $Re = 1.6 \times 10^5$, and $\overline{\Delta} = 0.0003$.[8,10] (*a*) Scheme of flow distribution along the exit section of the turn; (*b*) dependence of the coefficient ζ_{loc} on l_{el}/D_0.

● A further increase in the length of the insert leads to higher losses, due to more complete flow equalization over the cross section downstream of the first bend and to secondary excitation of transverse circulation and losses in the second bend. As a result, the total resistance coefficient increases, approaching $\zeta_{\text{loc}} = 2\zeta_{\text{is}}$ in the limit.

Similar situations are also observed at other parameters of combined bends.

47. The resistance coefficients of the paired branches (of the gooseneck type), of three bends joined in one plane and in space (see Diagrams 6-18 to 6-21) are determined from

$$\zeta \equiv \frac{\Delta p}{\rho w_0^2/2} = A\zeta'_{\text{loc}} + \lambda \frac{l_0}{D_h}$$

where ζ'_{loc} is determined as ζ_{loc} of a single bend and $A = f(l_{\text{el}}/D_h)$ is determined from corresponding curves obtained on the basis of the experimental data of Goldenberg,[8,10] Goldenberg and Umbrasas,[9] Klyachko et al.,[26] and Chun Sik Lee.[56]

48. In the case of sharply bent channels, the interaction between the paired elbows is mainly determined by the position and the magnitude of the separation zones downstream of the bend. Thus for a ⊓-shaped elbow made from a couple of 90° elbows with sharp corners and small relative distance ($l_{\text{el}}/b_0 \approx 0$), the flow separates from the inner wall only after the complete turn by the angle $\delta = 180°$. At such a large turning angle the flow separation is most intense and as a result the resistance coefficient is highest.

49. A significant increase in the relative distance l_{el}/b_0 (to $l_{\text{el}}/b_0 = 4$–5 and above) leads to almost complete speading of the flow over the linear segment after the first 90° turn, and the conditions of the subsequent 90° turn come to be nearly the same as those for the first turn. Thus, the total resistance coefficient of such a ⊓-shaped elbow will be close to twice the resistance coefficient of a right-angle elbow ($\delta = 90°$).

50. At some intermediate value of l_{el}/b_0 on the order of 1.0, the separation zone behind the first 90° turn has insufficient time to develop completely and, being concentrated at the inner wall before the second 90° turn, it creates the conditions for smooth rounding of the main flow. Under these conditions the second turn of the flow occurs almost without separation, and therefore the total resistance coefficient of such a ⊓-shaped elbow is a minimum.

51. Rounding of the corners of ⊓-shaped elbows decreases the difference between the values of ζ corresponding to different l_{el}/b_0, but the flow and the character of the resistance curves remain similar to those for elbows with sharp corners.

52. In the case of a pair of 90° elbows joined Z-shaped (Figure 6-15), the increase in the relative distance l_{el}/b_0 between the axes of two single elbows first leads to a sharp increase of the total resistance coefficient and then, when a certain maximum is reached, to its gradual decrease to a value roughly equal to twice the resistance coefficient of a single right-angle elbow ($\delta = 90°$).

Figure 6-15 Flow pattern in a Z-shaped bend.

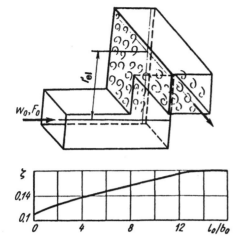

Figure 6-16 Flow in a combined elbow with a 90° turn in two mutually perpendicular planes.

Figure 6-17 Dependence of the resistance coefficient ζ of a smooth bend on the relative length of the starting (inlet) section l_0/b_0.[1]

53. The resistance coefficient of a Z-shaped elbow reaches the maximum in the case where the second of the two single elbows is placed near the widest section of the eddy zone formed after the first 90° turn (see Figure 6-16). A maximum reduction of the stream cross section is then obtained at the second turn.

54. In the case of a combined elbow with flow turning in two mutually perpendicular planes (Figure 6-16), the total resistance coefficient increases with an increase in the relative distance l_{el}/b_0 between the axes of the two constituent right-angle elbows. This increase from an initial value equal to the resistance coefficient of a single right-angle elbow ($\delta = 90°$) reaches a maximum at some small relative distance l'_{el}/b_0. With a further increase in l'_{el}/b_0, the total resistance coefficient begins to decrease again, approaching a value approximately equal to twic the resistance coefficient of a right-angle elbow ($\delta = 90°$).

55. The resistance coefficient of curved channels can vary with the character of the velocity profile at the entrance. In turn, the shape of the velocity profile can also differ according to the conditions of flow supply to these channels.

56. In particular, when the flow is supplied via a straight section placed downstream of a smooth inlet nozzle, the resistance coefficient ζ of the bends and elbows increases up to a certain limit together with an increase in the relative length l_0/b_0 of the straight inlet section (Figure 6-17). There is no increase in ζ when the length of the inlet section is nearly the same as the of the starting section, i.e., of the section over which the velocity profile develops, which corresponds to this particular mode of flow.

57. An increase in the resistance coefficient of a curved channel with the development of the velocity profile, i.e., with thickening of the boundary layer, is apparently due to the influence of the latter both on intensity of flow separation from the walls and on the formation and development of the secondary flows (vortex pair).

58. A velocity profile that has been strongly distorted by a barrier or fitting before the flow entered a curved channel can have a more significant effect on the resistance coefficient of the curved channel, than a straight inlet section. The resistance coefficient can either increase or decrease depending on the character of the velocity profile. If the velocity has its maximum near the inner corner of the turn (Figure 6-18), then the resistance coefficient of the curved channel can become even smaller than in the case of uniform velocity distribution. With other positions of the velocity maximum, the resistance coefficient increases.

59. The resistance of an elbow can be lowered not only by rounding or beveling its corners, but also by installing guide vanes. In the former case the overall size of the channel becomes larger, while in the latter the compact form of the channel is preserved. The guide

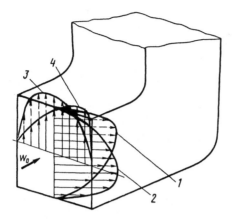

Figure 6-18 Different velocity profiles at the entrance into the elbow:[32] 1, w_{max} near the inner corner of the turn; 2, w_{max} near the outer corner of the turn; 3, w_{max} at the left wall of the elbow; 4, w_{max} at the right wall of the elbow.

vanes can be aerodynamically shaped (Figure 6-19a), simplified and bent along the surface of a cylinder (Figure 6-19b and c), and thin concentric (Figure 6-19d). The shape of the guide vane is chosen according to the following tabulation:

Symbols	Relative dimensions	Symbols	Relative dimensions
t_1	1.0	y_2	$0.215t_1$
x_1	$0.519t_1$	z_1	$0.139t_1$
x_2	$0.489t_1$	z_2	$0.338t_1$
r_1	$0.663t_1$	z_3	$0.268t_1$
r_2	$0.553t_1$	ρ	$0.033t_1$
y_1	0.463		

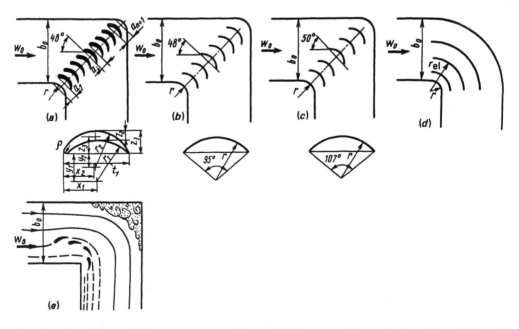

Figure 6-19 Guide vanes in elbows and turns; (a) shaped; (b) thin, along a 95° arc; (c) thin, along a 107° arc; (d) concentric; (e) slotted.

Turning vanes of identical shape and dimensions are usually mounted within the elbows and generally are installed along the line of bend of the channel (Figure 6-19a, b, and c).

60. To achieve smooth turning of the flow, a centrifugal fan is followed by bends.[3,4] The resistance coefficients of such bends depend on the operating conditions of the fan and on the angle of installation β, that is, on the angle between the velocity vectors at the inlet to the fan and at the exit from the bend reckoned in the direction of the rotation of the impellar (see Diagram 6-4). Under all the operating conditions of the fan, the resistance of the bend, installed downstream of it, is much higher than that under conventional flow conditions.

61. An aerodynamic grid, composed of guide vanes and placed in the elbow, deflects the flow to the inner wall due to the aerodynamic force developed in it. When the dimensions, number, and angle of the vanes are appropriately chosen, this flow departure prevents jet separation from the walls and formation of the eddy zone. The velocity distribution over the cross section downstream of the turn (Figure 6-20) is improved and the resistance of the elbow is decreased.

62. Since the main factor in decreasing the resistance and equalization of the velocity field is elimination of the eddy zone at the inner wall of the channel, the largest effect will be produced by the vanes placed closer to the inner curvature.

This suggests the possibility of reducing the number of vanes located near the outer wall of the elbow.[5,15]

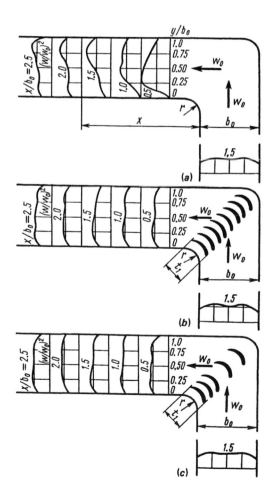

Figure 6-20 Distribution of dimensionless velocities (velocity pressures) in an elbow.[15] (a) without vanes; (b) with a normal number of vanes; (c) with a reduced number of vanes.

63. In the case where it is especially important to obtain a uniform velocity distribution directly after the turn, the "normal" number of vanes is used in the elbow, which is determined by the equation.*

$$n_{nor} = 2.13\left(\frac{r}{D_0}\right)^{-1} - 1 \tag{6-4}$$

In the majority of practical cases it is sufficient to use a reduced number of vanes ("most advantageous" or minimal):[15]

$$n_{adv} \approx 1.4\left(\frac{r}{D_0}\right)^{-1} - 1 \tag{6-5}$$

or

$$n_{min} \approx 0.9\left(\frac{r}{D_0}\right)^{-1} - 1 \tag{6-6}$$

In ordinary elbows, lower resistance and better distribution of the velocities are achieved with the optimum number of vanes determined by Equation (6-5).

The chord t_1 of the shaped vane is taken as the chord of a 90° arc of a circle, i.e., of the arc of the inner curvature of the elbow, and therefore

$$t_1 = r\sqrt{2} \tag{6-7}$$

or

$$t_1 = D_0\left(\frac{r}{D_0}\right)\sqrt{2} \tag{6-8}$$

Equations (6-4) to (6-6) are correct only for this relationship between the dimensions of the vane chord and the radius of curvature of the elbow.

64. If the curvature in the elbow is not smooth (there are sharp or beveled corners), then $t_1 = 0.15–0.60\, D_0$. Then the number of vanes can be determined by the following equations:[15]

$$n_{nor} = \frac{3D_0}{t_1} - 1 \tag{6-9}$$

$$n_{adv} \approx 2\frac{D_0}{t_1} \tag{6-10}$$

$$n_{min} \approx 1.5\frac{D_0}{t_1} \tag{6-11}$$

*For a right-angle elbow, D_0 in Equations (6-4) to (6-11) is replaced by b_0.

65. For elbows with a diverging section, in which the cross section past the turn is larger than that before it ($b_1 > b_0$), the numbers of vanes are determined, respectively, from

$$n_{nor} = 2.13 \frac{S}{t_1} - 1$$

$$n_{adv} \approx 1.4 \frac{S}{t_1}$$

$$n_{min} \approx 0.9 \frac{S}{t_1}$$

where

$$S = \sqrt{b_0^2 + b_1^2}$$

66. When the "normal" number of vanes is used, they are uniformly placed along the bending line of the elbow, so that the distance between the vane chords is $a_i = S/(n + 1)$.

If a reduced number of vanes is used, the author[15] recommends that the distance a between the chords be taken as varying according to an arithmetic progression, such that in the case of the optimum number of vanes $a_{n+1}/a_1 = 2$, and in the case of the minimum number of vanes $a_{n+1}/a_1 = 3$. Here, a_1 is the distance from the arc chord of the inner curvature of the elbow to the chord of the first vane (see Figure 6-19a); a_{n+1} is the distance between the chords of the last vane and the outer curvature.

The intermediate distances between the vanes are determined by the following equation:[16]

with an advantageous number of vanes

$$a_i = 0.67 \frac{S}{n + 1} \left(1 + \frac{i - 1}{n}\right)$$

with a minimum number of vanes

$$a_i = \frac{S}{n + 1} \left(0.5 + \frac{i - 1}{n}\right)$$

67. In the majority of practical cases the vanes used in elbows are simply thin shaped vanes selected for a 90° turn, on the average, along the arc of a circle $\varphi_1 = 95°$ independent of the elbow parameters (the relative curvature radius, the area ratio, etc.). The position and the angle of installation of such vanes are selected according to the same criteria used for profiled vanes. The resistance coefficient of elbows with such vanes is markedly higher than for elbows with profiled vanes.

68. A low value of resistance is obtained, coming close to the resistance of elbows with profiled vanes, when thin vanes are selected by Yudin's method.[50] The optimum angle of the vane arc and the vane angle depend on both the relative curvature radius of the elbow and its area ratio (see Diagram 6-30).

69. The installation of guide vanes in elbows is expedient as long as the relative curvature radius is comparatively small. For elbows of constant cross section, the installation of vanes

is justifiable as long as $r/b_0 \leqslant 0.4$–0.5. For diffuser elbows (i.e., with diverging exit cross section) the limiting value of r/b_0 increases up to about 1.0. In the case of converging elbows (with converging exit cross section), the value of r/b_0 is decreased to about 0.2.

70. The action of concentric vanes installed in turns is evidenced mainly in that they divide this bend into a number of bends with more elongated cross sections, which leads to a decrease in the pressure losses. The normal number, n_{ch}, of thin optimally installed concentric vanes in a bend is determined on the basis of the data of Khanzhonkov and Taliev:[46]

r/b_0	0–0.1	0.1–0.4	0.4–1.0	1.0
n_{ch}	3–4	2	1	0

The optimum position of the vanes in a bend is reached (see Figure 6-19d) when

$$r_i = 1.26 r_{i-1} + 0.07 b_0$$

71. The resistance coefficient of a rectangular bend with a normal number of optimally installed concentric vanes can be determined, approximately,[46] by the following equation:

$$\zeta \equiv \frac{\Delta p}{\rho w_0^2/2} = \left(0.46 \frac{R_0}{b_0} + 0.04\right)\zeta_{w.v.}$$

where $\zeta_{w.v.}$ is the resistance coefficient of the bend without vanes.

72. The normal number of vanes in a circular bend, according to the experiments of Ito and Imai,[68]

r_0/D_0	0–0.5	0.5–1.0	1.0
n_{ch}	2	1	0

With one vane installed, its optimum distance should be (see Figure 6-19d):

$$r_1 = r_0 \sqrt{1 + D_0/r_0}$$

In the case of two vanes, this distance is equal to

$$r_1 = r_0 \quad \sqrt[3]{1 + D_0/r_0} \quad \text{and} \quad r_2 = r_0 \quad \sqrt[3]{(1 + D_0/r_0)^2}$$

The values of the resistance coefficients of circular bends with guide concentric vanes and without them are given in Diagram 6-27.

73. When guide vanes are installed in combined elbows, the resistance coefficient is determined as the sum of the resistance coefficients of single elbows with vanes

$$\zeta = n_{is}\zeta_v$$

where ζ_v is the resistance coefficient of a single elbow with vanes and n_{is} is the number of turns in a combined elbow.

74. The coefficient of the local hydraulic resistance of a spatial (annular) turn through 180° depends on the relative distance h/D_0 from the entry edge of the inner tube up to the

end cover (hood) of the outer circular tube; on the area ratio $n_{ar} = F_1/F_0$ between the outer and inner tubes; on the relative thickness δ_{el}/D_0 or the curvature radius r/D_0 of the cut edge of the inner tube, as well as on the relative curvature radius R/D_1 of the cover (Figure 6-21).

75. The coefficient of local resistance ζ_{loc} is most strongly affected by the parameter h/D_0. When the ratio a increases from zero, the coefficient ζ_{loc} first decreases very sharply, reaching a minimum at some value of a, the increases somewhat sharply. Then it remains constant in some cases, and in others, it decreases to a certain value or smoothly increases.

76. Within certain limits of h/D_0 (following the first minimum of ζ_{loc}) and at some values of n_{ar} and r/D_0 (δ_{el}/D_0), one can observe marked oscillations (in time) of the coefficient ζ_{loc} caused by flow instability. This instability, which is typical of turns with small values of r/D_0 (δ_{el}/D_0), can be explained by periodic blowing-off and entrainment by the flow of the separating (eddy) zones 1 at the outer wall and zones 2 at the inner wall of the annular turn (Figure 6-22I) under certain conditions. This occurrence corresponds to a sharp decrease in the resistance. Following this, the vortices reappear and the resistance increases sharply in a contracted section behind the turn.

The curves $\zeta_{loc} = f(a, r/D_0$ or $\delta_{el}/D_0, n_{ar})$ of Diagrams 6-31 and 6-32 correspond to the time-average experimental values of ζ_{loc}.

77. Table 6-1 contains the values of ζ_{min} of annular turns corresponding to the first minimum of the resistance coefficient and to the optimum values of $(h/D_0)_{opt}$ for different r/D_0 (δ_{el}/D_0), R/D, and n_{ar}. The table also contains the values of $(h/D_0)_{tr}$ within the limits of which the flow is markedly unstable.

78. The relative thickness of the corner δ_{el}/D_0 of the inner tube of an annular turn, together with h/D_0, is also an important factor which influences the value of ζ_{min}, decreasing

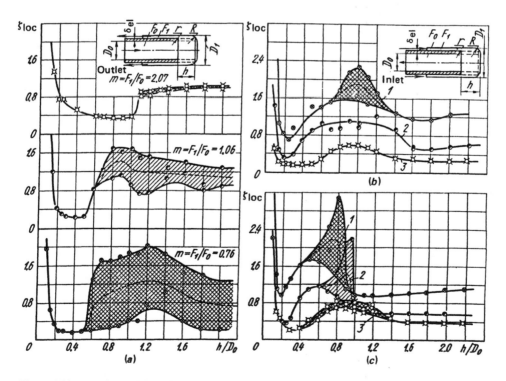

Figure 6-21 Dependence of the resistance coefficient ζ_{loc} of an annular turn on h/D_0 at $R/D_1 = 0.3$:[19] (a) pumping at $r/D_0 = 0.1$; (b) suction at $r/D_0 = 0.2$: 1, $n_{ar} = 0.80$; 2, $n_{ar} = 1.07$; 3, $n_{ar} = 2.1$; (c) suction at $r/D_0 = 0.1$: 1, $n_{ar} = 0.76$; 2, $n_{ar} = 1.06$; 3, $n_{ar} = 2.07$.

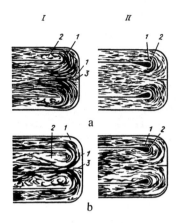

Figure 6-22 Flow patterns in a 180° turn without guide vanes (I) and with guide vanes and pairings (II):[47] I (*a*) pumping; (*b*) suction: 1, eddy zones at the outer wall; 2, eddy zones at the inner wall; 3, divider. II (*a*) pumping; (*b*) suction: 1, vane; 2, pairing.

it noticeably especially at $n_{ar} < 2$. At the same time, the rounding of this corner within $r/D_0 = 0.05–0.2$ barely reduces ζ_{min}. Therefore, in those cases where rounding of the corner is difficult, it may be left as is.

79. In the case of suction (entry through an annular tube), the optimum value of the parameter $m = F_1/F_0$ lies at all values of r/D_0 (δ_{el}/D_0) within 1.0–2.0; in the case of pumping (exit through an annular tube) it is different for different parameters. At $r/D_0 < 0.2$ an annular turn with the ratio $n_{ar} < 1.0$ is expedient. At $r/D_0 \geqslant 0.2$ ($\delta_{el}/D_0 \geqslant 0.4$), the optimum value of $n_{ar} = 1.0–1.5$.

80. In the case of suction, the optimum curvature radius of the end cover R/D_1 lies within 0.18–0.35, and in the case of pumping, with 0.2–0.45.

81. In order to better stabilize the flow in an annular turn, divider 3 can be used (see Figure 6-22I), which does not influence the losses appreciably.

The resistance of the annular turn can be decreased by installing guide vanes 1 in the vicinity of inner corners of the turn (Figure 6-22II).

82. A symmetrical 180° turn of the flow can also be achieved in a plane channel.[47] Plane symmetrical turns are often used, for example, in heating furnaces with closed-cycle circulation of gas flow. The resistance coefficient of such a turn depends on the same parameters as in an annular turn (paragraph 74).

83. Table 6-2 contains the values of ζ_{min} obtained at optimal geometric parameters of a plane 180° turn both in the absence and in the presence of divider 3 (Figure 6-22I) in the place of merging (division) of flows. At optimal values of $(h/a_0)_{opt}$ the divider moderately decreases the resistance coefficient of the turn.* However, the principal function of the divider is its stabilizing effect on the flow. Only a plane divider should be used in this case, as during suction it provides a somewhat greater reduction in the resistance than a profiled divider. During pumping, the effects of the plane and profiled dividers are practically the same. The resistance of the turn can be also reduced by installing fairing 2 on one of the sides of the inner channel (see Figure 6-22II). A still greater reduction in the resistance of a plane turn is achieved by the use of guide vanes (Figure 6-22II) installed in the vicinity of inner corners of the turn. The minimum values of the resistance coefficients of turns with guide vanes are obtained at noticeably lower ratios $(h/a_0)_{min}$ than without such vanes.

84. The right-angle turn with fairing and guide vanes is the best one among those studied. In the case of suction $(h/a_0)_{opt} \approx 0.45$ and $(h_0/a_0)_{opt} \approx 0.076$, and in the case of pumping $(h/a_0)_{opt} = 0.5–0.6$ and $(h_0/a_0)_{opt} = 0.076–0.175$.

85. Bent flexible glass-fabric air conduits, just as straight air conduits (see paragraph 72 of Section 2-1), have an elevated resistance. Some of the experimental data[53] on the resistance coefficients of such bends are given in Diagram 6-25.

---

*At small values of h/a_0, the divider may moderately increase the resistance of the turn.

Table 6-1 Characteristics of the spatial (annular) turn through 180°

Suction (inlet)

| Characteristics | δ_{el}/D_0 | | | | r/D_0 | |
of the turn	0.1	0.2	0.4	0.5	0.1	0.2
			$n_{ar} = \dfrac{F_2}{F_1} = 0.75\text{--}0.80$			
ζ_{min}	1.70	1.10	0.72	1.90	0.96	0.70
$(h/D_0)_{opt}$	0.23–0.27	0.22–0.28	0.03–0.38	0.18–0.22	0.18–0.23	0.22–0.30
$(h/D_0)_{tr}$	0.28–1.4	0.20–1.4	Stable	0.25–1.0	0.40–1.0	0.60–1.4
			$n_{ar} = 1.0\text{--}1.10$			
ζ_{min}	1.05	0.45	0.40	1.05	0.40	0.32
$(h/D_0)_{opt}$	0.27–0.34	0.23–0.33	0.26–0.36	0.24–0.33	0.20–0.29	0.18–0.28
$(h/D_0)_{tr}$	0.38–1.40	0.77–1.45	Stable	0.26–1.40	0.60–1.0	Stable
			$n_{ar} = 2.0\text{--}2.1$			
ζ_{min}	0.55	0.50	0.40	0.50	0.20	0.16
$(h/D_0)_{opt}$	0.35–0.45	0.22–0.48	0.26–0.40	0.33–0.60	0.28–0.40	0.17–0.50
$(h/D_0)_{tr}$	0.50–1.80	0.50–1.40	1.1–1.30	0.45–1.60	0.40–1.60	Stable

Pumping (exit)

| Characteristics | δ_{el}/D_0 | | | | r/D_0 | |
of the turn	0.1	0.2	0.4	0.5	0.1	0.2
			$n_{ar} = 0.75\text{--}0.80$			
ζ_{min}	0.24	0.22	0.36	0.19	0.16	0.30
$(h/D_0)_{opt}$	0.40 0.62	0.40–0.50	0.32–0.45	0.40–0.80	0.25–0.50	0.23–0.45
$(h/D_0)_{tr}$	0.60–20	0.55–2.0	Stable	0.75–2.0	0.40–2.0	Stable
			$n_{ar} = 1.0\text{--}1.1$			
ζ_{min}	0.40	0.26	0.26	0.40	0.23	0.20
$(h/D_0)_{opt}$	0.50–0.60	0.35–0.55	0.30–0.40	0.47–0.83	0.30–0.50	0.25–0.45
$(h/D_0)_{tr}$	0.55–2.0	0.90–2.0	0.75–1.0	0.80–2.0	0.60–2.0	Stable
			$n_{ar} = 2.0\text{--}2.1$			
ζ_{min}	0.34	0.32	0.30	0.34	0.32	0.40
$(h/D_0)_{opt}$	0.75–1.0	0.65–0.93	0.50–0.90	0.65–0.95	0.60–1.0	0.20–1.0
$(h/D_0)_{tr}$	1.0–2.0	0.55–2.0	0.30–1.8	0.30–2.0	1.1–2.0	1.0–2.0

86. During the pneumatic transport of pulverized materials, the highest resistance is produced in the places where the flow alters its direction, that is, in bent channels (elbows, bends, etc.).[69]

The overall resistance coefficient of bent channels with pulverized material in the flow is calculated as

$$\zeta \equiv \frac{\Delta p}{\rho w_0^2/2} = \zeta + \alpha(\zeta_1 - \zeta_0) \tag{6-40}$$

where ζ_0 and ζ_1 are the resistance coefficients of the bent channel without ($\alpha = 0$) and with ($\alpha = 1$) pulverized materials in the flow, respectively; $\alpha = m_{tot}/m_h$ is the coefficient of

Table 6-2 Characteristics of a symmetric plane turn through 180°

Type of device in the turning region	$(h/a_0)_{opt}$[a]	$(h_0/a_0)_{opt}$[a]	ζ_{min}[a]
Without divider, without fairing and guide vanes	0.40–0.60	–	4.0–4.2
	(0.55–0.70)	–	(4.0–4.2)
Without divider, guide vanes, but with fairing installed on the inside of the channel	0.40–0.60	–	3.4–3.5
	(0.45–0.60)	–	(2.3–2.5)
Without divider, but with fairing and with guide vanes	0.35–0.50	0.76	1.70–1.75
	(0.35–0.50)	(0.76–0.127)	(0.90–1.0)
Without divider, without fairing, but with guide vanes	0.40–0.55	0.127	1.75–1.80
	(0.45–0.57)	(0.127)	(1.30–1.35)
Without fairing, guide vanes, but with a plane divider	0.53–0.65	–	3.6–3.7
	(≥0.60)	–	(3.9–4.0)
With divider, fairing, but without guide vanes on the inside of the channel	0.50–0.65	–	3.3–3.4
	(0.55–0.70)	–	(2.2–2.3)
With divider, fairing, and guide vanes	0.35–0.55	0.76	1.2–1.3
	(0.40–0.65)	–	(0.90–1.0)
With divider, without fairing, but with guide vanes	0.45–0.60	0.127	1.2–1.3
	(0.50–0.70)	–	(1.30)
With divider, fairing, guide vanes, but with a burden	0.40–0.50	0.076	3.1–3.2
	(>0.40)	(0.076–0.127)	(2.6)

[a] Numbers not in parentheses refer to suction (inlet); those in parentheses to pumping (exit).

dust content (the ratio of the mass flow rate of the pulverized material to the mass flow rate of the gas flow).

87. When $2.5 \times 10^5 \leqslant \mathrm{Re} \leqslant 4.5 \times 10^5$ and $20 \leqslant \mathrm{Fr} \leqslant 36$, the overall resistance coefficient ζ is independent either of the Reynolds number $\mathrm{Re} = w_0 D_0/\nu_c$, or of the Froude number $\mathrm{Fr} = w_0/\sqrt{gD_0}$, where ν_c is the average value of the kinematic coefficient of the viscosity of the gas flow laden with pulverized material.

Pressure losses in the dust-laden flow are determined as

$$\Delta p = \zeta \rho w_0^2/2$$

where ρ is the average value of the density of a dust-laden gas flow.

88. The resistance coefficient of curved channels with dust laden flows is practically independent of whether the transported flow moves in the horizontal plane or changes its direction to the vertical, and vice versa.

The values of ζ are also independent of the size of particles of the pulverized material.

89. Rectangular bends differ from circular bends by a smaller local wear in motion of dust particles.

Elbows with sharp turning angles and without guiding devices are inapplicable for pneumatic systems, since dust is accumulated in outer corner elements and periodically returns to the main stream. In this case, the resistance and the wear of the system increase sharply.

Combined elbows occupy intermediate position between the elbow with a sharp turn and smooth bends.

90. Guide vanes or plates in elbows and bends not only decrease the resistance, but also diminish the wear, since the latter is distributed uniformly over these units.

During the pneumatic transport of not very hard material (e.g., sawdust) in large-diameter tubes, combined circular elbows can be used. When the material is transported in large-diameter tubes which produces appreciable wear, elbows with guide vanes should be used.

6-2 DIAGRAMS OF THE RESISTANCE COEFFICIENTS

Bends at $\frac{R_0}{D_0}\left(\frac{R_0}{b_0}\right) < 3.0$ and $0 < \delta \leqslant 180°$, $\frac{l_0}{D_h} \geqslant 10$*[1,17,31,61,64,77,78,91]	Diagram 6-1

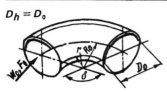

$D_h = D_0$

$D_h = \dfrac{2a_0 b_0}{a_0 + b_0}$

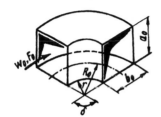

1) Smooth walls ($\Delta = 0$) and Re $= w_0 D_h/\nu \geqslant 2 \times 10^5$:

$$\zeta \equiv \frac{\Delta p}{\rho w_0^2/2} = \zeta_{loc} + \zeta_{fr} = \zeta_{loc} + 0.0175\,\delta\lambda\,\frac{R_0}{D_h}$$

$$\zeta_{loc} = A_1 B_1 C_1$$

$A_1 = f(\delta)$, see graph a or, tentatively, the corresponding formulas:

δ, degree	$\leqslant 70$	90	$\geqslant 100$
A_1	$0.9 \sin \delta$	1.0	$0.7 + 0.35\,\dfrac{\delta}{90°}$

$B_1 = f(R_0/D_0)$ or $f(R_0/b_0)$, see graphs b and c or, tentatively, the corresponding formulas:

$\dfrac{R_0}{D_0}\left(\dfrac{R_0}{b_0}\right)$	0.5–1.0	>1.0
B_1	$0.21(R_0/D_0)^{-2.5}$	$0.21(\sqrt{R_0/D_0})^{-0.5}$

$C_1 = f(a_0/b_0)$, see graph d for a circular or square cross section $C_1 = 1.0$ or, tentatively:

a_0/b_0	$\leqslant 4$	$\geqslant 4$
C_1	$0.85 + \dfrac{0.125}{a_0/b_0}$	$1.115 - \dfrac{0.84}{a_0/b_0}$

$$\zeta_{fr} = 0.0175\,\delta\lambda\,\frac{R_0}{D_h}$$

2) Rough walls ($\Delta > 0$) and Re $\geqslant 10^4$:

$$\zeta = k_\Delta k_{Re}\zeta_{loc} + 0.0175\,\delta\lambda\,\frac{R_0}{D_h}$$

$k = f(\overline{\Delta} = \Delta/D_h)$, see the tables; $k_{Re} = f(Re)$, see graph e or tentatively:

$R_0/D_0(R_0/b_0)$	0.50 − 0.55	$\geqslant$0.55 to 0.70	>0.70
k_{Re}	$1 + 4400/Re$	$5.45/Re^{0.131}$	$1.3 - 0.29\ln(Re \times 10^{-5})$

$\lambda = f(Re$ and $\overline{\Delta})$, see Diagrams 2-2 through 2-6; at $\lambda \approx 0.02$, $\zeta_{fr} = 0.00035\delta(R_0/D_h)$.

3) $3 \times 10^3 < Re < 10^4$

$$\zeta = \frac{A_2}{Re} + \zeta_{qu} + \zeta_{fr}$$

where for A_2, see the table (tentatively); ζ_{qu} is determined as ζ_{loc} at Re $> 2 \times 10^5$.

$R_0/D_0(R_0/b_0)$	0.50–0.55	>0.55–0.70	>0.70–1.0	>1.0–2.0	>2.0–2.5
r_0/D_0	0–0.05	>0.05–0.20	>0.2–0.5	>0.5–1.5	>1.5–2.0
$A_2 \times 10^{-3}$	4.0	6.0	4.0–2.0	1.0	0.6

*From here onward $l_0/D_h = 0$ means that an elbow (turn) is installed directly behind a smooth collector, while $l_0/D_h > 0$ means that it is installed downstream of a straight section (insert) behind the collector.

Diagram
6-1

Values of k_Δ

R_0/D_0 (R_0/b_0)	0.50–0.55		>0.55		
			Re		
$\overline{\Delta}$	3×10^3– 4×10^4	>4×10^4	3×10^3– 4×10^4	>4×10^4– 2×10^5	>2×10^5
0	1.0	1.0	1.0	1.0	1.0
0–0.001	1.0	$1 + 0.5 \times 10^3 \overline{\Delta}$	1.0	$\lambda_\Delta/\lambda_{sm}$	$1 + \overline{\Delta} \times 10^3$
>0.001	1.0	~1.5	1.0	~2.0	~2.0

where for λ_{sm}, see λ of commercially smooth tubes at the given Re in Diagrams 2-5 and 2-6; for λ_Δ, see λ of rough tubes ($\overline{\Delta} > 0$) at the given Re and $\overline{\Delta}$ in Diagrams 2-2 through 2-6.

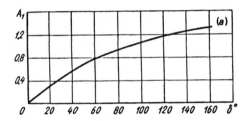

$\delta,°$	0	20	30	45	60
A_1	0	0.31	0.45	0.60	0.78
$\delta,°$	75	90	110	130	150	180
A_1	0.90	1.00	1.13	1.20	1.28	1.40

$R_0/D_0(R_0/b_0)$	0.50	0.60	0.70	0.80
B_1	1.18	0.77	0.51	0.37
$R_0/D_0(R_0/b_0)$	0.90	1.00	1.25	1.50
B_1	0.28	0.21	0.19	0.17

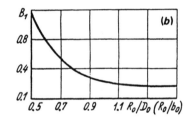

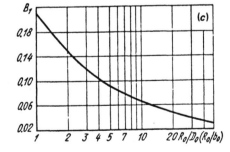

$R_0/D_0(R_0/b_0)$	2.0	4.0	6.0	8.0	10
B_1	0.15	0.11	0.09	0.07	0.07
$R_0/D_0(R_0/b_0)$	20		30		>40
B_1	0.15		0.11		>40

a_0/b_0	0.25	0.50	0.75	1.0	1.5	2.0
C_1	1.30	1.17	1.09	1.00	0.90	0.85
a_0/b_0	3.0	4.0	5.0	6.0	7.0	8.0
C_1	0.85	0.90	0.95	0.98	1.00	1.00

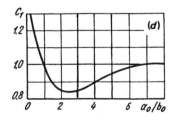

	Diagram 6-1

Values of k_{Re}

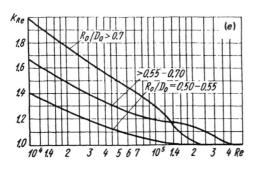

R_0/D_0	Re $\times$ 10^{-5}					
(R_0/b_0)	0.1	0.14	0.2	0.3	0.4	0.6
0.5–0.55	1.40	1.33	1.26	1.19	1.14	1.09
>0.55–0.70	1.67	1.58	1.49	1.40	1.34	1.26
>0.70	2.00	1.89	1.77	1.64	1.56	1.46

R_0/D_0	Re $\times$ 10^{-5}					
(R_0/b_0)	0.8	1.0	1.4	2.0	3.0	4.0
0.5–0.55	1.06	1.04	1.0	1.0	1.0	1.0
>0.55–0.70	1.21	1.19	1.17	1.14	1.06	1.0
>0.70	1.38	1.30	1.15	1.02	1.0	1.0

Tubes and channels (smooth), smoothly curved $\left(\dfrac{R_0}{D_0} \geqslant 3\right)$ with any angle of the turn (coils);[3,4,12,24,28,51,79,84] $l_0/D_0 \geqslant 10$

Diagram 6-2

1. Circular cross section

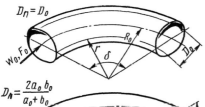

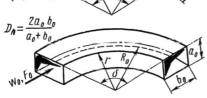

$$\zeta \equiv \frac{\Delta p}{\rho w_0^2/2} = 0.0175 \, \lambda_{el} \delta \frac{R_0}{D_h}$$

where $\lambda_{el} = f(Re, R_0/D_0)$, see curves, or for a circular cross section:

at $50 < Re \sqrt{\dfrac{D_0}{2R_0}} < 600$ $\quad \lambda_{el} = \dfrac{20}{Re^{0.65}} \left(\dfrac{D_0}{2R_0}\right)^{0.175}$

at $600 < Re \sqrt{\dfrac{D_0}{2R_0}} < 1400$ $\quad \lambda_{el} = \dfrac{10.4}{Re^{0.55}} \left(\dfrac{D_0}{2R_0}\right)^{0.225}$

at $1400 < Re \sqrt{\dfrac{D_0}{2R_0}} < 5000$ $\quad \lambda_{el} = \dfrac{5}{Re^{0.45}} \left(\dfrac{D_0}{2R_0}\right)^{0.275}$

$Re = \dfrac{w_0 D_h}{\nu}$

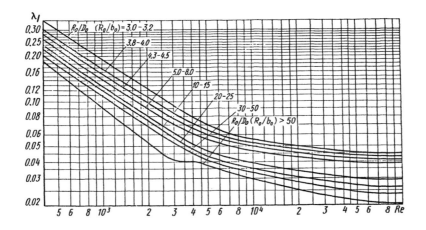

	Diagram 6-2

Values of λ_{el} (graph a)

R_0/D_0 (R_0/b_0)	Re $\times$ 10^{-3}						
	0.4	0.6	0.8	1	2	4	6
3.0–3.2	0.34	0.26	0.22	0.19	0.12	0.078	0.063
3.8–4.0	0.30	0.23	0.19	0.17	0.11	0.070	0.060
4.3–4.5	0.28	0.22	0.18	0.16	0.10	0.065	0.056
5.0 8.0	0.26	0.20	0.16	0.14	0.09	0.060	0.052
10–15	0.24	0.18	0.15	0.13	0.08	0.055	0.043
20–25	0.22	0.16	0.14	0.12	0.075	0.048	0.040
30–50	0.20	0.15	0.13	0.11	0.070	0.045	0.038
>50	0.18	0.135	0.105	0.090	0.052	0.040	0.035

R_0/D_0 (R_0/b_0)	Re $\times$ 10^{-3}					
	8	10	20	30	50	100
3.3–3.2	0.058	0.055	0.050	0.048	0.046	0.044
3.8–4.0	0.055	0.052	0.047	0.045	0.044	0.042
4.3–4.5	0.052	0.049	0.045	0.043	0.041	0.040
5.0–8.0	0.049	0.047	0.043	0.042	0.040	0.038
10–15	0.040	0.038	0.034	0.033	0.030	0.028
20–25	0.037	0.035	0.030	0.029	0.027	0.026
30–50	0.035	0.033	0.028	0.027	0.025	0.023
>50	0.032	0.030	0.025	0.023	0.022	0.020

2. Square cross-section

at $\mathrm{Re}\sqrt{a_0/(2R_0)} = 100 - 400$ or $\mathrm{Re} = \dfrac{100 - 400}{\sqrt{a_0/(2R_0)}}$

$\lambda_{el} = 16.5 \times (\mathrm{Re}\sqrt{a_0/(2R_0)})^{0.35}/\mathrm{Re}$, see graph b;

at $\mathrm{Re}\sqrt{a_0/(2R_0)} > 400$, for λ_{el} see graph b

Values of λ_{el} (graph b)

R_0/a_0	Re $\times$ 10^{-3}												
	0.4	0.6	0.8	1.0	1.5	2.0	2.5	3	4	6	8	10	20
1.70	0.272	0.210	0.172	0.160	0.140	0.148	0.140	0.136	0.132	0.120	0.112	0.108	0.092
3.40	0.240	0.180	0.152	0.132	0.112	0.112	0.108	0.104	0.096	0.088	0.080	0.076	0.072
6.85	0.212	0.160	0.136	0.116	0.092	0.080	0.072	0.068	0.061	0.052	0.048	0.044	0.040
13.7	0.188	0.142	0.120	0.104	0.080	0.068	0.060	0.056	0.048	0.044	0.040	0.038	0.034

Diagram
6-2

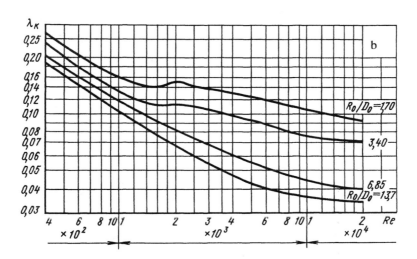

3. Rectangular cross-section

1) $\text{Re} = (0.5 - 6) \times 10^3$ (laminar regime)

$\lambda_{\text{el}} = [1.97 + 49.1(D_h/(2R_0))^{1.32}(b_0/a_0)^{0.37}]\text{Re}^{-0.46} = A_{\text{lam}}\text{Re}^{-0.46}$ or $\lambda_{\text{el}}/A_{\text{lam}} = \text{Re}^{-0.46}$

2) $\text{Re} = (7 - 38) \times 10^3$ (turbulent regime)

$\lambda_{\text{el}} = [0.316 + 8.65(D_h/(2R_0))^{1.32}(b_0/a_0)^{0.34}]\text{Re}^{-0.25} = A_{\text{turb}}\text{Re}^{-0.25}$ or $\lambda_{\text{el}}/A_{\text{turb}} = \text{Re}^{-0.25}$

Turns and bends;[22,90] $\text{Re} = w_0 D_0/\nu \geqslant 2 \times 10^5$

Diagram
6-3

Characteristics of the bend	Resistance coefficient $\zeta \equiv \dfrac{\Delta p}{\rho w_0^2/2}$			
$\delta = 30°$	D_0	½ in.	1 in.	1½ in.	2 in.

	D_0	½ in.	1 in.	1½ in.	2 in.
$\delta = 30°$	$\overline{\Delta} = \Delta/D_0$	0.02	0.01	0.0075	0.0050
	L mm	30	44	56	66
	ζ	0.81	0.52	0.32	0.19
$\delta = 45°$	L mm	36	52	68	81
	ζ	0.73	0.38	0.27	0.23
$\delta = 90°$ (knee bend)	L mm	30	40	55	65
	ζ	2.19	1.98	1.60	1.07

Diagram
6-3

$\delta = 90°; R_0/D_0 = 1.36–1.67$

L mm	45	63	85	98
ζ	1.20	0.80	0.81	0.58

$\delta = 90°; R_0/D_0 = 2–2.13$

L mm	55	85	116	140
ζ	0.82	0.53	0.53	0.35

$\delta = 180°$

L mm	38	102	102	127
ζ	1.23	0.70	0.65	0.58

Branch $\delta = 90°$; furrowed
$R_0/D_0 = 2.5$

D_0, mm	50	100	150	200	250	300	350
ζ	0.25	0.30	0.33	0.37	0.42	0.45	0.50

Circular section bends and elbows at high subsonic flow velocities[41,74]   Diagram 6-4

$$\zeta_\lambda \equiv \frac{\Delta p}{\rho_m w_m^2/2} = k_\lambda \zeta$$

where for ζ see corresponding diagrams of Chapter 6 for small velocities.

1. Small-diameter elbows and bends (25 mm), pure (not rusted) at $\lambda_c < 0.9$ and
   $10^5 < Re < 7 \times 10^5$:

$$k_\lambda = 1 + \alpha_1 \lambda_c^\beta$$

where $\lambda_c \equiv w_m/a_{cr}$; $w_m = 0.5(w_0 + w_1)$; $\zeta_m = 0.5(\rho_0 + \rho_1)$,
a_{cr} is the critical velocity of sound.

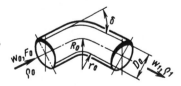

Circular section bends and elbows at high subsonic flow velocities[41,74]   Diagram 6-4

Values of α_1 and β

$\delta°$	R_0/D_0	α_1	β	$\Delta, \mu m$	Note
					Elbows
90	0.90	5.84	3.17	15	Butt-welding
90	0.90	6.86	3.17	1.5	Same
90	1.34	6.57	3.17	15	Same
90	1.34	6.76	3.17	1.5	Same
90	0.62	1.52	1.95	120	Threaded connection
90	0.62	2.56	1.95	1.5	Same
90	1.34	3.40	1.95	15	Butt-welding; transition from a 32-mm-diameter elbow to a straight 25-mm-diameter section of the tube
180	1.34	3.88	3.17	15	Butt-welding
180	1.34	5.02	3.17	1.5	Same
45	1.34	7.34	3.17	15	Same
45	1.34	7.53	3.17	1.5	Same
45	1.20	3.14	1.85	120	Threaded connection
					Bends
45	3.25	4.45	3.18	2.5	
89	2.48	13.47	3.17	2.5	
89	8.36	9.33	3.17	2.5	
90	29.29	8.24	3.17	2.5	
91	15.57	4.39	3.17	2.5	
180	4.80	4.45	3.17	2.5	

2. Standard bends and elbows

   $k_\lambda = f(\lambda_0)$, see the graph

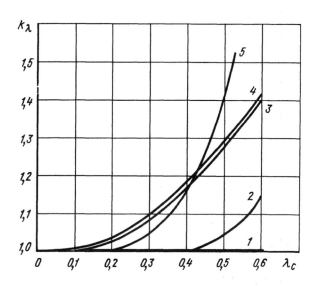

Circular section bends and elbows at high subsonic flow velocities[41,74]   Diagram 6-4

Values of k_λ

No.	Characteristics	λ_c								
		0.1	0.2	0.3	0.4	0.45	0.5	0.52	0.55	0.60
1.	Bend; $\delta = 45$–$90°$; $R_0/D_0 > 1$	1.0	1.0	1.0	1.0	1.0	1.0	1.0	1.0	1.0
2.	Bend; $\delta = 45°$ $R_0/D_0 = 1$	1.0	1.0	1.0	1.0	1.02	1.04	1.05	1.08	1.15
3.	Bend; $\delta = 90°$ $R_0/D_0 = 1$	1.0	1.02	1.08	1.17	1.22	1.28	1.30	1.34	1.40
4.	Bend; $\delta = 90°$; $0.75 \leqslant R_0/D_0 \leqslant 1$	1.0	1.03	1.10	1.19	1.24	1.30	1.32	1.35	1.42
5.	Elbow; $\delta = 90°$; $r_{in}/D_0 = 0$; $r_{out}/D_0 = 0$–0.5	1.0	1.0	1.05	1.16	1.26	1.41	1.50	–	–

Bends located downstream of centrifugal fans (Chapter 3, References 3, 4, 26)   Diagram 6-5

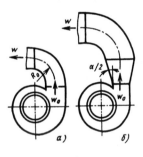

$$\zeta \equiv \frac{\Delta p}{\rho w_0^2/2}$$

Values of ζ

Turn	Angle of element installment, degree	Nominal operational conditions of the fan			Type of fan
		Q/Q_n $\eta^f \geqslant 0.9\,\eta^f_{max}$	$Q = Q_n$; $\eta^f = \eta^f_{max}$	$Q > Q_n$; $\eta^f \geqslant 0.9\,\eta^f_{max}$	
	Vanes bent backward				
Rectangular cross section (a) $R_0 = D_h$	90–270	0.6	0.2	0.3	Ts4-76
Circular cross section, $R_0 = 2D_h$	90–360	0.5	0.5	0.4	Ts4-76
Rectangular cross section, $R_0 = 1.5D_h$ with a pyramidal diffuser (b)	90–360	0.2	0.2	0.2	
	Vanes bent forward				
Rectangular cross section (a), $R_0 = D_h$	90–180	0.2	0.3	0.3	Ts14-76
	270–360	0.7	0.5	0.5	
Circular cross section, $R_0 = 2D_h$	90–360	0.3	0.4	0.4	
Rectangular cross section, $R_0 = 1.5\,D_h$ with a pyramidal diffuser (b)	90–180	0.4	0.2	0.2	

Note: η^f and η^f_{max} are the efficiency and the maximum efficiency of the fan, respectively.

Elbows with sharp corners ($r/b_0 = 0$) at $\delta = 90°$;   Diagram
$l_0/D_h \geq 0^{*36}$ 6-6

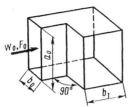

1. Smooth walls ($\Delta = 0$), $Re = \dfrac{w_0 D_h}{\nu} \geq 2 \times 10^5$;

$$\zeta \equiv \frac{\Delta p}{\rho w_0^2/2}$$

at $l_0/D_h = 0\text{-}2$; $\zeta = \zeta_{loc} = f\left(\dfrac{b_1}{b_0}, \dfrac{a_0}{b_0}\right)$, see graph a;

at $l_0/D_h \geq 10$, $\zeta \approx 1.05\zeta_{loc}$

$$D_h = \frac{2a_0 b_0}{a_0 + b_0}$$

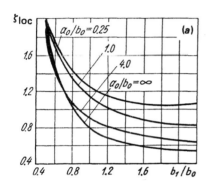

Values of ζ_{loc}

	b_1/b_0						
a_0/b_0	0.6	0.8	1.0	1.2	1.4	1.6	2.0
0.25	1.76	1.43	1.24	1.14	1.09	1.06	1.06
1.0	1.70	1.36	1.15	1.02	0.95	0.90	0.84
4.0	1.46	1.10	0.90	0.81	0.76	0.72	0.66
∞	1.50	1.04	0.79	0.69	0.63	0.60	0.55

2. Rough walls ($\Delta > 0$) and $Re \geq 10^4$:

$\zeta = k_\Delta k_{Re} \zeta_{loc}$

where $k_\Delta = f(Re$ and $\overline{\Delta} = \Delta/D_h)$, see the Table; k_{Re}), see graph b or, tentatively,

$k_{Re} \approx 4.06/Re^{0.118}$

Values of K_Δ

	$Re \times 10^{-3}$	
$\overline{\Delta}$	3–40	>40
0	1.0	1.0
0.001	1.0	$1 + 0.5 \times 10^3\,\overline{\Delta}$
0.001	1.0	≈ 1.5

$Re \times 10^{-4}$	1	1.4	2	3	4	6	8	10	14	≥ 20
k_{Re}	1.40	1.33	1.26	1.19	1.14	1.09	1.06	1.04	1.0	1.0

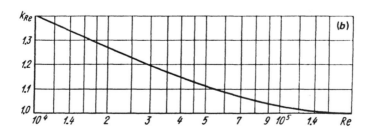

*Here and subsequently $l_0/D_h = 0$ means that the elbow (bend) is installed directly downstream of the smooth collector inlet.

Elbows with sharp corners ($r/b_0 = 0$) at $0 < \delta \le 180°$; $l_0/D_h \ge 10^{1,17,77,79,81,92}$

Diagram
6-7

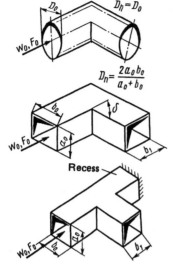

I. Elbow without recess

1) Smooth walls ($\Delta = 0$), Re $= w_0 D_h/\nu \ge 2 \times 10^5$:

$$\zeta \equiv \frac{\Delta p}{\rho w_0^2/2} = C_1 A \zeta_{loc}(\zeta_{fr} \approx 0)$$

$C_1 = f(a_0/b_0)$, see graph a (in the case of a circular or square section $C_1 = 1.0$) or, tentatively, $C_1 = 0.97 - 0.13\ln(a_0/b_0)$, $\zeta_{loc} = 0.95 \sin^2(\delta/2) + 2.05 \sin^4(\delta/2) = f(\delta)$, see graph b; $A = f(\delta)$, see graph b or tentatively $A \approx 0.95 + 33.5/\delta$;

2) Rough walls ($\Delta = 0$) and Re $\ge 10^4$:

$$\zeta = k_\Delta k_{Re} C_1 A \zeta_{loc}$$

k_Δ and k_{Re} are determined as a function of $\overline{\Delta} = \Delta/D_h$ and Re, respectively; see Diagram 6-6.

δ,°	0	20	30	45	60	75	90	110	130	150	180
ζ_{loc}	0	0.05	0.07	0.17	0.37	0.63	0.99	1.56	2.16	2.67	3.00
A	–	2.50	2.22	1.87	1.50	1.28	1.20	1.20	1.20	1.20	1.20

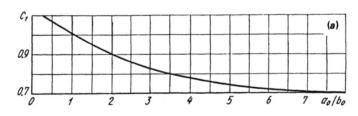

(a)

a_0/b_0	0.25	0.50	0.75	1.0	1.5	2.0	3.0	4.0	5.0	6.0	7.0	8.0
C_1	1.10	1.07	1.04	1.00	0.95	0.90	0.83	0.78	0.75	0.72	0.71	0.70

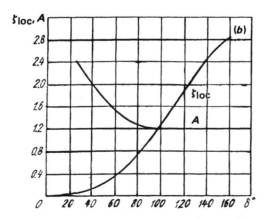

(b)

II. Elbow with recess

$$\zeta \equiv \frac{\Delta p}{\rho w_0^2/2} \approx 1.2\zeta_{w.r.}$$

where for $\zeta_{w.r.}$, see ζ for elbow without recess.

Elbows with rounded corners and diverging or converging exit[37] $(F_1/F_0 \geq 1.0)$; $0 < \delta \leq 180°$; $l_0/D_h \geq 10$	Diagram 6-8

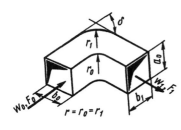

b_{con} is the width of the contracted section.

1) Smooth walls ($\Delta = 0$) and Re $= \dfrac{w_{con} b_{con}}{\nu} \geq 2 \times 10^3$;

$$\zeta \equiv \frac{\Delta p}{\rho w_{con}^2/2} = A_1 C_1 \exp\left(-\frac{k_1}{n_{ar}}\right) + \zeta_{fr} = AC_1\zeta' + \zeta_{fr}$$

where $\zeta' = \exp\left(-\dfrac{k_1}{n_{ar}}\right) = f\left(\dfrac{F_1}{F_0} \dfrac{r}{b_{con}}\right)$, see graph a;

$\zeta_{fr} = \left(1 + 0.0175 \dfrac{r}{D_h} \delta\right) \lambda$; for λ, see Diagrams 2-1 and 2-6; at $\lambda \approx 0.025 \zeta_{fr} = 0.02 + 0.00035 \delta \dfrac{r}{D_h}$;

$A_1 = f(\delta)$, see graph b; $C_1 = f\left(\dfrac{a_0}{b_{con}} = \dfrac{a_0}{b_0}\right)$, see, tentatively, graph d of Diagram 6-1;

$k_1 = 2.3 \lg \dfrac{1}{\zeta_0}$; ζ_0 is the resistance coefficient of the elbow at $n_{ar} = F_1/F_0 = 1.0$ and $\delta = 90°$; w_{con} is the mean velocity of flow in the contracted section.

2) Rough walls ($\Delta > 0$) and Re $\geq 10^4$:

$$\zeta = k_\Delta k_{Re} A_1 C_1 \zeta' + \zeta_{fr}$$

for k_Δ and k_{Re}, see Diagram 6-1.

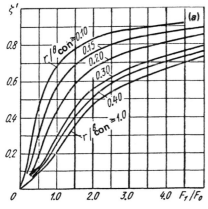

Values of ζ'

$\dfrac{r}{b_{con}}$	F_1/F_0							
	0.2	0.5	1.0	1.5	2.0	3.0	4.0	5.0
0.10	0.20	0.45	0.69	0.78	0.83	0.88	0.91	0.93
0.15	0.13	0.32	0.57	0.68	0.76	0.83	0.87	0.89
0.20	0.08	0.20	0.45	0.58	0.67	0.76	0.81	0.85
0.30	0.06	0.13	0.30	0.45	0.56	0.67	0.74	0.79
0.40	0.04	0.10	0.25	0.40	0.51	0.64	0.70	0.76
1.00	0.04	0.09	0.21	0.35	0.47	0.59	0.67	0.73

$\delta,°$	0	20	30	45	60	75	90	110	130	150	180
A_1	0	0.31	0.45	0.60	0.78	0.90	1.00	1.13	1.20	1.28	1.40

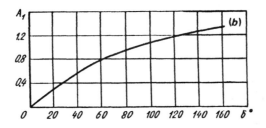

Elbows with rounded corners at $0.05 < r/D_0 \leq 0.5$ and $< \delta \leq 180°$; $l_0/D_h \geq 10$[1,17,31,61,64,77,79,91]	Diagram 6-9

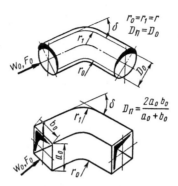

1) Smooth walls ($\Delta = 0$) and $Re = \dfrac{w_0 D_h}{\nu} \geq 2 \times 10^5$:

$$\zeta \equiv \frac{\Delta p}{\rho w_0^2/2} = \zeta_{loc} + \zeta_{fr}$$

where $\zeta_{loc} = A_1 B_1 C_1$; $\zeta_{fr} = (1 + 0.0175 \delta r/D_h) \lambda$; for λ, see Diagrams 2-1 and 2-6; at $\lambda \approx 0.02$, $\zeta_{fr} = 0.02 + 0.00035 \delta r/D_h$; $A_1 = f(\delta)$ and $C_1 = f(a_0/b_0)$ see Diagram 6-1; $B_1 = f(r/D_0)$, see the table or tentatively $B_1 \approx 0.155(r_0/D_0)^{-0.595}$.

2) Rough walls ($\Delta > 0$) and $Re \gtrsim 10^4$:

$$\zeta = k_\Delta k_{Re} \zeta_{loc} + \zeta_{fr}$$

for k_Δ and k_{Re}, see Diagram 6-1.

r/D_0 (r/b_0)	0.05	0.10	0.20	0.30	0.40	0.50	0.60
B_1	0.87	0.70	0.44	0.31	0.26	0.24	0.22

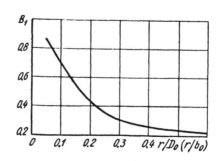

Elbows of rectangular cross section with different shapes of inner and outer corners of the turn at $\delta = 90°$; $l_0/D_h = 0-2$ [5,30,37]	Diagram 6-10

No.	Characteristics of the elbow	Resistance coefficient $\zeta \equiv \dfrac{\Delta p}{\rho w_0^2/2}$

1. Rounded inner corner, sharp outer corner:

$$D_h = \frac{4F_0}{\Pi_0}$$

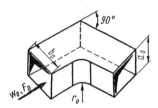

1) Smooth walls ($\Delta = 0$) and $Re = w_0 b_0/\nu > 2 \times 10^5$:

$$\zeta = C_1\zeta_{loc} + \zeta_{fr}$$

where $\zeta_{fr} = [1 + 1.57(r_0/b_0)]\lambda$; $\lambda = f(Re \text{ and } \overline{\Delta})$, see Diagrams 2-1 and 2-6; at $\lambda = 0.02$, $\zeta_{fr} = 0.02 + 0.031(r_0/b_0)$; $C_1 = f(a_0/b_0)$, see graph d of Diagram 6-1.

2) Rough walls ($\Delta > 0$) and $Re > 10^4$:

$$\zeta = k_\Delta k_{Re} C_1 \zeta_{loc} + \zeta_{fr}$$

where for k_Δ and k_{Re}, see Diagram 6-1; $\zeta_{loc} = f(r_0/b_0)$, see graph a or, tentatively, $\zeta_{loc} \approx 0.39(r_0/b_0)^{-0.352}$

r_0/b_0	0.05	0.1	0.2	0.3	0.5	0.7	1.0
ζ_{loc}	1.10	0.88	0.70	0.56	0.48	0.43	0.40

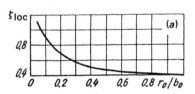

2. Rounded inner corner ($r_0/b_0 = 1.0$), beveled outer corner

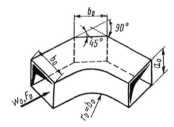

ζ is the same as under No. 1 at $\zeta_{loc} = 0.20$.

3. Beveled inner corner, sharp outer corner

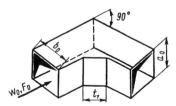

ζ is the same as under No. 1, but $\zeta_{loc} = f\left(\dfrac{t_1}{b_0}\right)$,

see graph b or $\zeta_{loc} \approx \dfrac{1}{0.72 + 1.85 t_1/b_0}$

t_1/b_0	0.1	0.2	0.3	0.4	0.5
ζ_{loc}	1.10	0.90	0.80	0.69	0.60

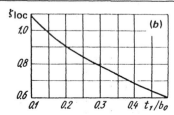

		Diagram 6-10

No.	Characteristics of the elbow	Resistance coefficient $\zeta \equiv \dfrac{\Delta p}{\rho w_0^2/2}$

| 4. | Inner corner cut by two chords; the outer corner is sharp | ζ is the same as under No. 1, but $\zeta_{loc} = 0.47$ |

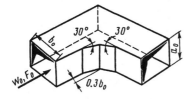

| 5. | Inner and outer corners are beveled | ζ is the same as under No. 1, but $\zeta_{loc} = 0.28$ |

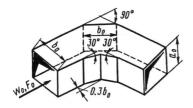

| 6. | Right-angle elbow ($\delta = 90°$) of rectangular cross section with circular fairing | a) $r_1/b_0 = 0$ ζ is the same as under No. 1, but ζ_{loc} is determined from graph c |

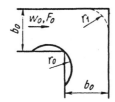

r_0/b_0	0.1	0.2	0.3	0.4	0.5	0.6	0.7
ζ_{loc}	1.13	0.88	0.69	0.57	0.55	0.58	0.65

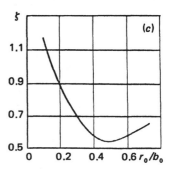

b) $r_0/b_0 = 0.45$;
   $r_1/b_0 = 0.45$
ζ is the same as under No. 1, but $\zeta_{loc} = 0.49$

Elbows composed of separate elements at different angles δ; circular cross section; $l_0/D_0 \geqslant 10$[22,6-71,6-81]	Diagram 6-11

No.	Characteristics of the elbow	Resistance coefficient $\zeta \equiv \dfrac{\Delta p}{\rho w_0^2/2}$

1. $\delta = 45°$; three elements at the angle 22.5°

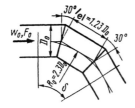

1) Smooth walls ($\Delta = 0$) and $\mathrm{Re} = w_0 D_0/\nu \geqslant 2 \times 10^5$:

$$\zeta = \zeta_{loc} + \zeta_{fr}$$

where $\zeta_{loc} = 0.11$; $\zeta_{fr} = \lambda l_{el}/D_0$; at $\lambda \approx 0.02$, $\zeta_{fr} = 0.02 l_{el}/D_0$.

2) Rough walls ($\Delta > 0$) and $\mathrm{Re} \geqslant 10^4$:

$$\zeta = k_\Delta k_{Re} \zeta_{loc} + \zeta_{fr}$$

for λ, k_Δ, k_{Re}, see Diagram 6-1

2. $\delta = 60°$; three elements at the angle 30°

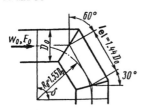

ζ is the same as under No. 1, but $\zeta_{loc} = 0.15$

3. $\delta = 60°$; four elements at the angle 20°

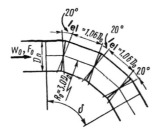

ζ is the same as under No. 1, but $\zeta_{fr} = 2(l_{el}/D_0)$; at $\lambda \approx 0.02$, $\zeta_{fr} = 0.04(l_{el}/D_0)$

4. $\delta = 90°$; three elements at the angles 60 and 30°

ζ is the same as under No. 1, but $\zeta_{loc} = 0.40$

5. $\delta = 90°$; three elements at the angles 45° welded with welding seams; $\mathrm{Re} > 10 \times 10^5$

D_0, mm	50	100	150	200	250	300	350
		0.80	0.60	0.45	0.38	0.32	0.30	0.30

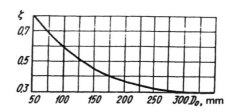

Segmented elbows of circular cross section at $\delta = 90°$; $l_0/D_0 > 10^{1.68}$

Diagram 6-12

No.	Elbow characteristics	Resistance coefficient $\zeta \equiv \dfrac{\Delta p}{\rho w_0^2/2}$

1. Made from five elements at the angle 22.5°

1) Smooth walls ($\Delta = 0$) and $\mathrm{Re} = w_0 D_0/\nu \geq 2 \times 10^5$:

$$\zeta = \zeta_{loc} + \zeta_{fr}$$

where $\zeta_{loc} = f(l_{el}/D_0)$, see graph a or

$$\zeta_{loc} = \sum_{i=0}^{n_i} a_i (R_0/D_0); \quad (1)$$

at $R_0/D_0 \leq 1.9$

$\begin{aligned}
a_0 &= 1.100609; & a_1 &= -0.2413919; \\
a_2 &= -2.257211; & a_3 &= 3.920123; \\
a_4 &= -3.270671; & a_5 &= 1.464781; \\
a_6 &= -0.2737305; & n_i &= 6;
\end{aligned}$

at $1.9 < R_0/D_0 < 10$

$\begin{aligned}
a_0 &= 0.6408985; & a_1 &= -0.5625683; \\
a_2 &= 0.2448837; & a_3 &= -0.5663924 \times 10^{-1}; \\
a_4 &= 0.7245266 \times 10^{-2}; & a_5 &= -0.4796866 \times 10^{-3}; \\
a_6 &= 0.1279164 \times 10^{-4}; & n_i &= 6;
\end{aligned}$

at $R_0/D_0 \geq 10$, $\quad \zeta_{loc} = 0.14$

$\zeta_{fr} = (n_{elem} - 1) l_{el}/D_0$; n_{elem} is the number of elements in the elbow.

2) Rough walls ($\Delta > 0$) and $\mathrm{Re} \geq 10^4$:

$$\zeta = k_\Delta k_{Re} \zeta_{loc} + \zeta_{fr}$$

for k_Δ and k_{Re}, see Diagram 6-1;

l_{el}/D_0	0.2	0.4	0.6	0.8	1.0	2.0	3.0	4.0	5.0	6.0
R_0/D_0	0.50	0.98	1.47	1.90	2.50	5.0	7.50	10.0	12.5	15.0
ζ_{loc}	0.75	0.45	0.34	0.15	0.12	0.16	0.42	0.14	0.14	0.14

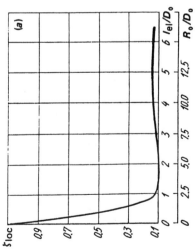

(a)

2.   Made from four elements at the angle 30°

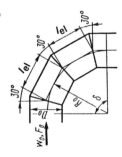

ζ is the same as under No. 1, but $\zeta_{loc} = f(l_{el}/D_0)$ is determined as a function of l_{el}/D_0 from graph b from formula (1):

at $R_0/D_0 < 7.5$ $a_0 = 1.110851$; $a_1 = -0.6822401$;

$$a_2 = 0.3342034; \quad a_3 = -0.2609621; \quad a_4 = 0.127691;$$

$$a_5 = -0.3035488 \times 10^{-1}; \quad a_6 = 0.339646 \times 10^{-2};$$

$$a_7 = 0.144361 \times 10^{-3}; \quad n_i = 7;$$

$$\text{at } R_0/D_0 \geqslant 7.5 \quad \zeta_{loc} = 0.2$$

l_{el}/D_0	0	0.2	0.4	0.6	0.8	1.0	2.0	3.0	4.0	5.0	6.0
R_0/D_0	0	0.37	0.75	1.12	1.50	1.85	3.70	5.55	7.40	9.25	11.0
ζ	1.10	0.92	0.70	0.58	0.40	0.30	0.16	0.19	0.20	0.2	0.20

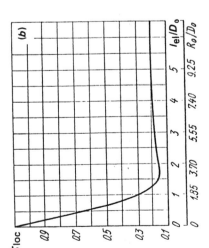

Diagram 6-12

No.	Elbow characteristics	Resistance coefficient $\zeta \equiv \dfrac{\Delta p}{\rho w_0^2/2}$

3. Made from three elements at the angle 45°

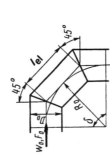

ζ is the same as under No. 1, but $\zeta_{loc} = f(R_0/D_0)$, see graph c or from formula (1):

at $R_0/D_0 < 4.5$ $a_0 = 1.118112$; $a_1 = -0.6977857$;

$a_2 = -0.4818015$; $a_3 = 0.7030898$; $a_4 = -0.2244795$;

$a_5 = -0.6968263 \times 10^{-3}$; $a_6 = 0.1058802 \times 10^{-1}$;

$a_7 = -0.1241125 \times 10^{-2}$; $n_i = 7$;

at $R_0/D_0 \geqslant 4.5$ $\zeta_{loc} = 0.4$

l_{el}/D_0	0	0.2	0.4	0.6	0.8	1.0	2.0	3.0	4.0	5.0	6.0
R_0/D_0	0	0.24	0.48	0.70	0.97	1.20	2.40	3.60	4.80	6.0	7.25
ζ	1.10	0.95	0.72	0.60	0.42	0.38	0.32	0.38	0.41	0.4	0.41

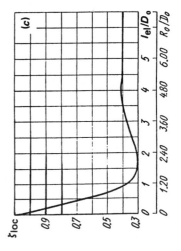

Diagram 6-13

Z-shaped elbows with sharp corners $(r_0/b_0 = 0)$[36,68,71]

$$D_h = \frac{4F_0}{\Pi_0}$$

No.	Elbow characteristics	Resistance coefficient $\zeta = \dfrac{\Delta p}{\rho w_0^2/2}$

1. Made from two 90° elbows; flow turning in one plane; $l_0/b_0 = 0-2$; rectangular cross section

1) Smooth walls ($\Delta = 0$) and $Re = w_0 b_0/\nu \geq 2 \times 10^5$:

$\zeta = G_1 \zeta_{loc} + \zeta_{fr}$

where $\zeta_{loc} = f(l_{el}/b_0)$, see graph a; $\zeta_{fr} = \lambda l'_{el}/b_0$; for λ, see Diagrams 2-1 through 2-6; at $\lambda \approx$ 0.02, $\zeta_{fr} = 0.02 l'_{el}/b_0$; for C_1, see, tentatively, graph a of Diagram 6-5.

2) Rough walls ($\Delta > 0$) and $Re \geq 10^4$:

$\zeta = k_\Delta k_{Re} C_1 \zeta_{loc} + \zeta_{fr}$

for k_Δ and k_{Re}, see Diagram 6-4

l'_{el}/b_0	0	0.4	0.6	0.8	1.0	1.2	1.4	1.6	1.8	2.0
ζ_{loc}	0	0.62	0.90	1.61	2.63	3.61	4.01	4.18	4.22	4.18
l'_{el}/b_0	2.4	2.8	3.2	4.0	5.0	6.0	7.0	9.0	10	∞
ζ_{loc}	3.65	3.30	3.20	3.08	2.92	2.92	2.80	2.70	2.45	2.30

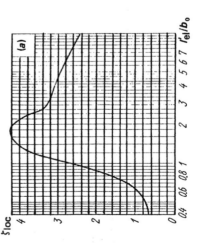

Diagram
6-13

$$D_h = \frac{4F_0}{\Pi_0}$$

Resistance coefficient $\zeta \equiv \dfrac{\Delta p}{\rho w_0^2/2}$

No.	Elbow characteristics
2.	Made from two 90° elbows; flow turning in two mutually perpendicular planes; $l_0/b_0 = 0\text{--}2$; rectangular cross section

ζ is the same as under No. 1, but at $\zeta_{loc} = f(l'_{el}/b_0)$, from graph b

l'_{el}/b_0	0	0.4	0.6	0.8	1.0	1.2	1.4	1.6	1.8	2.0
ζ_{loc}	1.15	2.40	2.90	3.31	3.44	3.40	3.36	3.28	3.20	3.11
l'_{el}/b_0	2.4	2.8	3.2	4.0	5.0	6.0	7.0	9.0	10	∞
ζ_{loc}	3.16	3.18	3.15	3.00	2.89	2.78	2.70	2.50	2.41	2.30

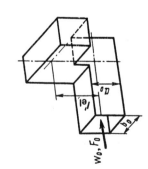

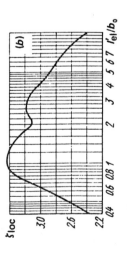

3. Made from two 30° elbows; turning of the flow in one plane; $l_0/b_0 > 10$; circular cross section

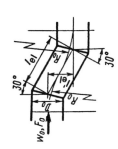

ζ is the same as under No. 1, but at $\zeta_{loc} = f[R_0/D_0(l_{el}/D_0)]$, from graph c or $\zeta_{loc} = \sum_{i=0}^{4} a_i(l_{el}/D_0)^i$

where $a_0 = 0.0095$; $a_1 = 0.22575$; $a_2 = -0.1177083$; $a_3 = 0.02475$; $a_4 = -0.1791667 \times 10^{-2}$. The formula is valid at $l_{el}/D_0 < 3$; at $l_{el}/D_0 \geqslant 3$, $\zeta_{loc} = 0.16$

l_{el}/D_0	0	1.0	2.0	3.0	4.0	5.0	6.0
R_0/D_0	0	1.85	3.70	5.55	7.40	9.25	11.3
ζ_{loc}	0	0.15	0.15	0.16	0.16	0.16	0.16

Z-shaped elbows with rounded corners[32] $(r/D_h > 0;\ l_0/D_0 \geqslant 10)$	Diagram 6-14

$$D_h = \frac{4F_0}{\Pi_0}$$

No.	Elbow characteristics	Resistance coefficient $\zeta \equiv \dfrac{\Delta p}{\rho w_0^2/2}$

1. Made from two 90° elbows; turning of the flow in one plane

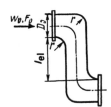

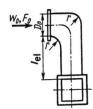

Normal turbulent velocity profile at the entrance at

$$Re = \frac{w_0 D_h}{\nu} \geqslant 10^4$$

$$\zeta \equiv \zeta'_{loc} + \zeta_{fr}$$

where $\zeta = f(l_{el}/D_h)$, see graph a; $\zeta'_{loc} = k_\Delta k_{Re}\zeta_{loc}$, see Diagram 6-1; $\zeta_{fr} \approx (5.0r/D_h + l_{el}/D_h)\lambda$; for λ, see Diagrams 2-1 through 2-6; at $\lambda \approx 0.02$,

$$\zeta_{fr} = 0.1 r/D_h + 0.02 l_{el}/D_h$$

Nonuniform velocity profile at the entrance

$$\zeta_{non} = k\overline{\zeta}\zeta'_{loc} + \zeta_{fr}$$

where for k, see below

No. of velocity profile from Figure 6-18	1	2	3	4
k_1 (at all l_{el}/D_h)	0.8	1.05	1.2	1.2

Values of $\overline{\zeta}$

r/D_0	l_{el}/D_h								
(r/b_0)	0.4	0.6	1.0	1.5	2.0	3.0	5.0	10	∞
0.2	1.20	1.45	1.45	1.12	1.08	1.02	1.04	1.0	1.0
0.5	–	–	0.85	0.73	0.77	0.79	0.83	0.90	1.0

2. Made from two 90° elbows; flow turning in two mutually perpendicular planes

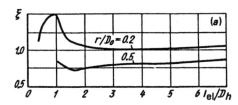

Normal turbulence velocity profile at the entrace at

$$Re \geqslant 10^4:$$

$$\zeta = \overline{\zeta}\zeta'_{loc} + \zeta_{fr}$$

where $\zeta = f(l_{el}/D_h)$, see graph b; $\zeta'_{loc} = k_\Delta k_{Re}\zeta_{loc}$, see Diagram 6-1; for ζ_{fr}, see No. 1.
Nonuniform velocity profile at the entrance:

Values of $k_1\zeta_{non} = k\overline{\zeta}_{loc} + \zeta_{fr}$

No. of velocity profile from Figure 6-18	l_{el}/D_h			
	1–3	4	5	$\geqslant 7$
1	0.85	0.87	0.89	0.94
2	1.10	1.15	1.20	1.32
3	1.05	1.13	1.18	1.34
4	1.15	1.17	1.20	1.26

Values of $\overline{\zeta}$

r/D_0	l_{el}/D_h								
(r/b_0)	0.4	0.6	1.0	1.5	2.0	3.0	5.0	10	∞
0.2	1.20	1.11	1.05	1.10	1.10	1.09	1.09	1.05	1.0
0.5	–	–	0.94	0.82	0.81	0.81	0.81	0.85	1.0

| ⌐-shaped elbows (180°) with sharp corners ($r/b_0 = 0$); rectangular cross section;[36] $F_1/F_0 \gtrless 1.0$; $l_0/b_0 = 0\text{–}2$ | Diagram 6-15 |

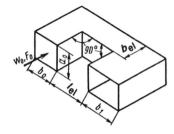

The resistance coefficient $\zeta \equiv \dfrac{\Delta p}{\rho w_0^2/2}$

1. $\dfrac{F_1}{F_0} = \dfrac{b_1}{b_0} = 0.5$

1) Smooth walls ($\Delta = 0$) and Re $= w_0 b_h/\nu \geqslant 2 \times 10^5$:

$$\zeta = C_1 \zeta_{loc} + \zeta_{fr}$$

where $\zeta_{loc} = f(l_{el}/b_0)$, see graph a; $\zeta_{fr} \approx \lambda(1 + l_{el}/b_0)$; for λ, see Diagrams 2-1 through 2-6; at $\lambda \approx 0.02$, $\zeta_{fr} = 0.02 + 0.02 l_{el}/b_0$; C_1, tentatively, see graph a of Diagram 6-7.

2) Rough walls ($\Delta > 0$) and Re $\geqslant 10^4$: $\zeta = k_\Delta k_{Re} C_1 \zeta_{loc} + \zeta_{fr}$, where for k_Δ and k_{Re}, see Diagram 6-6.

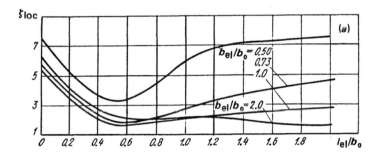

Values of ζ_{loc}

b_{el}/b_0	l_{el}/b_0										
	0	0.2	0.4	0.6	0.8	1.0	1.2	1.4	1.6	1.8	2.0
0.5	7.5	5.2	3.6	3.4	4.5	6.0	6.7	7.1	7.8	7.5	7.6
0.73	5.8	3.8	2.4	1.9	2.2	2.7	3.3	3.7	4.0	4.3	4.7
1.0	5.5	3.5	2.1	1.7	1.9	2.1	2.3	2.4	2.6	2.7	2.7
2.0	6.3	4.2	2.7	2.1	2.1	2.2	2.2	2.0	2.0	1.8	1.6

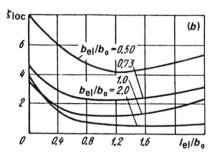

2. $\dfrac{F_1}{F_0} = \dfrac{b_1}{b_0} = 1.0$:

ζ is the same as under No. 1, but $\zeta_{loc} = f(l_{el}/b_0)$ from graph b.

Values of ζ_{loc}

b_{el}/b_0	l_{el}/b_0											
	0	0.2	0.4	0.6	0.8	1.0	1.2	1.4	1.6	1.8	2.0	2.4
0.5	7.9	6.9	6.1	5.4	4.7	4.3	4.2	4.3	4.4	4.6	4.8	5.3
0.73	4.5	3.6	2.0	2.5	2.4	2.3	2.3	2.3	2.4	2.6	2.7	3.2
1.0	3.6	2.5	1.8	1.4	1.3	1.2	1.2	1.3	1.4	1.5	1.6	2.3
2.0	3.9	2.4	1.5	1.0	0.8	0.7	0.7	0.6	0.6	0.6	0.6	0.7

Diagram
6-15

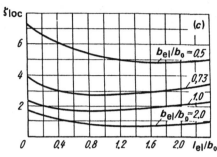

3. $\dfrac{F_1}{F_0} = \dfrac{b_1}{b_0} = 1.4$:

ζ is the same as under No. 1, but $\zeta_{loc} = f(l_{el}/b_0)$ from graph c.

Values of ζ_{loc}

$\dfrac{b_{el}}{b_0}$	l_{el}/b_0										
	0	0.2	0.4	0.6	0.8	1.0	1.2	1.4	1.6	1.8	2.0
0.5	7.3	6.6	6.1	5.7	5.4	5.2	5.1	5.0	4.9	4.9	5.0
0.73	3.9	3.3	3.0	2.9	2.8	2.8	2.8	2.9	2.9	3.0	3.2
1.0	2.3	2.1	1.9	1.8	1.7	1.7	1.8	1.8	1.9	2.0	2.1
2.0	1.7	1.4	1.2	1.0	0.9	0.8	0.8	0.7	0.7	0.8	0.8

4. $\dfrac{F_1}{F_0} = \dfrac{b_1}{b_0} = 2.0$:

ζ is the same as under No. 1, but $\zeta_{loc} = f(l_{el}/b_0)$ from graph d.

Values of ζ_{loc}

$\dfrac{b_{el}}{b_0}$	l_{el}/b_0										
	0	0.2	0.4	0.6	0.8	1.0	1.2	1.4	1.6	1.8	2.0
0.5	8.4	7.8	7.3	6.8	6.3	5.9	5.6	5.3	5.2	5.0	4.9
0.73	4.1	3.9	3.8	3.6	3.5	3.4	3.2	3.1	3.0	3.0	2.9
1.0	2.5	2.5	2.4	2.3	2.2	2.1	2.0	2.0	1.9	1.9	1.9
2.0	1.2	1.1	1.0	1.0	0.9	0.9	0.8	0.8	0.8	0.9	0.9

□-shaped elbows (180°) with rounded corners $(r/D_h > 0)$;[32]
$F_1/F_0 = 1.0$; $l_0/D_h \geqslant 10$

Diagram
6-16

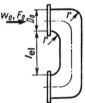

Normal turbulent velocity profile at the entrance

$$\mathrm{Re} = \frac{w_0 D_h}{\nu} \geqslant 10^4 \qquad \zeta \equiv \frac{\Delta p}{\rho w_0^2/2} = \bar{\zeta}\zeta'_{loc} + \zeta_{fr}$$

where $\bar{\zeta} = f(l_{el}/D_h)$, see the graph; $\zeta'_{loc} = k_\Delta k_{Re}\zeta_{loc}$, see Diagram 6-1; $\zeta_{fr} = (5.0r/D_h + l_{el}/D_h)\lambda$; for λ, see Diagrams 2-1 through 2-6; at $\lambda \approx 0.02$, $\zeta_{fr} = 0.1r/D_h + 0.02l_{el}/D_h$.

Nonuniform velocity profile at the entrance $\zeta_{non} = k\bar{\zeta}\zeta'_{loc} + \zeta_{fr}$

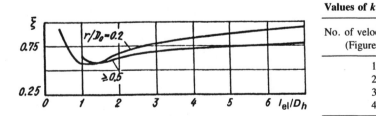

Values of k

No. of velocity profile (Figure 6-18)	l_{el}/D_h	
	1–3	$\geqslant 4$
1	0.80	0.80
2	1.15	1.05
3	1.20	1.15
4	1.20	1.15

Values of ζ

r/D_0 (r/b_0)	l_{el}/D_h								
	0.4	0.6	1.0	1.5	2.0	3.0	5.0	10	∞
0.2	0.93	0.75	0.57	0.60	0.67	0.77	0.86	0.97	1.0
$\geqslant 0.5$	–	–	0.63	0.58	0.58	0.63	0.74	0.85	1.0

U-shaped elbows (180°); rectangular cross section;[36]	Diagram
$F_1/F_0 \gtrless 1.0$; $l_0/b_0 = 0$–2	6-17

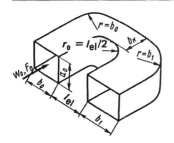

Resistance coefficient $\zeta \equiv \dfrac{\Delta p}{\rho w_0^2/2}$

1. $\dfrac{F_1}{F_0} = \dfrac{b_1}{b_0} = 0.5$

1) Smooth walls ($\Delta = 0$) and Re $= w_0 b_0/\nu \geq 2 \times 10^5$: $\zeta = C_1\zeta_{loc} + \zeta_{fr}$, where $\zeta_{loc} = f(l_{el}/b_0)$, see graph a; $\zeta_{fr} \approx (1.5 + 2l_{el}/b_0)\lambda$; for λ, see Diagrams 2-1 through 2-6; at $\lambda \approx 0.02$, $\zeta_{fr} = 0.03$–$0.04l_{el}/b_0$; C_1, tentatively, see graph a of Diagram 6-7.

2) Rough walls ($\Delta > 0$) and Re $\geq 10^4$:

$$\zeta = k_\Delta k_{Re} C_1 \zeta_{loc} + \zeta_{fr}$$

for k_Δ and k_{Re}, see Diagram 6-1;

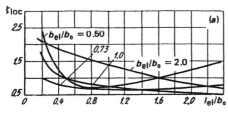

Values of ζ_{loc}

$\dfrac{B_{el}}{b_0}$					l_{el}/b_0					
	0.2	0.4	0.6	0.8	1.0	1.2	1.4	1.6	1.8	2.0
0.5	2.6	1.3	0.8	0.7	0.7	0.8	0.9	1.0	1.1	1.2
0.75	1.1	0.8	0.7	0.7	0.6	0.6	0.6	0.7	0.7	0.7
1.0	1.8	1.1	0.9	0.8	0.8	0.7	0.6	0.6	0.6	0.5
2.0	2.1	1.9	1.7	1.5	1.4	1.3	1.1	1.0	0.9	0.8

2. $\dfrac{F_1}{F_0} = \dfrac{b_1}{b_0} = 1.0$

ζ is the same as under No. 1, but $\zeta_{loc} = f(l_{el}/b_0)$ from graph b.

Values of ζ_{loc}

$\dfrac{B_{el}}{b_0}$					l_{el}/b_0					
	0.2	0.4	0.6	0.8	1.0	1.2	1.4	1.6	1.8	2.0
0.5	4.5	2.6	1.9	1.7	1.5	1.3	1.2	1.1	1.0	0.9
0.75	2.5	1.5	0.9	0.7	0.5	0.5	0.4	0.4	0.4	0.3
1.0	1.6	0.9	0.5	0.3	0.3	0.3	0.2	0.2	0.2	0.3
2.0	1.6	1.0	0.8	0.7	0.6	0.5	0.5	0.4	0.4	0.4

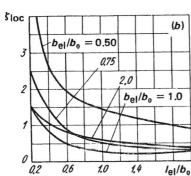

3. $\dfrac{F_1}{F_0} = \dfrac{b_1}{b_0} = 1.4$

ζ is the same as under No. 1, but $\zeta_{loc} = f(l_{el}/b_0)$ from graph c.

Values of ζ_{loc}

$\dfrac{B_{el}}{b_0}$					l_{el}/b_0					
	0.2	0.4	0.6	0.8	1.0	1.2	1.4	1.6	1.8	2.0
0.5	4.2	3.1	2.5	2.2	2.0	1.9	1.9	1.8	1.8	1.8
0.75	2.8	1.8	1.4	1.1	0.9	0.8	0.8	0.7	0.7	0.7
1.0	1.9	1.3	0.9	0.7	0.5	0.4	0.3	0.3	0.2	0.2
2.0	1.2	0.9	0.8	0.7	0.6	0.5	0.4	0.4	0.4	0.4

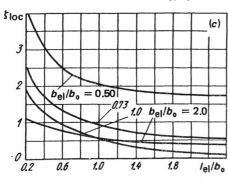

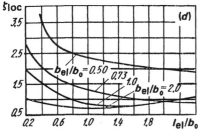

4. $\dfrac{F_1}{F_0} = \dfrac{b_1}{b_0} = 2.0$

ζ is the same as under No. 1, but $\zeta_{loc} = f(l_{el}/b_0)$ from graph d.

Values of ζ_{loc}

$\dfrac{B_{el}}{b_0}$					l_{el}/b_0					
	0.2	0.4	0.6	0.8	1.0	1.2	1.4	1.6	1.8	2.0
0.5	6.0	3.5	2.8	2.5	2.4	2.3	2.2	2.1	2.1	2.0
0.75	2.9	2.1	1.7	1.5	1.3	1.2	1.1	1.0	1.0	0.9
1.0	2.0	1.6	1.2	1.0	0.9	0.8	0.8	0.8	0.9	0.9
2.0	1.0	0.9	0.8	0.7	0.7	0.7	0.7	0.8	0.9	0.9

Doubly curved turns at different values of δ; $l_0/D_h \geqslant 10^{8\text{-}10,26}$	Diagram 6-18

S-shaped bend ("gooseneck"-type); flow in one plane

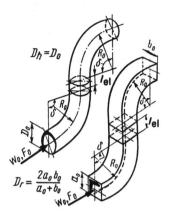

1) $\dfrac{R_0}{D_0} > 1.0$

$$\zeta \equiv \frac{\Delta p}{\rho w_0^2/2} = A\zeta'_{\text{loc}} + \zeta_{\text{fr}}$$

where for ζ'_{loc}, see ζ_{loc} of a single branch on Diagrams 6-1 and 6-2;

$$\zeta_{\text{fr}} = \lambda\left(\frac{l_{\text{el}}}{D_h} + 0.035\frac{R_0}{D_h}\delta\right); \text{ for } \lambda, \text{ see Diagrams 2-1}$$

through 2-6; at $\lambda \approx 0.02$, $\zeta_{\text{fr}} = 0.02\left(\dfrac{l_{\text{el}}}{D_h} + 0.0007\dfrac{R_0}{D_h}\delta\right)$;

$A = f(l_{\text{el}}/D_h)$, see Table 1 and graph a (correct at Re $= 2 \times 10^4$):

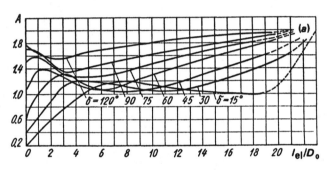

Values of A

$\delta,^\circ$	l_{el}/D_h														
	0	1	2	3	4	6	8	10	12	14	16	18	20	25	40–50
15	0.20	0.42	0.60	0.78	0.94	1.16	1.20	1.15	1.08	1.05	1.02	1.0	1.10	1.25	2.0
30	0.40	0.65	0.88	1.16	1.20	1.18	1.12	1.06	1.06	1.15	1.28	1.40	1.50	1.70	2.0
45	0.60	1.06	1.20	1.23	1.20	1.08	1.03	1.08	1.17	1.30	1.42	1.55	1.65	1.80	2.0
60	1.05	1.38	1.37	1.28	1.15	1.06	1.16	1.30	1.42	1.54	1.66	1.76	1.85	1.95	2.0
75	1.50	1.58	1.46	1.30	1.27	1.30	1.37	1.47	1.57	1.68	1.75	1.80	1.88	1.97	2.0
90	1.70	1.67	1.40	1.37	1.38	1.47	1.55	1.63	1.70	1.76	1.82	1.88	1.92	1.98	2.0
120	1.78	1.64	1.48	1.55	1.62	1.70	1.75	1.82	1.88	1.90	1.92	1.95	1.97	1.99	2.0

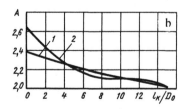

2) $R_0/D_0 = 0.8$ (circular cross-section)

$$\zeta = A\zeta_{\text{loc}} + \zeta_{\text{fr}}$$

where $\zeta_{\text{loc}} = f(\delta)$, see Table 2; $A = f(l_{\text{el}}/D_0)$, see Table 2 and graph b or

$$\zeta = 3.5\zeta_{\text{loc}}^{1.25} - (3 - \zeta_{\text{loc}}^{1.25})(\lambda l_{\text{el}}/D_0)^{0.33}\zeta_{\text{loc}} + \zeta_{\text{fr}}; \qquad (1)$$

for ζ_{fr} see para. 1.

Values of A

No. of curve	δ°	ζ_{loc}	l_{el}/D_0			
			0	5	10	15
1	45	0.23	2.39	2.26	2.13	2.0
2	90	0.35	2.66	2.20	2.11	2.02

Diagram
6-18

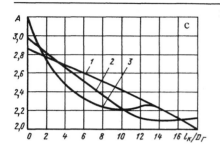

3) $\delta = 90°$ (rectangular cross section)
$\zeta_{loc} = f(R_0/b_0, b_0/a_0)$, see Table 3; $A = f(l_{el}/D_h)$, see Table 3 and graph c or formula (1) (D_0 is replaced by D_h); for ζ_{fr} see para. 1.

Values of A

No. of curve	R_0/b_0	b_0/a_0	ζ_{loc}	l_{el}/D_h			
				0	6	12	18
1	0.75	1.25	0.75	2.87	2.60	2.33	2.0
2	0.70	1.0	0.52	2.98	2.50	2.11	2.11
3	0.60	1.0	0.45	3.20	2.33	2.26	1.93

S-shaped joined bends; spatial (flow in two mutually perpendicular planes)[8-10,26]   Diagram 6-19

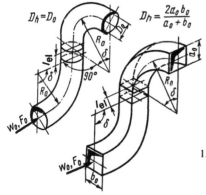

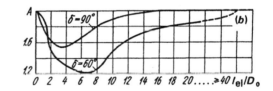

1. $R_0/D_0 \geqslant 1.0$:

$$\zeta \equiv \frac{\Delta p}{\rho w_0^2/2} = A\zeta'_{loc} + \zeta_{fr}$$

where for ζ'_{loc} see ζ_{loc} of a single bend on Diagrams 6-1 and 6-2; $\zeta_{fr} = \lambda(l_{el}/D_h + 0.035\,\delta R_0/D_h)$; for λ see Diagrams 2-1 through 2-6; at $\lambda \approx 0.02$, $\zeta = 0.02 l_{el}/D_h + 0.0007\,\delta R_0/D_h$; $A = f(l_{el}/D_h)$, from Table 1 and graph a (valid at Re $\geqslant 2 \times 10^4$)

2. $R_0/D_0 = 0.8$ (circular cross section)

$$\zeta = A\zeta_{loc} + \zeta_{fr}$$

where $\zeta_{loc} = f(\delta)$, see Table 2; $A = f(l_{el}/D_h)$, see Table 2 and graph b or

$$\zeta = 3.0\zeta_{loc}^{1.25} - 3.3(\zeta_{loc}^{0.5} + 2D_0/l_{el})\lambda l_{el}/D_0)\zeta_{loc}^2 + \zeta_{fr} \qquad (1)$$

for ζ_{fr} see para. 1.

Diagram 6-19

1. Values of *A*

δ,°	l_0/D_h												
	0	1	2	3	4	6	8	10	12	14	20	25	40
60	2.0	1.90	1.50	1.35	1.30	1.20	1.25	1.50	1.63	1.73	1.85	1.95	2.0
90	2.0	1.80	1.60	1.55	1.55	1.65	1.80	1.90	1.93	1.98	2.0	2.0	2.0

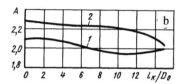

2. Values of *A*

No. of curve	δ°	ζ_{loc}	l_{el}/D_0			
			0	5	10	15
1	45	0.23	2.09	2.04	1.95	2.0
2	90	0.35	2.28	2.23	2.20	2.03

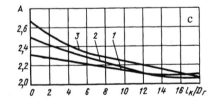

3. $\delta = 90°$ (rectangular cross section)$\zeta_{loc} = f(R_0/b_0, b_0/a_0)$, see Table 3; $A = f(l_{el}/D_h)$, see Table 3 and graph c or formula (1) (D_0 is replaced by D_h); for ζ_{fr} see para. 1.

3. Values of *A*

No. of curve	R_0/b_0	b_0/a_0	ζ_{loc}	l_{el}/D_h			
				0	6	12	18
1	0.75	1.25	0.75	2.33	2.21	2.11	2.06
2	0.70	1.0	0.52	2.50	2.27	2.11	2.11
3	0.60	1.0	0.45	0.67	2.34	2.20	2.06

Diagram 6-20

U-shaped joined bends and turns in one plane;[8,10.26] $l_0/D_h \geq 10$

U-shaped in one plane; smooth ($R_0/D_0 \geq 1.0$); $0 < \delta < 180°$

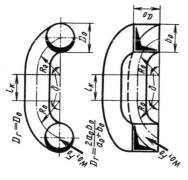

1. $R_0/D_0 \geq 1.0$

$$\zeta \equiv \frac{\Delta p}{\rho w_0^2/2} = A\zeta'_{loc} + \zeta_{fr}$$

where for ζ'_{loc}, see ζ_{loc} of a single branch on Diagrams 6-1 and 6-2;

$$\zeta_{fr} = \lambda\left(\frac{l_{el}}{D_h} + 0.035\frac{R_0}{D_h}\delta\right); \text{ for } \lambda, \text{ see Diagrams 2-1}$$

through 2-6; at $\lambda \approx 0.02$, $\zeta_{fr} = 0.02\left(\frac{l_{el}}{D_h} + 0.0007\frac{R_0}{D_h}\delta\right)$;

$A = f(l_{el}/D_h)$, see Table 1 and graph a

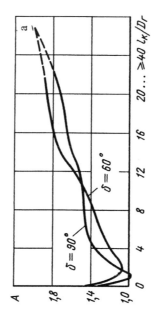

1. Values of A

$\delta°$	0	1	2	3	4	6	8	10	12	14	20	25	40–50
													l_{el}/D_h
60	1.50	1.15	1.05	1.10	1.20	1.30	1.35	1.46	1.57	1.73	1.85	1.95	2.0
90	1.37	0.95	1.10	1.25	1.35	1.45	1.45	1.50	1.50	1.60	1.70	1.90	2.0

Diagram 6-20

2. $R_0/D_0 = 0.8$ (circular cross-section)

$$\zeta = A\zeta_{loc} + \zeta_{fr}$$

where $\zeta_{loc} = f(\delta)$, see Table 2; $A = f(l_{el}/D_0)$, see Table 2 and graph b

or

$$\zeta = 1.2\zeta_{loc}^{0.5} + 1.87(\zeta_{loc}^{0.5} + 2D_0/l_{el})(\lambda l_{el}/D_0)\zeta_{loc}^{0.25} + \zeta_{fr} \quad (1)$$

for ζ_{fr} see para. 1.

2. Values of A

No. of curve	$\delta°$	ζ_{loc}	l_{el}/D_0			
			0	5	10	15
1	45	0.23	1.30	1.61	2.0	2.0
2	90	0.35	1.29	1.49	1.77	2.0

3. $\delta = 90°$ (rectangular cross section)
$\zeta_{loc} = f(R_0/b_0, b_0/a_0)$, see Table 3; $A = f(l_{el}/D_h)$, see Table 3 and graph c or formula (1) (D_0 is replaced by D_h); for ζ_{fr} see para. 1.

3. Values of A

No. of curve	R_0/b_0	b_0/a_0	ζ_{loc}	l_{el}/D_h			
				0	6	12	18
1	0.75	1.25	0.75	1.20	1.67	1.78	2.0
2	0.70	1.0	0.52	1.35	1.73	1.83	1.93
3	0.60	1.0	0.45	1.20	1.45	1.80	2.0

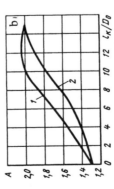

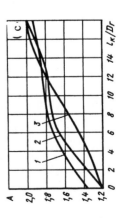

Joined gate-like bends, turns;[26] l_0/D_h Diagram 6-21

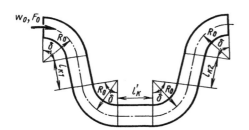

Connected in one plane

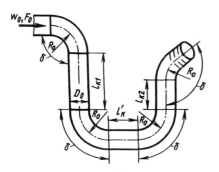

Connected in space

1. $0 < \delta < 180°$, $R_0/D_0 \geqslant 1.0$ (scheme 1)

$$\zeta \equiv \frac{\Delta p}{\rho w_0^2/2} \approx 2\zeta_1 + \zeta'_{fr} \text{ (tentatively)}$$

where ζ_1 is determined as ζ from para. 1 of Diagram 6-18;
$\zeta'_{fr} = \lambda l'_{el}/D_h$; for λ see Diagrams 2-1 through 2-6; at $\lambda \approx 0.02$, $\zeta'_{fr} = 0.02 l'_{el}/D_h$

2. $0 < \delta < 180°$, $R_0/D_0 \geqslant 1.0$ (scheme 2)

$$\zeta \equiv \frac{\Delta p}{\rho w_0^2/2} = \zeta_1 + \zeta_2 + \zeta'_{fr} \text{ (tentatively)},$$

where ζ_1 is determined as ζ from para. 1 of Diagram 6-18; ζ_2 is determined as ζ from para. 1 of Diagram 6-19; for ζ'_{fr} see para. 1

3. $\delta = 90°$, $R_0/D_0 = 0.8$ (circular cross section; scheme 1);

$$\zeta = 1.55 + \zeta_{fr}$$

where $\zeta_{fr} = \lambda(2l_{el}/D_0 + l'_{el}/D_0 + 5.04)$; at $\lambda \approx 0.02\zeta_{fr} = 0.1 + 0.04 l_{el}/D_0 + 0.02 l'_{el}/D_0$

4. $\delta = 90°$, $R_0/b_0 = 0.6$ (square cross section; scheme 1);
$\zeta = 4.12 + \zeta_{fr}$, where for ζ_{fr} see para. 3

Joined curved turns and elbows, $3 \times 90°$ and $4 \times 90°$ of rectangular cross section at $a_0/b_0 = 0.5$;[8,10,88] $l_{el}/b_0 \geqslant 10$ Diagram 6-22

Turns ($R_0/b_0 = 0.75$)

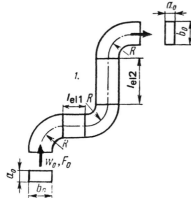

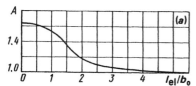

1) Smooth walls ($\Delta = 0$) and Re $= w_0 b_0/\nu \geqslant 4 \times 10^5$:

$$\zeta \equiv \frac{\Delta p}{\rho w_0^2/2} = \zeta_{loc} + \zeta_{fr}$$

2) Rough walls ($\Delta > 0$) and $10^4 <$ Re $< 4 \times 10^5$;

$$\zeta = k_\Delta k_{Re} \zeta_{loc} + \zeta_{fr}, \quad \zeta_{loc} = 1.5A$$

where $A = f(l_{el}/b_0)$, see graph a;

$$\zeta_{fr} = \left(\frac{l_{el_1}}{b_0} + \frac{l_{el_2}}{b_0} + 3.5\right)\lambda$$

for λ, see Diagrams 2-1 through 2-6; at $\lambda \approx 0.02$

$$\zeta_{fr} = 0.02\left(\frac{l_{el_1}}{b_0} + \frac{l_{el_2}}{b_0}\right) + 0.07$$

for k_Δ, see Diagram 6-1; $k_{Re} = f(\text{Re})$, see graph b.

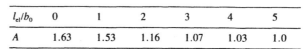

l_{el}/b_0	0	1	2	3	4	5
A	1.63	1.53	1.16	1.07	1.03	1.0

Joined curved turns and elbows, $3 \times 90°$ and $4 \times 90°$, of rectangular cross section at $a_0/b_0 = 0.5$;[8,10,88] $l_0/b_0 \geq 10$	Diagram 6-22

3. Turns, spatial (sharply curved)

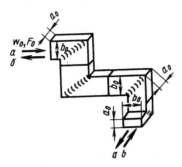

Without guide vanes:
flow direction a-a

$$\zeta = 12.5k_{Re};$$

flow direction b-b

$$\zeta = 8.7k_{Re};$$

With guide vanes:

$$\zeta = 0.4k_{Re};$$

Here for k_{Re} see graph b.

4. Turns, spatial (sharply curved)

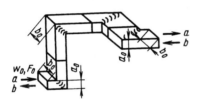

Without guide vanes: flow direction a-a

$$\zeta = 6.9k_{Re};$$

flow direction b-b

$$\zeta = 8.3k_{Re};$$

With guide vanes

$$\zeta = 0.4k_{Re};$$

Here for k_{Re} see graph b.

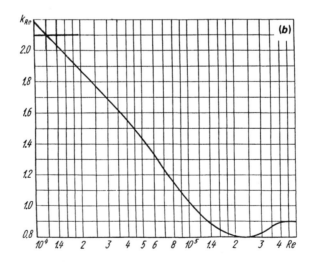

Re $\times 10^{-4}$	1	1.4	2	3	4	6	8	10	14	20	30	40
k_{Re}	2.20	2.03	1.88	1.69	1.56	1.34	1.14	1.02	0.89	0.80	0.83	1.0

	Diagram 6-22

5. Elbows at $r/b_0 = 0$ without vanes

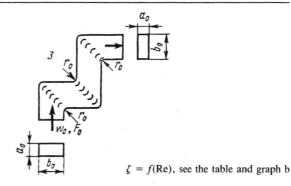

$\zeta = f(\text{Re})$, see the table and graph b

6. Elbows at $r/b_0 = 0.25$ with guide vanes

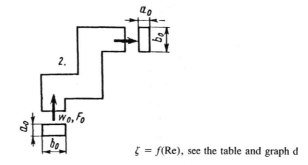

$\zeta = f(\text{Re})$, see the table and graph d

Values of ζ

	Re $\times$ 10^{-4}						
Scheme	2	3	4	6	10	20	40
5. Graph c	9.70	9.70	9.55	9.00	9.25	8.75	8.75
6. Graph d	1.0	1.0	0.77	0.61	0.53	0.46	0.38

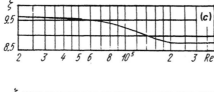

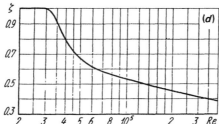

By-passes 4 × 90° (sharply curved) of rectangular cross section at $a_0/b_0 = 0.5;$[88] $l_0/b_0 > 10$		Diagram 6-23
By-pass characteristics	**Schemes**	**Resistance coefficients** $\zeta \equiv \dfrac{\Delta p}{\rho w_0^2/2}$
$\dfrac{r_1}{b_0} = \dfrac{r_2}{b_0} = \dfrac{r_3}{b_0} = \dfrac{r_4}{b_0} = 0$	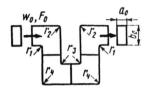	$6.77k_{Re}^{I}$
$\dfrac{r_1}{b_0} = \dfrac{r_2}{b_0} = \dfrac{r_3}{b_0} = 0;\quad \dfrac{r_4}{b_0} = 1.5$	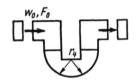	$6.38k_{Re}^{I}$
$\dfrac{r_1}{b_0} = \dfrac{r_3}{b_0} = 0.07;\quad \dfrac{r_2}{b_0} = \dfrac{r_4}{b_0} = 0$	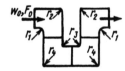	$5.30k_{Re}^{II}$
$\dfrac{r_1}{b_0} = \dfrac{r_2}{b_0} = 0;\quad \dfrac{r_3}{b_0} = 0.5;\quad \dfrac{r_4}{b_0} = 1.5$		$3.80k_{Re}^{II}$
$\dfrac{r_1}{b_0} = \dfrac{r_2}{b_0} = 0.25;\quad \dfrac{r_3}{b_0} = 0;\quad \dfrac{r_4}{b_0} = 1.5$ with guide vanes in elbows No. 1 and No. 4*		$1.65k_{Re}^{III}$
$\dfrac{r_1}{b_0} = \dfrac{r_2}{b_0} = 0.25;\quad \dfrac{r_3}{b_0} = 0.5:\quad \dfrac{r_4}{b_0} = 1.5$ with guide vanes in elbows No. 1 and No. 2*		$0.60k_{Re}^{IV}$
$\dfrac{r_1}{b_0} = \dfrac{r_2}{b_0} = \dfrac{r_3}{b_0} = \dfrac{r_4}{b_0} = 0.25$ with guide vanes in all the elbows*		$0.50k_{Re}^{IV}$

*Position and construction of vanes are described under paragraphs 64–72.

					Diagram 6-23

k_{Re}	\multicolumn{10}{c}{Re $\times 10^{-4}$}
	1	2	3	4	6	8	10	20	30	$\geqslant 60$
$k_{\mathrm{Re}}^{\mathrm{I}}$	1.28	1.15	1.10	1.06	1.04	1.02	1.01	1.0	1.0	1.0
$k_{\mathrm{Re}}^{\mathrm{II}}$	1.40	1.26	1.19	1.14	1.09	1.06	1.04	1.0	1.0	1.0
$k_{\mathrm{Re}}^{\mathrm{III}}$	1.86	1.60	1.46	1.37	1.24	1.15	1.10	1.0	1.0	1.0
$k_{\mathrm{Re}}^{\mathrm{IV}}$	–	2.65	2.20	1.95	1.65	1.52	1.40	1.23	1.11	1.0

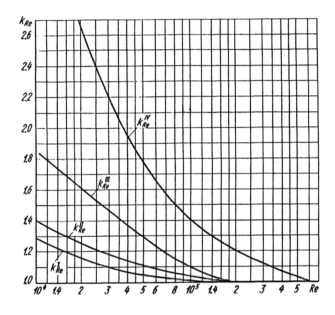

Joined elbows made from zinc-coated sheet at $R_0/D_0 = 1.0$; $D_0 = 100$ mm and corrugated elbows at $R_0/D_0 = 0.7$; $D_0 = 100$ mm; Re $= w_0 D_0/\nu \geq 1.5 \times 10^5$; $l_0/D_0 \geq 10^{58}$

Diagram 6-24

Resistance coefficient

$$\zeta \equiv \frac{\Delta p}{\rho w_0^2/2}$$

Elbow characteristics	Scheme	
Elbow; $\delta' = 45°$	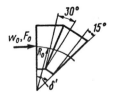	0.60

	Diagram 6-24

Elbow characteristics	Scheme	Resistance coefficient $\zeta \equiv \dfrac{\Delta p}{\rho w_0^2/2}$
Elbow; $\delta = 90°$		0.92
"Gooseneck," $2\delta = 2 \times 90°$		2.16
"Gooseneck" (turning in two planes); $\delta + \delta' = 90° + 45°$		1.50
"Gooseneck" (turning in two planes); $2\delta = 2 \times 90°$		1.60
Turns, $4\delta' = 4 \times 45°$		2.65
Elbow; $\delta' = 45°$		0.53
Elbow; $2\delta' = 2 \times 45°$		0.82

		Diagram 6-24

Elbow characteristics	Scheme	Resistance coefficient $\zeta \equiv \dfrac{\Delta p}{\rho w_0^2/2}$
Elbow; $\delta = 90°$		1.33
"Gooseneck"; $2\delta' = 2 \times 45°$		1.00
"Gooseneck"; $2\delta = 2 \times 90°$		3.30
"Gooseneck" (turning in two planes); $\delta + \delta' = 90° + 45°$		1.93
"Gooseneck" (turning in two planes); $\delta = 2 \times 90°$		2.56
Turn, $4\delta' = 4 \times 45°$		2.38

Flexible glass-cloth bends with furrowed surfaces;[53] $\mathrm{Re} \geqslant 10^5$	Diagram 6-25

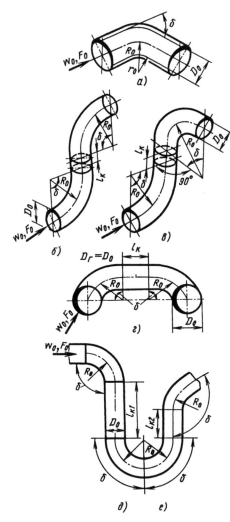

$$\zeta \equiv \frac{\Delta p}{\rho w_0^2/2} = 0.9 n_b \zeta_{\mathrm{loc}} + \zeta_{\mathrm{fr}}$$

where for ζ_{loc} see the tables; $\zeta_{\mathrm{fr}} = \lambda(l_{\mathrm{el}}/D_0 + 0.035 R_0/D_0)$,

$\lambda = 0.052(10 D_0)^{0.1/D_0}(0.05 b)^{0.2}$;

b is the width of the tape wound on the wire framework of a glass-cloth tube (see para. 72 of Section 2-1); D_0 is the diamater of the tube, m; n_b is the number of bends.

Values of ζ_{loc} at $R_0/D_0 = 1.5$ (scheme a)

D_0, m	$\delta°$			
	30	45	60	90
0.100	0.69	1.18	1.48	1.78
0.155	–	1.07	–	1.30
0.193	0.43	0.50	0.73	0.86
0.250	0.26	0.34	0.41	0.56

At $D_0 < 0.3$ m

$\zeta_{\mathrm{loc}} \approx 1.05 a \exp(-c D_0) \sin \delta$

where $a = 3.86$; $c = 7.8$ m^{-1}; at $D_0 \geqslant 0.3$

$\zeta_{\mathrm{loc}} \approx 0.4$

	Diagram 6-25

Values of ζ_{loc} at $\delta = 90°$ (numerator) and $\delta = 45°$ (denumerator) (scheme a)

D_0, m	R_0/D_0		
	0.75	1.5	3.0
0.100	2.28 / 1.25	1.78 / 1.18	1.70 / 1.04
0.155	1.30 / 1.12	1.30 / 1.07	1.18 / 1.05
0.193	1.12 / –	0.86 / –	–
0.250	0.90 / 0.44	0.71 / 0.39	0.52 / 0.25

Values of ζ_{loc} at $R_0/D_0 = 1.5$ and $\delta = 90°$

Scheme of the turn	Number of bends n_b	D_0, m	
		0.100	0.193
In one plane			
a	1	1.78	0.73
b	2	3.55	1.29
Spatial			
c	2	3.11	1.40
In one plane			
d	2	–	1.33
e	3	5.06	1.89
f	4	6.03	2.40

$$\sum_{}^{n_b} \zeta_{loc} = 0.9 n_b \zeta_{loc}$$

Elbows and turns ($\delta = 90°$) of rectangular cross section with guide vanes*[5,15]	Diagram 6-26

1. Elbow ($r_0 = r_1 = r$; $t_1 = r\sqrt{2}$) with profiled guide vanes;

$$Re = \frac{w_0 b_0}{\nu} = 2 \times 10^5$$

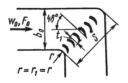

$$\zeta \equiv \frac{\Delta p}{\rho w_0^2 / p} = \zeta_{loc} + \zeta_{fr}$$

$$Re \gtrless 2 \times 10^5$$

$$\zeta = k_{Re} \zeta_{loc} + \zeta_{fr}$$

*Disposition and design of vanes are described under paragraphs 64–72.

Diagram 6-26

Normal number of vanes

$$n_{nor} = 2.13\left(\frac{r}{b_0}\right)^{-1} - 1$$

$$= 2.13\frac{S}{t_1} - 1$$

Reduced number of vanes

$$n_{adv} \approx 1.4\left(\frac{r}{b_0}\right)^{-1} - 1$$

$$= 1.4\frac{S}{t_1}$$

Minimal number of vanes

$$n_{min} \approx 0.9\left(\frac{r}{b_0}\right)^{-1} - 1$$

$$= 0.9\frac{S}{t_1}$$

where $\zeta_{loc} = f(r/b_0)$, see graph a; $\zeta_{fr} = (1 + 1.57r/b_0)\lambda$; for λ, see Diagrams 2-1 through 2-6; at $\lambda \approx 0.02$, $\zeta_{fr} = 0.02 + 0.31r/b_0$; $k_{Re} = f(Re)$, see, tentatively, graph b, or the formula $k_{Re} = 0.8 + 4.02 \times 10^4/Re$.

Values of ζ_{loc}

Number of vanes (see graph a)	r/b_0						
	0	0.1	0.2	0.3	0.4	0.5	0.6
Normal (curve 1)	0.33	0.23	0.17	0.16	0.17	0.22	0.31
Reduced (curve 2)	0.33	0.23	0.15	0.11	0.13	0.19	0.30
Minimal (curve 3)	0.45	0.33	0.27	0.22	0.17	0.15	0.17

Re $\times 10^{-4}$	3	4	5	6	8	10	14	20	30	$\geqslant 60$
k_{Re}	2.10	1.80	1.60	1.50	1.35	1.23	1.12	1.0	0.90	0.80

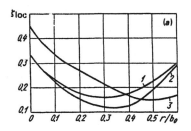

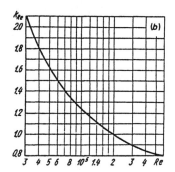

Diagram 6-26

2. The same as under No. 1, but guide vanes are thin at $\varphi_1 = 90\text{--}95°$ ζ is the same as under No. 1, but $\zeta_{loc} = f(r/b_0)$, according to graph c or the formulas.

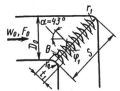

Values of ζ_{loc}

Number of vanes (see graph c)	r/b_0							ζ_{loc}
	0	0.05	0.10	0.15	0.20	0.25	0.30	
Normal (curve 1)	0.42	0.35	0.30	0.26	0.23	0.21	0.20	$1/(8.39r/b_0 + 2.58)$
Reduced (curve 2)	0.42	0.35	0.30	0.24	0.20	0.17	0.14	$0.4 \times 0.037r/b_0$
Minimal (curve 3)	0.57	0.48	0.43	0.39	0.35	0.31	0.28	$1/(5.43r/b_0 + 1.85)$

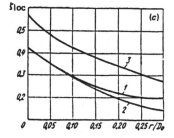

Turns ($\delta = 90°$) with concentric guide vanes[46,68]   Diagram 6-27

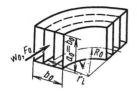

1. Turn of rectangular cross section ($r_0/b_0 = R_0/b_0 - 0.5$) with vanes at Re $= 10^5$

$$\zeta \equiv \frac{\Delta p}{\rho w_0^2/2} = \zeta_{\text{loc}} + \zeta_{\text{fr}}$$

at Re $\gtrsim 10^5$

$$\zeta = k_{\text{Re}}\zeta_{\text{loc}} + \zeta_{\text{fr}}$$

where $\zeta_{\text{loc}} = (0.46R_0/b_0 - 0.04)\zeta_{\text{w.v.}}$, see graph a; for $\zeta_{\text{w.v.}}$ see ζ without vanes from Diagram 6-1; $\zeta_{\text{fr}} = 1.57\lambda \dfrac{R_0}{b_0}$; for λ, see Diagrams 2-1 through 2-6; at $\lambda \approx 0.02$, $\zeta_{\text{fr}} = 0.03 \dfrac{R_0}{b_0}$; for k_{Re} see, tentatively, graph e of Diagram 6-1; distance between vanes: $r_i = 1.26r_{i-1} + 0.07b_0$

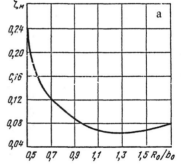

r_0/b_0	0.5	0.6	0.7	0.8	0.9	1.0	1.1	1.3	1.5
ζ_{loc}	0.24	0.15	0.12	0.10	0.09	0.08	0.07	0.06	0.07

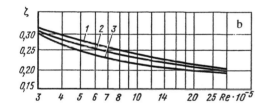

2. Turn of circular cross section with vanes

$$\zeta \equiv \frac{\Delta p}{\rho w_0^2/2} = f(\text{Re}, R_0/b_0), \text{ see graph b;}$$

$$\zeta \equiv \frac{\Delta p}{\rho w_0^2/2} = f(r_1/b_0, \text{Re}), \text{ see graph c}$$

Values of ζ at different R_0/b_0

R_0/b_0	Re $\times 10^{-4}$							
	3	4	6	8	10	15	20	30
1 (one vane)	0.32	0.3	0.29	0.25	0.24	0.23	0.22	0.2
1 (two vanes)	0.31	0.29	0.28	0.24	0.23	0.21	0.20	0.20
1.8 (one vane)	0.3	0.27	0.24	0.23	0.22	0.20	0.20	0.19

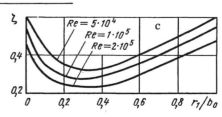

Values of ζ at $R_0/b_0 = 0.75$ and one vane ($i = 1$)

Re	r_1/b_0										
	0	0.1	0.2	0.3	0.4	0.5	0.6	0.7	0.8	0.9	1.0
5×10^{-4}	0.60	0.42	0.35	0.31	0.32	0.35	0.39	0.44	0.49	0.55	0.6
10^{-5}		0.54	0.34	0.29	0.27	0.28	0.30	0.35	0.39	0.44	0.49	0.54
2×10^{-5}	0.48	0.29	0.26	0.23	0.24	0.26	0.30	0.35	0.39	0.43	0.48

	Elbows of rectangular cross section at $\delta = 90°$ and with thin guide vanes* $(\varphi_1 = 95°)^{5.15}$		Diagram 6-28

No.	Elbow charcteristics	Scheme	Resistance coefficient
			$$\zeta \equiv \frac{\Delta p}{\rho w_0^2/2}$$

1. Inner corner is sharp $(t_1 = 0)$;
   $\alpha = 45°$; normal number of vanes:

   $$n_v = 2.13 \frac{S}{t_1} - 1$$

   $\zeta = 0.45 k_{Re} + \lambda^{**}$

   at $\lambda \approx 0.02$, $\zeta \approx 0.47 k_{Re}$; for λ, see Diagrams 2-1 through 2-6

2. The same as under No. 1, but
   $\alpha = 50°$

   $\zeta = 0.40 k_{Re} + \lambda$

   at $\lambda \approx 0.02$, $\zeta \approx 0.42 k_{Re}$

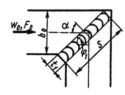

3. The same as under No. 1, but with reduced (most advantageous) number of vanes:

   $$n_v \approx 1.4 \frac{S}{t_1}$$

   $\zeta = 0.36 k_{Re} + \lambda$

   at $\lambda \approx 0.02$, $\zeta \approx 0.38 k_{Re}$

4. The same as under No. 1, but the inner corner is beveled $(t_1 = 0.25 b_0)$

   $\zeta = 0.32 k_{Re} + 1.28\lambda$

   at $\lambda \approx 0.02$, $\zeta \approx 0.35 k_{Re}$

5. Diverging elbow $(F_1/F_0 = 1.35)$ $r/b_0 = 1.18$; $\alpha \approx 53°$, normal number of vanes:

   $$n_v = 2.13 \frac{S}{t_1} - 1$$

   $t_1 = r\sqrt{2}$; $r_0 = r_1 = r$

   $\zeta = 0.40 k_{Re} + 1.28\lambda$

   at $\lambda \approx 0.02$, $\zeta \approx 0.43 k_{Re}$

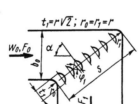

6. The same as under No. 5, but with reduced (minimal) number of vanes:

   $$n_v \approx 0.9 \frac{S}{t_1}$$

   $\zeta = 0.60 k_{Re} + 1.28\lambda$

   at $\lambda \approx 0.02$, $\zeta \approx 0.63 k_{Re}$

*Disposition of vanes is described under paragraphs 64–72.

**For k_{Re} see, tentatively, Diagram 6–26.

Smooth elbows of rectangular cross section at $\delta = 90°$ and with thin guide vanes[50]	Diagram 6-29

1. $\dfrac{F_1}{F_0} = 0.5$; $\dfrac{r}{b_0} = 0.2$; $\phi_1 = 103°$;

$r_0 = r_1 = r$

number of vanes (most advantageous) $n_{adv} = 11$

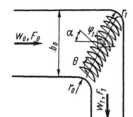

$$\zeta \equiv \frac{\Delta p}{\rho w_0^2/2} = k_{Re}\zeta_{loc} + \zeta_{fr}$$

where $\zeta_{fr} = \left(1 + 1.57\,\dfrac{r}{b_0}\right)\lambda$; for λ, see Diagrams 2-1 through 2-6; at

$\lambda \approx 0.02$, $\zeta_{fr} = 0.02 + 0.031\,\dfrac{r}{b_0}$

$k_{Re} = f(Re)$, see, tentatively, graph b of Diagram 6-26; $\zeta_{loc} = f(\theta)$, see graph a.

$\theta,°$	106	108	110	112	114	116	118
ζ_{loc}	0.52	0.46	0.43	0.42	0.44	0.48	0.52

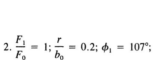

2. $\dfrac{F_1}{F_0} = 1$; $\dfrac{r}{b_0} = 0.2$; $\phi_1 = 107°$;

$r_0 = r_1 = r$

number of vanes (most advantageous) $n_{adv} = 5$

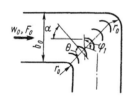

ζ is the same as under No. 1, but $\zeta_{loc} = f(\theta)$, see graph b

$\theta,°$	82	84	86	88	90	92	94	96	98
ζ_{loc}	0.50	0.30	0.22	0.17	0.14	0.12	0.11	0.12	0.14

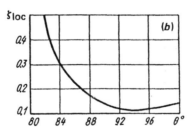

3. $\dfrac{F_1}{F_0} = 2$; $r_0 = r_1 = r$

(a) $r/b_0 = 0.2$; $\phi_1 = 154°$;

$\quad n_{adv} = 5$

(b) $r/b_0 = 0.5$; $\phi_1 = 138°$;

$\quad n_{adv} = 2$

(c) $r/b_0 = 1.0$; $\phi_1 = 90°$;

$\quad n_{adv} = 5$

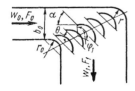

ζ is the same as under No. 1, but $\zeta_{loc} = f(\theta)$, see graph c.

Values of ζ_{loc}

	$\theta,°$							
Curve	68	70	72	74	76	78	80	82
1	0.39	0.36	0.34	0.33	0.34	0.37	0.40	0.44
2	0.32	0.29	0.27	0.26	0.26	0.25	0.25	0.25
3	0.40	0.26	0.21	0.21	0.25	0.32	0.52	0.67

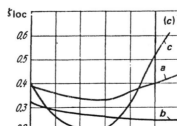

Elbows of circular cross section at $\delta = 90°$ with profiled guide vanes*[15]		Diagram 6-30

Elbow characteristics	Scheme	Resistance coefficient $\zeta \equiv \dfrac{\Delta p}{\rho w_0^2/2}$
Smooth turn ($r/D_0 = 0.18$); normal number of vanes: $$n_v = \frac{3D_0}{t_1} - 1$$	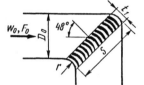	$\zeta = 2.3k_{Re} + 1.28\lambda$ at $\lambda = 0.02$, $\zeta \approx 0.26k_{Re}$; for λ, see Diagrams 2-1 through 2-6
Smooth turn ($r/D_0 = 0.18$); reduced number of vanes: $$n_v = \frac{2D_0}{t_1}$$ Vanes are installed according to arithmetic progression at $$\frac{a_{n+1}}{a_1} = 2$$		$\zeta = 0.15k_{Re} + 1.28\lambda$ at $\lambda \approx 0.02$, $\zeta = 0.18k_{Re}$
Beveled corners of the turn ($t_1/D_0 = 0.25$); normal number of vanes: $$n_v = \frac{3D_0}{t_1} - 1$$	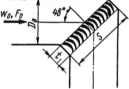	$\zeta = 0.30k_{Re} + 1.28\lambda$ at $\lambda \approx 0.02$, $\zeta \approx 0.33k_{Re}$
Beveled corners of the turn ($t_1/D_0 = 0.25$); reduced number of vanes: $$n_v = \frac{2D_0}{t_1}$$ Vanes are smoothly embedded and installed according to arithmetic progression at $$\frac{a_{n+1}}{a_1} = 2$$	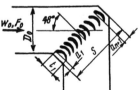	$\zeta = 0.23k_{Re} + 1.28\lambda$ at $\lambda \approx 0.02$, $\zeta \approx 0.26k_{Re}$
Beveled corners of the turn ($t_1/D_0 = 0.25$); reduced number of vanes (1st and 3rd vanes are removed from the outer wall)	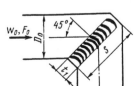	$\zeta = 0.21k_{Re} + 1.28\lambda$ at $\lambda \approx 0.02$, $\zeta \approx 0.24k_{Re}$

*Disposition and design of vanes are described under paragraphs 64–72. For k_{Re} see, tentatively Diagram 6-26.

Spatial (circular) turn through 180° (during suction);[19]	Diagram
$R/D_1 = 0.2\text{--}0.5$; $Re = w_0 D_0/\nu \geqslant 4 \times 10^4$	6-31

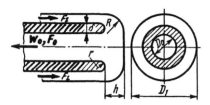

A. Rounded corners at the turn $(r/D_0 > 0)$

$$\zeta \equiv \frac{\Delta p}{\rho w_0^2/2} = f\left(\frac{h}{D_0}, \frac{r}{D_0}, n_{ar}\right)$$

See graph a.

$$n_{ar} = F_1/F_0$$

Values of ζ

r/D_0	n_{ar}	\multicolumn{16}{c}{h/D_0}
		0.10	0.15	0.20	0.25	0.30	0.40	0.50	0.60	0.70	0.80	0.90	1.0	1.20	1.40	1.60	1.80	2.00
	0.75	5.80	2.90	1.90	2.40	2.80	3.00	3.25	3.55	4.00	2.80	2.10	1.95	1.90	1.95	2.00	2.03	2.05
0.05	1.08	4.70	2.60	1.35	1.10	1.08	1.30	1.77	1.80	1.73	1.66	1.55	1.48	1.33	1.23	1.30	1.30	1.30
	2.05	3.45	1.50	1.00	0.73	0.60	0.50	0.50	0.70	1.20	1.37	1.37	1.30	0.80	0.60	0.55	0.55	0.55
	0.76	4.10	1.40	0.98	1.17	1.33	1.60	1.80	2.00	2.15	2.20	1.20	1.00	0.96	0.48	1.03	1.07	1.10
0.10	1.06	3.30	1.12	0.42	0.40	0.47	0.90	1.10	1.17	1.20	1.25	1.43	0.90	0.60	0.60	0.60	0.60	0.60
	2.07	2.20	0.60	0.40	0.30	0.22	0.23	0.35	0.52	0.66	0.75	0.77	0.75	0.63	0.46	0.40	0.40	0.40
	0.80	2.70	1.05	0.80	0.70	0.80	1.03	1.26	1.43	1.58	1.72	1.84	1.90	1.55	1.27	1.15	1.15	1.25
0.20	1.07	1.40	0.50	0.33	0.32	0.40	0.68	0.90	1.00	1.06	1.08	1.00	1.00	1.05	0.90	0.55	0.53	0.55
	2.10	0.50	0.23	0.20	0.18	0.16	0.16	0.18	0.28	0.43	0.55	0.58	0.53	0.45	0.32	0.27	0.26	0.25

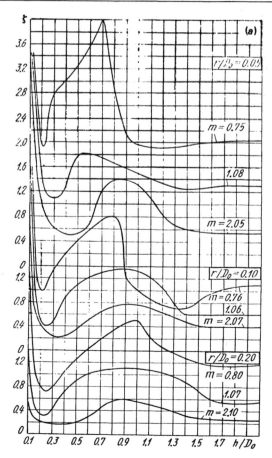

	Diagram 6-31

B. Thickened corners at the turn without rounding ($r/D_0 = 0$). For ζ, see graphs b–d.

Values of ζ

δ/D_0	n_{ar}	0.10	0.15	0.20	0.25	0.30	0.40	0.50	0.60	0.70	0.80	0.90	1.0	1.20	1.40	1.60	1.80	2.00
										h/D_0								
	0.75	8.70	3.90	2.20	1.70	2.80	3.10	3.40	3.70	4.25	3.40	2.30	2.00	1.90	1.95	2.00	2.00	2.00
0.10	1.08	–	3.90	1.75	1.20	1.00	1.40	2.10	2.66	2.66	2.10	1.60	1.30	1.20	1.16	1.17	1.18	1.20
	2.05	4.20	2.20	0.80	0.62	0.56	0.45	0.50	0.70	1.00	1.38	1.60	1.87	1.20	0.93	0.73	0.60	0.57
	0.76	8.26	3.00	1.50	1.10	1.90	2.50	2.85	3.20	3.45	3.55	3.30	2.60	1.60	1.30	1.25	1.27	1.30
0.20	1.06	5.75	1.60	0.80	0.50	0.46	0.90	1.30	1.67	1.98	2.26	2.53	2.63	1.10	0.83	0.80	0.83	0.85
	2.07	4.40	0.75	0.60	0.53	0.50	0.52	0.55	0.65	0.78	0.90	1.03	1.13	1.35	0.70	0.56	0.60	0.63
	0.80	8.26	2.40	1.25	0.90	0.78	2.50	3.40	3.90	4.30	4.25	4.05	3.65	2.42	2.00	1.83	1.77	1.75
0.40	1.07	3.90	2.00	0.70	0.46	0.40	0.60	1.40	2.00	2.46	2.66	2.72	2.65	1.70	1.30	1.13	1.03	0.95
	2.10	2.00	0.60	0.43	0.40	0.40	0.43	0.50	0.60	0.73	0.87	1.00	1.14	1.36	1.20	0.65	0.58	0.57

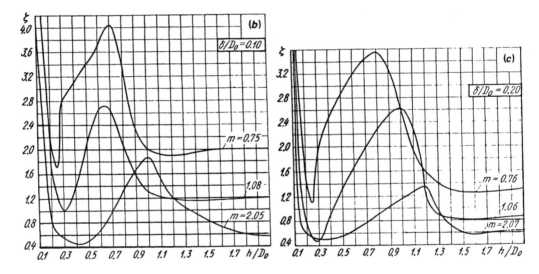

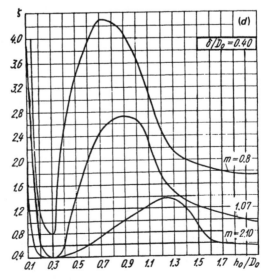

Spatial (circular) turn through 180° (with pumping);[19] $R/D_1 = 0.2$–0.5; $Re = w_0 D_0/\nu \geqslant 4 \times 10^4$	Diagram 6-32

A. Rounded corners of the turn ($r/D_0 > 0$)

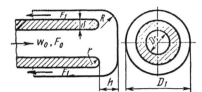

$$\zeta \equiv \frac{\Delta p}{\rho w_0^2/2} = f\left(\frac{h}{D_0}, \frac{r}{D_0}, n_{ar}\right)$$

see graph a.

$$n_{ar} = F_1/F_0$$

Values of ζ

r/D_0	n_{ar}	h/D_0							
		0.10	0.15	0.20	0.25	0.30	0.40	0.50	0.60
0.05	0.75	5.70	2.40	1.18	0.70	0.40	0.20	0.18	0.18
	1.08	7.60	2.60	1.45	0.90	0.70	0.52	0.42	0.40
	2.05	–	3.16	2.05	1.48	1.15	0.72	0.55	0.43
0.10	0.76	1.95	0.62	0.35	0.26	0.20	0.17	0.20	0.60
	1.06	2.80	1.20	0.40	0.30	0.25	0.23	0.28	0.80
	2.07	3.40	1.28	0.85	0.70	0.60	0.50	0.43	0.36
0.20	0.80	1.15	0.60	0.40	0.33	0.32	0.32	0.40	1.15
	1.07	1.20	0.50	0.32	0.23	0.20	0.20	0.20	0.30
	2.10	1.35	0.70	0.45	0.40	0.40	0.40	0.40	0.40

r/D_0	n_{ar}	h/D_0							
		0.70	0.80	0.90	1.00	1.20	1.40	1.60	1.80	2.00
0.05	0.75	0.19	0.20	0.75	1.08	1.10	1.00	0.80	0.60	0.40
	1.08	0.42	0.42	0.45	0.80	0.77	0.67	0.56	0.50	0.45
	2.05	0.38	0.35	0.38	0.60	0.88	0.72	0.70	0.88	0.85
0.10	0.76	0.90	1.00	1.10	1.18	1.25	1.20	1.00	0.80	0.75
	1.06	1.15	1.37	1.40	1.27	1.18	1.15	1.14	1.10	1.08
	2.07	0.35	0.33	0.33	0.35	0.70	0.75	0.77	0.80	0.80
0.20	0.80	1.53	1.70	1.76	1.55	1.37	1.37	1.37	1.36	1.35
	1.07	0.73	1.30	1.45	1.45	1.40	1.30	1.30	1.27	1.23
	2.10	0.40	0.40	0.40	0.40	0.20	0.15	0.10	0.10	0.10

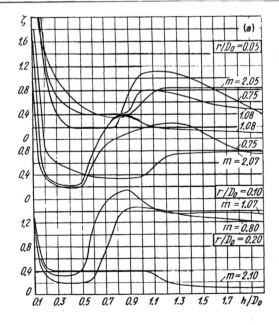

	Diagram 6-32

B. Thickened corners of the turn without rounding ($r/D_0 = 0$). For ζ, see graph b.

Values of ζ

δ/D_0	n_{ar}	h/D_0							
		0.10	0.15	0.20	0.25	0.30	0.40	0.50	0.60
	0.75	7.70	2.25	1.20	0.60	0.40	0.25	0.23	0.24
0.10	1.08	5.70	2.10	1.60	1.10	0.83	0.60	0.48	0.46
	2.05	6.60	3.90	2.50	2.60	1.32	0.80	0.56	0.45
	0.76	–	2.90	1.35	0.60	0.40	0.22	0.24	0.70
0.20	1.06	–	1.80	0.85	0.46	0.35	0.28	0.27	0.50
	2.07	4.10	3.00	1.60	1.10	0.90	0.65	0.50	0.45
	0.80	–	3.10	1.45	0.70	0.50	0.38	0.60	1.60
0.40	1.07	–	2.45	1.00	0.50	0.33	0.27	0.40	0.77
	2.10	2.40	0.80	0.56	0.48	0.45	0.40	0.36	0.35

δ/D_0	n_{ar}	h/D_0							
		0.70	0.80	0.90	1.00	1.20	1.40	1.60	1.80	2.00
	0.75	0.30	0.50	1.20	1.40	1.50	1.40	0.90	0.60	0.50
0.10	1.08	1.10	1.35	1.30	1.20	1.00	0.83	0.70	0.60	0.57
	2.05	0.40	0.35	0.34	0.35	0.82	0.92	0.90	0.87	0.88
	0.76	1.27	1.52	1.68	1.77	1.85	1.78	1.60	1.40	1.25
0.20	1.06	1.00	1.40	1.50	1.50	1.43	1.40	1.30	1.28	1.25
	2.07	0.40	0.40	0.40	0.60	0.75	0.75	0.73	0.72	0.70
	0.80	1.85	1.80	1.75	1.70	1.80	1.77	1.75	1.73	1.70
0.40	1.07	1.20	1.60	1.60	1.55	1.60	1.67	1.73	1.76	1.75
	2.10	0.33	0.30	0.33	0.56	0.80	0.88	0.93	1.00	1.00

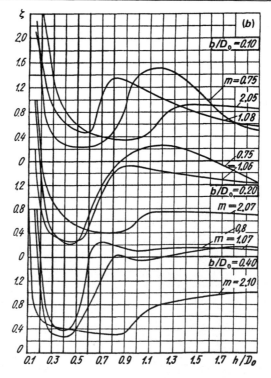

Symmetric turn through 180° in one plane (during suction);[47] $\mathrm{Re} = w_0 a_0/\nu \geqslant 0.8 \times 10^5$	Diagram 6-33

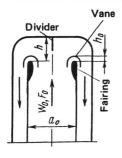

A. Without dividers. $\zeta \equiv \dfrac{\Delta p}{\rho w_0^2/2} = f\!\left(\dfrac{h}{a_0}\right)$, see graph a.

Values of ζ

Scheme and curve	h/a_0									
	0.20	0.25	0.30	0.35	0.40	0.45	0.50	0.55	0.60	0.65
1	–	9.5	7.9	5.5	4.5	4.1	4.0	4.0	4.2	5.2
2	10.5	7.5	5.7	4.7	3.9	3.5	3.4	3.7	4.5	–
3	7.9	6.3	5.0	4.4	4.0	3.8	3.9	4.0	5.0	–
4	–	4.2	2.6	1.8	1.6	1.5	1.5	1.6	1.8	2.1
5	3.8	2.3	1.7	1.5	1.4	1.5	1.6	1.8	2.2	–

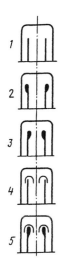

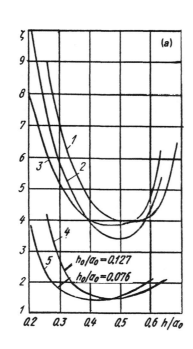

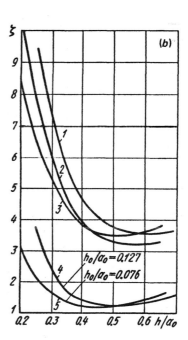

B. With plane dividers. For ζ, see graph b.

Values of ζ

Scheme and curve	h_0/a_0									
	0.20	0.25	0.30	0.35	0.40	0.45	0.50	0.55	0.60	0.65
1	–	9.5	7.5	5.6	4.6	4.1	3.8	3.6	3.6	3.6
2	10.5	8.0	6.0	4.6	4.0	3.5	3.3	3.2	3.3	3.3
3	8.6	6.7	5.3	4.3	3.8	3.6	3.5	3.5	3.6	3.8
4	–	3.6	2.3	1.7	1.4	1.3	1.3	1.3	1.4	1.5
5	3.0	2.1	1.6	1.3	1.2	1.2	1.3	1.3	1.5	1.6

Symmetric turn through 180° in one plane (with pumping);[47]   Diagram
Re $= w_0 a_0 / \nu \geqslant 0.8 \times 10^5$ 6-34

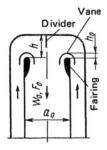

A. Without dividers. $\zeta \equiv \dfrac{\Delta p}{\rho w_0^2/2} = f\left(\dfrac{h}{a_0}\right)$, see graph a.

Values of ζ

	h/a_0										
Scheme	0.2	0.25	0.30	0.35	0.40	0.45	0.50	0.55	0.60	0.65	0.70
1	–	10	7.3	6.0	5.2	4.6	4.3	4.2	4.0	4.0	4.0
2	8.8	6.6	5.2	4.4	3.9	3.6	3.4	3.3	3.4	3.4	3.0
3	7.0	4.7	3.7	3.2	2.7	2.5	2.4	2.4	2.5	2.6	2.7
4	–	3.8	2.3	1.7	1.4	1.3	1.3	1.3	1.4	1.5	1.7
5	3.0	1.7	1.2	1.0	0.9	0.9	0.9	1.0	1.1	1.2	1.4

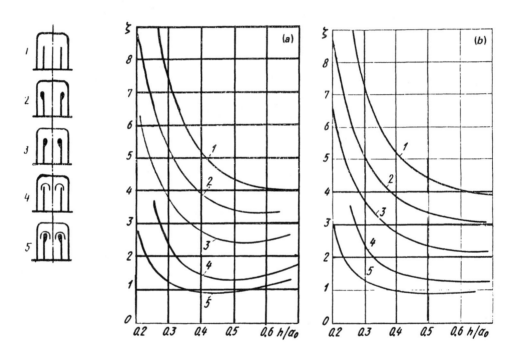

B. With plane dividers. For ζ, see graph b.

Values of ζ

	h/a_0										
Scheme	0.2	0.25	0.30	0.35	0.40	0.45	0.50	0.55	0.60	0.65	0.70
1	–	9.7	7.3	6.0	5.2	4.7	4.4	4.2	4.0	4.0	3.9
2	8.7	6.5	5.0	4.3	3.8	3.5	3.3	3.2	3.2	3.1	3.0
3	6.6	4.6	3.6	3.1	2.7	2.5	2.3	2.3	2.2	2.2	2.2
4	–	3.6	2.3	1.7	1.5	1.4	1.3	1.3	1.3	1.3	1.3
5	3.0	1.7	1.3	1.1	1.0	1.0	0.9	0.9	0.9	1.0	1.0

Turns and elbows in the system of pneumatic transport;[69]

Diagram 6-35

$Re = w_0 D_0/\nu_c > 2 \times 10^5$

$$\zeta \equiv \frac{\Delta p}{\rho w_0^2/2} = \zeta_0 + \varkappa(\zeta_1 - \zeta_0)$$

where ζ_0 is the resistance coefficient without the material transported; ζ_1 is the same during transportation of material with $\varkappa = 1$; $\varkappa = m_d/m_g$ is the dust content factor, kg/kg.

Name	Scheme	R_0/D_0	ζ_0	ζ_1
Turn of circular cross section		1.44	0.17	1.96
		3.33	0.15	1.34
		5.0	0.13	1.67
Elbow of circular cross section	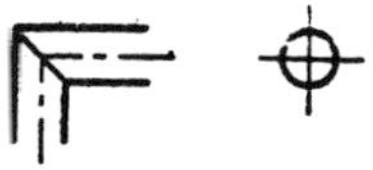	0	1.14	3.28
Composed elbow of circular cross section (n_{ele}, number of elements)	$n_{ele} = 2$ $n_{ele} = 3$ $n_{ele} = 5$	1.5	0.33	2.20
		1.5	0.22	2.05
		1.64	0.20	1.94
		3.0	0.20	1.92

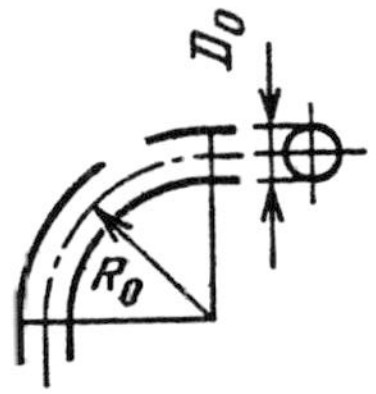

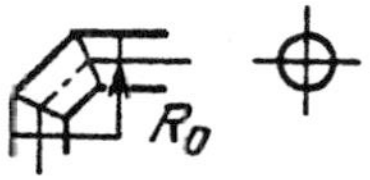

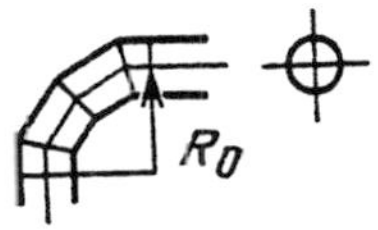

Diagram 6-35

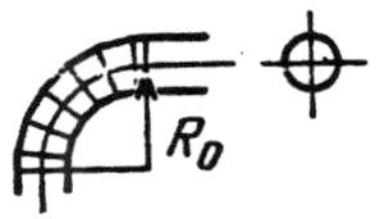

			ζ_0	ζ_1
		1.5	0.19	2.05
		3.0	0.15	1.84
Turn of square cross section with transition to an inscribed circle		1.5	0.23	1.98
		3.0	0.09	1.57

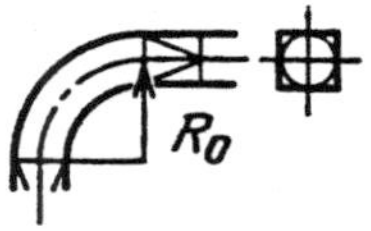

Name	Scheme	Geometric characteristics	ζ_0	ζ_1
Turn of rectangular cross section $A \times B$ with transition to equidimensional circle: $A \times B = \dfrac{\pi D_0^2}{4}$	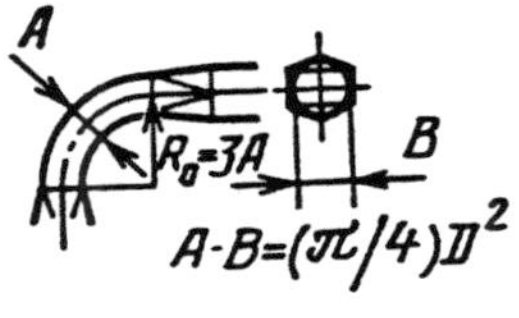	$\dfrac{B}{A} = 1.0$ $\dfrac{B}{A} = 1.8$	0.15 0.15	1.51 1.61
Turn of variable rectangular cross section with transition from square to inscribed circle	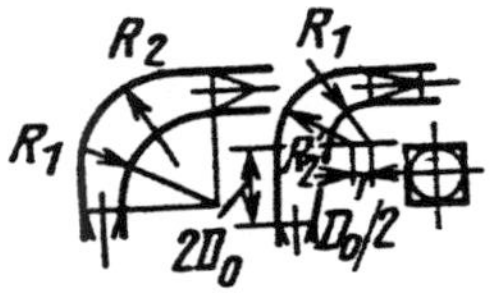	$R_1 = R_2 = 2D_0$ $R_1 = D_0$ $R_2 = 2D_0$	0.15 0.18	1.50 1.57

Elbow with transition from inscribed circle to square		$R_1 = R_2 = 0$ $R_1 = R_2 = \dfrac{D_0}{3}$	0.84 0.56	3.66 3.17
Elbow with guide vanes in transition from inscribed circle to square		$R_1 = R_2 = D_0/3$ Two vanes Five vanes	0.24 0.20	1.80 1.48
The same, but with guide plates		Two plates Four plates	0.35 0.33	1.87 1.82

REFERENCES

1. Abramovich, G. N., Aerodynamics of local resistances, *Prom. Aerodin. Tr. TsAGI*, vyp. 211, 65–160, 1935.
2. Agureikin, S. S., Spodyryak, N. T., and Ustimenko, B. P., Experimental investigation of the turbulent flow hydrodynamics in curvilinear channels, *Probl. Teploenerg. Prikl. Teplofiz.*, vyp. 5, 35–45, Nauka Press, Alma-Ata, 1969.
3. Aronov, I. Z., Heat Transfer and Hydraulic Resistance in Curved Tubes, thesis (Cand. Sci.), Kiev Polytechnical Institute, 1950, 130 p.
4. Aronov, I. Z., On the hydraulic similarity in fluid motion in curved tubes-coils, *Izv. VUZov Energ.*, no. 4, 52–59, 1962.
5. Baulin, K. K. and Idelchik, I. E., Experimental investigation of air flow in elbows, *Tekh. Zametki*, no. 24, 1934, 24 pp.
6. Berkutov, I. S. and Pakhmatulin, Sh. I., Experience in the reduction of hydraulic losses of bent channels, *Neft. Khoz.*, no. 1, 46–47, 1964.
7. Volkov, V. G., Khorun, S. P., and Yakovlev, A. I., Hydraulic resistance of plane channels with the reverse symmetric turning, in *Aerodynamics and Heat Transfer in Electrical Machines*, vyp. 1, pp. 98–105, Kharkov, 1972.
8. Goldenberg, I. Z., Study of the field of the axial flow velocity component in the ship pipeline behind a side branch, *Tr. Kaliningr. Tekh. Inst. Rybn. Prom.*, vyp. 22, 125–134, 1970.
9. Goldenberg, I. Z. and Umbrasas, M.-R. A., Relationship between the hydraulic losses and the secondary flow velocity in pipeline bends, *Tr. Kaliningrad. Tekh. Inst. Rybn. Promsti. Khoz.*, vyp. 58, pp. 36–42, 1975.
10. Goldenberg, I. Z., Experimental investigation of the effect of interaction of flow turns on hydraulic losses in pressure channels, *Tr. Kalingr. Inst. Rybn. Prom. Khoz.*, vyp. 19, 29–34, 1966.
11. Gontsov, N. G., Marinova, O. A., and Tananayev, A. V., Turbulent flow over the section of circular tube bend, *Gidrotekh. Stroit.*, no. 12, 24–28, 1984.
12. Dementiyev, K. V. and Aronov, I. Z., Hydrodynamics and heat transfer in rectangular curvilinear channels, *J. Eng. Phys.*, vol. 34, no. 6, 994–1000, 1978.
13. Zubov, V. P., Study of Pressure Losses in Wyes During the Separation and Merging of Flows, thesis, Cand. Sc., Eng., Moscow, 1978, p. 165.
14. Ivanov, K. F. and Finodeyev, O. V., Concerning certain aspects of the process of flow stabilization downstream of the bend, *Izv. VUZov, Energ.*, 1985.
15. Idelchik, I. E., Guide vanes in elbows of aerodynamic tubes, *Tekhzametki TsAGI*, no. 133, 35, 1936.
16. Idelchik, I. E., *Hydraulic Resistances (Physical and Mechanical Fundamentals)*, Gosenergoizdat, 1954, 316 p.
17. Idelchik, I. E., About the effect of the Re number and roughness on the resistance of curved channels, *Prom. Aerodin.*, no. 4, 177–194, BNI MAP, 1953.
18. Idelchik, I. E., On the separation flow modes in shaped parts of pipelines, in *Teplogazosnabzhen i Ventilyats*, pp. 43–49, Budivelnik Press, Kiev, 1966.
19. Idelchik, I. E. and Ginzburg, Ya. L., Hydraulic resistance of annular 180°-bends, *Teploenergetika*, no. 4, 87–90, 1968.
20. Ito, Nanbu, Flow in a rotating straight tube of circular cross section, *Trans. ASME* (Russian transl.), no. 3, pp. 46–56, Moscow, 1971.
21. Kazachenko, V. S., Local resistances of rectangular elbows, *Vodosnabzh. Sanit. Tekh*, no. 2, 7–11, 1962.
22. Kamershtein, A. G. and Karev, V. N., Investigation of hydraulic resistance of bent, welded, sharply bent and corrugated elbows-compensators, *VNIIStroineft i MIIGS*, pp. 52–59, 1956.
23. Karpov, A. I., Resistance of elbows of a small curvature radius under the conditions of pneumatic transport, *Izv. VUZov Energ.*, no. 8, 93–95, 1962.
24. Kvitkovsky, Yu. V., Hydraulic resistance of smoothly bent tubes, *Tr. Mosk. Inst. Inzh. Zhel.-Dor. Transp.*, vyp. 176, 61–63, 1963.
25. Klyachko, L. S., Refinement of the method of theoretical determination of the resistance coefficients of side branches of different outline, *Tr. Nauchn. Sess. LIOT*, vyp. 1, 79–137, 1955.
26. Klyachko, L. S., Makarenkova, T. G., and Pustoshnaya, V. F., Correlating formulas for determining the resistance coefficients of the arbitrary assemblies of units from the bends in ventilation systems, in *The Problems of the Design and Mounting of Sanitary-Technical Systems*, Trudy VNIIGS, pp. 3–8, Leningrad, 1980.
27. Koshelev, I. I., Eskin, N. B., and Abryutina, N. V., On the hydraulic resistance of bent small-diameter tubes of stainless steel with isothermal liquid flow, *Izv. VUZov, Energ.*, no. 2, 64–69, 1967.
28. Mazurov, D. Ya. and Zakharov, G. V., Study of some problems of the aerodynamics of tubular coils, *Teploenergetika*, no. 2, 39–42, 1969.

29. Maksimenko, A. V., Toward the problem of the regard for the effect of shaped parts in hydraulic calculation of ventilation systems, *Sudostroenie*, no. 8, 35–40, 1959.
30. Migai, V. K. and Gudkov, E. I., Some means for reducing losses in the elements of boiler gas-air pipelines, *Tr. TsKTI*, vyp. 110, 40–46, 1971.
31. Nekrasov, B. B., *Hydraulics*, 1954, 290 p.
32. Novikov, M. D., Aerodynamic resistance of twin turns of boiler gas-air pipelines, *Tr. TsKTI*, vyp. 110, 53–60, 1971.
33. Paraska, D. I., A Technique for Improving the Hydraulic Characteristics of Curved Forced Channels by Visualizing the Flows of Two-beam-refracting Fluid, thesis, Cand. Sc., Eng., Leningrad, 1982, p. 146.
34. Permyakov, B. A., The influence of the number of turns on the aerodynamics of coils made of helical tubes, *Prom. Teplotekh.*, vol. 6, no. 2, 21–22, 1984.
35. Polotsky, N. D., On inception of secondary flows during liquid motion along a curved channel, *Tr. Vses. Nauchno-Issled. Inst. Gidromashin.*, vyp. 29, 60–70, 1961.
36. *Industrial Aerodynamics*, Collected Papers No. 7, 1956, 154.
37. Rikhter, L. A., *Thrust and Blasting at Steam Electric Stations*, Gosenergoizdat, 1962, 200 p.
38. Rozovsky, I. L., Water motion at the turn of an open channel, *Izv. Akad. Nauk USSR*, pp. 41–47, Kiev, 1957.
39. Tatarchuk, G. T., Resistance of rectangular side branches, *Vopr. Otopl. Ventil. Tr. TsNIIPS*, pp. 17–28, Gosstroiizdat, 1951.
40. Topunov, A. M., Rubtsov, Yu. V., and Izmailovich, V. V., Reduction of hydraulic resistances in the elements of gas pipelines of power engineering equipment, *Teploenergetika*, no. 11, 43–46, 1981.
41. Trofimovich, V. V., Energy losses during turbulent motion of fluid in side branches, *Sanit. Tekh.*, vyp. 5, 156–164, 1967.
42. Uliyanov, I. E., Krumilina, N. N., and Vokar, N. V., *The Design of Air Conduits of the Aeroplane Power Units*, Moscow, 1979, p. 96.
43. Umbrasas, M.-R. A. and Goldenberg, I. Z., The influence of roughness on the magnitude of hydraulic losses in bends, in *Hydraulics, Hydraulic Transport of Fish and Pertinent Technical Means*, vyp. 69, pp. 62–69, Kaliningrad, 1977.
44. Umbrasas, M.-R. A., Evaluation of the Failure-Free Performance of Ship Pipelines with Bends when Designing Sea Water Systems, thesis, Cand. Sc., Eng., Sevastopol, 1984, p. 155.
45. Heckestad, Flow in a plane rectangular elbow, *Trans. ASME (Russian transl.)*, no. 3, 86–97, 1971.
46. Khazhonkov, V. I. and Taliev, V. I., Reduction of resistance in square side branches by means of guide vanes, *Tekhn. Otchyoty*, no. 110, 16, 1947.
47. Khanzhonkov, V. I., Aerodynamic resistance of plane channels with a reverse symmetrical turn, *Prom. Aerodin.*, vyp. 21, 151–166, Oborongiz, 1962.
48. Shchukin, V. K., Flow regimes and hydraulic resistance of radially rotating channels, *Izv. Akad. Nauk SSSR, Energ. Transp.*, no. 3, 152–159, 1980.
49. Shchukin, V. K., *Heat Transfer and Hydrodynamics of Internal Flows in the Fields of Body Forces*, Moscow, 1970, p. 331.
50. Yudin, E. Ya., Elbows with thin guide vanes, *Prom. Aerodin.*, no. 7, 55–80, 1956.
51. Adler, M., Strömung in gekrümmten Rohren, *Z. Angew. Math. Mech.*, vol. 14, 30–50, 1934.
52. Ajukawa, K., Pressure drop in the hydraulic conveyance of solid materials through a bend a vertical plane, *Bull. JSME*, vol. 12, no. 54, 57, 1969.
53. Bambach, Plötzliche Umlenkung (Stoss) von Wasser in geschlossenen unter Druck durchstromten Kanalen, no. 327, 1–60, VDI, 1930.
54. Benson, R. S. and Wollatt, D., Compressible flow loss coefficients at bends and T-functions, *Engineer*, vol. 221, no. 5740, 70–85, 1966.
55. Blenke, M., Bohner, K., and Mirner, W., Drucklust bei der 180°-Stromungsumlenkung in Schlaufenreaktor, *Verfarenstechnik*, vol. 3, no. 10, 444–452, 1960.
56. Chun Sik Lee, Stromungeswiderstände in 90°-Rohrkrummern, *Gesund. Ing.*, no. 1, 12–15, 1969.
57. Cross, Ph. and Pernes, P., Etude des pertes de charge singulieres dans les coudes brusques a 90° en polychlorure di vinyle, *Bull. Tech. Genie Rural*, no. 111, I–VII, 1–33, 1971.
58. Conn, H. G., Colborne, H. G., and Brown, W. G., Pressure losses in 4-inch diameter galvanized metal duct and fittings, *Heat./Piping/Air Cond.*, no. 1, 30–35, 1953.
59. Decock, P. and Pay, A., Mesure des pertes de charge localisus dans des accessoires de tuyauterie-coudes arrondis de 90°, *Chal. Clim.*, vol. 34, no. 398, 27–31, 1969.
60. Eastwood, W. and Sarginson, E. J., The effect of a transition curve on the loss of head at a bend in a pipeline, *Proc. Inst. Civ. Eng.*, vol. 16, no. 6, 129–142, 1960.
61. Fritzche, and Richter, H., Beltrag zur Kenntnis des Strömungswiderstandes gekrümmter rauher Rohrleitung, *Forsch. Geb. Ingenieurwes.*, vol. 4, no. 6, 40–90, 1933.

62. Haase, D., Strömung in einem 90°-Knie, *Ing. Arch.*, vol. 22, no. 4, 282–292, 1954.

63. Hassoon, H. M., Pressure drop in 180° pipe bends, *Build. Serv. Eng. Res. Technol.*, Vol. 3, no. 2, 70–74, 1982.

64. Hofmann, A., Der Verlust in 90°. Rohrkrümmern mit gleichbleibenden Kreisquerschnitt, *Mitt. Hydraul. Inst. Tech. Hochschule*, no. 3, 30–45, München, 1929.

65. Iguchi, M., Ohmi, M., and Nakajima, H., Loss coefficient of screw elbows in pulsatile flow, *Bull. JSME*, vol. 27, no. 234, 2722–2729, 1984.

67. Ito, H., *Trans. JSME, Ser. D.*, 82–1, pp. 131–136, 1963.

68. Ito, H. and Imai, K., Pressure losses in vaned elbows of a circular cross section, *Trans. ASME*, vol. D88, no. 3, 684–685, 1966.

69. Jung, R., Die Strömungsverluste in 90°-Umlenkungen beim pneumatischen Staubtransport, *Brennst. Waerme Kraft*, vol. 19, no. 9, 430–435, 1967.

70. Kamiyama, S., Theory of the flow through bends with turning vanes, *Sci. Rep. Res. Inst. Tohoku Univ., Ser. B, High Speed Mech.*, no. 20, 1–14, 1969.

71. Kirchbach, Der Energieverlust in Kniestücken, *Mitt. Hydraul. Inst. Tech. Hochschule Munchen*, no. 3, 25–35, 1929.

72. Markowski, M., Wspolczynniki oporow przeplywu dwufozowego czynnika przez luki przenolnikov powietrznych, *Arch. Budowy Maszyn.*, part 14, no. 2, 339–370, 1967.

73. Machne, G., Perdite di carico prodotte da curve isolate on cambiamento di diresione di 90° in tubazioni a serione circolare costante in moto turbolento, *Tec. Ital.*, vol. 22, no. 2, 77–91, 1957.

74. Morikawa, L., Druckverlust in pneumatischen Forderungen von kornigen Guten bei grossen Gutbelagen, *Bull. JSME*, vol. 11, no. 45, 469–477, 1968.

75. Morimune, T., Hirayama, N., and Maeda, T., Study of compressible high speed gas flow in piping system, *Bull. JSME*, vol. 23, no. 186, 1997–2012, 1980.

76. Murakami, M., Shimuzu, Y., and Shiragami, H., Studies on fluid flow in three-dimensional bend conduits, *Bull. JSME*, vol. 12, no. 54, 1369–1379, 1969.

77. Nippert, H., Über den Strömungsverlust in gekrümmten Kanalen, *Forschungsarb. Geb. Ingenieurwes*, no. 320, VDI, 1922, 85 pp.

78. Padmarajaiah, T. P., Pressure losses in 90°-bends in the region of turbulent flow, *J. Inst. Eng. (India) Civ. Eng. Div.*, vol. 45, par 1, no. 1, 103–111, 1964.

79. Richter, H., Der Druckabfall in gekrümmten glatten Rohrleitungen, *Forschungsarb. Geb. Ingenieurwes.*, no. 338, 30–47, VDI, 1930.

80. Richter, H., *Rohrhydraulik*, Berlin, 1954, 328 pp.

81. Schubart, Der Verlust in Kniestücken bei glatter und rauher Wandung, *Mitt. Hydraul. Inst. Tech. Hoschschule Munchen*, no. 3, 13–25, 1929.

82. Sharma, H. D., Varshney, D. V., and Chaturvedi, R. N., Energy loss characteristics in closed conduit bends (an air model study), *Proc. 42nd Annu. Res. Sess. Madras*, vol. 2B, 11–18, Jamil Nadu, 1972.

83. Shimizu, Y. and Sugino, K., Hydraulic losses and flow patterns of a swirling flow in U-bends, *Bull. JSME*, vol. 23, no. 183, 1443–1450, 1980.

84. Shiragami, N. and Inoue, I., Pressure losses in square section bends, *J. Chem. Eng. Jpn.*, vol. 14, no. 3, 173–177, 1981.

85. Smith, A. T. and Ward, The flow and pressure losses in smooth pipe bends of constant cross section, *J. R. Aeronaut. Soc.*, vol. 67, no. 631, 437–447, 1963.

86. Spalding, *Versuche über den Stomungsverlust in gekrümmten Leitungen*, no. 6, 1–17, VDI, 1933.

87. Spychala, F. A. S., Versuche zur Ermittlung von Druckverlusten in Rohrleitungen und Formstücken von Luftungsanlagen, *Schiffbauforschung*, vol. 7, no. 5–6, 216–222, 1968.

88. Sprenger, H., Druckverluste in 90° Krümmern für Rechteckrohre, *Schweiz. Bauztg. (SBZ)*, vol. 87, no. 13, 223–231, 1969.

89. Takami, T. and Sudou, K., Flow through curved pipes with elliptic sections, *Bull. JSME*, vol. 27, no. 228, 1176–1181, 1984.

90. Vuskovic, G., Der Strömungswidersland von Formstücken fur Gasroh leitungen (Fittings), *Mitt. Hydraul. Inst. Tech. Hochschule Munchen*, no. 9, 30–43, 1939.

91. Wasilewski, J., Verluste in glatten Rohrkrümmern mit kreisrundem Querschnitt bei weniger als 90° Ablenkung, *Mitt. Hydraul. Inst. Tech. Hochschule Munchen*, no. 5, 18–25, 1932.

92. Weisbach, J., *Lehrbuch der Ingenieur und Maschinenmechanik, II Aufl., 1850 u. Experimentalhydraulik*, 1855, 320 pp.

93. Werszko, D., Badania iloseiowego wplywu chropowatosci i liczby Reynoldsa nu wspolczynnik strat hydrauliznych 90° krzywakow kolowych, *Lesz. Nauk Politech. Wroclawski*, no. 173, 57–78, 1968.

94. Wolf, S. and Huntz, D. M., Losses in a compact 180-deg. return flow passage as a function of Reynolds number, *Trans. ASME*, vol. D92, no. 1, 193–194, 1970.

95. White, C. M., Streamline flow through curved pipes, *Proc. R. Soc. London Ser. A*, vol. 123, 20–31, 1929.

SEVEN

RESISTANCE IN THE CASES OF MERGING OF FLOW STREAMS AND DIVISION INTO FLOW STREAMS
Resistance Coefficients of Wyes, Tees, and Manifolds

7-1 EXPLANATIONS AND PRACTICAL RECOMMENDATIONS

1. Different types of wyes are considered in the present handbook: nonstandard wyes when $F_s + F_{st} = F_c$ (Figure 7-1a and b) and when $F_s + F_{st} > F_c$ (Figure 7-1c); normalized wyes of ordinary design (Figure 7-1d); and normalized wyes with branching assemblies of industrial construction (Figure 7-1e).

2. A wye is characterized by a branching angle α and the ratios of the cross-sectional areas of its branches F_s/F_c, F_{st}/F_c, and F_s/F_{st}. A wye can have different ratios of flow rates Q_s/Q_c and Q_{st}/Q_c and velocity ratios w_s/w_c and w_{st}/w_c. Wyes can be installed to merge or converge the flows or to diverge or separate the flows from the main passage.

3. The resistance coefficients of converging or merging wyes depend on the parameters named above, while those of diverging wyes of standard shape (without smooth rounding of the side branch and without divergence or convergence of both branches) depend only on the branching angle α and the velocity ratios w_s/w_c and w_{st}/w_c.

The resistance coefficients of wyes of rectangular cross section are assumed to be nearly independent of the aspect ratio of their cross section, unless such coefficients are refined later.

4. When two streams moving in the same direction, but with different velocities, merge (Figure 7-1a), turbulent mixing of streams (a shock) usually occurs, which is accompanied by nonrecoverable total pressure losses. In the course of this mixing, momentum exchange takes place between the particles of the medium moving with different velocities. This exchange favors equalization of the flow velocity field. In this case, the jet with higher velocity loses a part of its kinetic energy by transmitting it to the slower moving jet.

5. The total pressure difference between sections before and after mixing is always a large and positive quantity for a jet moving with a higher velocity. This difference increases the larger the part of its energy which it transmits to a jet moving at a lower velocity. Therefore, the resistance coefficient, which is defined as the ratio of the difference of total

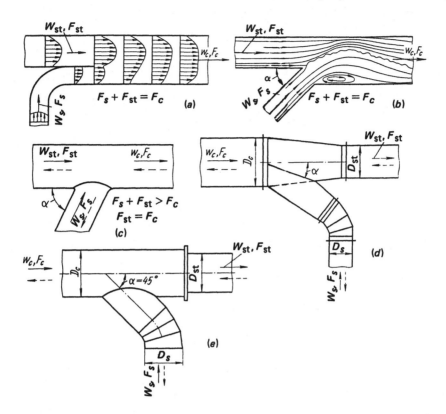

Figure 7-1 Schemes of wyes: (*a*) with the same direction of flows, $F_s + F_{st} = F_c$; (*b*) and (*c*) with flow at an angle α at $F_s + F_{st} = F_c$ and $F_s + F_{st} > F_c$, $F_{st} = F_c$, respectively; (*d*) normalized; (*e*) with branching assemblies of industrial-type construction.

pressures to the mean velocity pressure in the given section, also is always a positive quantity. The energy stored in the jet moving with a lower velocity also increases as a result of this mixing. Consequently, the difference between the total pressures, and, accordingly, the resistance coefficient of the branch in which the flow moves with a lower velocity, can also have negative values (see paragraph 2 of Section 1-1).

6. In practice, the branch is connected to the common channel on the side (side branching) at a certain angle α (see Figure 7-1*b* and *c*). In this case, losses due to turning of the stream are added to losses in a wye. The losses due to the turning of the flow are mainly due to the flow separation from the inner wall, flow contraction at the point of the turn, and its subsequent expansion (see Figure 7-1*b*). The contraction and expansion of the jet occur in the region of merging of streams and therefore influence the losses not only in a side branch, but also in the straight common passage.

7. When the branches are conical rather than cylindrical in shape or when there is a sudden expansion, there are losses due to flow expansion (diffuser or "shock" losses). If a side branch has a smooth turn, losses in this turn are also added.

In general, the principal losses in a converging wye are composed of (1) the losses due to turbulent mixing of two streams moving with different velocities (shock), (2) the losses due to flow turning when it passes from the side branch into the common channel, (3) the losses due to flow expansion in the diffuser part, and (4) the losses in a smooth branch.

8. The flow pattern in the diverging wye during flow separation into two jets (side branching and straight passage) varies with the ratio of velocities w_s/w_{st} or of flow rates Q_s/Q_{st}.[37]

9. When $Q_s < Q_{st}$, a large eddy zone is formed after the turn of the flow into the side branch (much larger than in the place of flow turning). This is due to the diffuser effect, that is, formation of a large positive pressure gradient at the place of wye branching, where the cross-sectional area increases sharply as compared with the main channel area. This large pressure gradient also causes partial flow separation from the opposite straight wall of the straight passage (Figure 7-2a). Both zones of flow separation from the wall create local jet contraction in both the side branch and the straight common passage. Flow contraction is followed by flow expansion.

10. When $Q_s \geq Q_{st}$, the flow separates more vigorously from the outer wall of the straight passage as well as from the wall of the side branch after turning (Figure 7-2b).

11. At $Q_s = 0$, an eddy zone forms at the entrance of the side branch (Figure 7-2c), which causes local contraction with subsequent expansion of the jet into the straight passage.

12. The distributions of velocities in side branches and in straight passages of the diverging wye with $\alpha = 90°$ and $F_s = F_{st} = F_c$ for the cases of $Q_s/Q_c = 0.5$ and $Q_s/Q_c = 1.0$ obtained by Aslaniyan et al.[1] are shown in Figures 7-3 and 7-4, respectively. These characteristics are given as the profiles and the fields of the axial velocity components in sections at different relative distances from the intersection of the wye axes.

13. The losses in the diverging wye are composed mainly of shock losses on sudden expansion at the place of flow division, losses due to flow turning into the side branch, losses in the smooth passage of the side branch, and losses due to a sudden contraction of the passage (an industrial wye).

14. At certain flow rate ratios Q_s/Q_c, the resistance coefficient of the straight passage can have a negative value, that is, the energy of the flow can rise in this passage. Due to flow division a portion of the slowly moving boundary layer adjacent to the wall passes into the side branch and the energy per unit volume of the fluid medium moving in the straight passage becomes higher than that in the side branch.

In addition, at the time of passing into the side branch, a part of the momentum is transferred to the flow in the straight passage.

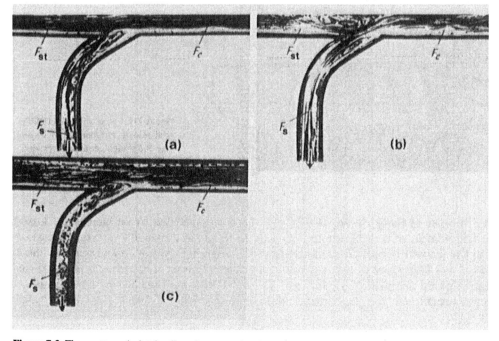

Figure 7-2 Flow patterns in intake diverging wyes: (a) $Q_s < Q_{st}$; (b) $Q_s \geq Q_{st}$; (c) $Q_s = 0$.[37]

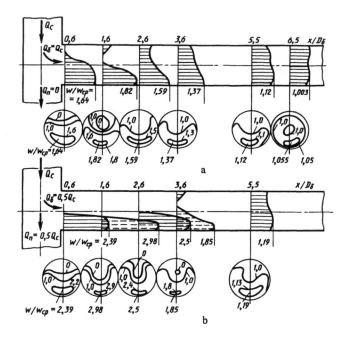

Figure 7-3 The profiles and fields of axial velocity components in a side branching of a straight, equally discharging wye:[1] (a) $Q_s = Q_c$; $Q_{st} = 0$; (b) $Q_s = 0.5 Q_c$; $Q_{st} = 0.5 Q_c$.

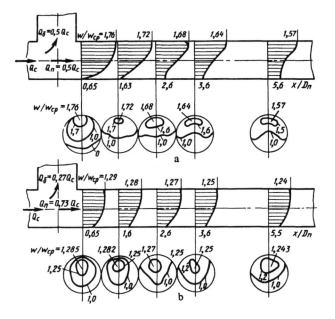

Figure 7-4 The profiles and fields of axial velocity components in the passage of a straight, equally discharging wye:[1] (a) $Q_s = 0.5 Q_c$; $Q_{st} = 0.5 Q_c$; (b) $Q_s = 0.27 Q_c$; $Q_{st} = 0.73 Q_c$.

An increase in energy in the straight passage is accompanied by an increase of losses in the side branch, so that the whole flow process results in irreversible pressure losses.

15. The resistance coefficients of nonstandard converging wyes of normal shape (without roundings and divergence or convergence of the side branch or of the straight passage) can be calculated by formulas of Levin[31] and Taliev.[43] These are obtained by comparing the predicted results with the experiments of Levin,[31] Gardel,[54] Kinne,[60] Petermann,[66] and Vogel.[78]

For the side branch:

$$\zeta_{c.s} \equiv \frac{\Delta p_s}{\rho w_c^2/2} = A\left[1 + \left(\frac{w_s}{w_c}\right)^2 - 2\frac{F_{st}}{F_c}\left(\frac{w_{st}}{w_c}\right)^2 - 2\frac{F_s}{F_c}\left(\frac{w_{st}}{w_c}\right)^2 \cos\alpha\right] + K_s$$

or

$$\zeta_{c.s} \equiv \frac{\Delta p_s}{\rho w_c^2/2} = A\left[1 + \left(\frac{Q_s}{Q_c}\frac{F_c}{F_s}\right)^2 - 2\frac{F_c}{F_{st}}\left(1 - \frac{Q_s}{Q_c}\right)^2\right.$$

$$\left. - 2\frac{F_c}{F_s}\left(\frac{Q_s}{Q_c}\right)^2 \cos\alpha\right] + K_s \tag{7-1}$$

For wyes of the type $F_s + F_{st} > F_c = F_c$, at all value of A is given in Table 7-1 compiled by Zubov on the basis of Gardel's[54] experiments. In all cases the value of K_s is zero. For wyes of the type $F_s + F_{st} = F_c$, the quantity $A = 1$ while the value of K_s is taken from Table 7-2.

Straight Passage

For wyes of the type $F_s + F_{st} > F_c$, $F_{st} = F_c$

$$\zeta_{c.st} \equiv \frac{\Delta p}{\rho w_c^2/2} = 1 - \left(1 - \frac{Q_s}{Q_c}\right)^2 - \left(1.4 - \frac{Q_s}{Q_c}\right)\left(\frac{Q_s}{Q_c}\right)^2 \sin\alpha$$

$$- 2K'_{st}\frac{F_c}{F_s}\frac{Q_s}{Q_c}\cos\alpha \tag{7-2}$$

where the values of K'_{st} are given in Table 7-3.

Table 7-1 Values of A

F_s/F_c	≤ 0.35	>0.35	>0.35
Q_s/Q_c	≤ 1.0	≤ 0.4	>0.4
A	1.0	$0.9\left(1 - \frac{Q_s}{Q_c}\right)$	0.55

Table 7-2 Values of K_s and K''_{st} for wyes of the type $F_s + F_{st} = F_c$

	F_s/F_c							
	0.10		0.20		0.33		0.5	
$\alpha,°$	K_s	K''_{st}	K_s	K''_{st}	K_s	K''_{st}	K_s	K''_{st}
15	0	0	0	0	0	0.14	0	0.40
30	0	0	0	0	0	0.17	0	0.35
45	0	0.05	0	0.14	0	0.14	0	0.30
60	0	0	0	0	0	0.10	0.10	0.25
90	0	0	0.10	0	0.20	0	0.25	0

Table 7-3 Values of K'_{st}

F_s/F_c	≤ 0.35		> 35
Q_s/Q_c	0–10	≤ 0.6	> 0.6
K'_{st}	$0.8Q_s/Q_c$	0.5	$0.8Q_s/Q_c$

For wyes of type $F_s + F_{st} = F_0$

$$\zeta_{c.st} \equiv \frac{\Delta p}{\rho w_c^2/2} = 1 + \left(\frac{w_{st}}{w_c}\right)^2 - 2\frac{F_{st}}{F_c}\left(\frac{w_{st}}{w_c}\right)^2 - 2\frac{F_s}{F_c}\left(\frac{w_s}{w_c}\right)^2 \cos\alpha + K''_{st}$$

or

$$\zeta_{c.st} \equiv \frac{\Delta p}{\rho w_c^2/2} = 1 + \left(\frac{F_c}{F_{st}}\right)^2\left(1 - \frac{Q_s}{Q_c}\right)^2 - 2\frac{F_c}{F_{st}}\left(1 - \frac{Q_s}{Q_c}\right)^2$$

$$- 2\frac{F_c}{F_s}\left(\frac{Q_s}{Q_c}\right)^2 \cos\alpha + K''_{st}$$

where for the values of K''_{st} see Table 7-2.

16. The resistance coefficients of nonstandard diversing wyes of normal shape with a turbulent flow can be calculated from the formulas of Levin[28] and Taliev[43] with correction factors obtained by comparing the predicted results with the experimental data of Levin,[28] Gardel,[54] Kinne,[60] Petermann,[66] and Vogel.[78]

For the side branch

$$\zeta_{c.s} \equiv \frac{\Delta p_s}{\rho w_c^2/2} = A'\left[1 + \left(\frac{w_s}{w_c}\right)^2 - 2\frac{w_s}{w_c}\cos\alpha\right] - K'_s\left(\frac{w_s}{w_c}\right)^2$$

or

$$\zeta_{c.s} \equiv \frac{\Delta p_s}{\rho w_c^2/2} = A'\left[1 + \left(\frac{Q_s}{Q_c}\frac{F_c}{F_s}\right)^2 - 2\frac{Q_s}{Q_c}\frac{F_c}{F_s}\cos\alpha\right] - K'_{st}\left(\frac{Q_s}{Q_c}\frac{F_c}{F_s}\right)^2$$

where K'_s is the coefficient of flow compressibility.

For wyes of the type $F_s + F_{st} > F_c$, $F_{st} = F_c$ the values of A' are given in Table 7-4, whereas the values of K'_s are taken to be equal to zero.

For wyes of the type $F_s + F_{st} = F_c$, $A' = 1.0$ and the values of K'_s are given in Table 7-5.

For wyes of the type $F_s + F_{st} > F_c$, $F_{st} = F_c$ (within the limits $w_{st}/w_c \leq 1.0$).

Table 7-4 Values of A'

F_s/F_c	≤ 0.35		< 0.35	
Q_s/Q_c	≤ 0.4	≥ 0.4	≤ 0.6	> 0.6
A'	$1.1-0.7Q_s/Q_c$	0.85	$1.0-0.6Q_s/Q_c$	0.6

Table 7-5 Values of K'_s

$\alpha°$	15	30	45	60	90
K'_s	0.04	0.16	0.36	0.64	1.0

$$\zeta_{c.st} \equiv \frac{\Delta p_{st}}{\rho w_c^2/2} = \tau_{st}(Q_s/Q_c)^2$$

where τ_{st} is given in Diagram 7-20.

For wyes of the type $F_s + F_{st} = F_c$, $\zeta_{c.st} = f(w_{st}/w_c)$, see Diagram 7-20.

17. Since the resistance coefficient of diverging wyes of normal shape is independent of the area ratios F_s/F_c and F_{st}/F_c, generalized curves can be plotted for this coefficient as a function of w_s/w_c and, respectively, of w_{st}/w_c rather than of Q_s/Q_c and Q_{st}/Q_c. Therefore, in some cases in Chapter 7, the curves of the resistance coefficient are given in the form $\zeta_{c.s} = f(w_{st}/w_c)$ and $\zeta_{c.st} = f(w_{st}/w_c)$, respectively, though most curves are given as $\zeta_{c.s} = f(Q_s/Q_c)$ and $\zeta_{c.st} = f(Q_s/Q_c)$.

18. The resistance coefficients of standard wyes and wyes with branches of industrial design can be calculated for turbulent flow from extrapolation formulas of Klyachko and Uspenskaya[21] (see Diagrams 7-15 through 7-17, 7-25, and 7-26).

19. There is a simple relationship* between the resistance coefficients of wyes based on the average velocity in the main channel and on the average velocity in branches:

$$\zeta_s \equiv \frac{\Delta p_s}{\rho w_s^2/2} = \frac{\zeta_{c.s}}{(w_{st}/w_c)^2} = \frac{\zeta_{c.s}}{[(Q_s/Q_c)(F_c/F_s)]^2}$$

and

$$\zeta_{st} = \frac{\Delta p_{st}}{\rho w_{st}^2/2} = \frac{\zeta_{c.st}}{(w_{st}/w_c)^2} = \frac{\zeta_{c.st}}{(1 - Q_s/Q_c)^2(F_c/F_{st})}$$

The total resistance coefficient of a wye based on the kinetic energy in the main channel[17,66] is

$$\zeta_{tot} = \frac{Q_s}{Q_c}\zeta_s + \frac{Q_{st}}{Q_c}\zeta_{st}$$

20. The resistance of wyes of normal shape can be markedly reduced by rounding the junction between the side branch and the main passage. In the case of converging wyes, only the outside corner has to be rounded (r_1, Figure 7-5). In the case of diverging wyes, both corners have to be rounded (r_2, Figure 7-5); this makes the flow more stable and reduces the possibility of flow separation from the inner corner.

Virtually, the rounding of the inner corners between the side branch and the main passage is sufficient when $r/D_c = 0.2–0.3$.[14]

21. The above formulas suggested for calculating the resistance coefficients of wyes and the corresponding graphic and turbulated data in Diagram 7-2 relate to very carefully

*For an incompressible fluid.

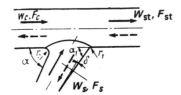

Figure 7-5 Schematic of an improved wye.

manufactured (turned) wyes. Industrial defects occurring in wyes during their production ("depressions" in the side branch and the "blocking" of its section by the miscut wall in the straight passage [common channel; main tube, to which a side branch is attached]) become the source of a sharp increase in the fluid resistance. The increase in the resistance of side branches is especially significant if the diameter of the cut-out in the main tube for the side branch is smaller than the diameter of the latter.

22. An increased resistance is also observed in wyes made of sheet steel with the flat seamed parts (see Diagrams 7-22 and 7-36).

23. The resistance of both the diverging and converging wyes is very effectively reduced if there is a gradual enlargement (diffuser) of the side branch. This noticeably reduces the losses both due to relative decrease in the flow velocity in the diverging section and due to decrease of the true angle of the flow turn at the same nominal angle of wye branchings ($\alpha_1 < \alpha$, Figure 7-5). Combination of rounding and beveling of corners and widening of the side branch gives a still larger reduction of the wye resistance.

The least resistance is achieved in wyes where the branch is smoothly bent (Figure 7-6); such branches with small branching angles ($<60°$) should be used wherever possible.

24. In converging wyes with $Q_s/Q_c \leq 0.8$ and threaded connection of branches, the values of the resistance coefficients are 10–10% higher than in the case of a smooth connection. When $Q_s/Q_c > 0.8$, the reverse phenomenon is observed: the resistance coefficient of the machined wye is 10–15% higher than in the case of a threaded connection of branches.[8,9] Probably, this is due to the fact that the enlargement of the section at the place of threaded connection (Figure 7-7) creates the condition like that in a stepped diffuser when a decrease in the resistance is observed as compared with a diffuser with straight walls (see Chapter 5).

In diverging wyes with threaded connection of branches the values of the coefficients $\zeta_{c.s}$ remain practically the same as for machined wyes. The values of $\zeta_{c.st}$ are correspondingly higher.[8,9]

25. The values of the resistance coefficients of wyes increase with the growth of the reduced velocity of the flow in the main channel $\lambda_c = w_c/a_{cr}$. The dependence of $\zeta_{c.s}$ and $\zeta_{c.st}$ on λ_c, presented in work by Uliyanov et al.[47] for certain wyes, are given in Diagram 7-24.

26. In the case of a turbulent flow ($Re_c = w_c/\nu \geq 4000$), the resistance coefficients of wyes depend little on the Reynolds number. A slight decrease of $\zeta_{c.s}$ with an increase in Re_c is observed only in converging wyes.[8,9]

27. In the course of transition from a turbulent to a laminar flow within the range $Re_c = 2 \times 10^3$ to 3×10^3 there occurs a sudden increase in the coefficient $\zeta_{c.s}$ for both

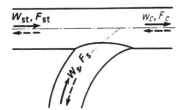

Figure 7-6 Schematic of a wye with a smoothly rounded branch.

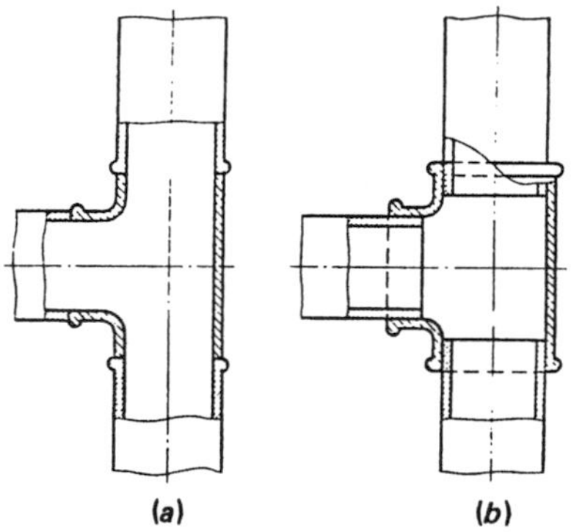

Figure 7-7 Schematic of an annular step in a standard wye: (a) welded wye; (b) wye with screwed pipes.

(a) (b)

converging and diverging wyes (Figure 7-8). The same occurs with the coefficient $\zeta_{c.st}$ of a diverging wye. For a converging wye, such a jump in $\zeta_{c.st}$ occurs at $\alpha > 60°$ and $F_s/F_c = 1$; when $\alpha = 45°$ and $F_s/F_c = 1$, the coefficient $\zeta_{c.st}$ does not increase; in this case it is independent of Re_c. When $\alpha = 30°$ and $F_s/F_c = 1.0$, even a sudden decrease in $\zeta_{c.st}$ occurs in transition from turbulent to laminar flow.[8,9]

28. In the case of laminar flow, the values of the resistance coefficients of wyes depend substantially on the relative length of the inlet section l_0/D_0 and increases with the increase in this length within the velocity profile stabilization as is the case for branches (see Chapter 6).[8,9]

29. The expression for the resistance coefficient of wyes with laminar flow has generally the form suggested by Zubov.[8,9]

$$\zeta^l \equiv \frac{\Delta p}{\rho w_c^2/2} = [(N - 1)k_1 + 1]\zeta^t + \frac{A}{Re_c} \qquad (7-5)$$

where $N = \dfrac{1}{F_c} \displaystyle\int_{F_c} \left(\dfrac{w}{w_c}\right)^3 dF$ is the coefficient of kinetic energy (of the Coriolis energy) of the flow in section c-c; k_1 is a correction factor; superscripts l and t refer to a laminar and a turbulent flow, respectively.

30. For a converging wye with a laminar flow $N = 2$, and for a side branch $k_1 = 1$, so that, according to Equation (7-5),

$$\zeta_{c.s}^l \equiv \frac{\Delta p}{\rho w_c^2/2} = 2\zeta_{c.s}^t + \frac{A}{Re_c} \qquad (7-6)$$

where $\zeta_{c.s}^t = \zeta_{c.s}$, see Equation (7-1); A is the quantity which depends on the parameters α, Q_s/Q_0, and F_s/F_c, but its numerical value has not as yet been established; tentatively $A \approx 150$.

According to the data of Zubov,[8,9] for a straight passage

$$\zeta_{c.st}^l = 2\zeta_{c.s}^l + a_0(1 - Q_s/Q_c)^2 - (1.6 - 0.3F_s/F_c) \times \left(\frac{F_c}{F_s} \cdot \frac{Q_s}{Q_c}\right)^2$$

where for $\zeta_{c.s}^l$, see Equation (7-6); for a_0 see Table 7-6.

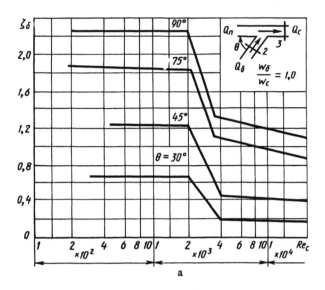

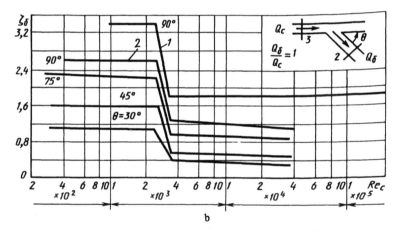

Figure 7-8 Dependence of the resistance coefficient ζ_s of wyes on data in Reference 8. (*a*) converging wyes; (*b*) diverging wyes.

31. According to Equation (7-5), for a diverging wye with laminar flow ($N = 2$), the resistance coefficient of a side branch is

$$\zeta'_{c.s} \equiv \frac{\Delta p}{\rho w_c^2/2} = (k_1 + 1)\zeta'_{c.s} + \frac{A}{\mathrm{Re}_c}$$

where $\zeta'_{c.s} = \zeta_{c.s}$, see Equation (7-3); tentatively $A \approx 150$; for k_1 see Table 7-7 (at $F_s/F_c = 1$).*

For a straight passage $N = 2$ and $k = 2$, so that, according to Equation (7-5), we have

$$\zeta'_{c.st} \equiv \frac{\Delta p}{\rho w_c^2/2} = 3\zeta'_{c.st} + \frac{A}{\mathrm{Re}_c}$$

where $\zeta'_{c.st} = \zeta_{c.st}$, see Equation (7-4); tentatively $A \approx 33$.

*For other values of F_s/F_c the coefficient k_1 is as yet unknown.

Table 7-6 Values of a_0

F_s/F_c	≤ 0.35		>0.35	
Q_s/Q_c	0–1.0	≤ 0.2		>0.2
a_0	$1.8 - Q_s/Q_c$	$1.8 - 4Q_s/Q_c$		$1.2 - Q_s/Q_c$

Table 7-7 Values of k_1

	$\alpha°$			
Q_s/Q_c	30	45	60	90
	At $F_s/F_c \leqslant 1$			
0	0.9	0.9	0.9	0.9
0.2	1.8	1.8	1.5	1.1
0.4	3.4	2.9	2.2	1.3
0.6	6.1	4.3	3.0	1.5
0.8	7.2	4.3	2.7	1.4
1.0	6.0	3.0	2.3	1.3
	At $F_s/F_c \geqslant 1$			
Up to 0.4	0.9	0.9	0.9	0.9
Above 0.4	0	0	0	0

32. In equilateral wyes which are used for joining two opposite streams (merging) (scheme of Diagram 7-29), the resistance coefficients of the two branches are practically equal.

33. When a partition is installed at the place of junction of a symmetrical wye, the two flows are independent of each other before converging into the common channel. This is followed by conventional turbulent mixing of two flows moving with different velocities. The losses in the wye in this case are made up of (1) the losses on mixing (shock losses) and (2) losses when the flow turns through 90°.

34. The resistance coefficient of a flow stream that moves in one of the branches with smaller velocity can have a negative value just as in a conventional diverging wye (due to the additional energy from the higher-velocity flow).

Without a partition the flow pattern in a symmetrical wye is less clearly defined. The pressure drops before and after merging of the flows mainly reflect the losses common to both branches. The value of these is positive at any velocity ratio (flow rate) between the branch and the common channel $w_s/w_c(Q_h/Q_c)$ and is approximately equal to the losses in a diverging elbow.

35. The resistance coefficient of each branch of a symmetrical wye at a junction can be calculated with the following formula of Levin:[32]

$$\zeta_{c.s} \equiv \frac{\Delta p_s}{\rho w_c^2/2} = 1 + \left(\frac{F_c}{F_s}\right)^2 + 3\left(\frac{F_c}{F_s}\right)^2\left[\left(\frac{Q_s}{Q_c}\right)^2 - \frac{Q_s}{Q_c}\right]$$

36. If a symmetrical wye is used for the division of flow, the conditions of flow passage in it are about the same as with a conventional turn. Therefore, the losses in this wye can be approximately determined from the data for elbows with different aspect ratios b_1/b_0.

The resistance coefficient of this wye can also be calculated with Levin's formula:[32]

$$\zeta_{c.s} \equiv \frac{\Delta p_s}{\rho w_c^2/2} = 1 + k_1 \left(\frac{w_s}{w_c}\right)^2$$

where $k_1 \approx 1.5$ for standard threaded malleable-iron wyes; $k_1 \approx 0.3$ for welded wyes.

37. A symmetrical wye can be fabricated to have smooth branches ("swallowtail"), reducing it resistance appreciably.

38. The resistance coefficient of converging symmetrical wyes at $\alpha < 90°$ and $F_c = 2F_s$ can be calculated from Levin's formula:[32]

$$\zeta_{c.s} \equiv \frac{\Delta p_s}{\rho w_c^2/2} = 4\frac{Q_s}{Q_c}(0.9 + \cos^2 \alpha) + \left(\frac{Q_s}{Q_c}\right)^4 \left[1 + \left(\frac{Q_c}{Q_s} - 1\right)^4\right](1 - \cos^2 \alpha)$$

$$- 4\left(\frac{Q_s}{Q_c}\right)^2 \cos^2 \alpha - 4(0.2 + 0.5 \cos^2 \alpha)$$

39. The resistance coefficient of diverging symmetrical wyes at $\alpha < 90°$ and $F_c = 2F_s$ can be calculated, approximately, just as for a side branch of a conventional wye of the type $F_s + F_{st} = F_c$ from Diagram 7-16.

40. Diagram 7-31 contains the values of the resistance coefficients of symmetrical wyes of the $F_s = F_{st} = F_c$ at $\alpha = 45°$. These data were obtained experimentally[57] for wyes with branches both butt jointed (Figure 7-9a) and threaded (Figure 7-9b and c). Two versions of the latter were tested: complete screw threading of branches (Figure 7-9b, $\delta = 0$) and incomplete threading (Figure 7-9c, $\delta/D_0 \approx 0.13$). In the case of butt jointing, the same work suggests approximating formulas for calculating the coefficients (see the diagram indicated).

41. The flow pattern in crosses is basically similar to that in wyes.

The resistance coefficients of double wyes of area $F_{st} = F_c$ at stream junction (see Diagrams 7-31 through 7-35) can be determined approximately:[29,30]

For one of the side branches (for example, No. 1):

$$\zeta_{1c.s} \equiv \frac{\Delta p_{1s}}{\rho w_c^2/2} = 1 + \left(\frac{Q_{1s}}{Q_c}\frac{F_c}{F_{1s}}\right)^2 - 8\left(\frac{Q_{1s}}{Q_c}\right)^2 \frac{[(Q_c/Q_{1s}) - (1 + Q_{2s}/Q_{1s})]^2}{4 - (1 + Q_{2s}/Q_{1s})(Q_{1s}/Q_c)}$$

$$- 2\left(\frac{Q_{1s}}{Q_c}\right)^2 \frac{F_c}{F_{1s}}\left[1 - \left(\frac{Q_{2s}}{Q_{1s}}\right)^2\right]\cos \alpha$$

For the other side branch ($\zeta_{2c.s}$) the subscripts 1 and 2 are interchanged.

For a straight passage:

$$\zeta_{c.st} \equiv \frac{\Delta p_{st}}{\rho w_c^2/2} = 1 + \left(\frac{Q_{st}}{Q_c}\right)^2 - \left(\frac{Q_{st}}{Q_c}\right)^2 \frac{1 + Q_{st}/Q_c}{(0.75 + 0.25Q_{st}/Q_c)^2}$$

$$- 2\left(\frac{Q_{1s}}{Q_c}\right)^2 \frac{F_c}{F_{1s}} \frac{1 + (Q_{2s}/Q_{1s})^2}{(1 + Q_{2s}/Q_{1s})^2}\left(\frac{Q_c}{Q_{st}} - 1\right)^2 \cos \alpha$$

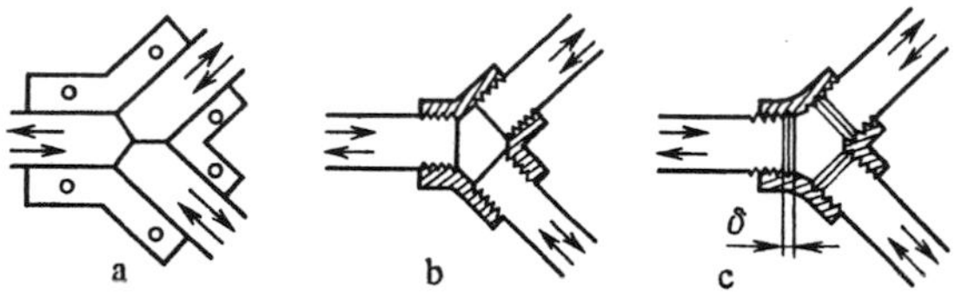

Figure 7-9 Symmetrically shaped wyes of the type $F_s = F_{st} = F_c$:[57] (a) butt-jointed branching; (b) threaded branching at $\delta = 0$; (c) threaded branching with $\delta/D_0 \approx 0.13$.

42. In order to determine the resistance coefficients of welded inflow (converging) crosses in cylindrical pipelines for steam, water, etc., with $\alpha = 90°$, the following formulas are recommended:[29,30]

For one of the side branches (for example, No. 1):

$$\zeta_{1c.s} \equiv \frac{\Delta p_{1s}}{\rho w_c^2/2} = 1.15 + \left(\frac{Q_{1s}}{Q_c}\frac{F_c}{F_{1s}}\right) - 8\left(\frac{Q_{1s}}{Q_c}\right)^2 \frac{[(Q_c/Q_{1s}) - (1 + Q_{2s}/Q_{1s})]^2}{4 - (1 + Q_{2s}/Q_{1s})(Q_{1s}/Q_c)}$$

For a straight passage:

$$\zeta_{c.st} \equiv \frac{\Delta p_{st}}{\rho w_c^2/2} = 1.2 + \left(\frac{Q_{st}}{Q_c}\right)^2 - \left(\frac{Q_{st}}{Q_c}\right)^2 \frac{1 + Q_{st}/Q_c}{(0.75 + 0.25 Q_{st}/Q_c)^2}$$

For standard crosses fabricated of malleable cast-iron at $Q_{st}/Q_c > 0.7$, the following quantity is added to the values of $\zeta_{c.st}$:

$$\Delta\zeta_{c.st} = 2.5\left(\frac{Q_{st}}{Q_c} - 0.7\right)$$

43. The resistance coefficients of crosses for flow division are determined approximately just as for diverging wyes from Diagrams 7-18 through 7-20.

For straight diverging double wyes ($\alpha = 90°$) fabricated of sheet steel (with the parts flat seamed), the values of the resistance coefficients obtained experimentally by Sosin and Neimark[40] for a turbulent flow are given in Diagrams 7-36 and 7-37.

44. When one side branch of the wye is close to the other, they influence each other. This especially refers to converging wyes. The extent of this effect of one branch on another branch depends on both the relative distance between them and the flow rate ratio Q_s/Q_c.

45. To date, there exist insufficient data on the correction factors for this interaction effect for all types of wyes; in order to approximately determine this effect in the case of suction, one can use the experimental results of Bezdetkina.[2]

The values of the correction factor k_2, expressed as the ratio of the resistance coefficient ζ_{s2} of the second side branch to the resistance coefficient ζ_{s1} of the first side branch, are summarized in Table 7-8 for different relative flow rates Q_s/Q_c and different relative distances l_{el}/D_c between adjacent branches.

46. At small relative flow rates ($Q_s/Q_c \leq 0.1$) the mutual effect of the branches of the wye is negligible ($k_2 \approx 1.0$, see Table 7-8). Therefore, if there are many side branches in which the ratios Q_s/Q_c for each single branch are small, the mutual effect can practically be neglected and the values of the resistance coefficients for each of them can be assumed such as for a single wye.

Some additional data on the mutual effect of a wye will be given in Chapter 12 (in the section "Mutual Effect of Local Fluid Resistances").

Table 7-8 Values of k_2

l_{el}/D_c	Q_s/Q_c			
	≤ 0.1	0.2	0.3	0.4
0–3	1.0	0.75	0.70	0.66
4	1.0	0.83	0.77	0.74
6	1.0	0.96	0.88	0.83
8	1.0	1.0	0.91	0.93
9	1.0	1.0	1.0	1.0

47. Outlet and inlet headers (collectors) also fall into the wye-type sections (see Diagrams 7-39 through 7-44. The primary requirements of such collectors are uniform outflow and, correspondingly, uniform inflow through all of their branches.

48. The degree of uniformity of the flow rate through the side branches of headers (collectors) depends, as the theory shows,[15-19] on a basic governing criterion, that is, "the characteristic of the header or collector" $A_{1,2}$, which is a function of a number of parameters:

$$A_{1,2} = \varphi(f, \mu \text{ or } \zeta_{br}, \zeta_{col})$$

where subscripts 1 and 2 refer, respectively, to supply and intake headers; $\bar{f} \equiv \Sigma_s/F_i \approx n_s f_s/F_{in}$ is the relative cross-sectional area n_s of the side branches; f_s is the area of the inlet section of one side branch, m²; F_{in} is the cross-sectional area of the header (initial for supply and final for intake), m²; $\mu = 1/\sqrt{(f_s/f_a)^2 + \zeta_{br}}$ is the coefficient of discharge through a side branch; f_a is the area of the outlet section of the final length of the side branch, m². $\zeta_{br} \equiv \Delta p_{br}/(\rho w_s^2/2)$ is the resistance coefficient of the whole branch, which includes the resistance of all the adjacent sections, apparatus, or other devices; it is reduced to the velocity w_s in the side branch

$$\zeta_{br} = \zeta_s + \zeta_{sec} + \zeta_{app}$$

where $\zeta_s \equiv \Delta p_s/(\rho w_s^2/2)$ is the resistance coefficient of the side branch alone; $\zeta_{sec} \equiv \Delta p_{sec}/(\rho w_s^2/2)$ is the resistance coefficient of all the sections of the side branch after flow division (up to its merging) except for the resistance for the resistance of an apparatus (device); $\zeta_{app} \equiv \Delta p_{app}/(\rho w_s^2/2)$ is the resistance coefficient of the apparatus (device) installed in the side branch; $\zeta_{coll} \equiv \Delta p_{coll}/(\rho w_{in}^2/2)$ is the resistance coefficient of the supplying (intake) part of the collector (header) reduced to the average velocity of the flow w_{in} in the section F_{in} of the header.

If there are no additional barriers along the channels it is assumed for practical calculations that

$$\zeta_{coll} \approx 0.5\lambda \frac{L}{D_{h,in}}$$

where L is the total length of the header, m; $D_{h,in} = 4F_{in}/\Pi_{in}$ is the hydraulic diameter of the initial cross section of the supplying channel, m.

49. With constant cross section of the header and with other conditions being equal, the degree of uniformity in the flow rate is higher the greater is F_{in} (the condition of completely uniform supply is $\bar{f} \rightarrow 0$).

In order to obtain uniform distribution of the flow rate without an increase in the cross-sectional area of the header, it should converge in the direction of the flow (header of variable cross section).

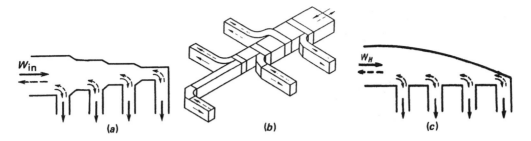

Figure 7-10 Headers of variable cross section: (*a*) stepwise change in the section with sharp branching; (*b*) stepwise change in the section with smooth branching; (*c*) with a shaped side wall.

This can be done in different ways: a linear change of the cross section (see dash-dotted lines in Diagrams 7-40 through 7-43), a stepwise change of the cross section (Figure 7-10*a*) or an appropriate shaping of one of the side walls (Figure 7-10*c*).

When $A_2 > 0.3$, the intake header should not have a variable cross section, since the flow distribution among the branches would be worse rather than better.*

When $A_2 < 0.3$, the intake header can be of variable cross section (to save metal), since it will not worsen uniformity of flow distribution among the branches.

50. The total resistance coefficient of isolated (single) headers of constant cross section and of variable cross section with a linear change in the cross section along the flow is determined from interpolation formulas based on experimental data[50] and given in Diagrams 7-40 through 7-43.

51. In the majority of cases the outlet and inlet headers operate jointly (joint headers). The flow in them can have opposite directions (Π-shaped collector, Diagram 7-42) or the same direction (Z-shaped collector, Diagram 7-49). When the resistance coefficients of both (outlet and inlet) headers are the same and $\zeta_{coll} < 1$, a Π-shaped collector provides a more uniform distribution of flow than a Z-shaped one. At $\zeta_{coll} > 1$, the situation is the reverse.

52. It is desirable that the outlet part of a Z-shaped header be of variable cross section (contraction in the flow direction) and the intake part of constant cross section at $A_4 > 0.3$.** (See paragraph 49.) In some cases a more uniform division of flow in a Π-shaped header may be achieved by contracting the cross section of the intake header in the direction toward its inlet and keeping the cross section of the outlet part constant.

53. The total resistance coefficient of joint Π- and Z-shaped headers with constant cross sections of both channels or with variable cross section of the outlet channel and constant cross section of the inlet channel is determined from the interpolation formulas[50] given in Diagrams 7-42 through 7-47.

54. In order to decrease the resistance of the side branches of the header, the transition sections for them can be made as shown in Diagram 7-39. Their design is simple and their resistance coefficients are minimal. These may be taken as standard.

The resistance of the side branches of a header decreases sharply if branching is smooth (see Figures 7-10*b* and 7-11).

55. The resistance coefficient of the *i*th branch $\zeta_{is} \equiv \Delta p_{is}/(\rho w^2_{(i-1)s}/2)$ of the outlet (inlet) box with transition sections made according to the scheme of Diagram 7-39 depends only on the velocity ratio $w_{is}/w_{(i-1)s}$.

---

*In the case of a dust-laden flow, the flow velocity along the length of the intake collector should not be smaller than a certain limiting value (10–15 m/s) to prevent dust from settling. In this case, the intake collector should be of variable cross section, though it entails worsening of flow distribution among the branches.

**A_4 is the characteristic of a Z-shaped collector.

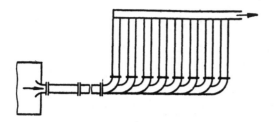

Figure 7-11 Π-shaped joint header with smooth branches of the supplying header.

This coefficient is virtually independent of the Reynolds number, at least from Re = 10^4, the aspect ratio of the cross section of the outlet box (within $h/b = 0.5$–1.0), and the area ratio F_s/F_c.

The resistance coefficient of the branch installed in the side of the outlet box is smaller than the resistance coefficient of the branch installed above or below this box, since in the latter case the flow successively turns twice through 90° in two mutually perpendicular directions (see Diagram 7-39).

7-2 DIAGRAMS OF THE RESISTANCE COEFFICIENTS

| Converging wye of the type $F_s + F_{st} > F_c$; $F_{st} = F_c$; $\alpha = 30°$[31,43] | | | | | | Diagram 7-1 |

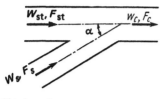

Side branch

$$\zeta_{c.s} \equiv \frac{\Delta p_s}{\rho w_c^2/2} = A\left[1 + \left(\frac{Q_s}{Q_c}\frac{F_c}{F_s}\right)^2\right.$$

$$\left. -2\left(1 - \frac{Q_s}{Q_c}\right)^2 - 1.7\frac{F_c}{F_s}\left(\frac{Q_s}{Q_c}\right)^2\right] = A\zeta'_{c.s}$$

For $\zeta'_{c.s}$, see the table and curves $\zeta'_{c.s} = f(Q_s/Q_c)$ at different F_s/F_c graph a $= f(F_s/F_c, Q_s/Q_c)$, see Table 7-1;

$$\zeta_s \equiv \frac{\Delta p_s}{\rho w_s^2/2} = \frac{\zeta_{c.s}}{[(Q_s Q_c)(F_c F_s)]}$$

Values of $\zeta_{c.s}$

$\dfrac{Q_s}{Q_c}$	F_s/F_c						
	0.1	0.2	0.3	0.4	0.6	0.8	1.0
0	−1.00	−1.00	−1.00	−1.00	−1.00	−1.00	−1.00
0.1	0.21	−0.46	−0.57	−0.60	−0.62	−0.63	−0.63
0.2	3.02	0.37	−0.07	−0.20	−0.28	−0.30	−0.31
0.3	7.45	1.50	0.50	0.20	−0.01	−0.04	−0.05
0.4	13.5	2.89	1.15	0.58	0.26	0.18	0.16
0.5	21.2	4.58	1.83	0.97	0.47	0.35	0.32
0.6	30.4	6.55	2.60	1.37	0.64	0.46	0.41
0.7	41.3	8.81	3.40	1.77	0.76	0.52	0.46
0.8	53.8	11.5	4.32	2.14	0.84	0.53	0.45
0.9	67.9	14.2	5.30	2.52	0.88	0.48	0.38
1.0	83.6	17.3	6.33	2.90	0.88	0.39	0.26

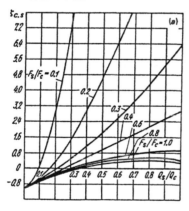

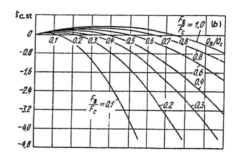

Passage

$$\zeta_{c.st} \equiv \frac{\Delta p_{st}}{\rho w_c^2/2} = 1 - \left(1 - \frac{Q_s}{Q_c}\right)^2$$

$$= -1.74\frac{F_c}{F_s}\left(\frac{Q_s}{Q_c}\right)^2$$

see the table and curves $\zeta_{c.st} = f(Q_s/Q_c)$ at different F_s/F_c (graph B);

$$\zeta_{st} \equiv \frac{\Delta p_{st}}{\rho w_{st}^2/2} = \frac{\zeta_{c.st}}{(1 - Q_s/Q_c)^2}$$

Values of $\zeta_{c.st}$*

$\dfrac{Q_s}{Q_c}$	F_s/F_c						
	0.1	0.2	0.3	0.4	0.6	0.8	1.0
0	0	0	0	0	0	0	0
0.1	+0.02	0.10	0.13	0.15	0.16	0.17	0.17
0.2	−0.34	+0.01	+0.13	0.19	0.24	0.27	0.29
0.3	−1.06	−0.27	−0.01	+0.12	0.22	0.30	0.35
0.4	−2.15	−0.75	−0.30	−0.06	0.17	0.29	0.36
0.5	−3.60	−1.43	−0.70	−0.35	0.00	0.21	0.32
0.6	−5.40	−2.29	−1.25	−0.73	−0.20	+0.06	0.21
0.7	−7.60	−3.35	−1.95	−1.20	−0.50	−0.15	+0.06
0.8	−10.2	−4.61	−2.74	−1.82	−0.90	−0.43	−0.15
0.9	−13.0	−6.06	−3.70	−2.55	−1.40	−0.77	−0.42
1.0	−16.4	−7.70	−4.80	−3.35	−1.90	−1.17	−0.75

*When a stream moves in the passage of a side branch past the free surface formed when $Q_s/Q_c = 0$, some loss of energy always takes place therefore, in real conditions at $Q_s/Q_c = 0$ the coefficient $\zeta_{c.s}$ is not equal to zero. Here and in subsequent tables $\zeta_{c.s} = 0$ is obtained by calculation from the formulas given.

Converging wye of the type $F_s + F_{st} > F_c$; $F_{st} = F_c$; $\alpha = 45°$ [31,43]

Diagram
7-2

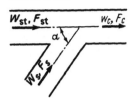

Side branch

$$\zeta_{c.s} \equiv \frac{\Delta p_s}{\rho w_c^2/2} = A\left[1 + \left(\frac{Q_s}{Q_c}\frac{F_c}{F_s}\right)^2\right.$$

$$\left. - 2\left(1 - \frac{Q_s}{Q_c}\right)^2 - 1.41\frac{F_c}{F_s}\left(\frac{Q_s}{Q_c}\right)^2\right] = A\zeta'_{c.s}$$

for $\zeta'_{c.s}$, see the table and curves $\zeta'_{c.s} = f(Q_s/Q_c)$ at different F_s/F_c (graph a); $A = f(F_s/F_c, Q_s/Q_c)$, see Table 7-1;

$$\zeta_s \equiv \frac{\Delta p_s}{\rho w_s^2/2} = \frac{\zeta_{c.s}}{[(Q_s/Q_c)(F_c/F_s)]^2}$$

Straight passage

$$\zeta_{c.st} \equiv \frac{\Delta p_{st}}{\rho w_c^2/2} = 1 - \left(1 - \frac{Q_s}{Q_c}\right)^2$$

$$- 1.41\frac{F_c}{F_s}\left(\frac{Q_s}{Q_c}\right)^2$$

see the table and curves $\zeta_{c.st} = f(Q_s/Q_c)$ at different F_s/F_c (graph b);

$$\zeta_{st} \equiv \frac{\Delta p_{st}}{\rho w_{st}^2/2} = \frac{\zeta_{c.st}}{(1 - Q_s/Q_c)^2}$$

Values of $\zeta'_{c.s}$

$\dfrac{Q_s}{Q_c}$	F_s/F_c						
	0.1	0.2	0.3	0.4	0.6	0.8	1.0
0	−1.00	−1.00	−1.00	−1.00	−1.00	−1.00	−1.00
0.1	0.24	−0.45	−0.56	−0.59	−0.61	−0.62	−0.62
0.2	3.15	0.54	−0.02	−0.17	−0.26	−0.28	−0.29
0.3	8.00	1.64	0.60	0.30	0.08	0	−0.03
0.4	14.0	3.15	1.30	0.72	0.35	0.25	0.21
0.5	21.9	5.00	2.10	1.18	0.60	0.45	0.40
0.6	31.6	6.90	2.97	1.65	0.85	0.60	0.53
0.7	42.9	9.20	3.90	2.15	1.02	0.70	0.60
0.8	55.9	12.4	4.90	2.66	1.20	0.79	0.66
0.9	70.6	15.4	6.20	3.20	1.30	0.80	0.64
1.0	86.9	18.9	7.40	3.71	1.42	0.80	0.59

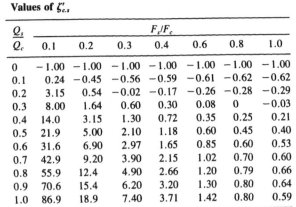

Values of $\zeta_{c.st}$

$\dfrac{Q_s}{Q_c}$	F_s/F_h						
	0.1	0.2	0.3	0.4	0.6	0.8	1.0
0	0	0	0	0	0	0	0
0.1	0.05	0.12	0.14	0.16	0.17	0.17	0.17
02	−0.20	0.17	0.22	0.27	0.27	0.29	0.31
0.3	−0.76	−0.13	0.08	0.20	0.28	0.32	0.40
0.4	−1.65	−0.50	−0.12	0.08	0.26	0.36	0.41
0.5	−2.77	−1.00	−0.49	−0.13	0.16	0.30	0.40
0.6	−4.30	−1.70	−0.87	−0.45	−0.04	0.20	0.33
0.7	−6.05	−2.60	−1.40	−0.85	−0.25	0.08	0.25
0.8	−8.10	−3.56	−2.10	−1.30	−0.55	−0.17	0.06
0.9	−10.00	−4.75	−2.80	−1.90	−0.88	−0.40	−0.18
1.0	−13.20	−6.10	−3.70	−2.55	−1.35	−0.77	−0.42

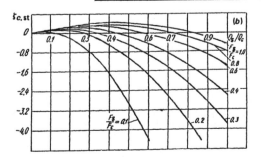

| Converging wye of the type $F_s + F_{st} > F_c$; $F_{st} = F_c$; $\alpha = 60°$ [31,43] | | | | | | | Diagram 7-3 |

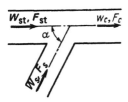

Side branch

$$\zeta_{c.s} \equiv \frac{\Delta p_s}{\rho w_c^2/2} = A\left[1 + \left(\frac{Q_s F_c}{Q_c F_s}\right)^2\right.$$

$$\left. -2\left(1 - \frac{Q_s}{Q_c}\right)^2 - \frac{F_c}{F_s}\left(\frac{Q_s}{Q_c}\right)^2\right] = A\zeta_{c.s}'$$

$A = f(F_s/F_c, Q_s/Q_c)$, see Table 7-1; for $\zeta_{c.s}'$ see the table and curves $\zeta_{c.s} = f(Q_s/Q_c)$ at different F_s/F_c (graph a);

$$\zeta_s \equiv \frac{\Delta p_s}{\rho w_s^2/2} = \frac{\zeta_{c.s}}{(Q_s F_c/Q_c F_s)^2}$$

Straight passage

$$\zeta_{c.st} \equiv \frac{\Delta p_{st}}{\rho w_c^2/2} = 1 - \left(1 - \frac{Q_s}{Q_c}\right)^2$$

$$- \frac{F_c}{F_s}\left(\frac{Q_s}{Q_c}\right)^2$$

see the table and curves $\zeta_{c.st} = f(Q_s/Q_c)$ at different F_s/F_c (graph B);

$$\zeta_{st} \equiv \frac{\Delta p_{st}}{\rho w_{st}^2/2} = \frac{\zeta_{c.st}}{(1 - Q_s/Q_c)^2}$$

Values of $\zeta_{c.s}''$

$\dfrac{Q_s}{Q_c}$	F_s/F_c						
	0.1	0.2	0.3	0.4	0.6	0.8	1.0
0	−1.00	−1.00	−1.00	−1.00	−1.00	−1.00	−1.00
0.1	0.26	−0.42	−0.54	−0.58	−0.61	−0.62	−0.62
0.2	3.35	0.55	0.03	−0.13	−0.23	−0.26	−0.26
0.3	8.20	1.85	0.75	0.40	0.10	0	−0.01
0.4	14.7	3.50	1.55	0.92	0.45	0.35	0.28
0.5	23.0	5.50	2.40	1.44	0.78	0.58	0.50
0.6	33.1	7.90	3.50	2.05	1.08	0.80	0.68
0.7	44.9	10.0	4.60	2.70	1.40	0.98	0.84
0.8	58.5	13.7	5.80	3.32	1.64	1.12	0.92
0.9	73.9	17.2	7.65	4.05	1.92	1.20	0.99
1.0	91.0	21.0	9.70	4.70	2.11	1.35	1.00

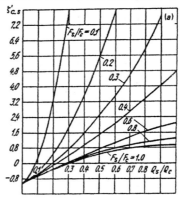

Values of $\zeta_{c.st}$

$\dfrac{Q_s}{Q_c}$	F_s/F_c						
	0.1	0.2	0.3	0.4	0.6	0.8	1.0
0	0	0	0	0	0	0	0
0.1	0.09	0.14	0.16	0.17	0.17	0.18	0.18
0.2	0	0.16	0.23	0.26	0.29	0.31	0.32
0.3	−0.40	0.06	0.22	0.30	0.32	0.41	0.42
0.4	−1.00	−0.16	0.11	0.24	0.37	0.44	0.48
0.5	−1.75	−0.50	−0.08	0.13	0.33	0.44	0.50
0.6	−2.80	−0.95	−0.35	−0.10	0.25	0.40	0.48
0.7	−4.00	−1.55	−0.70	−0.30	0.08	0.28	0.42
0.8	−5.44	−2.24	−1.17	−0.64	−0.11	0.16	0.32
0.9	−7.20	−3.08	−1.70	−1.02	−0.38	−0.08	0.18
1.0	−9.00	−4.00	−2.30	−1.50	−0.68	−0.28	0

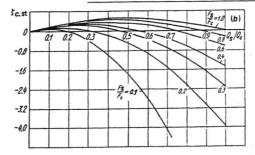

Converging wye of the type $F_s + F_{st} > F_c$; $F_{st} = F_c$;
$\alpha = 90°$[31,43]

Diagram
7-4

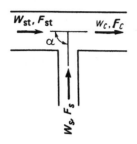

Side branch

$$\zeta_{c.s} \equiv \frac{\Delta p_s}{\rho w_c^2/2} = A\left[1 + \left(\frac{Q_s}{Q_c}\frac{F_c}{F_s}\right)^2 - 2\left(1 - \frac{Q_s}{Q_c}\right)^2\right] = A\zeta'_{c.s}$$

where $\zeta_{c.s} = f(Q_s/Q_c)$, see the table and graph a; $A = f(F_s/F_c, Q_s/Q_c)$, see Table 7-1.

$$\zeta_s \equiv \frac{\Delta p_s}{\rho w_s^2/2} = \frac{\zeta_{c.s}}{(Q_s F_c/Q_c F_s)^2}$$

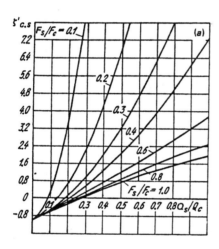

Values of $\zeta'_{c.s}$

$\frac{Q_s}{Q_c}$	F_s/F_c						
	0.1	0.2	0.3	0.4	0.6	0.8	1.0
0	−1.00	−1.00	−1.00	−1.00	−1.00	−1.00	−1.00
0.1	0.40	−0.37	−0.51	−0.54	−0.59	−0.60	−0.61
0.2	3.80	0.72	0.17	−0.03	−0.17	−0.22	−0.30
0.3	9.20	2.27	1.00	0.58	0.27	0.15	−0.11
0.4	16.3	4.30	2.06	1.30	0.75	0.55	0.44
0.5	25.5	6.75	3.23	2.06	1.20	0.89	0.77
0.6	36.7	9.70	4.70	2.98	1.68	1.25	1.04
0.7	42.9	13.0	6.30	3.90	2.20	1.60	1.30
0.8	64.9	16.9	7.92	4.92	2.70	1.92	1.56
0.9	82.0	21.2	9.70	6.10	3.20	2.25	1.80
1.0	101.0	26.0	11.90	7.25	3.80	2.57	2.00

Q_s/Q_c	0	0.1	0.2	0.3	0.4	0.5	0.6	0.7	0.8	0.9	1.0
$\zeta_{c.st}$	0	0.16	0.27	0.38	0.46	0.53	0.57	0.59	0.60	0.59	0.55

Straight passage

$$\zeta_{c.st} \equiv \frac{\Delta p_{st}}{\rho w_c^2/2} \approx 1.55\frac{Q_s}{Q_c}$$

$$-\left(\frac{Q_s}{Q_c}\right)^2$$

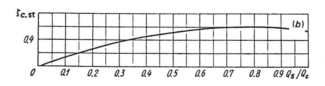

see the table and curve $\zeta_{c.st} = f(Q_s/Q_c)$, which is virtually correct for all values of F_s/F_c (graph B);

$$\zeta_{c.st} \equiv \frac{\Delta p_{st}}{\rho w_c^2/2} = \frac{\zeta_{c.st}}{(1 - Q_s/Q_c)^2}$$

Converging wye of the type $F_s + F_{st} = F_c$; $\alpha = 15°$[31,43]	Diagram 7-5

Side branch

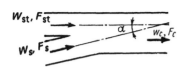

$$\zeta_{c.s} \equiv \frac{\Delta p_s}{\rho w_c^2/2} = 1 + \left(\frac{Q_s}{Q_c}\frac{F_c}{F_s}\right)^2 - 2\frac{F_c}{F_s}\left(1 - \frac{Q_s}{Q_c}\right)^2 - 1.94\frac{F_c}{F_s}\left(\frac{Q_s}{Q_c}\right)^2$$

see the table and curves $\zeta_{c.s} = f(Q_s/Q_c)$ for different F_s/F_c;

$$\zeta_s \equiv \frac{\Delta p_s}{\rho w_s^2/2} = \frac{\zeta_{c.s}}{(Q_s F_c/Q_c F_s)^2}$$

Straight passage

$$\zeta_{c.st} \equiv \frac{\Delta p_{st}}{\rho w_c^2/2} = 1 + \left(\frac{F_c}{F_s}\right)^2\left(1 - \frac{Q_s}{Q_c}\right)^2 - 2\frac{F_c}{F_{st}}\left(1 - \frac{Q_s}{Q_c}\right)^2 - 1.94\frac{F_c}{F_s}\left(\frac{Q_s}{Q_c}\right)^2 + K_{st}$$

see the table and curves $\zeta_{c.st} = f(Q_s/Q_c)$ for different F_s/F_c:

F_s/F_c	K_{st}
0–0.2	0
0.33	0.14
0.50	0.40

$$\zeta_{st} \equiv \frac{\Delta p_{st}}{\rho w_{st}^2/2} = \frac{\zeta_{c.st}}{(1 - Q_s/Q_c)^2(F_c/F_s)^2}$$

Values of $\zeta_{c.s}$ (in numerator) and $\zeta_{c.st}$ (in denominator)

F_s/F_c	Q_s/Q_c											
	0	0.03	0.05	0.10	0.2	0.3	0.4	0.5	0.6	0.7	0.8	1.0
0.06	−1.12	−0.70	−0.20	1.84	9.92	23.0	41.0	64.3	–	–	–	–
	0	0.06	0.04	−0.13	−0.95	−2.50	−4.60	−7.50				
0.10	−1.22	−1.00	−0.72	0.01	2.80	7.17	13.1	20.6	29.7	–	–	–
	0.01	0.10	0.12	0.02	−0.36	−1.20	−2.50	−4.10	−6.12			
0.20	−1.50	−1.40	−1.22	−0.84	0.02	1.20	2.55	4.20	6.12	8.20	10.7	–
	0.06	0.15	0.20	0.22	0.05	−0.28	0.89	−1.66	−2.63	−3.84	−5.22	
0.33	−2.00	−1.80	−1.71	−1.40	−0.67	−0.16	0.42	1.05	1.67	2.30	2.95	4.20
	0.40	0.42	0.45	0.47	0.42	0.24	−0.08	−0.52	−1.25	−1.80	−2.60	−4.66
0.50	−3.00	−2.80	−2.60	−2.24	−1.56	−1.00	−0.40	0.02	0.40	0.66	0.93	1.14
	1.40	1.40	1.39	1.37	1.24	1.01	0.78	−0.43	−0.10	−0.82	−1.08	−2.46

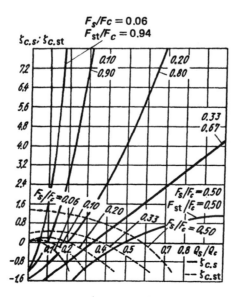

Converging wye of the type $F_s + F_{st} = F_c$; $\alpha = 30°$ [31,43]	Diagram 7-6

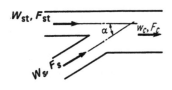

Side branch

$$\zeta_{c.s} \equiv \frac{\Delta p_s}{\rho w_c^2/2} = 1 + \left(\frac{Q_s}{Q_c}\frac{F_c}{F_s}\right)^2 - 2\frac{F_c}{F_{st}}\left(1 - \frac{Q_s}{Q_c}\right)^2 - 1.74\frac{F_c}{F_s}\left(\frac{Q_s}{Q_c}\right)^2$$

see the table and curves $\zeta_{c.s} = f(Q_s/Q_c)$ for different F_s/F_c;

$$\zeta_s \equiv \frac{\Delta p_s}{\rho w_0^2/2} = \frac{\zeta_{c.s}}{(Q_s F_c/Q_c F_s)^2}$$

Straight passage

$$\zeta_{c.st} \equiv \frac{\Delta p_{st}}{\rho w_c^2/2} = 1 + \left(\frac{F_c}{F_{st}}\right)^2\left(1 - \frac{Q_s}{Q_c}\right)^2 - 2\frac{F_c}{F_{st}}\left(1 - \frac{Q_s}{Q_c}\right)^2 - 1.74\frac{F_c}{F_s}\left(\frac{Q_s}{Q_c}\right)^2 + K_{st}$$

see the table and curves $\zeta_{c.st} = f(Q_s/Q_c)$ for different F_s/F_c:

F_s/F_c	K_{st}
0–0.2	0
0.33	0.14
0.50	0.40

$$\zeta_{st} \equiv \frac{\Delta p_{st}}{\rho w_{st}^2/2} = \frac{\zeta_{c.st}}{(1 - Q_s/Q_c)^2(F_c/F_s)^2}$$

Values of $\zeta_{c.s}$ (in numerator) and $\zeta_{c.st}$ (in denominator)

F_s/F_c					Q_s/Q_c							
	0	0.03	0.05	0.1	0.2	0.3	0.4	0.5	0.6	0.7	0.8	1.0
0.06	−1.13	−0.07	−0.30	1.82	10.1	23.3	41.5	65.2	–	–	–	–
	0	0.06	0.04	−0.10	−0.81	−2.10	−4.07	−6.60				
0.10	−1.22	−1.00	−0.76	0.02	2.88	7.34	13.4	21.1	29.4	–	–	–
	0.01	0.10	0.08	0.04	−0.33	−1.05	−2.14	−3.60	5.40			
0.20	−1.50	−1.35	−1.22	−0.84	0.05	1.40	2.70	4.46	6.48	8.70	11.4	17.3
	0.06	0.10	0.13	0.16	0.06	−0.24	−0.73	−1.40	−2.30	−3.34	−3.59	−8.64
0.33	−2.00	−1.80	−1.70	−1.40	−0.72	−0.12	0.52	1.20	1.89	2.56	3.30	4.80
	0.42	0.45	0.48	0.15	0.52	0.32	0.07	−0.32	−0.82	−1.47	−2.19	−4.00
0.50	−3.00	−2.80	−2.60	−2.24	−1.44	−0.91	−0.36	0.14	0.56	0.84	1.18	1.53
	1.40	1.40	1.40	1.36	1.26	1.09	0.86	0.53	0.15	−0.52	−0.82	−2.07

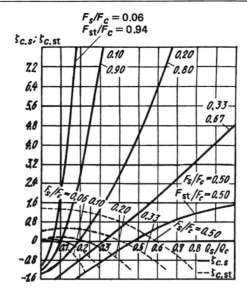

Converging wye of the type $F_s + F_{st} = F_c$; $\alpha = 45°$ [31,43]	Diagram 7-7

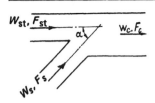

Side branch

$$\zeta_{c.s} \equiv \frac{\Delta p_s}{\rho w_c^2/2} = 1 + \left(\frac{Q_s}{Q_c}\frac{F_c}{F_s}\right)^2 - 2\frac{F_c}{F_s}\left(1 - \frac{Q_s}{Q_c}\right)^2 - 1.41\frac{F_c}{F_s}\left(\frac{Q_s}{Q_c}\right)^2$$

see the table and curves $\zeta_{c.s} = f(Q_s/Q_c)$ for different F_s/F_c;

$$\zeta_s \equiv \frac{\Delta p_s}{\rho w_s^2/2} = \frac{\zeta_{c.s}}{(Q_sF_c/Q_cF_s)^2}$$

Straight passage

$$\zeta_{c.st} \equiv \frac{\Delta p_{st}}{\rho w_c^2/2} = 1 + \left(\frac{F_c}{F_s}\right)^2\left(1 - \frac{Q_s}{Q_c}\right)^2 - 2\frac{F_c}{F_{st}}\left(1 - \frac{Q_s}{Q_c}\right)^2 - 1.41\frac{F_c}{F_s}\left(\frac{Q_s}{Q_c}\right)^2 + K_{st}$$

see the table and curves $\zeta_{c.st} = f(Q_s/Q_c)$ for different F_s/F_c:

F_s/F_c	K_{st}
0.10	0.05
0.20	0.14
0.33	0.14
0.50	0.30

$$\zeta_{st} \equiv \frac{\Delta p_{st}}{\rho w_{st}^2/2} = \frac{\zeta_{c.st}}{(1 - Q_s/Q_c)^2(F_c/F_s)^2}$$

Values of $\zeta_{c.s}$ (in numerator) and $\zeta_{c.st}$ (in denominator)

F_s/F_c	Q_s/Q_c											
	0	0.03	0.05	0.10	0.2	0.3	0.4	0.5	0.6	0.7	0.8	1.0
0.06	−1.12	−0.70	−0.20	1.82	10.3	23.8	42.4	64.3	–	–	–	–
	0.00	0.05	0.05	−0.05	−0.59	−1.65	−3.21	−5.13				
0.10	−1.22	−1.00	−0.78	0.06	3.00	7.64	13.9	22.0	31.9	–	–	–
	0.06	0.10	0.12	0.11	−0.15	−0.71	−1.55	−2.71	−3.73			
0.20	−1.50	−1.40	−1.25	−0.85	0.12	1.42	3.00	4.86	7.05	9.50	12.4	–
	0.20	0.25	0.30	0.30	0.26	0.04	−0.33	−0.86	−1.52	−2.40	−3.42	
0.33	−2.00	−1.82	−1.69	−1.38	−0.66	−0.10	0.70	1.48	2.24	3.10	3.95	5.76
	0.37	0.42	0.45	0.48	0.50	0.40	0.20	−0.12	−0.50	−1.01	−1.60	−3.10
0.50	−3.00	−2.80	−2.60	2.24	−1.50	−0.85	−0.24	−0.30	0.79	1.26	1.60	2.18
	1.30	1.30	1.30	1.27	1.20	1.10	0.90	0.61	0.22	−0.20	−0.68	−1.52

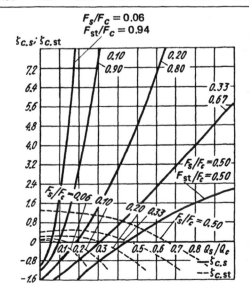

Converging wye of the type $F_s + F_{st} = F_c$; $\alpha = 60°$ [31,43]	Diagram 7-8

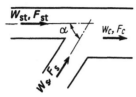

Side branch

$$\zeta_{c.s} \equiv \frac{\Delta p_s}{\rho w_c^2/2} = 1 + \left(\frac{Q_s}{Q_c}\frac{F_c}{F_s}\right)^2 - 2\frac{F_c}{F_s}\left(1 - \frac{Q_s}{Q_c}\right)^2 - \frac{F_c}{F_s}\left(\frac{Q_s}{Q_c}\right)^2 + K_s$$

see the table and curves $\zeta_{c.s} = f(Q_s/Q_c)$ for different F_s/F_c;

$$\zeta_s \equiv \frac{\Delta p_s}{\rho w_s^2/2} = \frac{\zeta_{c.s}}{(Q_s F_c/Q_c F_s)^2}$$

Straight passage

$$\zeta_{c.st} \equiv \frac{\Delta p_{st}}{\rho w_c^2/2} = 1 + \left(\frac{F_c}{F_s}\right)^2\left(1 - \frac{Q_s}{Q_c}\right)^2 - 2\frac{F_c}{F_{st}}\left(1 - \frac{Q_s}{Q_c}\right)^2 - \frac{F_c}{F_s}\left(\frac{Q_s}{Q_c}\right)^2 + K_{st}$$

see the table and curves $\zeta_{c.st} = f(Q_s/Q_c)$ for different F_s/F_c:

F_s/F_c	K_s	K_{st}
0–0.2	0	0
0.33	0	0.10
0.50	0.10	0.25

$$\zeta_{st} \equiv \frac{\Delta p_{st}}{\rho w_{st}^2/2} = \frac{\zeta_{c.st}}{(1 - Q_s/Q_c)^2(F_c/F_{st})^2}$$

Values of $\zeta_{c.s}$ (in numerator) and $\zeta_{c.st}$ (in denominator)

F_s/F_c	\multicolumn{12}{c}{Q_s/Q_c}												
	0	0.03	0.05	0.1	0.2	0.3	0.4	0.5	0.6	0.7	0.8	1.0
0.06	−1.12	−0.72	−0.20	2.00	10.6	24.5	43.5	68.0	–	–	–	–
	0.00	0.05	0.05	−0.03	−0.32	−1.10	−2.03	−3.42				
0.10	−1.22	−1.00	−0.68	0.10	3.18	8.01	14.6	23.0	33.1	–	–	–
	0.01	0.06	0.09	0.10	−0.03	−0.38	−0.96	−1.75	−2.75			
0.20	−1.50	−1.25	−1.19	−0.83	0.20	1.52	3.30	5.40	7.80	10.5	13.7	–
	0.60	0.10	0.14	0.19	0.20	0.09	−0.14	−0.50	−0.95	−1.50	−2.20	
0.33	−2.00	−1.81	−1.69	−1.37	−0.67	0.09	0.91	1.80	2.73	3.70	4.70	6.60
	0.33	0.39	0.41	0.45	0.49	0.45	0.34	0.16	−0.10	−0.47	−0.85	−1.90
0.50	−3.00	−2.80	−2.60	−2.13	−1.38	−0.68	−0.02	0.60	1.18	1.72	2.22	3.10
	1.25	1.25	1.25	1.23	1.17	1.07	0.90	0.75	0.48	0.22	−0.05	−0.78

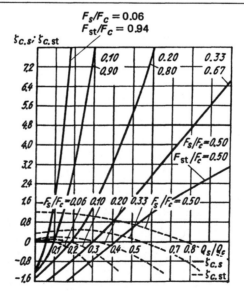

Converging wye of the type $F_s + F_{st} = F_c$; $\alpha = 90°$[31,43]	Diagram 7-9

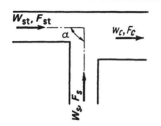

Side branch

$$\zeta_{c.s} \equiv \frac{\Delta p_s}{\rho w_c^2/2} = 1 + \left(\frac{Q_s}{Q_c}\frac{F_c}{F_s}\right)^2 - 2\frac{F_c}{F_s}\left(1 - \frac{Q_s}{Q_c}\right)^2 K_s$$

see the table and curves $\zeta_{c.s} = f(Q_s/Q_c)$ for different F_s/F_c;

$$\zeta_s \equiv \frac{\Delta p_s}{\rho w_c^2/2} = \frac{\zeta_{c.s}}{(Q_s F_c/Q_c F_s)^2}$$

Straight passage

$$\zeta_{c.st} \equiv \frac{\Delta p_{st}}{\rho w_c^2/2}$$

F_s/F_c	K_{st}
0.06	0
0.10	0
0.20	0.10
0.33	0.20
0.50	0.25

see the table and curves $\zeta_{c.st} = f(Q_s/Q_c)$ for different F_s/F_c;

$$\zeta_{st} \equiv \frac{\Delta p_{st}}{\rho w_{st}^2/2} = \frac{\zeta_{c.st}}{(1 - Q_s/Q_c)^2(F_c/F_s)^2}$$

Values of $\zeta_{c.s}$ (in numerator) and $\zeta_{c.st}$ (in denominator)

F_s/F_c						Q_s/Q_c						
	0	0.03	0.05	0.1	0.2	0.3	0.4	0.5	0.6	0.7	0.8	1.0
0.06	−1.12	−0.75	−0.20	2.06	11.2	25.0	46.2	72.5	–	–	–	–
	0.02	0.05	0.08	0.08	–	–	–	–				
0.10	−1.22	−1.00	−0.75	0.20	3.58	8.91	16.2	25.5	36.7	–	–	–
	0.04	0.08	0.10	0.20	–	–	–	–	–			
0.20	−1.40	−1.25	−1.10	−0.68	0.50	2.13	4.20	6.70	9.70	13.1	17.0	–
	0.08	0.12	0.18	0.25	0.34	0.32	–	–	–	–	–	
0.33	−1.80	−1.78	−1.50	−1.20	−0.45	0.56	1.59	2.70	4.05	5.42	6.93	10.4
	0.45	0.50	0.52	0.59	0.66	0.64	0.62	0.58	–	–	–	–
0.50	−2.75	−2.55	−2.35	−1.96	−1.15	−0.35	0.42	1.25	2.05	2.80	3.65	5.25
	1.00	1.04	1.06	1.16	1.25	1.28	1.22	1.10	0.88	0.70	–	–

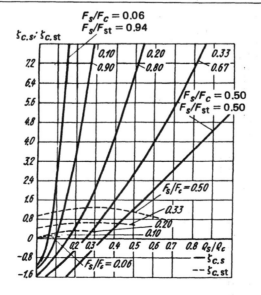

Threaded converging wye made of malleable iron of the type $F_s + F_{st} > F_c$; $F_{st} = F_c$; $\alpha = 90°$ [13]	Diagram 7-10

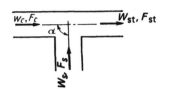

Side branch

$$\zeta_{c.s} \equiv \frac{\Delta p_s}{\rho w_c^2/2}$$

see the table and curves $\zeta_{c.s} = f(Q_s/Q_c)$ for different F_s/F_{st};

$$\zeta_s \equiv \frac{\Delta p_s}{\rho w_c^2/2} = \frac{\zeta_{c.s}}{(Q_s F_c/Q_c F_s)^2}$$

Straight passage

$$\zeta_{c.st} \equiv \frac{\Delta p_{st}}{\rho w_c^2/2}$$

see the table and curve $\zeta_{c.st} = f(Q_s/Q_c)$;

$$\zeta_{st} \equiv \frac{\Delta p_{st}}{\rho w_c^2/2} = \frac{\zeta_{c.st}}{(1 - Q_s/Q_c)^2}$$

Values of $\zeta_{c.s}$

F_s/F_c	Q_s/Q_c									
	0.1	0.2	0.3	0.4	0.5	0.6	0.8	0.9	1.0	
0.09	−0.50	2.97	9.90	19.7	32.4	48.8	66.5	86.9	110	136
0.19	−0.53	0.53	2.14	4.23	7.30	11.4	15.6	20.3	25.8	3.18
0.27	−0.69	0	1.11	2.18	3.76	5.90	8.38	11.3	14.6	18.4
0.35	−0.65	−0.09	0.59	1.31	2.24	3.52	5.20	7.28	9.23	12.2
0.44	−0.80	−0.27	0.26	0.84	1.59	2.66	4.00	5.73	7.40	6.60
0.55	−0.88	−0.48	0	0.53	1.15	1.89	2.92	4.00	5.36	6.00
1.0	−0.65	−0.40	−0.24	0.10	0.50	0.83	1.13	1.47	1.86	2.30

Values of $\zeta_{c.st}$

For all F_s/F_c	0.70	0.64	0.60	0.65	0.75	0.85	0.92	0.96	0.99	1.00

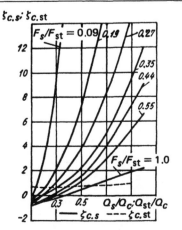

Diagram 7-11

Converging wye of improved shape of the type $F_s + F_{st} > F_c$; $F_{st} = F_c^{.66}$ $\alpha = 45°$

N1 $\dfrac{r_1'}{D_s} = 0.1$ w_n, F_n w_c, F_c α w_s, F_s

N2 $\dfrac{r_1'}{D_s} = 0.2$ r_1'

N3 $\delta' = 8°$

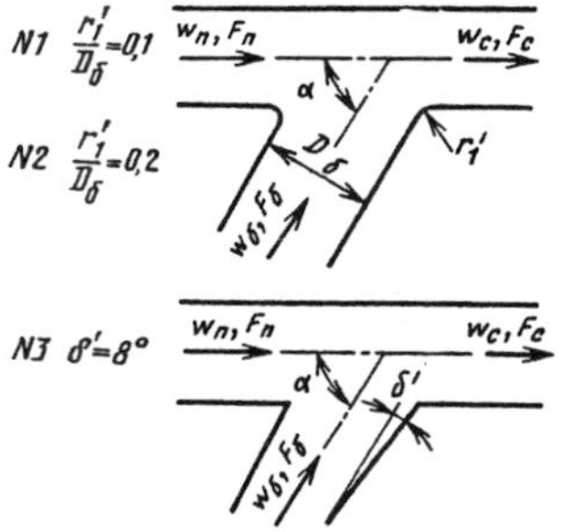

Side branch

$$\zeta_{c.s} \equiv \frac{\Delta p}{\rho w_c^2/2}$$

see the table and the curves $\zeta_{c.s} = f(Q_s/Q_c)$ of graph a for different F_s/F_c;

$$\zeta_s \equiv \frac{\Delta p}{\rho w_s^2/2} = \frac{\zeta_{c.s}}{(Q_s/Q_c F_c/F_s)^2}$$

Values of $\zeta_{c.s}$

Q_s/Q_c	N1 ($r_1'/D_s = 0.1$)		N2 ($r_1'/D_s = 0.2$)		N3 ($\delta' = 8°$)	
	F_s/F_c					
	0.122	0.34	1.0	1.0	0.122	0.34
0.1	0.00	-0.47	-0.62	-0.62	-0.04	-0.58
0.3	4.30	+0.30	-0.17	-0.17	+1.80	0.000
0.6	19.5	2.10	+0.22	+0.22	0.50	0.90
1.0	53.7	5.40	0.30	0.38	22.5	2.10

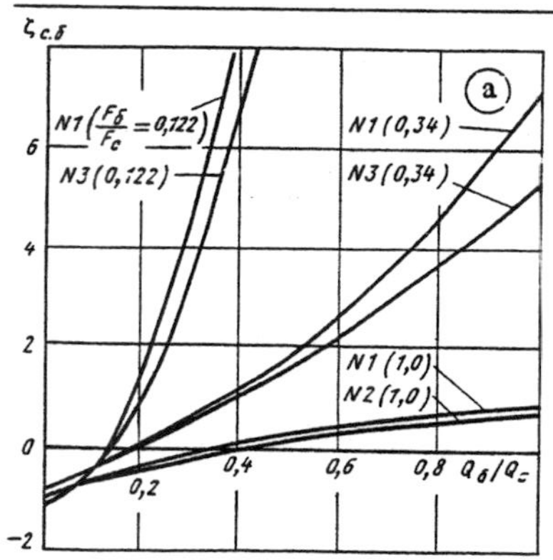

Straight passage

$$\zeta_{c.st} \equiv \frac{\Delta p}{\rho w_c^2/2}$$

see the table and the curves $\zeta_{c.st} = f(Q_s/Q_c)$ of graph b for different F_s/F_c;

$$\zeta_{st} \equiv \frac{\Delta p}{\rho w_{st}^2/2} = \frac{\zeta_{c.st}}{(1 - Q_s/Q_c)^2}$$

Graph (a): $\zeta_{c.s}$ vs Q_s/Q_c

Axis $\zeta_{c.s}$: 6, 4, 2, 0, -2 ; axis Q_s/Q_c: 0,2 0,4 0,6 0,8

Curve labels: N1 (0,34); N3 (0,34); N1 ($\frac{F_s}{F_c} = 0,222$); N3 (0,222); N1 (1,0); N2 (1,0)

Converging wye of improved shape of the type $F_s + F_{st} > F_c$; $F_{st} = F_c^{.66}$ $\alpha = 45°$ Diagram 7-11

Values of $\zeta_{c.st}$

Q_s/Q_c	N1 ($r_1'/D_s = 0.1$)			N2 ($r_1'/D_s = 0.2$)	N3 ($\delta' = 8°$)	
	\multicolumn{6}{c}{F_s/F_c}					
	0.122	1.0	0.34	1.0	0.122	0.34
0.1	+0.10	0.14	0.10	0.14	0.10	0.10
0.3	-0.50	0.19	0.00	0.18	0.36	0.09
0.6	-3.20	0.19	0.00	0.18	2.20	0.40
1.0	-9.70	-0.58	-2.90	-0.61	-7.10	-1.95

Converging wye of improved shape of the type $F_s + F_{st} > F_c$; $F_{st} = F_c$; $\alpha = 60°$ Diagram 7-12

Graph b: $\zeta_{c.s}$ vs Q_6/Q_c; curves labeled N1(1,0), N2(1,0), N1(0,34), N3(0,22), N1(0,122), N3(0,34); abscissa 0, 0.2, 0.4, 0.6, 0.8, 1.0; ordinate 0, -0.2, -0.4, -0.6, -0.8.

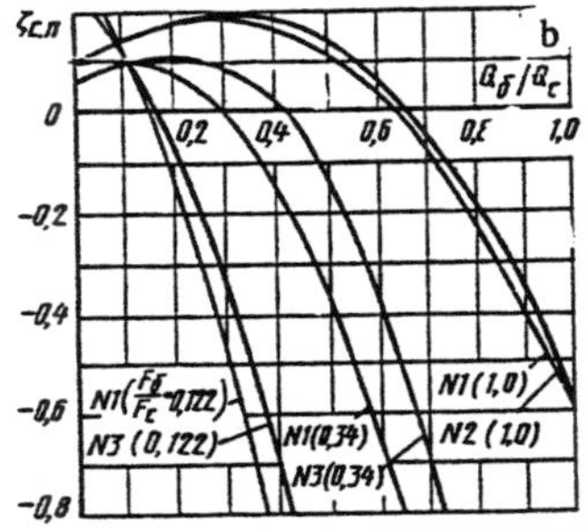

N°1 $\dfrac{r_1'}{D_6} = 0.1$ w_n, F_n w_c, F_c α D_6 w_6, F_6 r_1'

N°2 $\dfrac{r_1'}{D_6} = 0.2$

N°3 $\delta' = 8°$ w_n, F_n w_c, F_c α w_6, F_6 δ'

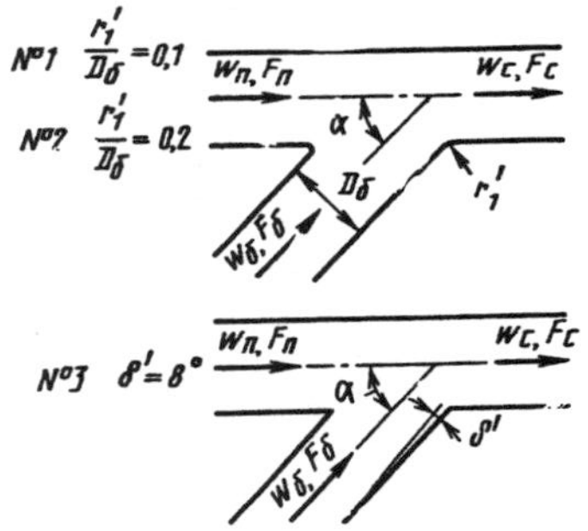

Side branch

$$\zeta_{c.s} = \frac{\Delta p}{\rho w_c^2/2}$$

see the table and the curves $\zeta_{c.s} = f(Q_s/Q_c)$ of graph a for different F_s/F_c;

$$\zeta_s = \frac{\Delta p}{\rho w_s^2/2} = \frac{\zeta_{c.s}}{(Q_s/Q_c \cdot F_c/F_s)^2}$$

Values of ζ_{st}

Q_s/Q_c	N1 ($r_i'/D_s = 0.1$)		N2 ($r_i'/D_s = 0.2$)		N3 ($\delta' = 8°$)	
	F_s/F_c					
	0.122	0.34	1.0	1.0	0.122	0.34
0.1	0.00	−0.43	−0.60	−0.60	−0.50	−0.56
0.3	5.50	+0.42	−0.14	−0.16	+1.40	0.00
0.6	21.9	2.30	+0.30	+0.26	7.50	0.87
1.0	60.0	6.18	0.53	0.50	21.1	2.00

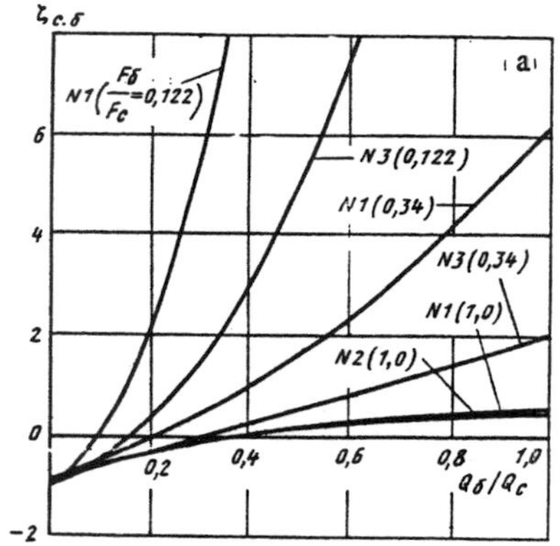

Straight passage

$$\zeta_{c.st} \equiv \frac{\Delta p}{\rho w_c^2/2}$$

$$\zeta_{st} \equiv \frac{\Delta p}{\rho w_{st}^2/2} = \frac{\zeta_{c.st}}{(1 - Q_s/Q_c)^2}$$

see the table and the curves $\zeta_{c.st} = f(Q_s/Q_c)$ of graph b for different F_s/F_c:

Values of $\zeta_{c.st}$

Q_s/Q_c	N1 ($r_i'/D_s = 0.1$)		N2 ($r_i'/D_s = 0.2$)		N3 ($\delta' = 8°$)	
	F_s/F_c					
	0.122	0.34	1.0	1.0	0.12	0.34
0.1	+0.10	0.15	0.13	0.13	0.15	0.15
0.3	−0.10	+0.19	0.23	0.23	0.00	0.25
0.6	−1.45	−0.26	+0.14	+0.13	−0.78	0.00
1.0	−6.14	−1.65	0.30	−0.35	−3.10	−0.75

Converging wye of improved shape of the type $F_s + F_{st} > F_c$; $F_{st} = F_c$; $\alpha = 60°$ Diagram 7-12

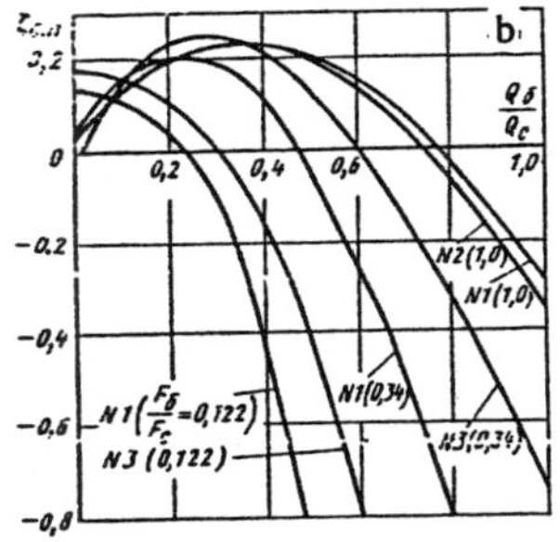

Converging wye of improved shape of the type $F_s + F_{st} > F_c$; $F_{st} = F_c^{.78}$; $\alpha = 90°$ Diagram 7-13

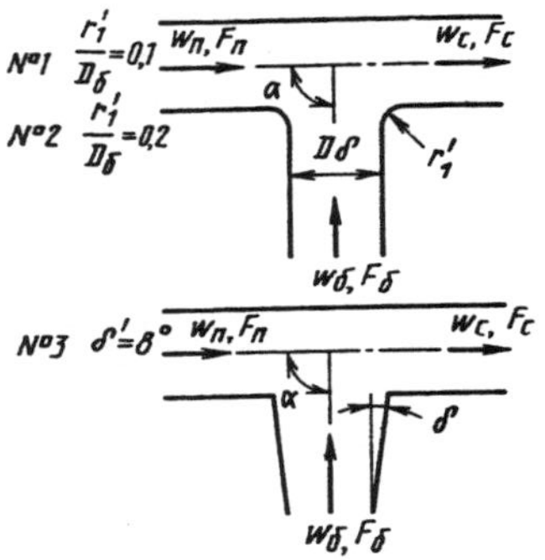

Side branch

$$\zeta_{c.s} = \frac{\Delta p}{\rho w_c^2/2}$$

see the table and the curves $\zeta_{c.s} = f(Q_s/Q_c)$ of graph a for different F_s/F_c:

$$\zeta_s = \frac{\Delta p}{\rho w_s^2/2} = \frac{\zeta_{c.s}}{(Q_s/Q_c \cdot F_c/F_s)^2}$$

Values of $\zeta_{c.s}$

Q_s/Q_c	N1 ($r_1'/D_s = 0.1$)		N2 ($r_1'/D_s = 0.2$)		N3 ($\delta' = 8°$)	
			F_s/F_c			
	0.122	0.34	1.0	1.0	0.122	0.34
0.1	−0.50	−0.36	−0.60	−0.64	−0.50	−0.43
0.3	+4.60	+0.54	−0.10	−0.15	+3.24	+0.49
0.6	23.6	2.62	+0.43	+0.31	19.2	2.20
1.0	—	7.11	0.87	0.71	62.0	5.38

Straight passage

$$\zeta_{c.st} \equiv \frac{\Delta p}{\rho w_c^2/2}, \text{ see the table and the curves}$$

$$\zeta_{c.s} = f(Q_s/Q_c) \text{ of graph b for different } F_s/F_c;$$

$$\zeta_{st} \equiv \frac{\Delta p}{\rho w_{st}^2/2} = \frac{\zeta_{c.st}}{(1 - Q_s/Q_c)^2}$$

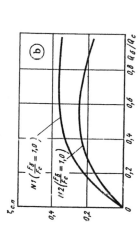

Values of $\zeta_{c.st}$

Q_s/Q_c	N1 ($r_i'/D_s = 0.1$)	N2 ($r_i'/D_s = 0.2$)
	F_s/F_c	
	1.0	1.0
0.1	0.12	0.08
0.3	0.29	0.21
0.6	0.36	0.25
1.0	0.35	0.17

Converging smooth wye ($r/b_s = 1.0$) of the type $F_s + F_{st} \geqslant F_c$ of rectangular cross section; $\alpha = 90°$[44,49]	Diagram 7-14

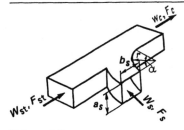

Side branch

$$\zeta_{c.s} \equiv \frac{\Delta p_s}{\rho w_c^2/2} = a_0\left(\frac{Q_s}{Q_c}\right)^2 + b_1\frac{Q_s}{Q_c} + c_1$$

see the table and graph a; for a_0, b_1, and c_1, see the table

$$\zeta_s \equiv \frac{\Delta p_c}{\rho w_s^2/2} = \frac{\zeta_{c.s}}{(Q_s F_c/Q_c F_s)^2}$$

Values of $\zeta_{c.s}$

$\dfrac{F_s}{F_{st}}\dfrac{F_s}{F_c}$	Q_s/Q_c								
	0.1	0.2	0.3	0.4	0.5	0.6	0.7	0.8	0.9
0.25 (0.25)	−0.50	0	0.50	1.20	2.20	3.70	5.80	8.40	11.40
0.33 (0.25)	−1.20	−0.40	0.40	1.60	3.00	4.80	6.80	8.90	11.00
0.50 (0.50)	−0.50	−0.20	0	0.25	0.45	0.70	1.00	1.50	2.00
0.67 (0.50)	−1.00	−0.60	−0.20	0.10	0.30	0.60	1.00	1.45	2.00
1.00 (0.50)	−2.15	−1.45	−0.95	−0.50	0	0.40	0.80	1.30	1.90
1.00 (1.00)	−0.60	−0.30	−0.10	−0.04	0.13	0.21	0.29	0.36	0.42
1.33 (1.00)	−1.20	−0.80	−0.40	−0.20	0	0.16	0.24	0.32	0.38
2.00 (1.00)	−2.10	−1.40	−0.90	−0.50	−0.20	0	0.20	0.25	0.30

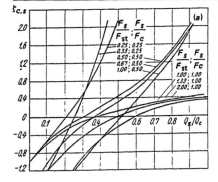

Straight passage

$$\zeta_{c.st} \equiv \frac{\Delta p_{st}}{\rho w_c^2/2} = a_2\left(\frac{Q_s}{Q_c}\right)^2 + b_2\frac{Q_s}{Q_c} + c_2$$

See the table and graph b; for a_2, b_2, and c_2, see the table

$$\zeta_{st} \equiv \frac{\Delta p_{st}}{\rho w_{st}^2/2} = \frac{\zeta_{c.st}}{(1 - Q_s/Q_c)^2(F_c/F_{st})^2}$$

Values of $\zeta_{c.st}$

$\dfrac{F_{st}}{F_c}\dfrac{F_s}{F_c}$	Q_s/Q_c								
	0.1	0.2	0.3	0.4	0.6	0.7	0.8	0.9	
0.75 (0.25)	0.30	0.30	0.20	−0.10	−0.45	−0.92	−1.45	−2.00	−2.60
1.00 (0.50)	0.17	0.16	0.10	0	−0.08	−0.18	−0.27	−0.37	−0.46
0.75 (0.50)	0.27	0.35	0.32	0.25	0.12	−0.03	−0.23	−0.42	−0.58
0.50 (0.50)	1.15	1.10	0.90	0.65	0.35	0	−0.40	−0.80	−1.30
1.00 (1.00)	0.18	0.24	0.27	0.26	0.23	0.18	0.10	0	−0.12
0.75 (1.00)	0.75	0.36	0.38	0.35	0.27	0.18	0.05	−0.08	−0.22
0.50 (1.00)	0.80	0.87	0.80	0.68	0.55	0.40	0.25	0.08	−0.10

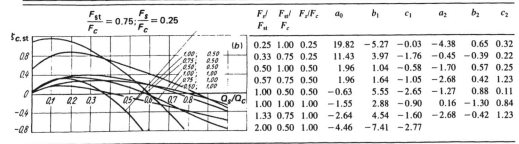

$\dfrac{F_s}{F_{st}}$	$\dfrac{F_{st}}{F_c}$	F_s/F_c	a_0	b_1	c_1	a_2	b_2	c_2
0.25	1.00	0.25	19.82	−5.27	−0.03	−4.38	0.65	0.32
0.33	0.75	0.25	11.43	3.97	−1.76	−0.45	−0.39	0.22
0.50	1.00	0.50	1.96	1.04	−0.58	−1.70	0.57	0.25
0.57	0.75	0.50	1.96	1.64	−1.05	−2.68	0.42	1.23
1.00	0.50	0.50	−0.63	5.55	−2.65	−1.27	0.88	0.11
1.00	1.00	1.00	−1.55	2.88	−0.90	0.16	−1.30	0.84
1.33	0.75	1.00	−2.64	4.54	−1.60	−2.68	−0.42	1.23
2.00	0.50	1.00	−4.46	−7.41	−2.77			

Diagram 7-15

Converging wye of normalized construction;[21] $\alpha = 30°$

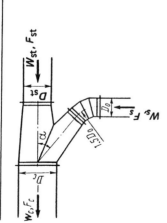

Side branch with $\bar{f}_{st} = \dfrac{F_{st}}{F_c} \geq 0.5$:

$$\zeta_{c.s} \equiv \frac{\Delta p_s}{\rho w_c^2/2} = x_s - 0.1/x_s - 0.3 + \beta, \text{ where } x_s = c_s x \bar{f}_s^\gamma x_{st} x (4\bar{f}_s + 0.024\bar{f}_s)^8$$

$$\gamma = \frac{0.2 - c_s}{c_s^{1.2} + 0.5}; \quad \sigma = \frac{\bar{f}_s - c_s + 0.3}{c_s^{0.8} + 2.2\bar{f}_s};$$

$$c_s = \left(\frac{w_s}{w_c}\right)^2 \bar{f}_{st} = \left(\frac{Q_s F_c}{Q_c F_s}\right)^2 \frac{F_{st}}{F_c}; \quad \bar{f}_s = \frac{F_s}{F_c}; \quad \beta_s = \left(\frac{Q_s F_c}{Q_c F_s}\right)^2 [0.95\exp(-15(\bar{f}_s - 0.38)^2 - 0.5]$$

Straight passage with $c_{st}\bar{f}_{st} = \left(\dfrac{Q_{st}}{Q_c}\right)^2 \bar{f}_{st} \leq 0.5$:

$$\zeta_{c.st} \equiv \frac{\Delta p_{st}}{\rho w_c^2} = \frac{0.4 - 0.13x_{st}^{-0.5}}{\bar{f}_{st}} - \beta_{st}; \quad \tau = \frac{x_{st} - 0.02}{x_{st}^3 + 0.11}; \quad x_{st} = c_{st} x \bar{f}_{st} x (2\bar{f}_s)^\psi;$$

$$\psi = \frac{0.12 - c_{st}\bar{f}_{st}}{0.02 + c_{st}\bar{f}_{st}}; \quad \beta_{st} = \frac{1 - \bar{f}_{st}}{1 + 10\bar{f}_s^5};$$

$$\zeta_s \equiv \frac{\Delta p_s}{\rho w_s^2/2} = \frac{\zeta_{c.s}}{\left(\frac{Q_s F_c}{Q_c F_s}\right)^2}; \quad \zeta_{st} \equiv \frac{\Delta p_{st}}{\rho w_{st}^2/2} = \frac{\zeta_{c.st}}{\left(1 - \frac{Q_s}{Q_c}\right)^2 \left(\frac{F_c}{F_{st}}\right)^2}$$

Converging wye of normalized construction; $\alpha = 30°$[21]

Diagram 7-15

Values of ζ_s (in numerator) and ζ_{st} (in denominator)

Q_r/Q_c

F_s/F_c	$\bar{f}_{st.av} = F_{st}/F_c = 1.0$						$\bar{f}_{st.av} = 0.8$						$\bar{f}_{st.av} = 0.63$					$\bar{f}_{st.av} = 0.5$			
	0.5	0.4	0.3	0.2	0.1	0.05	0.6	0.5	0.4	0.3	0.2	0.1	0.7	0.6	0.5	0.4	0.3	0.7	0.6	0.5	0.4
0.80	$\frac{-0.21}{0.33}$	$\frac{-1.02}{0.35}$	$\frac{-3.65}{0.32}$	–	–	–	$\frac{-0.05}{0.10}$	$\frac{-0.45}{0.27}$	$\frac{-1.49}{0.33}$	$\frac{-4.76}{0.32}$	$\frac{-9.46}{0.28}$	–	$\frac{0.38}{-0.86}$	$\frac{0.28}{-0.14}$	$\frac{0.04}{0.16}$	$\frac{-0.58}{0.30}$	$\frac{-2.53}{0.30}$	–	–	–	–
0.63	$\frac{0.32}{0.26}$	$\frac{-0.04}{0.31}$	$\frac{-1.29}{0.30}$	$\frac{-7.40}{0.28}$	–	–	$\frac{0.38}{-0.03}$	$\frac{0.21}{0.21}$	$\frac{-0.27}{0.30}$	$\frac{-1.83}{0.31}$	$\frac{-3.94}{0.27}$	–	$\frac{0.79}{-1.21}$	$\frac{0.76}{-0.28}$	$\frac{0.65}{0.08}$	$\frac{0.35}{0.25}$	$\frac{-0.61}{0.29}$	–	–	–	–
0.50	$\frac{0.79}{0.13}$	$\frac{0.63}{0.26}$	$\frac{0.02}{0.28}$	$\frac{-2.97}{0.27}$	–	–	$\frac{0.80}{-0.24}$	$\frac{0.74}{0.12}$	$\frac{0.51}{0.25}$	$\frac{-0.25}{0.28}$	$\frac{-1.37}{0.25}$	–	–	$\frac{0.98}{-0.47}$	$\frac{0.94}{-0.04}$	$\frac{0.79}{0.18}$	$\frac{0.29}{0.26}$	$\frac{0.74}{-1.20}$	$\frac{0.68}{-0.32}$	$\frac{0.53}{0.12}$	$\frac{0.15}{0.31}$
0.40	$\frac{1.03}{-0.08}$	$\frac{0.95}{0.17}$	$\frac{0.65}{0.24}$	$\frac{-0.88}{0.25}$	$\frac{-21.44}{0.23}$	–	$\frac{1.02}{-0.55}$	$\frac{0.99}{-0.01}$	$\frac{0.89}{0.18}$	$\frac{0.50}{0.24}$	$\frac{-0.19}{0.22}$	$\frac{-13.05}{0.22}$	–	$\frac{1.01}{-0.71}$	$\frac{0.99}{-0.17}$	$\frac{0.91}{0.09}$	$\frac{0.64}{0.21}$	$\frac{0.96}{-1.48}$	$\frac{0.94}{-0.47}$	$\frac{0.86}{0}$	$\frac{0.66}{0.26}$
0.32	$\frac{1.07}{-0.47}$	$\frac{1.04}{0.04}$	$\frac{0.87}{0.18}$	$\frac{0.08}{0.21}$	$\frac{-10.19}{0.21}$	–	$\frac{1.05}{-1.02}$	$\frac{1.04}{-0.20}$	$\frac{0.98}{0.08}$	$\frac{0.78}{0.19}$	$\frac{0.35}{0.17}$	$\frac{-5.58}{0.19}$	–	–	$\frac{0.95}{-0.35}$	$\frac{0.90}{-0.04}$	$\frac{0.75}{0.12}$	–	–	–	–
0.25	$\frac{1.07}{-1.05}$	$\frac{1.04}{-0.21}$	$\frac{0.94}{0.06}$	$\frac{0.52}{0.15}$	$\frac{-432}{0.18}$	–	–	$\frac{1.01}{-0.51}$	$\frac{0.98}{-0.07}$	$\frac{0.85}{0.10}$	$\frac{0.58}{0.10}$	$\frac{-2.42}{0.19}$	–	–	–	–	–	–	–	–	–
0.20	–	$\frac{1.09}{-0.60}$	$\frac{0.99}{-0.11}$	$\frac{0.71}{0.07}$	$\frac{-1.75}{0.14}$	–	–	–	$\frac{1.00}{-0.26}$	$\frac{0.90}{-0.01}$	$\frac{0.75}{0.01}$	$\frac{-0.86}{0.09}$	–	–	–	–	–	–	–	–	–
0.16	–	–	$\frac{1.12}{-0.39}$	$\frac{0.88}{-0.06}$	$\frac{-0.51}{0.06}$	$\frac{-14.68}{0.09}$	–	–	$\frac{1.11}{-0.55}$	$\frac{1.00}{-0.15}$	$\frac{0.97}{-0.12}$	$\frac{0.01}{0.01}$	–	–	–	–	–	–	–	–	–
0.125	–	–	$\frac{1.38}{-0.95}$	$\frac{1.12}{-0.32}$	$\frac{0.25}{-0.07}$	$\frac{-5.92}{0}$	–	–	–	$\frac{1.21}{-0.39}$	$\frac{0.97}{-0.12}$	$\frac{0.01}{0.01}$	–	–	–	–	–	–	–	–	–
0.10	–	–	–	$\frac{1.35}{-0.75}$	$\frac{0.66}{-0.28}$	$\frac{-2.33}{-0.15}$	–	–	–	–	–	–	–	–	–	–	–	–	–	–	–

Converging wye of normalized construction;[21] $\alpha = 45°$

Diagram
7-16

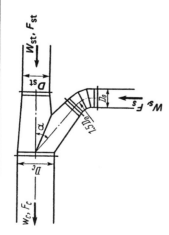

Side branch with $\overline{f}_{st} = \dfrac{F_{st}}{F_c} \geqslant 0.5$;

$$\zeta_{c.s} \equiv \frac{\Delta p_s}{\rho w_c^2/2} = x_s - \frac{0.1}{x_s} - 0.3 \quad \text{where for } x_s, \text{ see Diagram 7-15.}$$

Straight passage with $c_{st}\overline{f}_{st} = \left(\dfrac{Q_{st}}{Q_c}\right)^2 \dfrac{\overline{f}_s}{f_{st}} \leq 0.5$

$$\zeta_{c.st} \equiv \frac{\Delta p_{st}}{\rho w_c^2/2} = \frac{0.4 - 0.13x_{st}^{-0.5}}{\overline{f}_{st}^{\tau}}$$

where for x_{st} and τ see Diagram 7-15;

$$\zeta_s \equiv \frac{\Delta p_s}{\rho w_c^2/2} = \frac{\zeta_{c.s}}{(Q_s F_c/Q_c F_s)^2}$$

$$\zeta_{st} \equiv \frac{\Delta p_{st}}{\rho w_{st}^2/2} = \frac{\zeta_{c.st}}{(1 - Q_s/Q_c)^2(F_c/F_{st})^2}$$

Converging wye of normalized construction;[21] $\alpha = 45°$

Diagram 7-16

Values of ζ_s (in numerator) and ζ_{st} (in denominator)

Each cell is given as ζ_s / ζ_{st} (numerator / denominator).

F_s/F_c	$\bar f_{st.av}=F_{st}/F_c=1.0$						$\bar f_{st.av}=0.8$						$\bar f_{st.av}=0.63$					$\bar f_{st.av}=0.5$			
Q_s/Q_c	0.5	0.4	0.3	0.2	0.1	0.05	0.6	0.5	0.4	0.3	0.2	0.1	0.7	0.6	0.5	0.4	0.3	0.7	0.6	0.5	0.4
0.8	0.23/0.33	−0.58/0.35	−3.21/0.32	–	–	–	0.39/0.29	−0.01/0.39	−1.05/0.41	−4.32/0.38	–	–	–	–	–	–	–	–	–	–	–
0.63	0.45/0.26	0.09/0.31	−1.16/0.30	−7.27/0.28	–	–	0.51/0.16	0.34/0.33	−0.14/0.38	−1.70/0.37	−9.33/0.33	–	0.51/−0.12	0.41/0.28	0.17/0.43	−0.45/0.48	−2.40/0.44	–	–	–	–
0.50	0.53/0.13	0.37/0.26	−0.24/0.28	−3.23/0.27	–	–	0.54/−0.05	0.48/0.24	0.25/0.33	−0.51/0.34	−4.20/0.32	–	0.53/−0.47	0.50/0.14	0.39/0.35	0.09/0.43	−0.87/0.43	0.48/−0.14	0.42/0.27	0.27/0.50	−0.11/0.57
0.40	0.59/−0.08	0.51/0.17	0.21/0.24	−1.32/0.25	−21.88/0.23	–	0.58/−0.36	0.55/0.11	0.45/0.26	0.06/0.30	−1.81/0.30	–	–	0.54/−0.05	0.50/0.23	0.35/0.36	−0.15/0.40	0.52/−0.42	0.50/0.12	0.42/0.38	0.22/0.52
0.32	0.67/−0.41	0.64/0.04	0.47/0.18	−0.32/0.21	−10.59/0.21	–	0.65/−0.83	0.64/−0.08	0.58/0.16	0.38/0.25	−0.59/0.27	−13.45/0.25	–	0.61/−0.29	0.59/0.10	0.51/0.27	0.24/0.35	–	–	–	–
0.25	0.83/−1.05	0.80/−0.21	0.70/0.06	0.28/0.15	−4.56/0.18	–	–	0.77/−0.39	0.74/0.01	0.61/0.16	0.11/0.22	−5.82/0.23	–	–	0.71/−0.08	0.66/0.14	0.51/0.26	–	–	–	–
0.20	–	1.01/−0.60	0.91/−0.11	0.63/0.08	−1.87/0.14	–	–	–	0.92/−0.18	0.82/0.05	0.50/0.15	−2.50/0.19	–	–	–	–	–	–	–	–	–
0.16	–	–	1.17/−0.39	0.93/−0.06	−0.46/0.06	−14.63/0.09	–	–	1.16/−0.47	1.05/−0.09	0.80/0.06	−0.81/0.13	–	–	–	–	–	–	–	–	–
0.125	–	–	1.52/−0.95	1.26/−0.32	0.39/−0.07	−5.78/0.00	–	–	–	1.35/−0.33	1.11/−0.07	0.15/0.05	–	–	–	–	–	–	–	–	–
0.10	–	–	–	1.56/−0.75	0.87/−0.28	−2.12/−0.15	–	–	–	–	–	–	–	–	–	–	–	–	–	–	–

Diagram
7-17

Converging wye of industrail construction;[21] $\alpha = 45°$

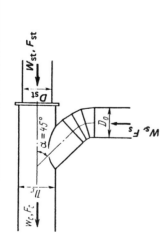

$\psi = \dfrac{0.12 - c_{st}\bar{f}_{st}}{0.02 + c_{st}\bar{f}_{st}}$;

Side branch with $\bar{f}_{st} = \dfrac{F_{st}}{F_c} \geq 0.5$

$$\zeta_{c.s} \equiv \frac{\Delta p_s}{\rho w_c^2/2} = x_s - \frac{0.1}{x_s} - 0.3$$

where $x_s = c_s \bar{f}_{st}^{\gamma}(5\bar{f}_s)^{\sigma}$; $\gamma = \dfrac{0.8 - c_s}{0.86c_s + 0.2}$;

$$c_s = \left(\frac{w_s}{w_c}\right)^2 \bar{f}_{st} = \left(\frac{Q_s}{Q_c}\frac{F_c}{F_{st}}\right)^2 \frac{F_{st}}{F_c}; \quad \bar{f}_s = \frac{F_s}{F_c}$$

Straight passage with $c_{st}\bar{f}_{st} = \left(\dfrac{Q_{st}}{Q_c}\right)^2 \dfrac{\bar{f}_s}{\bar{f}_{st}} \leq 0.5$

$$\zeta_{c.st} \equiv \frac{\Delta p_{st}}{\rho w_c^2/2} = \frac{0.4 - 0.13x_{st}^{-0.5}}{\bar{f}_{st}^{\tau}}; \quad \tau = \frac{x_{st} - 0.02}{x_{st}^3 + 0.11}; \quad x_{st} - c_{st}\bar{f}_{st}(2\bar{f}_s)^{\psi};$$

$$\zeta_s \equiv \frac{\Delta p_s}{\rho w_s^2/2} = \frac{\zeta_{c.s}}{(Q_sF_c/Q_cF_s)^2}; \quad \zeta_{st} \equiv \frac{\Delta p_{st}}{\rho w_{st}^2/2} = \frac{\zeta_{c.st}}{(1 - Q_s/Q_c)^2(F_c/F_{st})^2}$$

Values of ζ_s (in numerator) and ζ_{st} (in denominator)

	Q_s/Q_c																				
	$\bar{f}_{st.av} = F_{st}/F_c = 1.0$						$\bar{f}_{st.av} = 0.8$						$\bar{f}_{st.av} = 0.63$					$\bar{f}_{st.av} = 0.5$			
F_s/F_c	0.5	0.4	0.3	0.2	0.1	0.05	0.6	0.5	0.4	0.3	0.2	0.1	0.7	0.6	0.5	0.4	0.3	0.7	0.6	0.5	0.4
0.8	1.17/0.33	1.45/0.35	1.16/0.32	—	—	—	0.66/0.29	0.61/0.39	0.19/0.41	−1.86/0.38	—	—	—	—	—	—	—	—	—	—	—
0.63	0.79/0.26	0.98/0.31	0.85/0.31	−1.47/0.28	—	—	0.58/0.16	0.55/0.33	0.37/0.38	−1.61/0.37	−7.00/0.33	—	0.45/−0.12	0.38/0.28	0.19/0.43	−0.40/0.48	−2.80/0.44	—	—	—	—
0.50	0.70/0.13	0.74/0.26	0.69/0.28	−0.52/0.27	—	—	0.61/−0.05	0.58/0.24	0.47/0.33	−0.01/0.34	−3.26/0.32	—	0.54/−0.47	0.45/0.14	0.38/0.35	0.09/0.43	−1.02/0.43	0.42/−0.14	0.32/0.27	0.13/0.50	−0.38/0.57
0.40	0.75/−0.08	0.73/0.17	0.67/0.24	−0.01/0.25	−13.64/0.23	—	0.70/−0.36	0.65/0.11	0.58/0.26	0.31/0.30	−1.37/0.30	—	—	0.60/−0.05	0.52/0.23	0.35/0.36	−0.19/0.40	0.55/−0.42	0.47/0.12	0.35/0.38	0.08/0.52
0.32	0.84/−0.41	0.81/0.04	0.74/0.18	0.32/0.21	−7.26/0.21	—	0.81/−0.83	0.77/−0.08	0.70/0.16	0.52/0.25	−0.36/0.27	−17.56/0.26	—	0.74/−0.29	0.66/0.10	0.53/0.27	0.21/0.35	—	—	—	—
0.25	0.95/−1.05	0.93/−0.21	0.87/0.06	0.61/0.15	−3.34/0.18	—	—	0.91/−0.39	0.85/0.01	0.72/0.16	0.24/0.22	−7.70/0.23	—	—	0.84/−0.08	0.73/0.14	0.52/0.26	—	—	—	—
0.20	—	1.04/−0.60	1.00/−0.11	0.83/0.07	−1.37/0.14	—	—	—	1.00/−0.18	0.90/0.05	0.58/0.15	−3.28/0.19	—	—	—	—	—	—	—	—	—
0.16	—	—	1.13/−0.39	1.03/−0.06	−0.23/0.06	−16.86/0.09	—	—	1.12/−0.47	1.07/−0.09	0.84/0.06	−1.10/0.13	—	—	—	—	—	—	—	—	—
0.125	—	—	1.23/−0.95	1.23/−0.32	0.49/−0.07	−7.42/0	—	—	—	1.22/−0.33	1.11/−0.07	0.03/0.05	—	—	—	—	—	—	—	—	—
0.10	—	—	—	1.36/−0.75	0.83/−0.28	−3.00/−0.15	—	—	—	—	—	—	—	—	—	—	—	—	—	—	—

Diverging wye of the type $F_s + F_{st} > F_c$; $F_{st} = F_c$; $\alpha = 0–90°$. Side branching.[28]	Diagram 7-18

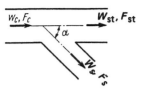

1. $0 < \alpha < 60°$ and $\alpha = 90°$ at $h_s/h_c \leq 2/3$:

$$\zeta_{c.s} \equiv \frac{\Delta p_s}{\rho w_c^2/2} = A'\left[1 + \left(\frac{w_s}{w_c}\right)^2 - 2\frac{w_s}{w_c}\cos\alpha\right] = A'\zeta'_{c.s}$$

where for A' see para. 16 of see Figure 7-1. At $\alpha = 90°$, A' is taken to be 1.0

2. $\alpha = 90°$ and $h_s/h_c = 1.0$ (up to $w_s/w_c \approx 2.0$):

$$\zeta_{c.s} \equiv \frac{\Delta p_s}{\rho w_c^2/2} = \zeta'_{c.s}\left[1 + 0.3\left(\frac{w_s}{w_c}\right)^2\right]$$

where for $\zeta'_{c.s}$, see the table and curves $\zeta'_{c.s} = f(w_s/w_c)$ at different α.

h_s is the height of the cross section of the side branch; h_c is the height of the cross section of the common straight channel

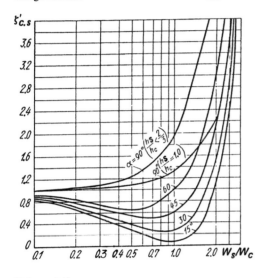

$$\zeta_s \equiv \frac{\Delta p_s}{\rho w_c^2/2} = \frac{\zeta_{c.s}}{(w_s/w_c)^2}$$

$$\frac{w_s}{w_c} = \frac{Q_s}{Q_c}\frac{F_c}{F_s}$$

Values of $\zeta'_{c.s}$

$\frac{w_s}{w_c}$	$\alpha,°$				$\alpha' = 90°$	
	15	30	45	60	$h_s/h_c \leq 2/3$	$h_s/h_c = 1.0$
0	1.0	1.0	1.0	1.0	1.0	1.0
0.1	0.82	0.84	0.87	0.91	1.01	1.0
0.2	0.65	0.70	0.75	0.84	1.04	1.01
0.4	0.38	0.46	0.60	0.76	1.16	1.05
0.6	0.20	0.31	0.50	0.65	1.35	1.11
0.8	0.09	0.25	0.51	0.80	1.64	1.19
1.0	0.07	0.27	0.58	1.00	2.00	1.30
1.2	0.12	0.36	0.74	1.23	2.44	1.43
1.4	0.24	0.70	0.98	1.54	2.96	1.59
1.6	0.46	0.80	1.30	1.98	3.54	1.77
2.0	1.10	1.52	2.16	3.00	4.60	2.20
2.6	2.75	3.23	4.10	5.15	7.76	–
3.0	7.20	7.40	7.80	8.10	9.00	–
4.0	14.1	14.2	14.8	15.0	16.0	–
5.0	23.2	23.5	23.8	24.0	25.0	–
6.0	34.2	34.5	35.0	35.0	36.0	–
8.0	62.0	62.7	63.0	63.0	64.0	–
10	98.0	98.3	98.6	99.0	100	–

Diverging wye of the type $F_s + F_{st} = F_c$; $\alpha = 0{-}90°$. Side branching[28]	Diagram 7-19

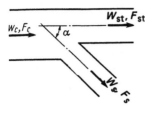

$$\zeta_{c.s} \equiv \frac{\Delta p_s}{\rho w_c^2/2} = 1 + \left(\frac{w_s}{w_c}\right)^2 - 2\frac{w_s}{w_c}\cos\alpha - K_s'\left(\frac{w_s}{w_c}\right)^2$$

$\alpha,°$	15	30	45	60	90
K_s	0.04	0.16	0.36	0.64	1.00

for $\zeta_{c.s} \equiv f(w_s/w_c)$ at different α, see also the table and the graph.

$$\zeta_s \equiv \frac{\Delta p_s}{\rho w_s^2/2} = \frac{\zeta_{c.s}}{(w_s/w_c)^2}$$

$$\frac{w_s}{w_c} = \frac{Q_s}{Q_c}\frac{F_c}{F_s}$$

Values of $\zeta_{c.s}$

	w_s/w_c												
$\alpha,°$	0.1	0.2	0.3	0.4	0.5	0.6	0.8	1.0	1.2	1.4	1.6	1.8	2.0
15	0.81	0.65	0.51	0.38	0.28	0.20	0.11	0.06	0.14	0.30	0.51	0.76	1.00
30	0.84	0.69	0.56	0.44	0.34	0.26	0.19	0.15	0.15	0.30	0.51	0.76	1.00
45	0.87	0.74	0.63	0.54	0.45	0.38	0.29	0.24	0.23	0.30	0.51	0.76	1.00
60	0.90	0.82	0.79	0.66	0.59	0.53	0.43	0.36	0.33	0.39	0.51	0.76	1.00
90	1.00	1.00	1.00	1.00	1.00	1.00	1.00	1.00	1.00	1.00	1.00	1.00	1.00

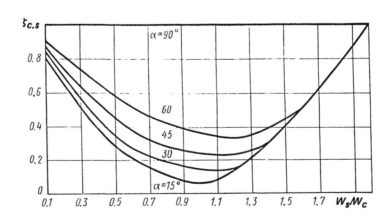

Diverging wye of the type $F_s + F_{st} > F_c$; $F_{st} = F_c$ (No. 1) and
$F_s + F_{st} = F_c$ (No. 2) $\alpha = 0$–90°. Passage[8.28]

Diagram
7-20

№1

No. 1. $F_s + F_{st} > F_c$; $F_{st} = F_c$

$$\zeta_{c.st} = \frac{\Delta p}{\rho w_c^2/2} = \tau_{st}(Q_s/Q_c)$$

where for τ_{st} see the table; for $\zeta_{c.st}$ see also Table 1 and graph a.

F_s/F_c	Q_s/Q_c	τ_{st}
≤0.4	0–1.0	0.4
>0.4	≤0.5	$2(2Q_s/Q_c - 1)$
	>0.5	$0.3(2Q_s/Q_c - 1)$

1. Values of $\zeta_{c.st}$

Q_s/Q_c	0	0.1	0.2	0.3	0.4	0.5	0.6	0.7	0.8	0.9	1.0
1. $F_s/F_c \le 0.4$	0	0.004	0.016	0.036	0.064	0.100	0.144	0.196	0.256	0.324	0.40
2. $F_s/F_c > 0.4$	0	−0.016	−0.048	−0.072	−0.064	0	—	—	—	—	—
3. $F_s/F_c > 0.4$	—	—	—	—	—	0	0.21	0.059	0.115	0.194	0.30

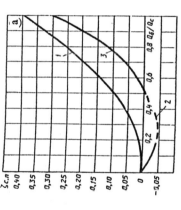

Diagram
7-20

Diverging wye of the type $F_s + F_{st} > F_c$; $F_{st} = F_c$ (No. 1) and
$F_s + F_{st} = F_c$ (No. 2) $\alpha = 0$–$90°$. Passage[8.28]

No. 2. $F_s + F_{st} = F_c$ at $w_{st}/w_c \gtrless 1.0$

$\zeta_{c.st} \equiv \dfrac{\Delta p}{\rho w_c^2/2}$, see the table and graph b;

$\zeta_{st} \equiv \dfrac{\Delta p}{\rho w_{st}^2/2} = \dfrac{\zeta_{c.st}}{(w_{st}/w_c)^2}$; $\dfrac{w_{st}}{w_c} = \dfrac{Q_{st}}{Q_c}\dfrac{F_c}{F_{st}}$

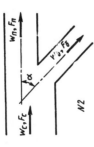

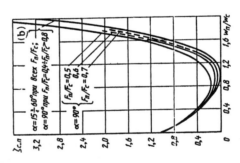

2. Values of $\zeta_{c.st}$

$\dfrac{w_{st}}{w_c}$	α					
	15–60°	90°				
		F_{st}/F_c				
	0–1.0	0–0.4	0.5	0.6	0.7	≥0.8
0	1.00	1.00	1.00	1.00	1.00	1.00
0.1	0.81	0.81	0.81	0.81	0.81	0.81
0.2	0.64	0.64	0.64	0.64	0.64	0.64
0.3	0.50	0.50	0.52	0.52	0.50	0.50
0.4	0.36	0.36	0.40	0.38	0.37	0.36
0.5	0.25	0.25	0.30	0.28	0.27	0.25
0.6	0.16	0.16	0.23	0.20	0.18	0.16
0.8	0.04	0.04	0.17	0.10	0.07	0.04
1.0	0.00	0.00	0.20	0.10	0.05	0.00
1.2	0.07	0.07	0.36	0.21	0.14	0.07
1.4	0.39	0.39	0.79	0.59	0.39	–
1.6	0.90	0.90	1.40	1.16	–	–
1.8	1.78	1.78	2.44	–	–	–
2.0	3.20	3.20	4.00	–	–	–

Threaded wyes of the type $F_s + F_c > F_c$; $F_{st} = F_c$; made of malleable iron,[13] $\alpha = 90°$	Diagram 7-21

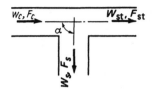

Side branch

$$\zeta_{c.s} \equiv \frac{\Delta p_s}{\rho w_s^2/2}$$

see the table and curves $\zeta_{c.s} = f(Q_s/Q_c)$ at different F_s/F_{st};

$$\zeta_s \equiv \frac{\Delta p_s}{\rho w_s^2/2} = \frac{\zeta_{c.s}}{(Q_s F_c/Q_c F_s)^2}$$

Straight passage

$$\zeta_{c.st} \equiv \frac{\Delta p_{st}}{\rho w_c^2/2}$$

see the table and curves $\zeta_{c.st} = f(Q_{st}/Q_c)$ at all F_s/F_c;

$$\zeta_{st} \equiv \frac{\Delta p_{st}}{\rho w_{st}^2/2} = \frac{\zeta_{c.st}}{(1 - Q_s/Q_c)^2(F_c/F_{st})^2}$$

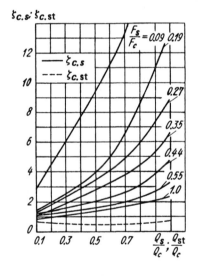

Values of $\zeta_{c.s}$ and $\zeta_{c.st}$

F_s/F_c	$Q_s/Q_c(Q_{st}/Q_c)$									
	0.1	0.2	0.3	0.4	0.5	0.6	0.7	0.8	0.9	1.0
0.09	2.80	4.50	6.00	7.88	9.40	11.1	13.0	15.8	20.0	24.7
0.19	1.41	2.00	2.50	3.20	3.97	4.95	6.50	8.45	10.8	13.3
0.27	1.37	1.81	2.30	2.83	3.40	4.07	4.80	6.00	7.18	8.90
0.35	1.10	1.54	1.90	2.35	2.73	3.22	3.80	4.32	5.28	6.53
0.44	1.22	1.45	1.67	1.89	2.11	2.38	2.58	3.04	3.84	4.75
0.55	1.09	1.20	1.40	1.59	1.65	1.77	1.94	2.20	2.68	3.30
1.00	0.90	1.00	1.13	1.20	1.40	1.50	1.60	1.80	2.06	2.80
				Values of $\zeta_{c.st}$						
At all F_s/F_c	0.70	0.64	0.60	0.57	0.55	0.51	0.49	0.55	0.62	0.70

Diverging wye ($\alpha = 90°$) with conical branches roughly made from roofing steel sheets (α_1 = var);[35] Re = $w_c D_c/\nu > 10^4$

Diagram 7-22

Side branch $F_s/F_c = 0.67$:

$$\zeta_{c.s} \equiv \frac{\Delta p}{\rho w_c^2/2}, \quad \text{see the table and graph a.}$$

Values of $\zeta_{c.s}$ (graph a)

$\alpha_1°$	w_s/w_c									
	0	0.2	0.4	0.6	1.0	1.4	1.6	1.8	2.0	2.2
0	1.08	1.01	1.0	1.02	1.22	1.57	1.8	2.05	2.45	2.8
15	1.05	0.90	0.77	0.70	0.75	0.90	1.0	1.2	1.4	1.6
30	1.05	0.90	0.77	0.70	0.70	0.80	0.90	1.02	1.20	1.4
45	1.05	0.90	0.77	0.70	0.68	0.70	0.80	0.90	1.05	1.25

Straight passage $F_{st}/F_c = 1.0$; $F_s/F_c = 0.67$:

$$\zeta_{c.s} \equiv \frac{\Delta p}{\rho w_c^2/2}, \quad \text{see the table and graph b.}$$

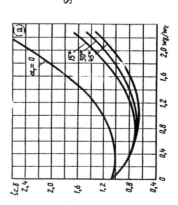

Diverging wye ($\alpha = 90°$) with conical branches roughly made from roofing steel sheets ($\alpha_1 = \mathrm{var}$);[35] $\mathrm{Re} = w_c D_c/\nu > 10^4$

Diagram 7-22

Values of $\zeta_{c.st}$ (graph b)

$\alpha_1°$	w_s/w_c										
	0	0.1	0.2	0.3	0.4	0.5	0.6	0.7	0.8	0.9	1.0
0.30	0.272	0.263	0.250	0.225	0.200	0.163	0.125	0.100	0.063	0.050	0.082
15.45	0.243	0.236	0.215	0.185	0.160	0.135	0.100	0.060	0.032	0.065	0.050

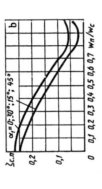

Straight passage $F_{st}/F_c = 0.67$; $F_s/F_c = 0.67$:

$$\zeta_{c.st} = \frac{\Delta p}{\rho w_c^2/2}, \quad \text{see the table and graph c.}$$

Values of $\zeta_{c.st}$ (graph c)

$\alpha_1°$	w_{st}/w_c											
	0	0.2	0.4	0.6	0.8	1.0	1.2	1.4	1.6	1.8	2.0	2.2
0	0.467	0.445	0.400	0.361	0.310	0.275	0.175	0.125	0.080	0.075	0.125	0.212
15	0.325	0.325	0.325	0.300	0.260	0.220	0.167	0.09	0.067	0.050	0.050	0.125
30	0.375	0.367	0.333	0.300	0.250	0.200	0.150	0.10	0.067	0.06	0.075	0.150
45	0.425	0.400	0.355	0.325	0.250	0.190	0.133	0.10	0.05	0.006	0.075	0.15

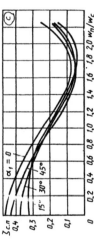

Diverging wye of the type $F_s + F_{st} > F_c$; $F_{st} = F_c$ of improved shape[60,66,78]

Diagram
7-23

N1 $\frac{r'_1}{D_6} = 0,1$
N2 $\frac{r'_2}{D_6} = 0,2$

N3. $\delta' = 8°$

Side branch

$\zeta_{c.s} \equiv \dfrac{\Delta p}{\rho w_c^2/2}$, see the table and the curves

$\zeta_{c.s} = f(Q_s/Q_c)$ of graphs a, b, and c;

$\zeta_s \equiv \dfrac{\Delta p}{\rho w_s^2/2} = \dfrac{\zeta_{c.s}}{(Q_s/Q_c \, F_c/F_s)^2}$

Values of $\zeta_{c.s}$ ($\alpha = 45°$)

Q_s/Q_c	No. 1 ($r'_1/D_s = 0.1$)		No. 2 ($r'_2/D_s = 0.2$)		No. 3 ($\delta' = 8°$)	
			F_s/F_c			
	0.122	0.34	1.0	1.0	0.122	0.34
0.1	0.40	0.62	0.77	0.77	0.40	0.62
0.3	1.90	0.35	0.56	0.56	0.90	0.35
0.6	9.60	0.90	0.32	0.32	5.40	0.60
1.0	30.6	3.55	0.32	0.32	17.4	2.00

Diverging wye of the type $F_s + F_{st} > F_c$; $F_{st} = F_c$ of improved shape[60,66,78]

Diagram
7-23

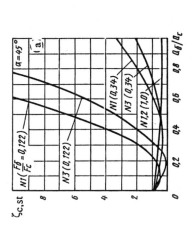

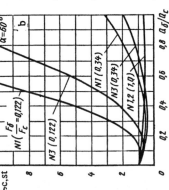

Values of $\zeta_{c.s}$ ($\alpha = 60°$)

Q_s/Q_c	No. 1 ($r_1'/D_s = 0.1$)		No. 2 ($r_2'/D_s = 0.2$)		No. 3 ($\delta' = 8°$)	
	F_s/F_c					
	0.122	0.34	1.0	1.0	0.122	0.34
0.1	0.90	0.77	0.84	0.84	0.70	0.67
0.3	2.70	0.60	0.67	0.67	1.30	0.44
0.6	12.0	1.10	0.53	0.53	5.40	0.68
1.0	36.7	3.16	0.62	0.62	16.6	1.85

Values of $\zeta_{c.s}$ ($\alpha = 90°$)

Q_s/Q_c	No. 1 ($r_1'/D_s = 0.1$)		No. 2 ($r_2'/D_s = 0.2$)		No. 3 ($\delta' = 8°$)	
			F_s/F_c			
	0.122	0.34	1.0	0.85	0.122	0.34
0.1	1.20	1.15	0.85	0.85	0.90	1.10
0.3	4.00	1.42	0.77	0.74	3.40	1.30
0.6	17.8	2.65	0.78	0.69	17.3	2.17
1.0	–	6.30	1.00	0.91	–	5.20

Straight passage

$$\zeta_{c.st} \equiv \frac{\Delta p}{\rho w_c^2/2}, \quad \text{see Diagram 7-20.}$$

Side branch with $\alpha = 90°$ and $F_s/F_c = 1.0$

$$\zeta_{c.s} \equiv \frac{\Delta p}{\rho w_c^2/2}, \quad \text{see the tables and the curves } \zeta_{c.s} = f(Q_s/Q_c, r/D_c) \text{ of graph d.}$$

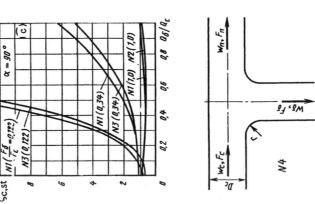

Diverging wye of the type $F_s + F_{st} > F_c$; $F_{st} = F_c$ of improved shape[60,66,78]

Diagram
7-23

Values of $\zeta_{c.s}$ (No. 4)

r/D_c	$Q_s/Q_c = w_s/w_c$										
	0	0.1	0.2	0.3	0.4	0.5	0.6	0.7	0.8	0.9	1.0
0.07	0.89	0.84	0.81	0.78	0.76	0.75	0.76	0.79	0.84	0.91	1.0
0.22	0.88	0.78	0.71	0.66	0.64	0.63	0.63	0.65	0.71	0.78	0.8

Straight passage with $\alpha = 90°$ and $F_s/F_c = 1.0$

$$\zeta_{c.st} \equiv \frac{\Delta p}{\rho w_c^2/2} \, ,$$ see the tables and the curves $\zeta_{c.s} = f(Q_s/Q_c, r/D)$ of graph d.

Values of $\zeta_{c.st}$ (No. 4)

r/D_c	$Q_s/Q_c = w_s/w_c$										
	0	0.1	0.2	0.3	0.4	0.5	0.6	0.7	0.8	0.9	1.0
0.07	0.13	0.07	0.03	0	0.01	0.04	0.08	0.16	0.24	0.34	0.45
0.22	0.10	0.06	0.02	0	0.03	0.09	0.15	0.23	0.30	0.40	0.50

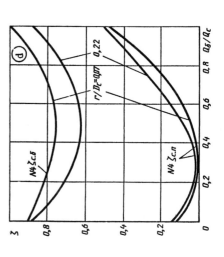

Wyes of improved shape ($\alpha = 90°$) at high velocities,[47] $\mathrm{Re} > 2 \times 10^5$

Diagram 7-24

Side branch

$$\zeta_{c.s} \equiv \frac{\Delta p}{\rho w_c^2/2}, \quad \text{see the tables and the curves of graphs a, b and c.}$$

a. Symmetrical wyes of the type $F_s = F_{st} = F_c$; $r/D_c = 0.5$

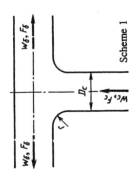

Scheme 1

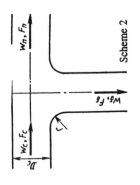

Scheme 2

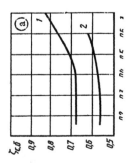

Wyes of improved shape ($\alpha = 90°$) at high velocities,[47] Re $> 2 \times 10^5$ Diagram 7-24

Values of $\zeta_{c.s}$

No. of the curve	σ_s/σ_c	$\lambda_c = w_c/a_{cr}$					
		0.2	0.3	0.4	0.5	0.6	0.7
1	0.2–0.8	0.68	0.68	0.64	0.71	0.77	0.83
2	1.0	0.57	0.57	0.58	0.60	0.62	0.68

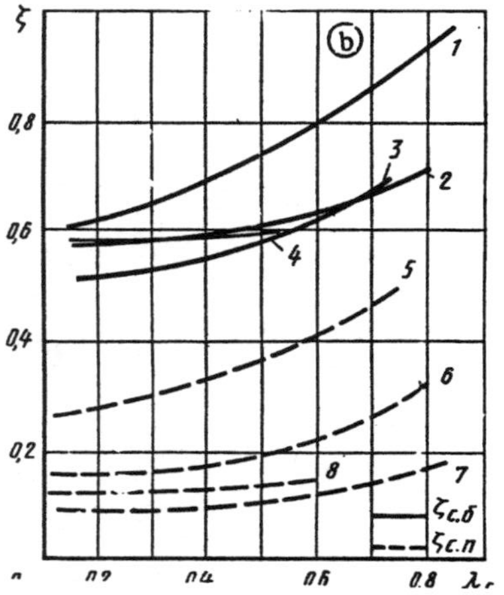

b. Flow-dividing wyes of the type $F_s + F_{st} > F_c$; $F_s = F_{st} = F_c$; $r/D_c = 0.5$ (scheme d, graph b)

Values of $\zeta_{c.s}$

No. of the curve	σ_s/σ_c	$\lambda_c = w_c/a_{cr}$							
		0.2	0.3	0.4	0.5	0.6	0.7	0.8	0.9
1	0.2	0.62	0.65	0.69	0.73	0.80	0.87	0.95	1.05
2	0.5	0.58	0.59	0.60	0.62	0.63	0.67	0.82	–
3	0.8	0.51	0.52	0.54	0.59	0.62	0.68	0.77	–
4	1.0	0.58	0.59	0.59	0.6	0.61	0.61	–	–

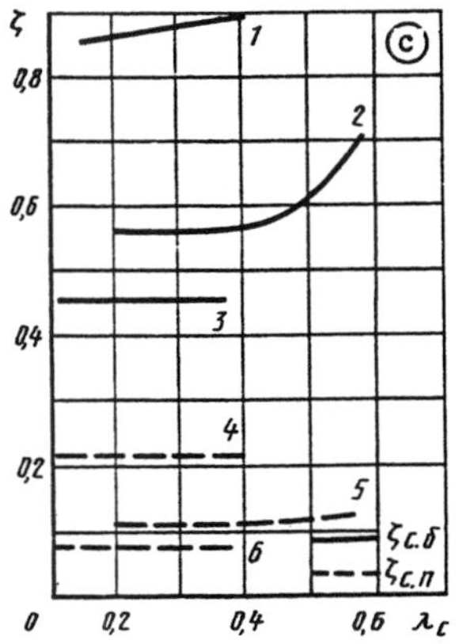

c. Flow-dividing wyes of the type $F_s + F_{st} = F_c$; $F_s = F_{st}$; $r/D_c = 0.5$ (scheme, graph c)

Values of $\zeta_{c.s}$

No. of the curve	σ_s/σ_c	$\lambda_c = w_c/a_{cт}$				
		0.2	0.3	0.4	0.5	0.6
1	0.25	0.87	0.88	0.90	–	–
2	0.5	0.57	0.57	0.57	0.61	0.73
3	0.8	0.46	0.46	0.47	–	–

Straight passage

$\zeta_{c.st} \equiv \dfrac{\Delta p}{\rho w_c^2/2}$, see the tables and the curves of graphs b and c.

a. Flow-divinding wyes of the type $F_s + F_{st} > F_c$; $F_s = F_{st} = F_c$; $r/D_c = 0.5$ (scheme 2, graph b).

Wyes of improved shape ($\alpha = 90°$) at high velocities,[47] $\text{Re} > 2 \times 10^5$

Diagram 7-24

Values of $\zeta_{c.st}$

No. of the curve	σ_{st}/σ_c	$\lambda_c = w_c/a_{ct}$							
		0.2	0.3	0.4	0.5	0.6	0.7	0.8	0.9
5	0.2	0.28	0.31	0.33	0.37	0.41	0.47	0.55	–
6	0.5	0.16	0.17	0.18	0.20	0.22	0.27	0.32	–
7	0.8	0.10	0.10	0.10	0.1	0.12	0.13	0.17	0.22
8	1.0	0.12	0.12	0.13	0.14	0.15	–	–	–

b. Flow-dividing wyes of the type $F_s + F_{st} = F_c$; $F_s \neq F_{st}$; $r/D_c = 0.5$ (scheme 2, graph c)

Diverging wye of normalized construction; $\alpha = 45°$ [21]

Diagram 7-25

Values of $\zeta_{c.st}$

No. of the curve	σ_{st}/σ_c	$\lambda_c = w_c/a_{ct}$				
		0.2	0.3	0.4	0.5	0.6
4	0.25	0.22	0.22	0.22	0.22	–
5	0.5	0.11	0.11	0.11	0.12	0.13
6	0.8	0.08	0.08	0.08	0.08	–

Side branch with $\bar{w}_s = w_s/w_c \leq 3$:

$$\zeta_{c.s} \equiv \frac{\Delta p_s}{\rho w_c^2/2} = 1 - 1.38\,\frac{w_s}{w_c} + \left(\frac{w_s}{w_c}\right)^2 - 0.06\left(\frac{w_s}{w_c}\right)^2$$

Straight passage with $\bar{w}_{st} = w_{st}/w_c < 2$:

$$\zeta_{c.st} \equiv \frac{\Delta p_{st}}{\rho w_c^2/2} = 0.28 - 0.9\,\frac{w_{st}}{w_c} + 0.955\left(\frac{w_{st}}{w_c}\right)^2 - 0.157\left(\frac{w_{st}}{w_c}\right)^2$$

$$\zeta_s \equiv \frac{\Delta p_s}{\rho w_s^2/2} = \frac{\zeta_{c.s}}{(Q_s F_c/Q_c F_s)^2}$$

$$\zeta_{st} \equiv \frac{\Delta p_{st}}{\rho w_{st}^2/2} = \frac{\zeta_{c.st}}{(1 - Q_s/Q_c)^2(F_c/F_{st})^2}$$

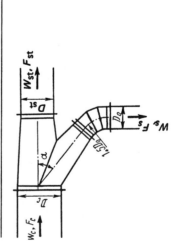

Values of ζ_s (in numerator) and ζ_{st} (in denominator)

F_s/F_c	$\bar{f}_{st.av} = F_{st}/F_c = 1.0$						$\bar{f}_{st.av} = 0.8$						$\bar{f}_{st.av} = 0.63$					$\bar{f}_{st.av} = 0.5$			
	Q_s/Q_c																				
	0.5	0.4	0.3	0.2	0.10	0.05	0.6	0.5	0.4	0.3	0.2	0.10	0.7	0.6	0.5	0.4	0.3	0.7	0.6	0.5	0.4
0.8	1.31/0.20	2.21/0.14	4.41/0.13	–	–	–	0.89/0.20	1.31/0.13	2.21/0.14	4.41/0.15	–	–	–	–	–	–	–	–	–	–	–
0.63	0.80/0.20	1.30/0.14	2.48/0.13	6.44/0.15	–	–	0.60/0.20	0.80/0.13	1.27/0.14	2.48/0.15	6.44/0.18	–	0.50/0.23	0.60/0.13	0.80/0.14	1.27/0.17	2.48/0.20	–	–	–	–
0.50	0.56/0.20	0.79/0.14	1.44/0.13	3.78/0.14	–	–	0.47/0.20	0.56/0.13	0.79/0.14	1.44/0.15	3.78/0.18	19.09/0.20	0.44/0.23	0.47/0.13	0.56/0.14	0.79/0.17	1.44/0.20	0.44/0.14	0.47/0.14	0.56/0.18	0.79/0.21
0.40	0.46/0.20	0.56/0.14	0.89/0.13	2.21/0.14	11.46/0.16	–	0.43/0.20	0.46/0.13	0.56/0.14	0.89/0.15	2.21/0.18	11.47/0.20	–	0.43/0.13	0.46/0.14	0.56/0.17	0.89/0.20	0.43/0.14	0.43/0.14	0.46/0.18	0.56/0.21
0.32	0.43/0.20	0.46/0.14	0.61/0.13	1.31/0.14	6.81/0.16	–	0.44/0.20	0.43/0.13	0.46/0.14	0.61/0.15	1.31/0.18	6.80/0.20	–	0.44/0.13	0.43/0.14	0.46/0.17	0.61/0.20	–	–	–	–
0.25	0.44/0.20	0.43/0.14	0.47/0.13	0.79/0.14	3.78/0.16	19.09/0.17	–	0.44/0.13	0.43/0.14	0.47/0.15	0.79/0.18	3.78/0.20	–	–	0.44/0.14	0.43/0.17	0.47/0.20	–	–	–	–
0.20	–	0.44/0.14	0.43/0.13	0.56/0.14	1.90/0.16	11.46/0.17	–	–	0.44/0.14	0.43/0.15	0.56/0.18	1.90/0.20	–	–	–	–	–	–	–	–	–
0.16	–	–	0.44/0.13	0.46/0.14	1.31/0.16	6.81/0.17	–	–	0.46/0.22	0.44/0.15	0.46/0.18	1.31/0.20	–	–	–	–	–	–	–	–	–
0.125	–	–	0.45/0.13	0.43/0.14	0.79/0.16	3.78/0.17	–	–	–	0.45/0.15	0.43/0.18	0.79/0.20	–	–	–	–	–	–	–	–	–
0.10	–	–	–	0.44/0.14	0.56/0.16	2.21/0.17	–	–	–	–	0.43/0.18	–	–	–	–	–	–	–	–	–	–

Diverging wye of normalized construction; $\alpha = 45°$[21]

Diagram 7-26

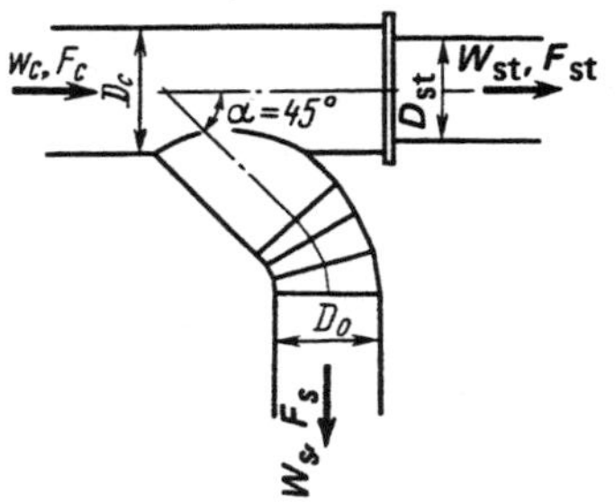

Side branch with $\bar{w}_s = w_s/w_c \leq 3$:

$$\zeta_{c.s} \equiv \frac{\Delta p_s}{\rho w_c^2/2} = 1 - 1.38\,\frac{w_s}{w_c} + \left(\frac{w_s}{w_c}\right)^2 - 0.06\left(\frac{w_s}{w_c}\right)^3$$

Straight passage with $\bar{w}_{st} = w_{st}/w_c < 2$:

$$\zeta_{c.st} \equiv \frac{\Delta p_{st}}{\rho w_c^2/2} = 0.28 - 0.9\,\frac{w_{st}}{w_c} + \frac{0.955}{\bar{f}_{st}}\left(\frac{w_{st}}{w_c}\right)^2 - \frac{0.157}{\bar{f}_{st}}\left(\frac{w_{st}}{w_c}\right)^2$$

$$\bar{f}_{st} = \frac{F_{st}}{F_c} \qquad \zeta_s \equiv \frac{\Delta p_s}{\rho w_s^2/2} = \frac{\zeta_{c.s}}{(Q_sF_c/Q_cF_s)^2} \qquad \zeta_{c.st} \equiv \frac{\Delta p_{st}}{\rho w_{st}^2/2} = \frac{\zeta_{c.st}}{(1 - Q_s/Q_c)^2(F_c/F_{st})^2}$$

Diverging smooth wye ($r/b_2 = 1.0$) of the type $F_s + F_{st} \geqslant F_c$ and of rectangular cross section; $\alpha = 90°$ [44,49]	Diagram 7-27

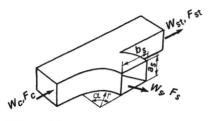

Side branch

$$\zeta_{c.s} \equiv \frac{\Delta p_s}{\rho w_c^2/2} = a_0 \left(\frac{Q_s}{Q_c}\right)^2 + b_1 \frac{Q_s}{Q_c} + c_1$$

see graph a; for a_0, b_1, and c_1, see the table;

$$\zeta_s \equiv \frac{\Delta p_s}{\rho w_s^2/2} = \frac{\zeta_{c.s}}{(Q_s F_c/Q_c F_s)^2}$$

Values of $\zeta_{c.s}$

$\dfrac{F_s}{F_{st}} \left(\dfrac{F_s}{F_c}\right)$	Q_s/Q_c								
	0.1	0.2	0.3	0.4	0.5	0.6	0.7	0.8	0.9
0.25 (0.25)	0.55	0.50	0.60	0.85	1.20	1.80	3.10	4.35	6.00
0.33 (0.25)	0.35	0.35	0.50	0.80	1.30	2.00	2.80	3.75	5.00
0.50 (0.50)	0.62	0.48	0.40	0.40	0.48	0.60	0.78	1.08	1.50
0.67 (0.50)	0.52	0.40	0.32	0.30	0.34	0.44	0.62	0.92	1.38
1.00 (0.50)	0.44	0.38	0.38	0.41	0.52	0.68	0.92	1.21	1.57
1.00 (1.00)	0.67	0.55	0.46	0.37	0.32	0.29	0.29	0.30	0.37
1.33 (1.00)	0.70	0.60	0.51	0.42	0.34	0.28	0.26	0.26	0.29
2.00 (1.00)	0.60	0.52	0.43	0.33	0.24	0.17	0.15	0.17	0.21

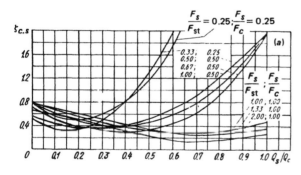

Straight passage

$$\zeta_{c.st} \equiv \frac{\Delta p_{st}}{\rho w_c^2/2}$$

$$= a_2 \left(\frac{Q_s}{Q_c}\right)^2 + b_2 \frac{Q_s}{Q_c} + c_2$$

see graph b; for a_2, b_2, and c_2, see the table;

$$\zeta_{st} \equiv \frac{\Delta p_{st}}{\rho w_{st}^2/2}$$

$$= \frac{\zeta_{c.st}}{(1 - Q_s/Q_c)^2 (F_c/F_{st})^2}$$

Values of $\zeta_{c.st}$

$\dfrac{F_{st}}{F_c} \left(\dfrac{F_s}{F_c}\right)$	Q_s/Q_c								
	0.1	0.2	0.3	0.4	0.5	0.6	0.7	0.8	0.9
1.00 (0.25)	−0.01	−0.03	−0.01	0.05	0.13	0.21	0.29	0.38	0.46
0.75 (0.25)	0.08	0.00	−0.02	−0.01	0.02	0.08	0.16	0.24	0.34
1.00 (0.50)	−0.03	−0.06	−0.05	0.00	0.06	0.12	0.19	0.27	0.35
0.75 (0.50)	0.04	−0.02	−0.04	−0.03	−0.01	0.04	0.12	0.23	0.37
0.50 (0.50)	0.72	0.48	0.28	0.13	0.05	0.04	0.09	0.18	0.30
1.00 (1.00)	−0.02	−0.04	−0.04	−0.01	0.06	0.13	0.22	0.30	0.38
0.75 (1.00)	0.10	0	0.01	−0.03	−0.01	0.03	0.10	0.20	0.30
0.50 (1.00)	0.62	0.38	0.23	0.13	0.08	0.05	0.06	0.10	0.20

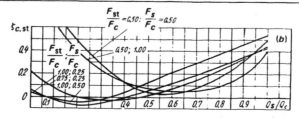

| Diverging smooth wye ($r/b_2 = 1.0$) of the type $F_s + F_{st} \geqslant F_c$ and of rectangular cross section; $\alpha = 90°$ [44,49] | | | | | | | | | Diagram 7-27 |

$\dfrac{F_s}{F_{st}}$	$\dfrac{F_{st}}{F_c}$	$\dfrac{F_s}{F_c}$	a_1	b_1	c_1	a_2	b_2	c_2
0.25	1.00	0.25	12.50	−5.80	1.07	0.64	−0.15	−0.03
0.33	0.75	0.25	8.57	−2.77	0.55	1.18	−0.83	0.14
0.50	1.00	0.50	3.75	−2.68	0.56	0.64	−0.15	−0.03
0.67	0.75	0.50	3.89	−2.88	0.79	1.36	−0.95	0.12
1.00	0.50	0.50	3.00	−1.60	0.57	2.80	−3.32	1.02
1.00	1.00	1.00	1.39	−1.74	0.84	0.75	−0.22	−0.02
1.33	0.75	1.00	1.09	−1.59	0.86	1.34	−1.07	0.18
2.00	0.50	1.00	1.04	−1.60	0.77	2.13	−2.63	0.85

| Nonsymmetric convergent wyes of the type $F_s + F_{st} \geqslant F_c$; $F_s = F_{st} = F_c$ with smooth branching [53] ($R_0/D_c = 2.0$); $\alpha = 90°$; $Re = w_c D_c/\nu \geqslant 10^4$ | Diagram 7-28 |

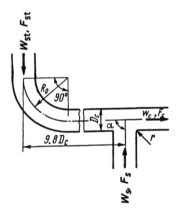

Side branch

$$\zeta_{c.s} \equiv \frac{\Delta p_s}{\rho w_c^2/2}$$

see the table and curve $\zeta_{c.s} = f(Q_s/Q_c)$;

$$\zeta_s \equiv \frac{\Delta p_s}{\rho w_s^2/2} = \frac{\zeta_{c.s}}{(Q_s/Q_c)^2}$$

1. The edge of the side branch is slightly rounded ($r/D_c = 0.1$)

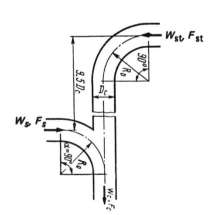

Straight passage

$$\zeta_{c.st} \equiv \frac{\Delta p_{st}}{\rho w_c^2/2}$$

see the table and curve $\zeta_{c.st} = f(Q_s/Q_c)$;

$$\zeta_{st} \equiv \frac{\Delta p_{st}}{\rho w_{st}^2/2} = \frac{\zeta_{c.st}}{(1 - Q_s/Q_c)^2}$$

2. Side branch is smooth ($R_0/D_c = 2$)

Nonsymmetric convergent wyes of the type $F_s + F_{st} \geqslant F_c$; $F_s = F_{st} = F_c$ with smooth branching[53] ($R_0/D_c = 2.0$); $\alpha = 90°$; $Re = w_c D_c/\nu \geqslant 10^4$	Diagram 7-28

Values of $\zeta_{c.s}$ (in numerator) and $\zeta_{c.st}$ (in denominator)

Scheme	\multicolumn{11}{c}{Q_s/Q_c}
	0	0.1	0.2	0.3	0.4	0.5	0.6	0.7	0.8	0.9	1.0
1	$\dfrac{-0.80}{0.11}$	$\dfrac{-0.59}{0.15}$	$\dfrac{-0.35}{0.19}$	$\dfrac{-0.15}{0.22}$	$\dfrac{0.02}{0.24}$	$\dfrac{0.18}{0.24}$	$\dfrac{0.31}{0.23}$	$\dfrac{0.40}{0.21}$	$\dfrac{0.54}{0.20}$	$\dfrac{0.70}{0.19}$	$\dfrac{0.90}{0.17}$
2	$\dfrac{-0.60}{0.28}$	$\dfrac{-0.40}{0.30}$	$\dfrac{-0.27}{0.29}$	$\dfrac{-0.14}{0.28}$	$\dfrac{-0.02}{0.25}$	$\dfrac{0.05}{0.20}$	$\dfrac{0.12}{0.15}$	$\dfrac{0.15}{0.10}$	$\dfrac{0.20}{0.05}$	$\dfrac{0.24}{-0.02}$	$\dfrac{0.27}{-0.08}$

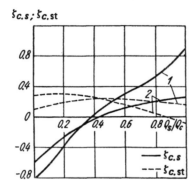

Symmetrical (equilateral) wye with a sharp 90° turn[27,29]	Diagram 7-29

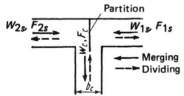

Merging of streams (countercurrent)
(a) without partition

$$\zeta_{1c.s} \equiv \frac{\Delta p_{1s}}{\rho w_c^2/2}$$

$$= A\left\{1 + \left(\frac{F_c}{F_{1s}}\right)^2 + 3\left(\frac{F_c}{F_{1s}}\right)^2\left[\left(\frac{Q_{1s}}{Q_c}\right)^2 - \left(\frac{Q_{1s}}{Q_c}\right)\right]\right\} = A\zeta'_{1c.s}$$

see the table and the curves $\zeta_{1c.s} = f(Q_{1s}/Q_c)$ at different F_{1s}/F_c on graph a; for A see Table 7-1, para. 7-1.

$$\zeta_{1s} \equiv \frac{\Delta p_{1s}}{\rho w_s^2/2} = \frac{\zeta_{1c.s}}{(Q_{1s}F_c/Q_cF_{1s})^2}$$

For the other side branch, subscript 1 is to be replaced by 2.

Symmetrical (equilateral) wye with a sharp 90° turn[27,29]	Diagram 7-29

Values of $\zeta'_{1c.s}$ and $\zeta_{1c.s}$

$\dfrac{F_{1s}}{F_c}$	Q_s/Q_c										
	0	0.10	0.20	0.30	0.40	0.50	0.60	0.70	0.80	0.90	1.0
					Without partition ($\zeta'_{1c.s}$)						
0.25	17.0	12.7	9.30	6.92	5.48	5.00	5.48	6.92	9.32	12.7	17.0
0.50	5.02	3.94	3.10	2.50	2.14	2.00	2.14	2.50	3.10	3.94	5.00
0.75	2.78	2.30	1.92	1.66	1.50	1.57	1.56	1.66	1.92	2.30	2.78
1.0	2.00	1.73	1.52	1.37	1.28	1.25	1.28	1.37	1.52	1.73	2.00
					With partition ($\zeta_{1c.s}$)						
1.0	-3.25	-2.40	-1.51	-0.80	0	0.75	1.45	2.15	2.85	3.50	4.15

(b) with partition

$\zeta_{1c.s} \equiv f(Q_s/Q_c)$; see dashed line of graph a.

Division of flow (cocurrent flow)

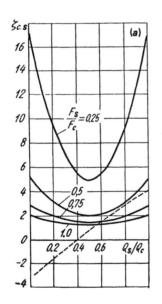

$\zeta_{c.s} \equiv \dfrac{\Delta p_{1s}}{\rho w_c^2/2} = 1 + k_{1,2}\left(\dfrac{w_s}{w_c}\right)^2$, see the table and the curves $\zeta_{c.s} = f(w_s/w_c)$ of graph b, where $k_1 \approx 1.5$ for standard threaded wyes made of malleable iron; $k_2 \approx 0.3$ for welded wyes.

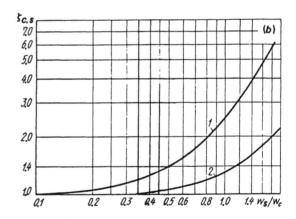

Values of $\zeta_{c.s}$

Type of wye	w_s/w_c													
	0.1	0.2	0.3	0.4	0.5	0.6	0.7	0.8	0.9	1.0	1.2	1.4	1.6	2.0
Standard made of iron (curve 1)	1.02	1.06	1.14	1.24	1.38	1.54	1.74	1.96	2.22	2.50	3.16	3.94	4.84	7.0
Welded (curve 2)		1.0	1.01	1.03	1.05	1.08	1.11	1.15	1.19	1.24	1.30	1.43	1.59	1.77	2.2

Symmetrical wye of the type $F_c = F_{1s} + F_{2s} = 2F_s$ with sharp turn corners; $\alpha = 15\text{--}45°$	Diagram 7-30

1) Merging of streams (converging wye)

$$\alpha = 15°; \quad \zeta_{1c.s} \equiv \frac{\Delta p_{1s}}{\rho w_c^2/2} = 7.3\frac{Q_{1s}}{Q_c} + 0.07\left[\left(\frac{Q_{1s}}{Q_c}\right)^4 + \left(1 - \frac{Q_{1s}}{Q_c}\right)^4\right] - 3.7\left(\frac{Q_{1s}}{Q_c}\right)^2 - 2.64$$

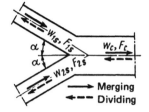

$$\alpha = 30°;$$

$$\zeta_{1c.s} \equiv \frac{\Delta p_{1s}}{\rho w_c^2/2}$$

$$= 6.6\frac{Q_{1s}}{Q_c} + 0.25\left[\left(\frac{Q_{1s}}{Q_c}\right)^4 + \left(1 - \frac{Q_{1s}}{Q_c}\right)^4\right] - 3.0\left(\frac{Q_{1s}}{Q_c}\right)^2 - 2.30$$

$$\alpha = 45°; \quad \zeta_{1c.s} \equiv \frac{\Delta p_{1s}}{\rho w_c^2/2} = 5.6\left(\frac{Q_{1s}}{Q_c}\right) + 0.50\left[\left(\frac{Q_{1s}}{Q_c}\right)^4 + \left(1 - \frac{Q_{1s}}{Q_c}\right)^4\right] - 2.0\left(\frac{Q_{1s}}{Q_c}\right)^2 - 1.80;$$

for $\zeta_{1c.s}$ see the table and the graph.

2) Flow division (diverging wye); $\zeta_{1c.s} \equiv \Delta p_{1s}/(\rho w_c^2/2)$ is determined tentatively as for a side branch of a conventional wye of the type $F_c = F_s + F_{st}$ from Diagram 7-19.

Values of $\zeta_{1c.s}$

$\alpha,°$	Q_{1s}/Q_c										
	0	0.10	0.20	0.30	0.40	0.50	0.60	0.70	0.80	0.90	1.0
15	−2.56	−1.89	−1.30	−0.77	−0.30	0.10	0.41	0.67	0.85	0.97	1.04
30	−2.05	−1.51	−1.00	−0.53	−0.10	0.28	0.69	0.91	1.09	1.37	1.55
45	−1.30	−0.93	−0.55	−0.16	0.20	0.56	0.92	1.26	1.61	1.95	2.30

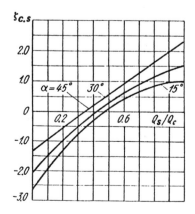

Symmetrical wye of the type $F_s = F_{st} = F_c$ [57]

Diagram 7-31

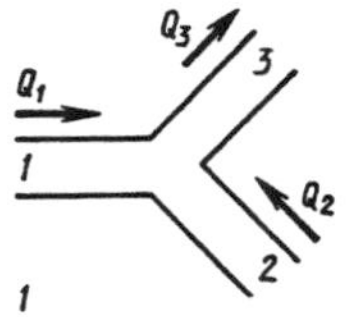

1. Merging of flows (converging wyes) under the angles of 45° and 90° (schemes 1 and 2):

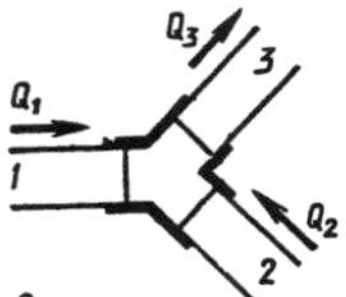

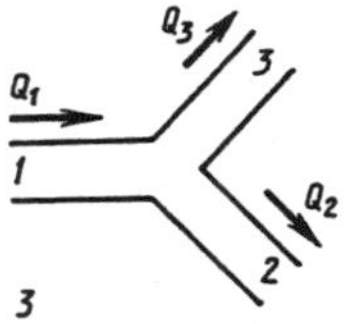

1) Butt-jointed branching:

$\zeta_{1\text{-}3} \equiv \dfrac{\Delta p}{\rho w_3^2/2}$, see the table and curve 1 of graph a, or it is determined from the formulas:

at $0 \leqslant Q_2/Q_3 \leqslant 0.4$

$\zeta_{1\text{-}3} = 0.33 + 0.51(Q_2/Q_3)^2$;

at $0.4 \leqslant Q_2/Q_3 \leqslant 1.0$

$\zeta = 0.26 + 0.38 Q_2/Q_3$;

2) Threaded branching with $\delta = 0$ (for δ see Figure 7-9):

$\zeta_{1\text{-}3} \equiv \dfrac{\Delta p}{\rho w_3^2/2}$, see the table and curve 2 of graph a;

3) Threaded branching with $\delta/D_0 \approx 0.13$:

$\zeta_{1\text{-}3} \equiv \dfrac{\Delta p}{\rho w_3^2/2}$, see the table and curve 3 of graph a.

Values of ζ_{1-3}

No. of the curve	Branching	Q_2/Q_3										
		0	0.1	0.2	0.3	0.4	0.5	0.6	0.7	0.8	0.9	1.0
1	Butt jointed	0.32	0.34	0.36	0.38	0.41	0.45	0.50	0.53	0.56	0.60	0.66
2	Threaded connection with $\delta = 0$	0.94	0.71	0.54	0.50	0.50	0.54	0.59	0.60	0.64	0.72	0.84
3	Threaded connection with $\delta/D_0 = 0.13$	1.15	1.12	0.68	0.60	0.63	0.64	0.63	0.60	0.73	0.85	0.87

2. Flow division (diverging wyes) under the angle of 45° (schemes 3 and 4):

   1) Butt-jointed branching:

   $$\zeta_{1\text{-}3} \equiv \frac{\Delta p}{\rho w_1^2/2}, \quad \text{see the table and curve 1 of graph b, or it is determined from the formulas:}$$

   at $0 \leqslant Q_2/Q_1 \leqslant 0.7$

   $$\zeta_{1\text{-}3} = 0.33 - 0.45 Q_2/Q_1 + 0.85(Q_2/Q_1)^2;$$

   at $0.7 \leqslant Q_2/Q_1 \leqslant 1.0$

   $$\zeta_{1\text{-}3} = 0.44 + 1.70 Q_2/Q_1 - 0.65(Q_2/Q_1)^2;$$

   2) Threaded branching with $\delta = 0$:

   $$\zeta_{1\text{-}3} \equiv \frac{\Delta p}{\rho w_1^2/2}, \quad \text{see the table and curve 2 of graph b;}$$

   3) Threaded branching with $\delta/D_0 \approx 0.13$:

   $$\zeta_{1\text{-}3} \equiv \frac{\Delta p}{\rho w_1^2/2}, \quad \text{see the table and curve 3 of graph b.}$$

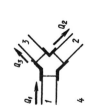

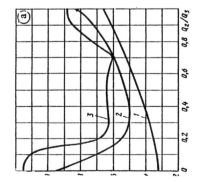

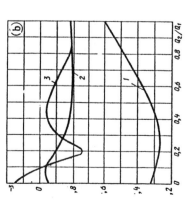

Symmetrical wye of the type $F_s = F_{st} = F_c^{57}$

Diagram 7-31

Values of ζ_{1-3}

No. of the curve	Branching	Q_2/Q_1										
		0	0.1	0.2	0.3	0.4	0.5	0.6	0.7	0.8	0.9	1.0
1	Butt jointed	0.32	0.30	0.27	0.27	0.29	0.32	0.37	0.43	0.49	0.54	0.60
2	Threaded connection with $\delta = 0.13$	0.94	0.96	0.90	0.85	0.83	0.81	0.82	0.82	0.82	0.82	0.82
3	Threaded connection with $\delta/D_0 \times 0.13$	1.15	0.99	0.74	0.90	0.95	0.95	0.91	0.88	0.82	0.82	0.82

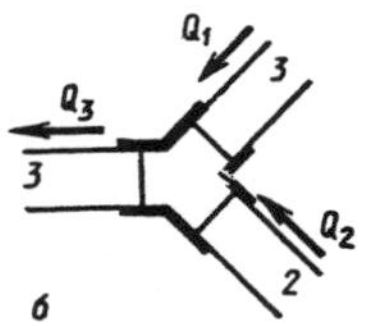

3. Merging of streams (converging wyes) under the angle of 45° (schemes 5 and 6):

1) Butt-jointed branching:

$$\zeta_{1-3} \equiv \frac{\Delta p}{\rho w_3^2/2}, \quad \text{see the table and curve 1 of graph c, or it is determined from the formula}$$

at $0 \leq Q_2/Q_1 \leq 0.7$

$$\zeta_{1-3} = 0.33 + 0.071 Q_2/Q_3 + 0.80(Q_2/Q_3)^2;$$

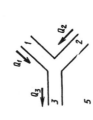

2) Threaded branching with $\delta = 0$:

$$\zeta_{1-3} \equiv \frac{\Delta p}{\rho w_3^2/2}, \text{ see the table and curve 2 of graph c;}$$

3) Threaded branching with $\delta/D_0 \approx 0.3$:

$$\zeta_{1-3} \equiv \frac{\Delta p}{\rho w_3^2/2}, \text{ see the table and curve 3 of graph c.}$$

Values of ζ_{1-3}

No. of the curve	Branching	Q_2/Q_3										
		0	0.1	0.2	0.3	0.4	0.5	0.6	0.7	0.8	0.9	1.0
1	Butt jointed	0.34	0.35	0.32	0.27	0.23	0.17	0.09	0	-0.12	-0.25	-0.40
2	Threaded connection with $\delta = 0$	0.90	0.87	0.54	0.49	0.45	0.36	0.25	0.14	0	0	-0.15
3	Threaded connection with $\delta/D_0 = 1.20$	1.20	1.20	0.60	0.52	0.53	0.45	0.34	0.20	0.09	0.14	0

Symmetrical wye of the type $F_s = F_{st} = F_c$ [57]

Diagram 7-31

4. Division of flow (diverging wyes) under the angles of 45° and 90° (schemes 7 and 8):

1) Butt-jointed branching:

$\zeta_{1-3} \equiv \dfrac{\Delta p}{\rho w_1^2/2}$, see the table and curve 1 of graph d, or it is determined from the formulas:

at $0 \le Q_2/Q_1 \le 0.7$

$\zeta_{1-3} = 0.33 - 0.72 Q_2/Q_1 + 0.97(Q_2/Q_1)^2$;

at $0.7 \le Q_2/Q_1 \le 1.0$

$\zeta_{1-3} = -0.58 + 1.77 Q_2/Q_1 - 0.73(Q_2/Q_1)^2$;

2) Threaded branching with $\delta = 0$:

$\zeta_{1-3} \equiv \dfrac{\Delta p}{\rho w_1^2/2}$, see the table and curve 2 of graph d;

3) Threaded branching with $\delta/D_0 \approx 0.13$:

$\zeta_{1-3} \equiv \dfrac{\Delta p}{\rho w_1^2/2}$, see the table and curve 3 of graph d.

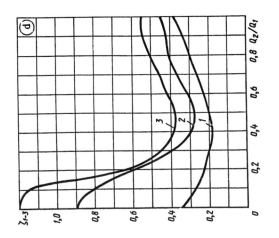

Values of ζ_{1-3}

No. of the curve	Branching	Q_2/Q_1										
		0	0.1	0.2	0.3	0.4	0.5	0.6	0.7	0.8	0.9	1.0
1	Butt jointed	0.34	0.27	0.23	0.20	0.18	0.20	0.23	0.27	0.30	0.33	0.38
2	Threaded connection with $\delta = 0.90$	0.90	0.81	0.60	0.41	0.30	0.28	0.31	0.36	0.41	0.42	0.48
3	Threaded connection with $\delta/D_0 \approx 0.13$	1.20	1.18	0.63	0.45	0.40	0.38	0.43	0.45	0.50	0.54	0.55

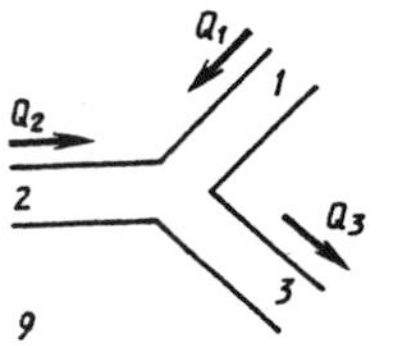

5. Merging of streams (converging wyes) under the angles of 45° and 90° (schemes 9 and 10):

1) Butt-jointed branching:

$$\zeta_{1-3} \equiv \frac{\Delta p}{\rho w_3^2/2},$$ see the table and curve 1 of graph e, or it is determined from the formula

$$\zeta_{1-3} = 1.13 - 1.38 Q_2/Q_3 - 0.05(Q_2/Q_3)^2;$$

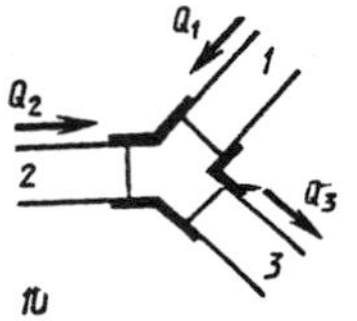

9

10

Symmetrical wye of the type $F_s = F_{st} = F_c$[57]

Diagram 7-31

2) Threaded branching with $\delta = 0$:

$$\zeta_{1\text{-}3} \equiv \frac{\Delta p}{\rho w_3^2/2}\ ,\quad \text{see the table and curve 2 of graph e;}$$

3) Threaded branching with $\delta/D_0 \approx 0.13$:

$$\zeta_{1\text{-}3} \equiv \frac{\Delta p}{\rho w_3^2/2}\ ,\quad \text{see the table and curve 3 of graph e.}$$

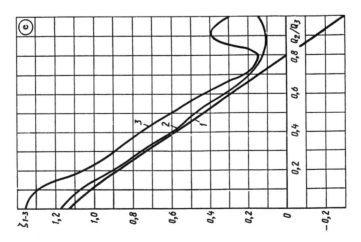

Values of ζ_{1-3}

No. of the curve	Branching						Q_2/Q_3					
		0	0.1	0.2	0.3	0.4	0.5	0.6	0.7	0.8	0.9	1.0
1	Butt jointed	1.3	1.01	0.88	0.70	0.60	0.44	0.30	0.14	0	-0.15	-0.30
2	Thread connection with $\delta = 0$	1.17	1.08	0.90	0.73	0.62	0.48	0.32	0.18	0.15	0.10	0.14
3	Threaded connection with $\zeta/D_0 \approx 0.13$	1.36	1.30	1.06	0.90	0.77	0.60	0.44	0.21	0.14	0.40	0.30

6. Flow division (diverging wyes) under the angles of 90° and 45° (schemes 11 and 12):

1) Butt-jointed branching:

$$\zeta_{1-3} \equiv \frac{\Delta p}{\rho w_1^2/2}, \quad \text{see the table and curve 1 of graph f, or it is determined from the formula}$$

$$\zeta_{1-3} = 1.13 - 1.40Q_2/Q_1 + 1.03(Q_2/Q_1)^2;$$

2) Threaded branching with $\delta = 0$:

$$\zeta_{1-3} \equiv \frac{\Delta p}{\rho w_1^2/2}, \quad \text{see the table and curve 2 of graph f;}$$

3) Threaded branching with $\delta/D_0 \approx 0.13$:

$$\zeta_{1-3} \equiv \frac{\Delta p}{\rho w_1^2/2}, \quad \text{see the table and curve 3 of graph f.}$$

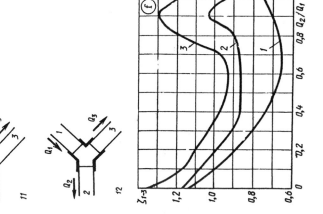

Symmetrical wye of the type $F_s = F_{st} = F_c$ [57]   Diagram 7-31

Values of ζ_{1-3}

No. of the curve	Branching	Q_2/Q_1										
		0	0.1	0.2	0.3	0.4	0.5	0.6	0.7	0.8	0.9	1.0
1	Butt jointed	1.13	1.00	0.90	0.81	0.74	0.89	0.66	0.65	0.67	0.70	0.75
2	Threaded connection with $\delta = 0$	1.17	1.08	1.00	0.91	0.87~	0.87	0.87	0.87	0.90	1.13	1.05
3	Threaded connection with $\delta/D_0 \approx 0.13$	1.36	1.17	1.10	1.02	0.97	0.93	0.93	0.96	1.30	1.40	1.20

Symmetrical wye with smooth turn through 90°[44-53]	Diagram 7-32

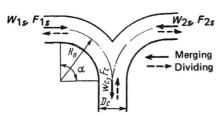

Circular cross section at

$$\zeta_{1c.s} \equiv \frac{\Delta p_{1s}}{\rho w_c^2/2} \text{ is determined:}$$

(a) for merging and $R_0/D_c = 2$ see the table and the curve $\zeta_{1c.s} = f(Q_s/Q_c)$;

(b) for division and $F_{1s}/F_c = 0.5$; $Q_{1s}/Q_c = 0.5$ see below the table of the values of $[\zeta_{1c.s} = f(R_0/D_c)]$.

For the other side branch, subscript 1 is to be replaced by 2.

Q_{1s}/Q_c	0	0.10	0.20	0.30	0.40	0.50	0.60	0.70	0.80	0.90	1.0
$\zeta_{1c.s}$	-0.13	-0.10	-0.07	-0.03	0	0.03	0.30	0.03	0.03	0.05	0.08

$\dfrac{R_0}{D_c}$	0.50	0.75	1.0	1.5	2.0
$\zeta_{1c.s}$	1.10	0.60	0.40	0.25	0.20

$$\zeta_{1s} \equiv \frac{\Delta p_{1s}}{\rho w_s^2/2} = \frac{\zeta_{1c.s}}{(Q_{1s}F_c/Q_cF_{1s})^2}$$

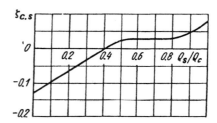

Rectangular cross section at $R_0/b_0 = 1.5$ and $Q_{1s}/Q_c = 0.5$

$$\zeta_{1c.s} \equiv \frac{\Delta p_{1s}}{\rho w_c^2/2}, \text{ see below.}$$

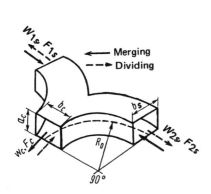

Values of $\zeta_{1c.s}$

State of the flow	F_{1s}/F_c	
	0.50	1.0
Merging	0.23	0.07
Division	0.30	0.25

Four-way wye piece of the type $F_{1s} = F_{2s} = F_s$; $F_{st} = F_c$; $\alpha = 15°$[29,30]	Diagram 7-33

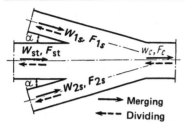

→ Merging
←--- Dividing

1. Merging of streams (outlet four-way piece)
Side branch

$$\zeta_{1c.s} \equiv \frac{\Delta p_{1s}}{\rho w_c^2/2} = 1 + \left(\frac{Q_{1s}}{Q_c}\frac{F_c}{F_{1s}}\right)^2 - 8\left(\frac{Q_{1s}}{Q_c}\right)^2$$

$$\times \frac{[Q_c/Q_{1s} - (1 + Q_{2s}/Q_{1s})]^2}{4 - (1 + Q_{2s}/Q_{1s})Q_{1s}/Q_c}$$

$$- 1.93\left(\frac{Q_{1s}}{Q_c}\right)^2\frac{F_c}{F_{1s}}\left[1 + \left(\frac{Q_{2s}}{Q_{1s}}\right)^2\right]$$

see the table and the curves $\zeta_{1c.s} = f(Q_{st}/Q_c, Q_{2s}/Q_{1s})$ at different F_{1s}/F_c.
For the other side branch subscripts 1 and 2 change places.
Main passage

$$\zeta_{c.st} \equiv \frac{\Delta p}{\rho w_c^2/2} = 1 + \left(\frac{Q_{st}}{Q_c}\right)^2 - \left(\frac{Q_{st}}{Q_c}\right)^2\frac{1 + Q_{st}/Q_c}{(0.75 + 0.25Q_{st}/Q_c)^2} - 1.93\left(\frac{Q_{st}}{Q_c}\right)^2\frac{F_c}{F_{1s}}\frac{1 + (Q_{2s}/Q_{1s})^2}{(1 + Q_{2s}/Q_{1s})^2}\left(\frac{Q_c}{Q_{st}} - 1\right)^2$$

see the table and the curves $\zeta_{c.st} = f(Q_{st}/Q_c, Q_{2s}/Q_{1s})$ at different F_{1s}/F_c.

2. Division of flow (intake four-way piece); $\zeta_{1c.s}$ and $\zeta_{c.st}$ are determined tentatively similar to diverging wyes from Diagrams 7-18 and 7-20.

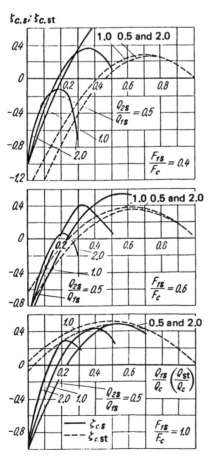

$\zeta_{c.s}$; $\zeta_{c.st}$

Values of $\zeta_{c.s}$

$\dfrac{Q_{2s}}{Q_{1s}}$	Q_{1s}/Q_c						
	0	0.1	0.2	0.3	0.4	0.5	0.6
			$F_{1s}/F_c = 0.2$				
0.5	−1.0	−0.37	0.46	1.48	2.69	4.07	5.62
1.0	−1.0	−0.29	0.43	1.23	1.80	2.81	−
2.0	−1.0	−0.32	−0.31	−1.13	−	−	−
			$F_{1s}/F_c = 0.4$				
0.5	−1.0	−0.50	−0.05	0.34	0.65	0.90	1.04
1.0	−1.0	−0.39	0.06	0.31	0.35	0.14	−
2.0	−1.0	−0.27	−0.10	−0.65	−	−	−
			$F_{1s}/F_c = 0.6$				
0.5	−1.0	−0.51	−0.11	−0.21	0.42	0.55	0.53
1.0	−1.0	−0.39	0.05	0.40	0.31	0.09	−
2.0	−1.0	−0.22	+0.08	−0.18	−	−	−
			$F_{1s}/F_c = 1.0$				
0.5	−1.0	−0.51	−0.12	0.20	0.39	0.49	0.37
1.0	−1.0	−0.38	0.09	0.36	0.44	0.28	−
2.0	−1.0	−0.18	0.27	0.19	−	−	−

| Four-way wye piece of the type $F_{1s} = F_{2s} = F_s$; $F_{st} = F_c$; $\alpha = 15°$[29,30] | | | | | | | | | | | Diagram 7-33 |

Values of $\zeta_{c.st}$

$\dfrac{Q_{2s}}{Q_{1s}}$	Q_{st}/Q_c										
	0	0.1	0.2	0.3	0.4	0.5	0.6	0.7	0.8	0.9	1.0
				$F_{1s}/F_c = 0.2$							
0.5–2.0	−4.37	−2.93	−2.04	−1.44	−1.08	−0.58	−0.22	0.03	0.16	0.14	0
1.0	−3.84	−2.93	−2.13	−1.44	−0.89	−0.45	−0.13	0.08	0.17	0.14	0
				$F_{1s}/F_c = 0.4$							
0.5–2.0	−1.70	−1.19	−0.76	−0.40	−0.12	0.08	0.21	0.27	0.25	0.16	0
1.0	−1.42	−0.96	−0.58	−0.26	−0.02	0.15	0.26	0.29	0.26	0.16	0
				$F_{1s}/F_c = 0.6$							
0.5–2.0	−0.81	−0.47	−0.19	0.04	0.20	0.30	0.36	0.35	0.29	0.17	0
1.0	−0.16	−0.31	−0.05	0.13	0.27	0.35	0.39	0.37	0.29	0.17	0
				$F_{1s}/F_c = 1.0$							
0.5–2.0	−0.35	0.11	0.10	0.26	0.36	0.42	0.43	0.39	0.31	0.18	0
1.0	−0.21	0.02	0.19	0.33	0.41	0.45	0.45	0.41	0.31	0.18	0

| Four-way wye piece of the type $F_{1s} = F_{2s} = F_s$; $F_{st} = F_c$; $\alpha = 30°$[29,30] | Diagram 7-34 |

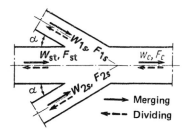

1. Merging of streams (outlet four-way piece)
Side branch

$$\zeta_{1c.s} \equiv \frac{\Delta p_{1s}}{\rho w_c^2/2} = 1 + \left(\frac{Q_{1s}}{Q_c}\frac{F_c}{F_{1s}}\right)^2 - 8\left(\frac{Q_{1s}}{Q_c}\right)^2$$

$$\times \frac{[Q_c/Q_{1s} - (1 + Q_{2s}/Q_{1s})]^2}{4 - (1 + Q_{2s}/Q_{1s})Q_{1s}/Q_c}$$

$$- 1.73\left(\frac{Q_{1s}}{Q_c}\right)^2 \frac{F_c}{F_{1s}}\left[1 + \left(\frac{Q_{2s}}{Q_{1s}}\right)^2\right]$$

Merging →
Dividing ◄- -

see the table and the curves $\zeta_{1c.s} = f(Q_{1s}/Q_c, Q_{2s}/Q_{1s})$ at different F_{1s}/F_c.
For the other side branch subscripts 1 and 2 change places.
Main passage

$$\zeta_{c.st} \equiv \frac{\Delta p}{\rho w_c^2/2} = 1 + \left(\frac{Q_{st}}{Q_c}\right)^2 - \left(\frac{Q_{st}}{Q_c}\right)^2 \frac{1 + Q_{st}/Q_c}{(0.75 + 0.25 Q_{st}/Q_c)^2} - 1.73\left(\frac{Q_{st}}{Q_c}\right)^2 \frac{F_c}{F_{1s}} \frac{1 + (Q_{2s}/Q_{1s})^2}{(1 + Q_{2s}/Q_{1s})^2}\left(\frac{Q_c}{Q_{st}} - 1\right)^2$$

see the table and the curves $\zeta_{c.st} = f(Q_{st}/Q_c, Q_{2s}/Q_{1s})$ at different F_{1s}/F_c.

2. Division of flow (intake four-way piece); $\zeta_{c.s}$ and $\zeta_{c.st}$ are determined tentatively as for diverging wyes from Diagrams 7-18 and 7-20.

Four-way wye piece of the type $F_{1s} = F_{2s} = F_s$; $F_{st} = F_c$; $\alpha = 30°$[29,30]	Diagram 7-34

$\zeta_{c.s}$; $\zeta_{c.st}$

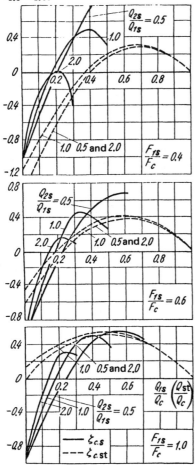

Values of $\zeta_{c.s}$

$\dfrac{Q_{2s}}{Q_{1s}}$	Q_{1s}/Q_c						
	0	0.1	0.2	0.3	0.4	0.5	0.6
			$F_{1s}/F_c = 0.2$				
0.5	−1.0	−0.36	+0.51	1.59	2.89	4.38	6.10
1.0	−1.0	−0.27	0.51	1.41	2.12	2.91	−
2.0	−1.0	−0.27	0.11	−0.72	−	−	−
			$F_{1s}/F_c = 0.4$				
0.5	−1.0	−0.49	−0.03	0.40	0.75	1.06	1.44
1.0	−1.0	−0.38	0.10	0.40	0.51	0.34	−
2.0	−1.0	−0.25	0.01	−0.42	−	−	−
			$F_{1s}/F_c = 0.6$				
0.5	−1.0	−0.51	−0.10	0.25	0.50	0.65	0.68
1.0	−1.0	−0.38	0.08	0.45	0.42	0.25	−
2.0	−1.0	−0.21	0.15	0.08	−	−	−
			$F_{1s}/F_c = 1.0$				
0.5	−1.0	−0.51	−0.11	0.22	0.43	0.55	0.55
1.0	−1.0	−0.37	0.10	0.40	0.51	0.38	−
2.0	−1.0	−0.17	0.31	0.28	−	−	−

Values of $\zeta_{c.st}$

$\dfrac{Q_{2s}}{Q_{1s}}$	Q_{st}/Q_c										
	0	0.1	0.2	0.3	0.4	0.5	0.6	0.7	0.8	0.9	1.0
				$F_{1s}/F_c = 0.2$							
0.5–0.2	−3.81	−2.51	−1.81	−1.20	−0.86	−0.44	−0.13	0.08	0.18	0.14	0
1.0	−3.34	−2.53	−1.81	−1.20	−0.71	−0.32	−0.05	0.12	0.18	0.14	0
				$F_{1s}/F_c = 0.4$							
0.5–0.2	−1.42	−0.97	−0.58	−0.26	0.02	0.15	0.26	0.30	0.26	0.17	0
1.0	−1.16	−0.76	−0.48	−0.14	0.07	0.21	0.30	0.31	0.27	0.17	0
				$F_{1s}/F_c = 0.6$							
0.5–2.0	−0.52	−0.32	−0.07	0.13	0.27	0.35	0.39	0.37	0.29	0.17	0
1.0	−0.45	−0.18	0.04	0.21	0.33	0.39	0.41	0.39	0.30	0.18	0
				$F_{1s}/F_c = 1.0$							
0.5–2.0	−0.03	0.21	0.34	0.45	0.50	0.52	0.49	0.43	0.32	0.18	0
1.0	0.13	0.29	0.41	0.49	0.54	0.54	0.51	0.44	0.32	0.18	0

Four-way wye piece of the type $F_{1s} = F_{2s} = F_s$; $F_{st} = F_c$; $\alpha = 45°$ [29,30]   Diagram 7-35

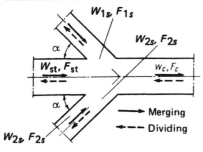

1. Merging of streams (outflow four-way piece)

Side branch

$$\zeta_{1c.s} \equiv \frac{\Delta p_{1s}}{\rho w_c^2/2} = 1 + \left(\frac{Q_{1s}}{Q_c}\frac{F_c}{F_{1s}}\right)^2 - 8\left(\frac{Q_{1s}}{Q_c}\right)^2$$

$$\times \frac{[Q_c/Q_{1s} - (1 + Q_{2s}/Q_{1s})]^2}{4 - (1 + Q_{2s}/Q_{1s})Q_{1s}/Q_c}$$

$$- 1.42\left(\frac{Q_{1s}}{Q_c}\right)^2 \frac{F_c}{F_{1s}}\left[1 + \left(\frac{Q_{2s}}{Q_{1s}}\right)^2\right]$$

see the table and the curves $\zeta_{1c.s} = f(Q_{1s}/Q_c, Q_{2s}/Q_{1s})$ at different F_{1s}/F_c. For the other side branch subscripts 1 and 2 change places.

Main passage

$$\zeta_{c.st} \equiv \frac{\Delta p}{\rho w_c^2/2} = 1 + \left(\frac{Q_{st}}{Q_c}\right)^2 - \left(\frac{Q_{st}}{Q_c}\right)^2 \frac{1 + Q_{st}/Q_c}{(0.75 + 0.25Q_{st}/Q_c)^2} - 1.42\left(\frac{Q_{st}}{Q_c}\right)^2 \frac{F_c}{F_{1s}}\frac{1 + (Q_{2s}/Q_{1s})^2}{(1 + Q_{2s}/Q_{1s})^2}\left(\frac{Q_c}{Q_{st}} - 1\right)^2$$

see the table and the curves $\zeta_{c.st} = f(Q_{st}/Q_c, Q_{2s}/Q_{1s})$ at different F_{1s}/F_c.

2. Division of flow (diverging four-way piece); $\zeta_{c.s}$ and $\zeta_{c.st}$ are determined tentatively as for wyes from Diagrams 7-18 and 7-20.

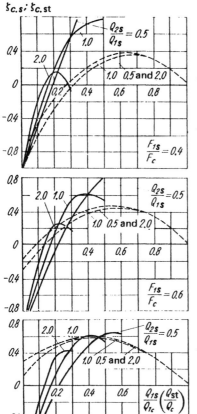

Values of $\zeta_{c.s}$

$\dfrac{Q_{2s}}{Q_{1s}}$	Q_{1s}/Q_c						
	0	0.1	0.2	0.3	0.4	0.5	0.6
			$F_{1s}/F_c = 0.2$				
0.5	−1.0	−0.36	0.59	1.77	3.20	4.88	6.79
1.0	−1.0	−0.24	0.63	1.70	2.64	3.73	−
2.0	−1.0	−0.19	0.21	0.04	−	−	−
			$F_{1s}/F_c = 0.4$				
0.5	−1.0	−0.48	−0.02	0.58	0.92	1.31	16.3
1.0	−1.0	−0.36	0.17	0.55	0.72	0.78	−
2.0	−1.0	−0.18	0.16	−0.06	−	−	−
			$F_{1s}/F_c = 0.6$				
0.5	−1.0	−0.50	−0.07	0.31	0.60	0.82	0.92
1.0	−1.0	−0.37	0.12	0.55	0.60	0.52	−
2.0	−1.0	−0.18	0.26	0.16	−	−	−
			$F_{1s}/F_c = 1.0$				
0.5	−1.0	−0.51	−0.09	0.25	0.50	0.65	0.64
1.0	−1.0	−0.37	0.13	0.46	0.61	0.54	−
2.0	−1.0	−0.15	0.38	0.42	−	−	−

Four-way wye piece of the type $F_{1s} = F_{2s} = F_s$; $F_{st} = F_c$; $\alpha = 45°$[29,30]

Diagram 7-35

Values of $\zeta_{c.st}$

$\dfrac{Q_{2s}}{Q_{1s}}$	Q_{st}/Q_c										
	0	0.1	0.2	0.3	0.4	0.5	0.6	0.7	0.8	0.9	1.0
				$F_{1s}/F_c = 0.2$							
0.5–2.0	−2.92	−1.87	−1.29	−0.80	−0.56	−0.23	−0.01	0.16	0.22	0.15	0
1.0	−2.54	−1.87	−1.30	−0.80	−0.42	−0.12	0.08	0.20	0.22	0.15	0
				$F_{1s}/F_c = 0.4$							
0.5–2.0	−0.98	−0.61	−0.30	−0.05	0.14	0.26	0.33	0.34	0.28	0.17	0
1.0	−0.77	−0.44	−0.16	0.05	0.21	0.31	0.36	0.35	0.29	0.17	0
				$F_{1s}/F_c = 0.6$							
0.5–2.0	−0.32	0.08	0.11	0.27	0.37	0.43	0.44	0.40	0.31	0.18	0
1.0	−0.18	−0.04	0.21	0.34	0.42	0.46	0.46	0.41	0.31	0.18	0
				$F_{1s}/F_c = 1.0$							
0.5–2.0	0.11	0.36	0.46	0.53	0.57	0.56	0.52	0.44	0.33	0.18	0
1.0	0.29	0.42	0.51	0.57	0.59	0.58	0.54	0.45	0.33	0.18	0

Four-way wye piece of the type $F_{1s} = F_{2s} = F_s$; $F_{st} = F_c$: $\alpha = 60°$[29,30]

Diagram 7-36

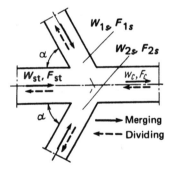

1. Merging of streams (outlet four-way piece)
Side branch

$$\zeta_{1c.s} \equiv \frac{\Delta p_{1s}}{\rho w_c^2/2} = 1 + \left(\frac{Q_{1s}}{Q_c}\frac{F_c}{F_{1s}}\right) - 8\left(\frac{Q_{1s}}{Q_c}\right)^2$$

$$\times \frac{[Q_c/Q_{1s} - (1 + Q_{2s}/Q_{1s})]^2}{4 - (1 + Q_{2s}/Q_{1s})Q_{1s}/Q_c}$$

$$- \left(\frac{Q_{1s}}{Q_c}\right)^2\frac{F_c}{F_{1s}}\left[1 + \left(\frac{Q_{2s}}{Q_{1s}}\right)^2\right]$$

see the table and the curves $\zeta_{1c.s} = f(Q_s/Q_c, Q_{2s}/Q_{1s})$ at different F_{1s}/F_c.
For the other side branch subscripts 1 and 2 change places.
Main passage

$$\zeta_{c.st} \equiv \frac{\Delta p}{\rho w_c^2/2} = 1 + \left(\frac{Q_{st}}{Q_c}\right)^2 - \left(\frac{Q_{st}}{Q_c}\right)^2\frac{1 + Q_{st}/Q_c}{(0.75 + 0.25Q_{st}/Q_c)} - \left(\frac{Q_{st}}{Q_c}\right)^2\frac{F_c}{F_{1s}}\frac{1 + (Q_{2s}/Q_{1s})^2}{(1 + Q_{2s}/Q_{1s})^2}\left(\frac{Q_c}{Q_{st}} - 1\right)^2$$

see the table and the curves $\zeta_{c.st} = f(Q_{st}/Q_c, Q_{2s}/Q_{1s})$ at different F_{1s}/F_c.

2. Division of flow (diverging four-way piece); $\zeta_{c.s}$ and $\zeta_{c.st}$ are determined tentatively as for diverging wyes from Diagrams 7-18 and 7-20.

Four-way wye piece of the type $F_{1s} = F_{2s} = F_s$; $F_{st} = F_c$; $\alpha = 60°$ [29,30]	Diagram 7-36

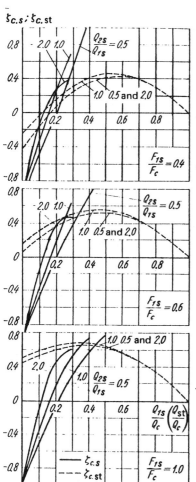

Values of $\zeta_{c.s}$

$\dfrac{Q_{2s}}{Q_{1s}}$	Q_{1s}/Q_c						
	0	0.1	0.2	0.3	0.4	0.5	0.6
	$F_{1s}/F_c = 0.2$						
0.5	−1.0	−0.31	0.59	2.00	3.62	5.54	7.72
1.0	−1.0	−0.20	0.80	2.07	3.30	4.77	−
2.0	−1.0	−0.09	0.62	0.97	−	−	−
	$F_{1s}/F_c = 0.4$						
0.5	−1.0	−0.47	−0.06	0.60	1.12	1.63	2.10
1.0	−1.0	−0.34	0.25	0.73	1.10	1.31	−
2.0	−1.0	−0.15	0.27	0.41	−	−	−
	$F_{1s}/F_c = 0.6$						
0.5	−1.0	−0.50	0.04	0.38	0.74	1.03	1.23
1.0	−1.0	−0.36	0.18	0.67	0.82	0.87	−
2.0	−1.0	−0.15	0.40	0.47	−	−	−
	$F_{1s}/F_c = 1.0$						
0.5	−1.0	−0.50	−0.07	0.30	0.58	0.79	0.88
1.0	−1.0	−0.36	0.16	0.53	0.74	0.75	−
2.0	−1.0	−0.13	0.46	0.61	−	−	−

Values of $\zeta_{c.st}$

$\dfrac{Q_{2s}}{Q_{1s}}$	Q_{st}/Q_c										
	0	0.1	0.2	0.3	0.4	0.5	0.6	0.7	0.8	0.9	1.0
				$F_{1s}/F_c = 0.2$							
0.5–2.0	−1.77	−1.02	−0.64	−0.30	−0.15	0.06	0.20	0.26	0.26	0.16	0
1.0	−1.50	−1.03	−0.64	−0.30	−0.05	0.13	0.24	0.29	0.26	0.16	0
				$F_{1s}/F_c = 0.4$							
0.5–2.0	−0.40	−0.14	0.07	0.24	0.35	0.41	0.42	0.39	0.30	0.18	0
1.0	−0.25	−0.02	0.16	0.31	0.40	0.44	0.45	0.40	0.31	0.18	0
				$F_{1s}/F_c = 0.6$							
0.5–2.0	0.06	0.23	0.36	0.46	0.51	0.52	0.50	0.43	0.32	0.18	0
1.0	0.16	0.32	0.43	0.51	0.55	0.55	0.51	0.44	0.33	0.18	0
				$F_{1s}/F_c = 1.0$							
0.5–2.0	0.44	0.54	0.60	0.65	0.65	0.62	0.56	0.47	0.34	0.18	0
1.0	0.50	0.59	0.64	0.67	0.67	0.63	0.57	0.47	0.34	0.18	0

Cross of the type $F_{1s} = F_{2s} = F_s$; $F_{st} = F_c$;   Diagram
$\alpha = 90°$ [29,30]   7-37

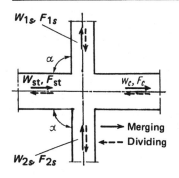

Main passage

$\zeta_{c.s}$; $\zeta_{c.st}$

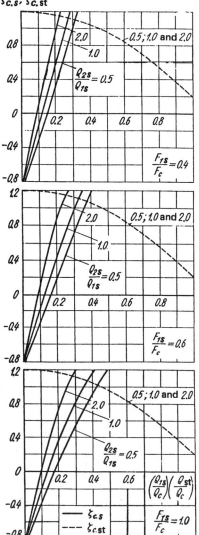

1. Merging of streams (converging cross)
Side branch

$$\zeta_{1c.s} \equiv \frac{\Delta p_{1s}}{\rho w_c^2/2} = 1 + \left(\frac{Q_{1s}}{Q_c}\frac{F_c}{F_{1s}}\right)^2$$
$$- 8\left(\frac{Q_{1s}}{Q_c}\right)^2 \frac{[Q_c/Q_{1s} - (1 + Q_{2s}/Q_{1s})]^2}{4 - (1 + Q_{2s}/Q_{1s})Q_{1s}/Q_c}$$

see the table and the curves $\zeta_{1c.s} = f(Q_{1s}/Q_c, Q_{2s}/Q_{1s})$ at different F_{1s}/F_c.

For the other side branch subscripts 1 and 2 change places.

$$\zeta_{c.st} \equiv \frac{\Delta p}{\rho w_c^2/2} = 1 + \left(\frac{Q_{st}}{Q_c}\right)^2 - \left(\frac{Q_{st}}{Q_c}\right)^2 \frac{1 + Q_{st}/Q_c}{(0.75 + 0.25 Q_{st}/Q_c)^2}$$

see the table and the curves $\zeta_{c.st} = f(Q_{st}/Q_c, Q_{2s}/Q_{1s})$ at all F_{1s}/F_c and Q_{2s}/Q_{1s}.

For standard crosses made of malleable iron at $Q_{st}/Q_c > 0.7$

$$\zeta'_{1c.s} \equiv \frac{\Delta p_{st}}{\rho w_c^2/2} = \zeta_{c.st} + 2.5\left(\frac{Q_{st}}{Q_c} - 0.7\right)$$

2) Flow division (diverging cross); $\zeta_{c.s}$ and $\zeta_{c.st}$ are determined tentatively as for diverging wyes from Diagrams 7-18 and 7-20.

Values of $\zeta_{c.s}$

$\dfrac{Q_{2s}}{Q_{1s}}$	Q_{1s}/Q_c						
	0	0.1	0.2	0.3	0.4	0.5	0.6
			$F_{1s}/F_c = 0.2$				
0.5	−0.85	−0.10	1.09	2.72	4.77	7.25	10.1
1.0	−0.85	−0.05	1.35	3.12	5.05	7.40	–
2.0	−0.85	−0.31	1.77	3.37	–	–	–
			$F_{1s}/F_c = 0.4$				
0.5	−0.85	−0.29	0.34	1.03	1.77	2.56	3.37
1.0	−0.85	−0.14	0.60	1.33	2.05	2.71	–
2.0	−0.85	0.12	1.02	1.68	–	–	–
			$F_{1s}/F_c = 0.6$				
0.5	−0.85	−0.32	0.20	0.72	1.22	1.70	2.13
1.0	−0.85	−0.18	0.46	1.02	1.50	1.85	–
2.0	−0.85	0.09	0.88	1.37	–	–	–
			$F_{1s}/F_c = 0.8$				
0.5	−0.85	−0.33	0.13	0.61	1.02	1.38	1.68
1.0	−0.85	−0.18	0.41	0.91	1.30	1.54	–
2.0	−0.85	0.08	0.83	1.26	–	–	–
			$F_{1s}/F_c = 1.0$				
0.5	−0.85	−0.34	0.13	0.56	0.93	1.25	1.48
1.0	−0.85	−0.19	0.39	0.86	1.21	1.40	–
2.0	−0.85	0.07	0.81	1.21	–	–	–

(Q_{st}/Q_c)	0	0.1	0.2	0.3	0.4	0.5	0.6	0.7	0.8	0.9	1.0
$\zeta_{c.st}$	1.20	1.19	1.17	1.12	1.05	0.96	0.85	0.72	0.56	0.39	0.20

Diagram 7-38

Straight diverging crosses with $\alpha = 90°$ made of roofing sheets,[40] Re $> 10^4$

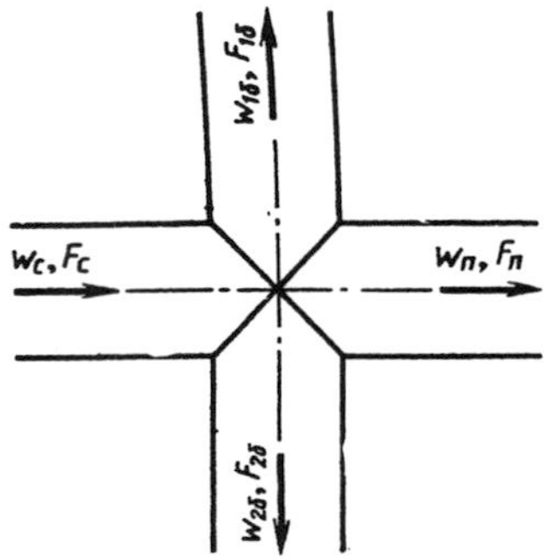

Side branching

$$\zeta_{c.s} \equiv \frac{\Delta p}{\rho w_c^2/2},$$ see the tables and graphs a and b.

Values of $\zeta_{c.s}$ at $Q_{1s}/Q_{2s} = 1$ (graph a)

F_s/F_c	F_{1s}/F_{2s}	w_s/w_c											
		0	0.2	0.4	0.48	0.6	0.8	1.0	1.1	1.2	1.4	1.6	1.8
1	0.445	1.0	0.80	1.4	2.1	–	–	–	–	–	–	–	1.8
0.445	0.445–1	1.0	0.80	0.80	0.80	0.85	1.4	3.0	5.6	–	–	–	–
0.284	0.84–1	1.0	0.80	0.78	0.80	0.83	0.95	1.2	1.4	1.7	2.6	5.0	7.6

Values of $\zeta_{c.s}$ at $Q_{1s}/Q_{2s} \neq 1$ (graph b)

F_s/F_c	F_{1s}/F_{2s}	w_s/w_c											
		0	0.4	0.8	1.2	1.4	1.6	1.8	2.0	2.2	2.4	2.8	3.4
0.445	0.64–1	0.5	0.75	0.90	1.3	1.4	1.6	1.8	2.0	2.2	2.4	–	3.4
0.284	0.64–1	0.5	0.75	0.90	1.3	1.5	1.75	2.2	2.6	3.0	3.4	4.2	5.4

Straight diverging crosses with $\alpha = 90°$ made of roofing sheets;[40] $Re > 10^4$ Diagram 7-38

Main passage

$$\zeta_{c.st} \equiv \frac{\Delta p}{\rho w_c^2/2}, \quad \text{see the tables and graph c and d.}$$

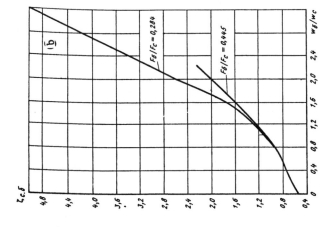

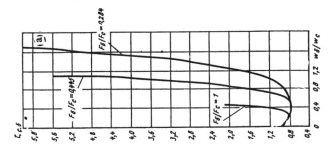

Values of $\zeta_{c.st}$ at F_{st} = const., at any F_{1s}/F_{2s} and any F_s/F_c (graph c)

w_{st}/w_c	0	0.1	0.2	0.3	0.4	0.5	0.6	0.7	0.8	0.9	1.0
$\zeta_{c.st}$	0.63	0.62	0.40	0.15	0	-0.05	-0.08	-0.08	-0.05	0	+0.05

Values of $\zeta_{c.st}$ in the presence of a conical transition in the main passage (graph d)

w_{st}/w_c	0	0.2	0.4	0.6	0.8	1.0	1.2	1.4	1.6	1.8	2.0	2.2
$\zeta_{c.st}$	0.6	0.55	0.45	0.25	0.10	0.05	0.05	0.05	0.07	0.10	0.17	0.2

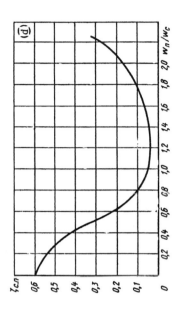

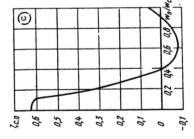

Header (diverging) box with transition sections[61]	Diagram 7-39

$\zeta_{i.s} \equiv \dfrac{\Delta p_{1s}}{\rho w_c^2/2}$, see the curves $\zeta_{i.s} = f\left(\dfrac{w_s}{w_{(i-1)c}}\right)$, where $w_{(i-1)c}$ is average velocity in the box before the ith branch.

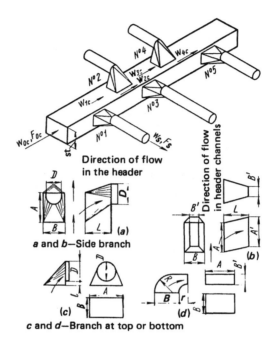

Direction of flow in the header

a and *b*—Side branch

c and *d*—Branch at top or bottom

Dimensions in the Scheme (h is the Height of the Box Cross Section)

Scheme	D	A'	B'	A	B	L	l	R
a	0.6–0.9h	–	–	≈1.7D	D	1–1.3D	–	–
b	–	1.15–1.25h	0.30–0.45h	1–1.5h	0.6–0.9h	0.6–1.1h	–	–
c	0.6–0.9h	–	–	≈1.7D	D	–	0.2D	–
d	–	1.15–1.25h	0.35–0.45h	1.15–1.25h	0.6–0.9h	–	–	0.6–0.9h 0.3–0.4h

Values of $\zeta_{i.s}$

Branching	$w_s/w_{(i-1)c}$							
	0.4	0.6	0.8	1.0	2.0	3.0	4.0	5.0
Side	4.30	1.60	0.88	0.60	0.24	0.20	0.19	0.18
Upper or lower	–	3.00	1.80	1.43	0.92	0.90	1.12	1.67

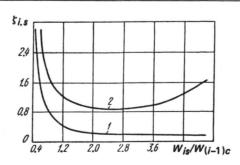

Outlet headers at $\alpha = 90°$ and $L/D_{h,in} < 150$ (without additional barriers in the channel);[50] $Re = w_{in}D_{h,in}/\nu \geq 10^4$	Diagram 7-40

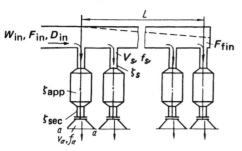

$$D_h = \frac{4F_{in}}{\Pi_{in}}$$

$0.9 \leq A_1' \leq 2.6$
$0 < K_1 < 0.3$:
$$\zeta \equiv \frac{\Delta p}{\rho w_{in}^2/2} \approx 2.63 - 0.54A_1'$$

$0.3 \leq K_1 < 0.6$:
$$\zeta \approx 2.28 - 0.51A_1' + 0.40K_1 + 0.0066L/D_{h,in} - 0.0015A_1'L/D_{h,in}$$

$0.6 \leq K_1 \leq 0.9$:
$$\zeta \approx 2.20 - 0.57A_1' + 0.60K_1 + 0.0086L/D_{h,in} - 0.002A_1'L/D_{h,in} = f(A_1'K_1L/D_{h,in})$$

where $A_1' = \overline{f}\, \dfrac{1}{\sqrt{0.6 + (f_s/f_a)^2 + \zeta_{sec} + \zeta_{app}}}$

$\zeta_{sec} \equiv \Delta p_{sec}/(\rho w_s^2/2)$; see the data of the handbook for corresponding section connected to side branches before and after the apparatus;

$\zeta_{app} \equiv \Delta p_{app}/(\rho w_0^2/2)$; see Chapter 12 or other literature sources of data for this type of apparatus (devices), adjacent to side branches; $\overline{f} = n_0f_s/F_{in}$ (n_0 is the number of branches); $K_1 = 1 - f_{fin}/F_{in}$.

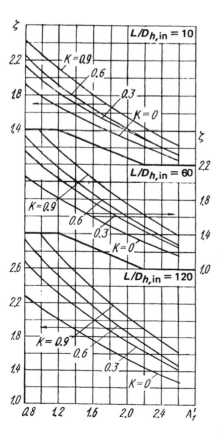

Values of ζ

K_1	\multicolumn{6}{c}{A_1'}
	0.4	0.6	0.8	1.0	1.2	1.4
\multicolumn{7}{c}{$L/D_{h,in} = 5-10$}
0	2.40	2.10	2.00	1.80	1.65	1.60
0.3	2.30	2.20	2.13	1.97	1.83	1.70
0.6	2.40	2.28	2.23	2.07	1.90	1.77
0.9	2.60	2.50	2.43	2.26	2.10	1.94
\multicolumn{7}{c}{$L/D_{h,in} = 60$}
0	2.30	2.10	2.05	1.93	1.80	1.70
0.3	2.40	2.30	2.20	2.18	2.04	1.90
0.6	2.70	2.55	2.45	2.33	2.16	2.00
0.9	3.00	2.85	2.70	2.56	2.37	2.20
\multicolumn{7}{c}{$L/D_{h,in} = 120$}
0	2.30	2.10	2.25	2.13	2.00	1.87
0.3	2.70	2.60	2.55	2.48	2.31	2.15
0.6	3.05	2.80	2.77	2.71	2.51	2.33
0.9	3.45	3.30	3.10	2.97	2.75	2.55

K_1	\multicolumn{6}{c}{A_1'}
	1.6	1.8	2.0	2.2	2.4	2.6
\multicolumn{7}{c}{$L/D_{h,in} = 5-10$}
0	1.50	1.38	1.30	1.20	1.13	1.07
0.3	1.59	1.48	1.39	1.29	1.20	1.12
0.6	1.65	1.59	1.41	1.31	1.20	1.12
0.9	1.80	1.67	1.54	1.43	1.33	1.23
\multicolumn{7}{c}{$L/D_{h,in} = 60$}
0	1.60	1.50	1.40	1.31	1.23	1.15
0.3	1.77	1.65	1.54	1.44	1.34	1.25
0.6	1.86	1.72	1.59	1.48	1.37	1.27
0.9	2.04	1.89	1.75	1.62	1.50	1.39
\multicolumn{7}{c}{$L/D_{h,in} = 120$}
0	1.75	1.65	1.55	1.44	1.35	1.27
0.3	2.01	1.87	1.75	1.63	1.52	1.41
0.6	2.16	2.00	1.85	1.72	1.59	1.47
0.9	2.37	2.19	2.03	1.88	1.75	1.62

Intake headers at $\alpha = 90°$;[50]	Diagram
$L/D_{h,in} < 150$; $Re = w_{in}D_{h,in}/\nu \geqslant 10^4$	7-41

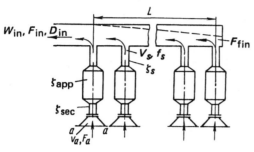

$D_{h,in} = \dfrac{4F_{in}}{\Pi_{in}}$

$0.2 \leqslant A_2' \leqslant 1.4$:

$$\zeta \equiv \frac{\Delta p}{\rho w_{in}^2/2} \approx \frac{1}{th^2\varphi} - 1$$

see the curves $\zeta = f(A_2', K_1)$, where $\varphi = 0.09 + 0.50A_2' + 0.02K_1 - 0.09A_2'K_1$

$$A_1' = \overline{f}\,\frac{1}{\sqrt{0.6 + (f_s/f_a)^2} + \zeta_{sec} + \zeta_{app}}$$

$\zeta_{sec} \equiv \Delta p_{sec}/(\rho w_s^2/2)$; see the data of the handbook for corresponding sections connected to side branches before and after the apparatus;

$\zeta_{app} \equiv \Delta p_{app}/(\rho w_s^2/2)$; see Chapter 12 or any other sources of data on apparatus (devices), adjacent to side branches; $\overline{f} = n_0 f_s/f_{in}$ (n_0 is the number of branches); $K_1 = 1 - F_{fin}/F_{in}$.

Values of ζ

K	A_2'							
	0.2	0.3	0.4	0.6	0.8	1.0	1.2	1.4
0	27.5	17.0	11.8	6.30	3.90	2.52	1.76	1.30
0.3	27.2	17.3	12.0	6.60	4.12	2.78	1.97	1.44
0.6	27.0	17.5	12.4	7.00	4.43	3.02	2.16	1.59
0.9	27.0	18.0	12.8	7.42	4.77	3.28	2.37	1.77

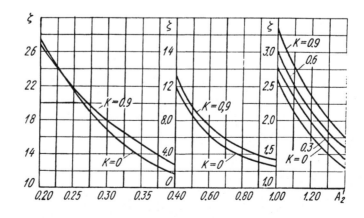

Π-shaped headers at $\alpha = 90°$; $L/D_{h,in} \leqslant 5.0$; $0.5 \leqslant F_{in}/F_{in}^* \leqslant 1.0$; $K_1 \leqslant 0.9$ for supply and $K = 0$ for intake channels;[50] $Re = w_{in}D_{h,in}/\nu \leqslant 10^4$	Diagram 7-42

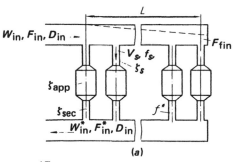

(a)

$$D_{h,in} = \frac{4F_{in}}{\Pi_{in}}$$

$\bar{f} = n_0 f_s/f_{in}$ (n_0 is the number of branches); $K_1 = 1 - F_{fin}/F_{in}$.

$0.54 \leqslant A_3' \leqslant 1.6$:

$$\zeta \equiv \Delta p/(\rho w_{in}^2/2) \approx 1/(0.788A_3' + 0.029K_1 + 0.115F_{in}/F_{in}^* - 0.130A_3'K_1 - 0.353A_3'F_{in}/F_{in}^* - 0.090)$$

$$\zeta = f(A_3', K_1, F_{in}/F_{in}^*)$$

$$A_3' = \bar{f}\frac{1}{\sqrt{0.6 + (f_s/f_s^*)^2 + \zeta_{sec} + \zeta_{app}}}$$

$\zeta_{sec} \equiv \Delta p_{sec}/(\rho w_s^2/2)$; see the data of the handbook for corresponding sections adjacent to side branches before and after the apparatus (device); $\zeta_{app} \equiv \Delta p_{app}/(\rho w_0^2/2)$; see Chapter 12 or other sources of data on apparatus (devices), adjacent to side branches;

Values of ζ

K_1	A_3'						
	0.5	0.6	0.8	1.0	1.2	1.4	1.6
	$F_{in}/F_{in}^* = 0.5$						
0	3.66	3.00	2.19	1.73	1.43	1.21	1.06
0.3	3.80	3.13	2.30	1.82	1.51	1.29	1.12
0.6	3.97	3.28	2.43	1.93	1.60	1.37	1.19
0.9	4.15	3.44	2.57	2.05	1.70	1.46	1.27
	$F_{in}/F_{in}^* = 0.75$						
0	3.88	3.22	2.41	1.92	1.60	1.37	1.20
0.3	4.05	3.38	2.55	2.04	1.71	1.46	1.28
0.6	4.23	3.56	2.70	2.18	1.82	1.57	1.38
0.9	4.44	3.76	2.88	2.33	1.96	1.69	1.49
	$F_{in}/F_{in}^* = 1.0$						
0	4.12	3.50	2.68	2.17	1.83	1.58	1.39
0.3	4.32	3.69	2.85	2.33	1.96	1.70	1.60
0.6	4.53	3.90	3.05	2.50	2.12	1.84	1.63
0.9	4.76	4.13	3.27	2.71	2.31	2.01	1.79

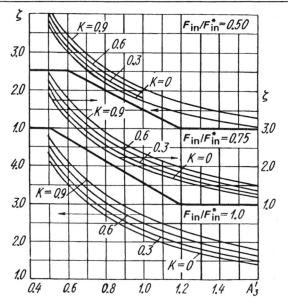

Z-shaped headers at $\alpha = 90°$ and $L/D_{h,\text{in}} \leqslant 50$; $0.5 \leqslant F_{\text{in}}/F_{\text{in}}^* \leqslant 1.0$; $K_1 \leqslant 0.9$ for supply   Diagram
and $K_1 = 0$ for intake channels;[50] $\text{Re} = w_{\text{in}}D_{h,\text{in}}/\nu \geqslant 10^4$ 7-43

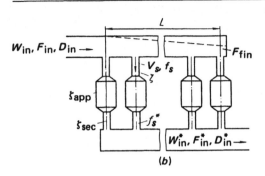

(b)

$$D_{h,\text{in}} = \frac{4F_{\text{in}}}{\Pi_{\text{in}}}$$

$0.54 \leqslant A_4' \leqslant 1.6$:

$$\zeta \equiv \Delta p/(\rho w_{\text{in}}^2/2) \approx 1/(0.692A_4' - 0.073K_1$$
$$+ 0.128F_{\text{in}}/F_{\text{in}}^* - 0.424A_4'F_{\text{in}}^* - 0.013)$$

$$\zeta = f(A_4', K_1, F_{\text{in}}/F_{\text{in}}^*)$$

$$A_4' = \overline{f}\ \frac{1}{\sqrt{0.6 + (f_s/f_s^*)^2 + \zeta_{\text{sec}} + \zeta_{\text{app}}}}$$

where $\zeta_{\text{sec}} \equiv \Delta p_{\text{sec}}/(\rho w_s^2/2)$, see the data of the handbook for corresponding sections adjacent to side branches before and after the apparatus (device); $\zeta_{\text{app}} \equiv \Delta p_{\text{app}}/(\rho w_s^2/2)$; see Chapter 12 or other sources of data for the given apparatus (devices) adjacent to side branches; $\overline{f} = n_0 f_s/F_{\text{in}}$ (n_0 is the number of branches); $K_1 = 1 - F_{d\text{in}}/F_{\text{in}}$.

Values of ζ

K_1	A_4'						
	0.5	0.6	0.8	1.0	1.2	1.4	1.6
$F_{\text{in}}/F_{\text{in}}^* = 0.5$							
0	3.44	2.95	2.30	1.88	1.59	1.38	1.22
0.3	3.72	3.15	2.42	1.96	1.65	1.43	1.25
0.6	4.05	3.39	2.56	2.05	1.71	1.47	1.29
0.9	4.44	3.66	2.71	2.15	1.78	1.52	1.33
$F_{\text{in}}/F_{\text{in}}^* = 0.75$							
0	3.70	3.25	2.62	2.19	1.88	1.65	1.47
0.3	4.03	3.50	2.78	2.30	1.96	1.71	1.52
0.6	4.42	3.79	2.96	2.42	2.05	1.78	1.57
0.9	4.89	4.14	3.16	2.56	2.15	1.85	1.62
$F_{\text{in}}/F_{\text{in}}^* = 1.0$							
0	4.02	3.63	3.04	2.61	2.29	2.04	1.84
0.3	4.40	3.94	3.25	2.71	2.41	2.14	1.92
0.6	4.87	4.31	3.50	2.95	2.55	2.24	2.00
0.9	5.46	4.76	3.79	3.15	2.70	2.36	2.09

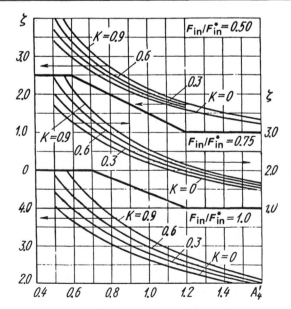

REFERENCES

1. Aslaniyan, O. I., Goldenberg, I. Z., Zyuban, V. A., et al., Study of the axial velocity fields in uptake wyes, *Izv. VUZov, Energ.*, no. 11, 110–116, 1987.
2. Bezdetkina, E. V., Specific features of operation of normalized wyes in industrial conditions, *Nauchn. Tr. Po Sanit. Tekh.*, vyp. 111, 83–88, Nizhne-Volzhsk. Izd., Volgograd, 1971.
3. Vasilevskiy, V. P., Determination of the resistance coefficient for two flows converging at different velocities by the method of the theory of turbulent jets, in *Technological Progress in the Design and Usage of Water Routes and Hydroengineering Constructions*, vyp. 176, pp. 15–19, Leningrad, 1983.
4. Gusev, V. M. and Rienas, F. R., Investigation of the paired installation of standard wyes having an orifice plate, in *Investigation in the Field of Heating, Ventilation and Air Conditioning* (Sb. Trudov LISI), no. 110, pp. 18–26, 1975.
5. Dashkiyev, Yu. G. and Polupan, G. P., The hydraulic resistance of diverging and converging wyes of type $F_c = F_{st} - F_s - F_w$, *Teploenergetika*, no. 7, 44–46, 1983.
6. Dergachev, B. A., The cases of the increase in the total head in the developed flow of a real fluid, *Collected Papers on Hydraulics*, vyp. 3, pp. 64–69, Moscow, 1980.
7. Dergachev, B. A., The specific energy balance equation in the case of the forced liquid flow division, *Tr. Leningr. Politekh. Inst.*, no. 333, 76–79, 1973.
8. Zubov, V. P., Investigation of Pressure Losses in Wyes with Converging and Diverging Flows, thesis (Cand. Sc. Eng.), Moscow, 1978, p. 165.
9. Zubov, V. P., Concerning the resistance of an ordinary wye with converging flows, *The Problems of Hydraulics (Sb. Tr. MISI)*, no. 124, 55–60, 1974.
10. Zubov, V. P., The physical meaning of the resistance coefficients of wyes with converging liquid flows, *Stroit. Arkhit. VNIIIC*, no. C, 25, 1981.
11. Zubov, V. P. and Drozdov, Ye. V., Investigation of the dependence of the resistance coefficients of wyes on Reynolds number, in *The Hydraulics of Blade Machines and the General Mechanics (Trudy VPI)*, pp. 107–112, Voronezh, 1974.
12. Zubov, V. P., Drozdov, Ye. V., and Kurganov, A. M., Concerning the negative resistance coefficient of diverging flows, in *Sb. Tr. LISI*, no. 5, pp. 56–62, Leningrad, 1976.
13. Zusmanovich, V. M., Resistance of wyes of sewage gas-water supplying pipes, *Vopr. Otoplen. Ventilyats.*, pp. 10–30, Gosstroiizdat, 1953.
14. Zyuban, V. A. and Goldenberg, I. Z., Investigation of head losses in intake wyes, "Bibl. Ukazaztel VINITI-deponir. n.r.", no. 80 (144), p. 130, 1983.
15. Idelchik, I. E., *Aerodynamics of Industrial Apparatus (Supply, Outflow and Uniform Distribution of the Flow)*, Energiya Press, Moscow, 1964, 289 p.
16. Idelchik, I. E., *The Aerohydrodynamics of Technological Apparatus*, Moscow, 1983, p. 350.
17. Idelchik, I. E., Towards determination of the hydraulic resistance of sections with division and joining of two-phase (multiphase) flows, *Izv. Vyssh. Uchebn. Zaved. Energ.*, no. 7, 1975.
18. Idelchik, I. E., Formulas for calculation of flow delivery along contracting, filtering and other Z-shaped apparatus and collectors, *Teor. Osn. Khim. Tekhnol.*, vol. 6, no. 2, 253–260, 1970.
19. Idelchik, I. E. and Shteinberg, M. E., Towards the methods of calculation of flow distribution along the channels with flow delivery along the path, *Teor. Osn. Khim. Tekhnol.*, vol. 6, no. 4, 603–610, 1972.
20. Kiselev, P. G., About the magnitude of the lost head in merging of flows, in *The Problems of Hydraulics and Water Supply, MISI*, no. 174, pp. 5–9, Moscow, 1980.
21. Klyachko, L. S. and Uspenskaya, L. B., Calculation formulas for normalized ventilation wyes and branching units of industrial air pipelines, *Tr. VNIIGSa*, vyp. 28, 25 45, 1970.
22. Klyachko, L. S. and Pustoshnaya, V. F., Investigation of the effect of some constructional elements of rectangular wyes on their aerodynamic characteristics, *Tr. VNIIGSa*, vyp. 28, 46–53, 1970.
23. Kozhevnikova, Ye. N., Mixing of Fluids in Pipelines with Different Means of Admixture Supply, thesis (Cand. Sc., Eng.), Leningrad, 1983, p. 168.
24. Kozhevnikova, Ye. N. and Loktionova, Ye. A., Losses of Head in Converging of Two Flows, *Tr. Leningr. Politekh. Inst.*, no. 401, 43–46, 1984.
25. Krivitskaya, N. A., Allowance for pressure losses in wyes in gas-distributing pipelines with a great number of branches,
26. Kuzmenko, L. M., Generalization of the Borda-Carnot formula to the case of merging of two flows with a nonuniform velocity field, in *Hydromechanics*, vyp. 40, pp. 39–43, Kiev, 1979.
27. Levin, S. R., Hydraulic resistance of welded crosses and wyes, *Vodosnabzh. Sani. Tekh.*, no. 4, 10–33, 1961.
28. Levin, S. R., Flow division in pipelines, *Tr. LTI im. S. M. Kirova*, no. 1(3), 86–103, 1948.

29. Levin, S. R., A new method of theoretical determination of hydraulic resistances during mixing of flows in pipelines, *Tr. LTI im. S. M. Kirova*, no. 6, 119–140, 1955.
30. Levin, S. R., Mixing of flows in crosses of pipelines, *Tr. LTI im. S. M. Kirova*, no. 5, 80–95, 1945.
31. Levin, S. R., Resistance of wyes of outlet air pipelines, *Otoplenie Vent.*, no. 10/11, 5–10, 1940.
32. Levin, S. R., Collision of incompressible fluid flows in pipelines, *Tr. LTI im. S. M. Kirova*, no. 8, 89–103, 1958.
33. Lyubanov, V. and Chakrov, T., Mazes correlated flow, *Teor. Prilozhno Mekhanika*, no. 2, 54–57, 1980.
34. Neikov, O. D., Alekseyev, A. G., and Koval, V. I., Local resistances and turbulence in joining and division of air flows, *Tr. Nauchno-Issled. Inst. Po Ventil. Ochistke Vozdukha Na Gornorudn. Predpr.*, vyp. 5, 37–45, 1969.
35. Neimark, L. I., Investigation of the resistance of wyes of high-velocity intake systems of air conditioning, *Tr. Nauchno-Issled. Inzh. Sanit. Tekh*, vyp. 18, 139–150, 1966.
36. Petrov, G. A., Hydraulics of the Variable Mass (Motion of Fluid with Flow Rate Variation Along the Path). Kharkov, 1964, p. 224.
37. Pruzner, A. S., Resistance of wyes during intake operation, *Sovrem. Vopr. Ventil.*, pp. 41–60, Stroiizdat, 1941.
38. Rekin, A. D., Hydraulic resistance in the course of flow separation into two parallel channels with an arbitrary flow rate ratio, *J. Eng. Phys.*, vol. 11, no. 5, 842–847, 1981.
39. Sekundov, A. N., Universal relationship between the losses, turbulization and mixing in a cylindrical channel, in *Turbulent Jet Flows*, pp. 104–108, Tallinn, 1982.
40. Sosin, M. L. and Neimark, L. I., Aerodynamic characteristics of straight intake crosses, *Issled. Raschyot. Proektir. Sanit. Tekh. Sistem, Akad. Nauk SSSR*, vyp. 2, 150, 1970.
41. Taliev, V. N., *Aerodynamics of Ventilation*, Gosstroiizdat, 1967, 288 pp.
42. Taliev, V. N., Pressure losses in an air conduit in the course of pressure division into two differently directed flows, *Izv. VUZov, Stroit. Arkhit.*, no. 5, 100–102, 1983.
43. Taliev, V. N., *Calculation of Local Resistances of Wyes*, Gosstroiizdat, 1952, 35 pp.
44. Taliev, V. N. and Tatarchuk, G. T., Resistance of rectangular wyes, *Vopr. Otopl. Ventil.*, pp. 50–80, Gosstroiizdat, 1951.
45. Tatarchuk, G. T., Local resistances of iron crosses, *Vopr. Otopl. Ventil.*, pp. 31–45, Gosstroiizdat, 1956.
46. Terentiev, N. I., Investigation of the mutual effect of wyes and side branches on local pressure losses in pipelines of central pumping installations, Transport, *Tr. TsNII MPS*, vyp. 43, 40–47, 1971.
47. Uliyanov, I. Ye., Krumilina, N. N., and Vokar, N. V., *Design of the Air Ducts of the Aeroplane Power Units*, Moscow, 1979, p. 96.
48. Uspenskaya, L. B., The resistance coefficient of normalized ventilation wyes in intake air pipelines, *Vodosnabzh. Sanit. Tekh.*, no. 2, 10–15, 1963.
49. Tsal, R. Ya. and Chechik, E. N., *Digital Machines Used for Calculations of Sanitary Systems*, Kiev, Budivelnik Press, 1968, 143 pp.
50. Shteinberg, M. E. and Idelchik, I. E., Investigation of the hydraulic resistance of collectors of variable cross section of gas purifying and other installations, *Prom. Sanit. Ochistka Gaz.*, no. 2, 1–5, 1973.
51. Boyar, R. E., Brown, W. K., Jr., and Nguyen, M. D., Friction loss characteristics of branch duct fittings with a fixed duct configuration, *Trans. ASHRAE*, vol. 72, part 1, 346–357, 1966.
52. Forney, L. J. and Lee, H. C., Optimum dimensions for pipeline mixing at a T-junction, *AIChE J.*, vol. 28, no. 6, 980–987, 1982.
53. Franke, P., Die zusätzlichen Verluste bei der Vereinigung von zwei Wasserströmen in einem gemeinsamen Steigschacht., *VDIZ.*, vol. 97, no. 24, 841–843, 1955.
54. Gardel, A., Les pertes de charge dans les branchements en Te des conduites de section circulaire, *Bull. Tech. Suisse Romande*, 96 year, no. 25, 363–391, 1970.
55. Haggenmuller, K., Beitrag ruz strömungs-und festigkeitsgünstigen Ausbildung von Abzweigen und Beileitungen, Bd. 133, 1973.
56. Ito, H., Sato, M., and Oka, K., Complete characteristics of energy losses due to division and combination of flow at a sorewed tee, *Trans. Jpn. SME*, vol. 44, no. 387, 3902–3907, 1978.
57. Ito, H., Sato, M., and Oka, K., Energy losses due to division and combination of flow at 90° wyes, *Trans. JSME*, vol. 50, no. 450, 342–349, 1984.
58. Iwanami, S., Suu Tetsuo, and Kato Kiroshi, Study of flow characteristics in right-angled pipe fittings, Ist. rept. on case of mater flow, *Bull. JSME*, vol. 12, no. 53, 1041–1050, 1969.
59. Kalis, J., Hydraulicke ztraty v odbocnicich rozdelovacich potrubi vodnich elektraren. *Vodohospod. Cas.*, vol. 12, no. 1, 48–77, 1964.
60. Kinne, E., Der Verlust in 60° Rohrverzweigungen, *Mitt. Hydraul. Inst. Tech. Hochschule, Munchen*, no. 4, 90–105, 1931.

61. Konzo, S. A. S., Investigation of the pressure losses of takeoffs for extended-plenum type air conditioning duct systems, *Univ. Ill. Bull. Bull. Ser.,* no. 415, 110–116, 1953.
62. Kramer, K., Der Druckabfall in einem laminar durch strömten, regelmássig verzweigten Rohrleitungssystem mit Anwendung auf den Blutkreislauf des Menschen, *Arch. Kreislaufforsch.,* vol. 52, no. 1–2, 79–95, 1967.
63. Kubo Toshisuke and Ueda Tatsuhiro, On the characteristics of divided flow and confluent flow in headers, *Bull. JSME,* vol. 12, no. 52, 802–809, 1969.
64. Lakshmana, R. N. S., Pressure losses at pipe trifurcations, *Water Power,* vol. 21, no. 8, 309–313, 1969.
65. Marchetti, M. and Noseda, G., Perdite di carico nelle biforcazioni simmetriche a diametro costante, della condotte forzate, *Energ. Elletr.,* vol. 37, no. 4, 289–301, 1960.
66. Petermann, F., Der Verlust in schiefwinkligen Rohrverzweigungen, *Mitt. Hydraul. Inst. Tech. Hochschule, Munchen,* no. 3, 100–120, 1929.
67. Platzer, B., Berechung von Druckverlusbeiwerten in rechtwinkligen Kreuzverzweigungen, Luft-und Kalte-technik, Bd. 18, n.4, 219–220, 239, 240, 1982.
68. Price, J. T., Chimney flow improvement, *Power Engineering,* pp. 52–55, September, 1967.
69. Rao, N. S., Lakshmana, R. B. C. S., and Ramaswamy, R. I., Pressure losses at trifurcations in closed conduits, *J. Hydraul. Div. Proc. ASCE,* vo. 93, no. 3, 51–64, 1967.
70. Rao, B. C. S., Lakshmana, R. N. S., and Shivaswamy, M. S., Distribution of energy losses at conduit trifurcations, *J. Hydraul. Div. Proc. ASCE,* vo. 94, no. 6, 1363–1374, 1968.
71. Rao, P. V. and Sharma, S. N. P., Energy loss at abrupt pipe trifurcations, *Univ. Roorkee Res. J.,* vol. 10, no. 3–4, part 1, 43–53, 1968.
72. Ruus, E., Head losses in wyes and manifolds, *J. Hydraul. Div. Proc. ASCE,* vol. 96, no. 3, 593–608, 1970.
73. Spielbauer, M., Die spezifischen Widerstände von Rohrverzweigungen und ihre Bedeutung fur dieintegration der Leistungsverluste sowie für die Querschnittsoptimierung, *Bautechnik,* vol. 40, no. 1, 19–26, 1963.
74. Spychala, F. U. S., Versuche zur Ermittlung von Druckverlusten in Rohrleitungen und Formstücken von Lüftungsanlagen, *Schifflauforschung,* vol. 7, no. 5–6, 216–222, 1968.
75. Shisholm, D., Calculate pressure losses in bends and tees during steamwater flow, *Eng. Boiler House Rev.,* vol. 82, no. 8, 235–237, 1967.
76. Tsao, S. and Rodgers, W., Numerical solutions of transients in pneumatic networks. Part 3. Network problems with branching, *Trans. ASME,* vol. 36, no. 3, 594–597, 1969.
77. Turton, R. K., Design of slurry distribution manifolds, *The Engineer Technical Contributors Section,* April, 29, 641–643, 1966.
78. Vogel, C., Untersuchungen über den Verlust in rechtwinkligen Rohrverzweigungen, *Mitt. Hydraul. Inst. Tech. Hochschule, Munchen,* no. 1, 1926, no. 2, 85–105, 1928.
79. Williamson, J. and Rhone, T. J., Dividing flow in branches and wyes, *J. Hydraul. Div.,* pp. 747–769, May, 1973.

RESISTANCE TO FLOW THROUGH BARRIERS UNIFORMLY DISTRIBUTED OVER THE CHANNEL CROSS SECTION
Resistance Coefficients of Grids, Screens, Porous Layers, and Packings

8-1 EXPLANATIONS AND PRACTICAL RECOMMENDATIONS

1. Barriers that are distributed uniformly over the cross section of tubes and channels and the create uniform resistance to flow consist of grids, screens, beds, fabrics, packings of Raschig rings, lumped or loose material, crosswise bundles of tubes, and so on.

2. The resistance created by plane grids (perforated sheets) placed in a straight tube is the same as that of flow passage through an orifice plate. When approaching the grid, the fluid contracts during its passage through the grid orifices and leaves the grid as separate jets entering the tube with higher velocity. Thus, there appear losses that are associated both with the entry into orifices and with the sudden expansion at their exit (Figure 8-1).

The resistance coefficient of a perforated plate (grid) depends on the free-area coefficient $\bar{f} = \Sigma f_{or}/F_{gr} = F_0/F_1$, the shape of the orifice edges, and the Reynolds number $\text{Re} = w_{or}d_{or}\nu$. It is calculated by the same equations that are used for an orifice plate, that is, Equations (4-7) through (4-27), respectively:

$$\zeta \equiv \frac{\Delta p}{\rho w_1^2/2} = f\left(\bar{f}, \frac{r}{d_{or}}, \frac{l}{d_{or}}, \text{Re}\right)$$

3. At small values of the free-area coefficient $\bar{f}$ of the perforated plate (grid), the velocity of the flow in the orifices and especially in the narrowest section of the jets in the orifices can turn out to be very high even at low inlet velocities. In some cases the velocity of the flow in the contracted section of the jets can approach sonic velocity (Mach numbers close to unity). Under these conditions the resistance coefficient of the grid becomes a function of the Mach number $\text{Ma}_1 = w_1/a$ (see paragraph 38 of Chapter 4), that is,

$$\zeta_M \equiv \frac{\Delta p}{\rho_1 w_1^2/2} = k_M\zeta$$

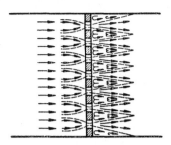

Figure 8-1 Pattern of flow through grid, perforated plate, and screen.

where k_M is the correction for the effect of the Mach number obtained on the basis of the experimental data of Cornell[63] (see Diagram 8-7), ζ is determined as in the case of $M_1 \approx 0$ by equations of Chapter 4, and w_1 is the average velocity of the flow before the barrier (grids, screens, and the like, m/s).

4. When designing perforated grids, one can make use of the following relationship between the number of orifices n_{or}, their transverse, S_1, and longitudinal, S_2, pitches, their diameter d_{or}, and the free-area coefficient $\overline{f}$ of the grid.

The number of orifices

$$n_{or} = \frac{1.27 \overline{f} F_{gr}}{d_{or}^2}$$

The distance between the orifices:

With in-line (rectangular) configuration (Figure 8-2a):

$$S_1 = \frac{0.785 \, d_{or}^2}{S_2 \overline{f}}$$

$$S_2 = \frac{0.785 \, d_{or}^2}{S_1 \overline{f}} \tag{8-1}$$

In the first of Equation (8-1) the known quantity is the pitch S_2, and in the second, the pitch S_1; in the particular case when $S_1 = S_2$, we have

$$S_1 = \frac{0.89 \, d_0}{\sqrt{\overline{f}}} \tag{8-2}$$

With staggered (triangular pitch) configuration of orifices at an angle θ (Figure 8-2b):

$$S_1 = \frac{0.63 \, d_{or} \sqrt{\tan \theta}}{\sqrt{\overline{f}}}$$

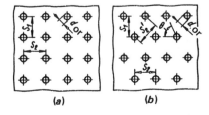

(a)   (b)

Figure 8-2 Disposition of orifices in a perforated plate (grid): (a) in-line, (b) staggered.

$$S_2 = \frac{1.25\, d_{or}}{\sqrt{f}\,\tan\theta}$$

In the particular case of equal distances between the orifices in both the transverse and diagonal direction ($S_2 = S_1'$; $\theta = 60°$) we obtain

$$S_1 = \frac{0.82\, d_{or}}{\sqrt{f}} \qquad S_2 = \frac{0.95\, d_{or}}{\sqrt{f}}$$

At $S_1 = S_2$, we obtain Equation (8-2).

5. The resistance coefficient of noncontaminated screens at large Reynolds numbers is

$$\zeta \equiv \frac{\Delta p}{\rho w_1^2/2} = k_0\left(1 - \frac{F_0}{F_1}\right) + \left(\frac{F_1}{F_0} - 1\right)^2 \tag{8-3}$$

For screens made of circular metal wires with a conventional (as received) surface (but neither rusty nor dusty) $k_0 = 1.3$ (according to Adamov); for new wire screens $k_0 = 1.0$; for silk-thread screens $k_0 = 2.1$.[49]

6. The resistance coefficients for circular-wire screens at Reynolds numbers $Re < 10^3$, and for silk-thread screens at $Re < 500$, can be determined from the following formulas.

● Screens made from circular wire

at $50 < Re < 10^3$

$$\zeta = k_{Re}'\zeta_{qu}$$

at $Re < 50$

$$\zeta \approx \frac{22}{Re} + \zeta_{qu}$$

● Screens made from silk threads

at $40 < Re < 500$

$$\zeta = k_{Re}''\zeta_{qu}$$

at $Re < 40$

$$\zeta \approx \frac{7}{Re} + \zeta_{qu}$$

where ζ_{qu} is determined as ζ from Equation (8-3); k_{Re}' and k_{Re}'' are determined from corresponding curves $k_{Re} = f(Re)$ of Diagram 8-6.

7. The resistance coefficient of two-plane screens (see Diagram 8-6) can be determined[34] as

$$\zeta \equiv \frac{\Delta p}{\rho w_0^2/2} = 1.28(1 - \overline{f})/\overline{f}$$

The nonuniform location of bars does not influence the resistance coefficient of the screen; it depends only on the total free area $\overline{f}$.[34]

8. The screens made of nichrome wire as a base, with a dielectric kapron thread of the same diameter ($d = 0.5$–1.2 mm) running crosswise, were investigated by Leibenzon[40] when installed at different angles to the flow ($\varphi = 0$–$75°$). With an increase in φ within 0–$45°$, the resistance coefficient of the screen grows relatively slightly. A sharp increase (almost double) occurs when φ increases from 45 to 60°. Then the coefficient ζ decreases again with a further growth of φ.

9. Just as in the case of grids, the stream velocity in the orifices of a screen with small free-area coefficients can approach the velocity of sound ($\mathrm{Ma}_1 = 1.0$). The effect of the Mach number Ma_1 is defined by

$$\zeta_\mathrm{M} \equiv \frac{\Delta p}{\rho_1 w_1^2/2} = k_\mathrm{M}'\zeta$$

where k_M' is the correction for the effect of the Mach number[67] (see Diagram 8-7).

10. a similar phenomenon can also be observed with other porous (filtering) materials. The values of the resistance coefficients of some of these obtained at very high pressures (up to 20 MPa) are given in Diagram 8-8 as a function of the Reynolds number.[58] This diagram also shows the curves $\overline{p} = \overline{p}_2/p_1$ vs. flow velocity w_1 for the same materials.

Neither the resistance coefficient ζ nor the pressure ratio $\overline{p}$ depends on the pressure p_1 in front of the porous material.

11. Theoretically, the installation of two screens close to each other should not lead to an increase in flow resistance, since if the wires of the two screens were accurately super-imposed, this would result in a screen of doubled thickness in the flow direction. In practice, however, the wires of both screens are partially displaced with respect to each other, and as a result the clear area decreases slightly and the resistance increases, but this increase is rarely twofold. When two screens are installed at some distance from each other (approx-imately above 15 wire diameters) the resistance of the screens doubles. Therefore, in practical calculations the total resistance coefficient of screens placed in series can be determined as a sum of the resistance coefficients of separate screens, that is,

$$\zeta_s = \sum_{i=1}^{n_s} \zeta_i$$

where n_s is the number of rows of screens.

12. When grids (screens) are used as bubbling trays (grid trays) in process apparatus where mass transfer occurs (rectification, sorption, wetting of gases, etc.; Figure 8-3), their resistance depends (1) on the conditions of tray operation (dry tray wetted by a liquid column over it with and without bubbling) and (2) on the physical properties of the working media and the tray dimensions.

13. The resistance coefficient of a dry tray is determined from the data given under paragraphs 2, 5, and 6 for an ordinary grid (screen).

The resistance of a wetted tray with small orifices is higher than the resistance of a dry tray, since a liquid forms in the orifices and its breaking requires a certain amount of energy of the gas (air) flow passing through the orifice.

The resistance coefficient of a wetted tray (with small orifices) can be calculated from the equation of Usyukin and Akselrod:[47]

$$\zeta \equiv \frac{\Delta p}{\rho_g w_0^2/2} = \zeta_\mathrm{dry}\left(\frac{F_0}{F_1}\right)^2 + 2 \times 10^{-4}\,\frac{\sigma/a_0}{\rho_g w_0^2/2}$$

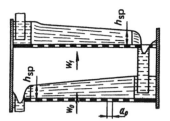

Figure 8-3 Screen trays in a rectification column.

where ζ_{dry} is the resistance coefficient of a dry tray determined as ζ for an ordinary grid (screen), see Diagrams 8-1 through 8-6; σ is the surface tension coefficient of a liquid at the gas-liquid interface, N/m; ρ_g is the gas density, kg/m³; a_0 is the radius of the circular orifice or the width of a slit in the tray, m; and w_0 is the average flow velocity in the clear area of the barrier (grid, screen, etc.), m/s.

14. The resistance coefficient of a tray under normal operating conditions with bubbling[47]

$$\zeta \equiv \frac{\Delta p}{\rho_g w_0^2/2} = \zeta_{dry}\left(\frac{F_0}{F_1}\right)^2 + \frac{2 \times 10^{-4}\ \sigma/a_0}{\rho_g w_0^2/2} + 4.9\frac{\rho_f}{\rho_w}\frac{h_{sp}}{\rho_g w_0^2/2}$$

$$+ 22.5\frac{\rho_f}{\rho_w}\left(\frac{Q_f}{l_{sp}}\right)^{2/3}\frac{1}{\rho_g w_0^2/2}$$

where ρ_w and ρ_f are the density of water and of the working fluid, kg/m³; h_{sp} and l_{sp} are the height and length of the spilling partition of the tray, m.

15. The resistance coefficient of bubbling trays without special spilling devices can be calculated, with sufficient accuracy for technical calculations, by the formula of Dilman et al.[44]

$$\zeta \equiv \frac{\Delta p}{\rho_g w_0^2/2} = 2\zeta_{dry}\left(\frac{F_0}{F_1}\right)^2\frac{1}{(1 - \bar{f})^3} + \frac{2\sigma/a_0}{\rho_g w_0^2/2}$$

The free-area coefficient $\bar{f}$ of the tray slits through which liquid flows down is

$$\bar{f}' = \frac{\sqrt[3]{(L_0/G_0)^2(\rho_g/\rho_f)[0.5/\zeta_{dry}(F_0/F_1)^2\rho_f^2]}}{1 + \sqrt[3]{(L_0/G_0)^2(\rho_g/\rho_f)[0.5/\zeta_{dry}(F_0/F_1)^2\mu_f^2]}}$$

where G_0 and L_0 are the mass flow rates of gas and liquid, respectively, kg/m² s; μ_f is the discharge coefficient of the liquid through a slit (orifice) of the tray.

16. Just as for ordinary thickened grids, the total losses in grids made of bars (bar gratings) with different cross-sectional shapes (see Diagrams 8-9 and 8-10) consist of the entrance losses, frictional losses, and losses for sudden expansion (shock losses) at the exit into the channel from the constricted cross section between the bars.

The resistance coefficient of gratings at $l/d_m = 5$ and $a_0/S_1 \geqslant 0.5$ can be determined from the equation of Kirschmer[69]

$$\zeta \equiv \frac{\Delta p}{\rho w_1^2/2} = \beta_1 k_1 \sin \theta \tag{8-4}$$

where β_1 is the coefficient of the shape of bars (see Diagram 8-9); $k_1 = (S_1/a_0 - 1)^{4/3}$, θ is the angle of bar inclination toward the flow; d_m is the width (diameter) of the midsection

of the grid bar, m; a_0 is the gap between two adjacent bars, m; S_1 is the distance between the axes of two adjacent bars, m; and l is the bar length, m.

17. The resistance coefficient of grids at any value of the free-area coefficient $f = F_{or}/F_0 = a_0/S_1$ and any relative depth of the gap (grid thickness) l/a_0 can be determined approximately from:

$$\zeta \equiv \frac{\Delta p}{\rho w_1^2/2} = \beta_2 \zeta' \sin \theta \tag{8-5}$$

where β_2 is the coefficient of the bar shape (see Diagram 8-9); ζ' is the resistance coefficient of an ordinary grid or orifice plate with thick-edged orifices, determined as ζ from the author's equation (4-12) or from Diagram 8-3.

18. When $a_0/S_1 \geq 0.5$, the resistance coefficient of a bar grating having any shape of the bar and placed immediately behind a flow turn at an angle of attack α_0^{22} is

$$\zeta \equiv \frac{\Delta p}{\rho w_1^2/2} = \sigma_1 \sigma_2 \tag{8-6}$$

where σ_1 is a coefficient that depends almost entirely on the angle of attack σ_0 (for the given shape of the bar, see graph a of Diagram 8-10); σ_2 is a coefficient that depends on the angle of attack σ_0 and on the free-area coefficient a_0/S_1 (see graph b of Diagram 8-10).

19. When bar gratings are used in hydraulic structures, the actual values of ζ for these gratings turn out to be higher than predicted, due to fouling of the gratings and their special design features. Therefore, Dulnev[15] recommends introducing into Equation (8-4), (8-5), and (8-6) the correction factor c', which allows for the nature and amount of rubbish contained in water, the method of cleaning the grid, the possibility of deposition of silt before the grid, and so on. In the case of mechanical cleaning of grids, $c' = 1.1–1.13$, and in the case of manual cleaning, $c' = 1.5–2.0$. It is recommended that the special design features be allowed for by the correction factor

$$c'' \approx \frac{1}{(1 - A/L)^2}$$

where L is the internal height of the grating, m; A is the total height of the transverse elements ($A = hn_1 + dn_2$), m; h and n_1 are the height and the number of intermediate support bars, m; and d and n_2 are the diameter and the number of bracing elements, m.

20. In the case of flow passage through a porous medium, a gradual transition is observed from a laminar to a turbulent regime. The smooth transition is due (1) to the tortuosity of the pores, contractions, and expansions and the surface roughness of the porous medium, which favors vortex formation and flow disturbances, and (2) to gradual propagation of turbulence from larger pores to smaller ones, which is associated with the size distribution of pores in the medium.

21. Porous media can be classified into three main groups:

- Cemented or bonded media (porous ceramics, coal, porous metal)
- Loose or unbonded media (powders, various lump materials, packings made from elements of regular geometric form: spheres, cylinders, rings)
- Gridlike or chordlike packings, packings of screens or meshes, tubes, corrugated strips, etc.

22. The porosity and magnitude of the gaps (the free-area coefficient) of a bed composed of identical spherical bodies are independent of the grain diameter; they are functions of the mutual disposition of grains, that is, of the angle θ (Figure 8-4):

$$\varepsilon' = 1 - \frac{\pi}{6(1 - \cos\theta)\sqrt{1 + 2\cos\theta}} \qquad \overline{f} = 1 - 0.25\pi/\sin\theta$$

23. For a layer of loose bodies or lumps of spherical or irregular shape the resistance coefficient can be calculated accurate to ± 20–35%* from the expression resulting from the verified[66] formula of Ergun:[64]

$$\zeta \equiv \frac{\Delta p}{\rho w_1^2/2} = \left[\frac{360(1 - \varepsilon')^2}{\varepsilon'^3 \mathrm{Re}_1} + \frac{B'(1 - \varepsilon')}{\varepsilon'^3}\right] l_0/d_{el} = \lambda l_0/d_{el} \tag{8-7}$$

where

$$\lambda \equiv \frac{\Delta p}{\rho w_1^2/2 l_0/d_{el}} = \frac{360(1 - \varepsilon')^2}{\varepsilon'^3 \mathrm{Re}_1} + \frac{B'(1 - \varepsilon')}{\varepsilon'^3} = \frac{A}{\mathrm{Re}_1} + B_1 \tag{8-8}$$

$\mathrm{Re}_1 = w_1 d_{el}/\nu$; $d_{el} = \varphi_1 d_{gr}$; d_{gr} is the mean size (diameter) of the body; φ_1 is the coefficient of the body shape; $B' = 1.8$ for bodies with a smooth surface; $B' = 4.0$ for bodies with a rough surface. The values of ε', d_m and φ_1 for bodies of different materials are given in Diagram 8-11.

24. The resistance coefficient of a bed made of bodies of irregular shape and also of rings, for which the hydraulic diameter of pores d_h is known, is

$$\zeta \equiv \frac{\Delta p}{\rho w_1^2/2} = \lambda \frac{1}{\varepsilon'^2} \frac{l_0}{d_h} \tag{8-9}$$

where, according to Ishkin and Kaganer[32] at $\mathrm{Re}_h \equiv (1/\varepsilon')(w_1 d_h/\nu) < 3$

$$\lambda = 180/\mathrm{Re}_h \tag{8-10}$$

and at $\mathrm{Re}_h > 3$

$$\lambda = 164/\mathrm{Re}_h + 7.68/\mathrm{Re}_h^{0.11} \tag{8-11}$$

Equations (8-9) through (8-11) can be used also for determining the resistance coefficient of the bounded porous material.

---

*This accuracy is relatively good if it is taken into account that the applicability of the proposed formula within the range of the Reynolds numbers from 10^{-1} to 10^3 varies the resistance coefficient by two orders (from 0.5 to 50).[4]

Figure 8-4 Relative position of spherical bodies in a packed bed.

Table 8-1 Values of ε' and $\bar{f}$

θ	60°	60°02′	61°18′	62°36′	64°03′	65°37′	
ε'	0.259	0.26	0.28	0.30	0.32	0.34	
f	0.0931	0.0977	0.1045	0.1155	0.1266	0.1337	
θ	67°21′	69°17′	71°28′	74°03′	77°10′	81°25′	90°00′
ε'	0.36	0.38	0.40	0.42	0.44	0.46	0.476
f	0.1491	0.1605	0.1719	0.1832	0.1946	0.2057	0.2146

25. The resistance of "regular" porous media, such as packings of Raschig rings laid in regular rows (Diagram 8-13) and chordlike packings of wooden laths laid in parallel (Diagram 8-14), is mainly determined by the frictional pressure losses in the absence of wetting by liquid.

The resistance coefficient of such packings can be calculated from Equation (8-19), where, according to the refined data,[16] within $0.4 \times 10^3 < \mathrm{Re}_{1h} < w_1 d_h / \nu \leqslant 8 \times 10^3$ (where Re_{1h} is based on the velocity upstream of the packing)

$$\lambda = \frac{3.2}{\mathrm{Re}_{1h}^{0.375}} \tag{8-12}$$

while for $\mathrm{Re}_{1h} > 8 \times 10^3$

$$\lambda \cong 0.11 = \text{const.} \tag{8-13}$$

where $d_h = 4\varepsilon'/\bar{s}$ is the hydraulic diameter of the gap between the rings, mm ($\bar{s}$ is the specific surface area of all the rings, m²/m³).

26. The resistance of packings of Raschig rings placed in staggered arrangement (see Diagram 8-13) and chordike packings placed crosswise (see Diagram 8-14), in the absence of wetting by liquid, is determined by both the frictional losses and the losses due to sudden contraction and expansion of the flow at the places of intersection of the packing rows.

27. The resistance coefficient of ceramic Raschig rings with outer-to-inner-diameter ratio $d_{\text{out}}/d_{\text{in}} \approx 1.2$ and relative height $l_r/d_{\text{out}} \approx 1.0$ with a staggered arrangement can be determined from Equation (8-9) where, within $0.4 \times 10^3 < \mathrm{Re}_{1h} \leqslant 6 \times 10^3$, λ is calculated from Zhavoronkov's equation[16] refined by the present author as

$$\lambda = \frac{9.6}{\mathrm{Re}_{1h}^{0.375}} \tag{8-14}$$

and for $\mathrm{Re}_{1h} > 6 \times 10^3$ by

$$\lambda \approx 0.36 = \text{const.} \tag{8-15}$$

With a certain approximation, Equations (8-14) and (8-15) can be extended to the rings of other dimensions as well.

28. The resistance coefficient of chordlike packings laid crosswise is calculated from Equation (8-9), in which, within $0.4 \times 10^3 < \mathrm{Re}_{1h} < 6 \times 10^3$, according to Zhavoronkov[16]

$$\lambda = \frac{k_1'}{\mathrm{Re}_{1h}^{0.375}} \tag{8-16}$$

and for $Re_{1h} > 6 \times 10^3$

$$\lambda = \lambda' = \text{const.} \tag{8-17}$$

where k_1' and λ' are taken as functions of the number of the grid (see Diagram 8-14).*

29. The resistance to the motion of a gas stream in a wetted packing is much higher than in a dry packing. The increase in resistance is due both to reduction of the free area by liquid and to gas bubbling through the liquid retained in the stagnant zones of the packing. The influence of the intensity of wetting on the resistance of packing increases with a decrease in the size of the elements in the packing.

30. When a gas moves in a counterflow direction through the wetted packing three regimes are observed: stable, when the liquid flows down completely; unstable, when at first entrainment (capturing) of the liquid occurs; and then liquid flow reversal, which leads to choking and expulsion of liquid out of the packing together with the gas. Retention and choking of the liquid occur at a gas stream velocity that becomes smaller, the larger the intensity A of wetting of the packing.[16]

31. The resistance coefficient of a wetted packing, ordered or disordered, before the onset of liquid retention—that is, at a velocity $w_1 \approx w_{1\text{lim}}$ at about $A = 50$ m³/(m² h)—can be approximately calculated on the basis of Zhavoronkov's[16] data by the formula

$$\zeta \equiv \frac{\Delta p}{\rho w_1^2 / 2} = \zeta_{\text{dry}}(1 + \tau' A) \tag{8-18}$$

where ζ_{dry} is the resistance coefficient of a dry packing determined as ζ from Equations (8-7)–(8-17); A is the intensity of wetting of the packing by the liquid, m³/(m² h); τ is a coefficent allowing for the effect of the type of packing on the increase in resistance due to wetting (see Diagrams 8-12 to 8-14); w_{lim} is the limiting velocity of the gas stream in a free section of the apparatus (before the packing) at which retention or choking of the liquid starts (see Diagrams 8-12 to 8-14).

32. The resistance of packings can increase sharply (by a factor of 2 to 3 or greater) if the gas passing through them is dust-laden; this should be taken into account in hydraulic calculations.

33. If the passage of a gas through the packing is accompanied by its cooling or heating, then the total resistance coefficient must include an additional term $\Delta\zeta_t$ allowing for acceleration (retardation) pressure losses by the flow within the bed as a result of the decrease (increase) in the density of the working medium:[43]

$$\zeta_t \equiv \frac{\Delta p}{\rho_m w_{1m}^2 / 2} = \zeta + \Delta\zeta_t$$

where ζ is determined from Equations (8-7)–(8-18) as

$$\Delta\zeta_t' = 2 \frac{T_{\text{ex}} - T_{\text{in}}}{T_m}$$

(for heating $\Delta\zeta_t$ is positive, while for cooling $\Delta\zeta_t$ is negative);

---

*For more detailed information on the geometry and resistance of granular beds and beds made from bodies of irregular shape, see the work of Aerov and Todes[3].

$$w_{1m} = w_1 \frac{T_m}{T_{in}} \qquad T_m = \frac{T_{in} + T_{ex}}{2}$$

$$\rho_m = \rho_0 \frac{273}{T_m} \qquad \mathrm{Re}_{1h} = \frac{w_{1m}d_h}{\nu}$$

w_{1m} is the flow velocity before the barrier front based on the arithmetic mean temperature T_m of the flow along this barrier, m/s; ρ_0 and ρ_m are the density of the passing medium at $T = 273$ K and that calculated on the basis of the arithmetic mean temperature T_m of the flow along the barrier, respectively, kg/m³; ν is taken depending on the arithmetic mean temperature T_m (t_m).

34. For dry filtration of gases (air) from highly dispersed dust, wide use is made of cloth filters. Unlike a cloth through which a clean (nondusty) gas passes, the resistance of the filtering cloth to a dust-laden gas increases with time. The explanation is that the pores of the cloth on the side of the dusty gas entrance are filled with dust particles, which form a "second" porous layer in the pores and on the cloth surface. As the pores are filled with dust particles the thickness of the dust layer on the surface increases, and the resistance of the filtering porous medium (cloth and dust) increases.

35. It is suggested[18] that the resistance of the dusty filtering cloth be considered as composed of two parts: $\Delta p'$, the resistance due to the dust left in the cloth, and $\Delta p''$, the resistance of the dust layer removed periodically when the cloth is cleaned.

Following this suggestion, Gordon and Aladzhalov[12] recommend that the total resistance of the dusty cloth be calculated from

$$\Delta p = (A_2 + B_2 p_d)\eta w_1$$

where A_2 is an experimental coefficient that depends on the kind of dust, type of cloth, and dust content*; B_2 is an experimental coefficient that depends on the bulk weight of dust and permeability of the dust layer l; p_d is the degree of dustiness of the gas, kg/m²; and w_1 is the filtration rate (specific loading on the cloth), m³/(m² s).

36. In certain cases the resistance of the dusty cloth is given in the form[50]

$$\Delta p = (A_3 + A_3')q^m$$

where A_3 and A_3' are proportionality factors that depend on the kind of dust, type of cloth, and dust content; $q = Q/F_1$ is the specific loading on the cloth, m³/m² s; and m is an experimentally determined quantity.

37. Porous materials used in contact, filtering, and other apparatus are frequently shaped in the form of a cylindrical layer (Figure 8-5). Specific losses, that is, pressure losses per unit thickness of the layer of a porous cylinder at the given liquid (gas) flow rate, vary with the thickness of the cylinder walls. In the case where the flow escapes outside, the flow velocity in the direction of escape decreases with an increase in the surface area of the cylindrical layer (diffuser effect), and consequently the specific losses become smaller. In the case of intake or suction, a reverse effect (converging passage effect) is observed.

---

*Some refinement of coefficients A_2 and B_2 is made by A. F. Grigoriev.[13]

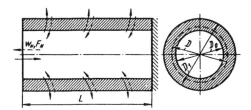

Figure 8-5 Layered (porous) cylinder.

38. In application to a cylindrical layer Equation (8-7) acquires[20,21,25] the following form:

$$\zeta_{in} \equiv \frac{\Delta p}{\rho w_{0in}^2/2} = \frac{\overline{f}(1 - \varepsilon')D_0}{\varepsilon'^3 d_{el}}$$

$$\times \left[\frac{180(1 - \varepsilon')}{Re_{in}} \ln \frac{D_1}{D_0} + \frac{\overline{f}B'D_0}{2D_1} \left(\frac{D_1}{D_0} - 1 \right) \right]$$

and

$$\zeta_{ex} \equiv \frac{\Delta p}{\rho w_{0ex}^2/2} = \frac{\overline{f}(1 - \varepsilon')D_1}{\varepsilon'^3 d_{el}}$$

$$\times \left[\frac{180(1 - \varepsilon')}{Re_{ex}} \ln \frac{D_1}{D_0} + \frac{\overline{f}B'}{2} \left(\frac{D_1}{D_0} - 1 \right) \right]$$

whereas Equations (8-10) and (8-11) become: at $Re_h < 3$, respectively,

$$\zeta_{in} \equiv \frac{\Delta p}{\rho w_{0in}^2/2} = \frac{90}{Re_{h,in}} \frac{D_0}{d_h} \ln \frac{D_1}{D_0}$$

or

$$\zeta_{ex} \equiv \frac{\Delta p}{\rho w_{0ex}^2/2} = \frac{90}{Re_{h,ex}} \frac{D_1}{d_h} \ln \frac{D_1}{D_0}$$

$3 < Re_h < 1000$:

$$\zeta_{in} \equiv \frac{\Delta p}{\rho w_{0in}^2/2} = \frac{82}{Re_{h,in}} \frac{D_0}{d_h} \ln \frac{D_1}{D_0} + \frac{4.31}{Re_{h,in}^{0.11}} \frac{D_0^{1.89}}{d_h D_1^{0.89}} \left[\left(\frac{D_1}{D_0} \right)^{0.89} - 1 \right]$$

or

$$\zeta_{ex} \equiv \frac{\Delta p}{\rho w_{0ex}^2/2} = \frac{82}{Re_{h,ex}} \frac{D_1}{d_h} \ln \frac{D_1}{D_0} + \frac{4.31}{Re_{h,ex}^{0.11}} \frac{D_1}{d_h} \left[\left(\frac{D_1}{D_0} \right)^{0.89} - 1 \right]$$

where

$$Re_{in} \equiv \frac{w_{0in}d_{el}}{\nu} ; \qquad Re_{ex} \equiv \frac{w_{0ex}d_{el}}{\nu}$$

$$Re_{hin} \equiv \frac{w_{0in}d_h}{\nu} ; \qquad Re_{hex} \equiv \frac{w_{0ex}d_h}{\nu}$$

w_{0in} and w_{0ex} are the mean flow velocities in the free area of the layer at the inlet to and exit from the layer, in m/s.

39. The above equations do not allow for a certain difference between the resistances of the cylindrical layer in the case of flow discharge and intake or suction. In the former, the resistance coefficient calculated at the same velocity is smaller (due to the diffuser effect) than in the second case (due to the converging passage effect). Experiments show that when the relative thickness of the layer is not very great, this difference can amount to 20% or more.

40. If the approach velocities are nonuniformly distributed over the cross section, then the barriers, uniformly distributed over the channel cross section, exert an equalizing effect on the incoming flow. The barriers (different grids, screens, beds of loose or lump materials, fabrics, etc.), creating a resistance, make the incoming medium (liquid, gas) spread over the front of the barrier and simultaneously cross it through orifices (channels).

41. The degree of the equalizing action of such barriers depends on their geometric parameters (free-area coefficient, relative thickness of the bed, etc). Since these parameters determine the resistance coefficient of the barriers, the resulting degree of equalizing action (the degree of flow medium spreading) is a function of the resistance coefficient. The higher the resistance coefficient of the barrier, the greater is the degree of flow medium spreading over its front. However, plane (thin-walled) grids (such as perforated sheets, wire or other screens, or fabric), unlike three-dimensional (deep) barriers (beds of loose or lumpy materials, tubular gratings, etc.) are notable for their specific features: when a certain (limiting or "critical") value of the resistance coefficient in the cross sections is attained at a finite distance downstream of a plane grid, the velocity profile becomes "overturned" ("reversed"), that is, there is a new nonuniformity of the flow at which the maximum of the velocities downstream of the grid corresponds to the maximum of the velocities in front of it and vice versa (Figure 8-6).[20,21,28,29]

42. This can be explained as follows. When the medium speads over the front of the grid, the streamlines become distorted. Since the grid is thin—that is, its orifices have no directing surfaces—then the transverse (radial) direction of streamlines is retained after the medium has passed through the orifices. This, however, causes further spreading of the medium, that is, motion in the radial direction. The higher the resistance coefficient of the grid, the sharper is the distortion of streamlines during spreading of the jet over the grid front, and consequently the greater is the departure of the jets issuing from the orifices to the periphery of the grid. With increases of the resistance coefficient of the grid up to a certain value, there arrives a time when all of the jets begin to depart to the periphery, moving further translationally only along the channel wall, while the central portion of the

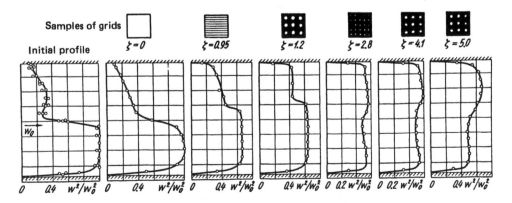

Figure 8-6 Flow profiles with regular nonuniform grids (according to Taganov).

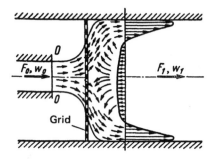

Figure 8-7 Flow schematic of incidence of a narrow jet on a perforated grid in a tube.

cross section not only becomes free of the translational velocity, but also contains reverse currents entrained by the circumferential jets (Figure 8-7). Thus the "overturned" velocity profile develops downstream of the grid.[20,21]

8-2 DIAGRAMS OF THE RESISTANCE COEFFICIENTS

Thin-walled grid of perforated sheets of strips with sharp-edged orifices $(l/D_h = 0\text{--}0.015);$[22-24,26,30] $\mathrm{Re} = w_0 d_h/\nu \geqslant 10^5$*	Diagram 8-1

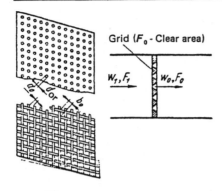

Grid (F_0 - Clear area)

$w_1, F_1 \quad w_0, F_0$

$$\zeta \equiv \frac{\Delta p}{\rho w_i^2/2} = [0.707(1 - \overline{f})^{0.375} + 1 - \overline{f}]^2 \frac{1}{\overline{f}^2} = f(\overline{f})$$

see the table and the graph.

$\overline{f}$	ζ	$\overline{f}$	ζ	$\overline{f}$	ζ
0.02	7083	0.22	41.8	0.50	4.37
0.03	3089	0.24	33.8	0.52	3.81
0.04	1716	0.26	27.7	0.55	3.10
0.05	1081	0.28	23.0	0.60	2.24
0.06	733	0.30	19.2	0.65	1.60
0.08	402	0.32	16.2	0.70	1.13
0.10	250	0.34	13.8	0.75	0.79
0.12	168	0.36	11.8	0.80	0.54
0.14	119	0.38	10.1	0.85	0.34
0.16	88.1	0.40	8.75	0.90	0.19
0.18	67.2	0.42	7.57	0.95	0.09
0.20	52.6	0.45	6.12		
		0.47	5.31	1.00	0

$$d_h = \frac{4 f_0}{\Pi_0}$$

$$\overline{f} = \frac{F_0}{F_1} = \frac{\Sigma f_{or}}{F_1}$$

f_{or} is the area of one orifice;
F_0 is the clear area of the grid.
Π_0 is the perimeter of the orifice.

*The author's formulas given in Diagrams 8-1 through 8-4 have been somewhat refined (see Chapter 4).

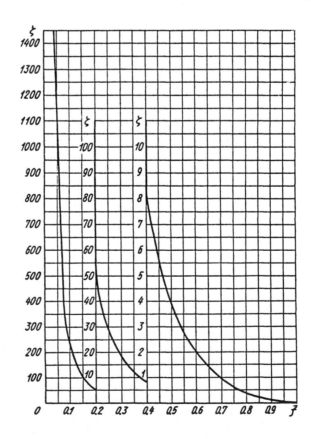

Grid with orifice edges beveled facing the flow or grid made with iron corners with the apex facing the flow;[22-24,26,30] Re $= w_0 d_h/\nu > 10^4$	Diagram 8-2

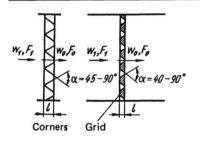

Corners Grid

$$\zeta \equiv \frac{\Delta p}{\rho w_1^2/2} = [\sqrt{\zeta'}(1 - \bar{f})^{0.375} + (1 - \bar{f})]^2/\bar{f}^2$$

where $\zeta' = f(l/d_h)$, see the table or graph a of Diagram 4-13;

$$\zeta = f\left(\bar{f}, \frac{l}{d_h}\right) \quad \text{see the graph.}$$

$$d_h = \frac{4f_{or}}{\Pi_0} \quad \bar{f} = \frac{F_0}{F_1} = \frac{\Sigma f_{or}}{F_1}$$

f_{or} is the area of one orifice;
F_0 is the clear area of the grid.
Π_0 is the perimeter of the orifice.

Values of ζ

l/d_h	ζ'	\multicolumn{17}{c}{$\bar{f}$}
		0.02	0.04	0.06	0.08	0.10	0.15	0.20	0.25	0.30	0.40	0.50	0.60	0.70	0.80	0.90	1.0
0.01	0.46	6840	1656	708	388	241	98.2	50.7	29.5	18.5	8.39	4.18	2.13	1.08	0.51	0.18	0
0.02	0.42	6592	1598	682	374	232	94.5	48.7	28.4	17.8	8.05	4.00	2.03	1.02	0.48	0.17	0
0.03	0.38	6335	1535	655	360	223	90.6	46.7	27.2	17.0	7.69	3.80	1.93	0.97	0.45	0.16	0
0.04	0.35	6140	1488	635	348	216	87.7	45.2	26.2	16.4	7.40	3.66	1.84	0.92	0.43	0.15	0
0.06	0.29	5737	1387	592	325	201	81.5	41.9	24.4	15.2	6.83	3.35	1.68	0.83	0.38	0.13	0
0.08	0.23	5300	1281	546	300	185	75.0	38.5	22.3	13.9	6.20	3.02	1.51	0.74	0.33	0.11	0
0.12	0.16	4748	1147	488	267	165	66.7	34.1	19.7	12.2	5.40	2.61	1.29	0.62	0.27	0.09	0
0.16	0.13	4477	1081	460	251	155	62.7	32.0	18.4	11.4	5.02	2.42	1.18	0.56	0.24	0.08	0

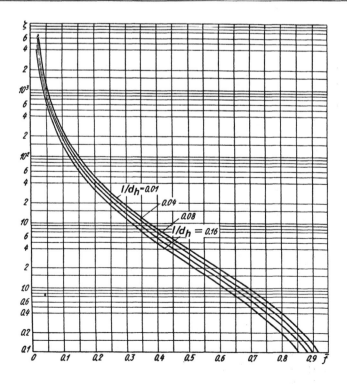

Grid made of thickened laths or perforated thick plate $(l/d_h > 0.015)$;[22-24,26,30] $Re = w_0 d_h/\nu \geqslant 10^5$	Diagram 8-3

Grid (F_0 - Clear area)

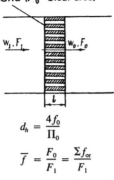

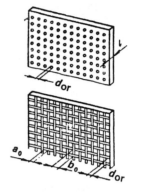

$$d_h = \frac{4 f_0}{\Pi_0}$$

$$\bar{f} = \frac{F_0}{F_1} = \frac{\Sigma f_{or}}{F_1}$$

f_{or} is the area of one orifice; F_0 is the clear area of the grid; Π_0 is the perimeter of the orifice.

Values of ζ_1 at $\lambda = 0.02$

$\bar{l} = \dfrac{l}{d_h}$	τ	$\bar{f}$															
		0.02	0.04	0.06	0.08	0.10	0.15	0.20	0.25	0.30	0.40	0.50	0.60	0.70	0.80	0.90	1.00
0	1.35	6915	1676	716	394	244	99.5	51.4	30.0	18.8	8.56	4.27	2.19	1.11	0.53	0.19	0
0.2	1.22	6613	1602	684	376	233	95.0	49.0	28.6	18.0	8.17	4.08	2.09	1.07	0.51	0.19	0
0.4	1.10	6227	1533	655	360	223	91.0	47.0	27.4	17.2	7.83	3.92	2.01	1.03	0.50	0.19	0.01
0.6	0.84	5708	1382	591	324	201	81.9	42.3	24.6	15.5	7.04	3.53	1.82	0.94	0.46	0.18	0.01
0.8	0.42	4695	1137	486	266	165	67.2	34.6	20.2	12.7	5.77	2.90	1.50	0.78	0.39	0.16	0.02
1.0	0.24	4268	1033	441	242	150	61.0	31.4	18.3	11.5	5.24	2.64	1.37	0.72	0.37	0.16	0.02
1.4	0.10	3948	956	408	224	139	56.4	29.1	17.0	10.7	4.86	2.45	1.29	0.68	0.36	0.16	0.03
2.0	0.02	3783	916	391	215	133	54.1	27.9	16.3	10.2	4.68	2.38	1.26	0.68	0.36	0.17	0.04
3.0	0	3783	916	391	215	133	54.3	28.0	16.4	10.3	4.75	2.43	1.30	0.71	0.39	0.20	0.06
4.0	0	3833	929	397	218	135	55.2	28.6	16.7	10.6	4.88	2.51	1.35	0.75	0.42	0.22	0.08
5.0	0	3883	941	402	221	137	56.0	29.0	17.0	10.8	5.00	2.59	1.41	0.79	0.45	0.24	0.10
6.0	0	3933	954	408	224	139	56.9	29.6	17.4	11.0	5.12	2.67	1.46	0.83	0.48	0.27	0.12
7.0	0	3983	966	413	227	141	57.8	30.0	17.7	11.2	5.25	2.75	1.52	0.87	0.51	0.29	0.14
8.0	0	4033	979	419	231	143	58.7	30.6	18.0	11.4	5.38	2.83	1.57	0.91	0.54	0.32	0.16
9.0	0	4083	991	424	234	145	59.6	31.0	18.3	11.6	5.50	2.91	1.63	0.96	0.58	0.34	0.18
10.0	0	4133	1004	430	237	147	60.5	31.6	18.6	11.9	5.62	3.00	1.68	0.99	0.61	0.37	0.20

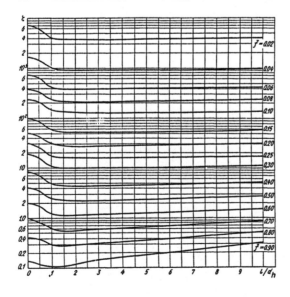

$$\zeta_1 \equiv \frac{\Delta p}{\rho w_1^2/2}$$

$$= \left[0.5(1 - \bar{f})^{0.75} + \tau(1 - \bar{f})^{1.375} + (1 - \bar{f})^2 + \lambda \frac{l}{d_h} \right] \Big/ \bar{f}^2$$

where for τ see the table or determine from the formula

$$\tau = (2.4 - \bar{l})^{\varphi(\bar{l})};$$

$$\varphi(\bar{l}) = 0.25 + 0.535\bar{l}^8/(0.05 + \bar{l}^7)$$

For $\zeta_1 = f(\bar{l}, \bar{f})$ at $\lambda = 0.02$ see the table and the graph

Grid with rounded orifice edges;[22-24,26,30]

Re $= w_0 d_h / \nu \geq 3 \times 10^3$

Diagram
8-4

$$\zeta_1 \equiv \frac{\Delta p}{\rho w_1^2/2} = [\sqrt{\bar{\zeta}'}(1 - \bar{f})^{0.75} + (1 - \bar{f})^2]/\bar{f}^2$$

where for ζ', see the table below, graph b of Diagram 4-13 or the formula

$$\zeta' = 0.03 + 0.47 \times 10^{-7.7\bar{r}}, \quad \bar{r} = r/d_h$$

$d_h = \dfrac{4f_0}{\Pi_0}$

$\bar{f} = \dfrac{F_0}{F_1} = \dfrac{\Sigma f_{or}}{F_1}$

f_{or} is the area of one orifice;
F_0 is the clear area of the grid.
Π_0 is the perimeter of the orifice.

Values of ζ_1

r/d_h	ζ'	$\bar{f}$																			
		0.02	0.04	0.06	0.08	0.10	0.15	0.20	0.25	0.30	0.35	0.40	0.45	0.50	0.55	0.60	0.65	0.70	0.75	0.80	0.90	1.0
0.01	0.44	6717	1628	695	382	236	96.4	49.7	29.0	18.2	12.0	8.24	5.75	4.10	2.91	2.08	1.49	1.05	0.73	0.49	0.18	0
0.02	0.37	6273	1520	648	356	221	89.7	46.2	26.9	16.8	11.1	7.59	5.29	3.75	2.65	1.90	1.35	0.95	0.66	0.44	0.15	0
0.03	0.31	5875	1421	607	332	206	83.6	43.0	25.0	15.6	10.3	7.01	4.87	3.45	2.43	1.74	1.23	0.86	0.59	0.40	0.14	0
0.04	0.26	5520	1336	570	312	193	78.3	40.2	23.4	14.6	9.54	6.51	4.51	3.19	2.24	1.60	1.13	0.79	0.54	0.36	0.12	0
0.06	0.19	4982	1206	513	281	174	70.3	36.0	20.8	12.9	8.46	5.76	3.97	2.79	1.96	1.38	0.97	0.67	0.46	0.30	0.10	0
0.08	0.15	4657	1125	479	262	162	65.3	33.4	19.3	12.0	7.80	5.29	3.63	2.55	1.78	1.25	0.88	0.60	0.41	0.26	0.08	0
0.12	0.09	4085	986	420	229	141	56.8	29.0	16.6	10.2	6.65	4.48	3.06	2.14	1.48	1.03	0.71	0.48	0.33	0.21	0.06	0
0.16	0.06	3745	902	384	210	129	51.8	26.3	15.0	9.26	5.99	4.02	2.73	1.90	1.31	0.91	0.62	0.42	0.28	0.17	0.05	0

Grid with rounded orifice edges;[22,24,26,30]

$Re = w_0 d_h / \nu \geq 3 \times 10^3$

Diagram
8-4

Grids with different shapes of orifice edges; transitional and laminar regions of flow (Re $= w_0 d_h/\nu < 10^4-10^5$), tentatively[30]	Diagram 8-5

Grid (F_0 - Clear area)

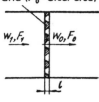

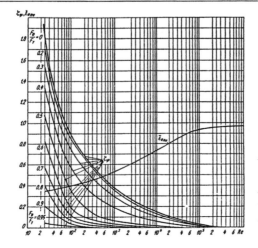

$$d_h = \frac{4f_{or}}{\Pi_0}$$

$$\overline{f} = \frac{F_0}{F_1} = \frac{\Sigma f_{or}}{F_1}$$

f_{or} is the area of one orifice;
F_0 is the clear area of the grid.
Π_0 is the perimeter of the orifice.

1. $30 < \text{Re} < 10^4-10^5$:

$$\zeta_1 \equiv \frac{\Delta p}{\rho w_1^2/2} = \frac{\zeta_\phi}{\overline{f}^2} + \overline{\varepsilon}_{0\text{Re}}\zeta_{1\text{qu}}$$

2. $10 < \text{Re} < 30$:

$$\zeta_1 = \frac{33}{(\text{Re }\overline{f}^2)} + \overline{\varepsilon}_{0\text{Re}}\zeta_{1\text{qu}}$$

3. $\text{Re} < 10$:

$$\zeta_1 = \frac{33}{(\text{Re }\overline{f}^2)}$$

where $\zeta_\phi = f_1(\text{Re}, F_1/F_0)$ and $\overline{\varepsilon}_{0\text{Re}} = f_2(\text{Re})$, see the tables, or determine from the formulas given below $\zeta_{1\text{qu}}$ is determined as ζ_1 at Re $> 10^4-10^5$ from Diagrams 8-1, and 8-4.

$$\zeta_\phi = [18.78 - 7.768/\overline{f} + 6.337/\overline{f}^2]\exp\{(-0.942 - 7.246\overline{f} - 3.878\overline{f}^2)\lg \text{Re}\}$$

Re	10	20	30	40	60	80	10^2	2×10^2	4×10^2	6×10^2	10^3	2×10^3
$\overline{\varepsilon}_{0\text{Re}}$	0.34	0.35	0.36	0.37	0.40	0.43	0.45	0.52	0.58	0.62	0.65	0.69

Re	4×10^3	6×10^3	10^4	2×10^4	4×10^4	6×10^4	10^5	2×10^5	3×10^5	4×10^5
$\overline{\varepsilon}_{0\text{Re}}$	0.74	0.76	0.80	0.82	0.85	0.87	0.90	0.95	0.98	1.0

Values of ζ_ϕ

$\dfrac{F_0}{F_1}$														
0	1.94	1.38	1.14	0.89	0.69	0.64	0.39	0.30	0.22	0.15	0.11	0.0	0.01	0
0.2	1.78	1.36	1.05	0.85	0.67	0.57	0.36	0.26	0.20	0.13	0.09	0.03	0.01	0
0.3	1.57	1.16	0.88	0.75	0.57	0.43	0.30	0.22	0.17	0.10	0.07	0.02	0.01	0
0.4	1.35	0.99	0.79	0.57	0.40	0.28	0.19	0.14	0.10	0.06	0.04	0.02	0.01	0
0.5	1.10	0.75	0.55	0.34	0.19	0.12	0.07	0.05	0.03	0.02	0.01	0.01	0.01	0
0.6	0.85	0.56	0.30	0.19	0.10	0.06	0.03	0.02	0.01	0.01	0	0	0	0
0.7	0.58	0.37	0.23	0.11	0.06	0.03	0.02	0.01	0	0	0	0	0	0
0.8	0.40	0.24	0.13	0.06	0.03	0.02	0.01	0	0	0	0	0	0	0
0.9	0.20	0.13	0.08	0.03	0.01	0	0	0	0	0	0	0	0	0
0.95	0.03	0.03	0.02	0	0	0	0	0	0	0	0	0	0	0

Screens[24,26,34,49]   Diagram
                                                                       8-6

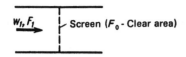

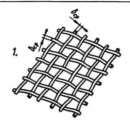

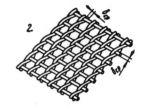

$$\overline{f} = \frac{F_0}{F_1} = \frac{\Sigma f_{or}}{F_1}$$

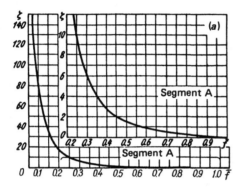

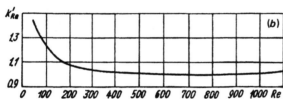

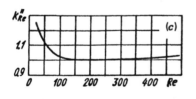

1. Circular metal wire

$$Re = \frac{w_0 \delta_m}{\nu} \geq 10^3$$

$$\zeta_{wir} \equiv \frac{\Delta p}{\rho w_1^2/2}$$

$$= 1.3(1 - \overline{f}) + \left(\frac{1}{\overline{f}} - 1\right)^2$$

see graph a; $50 < Re < 10^3$:

$$\zeta_{Re} \equiv \frac{\Delta p}{\rho w_1^2/2} = k'_{Re}\zeta_{wir}$$

$Re < 50$: $\zeta_{Re} \approx \dfrac{22}{Re} + \zeta_{wir}$

where for k'_{Re}, see graph b.

For n_{scr} number of rows of successively installed screens

$$\zeta_{scr} \equiv \frac{\Delta p}{\rho w_1^2/2} \approx \sum_{i=1}^{n_{scr}} \zeta_i \quad \text{or} \quad \zeta_{scr} \approx \sum_{1}^{n_{scr}} \zeta_{Rei}$$

2. Silk threads

$Re > 500$: $\zeta_{sil} \equiv \dfrac{\Delta p}{\rho w_1^2/2} = 1.62\zeta_{wir}$

$40 < Re < 500$: $\zeta_{Re} = k''_{Re}\zeta_{sil}$

$Re < 40$: $\zeta_{Re} \approx \dfrac{7}{Re} + \zeta_{sil}$

where for k''_{Re} see graph c.

$\overline{f}$	0.05	0.10	0.15	0.20	0.25	0.30	0.35	0.40	0.45
ζ_{wir}	363	82.0	33.4	17.0	10.0	6.20	4.10	3.00	2.20
$\overline{f}$	0.50	0.55	0.60	0.65	0.70	0.75	0.80	0.90	1.00
ζ_{wir}	1.65	1.26	0.97	0.75	0.58	0.44	0.32	0.14	0.00

Re	50	100	150	200	300	400	500	1000	1200
k'_{Re}	1.44	1.24	1.13	1.08	1.03	1.01	1.01	1.00	1.02

Re	40	80	120	300	350	400	500
k''_{Re}	1.16	1.05	1.01	1.00	1.01	1.01	1.03

Screens[24,26,34,49]

Diagram
8-6

Two-plane screen

3.

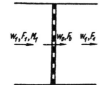

3. Two-plane screen made from bars of circular
cross section

$$\zeta \equiv \frac{\Delta p}{\rho w_0^2/2} = 1.28 \frac{1 - \bar{f}}{\bar{f}^2}$$

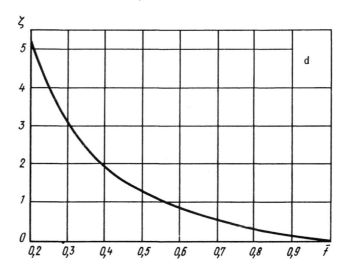

$\bar{f}$	0.2	0.3	0.4	0.5	0.6	0.7	0.8	0.9	0.95
ζ	5.12	2.99	1.92	1.28	0.85	0.55	0.32	0.14	0.07

Grids and screens at high subsonic flow velocities
(large Mach numbers)[67]

Diagram
8-7

Grids with sharp-edged inlet orifices

$$\zeta_M \equiv \frac{\Delta p}{\rho_1 w_1^2/2} = k_M \zeta$$

where for ζ see Diagram 8-1 at $Ma_1 \approx 0$; $k_M = f(Ma_1)$ at different $\bar{f}$, see tentatively
graph a. Grids with rounded or beveled orifice edges facing the flow and screens:
$\zeta_M = k'_M \zeta$, where for ζ, see Diagrams 8-2, 8-4, and 8-6 at $Ma_1 \approx 0$; $k'_M = f(Ma_1)$
at different $\bar{f}$ (for grids, tentatively) see graph b. $Ma_1 = w_1/a$ is the Mach number
before the front of the grid (screen).

Values of k_M

$\bar{f}$	Ma_1													
	0	0.05	0.10	0.15	0.20	0.25	0.30	0.35	0.40	0.45	0.50	0.55	0.60	0.65
0.2	1.00	1.09	1.30	–	–	–	–	–	–	–	–	–	–	–
0.3	1.00	1.03	1.13	1.51	–	–	–	–	–	–	–	–	–	–
0.4	1.00	1.00	1.03	1.14	1.41	–	–	–	–	–	–	–	–	–
0.5	1.00	1.00	1.00	1.03	1.10	1.27	1.85	–	–	–	–	–	–	–
0.6	1.00	1.00	1.00	1.00	1.04	1.12	1.30	1.77	–	–	–	–	–	–
0.7	1.00	1.00	1.00	1.00	1.03	1.08	1.16	1.35	1.68	–	–	–	–	–
0.8	1.00	1.00	1.00	1.00	1.01	1.03	1.07	1.12	1.20	1.37	1.63	2.01	–	–
0.9	1.00	1.00	1.00	1.00	1.00	1.00	1.02	1.04	1.07	1.13	1.21	1.33	1.50	1.75

Grids and screens at high subsonic flow velocities
(large Mach numbers)[67]

Diagram
8-7

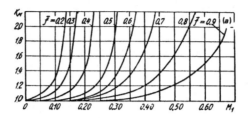

Values of k'_M

$\bar{f}$	0	0.05	0.10	0.15	0.20	0.25	0.30	0.35	0.40	0.45	0.50	0.55	0.60	0.65
0.35	1.00	1.01	1.04	1.12	1.30	–	–	–	–	–	–	–	–	–
0.4	1.00	1.00	1.02	1.10	1.25	1.55	–	–	–	–	–	–	–	–
0.45	1.00	1.00	1.01	1.07	1.19	1.40	1.82	–	–	–	–	–	–	–
0.50	1.00	1.00	1.00	1.04	1.13	1.30	1.64	–	–	–	–	–	–	–
0.55	1.00	1.00	1.00	1.00	1.04	1.17	1.42	1.93	–	–	–	–	–	–
0.60	1.00	1.00	1.00	1.00	1.02	1.11	1.32	1.68	–	–	–	–	–	–
0.65	1.00	1.00	1.00	1.00	1.01	1.07	1.22	1.47	1.90	–	–	–	–	–
0.70	1.00	1.00	1.00	1.00	1.00	1.05	1.16	1.33	1.60	2.12	–	–	–	–
0.75	1.00	1.00	1.00	1.00	1.00	1.03	1.12	1.23	1.42	1.73	2.40	–	–	–
0.80	1.00	1.00	1.00	1.00	1.00	1.01	1.06	1.15	1.28	1.49	1.81	–	–	–
0.85	1.00	1.00	1.00	1.00	1.00	1.00	1.00	1.01	1.08	1.20	1.40	1.80	2.71	–
0.90	1.00	1.00	1.00	1.00	1.00	1.00	1.00	1.00	1.00	1.01	1.08	1.32	1.75	2.65

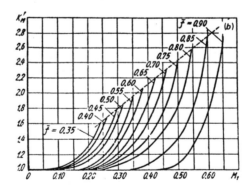

Filtering materials at high pressures of the flow medium (clean)[58]

Diagram
8-8

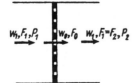

$\zeta \equiv \dfrac{\Delta p}{\rho_1 w_1^2/2}$, see the curves $\zeta = f(\text{Re})$ of graphs a and b; $\bar{p} = p_2/p_1$, see the curves $\bar{p} = f(w_1)$ of graph c; $\text{Re} = w_1\delta/\nu$

Filtering materials at high pressures of the flow medium (clean)[58]	Diagram 8-8

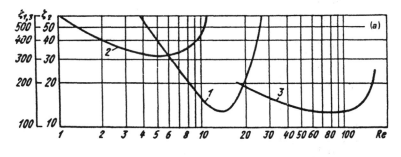

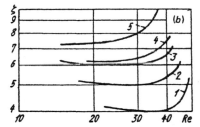

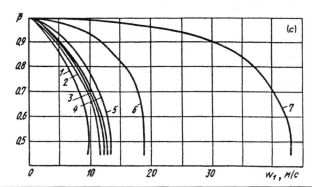

Name	Average size of thread (grain)δ, mm	Thickness of filter, mm	Graph (number of curve)	
			$\zeta = f(Re)$	$\bar{p} = f(w_1)$
Metallic streen 685/6250	0.048 (warp is 32 μm two 64-μm cleats) $\delta = \dfrac{\delta_{cl} + \delta_w}{2}$	0.128	$a(1)$	$c(7)$
Black chamois GOST 3717-84	0.024	1.5	$a(2)$	$c(2)$
Capron complex threads of cloth intertwining (material 23759)	0.300	0.275	$a(3)$	$c(6)$
Metal ceramic	0.100		b	c
		1	(1)	(1 and 5)
		2	(2)	(4)
		3	(3)	(3)
		1	(4)	(3)
		1	(5)	—

| Filtering materials at high pressures of the flow medium (clean)[58] | | | | | | | | | | | | | Diagram 8-8 | |

Values of ζ

Curve of graph a	Re													
	1	2	3	4	6	8	10	15	20	25	30	50	100	150
1	–	–	–	55	32	20	15	13	21	50	–	–	–	–
2	600	400	350	315	310	360	420	–	–	–	–	–	–	–
3	–	–	–	–	–	–	–	–	190	180	160	130	130	130

Values of ζ

Curve of graph b	Re							
	15	20	25	30	35	40	45	
1	–	4.2	4.1	4.0	4.0	4.0	4.7	
2	5.2	5.1	5.0	5.0	5.1	5.2	6.5	
3	6.1	6.0	6.0	6.0	6.2	6.2	6.6	–
4	–	6.1	6.2	6.3	6.9	7.4	–	–
5	7.1	7.2	7.4	8.0	9.5	–	–	–

| Grating made from bars with the angle of attack[15,26,69,82] $\alpha_0 = 0$; $\mathrm{Re} = w_0 a_0/\nu > 10^4$ | Diagram 8-9 |

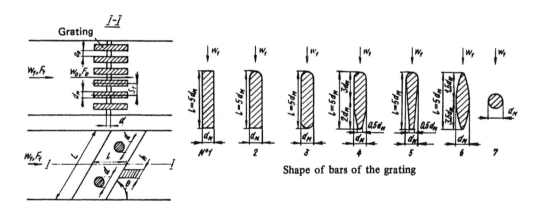

Shape of bars of the grating

1. Clean grating
    a) $l/d_m = 5$ and $a_0/S_1 > 0.5$:

    $$\zeta_1 \equiv \frac{\Delta p}{\rho w_1^2/2} = \beta_1 k_1 \sin \theta \ , \quad \text{where for } \beta_1 \text{ see the table;}$$

    $k_1 = (S_1/a_0 - 1)^{4/3}$ see the table and the graph $k_1 = f(a_0/S_1)$;
    b) arbitrary l/d_m and a_0/S_1:

    $$\zeta_1 \equiv \frac{\Delta p}{\rho w_1^2/2} = \beta_1 \zeta' \sin \theta \ , \quad \text{for } \beta_2 \text{ see the table;}$$

    ζ' is determined as ζ of a thickened grid from Diagram 8-3.

Grating made from bars with the angle of attack[15,26,69,82] $\alpha_0 = 0$; Re $= w_0 a_0/\nu > 10^4$							Diagram 8-9	

No. of the bar	1	2	3	4	5	6	7
β_1	2.34	1.77	1.77	1.00	0.87	0.71	1.73
β_2	1.0	0.76	0.76	0.43	0.37	0.30	0.74

$\dfrac{a_0}{S_1}$	0	0.1	0.2	0.3	0.4	0.5	0.6	0.7	0.8	0.9	1.0
k_1	∞	18.7	6.35	3.09	1.72	1.00	0.58	0.32	0.16	0.05	0

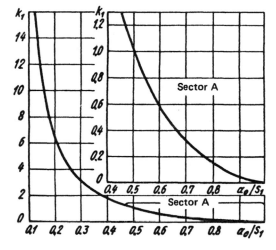

2. Contaminated grating (in hydroengineering systems)

$$\zeta_{con} = c'\zeta$$

where $c' = 1.1$–1.3 with mechanical cleaning of the grating; $c' = 1.5$–2.0 with manual cleaning of the grating.

3. Grating with an additional frame (in hydroengineering systems)

$$\zeta_{fr} = c''\zeta_{con}$$

where $c'' = 1/(1 - A/L)^2$; $A = hz_{n_1} + dz_{n_2}$ is the total height of transverse elements; n_1 is the number of intermediate supporting bars; n_2 is the number of binding elements; L is the internal height of the grating.

Grating made of bars with an angle of attack[15,26,69,82] $\alpha_0 > 0$ at $a_0/S_1 \geq 0.5$; Re $= w_0 a_0/\nu > 10^4$	Diagram 8-10

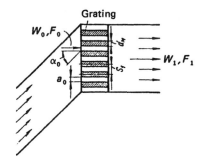

$$\zeta \equiv \frac{\Delta p}{\rho w_1^2/2} = \sigma_1 \sigma_2$$

where for σ_1, see graph a; for σ_2, see graph b.

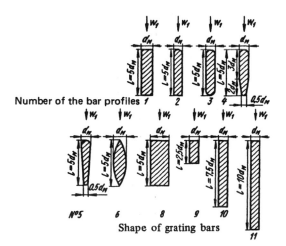

Number of the bar profiles

Shape of grating bars

Grating made of bars with an angle of attack[15,26,69,82] $\alpha_0 > 0$ at $a_0/S_1 \geqslant 0.5$; $Re = w_0 a_0/\nu > 10^4$	Diagram 8-10

Values of σ_1

No. of curve	α_0, degrees									
	0	5	10	15	20	25	30	40	50	60
1	1.00	1.00	1.00	1.00	1.00	1.00	1.00	1.00	1.00	1.00
2	0.76	0.65	0.58	0.54	0.52	0.51	0.52	0.58	0.63	0.62
3	0.76	0.60	0.55	0.51	0.49	0.48	0.49	0.57	0.64	0.66
4	0.43	0.37	0.34	0.32	0.30	0.29	0.30	0.36	0.47	0.52
5	0.37	0.37	0.38	0.40	0.42	0.44	0.47	0.56	0.67	0.72
6	0.30	0.24	0.20	0.17	0.16	0.15	0.16	0.25	0.37	0.43
8	1.00	1.08	1.13	1.18	1.22	1.25	1.28	1.33	1.31	1.20
9	1.00	1.06	1.10	1.15	1.18	1.22	1.25	1.30	1.22	1.00
10	1.00	1.00	1.00	1.01	1.02	1.03	1.05	1.10	1.04	0.82
11	1.00	1.04	1.07	1.09	1.10	1.11	1.10	1.07	1.00	0.92

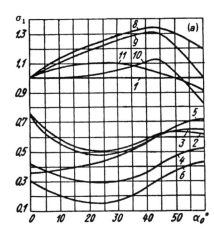 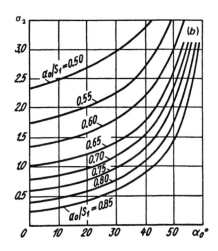

Values of σ_2

$\dfrac{a_0}{S_1}$	α_0, degrees									
	0	5	10	15	20	25	30	40	50	60
0.50	2.34	2.40	2.48	2.57	2.68	2.80	2.95	3.65	4.00	4.70
0.55	1.75	1.80	1.85	1.90	2.00	2.10	2.25	2.68	3.55	4.50
0.60	1.35	1.38	1.42	1.48	1.55	1.65	1.79	2.19	3.00	4.35
0.65	1.00	1.05	1.08	1.12	1.20	1.30	1.40	1.77	2.56	4.25
0.70	0.78	0.80	0.85	0.89	0.95	1.05	1.17	1.52	2.30	4.10
0.75	0.60	0.62	0.65	0.70	0.75	0.85	0.95	1.30	2.05	3.90
0.80	0.37	0.40	0.45	0.50	0.55	0.64	0.75	1.06	1.75	3.70
0.85	0.24	0.25	0.30	0.36	0.42	0.50	0.60	0.88	1.40	3.50

Packing – a bed of spherical or lumpy irregular-shape bodies[3,64,66]

Diagram 8-11

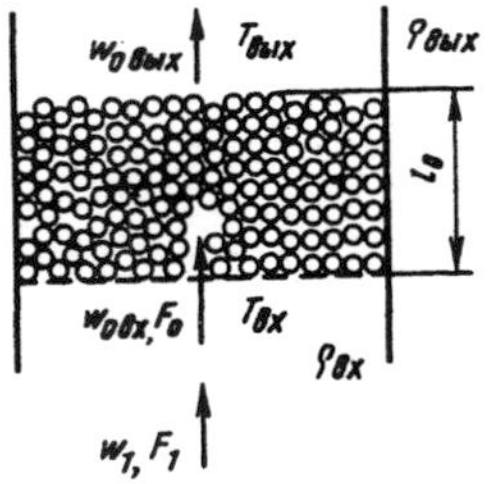

$$\zeta \equiv \frac{\Delta p}{\rho w_1^2/2} = \lambda l_0/d_{el} + \Delta\zeta_t,$$

where $\lambda = \dfrac{360(1-\varepsilon')^2}{\varepsilon'^3 Re_1} + \dfrac{B'(1-\varepsilon')}{\varepsilon'^3} = \dfrac{A_1}{Re_1} + B_1;$

$A_1 = 360(1-\varepsilon')/\varepsilon'^3$, see curve 1 of the graph;

$B_1 \equiv B'(1-\varepsilon')/\varepsilon'^3;$

$B' = 1.8$ for bodies with smooth surface (see curve 2);

$B' = 4.0$ for bodies with rough surface (see curve 3);

$Re_1 \equiv w_1 d_{el}/\nu;$

$d_{el} = \varphi_1 d_{gr};$ for d_{gr}, ε' and φ_1 see Tables 1 and 3;

$\Delta\zeta_t = 2\dfrac{T_{ex} - T_{in}}{T_m};$ $T_m = \dfrac{T_{in} + T_{ex}}{2};$

$\rho_m = \rho_0 \dfrac{273}{T_m};$ $w_m = w_1 T_m/T_{in};$ $\nu = f(T_m),$ see Section 1-2.

Spherical bodies

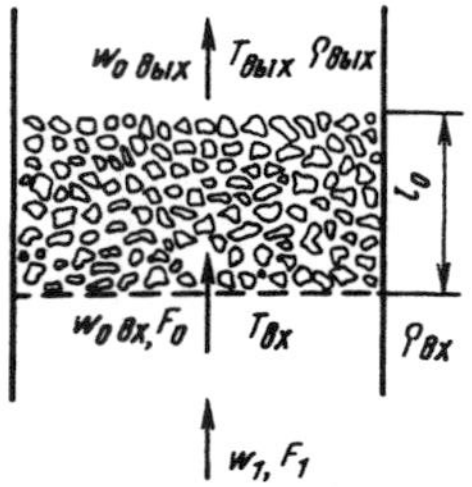

Bodies of irregular shape

1. Spherical bodies

$\theta°$	60	64	68	72	76	80	84	90
ε'	0.250	0.320	0.365	0.405	0.435	0.495	0.470	0.476

Packing – a bed of spherical or lumpy irregular-shape bodies[3,64,66]   Diagram 8-11

2. Values of A_1 and B_1

ε'	A_1	B_1 at B'	
		1.8	4.0
0.25	12960	86.4	192
0.30	6534	46.7	103.7
0.35	3547	27.3	60.6
0.40	3025	16.87	37.5
0.45	1195	10.9	24.1
0.50	720	7.20	16.0
0.55	438.1	4.87	10.8
0.60	266.8	3.33	7.4
0.65	160.56	2.25	5.1
0.70	98.32	1.58	3.5

3. Bodies and particles of irregular shape

	With smooth surface				With rough surface		
Material	d_{gr}, mm	ε'	φ	Material	d_{gr}, mm	ε'	φ_1
Polydisperse beach sand	2–3	0.35	0.66	Activated charcoal	1–2	0.500	0.64
	1.5	0.35	0.76		1.5	0.445	0.92
					1.5–4.5	0.400	0.79
Bank sand	2.5–5	0.445	0.80				
	1.2–2.5	0.390	0.76				
Activated alumina	1–3	0.500	0.68	Limestone	1.6	0.640	0.77
	3–5	0.500	0.49	Coke	5.25	0.480	0.77
	9–10	0.520	0.50	Quartz sand	0.2–0.3	0.430–0.460	0.63–0.70
					1.2–5	0.390–0.445	0.76–0.80
Alumina silica gel	2.5	0.520	0.56				
	3.5	0.480	0.68				
	4.5	0.500	0.49				
Anthracite	1.0	0.540	0.66	Silica gel KSM	3–5	0.490	0.50
	2.1	0.520	0.67	Shale	5–25	0.43–0.52	0.68–0.?
	3.5	0.510	0.66		2.6	0.480	0.77
	7–8	0.520	0.07	Crushed stone	30–25	0.500	0.62
	12–18	0.465	–		5–10	0.460–0.500	0.54
	18–25	0.475	–				
Gravel	3.7	0.470–0.540	0.73				
	12–20	0.370	0.68				

Packing – a bed of lumpy and loose bodies of irregular shape at the prescribed d_h[16,34]

Diagram 8-12

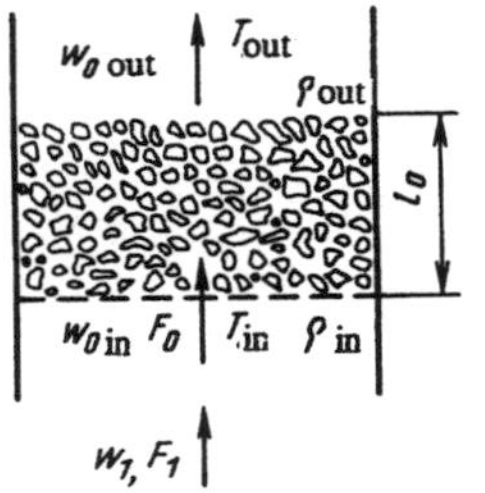

$A \times 10^2$ m³/m²s	$w'_{1\lim}$ m/s
0	8
0.14	0.8
0.28	0.7
0.7	0.6
1.4	0.5

Type of material	d_h, m	ε' m³/m³	$\bar{s}$, m²/m³
Andesite lumps 43.2 mm	0.0333	0.565	68
Circular gravel 42 mm	0.0193	0.388	80
Catalyst for ammonia synthesis 6.1 mm	0.00194	0.465	960
Catalyst for CO conversion made in 11.5 × 6 mm pellets	0.0033	0.380	460
Vanadium sulfuric acid catalyst made in 11 × 6.5 mm pellets	0.00415	0.430	415
Iron rings 35 × 35 × 2.5 mm	0.0372	0.830	147
50 × 50 × 5 mm	0.036	0.970	104
Ceramic rings 15 × 15 × 2 mm	0.0085	0.700	330
25 × 25 × 3 mm	0.0145	0.740	204
35 × 35 × 4 mm	0.0225	0.780	140
50 × 50 × 5 mm	0.0360	0.785	88
Porcelain rings 8 × 8 × 1.5 mm	0.0045	0.640	570
Ceramic saddle-shaped elements 12.5 mm	–	0.710–0.760	–
25 mm	–	0.710	–

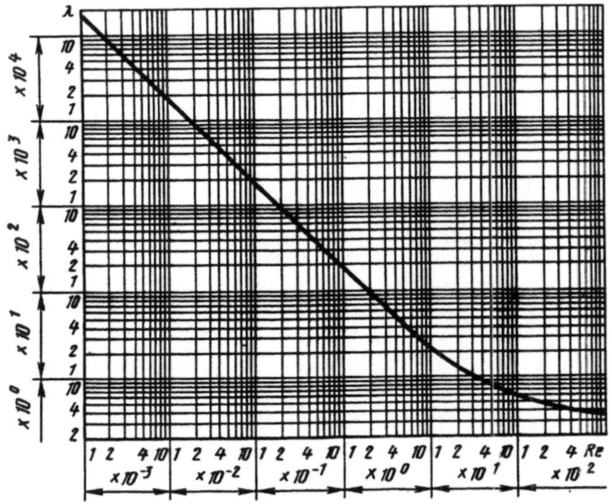

Dry packing

$$\zeta \equiv \frac{\Delta p}{\rho_m w_{1m}^2/2} = \lambda \frac{l_0}{d_h}\frac{1}{\varepsilon'^2} + \Delta\zeta_i = \zeta_{dry} + \Delta\zeta_i;$$

$$Re_h = \frac{w_{1m} d_h}{\nu}\frac{1}{\varepsilon'} < 3:$$

$\lambda = 180/Re_h = f(Re_h),$ see the graph:

$3 < Re_h < 1000:$

$\lambda = 164/Re_h + 7.68/Re_h^{0.11} = f(Re),$ see the graph.

Wetted packing (tentatively) at $A \le 1.4 \times 10^{-2}:$

$w_1 < w_{1lim};$ $5 < d_h < 30\text{-}35$ mm:

$\zeta \approx \zeta_{dry}(1 + 2.15 \times 10^2 A) + \Delta\zeta_i;$ $\tau' = 2.15 \times 10^2;$

A is the intensity of wetting by liquid, $m^3/m^2 s;$

$\Delta\zeta_i = 2\dfrac{T_{ex} - T_{in}}{T_m}$, for ν depending on T_m see Section 1-2;

$T_m = 0.5(T_{in} - T_{ex});$ $\rho_m = 273\rho_0/T_m;$ $w_{1m} = w_1 T_m/T_{in}$

Re	1×10^{-3}	5×10^{-3}	1×10^{-2}	5×10^{-2}	1×10^{-1}	5×10^{-1}	1	2	3
λ	180,000	36,000	18,000	3,600	1,800	360	180	90	61.5

Re	4	5	6	7	8	9	10	15	20	25	30	35
λ	47.9	39.7	33.7	29.6	26.5	24.3	22.4	16.8	13.7	12.0	10.7	9.90

Re	40	45	50	60	70	80	90	100	150	200	250	300	350
λ	9.24	8.70	8.30	7.62	7.16	6.80	6.52	6.27	5.62	5.12	4.84	4.65	4.49

Re	400	450	500	600	700	800	900	1,000
λ	4.37	4.29	4.21	4.07	3.97	3.96	3.81	3.74

Packing of ceramic Raschig rings[16] ($d_{ex}/d_{in} \approx 1.2$)	Diagram 8-13

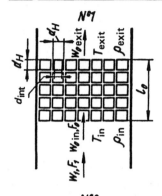

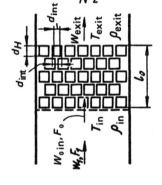

In-line arrangement

$A \times 10^2$, m³/m² s	$w_{1\,lim}$, m/s
0–0.28	2.0
0.42–0.70	1.5
0.83–1.40	1.0

Staggered arrangement

A, m³/m²s	$w_{1\,lim}$, m/s
0–0.28	1.5
0.42–0.56	1.2
0.83–1.40	0.8

d_{ex}, mm	d_h, m	ε'	$1/\varepsilon'$	$1/\varepsilon'^2$	$\bar{s}$, m²/m³
50	0.027	0.73	1.36	1.85	108
80	0.036	0.72	1.39	1.93	–
100	0.048	0.72	1.39	1.93	–
150	0.075	0.72	1.39	1.93	–
200	0.100	0.72	1.39	1.93	–

Values of λ

	$Re_h \times 10^{-2}$								
Curve	4	6	8	10	15	20	40	60	80
1	0.34	0.29	0.26	0.24	0.21	0.19	0.14	0.12	0.11
2	1.0	0.85	0.76	0.71	0.62	0.55	0.42	0.37	0.36

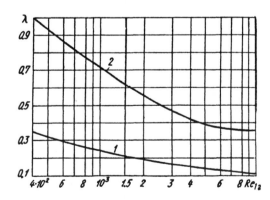

Dry packing

$$\zeta_1 \equiv \frac{\Delta p}{\rho_m w_{1m}^2/2} = \lambda \frac{l_0}{d_h} \frac{1}{\varepsilon'^2}$$

$$0.4 \times 10^3 < Re_{1h} = \frac{w_{1m} d_h}{\nu} < 8 \times 10^3$$

$$\lambda = \frac{3.2}{Re_{1h}^{0.375}} = f(Re_{1h}), \text{ see curve 1;}$$

$Re_{1h} > 8 \times 10^3$: $\lambda \approx 0.11 = $ const.
$0.4 \times 10^3 < Re_{1h} \leq 6 \times 10^3$

$$\lambda = \frac{9.6}{Re_{1h}^{0.375}} = f(Re_{1h}), \text{ see curve 2;}$$

$Re_{1h} > 6 \times 10^3$; $\lambda \approx 0.36 = $ const. Wetted packings (tentatively) (at $A \leq 1.4 \times 10^{-2}$; $w_1 \leq w_{1m}$)

$\zeta_1 \equiv \Delta p/(\rho_m w_{1m}^2/2) = \lambda(l_0/d_h)(1/\varepsilon'^2)(1 + 1.4 \times 10^2 A) + \Delta\zeta$, where A is the intensity of wetting, m³/m² s; $\tau' = 1.4 \times 10^2$; for ζ_1, T_m, ρ_m, w_{1m}, and ν see Diagram 8-12.

Packings of wooden laths (chordlike)[16]

Diagram
8-14

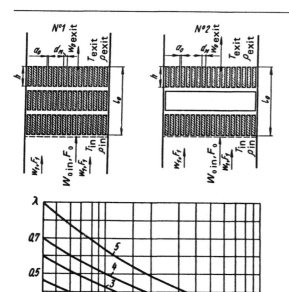

1) Parallel arrangement
2) Crosswise arrangement

Dry packing

$$\zeta_1 \equiv \frac{\Delta p}{\rho_m w_{1m}^2/2} = \lambda \frac{l_0}{d_h} \frac{1}{\varepsilon'^2}$$

1) $4 \times 10^2 < \mathrm{Re}_{1h} = w_{1m} d_h/\nu < 10^4$

$$\lambda = \frac{3.2}{\mathrm{Re}_{1h}^{0.375}} = f(\mathrm{Re}_{1h}), \text{ see curve 1;}$$

$\mathrm{Re}_{1h} > 10^4$: $\lambda \approx 0.10 = \mathrm{const.}$
2) $4 \times 10^2 < \mathrm{Re}_{1h} = w_{1m} d_h/\nu \leq 10^4$

$$\lambda = \frac{k_1'}{\mathrm{Re}_{1h}^{0.375}} = f(\mathrm{Re})$$

see curves 2–5; $\mathrm{Re}_{1h} > 10^4$; $\lambda = \lambda'$.

Basic characteristics of chords arranged crosswise

Curve	d_m, mm	α_0, mm	h, mm	d_h, mm	ε'	$1/\varepsilon'^2$	$\bar{s}$, m²/m³	k_1'	λ'
2	10	10	100	22	0.55	3.31	100	4.4	0.14
3	10	10	50	22	0.55	3.31	100	5.7	0.18
4	10	20	100	41	0.68	2.16	66	6.7	0.21
5	10	30	100	63	0.77	1.69	49	8.5	0.26

Wetted packing (tentatively) (at $A \leq 1.4 \times 10^{-2}$; $w_1 \leq w_{1\lim}$): $\zeta_1 = \lambda(l_0/d_h)(1/\varepsilon'^2) \times (1 + \tau'A) + \Delta\zeta$, where A is the intensity of wetting by liquid m³/m² s; $\tau' = 1.4 \times 10^2$ for scheme 1 and 2.15×10^2 for scheme 2; for $\Delta\zeta_1$, ρ_m, w_{1m}, and ν, see Diagram 8-12.

Values of $w_{1\lim}$, m/s

Scheme	$A \times 10^2$, m³/m² s		
	0–0.28	0.42–0.07	0.83–1.40
1	2.0	1.5	1.0
2	1.0	0.7	0.5

Values of λ

	Re_{1h}									
	4×10^2	6×10^2	8×10^2	10^3	1.5×10^3	2×10^3	4×10^3	6×10^3	8×10^3	10^4
	$\mathrm{Re}_{1h}^{0.375}$									
Curve	9.5	11.0	12.3	13.3	15.5	17.3	22.4	26.1	29.1	31.6
1	0.33	0.28	0.25	0.23	0.20	0.18	0.14	0.12	0.11	0.11
2	0.46	0.40	0.35	0.33	0.28	0.25	0.20	0.17	0.15	0.14
3	0.60	0.52	0.46	0.43	0.37	0.33	0.25	0.22	0.19	0.18
4	0.70	0.61	0.54	0.50	0.43	0.39	0.30	0.25	0.22	0.21
5	0.90	0.78	0.69	0.64	0.55	0.49	0.38	0.32	0.28	0.26

Filtering fabrics (according to Adamov)	Diagram 8-15

$$\Delta p \approx 9.81 A_0 q^m \text{ at } q > 0.6 \times 10^3 \text{ m}^3/\text{m}^2 \text{ h}$$

Fabric	m	$A_0 \times 10^4$
1. Calico (without nap)	1.347	2.0
2. Moleskin (without nap)	1.155	48
3. Cottonthread flannelette (medium nap on the two sides)	1.097	87

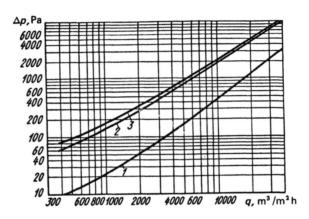

Values of Δp, numerator in kg$_f$/m², denominator in Pa

	q, numerator in m³/m² h, denominator in Pa							
	600	800	1000	2000	3000	4000	5000	6000
Fabric	0.167	0.222	0.28	0.556	0.833	1.11	2.39	1.67
1. Calico	1.40 / 13.7	1.80 / 17.7	2.30 / 22.6	5.20 / 51.0	8.70 / 85.3	12.6 / 124	17.0 / 167	21.0 / 206
2. Moleskin	9.00 / 88.3	10.9 / 107	13.8 / 135	29.5 / 289	46.0 / 452	66.0 / 648	83.0 / 815	105 / 1030
3. Cottonthread flannelette	10.9 / 107	13.9 / 137	17.0 / 167	35.0 / 343	53.0 / 520	73.0 / 716	93.0 / 912	115 / 1130

	q, numerator in m³/m² h, denominator in m³/m² s						
	7000	8000	9000	10,000	20,000	30,000	40,000
Fabric	1.94	2.22	2.50	2.78	5.56	8.33	11.1
1. Calico	27.0 / 265	32.0 / 314	39.0 / 383	45.0 / 442	126 / 1236	229 / 2250	369 / 3620
2. Moleskin	129 / 1270	145 / 1420	167 / 1640	195 / 1910	457 / 4480	759 / 7450	1080 / 10,600
3. Cottonthread flannelette	138 / 1355	160 / 1570	182 / 1785	209 / 2050	479 / 4700	767 / 7525	1110 / 11,900

D_0/D_{con}	1.2	1.4	1.8
ζ	0.3	0.7	2.2

At Re $< 10^4$ for all of the values $\zeta_{Re} = \dfrac{530(\zeta)1.25}{Re}$.*

*See the footnote in Diagram 3-1.

REFERENCES

1. Altshul, A. D. and Krasnov, N. S., Towards calculation of the effect of contamination on the hydraulic resistance of screens with square cells, in *Motion of Homogeneous and Inhomogeneous Liquids, Tr. MISI Kuibysheva*, vyp. 2, no. 55, 70–75, 1968.

2. Altshul, A. D., *Hydraulic Resistances*, Nedra Press, Moscow, 1970, 216 p.

3. Aerov, M. E. and Todes, O. M., *Hydraulic and Thermal Foundations Underlying Operation of Stationary and Fluidized Granular Bed Apparatus*, Khimiya Press, Moscow, 1968, 510 p.

4. Aerov, M. E., Todes, O. M., and Narinskiy, D. A., *Stationary Granular-Bed Apparatus*, Moscow, 1979, p. 175.

5. Basovskaya, A. A. and Reisig, V. A., Investigation of heat transfer and of hydraulic resistance in micronozzle grids, *J. Eng. Phys.*, vol. 39, no. 5, 798–801, 1980.

6. Basovskaya, A. A. and Reisig, V. A., Experimental investigation of heat transfer and hydraulic resistance to air flow through a wire mesh, *J. Eng. Phys.*, vol. 33, no. 4, 734–739, 1977.

7. Belov, S. V., *Porous Materials in Machine Building*, Moscow, 1981, p. 184.

8. Bernshtein, R. S., Pomerantsev, V. V., and Shagalova, S. L., A generalized method for calculating the aerodynamic resistance of loaded sections, in *Problems of Aerodynamics and Heat Transfer in Boiler-Furnace Processes*, Knorre, Ed., 267–289, Gosenergoizdat, 1958.

9. Voskresenskiy, A. K., Oblivin, A. N., and Sagal, S. Z., Hydrodynamic characteristics of porous bodies, in *The Problems of Heat Transfer* (Trudy Moskovsk. Lesotekhn. Inst., vyp. 130, 5–21, 1981.

10. Derbunovich, G. I., Zemskaya, A. S., Repik, Ye. U., and Sosedko, Yu. P., Hydraulic resistance of perforated grids, *Uch. Zap. TsAGI*, vol. 15, no. 2, 114–118, 1984.

11. Goldshtik, M. A., *Transfer Processes in a Granular Bed*, Inst. Teplofiz. SO AN SSSR, Novosibirsk, 1984, p. 163.

12. Gordon, G. M. and Aladzhalov, I. A., *Bag Filter Gas Cleaning in Nonferrous Metallury*, Metallurgizdat, Moscow, 1956, 180 p.

13. Grigoriev, A. F., Dependence of the hydraulic resistance of a bag filter on dust content in fabric, *Sb. Nauchn. Tr. Sanitarn. Tekh.*, vyp. 3, 72–76, Volgograd, 1971.

14. Dryabin, V. A., Galershtein, D. M., and Zabrodskiy, S. S., Hydraulic resistance of a stationary granular bed to a descending dust-laden gas flow, *J. Eng. Phys.*, vol. 34, no. 5, 828–832, 1978.

15. Dulnev, V. B., Determination of pressure head losses in grids, *Gidrotekh. Stroit.*, no. 9, 31–35, 1956.

16. Zhavoronkov, N. M., *Hydraulic Foundations of a Scrubbing Process and Heat Transfer in Scrubbers*, Sovetskaya Nauka, 1944, 224 p.

17. Zhavoronkov, N. M., et al., Hydro- and aerodynamics of packings of scrubber and rectifier columns. Critical phenomena in sprayed non-ordered packings, *Khim. Prom.*, no. 3, 75–79, 1949.

18. Zaitsev, M. M., Calculation of a bag filter, *Tr. NIItsement*, vyp. 3, 80–89, 1950.

19. Zindra, N. N. and Sukharev, M. I., Study of increase in the resistance of cloth filters in cleaning of aerosols, *Tr. Leningr. Inst. Tekstil. iLyogk. Prom.*, vyp. 10, 31–35, 1969.

20. Idelchik, I. E., *Aerohydrodynamics of Technological Apparatus*, Moscow, 1983, p. 351.

21. Idelchik, I. E., *Aerodynamics of Industrial Apparatus*, Energiya Press, Moscow, 1964, 286 p.

22. Idelchik, I. E., Equalization action of a barrier placed behind a diffuser, *Tr. BNT MAP*, no. 662, 25–52, 1948.

23. Idelchik, I. E., Hydraulic resistance during inlet of flows into channels and passage through orifices, *Prom. Aeordin.*, no. 2, 27–57, 1944.

24. Idelchik, I. E., *Hydraulic Resistances (Physical and Mechanical Fundamentals)*, Gosenergoizdat, Moscow, 1954, 316 p.

25. Idelchik, I. E., Towards calculation of the hydraulic resistance of contracting and filtering apparatus of cylindrical shape, *Khim. Prom.*, no. 11, 60–62, 1964.

26. Idelchik, I. E., Determination of the resistance coefficients during discharge through orifices, *Gidrotekh. Stroit.*, no. 5, 31–36, 1953.

27. Idelchik, I. E., Calculation of the hydraulic resistance of dry grid trays and partitions, *Khim. Prom.*, no. 3, 247–251, 1960.

28. Idelchik, I. E., Means of uniform gas flow distribution in industrial apparatus, *Khim. Prom.*, no. 6, 31–37, 1955.

29. Idelchik, I. E., Forced flow delivery in gas-cleaning, heat exchanging and other apparatus, *Tr. NIIOGAZ*, no. 1, 151–207, Goskhimizdat, Moscow, 1957.

30. Idelchik, I. E., Account for the effect of viscosity on the hydraulic resistance of diaphragms and grids, *Teploenergetika*, no. 9, 75–80, 1960.

31. Iljin, Yu. V., Gas flow through porous metallic walls, *Izv. VUZov, Aviats. Tekh.*, no. 1, 65–73, 1959.

32. Ishkin, N. P. and Kaganer, M. G., Hydraulic resistance of porous media, *Kislorod.*, no. 3, 25–36, 1952.
33. Derbunovich, G. I., Zemskaya, A. S., Repik, Ye. U., and Sosedko, Yu. P., Concerning the hydraulic resistance of screens, *Uch. Zap. TsAGI*, vol. 2, no. 2, 133–136, 1980.
34. Konobeyev, B. I., Malyusov, V. A., and Zhavoronkov, N. M., Hydraulic resistance and film thickness during reversed liquid flow under the action of gas in vertical tubes, *Khim. Prom.*, no. 3, 21–26, 1957.
35. Kollerov, D. K., Hydrodynamics of porous media, *Khim. Prom.*, no. 2, 18–23, 1959.
36. *Handbook: Construction Materials and Carbon-Based Items*, Moscow, 1980, p. 63.
37. Krasnov, N. S., On the resistance coefficient of screens with square cells in the region of small Reynolds numbers, *Vyssh. Shkola (Tr. Kolomensk. Fil. VZPI)*, vyp. 5, 64–66, 1971.
38. Kuzmin, Yu. M., Formula for determination of the pressure head losses in metallic screens, *Vodosnabzh. Sanit. Tekh.*, no.2, 27–29, 1966.
39. Kurbanov, A. Z., Kreinin, Ye. V., and Bergauz, A. L., Investigation of the hydrodynamics and heat transfer of single screens, *J. Eng. Phys.*, vol. 40, no. 5, 916–918, 1981.
40. Leibenzon, L. S., *Motion of Natural Liquids and Gases in a Porous Medium*, Gostekhizdat, Moscow, 1947, 150 p.
41. Minsky, E. M., On turbulent filtration in porous media, *Dokl. Akad. Nauk SSSR*, vol. 78, no. 3, 85–93, 1951.
42. Mints, D. M. and Shubert, S. A., Hydraulics of granular materials, *Izd. Ministr. Kommun. Khoz. RSFSR*, 1955, 112 p.
43. Mikheleyev, M. A. and Mikheyeva, I. M., *Fundamentals of Heat Transfer*, Moscow, 1977, p. 344.
44. Dilman, V. V., Darovskikh, Ye. P., Aerov, M. E., and Akselrod, Z. S., Concerning the hydraulic resistance of grid and hole trays, *Khim. Promst.*, no. 3, 156–161, 1956.
45. Petryanov, I. V., et al., *Fibrous Filtering Materials*, Znaniye Press, 1968, 90. p.
46. Rekk, E. E., Comparative estimation of fabrics used for cleaning air of dust in ventilation filters, *Otoplenie Vent.*, no. 4, 10–15, 1934.
47. Usyukin, I. P. and Akselrod, L. S., Fundamentals of hydraulic calculation of screened rectifying columns, *Kislorod*, no. 1, 60–65, 1949.
48. Uchastkin, P. V., Investigation of the efficiency and hydrodynamic resistance of eliminators, *Otoplenie Vent.*, no. 6, 21–30, 1940.
49. Khanzhonkov, V. I., Resistance of screens, *Prom. Aerodin.*, no. 2, 101–114, 1944.
50. Khovansky, O. M., On the coefficient of hydrodynamic pressure head loss in perforated grids and screens of square weaving, *Izv. VUZov Mashinostr.*, no. 2, 101–106, 1963.
51. Tsirlin, A. M., Voronin, B. D., and Khoiov, G. Ya., Hydraulic resistance of tubes with a nozzle of irregular shape during high-temperature gas passage, *J. Eng. Phys.*, vol. 7, no. 8, 103–107, 1964.
52. Chertkov, B. A., Hydrodynamic regime on screen-type trays at small spraying moisture content, *Protsessy Khim. Tekh.*, 36–43, Nauka Press,Moscow-Leningrad, 1965.
53. Chukin, V. V. and Kuznetsov, R. F., Hydraulic resistance of a packed bed of lumped materials, *Khim. Tekh. Topl. Masel*, no. 8, 10–12, 1967.
54. Shevyakova, S. A. and Orlov, V. K., Investigation of the hydraulic resistance and heat transfer in heat exchangers made of perforated plates, *J. Eng. Phys.*, vol. 45, no. 1, 32–36, 1983.
55. Shemurin, V. A., On the dependence between the filtration coefficient and specific resistance of sandclay species, *Gidrotekh. Stroit.*, no. 9, 35–40, 1962.
56. Shepelev, I. A., *Fundamentals of Calculation of Air Screens, Intake Jets and Porous Filters*, Stroiizdat, Moscow, 1950, 139 p.
57. Shimansky, Yu. N., On the resistance coefficient of a bed of solid particles, *Khim. Prom.*, no. 6, 476–477, 1966.
58. Idelchik, I. E., Voronin, I. B., Gordeyev, I. V., and Matveyev, Yu. P., Experimental determination of the hydraulic characteristics of porous materials at high pressures, *Teploenergetika*, no. 1, 81–83, 1973.
59. Benton, E. R. and Knapton, D. A., Supersonic drag of porous wire screens, *ARS J.*, vol. 32, no. 10, 1608–1610, 1962.
60. Bernt, J., Heidenreich, E., and Tittel, R., Zur Bestimmung des Druckverlustes bei Filtermitteln, *Chem. Tech.*, Bd. 26, Heft 11, 692–693, 1974.
61. Böhlen, B., Rurki, H. U., and Guyer, A., Über den Druckverlust strömender Gase in Schuttschichten bei erhohtem Druck, *Helv. Chim. Acta*, vol. 48, no. 1, 1270–1278, 1965.
62. Bruniak, R. and Sockel, H., Widerstandsmessungen an Rohren und Gerüstteilen, *Österr. Ing. Z.*, vol. V4, no. 9, 320–325, 1961.
63. Cornell, W. G., Losses in flow normal to plane screens, *Trans. ASME*, no. 4, 45–53, 1958.
64. Ergun, S., Fluid flow through packed columns, *Chem. Eng. Prog.*, vol. 48, no. 2, 89–94, 1952.
65. Flachsbart, O., Widerstand von Seidengauzefiltern Rundracht und Blechstreifensieben mit quadratischen Marchen, *Ergeb. Aerodyn. Versuchsanstalt Göttingen. IV Lieferung*, 30–40, 1932.

66. MacDonald, I. F., El-Sayed, M. S., Mow, K., and Dullien, A. L., Flow through porous media — the Ergus equation revised, *Ind. Eng. Chem. Fundam.*, vol. 18, no. 3, 199–208, 1979.

67. Huesmann, K., Druckverlust und Durchflusskoeffizienten von parallel engestromten perforierten Platten, *Gesund. Ing.*, vol. 87, no. 6, 158–160, 1966.

68. Ingmanson, W. L., Resistance of wire screens to flow of water, *Tappi*, vol. 44, no. 1, 47 54, 1961.

69. Kirschmer, O., Untersuchungen uber den Gefallsverlust an Rechen, *Mitt. Hydraul. Inst. Tech. Hochschule, Munchen*, no. 1, 91–100, 1926.

70. Klinger, J., Zur Bestimmung des Widerstandswerters von Drahtseibgeweben, *Wiss. Z. Tehc. Univ. Dresden*, vol. 15, H.i, 93 99, 1966.

71. Mathur, M. L. and Kachhara, N. L., Pressure losses in flow through screens, *Indian Eng.*, vol. 12, no. 10, 19–27, 1968.

72. Milton, P. and Francis, J. R., The aerodynamic drag of perforated plates at zero incidence, *J. R. Aeronaut. Soc.*, vol. 62, no. 568, 301–303, 1958.

73. Monahan, R. E., The resistance to flow of perforated plates and wire screens, *Pulp Paper Mag. Can.*, vol. 66, no. 1, T33–T38, 1965.

74. Morgan, P. G., Fluid flow through screens of flow solidity, *J. R. Aeronaut. Soc.*, vol. 66, no. 613, 54–56, 1962.

75. Osborn, J. F., Rectangular-bar trashrack and baffle headlosses, *J. Power Div. Proc. Am. Soc. Civil Eng.*, vol. 94, no. 2, 111–123, 1968.

76. Pinker, R. A. and Herbert, M. V., Pressure loss associated with compressible flow through square-mesh wire gauzes, *J. Mech. Eng. Sci.*, vol. 9, no. 1, 11–23, 1967.

77. Rummer, R. R. and Drinker, P. A., Resistance to laminar flow through porous media, *J. Hydraul. Div. Proc. Am. Soc. Civil Eng.*, vol. 92, no. 5, 155 163, 1966.

78. Sakra, T., Kuchier, M., and Lecjaks, L., Tlakove straty pri prutoku tekutin sily, *Sb. Ved. Pr. Vys. Sk. Chemickotechnol. Pardubice*, sv. 2, 189–203, 1967.

79. Sharan, V. R., Characteristics of flow through two-dimensional screens and perforated plates, *J. Sci. Ind. Res.*, vol. 34, no. 2, 89–92, 1975.

80. Smith, P. L.and Van Winkle, M., Discharge coefficients through perforated plates at Reynolds numbers of 400 to 3000, *AIChe J.*, vol. 4, no. 5, 266–268, 1958.

81. Sockel, H., Abströmung hinter Schaufelgittern, *Brennst. Waermewirtsch.*, vol. 19, no. 8, 393–395, 1967.

82. Spandler, I., Untersuchungen über den Verlust an Rechen beischrager Zuströmung, *Mitt. Hydraul. Inst. Tech. Hochsch. Müunchen*, no. 2, 63–70, 1928.

83. Stengel, H. and Fischer, H. Y., Ergebnisse von strömungstechnischen Untersuchungen an Netztuchern im Windkanal, *Schiffbautechnik*, vol. 14, no. 7, 374–381, 1964.

84. Wen, C. Y., O'Brien, W. S., and Fan, L., Pressure drop through packed beds operated cocurrently, *J. Chem. Eng. Data*, vol. 8, no. 1, 47–51, 1963.

85. Zabeltitz, Ch., Gleichungen für Widerstandsbeiwerte zur Berechungng der Strömungswidwestände von Kugeln und Schuttschichten, *Grundlag. Landtechn.*, vol. 17, no. 4, 148–154, 1967.

RESISTANCE TO FLOW THROUGH PIPE FITTINGS AND LABYRINTH SEALS
Resistance Coefficients of Throttling Devices, Valves, Plugs, Labyrinth Seals, and Compensators

9-1 EXPLANATIONS AND PRACTICAL RECOMMENDATIONS

1. The resistance coefficient of flow-stopping, throttling, or controlling devices depends on their design and the shape of the internal parts that determine the uniformity of the flow, uniformity of the cross section, and so on. The quality of the inner surface finish also influences the resistance coefficient of the device.

2. The length of some types of globe and gate valves does not vary in proportion to their flow section; therefore, when the diameter of this section is changed, complete geometric similitude is not preserved. Moreover, the smaller the size of the casting, the greater is its roughness. As a result, the resistance of some globe and gate valves varies with the flow cross-sectional diameter; the resistance coefficient ζ of globe valves of large dimensions increases with the flow cross-sectional diameter, while in globe valves of small dimensions it increases with a decrease in the diameter.

3. The resistance of gate valves is similar to the resistance of flow obstructions in which a sudden contraction of the flow is followed by a sudden expansion (Figure 9-1a). The phenomenon in butterfly valves, taps (faucets), and globe valves is more complex (Figure 9-1b, c, and d). Here, in addition to abrupt contractions and expansions, there are complex bypasses and turns of the flow. All this is associated with the local increase in velocities and flow separations and, consequently, eddy formation, which increases the resistance of these elements.

The resistance of each type of throttling device depends on the position of the shutoff component.

4. The resistance coefficient of open gate valves of different dimensions and designs differs in magnitude. This difference is mainly due to the relative dimensions of the valve disk cavity or recess. The smaller the diameter of the gate opening, the larger are the relative dimensions of the recess. Therefore, the resistance coefficients of open gate valves of the same type of design are smaller for large disk or gate diameters.

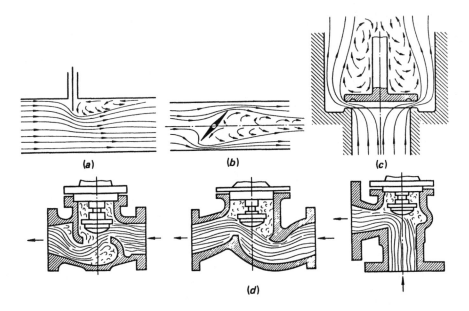

Figure 9-1 Flow pattern in throttling and control devices: (*a*) gate valve, (*b*) butterfly valve, (*c*) disk valve, and (*d*) globe valves.

5. When the valve disk is installed on one side of the gate opening, this distorts the symmetry of the flow. As a result, pressure fluctuations and vibrations of the pipeline increase substantially. From this point of view, a rectangular gate with valve disks on two sides moving simultaneously is advantageous.[35,36]

6. In order to reduce the size of the gate valve, as well as the magnitude of forces and torques required to control it, the flow section in the valve casing is usually contracted. The contraction is usually symmetrical, but for a one-side motion of liquid it can also be asymmetric.[11] The contraction of the passage increases the resistance coefficient of the gate valve.

7. Gate valves and various plugs (conical, spherical, segmented, rollerlike) used in water supply systems, pressure delivery pipes of hydroelectric stations, and gas and petroleum pipelines and other structures and plants can operate both within the system and at its exit (terminal). In the first case they are installed in the straight pipe, in converging-diverging transition units, or in a converging transition unit (see respective schemes on Diagrams 9-5, 9-7 to 9-13, and 9-20). The values of ζ given in these diagrams do not allow for the additional losses of velocity pressure at the exit and, correspondingly, the losses in transition pieces.[33,34]

The total resistance coefficient of the terminal (end) gate valves and plugs, and similarly for gate valves and plugs installed in transition pieces, is determined as $\zeta_{tot} = \zeta + 1$, and, correspondingly, $\zeta_{ov} = \zeta + \zeta_{tr}$, where the ζ's are the values of these coefficients for the terminal gate valves and plugs and ζ_{tr} is determined as ζ of the converging-diverging and other transition pieces in Diagrams 5-25 and 5-26.

8. Flow-stopping devices display the same three characteristic regions of the flow regime (Figure 9-2) as do orifice plates (see paragraphs 32 and 33 of Chapter 4): purely laminar, transient, and purely turbulent (quadratic) regimes.[4-6] Equation (1-3) also holds for these devices

$$\zeta = \frac{A}{Re} + \zeta_{qu}$$

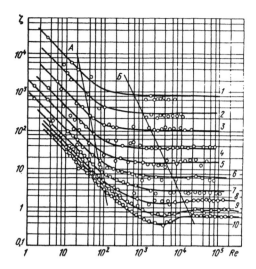

Figure 9-2 Function $\zeta = f(\text{Re})$ for a disk throttle ($\alpha = 90° - \delta$).[5] 1, $\alpha = 9°$; 2, $\alpha = 18°$; 3, $\alpha = 27°$; 4, $\alpha = 36°$; 5, $\alpha = 45°$; 6, $\alpha = 54°$; 7, $\alpha = 63°$; 8, $\alpha = 72°$; 9, $\alpha = 81°$; 10, $\alpha = 90°$. Left side of line A, laminar region; between lines A and B, transition region; right side of line B, turbulent region.

which characterizes the law of resistance for a wide range of the Reynolds number [where ζ_{qu} is the resistance coefficient in the (square law) quadratic region and A is a coefficient that depends on the type of stopping device].

9. For a regulating valve (at $D_0 = 0.05$ m), Arzumanov and Vizeryan[5,6] suggest the following equations for calculating the resistance coefficient.*

- For an angular single-seat valve within $1.7 \leqslant h/D_h \leqslant 30$

$$\zeta \equiv \frac{\Delta p}{\rho w_h^2/2} = \frac{4.1\ h/D_h + 23}{\text{Re}_h} + \left(1 - \frac{F_h}{F_0}\right)^2 + 0.18$$

With complete opening of the valve ($h/D_h \leqslant 1.7$)

$$\zeta \equiv \frac{30}{\text{Re}_h} + \left(1 - \frac{F_h}{F_0}\right)^2 + 0.18$$

- For a double-seat valve within $4.0 < h/D \leqslant 6.0$

$$\zeta \equiv \frac{\Delta p}{\rho w_h^2/2} = \frac{0.5\ h/D_h + 27}{\text{Re}_h} + \left(1 - \frac{F_h}{F_0}\right)^2 + 4.7\left(\frac{F_h}{F_0}\right)^2$$

With complete opening of the valve

$$\zeta \equiv \frac{30}{\text{Re}_h} + \left(1 - \frac{F_h}{F_0}\right)^2 + 4.7\left(\frac{F_h}{F_0}\right)^2$$

where $\text{Re}_h = w_h R_h/\nu = w_h D_h/4\nu$ and $D_h = 4F_h/\Pi_h$

10. The relative depth of the plunger stroke (depth of the channel in a throttling device; see scheme of Diagram 9-21) h/D_h for different types and dimensions of valves is different

---

*Quantities with subscript h at w, Re, F, and Π refer to the flow cross section of the stopping device.

and depends on the degree of opening of the regulating valve $\overline{H} = H/H_{max}$, where H and H_{max} are the instantaneous and maximum values of the plunger stroke, respectively.[5]

The value of h is assumed to be equal to the height of the seat h_s for the case when a shaped part of the plunger with full opening of the valve ($\overline{H} = 1.0$) leaves the seat completely or when the profiled part of the plunger is at the upper edge of the seat during intermediate positions.

11. The best design of a stopping device, with respect to hydraulic resistance, is that of a straightway globe valve. The resistance coefficient of such a valve as a function of the valve lift h/D_h at $Re = w_0 D_h/\nu \geqslant 3 \times 10^5$ can be determined from the following equations of Murin:[22]

At $D_0 = 38$ mm

$$\zeta \equiv \frac{\Delta p}{\rho w_0^2/2} = 1.28 + \frac{0.084}{(h/D_0)^2}$$

At $D_0 = 200$ mm

$$\zeta = \frac{0.51}{(h/D_0)^2}$$

With full opening of the valve within $D_0 = 25$–200 mm

$$\zeta = \frac{5.2}{D_0^{0.5}}$$

12. The resistance coefficient of throttling valves with disk seal gates in a circular tube can be calculated for the entire range of Reynolds numbers from the equations.[5,6]

$$\zeta \equiv \frac{\Delta p}{\rho w_0^2/2} = \frac{A}{Re} + \left(1 - \frac{50}{Re}\right)\zeta_{qu} \qquad (9\text{-}1)$$

where

$$A = \frac{120}{2} \frac{1 + 0.5 \overline{D}_d(1 + \sin \delta)}{(1 - \overline{D}_d^2 \sin \delta)^2} \qquad (9\text{-}2)$$

δ is the angle of valve opening, in degrees; $\overline{D}_d = D_d/D_0$; D_d is the disk diameter, in meters; $Re = w_0 D_0/\nu$; at $Re \leqslant 50$, the value of $(1 - 50/Re)$ is assumed to be equal to zero.

At $\delta > 20°$

$$\zeta_{qu} = \left(\frac{1.56}{1 - \overline{D}_d \sin \delta} - 1\right)^2 \qquad (9\text{-}3)$$

13. In the range of variation of the quantity δ from 0 to 30°, the resistance coefficient of a throttling device is noticeably affected by its shape and size (relative thickness b/D_0, state of its edges, etc.). Within these limits, the actual values of ζ are higher than those calculated from Equation (9-3). Within the above limits of the values of δ, the stability of

the characteristics of the valve operator is also degraded. Therefore, it is recommended that the working range of application of throttling devices used for automatic control be bounded by the limits of δ from 30 to 90°, at which the throughput capacity is almost independent of the design features of the valve.

14. To determine the resistance coefficient of throttling valves in a rectangular tube at small Reynolds numbers, one can make use of Equation (9-1) to determine with definite accuracy the values of A from Equation (9-2) for the case of a circular cross section.

15. The resistance coefficient of certain types of lifting valves can be determined from the equations suggested by Bach:[37]

- For a tray valve without bottom guides within $0.1 < h/D_0 < 0.25$ and $0.1 < b_{tr}/D_0 < 0.25$

$$\zeta \equiv \frac{\Delta p}{\rho w_0^2/2} = 0.15 + 4\frac{b_{tr}}{D_0} + \frac{0.155}{(h/D_0)^2}$$

where b_{tr} is the width of the tray flange, in meters.
- For a tray valve with bottom guides within $0.125 < h/D_0 < 0.25$ and $0.1 < b_{tr}/D_0 < 0.25$

$$\zeta = (0.8-1.6)\left(0.15 + 4\frac{b_{tr}}{D_0} + \frac{0.73}{(h/D_0)^2(\pi - iS_{sh}/D_0)^2}\right)$$

where S_{sh} is the width of the guide shoulder (Diagram 9-24) and i is the number of guide ribs.
- For a conical valve with a flat seat within $0.1 < h/D_0 < 0.25$ and at $b_{tr}/D_0 = 0.1$

$$\zeta = 2.6 - \frac{0.8}{h/D_0} + \frac{0.14}{(h/D_0)^2}$$

- For a conical valve with a conelike supporting surface within $0.125 < h/D_0 < 0.4$

$$\zeta = 0.6 + \frac{0.15}{(h/D_0)^2}$$

- For a spherical valve with a spherical seat within $0.1 < h/D_0 < 0.25$

$$\zeta = 2.7 - \frac{0.8}{h/D_0} + \frac{0.14}{(h/D_0)^2}$$

16. In some cases, for example, in bag filters with the reverse blow-through (BFR), the gas stream from the outlet header (supplying section, see Diagram 9-27) enters the sections to be filtered. The cleaned gas is directed through outlet tray valves into the intake header (outlet channel) and is withdrawn from the apparatus. When the regeneration of any section is required, it must be separated from the main stream with the help of a discharge valve and connected with the blowing bellmouth by opening the blowing valve.

The values of the resistance coefficients of a tray valve operating according to the schemes given in Diagram 9-27 were obtained experimentally by Koryagin et al.[16] and are presented in the same diagram.

17. Since the motion of a gas through a throttling device is accompanied by appreciable pressure losses, the density of the gas can also vary considerably. This should be considered when determining the resistance of the device from the equation:[11]

$$\Delta p = k_{com} \frac{\rho_{in} w_{0in}^2}{2}$$

where w_{0in} is the mean stream velocity before the throttling device at a pressure p_0, m/s; ρ_{in} is the gas density before the throttling device, kg/m³, k_{com} is the correction for gas compressibility, which depends on the ratio between the pressure p_0 before the throttling device and the pressure p_1 following it:

$$\frac{p_1}{p_0} = 1 - \frac{\Delta p}{p_0}$$

Then the values of the correction will be

- At $p_1/p_0 > 0.9$ or $\Delta p < 0.1 p_0$

    $$k_{com} \approx 1.0$$

- At $(p_1/p_0)_{cr} < p_1/p_0 < 0.9$ or $1 - (p_1/p_0)_{cr} > \Delta p/p_0 > 0.1$

    $$k_{com} = \frac{\Delta p}{p_0} \frac{k-1}{k[(p_1/p_0)^{2/k} - (p_1/p_0)^{(k+1)/k]}}$$

    or approximately[7]

    $$k_{com} = \frac{1}{(1 - 0.46 \, \Delta p/p_0^2}$$

where $(p_1/p_0)_{cr}$ is the critical ratio of pressures before and after the throttling device at which the flow velocity in the constricted section becomes equal to the local speed of sound; for air and a diatomic gas $(p_1/p_0)_{cr} = 0.53$ and $1 - (p_1/p_0)_{cr} = 0.47$.

The values of Δp, p_1/p_0, and k_{com} are calculated by the method of successive approximations.

18. The resistance coefficient of a conical gate installed in a spillway is independent of the tailwater level h_t (Figure 9-3a), that is, it is the same in the case of discharge into the atmosphere and discharge under water.[25] When a conical gate is installed in a special chamber, which ensures reliable dissipation of the kinetic energy of the flow in the tailwater (Figure 9-3b), its resistance coefficient varies somewhat (see Diagram 9-9).

19. The total resistance coefficient of stopping devices, placed one after the other or after bends, is lower than the sum of the single resistance coefficients of these elements taken separately (in the absence of their interaction effect).

The degree of the interaction effect of curved parts depends on the relative distance l_{el}/D_0 between them. The larger l_{el}/D_0, the smaller is the effect of this parameter. This effect virtually disappears at $l_{el}/D_0 = 30–40$.

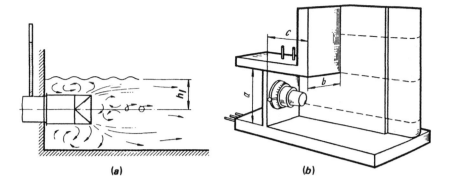

Figure 9-3 Cone plug in a spillway: (*a*) flow pattern and (*b*) plug design.

20. The interaction effect of the stopping device (fitting) during complete opening can be defined by the formulas suggested by Skobeltsyn and Khomutov:[26]

At Re < 160

$$\zeta_{1+2} = \frac{31.2}{Re^{0.785}} (\zeta_{1qu} + \zeta_{2qu})(2 - \beta)$$

At $160 \leqslant Re \leqslant 500$

$$\zeta_{1+2} = \frac{1.31}{Re^{0.159}} (\zeta_{1qu} + \zeta_{2qu})(2 - \beta)$$

In the quadratic region at Re > 500

$$\zeta_{1+2} = 0.5(\zeta_{1qu} + \zeta_{2qu})(2 - \beta)$$

where ζ_{1+2} is the total resistance coefficient of a pair of stopping lock devices that influence each other; ζ_{1qu} and ζ_{2qu} are the single resistance coefficients of stopping devices that comprise a pair in the quadratic region of the resistance (Re > 500); and β is a coefficient that depends on the relative distance between the stopping devices.

The coefficient β for the straightway stopping fitting is

$$\beta = 22.2 \times 10^{-5}\left(\frac{l_{el}}{D_0}\right)^2 - 26.7 \times 10^{-3} \frac{l_{el}}{D_0} + 0.8$$

For the remaining types of stopping devices it is

$$\beta = 4.17 \times 10^{-5}\left(\frac{l_{el}}{D_0}\right)^2 - 5 \times 10^{-3} \frac{l_{el}}{D_0} + 0.15$$

21. In a labyrinth seal, in which baffles are interstitially located on one side and on one level, the flow passes uniformly. Entering the first gap (Figure 9-4a), the flow contracts in the same way as in the case of entrance into a straight channel mounted flush with the wall, or as in the case of passage through an orifice in a thin wall. When the flow enters the

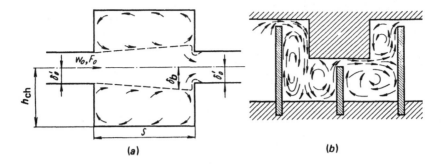

Figure 9-4 Flow pattern in labyrinths: (*a*) cell of a simple labyrinth and (*b*) labyrinth with complex flow passage.

labyrinth chamber it expands and, due to turbulent agitation, additional fluid is entrained at the expense of the surrounding medium. When the relative dimensions of the chamber are sufficiently large (as compared with the gap), a core of constant mass separates from the jet at the chamber end and, contracting, enters the second gap. The entrained masses of the surrounding medium separate from the core at the chamber end and move with a circulatory motion in the chamber until they become once more mixed with the flow. Since the constant-mass core has a high kinetic energy before it enters the second gap, it will contract less than in the first gap.

22. The resistance of the labyrinth cell (Figure 9-4*b*) is due to the frictional losses in the gap and the energy losses in the constant-mass core. The latter are made up of two parts: the difference between the energy stored in the constant-mass core at the beginning and at the end of the cell, and the losses at the entrance into the next gap.

If the dimensions of the chamber are relatively small, so that

$$\frac{h_{ch}}{\delta_0'} < \frac{\delta_b}{\delta_0'}$$

then the jet issuing from the gap into the chamber will fill the entire section. The resistance in this case is made up of the frictional losses in the gap, the losses at a sudden expansion, and the losses at entering the next gap, where δ_0' is the half-width of the labyrinth gap with recesses on both sides, or the width of the jet in the labyrinth with a recess on one side; δ_b is the half-width of the free jet at the end of the chamber (or, correspondingly, the width of the jet), in meters; and h_{ch} is the height of the chamber of the labyrinth cell.

According to Abramovich.[2]

$$\frac{\delta_b}{\delta_0'} = 2.4 \frac{a_{str}S}{\delta_0'} + 1$$

where S is the length of a free jet (the length of the chamber of a labyrinth cell), m, and a_{str} is the coefficient of the structure (turbulence) of flow, taken, in this case, to be equal to 0.1.

23. In labyrinth seals with protuberances or with a staggered arrangement of baffles and with large chamber dimensions between the baffles, the jet, being compressed in the gap, moves toward the protuberances of the labyrinth (Figure 9-4*b*). Here, it deflects through 90° and moves directly to the lower wall of the chamber. It then circulates in the chamber and moves along the second chamber toward the second gap. The jet, flowing in the labyrinth chamber, entrains stationary masses from the surrounding space, causing them to move with

eddy zones forming as a result. Protrusions between the baffles of the labyrinth lengthen the path of the free jet, which contributes to its attenuation. Labyrinths with tortuous flow paths are more efficient, since their jet path length, and correspondingly their resistance, is markedly larger than in labyrinths with straight flow passage.

24. The resistance coefficient of labyrinths with an oblong gap is calculated from the author's equations:[13,14]

- At $h_{ch}/\delta_0' \geqslant \delta_b/\delta_0'$

$$\zeta \equiv \frac{\Delta p}{\rho w_0^2/2} = 1 + \zeta' + z(a_0 + \zeta'b_1 + \zeta_{fr})$$

where a_0 and b_1 are coefficients that depend on the relative length of the labyrinth cell (see Diagram 9-28); $\zeta_{fr} = \lambda(l/\delta_0')$ is the friction coefficient of the gap; λ, (see Diagrams 2-1 through 2-6); ζ' is a coefficient that considers the effect of the inlet edge shape of the gap (it is determined in Diagrams 3-4 and 3-7 as a function of the degree of the inlet edge rounding or beveling).

- At $h_{ch}/\delta_0' < \delta_b/\delta_0'$

$$\zeta = 1 + \zeta' + z(a_2 + \zeta'b_2 + \zeta_{fr})$$

where

$$a_2 = \left(1 - \frac{F_0}{F_{ch}}\right)^2 \quad b_2 = 1 - \frac{F_0}{F_{ch}}$$

25. The flow pattern in fittings, parts of tubes of complex shape, and channels having a number of closely spaced sharp turns, abrupt expansions and contractions, by passes, and so on, as well as the entry and exit of an infinite space (see Diagrams 9-29 through 9-31), is in many respects similar to the flow structure in curved channels, valves, and labyrinth seals with large gaps.

When estimating the resistance of such complex shaped parts it is necessary to consider the mutual interaction effect of separate elements of fittings, which substantially increases the total resistance over a simple sum of the resistances of its separate elements. In many cases this resistance increases by a factor of 3 to 5.

26. When a complex fitting is used as a labyrinth seal, its resistance is useful, since it is more efficient in operation as the resistance increases (air passage through it is reduced). In the remaing cases—for example, when the complexity of the fitting is dictated by a limited overall size of the device—the resistance is detrimental and it should be lowered. The losses in such fittings can be substantially reduced by enlarging its separate cross sections. The resistance can also be decreased very efficiently by installing guide vanes at sharp-corner turns (see Section 6-1). This does not entail a change in the dimensions of the shaped part. The resistance can also be reduced markedly by rounding the corners of the turns.

The installation of fairings is very useful when the obstructions placed in the stream have an irregular shape.

9-2 DIAGRAMS OF THE RESISTANCE COEFFICIENTS

Various globe and gate valves;[26,35,37] $\mathrm{Re} = w_0 D_h/\nu > 10^4$	Diagram 9-1

$$\zeta \equiv \frac{\Delta p}{\rho w_0^2/2}$$

$\mathrm{Re} = w_0 D_h/\nu$

"Rey"-type globe valve

$\zeta = 3.4$

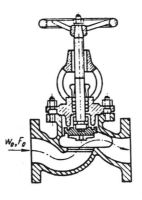

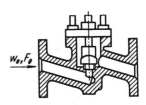

Forged globe valve

$\zeta = 7.8$

$\mathrm{Re} > 10^4$

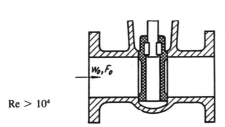

Wedge-type gate valve

$\zeta = 0.2$

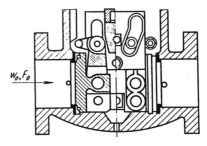

Steam gate valve with lever gate

$\zeta = 0.75$

$\mathrm{Re} > 10^4$

Conduit-type gate valve

$\zeta = 0.1$

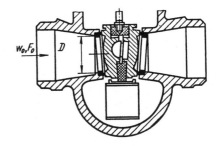

With two successively installed globe valves (gate valves) the total resistance coefficient is[26]

$$\zeta_{1+2} = 0.5(\zeta_1 + \zeta_2)(2 - \beta)$$

where for ζ_1, see ζ of the first stopping device; for ζ_2, see ζ of the second stopping device; $\beta = 4.2 \times 10^{-5}$ $(l/D_0)^2 = 5 \times 10^{-3}$ $l/D_0 + 0.15$; l is the distance between two stopping devices.

"Kosva" angle globe valve at complete opening;*[34,37]	Diagram
$Re = w_0 D_h / \nu \geq 10^4$	9-2

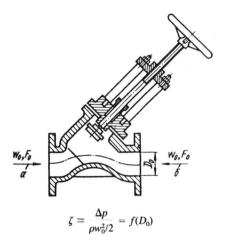

$$\zeta = \frac{\Delta p}{\rho w_0^2 / 2} = f(D_0)$$

With a 30% contracted section of the seat (along arrow A)

D_0, mm	60	80	100	150	200	250	300	350
ζ	2.70	2.40	2.20	1.86	1.65	1.50	1.40	1.30

With full seat section

D_0, mm	(inches)	ζ (flow along arrow A)	ζ (flow along arrow B)
25	(1)	1.80	1.70
32	($1^{1}/_{4}$)	2.00	1.90
40	($1^{1}/_{2}$)	1.70	1.60

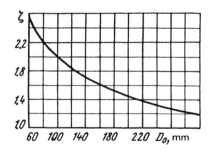

*For two consecutively installed globe valves ζ is taken from Diagram 9-1.

Direct-flow angle globe valve*[22]	Diagram 9-3

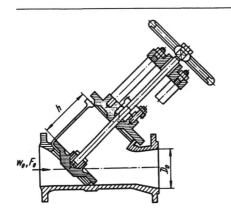

1. $\mathrm{Re} = \dfrac{w_0 D_h}{\nu} \geqslant 3 \times 10^5$

   Incomplete opening
   a) $D_0 = 38$ mm and $0.2 < h/D_0 < 0.8$

   $$\zeta \equiv \frac{\Delta p}{\rho w_0^2/2} = 1.28 + \frac{0.084}{(h/D_0)^2} \quad \text{see graph a}$$

   b) $D_0 = 200$ mm and $0.2 < h/D_0 < 1.0$

   $$\zeta \equiv \frac{0.51}{(h/D_0)^2} \quad \text{see graph a}$$

   Complete openig for diameters $D_0 = 25{-}250$

   $$\zeta \approx \frac{5.2}{\sqrt{D_0}} \quad \text{see graph b}$$

2. $\mathrm{Re} < 3 \times 10^5$

   $$\zeta_{\mathrm{Re}} = k_{\mathrm{Re}} \zeta$$

   where for k_{Re}, see graph c

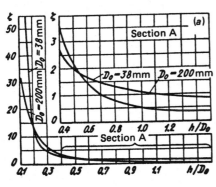

Values of ζ

D_0, mm	h/D_0									
	0.2	0.3	0.4	0.5	0.6	0.7	0.8	1.0	1.2	1.4
38	12.0	4.40	2.60	2.00	1.70	1.50	1.30	1.11	0.95	0.85
200	13.0	5.80	3.20	2.00	1.40	1.00	0.80	0.50	0.40	0.36

D_0, mm	25	38	50	65	75	100	125	150	200	250
ζ	1.04	0.85	0.73	0.65	0.60	0.50	0.46	0.42	0.36	0.32

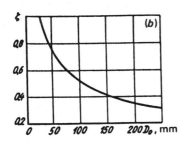

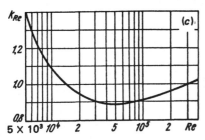

Re	5×10^3	10^4	2×10^4	5×10^4	10^5	2×10^5	3×10^5
k_{Re}	1.40	1.07	0.94	0.88	0.91	0.96	1.0

*For two consecutively installed valves ζ is taken from Diagram 9-1.

| Standard globe valve with dividing walls at complete opening;*[34,37] | Diagram |
| Re $= w_0 D_h/\nu \geqslant 10^4$ | 9-4 |

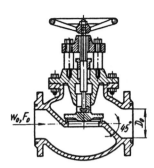

$$\zeta \equiv \frac{\Delta p}{\rho w_0^2/2} = f(D_0), \quad \text{see the table, or according to the formula**}$$

$$\zeta = \sum_{i=0}^{n_1} a_i D_0;$$

at $D_0 < 0.08$ m

$a_0 = 17.73064;$ $a_1 = -685.2598;$

$a_2 = 11634.4;$ $a_3 = -65479.38$

$n_1 = 3;$

at $D_0 \geqslant 0.08$ m

$a_0 = 3.277272;$ $a_1 = 8.66666;$

$a_2 = -6.060605,$ $n_1 = 2$

1. Dividing walls at angle 45° (curve 1)

D_0, mm	13	20	40	80	100	150	200	250	300	350
ζ	10.8	8.00	4.90	4.00	4.10	4.40	4.70	5.10	5.40	5.50

2. Vertical dividing walls (curve 2)

D_0, mm	13	20	25	30	40	50
ζ	15.9	10.5	9.30	8.60	7.60	6.90

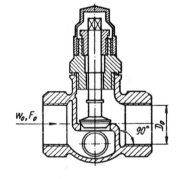

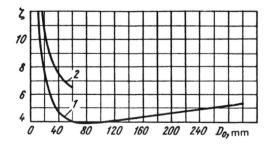

If two globe valves are installed successively, then the overall resistance coefficient is

$$\zeta_{1+2} = 0.5(\zeta_1 + \zeta_2)(2 - \beta)$$

where ζ_1 is determined as ζ of the first globe valve, ζ_2 as ζ of the second;

$$\beta = 4.2 \times 10^{-5}\left(\frac{l_{con}}{D_0}\right)^2 - 5 \times 10^{-3}\frac{l_{con}}{D_0} + 0.15$$

(l_{con} is the distance between two stopping devices).

*For two consecutively installed globes ζ is taken from Diagram 9-1.

**See the footnote on Diagram 3-1.

Gate valves in a straight tube (without a recess for the valve disk);[12,14,17,35] $Re = w_0 D_h/\nu > 10^4$	Diagram 9-5

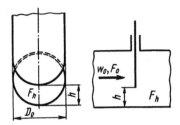

Circular cross section

$$\zeta \equiv \frac{\Delta p}{\rho w_0^2/2}$$

see the curves $\zeta = f(h/D_0 \text{ or } h/a_0)$

or determine from the formula

$$\zeta = \exp\left[2.3 \sum_{i=0}^{6} a_i (h/D_0)^i\right]$$

where a_i is given below.

At $0.2 \leqslant h/D_0 < 0.9$

$a_0 = 7.661175;$ $a_1 = -72.63827;$
$a_2 = 345.7625;$ $a_3 = -897.8331;$
$a_4 = 1275.939;$ $a_5 = -938.8331;$
$a_6 = 278.8193.$

At $h/D_0 \geqslant 0.9$

$$\zeta = 0.6\text{--}0.6(h/D_0)$$

$$D_h = \frac{4F_0}{\Pi_0}$$

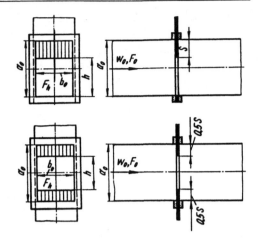

Rectangular cross section

Values of ζ for single disk gate valves (graph a)

	h/D_0 (h/a_0)									
	0.10	0.15	0.20	0.30	0.40	0.5	0.6	0.7	0.8	0.9
$\dfrac{a_0}{b_0}$ $(a_0 \times b_0)$	F_h/F_0 for circular cross section									
	–	–	0.25	0.38	0.50	0.61	0.71	0.81	0.90	0.96
	Circular cross section ($D_0 = 25$ mm)									
Curve 1	–	–	35.0	10.0	4.60	2.06	0.98	0.44	0.17	0.06
	Rectangular cross section									
0.5 (25 × 50). Curve 2	193	–	44.5	17.8	8.12	4.02	2.08	0.95	0.39	0.09
0.5 (150 × 300 mm). Curve 3	105	51.5	30.6	13.5	6.85	3.34	1.73	0.83	0.32	0.09
1.0 (150 × 150 mm). Curve 4	155	72.0	42.3	18.5	8.78	4.54	2.43	1.23	0.55	0.17
1.0 (225 × 150 mm). Curve 5	330	122	58.2	19.6	9.10	4.68	2.66	1.23	0.47	0.11
2.0 (300 × 150 mm). Curve 6	203	86.5	48.7	17.9	8.78	4.47	2.25	1.12	0.51	0.13

Gate valves in a straight tube (without a recess for the valve disk);[12,14,17,35] Re $= w_0 D_h/\nu > 10^4$	Diagram 9-5

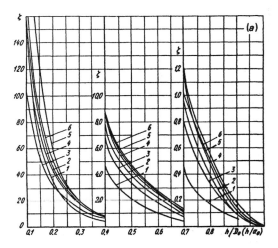

Values of ζ for two-part disk gate valve of rectangular cross section (graph b)

$\dfrac{a_0}{b_0}$ $(a_0 b_0)$	h/a_0								
	0.1	0.2	0.3	0.4	0.5	0.6	0.7	0.8	0.9
0.5 (150 × 300 mm). Curve 1	112	30.6	13.1	6.64	3.26	1.52	0.71	0.28	0.06
1.0 (150 × 150 mm). Curve 2	95.3	31.7	14.1	6.95	3.63	1.83	0.91	0.36	0.08
1.5 (225 × 150 mm). Curve 3	287	50.1	17.9	8.31	4.22	2.22	1.02	0.39	0.10
2.0 (300 × 160 mm). Curve 4	215	48.7	18.5	8.48	4.17	2.14	1.02	0.42	0.12

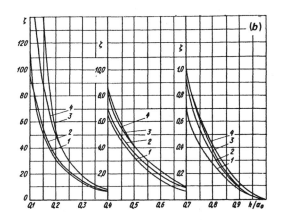

Plane-parallel gate valves of the Ludlow type, with a recess for the valve disk, in a straight tube of a circular cross section;[95] Re $= w_0 D_0/\nu > 10^4$	Diagram 9-6

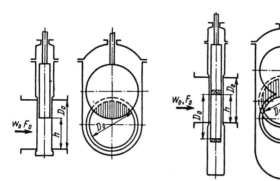

1. Gate valve in the system:

$$\zeta \equiv \frac{\Delta p}{\rho w_0^2/2}$$

see the curves $\zeta = f(h/D_0)$ or determine from the formula

$$\zeta = \exp\left[2.3 \sum_{i=0}^{7} a_i \left(\frac{h}{D_0}\right)^i\right],$$

where at $0.1 \leq h/D_0 \leq 1$

$a_0 = 3.229274$; $a_1 = -7.258083$;
$a_2 = -44.79518$; $a_3 = 337.6749$;
$a_4 = -967.6142$; $a_5 = 1404.989$;
$a_6 = -1022.979$; $a_7 = 295.2782$.

2. Exit gate valve (tentatively)

$$\zeta_{tot} \equiv \frac{\Delta p}{\rho w_0^2/2} = \zeta + 1$$

Values of ζ

Position of the gate valve	h/D_0										
	0.10	0.15	0.20	0.30	0.40	0.50	0.60	0.70	0.80	0.90	1.0
	With a recess for the valve disk (graph a)										
In the system (the gate valve is followed by a straight tube), Curve 1	200	77.0	33.0	11.0	4.70	2.35	1.23	0.67	0.31	0.11	0.05

Position of the gate valve	h/D_0										
	0.10	0.15	0.20	0.30	0.40	0.50	0.60	0.70	0.80	0.90	1.0
Terminal (gate valve at the exit), Curve 2	200	64.0	36.0	14.2	7.10	3.85	2.30	1.40	0.75	0.21	0.11
	With a hollow ring on the valve (graph b)										
In the system, Curve 1	400	–	43.0	12.8	5.30	2.48	1.19	0.51	0.22	0.08	0.03
Terminal, Curve 2	3900	–	260	70.0	22.0	87.0	4.00	1.85	0.78	0.15	0

Plane-parallel gate valves of the Ludlow type, with a recess for the valve disk, in a straight tube of a circular cross section;[95] Re $= w_0 D_0/\nu > 10^4$	Diagram 9-6

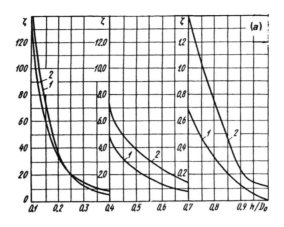

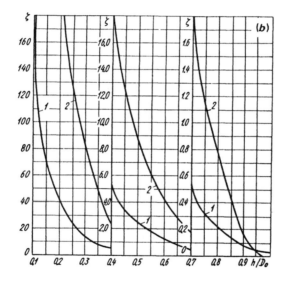

Plane-parallel gate valves of the Ludlow type, with a recess for the valve disk, in a converging-diverging transition piece of circular cross section;[14.36] Re $= w_0 D_0/\nu > 10^4$	Diagram 9-7

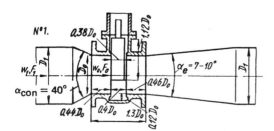

Asymmetric transition

$$\zeta \equiv \frac{\Delta p}{\rho w_0^2/2} = f\left(\frac{h}{D_0}\right)$$

$$\zeta_{ov} \equiv \frac{\Delta p}{\rho w_0^2/2} = \zeta + \zeta_{tr}$$

where ζ_{tr} is determined as ζ from Diagram 5-25.

Plane-parallel gate valves of the Ludlow type, with a recess for the valve disk, in a converging-diverging transition piece of circular cross section;[14,36] $Re = w_0 D_0/\nu > 10^4$	Diagram 9-7

Values of ζ for an asymmetric transition*

$\dfrac{D_1}{D_0}$	h/D_0										
	0.10	0.15	0.20	0.30	0.40	0.50	0.60	0.70	0.80	0.90	1.0
1.5 (curve 1)	200	77.0	34.0	12.5	6.50	3.65	2.15	1.35	0.71	0.24	0.07
1.5 (curve 2)	200	77.0	33.0	12.5	6.10	3.15	1.85	1.10	0.58	0.18	0.06

*Values of ζ for a gate valve in a converging-diverging transition piece do not allow for the losses in these transition pieces.

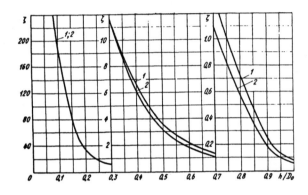

2.   Symmetrical transition.** Complete opening.

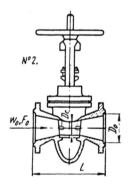

$$\zeta \equiv \frac{\Delta p}{\rho w_c^2/2}$$

where w_c is the velocity in the narrow section of the gate valve. For Case 1[27]

$$\zeta = 7 \tan \phi [1 - (h/D_0)^2]^2/(h/D_0)^4 \qquad (1)$$

at $Re < 10^4$

$$\zeta_{Re} = \zeta + 530\zeta^{1.25}/Re$$

where ζ is determined from formula (1).[13]

D_0, mm	300	300	200	250
D_c/D_0	0.67	0.67	0.75	0.80
L/D_0	2.50	1.68	1.33	1.50
ζ (without a guide pipe)	0.30	0.36	0.19	0.16
ζ (with a guide pipe)	0.25	0.28	0.18	0.15

**Values of ζ of the gate valve with symmetrical transition allow for the contraction and subsequent expansion losses.

Rolling seal gates;[35,36] $Re = w_0 D_0/\nu > 10^4$

Diagram
9-8

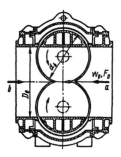

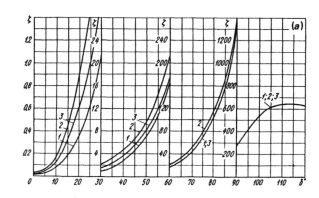

1. Seal gate in the system:

$$\zeta \equiv \frac{\Delta p}{\rho w_0^2/2},$$

   see the table and the curves $\zeta = f(\delta)$
2. Exit seal gate (tentatively):

$$\zeta \equiv \frac{\Delta p}{\rho w_0^2/2} = \zeta + 1$$

3. Seal gate in a transition piece (tentatively):
   $\zeta = \Delta p/(\rho w_0^2/2) - \zeta + \zeta_{fr}$ where ζ_{tr} is determined as ζ from Diagrams 5-25 and 5-26.

Values of ζ

D_1/D_0; place of installation of the breechlock	δ, degrees											
	0	10	20	30	40	50	60	70	80	90	100	115
Straight flow (direction A-B; graph a)												
1.0; in the system ($l_1^* > 0$); curve 1	0.02	0.08	0.36	1.08	2.80	6.80	16.9	44.0	108	277	540	620
1.0; at exit ($l_1 = 0$); curve 2	0.03	0.17	0.90	2.13	4.70	9.50	21.6	49.0	112	277	540	620
1.25–1.5; in converging-diverging transition piece ($l_1 > 0$); curve 3	0.02	0.13	0.60	1.60	3.70	7.5	18.0	44.0	106	277	540	620
Reverse flow (direction B-A; graph b)												
1.0; in the system ($l_1 > 0$); curve 1	0.01	0.19	0.70	1.70	3.8	7.70	15.8	35.0	81.0	191	549	820
1.0; at exit ($l_1 = 0$); curve 2	0.03	0.24	1.00	2.60	5.50	10.8	21.5	44.0	92.0	191	540	820

*For l_1, see scheme a of Diagram 9-20.

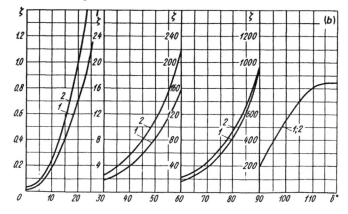

Circular outlet seal gates;[35,36] Re $= w_0 D_0/\nu > 10^4$ | Diagram 9-9

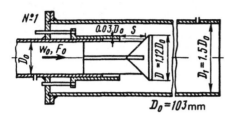

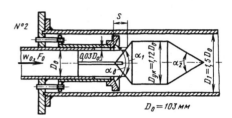

1. With a thrust cone

$$\zeta \equiv \frac{\Delta p}{\rho w_0^2/2}$$

see the curves $\zeta = f(s/D_0)$ of graph a.

2. With a streamlined thrust element for ζ, see the curves $\zeta = f(s/D_0)$ of graph b.

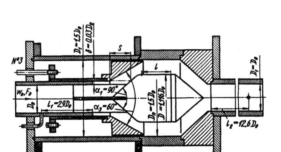

3. Discharge tube is contracted at the exit at complete opening

$$\zeta \equiv \frac{\Delta p}{\rho w_0^2/2} = 0.3$$

Values of ζ (scheme 1, graph a)

$\dfrac{D_1}{D_0}$	$\dfrac{s}{D_0}$				
	0.40	0.50	0.60	0.70	0.80
1.5 (curve 1)	1.80	1.50	1.35	1.30	1.26
1.75–2.0 (curve 2)	1.44	1.15	0.97	0.88	0.82
3.0 (curve 3)	1.58	1.20	1.05	0.95	0.90
∞ (curve 4)	1.83	1.50	1.30	1.19	1.12

Circular outlet seal gates;[35,36] Re $= w_0 D_0/\nu > 10^4$						Diagram 9-9

Values of ζ (scheme 2, graph b)

$\dfrac{D_1}{D_0}$	$\dfrac{s}{D_0}$						
	0.1	0.2	0.3	0.4	0.5	0.7	1.0
1.5 (curve 1)	13.0	3.10	1.04	0.51	0.39	0.33	0.32
1.75 (curve 2)	13.8	3.08	1.45	0.85	0.59	0.41	0.35
2.0 (curve 3)	9.42	3.50	1.50	1.01	0.76	0.58	0.51
2.5 (curve 4)	11.9	4.31	2.17	1.44	1.10	0.84	0.76
3.0 (curve 5)	16.0	4.92	2.51	1.66	1.28	1.00	0.86

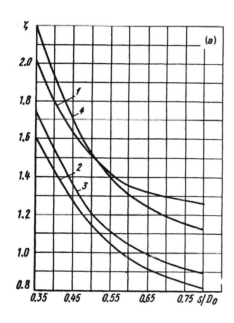

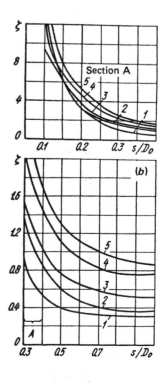

Revolving, conical seal gates;[35,36] $Re = w_0 D_h / \nu > 10^4$ Diagram 9-10

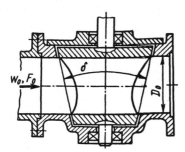

1. Seal gate in the system:

$$\zeta \equiv \frac{\Delta p}{\rho w_0^2/2} \, , \quad \text{see the curve } \zeta = f(\delta)$$

2. Seal gate at exit (tentatively):

$$\zeta_{ex} \equiv \frac{\Delta p}{\rho w_0^2/2} = \zeta + 1$$

3. Seal gate in the transition piece (tentatively):

$$\zeta_{ov} \equiv \frac{\Delta p}{\rho w_0^2/2} = \zeta + \zeta_{tr}$$

where ζ_{tr} is determined as ζ from Diagrams 5-24 and 5-25

Values of ζ

D_1/D_0; place of installation of the seal gate	δ, degrees									
	0	10	20	30	40	50	60	70	80	85
Seal gate in a straight tube										
1.0; in the system ($l_1^* > 0$), curve 1	0.04	0.36	1.60	5.00	15.0	42.5	130	800	2500	6000
1.0; at exit ($l_1 = 0$), curve 2	0.05	0.51	2.75	7.70	17.5	48.5	150	810	2500	6000
Seal gate in a converging-diverging transition piece: $\alpha_{con} = 40°$; $\alpha_{div} = 7°$										
1.25–1.5; in the system, curve 2	0.04	0.36	1.60	5.20	16.0	45.0	110	250	490	2500

*For l_1, see scheme a of Diagram 9-20.

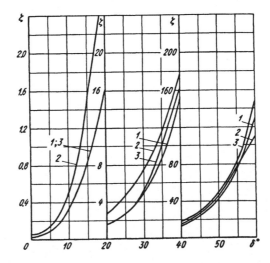

Spherical seal gates with one-sided sealing of the valve.[35,36]
$Re = w_0 D_0 / \nu > 10^4$

Diagram 9-11

1. Seal gate in the system:

$$\zeta \equiv \frac{\Delta p}{\rho w_0^2 / 2}$$

see the curve $\zeta = f(\delta)$

2. Seal gate at exit (tentatively):

$$\zeta_{tot} \equiv \frac{\Delta p}{\rho w_0^2 / 2} = \zeta + 1$$

Values of ζ

Place of installation of the seal gate	δ, degrees									
	0	10	20	30	40	50	60	70	80	85
Straight flow (direction A-B; graph a)										
In the system ($l_i{}^* > 0$), curve 1	0.02	0.23	0.98	2.70	6.40	14.8	35.7	116	815	4450
At exit ($l_i = 0$), curve 1	0.04	0.44	1.52	3.70	8.10	17.5	38.6	118	815	4450
Reverse flow (direction B-A; graph b)										
In the system ($l_i > 0$), curve 1	0.02	0.22	0.93	2.30	6.00	13.5	30.0	74.5	288	425
At exit ($l_i = 0$), curve 1	0.04	0.41	1.40	3.25	6.95	15.0	31.5	74.5	288	425

*For l_i, see scheme a of Diagram 9-20

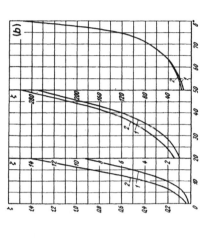

(a)

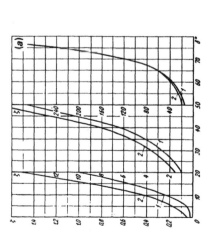

(b)

Spherical seal gates with two-sided sealing of the valve;[35,36] $Re = w_0 D_h / \nu > 10^4$	Diagram 9-12

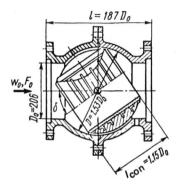

1. Seal gate in the system:

$$\zeta \equiv \frac{\Delta p}{\rho w_0^2/2} \,, \quad \text{see the curves } \zeta = f(\delta)$$

2. Seal gate at exit (tentatively):

$$\zeta_{tot} \equiv \frac{\Delta p}{\rho w_0^2/2} = \zeta + 1$$

Values of ζ

Place of installation of the seal gate	δ, degrees								
	0	10	20	30	40	50	60	70	80
In the system ($l_1^* > 0$), curve 1	0.02	0.29	1.10	3.50	9.50	21.7	59.0	278	10,000
At exit ($l_1 = 0$), curve 2	0.04	0.50	1.80	4.30	10.3	22.8	59.0	278	10,000

*For l_1, see scheme a of Diagram 9-20.

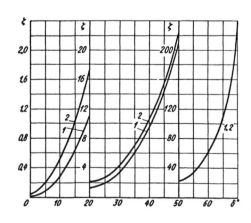

Spherical seal gates with a spherical valve disk and seat;[35,36] $Re = w_0 D_0/\nu > 10^4$	Diagram 9-13

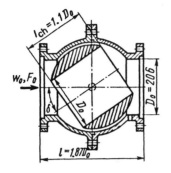

1. Seal gate in the system:

$$\zeta \equiv \frac{\Delta p}{\rho w_0^2/2}, \quad \text{see the curves } \zeta = f(\delta)$$

2. Seal gate at exit (tentatively):

$$\zeta_{tot} \equiv \frac{\Delta p}{\rho w_0^2/2} = \zeta + 1$$

3. Seal gate in a transition piece (tentatively):

$$\zeta_{ov} = \frac{\Delta p}{\rho w_0^2/2} = \zeta + \zeta_{tr}$$

where ζ_{tr} is determined as ζ from Diagrams 5-25 and 5-26

Values of ζ

D_1/D_0; place of installation of a seal gate	δ, degrees									
	0	10	20	30	40	50	60	70	75	85
Seal gate in a straight tube (graph a)										
1.0; in the system $(l_1^* > 0)$, curve 1	0.02	0.21	1.07	3.35	9.20	24.0	65.0	204	330	624
1.0; at exit $(l_1 = 0)$, curve 2	0.03	0.47	1.90	4.75	12.4	27.5	65.0	204	–	625
Seal gate in a converging-diverging transition piece (curve b) $\alpha_{con} = 40°$; $\alpha_{div} = 7°$										
1.25; in the system curve 1	0.04	0.38	1.70	4.35	10.9	25.5	70.0	204	330	624
1.5; in the system, curve 2	0.06	0.57	2.00	5.00	11.5	28.0	70.0	204	330	624

*For l_1, see scheme a of Diagram 9-20.

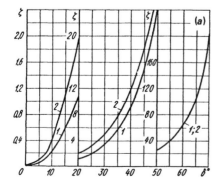

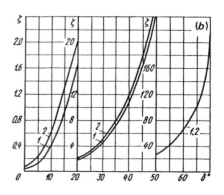

Sector gate valves; Re $= w_0 D_h/\nu > 10^4$	Diagram 9-14

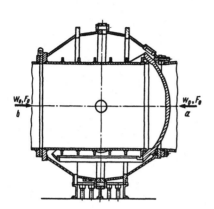
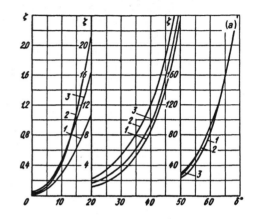

1. Gate valve in the system

$$\zeta \equiv \frac{\Delta p}{\rho w_0^2/2}$$

see the table and the curves
$\zeta = f(\delta)$

2. Exit gate valve (tentatively):

$$\zeta_{tot} \equiv \frac{\Delta p}{\rho w_0^2/2} = \zeta + 1$$

3. Gate valve in transition piece: (tentatively):

$$\zeta_{ov} \equiv \frac{\Delta p}{\rho w_0^2/2} = \zeta + \zeta_{tr}$$

where ζ_{tr} is determined as ζ from Diagrams 5-25 and 5-26

Values of ζ

D_1/D_0; place of installation of the gate valve	δ, degrees								
	0	10	20	30	40	50	60	70	80
Straight flow (direction A-B; graph a)									
1.0; in the system ($l_1{}^* > 0$), curve 1	0.02	0.27	1.10	3.20	8.70	23.5	79.5	272	624
1.0; at exit ($l_1 = 0$), curve 2	0.03	0.44	2.10	5.25	12.0	30.5	91.0	277	624
1.25–1.50; in a converging-diverging transition piece ($l_1 > 0$); curve 3	0.05	0.47	1.64	3.94	9.40	28.3	90.0	277	624
Reverse flow (direction B-A; graph b)									
1.0; in the system ($l_1 > 0$); curve 1	0.02	0.12	0.59	1.82	5.62	18.8	79.5	398	773
1.0; at exit ($l_1 = 0$); curve 2	0.04	0.53	1.60	3.42	8.65	18.8	73.5	398	773

*For l_1, see scheme a of Diagram 9-20.

Sector gate valves; Re $= w_0 D_h/\nu > 10^4$

Diagram
9-14

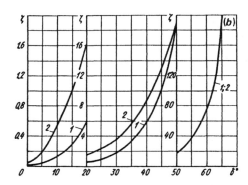

Flap (in the system);[7] Re $= w_0 D_h/\nu > 10^4$

Diagram
9-15

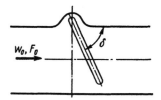

$$\zeta \equiv \frac{\Delta p}{\rho w_0^2/2} \approx 0.35\exp(0.0744\delta)$$

from the curve $\zeta = f(\delta)$

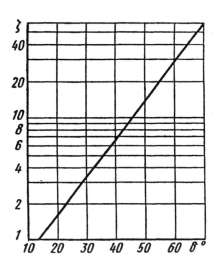

δ, degrees	20	30	40	50	60	70	75
ζ	1.7	3.2	6.6	14	30	62	90

Cylindrical valve in the system[47]	Diagram
$Re = w_0 D_h/\nu > 10^4$	9-16

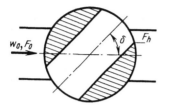

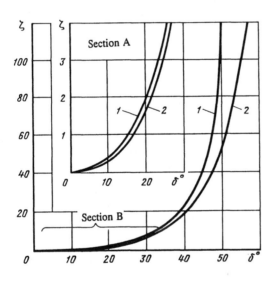

$$\zeta \equiv \frac{\Delta p}{\rho w_0^2/2} \; , \quad \text{see the curves } \zeta = f(\delta)$$

1. Cylindrical tube

$\delta°$	5	10	20	30	40	50	55	67
F_h/F_0	0.93	0.85	0.69	0.52	0.35	0.19	0.11	0
ζ	0.05	0.31	1.84	6.15	20.7	95.3	275	∞

2. Rectangular tube

$\delta°$	5	10	20	30	40	50	60	82
F_h/F_0	0.93	0.85	0.69	0.53	0.38	0.25	0.14	0
ζ	0.05	0.29	1.56	5.47	17.3	52.6	206	–

Butterfly valves (throttling, plane disks) in a tube of circular cross section at different $Re = w_0 D_0/\nu^5$	Diagram 9-17

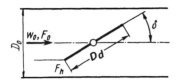

Curve 1:

$$D_0 = 25\text{--}40 \text{ mm}$$

$$\overline{D}_d = \frac{D_d}{D_0} = 0.98$$

$$\overline{f} = \frac{F_h}{F_0} \approx 0.92 \quad (\text{at } \delta = 0°)$$

Curve 2:

$$\overline{D}_d = 1.0$$

$$\overline{f} \approx 0.99 \quad (\text{at } \delta = 0°)$$

$$\zeta \equiv \frac{\Delta p}{\rho w_0^2/2} \approx \frac{120}{Re} \frac{1 + 0.5\overline{D}_d(1 + \sin \delta)}{(1 - \overline{D}_d^2 \sin \delta)^2}$$

$$+ \left(1 - \frac{50}{Re}\right)\left(\frac{1.56}{1 - \overline{D}_d^2 \sin \delta} - 1\right)^2$$

$$= \frac{1}{Re} + \left(1 - \frac{50}{Re}\right)\zeta_{qu}$$

where $A \approx 120\left[\dfrac{1 + 0.5\overline{D}_d(1 + \sin \delta)}{(1 - \overline{D}_d^2 \sin \delta)^2}\right]$; $\quad Re = \dfrac{w_0 D_0}{\nu}$

at $\delta > 25°$:

$$\zeta_{qu} \equiv \left(\frac{1.56}{1 - \overline{D}_d^2 \sin \delta} - 1\right)^2$$

for all δ: $\zeta_{qu} = f(\delta)$, see the graph; at $Re \leq 50$, the value of $1 - 50/Re$ is assumed to be equal to zero.

Values of ζ_{qu}

Curve	δ, degrees								
	0	10	20	30	40	50	60	70	75
1	0.60	0.85	1.70	4.00	9.40	24.0	67.0	215	400
2	–	0.52	1.54	4.50	11.0	29.0	108	625	–

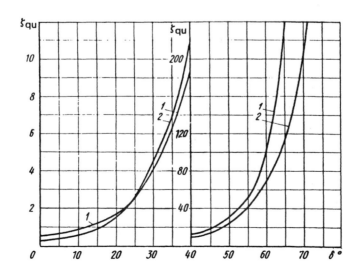

Throttling butterfly valves in a tube of rectangular cross section at any Re $= w_0 D_h/\nu^{6,28,35}$	Diagram 9-18

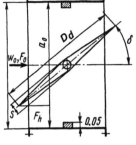

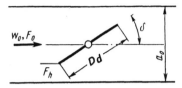

1. Plane valve   2. Beveled plane valve

$$\zeta \equiv \frac{\Delta p}{\rho w_0^2/2} \approx \frac{120}{Re}$$

$$\overline{f} = \frac{F_h}{F_0} \approx 0.99 \quad (\text{at } \delta = 0°) \qquad \overline{f} = \frac{F_h}{F_0}$$

$$\times \left[\frac{1 + 0.5(1 + \sin \delta)}{(1 - \sin \delta)^2} \right]$$

$$= 0.725 \quad (\text{at } \delta = 0°)$$

$$\overline{D}_d = \frac{D_d}{a_0} = 1.0 \qquad\qquad \overline{D}_d = 1.0$$

$$+ \left(1 - \frac{50}{Re} \right) \zeta_{qu}$$

at Re $\le$ 50, the value of $1 - 50/Re$ is assumed to be equal to zero; $\zeta_{qu} = f(\delta)$, see the graph.

Values of ζ_{qu}

$\dfrac{a_0}{b_0}$ (a_0)	δ, degrees								
	0	10	20	30	40	50	60	65	70
1. Thin plane valve									
0.5–1.0 (150–300 mm) curve 1	0.04	0.30	1.10	3.00	8.00	23.0	60	100	190
1.5–2 (150–300 mm) curve 2	0.04	0.35	1.25	3.60	10.0	29.0	80.0	–	230
0.5 (25–40 mm) curve 3	–	0.45	1.34	3.54	9.30	25.0	77.0	158	368
2. Beveled plane valve									
0.5–1.0 (200–400 mm) curve 4	0.50	0.65	1.60	4.00	9.40	24.0	67.0	120	215

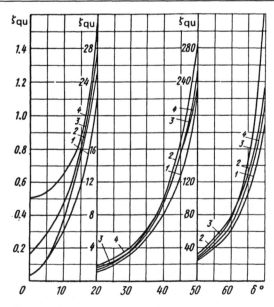

Thin-walled disk throttling valves, with parallel and nonparallel flaps, in a tube of square cross section at any value of Re $= w_0 D_h / \nu^{6.29}$	Diagram 9-19

$$\bar{f} = \frac{F_h}{F_0} = 0.99 \quad (\text{at } \delta = 0°)$$

$$\bar{f} = 0.725 \quad (\text{at } \delta = 0°)$$

$$\zeta \equiv \frac{\Delta p}{\rho w_0^2 / 2} \approx \frac{120}{\text{Re}} \left[\frac{1 + 0.5(1 + \sin \delta)}{(1 - \sin \delta)^2} \right] + \left(1 - \frac{50}{\text{Re}} \right) \zeta_{qu}$$

at Re ≤ 50, the value of $1 - 50/\text{Re}$ is taken to be equal to zero; $\zeta_{qu} = f(\delta)$, see the graph.

Values of ζ_{qu}

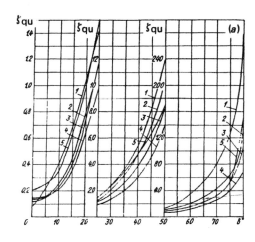

Number of flaps (no. of curve)	δ, degrees				
	0	10	20	30	40
Parallel flaps (scheme 1, graph a)					
2 (Curve 1)	0.07	0.40	1.10	2.20	5.50
3 (Curve 2)	0.14	0.25	0.80	2.00	4.50
4 (Curve 3)	0.12	0.22	0.73	1.70	4.00
5 (Curve 4)	0.15	0.20	0.65	1.50	3.00
6 (Curve 5)	0.20	0.35	1.00	2.30	4.80
Nonparallel flaps (scheme 2, graph b)					
2 (Curve 1)	0.70	0.95	1.50	3.00	7.50
Parallel flaps on a side branch (scheme 3, graph b)					
3 (Curve 2)	0.28	0.40	1.10	2.50	5.00
Streamlined (scheme 4, graph b)					
2 (Curve 3)	–	0.57	0.92	2.50	5.80

Number of flaps (no. of curve)	δ, degrees			
	50	60	70	80
Parallel flaps (scheme 1, graph a)				
2 (Curve 1)	11.5	30.0	80.0	300
3 (Curve 2)	10.0	20.0	40.0	140
4 (Curve 3)	8.00	14.0	30.0	110
5 (Curve 4)	7.00	13.0	35.0	70
6 (Curve 5)	8.50	16.0	35.0	150
Nonparallel flaps (scheme 2, graph b)				
2 (Curve 1)	20.0	55.0	180.0	800
Parallel flaps on a side branch (scheme 3, graph b)				
3 (Curve 2)	10.0	18.0	42.0	200
Streamlined (scheme 4, graph b)				
2 (Curve 3)	12.5	28.0	58.0	130

Throttling valves in a tube of circular cross section with disk gates of different shape at complete opening ($\delta = 0°$),[35] $Re = w_0 D_0/\nu > 10^5$

Diagram 9-20

Values of $\zeta_{tot} = \dfrac{\Delta p}{\rho w_0^2/2} = \zeta + 1$ for terminal valves (tentatively)

Values of $\zeta = \dfrac{\Delta p}{\rho w_0^2/2}$

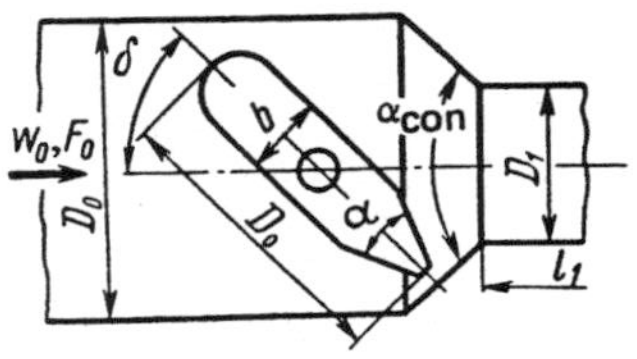

D_0/D_1; place of valve installation	b/D_0					
	0.10	0.15	0.20	0.25	0.30	0.35
1.0; in the system ($l_1 > 0$)	0.06	0.098	0.175	0.315	0.525	0.800
1.4–1.8; in the system ($l_1 = 0$)	–	0.082–0.085	0.090–0.100	0.110–0.125	0.180–0.200	0.250–0.200
1.35; at exit ($l_1 = 0$)	–	0.085	–	0.195	–	0.275
1.0; at exit ($l_1 = 0$)	–	–	–	0.405	–	–

Plane disk with stationary fairings, $\alpha_2 = 20°$; $D_0/D_1 = 1.0$

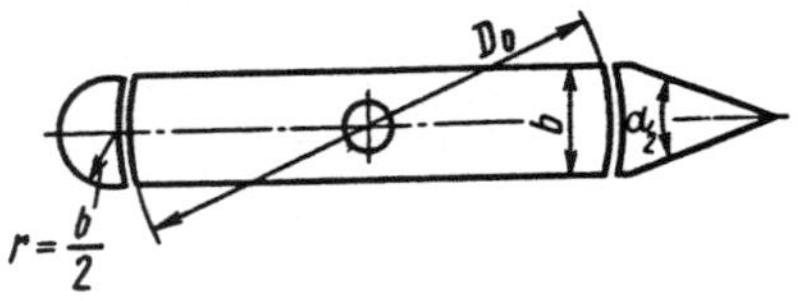

In the system ($l_1 > 0$)	0.05	0.07	0.09	0.13	0.17	0.23
At exit ($l_1 = 0$)	–	0.100	–	0.150	–	0.315

Beveled disk; $D_0/D_1 = 1.0$

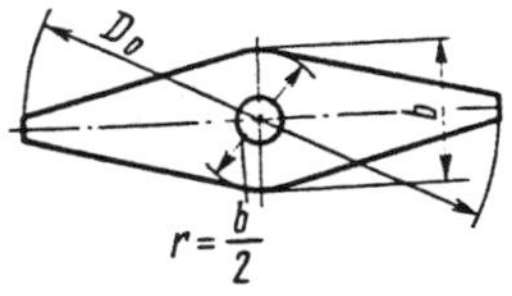

In the system ($l_1 > 0$)	0.08	0.15	0.33	0.53	0.70	–

Regulating valves at any Re	Diagram
$(D_0 = 50 \text{ mm})^{5,6}$	9-21

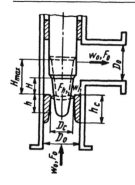

1. Angular single-seat valve within $1.7 < h/D_h \leq 30$:

$$\zeta \equiv \frac{\Delta p}{\rho w_h^2/2} = \frac{A_1}{Re_h} + \zeta_{1qu}$$

where

$$A_1 = 4.1 \frac{h}{D_h} + 23 \qquad \zeta_{1qu} = \left(1 - \frac{F_h}{F_0}\right)^2 + 0.18$$

$$\zeta_0 \equiv \frac{\Delta p}{\rho w_0^2/2} = \zeta\left(\frac{F_0}{F_h}\right)^2 = \frac{A_1}{Re_h}\left(\frac{F_0}{F_h}\right)^2 + \zeta_{01qu}$$

where $\zeta_{01qu} = \zeta_{1qu}\left(\frac{F_0}{F_h}\right)^2$ see the curve $\zeta_{01qu} = f\left(\frac{F_h}{F_0}\right)$

at complete opening of the valve $h/D_h \leq 1.7$:

$$\zeta = \frac{30}{Re_h} + \zeta_{1qu} \qquad \zeta_0 = \frac{30}{Re_h}\left(\frac{F_0}{F_h}\right)^2 + \zeta_{01qu}$$

2. Double-seat valve within $4.0 \leq h/D_h \leq 60$:

$$\zeta \equiv \frac{\Delta p}{\rho w_h^2/2} = \frac{A_2}{Re_h} + \zeta_{2qu}$$

where

$$A_2 = 0.5 \frac{h}{D_h} + 27 \qquad \zeta_{2qu} = \left(1 - \frac{F_h}{F_0}\right)^2 + 4.7\left(\frac{F_h}{F_0}\right)^2$$

$$\zeta_0 \equiv \frac{\Delta p}{\rho w_0^2/2} = \zeta\left(\frac{F_0}{F_h}\right)^2 = \frac{A_2}{Re_h}\left(\frac{F_0}{F_h}\right)^2 + \zeta_{02qu}$$

where $\zeta_{02qu} = \zeta_{2qu}\left(\frac{F_0}{F_h}\right)^2$ see the curve $\zeta_{02qu} = f\left(\frac{F_h}{F_0}\right)$

at complete opening of the valve $h/D_h \leq 4.0$:

$$\zeta = \frac{30}{Re_h} + \zeta_{2qu} \qquad \zeta_0 = \frac{30}{Re_h}\left(\frac{F_0}{F_h}\right)^2 + \zeta_{02qu}$$

F/F_0	0.1	0.2	0.3	0.4	0.5	0.6	0.7	0.8	0.9	1.0
ζ_{01qu}	99.0	20.5	7.50	3.40	1.72	0.95	0.55	0.34	0.24	0.18
ζ_{02qu}	86.0	21.0	10.5	7.20	5.70	5.20	4.90	4.75	4.70	4.70

Check valve and suction valve with screen[15]   Diagram 9-22

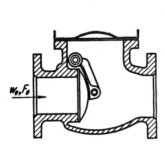
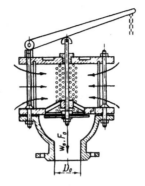

1. Check valve

2. Suction valve with a screen
   a) $Re \geq 10^4$

$$\zeta \equiv \frac{\Delta p}{\rho w_0^2/2} = f(D_0), \quad \text{see the graph, table or determine from the}$$

formulas (D_0 in mm):

Scheme 1

$$\zeta = 1.0755 + 5.161422D_0 = 6.714641D_0^2 + 4.934111D_0^3 \qquad (1)$$

Scheme 2

$$\zeta = \sum_{i=0}^{7} a_i D_0^i \qquad (2),$$

where $a_0 = 22.1298$; $a_1 = -382.4438$; $a_2 = 3320.882$;
$a_3 = -22160.76$; $a_4 = 70762.35$; $a_5 = -126777.8$;
$a_6 = 118352.6$; $a_7 = -44643.31$

Values of ζ

Scheme	D_0, mm						
	40	70	100	200	300	500	750
1	1.3	1.4	1.5	1.9	2.1	2.5	2.9
2	1.2	8.5	7.0	4.7	3.7	2.5	1.6

b) $Re < 10^4$

$$\zeta_{Re} = \zeta + 530 \, (\zeta)^{1.25}/Re,$$

where ζ is determined from formulas (1) and (2).

Disk valve without bottom guides[30,37]   Diagram 9-23

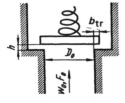

$$\zeta \equiv \frac{\Delta \rho}{\rho w_0^2/2} = \alpha_0 + \beta_0$$

where $\alpha_0 = 0.55 + 4[(b_{tr}/D_0) - 0.1]$, see graph a: $b_0 = 0.155/(h/D_0)^2$, see graph b. The formula is valid within

$$0.1 < \frac{h}{D_0} < 0.25 \qquad 0.1 < \frac{b_{tr}}{D_0} < 0.25$$

| Disk valve without bottom guides[30,37] | | | | | | | Diagram 9-23 | | |

b_{tr}/D_0	0.10	0.12	0.14	0.16	0.18	0.20	0.22	0.24	0.25
α_0	0.55	0.63	0.71	0.79	0.87	0.95	1.03	1.11	1.15

h/D_0	0.10	0.12	0.14	0.16	0.18	0.20	0.22	0.24	0.25
β_0	15.5	10.8	7.90	6.05	4.78	3.87	3.20	2.69	2.48

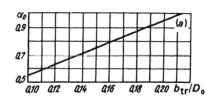
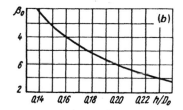

| Disk valve with bottom guides[30,37] | | | Diagram 9-24 |

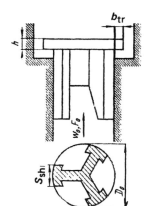

$$\zeta \equiv \frac{\Delta p}{\rho w_0^2/2} = \gamma_0\alpha_0 + \frac{\beta_1}{(\pi - iS_{sh}/D_0)}$$

where $\alpha_0 = 0.55 + 4\left(\frac{b_{tr}}{D_0} - 0.1\right)$, see graph a; for γ_0, see graph b;

$\beta_1 = \frac{1.73}{(h/D_0)^{-2}}$, see graph c; i is the number of fins; F_{fl} is the true flow area.

The formula is valid within

$$0.125 < \frac{h}{D_0} < 0.25 \qquad 0.10 < \frac{b_{tr}}{D_0} < 0.25$$

b_{tr}/D_0	0.10	0.12	0.14	0.16	0.18	0.20	0.22	0.24	0.25
α_0	0.55	0.63	0.71	0.79	0.87	0.95	1.03	1.11	1.15

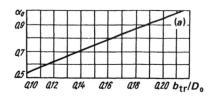

| Disk valve with bottom guides[30,37] | | | | | | Diagram 9-24 | |

F_n/F_0	0.80	0.81	0.82	0.83	0.84	0.85	0.86	0.87
γ_0	1.60	1.48	1.36	1.23	1.14	1.02	0.92	0.80

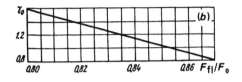

h/D_0	0.125	0.14	0.16	0.18	0.20	0.22	0.24	0.25
β_1	111	88.4	67.5	53.5	43.3	35.8	30.0	2.77

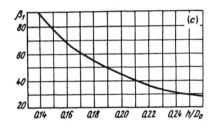

| Conical valve on a conical seat[30,37] | Diagram 9-25 |

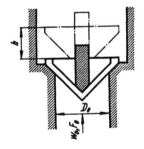

$$\zeta \equiv \frac{\Delta p}{\rho w_0^2/2} = 0.6 + \frac{0.15}{(h/D_0)^2} = f\left(\frac{h}{D_0}\right)$$

see the graph. The formula is valid within $0.125 < h/D_0 < 0.4$

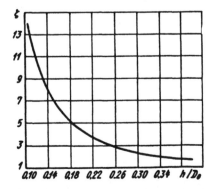

h/D_0	0.10	0.15	0.20	0.25	0.30	0.35	0.40
ζ	15.6	7.27	4.35	3.00	2.27	1.82	1.54

Conical valve on a flat seat and ball valve on a spherical seat[30,37]	Diagram 9-26

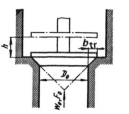 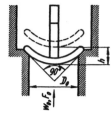

$$\zeta \equiv \frac{\Delta p}{\rho w_0^2/2} = 2.7 - \beta_2 + \beta_3$$

where

$$\beta_2 = \frac{0.8}{h/D_0} = f_1\left(\frac{h}{D_0}\right) \qquad \beta_3 = \frac{0.14}{(h/D_0)^2} = f_2\left(\frac{h}{(D_0)}\right)$$

The formula is valid within

$$0.1 < \frac{h}{D_0} < 0.25 \qquad \frac{b_{tr}}{D_0} = 0.1$$

1. Conical valve   2. Ball valve

h/D_0	0.10	0.12	0.14	0.16	0.18	0.20	0.22	0.24	0.25
β_2	8.00	6.66	5.71	5.00	4.44	4.00	3.63	3.33	3.20
β_3	14.0	9.73	7.15	5.46	4.32	3.50	2.90	2.43	2.24

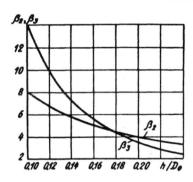

Disk valve under complex conditions[16] Re $\geq 10^4$	Diagram 9-27

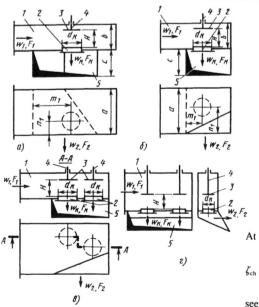

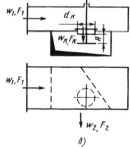

At $0.15 < H/d_{ch} < 0.6$

$$\zeta_{ch} \equiv \frac{\Delta p}{\sigma w_{ch}^2} \approx 0.122 (H/d_{ch})^{-2} + 0.195(H/d_{ch})^{-1} + c_i,$$

see curves 1–4;

$$\zeta_{ch} \equiv \frac{\Delta p}{\sigma w_{ch}^2/2} \approx 0.075 (H/d_{ch})^{-2} + 0.286(H/d_{ch})^{-1} + 2.42,$$

see curve 5

Disk valve under complex conditions[16] $Re \geqslant 10^4$	Diagram 9-27

a–d,	the valve is open in the direction of the high-pressure volume;
e,	the valve is open in the direction of the low-pressure volume;
a)	blow-down valve: $b = 0.9$–2.0; $c = 1.1$–3.3; $a = 2.5$–2.8; $m_1 = 1.2$–2.0; $n_1 = 0.6$–1.7
b)	discharge valve: $b = 1.1$–2.0, $c = 0.8$–3.5; $a = 2.2$, $m_1 = 0.7$, $n_1 = 1.4$
c)	discharge valves;
d)	intake valves
1)	supplying section; 2) seat; 3) tray of the valve;
4)	movable rod; 5) discharge channel

Values of ζ_{ch}

No. of the curve	Scheme	c_i	\multicolumn{8}{c}{H/d_{ch}}

No. of the curve	Scheme	c_i	0.15	0.2	0.3	0.4	0.5	0.6	0.7	0.8
1	d	4.41	–	8.85	5.35	5.40	6.20	5.15	5.12	5.10
2	c	3.71	–	8.00	5.80	5.00	4.60	4.45	4.45	4.45
3	a	2.81	8.50	6.05	5.00	4.15	3.75	3.50	3.50	3.50
4	b	2.56	8.50	6.05	4.75	3.90	3.95	3.25	3.20	3.20
5	e	2.42	7.60	5.65	4.30	3.60	3.35	3.15	3.05	3.05

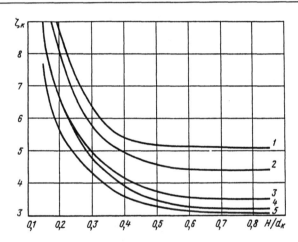

Labyrinth seal with an enlarged gap[13,14]	Diagram 9-28

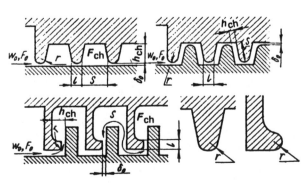

$$\frac{h_{ch}}{\delta_0'} > \frac{\delta_b}{\delta_0'}$$

$$\zeta \equiv \frac{\Delta p}{\rho w_0^2/2} = 1 + \zeta' + n_c(a_0 + \zeta' b_1 + \zeta_{tr})$$

$$\frac{h_{ch}}{\zeta_0'} < \frac{\delta_b}{\zeta_0'}:$$

$$\zeta = 1 + \zeta' + n_c(a_2 + \zeta' b_2 + \zeta_{tr})$$

where

$$\frac{\delta_b}{\zeta_0'} = 0.24 \frac{S}{\delta_0'} + 1; \qquad a_0 = F_1\left(\frac{S}{\delta_0'}\right);$$

Labyrinth seal with an enlarged gap[13,14]	Diagram 9-28

and $b_1 = f_2(S/\zeta_0')$, see graph a; $a_2 = [1 - (F_0/F_{ch})]^2$ and $B_2 = 1 - (F_0/F_{ch})$, see graph b; ζ' is determined as $\zeta = f(r/D_0)$ from Diagram 3-4; at $r_i/\zeta_0' = 0$; $\zeta' = 0.5$; $\zeta_0 = \lambda l/D_h$; for λ see Diagrams 2-1 through 2-6; n_c is the number of cells of the labyrinth, D_h is the hydraulic diameter of the gap; F_0 is the sectional area of the gap; F_{ch} is the area of the chamber cross section.

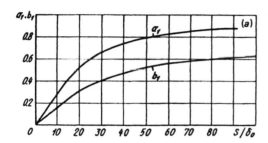

s/ζ_0'	a_0	b_1
0	0	0
5	0.15	0.08
10	0.28	0.16
20	0.53	0.91
30	0.65	0.40
40	0.73	0.47
50	0.78	0.52
60	0.82	0.55
70	0.84	0.58
80	0.87	0.59
90	0.87	0.61
100	0.87	0.63

$\dfrac{F_0}{F_{ch}} = \dfrac{\delta_0'}{h_{ch}}$	0	0.1	0.2	0.3	0.4	0.5	0.6	0.7	0.8	0.9	1.0
a_2	1.0	0.81	0.64	0.49	0.36	0.25	0.16	0.09	0.04	0.01	0
b_2	1.0	0.90	0.80	0.70	0.60	0.50	0.40	0.30	0.20	0.10	0

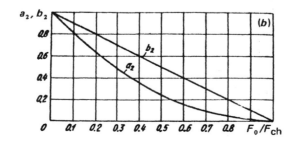

Labyrinth with flow passage from one volume into another through a 90° turn (data of the author)	Diagram 9-29

Elbow characteristic	Scheme	Resistance coefficient $\zeta \equiv \dfrac{\Delta p}{\rho w_0^2/2}$
With beveled inlet (exit) section without vanes	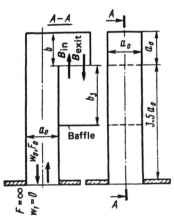	$\zeta_{in} \approx 4.8$ $\zeta_{exit} \approx 3.7$
The same but with vanes		$\zeta_{in} \approx 2.8$ $\zeta_{exit} \approx 2.3$
With inlet (exit) length $l_0 = a_0$, without vanes		$\zeta_{in} \approx 4.3$ $\zeta_{exit} \approx 3.7$
The same with vanes		$\zeta_{in} \approx 2.3$ $\zeta_{exit} \approx 1.7$

Labyrinth with flow passage from one volume into another through an oblong 180° turn (data of the author)	Diagram 9-30

$$\zeta \equiv \frac{\Delta p}{\rho w_0^2/2} = f\!\left(\frac{b}{a_0}\right)$$

Values of ζ with a baffle; $b/a_0 = 1.0$ (see graph a)

Flow direction	b_8/a_0							
	0.2	0.4	0.8	1.2	1.6	2.0	2.4	2.6
Inlet (curve 1)	7.3	4.6	4.3	4.3	4.3	4.3	4.4	4.4
Exit (curve 2)	13	7.6	6.8	6.6	6.3	6.1	6.0	5.9

Values of ζ without baffle (see graph b)

Flow direction	b/a_0					
	0.5	0.6	0.8	1.0	1.2	1.4
Inlet (curve 1)	9.5	8.0	5.8	4.4	3.6	3.2
Exit (curve 2)	12.0	10.1	7.4	5.7	4.6	4.1

Labyrinth with flow passage from one volume into another through an oblong 180° turn (data of the author)	Diagram 9-30

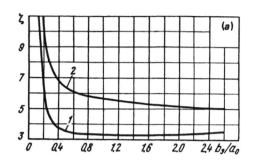

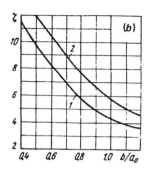

Labyrinth with flow passage from one volume into another through different elbow turns (data of the author)	Diagram 9-31

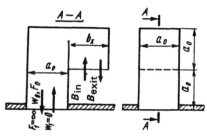

$$\zeta \equiv \frac{\Delta p}{\rho w_0^2/2} = f\left(\frac{b}{a_0}\right) \quad \text{see the graphs}$$

a) Short 180° turn

a) Values of ζ

	b_{ch}/a_0					
Flow direction	0.5	0.6	0.8	1.0	1.2	1.4
Inlet (curve 1)	11.0	9.0	6.7	5.5	4.9	4.5
Exit (curve 2)	17.2	14.5	10.2	7.4	5.8	5.1

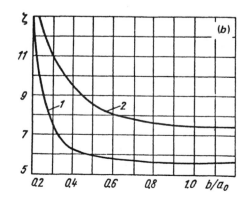

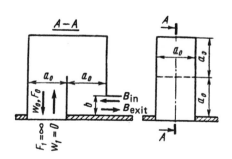

b) Hood with three-sided inlet (exit)

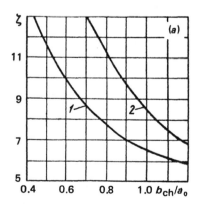

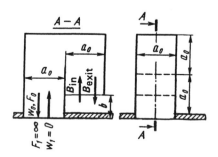

c) Hood with a straight section at the inlet (exit)

Labyrinth with flow passage from one volume into another through different elbow turns (data of the author)	Diagram 9-31

b) Values of ζ

Flow direction	b/a_0					
	0.18	0.2	0.4	0.6	0.8	1.0
Inlet (curve 1)	13.3	12.4	6.2	5.7	5.7	5.5
Exit (curve 2)	14.2	13.9	9.4	8.0	7.5	7.0

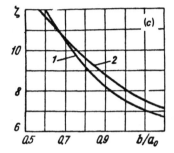

c) Values of ζ

Flow direction	b/a_0					
	0.5	0.6	0.8	1.0	1.2	1.4
Inlet curve 1)	13.5	12.0	9.0	7.4	6.6	6.9
Exit (curve 2)	13.0	11.7	9.5	8.0	7.1	6.3

Expansion joints[34]	Diagram 9-32

Type	Scheme	Resistance coefficient $\zeta \equiv \dfrac{\Delta p}{\rho w_0^2/2}$
Stuffing box	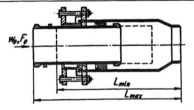	$\zeta = 0.2$
Lyre-shaped, smooth $R_0/d = 6$ $r/d \approx 5$	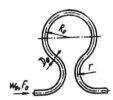	$\zeta = 1.6 + 2D_0$ (D_0, in m)
Lyre-shaped with folds $R_0/d \approx 6$ $r/d \approx 6$	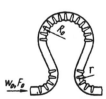	$\zeta \times 1.9 + 3D_0$ (D_0, in m)

For "Lyre-shaped, smooth":

D_0, mm	50	100	200	300	400	500
ζ	1.7	1.8	2.0	2.2	2.4	2.6

For "Lyre-shaped with folds":

D_0, mm	80	100	200	300	400	500
ζ	2.1	2.2	2.5	2.8	3.1	3.5

Expansion joints[34]		Diagram 9-32

Type	Scheme	Resistance coefficient $\zeta \equiv \dfrac{\Delta p}{\rho w_0^2/2}$

Lyre-shaped, made from corrugated tube

$R_0/d \approx 5$
$r/d \approx 3.0$

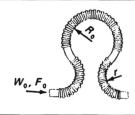

$\zeta \approx 2.875 + 4.25 D_0$ (D_0, in m)

D_0, mm	50	100	200	300	400	500
ζ	3.1	3.3	3.7	4.2	4.6	5.0

II-shaped

$\zeta = 1.9 + 2D_0$ (D_0, in m)

D_0, mm	50	100	200	300	400	500
ζ	2.0	2.1	2.3	2.5	2.7	2.9

Wavy, sealing, lenslike, angular, axial

$\zeta = 0.3$

Coils[3,4]		Diagram 9-33

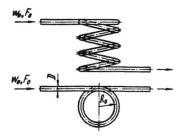

$\zeta \equiv \dfrac{\Delta p}{\rho w_0^2/2}$ see Diagram 6-2

REFERENCES

1. Abelev, S. A., Hydraulics of gates and valves, *Gidravlich. Issled.*, 30–40, 1962.
2. Abramovich, G. N., *Theory of Turbulent Jets*, Fizmatgiz, Moscow, 1960, 715 p.
3. Altshul, A. D. and Kalitsun, V. I., On pressure head losses in converging-diverging units with a gate valve, *Gazov. Prom.*, no. 2, 35–39, 1960.
4. Altshul, A. D. and Arzumanov, E. S., Pressure losses in regulating valves during flow of viscous liquids, *Neft. Khoz.*, no. 7, 51–56, 1967.
5. Arzumanov, E. S., *Calculation and Choice of Regulators of Automatic Systems*, Energiya Press, Moscow, 1971, 112 p.
6. Arzumanov, E. S. and Viziryan, R. E., Pressure losses in valve gates during flow of viscous liquids in pipelines, *Neft. Khoz.*, no. 9, 66–68, 1971.
7. Aronovich, V. V. and Slobodkin, M. S., *Regulating and Locking Fitting*, Mashgiz, 1953.
8. Balanin, V. V., Hydraulic characteristics of disk valve gates with fairings, *Tr. Leningr. Inst. Vodnogo Transp.*, vyp. 112, 4–17, 1967.
9. Baulin, K. K., Testing of labyrinth seals, *Tr. VIGM*, vyp. 10, 50–65, 1940.
10. Gubarev, P. S., Local resistances of fittings of high-pressure air pipelines, *Sudostroenie*, no. 3, 41–44, 1957.
11. Gurevich, D. F., *Fundamentals of Calculation of Pipeline Fitting*, Mashgiz, Leningrad, 1956, 230 p.
12. Idelchik, I. E., Hydraulic resistances during entry of flow into channels and passage through orifices, *Prom. Aerodin.*, no. 2, 27–56, 1944.
13. Idelchik, I. E., Towards calculation of labyrinth seals, *Kotloturbostroenie*, no. 3, 40–45, 1953.
14. Idelchik, I. E., *Hydraulic Resistances (Physical and Mathematical Fundamentals)*, Gosenergoizdat, Moscow, 1954, 316 p.
15. Kokaya, N. V., The hydraulics of conical seals and the chambers for suppressing hydraulic energy, in *The Methods of Investigations and Hydraulic Calculations of Water Spilling Hydrotechnical Constructions, Proceedings of Conferences and Meetings on Hydrotechnique*, pp. 186–188, Leningrad, 1985.
16. Koryagin, V. S., Ginzburg, Ya. L., and Shteinberg, M. O., The coefficients of hydraulic resistance of tray valves operating in constricted conditions, *Teploenergetika*, no. 3, 73–74, 1981.
17. Kremis, S. A., Towards determination of hydraulic resistances in reverse valves, *Izv. ZUVov Stroitel Arkhitekt.*, no. 1, 65–70, 1963.
18. Kuznetsov, L. A. and Rudomino, B. V., *Design and Calculation of Pipelines of Heat Power Plants*, Mashgiz, Moscow, 1949, 215 p.
19. Levkoeva, I. V., Concerning determination of pressure head losses in local resistances, in *Investigations in the Field of Theoretical and Applied Aerodynamics*, Tr. MAI, vyp. 111, 155–160, 1959.
20. Levkoeva, N. V., Dependence of the local resistance coefficients of pipeline fitting on the Reynolds number, *Tr. MAI*, vyp. 143, 131–139, 1961.
21. Lyzhin, O. V., Throttling devices in a compressible gas flow, *Inzh. Zh.*, no. 4, 641–649, 1965.
22. Murin, G. A., Hydraulic resistance of direct-flow valves, *Otoplenie Vent.*, no. 5, 25–30, 1941.
23. Pavlukhin, A. V., On calculation of aerodynamic resistances of a combination of flap valves with other local resistances, *Tr. Inst. Okhrany Truda VTsSPS*, vyp. 48, 130 145, 1967.
24. Poluboyarinov, Yu. G. and Yakovlev, N. A., Local resistance coefficients of non-direct-flow conical valves in laminar liquid flow, *Tr. LPI*, no. 274, 120–128, 1966.
25. Rolle, N. L., Resistance and discharge coefficients of a circular valve, *Gidrotekh. Stroit.*, no. 4, 18–23, 1953.
26. Skobeltsyn, Ya. A. and Khomutov, P. V., Mutual effect of shutters with differently shaped passages at low Reynolds numbers, *Transp. Khranenie Nefti Nefteprod.*, no. 7, 62–65, 1972.
27. Kotelevskiy, Yu. M., Ed., *Modern Constructions of Pipeline Fittings, Handbook*, Moscow, 1970, p. 250.
28. Sotnikov, A. G. and Saidova, D. Z., Investigation of separate units in the air-conditioning systems, *Sanit. Tekh. Tr. LISI*, 115–120, 1967.
29. Teterevnikov, V. N., Hydraulic characteristics of flap valves, *Tr. LIOT*, 53–54, 1955.
30. Frenkel, N. A., *Hydraulics*, Gosenergoizdat, Moscow, 1956, 456 p.
31. Chebysheva, K. V., Towards the problem of calculation of a labyrinth sealing, *Tekh. Zametki TsAGI*, no. 142, 25, 1937.
32. Churakova, S. V. and Yurkina, M. P., On the magnitude of the resistance coefficient of lense compensators, *Energomashinostroenie*, no. 8, 21–24, 1962.
33. Elterman, E. M., Local resistance coefficients of conical diaphragms, *Tr. Inst. Okhrany Truda VTsSPS*, 45–50, 1963.
34. Erlikh, A. M., *Steam Pipelines, Their Fittings and Other Units*, ONTI Press, 1937, 256 p.
35. Yanshin, B. I., *Hydrodynamic Characteristics of Valve Gates and Elements of Pipelines*, Mashinestroenic Press, Moscow, 1965, 260 p.

36. Yanshin, B. I., *Valve Gates and Transition Units of Pipelines*, Mashgiz, Moscow, 1962, 179 p.
37. Bach, C., *Versuche über Ventilbelassung und Ventilwiederstand*, 1884, 310, S.
38. Baumann, H. D., Die Einfürung eines kritischen Koeffizienten für die Bestimung des Durchflusses von Stellventilen, *Regelungstechnik*, Heft 11, 495–499, 1963.
39. Hearly, J. H., Patterson, M. N., and Brown, E. I., Pressure losses through fittings used in return air duct systems, *ASHRAE J.*, vol. 4, no. 5, 70–76, 1962.
40. Hörnig, G., Druckerluste in Schnellkuplungsrohren, formstücken und armaturen beim Fliesen von Klarschlamm, *Wasserwirtsch. Wassertech.*, vol. 1, no. 11, 374–377, 1969.
41. Kearton, W. J., The flow of air through radial labyrinth glands, *Proc. Inst. Mech. Eng.*, vol. 169, no. 30, 539–552, 1955.
42. Komotori, L., Probleme bei Labyrintstopfluchsen, *Proc. Fujihara Mem. Fac. Eng. Keio Univ.*, vol. 14, no. 54, 73–120, 1961.
43. Komotori, K., Flow observations in the labyrinth packing, *Proc. Fujihara Mem. Fac. Eng. Keio Univ.*, vol. 9, no. 33, 33–41, 1956.
44. Maione, U., Perdite di carico delle strozzature a spidolo vivo dedei possipiezometrici. Reicrca sperim, *Energ. Elettr.*, vol. 45, no. 4, 237–253, 1968.
45. Reichert, V., Theoretisch-experimentelle Untersuchun en zur Widerstandscharakteristik von Hydralikventilen, Wissenschaftliche Zeit der Technischen Univer. Dresden, Bd. 31, Heft 2, 149–155, 1982.
46. Skalička, J., Hydraulicke ztraty skriticich organech na potrubi a jejich zavislost na reynoldsove cisle, *Sb. Vys. Uceni Tech. Brne.*, no. 1, 57–63, 1965.
47. Weisbach, J., *Lehrbuch der technischen Mechanik*, Berlin, 1875, 320 p.

RESISTANCE TO FLOW PAST OBSTRUCTIONS IN A TUBE
Resistance Coefficients of Sections with Proturberances, Trusses, Girders, and other Shapes

10-1 EXPLANATIONS AND PRACTICAL RECOMMENDATIONS

1. The resistance of tubes and channel segments containing bodies over which the flow moves is made up of the resistance of the section proper, ζ_{sec} (friction resistance in the case of a straight section), and the resistance of the body, ζ:

$$\zeta_{ov} \equiv \frac{\Delta p}{\rho w_0^2/2} = \zeta_{sec} + \zeta \tag{10-1}$$

2. The power required to overcome the flow resistance of the body in the tube is expressed in terms of the drag coefficient P_{dr} of this body[3] as

$$\Delta N = P_{dr} w_{loc} \tag{10-2}$$

The drag force is

$$P_{dr} = c_x S_m \frac{\rho w_{loc}^2}{2} \tag{10-3}$$

where

$$w_{loc} = \frac{w}{1 - \tau(S_m/F_0)} \tag{10-4}$$

c_x is the drag coefficient of the body, which depends on the shape of the body, the Reynolds number $\mathrm{Re}' = w_0 d_m/\nu$, and other parameters, and is determined from Diagrams 10-1 through 10-15; S_m is the mid-sectional area (m²) and d_m is the diameter or maximum width (m) of the body; w_{loc} is the local velocity of the flow [in the free area $(F_0 - S_m)$], that is, the velocity based on the tube net cross-sectional area, m/s; w is the flow velocity at a given point of the cross section in front of the body, m/s and τ is a correction factor for the effect of the body shape and contraction of the transverse cross section of the tube; for smooth bodies $\tau \leqslant 1.0$, for nonsmooth bodies $\tau > 1.0$.[3]

In diagrams of Chapter 10 the values of τ are taken approximately with allowance for the results of the experiments described in References 3 and 4.

3. The power indicated under paragraph 2 can be expressed in terms of the local hydraulic resistance coefficient of a tube section with a body in it by the equation

$$\Delta N = \zeta \frac{\rho w_0^2}{2} w_0 F_0 \tag{10-5}$$

Simultaneous solution of Equations (10-1) to (10-3) provides the relationship between the local resistance coefficient ζ and the drag coefficient of the body c_x:

$$\zeta = c_x \frac{S_m}{F_0} \left(\frac{w_{\text{loc}}}{w_0}\right)^3 \tag{10-6}$$

4. In the general case, the flow velocity in the tube is distributed nonuniformly over the cross section; therefore the body resistance also depends on the relative location of the body.

For a stabilized laminar flow, the velocity profile is expressed by

$$\frac{w}{w_0} = k_1 \left[1 - \left(\frac{2y}{D_0}\right)^2\right] \tag{10-7}$$

where for a three-dimensional flow (circle, rectangle at $a_0/b_0 = 0.5-2.0$) $k_1 = 2$, while for a two-dimensional flow (plane or annular slit) $k_1 = {}^3/_2$; y is the distance between the axes (centers) of the body and the tube (Figures 10-1a and b); in the case of an annular cross section of the tube it is the distance between the body axis and the average circle of the annulus (Figure 10-1c), m.

On the basis of Equations (10-4), (10-6), and (10-7), we obtain

$$\zeta \equiv \frac{\Delta p}{\rho w_0^2/2} = c_x \frac{S_m/F_0 \; K_1^3[1 - (2y/D_0)^2]^3}{(1 - \tau S_m/F_0)^3} = k_2 \frac{c_x \; S_m/F_0[1 - (2y/D_0)^2]^3}{(1 - \tau S_m/F_0)^3}$$

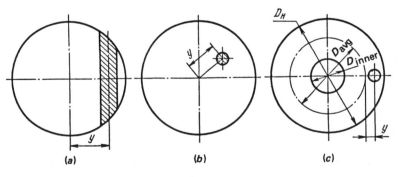

(a)   (b)   (c)

Figure 10-1 Location of the flow obstacle: (a) and (b) plane-parallel and three-dimensional flow around a body in a tube; (c) three-dimensional flow around a body in an annular tube.

Table 10-1 Values of m and k_1

Coefficients	Re					
	4×10^3	4×10^3	2.5×10^4	2×10^5	6×10^5	3×10^6
m	5	6	7	8	9	10
k_1	1.32	1.26	1.23	1.20	1.17	1.15

5. For a stabilized turbulent flow, the velocity profile can be expressed approximately as

$$\frac{w}{w_0} = k_1 \left(1 - \frac{2y}{D_0} \right)^{1/m} \tag{10-8}$$

where for a three-dimensional flow[9]

$$k_1 = \frac{(2m + 1)(m + 1)}{2m^2}$$

and for a two-dimensional flow

$$k_1 = \frac{m + 1}{m}$$

m is an exponent which can generally vary over a wide range (see Chapter 4).
According to Equations (10-4), (10-6), and (10-8), we obtain

$$\zeta \equiv \frac{\Delta p}{\rho w_0^2/2} = \frac{c_x \, S_m/F_0 \, k_1^3 (1 - 2y/D_0)^{3/m}}{(1 - \tau \, S_m/F_0)^3} = k_2 \frac{c_x \, S_m/F_0 (1 - 2y/D_0)^{3/m}}{(1 - \tau \, S_m/F_0)^3}$$

6. For a turbulent flow in a straight tube the values of m and k_1 are given in Table 10-1 as functions of $Re' = w_0 d_m/\nu$. In particular, at $Re' = 6 \times 10^5$, $m = 9$ and $k_1 = 1.17$, $k_2 = k_1^3 = 1.6$.

The last value of k_2 is valid for bodies in a three-dimensional flow at very small ratios S_m/F_0, the midsectional body area to that of the tube. With an increase of S_m/F_0, the value of k_2 decreases, approaching unity. The diagrams in the present chapter show values of k_2 that are calculated approximately, considering the above circumstances and experimental results.[4]

7. The drag coefficient of an oblong body is determined by two factors: the frictional resistance and the shape resistance. The latter is due to flow separation from the body surface and subsequent formation of vortices. The relationship between the magnitudes of the frictional resistance and the shape resistance depends on the body shape and its position in the flow (angle of attack, slip angle), the roughness of its surface, the Reynolds number, and the degree and scale of turbulence of the incident flow.* For bodies having a poorly streamlined shape, the frictional resistance is very small in comparison with the total drag. For streamlined bodies, the frictional resistance is comparable to the shape resistance.

8. The dependence of the drag coefficient of such bodies as a sphere or a cylinder on the Reynolds number is very complex (see Diagram 10-1 and graph a of Diagram 10-7).

---

*The effect of flow contraction (Mach number) on the drag coefficients of various bodies is not considered here. For detailed information, see the literature.[10,24,34]

The coefficient c_x has its maximum value at very small Reynolds numbers Re'. As Re' increases, the drag coefficient decreases, reaching the first minimum at a certain value of Re' (of the order of $2-5 \times 10^3$). With further increase in Re', there is a small increase in c_x to a certain constant value, which is retained up to about Re' $= 10^5-2 \times 10^5$. As soon as Re' attains this value (the critical Reynolds number), the value of c_x drops sharply down to the second minimum, which corresponds to Re' $= 3 \times 10^5-5 \times 10^5$. This is followed by the next slight increase in c_x. But at about Re' $= 10^6$, the drag coefficient acquires an almost constant value.

9. The complex dependence of the drag coefficient of cylindrical (spherical) barriers on the Reynolds number is due to the highly variable pattern of flow past these barriers with increases in Re', from very small values (Re' $\ll 1$) to very large values (Re' $= 10^6-10^7$).

The most important transition is that from a steady-state flow past a barrier to an oscillating flow, the latter being observed for cylindrical bodies within Re' $= 30-50$ and for spherical bodies within Re' $= 130-200$. A very important phenomenon observed during the growth of Re' is the formation and development of the nearest aerodynamic wake and then of the body boundary layer.

10. At small and moderate Reynolds numbers (Re' $\leqslant 40-50$) there occurs a consecutive replacement of one pattern of flow past barriers of the types under consideration by another (Figure 10-2):

- Re' $\ll 1$. At very small Reynolds numbers the flow inertia is negligibly small, therefore the flow past the barrier is ideally smooth and is symmetrical upstream as well as downstream of the body (Figure 10-2a).
- $0.05 <$ Re' $< (5-10)$ for a cylinder and Re' $< (10-24)$ for a sphere. In this case, the inertia forces become noticeable. The streamlines become more curved as they approach the body from the upstream direction. As a result, there appears an asymmetry of the streamlines between the upstream and downstream sides of the barrier.

  An extensive parabolic stagnant zone (a noncirculation wake, Figure 10-2b) is formed behind the barrier. At each point of this zone the flow velocity is noticeably smaller than at the symmetrical point of a less stagnant nose zone formed upstream of the barrier. With an incraese in Re, the asymmetry of the streamlines increases, while the length and width of the stagnant zone decrease.
- $(5-10) <$ Re' $< (40-50)$ for a cylinder and Re' < 130 for a sphere. A pair of opposite vortices (Figure 10-2c) appear behind the cylinder and form a steady recirculating wake [one toroidal vortical wake appears behind a sphere at Re' $> (10-24)$]. The flow velocity in each vortex increases from the center to the periphery by a linear law. With increases in Re, the length of the attached wake increases continuously up to the moment of loss of stability.

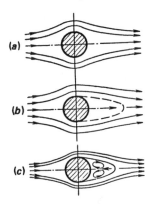

(a)

(b)

(c)

Figure 10-2 Flow patterns in the wake behind a spherical body with different modes of flow within the ranges of small and moderate Reynolds numbers: (a) Re' $\leqslant 1$; (b) $0.05 <$ Re' $< (5-10)$; (c) $(5-10) <$ Re' $< (40-50)$.

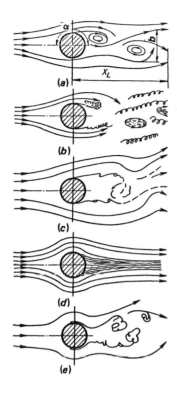

Figure 10-3 Flow patterns in a wake behind a spherical body with different modes of flow at Re' > 50: (a) (40–50) < Re' < (150–200); (b) (150–200) < Re' < 1500; (c) 1500 < Re' < 2 × 10⁵; (d) 2 × 10⁵ < Re' < 3.5 × 10⁶; (e) 3.5 < Re' < 8 × 10⁶.

Five flow modes can be distinguished for Reynolds numbers exceeding Re' ≈ 50 (for a cylinder) (Figure 10-3); see paragraphs 10-14.

11. (40–50) < Re' < (150–200). At the beginning of this range the mode of flow changes sharply; the elongated vortices of the attached wake lose their stability, start to shed from the cylinder alternately from each side, and are entrained by the flow (the Karman vortex street, Figure 10-3a); from this moment the flow past the cylinder acquires an oscillating character since the flow pressure on the body varies with each separation of a vortex.

The angle α at which the flow starts to separate increases with the Reynolds number and, within the range of Re' considered, amounts to 115–130°. The length of the wake x_L at Re' = 50 is equal to $2.5d_m$ and afterwards increases in proportion to Re'; the width of the wake is $b \approx 0.85$–$1.05d_m$. The velocity of the reverse flow in the wake at the boundary between the vortices increases from about 10 to 30–50% of the velocity of flow incidence on the cylinder.

The side boundaries of the wake are unstable; random vortices appear on them, which afterwards lead to more and more intensive turbulent agitation of the adjacent flow layers and to mass exchange with the outer flow.

The attached wake of spherical and other three-dimensional bodies of rotation is characterized by the formation of a single toroidal vortex (rather than a pair of vortices) separating in spiral threads. The length of this vortex is less than that for a cylinder, while the frequency of its separation is twice as large.

12. (150–200) < Re' < 1500. The stagnant region in front of the barrier becomes gradually thinner and small compared with the barrier size.

As a result, only a thin film of the stagnant flow remains on the upstream side of the barrier which forms a laminar boundary layer on both its sides (Figure 10-3b). Reaching some point near the mid-section of the body ($\alpha \approx 80°$), the boundary layer separates from the body surface and moves along the external boundary of the attached wake. On reaching the final point of the wake, it joins the boundary layer which has separated from the other side of the body. The boundary-layer separation is due to increased pressure along the body surface.

This phenomenon results in an increase in the bottom pressure. At the same time, an irregular flow appears in the near wake, which develops into a clearly defined turbulent flow downstream of the channel.

13. $1500 < Re' < 2 \times 10^5$. The turbulence behind the body appears closer and closer to it. As a result, the point of transition from the laminar to the turbulent boundary layer shifts closer to the near of the cylinder (sphere).

The process of transition, which is not accompanied by the shedding of vortices, starts with sinusoidal oscillations that become stronger with increasing Reynolds number up to the transition point. In this case the bottom pressure drops appreciably especially within $Re' = 2 \times 10^3$–10^4. The velocity at the external boundary of the separated (free) jet increases, while the distance up to the point of the joining of layers becomes shorter. In this case, transition to a turbulent flow occurs very close to the point of the boundary layer separation.

This results in very intensive velocity fluctuations near the rear part of the body, the strength of which exceeds that of the averaged flow velocity at the same points of the wake already at $Re' \approx 8 \times 10^3$.

When $Re' > 5 \times 10^3$, complete turbulent mixing develops behind the cylinder (Figure 10-3c).

14. $2 \times 10^5 < Re' < 3.5 \times 10^6$. This critical range of Reynolds numbers is distinguished by the transition from a laminar boundary layer to a turbulent one. The boundary layer starts to separate in the laminar mode of flow, almost in the same place on the frontal portion of the cylinder at which it separates at smaller values of Re'. This separation is followed by the transition of the mode of flow and then by a second, but turbulent ("bubble"), separation on the rear portion of the cylinder. Regularity in the boundary layer separation is not so marked as in the case of smaller and larger Reynolds numbers. The bottom pressure increases sharply, while the zone of separation becomes narrower ($\alpha = 110$–$120°$, Figure 10-3d). As a result, at $Re' \approx 5 \times 10^5$, there occurs a sudden critical decrease in the drag resistance of the cylinder which was mentioned earlier. This critical resistance for a sphere corresponds to $Re' \approx 3 \times 10^5$.

15. $3.5 \times 10^6 < Re' < 8 \times 10^6$. Shedding of vortices becomes regular again, but this time with a turbulent boundary layer (Figure 10-3e).

All further variations, associated with an increase in the Reynolds number and accompanied by a shift in the flow mode transition point to the stagnation transition point, are assumed to be relatively weak.

16. All the characteristic ranges of the Reynolds numbers described under paragraphs 10 to 15 for different modes of flow past a cylinder (sphere) are valid only in the case when the flow is laminar or slightly turbulent ($\varepsilon_t < 0.01\%$, where $\varepsilon_t = \sqrt{w'^2}/w_0$ is the degree of flow turbulence; w' is the longitudinal oscillating velocity of the flow, m/s).

An increase in the degree of turbulence of the incident flow in each mode of flow makes the point of transition from laminar to turbulent boundary layer approach the wake region of the body. It thereby displaces the characteristic range of the Reynolds numbers and, in particular, the critical region in which a sharp decrease in the coefficient c_x is observed toward smaller values of Re' (see graph b of Diagram 10-7).

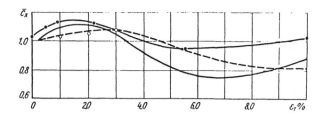

Figure 10-4 Drag $\bar{c}_x$ of cubic and prismatic bodies vs. different levels of turbulence of the incident flow.[10]

17. The position of the point of transition of the laminar into the turbulent boundary layer is also affected by the condition of the body surface (the degree of its roughness $\overline{\Delta}$). The effect of different surface irregularities shows itself in perturbation of the laminar flow, displacement of the point of transition forward (to the frontal portion of the body), and increased length of the turbulent boundary layer.

In the case of a cylinder (sphere), the resistance crisis occurs earlier, that is, at a lower Reynolds number, for larger degrees of roughness. At the same time, the higher the value of $\overline{\Delta}$, the larger are the values of $c_{x\min}$ and c_x in the postcritical region (see Diagram 10-2).

18. The initial turbulence of the incident flow also markedly influences the drag resistance of poorly streamlined bodies (with sharp edges especially in the range of $\varepsilon_T \leqslant 10\%$).

For cubic and prismatic bodies, as well as for a flat plate placed normal to the flow, the dependence of c_x, or equally, of $\bar{c}_x = c_{x\varepsilon t>0}/c_{x\varepsilon t=0}$, on ε_t is qualitatively identical and of a critical nature with respect to ε_t (see Reference 7 in Chapter 4). This is also due to a change in the mode of flow. When the intensity of turbulence of the incident flow increases only slightly, the resistance coefficient $\bar{c}_x$ increases (Figure 10-4) due to the enlargement of the flow separation zone behind the body. With further increase in the turbulence intensity the separation zone becomes stabilized or contracts slightly as a result of energy accumulation from the main stream. This leads to a constant drag resistance or to its decrease compared with an incident flow of low turbulence.

19. The drag coefficient of a cylinder at $\mathrm{Re'} \leqslant 0.5$ can be calculated from Lamb's equation:[23]

$$c_x = \frac{8\pi}{(2.002 - \ln \mathrm{Re'})\mathrm{Re'}}$$

At $\mathrm{Re'} > 0.5$, the value of c_x is determined on the basis of the data of Diagram 10-1.

20. The drag coefficient of a sphere at $\mathrm{Re'} < 0.5$ can be calculated from the Stokes formula

$$c_x = \frac{24}{\mathrm{Re'}}$$

while for $0.5 \leqslant \mathrm{Re'} \leqslant 1.0$, by Oseen's formula

$$c_x = \frac{24}{\mathrm{Re'}} + 4.5$$

In the range $0.1 < \text{Re}' < 10^3$, an almost satisfactory agreement with experiments (at $\text{Re}' = 3\text{--}400$; the error is $<2\%$) is given by the empirical formula of Klyachko[18]*

$$c_x = \frac{24}{\text{Re}'} + 4/(\text{Re}')^{1/3}$$

21. The effect of the degree of turbulence on the resistance coefficient of a sphere can be evaluated from the formula of Claymen and Guavin[17]

$$c_x = \frac{3990}{(\lg \text{Re}')^{6.1}} - \frac{4.47 \times 10^5}{\text{Re}'^{1.8} \, \varepsilon_t^{0.97}}$$

which is valid within $400/\varepsilon_t < \text{Re}' < 3 \times 10^4$ at $\varepsilon_t = 0.7\text{--}3.5$, for cases when the turbulence degree is small compared with the sphere diameter.

Up to $\text{Re}' = 8 \times 10^4$, a close coincidence with the experiment is given by the formula suggested by Kheven and Kyakhov:[37]

$$c_x = A \exp[(n_1 + k_1 \ln \text{Re}') \ln \text{Re}']$$

where $A = 26.555$; $n_1 = -0.91528$; $k_1 = 0.049274$.

22. In order to determine the drag coefficient of particles of any isometric sphere (the shape of an equilateral polyhedron) for any mode of flow, Vakhrushev[6] suggests the following generalized formula

$$
\begin{aligned}
c_x = &\left(\frac{28.47}{\text{Re}' \lg 15.38/\phi} + \frac{4.565\phi}{3\sqrt{\text{Re}'}} - \frac{0.491\phi}{\sqrt{\text{Re}'}} \right) \\
&\times \{1 - \text{th}\,[0.01282\,\text{Re}'(\phi - 0.9805)]\} \\
&+ 2.86(\phi - 0.8531)\,\text{th}\,[0.01282\,\text{Re}' \times (\phi - 0.9805)] \\
&+ \left(7.76 - 2.86\phi - \frac{488}{\phi} \right) \times \text{th}\,[0.00104\,\text{Re}'(\phi - 0.9038)]
\end{aligned}
\tag{10-9}
$$

---

*Satisfactory agreement with experiments (with an average error of $\pm 10\%$ and, for the range $10 < \text{Re}' < 10^2$, with an error up to 36.9%) is provided by Adamov's[1] formula for the whole range of Reynolds numbers up to the onset of the critical resistance:

$$c_x = \frac{24}{\text{Re}'}\,[1 + (0.0167\,\text{Re}')^{1/n}]^n \quad \text{for bodies of any shapes}$$

$$c_x = \frac{24}{\text{Re}'}\,[1 + (0.065\,\text{Re}')^{3/2}]^{3/2} \quad \text{for spherical bodies}$$

Within $0.1 < \text{Re}' < 20$, the following formula[54] gives close agreement with experiment:

$$c_x = \frac{24}{\text{Re}'} + 1.66$$

while for $0.5 < \text{Re}' < 10^3$, close agreement is provided by the formula of Rumpf[60]

$$c_x = \frac{21}{\text{Re}'} + \frac{6}{\sqrt{\text{Re}'}} + 0.28$$

Similar formulas can also be found in other works, for example, in the work of Tanaka.[63]

where ϕ is the coefficient of nonsphericity of the particles. This is equal to the area ratio of the particle surface to the surface of the sphere of the same volume. The diameter of this sphere, d_e, which enters the Reynolds number $Re' = w_0 d_e/\nu$, is taken as the determining size of the particles.

23. At $\phi = 1$ (a sphere), Equation (10-9) takes on the form

$$c_x = \left(\frac{24}{Re'} + \frac{4.565}{3\sqrt{Re'}} - \frac{0.491}{\sqrt{Re'}}\right)(1 - \text{th } 0.00025 \, Re')$$

$$+ 0.42 \text{ th } 0.00025 \, Re' + 0.02 \text{ th } 0.0001 \, Re'$$

This formula is valid for the whole range of Reynolds numbers, practically from 0 to Re'_{cr}.

For the range $0 < Re' \leqslant 53.5/(\phi - 0.9732)$, one can use the following formula with an accuracy up to 10%

$$c_x = \frac{28.47}{Re' \lg 15.38/\phi} + \frac{4.565\phi}{3\sqrt{Re'}} - \frac{0.491\phi}{\sqrt{Re'}}$$

For a sphere, the range is $0 < Re' < 2000$.

24. When $Re' \geqslant 150/(\phi - 0.9732)$, one can use the following formula with an accuracy up to 5%:

$$c_x = 2.86(\phi - 0.8531) \text{ th } [0.01282 \, Re'(\phi - 0.9805)]$$

$$+ \left(7.76 - 2.86\phi - \frac{4.88}{\phi}\right) \text{ th } [0.00104 \, Re'(\phi - 9038)]$$

25. The effect of the degree of turbulence on the drag coefficient of a cylinder can be approximated by

$$c_{x\varepsilon_t<0} = \bar{c}_x \, c_{x\varepsilon_t\approx 0}$$

where $c_x = f_1(Re')$ and $\bar{c}_x = f(Re')$ are taken from the respective graphs of Diagram 10-1.

The value of $\bar{c}_x$ is determined from the curves $c_x = f_1(Re')$ obtained at $\bar{l} = t/d_m = 7.7$ and different $\varepsilon, \%$ and from the curve $c_x = f(1/\bar{l})$.[7-10]

26. The drag coefficient of a cylinder and other oblong bodies depends on the aspect ratio $\bar{l} = t/d_m$. An increase in $\bar{l}$ leads to an increase of the drag coefficient.

27. The drag coefficient of a flat plate placed across the flow is virtually constant at $Re' = w_0 D_0/\nu$ and $(w_0 a_0/\nu) > 1000$ and amounts to $c_x = 1.12\text{--}1.16$.

For a rectangular plate, the drag coefficient depends on the aspect ratio d_m/l_1 and changes from $c_x = 1.12\text{--}1.16$ (at $d_m/l_1 = 1$) to $c_x \approx 2.0$ (at $d_m/l_1 = 0$).

In case there is an orifice in the circular plate, c_x changes almost parabolically from 1.12–1.16 (at $d = 0.2D_0$) up to 1.78 (at $d = 0.8D_0$).

28. When several bodies (a complex of bodies of different shapes and dimensions) are placed at the same location in the tube, then the overall coefficient of local resistances of these bodies is calculated by the author's formula,[3] which is valid at $S_m/F_0 < 0.3$ and $Re > 10^4$:

$$\zeta = \frac{\Delta p}{\rho w_0^2/2} = k \sum_{i=1}^{n} c_{xi} \frac{(S_{mi}/F_0)(1 - 2y/D_0)^{3/m}}{(1 - \sum_{i=1}^{m} \tau \, S_{mi}/F_0)^3}$$

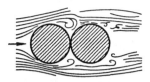

Figure 10-5 Flow past two cylinders placed close to each other.

where i is the ordinal number of the body of the given complex; n_b is the total number of bodies in the complex.

29. The drag resistance of two bodies (spheres, cylinders, plates, etc.) placed one behind the other in the flow is not equal to twice the drag resistance of a single body; the drag coefficient of each of these bodies and their total drag coefficient depend on the relative distance (longitudinal spacing) $\bar{l} = l_2/d_m$ between the bodies.

30. When two cylinders are placed close to each other in the flow, then the rear cylinder will be completely covered by the vortex zone created by the first cylinder (Figure 10-5) and will not create any drag. In this case, the rarefaction behind the first cylinder will be larger than that behind the second cylinder. This difference of pressures at the second cylinder will cause the appearance of a force opposing the flow, with the result that c_x of the second cylinder will become negative, causing the total drag coefficient of the two cylinders to be smaller. With increase in the relative distance between the cylinders, the effect of "suction" of the rear cylinder toward the front one decreases. However, since the rear cylinder remains in the aerodynamic "shadow," that is, in a stagnant and strongly turbulized zone of the first cylinder, then, with further increase in $\bar{l}$, its drag coefficient remains lower than c_x of an isolated cylinder, slowly approaching this value.

A lower value of c_x is obtained not only for cylinders, but also for any bodies located in the aerodynamic "shadow" of another body.

31. The mean value of the drag coefficient c_{xm} and correspondingly the coefficient of the local hydraulic coefficient ζ_1 of one body placed in a longitudinal row of bodies increase with a decrease of the number n_b of these bodies in the row starting approximately from n_b = 5. At $n_b > 6$–50 almost constant mean values of c_{xm} and ζ_1 are established corresponding to the given relative distance l_2/d_m between the bodies of the longitudinal row (see graphs of Diagrams 10-12 and 10-13).

32. The value of ζ_1 for cylinders installed over the tube diameter in one longitudinal row can be calculated from the formulas suggested by Bystrov and Mikhailov[5] and given in Diagram 10-13.

33. If several groups of bodies are placed in the flow channel, arranged in longitudinal rows, the local resistance coefficient λ_m of a group over the tube length of one hydraulic diameter of the tube cross section is calculated from the author's formula,[3] valid at about $S_m/F_0 < 0.3$ and $\mathrm{Re}' > 10^4$:

$$\lambda_m \equiv \frac{\Delta p}{(\rho w_0^2/2)(L/D_h)} = k_2 \sum_{i=1}^{n_r} c_{x1i} \frac{1}{(d_m/D_h)_i \bar{l}_i} \frac{(S_{mi}/F_0)(1 - 2y/D_0)^{3/m}}{(1 - \sum_{i=1}^{n_r} \tau_i \, S_{mi}/F_0)^3}$$

where i is the ordinal number of a body in the given complex or the ordinal number of the given longitudinal row of several bodies; n_r is the total number of longitudinal rows; c_{x1i} is the drag coefficient of a single body in the ith longitudinal row, which depends on the shape of the body profile, the Reynolds number Re', and other parameters (see Diagrams of Chapter 10).

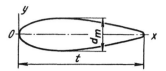

Figure 10-6 Profile of a streamlined body.

34. The hydraulic resistance coefficient of a group of bodies over the calculated length L of the tube is

$$\zeta \equiv \frac{\Delta p}{\rho w_0^2/2} = \lambda_m \frac{L}{D_h}$$

The friction coefficient of a straight tube section is

$$\zeta_{sec} = \zeta_{fr} = \frac{\Delta p}{\rho w_0^2/2} = \lambda_{fr} \frac{L}{D_h}$$

Whence

$$\zeta \equiv \frac{\Delta p}{\rho w_0^2/2} = (\lambda_m + \lambda_{fr}) \frac{L}{D_h}$$

where λ_{fr} is the coefficient of hydraulic friction determined as λ from Diagrams 2-1 through 2-6.

35. An important factor influencing the drag coefficient of a body is the shape of its profile. The more streamlined the body, the weaker is separation of the flow and formation of vortices and, therefore, the smaller is the drag coefficient. Therefore, wherever possible, one should use streamlined shapes. The streamlined shape of the body is characterized by a smoothly rounded nose part and a tapering trailing edge (Figure 10-6).

The sharper the contraction of the profile behind the body midsection (and, consequently, retardation of the flow), the earlier the flow will separate from the body and the more vigorous will be the formation of vortices behind the body. By adequately selecting the profile of the trailing part of the body, it is possible to avoid the flow separation.

36. As a guide for constructing some of the profiles of streamlined bodies, one can use the values of their dimensionless coordinates (see Figure 10-6) presented in Table 10-2.

37. The class of streamlined bodies also incorporates elliptical cylinders and circular cylinders with tail fairings. The drag coefficient of these bodies is higher than that of bodies whose profiles are constructed according to Table 10-2. However, they are frequently used in practice because of the greater simplicity of their construction.

38. The drag resistance of poorly streamlined bodies (Figure 10-7) can be substantially reduced (by 40%)[32] by arranging recesses on its trailing part (Figure 10-7, model 2). One

Table 10-2 Coordinates $2y/d_m$ of the streamlined profiles

Profile	0	0.05	0.10	0.20	0.3	0.4	0.5	0.6	0.7	0.8	0.9	1.0
					x/t							
1	0	0.528	0.720	0.917	0.987	1.00	0.960	0.860	0.737	0.568	0.340	0
2	$r = 0.08^a$	0.490	0.750	0.960	1.00	0.980	0.930	0.840	0.720	0.560	0.370	$r = 0.10^a$
3	0	0.530	0.720	0.940	1.00	0.995	0.940	0.860	0.910	0.520	0.300	0

[a] r is the radius of curvature of the nose and tail (leading and trailing edge) parts of the profile.

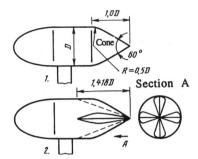

Figure 10-7 A badly streamlined body of revolution:[32] (1) without recesses; (2) with recesses through 90° respresenting a dihedral angle.

of the reasons for this reduction of resistance can be the destruction of vortices developing in the separated boundary layer by the flow disturbances produced by the recesses.

39. The drag resistance of poorly streamlined bodies (Table 10-3) is reduced substantially when smooth fairings are placed in front and behind the body and also when corresponding screens are installed upstream and even downstream of the body.[28]

40. The drag coefficient of systems of interconnected bodies, such as beams or trusses, depends on the shape of their cross section, the method of their connection, the direction of the incident flow, and the Reynolds number. The effect of the incident flow direction in such systems is more complex than for a single body, since in this case the trailing edges are oriented differently with respect to the aerocynamic shadow of the front elements of the system (Figure 10-8).

41. The local resistance coefficient of a truss placed in a tube is

$$\zeta \equiv \frac{\Delta p}{\rho w_0^2/2} = (1 - 1.15)c_{x\alpha}^* \frac{S_m/F_0}{(1 - S_m/F_0)^3}$$

Where S_m/F_0 is the degree of filling of the tube cross section with the truss elements; S_m is the total midsectional area of all the truss elements.

The drag coefficient of the truss at the given Reynolds number $\text{Re}' = w_0 d_m/\nu$ and at the given angle, α, of the incident flow direction[36] is

$$c_{x\alpha}^* = c_{x\alpha} \frac{c_{x0}^*}{c_{x0}}$$

where c_{x0}, c_{x0}^*, and $c_{x\alpha}$ are the drag coefficients of the truss, respectively, at $\alpha = 0$ and $\text{Re}' = \text{Re}_1'$, at $\alpha = 0$ and at the unknown value of Re, and at the unknown value of α and at the Re_1' at which the relationship $c_{x\alpha} = f(\alpha)$ has been obtained.

42. Calculations for mine shafts and excavations are based on the dimensional coefficient of the aerodynamic resistance expressed in terms of λ in kg·s²/m⁴

$$\alpha_{sh} = \frac{\rho}{2g} \frac{\lambda}{4}$$

The resistance of a portion of the mine (excavation) is expressed in terms of the coefficient α_{sh} (in Pa) as

$$\Delta p = 9.8\alpha_{sh} w_0^2 \frac{2L}{D_h} = 9.8\alpha_{sh} \left(\frac{Q}{F_0}\right)^2 \frac{\Pi_0}{F_0} L$$

Table 10-3 Coefficients of the reduction of drag of badly streamlined bodies

Shape of the body	$\bar{c}_x = c_x/c_{x0}$	Shape of the body	$\bar{c}_x = c_x/c_{x0}$	Shape of the body	$\bar{c}_x = c_x/c_{x0}$
	1,0		0,65		0,25
	0,85		0,46		0,33
	0,19		0,26		0,56
	0,78		0,53		0,43
	0,63		0,27		0,34
	0,67		0,46		0,43

Table 10-3 Coefficients of the reduction of drag of badly streamlined bodies (continued)

Shape of the body	$\bar{c}_x = c_x/c_{x0}$	Shape of the body	$\bar{c}_x = c_x/c_{x0}$	Shape of the body	$\bar{c}_x = c_x/c_{x0}$
	1,16		0,40		0,35
	0,34		0,39		0,31
	0,47		0,29		0,30
	0,30		0,62		0,27
	1,07		0,37		0,75
	0,11		0,36		0,80

Note: c_{x0} is the coefficient of drag of a plate positioned normally to the flow

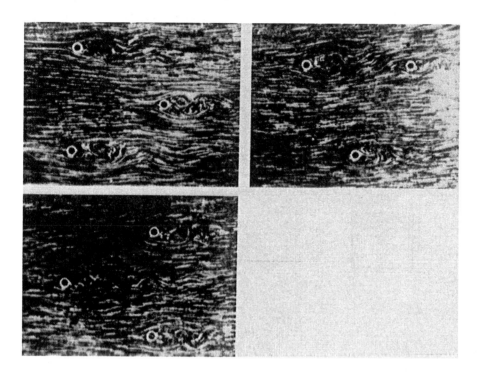

Figure 10-8 Patterns of flow past truss systems.[36]

10-2 DIAGRAMS OF THE RESISTANCE COEFFICIENTS

Circular smooth cylinder in a tube: plane-parallel flow;[10,48,58] $S_m/F_0 < 0.3$	Diagram 10-1

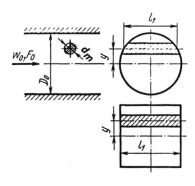

At Re$'$ > 5 × 10^5:

$$\zeta \equiv \frac{\Delta p}{\rho w_0^2/2} = c_x \frac{S_m/F_0}{(1 - 0.5\, S_m/F_0)^3} \left(1 - \frac{2y}{D_0}\right)^{1/3}$$

where at $\varepsilon_t \leq 0.01\%$, $c_x = f_1(\text{Re}')$, see graph a; at $\varepsilon_t > 0$

$$c_{x\varepsilon_t > 0} = \bar{c}_x c_x; \qquad \bar{c}_x = \frac{c_{x\varepsilon_t > 0.01}}{c_{x\varepsilon_t \leq 0.01}}, \quad \text{see the curves}$$

$\bar{c}_x = f_2(\text{Re}')$ of graph b;

At Re$'$ ≥ 2 × 10^4

$$D_h = \frac{4F_0}{\Pi_0}; \qquad S_m = d_m l_1$$

$\zeta' = c_{x0} S_m/F_0 \, (1 - 2y/D_0)^{1/3}$, where for c_{x0} see graph c; $\varepsilon_t \approx 0.01\%$

$$\text{Re}' = \frac{w_0 d_m}{\nu}; \qquad \text{Re} = \frac{w_0 D_h}{\nu}$$

$\varepsilon_t = \dfrac{\sqrt{\overline{w'^2}}}{w_0}$ is the degree of turbulence.

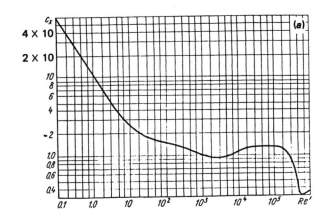

$\varepsilon_t \approx 0.1\%$

Re$'$	0.1	0.5	1.0	5	10	5 × 10	10^2	5 × 10^2	10^3	5 × 10^3	10^4
c_x	59.0	22.5	10.0	4.50	2.65	1.65	1.50	1.20	1.00	0.90	1.05

Re$'$	5 × 10^4	10^5	2 × 10^5	3 × 10^5	4 × 10^5	5 × 10^5	6 × 10^5	7 × 10^5	8 × 10^5	10^6
c_x	1.25	1.25	1.20	1.10	0.80	0.60	0.32	0.30	0.32	0.35

Circular smooth cylinder in a tube: plane-parallel flow;[10,48,58]
$S_m/F_0 < 0.3$

Diagram
10-1

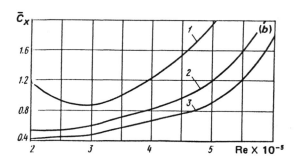

Values of $\bar{c}_x$

No. of curve (ε_i, %)	Re' $\times 10^{-5}$							
	2.0	2.5	3.0	3.5	4.0	4.5	5.5	6.0
1 (0.3)	0.84	0.69	0.67	0.74	0.88	1.08	1.30	2.80
2 (0.8)	0.36	0.38	0.40	0.42	0.48	0.59	0.80	1.57
3 (5.5)	0.28	0.29	0.32	0.36	0.42	0.50	0.62	1.25

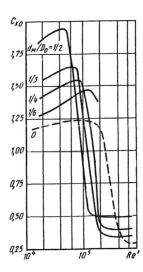

Values c_{x0} ($\varepsilon_i \approx 0.01\%$)[58]

d_m/D_0	S_m/F_0	Re' $\times 10^{-5}$							
		0.2	0.4	0.6	0.8	1	2	4	6
0.50	0.25	1.95	1.92	1.75	1.38	0.88	0.50	0.50	0.50
0.33	0.111	1.54	1.60	1.63	1.62	0.32	0.35	0.34	0.34
0.25	0.0625	1.41	1.49	1.52	1.53	1.50	0.40	0.38	0.38
0.167	0.028	1.28	1.35	1.39	1.42	1.44	1.35	–	–

Circular rough cylinder in a tube; plane-parallel flow
(initial turbulence is slightly increased); $S_m/F_0 < 0.3^{50}$

Diagram 10-2

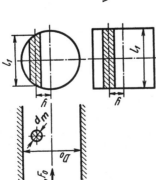

$$\zeta \equiv \frac{\Delta p}{\rho w_0^2/2} = c_x \frac{S_m/F_0}{(1 - 0.5\, S_m/F_0)^3}\left(1 - \frac{2y}{D_0}\right)^{1/3}$$

where $c_x = f(Re', \bar{\Delta})$, see the graph.

$S_m = d_m l_f$; $Re' = \dfrac{w_0 d_m}{\nu}$

Values of c_x

$\bar{\Delta} \times 10^4$	Re $\times 10^{-5}$																	
	1.0	2.0	2.5	3.0	3.5	4.0	4.5	5.0	5.5	6.0	6.5	7.0	8.0	9.0	10	15	20	40
0 (curve 1)	1.05	1.18	1.21	1.23	1.24	1.25	1.25	1.25	1.25	1.25	1.25	1.25	1.25	1.23	1.20	1.00	0.60	–
5 (curve 2)	1.05	1.18	1.20	1.22	1.24	1.25	1.25	1.25	1.25	1.25	1.25	1.21	1.18	1.15	1.10	0.80	0.40	0.55
20 (curve 3)	1.05	1.18	1.21	1.23	1.24	1.25	1.24	1.23	1.22	1.20	1.18	1.15	1.10	1.06	1.00	0.42	0.60	0.82
40 (curve 4)	1.05	1.18	1.20	1.20	1.20	1.20	1.10	1.17	1.15	1.12	1.07	1.00	0.60	0.65	0.70	0.83	0.90	0.98
70 (curve 5)	1.05	1.15	1.15	1.15	1.15	1.13	1.10	0.90	0.80	0.76	0.75	0.77	0.78	0.80	0.82	0.90	0.98	1.00
90 (curve 6)	1.05	1.15	1.15	1.15	1.10	1.06	0.83	0.79	0.80	0.81	0.82	0.83	0.84	0.85	0.85	–	–	–
200 (curve 7)	1.05	1.15	1.15	1.12	1.00	0.85	0.86	0.87	0.88	0.90	0.91	0.92	0.93	0.94	0.95	–	–	–

Single circular cylinders with fins or laths in a tube; plane-parallel flow; $S_m/F_0 < 0.3^8$	Diagram 10-3

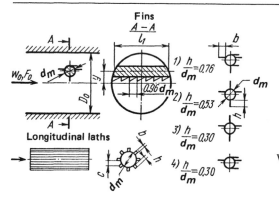

$$\zeta \equiv \frac{\Delta p}{\rho w_0^2/2}$$

$$= (1-1.1) c_x \frac{S_m/F_0}{(1 - 0.5\, S_m/F_0)^3} \times \left(1 - \frac{2y}{D_0}\right)^{1/3}$$

With fins, $c_x = f(Re')$, see graph a.

Values of c_x at $\alpha = 0°$;
$b/d_m = 1$

No. of curve and no. of fin	Re' × 10⁻⁵				
	1	2	3	4	5
1	1.70	1.40	1.40	1.47	1.46
2	1.40	1.25	1.27	1.26	1.26
3	1.0	1.05	1.08	1.11	1.12
4	0.55	0.59	0.59	0.59	0.61

No. of curve and no. of fin	Re' × 10⁻⁵			
	6	7	8	10
1	1.45	1.46	1.48	1.48
2	1.28	1.29	1.29	1.29
3	1.13	1.14	1.15	1.16
4	0.62	0.63	0.64	0.65

Values of c_x at $c/h = 0.33$

$\dfrac{h}{d_m}\ \dfrac{b}{d_m}$	Re' × 10⁻⁵							
	0.5	0.6	0.8	1.0	1.5	2	3	≥4
0.027 (0.055)	1.05	0.92	0.66	0.80	0.88	0.93	0.97	0.99
0.041 (0.083)	0.88	0.90	0.94	0.95	0.98	1.00	1.02	1.03
0.055 (0.110)	1.15	1.08	0.85	0.94	1.00	1.01	1.04	1.05
0.087 (0.174)	0.85	0.61	0.70	0.93	0.99	1.01	1.05	1.06

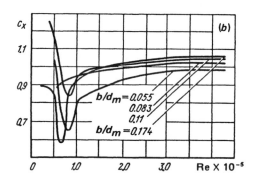

With longitudinal laths $c_x = f(Re')$, see graph b.

Spacers in a tube; plane-parallel flow; $S_m/F_0 < 0.3$[1,21,22,44,48]	Diagram 10-4

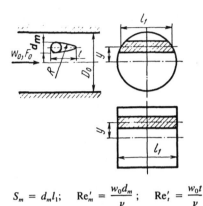

$$\zeta \equiv \frac{\Delta p}{\rho w_0^2/2} = k_2 c_x \frac{S_m/F_0}{(1 - \tau S_m/F_0)^3}\left(1 - \frac{2y}{D_0}\right)^{1/3}$$

$$S_m = d_m l_1; \quad \mathrm{Re}'_m = \frac{w_0 d_m}{\nu}; \quad \mathrm{Re}'_t = \frac{w_0 t}{\nu}$$

Name of a spacer and scheme	Drag coefficient c_x

Circular cylinder with fairing, $\mathrm{Re}'_m > 10^6$

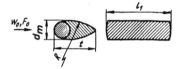

Curve 1 of graph a ($\tau \approx 0.5$; $k_2 = 1.0$)

t/d_m	2	3	3.5	4.0
R/d_m	0	4.0	6.0	8.0
c_x	0.20	0.10	0.07	0.06

Shaped spacer, $\mathrm{Re}'_m > 10^6$

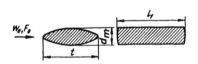

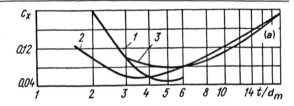

Curve 2 of graph a ($\tau \approx 0.5$; $k_2 = 1.0$)

t/d_m	2	3	4	5	6	8	12	14	20
c_x	0.09	0.06	0.06	0.07	0.08	0.10	0.14	0.16	0.19

Plate with rounded edges; $r/d_m = 0.5$

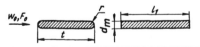

Re'_m	5×10^5	2×10^6	$\tau \approx 0.5$
c_x	0.78	0.66	$k_2 = 1.0$

Wedge-shaped plate; $d_1/t = 0.0417$; $d_2/t = 0.025$

Re'_t	5×10^5	2×10^6	$\tau \approx 0.5$
c_x	0.53	0.46	$k_2 = 1.0$

Profiles of different length; $\mathrm{Re}'_m \approx 10^6$

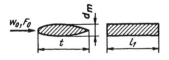

Curve 3 of graph a ($\tau \approx 0.5$; $k_2 = 1.0$)

t/d_x	3.0	5.0	8.0	12	18
c_x	0.10	0.080	0.096	0.13	0.193

Name of a spacer and scheme	Drag coefficient c_x

Square beam

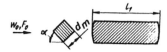

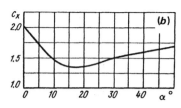

α, deg	0	10	20	30	40	50	$\tau \approx 0.5$
c_x	2.00	1.43	1.35	1.50	1.52	1.54	$k_2 = 1.0$

Profiled steel tube (drop-like profile);
$Re_m' > 5 \times 10^4$

t/d_m	3.0	5.0
c_x	0.1	0.2
	$\tau = 0.5$; $k_2 = 1.0$	

Profiled wire; $Re_m' = 3 \times 10^3$–10^4

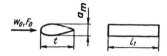

$$c_x = 0.3\text{–}0.4$$
$$\tau \approx 0.5; \quad k_2 \approx 1.0$$

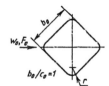

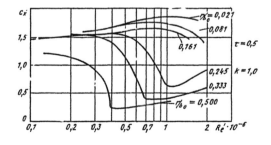

$\tau \approx 0.5$; $k \approx 1.0$
$\tau = 0.5$; $k = 1.0$

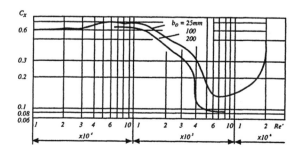

Spacers in a tube; plane-parallel flow; $S_m/F_0 < 0.3$[1,21,22,44,48]

Diagram 10-4

$$Re' = w_0 d_m/2 = 10^5$$

Scheme of the spacer	c_0/b_0	r/b_0	c_x	τ	k_2
	1:2	—			
	1:2	—	1.6	0.5	1.0
	1:2	—			
	2:1	—			
	2:1	—	0.6	0.5	1.0
	2:1	—			
	1:2	0.021			
	1:2	0.021	2.5	0.8	1.0
	1:2	0.021			
	1:2	0.083	1.9	0.8	1.0
	1:2	0.250			
	1:2	0.250	1.6	0.5	1.0

Scheme of the spacer	c_0/b_0	r/b_0	c_x	τ	k_2
	1:2 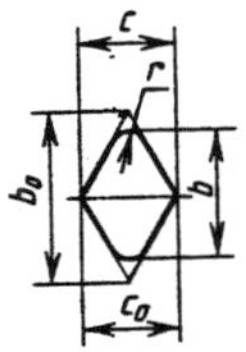 	0.021			
	1:2	0.021	1.8	~1.0	~1.1
	1:2	0.021			
	2:1	0.083	1.7	~1.0	~1.1
	2:1	0.167	1.7	~1.0	~1.1
	2:1	0.167			
	1:1	0.015			
	1:1	0.015	1.5	~0.5	~1.0
	1:1	0.015			
	1:1	0.118	1.5	~0.5	~1.0
	1:1	0.235			
	1:1	0.235	1.5	~0.5	~1.0

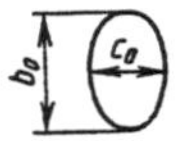

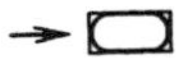

Scheme of the spacer	c_0/b_0	r/b_0	c_x	τ	k_2
	0.5	—	1.6–1.7	~0.5	~1.0
	1.5	0.10	0.5–0.6	0.5	1.0
	0.67	0.16	1.5	~1.0	~1.1
	0.67	—	1.5	~1.0	~1.1
30°	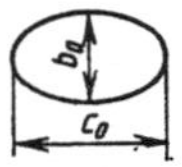  1.85	—	1.0	0.5	1.0
 60°	1.00	—	1.3–1.45	~0.5	~1.0
 90°	0.50	—	1.6	~1.0	~1.1
120°	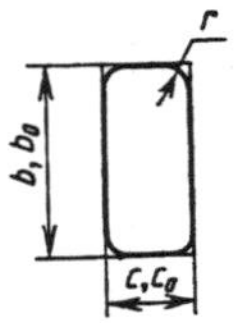 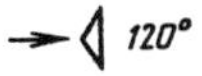 0.29	—	1.85	~1.0	~1.1
120°	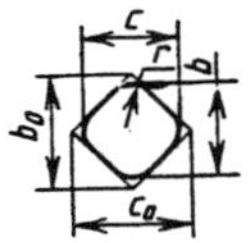 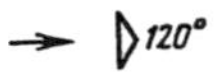 1.85	—	1.8	~1.0	~1.1
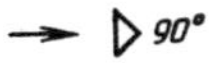 90°	1.00	—	2.0	~1.0	~1.1
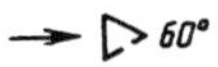 60°	0.5	—	2.1	~1.0	~1.1
 30°	0.29	—	2.0–2.1	1.0	1.1

Flow past obstructions of various cross-sectional shapes (rotated data tables).

Shape	ratio	r/D_g	ζ		
ellipse, flow ↑	4	–	~0.28	0.5	1.0
ellipse, flow ↑	8	–	~0.2	0.5	1.0
semicircle	1	–	1.2–1.3	0.5	1.0
semicircle with circle	1	–	1.3–2.3	0.5	1.0

Triangle inscribed in square (b, b₀, c, c_g):

	ratio	r/D_g	ζ		
	1:1	0.021	–		
	1:1	0.021	1.2	0.5	1.0
	1:1	0.021	1.3	0.5	1.0
	1:1	0.083	1.1	0.5	1.0
	1:1	0.250	–		
	1:1	0.250	–		

Teardrop triangle (b, b₀, c, c_g):

	ratio	r/D_g	ζ		
	1:1	0.021	–		
	1:1	0.021	2.0	1.0	1.0
	1:1	0.021	1.9	1.0	1.0
	1:1	0.083	1.8	1.0	1.0
	1:1	0.250	–		
	1:1	0.250	–		

Shape	ratio	r/D_g	ζ		
square, flow ↑	–	0.37	0.75	0.5	1.0
ellipse, flow ↑	2	–	0.5	0.5	1.0

Rounded square (r, c,c_g, b,b₀):

ratio	r/D_g	ζ		
1:1	0.021	2.0	0.5	1.0
1:1	0.021			
1:1	0.021			
1:1	0.167	1.2	0.5	1.0
1:1	0.333	1.0	0.5	1.0
1:1	0.333			
2:1	0.042	1.4	0.5	1.0
2:1	0.042			
2:1	0.042			
2:1	0.167	0.7	0.5	1.0
2:1	0.500	0.4	0.5	1.0
2:1	0.500			

Diamond / rhombus (b, c, c_g, b₀):

ratio	r/D_g	ζ		
2:1	0.042	1.1	0.5	1.0
2:1	0.042			
2:1	0.042			
2:1	0.167	1.1	0.5	1.0
2:1	0.333	1.1	0.5	1.0
2:1	0.333			

Pair of circular cylinders in a tube; plane-parallel flow; Re$' = w_0 d_m/\nu > 10^5$; $S_m/F_0 < 0.3$[21,22]	Diagram 10-5

$$\zeta \equiv \frac{\Delta p}{\rho w_0^2/2} = c_{x tot} \frac{S_m/F_0}{(1 - 0.5\, S_m/F_0)^3}\left(1 - \frac{2y}{D_0}\right)^{1/3} \text{ where } \tau = f(S_m/F_0), \text{ see Diagram 10-1.}$$

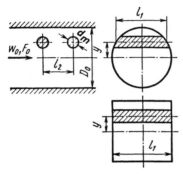

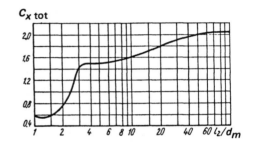

$$S_m = d_m l_1$$

l_2/d_m	1.0	1.5	2.0	2.5	3.0	4.0	5.0	10	20	30	50	100
$c_{x tot}$	0.60	0.60	0.76	1.10	1.44	1.50	1.52	1.62	1.82	1.92	2.0	2.06

Rolled and shaped profiles in a tube; plane-parallel flow;[3,48] $S_m/F_0 < 0.3$; Re$' = w_0 d_m/\nu > 10^5$	Diagram 10-6

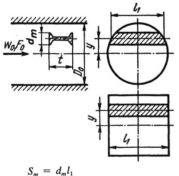

$$\zeta \equiv \frac{\Delta p}{\rho w_0^2/2} = k_2\, c_x \frac{S_m/F_0}{(1 - \tau\, S_m/F_0)^3}\left(1 - \frac{2y}{D_0}\right)^{1/3}$$

where for c_x and τ, see the table for a given profile at the given angle of attack α

$$S_m = d_m l_1$$

| Rolled and shaped profiles in a tube; plane-parallel flow;[3,48] $S_m/F_0 < 0.3$; $Re' = w_0 d_m/\nu > 10^5$ | | | | | Diagram 10-6 | | | | |

Profile	t/d_m	c_x	τ	k_2	Profile	t/d_m	c_x	τ	k_2
	1.0	2.76	~1.0	~1.0		2.1–2.2	1.2	~1.0	~1.1
	0.5	2.68	~1.0	~1.1		2.2	2.08	~1.0	~1.1
	1.08	2.66	~1.0	~1.1		0.65 2.2	1.8 0.9	~0.5	1.0
	0.46	1.66	~1.0	~1.1		2.2	0.15	0.5	1.0
	1.0	1.76	~1.0	~1.1		2.2	0.5	~1.0	~1.1
$\frac{b}{d_m}=0.29$; $\frac{c}{d_m}=0.42$	0.63	2.2	~1.0	~1.1		2.2	0.3	~0.5	~1.0
						0	2.40	~1.0	~1.1

Sphere in a tube; three-dimensional flow, $S_m/F_0 < 0.3$[6,17,48]	Diagram 10-7

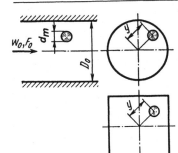

$$\zeta \equiv \frac{\Delta p}{\rho w_0^2/2} = c_x \frac{S_m/F_0}{(1 - 0.5\, S_m/F_0)^3}\left(1 - \frac{2y}{D_0}\right)^{1/3}$$

1. $\varepsilon_t = \dfrac{\sqrt{\overline{w'^2}}}{w_0} \approx 0$ (where ε_t is the degree of turbulence):

a) $Re' = \dfrac{w_0 d_m}{\nu} \le 1.0$: $c_x = \dfrac{24}{Re'}$;

b) $0.1 < Re' < 10^3$: $c_x = \dfrac{24}{Re'} + \dfrac{4}{(Re')^{1/3}}$

c) $0 < Re' < 5 \times 10^5$: $c_x = \left(\dfrac{24}{Re'} + \dfrac{4.565}{3\sqrt{Re'}} - \dfrac{0.491}{\sqrt{Re'}}\right)$

$\times\ (1 - \text{th}\, 0.00025\, Re') + 0.42\, \text{th}\, 0.00025\, Re'$

$+\ 0.02\, \text{th}\, 0.0001\, Re'$; for $c_x = f(Re')$, see graph a.

$S_m = \dfrac{\pi d_m^2}{4}$; $Re' = \dfrac{w_0 d_m}{\nu}$

2. $\varepsilon_t = 0.07\text{--}0.35$ and $\dfrac{400}{\varepsilon_t} < Re' < 3 \times 10^4$:

$$c_x = \frac{3990}{(\lg Re')^{6.1}} - \frac{4.47 \times 10^5}{Re'^{1.8}\, \varepsilon_t^{0.97}} = f(Re'\,\varepsilon_t), \text{ see graph b,}$$

Re'	10^{-3}	5×10^{-3}	10^{-2}	5×10^{-2}	10^{-1}	5×10^{-1}
c_x	2.4×10^4	4.8×10^3	2.4×10^3	4.8×10^2	24.4×10	50.70

Re'	1.0	2.0	3.0	4.0	5	10	20
c_x	26.90	14.80	10.65	8.45	7.12	4.32	2.74

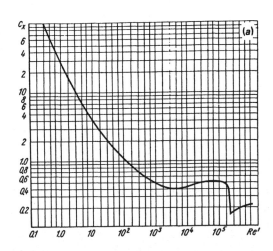

Sphere in a tube; three-dimensional flow, $S_m/F_0 < 0.3^{6,17,48}$		Diagram 10-7

Re'	30	40	50	80	10^2	1.5×10^2	2×10^2	3×10^2	5×10^2	10^3	5×10^3	10^4
c_x	2.14	1.80	1.58	1.23	1.09	0.90	0.79	0.68	0.57	0.47	0.38	0.40

Re'	5×10^4	10^5	2×10^5	3×10^5	4×10^5	5×10^5	6×10^5	7×10^5	8×10^5	9×10^5	10^6
c_x	0.49	0.50	0.49	0.40	0.18	0.19	0.20	0.21	0.21	0.22	0.22

Values of c_x

ε_t	Re' × 10⁻³										
	0.4	0.6	0.8	1	1.15	1.34	1.6	1.7	1.9	2.11	2.36
0.11	–	–	–	–	–	–	–	0.42	0.33	0.29	0.20
0.13	–	–	–	–	–	–	0.40	0.35	0.25	0.20	0.19
0.15	–	–	–	–	–	–	0.35	0.35	0.23	0.18	0.19
0.17	–	–	–	–	0.50	0.40	0.29	0.23	0.18	0.18	0.29
0.19	–	–	–	0.58	0.40	0.30	0.23	0.18	0.16	0.31	0.51
0.21	–	–	–	0.42	0.33	0.25	0.16	0.14	0.33	0.52	0.68
0.23	–	–	0.60	0.34	0.25	0.18	0.14	0.35	0.54	0.70	0.83
0.25	–	–	0.40	0.24	0.17	0.12	0.36	0.57	0.73	0.85	0.95
0.30	–	0.40	0.14	0.10	0.17	0.45	0.84	0.97	1.07	1.14	1.19
0.35	0.80	0.20	0.09	0.25	0.53	0.91	1.18	1.26	1.31	1.35	1.36

ε_t	Re' × 10⁻³										
	2.67	3.08	3.64	4.44	5.7	8	10	15	20	25	30
0.07	–	–	–	–	0.23	0.43	0.48	0.48	0.41	0.41	0.38
0.09	–	–	–	0.24	0.45	0.55	0.56	0.52	0.46	0.42	0.39
0.11	0.20	0.24	0.25	0.46	0.59	0.63	0.61	0.54	0.48	0.43	0.40
0.13	0.21	0.26	0.47	0.61	0.69	0.68	0.65	0.56	0.49	0.44	0.40
0.15	0.28	0.49	0.64	0.73	0.76	0.72	0.67	0.57	0.50	0.44	0.40
0.17	0.49	0.65	0.76	0.82	0.82	0.75	0.69	0.58	0.50	0.45	0.41
0.19	0.67	0.79	0.86	0.89	0.86	0.78	0.71	0.59	0.51	0.45	0.41
0.21	0.81	0.89	0.94	0.94	0.90	0.80	0.72	0.59	0.51	0.45	0.41
0.23	0.92	0.98	1.01	0.99	0.93	0.81	0.73	0.60	0.51	0.46	0.41
0.25	1.02	1.06	1.06	1.03	0.95	0.83	0.74	0.60	0.52	0.46	0.41
0.30	1.21	1.21	1.17	1.10	1.00	0.85	0.76	0.61	0.52	0.46	0.42
0.35	1.35	1.31	1.25	1.16	1.04	0.87	0.77	0.62	0.53	0.46	0.42

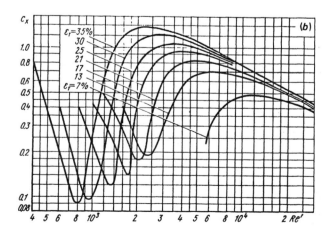

Bodies of isometric shape; three-dimensional flow;   Diagram
$S_m/F_0 < 0.3^6$ 10-8

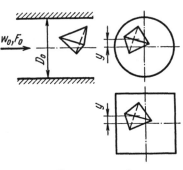

$$\zeta \equiv \frac{\Delta p}{\rho w_0^2/2} \approx c_x \frac{S_m/F_0}{(1 - S_m/F_0)^3}\left(1 - \frac{2y}{D_0}\right)^{1/3}$$

$$c_x = \left(\frac{28.47}{\text{Re}' \lg 15.38/\phi} + \frac{4.565\phi}{3\sqrt{\text{Re}'}} - \frac{0.491\phi}{\sqrt{\text{Re}'}}\right)$$

$\times \{1 - \text{th}\,[0.01282\,\text{Re}'(\phi - 0.9805)]\} + 2.86(\phi - 0.8531)$

$\times \text{th}\,[0.01282\,\text{Re}'(\phi - 0.9805)] + (7.76 - 2.86\phi - 4.88/\phi)$

$\times \text{th}\,[0.00104\,\text{Re}'(\phi - 0.9038)]$ see the curves $c_x = f(\text{Re}')$;

$\phi = 1.182$ for octahedrons; $\phi = 1.104$ for cubic octahedrons;
$\phi = 1.50$ for tetrahedrons

$$S_m = \frac{\pi d_e^2}{4} \quad \text{Re}' = \frac{w_0 d_m}{\nu}$$

for d_e see para. 22

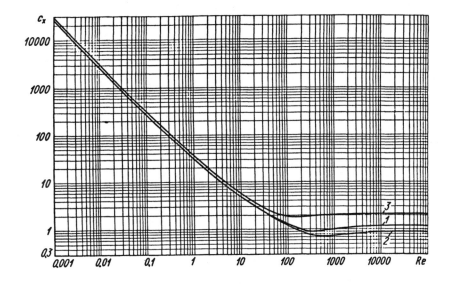

Values of c_x

Curve	Re'						
	10^{-3}	10^{-2}	10^{-1}	5×10^{-1}	1.0	2.0	5.0
1 (octahedrons)	2.5×10^4	2.5×10^3	2.5×10^2	5.2×10	30	15	8.0
2 (cubic octahedrons)	2.5×10^4	2.5×10^3	2.5×10^2	5.5×10	29	16	7.4
3 (tetrahedrons)	2.9×10^4	2.9×10^3	2.9×10^2	5.6×10	33	19	9.0

Curve	Re'							
	10	5×10	10^2	5×10^2	10^3	5×10^3	10^4	5×10^4	10^5
1 (octahedrons)	5.0	1.8	1.25	0.93	1.0	1.20	1.25	1.25	1.25
2 (cubic octahedrons)	4.5	1.7	1.15	0.72	0.75	0.86	0.90	0.90	0.90
3 (tetrahedrons)	5.6	2.2	1.80	1.90	2.0	2.05	2.05	2.05	2.05

Bodies of different shapes in a tube; three-dimensional flow; $S_m/F_0 < 0.3^{38,48}$	Diagram 10-9

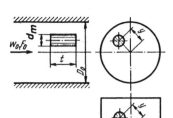

$$\zeta \equiv \frac{\Delta p}{\rho w_0^2/2} = k_2 c_x \frac{S_m/F_0}{(1 - \tau S_m/F_0)^3} \left(1 - \frac{2y}{D_0}\right)^{1/3}$$

$$Re' = \frac{w_0 d_m}{\nu}$$

Name of a body and scheme	Drag coefficient c_x
Convex hemisphere-cup (without end plane) $S_m = \dfrac{\pi d_m^2}{4}$	$Re' = 4 \times 10^5$; $c_x = 0.36$; $Re' = 5 \times 10^5$; $c_x = 0.34$
Hemisphere-cone $S_m = \dfrac{\pi d_m^2}{4}$ 	$Re' = 1.35 \times 10^5$; $c_x = 0.088$
Concave hemisphere-cup (without end plane) $S_m = \dfrac{\pi d_m^2}{4}$ 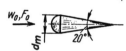	$Re' = 4 \times 10^5$; $c_x = 1.44$; $Re' = 5 \times 10^5$; $c_x = 1.42$
Cone-hemisphere-cone $S_m = \dfrac{\pi d_m^2}{4}$ 	$Re' = 1.35 \times 10^5$; $c_x = 0.16$

t/d_m	0.5	1	2	3	4	5	6	7
c_x	1.0	0.91	0.85	0.85	0.87	0.90	0.95	0.99

Circular smooth cylinder in a flow parallel to the axis, $S_m = \dfrac{\pi d_m^2}{4}$

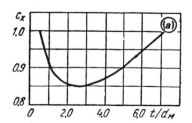

| Bodies of different shapes in a tube; three-dimensional flow; $S_m/F_0 < 0.3$[38,48] | | | | | | | | Diagram 10-9 |

Name of body and scheme	Drag coefficient c_x							
	Curve 1 of graph b							
	l_1/d_m	1.0	2.0	5.0	10	40	∞	
	c_x	0.63	0.68	0.74	0.82	0.98	1.20	~1.0 ~1.1
	$\tau \approx 1.0$							

Circular smooth cylinder in a flow normal to the axis; $S_m = \dfrac{d_m}{l_1}$; $Re' = 8.8 \times 10^4$

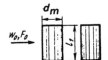

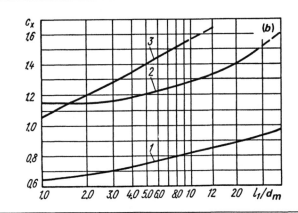

Cone (with the plane at the base); $S_m = \dfrac{\pi d_m^2}{4}$; $Re' = 2.7 \times 10^5$

α, deg	30	60		
c_x	0.35	0.61	0.5	1.0

α, deg	0	10	20	30	40	50		
c_x	1.58	1.12	0.80	0.87	0.89	0.90	0.5	1.0

Square beam; $S_m = d_m l_1$; $\dfrac{l_1}{d_m} = 5$

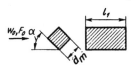

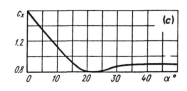

Cube ($t/d_m = l_1/d_m = 1$); $Re' = 8 \times 10^5$

$c_x = 1.05$ 0.5   1.0

Bodies of different shapes in a tube; three-dimensional flow; $S_m/F_0 < 0.3$[38,48]								Diagram 10-9

Name of body and scheme	Drag coefficient c_x							

Rectangular plate; $S_m = d_m l_1$; Re' $= 6 \times 10^5$

Curve 2 of graph b ($\tau = 1.5$)

l_1/d_m	1.0	2.0	2.8	4.0	5.0	10	20	∞
c_x	1.16	1.16	1.18	1.19	1.21	1.29	1.40	2.0
d/D	0	0.1	0.2	0.3	0.4	0.5		
c_x	1.16	1.16	1.16	1.18	1.20	1.22	~1.0	~1.1
d/D	0.6	0.7	0.8	0.9	1.0			
c_x	1.25	1.40	1.78	1.92	2.00			

Washer; $S_m = \dfrac{\pi}{4}(D^2 - d^2)$

Re' $= 3.6 \times 10^5$

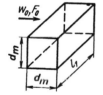

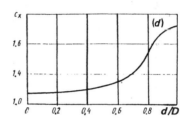

Prismatic body of square cross section; Re' $> 5 \times 10^5$

Curve 3 of graph b

l_1/d_m	0.15	0.20	0.3	0.5	1.0	2.0	5.0	∞
c_x	0.57	0.67	0.77	0.90	1.05	1.20	1.40	2.0

~1.0 ~1.0

Circular or square disk; Re' $= 6.2 \times 10^5$

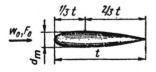

$c_x = 1.16$ ~1.0 ~1.0

Body of revolution; Re' $= (5–6) \times 10^5$ angle of attack $\alpha = 0–20°$

$\bar{l} = t/d_m$	3	4	5	6
c_x	0.05–0.10	0.05–0.12	0.06–0.15	0.075–0.18

0.5 1.0

Eliptical smooth cylinder or ellipsoid in a tube; three-dimensional flow; $S_m/F_0 < 0.3$	Diagram 10-10

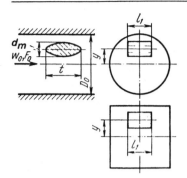

$$\zeta \equiv \frac{\Delta p}{\rho w_0^2/2} = c_x \frac{S_m/F_0}{(1 - 0.5\, S_m/F_0)^3} \left(1 - \frac{2y}{D_0}\right)^{1/3}$$

$$S_m = d_m l_1, \quad \mathrm{Re}' = \frac{w_0 d_m}{\nu}$$

Elliptical cylinder: $c_x = f(\mathrm{Re}')$, see graph a

Values of c_x (graph a)

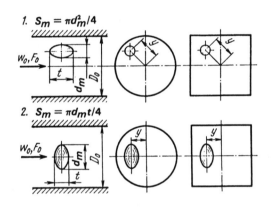

1. $S_m = \pi d_m^2/4$

2. $S_m = \pi d_m t/4$

$\dfrac{l_1}{d_m}$	$\mathrm{Re}' \times 10^{-5}$			
	0.3	0.4	0.5	0.6
2.5	0.38	0.31	0.26	0.22
3.0	0.32	0.26	0.22	0.19
3.5	0.28	0.24	0.21	0.18
4.0	0.25	0.21	0.18	0.16

$\dfrac{l_1}{d_m}$	$\mathrm{Re}' \times 10^{-5}$			
	0.7	0.8	0.9	1.0
2.5	0.18	0.16	0.14	0.13
3.0	0.16	0.14	0.12	0.11
3.5	0.16	0.14	0.12	0.11
4.0	0.15	0.14	0.13	0.13

Ellipsoid: $c_x = f(\mathrm{Re}')$, see graph b

Values of c_x (graph b)

$\dfrac{t}{d_m}$	$\mathrm{Re}' \times 10^{-5}$							
	0.2	0.5	1.0	2	3	4	5	6
0.75	–	–	0.62	0.59	0.58	0.57	0.31	0.20
1.33	–	–	0.26	0.10	–	0.12	–	–
1.80	0.32	0.22	0.10	0.05	0.06	0.07	0.08	0.08
3.00	–	–	0.07	0.05	0.05	0.06	–	–

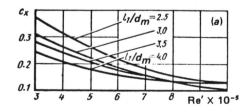

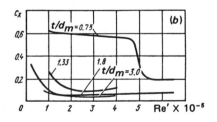

Rectangular plate and a pair of circular plates in a tube; three-dimensional flow:[10,38,48] $S_m/F_0 < 0.3$; Re' $= w_0 d_m/\nu = (4-6) \times 10^5$	Diagram 10-11

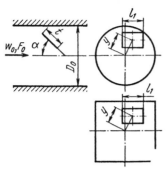

$$\zeta \equiv \frac{\Delta p}{\rho w_0^2/2} = 1.1\, c_x\, \frac{S_m/F_0}{(1 - S_m/F_0)^3}\left(1 - \frac{2y}{D_0}\right)^{1/3}$$

$S_m = l_1 t \sin \alpha$

1. Rectangular plate: $c_x = f(\alpha)$, see graph a.

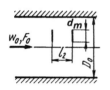

Values of c_x (graph a)

Curve	α, degrees						
(l_1/t)	5	10	20	30	40	50	60
1 (0.2)	0.02	0.03	0.17	0.44	0.76	1.02	1.08
2 (1.0)	0.04	0.09	0.30	0.70	1.10	1.13	0.98
3 (5.0)	0.05	0.14	0.30	0.47	0.64	0.80	0.90

2. A pair of circular plates: $c_x = c_{xov} = f(l_2/d_m)$, see graph b.

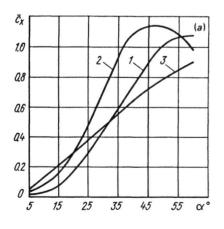

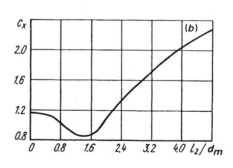

l_2/d_m	0	0.25	0.5	0.75	1.0	1.25	1.5	1.75	2.0	2.5	3.0	3.5	4.0	4.5
c_{xtot}	1.16	1.15	1.13	1.05	0.93	0.86	0.85	0.93	1.11	1.38	1.63	1.85	2.05	2.22

Shaped profiles placed in one longitudinal row in a tube; plane-parallel flow;[8] $S_m/F_0 < 0.3$; $Re' = w_0 d_m/\nu > 10^5$	Diagram 10–12

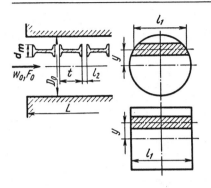
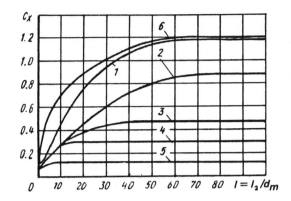

$$S_m = d_m l_1; \quad D_h = \frac{4F_0}{\Pi_0}; \quad \bar{l} = l_2/d_m \quad \zeta \equiv \frac{\Delta p}{\rho w_0^2/2} \approx k_2 \frac{c_x}{d_m D_h} \frac{1}{\bar{l}} \frac{S_m/F_0}{(1 - \tau S_m/F_0)} \times \left(1 - \frac{2y}{D_0}\right)^{1/3} \frac{L}{D_h} + \lambda \frac{L}{D_h}$$

where $c_x = f(\bar{l})$, see the graph; for λ, see Diagrams 2-1 through 2-6

Values of c_{x1}

Scheme of profile	k_2	τ	$\bar{l}$										
			0	2	5	10	20	30	40	50	60	70	100
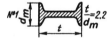 N°1 $\frac{t}{d_m}=2.2$	~1.1	≈1.0	≈0.10	0.10	0.24	0.44	0.75	0.95	1.06	1.14	1.18	1.18	1.18
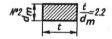 N°2 $\frac{t}{d_m}=2.2$	~1.1	≈1.5	≈0.10	0.10	0.17	0.28	0.45	0.60	0.71	0.80	0.85	0.88	0.88
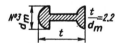 N°3 $\frac{t}{d_m}=2.2$	1.0	~1.0	≈0.10	0.10	0.17	0.27	0.37	0.43	0.46	0.47	0.47	0.47	0.47
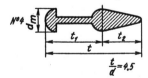 N°4 $\frac{t}{d}=4.5$	1.0	0.5	≈0.10	0.10	0.17	0.26	0.30	0.30	0.30	0.30	0.30	0.30	0.30
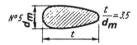 N°5 $\frac{t}{d_m}=3.5$	1.0	0.5	0.08	0.08	0.11	0.12	0.12	0.12	0.12	0.12	0.12	0.12	0.12
N°6	1.0	0.5	≈0.20	0.40	0.53	0.70	0.88	1.0	1.10	1.17	1.20	1.20	1.20

$Re' = 5.10^4 - 2.10^5$

Smooth cylinders in a tube arranged in one central longitudinal row; plane-parallel flow[5]	Diagram 10-13

$$\zeta \equiv \frac{\Delta p}{\rho w_0^2/2} = n_t \left\{ \frac{85(1 - 1.18 d_m/D_0)[2 \lg(l_2/d_m + 1)(d_m/D_0)^{1/4}]^{2.5}}{[(Re')^{0.25}(1 + 0.25 l_2/d_m)^{10 \cdot 5 Re'}} \right.$$

$$\left. + (2 \lg(l_2/d_m) + 1)(d_m/D_0)^{1.4} \right\} \lambda L/D_0 = n_t \zeta_1 + \zeta_{tr},$$

where n_t is the number of tubes in the longitudinal row;
$Re' = w_0 d_m/\nu$; for ζ see the graph and the table; for λ see Diagrams 2-1 through 2-4. The formula is valid within $0.08 < d_m/D_0 \leq 0.35$; $1.3 \leq l_2/d_m \leq 4.5$; $2.5 \times 10^4 < Re < 4 \times 10^5$.

At $d_m/D_0 \leq 0.15$ and $\lg Re > 5.35 + \dfrac{17.5 d_m/D_0 - 2.6}{l_2/d_m}$

and at $d_m/D_0 > 0.15$ and $\lg Re > 5.35 + \dfrac{5 \, d_m/D_0 - 0.75}{l_2/d_m}$

$$\zeta = n_t \, [2 \lg l_2/d_m) + 1] \, (d_m/D_0)^{1.4}$$

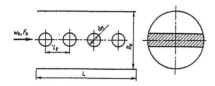

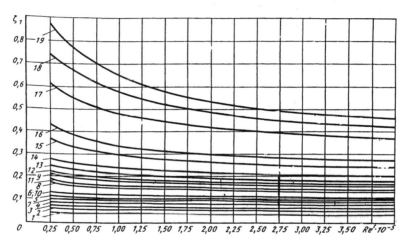

Values of ζ_1

No. of the curve	d_m/D_0	l_2/d_m	Re' × 10⁻⁵				
			0.25	1.0	1	3	4
1	0.08	1.5	0.026	0.026	0.035	0.039	0.039
2	0.08	3.0	0.070	0.070	0.072	0.073	0.074
3	0.08	4.5	0.079	0.079	0.079	0.079	0.079
4	0.12	2.0	0.087	0.087	0.087	0.087	0.087
5	0.12	3.0	0.096	0.096	0.096	0.096	0.096
6	0.12	4.0	0.132	0.122	0.122	0.122	0.122
7	0.15	1.5	0.097	0.097	0.097	0.097	0.097
8	0.15	3.0	0.157	0.140	0.140	0.140	0.140
9	0.15	4.5	0.180	0.157	0.157	0.157	0.157
10	9.18	1.3	0.109	0.109	0.109	0.104	0.104
11	0.18	2.0	0.210	0.183	0.174	0.174	0.174
12	0.18	2.7	0.220	0.190	0.183	0.183	0.183
13	0.18	3.3	0.235	0.210	0.210	0.205	0.205
14	0.22	2.0	0.270	0.235	0.225	0.225	0.225
15	0.22	3.0	0.350	0.300	0.260	0.250	0.250
16	0.22	4.0	0.420	0.340	0.300	0.295	0.295
17	0.34	2.0	0.600	0.480	0.530	0.400	0.383
18	0.34	2.7	0.750	0.570	0.490	0.450	0.445
19	0.34	3.3	0.900	0.650	0.550	0.500	0.470

Tube reinforced by various spacers and braces across the section and along the channel;[3] $S_m/F_0 < 0.3$; $Re' = w_0 d_m/\nu > 10^5$	Diagram 10-14

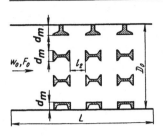

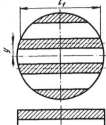

$$\zeta \equiv \frac{\Delta p}{\rho w_0^2/2} \approx 1.15 \sum_{i=1}^{h}$$

$$\times \frac{c_{x1i} S_{mi}/F_0 (1 - 2y/D_0)^{1/3}}{(d_m/D_h)_i \bar{l}_i (1 - \Sigma_{i=1}^n \tau_i S_{mi}/F_0)^3}$$

$$\times \frac{L}{D_h} + \lambda \frac{L}{D_h}$$

$$D_h = \frac{4F_0}{\Pi_0}$$

$$\bar{l} = \frac{l_2}{d_m}$$

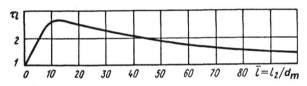

where i is the ordinal number of the reinforcement, n is the number of rows of reinforcement, c_{x1i} is determined as c_{x1} for the given profile as a function of $\bar{l} = \bar{l}_2/d_m$ from Diagram 10-12; for λ, see Diagrams 2-1 through 2-6; τ_i is determined as a function of the profile shape: (a) for an I-beam, channel, angle, plates with frontal incidence of the flow, rectangle, etc., from the curve $\tau_i = f(\bar{l})$; (b) for sections of streamlined shape, $\tau_i \times 0.5$.

$\bar{l}$	0	2	4	6	8	10	15	20	30	40	50	60	80	100
τ_i	1.00	1.35	1.70	2.10	2.40	2.60	2.60	2.50	2.30	2.10	1.90	1.75	1.55	1.40

Truss in a tube; plane-parallel flow; $S_m/F_0 < 0.3$[36]	Diagram 10-15

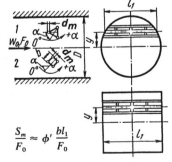

$$\frac{S_m}{F_0} \approx \phi' \frac{bl_1}{F_0}$$

$$\zeta \equiv \frac{\Delta p}{\rho w_0^2/2} = c_{x\alpha}^* \frac{S_m/F_0}{(1 - 0.5 S_m/F_0)^3}$$

where $c_{x\alpha}^* = c_{x\alpha} c_{x0}^*/c_{x0}$

Triangular truss: $c_{x\alpha} = f(\alpha)$, see graph a (Re' $= w_0 d_m/\nu) = 1.18 \times 10^5$, for c_{x0}^*, see the curves $c_{x0} = f(\text{Re}')$ of graph b obtained at $\alpha = 0$; for c_{x0}, see graph a at $\alpha = 0$

b is the width of the profile.
ϕ' is the coefficient of filling of the truss.

Welded lattice truss without cross stays

Welded lattice truss with cross stays

Lattice truss with cross stays and balle

Lattice truss with cross stays and corner plates

Truss in a tube; plane-parallel flow; $S_m/F_0 < 0.3^{36}$	Diagram 10-15

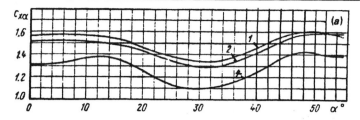

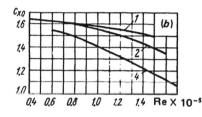

Values of $c_{x\alpha}$

Truss and curves	α, degrees										
	0	10	15	20	25	30	35	40	45	50	60
1	1.32	1.37	1.37	1.25	1.13	1.00	1.15	1.25	1.39	1.42	1.40
2	1.52	1.52	1.49	1.43	1.35	1.30	1.32	1.42	1.53	1.58	1.58
4	1.57	1.57	1.54	1.47	1.39	1.35	1.37	1.46	1.57	1.60	1.55

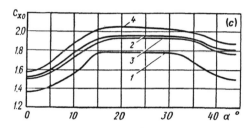

Values of c_{x0}

Truss and curves	$Re' \times 10^{-5}$						
	0.5	0.6	0.8	1.0	1.2	1.5	1.6
1	1.65	1.63	1.61	1.58	1.55	1.50	–
2	1.65	1.63	1.60	1.55	1.50	1.40	1.35
4	–	1.55	1.50	1.41	1.32	1.17	1.12

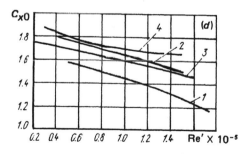

Square truss: $c_{x\alpha} = f(\alpha)$, see graph c ($Re' = w_0 d_m/\nu = 1.18 \times 10^5$); c_{c0}^* see the curves $c_{x0}^* = f(Re')$ of graph d obtained at $\alpha = 0$; for c_{x0}, see graph c at $\alpha = 0$

Values of $c_{x\alpha}$

Truss and curves	α, degrees								
	0	5	10	15	20	30	35	40	45
1	1.35	1.42	1.55	1.78	1.79	1.78	1.67	1.54	1.50
2	1.50	1.60	1.78	1.93	1.95	1.95	1.93	1.83	1.81
3	1.49	1.56	1.73	1.89	1.93	1.93	1.91	1.80	1.77
4	1.59	1.68	1.88	2.03	2.05	2.03	1.99	1.90	1.88

Values of c_{x0}^*

Truss and curves	$Re' \times 10^{-5}$						
	0.4	0.6	0.8	1.0	1.2	1.4	1.6
1	–	1.55	1.50	1.44	1.38	1.30	1.22
2	1.80	1.74	1.70	1.65	1.6	1.54	–
3	1.72	1.68	1.64	1.59	1.55	1.51	1.46
4	1.84	1.77	1.73	1.70	1.68	1.66	–

REFERENCES

1. Abramov, F. A., et al., *Aerodynamic Resistance of Underground Workings*, Nedra Press, Moscow, 1964, 186 p.
2. Abramov, F. A., Dolinskiy, V. A., Idelchik, I. E., Kersten, I. O., and Tsodikov, V. Ya., *Aerodynamic Resistance of Headings*, Moscow, 1964, p. 186.
3. Skochinskiy, A. A., Ksenofontova, A. I., Kharev, A. A., and Idelchik, I. E., *Aerodynamic Resistance of Shafts and the Means of Its Reduction*, Moscow, 1953, p. 363.
4. Budarin, V. A., Investigation of the Forced Coupling of a Liquid Flow with a Poorly Streamlined Body in a Circular Tube, thesis (Cand. Sc., Eng.), Moscow, 1982, p. 166.
5. Bystrov, P. I. and Mikhailov, V. S., Hydrodynamics of Collecting Heat Exchanging Apparatus, Moscow, 1982, p. 223.
6. Gorlin, S. M. and Khudyakov, G. E., Effect of the initial flow turbulence on the aerodynamic resistance of poorly streamlined sharp-edged bodies, *Izv. Akad. Nauk SSSR Mekh. Shid. Gaza*, no. 2, 120–128, 1969.
7. Gorlin, S. M., *Experimental Aeromechanics*, Vysshaya Shkola Press, Moscow, 1970, 423 p.
8. Dunchevsky, G. M., Study of the flow past a cylinder in a circular tube, *Gidravl. Gidrotekh. (Mezhved. Respubl. Nauch. Tekh. Sb. No. 4)*, 110–117, Tekhnika Press, Kiev, 1966.
9. Idelchik, I. E., Shock losses in a flow with non-uniform velocity distribtuion, *Tr. BNT MAP*, vyp. 662, 1–24, 1948.
10. Idelchik, I. E., *Hydraulic Resistance (Physical and Mechanical Fundamentals)*, Gosenergoizdat, Moscow-Leningrad, 1954, 316 p.
11. Grabovskiy, A. M. and Budarin, V. A., Concerning the calculation of the drag and local resistance coefficients of poorly streamlined bodies, *Izv. VUZov. Energ.*, no. 12, 60–64, 1980.
12. Devnin, S. I., *Aerohydrodynamic Calculation of Poorly Streamlined Ship Constructions*, Leningrad, 1967, p. 223.
13. Klyachko, L. S., Equation of motion of dust particles in dust collectors, *Otoplenie Vent.*, no. 4, 27–32, 1934.
14. Korepanov, K. V., Ventilation resistance of trucks and trains moving in underground working, *Razrab. Mestorozhd. Polezn. Iskop.*, vyp. 4, 18–27, Tekhnika Press, Kiev, 1965.
15. Krapivin, A. M., et al., Hydraulic resistance of a one-row longitudinal tube bundle in a plane parallel gas flow, *Teploenergetika*, no. 6, 30–34, 1972.
16. Kuznetsov, B. Ya., Aerodynamic investigations of cylinders, *Tr. TsAGI*, vyp. 98, 50, 1931.
17. Kuznetsov, B. Ya., Drag resistance of ropes, wires, tenders and aircraft strips, *Tr. TsAGI*, vyp. 97, 45, 1931.
18. Lamb, G., *Hydrodynamics*, Gostekhizdat, Moscow, 1947, 690 p.
19. Loitsyansky, L. G., *Liquid and Gas Mechanics*, Nauka Press, Moscow, 1973, 904 p.
20. Malevich, Yu. A. and Lyogky, V. M., Aerodynamic resistance of single finned tubes in a transverse air flow, *Izv. VUZov Energ.*, no. 7, 116–120, 1966.
21. Maseyev, M. M., Bat, A. A., and Khokhlova, L. N., Aerodynamic resistance of a group of cylinders, *Nauch. Tr. Inst. Mekh, MGU*, no. 4, 23–32, 1970.
22. Pevz, G. D. and Derzhinkevich, I. B., Study of the drag resistance of a new type of stulls of shaft wells, *Razrab. Rudn. Mestorozhd. (Resp. Mezhved. Sb. Nauch. Tr.)*, vyp. 2(27), 60–68, 1969.
23. Retter, E. I., Aerodynamics of shapeless industrial buildings, *Mikroklimat Zdanii Zadachi Teplofiz.*, 6–25, Gosstroiizdat, Moscow, 1963.
24. Sarpkaya, T. and Garrison, Ts., Vortex formation and resistance in a transient flow, *Prikl. Mekh.*, vol. 30, no. 1, 75–85, Mir Press, 1963.
25. Lyatkher, V. M. and Prudovskiy, A. M., *Hydraulic Modelling*, Moscow, 1984, p. 392.
26. Ustinov, A. M. and Kaliev, S. T., Determination of the coefficients of aerodynamic resistance of workings with stulls of new type, *Tr. Karagandinsk. Nauch.-Issled. Ugol. Inst.*, vyp. 16, 140–145, 1964.
27. Fabrikant, N. Ya., *Aerodynamics*, Nauka Press, Moscow, 1964, 530 p.
28. Migai, V. K. and Nosova, I. S., About the decrease of resistance of poorly streamlined bodies, *Teploenergetika*, no. 8, 60–63, 1980.
29. Khudyakov, G. E., Effect of elongation of the aerodynamic characteristics of prismatic bodies of square cross section, *Tr. Inst. Mekh. MGU*, vol. 4, no. 14, 28–32, 1970.
30. Chernov, A. P., Dust-laden flow past a fixed cylinder, *Tr. Inst. Energ. Akad. Nauk Kaz. SSR*, no. 3, 63–69, 1961.
31. Shapoval, G. T., Study of the resistance coefficients of load-carrying cylinders moving in tubes, *Izv. VUZov Gorn. Zh.*, no. 3, 129–135, 1964.
32. Kvass, B., Howard, F., Weinstein, L., and Bushnell, D., Reduction of the resistance of poorly streamlined bodies with the aid of longitudinal recesses, *Rocket Technol. Aeronaut.*, vol. 19, no. 6, 124–126, 1981.
33. Shterenlikht, D. V., Drag resistance of cylinders with longitudinal fins, *Tr. Vses. Nauch.-Issled. Inst. Gidrotekh.*, vyp. 4, 230–235, 1962.

34. Yuriev, B. N. and Lesnikova, M. P., *Aerodynamic Investigations (Tr. TsAGI)*, vyp. 33, 1928, 230 p.
35. Fedyayevskiy, K. K. and Blyumina, L. Kh., *Hydroaerodynamics of Separated Flow Past Bodies*, Moscow, 1977, p. 120.
36. Brenner, H. and Cox, R. G., The resistance to a particle of arbitrary shape in translational motion at small Reynolds numbers, *J. Fluid Mech.*, vol. 17, no. 4, 561–595, 1963.
37. Khenven, A. R. and Lyakhov, D. M., About the coefficients of hydraulic resistance of a sphere and a layer of spherical elements, *Teplofiz. Vysok. Temp.*, vol. 20, no. 6, 1119–1123, 1982.
38. *Ergebnisse der aerodynamischen Versuchsanstalt zu Göttingen*, Lieferung III, 1927, 280 S.
39. Cheng, P., *Separation Flows*, vol. 1, Moscow, 1972, p. 300.
40. Fage, A. and Warsap, J., The effects of turbulence and surface roughness on the drag of circular cylinders, *ARCRM*, no. 93, 1283, 1963.
41. Goin, K. L. and Lawrence, W. B., Subsonic drag of spheres at Reynolds number from 200 to 10,000, *AIAA J.*, vol. 6, no. 5, 961–962, 1968.
42. Hori, Ei-ichi, Experiments of flow around a pair of parallel circular cylinders, *Proc. 9th Jpn. Nat. Cong. Appl. Mech., Tokyo*, 231–234, 1960.
43. Young, D. F., Drag and lift on spheres within cylindrical tubes, *J. Hydraul. Div. Proc. Am. Soc. Civil Eng.*, vol. 86, no. 5, part 1, 47–57, 1960.
44. Kafkova, D. and Smutek, R., L'influence du mouvement oscillatoire d'un fluide sur le mouvement d'une particle spherique, *Acta Tech.*, vol. 14, no. 5, 610–629, CSAV, 1969.
45. Koch, L., Solids in pipes, *Int. Sci. Technol.*, no. 26, 68–72, 1964.
46. Livesey, J. L. and Turner, I. T., The influence of velocity profile characteristics on the drag of short circular struts spanning two-dimensional channels, *J. R. Aeronaut. Soc.*, vol. 71, no. 680, 569–573, 1967.
47. Robertson, J. and Rutherford, G. S., Turbulence effect on drag of angular blunt bodies, *J. Hydraul. Div. Proc. Am. Soc. Civ. Eng.*, vol. 95, no. 2, 781–785, 1969.
48. Rumpf, H., Über das Ansetzen fein verteilter Stoffe an den wänden von Strömungs Kanalen, *Chem. Ing. Tech.*, vol. 25, no. 6, 317–327, 1953.
49. Smythe, W. R., Flow around a sphere in a circular tube, *Phys. Fluids*, vol. 4, no. 6, 756–759, 1961.
50. Strordeur, A. N., Drag coefficients for fuel-element spacers, *Nucleonics*, vol. 19, no. 6, 74–76, 1961.
51. Tanaka, Z. and Jinoya, K., New approximate equation of drag coefficient for spherical particles, *J. Chem. Eng. Jpn.*, vol. 3, no. 2, 261–262, 1970.
52. Torobin, L. B. and Gauvin, W. H., The drag coefficients of single spheres moving in steady and accelerated motion in a turbulent fluid, *AIChE J.*, vol. 7, no. 4, 615–619, 1961.
53. Wentz, Ch. A. and Thodos, G., Total and form drag friction factors for the turbulent flow of air through packed and distended beds of spheres, *AIChe J.*, vol. 9, no. 3, 358–361, 1963.
54. Morel, T. and Bohn, M., Flow over two circular disks in tandem, *J. Fluids Eng. Trans. ASME*, vol. 102, no. 1, 104–111, 1980.
55. Richter, A. and Naudascher, E., Fluctuating forces on a rigid circular cylinder in confined flow, *J. Fluid Mech.*, vol. 78, no. 3, 561–576, 1976.

RESISTANCE TO FLOW AT THE EXIT
FROM TUBES AND CHANNELS
Resistance Coefficients of Exit Sections

11-1 EXPLANATIONS AND PRACTICAL RECOMMENDATIONS

1. When fluid flow leaves the system, the kinetic energy of the discharged jet is always lost to this system. Therefore, in the general case, the exit losses consist of the internal losses in the exit section Δp_{int} and the velocity (dynamic) pressure Δp_{vel} of the jet issuing from the system

$$\Delta p = \Delta p_{\text{int}} + \Delta p_{\text{vel}}$$

The resistance coefficient of the discharge, reduced to the velocity in the smallest cross section, is

$$\zeta \equiv \frac{\Delta p}{\rho w_0^2/2} = \frac{\Delta p_{\text{int}}}{\rho w_0^2/2} + \frac{\Delta p_{\text{vel}}}{\rho w_0^2/2} = \zeta_{\text{int}} + \zeta_{\text{vel}}$$

In the general case the velocity field at the exit is not uniform; therefore, the velocity pressure is determined by the prescribed distribution of velocities:

$$\Delta p_{\text{vel}} = \frac{1}{Q} \int_{F_{\text{ex}}} \frac{\rho w^3}{2} \, dF$$

and

$$\zeta_{\text{vel}} \equiv \frac{\Delta p_{\text{vel}}}{\rho w_0^2/2} = \frac{1}{F_0} \int_{F_{\text{ex}}} \left(\frac{w}{w_0}\right)^3 dF = \frac{1}{n_1^2} \frac{1}{F_{\text{ex}}} \int_{F_{\text{ex}}} \left(\frac{w}{w_{\text{ex}}}\right)^3 dF = \frac{1}{n_1^2} N$$

where $n_1 = F_{\text{ex}}/F_0$ is the degree of divergence of the exit section; $N = (1/F_{\text{ex}}) \int_{F_{\text{ex}}} (w/w_{\text{ex}})^3 \, dF$ is the kinetic energy coefficient of the flow (the Coriolis coefficient) at a certain location in the exit section.

2. In the case of free discharge of the flow from a straight section of the tube (channel) of constant cross section into a large volume, the total losses are reduced only to the losses of the velocity pressure at the exit, and since in this case $F_0 = F_{ex}$ ($n_1 = 1$), the total resistance coefficient is

$$\zeta \equiv \frac{\Delta p}{\rho w_0^2/2} = \frac{\Delta p_{vel}}{\rho w_0^2/2} = N$$

The coefficient N depends on the nature of the velocity distribution at the exit. In the case of uniform distribution of velocities it is equal to unity, and in the remaining cases it is always larger than unity.

3. If the velocities at the exit are distributed according to the exponential law (see paragraph 6-9, Section 4-1)

$$\frac{w}{w_{max}} = \left(1 - \frac{y}{R_0}\right)^{1/m}$$

where w and w_{max} are the velocity at the given point and the maximum velocity over the cross section, respectively, m/s; R_0 is the radius of the cross section, m; y is the distance from the tube (channel) axis, m; and $m \geq 1$ is the exponent, then the resistance coefficient of the discharge from a tube of circular or square cross section is calculated from the author's equation[15,17]

$$\zeta \equiv \frac{\Delta p}{\rho w_0^2/2} = \frac{(2m + 1)^3(m + 1)^3}{4m^2(2m + 3)(m + 3)}$$

and the resistance coefficient of the discharge from a plane tube is calculated from

$$\zeta \equiv \frac{\Delta p}{\rho w_0^2/2} = \frac{(m + 1)^3}{m^2(m + 3)}$$

When velocities at the exit from a plane tube are distributed according to a sinusoidal function (see paragraph 10 of Section 4-1),

$$\frac{w}{w_0} = 1 + \frac{\Delta w}{w_0} \sin (4k_1\pi y/b_0)$$

(where Δw is the deviation of the velocity at the given point from the section-averaged velocity, m/s; k_1 is an integer; $\pi = 3.14 \ldots$), the resistance coefficient of the discharge is

$$\zeta \equiv \frac{\Delta p}{\rho w_0^2/2} = 1 + \frac{3}{2}\left(\frac{\Delta w}{w_0}\right)^2$$

4. When the exit section is made flush with the wall along which the flow passes with velocity w_∞ (irrespective of the flow in the channel), there occurs the same phenomenon as in the case of jet entry through an orifice in a thin wall (see Chapter 4, paragraphs 41–48).

In case of a flow in straight channels, the jet leaves them without contraction, owing to which the velocity pressure losses do not exceed the value obtained on the basis of the mean velocity over the channel cross section. At certain velocity ratios $w_\infty/w_0 > 0$, the total pressure losses can even become smaller than the velocity pressure mentioned above ($\zeta < 1$), due (see paragraphs 41–48 of Chapter 4) to the phenomenon of higher rarefaction in the eddy zone on the downstream side of the jet issuing from the channel.[27]

5. The resistance of diffusers for a free discharge into a large volume (diffusers installed at the exit from the system) is composed of the losses in the diffuser proper and the velocity pressure losses at its exit. For more detailed information about the effect of the basic parameters on the resistance of diffusers and their flow structure, the reader is referred to Chapter 5. The values of the resistance coefficients obtained experimentally[21] for diffusers installed at the exit from the system are given in Diagrams 11-3 through 11-6 as functions of α, n_1, inlet conditions, and the Reynolds number Re $= w_0 D_0/\nu$.

6. The values of the pressure reduction coefficients $\bar{p} = p_1/p_0^* = p_a/p_0^*$ (where p_a is the atmospheric pressure and p_0^* is the total pressure at section 0-0) are given in Diagram 11-4 as functions of the relative velocity $\lambda_c \equiv w_0/a_{cr}$ (and the Reynolds number) at different n_1 and l_0/D_0 and large subsonic velocities[7] for diffusers installed at the exit from the system.

The coupling between the resistance coefficient of diffusers and the pressure reduction coefficient can be derived from equations similar to those given under paragraph 55 of Chapter 5, but with $\bar{p}_0$ replaced by $\bar{p}$.

7. When the flow issuing from a tube impinges on a baffle, the magnitude of the losses depends on the relative spacing between the baffle and the end of the tube. In some cases the baffle increases the losses; in others it decreases them. Thus, a baffle placed downstream from a cylindrical section or a rectilinear diffuser with a divergence angle up to $\alpha = 30°$ will always increase the losses. A baffle placed downstream from a curved diffuser or a rectilinear diffuser with a divergence angle above 30° can decrease the total losses appreciably, provided a proper choice of the distance between the baffle and the diffuser has been made.

8. A baffle placed downstream from a diffuser creates an additional pressure that causes the flow to spread over the cross section. This leads to a decrease in the flow separation region and thus to more efficient flow spreading. This is accompanied by decreases in both the losses inside the diffuser and the velocity pressure losses at the exit. The baffle also makes the flow turn radially (through 90°) before it leaves the system. If the outlet edge of the diffuser is not smoothly rounded, this turning of the flow is accompanied by a considerable contraction of the jet (Figure 11-1a) and, consequently, by an increase in its kinetic energy.

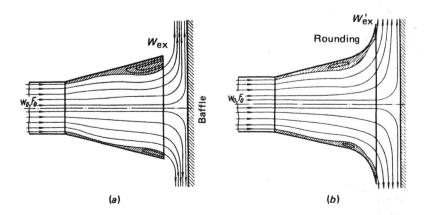

Figure 11-1 Flow pattern at the diffuser exit onto a baffle: (*a*) without rounding of the exit edges of the diffuser; (*b*) with rounded exit edges of the diffuser.

Therefore, when a baffle is placed downstream from a diffuser with a small divergence angle so that the average flow velocity at the place of flow turning is large, the advantage provided by spreading and more complete expansion of the jet in the diffuser can be smaller than the additional losses due to jet contraction at the exit. In the case of large divergence angles of the diffuser, the losses due to turning of the flow become relatively small and the baffle exhibits a more beneficial effect.

9. Smooth rounding of the exit edge of the diffuser or of the straight section (1) reduces the jet contraction (Figure 11-1b) and (2) leads to the formation of an annular diffuser in which an additional expansion of the jet occurs, which, in turn, transforms kinetic energy into pressure energy. Therefore, the installation of a baffle downstream from a diffuser with rounded edges is advantageous at both large and small expansion ratios of the diffuser ($n_1 = 1$ inclusive, i.e., the straight section).

10. For both straight diffusers with large divergence angles and diffusers or straight sections with rounded edges, there is an optimum distance $(h/D_h)_{opt}$ between the baffle and the exit orifice at which the resistance coefficient of the section with jet discharge onto the baffle is a minimum. When the baffle is placed at a large distance from the exit orifice (on the order of $h/D_h > 0.6$), the baffle does not exhibit any influence and the losses are equal to those without a baffle. When the baffle is placed very close to the exit orifice, at about $h/D_h < 0.15$, the flow velocity between the baffle and the exit edge increases and the losses increase sharply. The optimum distance of $(h/D_h)_{opt}$, which falls between 0.15 and 0.25, corresponds to more favorable conditions, when a substantial decrease in the flow velocity is accompanied by smaller vortex formation due to separation of the flow during its turning and expansion.

11. Adoption[13] of the following parameters for a diffuser with rounded edges and a baffle: $l_d/D_h = 2.5$; $\alpha = 14–16°$; $R_0/D_h = 0.6–0.7$; $D/D_h = 3.0$; $h/D_h = 0.24–0.26$, results in a total resistance coefficient for such a diffuser of F

$$\zeta \equiv \frac{\Delta p}{\rho w_0^2/2} = 0.25–0.35$$

12. A smaller value of ζ is obtained when the diffuser surface is highly polished or when there is a very smooth transition from the inlet collector to the diffuser (see the scheme of Diagram 11-8).

The resistance coefficient of such carefully manufactured diffusers with flow discharging onto the baffle is

$$\zeta \equiv \frac{\Delta p}{\rho w_0^2/2} = 1 - \eta_d$$

where η_d represents the diffuser performance determined on the basis of experimental data;[41] see Diagram 11-8.

13. When an exit diffuser is placed downstream from a centrifugal fan, the recommendations given under paragraphs 77–80 of Chapter 5 should be taken into account. Installation of the diffuser behind an induced-draft fan with flow discharge into a large volume is especially necessary, since then the exit losses can be reduced by a factor of 3 to 4, as shown by the data of Lokshin and Gazirbekova.[24]

It is advisable that the relative length of a pyramidal diffuser, placed downstream from a centrifugal fan (induced-draft fan), not be larger than $l_d/b_0 = 2.5–3.0$ at angles of divergence $\alpha = 8–12°$, and that the relative length of a plane diffuser not be larger than $l_d/b_0 = 4–5$ at $\alpha = 15–25°$. The resistance coefficients of diffusers installed downstream from centrifugal fans are determined from the data of Diagrams 11-11 to 11-15.

14. In some cases the flow from a centrifugal fan is discharged through a diffuser or a branch into a duct[6] (see Diagram 11-14). This diagram also contains the resistance coefficients of the constituent elements (diffuser, branch, duct) downstream from a fan with backward curved blades.

15. The resistance coefficients of conical diffusers installed downstream from axial fans[6] (also see Reference 3 in Chapter 3) are given in Diagram 11-15.

16. The total resistance coefficient ζ_{tot} of an annular diffuser with rectilinear boundaries (see paragraphs 82 and 83 of Chapter 5) installed downstream from an axial fan with a diverging back fairing during free discharge of flow into a large volume is determined from experimental data obtained by Dovzhik and Morozov.[12] It is given in Diagram 11-9 in the form of the dependence of ζ_{tot} on the angle α_1 at different α_2 for diffusers with $d_0 = 0.688$ and $l_d = 0.5$ and 1.0.

When the velocity field at the entrance into the diffuser is nonuniform or when the diffuser is installed downstream from an operating axial machine, the resistance coefficient is

$$\zeta \equiv \frac{\Delta p}{\rho w_0^2/2} = k_d \zeta_{tot}$$

where k_d is a correction factor determined from Diagram 5-1 or, alternatively, from Diagram 5-19.

The total resistance coefficients of radial discharge annular and axial-inlet radial discharge annular (combined) diffusers installed in the outlet pipes of turbomachines (see paragraphs 84–89 of Chapter 5) with induced draft and flow discharge into a large volume are given in Diagram 11-10.

17. The analysis of experimental data carried out by Brusilovskiy[4] has shown that the resistance coefficient ζ_{tot} of an axial-inlet diffuser can be also determined, with an accuracy suitable for engineering calculations, as ζ_{tot}^{pl}, the values of which are given in Diagram 11-9 (graphs d and e) for plane diffusers as functions of $n_1 = F_1/F_2$ and of the reduced length

$$\bar{l}_{red} = \frac{2 \lg[(1 + \bar{D}_1)/\cos \alpha_1 + (\bar{d}_0 + \bar{d}_1)/\cos \alpha_2]}{1 - \bar{d}_0^2} \tag{11-1}$$

in this case $\bar{l}_{red} = 2\bar{l}_{pl}$, where $\bar{l}_{pl} = l_{pl}/h_0$ is the relative length of the plane diffuser boundary, the value of which over the entire domain of the graphs considered usually differs from the relative axial length of the diffuser by no larger than 1%; h_0 is the width of the inlet section of the diffuser; the remaining symbols are given in Diagram 11-9.

18. Another type of discharge exists in the outlet sections of exhaust shafts having the same shapes and parameters as supply shafts. Their selection should be based on recommendations given in Chapter 3, paragraph 27.

19. Inlet nozzles (with respect to the room into which air is fed, but not with respect to the system that supplies the air to the room) also belong to the category of discharge units. The main requirements of such inlet nozzles are to ensure a rapid attenuation of the jet issuing from the nozzle or, conversely, to give a concentrated jet. The nature of the losses in such nozzles is the same as in the cases considered above of flow discharge from the system. They are generally reduced to loss of kinetic energy at the given degree of contraction or expansion of the jet.

20. This handbook presents resistance coefficients not only for the most effective types of nozzles, but also for nozzles of simpler shapes, which include nozzles such as ordinary elbows or side branches.

21. In certain cases the supplied air is distributed through air ducts with perforated surfaces (see Diagram 11-19). This ensures rapid attenuation of jet velocities, which is very desirable in many cases. At the same time, if the ratio of the total area of the orifices to the area of the duct cross section is large ($\bar{f}_0 = F_{or}/F_0 > 0.5$), uniform distribution of the flow along the duct will not occur.

Tapered air ducts ensure a more uniform distribution of the flow along the perforated surface than straight ducts, provided the ratio of the final to the initial area stays within $F_1/F_0 = 0.15-1.0$.

22. The total resistance coefficient of an inlet nozzle with a perforated surface when $0.5 < \bar{f}_0 < 3.0$ and $0 < F_1/F_0 < 1.0$, can be calculated from Grimitlin's[9] formula

$$\zeta \equiv \frac{\Delta p}{\rho w_0^2/2} \approx \frac{1.8}{\bar{f}_0^2} + \left(\frac{l}{D_h}\right)^{0.15} \tag{11-2}$$

When $F_1/F_0 > 0$, this formula exceeds the values by about 20%.

More accurate results are obtained from another formula of Grimitlin:

$$\zeta \equiv \frac{\Delta p}{\rho w_0^2/2} = 1.62 \bar{f}_0^{-2.2} \left(\frac{F_1}{F_0}\right)^{0.25 \bar{f}_0} \left(\lambda \frac{l}{D_h}\right)^{-0.05} + 1$$

Graph a of Diagram 11-19 has been plotted on the basis of the more simplified Equation (11-1).

23. Ordinary elbows and side branches (bends) with flow discharge into a large volume are frequently used as inlet nozzles. The resistance of such elbows and side branches depends substantially on the length of the discharge section. At first, when the length of this section is increased, the losses become somewhat higher, but they drop sharply and, starting with some value of l_0/b_0, become constant. This behavior of the resistance curve is due to the shape and magnitude of the eddy zone formed at the inner wall of the elbow after the turn.

24. The eddy zone in the elbow starts to form ner the corner of the turn, gradually expands, and at some distance from the turn attains its maximum width. Afterwards the eddy zone starts to contract again until the flow spreads entirely over the cross section. Thus, when the discharge section of the elbow is made of such a length that it ends at the cross section where the eddy zone is widest, that is, where the free area is most contracted, the flow will exit into the large volume at its maximum velocity and with the maximum loss of energy. This corresponds to the maximum of ζ of the graphs of Diagrams 11-16 through 11-18.

25. If there is no discharge section after the turn in the elbow, the eddy zone will be absent and the flow will exit into the large volume at lower velocity, and consequently the resistance coefficient ζ will be lower. Nevertheless, it will not decrease substantially. This is due to the fact that inertia compresses the flow to the upper wall, with the result that the velocity at the exit becomes considerably higher than the cross-section averaged velocity.

26. When the discharge section is made sufficiently long, this provides a complete spreading of the flow over the cross section and the resistance coefficient ζ has the minimum value. This, however, increases with l_1/b_0 due to higher friction losses in the straight section.

For elbows with free discharge of the flow and with the discharge cross section made twice as large as the inlet cross section, the resistance coefficient is lower by 40–50%.

27. Guide vanes can be used to decrease the resistance of elbows placed at the exit into a large volume. This provides even larger reduction of the resistance than the use of elbows with long downstream discharge sections, since the absolute resistance of the discharge elbows alone is much larger than that of elbows with downstream discharge sections.

28. The resistance coefficient of a straight exit section with a perforated plate (grid) or an orifice at the exit (discharge from an orifice into an infinite space $F_2 = \infty$; see scheme of Diagram 11-22) at $\mathrm{Re} = w_0 d_h / \nu > 10^5$ is generally calculated from the author's equation (4-10)

$$\zeta \equiv \frac{\Delta p}{\rho w_0^2/2} = \left[1 + \zeta'(1 - \overline{f})^{0.75} + \tau(1 - \overline{f})^{0.375} + \lambda \frac{l}{d_h} \right] \frac{1}{\overline{f}^2} \qquad (11\text{-}3)$$

where ζ' is the inlet resistance coefficient that is determined as ζ from Diagram 3-4 and 3-7; τ is a coefficient allowing for the effect of the plate or orifice thickness, the shape of the inlet edge of the orifice, and the conditions of flow through it; λ is the friction coefficient in the orifices of the grid or orifice; and $\overline{f} = F_{or}/F_{gr}$ is the clear flow area coefficient of the grid or orifice.

The general case is reduced to a number of particular cases:

- Sharp-edged orifices ($l/d_h = 0$) for which $\zeta' = 0.5$; $\tau = 1.41$, and $\lambda l/d_h = 0$ and Equation (11-3) reduces to the following author's formula:

$$\zeta \equiv \frac{\Delta p}{\rho w_0^2/2} = [1 + 0.5(1 - \overline{f})^{0.75} + 1.41(1 - \overline{f})^{0.375}] \cdot \overline{f}^{-2} \qquad (11\text{-}4)$$

- Thick-walled orifices for which $\zeta' = 0.5$ and $\tau = f(l/d_h)$ is determined from Diagram 11-23 (graph a).
- Beveled or rounded (in the flow direction) edges of orifices for which it is assumed that $\lambda = l/d_h = 0$ and $\tau \approx 2\sqrt{\zeta'}$, while

$$\zeta \equiv \frac{\Delta p}{\rho w_0^2/2} = [1 + \zeta'(1 - \overline{f}^2)^{0.75} + 2\sqrt{\zeta'}(1 - \overline{f})^{0.375}] \overline{f}^{-2} \qquad (11\text{-}5)$$

For beveled edges ζ' is determined as ζ for a conical nozzle (collector) having the end-face wall a function of the angle of convergence α and relative length l/d_h from graph b of Diagram 11-23.

For rounded edges ζ' is determined as ζ for a circular nozzle (collector) having the end-face wall a function of r/d_h from graph b of the same diagram.

29. For the transient and laminar regions of the flow, the resistance coefficient can be determined from the following approximate formulas (in accordance with paragraphs 36 and 37 of Chapter 4):

At $30 < \mathrm{Re} < 10^4 – 10^5$

$$\zeta \equiv \frac{\Delta p}{\rho w_0^2/2} = \frac{\zeta \phi}{\overline{f}^2} + \overline{\varepsilon}_{0\mathrm{Re}} \zeta_{qu}$$

At $10 < \mathrm{Re} < 30$

$$\zeta = \frac{33}{\mathrm{Re}} \frac{1}{\overline{f}^2} + \overline{\varepsilon}_{0\mathrm{Re}} \zeta_{qu}$$

At Re < 10

$$\zeta = \frac{33}{\text{Re}} \frac{1}{\bar{f}^2}$$

where $\zeta_\phi = f_1(\text{Re}, F_0/F_1)$ $(\bar{f} = F_{or}/F_0$ corresponds to $F_0/F_1)$ and $\varepsilon_{0\text{Re}} = f_2(\text{Re})$ are determined from Diagram 4-19; ζ_{qu} is the resistance coefficient of the given type of a grid and is determined from Equations (11-4) and (11-5).

30. The resistance of the side discharge from the terminal section of the tube or duct (see the scheme of Diagram 11-25) is higher than that of straight discharge through an orifice or a grid (see Diagram 11-29), since this is associated with an additional 90° turn of the flow with a change in the jet momentum. The larger the value of $\bar{f} = F_{or}/F_0$, the larger is this difference.

A relative increase in the resistance with $\bar{f}$ is also influenced by the fact that with the increase of this area ratio, the relative velocity of the flow in the tube increases, thus increasing the skewness and contraction of the jet during discharge from the orifice (Figure 11-2).

A side discharge through two opposite orifices increases the resistance of the discharge, and this increase is higher with larger $\bar{f}$.

31. The resistance coefficient of gratings with fixed louvers, when placed at the exit from a straight channel (see Diagram 11-26), can be calculated approximately from the following formulas:

a) $$\frac{l}{b_1'} \geqslant \left(\frac{l}{b_1'}\right)_{\text{opt}}$$

$$\zeta \equiv \frac{\Delta p}{\rho w_0^2/2} = \left[1 + 0.85\left(1 - \bar{f}\frac{F_{gr}}{F_0}\right) + \zeta_{fr}\right]\frac{k_1}{\bar{f}^2}\left(\frac{F_0}{F_{gr}}\right)^2$$

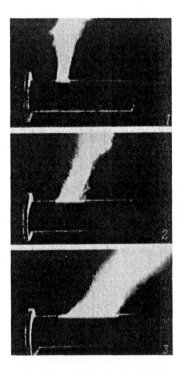

Figure 11-2 Flow patterns of smoke discharging from a side orifice at the terminal section of the tube:[36] 1, $\bar{f} = 0.29$; 2, $\bar{f} = 0.62$; 3, $\bar{f} = 1.15$.

b) $\dfrac{l}{b'_1} < \left(\dfrac{l}{b'_1}\right)_{\text{opt}}$

$$\zeta \equiv \frac{\Delta p}{\rho w_0^2/2} = \left[1 + 0.85\left(1 - \overline{f}\,\frac{F_{\text{gr}}}{F_0}\right) + \zeta_{\text{fr}}\right] \frac{k_1}{\overline{f}^2}\left(\frac{F_0}{F_{\text{gr}}}\right)^2 + \Delta\zeta$$

where $\Delta\zeta \approx 0.5[11(1 - \overline{f}) - l/b'_1]$ and $\zeta_{\text{fr}} = \lambda l/b'_1$; $k_1 = 1.0$ for a standard grating (inlet edges cut vertically); $k_1 = 0.6$ for an improved grating (inlet edges cut horizontally); $\overline{f} = F_{\text{or}}/F_0$ is the clear area coefficient of the grating; and λ is the friction coefficient of the louver channels, which is determined as a function of $\mathrm{Re} = w_{\text{or}}b'_1/\nu$ from Diagrams 2-1 through 2-6.

32. The kinetic energy of a submerged free jet issuing into an infinite volume is lost to the given system. Tables 11-1 and 11-2 contain the formulas for calculating the corresponding parameters of the free jet for both its starting section and main section (data of Abramovich.[1] The starting section is defined as that part of the jet in which, starting from the exit orifice of the channel, the velocity at the axis remains constant and equal to the initial velocity. The main section is defined as the remaining part of the jet in which the velocity at the axis decreases gradually and attenuates. The region separating the two parts is called the transition region (Figure 11-3).

33. The dimensionless velocity profile of the axisymmetric and two-dimensional free jets can be described by the following equations of Schlichting:[1]

for the starting length

$$\frac{w_0 - w}{w_0} = \left[1 - \left(\frac{y - y_2}{R_s}\right)^{1.5}\right]^2 = (1 - \eta_{\text{in.c}}^{1.5})^2,$$

$$\eta_{\text{in.c}} = \frac{y - y_2}{R_s},$$

for the main section

$$w/w_m = [1 - (y/R_s)^{1.5}]^2 = (1 - \eta_c^{1.5})^2,$$

$$\eta_c = y/R_s$$

For the jet starting length $R_s = b_{\text{tot.}l.}$ is the total thickness of the boundary layer (Figure 11-3); y is the distance from the given point to the boundary layer contact with the constant velocity core; y_1 is the boundary of the constant velocity core; y_2 is the common (outer) boundary of the jet. For the main section R_s is the jet cross-section radius.

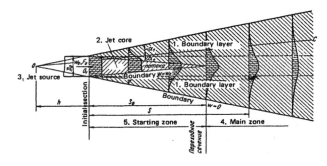

Figure 11-3 Flow pattern of a free jet.

Table 11-1 Parameters of an axisymmetric free submerged jet.

Parameters	Jet sections	
	Initial	Main ($\bar{s} > 12$)
1	2	3
	Axisymmetric jet	
Tangent of the angle of the one-sided expansion of the outer edge	tg $\alpha_1 = 0.144$ $\alpha_2 \approx 8°20'$	tg $\alpha_1 = 0.22$ $\alpha_1 = 12°30'$
Tangent of the angle of one-sided contraction of the constant velocity core	tg $\alpha_2 = 0.126$ $\alpha_2 = 7°10'$	— —
Relative diameter of the outer edge	$\bar{D} \equiv D_s/D_0 = 1 + 0.144\bar{s}$; $\bar{s} = s/R_0; R_0 = D_0/2$	$\bar{D}_s = 0.22\bar{s}$
Relative area of the jet cross section	$\bar{F}_s \equiv F_s/F_0 = (1 + 0.144\bar{s})^2$	$\bar{F} = (0.22\bar{s})^2$
Relative thickness of the boundary layer	$\bar{b}_{b.l.} \equiv b_{b.l.}/R_0 = 0.27\bar{s}$	$R_s = \bar{b}_{b.l.} = 0.22\bar{s}$
Relative width of the initial mass core	$\bar{R}_{in.m.} \equiv R_{in.m.}/R_0 = 1 + 0.0186\bar{s} + 0.00012\bar{s}^2$	$\bar{R}_{in.m.} = 0.22\bar{s}\eta_c$, where $\eta_c = f(\bar{s})$
Relative length of the initial section	$\bar{s}_{in} \equiv s_{in}/R_0 \approx 8$	See Figure 11-4
Relative thickness of the jet at the end of the initial section	$R_{in} \equiv R_{in}/R_0 = 2.16$	—
Relative velocity at the jet axis	$\bar{w}_m \equiv w_m/w_0 = 1$	$\bar{w}_m = 12.4/\bar{s}$
Relative arithmetic — mean (with respect to area) velocity	$\bar{w}_{av} \equiv \bar{w}_{av}/w_m = Q/w_0 F_s =$ $\dfrac{1 + 0.073\bar{s} + 0.002\bar{s}^2 - 0.0001\bar{s}^3 + ... + 0.000002\bar{s}^4}{1 + 0.316\bar{s} + 0.022\bar{s}^2 - 0.00047\bar{s}^3 + ... + 0.000002\bar{s}^4}$	$\bar{w}_{av} = 0.52 =$ const.
Relative mean — square (based on flow rate) velocity	$w_{av} \equiv w'_{av}/w_m = \dfrac{\int_m w\,dm}{w_m ms} = (1 + 0.073\bar{s} + 0.002\bar{s}^2 - 0.0001\bar{s}^3$ $+ 0.0000025\bar{s}^4)$	
Relative fluid discharge through the given cross section	$\bar{q} \equiv Q/Q_0 = 1 + 0.073\bar{s} + 0.002\bar{s}^2 + 0.0001\bar{s}^3$ $+ 0.0000025\bar{s}^4$	$\bar{q} = 0.155\bar{s}$

Relative residue of kinetic energy in the given cross section	$\bar{e} \equiv 2E/m_0 w_0^2 = 1 - 0.036\bar{s} - 0.0008\bar{s}^2 + 0.00006\bar{s}^3 + 0.0000002\bar{s}^4$	$\bar{q} = 0.155\bar{s}$
Relative residue of the energy of constant mass jet in the given cross section	$\bar{e}_c \equiv 2E_c/m_0 w_0^2 = (1 - 0.125\bar{s})^2 + 0.54\bar{s}(1 + 0.144\bar{s})K_1 - 0.27\bar{s}K_2$ where for $K_1 = f_1(\eta_{in.c})$ and $K_2 = f_2(\eta_{in.c})$ see Table 11-3 or Equation (11-5); $\eta_{in.c} = 0.515 - 0.006\bar{s}$	$\bar{e}_c = 92H_1/\bar{s}$, where for $H_1 = f_1(\eta_c)$ see Table 11-3 or Equation (11-6a) $\eta_c = f(s)$ is given in Figure 11-4
Coefficient of resistance (of energy loss)	$\zeta \equiv \dfrac{\Delta p}{\rho w_0^2/2} = 1 - \bar{e}$	$\zeta = 1 - \bar{e}$
Coefficient of momentum	$M_s \equiv \dfrac{1}{F_s}\int_{F_s}\left(\dfrac{w}{w_{av}}\right)^2 dF = \dfrac{1}{\bar{q}w_{av}}$	$M_s = \dfrac{1}{\bar{q}\overline{w_m}\,\overline{w}_{av}} = 2.06$
Coefficient of kinetic energy	$N_s \equiv \dfrac{1}{F_s}\int_{F_s}\left(\dfrac{w}{w_{av}}\right)^3 dF = \dfrac{\bar{e}}{\bar{q}w_{av}^2}$	$N_s = \dfrac{\bar{e}}{\bar{q}\overline{w_m^2}\,\overline{w}_{av}^2} = 4.88$

Plane jet

Tangent of the angle of one-sided expansion of the outer edge	$tg\ \alpha_1 = 0.158$ $\alpha_1 \approx 9°$	$tg\ \alpha_1 = 0.22$ $\alpha_1 \approx 12°30'$
Tangent of the angle of one-sided contraction of the constant-velocity core	$tg\ \alpha_2 = 0.112$ $\alpha_2 = 6°30'$	—
Relative half-width	$\bar{b}_s = b_s/b_0 = 1 + 0.158\bar{s}$	$\bar{b}_s = 0.22\bar{s}$
Relative cross-sectional area	$\bar{F}_s \equiv F_s/F_0 = 1 + 0.158\bar{s}$	$\bar{F}_s = 0.22\bar{s}$
Relative boundary-layer thickness	$\bar{b}_{b.l} = b_{b.l}/b_0 = 0.275\bar{s}$	$\bar{b}_{b.l.} = 0.22\bar{s}$
Relative width of the initial mass core	$\bar{b}_{in.m} \equiv b_{in.m}/b_0 = 1 + 0.019\bar{s}$	$\bar{b}_{in.m} = 0.22\eta_c\bar{s}$ where $\eta_c = f(\bar{s})$, see Figure 11-4
Relative length of the initial section	$\bar{s}_{in} = s/b_0 = 9$	—
Relative thickness of the jet at the end of the initial section	$\bar{b}_{in} = b_{in}/b_0 = 2.43$	—
Relative velocity at the axis	$\bar{w}_m = w_m/w_0 = 1$	$\bar{w}_m \cong 3.8/\bar{s}$
Relative arithmetic — mean (with respect to the area) velocity	$\bar{w}_{av} \equiv Q/w_m F_0 = \dfrac{1 + 0.0036\bar{s}}{1 + 0.158\bar{s}}$	$\bar{w}_{av} = 0.45 = $ const.

Table 11-1 Parameters of an axisymmetric free submerged jet. (continued)

Parameters	Jet sections	
	Initial	Main ($\bar{s} > 12$)
1	2	3
Relative mean-square (with respect to flow rate) velocity	$\bar{w}'_{av} \equiv \dfrac{\int_{F_m} w \, dm}{w_m m_s} = \dfrac{1}{1 + 0.036\bar{s}}$	$\bar{w}'_{av} = 0.7 = \text{const.}$
Relative discharge of fluid through the given cross section	$\bar{q} = Q/Q_0 = 1 + 0.036\bar{s}$	$\bar{q} = 0.375\sqrt{\bar{s}}$
Relative residue of the kinetic energy of the jet at the given cross section	$\bar{e} \equiv 2E/m_0 w_0^2 = 1 - 0.019\bar{s}$	$\bar{e} \approx 3.1/\sqrt{\bar{s}}$
Relative residue of the energy of the constant-mass jet at the given cross-section	$\bar{e}_c \equiv \dfrac{2E_c}{m_0 w_0^2} = 1 - 0.27s(0.416 - K_1)$ where $K_1 = f(\eta_c)$, see Table 11-3 or Equation (11-6a)	$\bar{e}_c = 12H_2/\sqrt{\bar{s}}$ where $H_2 = f_2(\eta_c)$, see Table 11-3 or Equation (11-7b); for η_c see Figure 11-4
Coefficient of resistance (of energy loss)	$\zeta = 1 - \bar{e}$	$\zeta = 1 - \bar{e}$

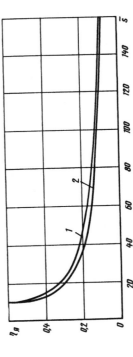

Figure 11-4 The junction $\eta_c = f(\bar{s})$:[1] (1), axisymmetrical jet; (2), plane jet.

Note: According to the new theory of G. I. Abramovich,[1] a kind of discontinuity in the jet boundaries occurs in the transition section ($\alpha_1 > \alpha_{1in}$). Actually, the slope of the jet boundaries in the transition section varies from α_{1in} to α_1.

Table 11-2 Values of $\eta_c = f(\bar{s})$ (Figure 11-4)

					$\bar{s}$					
12.4	15	17.5	20	30	40	60	80	100	120	160
					1. Axisymmetric jet					
0.6	0.4	0.34	0.32	0.25	0.22	0.18	0.16	0.14	0.12	0.10
					2. Plane jet					
0.6	0.35	0.32	0.30	0.23	0.20	0.16	0.14	0.12	0.10	0.09

Table 11-3 Values of $K = f(\eta_{in.c})$ and $H = f(\eta_c)$ (Equations (11-6) and (11-7))

Parameters	$\eta_{in.c}$, η_c								
	0.10	0.15	0.20	0.25	0.30	0.35	0.40	0.5	0.6
K_1	0.347	0.347	0.346	0.346	0.346	0.345	0.340	0.338	0.300
K_4	0.275	0.275	0.275	0.275	0.275	0.275	0.270	0.265	0.250
H_1	0.012	0.020	0.024	0.036	0.050	0.058	0.070	0.078	0.085
H_2	0.078	0.130	0.158	0.187	0.210	0.218	0.23	0.245	0.250

$$K_1 = \int_{\eta_{in.c}}^{1} \left(\frac{w}{w_0}\right)^3 d\eta = 0.347 - (1.456\eta_{in.c}^{5.5} - 1.715\eta_{in.c}^{7} + 0.706\eta_{in.c}^{8.5} - 0.1\eta_{in.c}^{10}); \qquad \text{(a)}$$

$$K_2 = \int_{\eta_{in.c}}^{1} \left(\frac{w}{w_0}\right)^3 \eta \, d\eta = 0.274 - (1.232\eta_{in.c}^{6.5} - 1.5\eta_{in.c}^{8} + 0.632\eta_{in.c}^{9.5} - 0.09\eta_{in.c}^{11}); \qquad \text{(b)} \qquad (11\text{-}6)$$

$$H_1 = \int_{0}^{\eta_c} (1 - \eta^{1.5})^6 \, \eta \, d\eta = \eta_c - 2.4\eta_c^{2.5} + 3.75\eta_c^{4} - 3.64\eta_c^{5.5}$$

$$+ 2.14\eta_c^{7} - 0.706\eta_c^{8.5} + 0.1\eta_c^{10}; \qquad \text{(a)} \qquad (11\text{-}7)$$

$$H_2 = 2\int_{0}^{\eta_c} (1 - \eta^{1.5})^6 \, \eta \, d\eta = \eta_c^{2} - 3.428\eta_c^{3.5} - 6.0\eta_c^{5} - 6.154\eta_c^{6.5}$$

$$+ 3.75\eta_c^{8} - 1.263\eta_c^{2.5} + 0.182\eta_c^{11}; \qquad \text{(b)}$$

$$\eta_{in.c} = 0.515 - 0.006\bar{s} \qquad (11\text{-}8)$$

For η_c, see Table 11-2.

11-2 DIAGRAMS OF THE RESISTANCE COEFFICIENTS

Free discharge from a straight tube at different velocity distributions[15,17]	Diagram 11-1

Velocity distribution and scheme	Resistance coefficient $\zeta \equiv \dfrac{\Delta p}{\rho w_0^2/2}$

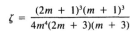

$\zeta = 1.0$

Uniform

Tube of circular or square cross section:

$$\zeta = \frac{(2m + 1)^3(m + 1)^3}{4m^4(2m + 3)(m + 3)}$$

see curve 1 of graph a

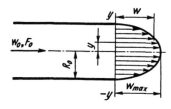

Exponential

$$\frac{w}{w_{max}} = \left(1 - \frac{y}{R_0}\right)^{1/m}$$

$$m \geq 1.0$$

Plane tube: $\zeta = \dfrac{(m + 1)^3}{m^2(m + 3)}$, see curve 2 of graph a

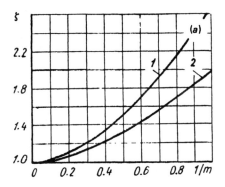

Values of ζ

Tube	m						
	1.00	1.35	2.00	3.00	4.00	7.00	∞
1. Circular	2.70	2.00	1.50	1.25	1.15	1.06	1.00
2. Plane	2.00	1.63	1.35	1.19	1.12	1.04	1.00

Free discharge from a straight tube at different velocity distributions[15,17]			Diagram 11-1	

$$\zeta = 1 + \left(\frac{\Delta w}{w_0}\right)^2; \quad \text{see graph b}$$

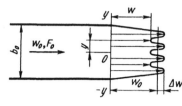

$\Delta w/w_0$	0.1	0.2	0.3	0.4	0.5
ζ	1.02	1.06	1.13	1.24	1.38
$\Delta w/w_0$	0.6	0.7	0.8	0.9	1.0
ζ	1.54	1.74	1.96	2.20	2.50

Sinusoidal distribution
in a plane tube:

$$\frac{w}{w_0} = 1 + \frac{\Delta w}{w_0}\sin 2k_1\pi\frac{y}{b_0}$$

k_1 is an integer.

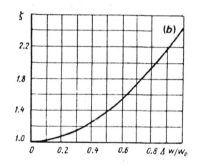

Asymmetrical distribution
in a plane tube:

$$\frac{w}{w_0} = 0.585 + 164\sin\left(0.2 + 3.9\frac{y}{b_0}\right)$$

$$\zeta = 3.67$$

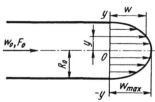

Tube of circular or square cross section: $\zeta = 2.0$
Plane tube: $\zeta = 1.55$

Parabolic:

$$\frac{w}{w_0} = 1 - \left(\frac{y}{R_0}\right)^2$$

Discharge from a tube made flush with the wall in the presence of a passing stream ($w_\infty > 0$);[27] Re $= w_0 D_h/\nu \geqslant 10^4$	Diagram 11-2

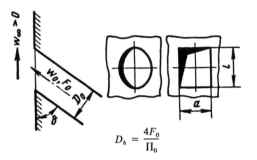

$$\zeta \equiv \frac{\Delta p}{\rho w_0^2/2} = f\left(\frac{w_\infty}{w_0}\right)$$

$$D_h = \frac{4F_0}{\Pi_0}$$

Values of ζ for orifices of circular and rectangular cross sections (rounded up to 10%)

b/a	δ, degrees	(no. of curve)	\multicolumn{5}{c}{w_∞/w_0}
			0	0.5	1.0	1.5	2.0
0.5; 1; 2	30–45	(1)	1.00	1.00	1.10	1.33	1.55
(graph a)	60	(2)	1.00	0.90	1.05	1.35	1.60
0.1–0.2	90	(3)	1.00	0.80	0.95	1.35	1.65
(graph b)	120–135	(4)	1.00	0.80	0.95	1.25	1.65
5–10	150	(5)	1.00	0.82	0.83	1.00	1.25
(graph c)	30–90	(6)	1.00	0.95	1.15	1.45	1.80
	120	(7)	1.00	0.92	1.07	1.40	1.90
	150	(8)	1.00	0.75	0.95	1.35	1.75
	45	(9)	1.00	0.92	0.93	1.10	1.30
	60	(10)	1.00	0.87	0.87	1.03	1.25
	90	(11)	1.00	0.82	0.80	0.97	1.20
	120	(12)	1.00	0.80	0.76	0.90	0.98

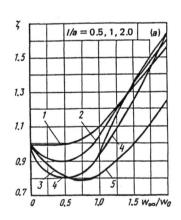

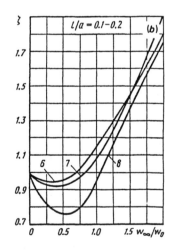

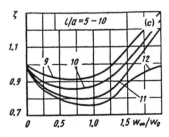

Free discharge from a circular straight wall diffuser[19-22]	Diagram 11-3

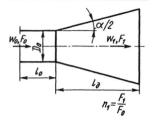

$$n_1 = \frac{F_1}{F_0}; \quad Re = \frac{w_0 D_0}{\nu}$$

Uniform velocity field at the entrance into the diffuser ($w_{max}/w_0 \approx 1.0$):

$$\zeta \equiv \frac{\Delta p}{\rho w_0^2/2} = \zeta_{tot} = f(\alpha, n_1, Re), \quad \text{see graph a}$$

Nonuniform velocity field at the entrance into the diffuser ($w_{max}/w_0 \geq 1.0$, see Diagram 5-1):

$$\zeta = k_{tot}\zeta_{tot}$$

a)   For diffusers downstream of a straight section having $l_0/D_0 \geq 10$, $k_{tot} = f(\alpha, n_1, Re)$, see graph b.

b)   For diffusers with $\alpha = 6\text{--}14°$ placed downstream of a shaped (curved) portion, k_{tot} is determined as $k_d = f(w/w_0)$ from Diagram 5-1.

c)   For diffusers with $\alpha > 20°$ downstream of the shaped portion, the order of magnitude of k_{tot} is assumed to be tentatively equal to N_0 from Tables 12-1 to 12-7.

Values of ζ_{tot} at $w_{max}/w_0 \approx 1.0$; $l_0/D_0 \approx 0$

Re × 10⁻⁵	α, degrees												
	3	4	6	8	10	12	14	16	20	30	45	60	≥90
						$n_1 = 2$							
1	0.409	0.369	0.342	0.357	0.326	0.342	0.365	0.400	0.506	0.902	1.049	1.037	1.02
2	0.355	0.342	0.324	0.320	0.310	0.320	0.333	0.355	0.440	0.740	0.969	0.994	1.0
3	0.360	0.342	0.320	0.321	0.302	0.313	0.323	0.329	0.360	0.527	0.898	0.995	1.0
4	0.346	0.325	0.310	0.315	0.302	0.303	0.315	0.344	0.418	0.578	0.782	0.982	1.0
≥6	0.360	0.320	0.295	0.291	0.293	0.306	0.329	0.360	0.458	0.635	0.858	0.969	1.0
						$n_1 = 4$							
1	0.213	0.209	0.217	0.235	0.213	0.240	0.280	0.320	0.400	0.697	0.986	1.004	1.0
2	0.190	0.186	0.186	0.200	0.182	0.204	0.240	0.280	0.355	0.542	0.938	0.995	1.0
3	0.184	0.173	0.169	0.182	0.173	0.190	0.226	0.247	0.298	0.440	0.760	0.995	1.0
4	0.178	0.167	0.160	0.167	0.167	0.199	0.233	0.275	0.360	0.555	0.782	0.982	1.0
≥6	0.184	0.160	0.157	0.155	0.157	0.180	0.239	0.295	0.422	0.637	0.858	0.969	1.0
						$n_1 = 6$							
1	0.171	0.169	0.180	0.200	0.186	0.217	0.257	0.293	0.373	0.666	0.986	1.006	1.0
2	0.155	0.153	0.155	0.164	0.160	0.186	0.222	0.253	0.320	0.493	0.938	0.980	1.0
3	0.150	0.146	0.146	0.160	0.153	0.173	0.200	0.233	0.280	0.400	0.760	0.989	1.0
4	0.133	0.129	0.129	0.146	0.138	0.160	0.209	0.249	0.346	0.520	0.782	0.982	1.0
≥6	0.150	0.127	0.122	0.127	0.129	0.159	0.218	0.273	0.384	0.618	0.858	0.969	1.0
						$n_1 = 10$							
1	0.155	0.159	0.169	0.175	0.164	0.182	0.237	0.275	0.359	0.680	0.986	1.006	1.0
2	0.133	0.131	0.138	0.146	0.127	0.150	0.190	0.226	0.295	0.498	0.938	0.715	1.0
3	0.129	0.126	0.127	0.133	0.115	0.138	0.180	0.209	0.266	0.400	0.760	0.989	1.0
4	0.117	0.115	0.117	0.120	0.114	0.133	0.186	0.239	0.320	0.520	0.782	0.982	1.0
≥6	0.133	0.109	0.102	0.104	0.110	0.142	0.200	0.266	0.384	0.613	0.858	0.969	1.0
						$n_1 = 16$							
1	0.144	0.142	0.164	0.164	0.155	0.159	0.200	0.253	0.355	0.657	0.986	1.006	1.0
2	0.122	0.119	0.123	0.133	0.115	0.135	0.173	0.200	0.270	0.493	0.938	0.997	1.0
3	0.117	0.110	0.115	0.120	0.104	0.133	0.160	0.190	0.253	0.400	0.760	0.989	1.0
4	0.106	0.102	0.099	0.106	0.102	0.120	0.175	0.219	0.298	0.499	0.782	0.982	1.0
≥6	0.113	0.095	0.089	0.090	0.099	0.122	0.175	0.235	0.360	0.600	0.858	0.969	1.0

Free discharge from a circular straight wall diffuser[19-22]	Diagram 11-3

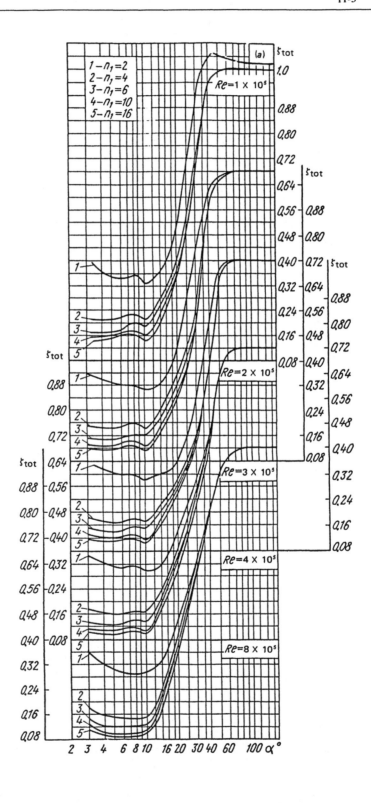

Free discharge from a circular straight wall diffuser[19-22]	Diagram 11-3

Values of k_{tot} at $w_{max}/w_0 > 1.0$ ($l_0/D_0 \geqslant 10$)

Re × 10^{-3}	α, degrees											
	4	6	8	10	12	14	16	20	30	45	60	90
					$n_1 = 2$							
0.5	1.30	1.40	1.50	1.70	1.60	1.35	1.30	1.22	1.10	1.05	1.00	1.0
1.0	1.33	1.50	1.65	1.82	1.85	1.75	1.60	1.40	1.12	1.06	1.05	1.0
2.0	1.33	1.55	1.70	1.87	2.00	2.00	1.87	1.60	1.12	1.10	1.10	1.0
≥3.0	1.33	1.57	1.75	1.88	2.00	2.03	2.03	1.95	1.55	1.30	1.10	1.0
					$n_1 = 4\text{–}6$							
0.5	1.52	1.55	1.70	2.00	1.96	1.90	1.80	1.65	1.20	1.05	1.00	1.0
1.0	1.52	1.68	2.00	2.30	2.23	2.12	2.00	1.85	1.23	1.05	1.00	1.0
2.0	1.52	1.85	2.28	2.60	2.52	2.42	2.30	2.15	1.60	1.10	1.05	1.0
≥3.0	1.52	1.90	2.35	2.65	2.63	2.60	2.50	2.35	1.90	1.40	1.10	1.0
					$n_1 \geqslant 10$							
0.5	1.70	1.73	1.80	2.15	2.10	1.95	1.88	1.68	1.20	1.05	1.00	1.0
1.0	1.70	1.73	2.15	2.60	2.40	2.17	2.02	1.85	1.20	1.05	1.03	1.0
≥2.0	1.80	1.93	2.40	3.05	2.75	2.53	2.30	2.10	1.60	1.12	1.08	1.0

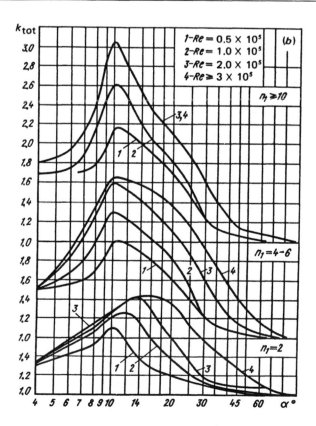

Free discharge from conical diffusers at high subsonic velocities (pressure reduction factors)[7]	Diagram 11-4

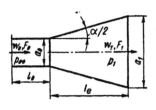

$$\bar{p} = \frac{p_1}{p_0^*} = \frac{p_0}{p_0^*} = f\left(\lambda_c, \alpha, n_1, \frac{l_0}{D_0}\right), \quad \text{see the graph;}$$

$$\zeta_{\text{tot}} \equiv \frac{\Delta p}{\rho_0^* w_0^2/2} = \frac{k+1}{k} \frac{1}{\lambda_c^2} \ln \frac{1}{\bar{p}};$$

$$\lambda_c = \frac{w_0}{a_{\text{cr}}} \quad a_{\text{cr}} = \sqrt{\frac{2k}{k+1} RT_0^*}$$

$n_1 = F_1/F_0$

Values of $\bar{p}$ at $\alpha = 4°$ (graph a)

	λ_c										
	0.1	0.2	0.3	0.4	0.5	0.6	0.7	0.8	0.9	0.94	0.945
						Re $\times 10^{-5}$					
n_1	1.7	3.2	4.6	6.0	7.3	8.6	9.8	10.8	11.7	12.1	12.2
					$\frac{l_0}{D_0} = 0$						
2	0.999	0.994	0.982	0.971	0.958	0.943	0.926	–	–	–	–
4	0.999	0.996	0.992	0.986	0.979	0.971	0.963	0.955	0.945	0.940	0.920
6	0.999	0.997	0.993	0.988	0.983	0.977	0.970	0.963	0.956	0.945	0.930
10–16	0.999	0.997	0.993	0.990	0.985	0.980	0.975	0.969	0.964	0.955	0.940
					$\frac{l_0}{D_0} = 2$						
2	0.999	0.991	0.980	0.966	0.952	0.936	0.920	–	–	–	–
4	0.999	0.996	0.990	0.984	0.977	0.970	0.961	0.953	–	–	–
6	0.999	0.998	0.993	0.987	0.980	0.974	0.970	0.963	–	–	–
10–16	0.999	0.999	0.995	0.990	0.984	0.978	0.975	0.969	–	–	–
					$\frac{l_0}{D_0} = 5$						
2	0.998	0.990	0.980	0.966	0.952	0.937	0.922	–	–	–	–
4	0.999	0.997	0.991	0.983	0.975	0.966	0.956	0.946	–	–	–
6	0.999	0.998	0.994	0.987	0.980	0.974	0.965	0.956	–	–	–
10–16	0.999	0.999	0.995	0.990	0.984	0.977	0.969	0.960	–	–	–

Free discharge from conical diffusers at high subsonic velocities (pressure reduction factors)[7]									Diagram 11-4		

	λ_c										
	0.1	0.2	0.3	0.4	0.5	0.6	0.7	0.8	0.9	0.94	0.945
	$Re \times 10^{-5}$										
n_1	1.7	3.2	4.6	6.0	7.3	8.6	9.8	10.8	11.7	12.1	12.2

$$\frac{l_0}{D_0} \geq 10$$

	0.1	0.2	0.3	0.4	0.5	0.6	0.7	0.8	0.9	0.94	0.945
2	0.998	0.990	0.978	0.962	0.945	0.927	–	–	–	–	–
4	0.999	0.994	0.987	0.978	0.968	0.957	0.944	0.930	–	–	–
6	0.999	0.995	0.989	0.983	0.975	0.965	0.954	0.942	–	–	–
10–16	0.999	0.996	0.990	0.984	0.977	0.968	0.957	0.946	–	–	–

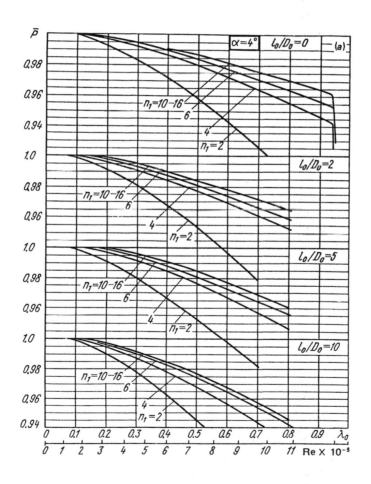

Free discharge from conical diffusers at high subsonic velocities (pressure reduction factors)[7]	Diagram 11-4

Values of $\bar{p}$ at $\alpha = 6°$ (graph b)

						λ_c					
	0.1	0.2	0.3	0.4	0.5	0.6	0.7	0.8	0.9	0.94	0.95
						Re $\times$ 10^{-5}					
n_1	1.7	3.2	4.6	6.0	7.3	8.6	9.8	10.8	11.7	12.1	12.2

$$\frac{l_0}{D_0} = 0$$

2	0.999	0.994	0.985	0.974	0.958	0.947	0.932	–	–	–	–
4	0.999	0.997	0.992	0.985	0.978	0.970	0.963	0.954	0.946	0.940	0.930
6	0.999	0.999	0.995	0.989	0.983	0.977	0.970	0.963	0.955	0.950	0.930
10	0.999	0.999	0.996	0.990	0.985	0.979	0.974	0.968	0.961	0.950	0.930
16	0.999	0.999	0.997	0.992	0.987	0.982	0.976	0.970	0.963	0.950	0.930

$$\frac{l_0}{D_0} = 2$$

2	0.988	0.990	0.980	0.968	0.953	0.937	0.920	–	–	–	–
4	0.999	0.995	0.989	0.982	0.973	0.963	0.953	0.940	–	–	–
6	0.999	0.997	0.991	0.985	0.978	0.970	0.960	0.950	0.938	–	–
10–16	0.999	0.997	0.993	0.988	0.983	0.976	0.968	0.962	0.953	0.941	–

$$\frac{l_0}{D_0} = 5$$

2	0.998	0.990	0.980	0.967	0.951	0.931	–	–	–	–	–
4	0.999	0.995	0.988	0.980	0.970	0.959	0.947	0.933	–	–	–
6	0.999	0.996	0.990	0.983	0.977	0.968	0.958	0.947	–	–	–
10–16	0.999	0.996	0.992	0.986	0.979	0.971	0.962	0.952	–	–	–

| Free discharge from conical diffusers at high subsonic velocities (pressure reduction factors)[7] | | | | | | | | | | Diagram 11-4 |

	λ_c										
	0.1	0.2	0.3	0.4	0.5	0.6	0.7	0.8	0.9	0.94	0.95
	$Re \times 10^{-5}$										
n_1	1.7	3.2	4.6	6.0	7.3	8.6	9.8	10.8	11.7	12.1	12.2

$$\frac{l_0}{D_0} \geqslant 10$$

n_1											
2	0.997	0.988	0.977	0.961	0.941	0.918	–	–	–	–	–
4	0.998	0.993	0.985	0.976	0.965	0.952	0.938	0.924	–	–	–
6	0.999	0.995	0.988	0.980	0.970	0.958	0.945	0.932	–	–	–
10–16	0.999	0.996	0.990	0.982	0.973	0.962	0.950	0.937	–	–	–

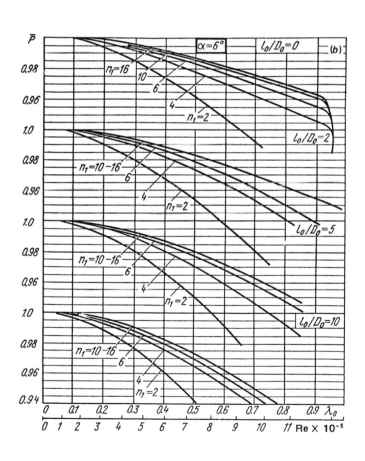

| Free discharge from conical diffusers at high subsonic velocities (pressure reduction factors)[7] | | | | | | | | | | Diagram 11-4 |

Values of $\bar{p}$ at $\alpha = 8°$ (graph c)

	λ_c										
	0.1	0.2	0.3	0.4	0.5	0.6	0.7	0.8	0.9	0.94	0.95
	Re $\times 10^{-5}$										
n_1	1.7	3.2	4.6	6.0	7.3	8.6	9.8	10.8	11.7	12.1	12.2

$$\frac{l_0}{D_0} = 0$$

2	0.999	0.995	0.986	0.972	0.957	0.942	0.927	0.910	–	–	–
4	0.999	0.997	0.993	0.986	0.978	0.970	0.960	0.950	0.937	0.931	0.920
6	0.999	0.998	0.994	0.988	0.982	0.974	0.967	0.959	0.951	0.947	0.930
10–16	0.999	0.998	0.995	0.986	0.985	0.979	0.972	0.965	0.959	0.953	0.940

$$\frac{l_0}{D_0} = 2$$

2	0.998	0.990	0.979	0.966	0.950	0.932	–	–	–	–	–
4	0.999	0.993	0.987	0.979	0.970	0.960	0.948	0.932	–	–	–
6	0.999	0.994	0.990	0.983	0.975	0.965	0.954	0.943	0.930	–	–
10–16	0.999	0.995	0.996	0.985	0.979	0.971	0.962	0.952	0.938	–	–

$$\frac{l_0}{D_0} = 5$$

2	0.998	0.990	0.977	0.961	0.943	0.925	–	–	–	–	–
4	0.999	0.993	0.986	0.975	0.963	0.951	0.938	0.924	–	–	–
6	0.999	0.995	0.988	0.980	0.971	0.960	0.948	0.934	–	–	–
10–16	0.999	0.995	0.989	0.983	0.976	0.966	0.954	0.941	–	–	—

Free discharge from conical diffusers at high subsonic velocities (pressure reduction factors)[7]									Diagram 11-4	
					λ_c					
	0.1	0.2	0.3	0.4	0.5	0.6	0.7	0.8	0.9	0.94	0.95
						$Re \times 10^{-5}$				
n_1	1.7	3.2	4.6	6.0	7.3	8.6	9.8	10.8	11.7	12.1	12.2

$$\frac{l_0}{D_0} \geq 10$$

	0.1	0.2	0.3	0.4	0.5	0.6	0.7	0.8	0.9	0.94	0.95
2	0.998	0.990	0.975	0.959	0.940	0.920	–	–	–	–	–
4	0.998	0.932	0.983	0.970	0.957	0.942	0.925	–	–	–	–
6	0.999	0.994	0.987	0.975	0.963	0.950	0.933	–	–	–	–
10–16	0.999	0.994	0.998	0.978	0.967	0.956	0.942	–	–	–	–

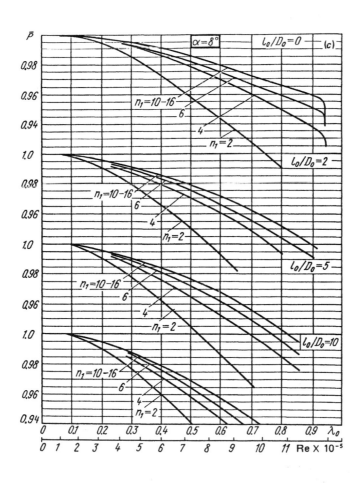

| Free discharge from conical diffusers at high subsonic velocities (pressure reduction factors)[7] | | | | | | | | Diagram 11-4 | |

Values of $\bar{p}$ at $\alpha = 10°$ (graph d)

	λ_c									
	0.1	0.2	0.3	0.4	0.5	0.6	0.7	0.8	0.9	0.95
	Re $\times 10^{-5}$									
n_1	1.7	3.2	4.6	6.0	7.3	8.6	9.8	10.8	11.7	12.2

$$\frac{l_0}{D_0} = 0$$

2	0.998	0.994	0.984	0.972	0.959	0.945	0.930	0.913	–	–
4	0.999	0.996	0.991	0.985	0.977	0.968	0.959	0.950	0.940	0.933
6	0.999	0.996	0.993	0.987	0.981	0.973	0.966	0.958	0.951	0.940
10–16	0.999	0.997	0.994	0.989	0.984	0.977	0.970	0.963	0.956	0.951

$$\frac{l_0}{D_0} = 2$$

2	0.997	0.991	0.978	0.963	0.948	0.933	0.914	–	–	–
4	0.998	0.994	0.987	0.976	0.964	0.950	0.933	0.910	–	–
6	0.998	0.994	0.987	0.978	0.968	0.958	0.943	0.923	–	–
10–16	0.998	0.995	0.988	0.981	0.973	0.964	0.952	0.934	–	–

$$\frac{l_0}{D_0} = 5$$

2	0.997	0.989	0.976	0.960	0.940	0.918	–	–	–	–
4	0.998	0.993	0.982	0.968	0.953	0.936	–	–	–	–
6	0.998	0.994	0.985	0.973	0.960	0.948	0.934	–	–	–
10–16	0.999	0.994	0.986	0.976	0.965	0.952	0.939	–	–	–

| Free discharge from conical diffusers at high subsonic velocities (pressure reduction factors)[7] | | | | | | | | Diagram 11-4 | | |

	λ_c										
	0.1	0.2	0.3	0.4	0.5	0.6	0.7	0.8	0.9	0.95
	Re $\times$ 10^{-5}										
n_1	1.7	3.2	4.6	6.0	7.3	8.6	9.8	10.8	11.7	12.2

$$\frac{l_0}{D_0} \geqslant 10$$

2	0.996	0.988	0.973	0.956	0.935	–	–	–	–	–
4	0.998	0.992	0.982	0.968	0.953	0.937	0.918	–	–	–
6	0.998	0.993	0.984	0.971	0.959	0.942	0.922	–	–	–
10	0.998	0.993	0.984	0.974	0.961	0.945	0.928	–	–	–
16	0.999	0.994	0.985	0.976	0.964	0.949	0.934	–	–	–

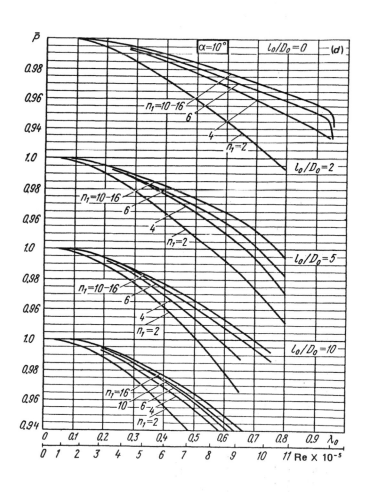

| Free discharge from conical diffusers at high subsonic velocities (pressure reduction factors)[7] | | | | | | | Diagram 11-4 | |

Values of $\bar{p}$ at $\alpha = 14°$ (graph e)

	λ_c								
	0.1	0.2	0.3	0.4	0.5	0.6	0.7	0.8	0.9
	Re $\times$ 10^{-5}								
n_1	1.7	3.2	4.6	6.0	7.3	8.6	9.8	10.8	11.7

$$\frac{l_0}{D_0} = 0$$

2	0.998	0.993	0.983	0.968	0.953	0.932	0.915	0.895	–
4	0.998	0.995	0.988	0.978	0.967	0.953	0.940	0.926	0.910
6	0.999	0.995	0.988	0.980	0.969	0.958	0.943	0.930	0.915
10	0.999	0.996	0.990	0.981	0.971	0.960	0.948	0.936	0.923
16	0.999	0.996	0.991	0.983	0.975	0.965	0.954	0.942	0.930

$$\frac{l_0}{D_0} = 2$$

2	0.998	0.987	0.974	0.954	0.932	0.909	–	–	–
4	0.998	0.990	0.979	0.965	0.947	0.925	–	–	–
6	0.998	0.990	0.980	0.968	0.952	0.930	–	–	–
10	0.999	0.991	0.981	0.970	0.955	0.935	–	–	–
16	0.999	0.993	0.983	0.973	0.960	0.940	–	–	–

$$\frac{l_0}{D_0} = 5$$

2	0.996	0.986	0.970	0.950	0.930	0.906	–	–	–
4	0.997	0.988	0.976	0.960	0.942	0.922	–	–	–
6	0.997	0.989	0.977	0.963	0.948	0.930	–	–	–
10	0.997	0.989	0.978	0.965	0.950	0.933	–	–	–
16	0.998	0.991	0.980	0.968	0.953	0.937	–	–	–

| Free discharge from conical diffusers at high subsonic velocities (pressure reduction factors)[7] | | | | | | | Diagram 11-4 | |

	λ_c								
	0.1	0.2	0.3	0.4	0.5	0.6	0.7	0.8	0.9
	Re $\times$ 10^{-5}								
n_1	1.7	3.2	4.6	6.0	7.3	8.6	9.8	10.8	11.7

$$\frac{l_0}{D_0} \geq 0$$

2	0.996	0.985	0.968	0.948	0.927	–	–	–	–
4	0.997	0.987	0.972	0.955	0.936	0.910	–	–	–
6	0.997	0.987	0.973	0.958	0.940	0.917	–	–	–
10	0.998	0.988	0.975	0.960	0.944	0.927	–	–	–
16	0.998	0.989	0.977	0.962	0.947	0.931	–	–	–

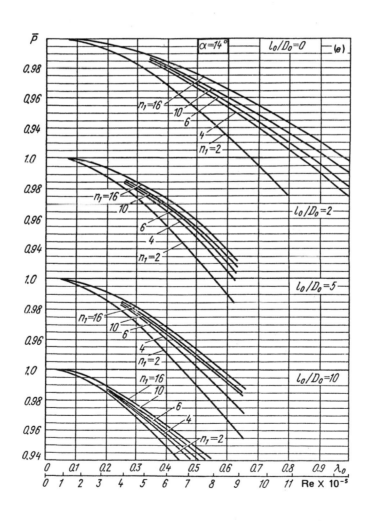

Free discharge from a rectilinear (straight wall) diffuser of rectangular (square) cross section [19-22]	Diagram 11-5

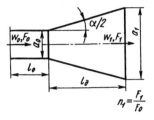

$n_1 = F_1/F_0$

$Re = \dfrac{w_0 D_0}{\nu}$

$D_h = 4F_0/\Pi_0$

1. Uniform velocity field at the entrance into the diffuser ($w_{max}/w_0 \approx 1.0$):

$$\zeta \equiv \frac{\Delta p}{\rho w_0^2/2} = \zeta_{tot} = f(\alpha, n_1, Re), \quad \text{see graph a.}$$

2. Nonuniform velocity field at the entrance into the diffuser ($w_{max}/w_0 \geqslant$ 1.1, see Diagram 5-1):
   a) For diffuser downstream of straight section $l_0/D_0 > 10$

   $$\zeta = \zeta_{tot} = f(\alpha, n_1, Re), \quad \text{see graph b.}$$

   b) For diffusers with $\alpha = 6-14°$, downstream the shaped (curved) part

   $$\zeta = k_{tot}\zeta_{tot}$$

   where for ζ_{tot}, see graph a; k_{tot} is determined as k_d from Diagram 5-1.
   c) For diffusers with $\alpha > 20°$ downstream of the shaped section, $\zeta = k_{tot}\zeta_{tot}$, where k_{tot} is assumed to be equal to N_0 from Tables 12-1 to 12-7.

Values of ζ_{tot} at $w_{max}/w_0 \times 1.1$ ($l_0/D_h \approx 0$)

Re $\times 10^{-5}$	\multicolumn{9}{c}{α, degrees}
	4	6	8	10	14	20	30	45	$\geqslant$60
	\multicolumn{9}{c}{$n_1 = 2$}
0.5	0.40	0.40	0.43	0.47	0.58	0.70	0.86	1.01	1.10
1	0.38	0.39	0.42	0.46	0.58	0.70	0.86	1.01	1.10
2	0.36	0.37	0.39	0.44	0.58	0.70	0.86	1.01	1.10
$\geqslant$4	0.34	0.36	0.38	0.43	0.58	0.70	0.86	1.01	1.10
	\multicolumn{9}{c}{$n_1 = 4$}
0.5	0.25	0.27	0.32	0.30	0.48	0.61	0.76	0.94	1.06
1	0.22	0.24	0.28	0.34	0.48	0.61	0.76	0.94	1.06
2	0.20	0.22	0.25	0.31	0.48	0.61	0.76	0.94	1.06
$\geqslant$4	0.18	0.20	0.23	0.30	0.48	0.61	0.76	0.94	0.06
	\multicolumn{9}{c}{$n_1 = 6$}
0.5	0.23	0.24	0.28	0.34	0.47	0.62	0.74	0.94	1.05
1	0.19	0.21	0.25	0.31	0.47	0.62	0.74	0.94	1.05
2	0.16	0.185	0.22	0.29	0.47	0.62	0.74	0.94	1.05
$\geqslant$4	0.145	0.16	0.20	0.28	0.47	0.62	0.74	0.94	1.05

| Free discharge from a rectilinear (straight wall) diffuser of rectangular (square) cross section [19-22] | | | | | | | | Diagram 11-5 | |

Re $\times$ 10^{-5}	α, degrees								
	4	6	8	10	14	20	30	45	$\geqslant$60
				$n_1 = 10$					
0.5	0.20	0.23	0.26	0.34	0.47	0.60	0.73	0.89	1.04
1	0.17	0.19	0.24	0.30	0.46	0.60	0.73	0.89	1.04
2	0.14	0.17	0.21	0.26	0.45	0.60	0.73	0.89	1.04
$\geqslant$4	0.13	0.15	0.18	0.25	0.44	0.60	0.73	0.89	1.04

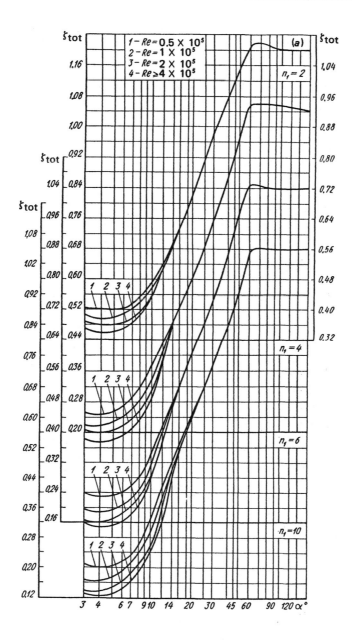

Free discharge from a rectilinear (straight wall) diffuser of rectangular (square) cross section [19-22]	Diagram 11-5

Values of ζ_{tot} at $w_{max}/w_0 \geq 1.1$ ($l_0/D_0 \geq 10$)

	α, degrees									
Re $\times$ 10^{-5}	4	6	8	10	14	20	30	45	60	$\geq$90

					$n_1 = 2$					
0.5	0.550	0.600	0.645	0.680	0.740	0.820	0.920	1.05	1.10	1.08
1	0.510	0.560	0.610	0.655	0.730	0.810	0.900	1.04	1.09	1.08
2	0.470	0.510	0.565	0.610	0.700	0.790	0.890	1.04	1.09	1.08
$\geq$4	0.416	0.460	0.500	0.555	0.640	0.760	0.880	1.02	1.07	1.08
					$n_1 = 4$					
0.5	0.380	0.460	0.530	0.595	0.685	0.780	0.895	1.02	1.07	1.09
1	0.330	0.390	0.485	0.550	0.660	0.775	0.895	1.02	1.07	1.09
2	0.265	0.340	0.420	0.500	0.620	0.740	0.870	1.00	1.06	1.08
$\geq$4	0.220	0.295	0.360	0.440	0.560	0.700	0.840	0.990	1.06	1.08
					$n_1 = 6$					
0.5	0.335	0.420	0.495	0.570	0.660	0.770	0.910	1.02	1.07	1.08
1	0.300	0.385	0.465	0.535	0.630	0.760	0.980	1.02	1.07	1.08
2	0.240	0.335	0.420	0.480	0.600	0.730	0.880	1.00	1.06	1.08
$\geq$4	0.180	0.265	0.340	0.435	0.560	0.725	0.855	0.98	1.06	1.08

					α, degrees					
Re $\times$ 10^{-5}	4	6	8	10	14	20	30	45	60	$\geqslant$90
					$n_1 = 10$					
0.5	0.300	0.370	0.450	0.530	0.640	0.740	0.850	0.970	1.19	1.12
1	0.250	0.320	0.400	0.480	0.620	0.730	0.850	0.970	1.10	1.12
2	0.200	0.260	0.340	0.440	0.560	0.690	0.820	0.950	1.10	1.11
$\geqslant$4	0.160	0.215	0.280	0.400	0.545	0.670	0.800	0.930	1.09	1.11

Free discharge from a rectilinear (straight wall) diffuser of rectangular (square) cross section [19-22]

Diagram 11-5

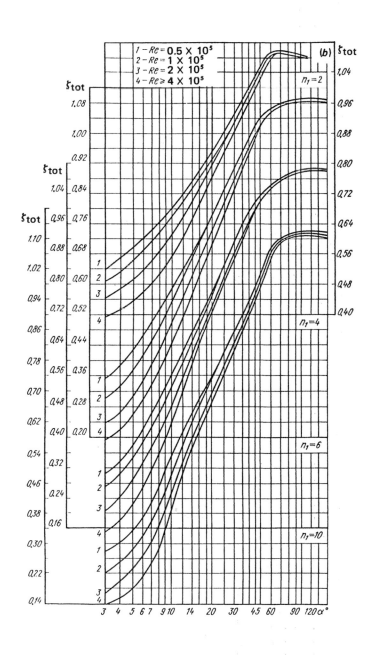

Free discharge from a straight wall plane (rectangular) diffuser; with ratio $a_0/b_0 = 0.5-2.0$[19-22]	Diagram 11-6

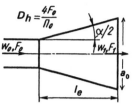

$$D_h = \frac{4F_0}{\Pi_0}$$

$$n_1 = \frac{F_1}{F_0} \qquad \mathrm{Re} = \frac{w_0 D_0}{\nu}$$

$$D_h = 4F_0/\Pi_0$$

1. Uniform velocity field at the entrance into the diffuser ($w_{max}/w_0 \approx 1.0$):
   $\zeta \equiv \Delta p/(\rho w_0^2/2) = \zeta_{tot} = f(\alpha, n_1, \mathrm{Re})$, see graph a.

2. Nonuniform velocity field at the entrance into the diffuser ($w_{max}/w_0 \geqslant 1.1$, see Diagram 5-1):
   a) For diffusers with straight section $l_0/D_0 > 10$, $\zeta = \zeta_{tot} = f(\alpha, n_1, \mathrm{Re})$, see graph b.
   b) For diffusers with $\alpha = 6-20°$, behind a shaped (curved) part: $\zeta = k_{tot}\zeta_{tot}$, where for ζ_{tot}, see graph a; k_{tot} is determined as k_d from Diagram 5-1.
   c) For diffusers with $\alpha > 20°$ downstream of the shaped section, $\zeta = k_{tot}\zeta_{tot}$, where k_{tot} is assumed to be equal to N_0 from Tables 12-1 to 12-7.

Values of ζ_{tot} at $w_{max}/w_0 \approx 1.0$ ($l_0/D_0 \approx 0$)

Re × 10⁻⁵	α, degrees									
	4	6	8	10	14	20	30	45	60	≥90
	$n_1 = 2$									
0.5	0.46	0.43	0.42	0.42	0.42	0.47	0.56	0.76	0.90	1.06
1	0.44	0.41	0.40	0.39	0.39	0.42	0.50	0.75	0.90	1.06
2	0.42	0.39	0.38	0.37	0.36	0.38	0.50	0.75	0.90	1.06
4	0.40	0.37	0.36	0.36	0.36	0.37	0.50	0.75	0.90	1.06
≥6	0.38	0.36	0.34	0.34	0.34	0.38	0.57	0.76	0.90	1.06

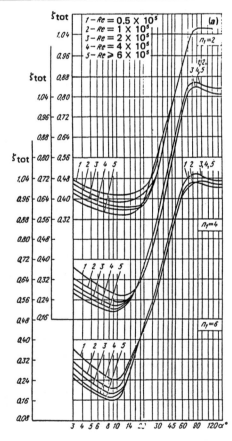

| Free discharge from a straight wall plane (rectangular) diffuser; with ratio $a_0/b_0 = 0.5$–2.0[19-22] | | | | | | | | | | Diagram 11-6 |

Re $\times 10^{-5}$	α, degrees									
	4	6	8	10	14	20	30	45	60	$\geqslant 90$
$n_1 = 4$										
0.5	0.34	0.30	0.28	0.26	0.26	0.34	0.50	0.79	0.96	1.07
1	0.30	0.27	0.24	0.23	0.25	0.34	0.50	0.79	0.96	1.07
2	0.28	0.24	0.22	0.21	0.25	0.37	0.57	0.82	1.00	1.09
4	0.26	0.22	0.21	0.20	0.25	0.37	0.57	0.82	1.00	1.09
$\geqslant 6$	0.24	0.21	0.20	0.20	0.25	0.37	0.57	0.82	1.00	1.09
$n_1 = 6$										
0.5	0.33	0.28	0.25	0.24	0.33	0.44	0.61	0.83	0.96	1.02
1	0.28	0.24	0.21	0.21	0.31	0.45	0.64	0.87	0.98	1.02
2	0.26	0.22	0.19	0.19	0.28	0.47	0.64	0.87	1.00	1.06
4	0.24	0.19	0.18	0.18	0.28	0.47	0.64	0.87	1.00	1.06
$\geqslant 6$	0.22	0.18	0.16	0.17	0.28	0.47	0.64	0.87	1.00	1.06

Values of ζ_{tot} at $w_{max}/w_0 \geqslant 1.1$ ($l_0/D_0 > 10$)

Re $\times 10^{-5}$	α, degrees									
	4	6	8	10	14	20	30	45	60	90
$n_1 = 2$										
0.5	0.51	0.50	0.50	0.51	0.56	0.63	0.80	0.96	1.04	1.09
1	0.48	0.47	0.48	0.50	0.56	0.62	0.80	0.96	1.04	1.09
2	0.42	0.42	0.44	0.46	0.53	0.63	0.74	0.93	1.02	1.08
$\geqslant 4$	0.38	0.38	0.40	0.42	0.50	0.62	0.74	0.93	1.02	1.08
$n_1 = 4$										
0.5	0.35	0.32	0.34	0.38	0.48	0.63	0.76	0.91	1.03	1.07
1	0.31	0.30	0.30	0.36	0.45	0.59	0.72	0.88	1.02	1.07
2	0.26	0.26	0.26	0.31	0.40	0.53	0.67	0.83	0.96	1.06
$\geqslant 4$	0.21	0.21	0.22	0.27	0.39	0.53	0.67	0.83	0.96	1.06
$n_1 = 6$										
0.5	0.34	0.34	0.32	0.34	0.41	0.56	0.70	0.84	0.96	1.08
1	0.32	0.28	0.27	0.30	0.41	0.56	0.70	0.84	0.96	1.08
2	0.26	0.24	0.24	0.26	0.36	0.52	0.67	0.81	0.94	1.06
4	0.21	0.20	0.20	0.24	0.36	0.52	0.67	0.81	0.94	1.06
$\geqslant 6$	0.21	0.19	0.18	0.23	0.34	0.50	0.67	0.81	0.94	1.05

Free discharge from a straight wall plane (rectangular) diffuser; with ratio $a_0/b_0 = 0.5{-}2.0$[19-22]	Diagram 11-6

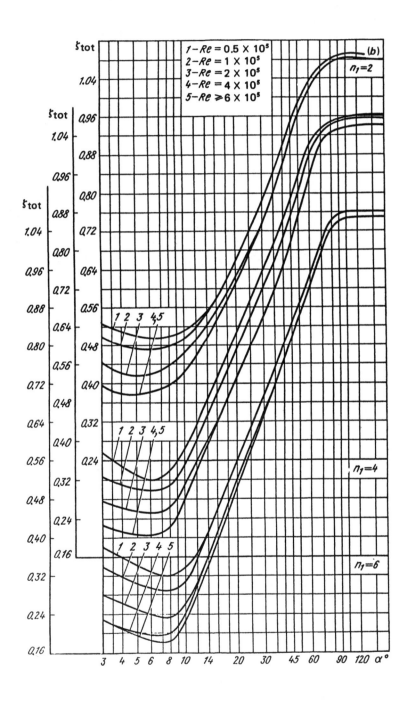

Discharge from a tube (channel) onto a baffle[13,25,34]	Diagram 11-7

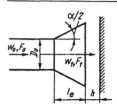

$$D_h = \frac{4F_0}{\Pi_0} \qquad n_1 - \frac{F_1}{F_0}$$

1. Straight wall diffuser at $l_d/D_h = 1.0$

$$\zeta \equiv \frac{\Delta p}{\rho w_0^2/2} = f\left(\frac{h}{D_0}\right), \quad \text{see graph a.}$$

Values of ζ

α, degrees (n_1)	h/D_0									
	0.10	0.15	0.20	0.25	0.30	0.40	0.50	0.60	0.70	1.0
0 (1.0)	–	–	–	–	–	–	1.37	1.20	1.11	1.00
15 (1.59)	–	–	–	1.50	1.06	0.72	0.61	0.59	0.58	0.58
30 (2.37)	–	–	1.23	0.79	0.66	0.64	0.66	0.66	0.67	0.67
45 (3.34)	–	1.50	0.85	0.73	0.75	0.79	0.81	0.82	0.82	0.82
60 (4.65)	–	0.98	0.76	0.80	0.90	0.96	1.00	1.01	1.02	1.02
90 (9.07)	1.50	0.72	0.74	0.83	0.89	0.94	0.96	0.98	1.00	1.00

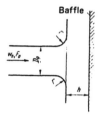

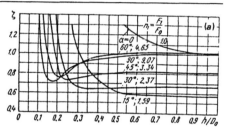

2. Straight section with rounded edges

$$\zeta = f\left(\frac{h}{D_0}\right), \quad \text{see graph b.}$$

Values of ζ

$\dfrac{r}{D_0}$	h/D_0											
	0.05	0.07	0.10	0.15	0.20	0.25	0.30	0.35	0.40	0.50	0.60	1.0
0.2	–	2.30	0.90	0.52	0.51	0.62	0.75	0.82	0.85	0.86	0.85	0.85
0.3	–	1.60	0.75	0.47	0.48	0.55	0.66	0.73	0.78	0.81	0.82	0.82
0.5	2.50	1.30	0.63	0.44	0.41	0.49	0.58	0.65	0.71	0.76	0.87	0.78

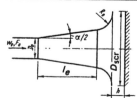

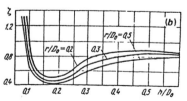

3. Diffuser with optimum characteristic parameters
   $(l_d/D_0 \approx 2.5; \ \alpha = 14°; \ R_0/D_0 \approx 0.7; \ D_e/D_0 \approx 3.0)$.
   $\zeta = f(h/D_0)$, see graph c.

h/D_0	0.10	0.15	0.20	0.25	0.30
ζ	0.78	0.46	0.36	0.32	0.32
h/D_0	0.35	0.40	0.50	0.60	1.0
ζ	0.33	0.33	0.34	0.34	0.36

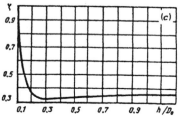

Discharge from a diffuser (with a smooth rounded inlet) onto a baffle;[41] $Re \equiv w_0 D_0/\nu \geqslant 2 \times 10^5$	Diagram 11-8

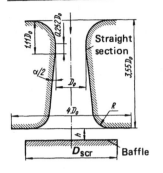

$$\zeta \equiv \frac{\Delta p}{\rho w_0^2/2} = 1 - \eta_d$$

where $\eta_d = f\left(\dfrac{h}{D_0}, \alpha, \dfrac{R}{D_0}\right)$, see the graph.

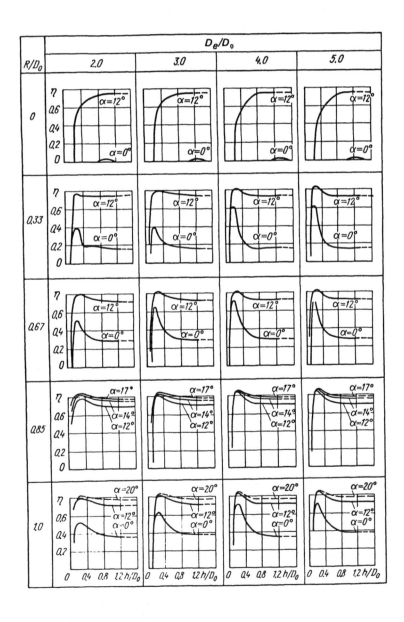

Free discharge from an annular diffusers;[5,12] $d_0 = 0.688$	Diagram 11-9

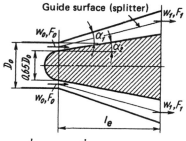

$$\zeta \equiv \frac{\Delta p}{\rho w_0^2/2} = k_d \zeta_{tot}$$

where ζ_{tot} is determined as a function of α_1 and α_2 from graphs a-c (at $\bar{d}_0 = 0.688$) or as a function of n_1 and $\bar{l}_{lim}$ (at $\Delta_0^* = 0.015$ and 0.03) from graphs d and e, where $\bar{l}_{lim}$ is calculated from Equation (11-1); for k_d see Diagram 5-1 or 5-18 (when placed downstream of an operating compressor)

$$\bar{l}_d = \frac{l_d}{D_0} \qquad \bar{d}_0 = \frac{d_0}{D_0}$$

$$n_1 = \frac{F_1}{F_0} = 1 + \frac{4\bar{l}_d}{1 - \bar{d}_0}(\tan^2 \alpha_1 - \tan^2 \alpha_2) + \frac{4\bar{l}_d}{1 - \bar{d}_0^2}(\tan \alpha_1 - \bar{d}_0 \tan \alpha_2)$$

Values of ζ_{tot} at $\bar{l}_d = 0.5$ (without guide surface)

α_2, degrees	α_1, degrees								
	-4	-2	0	2	4	6	8	10	12
8	0.45	0.46	0.48	0.51	0.57	0.65	0.77	–	–
10	0.45	0.45	0.45	0.47	0.49	0.54	0.61	0.72	–
12	0.47	0.46	0.45	0.44	0.44	0.47	0.50	0.58	0.68
14	0.54	0.51	0.50	0.48	0.47	0.46	0.47	0.50	0.56
16	0.61	0.58	0.56	0.54	0.51	0.48	0.47	0.46	0.48

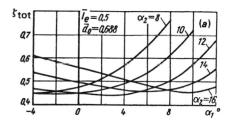

Values of ζ_{tot} at $\bar{l}_d = 1.0$ (without guide surface)

α_2, degrees	α_1, degrees								
	-4	-2	0	2	4	6	8	10	12
8	0.34	0.33	0.33	0.34	0.38	0.47	–	–	–
10	0.38	0.35	0.33	0.32	0.32	0.35	0.42	0.55	–
12	0.44	0.38	0.35	0.32	0.30	0.30	0.32	0.38	0.52
14	0.50	0.44	0.40	0.36	0.33	0.31	0.30	0.32	0.36
16	0.55	0.50	0.45	0.41	0.38	0.35	0.32	0.30	0.31

Values of ζ_{tot} at $\bar{l}_d = 0.5$ (with guide surface)

α_2, degrees	α_1, degrees						
	-4	-2	0	2	4	6	8
12	0.43	0.42	0.42	0.44	0.47	0.50	0.57
14	0.44	0.43	0.42	0.43	0.45	0.47	0.52
16	0.45	0.43	0.42	0.42	0.43	0.44	0.47

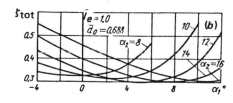

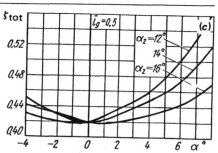

Free discharge from an annular diffusers;[5,12] $d_0 = 0.688$	Diagram 11-9

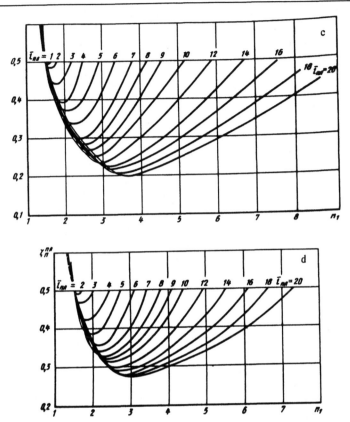

Free discharge from axial-annular-radial-diffusers[11,12]	Diagram 11-10

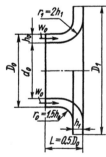

Annular radial diffuser with circular arc at $r_0/h_0 = 1.5$ and $r_1/h_1 = 2$, $\overline{d}_0 = 0.688$

$$\zeta \equiv \frac{\Delta p}{\rho w_0^2/2} = f(n_1, \overline{D}_1), \quad \text{see graphs a and b.}$$

$$n_1 = 2\frac{h_1}{h_0}\overline{D}_1 \frac{1}{1 + \overline{d}_0}$$

$$\overline{D}_1 = \frac{D_1}{D_0}; \quad \overline{d}_0 = \frac{d_0}{D_0}$$

$$w_0 = \frac{Q}{(\pi/4)(D_0^2 - D_0^2)}$$

$$\overline{w}_0 = w_0/u$$

Q is the flow rate, m³/s;
u is the velocity at outer radius, m/s.

Free discharge from axial-annular-radial-diffusers[11,12]						Diagram 11-10

Values of ζ

	n_1						
	1.1	1.8	2.2	2.6	3.0	3.4	3.8

Diffuser downstream of an operating compressor
$\overline{w}_0 \approx 0.5$ (see graph a)

1.5	–	0.76	0.76	0.76	0.76	–	–
1.7	–	0.65	0.69	0.71	0.72	0.73	–
1.9	–	–	0.58	0.64	0.67	0.71	0.72
2.2	–	–	–	0.49	0.55	0.61	0.66

Diffuser with an idle compressor (see graph b)

1.4	0.82	0.72	0.69	0.70	0.71	–	–
1.6	0.76	0.64	0.61	0.61	0.63	0.64	–
1.8	0.70	0.57	0.54	0.53	0.55	0.57	0.58
2.0	–	0.51	0.46	0.45	0.48	0.48	0.50

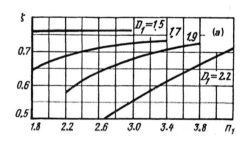

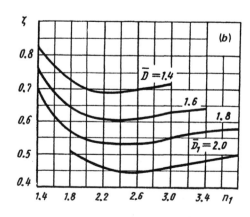

Free discharge from axial-annular-radial-diffusers[11,12]	Diagram 11-10

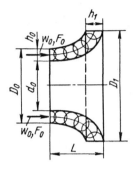

Annular radial diffuser with an elliptical arc and $\bar{d}_0 = 0.7$:

$\zeta = f(h_1/h_0)$, see graph c

Values of ζ

$\bar{D}_1$	h_1/h_0								
	0.8	0.9	1.0	1.1	1.2	1.4	1.6	1.8	2.0
1.5	0.85	0.78	0.73	0.70	0.69	0.67	0.66	0.66	0.66
1.8	0.72	0.66	0.63	0.61	0.61	0.62	0.63	0.64	0.65
2.1	0.61	0.65	0.52	0.52	0.54	0.57	0.59	0.61	0.62

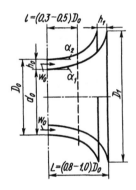

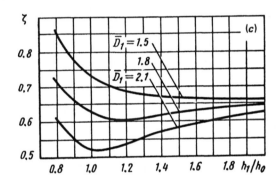

Axial annular radial diffuser at $\bar{D}_1 = 2.06$; $\bar{d}_0 = 0.688$; $\alpha_2 = 8°$; $\bar{w}_0 = 0.5$:

$\zeta = f(n_1, \bar{D}_1)$, see graph d

Values of ζ

α_1, degrees	n_1							
	1.4	1.8	2.2	2.6	3.0	3.4	3.6	4.0
−2	0.61	0.54	0.52	0.50	0.49	0.49	0.49	0.49
2	0.56	0.45	0.43	0.42	0.43	0.44	0.45	0.47
4	0.52	0.39	0.34	0.33	0.35	0.38	0.40	0.46

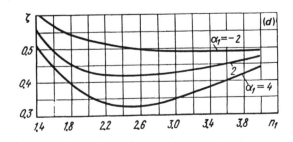

Free discharge from rectangular diffusers downstream of a centrifugal induced-draft fan[24]	Diagram 11-11

Plane asymmetrical diffuser

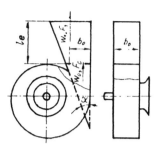

$$\zeta \equiv \frac{\Delta p}{\rho w_0^2/2} = f(n_1), \quad \text{see graph a}$$

$\alpha°$	Formulas
10	$\zeta = 0.827\, n_1^{-1} - 0.059$
15	$\zeta = n_1\,(6.72\, n_1 - 7.5)^{-1}$
20	$\zeta = n_1\,(5.6\, n_1 - 5.79)^{-1}$
25	$\zeta = n_1\,(3.95\, N_1 - 3.31)^{-1}$
35	$\zeta = n_1\,(2.28\, n_1 - 1.07)^{-1}$

$$n_1 = \frac{F_1}{F_0}$$

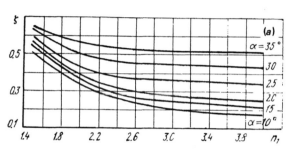

Values of ζ

$\alpha,°$	n_1					
	1.5	2.0	2.5	3.0	3.5	4.0
10	0.51	0.34	0.25	0.21	0.18	0.17
15	0.54	0.36	0.27	0.24	0.22	0.20
20	0.55	0.38	0.31	0.27	0.25	0.24
25	0.59	0.43	0.37	0.35	0.33	0.33
30	0.63	0.50	0.46	0.44	0.43	0.42
35	0.65	0.56	0.53	0.52	0.51	0.50

Pyramidal diffuser

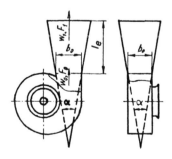

$$\zeta = f(n_1), \quad \text{see graph b}$$

$\alpha°$	Formulas
10	$\zeta = n_1\,(4.05\, n_1 - 3.32)^{-1}$
15	$\zeta = n_1\,(2.34\, n_1 - 1.23)^{-1}$
20	$\zeta = n_1\,(1.71\, n_1 - 0.52)^{-1}$
25	$\zeta = 0.641 - 0.22\, n_1^{-1}$
35	$\zeta = n_1\,(1.44\, n_1 - 0.36)^{-1}$

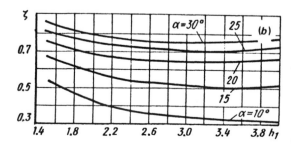

Values of ζ

$\alpha,°$	n_1					
	1.5	2.0	2.5	3.0	3.5	4.0
10	0.54	0.42	0.37	0.34	0.32	0.31
15	0.67	0.58	0.53	0.51	0.50	0.51
20	0.75	0.67	0.65	0.64	0.64	0.65
25	0.80	0.74	0.72	0.70	0.70	0.72
30	0.85	0.78	0.76	0.75	0.75	0.76

Discharge (free) nonsymmetrical diffuser downstream of a centrifugal intake fan;[6] $\alpha_1 = $ var., $\alpha_2 = 0°$	Diagram 11-12

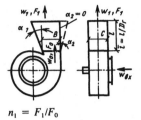

$n_1 = F_1/F_0$

$$\zeta \equiv \frac{\Delta p}{\rho w_0^2/2};$$ η^f is the efficiency of the fan

The vanes of the fan rotor are bent backward

Values of ζ

	n_1						
l/D_h	1.2	1.4	1.6	1.8	2.0	2.2	2.4

Nominal regime $\eta^f = \eta^f_{max}$, $Q = Q_n$

1	0.06	0.10	0.20	0.40	–	–	–
1.5	0.06	0.15	0.23	0.30	0.40	–	–
2.5	–	–	0.13	0.13	0.14	0.20	0.33

Regime with $\eta^f \geqslant 0.9\, \eta^f_{max}$, $Q > Q_n$

1.0	0.08	0.13	0.30	–	–	–	–
1.5	0.15	0.18	0.24	0.33	0.45	–	–
2.5	–	0.10	0.13	0.19	0.25	0.32	0.40

The vanes of the fan rotor are bent forward

Values of ζ

	n_1							
l/D_h	1.2	1.4	1.6	1.8	2.0	2.2	2.4	2.6

Regime with $\eta^f \geqslant 0.9\, \eta^f_{max}$, $Q < Q_n$

1.0	0.22	0.28	0.34	0.43	–	–	–	–
1.5	0.08	0.18	0.22	0.23	–	–	–	–
5.3	–	0.09	0.10	0.12	0.15	0.18	0.21	0.27

Nominal regime with $\eta^f = \eta^f_{max}$, $Q = Q_n$

1.0	0.08	0.16	0.28	0.48	–	–	–	–
1.5	–	0.09	0.15	0.23	0.35	–	–	–
2.5	–	–	0.11	0.12	0.15	0.22	0.32	0.50
5.3	–	–	0.15	0.15	0.15	0.17	0.19	0.20

Regime with $\eta^f \geqslant 0.9\, \eta_{max}$, $Q > Q_n$

0.9	0.11	0.27	0.41	0.60	–	–	–	–
1.5	0.10	0.16	0.23	0.36	0.53	–	–	–
2.5	–	0.09	0.15	0.25	0.36	0.48	0.58	0.64
5.3	–	0.16	0.15	0.15	0.17	0.20	0.25	0.30

Discharge (free) pyramidal diffuser downstream of a centrifugal intake fan[6]	Diagram 11-13

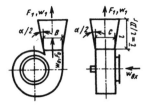

$$\zeta \equiv \frac{\Delta p}{\rho w_0^2/2}$$

$n_1 = F_1/F_0$

The vanes of the fan rotor are bent backward

Values of ζ

	n_1							
l/D_h	1.2	1.4	1.6	1.8	2.0	2.2	2.4	2.6
	Regime with $\eta^f \geqslant 0.9\, \eta^f_{max}$, $Q < Q_n$							
1.0	1.08	1.10	1.12	1.18	1.22	1.33	1.45	1.6
	Nominal regime with $\eta^f = \eta^f_{max}$, $Q = Q_n$							
1.5	–	0.25	0.22	0.20	0.22	0.30	0.48	–
1.5	–	0.12	0.12	0.15	0.20	0.28	0.38	0.5
	Regime with $\eta^f \geqslant 0.9\, \eta^f_{max}$, $Q > Q_n$							
1.0	–	–	–	–	0.15	0.20	0.30	0.42
1.5	–	0.12	0.12	0.12	0.13	0.13	0.15	0.20

The vanes of the fan rotor are bent forward

Values of ζ

	n_1											
l/D_h	1.4	1.6	1.8	2.0	2.2	2.4	2.6	2.8	3.0	3.2	3.6	4.0
	Regime with $\eta^f \geqslant 0.9\, \eta^f_{max}$, $Q < Q_n$											
1.0	0.20	0.50	0.66	0.75	–	–	–	–	–	–	–	–
1.5	–	0.28	0.40	0.55	0.65	0.78	0.88	–	–	–	–	–
2.5	–	–	–	–	0.37	0.40	0.42	0.48	0.55	0.62	0.8	1.0
	Nominal regime with $\eta^f = \eta^f_{max}$											
1.0	0.10	0.26	0.32	0.38	–	–	–	–	–	–	–	–
1.5	–	–	0.22	0.35	0.40	0.44	–	–	–	–	–	–
2.5	–	–	–	–	0.20	0.28	0.35	0.40	0.46	0.52	0.56	0.56
	Regime with $\eta^f \geqslant 0.9\, \eta^f_{max}$, $Q > Q_n$											
1.0	0.15	0.30	0.40	0.48	–	–	–	–	–	–	–	–
1.5	–	0.18	0.28	0.35	0.42	0.50	0.54	–	–	–	–	–
2.5	–	–	–	–	0.20	0.28	0.36	0.40	0.45	0.50	0.56	0.62

Outlet elements installed downstream of centrifugal fans[6]

Diagram 11-14

$$D_h = 4F_0/\Pi_0 \qquad \zeta \equiv \frac{\Delta p}{\rho w_0^2/2}, \quad \eta^f \text{ is the efficiency of a fan}$$

Values of ζ

Scheme of the element	Characteristics of the element	Working regime of the fan with the vanes bent backward		
			Nominal	
		$Q < Q_n$ $\eta^f \geq 0.9\eta^f_{max}$	$Q = Q_n$ $\eta^f = \eta^f_{max}$	$Q > Q_n$ $\eta^f \geq 0.9\,\eta^f_{max}$
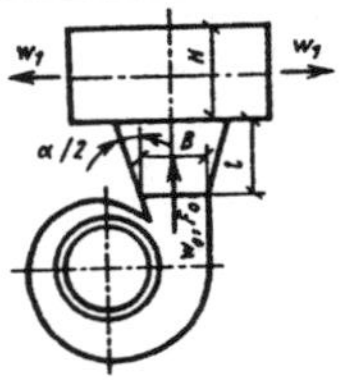 Pyramidal diffuser with $\underline{l} = l/D_h = 1-1.5$ $N_1 = 1.5-2.6$	A duct with ($\overline{H} = H/D_h = 1-2$) with flow discharge in two sides	1.9	0.7	0.6
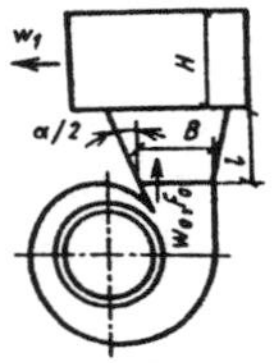 Pyramidal diffuser with $\underline{l} = 1-1.3$; $n_1 = 1.5-2.6$	A duct ($\overline{H} = 1-2$) with flow discharge in one side	2	0.8	0.6
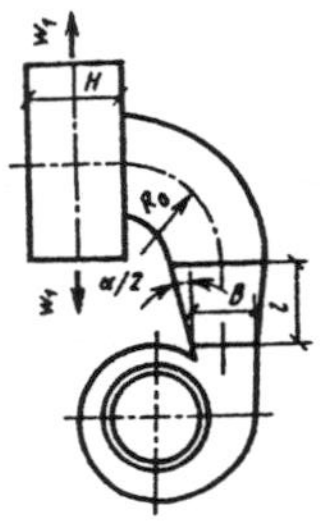 Pyramidal diffuser with $\underline{l} = 1-5$; $n_1 = 2.6$; a turn ($R_0/D_h = 1.0$)	A duct ($\overline{H} = 1-2$) with flow discharge in two sides	1.6	0.7	0.5
Pyramidal diffuser with $\underline{l} = 1-1.5$; $n_1 = 2.6$; a turn ($R_0/D_h = 1.0$)	A duct ($\overline{H} = 1-2$) with flow discharge in one side	1.9	0.8	0.6

Values of ζ

$$\zeta \equiv \frac{\Delta p}{\rho w_0^2/2}$$

Scheme of the element	Characteristics of the element	Angle of installation $\beta°$	Working regime of the fan					
			Vanes bent backward			Vanes bent forward		
			$Q < Q_n$ $\eta^f \geq 0.9\eta^f_{max}$	$Q = Q_n$ $\eta^f = \eta^f_{max}$	$Q \geq Q_n$ $\eta^f \geq 0.9\eta^f_{max}$	$Q < Q_n$ $\eta^f \geq 0.9\eta^f_{max}$	$Q = Q_n$ $\eta^f = \eta^f_{max}$	$Q > Q_n$ $\eta^f \geq 0.9\eta^f_{max}$
Turn of rectangular cross section $(R_0/D_h = 1)$		90;180;360 270	0.6 0.6	0.2 0.2	0.3 0.3	0.2 0.7	0.3 0.5	0.3 0.5
Turn of circular cross section $(R_0/D_h = 2)$		90–360	0.5	0.5	0.4	0.3	0.4	0.4
Turn of rectangular cross section with a pyramidal diffuser $(R_0/D_h = 1.5)$		90–180 270–360	0.2 0.2	0.2 0.2	0.2 0.2	0.4 –	0.2 –	0.2 –
Adapter from square to circular cross section of equidimensional area		–	0.1	0.1	0.1	0.2	0.2	0.2

Discharge diffusers downstream of axial fans[6] (also Reference 3 in Chapter 3)	Diagram 11-15

$$\zeta \equiv \frac{\Delta p}{\rho w_0^2/2}$$

Q, η^f are the capacity and efficiency of the fan
Conical diffusers

Values of ζ

l/D_0	n_1						
	1.5	2.0	2.5	3.0	3.5	4.0	4.5

Regime with $\eta^f > 0.9\ \eta^f_{max}$, $Q > Q_n$

l/D_0	1.5	2.0	2.5	3.0	3.5	4.0	4.5
1.0	1.0	0.94	0.96	1.03	–	–	–
1.75	1.0	1.0	1.0	1.0	1.0	1.0	1.0

Nominal regime with $\eta^f = \eta^f_{max}$, $Q = Q_n$

l/D_0	1.5	2.0	2.5	3.0	3.5	4.0	4.5
1.0	0.30	0.30	0.40	0.55	–	–	–
1.75	–	0.35	0.40	0.43	0.46	0.50	0.55

Regime with $\eta^f \geqslant 0.9\ \eta^f_{max}$, $Q < Q_n$

l/D_0	1.5	2.0	2.5	3.0	3.5	4.0	4.5
1.0	0.25	0.26	0.38	–	–	–	–
1.5	0.22	0.24	0.28	0.35	0.43	0.54	0.65

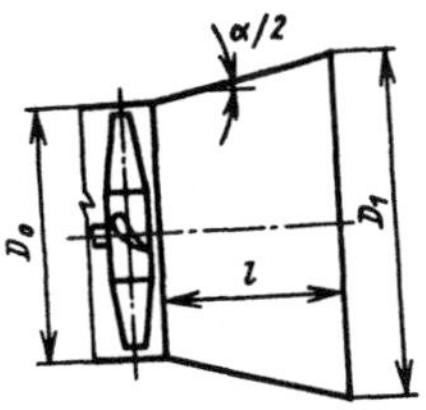

Step diffusers

l/D_0	n_1				
	1.0	1.5	2.0	2.5	3.0

Regime with $\eta^f \geqslant 0.9\ \eta^f_{max}$, $Q < Q_n$

l/D_0	1.0	1.5	2.0	2.5	3.0
1.0	–	0.65	0.51	0.64	0.95
1.5	–	0.72	0.66	0.72	0.79

Nominal regime with $\eta^f = \eta^f_{max}$, $Q = Q_n$

l/D_0	1.0	1.5	2.0	2.5	3.0
1.0	0.23	0.27	0.32	0.40	0.54
1.5	–	0.23	0.23	0.30	0.38

Regime with Q_{max}

l/D_0	1.0	1.5	2.0	2.5	3.0
1.0	0.18	0.16	0.32	0.55	–
1.5	0.13	0.16	0.25	0.38	0.53

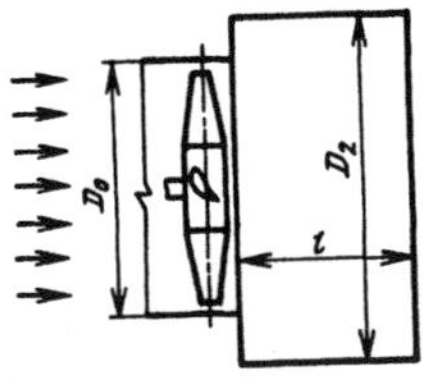

Discharge from a straight walled elbow ($\delta = 90°$) with a sharp corner in the turn[28]

Diagram
11-16

$$\zeta \equiv \frac{\Delta p}{\rho w_0^2/2} = \zeta_{loc} + \lambda \frac{l_1}{b_1}\left(\frac{b_0}{b_1}\right)^2, \quad \text{where for } \lambda, \text{ see Diagrams 2-1 through 2-6}$$

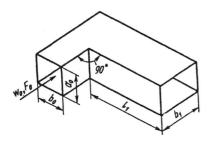

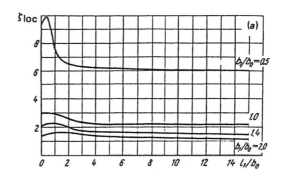

Elbow of square cross section ($\alpha_0/b_0 = 1.0$)

$\zeta_{loc} = f\left(\frac{l_1}{b_0}\right)$, see graph a

Values of ζ_{loc} (graph a)

$\frac{b_1}{b_0}$	$\frac{l_1}{b_0}$								
	0	0.5	1.0	1.5	2.0	4.0	6.0	8.0	15.0
0.5	9.0	10	7.6	6.7	6.5	6.2	6.2	6.1	5.9
1.0	2.9	3.0	2.9	2.8	2.6	2.2	2.2	2.2	2.2
1.4	2.0	2.2	2.2	2.1	1.9	1.7	1.6	1.5	1.5
2.0	1.3	1.5	1.6	1.6	1.6	1.4	1.3	1.2	1.1

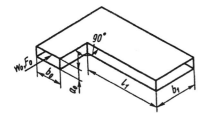

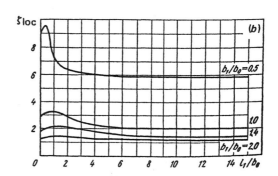

Plane elbow ($\alpha_0/b_0 = 0.25$)

$\zeta_{loc} = f\left(\frac{l_1}{b_0}\right)$, see graph b

| Discharge from a straight walled elbow ($\delta = 90°$) with a sharp corner in the turn[28] | | | | | | | Diagram 11-16 | |

Values of ζ_{loc}

$\dfrac{b_1}{b_0}$	$\dfrac{l_1}{b_0}$								
	0	0.5	1.0	1.5	2.0	4.0	6.0	8.0	15.0
0.5	8.8	9.5	7.2	6.6	6.3	6.0	5.9	5.8	5.8
1.0	2.7	3.2	3.3	3.1	2.9	2.3	2.1	2.0	2.0
1.4	1.8	2.1	2.2	2.2	2.1	1.8	1.6	1.4	1.4
2.0	1.3	1.5	1.6	1.5	1.5	1.4	1.3	1.2	1.1

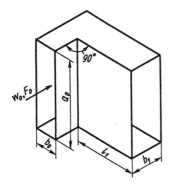

Elbow of rectangular cross section ($a_0/b_0 = 4$)

$$\zeta_{loc} = f\left(\frac{l_1}{b_0}\right), \quad \text{see graph c}$$

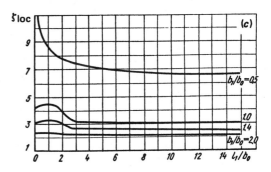

Values of ζ_{loc} (graph c)

$\dfrac{b_1}{b_0}$	$\dfrac{l_1}{b_0}$								
	0	0.5	1.0	1.5	2.0	4.0	6.0	8.0	15.0
0.5	9.9	8.5	7.6	7.1	6.8	6.2	5.9	5.7	5.6
1.0	3.2	3.3	3.5	3.4	3.0	2.1	2.1	2.1	2.0
1.4	2.0	2.2	2.3	2.2	2.0	1.7	1.6	1.6	1.5
2.0	1.3	1.4	1.4	1.3	1.2	1.2	1.2	1.1	1.1

Discharge from a smooth elbow at $\delta = 90°$[38]

Diagram
11-17

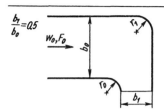

$r_0 = r_1 = r$

Elbow with $r/b_0 = 0.2$:

$$\zeta \equiv \frac{\Delta p}{\rho w_0^2/2} = f\left(\frac{b_1}{b_0}\right),$$

see graph a.

b_1/b_0	0.5	1.0	2.0
ζ	4.92	2.80	1.3

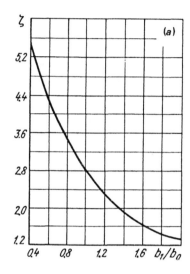

Elbow with $r/b_0 = $ var.

$$\zeta = f\left(\frac{r}{b_0}\right), \quad \text{see graph b.}$$

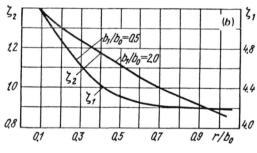

Values of ζ (ζ_1 and ζ_2)

b_1/b_0	r/b_0			
	0.1	0.2	0.3	0.4
0.5	5.20	4.92	4.64	4.44
2.0	1.40	1.30	1.23	1.17

b_1/b_0	r/b_0			
	0.5	0.6	0.8	1.0
0.5	4.31	4.24	4.20	4.18
2.0	1.11	1.05	0.95	0.87

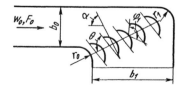

Elbow with $\delta = 90°$ ($b_1/b_0 = 2.0$) with five thin guide vanes

$$\zeta = f\left(\frac{r}{b_0}\right), \quad \text{see graph c}$$

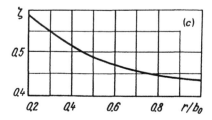

Characteristics	r/b_0		
	0.2	0.5	1.0
θ, degrees	70	72–74	72–74
ϕ_1, degrees	154	99	90
ζ	0.59	0.49	0.44

Discharge from a bend and a composite elbow at $\delta = 90°$[3.37]	Diagram 11-18

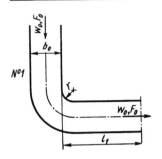

$$\zeta \equiv \frac{\Delta p}{\rho w_0^2/2} = \zeta_{loc} + \lambda \frac{l_1}{b_0}$$

where $\zeta_{loc} = f(r/b_0, l_1/b_0)$. For λ, see Diagrams 2-1 through 2-6

Values of ζ_{loc}

$\frac{r}{b_0}$	$\frac{l_1}{b_0}$									
	0	0.5	1.0	1.5	2.0	3.0	4.0	6.0	8.0	12.0
0.0	2.95	3.13	3.23	3.00	2.72	2.40	2.24	2.10	2.05	2.00
0.2	2.15	2.15	2.08	1.84	1.70	1.60	1.56	1.52	1.49	1.48
0.5	1.80	1.54	1.43	1.36	1.32	1.26	1.22	1.19	1.19	1.19
1.0	1.46	1.19	1.11	1.09	1.09	1.09	1.09	1.09	1.09	1.09
2.0	1.19	1.10	1.06	1.04	1.04	1.04	1.04	1.04	1.04	1.04

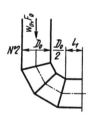

Composite elbow

$\frac{l_1}{D_0}$	0.4	0.8
ζ	1.52	1.41

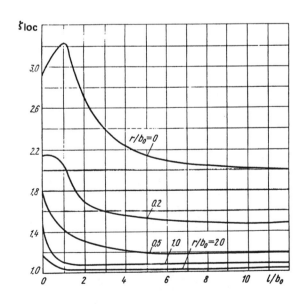

Air distributors with perforated outlet[3,9,23]	Diagram 11-19

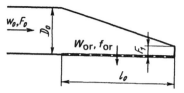

$$D_h = \frac{4F_0}{\Pi_0}$$

$$0.5 < \bar{f}_0 = \frac{F_{or}}{F_0} < 3.0$$

$$0 < \frac{F_1}{F_0} < 1.0$$

Thin-walled distributor with perforated lateral outlet

$$\zeta \equiv \frac{\Delta p}{\rho w_0^2/2} \approx \frac{1.8}{\bar{f}_0^2} + \left(\frac{l_0}{D_h}\right)^{0.15} = f(\bar{f}_0)$$

Values of ζ

$\dfrac{l_0}{D_h}$	$\bar{f}_0$							
	0.5	0.6	0.8	1.0	1.5	2.0	2.5	3.0
10	8.61	6.41	4.22	3.21	2.21	1.86	1.69	1.61
20	8.77	5.57	4.38	3.37	2.37	2.02	1.85	1.77
30	8.87	6.67	4.48	3.47	2.47	2.12	1.95	1.87
40	8.94	6.74	4.55	3.54	2.54	2.19	2.02	1.94

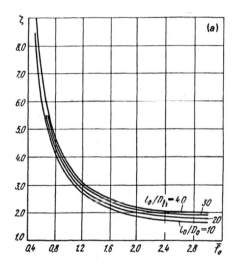

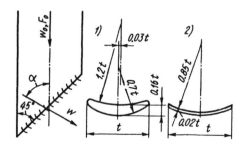

Vaned distributor

$$\zeta = f(\alpha)$$

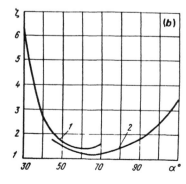

Values of ζ

Vanes	α, degrees								
	30	40	50	60	70	80	90	100	110
1. Profiled airfoils	6.4	2.7	1.7	1.4	1.6	–	–	–	–
2. Simplified curvatuve	–	–	1.5	1.2	1.2	1.4	1.8	2.4	3.5

Air distributors with perforated outlet[3,9,23]	Diagram 11-19

Characteristics of the device and scheme	$\zeta \equiv \dfrac{\Delta p}{\rho w_0^2 / 2}$

Two-jet, six-diffuser of the VDSh type of the NIIS T design*	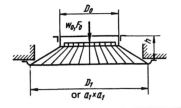	1.9

Non-standard perforated distributor (rectangular or circular) $\overline{f} = \dfrac{F_{or}}{F_0} = 0.04\text{–}0.10$	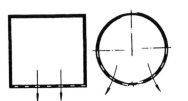	2.4

Standardized, perforated distributor of circular cross-section:

1) VK-1 (6 rows of orifices)*
2) VK-2 (12 rows of orifices)*

1.7–2.0
(ζ is based on the area

$$F_0 = \frac{\pi D_0^2}{4}$$

where D_0 is the diameter of the attached pipe)

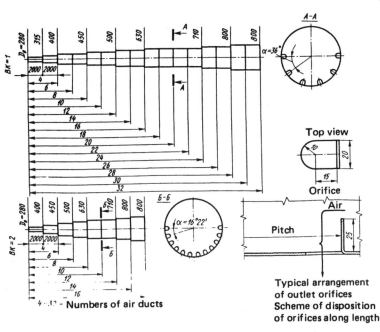

Top view

Orifice

Air

Pitch

Typical arrangement of outlet orifices
Scheme of disposition of orifices along length

4 · 32 - Numbers of air ducts

*These are Russian designations of particular configurations.

Air distributors with perforated outlet[3,9,23]	Diagram 11-19

Characteristics of the device and scheme	$\zeta \equiv \dfrac{\Delta p}{\rho w_0^2/2}$

At the wall, of the VP type*

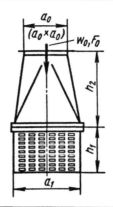

6.8

Static (volute-type) centrifugal distributor (a) inlet; (b) inlet exhaust.

Optimum characteristics:
$R_0 = 0.5 d_0 \exp(\phi/2\pi)$
(logarithmic coil);
$h/a_0 = 1.05$

$\dfrac{a}{b} = 0.8{-}0.9$

$\dfrac{ab}{d_0^2} = 0.85{-}0.90$

$\dfrac{D_{dis}}{d_0} = 1.3{-}1.5$

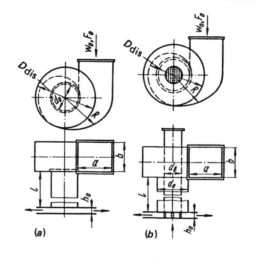

6.5

With three diffusers

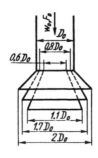

1.1

*Russian design designations.

Air distributors with perforated outlet[3,9,23]	Diagram 11-19

Characteristics of the device and scheme	$\zeta \equiv \dfrac{\Delta p}{\rho w_0^2/2}$

Slotted, with parallel guide vanes at $\bar{f} = \dfrac{F_{\text{open}}}{F_0} \geq 0.8$	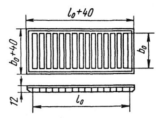	1.5

Rectangular, in the form of a grating with parallel guide vanes	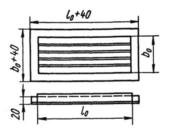	1.8

Spray; branch pipe*	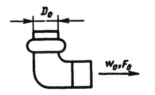	0.75

With revolving out of the PP type*	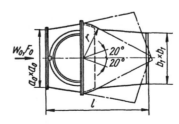	1.1

*Russian design designations.

Air distributors with perforated outlet[3,9,23]	Diagram 11-19
Characteristics of the device and scheme	$\zeta \equiv \dfrac{\Delta p}{\rho w_0^2/2}$

Combined inlet-exhaust dome of the VK type

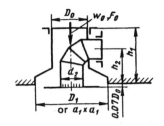

2.0

In the form of a ceiling dome:

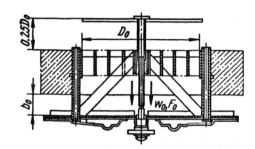

$b_0/D_0 = 0.2$ 4.0
$b_0/D_0 = 0.3$ 2.3
$b_0/D_0 = 0.4$ 1.9

With a universal tray dome of the VU type

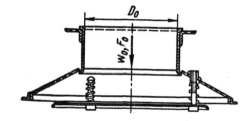

a) With a raised disk   3.0
b) With a lowered disk   1.9

In the form of a hemisphere with orifices:

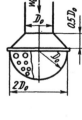

$F_{or}/F_0 = 0.56$ 11.0
$F_{or}/F_0 = 3.9$ 1.0

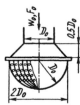

Air distributors with perforated outlet[3,9,23]	Diagram 11-19

Characteristics of the device and scheme	$\zeta \equiv \dfrac{\Delta p}{\rho w_0^2/2}$

In the form of a hemisphere with slots $F_{or}/F_0 = 1.4$

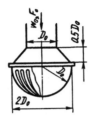

2.0

With fan grating of the RB type, of the VNIIST design:* ($\beta = 45°$, $\beta = 60°$, $\beta = 90°$)

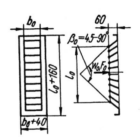

1.0

With a regulating grating

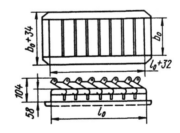

Type of grating	A, B, D	B
ζ	2.2	3.3

In the form of a cylinder with perforated surface $F_{or}/F_0 = 4.7$

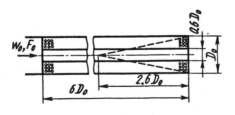

0.9

*Russian design designatons.

Straight and circular exhaust vents[32]	Diagram
$Re = w_0/D_0 \nu > 10^4$	11-20

No. of curve	Vent type	Scheme	Resistance coefficient $\zeta \equiv \dfrac{\Delta p}{\rho w_0^2/2}$

| 1 | With plane baffle | 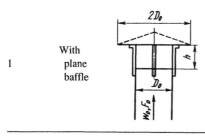 | |

Values of ζ

	h/D_0				
Vent	0.10	0.20	0.25	0.30	0.35
1	–	–	3.40	2.60	2.10
2	–	--	–	–	–
3	4.00	2.30	1.90	1.60	1.40
4	–	2.90	2.30	1.90	1.70
5	2.60	1.20	1.00	0.80	0.70

| 2 | With split canopy | 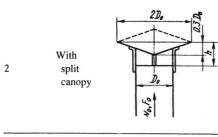 | |

	h/D_0				
Vent	0.40	0.50	0.60	0.80	1.0
1	1.70	1.40	1.20	1.10	1.00
2	3.50	2.00	1.50	1.20	1.10
3	1.30	1.15	1.10	1.00	1.00
4	1.50	1.30	1.20	1.10	1.00
5	0.65	0.60	0.60	0.60	0.60

| 3 | With hood | | |

| 4 | With hood and split canopy | | |

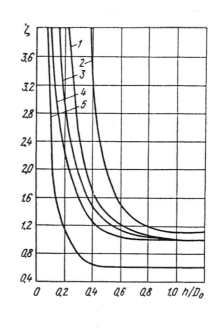

| 5 | With diffuser and hood | 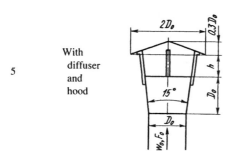 | |

Exhaust vents of rectangular cross section; lateral openings with and without fixed louvers[26]	Diagram 11-21

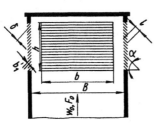 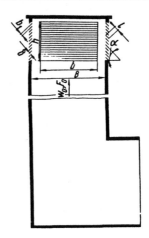

$$\frac{h}{B} = 0.5 \qquad \overline{f} = \frac{n_{obh}}{F_0}$$

Straight vents

No. of openings	Layout of openings Without louvers	Layout of openings With louvers	$\overline{f}$	b/h	Resistance coefficient $\zeta \equiv \dfrac{\Delta p}{\rho w_0^2/2}$ Without louvers	$\alpha = 30°$ $b_1'/h = 0.029$ $l/b_1' = 1.6$ $\delta/b_1' = 0.058$	$\alpha = 45°$ $b_1'/h = 0.024$ $l/b_1' = 1.4$ $\delta/b_1' = 0.07$
One			0.36	1.5	15.5	22.0	–
Two			0.36	1.5	5.00	7.20	–
Three			0.36	1.5	3.50	5.00	–
Four			0.36	1.5	2.20	2.60	3.50
			0.24	1.0	5.30	7.00	10.0
			0.12	0.5	15.6	19.6	29.0

Exhaust vents of rectangular cross section; lateral openings with and without fixed louvers[26]	Diagram 11-21

Shafts with a turn

						Resistance coefficient $\zeta \equiv \dfrac{\Delta p}{\rho w_0^2/2}$	
	Layout of openings						$\alpha = 30°$ $b_1'/h = 0.029$ $l/b_1' = 1.6$ $\delta/b_1' = 0.058$	$\alpha = 45°$ $b_1'/h = 0.024$ $l/b_1' = 1.4$ $\delta/b_1' = 0.007$
No. of openings	Without louvers	With louvers	$\bar{f}$	b/h	Without louvers		
One			0.36	1.5	14.0	18.6	–
			0.36	1.5	17.6	26.0	–
Two			0.36	1.5	5.20	6.60	–
			0.36	1.5	7.00	9.30	–
Three			0.36	1.5	4.00	4.60	–
			0.36	1.5	7.00	9.00	–
Four			0.36	1.5	4.00	4.20	5.00
			0.24	1.0	6.60	8.00	10.7
			0.12	0.5	16.0	20.0	29.5

Discharge from a straight tube through an orifice or a perforated plate (grid) with sharp-edged orifices ($l/d_h = 0{-}0.015$);[16-18] $Re = w_0 d_h/\nu \geqslant 10^5$	Diagram 11-22

$$\zeta \equiv \frac{\Delta p}{\rho w_0^2/2} = (1 + 0.707\sqrt{1 - \overline{f}})^2 \frac{1}{\overline{f}^2}, \text{ see the graph}$$

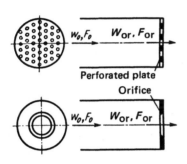

$$d_h = \frac{4f_0}{\Pi_{or}}$$

$$\overline{f} = F_{or}/F_0$$

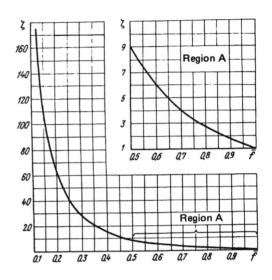

$\overline{f}$	0.05	0.10	0.15	0.20	0.25	0.30	0.35	0.40	0.45
ζ	1107	273	119	66	41.4	28.2	20.3	15.2	11.8

$\overline{f}$	0.50	0.55	0.60	0.65	0.70	0.75	0.80	0.85	0.9	0.95	1.0
ζ	9.30	7.49	6.12	5.05	4.20	3.52	2.95	2.47	2.06	1.63	1.0

Discharge from a straight tube through an orifice or a perforated plate[16-18] (grid) with differently shaped orifice edges; Re $= w_{or}d_h/\nu > 10^4$	Diagram 11-23
Scheme and graph	Resistance coefficient

$$\zeta \equiv \frac{\Delta p}{\rho w_0^2/2}$$

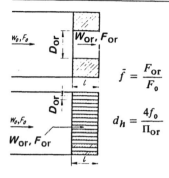

$$\bar{f} = \frac{F_{or}}{F_0}$$

$$d_h = \frac{4f_0}{\Pi_{or}}$$

$$\zeta = \left[1 + 0.5(1 - \overline{f})^{0.75} + \tau(1 - \overline{f})^{0.375} + \lambda \frac{l}{d_h} \right] \frac{1}{\overline{f}^2}$$

were for λ, see Diagrams 2-1 through 2-6; $\tau = f(l/d_h)$

Thick walled orifices

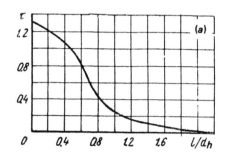

(a)

$\frac{l}{d_h}$	0	0.2	0.4	0.6	0.8
τ	1.35	1.22	1.10	0.84	0.42
$\frac{l}{d_h}$	1.0	1.2	1.6	2.0	2.4
τ	0.24	0.16	0.07	0.02	0

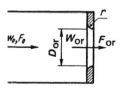

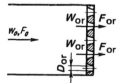

$$\zeta = \left[1 + \zeta'(1 - \overline{f})^{0.75} + 2\sqrt{\zeta'} \times (1 - \overline{f})^{0.375} \right] \frac{1}{\overline{f}^2}$$

where $\zeta' = f(l/d_h)$

Orifice edges beveled in the flow direction

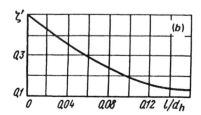

(b)

$\frac{l}{d_h}$	0.01	0.02	0.03	0.04
ζ'	0.46	0.42	0.38	0.35
$\frac{l}{d_h}$	0.06	0.08	0.12	0.16
ζ'	0.29	0.23	0.16	0.13

Discharge from a straight tube through an orifice or a perforated plate[16-18] (grid) with differently shaped orifice edges; Re $= w_{or}d_h/\nu > 10^4$	Diagram 11-23

Scheme and graph	Resistance coefficient $\zeta \equiv \dfrac{\Delta p}{\rho w_0^2/2}$

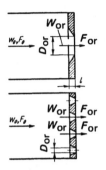

$$\zeta = \left[1 + \zeta'(1 - \overline{f})^{0.75} + 2\sqrt{\zeta'}(1 - \overline{f})^{0.375} \right]\frac{1}{\overline{f}^2}$$

where $\zeta' = f\left(\dfrac{r}{d_h}\right)$

Orifice edges rounded in the flow direction

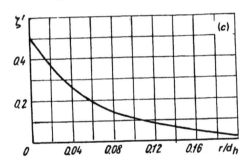

$\dfrac{r}{d_h}$	0	0.01	0.02	0.03	0.04	0.05
ζ'	0.50	0.44	0.37	0.31	0.26	0.22
$\dfrac{r}{d_h}$	0.06	0.08	0.12	0.16	0.20	
ζ'	0.19	0.15	0.09	0.06	0.03	

Discharge from a tube through an orifice or a perforated plate (grid) with differently shapes orifice edges in transition and laminar regions (Re $= w_{or}D_h/\nu > 10^4-10^5$, tentatively)[16-18]	Diagram 11-24

w_0, F_0 W_{or}, F_{or}

Perforated plate

Orifice

w_0, F_0 W_{or}, F_{or}

$D_h = \dfrac{4F_{or}}{\Pi_{or}}$

$\overline{f} = \dfrac{F_{or}}{F_0}$

1) $25 < \text{Re} < 10^4-10^5$:

$$\zeta \equiv \frac{\Delta p}{\rho w_0^2/2} = \zeta_\phi \frac{1}{\overline{f}^2} + \overline{\varepsilon}_{0Re}\zeta_{qu}$$

2) $10 < \text{Re} < 25$:

$$\zeta = \frac{33}{\text{Re}}\frac{1}{\overline{f}^2} + \overline{\varepsilon}_{0Re}\zeta_{qu}$$

3) $\text{Re} < 10$:

$$\zeta = \frac{33}{\text{Re}}\frac{1}{\overline{f}^2}$$

where $\overline{\varepsilon}_{0Re} = f_2(\text{Re})$ and $\zeta_\phi = f_1(\text{Re}, F_0/F_1)$, see Diagram 4-19 (it is assumed that $\overline{f} = F_{or}/F_0$ corresponds to F_0/F_1); ζ_{qu} is determined as at Re $> 10^4-10^5$ from Diagrams 11-22 and 11-23.

Side discharge from the end orifice of a circular pipe (data of the author and of Reference 36)	Diagram 11-25

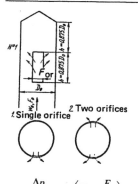

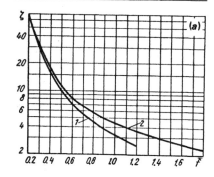

$$\zeta = \frac{\Delta p}{\rho w_0^2/2} = f\left(\overline{f} = \frac{F_{or}}{F_0}\right)$$

Values of ζ

Number of orifices	$\overline{f}$												
	0.2	0.3	0.4	0.5	0.6	0.7	0.8	0.9	1.0	1.2	1.1	1.6	1.8
One (curve 1)	65.7	30.0	16.4	10.0	7.30	5.50	4.48	3.67	3.16	2.44	–	–	–
Two (curve 2)	67.7	33.0	17.2	11.6	8.45	6.80	5.86	5.00	4.38	3.47	2.90	2.52	2.25

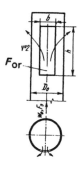

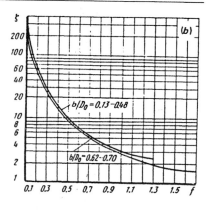

Values of ζ

$\dfrac{b}{D_0}$	$\overline{f}$							
	0.1	0.2	0.3	0.4	0.5	0.6	0.7	0.8
0.13	253	63.3	28.1	15.9	–	–	–	–
0.26	248	62.0	27.7	15.7	10.2	7.22	5.43	–
0.38	244	61.0	27.1	15.5	10.1	7.12	5.36	4.25
0.48	240	60.0	26.6	15.3	9.90	7.00	5.26	4.17
0.62	228	57.0	25.6	14.6	9.60	6.80	5.15	4.07
0.7	220	55.0	24.8	14.3	9.30	6.60	5.05	4.00

$\dfrac{b}{D_0}$	$\overline{f}$								
	0.9	1.0	1.1	1.2	1.3	1.4	1.5	1.6	1.7
0.13	–	–	–	–	–	–	–	–	–
0.26	–	–	–	–	–	–	–	–	–
0.38	3.56	3.00	–	–	–	–	–	–	–
0.48	3.46	2.93	2.93	2.56	2.29	–	–	–	–
0.62	3.36	2.85	2.48	2.22	2.01	1.86	1.73	–	–
0.70	3.31	2.80	2.44	2.18	1.92	1.82	1.69	1.56	1.52

Discharge from a straight channel through a fixed louver grating[39,40]	Diagram 11-26

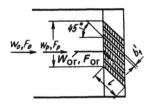

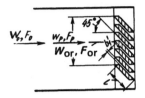

No. 1 Inlet edges are cut vertically　　　　　　　No. 2. Inlet edges are cut horizontally

1) $\dfrac{l}{b_1'} \geq \left(\dfrac{l}{b_1'}\right)_{opt} \left[\text{where } \left(\dfrac{l}{b_1'}\right)_{opt} \approx 11(1 - \overline{f}) \right]$

$\zeta \equiv \dfrac{\Delta p}{\rho w_0^2/2} = k\left[1 + 0.85\left(1 - \overline{f}\,\dfrac{F_{gr}}{F_0}\right) + \zeta_{fr}\right]\dfrac{k_1}{\overline{f}^{\,2}}\left(\dfrac{F_0}{F_{gr}}\right)^2 = k_1\zeta'$

2) $\dfrac{l}{b_1'} < \left(\dfrac{l}{b_1'}\right)_{opt}: \quad \zeta = k_1\zeta' + \Delta\zeta$

where $k = 1.0$ for No. 1; $k = 0.6$ for No. 2.

$\Delta\zeta \approx 0.5\left[11(1 - \overline{f}) - \dfrac{l}{b_1'}\right] \quad \zeta_{fr} = \lambda\dfrac{l}{b_1'}; \quad$ for λ, see Diagrams 2-1 through 2-6.

At $\dfrac{l}{b_1'} = \left(\dfrac{l}{b_1'}\right)_{opt}, \quad \overline{f} = \dfrac{F_{or}}{F_{gr}} = \dfrac{F_{or}}{F_0}$ and $\lambda = 0.064$ (at $Re = w_0 b_1'/\nu = 10^3$)

For values of $\zeta' = f(\overline{f})$, see the graph.

$\overline{f}$	0.1	0.2	0.3	0.4	0.5
ζ'	247	55.0	23.8	12.3	7.00

$\overline{f}$	0.6	0.7	0.8	0.9	1.0
ζ'	4.60	3.00	2.06	1.43	1.00

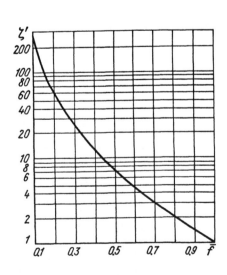

Discharge sections under different conditions		Diagram 11-27

		Resistance coefficient
Discharge conditions	Scheme	$\zeta \equiv \dfrac{\Delta p}{\rho w_0^2/2}$
From a straight tube (channel) with screen at the exit	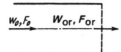	$\zeta = 1 + \zeta_{sc}$ where ζ_{sc} is determined as ζ of the screen from Diagram 8-6 (approximately)
From a vent pipe with screen $\bar{f} = \dfrac{F_{or}}{F_{gr}} = 0.8$	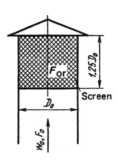	$\zeta = 1.1$ (approximately)
Through a stamped standard louver grating at $\bar{f} = F_{or}/F_{gr} \approx 0.8$ with completely opened adjustable slats	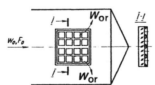	$\zeta \approx 3\text{--}3.5$ (approximately)
Through stamped or cast shaped grids	See scheme of Diagram 3-21	$\zeta = f(\bar{f})$ (see Diagram 11-18 (approximately)
Through a smoothly converging nozzle	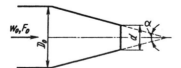	$\zeta = 1.05 \left(\dfrac{D_0}{d}\right)^4$

Free jet of circular cross-section[1]

Diagram
11-28

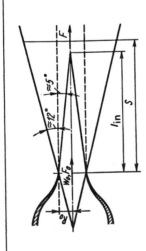

$$\zeta \equiv \frac{\Delta p}{\rho w_0^2/2} = 1 - \bar{e}$$

1. Starting section ($\bar{s} \leq 9$):*

$$\bar{q} \equiv Q/Q_0 = 1 + 0.073\bar{s} + 0.0025\bar{s}^2 - 0.0001\bar{s}^3 + 0.000002\bar{s}^4;$$

$$\bar{e} \equiv 2E/m_0 w_0^2 = 1 - 0.036\bar{s} - 0.0008\bar{s}^2 + 0.00006\bar{s}^3 + 0.000002\bar{s}^4;$$

$$\bar{e}_c = (1 - 0.25\bar{s})^2 + 0.545(1 - 0.44\bar{s})K_1 - 0.27\bar{s}K_2$$

where for K_1 and K_2 see Table 11-3 or equations (11-6);

$$\bar{F}_s \equiv F_s/F_0 = (1 + 0.144\bar{s})^2; \ \bar{w}_m = w_m/w_0 = 1.$$

2. Main section ($\bar{s} > 12$):

$$\bar{q} \equiv Q/Q_0 = 0.155\bar{s}; \ \bar{e} = 7.75/\bar{s}; \ \bar{e}_c = 92H_1/\bar{s} \text{ where for } H_1 \text{ see Table 11-3 or equation (11-7a);}$$

$$\bar{w}_m = w_m/w_0 \approx 12.4/\bar{s}; \ \bar{F}_s = (0.225\bar{s})^2$$

$\bar{q}$ is the relative discharge through the given cross section of the jet; $\bar{e}$ is the relative energy residue in the given cross section of the jet; $\bar{F}_s$ is the relative area of the given cross section of the jet

Parameters	$\bar{s} = s/R_0$														
	0	2	4	6	9	10	11	12	12.5	15	20	25	30	40	50
$\bar{q}$	1.0	1.15	1.32	1.49	1.76	1.85	1.90	2.0	1.94	2.33	3.10	3.88	4.65	6.20	7.75
$\bar{e}$	1.0	0.93	0.86	0.77	0.67	0.60	0.58	0.55	0.53	0.52	0.39	0.31	0.26	0.19	0.16
$\bar{e}_{cor}$	1.0	0.87	0.76	0.66	0.53	0.50	0.46	0.43	0.41	0.34	0.25	0.18	0.13	0.07	0.05
$\dfrac{w_m}{w_0}$	1.0	1.0	1.0	1.0	1.0	1.0	1.0	1.0	0.99	0.83	0.62	0.50	0.41	0.31	0.25
F_s	1.0	1.66	2.48	3.48	5.27	6.25	6.5	7.0	7.50	10.9	19.4	30.3	43.6	77.5	121

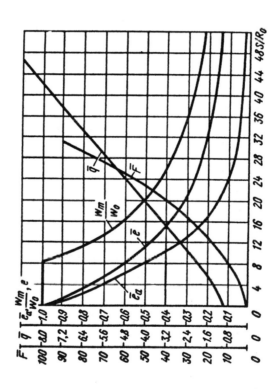

*See the footnote to para. 33 of Section 11-1.

Plane-parallel free jet[1]

Diagram
11-29

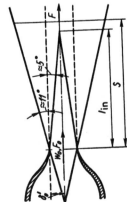

$$\zeta \equiv \frac{\Delta p}{\rho w_0^2/2} = 1 - \bar{e}$$

1. Starting section ($\bar{s} \le 9$):*
   $\bar{q} \equiv Q/Q_0 = 1 + 0.036\bar{s}$; $\bar{e} \equiv 2E/(m_0 w_0^2) = 1 - 0.019\bar{s}$;
   $\bar{e}_c = 1 - 0.27\bar{s}(0.416 - K_1)$ where for K_1, see Table 11-3 or equation (11-6a)

2. Main section ($\bar{s} > 12$)
   $\bar{q} = 0.375\sqrt{\bar{s}}$; $\bar{e} \equiv 3/\sqrt{\bar{s}}$; $w_m \equiv w_m/w_0 = 3.8/\sqrt{\bar{s}}$;
   $\bar{F}_s \equiv F_s/F_0 = 0.22\bar{s}$; $\bar{e}_c = 12H_2/\sqrt{\bar{s}}$ where for H_2 see Table 11-3 or equation (11-7b); for the nomenclature see Diagram 11-28

Parameters	\multicolumn{15}{c}{$\bar{s} = s/b_0$}
	0	2	4	6	9	10	11	12	12.5	15	20	25	30	40	50
$\bar{q}$	1.0	1.07	1.14	1.216	1.32	1.35	1.38	1.40	1.42	1.45	1.68	1.875	2.05	2.372	2.651
$\bar{e}$	1.0	0.96	0.92	0.89	0.83	0.81	0.80	0.78	0.76	0.73	0.67	0.60	0.55	0.48	0.43
$\bar{e}_{cor}$	1.0	0.95	0.89	0.84	0.77	0.75	0.73	0.71	0.71	0.65	0.55	0.47	0.40	0.33	0.26
$\bar{w}_m$	1.0	1.0	1.0	1.0	1.0	0.99	0.98	0.96	0.95	0.92	0.85	0.76	0.69	0.60	0.54
$\bar{F}_s$	1.0	1.32	1.63	1.95	2.42	2.50	2.60	2.70	2.90	3.30	4.40	5.50	6.60	8.80	11.0

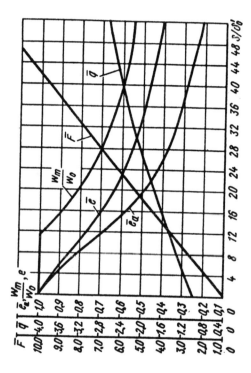

*See the footnote to para. 33 of Section 11-1.

REFERENCES

1. Abramovich, G. N., *Theory of Turbulent Jets*, Firmatgiz, Moscow, 1960, 715 p.
2. Averiyanov, A. G., et al., *Ventilation of Shops of Shipbuilding Works*, Sudostroenic Press, Moscow, 1969, 268 p.
3. Barurin, V. V. and Shepelev, I. A., Aerodynamic characteristics of intake nozzles, *Sovrem. Vopr. Ventilyatsii*, 23–35, Stroiizdat, Moscow, 1941.
4. Brusilovskiy, I. V., Determination of the optimal parameters of the diffusers of axial fans and of their energetic characteristics from experimental data, *Prom. Aerodin.*, vyp. 2(34), 118–133, Moscow, 1987.
5. Bushel, A. R., Reduction of inner losses in a shaft installation having an axial ventilator, *Tr. MAP*, no. 673, 50, 1948.
6. Bychkova, L. A., *Recommendations on the Calculation of Hydraulic Resistances of the Complex Elements of Ventilation Systems*, Moscow, 1981, p. 32.
7. Ginzburg, Ya. A. and Idelchik, I. E., Experimental determination of the pressure reduction coefficients in conical diffusers at large subsonic velocities and under different inlet conditions, *Uch. Zap. TsAGI*, vol. IV, no. 3, 23–31, 1973.
8. Gorelov, G. M. and Freidin, A. S., Some results of an experimental investigation of a diffuser with flow backing at the exit, *Tr. Kuibyshev. Aviats. Inst.*, vyp. 15, part 2, 35–42, 1963.
9. Grimitlin, M. I., Air delivery through perforated air pipelines, *Tr. LIOT*, 190, Leningrad, 1960.
10. Deich, M. E. and Zaryankin, A. E., *Gas Dynamics of Diffusers and Exhaust Pipes of Turbomachines*, Energiya Press, Moscow, 1970, 384 p.
11. Dovzhik, S. A. and Guinevsky, A. S., Experimental investigation of pressure head pipes of stationary axial turbomachines, *Tekh. Otchyoty*, no. 130, 13, 1955.
12. Dovzhik, S. A. and Morozov, V. I., Experimental investigation of circular diffusers of axial turbomachines, *Promaerodinamika*, vyp. 20, 168–201, Oborengiz, Moscow, 1961.
13. Idelchik, I. E., Flow aerodynamics and pressure head losses in diffusers, *Prom. Aerodin.*, no. 3, 132–209, 1947.
14. Idelchi, I. E., Hydraulic resistance during flow inlet into channels and passage through orifices, *Prom. Aerodin.*, no. 2, 27–57, 1944.
15. Idelchi, I. E., *Hydraulic Resistances (Physical and Mechanical Fundamentals)*, Grosenergoizdat, Moscow, 1954, 316 p.
16. Idelchik, I. E., Determination of the resistance coefficients in discharge through orifices, *Gidrotekh. Stroit.*, no. 5, 31–36, 1953.
17. Idelchik, I. E., Shock losses in the flow with nonuniform velocity distribution, *Tr. MAP*, vyp. 662, 1–24, 1948.
18. Idelchik, I. E., Account for the viscosity effect on the hydraulic resistance of diaphragms and grids, *Teplo-energetika*, no. 9, 75–80, 1960.
19. Idelchik, I. E. and Ginzburg, Ya. L., About the investigation of the Reynolds number and inlet conditions effect on the laws governing flow motion in diffusers, *Probl. Ventilyats. Kondits. Vozdukha*, 224–231, Vyssh. Shkola Press, Minsk, 1969.
20. Idelchi, I. E. and Ginzburg, Ya. L., About the mechanism of the effect of inlet on the resistance of diffusers, *J. Eng. Phys.*, vol. 16, no. 3, 413–416, 1969.
21. Idelchik, I. E. and Ginzburg, Ya. L., Basic results of new experimental investigations of conical diffusers, *Mekh. Ochistka Promysh. Gazov*, 178–210, NIIOGAZ.
22. Idelchik, I. E. and Ginzburg, Ya. L., Simple means to reduce the resistance of short diffusers with large divergence angles, *Vodosnabzh. Sanit. Tekh.*, no. 10, 27–30, 1971.
23. Klyachko, L. S., Pustoshnaya, V. F., and Chemodanova, O. V., Static (snail-like) centrifugal air distributor, *Vopr. Proekt. Montazha Sanit-Tekh. Sistem*, 16–25, (Trudy VNIIGS vyp. 28), Stroiizdat, Moscow, 1970.
24. Lokshin, I. L. and Gazirbekova, A. Kh., Operation of diffusers installed behind centrifugal fans, *Prom. Aerodin.*, no. 6, 127–152, 1955.
25. Nosova, M. M., Resistance of entry and exit pipes with baffles, *Prom. Aerodin.*, no. 7, 95–100, 1956.
26. Nosova, M. M. and Tarasov, N. F., Resistance of intake shafts, *Prom. Aerodin.*, 197–215, Oborengiz, Moscow, 1959.
27. Nosova, M. M. and Barnakova, T. S., Resistance of inlet and outlet orifices in the presence of the passing stream, *Prom. Aerodin.*, no. 15, 20–38, Oborengiz, Moscow, 1959.
28. *Industrial Aerodynamics*, no. 6, BNI MAP, 1956, 181 p.
29. Fedotkin, M. P., On pressure head losses in two-phase flow discharge from tubes, *Izv. VUZov Energ.*, no. 8, 69–77, 1966.
30. Khanzhonkov, V. I., Aerodynamic characteristics of a square ventilation deflector of the Central Aerodynamic Hydrodynamic Institute and of its modifications, *Prom. Aerodin.*, vyp. 1(33), 88–106, Moscow, 1986.

31. Khanzhonkov, V. I., Resistance to discharge through orifices in a wall in the presence of a passing stream, *Prom. Aerodin.*, no. 15, 5–19, Oborengiz, Moscow, 1959.
32. Khanzhonkov, V. N., Resistance of intake shafts, *Prom. Aerodin.*, no. 3, 214–219, 1947.
33. Khanzhonkov, V. N., Resistance of screens, *Prom. Aerodin.*, no. 2, 101–115, 1944.
34. Khanzhonkov, V. N., Improvement of the efficiency of diffusers with large divergence angles by means of plane baffles, *Prom. Aerodin.*, no. 3, 210–214, 1947.
35. Khanzhonkov, V. N., Reduction of the aerodynamic resistance of orifices by circular fins and recesses, *Prom. Aerodin.*, no. 12, 181–198, Oborengiz, Moscow, 1959.
36. Khanzhonkov, V. I. and Davydenko, N. I., Resistance of side orifices of the terminal section of a pipeline, *Prom. Aerodin.*, no. 15, 38–46, 1959.
37. Khanzhonkov, N. N. and Taliev, V. N., Reduction of resistance of square side branches by means of guide vanes, *Tekh. Otchyoty*, no. 10, 16, 1947.
38. Yudin, E. Ya., Elbows with thin guide vanes, *Prom. Aerodin.*, no. 7, 55–80, 1956.
39. Bevier, C. W., Resistance of wooden louvers to fluid flow, *Heat. Piping Air Cond.*, 25–33, May 1955.
40. Cobb, P. R., Pressure loss of air through 45-degree wooden louvers, *Heat. Piping Air Cond.*, 41–45, December 1953.
41. Hofmann, A., Die Energieumsetzung in saugrohrähnlicherweiterten Düsen, *Mitteilungen*, no. 4, 90–95, 1931.

TWELVE

RESISTANCE TO FLOW THROUGH VARIOUS TYPES OF APPARATUS
Resistance Coefficients of Apparatus and other Equipment

12-1 EXPLANATIONS AND PRACTICAL RECOMMENDATIONS; GAS OR AIR SCRUBBERS

1. Gas or air scrubbers can be divided into several groupings according to the principles used for separating the fluid from suspended particles. The resistance of the following is considered here: inertial louver-type dust separators, ordinary and battery-type cyclones, wet scrubbers, porous and cloth filters, and electrostatic filters.

2. In inertial louver-type dust separators, the entering gas flow is split by the louver slats into fine jets and they turn sharply about these slats (Figure 12-1). This gives rise to centrifugal forces under the action of which the dust particles separate from the flow. The impact of the dust particles on the slats and their reflection aids this separation.

The degree to which the gas is cleaned depends on the flow velocity at the moment it reaches the louver slats, the dust particle size and density, the gas viscosity and density, the curvature radius of the trajectory of the jet passing through the louver grating, and the design of the dust separator.

3. The process of separation of suspended particles from the flow in cyclones is based on the utilization of inertial forces during helical motion of the flow in the body of the cyclone, starting at the tangential inlet and ending at the dust discharge orifice in the bottom of the body (Figure 12-2). As the flow moves along the descending (outer) spiral, part of it is directed at decreasing velocity toward the exhaust pipe, while the particles suspended in it are thrown to the wall of the body and continue to move with the remaining part of the flow toward the dust discharge orifice.

A certain portion of the flow that moves along the outer spiral passes through the dust discharge orifice into a receptacle, carrying the suspended particles with it. In the receptacle, the flow gradually loses its velocity, with the result that the particles suspended in it settle out.

The cleaned gas stream then reenters the dust separator body through the same discharge orifice, but along the ascending (inner) spiral. The flow moves along this spiral until it

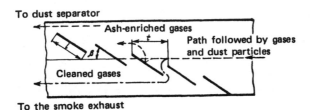

To dust separator

Ash-enriched gases

Path followed by gases
and dust particles

Cleaned gases

To the smoke exhaust

Figure 12-1 Scheme of operation of a louver-type dust separator.

enters the exhaust pipe and continues in this pipe. During this motion the flow recombines
with the part of the flow that is being separated from the descending spiral.

4. The degree to which the flow is cleaned in cyclones depends on the design and
dimensions of the cyclone, velocity of the dust-laden flow, physical properties of the dust
and size of its particles, physical properties of the moving medium, dust concentration, and
other factors. As a rule, cyclones are most effective when dust particles are larger than
5 μm.

5. The capacity or output of a cyclone is a direct function of its hydraulic resistance.
The smaller the resistance coefficient of a cyclone, the larger is its output capacity. Theoretically, the resistance coefficient of a cyclone can be estimated by the method of Klyachko[47]
or of Minksy and Korchazhkin.[62]

The values of the resistance coefficients of different types of cyclones, given in this
handbook, have been determined experimentally.

For the purpose of comparing the operating performance of different types of cyclones,
the most typical characteristic is flow velocity in the body of the cyclone. However, for
calculations it is more convenient to use the inlet velocity. Therefore, two resistance coefficients are given for the cyclones: one utilizing the average inlet velocity [$\zeta_0 \equiv 2\Delta p/(\rho w_0^2)$]
and the other using the average velocity over the body cross section [$\zeta_1 \equiv 2\Delta p/(\rho w_1^2)$].

6. In the case of a cyclone operating in a system where the moving medium discharges
from it into a gas pipeline through a comparatively long straight section ($l/d > 10$) with a
diameter, d, equal to the diameter of the cyclone exhaust pipe, the total pressure losses in

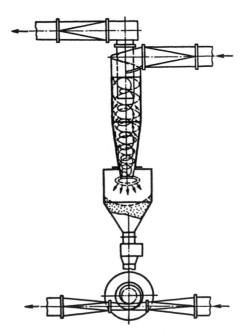

Figure 12-2 Pattern of flow in the body of the cyclone
with a driving volute at the exit.

the cyclone proper are combined with the swirl of losses of the flow and its straightening downstream from the cyclone. In this case, friction losses also increase since the rotational motion increases the velocity gradient in the wall region. All the losses are an inseparable part of the "local" losses in the cyclone.

7. When the cyclone flow discharges into a large volume or into the atmosphere, the whole kinetic energy of the rotating medium issuing from the cyclone into the large volume is lost for this cyclone. This energy is greater than that lost in a straight exit section during deswirling of the jet. It is approximately equal to the value of the kinetic energy based on the average velocity w_{ex} at the cross section of the exit pipe. Therefore, when for the first case (cyclone in the system)

$$\Delta p_{sys} \equiv \zeta_{1sys} \frac{\rho w_1^2}{2}$$

then for the second case (total losses)

$$\Delta p_{tot} = \Delta p_{sys} + \frac{\rho w_{ex}^2}{2} = \Delta p_{sys} + \left(\frac{D_1}{d}\right)^4 \frac{\rho w_1^2}{2}$$

and hence

$$\zeta_{1tot} = \zeta_{1sys} + \left(\frac{D_1}{d}\right)^4$$

where $\zeta_{1sys} \equiv 2\Delta p_{sys}/(\rho w_1^2)$ is the resistance coefficient of a single cyclone operating in the system, and $\zeta_{1tot} \equiv 2\Delta p_{tot}/(\rho w_1^2)$ is the total resistance coefficient of a single cyclone with flow discharge into a large volume.

8. The resistance coefficient of a cyclone ζ_1 depends on the Reynolds number Re $= w_1 D_1/\nu$, but, unlike the conventional friction coefficient, it increases with Re within certain limits, and conversely, decreases with this number. This means that the resistance coefficient also increases with flow velocity w_1 in the cyclone at constant D_1 and ν or with the diameter of the cyclone at constant w_1 and ν. This change in ζ_1 is due to the effect of the friction resistance in a cyclone on the intensity of flow rotation.[30,32] The smaller Re, the higher is the surface friction coefficient λ and, consequently, the stronger the cyclone walls retard the flow during its rotation. Since the major losses in the cyclone are associated with the rotational motion of the medium, a decrease in the intensity of rotation leads to a reduction in the total resistance coefficient of the cyclone.

9. The relative roughness of the cyclone walls and the relative size of the local asperities (protuberances due to welding, seams, etc.) also influence ζ in the same way as Re.

If the absolute roughness of the cyclone walls is constant, the resistance coefficient ζ_1 increases significantly with the cyclone diameter, since in this case the relative roughness decreases and, consequently, the friction coefficient and its retarding effect decrease.

For cyclones of the TsN* type the coefficient ζ_1 increases with the diameter of the cyclone almost up to $D_1 = 500$ mm, after which it can be assumed to be essentially constant.**

---

*This is a specific Russian type.

**Some experiments show that for the cyclones of other types, for example, of the SDK type, the resistance coefficient increases steadily with D_1 (SDK is a Russian pump designation.) The technical data for the types and dimensions of TsN-15 cyclones and also of the cyclones of other types not described in this handbook are given in Reference 15.

10. Increased concentration of suspended particles decreases the cyclone resistance. This is attributable to a large number of factors: lower turbulence of flow in the presence of suspended particles; smaller portion of energy spent for transportation of solid (or liquid) particles and for swirling of the moving medium; and additional retardation of the rotational motion of the medium by the settling solid (or liquid) particles.[30,32] The greater (within certain limits) the concentration of suspended particles in the flow, the greater is the decrease in resistance of the cyclone.*

11. The cyclone resistance decreases significantly if the flow in the exhaust pipe has less swirl. The latter is achieved by installing either a special flow straightener (see scheme a of Diagram 12-2) upstream of the exhaust pipe, or a circular diffuser at the exit from the pipe. A circular diffuser is effective during both operation of a cyclone with discharge into a large volume (see scheme b of Diagram 12-2) and operation in a piping system (see scheme c of Diagram 12-2). Simultaneous use of the flow straightener and the circular diffuser is not efficient.

12. A slight decrease in the cyclone resistance is also provided by a volute casing (see Figure 12-2 and scheme d of Diagram 12-2), which also allows a simultaneous change in direction of the flow by 90°. A change in the flow direction is also provided by an ordinary elbow (see schemes c and e of Diagram 12-2). When an elbow with a 90° turn and $R_0/d = 1.5$ is installed adjacent to the cyclone, the resistance of the latter does not increase. Only when the elbow is installed far downstream from the cyclone (at a distance $l/d > 12$) must its additional resistance be considered.[38]

13. The larger the cyclone diameter, the greater is its output, but with an increase in the diameter the degree of separation decreases. Therefore, in the case of large fluid quantities it is more expedient to use a group of cyclones of smaller diameter, or a battery-type cyclone, instead of a single cyclone of large diameter. Battery-type cyclones differ from grouped cyclones not only in considerably smaller dimensions of the cyclone elements, but also in design. Thus, to ensure rotational motion of the flow in the cyclone elements of a battery-type cyclone, special guide devices are installed (swirlers with blades set at angles of 25–30° toward the cyclone axis or screw vanes, Figure 12-3).

14. The total hydraulic resistance of group-type and battery-type cyclones includes the resistance not only of the cyclone elements, but also of the supply and discharge sections (from section 0–0 to section 2–2; see schemes of Diagrams 12-5 and 12-6). Moreover, the total resistance also accounts for the effect of the inlet conditions into the cyclone elements.

The resistance coefficients ζ_{1gr} of group-type cyclones are calculated with the formulas given in Diagram 12-5, while the coefficients ζ_{1b} for battery-type cyclones are given by the formulas in Diagram 12-6.

15. In many cases it is expedient to use direct-flow cyclones, which have moderate overall dimensions with relatively low resistance coefficients.

Some of these cyclones ensure sufficiently high cleaning or separation (see Diagram 12-7). The efficiency of cleaning depends substantially on the degree of suction $\bar{q} = q/Q$ of a dust-gas mixture from the cyclone receptacle (where q is the quantity of the absorbed dust-gas mixture, m³/s).

16. Diagram 12-7 shows the optimum velocities of the flow in the cross-sectional area of a direct-flow cyclone body at which nearly maximum cleaning efficiency is attained without further increase in the velocity and, hence, in the resistance. The lowest resistance coefficient ($\zeta = 1.5–1.7$) is provided by a cyclone designed by Barakhtenko and Idelchik.[9]

17. Direct-flow cyclones, especially those with blade swirlers, can be easily arranged in groups (batteries). The resistance coefficient of a battery of direct-flow cyclones remains nearly the same as that for a single cyclone.

---

*As long as the energy losses for the transportation of suspended particles do not exceed the resistance mentioned.

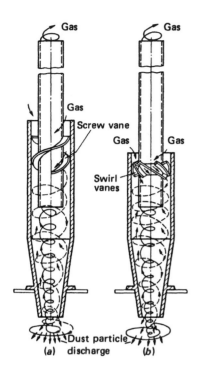

Figure 12-3 Elements of a battery-type dust separator: (*a*) with screw vanes; (*b*) with swirl vanes.

18. Wet-scrubbing apparatus is often used to increase the removal of suspended para-ticles. Improved capture of particles is achieved in wet scrubbers by nozzle spraying the flow with liquid or by a water film on the scrubber surface.

Diagrams 12-8 through 12-12 present values of the resistance coefficients ζ or absolute values of the resistance Δp for various types of wet-scrubbing apparatus.

19. A high-performance type of wet scrubber is the Venturi scrubber, consisting of two main types: a tube-sprayer 1, made in the form of a Venturi tube, and a drop-catcher 2 (Figure 12-4). This apparatus is characterized by a high flow velocity at its throat (60–150 m/s).

The liquid, introduced into the Venturi tube in the form of jets or drops, is fragmented into very minute particles with large total surface area (large number of particles per unit volume) by the high gas flow velocity at the throat. Moreover, the high velocity leads to an increase of the flow turbulence. These factors increase the probability that the liquid and solid particles will collide in a dust-laden gas. Consequently, the process of cleaning in this kind of apparatus can be considered essentially as a coagulation process. The coagulated

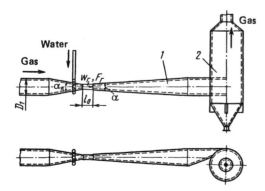

Figure 12-4 Venturi scrubber: (1) Venturi tube; (2) scrubber.

particles are then trapped by the second part of the Venturi scrubber, that is, by the drop-catcher.

20. The resistance coefficient of the Venturi scrubber[64,76,83,84,88] is

$$\zeta \equiv \frac{\Delta p}{\rho_g w_g^2/2} = \zeta_g + \zeta_l \frac{\rho_l}{\rho_g} m_0$$

where $\zeta_g \equiv 2\Delta p_g/(\rho_g w_g^2)$ is the resistance coefficient of the Venturi tube without wetting; $\zeta_l \equiv 2\Delta p_l/(\rho_g w_g)$ is the resistance coefficient of the Venturi tube allowing for the effect of wetting; w_g is the mean velocity of the working gas in the throat of the tube-sprayer, m/s; ρ_g and ρ_l are the densities of the working gas and of the sprayed liquid in the throat of the tube-sprayer, kg/m³; and m_0 is the specific discharge of the wetting liquid, m³/m³.

21. The resistance coefficient of a "dry" Venturi scrubber (without wetting) can be calculated with an approximate formula of Dubinskaya[22,23] derived on the basis of experimental data:

$$\zeta_g = 0.165 + 0.34 \frac{l_0}{D_h} - 3 \times 10^{-3} w_g \left[0.06 + 0.028 \left(\frac{l_0}{D_h} \right) \right] \tag{12-1}$$

where D_h is the hydraulic diameter of the Venturi tube throat, m; l_0 is the length of the throat, m; and the coefficient 3×10^{-3} is dimensional (s/m).

Equation (12-1) is applicable for Venturi tubes of circular and rectangular (slit) cross section with the inner surface finish not more than Ra = 3.2 μm and is valid at $w_g \leqslant 150$ m/s and $0.15 \leqslant l_0/D_h \leqslant 10$.

22. The resistance coefficient of the Venturi scrubber, allowing for wetting, can be calculated from the following empirical formulas derived by Dubinskaya:[22,23]

At $w_g \leqslant 60$ m/s:

$$\zeta_l = 3.5 \left(\frac{l_0}{D_h} \right)^{-0.266} \zeta_g m_0^{B_1} \tag{12-2}$$

At $w > 60$ m/s:

$$\zeta_l = 1.68 \left(\frac{l_0}{D_h} \right)^{0.29} \zeta_g m_0^{B_2} \tag{12-3}$$

where

$$B_1 = 1 - 0.98 \left(\frac{l_0}{D_h} \right)^{+0.026} \tag{12-4}$$

$$B_2 = 1 - 1.12 \left(\frac{l_0}{D_h} \right)^{-0.045} \tag{12-5}$$

Equations (12-2) to (12-5) have been obtained for the cases where wetting liquid is supplied through a sprayer or tip into the converging portion of Venturi tubes of circular or rectangular (slit) cross section at $0.15 \leqslant l_0/D_h \leqslant 12$.

23. Due to design and practical considerations, use is frequently made of battery turbulent scrubbers composed of several tens of small Venturi scrubbers. To calculate the resistance coefficient ζ_l of a battery of Venturi tubes of circular cross section (at $D_h \approx 90–100$ mm, $\alpha_{con} \approx 60–65°$, $\alpha \approx 7°$, $l_0/D_h = 0.15$) with liquid supplied to a converging portion of each Venturi tube through mechanical sprayers of various types, Dubinskaya[22,23] recommends the following empirical formula:

$$\zeta_l = 0.215 \zeta_g m_0^{-0.54}$$

24. The hydraulic resistance of the drop-catcher is determined depending on the selected type of this apparatus.

25. A wet dust-catcher supplied with perforated plates (see the scheme of Diagram 12-10) displays different hydrodynamic regimes on interaction of the gas with the liquid:

- Regime of a wetted perforated plate
- Bubbling regime
- Foam regime
- Wavy regime

Usually, the dust-catcher operates in a foam regime.

26. The resistance of the perforated plate with a layer of foam is determined from the formula suggested by Waldberg[66,76,88]

$$\Delta p = 0.5 \, A^2 \frac{\rho_g w_g^2}{2\bar{f}^2} + \Delta p_\sigma$$

where

$$A = 39 L^{-0.57} \left[\left(\frac{L}{G} \right)^{0.7} \left(\frac{\rho_g}{\rho_l} \right) \right]^{0.35}$$

$\bar{f} = F_{or}/F_{gr}$ is the clear area coefficient of the grid (perforated plate); w_g is the gas flow velocity in a free cross-section of the apparatus, m/s; L and G are mass flow rates of liquid and gas, respectively, through a unit surface of the grid, kg/m² s; and Δp_σ is the hydraulic resistance induced by the surface tension forces, Pa.

For slit grids

$$\Delta p_\sigma = \frac{2\sigma}{b_{sl}}$$

For hole grids (from the formula suggested by D. S. Artamonov)

$$\Delta p_\sigma = \frac{4\sigma}{1.3 d_{or} + 0.08 d_{or}^2}$$

where σ is the surface tension at the gas-liquid interface, N/m; d_{or} is the diameter of the grid orifice, m; and b_{sl} is the width of the grid slit, m.*

27. Oil-type filters are used for removal of relatively large particles (above 10 μm) from air supplied to the room. Air is cleaned as a result of inertial separation of dust particles on the surface of a porous layer and binding of the particles on these surfaces by oil films.

The hydraulic resistance of unified cell filters of the F_c** type are given in Diagram 12-13 (F_cR** is a filter of the Rekk** design filled with corrugated viniplast screen; F_cPF** is a filter treated with polyurethane foam; F_cEG** is treated with the filtering material GFE**, which is an elastic fiberglass.[70,77]

28. In bag-type filters gas cleaning is achieved by filtering through a cloth that captures the dust. The main pressure losses in bag-type filters occur in cloth filters. Their resistance can therefore be estimated on the basis of the resistance of various types of cloth.

Diagrams 12-14 through 12-17 show the characteristics and resistances of various types of filters (FVK, VRU, FRP, FYaL, and AFA).**

More detailed information on bag-type and other filters are presented in References 15 and 17.

29. Secondary (fine) ventilation filters provide cleaning of the inflow and outflow air, as well as of the air-conditioning and recirculation systems.[68] Among them the most common design is the LAKI** frame filter (from the Laboratory of Aerosols of the Karpov Physicochemical Institute) (Diagram 12-16).

Within the filtration rate limits $w = 0.01-0.1$ m/s, the resistance of the LAKI filter is about twice the resistance of filtering material FP (the filtering material of Petryanov), which is equipped with this material.

30. Within filtration rates up to $w = 10-20$ m/s the proportionality of the resistance Δp to the rate w is preserved for FP** materials

$$\Delta p = \Delta p_0 w$$

where Δp_0 is the standard resistance, i.e., the resistance in Pa at $w = 1$ m/s.

The resistance of filtering materials (Pa) can be determined from the formula of Fuks-Stechkina:

$$\Delta p = 9.81 \frac{4w\mu m_1}{a^2\rho_p(-1.15 \lg \beta - \varepsilon)}$$

where m_1 is the density of filters; ρ_p is the density of a polymer of the material fibers; β is the density of packing (a fraction of the layer volume occupied by fibers); a is the fiber radius; and ε is a coefficient, which equals 0.75 for parallel fibers and 0.4 for a system of isotropically distributed fibers (similar to the FP materials).

The formula is valid only in the case when the radius of the filter fibers is much larger than the mean free path of the gas molecules.

31. The FP materials are also used in analytical aerosol filters AFA intended to control and analyze the contamination of air with aerosol admixtures. Such filters are characterized by high retentivity, which allows them to capture practically all the particles in the air irrespective of their size.

32. In order to capture dust, use is also made of bed filters made of loose or lump materials (sand, gravel, slag, Raschig rings, etc.), filters made of sets of metallic wire cloth screens or specially prepared porous materials, paper filters, etc.

*Technical data on other particular types of scrubbers are given in Reference 15.
**Russian designations.

The hydraulic resistance of such filters can be determined from the same data used for nozzles and screens (see Chapter 8).

33. In industrial electrostatic filters of almost all types the pressure losses mainly consist of (1) losses at the entry into the working chamber (electric fields), (2) losses at the exit from the working chamber (last electric field), and (3) losses during passage through the interelectrode space (in the case of an electrostatic filter the losses between the settling plates, and in the case of a pipe electrostatic filter the losses along the settling pipes).

The total resistance coefficient of an electrostatic filter is

$$\zeta \equiv \frac{2\Delta p}{\rho w_0^2} = \zeta_{in} + \zeta_{ex} + \zeta_{ch}$$

where ζ_{in} is the resistance coefficient of the inlet section of the apparatus; ζ_{ex} is the resistance coefficient of the exit section; and ζ_{ch} is the resistance coefficient of the working chamber (electric fields) of the apparatus with settling elements. All of the coefficients are based on the velocity w_0.

34. In electrostatic filters, similar to other industrial apparatus, the gas expands suddenly upon entering the working chamber* (see the schemes of Diagram 12-19). Therefore, the resistance coefficient of the inlet, in the absence of gas-distributing devices, can be determined from

$$\zeta_{in} \equiv \frac{\Delta p_{in}}{\rho w_0^2/2} = N_0 \left(1 - \frac{2}{3n_1}\right) + \frac{1}{n_1^2}\frac{4}{3n_1}$$

where $n_1 = F_{ch}/F_0$ is the area ratio of the apparatus (ratio of the working chamber area to the inlet orifice area); $N_0 = (1/F) \int_{F_0} (w/w_0)^3 \, dF$ is the kinetic energy coefficient, characterizing the velocity distribution at the inlet.

The values of this coefficient, as well as of the momentum coefficient $M_0 = (1/F_0) \int_{F_0} (w/w_0)^2 \, dF$ (very approximately) are given in Tables 12-1 through 12-7 for different cases of flow entrance into the apparatus.

35. The resistance coefficient of discharge from an apparatus (electrostatic filter) through a converging nozzle or discharge with a sudden contraction (see schemes of Diagram 12-19) can be determined on the basis of Equation (3-1) as

$$\zeta_{ex} \equiv \frac{\Delta p_{ex}}{\rho w_0^2/2} = \zeta' \left(1 - \frac{F_{ex}}{F_{ch}}\right)\left(\frac{F_0}{F_{ex}}\right)^2$$

where ζ' is a coefficient determined as ζ of the inlet section from Diagrams 3-1, 3-2, 3-4, and 3-7; F_{ex} is the area of the narrowest cross section of the exit length, m².

36. The resistance coefficient of the working chamber in the form of a tubular electrostatic filter is

$$\zeta_{ch} = \zeta_{el} = \frac{\Delta p_{ch}}{\rho w_0^2/2} = \zeta'_{in} + \zeta'_{ex} + \zeta_{fr},$$

where $\zeta'_{in} = 0.5(1 - F_{el}/F_{ch})(F_0/F_{el})^2$ is the resistance coefficient of the inlet to settling tubes; $\zeta'_{ex} = (1 - F_{el}/F_{ch})^2(F_0/F_{el})^2$ is the resistance coefficient of discharge from settling

*In cases when the flow enters through diffusers (horizontal electrostatic filters), it is possible to consider that there is a sudden expansion, since the diffuser divergence angle generally exceeds 60–90°.

Table 12-1 Elbow $\delta = 45°$; $r/b_0 = 0$

Coefficients	$\dfrac{x}{b_0'}$		
	0–1.2	3.25	$\geqslant 5.0$
M_0	1.12	1.08	1.02
N_0	1.36	1.25	1.06

Table 12-2 Elbow $\delta = 90°$; $r/b_0 = 0$; $b_0'/b_0 = 1.0$

Coefficients	$\dfrac{x}{b_0'}$			
	1.2	3.0	6.0	10
M_0	1.80	1.50	1.10	1.02
N_0	3.50	2.80	1.30	1.06

Table 12-3 Elbow $\delta = 90°$; $r/b_0 = 0.1$; $b_0'/b_1 = 1$

Coefficients	$\dfrac{x}{b_0}$				
	0–0.5	1.5	3.0	6.0	8.0
M_0	1.40	1.25	1.12	1.06	1.02
N_0	2.30	1.75	1.36	1.18	1.06

Table 12-4 Elbow $\delta = 90°$; with expansion ($F_0'/F_0 = 1.3$); $r/b_0 = 0.18$

Coefficients	$\dfrac{x}{b_0'}$				
	0–0.5	1.5	3.0	6.0	10
M_0	1.70	1.40	1.25	1.10	1.02
N_0	3.20	2.30	1.75	1.30	1.06

Table 12-5 Bend $\delta = 90°$; $r/b_0 = 0.5$; $R_0/b_0 = 1.5$

Coefficients	$\dfrac{x}{b_0}$				
	0–0.5	1.0	2.0	3.0	4.0
M_0	1.25	1.13	1.07	1.03	1.02
N_0	1.80	1.40	1.21	1.10	1.06

Table 12-6 Diffuser of circular or rectangular cross section with expansion in two planes

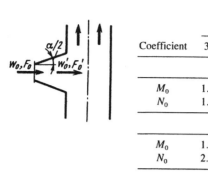

Coefficient								
	3.0	4.0	6.0	10	3.0	4.0	6.0	10
	$\alpha = 6°$				$\alpha = 10°$			
M_0	1.15	1.20	1.40	1.25	1.20	1.30	1.90	1.40
N_0	1.45	1.60	2.20	1.75	1.60	1.90	3.70	2.20
	$\alpha = 15°$				$\alpha = 30°$			
M_0	1.50	1.85	2.30	1.80	2.00	2.50	3.10	2.55
N_0	2.50	3.50	4.80	3.40	4.00	5.30	7.20	5.70
	$\alpha = 45°$				$\alpha = 60°$			
M_0	2.50	2.90	3.90	4.50	2.70	3.30	4.50	5.90
N_0	6.00	6.90	9.70	11.5	5.80	8.00	11.5	15.7
	$\alpha = 90°$				$\alpha = 180°$			
M_0	2.80	3.75	5.20	7.00	4.00	5.10	7.30	9.00
N_0	6.90	9.00	13.5	19.0	10.0	13.0	20.0	25.0

Header above table: $n_1 = \dfrac{F_0'}{F_0}$

Table 12-7 Plane diffuser

$$n_1 = F_0'/F_0$$

Coefficients	1.21	1.40	1.60	1.86	2.07	2.28
			$\alpha°$			
	2	4	6	8	10	12
M_0	1.0	1.07	1.11	1.15	1.20	1.27
N_0	1.0	1.28	1.33	1.45	1.60	1.86

Table 12-7 Plane diffuser

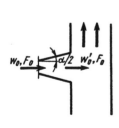

Header above table: $n_1 = \dfrac{F_0'}{F_0}$

Coefficients	3.0	4.0	6.0	10	3.0	4.0	6.0	10
	$\alpha = 6°$				$\alpha = 10°$			
M_0	1.10	1.15	1.35	1.15	1.12	1.20	1.60	1.30
N_0	1.30	1.45	2.05	1.45	1.36	1.60	2.80	1.90
	$\alpha = 15°$				$\alpha = 30°$			
M_0	1.40	1.50	1.70	1.40	1.80	2.50	2.20	1.80
N_0	2.20	2.50	3.10	2.20	3.40	5.40	4.60	3.40
	$\alpha = 45°$				$\alpha = 60°$			
M_0	2.00	2.60	2.30	2.00	2.10	2.90	3.70	3.50
N_0	4.00	5.80	4.90	4.00	4.30	7.00	9.00	8.50
	$\alpha = 90°$				$\alpha = 180°$			
M_0	2.25	3.20	4.80	6.60	3.00	4.50	7.00	8.00
N_0	5.10	7.80	13.5	17.0	7.00	11.5	19.0	22.0

tubes; $\zeta_{fr} = \; = \lambda l_{el}/D_{el}(F_0/F_{el})^2$ is the friction coefficient of settling tubes; F_{el} is the total cross-sectional area of the settling tubes; D_{el} and l_{el} are their diameter and length.

37. The resistance coefficient of a plate electrostatic filter can be determined from the author's formula:

$$\zeta_{ch} = \zeta_{el} = \frac{\Delta p}{\rho w_0^2/2} = n_f k_{pr}(\zeta_{elec} + 0.5 n_{el})(F_0/F_{ch})^2$$

where ζ_{elec} is the resistance coefficient of the interelectrode channel which depends on the shape of settling electrodes, the shape of the corona electrodes, and of the supports in the frame of their fixturing; calculations show that the value of this coefficient lies within the range 0.2–0.3; n_{el} is the number of elements of the settling electrodes in one electric field; n_f is the number of electric fields; $k_{pr} \equiv \zeta_{el}^{pr}/\zeta_{el}^{abs}$ is the ratio of the resistance coefficient of the interelectrode channel in the presence of the corona discharge to this coefficient in the absence of this discharge; this ratio depends on the gas flow velocity in the electrostatic filter: it is the higher, the smaller the velocity (Figure 12-5).

38. Many devices besides electrostatic filters are provided with gas-distributing grids to ensure uniform distribution of the flow after its entrance into the working chamber. The entire portion, from the final section of the inlet pipe, including the perforated plate (grid), can be considered as a single unit.

The flow into the working chamber in the majority of industrial devices can be categorized into three types of flow impingement on the perforated plates (grid): (1) central (frontal) (Figure 12-6a); (2) peripheral (Figure 12-6b); and (3) lateral (Figure 12-6c) impingement.

Either a single grid or a system of grids in series is used depending on the ratio F_{ch}/F_0.[27,28]

39. The resistance coefficient of the inlet section of apparatus with frontal incidence of the flow on the perforated plate (grid)* is calculated from the author's formula:[27,28]

$$\zeta_{in} = \zeta \equiv \frac{\Delta p}{\rho w_0^2/2}$$

$$= \zeta'_{0be} + N_0 + 0.7 \zeta_{gr} \left(\frac{F_0}{F_{ch}}\right)^2 + \frac{0.013}{(H_{gr}/D_0)^2} \sqrt[3]{\zeta_{gr}} - 3\sqrt{\zeta_{gr}} \qquad (12\text{-}6)$$

*This includes not only a plane grid (perforated sheet), but also other types of uniformly distributed resistances (different nozzles or layers of lumped or loose materials, etc.).

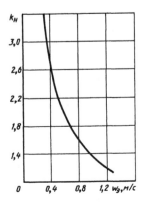

Figure 12-5 Dependence of the coefficient k_n on w_e for the electric field length $L = 6$ m and electric voltage of 45 kV.[87]

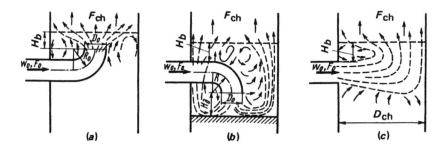

Figure 12-6 Different methods of flow supply introduction to the apparatus: (*a*) central impingement of flow on a gas-distributing grid; (*b*) peripheral impingement of flow on a gas-distributing grid; (*c*) lateral impingement of flow on a gas-distributing grid.

where $\zeta'_{0be} = 0.5\zeta_{0be}$; ζ_{0be} is the resistance coefficient of the bend through which the flow is discharged against the grid, and is determined as ζ from the corresponding diagrams of Chapter 6; ζ_{gr} is the resistance coefficient of the grid determined as ζ from Diagrams of Chapter 8; and H_{gr} is the distance from the exit orifice of the intake bend to the grid, m.

The last term on the right-hand side of Equation (12-6) applies only for $H_{gr}/D_0 < 1.2$.

40. The resistance coefficient of the inlet section of the apparatus with peripheral incidence of the flow on the grid[28] is

$$\zeta_{in} = \zeta \equiv \frac{\Delta p}{\rho w_0^2/2} = \zeta'_{0be} + 0.9\left[N_0 + 0.7\zeta_{gr}\left(\frac{F_0}{F_{ch}}\right)^2\right] + \frac{0.05}{(H_b/D_0)^2} \qquad (12\text{-}7)$$

where H_b is the distance from the exit orifice of the intake bend to the bottom of the apparatus or to a baffle (if a baffle is installed behind the bend).

The last term on the right-hand side of Equation (12-7) applies only for $H_b/D_0 < 1.2$.

41. The resistance coefficient of the inlet section of the apparatus with lateral incidence of the flow on the grid[27,28] is

$$\zeta_{in} = \zeta \equiv \frac{\Delta p}{\rho w_0^2/2} - N_0 + 0.7\zeta_{gr}\left(\frac{F_0}{F_{ch}}\right)^2 + 0.1 + \left(2 - 20\frac{H_{gr}}{D_{ch}}\right) \qquad (12\text{-}8)$$

where D_{ch} is the diameter or large side of the chamber cross section, m.

The last term on the right-hand side of Equation (12-8) applies only for $H_{gr}/D_{ch} < 0.1$.

42. In the case of a series of perforated plates (grids), the resistance coefficient of the inlet section is determined from Equations (12-6) to (12-8), but with ζ_{gr} replaced by the sum of the resistance coefficients of all the grids of the series reduced to the same velocity w_{ch}[27]

$$\sum_{i=1}^{m_{gr}} \zeta_{ch,gr,i} = \zeta_{ch,gr,1} + \zeta_{ch,gr,2} + \dots + \zeta_{ch,gr,m}$$

$$= \zeta_{gr,1}\left(\frac{F_{ch}}{F_1}\right)^2 + \zeta_{gr,2}\left(\frac{F_{ch}}{F_2}\right)^2 + \dots \zeta_{gr,i}\left(\frac{F_{ch}}{F_i}\right)^2 + \dots \zeta_{gr,m}$$

where m_{gr} is the number of grids in the series.

43. Flow supply to the electrostatic filters is often accomplished according to the schemes shown in Figure 12-7a–d. For a more uniform distribution of the flow and its passage parallel to the axis of the filter in the places of its turning to the working chamber (electrodes),

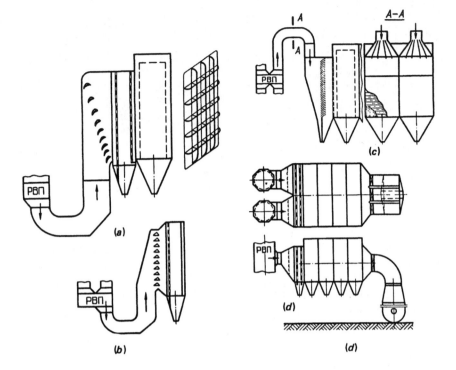

Figure 12-7 Different methods of flow supply introduction to electrostatic filters: (*a*) and (*b*) from below with a 90° turn; distributors are of the NIIOGAZ and MEI design, respectively; (*c*) from above with a 90° turn; (*d*) frontal through a double diffuser.

guide vanes are installed (the NIIOGAZ* scheme, Figure 12-7*a*) or spatial corners (MEF* scheme, Figure 12-7*b*). In the case of the frontal (central) supply of the flow to the electrostatic filter (Figure 12-7*d*) dividing walls are installed to have a better velocity distribution in the diffuser (see Figure 5-19*d* and *e*). In this case the inlet resistance coefficient ζ_{in} decreases noticeably (by 20–30%) compared with the value given by Equation (12-8).[34,35] Information on specific types of electrostatic filters is given in References 15 and 101.

Heat Exchangers

1. The total pressure losses in honeycomb radiators, used for cooling air, are made up of the losses at the entry into the radiator tube, the frictional losses in the tubes, and the losses at sudden expansion of flow during discharge from the tubes into the common channel. The resistance coefficient of a honeycomb radiator is determined from Mariyamov's[61] formula:

$$\zeta \equiv \frac{\Delta p}{\rho_{in} w_1^2/2} = \lambda\left(3 + \frac{l_0}{d_h}\right)\left(\frac{F_1}{F_0}\right)^2 + \left(\frac{F_1}{F_0} - 1\right)^2 + \left(1.7 + \lambda\frac{l_0}{d_h}\right)\left(\frac{F_1}{F_0}\right)^2 \overline{T}$$

$$= \lambda\left(3 + \frac{l_0}{d_h}\right)\left(\frac{F_1}{F_0}\right)^2 + \zeta_{el} + \Delta\zeta_t$$

*Russian designations. NIIOGAZ = Scientific Research Institute for Gas; MEI = Moscow Power Engineering Institute.

where $\zeta_{el} = (F_1/F_0 - 1)^2$; $\Delta\zeta_t = [1.7 + \lambda(l_0/d_h)](F_1/F_0)^2\,\overline{T}$; $d_h = 4F_0/\Pi_0$; $\overline{T} = (T_{ex} - T_{in})/T_{in}$ is the ratio of the difference between the temperatures of the outflowing and incoming streams to the temperature of the incoming stream; $\lambda = 2\Delta p/(\rho w_0^2)(l_0/d_h)$ is the linear friction coefficient along the tube length (depth) of the radiator; and the subscript "0" shows that the corresponding quantities refer to the tube of the radiator.

2. For honeycomb radiators with circular and hexagonal tubes the friction coefficient[61] is

$$\lambda = 0.375\mathrm{Re}^{*-0.1}\,\overline{\Delta}^{0.4}$$

within $35 < \mathrm{Re}^* \leqslant 275$;

$$\lambda = 0.214\,\overline{\Delta}^{0.4}$$

within $275 \leqslant \mathrm{Re}^* \leqslant 500$, where $\mathrm{Re}^* = W_{0in}\,\Delta/\nu$; $\overline{\Delta} = \Delta/d_h$ is the relative roughness of the radiator tubes.

3. The total pressure losses in tubular-finned and tubular-plate radiators are made up of the frictional losses and the losses at contraction and expansion of the flow during its passage from one row of tubes to another.

The resistance coefficient of such radiators[60] is

$$\zeta \equiv \frac{\Delta p}{\rho_{in}w_1^2/2} = \left(z\zeta_c + \lambda\frac{l_0}{d_h}\right)\left(\frac{F_1}{F_0}\right)^2 + \left(1.7 + \lambda\frac{l_0}{d_h}\right)\left(\frac{F_1}{F_0}\right)^2\overline{T}$$

$$= \left(z\zeta_c + \lambda\frac{l_0}{d_h}\right)\left(\frac{F_1}{F_0}\right)^2 + \Delta\zeta_t$$

where $\zeta_c = 1.5(1 - F_0/F_0')^2$; $\Delta\zeta_t = [1.7 + \lambda(l_0/d_h)](F_1/F_0)^2\,\overline{T}$; $d_h = 2b_0h_2/(b_0 + h_2)$; F_0' is the area of the narrowest cross section of the radiator (between the tubes), m²; F_0 is the cross-sectional area of the channels between the plates in the zone between the rows, m²; z_r is the number of rows of tubes; b_0 is the mean gap between the fins or plates, m; and h_2 is the gap between adjacent tubes of the radiator, m.

4. The friction coefficient for the tubular-finned radiators within $3000 < \mathrm{Re} = w_{0in}d_h/\nu < 25{,}000$[60] is

$$\lambda = \frac{0.77}{\sqrt[3]{\mathrm{Re}}}$$

5. The friction coefficient for the tubular-plate radiators within $4 \times 10^3 \leqslant \mathrm{Re} = w_{0in}d_h/\nu \leqslant 10^4$ is[60]

$$\lambda = \frac{0.98}{\sqrt[3]{\mathrm{Re}}}$$

and at $\mathrm{Re} > 10^4$

$$\lambda = \frac{0.21}{\sqrt[6]{\mathrm{Re}}}$$

6. The resistance of heaters is similar to the resistance of radiators (coolers). It also consists of the losses at the entrance, the frictional losses, and the shock losses at discharge from the narrow section between the tubes and plates of the heater. The main parameter used for the selection of a heater is the mass velocity at its clear cross section $\rho_m w$ (where ρ_m is the mean density of the heated air passing through the heater, kg/m³). Therefore, the resistance of heaters is given in the form of the dependence of Δp (Pa) on $\rho_m w_0$ (kg/m² s).

The technological characteristics and constructional dimensions of modern heaters are given in the work of Staroverov.[77]

7. In cross flow, heat exchanger tubes are arranged in both in-line and staggered configurations. With a flow through a bundle of tubes arranged in an in-line fashion, the jets discharge from the space between the tubes of the first row, expanding in the intrarow space (Figure 12-8). The main core of the flow entrains the fluid masses from the shadow regions. On approaching the second row of tubes, the jets separate. The main core of the flow passes the second row of tubes while the entrained masses form a closed circulating flow (eddy zone) in the shadow regions. The pattern of flow in the subsequent intrarow spaces is similar to that described above.* Thus, the nature of the pressure losses in a tube bundle is similar to that in a free jet.[1]

8. The values of the resistance coefficients of tube bundles depend on the number of rows and the distribution of tubes, as well as on the Reynolds number Re. Their flow velocity is determined on the basis of the contracted section of the fluid passage located in the axial plane of tubes normal to the flow. The resistance coefficient of the bundle of tubes also considers the resistance at the inlet to and exit from the rows of tubes.

9. The resistance coefficient of a staggered smooth-wall bundle of tubes within $3 \times 10^3 < \mathrm{Re}_m < 10^5$ is calculated from the following equations:[6,58]

1) $S_1/d_{\mathrm{ch}} < 1.44$ and $0.1 \leqslant \bar{s} < 1.7$:

$$\zeta \equiv \frac{\Delta p}{\rho_m w_{0m}^2/2} = \{3.2 + 0.66(1.7 - \bar{s})^{1.5}$$

$$+ (13.1 - 9.1 S_1/d_{\mathrm{out}})[0.8 + 0.2(1.7 - \bar{s})^{1.5}]\}\mathrm{Re}_m^{-0.27}(z_p + 1); \qquad (12\text{-}9)$$

2) $S_1/d_{\mathrm{out}} \geqslant 1.44$ and $0.1 \leqslant \bar{s} < 1.7$:

$$\zeta = 3.2 + 0.66(1.7 - \bar{s})^{1.5}\,\mathrm{Re}_m^{-0.27}(z_p + 1); \qquad (12\text{-}10)$$

3) $S_1/d_{\mathrm{out}} < 1.44$ and $1.7 \leqslant \bar{s} \leqslant 6.5$:

$$\zeta = (1.88 - S_1/d_{\mathrm{out}})(\bar{s} + 1)^2\,\mathrm{Re}_m^{-0.27}(z_p + 1); \qquad (12\text{-}11)$$

4) $1.44 \leqslant S_1/d_{\mathrm{out}} \leqslant 3.0$ and $1.7 \leqslant \bar{s} \leqslant 6.5$:

$$\zeta = 0.44(\bar{s} + 1)^2\mathrm{Re}_m^{-0.27}(z_p + 1); \qquad (12\text{-}12)$$

5) $3 < S_1/d_{\mathrm{out}} \leqslant 10$ and $\bar{s} > 1.7$:

$$\zeta = 1.83(S_1/d_{\mathrm{out}})^{-1.46}\mathrm{Re}_m^{-0.27}(z_p + 1); \qquad (12\text{-}13)$$

---

*Actually, the flow, on passing the first transverse row of tubes, becomes turbulent and thereby slightly alters the conditions of flow past the subsequent rows.

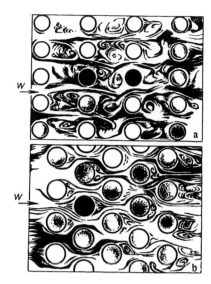

Figure 12-8 Tube bundle: (a) in-line; (b) staggered.

where $w_{0m} = w_{in}T_m/T_{in}$; $T_m = (T_{in} + T_{ex})/2$; $\rho_m = 273\,\rho_0/T_m$; $\mathrm{Re}_m = w_{0m}d_{out}/\nu$; $\bar{s} = (S_1 - d_{out})/(s_2' - d_{out})$; where z_r is the number of rows of tubes over the tube depth; ν is taken with respect to the arithmetic mean temperature T_m from Section 1-2.

The resistance coefficient reduced to the velocity upstream of the tube bundle is given in terms of the coefficient ζ:

$$\zeta_1 \equiv \frac{\Delta p}{\rho_1 w_1^2/2} = \zeta\left(\frac{\rho_1}{\rho_m}\right)^2\left(\frac{F_1}{F_0}\right)^2$$

10. The resistance coefficient of an in-line smooth-wall bundle of tubes within $3 \times 10^3 < \mathrm{Re}_m < 10^{5*}$ is [12,58]

$S_1/d_{out} \leq S_2/d_{out}$ and $0.06 \leq \bar{s}_1 \leq 1.0$:

$$\zeta \equiv \frac{\Delta p}{\rho_m w_{0m}^2/2} = 1.8\left(\frac{S_1}{d_{out}} - 1\right)^{-0.5}\mathrm{Re}_m^{-0.2}z_r \tag{12-14}$$

$S_1/d_{out} > S_2/d_{out}$:
$1.0 < \bar{s}_1 \leq 8.0$:

$$\zeta = 0.34\left(\bar{s}_1 - 0.94\right)^{-0.59}\left(\frac{S_1}{d_{out}} - 1\right)^{-0.5}\mathrm{Re}_m^{-0.2}\,\bar{s}_1^2 z_r \tag{12-15}$$

where $\bar{s}_1 = (S_1 - d_{out})/(S_2 - d_{out})$.

If the pitches S_1 and S_2 vary within the bundle, the resistance is calculated from their average value.

11. It is recommended[65] that calculation of bundles with nonuniform transverse pitches (Figure 12-9) be based on the mean resistance coefficient ζ_m which is determined from Equation (12-16) and which takes into account the difference of both the geometries of the channels and flow velocities in the channels of different cross sections.

---

*Equations (12-14) and (12-15) are somewhat refined as recommended in Reference 65.

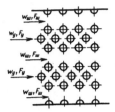

Figure 12-9 Tube bundle with a variable pitch.

The formula for determining the value of ζ_m reduced to the mean discharge flow velocity has the form

$$\zeta_m = \zeta_{\text{nar}} \left[\frac{F}{F_{\text{nar}} + F_{\text{br}}\sqrt{\zeta_{\text{nar}}/\zeta_{\text{br}}}} \right]$$

$$= \zeta_{\text{nar}} \left\{ \frac{n_{\text{pas}}[(s_1/d_{\text{out}})_m - 1]}{n_{\text{nar}}[(s_1/d_{\text{out}})_{\text{nar}} - 1] + n_{\text{br}}[(s_1/d_{\text{out}})_{\text{br}} - 1]\sqrt{\zeta_{\text{nar}}/\zeta_{\text{br}}}} \right\} \quad (12\text{-}16)$$

where F is the axial cross section of the transverse row of tubes for flow passage; n_{pas} is the number of passages between the transverse rows of tubes; ζ_{nar} and ζ_{br} are the resistance coefficients of the bundles with "narrow"$[(s_1/d_{\text{out}})_{\text{nar}}]$ and "broad" $[(s_1/d_{\text{out}})_{\text{br}}]$ transverse pitches. The latter two are calculated not only as functions of the actual pitches s_1/d_{out} and parameters $\bar{s}$ and $\bar{s}_1$, but also with respect to the number Re based on the mean flow velocity.

12. In the case of heat transfer in a bundle of tubes, the values of ζ in Equations (12-9) to (12-16) should be supplemented with the term $\Delta\zeta_t$, which allows for the acceleration (deceleration) pressure losses within the bundle due to a decrease (increase) of the density of the working medium:[63]

$$\Delta\zeta_t = 2\frac{T_{\text{ex}} - T_{\text{in}}}{T_m}$$

(see paragraph 33 of Chapter 8).

13. With oblique fluid flow over a bundle of tubes its resistance decreases,[42] since the condition of the flow past the tubes is thus improved. The degree of reduction of the resistance (the flow "direction" coefficient) $\psi = \zeta_\theta/\zeta_{90°}$ depends on both the angle of inclination θ and the other parameters of the bundle. However, the effect of other parameters can be neglected in practical calculations by assuming the average value of ψ to be constant for each inclination angle. Average values of ψ are given below:

In-line bundle   *Staggered bundle*
$\theta = 60°, \psi = 0.82$ $\theta = 60°, \psi = 0.80$
$\theta = 45°, \psi = 0.54$ $\theta = 45°, \psi = 0.57$
$\theta = 30°, \psi = 0.30$ $\theta = 30°, \psi = 0.34$

14. In order to increase the heating (cooling) surface it is a frequent practice to use finned and tailed tubes.

The resistance coefficient of a bundle of staggered finned tubes (see scheme of Diagram 12-30)[6] is

$$\zeta \equiv \frac{\Delta p}{\rho_m w_{0m}^2/2} = c_z c_s \text{Re}_l^{-0.25} z$$

where $c_z = f(z_r)$ is the correction for the number of rows or tubes with few rows ($z_r \leqslant 5$); at $z_r \geqslant 6$, $c_z = 1.0$ (see Diagram 12-30).

At $l/d_h = 0.16\text{--}6.55$ and $\text{Re}_l = 2.2 \times 10^3\text{--}1.8 \times 10^5$

$$c_s = 5.4\left(\frac{l}{d_h}\right)^{0.3}$$

At $\text{Re}_l > 1.8 \times 10^5$

$$\zeta = 0.26 \left(\frac{l}{d_h}\right)^{0.3} c_z(z_r + 1)$$

where $\text{Re}_l = w_{0m}l/\nu$.

For tubes with round fins

$$l = \frac{(D^2 - d_{\text{out}}^2)m_f}{2L\beta} + \frac{(D^2 + d_{\text{out}}^2)m_f}{2d_{\text{out}}L\beta}\sqrt{0.785(D^2 - d_{\text{out}}^2)} \tag{12-17}$$

where D is the diameter with respect to the tips of fins (fin diameter), m; L is the tube length, m; β is the fin coefficient (ratio of the total surface area to the surface area of the smooth tube of diameter d_{out}); and m is the number of fins per tube with total surface area H_{fin}.

The hydraulic diameter is

$$d_h = \frac{4F_0}{\Pi_0} = \frac{2[S_{f\delta}(S_1 - d_{\text{out}}) - 2\delta h]}{2h + S_{f\delta}} \tag{12-18}$$

where h and δ are the height and thickness of the fins, respectively, m; and $S_{f\delta}$ is the distance between medium planes of the two neighboring fins, m.

For tubes with square fins

$$l = \frac{\pi d_{\text{out}}^2(S_{f\delta} - \delta)}{H/m_f} + \frac{2[(2h + d_{\text{out}})^2 - 0.785d_{\text{out}}^2] + 4(2h + d_{\text{out}})\delta}{H/m_f}$$
$$\times \sqrt{(2h + d_{\text{out}})^2 - 0.785d_{\text{out}}^2} \tag{12-19}$$

where

$$\frac{H}{m_f} = \pi d_{\text{out}}(S_{f\delta} - \delta) + 2[(2h + d_{\text{out}})^2 - 0.785d_{\text{out}}^2] + 4(2h + d_{\text{out}})\delta \tag{12-20}$$

H is the total surface area of a finned tube, m².

15. The resistance coefficient of a bundle with an in-line arrangement of finned tubes[6] is

$$\zeta \equiv \frac{\Delta p}{\rho_m w_{0m}^2/2} = c_z' c_s' \, \text{Re}_l^{-0.08} z_r$$

where $c_z' = f(z_r)$ is the correction for the number of rows for a bundle with few rows ($z_r \leq 5$); at $z_r \geq 6$, $c_z = 1.0$ (see Diagram 12-30). At $l/d_h = 0.9$–11.0, $\bar{S}_1 = 0.5$–2.0 and $Re_1 = 4.3 \times 10^3$–1.6×10^5

$$c_s' = 0.52 \left(\frac{l}{d_h}\right)^{0.3} (\bar{S}_1)^{-0.68}$$

16. To decrease the resistance of a tube bundle in cross flow, streamlined tubes are often used. Information that can be used to determine the resistance coefficients of streamlined and other types of tubes in a bundle is given in Diagram 12-31.

17. In multipass heat exchangers the transverse flow past tubes turns sharply through $180°$ on moving from one bundle into the next. The phenomenon is similar to that taking place in a Π-shaped elbow without bundles of tubes; i.e., an eddy zone is created at the inner wall after the second $90°$ turn, but is reduced slightly due to the smoothing effect of the tube bundles.

Reduction or elimination of this eddy zone increases the efficiency of the heat exchanger. This is achieved with guide vanes installed at the point of the flow turn (simplified circular arc). A device[102] in the form of a partition is sometimes used, either straight or bent against the flow direction at the point of turning (see the scheme of Diagram 12-32).

Deflectors and Ventilating Hoods

1. Deflectors are used in cases where it is desirable to use wind energy to enhance ventilation. When the wind blows on the deflector, a negative pressure is created on part of its surface, and this negative pressure contributes to the aspiration of room air to the outside. The total pressure losses in the deflector are made up of the losses in the duct proper and the velocity pressure losses at the exit.

Of greatest interest are the deflectors of the TsAGI, Chanard-Etoile, and Grigorovich* types. The resistance coefficients of these deflectors are given in Diagram 12-35.

2. Dome ventilators are installed on the roof of industrial buildings of natural elimination of polluted air. The most efficient types of such ventilators are the ventilator house, the LenPSP ventilators, and the KTIS, double-level, Giprotis, and Ryukin-Ilinsky ventilators.*

Rectangular ventilators with panels, as well as Baturin-Brandt, LenPSP, KTIS, PSK-2, and Giprotis ventilators and the ventilator house, belong to the category of practically draft-proof ventilators.

Values of the resistance coefficients of different types of dome ventilators are given in Diagrams 12-36 and 12-37.

The resistance coefficients of rectangular ventilators with panels can be calculated from the following equation from the data of Taliev[80] and Frukht:[92,93]

$$\zeta \equiv \frac{2\Delta p}{\rho w_0^2} = 3(h/l) + 0.2h/l + a$$

where w_0 is the mean velocity in the gaps of ventilators, m/s; l is the distance from the panel to the outer edge of the flap, m; h is the height of all the gaps on one side of the flap, m; for the coefficient a which depends on the angle α of opening of the ventilator flap (see Diagram 12-37).

*Russian designations.

3. It is often the case that the spacing between adjacent shaped components, barriers, flow-stopping or regulating devices, etc., in common hydraulic (air) systems is small (or sometimes is absent) and the rectilinear sections available are insufficient for the flow to be stabilized. In these cases the mutual effect of the local resistances is observed. As a result, the degree of flow deformation in the second and subsequent elements alters. Accordingly, the coefficients of local resistances of the interacting elements varies as compared to those of isolated elements.

4. Depending on the type of the shaped parts and other elements that comprise the considered system (assembly) and on their mutual position, the total resistance coefficient of the assembly can be higher or lower than the sum of the isolated elements of the given system (assembly). Therefore, the system which consists of several shaped parts and other barriers connected by short segments (less than $10–20/D_0$) should be considered as the joint local resistance with its own resistance coefficient. As a rule, it can be determined only experimentally. Nevertheless, given below is some information to allow for the mutual effect of some shaped parts and regulating devices. In particular, on the basis of the studies of the mutual effect of locking devices, the authors of works in References 14, 18, 19, 26, 48, 49, and 90 suggest the following formula:

$$\psi = \frac{\zeta_{1+2}}{\zeta_1 + \zeta_2} = \frac{\zeta_\Sigma}{\Sigma\zeta} = 0.5(2 - \beta) \tag{12-21}$$

where $\zeta_\Sigma = \zeta_{1+2}$ is the overall resistance coefficient of two locking devices. It is obtained experimentally when both elements operate simultaneously; $\Sigma\zeta = \zeta_1 + \zeta_2$ are the resistance coefficients of the first and second locking device, respectively, operating separately; β is the coefficient which depends on the relative distance l/D_0 between the locking devices and which can be determined for all their types (except a single-pass one) from the equation[74]

$$\beta = 4.17 \times 10^{-5} (l/D_0)^2 - 5 \times 10^{-3} l/D_0 + 0.15 \tag{12-22}$$

which is valid within $0 \leqslant l/D_0 \leqslant 60$ and $Re = w_0 D_0/\nu > 500$.

For the pipe fittings whose construction is close to the single-pass one, the following formula is suggested:[69]

$$\beta = 22.2 \times 10^{-5} (l/D_0)^2 - 2.67 \times 10^{-3} l/D_0 + 0.8 \tag{12-23}$$

5. According to the same authors, Equations (12-21) through (12-23) can be applied with sufficient practical accuracy to also take into account the mutual effect of other pairs of shaped elements, for example: sudden contraction + a locking device; a throttle + an elbow, etc.

6. The mutual effect ψ for other shaped elements (a wye + a wye; a wye + fittings; a bend + a wye; a wye + a bend; a bend + a bend; a bend + fittings; fittings + a bend; fittings + a wye, etc.), obtained on the basis of the experiments in References 14, 18, 19, 26, 48, 49, and 90, is presented in Diagrams 12-39 through 12-44 as a function of the basic parameters of the shaped elements, relative distance l/D_0 between them and of their mutual orientation.

12-2 DIAGRAMS OF THE RESISTANCE COEFFICIENTS

| The "NIIGOAZ" cyclones of the "TsN" type (without flow straighteners); $w_1 \geqslant 3$ m/s[28,29,31,33,38,97] | | | Diagram 12-1 | |

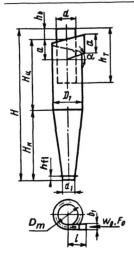

	Cyclone type			
Parameters	TsN-15	TsN-15y	TsN-24	TsN-11
	$d = 0.59D_1$; $d_1 = 0.3{-}0.4D_1$; $b = 0.2D_1$; $b_1 = 0.26D_1$; $l = 0.6D_1$; $D_m = 0.8D_1$ (diameter along the middle line of the cyclone); $h_n = 0.1D_1$, mm			
α, degrees	15	15	24	11
a	$0.66D_1$	$0.66D_1$	$0.11D_1$	$0.48D_1$
h_t	$1.74D_1$	$1.50D_1$	$2.11D_1$	$1.55D_1$
H_c	$2.26D_1$	$1.51D_1$	$2.11D_1$	$2.06D_1$
H_k	$2.0D_1$	$1.50D_1$	$1.75D_1$	$2.0D_1$
h_b	$0.3D_1$	$0.3D_1$	$0.4D_1$	$0.3D_1$
H	$4.56D_1$	$3.31D_1$	$4.26D_1$	$4.38D_1$
$\zeta_{1sys(500)}$	155	165	75	245
$\zeta_{1tot(500)}$	163	170	80	250

$\zeta_{1sys(500)} = \Delta p/(\rho w_1^2/2)$ is the resistance coefficient of a cyclone of diameter $D_1 > 500$ mm when it operates in a system with a clean flow; $\zeta_{1tot(500)}$ is the same with flow discharge into a large volume.

At smaller D_1 and with dust-laden flow

$$\zeta_{1sys} = \frac{\Delta p_{sys}}{\rho w_1^2/2} = k_1 k_2 \zeta_{1sys(500)}; \qquad \zeta_{1tot} = \frac{\Delta p_{tot}}{\rho w_1^2/2} = k_1 k_2 \zeta_{1tot(500)};$$

$$\zeta_{0sys} = \frac{\Delta p_{sys}}{\rho w_1^2/2} = \zeta_{1sys}\left(\frac{F_0}{F_1}\right)^2; \qquad \zeta_{0tot} = \frac{\Delta p_{tot}}{\rho w_0^2/2} = \zeta_{1tot}\left(\frac{F_0}{F_1}\right)^2; \qquad w_1 = \frac{Q}{F_1} \text{ m/s}; \qquad F_1 = \frac{\pi D_1^2}{4}$$

(Q is the discharge, m³/2)

Values of k_1

Cyclone type	D_1, mm				
	150	200	300	450	>500
TsN-15	0.85	0.90	0.93	1.0	1.0
TsN-25y	0.85	0.90	0.93	1.0	1.0
TsN-24	0.85	0.90	0.93	1.0	1.0
TsN-11	0.94	0.95	0.96	0.99	1.0

Values of k_2

Cyclone type	Dust content $z \times 10^3$ kg/m³						
	0	>10–20	>20–40	>40–80	>80–120	>120–150	>150
TsN-15	1.0	0.93	0.92	0.91	0.90	0.87	0.86
TsN-25y	1.0	0.93	0.92	0.91	0.89	0.88	0.87
TsN-24	1.0	0.95	0.93	0.92	0.90	0.87	0.86
TsN-11	1.0	0.96	0.94	0.92	0.90	0.87	0.86

The "NIIOGAZ" cyclones of the "TsN" type (with flow straighteners); $w_1 \geqslant 3$ m/s[28,29,31,33,38,97]	Diagram 12-2

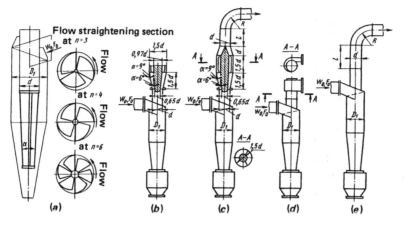

(a) (b) (c) (d) (e)

Values of ζ_1 at $D_1 = 500$ mm

Type of cyclone	With straightener (scheme a)		With annular diffuser (schemes b and c)		With exit volute (scheme d)	With bend at $\delta = 90°$ $R/d = 1.5$ (scheme e)	
	$\zeta_{1sys(500)}$	$\zeta_{1tot(500)}$	$\zeta_{1sys(500)}$	$\zeta_{1tot(500)}$	$\zeta_{1sys(500)}$	$\zeta_{1sys(500)}$ $l/d = 0\text{-}12$	$\zeta_{1sys(500)}$ $l/d > 12$
TsN-15	115	121	132	140	150	155	160
TsN-15y	148	152	140	148	158	165	170
TsN-24	61	66	64	70	73	75	80
TsN-11	–	–	207	215	235	245	250

$$\zeta_{1sys} = \frac{\Delta p_{sys}}{\rho w_1^2/2} = k_1 k_2 \zeta_{1sys(500)}; \quad \zeta_{1tot} = \frac{\Delta p_{tot}}{\rho w_1^2/2} = k_1 k_2 \zeta_{1tot(500)}; \quad \zeta_{0sys} = \frac{\Delta p_{sys}}{\rho w_0^2/2} = \zeta_{1sys}\left(\frac{F_0}{F_1}\right)^2;$$

$$\zeta_{0tot} = \zeta_{1tot}\left(\frac{F_0}{F_1}\right)^2 \quad \text{where for } k_1 \text{ and } k_2, \text{ see Diagram 12-1; } w_1 = Q/F_1; \; F_1 = \pi D_1^2/4 \; (Q \text{ is the discharge, m}^3/\text{s})$$

The "NIIOGAX" cyclones of the "SDK-TsN-33" "SK-TsN-34" and STsN-40 types; $w_1 \geqslant 3$ m/s[28,31,33,38,45,97]	Diagram 12-3

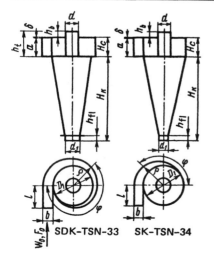

SDK-TSN-33 SK-TSN-34

Symbol	Type of cyclone	
	SDK-TsN-33	SK-TsN-34
H_c	$0.535D_1$	$0.515D_1$
H_k	$3.0D_1$	$2.11D_1$
d	$0.334D_1$	$0.340D_1$
d_1	$0.334D_1$	$0.229D_1$
b	$0.264D_1$	$0.214D_1$
h_b	$0.2\text{-}0.3D_1$	$0.515D_1$
h_{fl}	$0.1D_1$	$0.1D_1$
a	$0.535D_1$	$0.2\text{-}0.3D_1$
l	$0.6D_1$	$0.6D_1$
h	$a + h_B + \delta$	$a + h_B + \delta$
ρ	$D_1/2 + b(L/2\pi)$	$D_1/2 + b(L/\pi)$
$\zeta_{1sys(500)}$	520	1050
	500 (with volute)	–
	500 (with bend)	–
$\zeta_{1tot(500)}$	600	1150

The "NIIOGAX" cyclones of the "SDK-TsN-33" "SK-TsN-34" and STsN-40 types; $w_1 \geq 3$ m/s[28,31,33,38,45,97]	Diagram 12-3

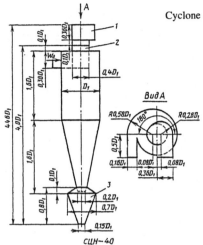

Cyclone STsN-40: $D_1 = 300–3000$ m 1, volute; 2, exhaust pipe; 3, hopper

$$\zeta_{0.c} \equiv \frac{\Delta p}{\rho w_0^2/2} = 6.9; \quad \zeta_{1c} \equiv \frac{\Delta p}{\rho w_1^2/2} = 1150;$$

$$\zeta_{1c} \equiv \frac{\Delta p_c}{\rho w_1^2/2} = k_2\zeta_{1c}(500); \quad \zeta_{1tot} \equiv \frac{\Delta p_{tot}}{\rho w_1^2/2} = k_2\zeta_{1tot}(500);$$

$$\zeta_{0c} \equiv \frac{\Delta p_c}{\rho w_0^2/2} = \zeta_{1c}\left(\frac{F_0}{F_1}\right)^2; \quad \zeta_{0tot} \equiv \frac{\Delta p_{tot}}{\rho w_0^2/2} = \zeta_{1tot}\left(\frac{F_0}{F_1}\right)^2;$$

$$w_1 = Q/F_1, \text{ m/s}; \quad F_1 = \pi D_1^2/4; \quad Q \text{ is the discharge, m}^3/\text{s}$$

Values of k_2 with dust content $z \times 10^3$ kg/m³

Type of cyclone	0	>10–20	>20–40	>40–80	>80–120	>80–120	>120–150
SDK-TsN-33	1.0	0.81	0.79	0.78	0.77	0.76	0.75
SK-TsN-34	1.0	0.98	0.95	0.93	0.92	0.91	0.90
STsN-40	1.0	0.98	0.96	0.94	–	–	–

Countercurrent cyclones of various types[16,25,51,52,69,70]	Diagram 12-4

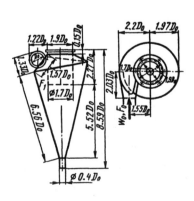

"SIOT" type (conical)

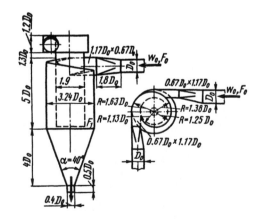

"LIOT" type (shortened, with a straightening volute)

Countercurrent cyclones of various types[16,25,51,52,69,70]		Diagram 12-4

	Resistance coefficients	
Type of cyclone	$\zeta_0 \equiv \Delta p/\rho w_0^2/2$	$\zeta_1 \equiv \Delta p/\rho w_i^2/2$
SIOT (conical):		
With volute	4.2	–
Without volute	6.0	–
LIOT (shortened):		
With volute	3.7	411
Without volute	4.2	460
"Klaipeda" of "Giprodrevprom" design	5.0	–
Ts of "Giprodrevprom" design	5.4	–
"UTs-38" ($D_0 = 0.6$ m):		
Without volute	11.9	1730
With volute	10.7	1560
"UTs-38" ($D_0 = 0.7$ m):		
Without volute	12.5	1990
With volute	11.7	1800
"4BTsSh" ($D_0 = 0.3$ m):		
Without volute	3.7	190
With volute	3.9	200
"STsK-TsN-38" ($D_0 = 0.45$ m):		
Without volute	11.0	1640
With volute	12.8	1920
"VTsNIIOT" ($D_0 = 0.37$ m):		
Without volute	9.3	–
With volute	10.4	–
"T-4/630" ($D_0 = 0.63$ m)		
Without volute	10.1	–

The "NIIOGAZ" cyclones (grouped)[31,97]		Diagram 12-5
Arrangement of the cyclones	Scheme	Resistance coefficient of the cyclone over the length from 0–0 to 2–2 $\zeta_{1gr} \equiv \Delta p_{gr}/(\rho w_g^2/2)$
		$\zeta_{1gr} = k_1 k_2 \zeta_{1c(500)} + 35$
Rectangular; uniform supply; cyclone elements are located in one plane; gas is discharged from the common clean gas chamber	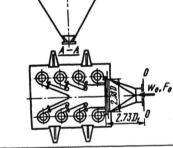	
Stepwise supply; the same conditions as above	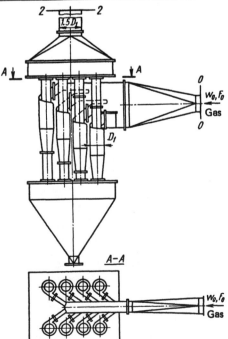	

The "NIIOGAZ" cyclones (grouped)[31,97]		Diagram 12-5
Arrangement of the cyclones	Scheme	Resistance coefficient of the cyclone over the length from 0–0 to 2–2 $$\zeta_{1gr} \equiv \Delta p_{gr}/(\rho w_g^2/2)$$
		$$\zeta_{1gr} = k_1 k_2 \zeta_{1c(500)} + 28$$
Rectangular; conditions are the same as above, but the gas from the cyclone elements is discharged through a volute	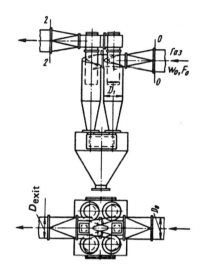	
Rectangular; flow is fed into the common chamber	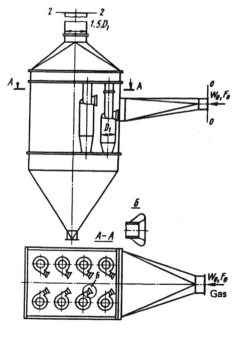	

The "NIIOGAZ" cyclones (grouped)[31,97]		Diagram 12-5

Arrangement of the cyclones	Scheme	Resistance coefficient of the cyclone over the length from 0–0 to 2–2 $$\zeta_{1gr} \equiv \Delta p_{gr}/(\rho w_g^2/2)$$
		$$\zeta_{1gr} = k_1 k_2 \zeta_{1c(500)} + 60$$

Circular; gas is fed from below

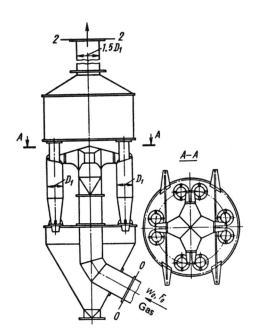

For $\zeta_{1c(500)}$, see Diagrams 12-1 through 12-3; for k_1 and k_2, see Diagrams 12-1 and 12-2, respectively; $w_1 = Q/m_{cyc}F_1$ m/s; $F_1 = \pi D_1^2/4$; m_{cyc} is the number of cyclone elements in the group; Q is the overall discharge, m³/s.

Battery cyclone of the "BTs" type[11]		Diagram 12-6

Characteristic of the cyclone	Scheme	Resistance coefficient of the cyclone over the length from 0–0 to 2–2
		$$\zeta_1 \equiv \frac{\Delta p}{\rho w_1^2/2}$$

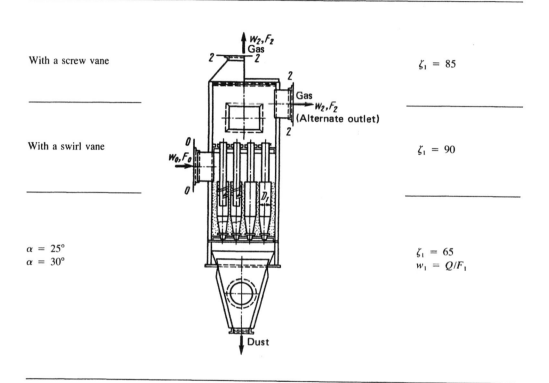

With a screw vane	$\zeta_1 = 85$
With a swirl vane	$\zeta_1 = 90$
$\alpha = 25°$ $\alpha = 30°$	$\zeta_1 = 65$ $w_1 = Q/F_1$

The total resistance coefficient of a battery cyclone over the length from section 0–0 to section 2–2 is

$$\zeta_{1b} = \zeta_1 + \zeta_{ex}\left(\frac{F_1}{F_2}\right)^2 = \zeta_1 + \zeta'\left(1 - \frac{F_2}{F}\right)\left(\frac{F_1}{F_2}\right)^2$$

ζ' is determined as ζ from Diagram 3-7;

$$w_1 = \frac{Q}{m_{cyc}F_1} \ \text{m/s} \qquad F_1 = \frac{\pi D_1^2}{4}$$

F_b is the area of the body of the apparatus; Q is the overall discharge, m³/s; m_{cyc} is the number of cyclone elements in the battery.

Direct-flow cyclones[9,25,36,44,46]   Diagram
12-7

Characteristic and scheme	Basic dimensions			Optimum average flow velocity in the body of the cyclone w_1 (m/s)	Fractional coefficient of cleaning η_{fr} (%) at $\bar{q}=15\%$ and free fall velocity of particles $w_{fr,f}$ (m/s)					The resistance coefficient $\zeta \equiv \Delta p/(\rho w_1^2/2)$ at the degree of suction $\bar{q}$ (%)			
	D_1 (mm)	$\bar{L}=L/D_1$	$\bar{d}=d/D_1$		$0-0.001$	$>0.001-0.008$	$>0.008-0.012$	$>0.012-0.100$	>0.100	0	5	10	15
Four-blade swirler with dust discharge through a volute (of "NIIOGAZ" type)	100	2.5	0.6–0.7	11–13	–	–	–	–	–	–	–	–	9.5
Four-blade swirler with an impingement orifice	350	1.0	0.7	9.0	–	–	–	–	–	–	–	–	6–7
Radial swirler with an impingement orifice	150	4.7	0.8	16.4	45	82	93.5	98	100	10.5	8.1	7.1	7.0
Six-swirler conical inlet with an impingement (of the "Butakov-Barakhtenko" orifice design)	150	0.73	0.8	16–18	57	86	95	98.5	100	1.7	1.6	1.55	1.5
Twelve-blade swirler with dust exit through an annular diffuser	50	5.0	0.8	11.8	13	82	98	100	100	–	–	–	1.5
Tangential conical inlet (of the "Amerklon" type)	100	1.3	0.65	20–24	–	–	–	–	–	–	–	–	5.9

Direct-flow cyclones with water film[9,46]				Diagram 12-8
Type of cyclone	Scheme	Optimum average flow velocity in the cyclone body w_1 (m/s)	Water flow rate, m_0 (liter/m³)	Resistance coefficient $\zeta \equiv \dfrac{\Delta p}{\rho w_1^2/2}$

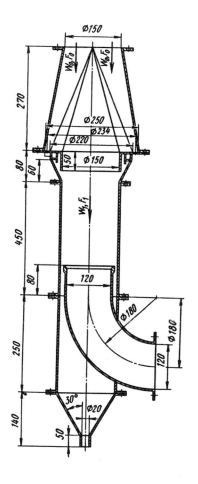

Type of cyclone	w_1 (m/s)	m_0	ζ
"Butakov-Barakhtenko"	20–22	0.10	1.8
"TsKTI"	4.0	0.15	13.0
"Tsentrgiproshakhta"	6.0–7.0	0.12	22.0

Turbulent wet scrubber (Venturi tube)[13,22,23]	Diagram 12-9

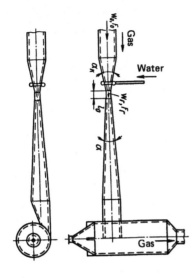

Single Venturi tube

$$\zeta \equiv \frac{\Delta p}{\rho_g w_g^2/2} = \zeta_g + \zeta_l \frac{\rho l}{\rho g} m_1$$

where $\zeta_g = 0.165 + 0.034 \dfrac{l_0}{D_h}$

$$- \left[0.06 + 0.028 \left(\frac{l_0}{D_h}\right) \right] \times 3 \times 10^{-3} w_g$$

the formula is valid at $w_g \leqslant 150$ m/s and $0.15 \leqslant l_0/D_h \leqslant 10$, where $D_h = 4F_0/\pi_0$; at $w_g \leqslant 60$ m/s

$$\zeta_l = 3.5 \left(\frac{l_0}{D_h}\right)^{-0.266} \zeta_g m_1^{B_1}$$

at $w_g > 60$ m/s

$$\zeta_l = 1.68 \left(\frac{l_0}{D}\right)^{0.29} \zeta_g m_1^{B_2}$$

The formulas of ζ_l are valid at $0.15 \leqslant l_0/D_h \leqslant 12$;

$$B_1 = 1 - 0.98 \left(\frac{l_0}{D_h}\right)^{+0.026} \quad \text{and} \quad B_2 = 1 - 1.12 \left(\frac{l_0}{D_h}\right)^{-0.045}$$

see the curves of graph a; $(l_0/D_h)^{-0.266}$ and $(l_0/D_h)^{0.29}$, see the curve of graph B.

A battery of Venturi tubes
For ζ_g see para. 1; $\zeta_l = 0.215 \zeta_g \, m_1^{-0.54}$ where for $m_1^{-0.54}$, see the curve of graph c.

$\dfrac{l_0}{D_h}$	0.15	0.2	0.3	0.4	0.5	0.6	0.8	1.0	1.5
$B_1 \times 10^2$	6.7	6.0	5.0	4.3	3.8	3.3	2.6	2.0	1.0
B_2	−0.22	−0.21	−0.18	−0.17	−0.16	−0.15	−0.13	−0.12	−0.10
$\left(\dfrac{l_0}{D_h}\right)^{-0.266}$	1.66	1.53	1.38	1.28	1.20	1.15	1.06	1.00	0.90
$\left(\dfrac{l_0}{D_h}\right)^{0.29}$	0.58	0.63	0.70	0.77	0.82	0.86	0.94	1.00	1.12

Turbulent wet scrubber (Venturi tube)[13,22,23]								Diagram 12-9	
$\dfrac{l_0}{D_h}$	2.0	3.0	4.0	5.0	6.0	7.0	8.0	9.0	10
$B_1 \times 10^2$	0.2	−0.8	−1.6	−2.2	−2.7	−3.1	−3.4	−3.8	−4.0
B_2	−0.09	−0.07	−0.05	−0.04	−0.03	−0.03	−0.02	−0.02	−0.01
$\left(\dfrac{l_0}{D_h}\right)^{-0.266}$	0.83	0.75	0.69	0.65	0.62	0.60	0.58	0.56	0.54
$\left(\dfrac{l_0}{D_h}\right)^{0.29}$	1.22	1.38	1.48	1.58	1.68	1.76	1.83	1.90	1.95

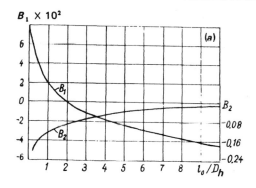

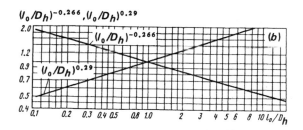

m_1	0.4	0.6	0.8	1.0	1.4	2.0	3.0	4.0	5.0	6.0
$m_1^{-0.54}$	1.64	1.32	1.13	1.00	0.84	0.69	0.55	0.47	0.42	0.38

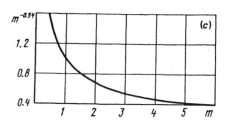

Dust-trapper (scrubber) with perforated plates in a foam regime[76,81]	Diagram 12-10

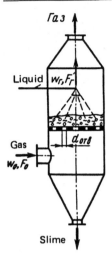

$$\Delta p = \frac{A^2}{\bar{f}^2} \frac{\rho_g w_g^2}{2} + \Delta p\sigma$$

where $A = 39L^{-0.57}[(L/G)^2(\rho_g/\rho_{liq})]^{0.35} = 39a_1 b_1$ (see graph b); $a_1 = L^{-0.57}$, see graph a; $b_1 = [(L/G^2(\rho_g/\rho_{liq})]^{0.35}$, see graph b; $\Delta p_\sigma = 4\sigma/(1.3d_{or} + 0.08d_{or}^2)$ for grids with holes; $\Delta p_\sigma = 2\sigma/b_{sl}$ for grids with slots; G is the mass gas flow rate through the grid unit surface, kg/m^2 s; L is the mass flow rate of liquid through the grid unit surface, kg/m^2 s; d_{or} is the grid orifice diameter, m; b_{sl} is the grid slot width,m; $\bar{f} = F_{or}/F_{gr}$ is the clear area coefficient of the grid; w_g is the gas flow velocity in the free section of the apparatus, m/s; σ is the surface tension at the gas-liquid interface, N/m^2.

L, kg/m^2 s	0.3	0.6	1.0	1.5	2.0
$a_1 = L^{-0.57}$	1.99	1.34	1.00	0.79	0.67

L, kg/m^2 s	2.5	3.0	3.5	4.0	4.5	5.0
$a_1 = L^{-0.57}$	0.59	0.53	0.49	0.45	0.42	0.40

Values of A at $L = 0.3$–5.0 kg/(m^2·s)

$\left(\dfrac{L}{G}\right)^2 \dfrac{\rho_g}{\rho_{liq}} \times 10^3$	0.15	0.4	0.8	1.2	1.6	2.0	2.4
$b_1 \times 10^2$	4.59	6.47	8.24	9.50	10.5	11.4	12.1
$L = 0.3$ kg/m^2 s	3.55	5.01	6.38	7.36	8.13	8.83	9.37
$L = 0.6$ kg/m^2 s	2.40	3.38	4.30	4.96	5.48	5.95	6.31
$L = 1.0$ kg/m^2 s	1.79	2.52	3.21	3.70	4.10	4.45	4.72
$L = 1.5$ kg/m^2 s	1.42	1.99	2.55	2.94	3.25	3.54	3.74
$L = 2.0$ kg/m^2 s	1.21	1.70	2.16	2.50	2.76	3.00	3.18
$L = 2.5$ kg/m^2 s	1.06	1.50	1.91	2.20	2.43	2.64	2.80
$L = 3.0$ kg/m^2 s	0.95	1.35	1.72	1.98	2.19	2.38	2.52
$L = 3.5$ kg/m^2 s	0.88	1.23	1.57	1.81	2.01	2.18	2.31
$L = 4.0$ kg/m^2 s	0.80	1.13	1.46	1.68	1.86	2.02	2.14

Dust-trapper (scrubber) with perforated plates in a foam regime[76,81]						Diagram 12-10	
$L = 4.5$ kg/m² s	0.75	1.06	1.36	1.57	1.74	1.88	2.00
$L = 5.0$ kg/m² s	0.71	1.01	1.28	1.48	1.64	1.78	1.9

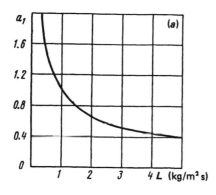

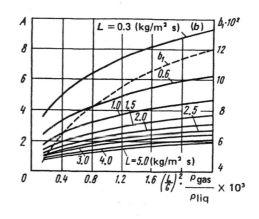

Scrubber with wooden packing[25]	Diagram 12-11

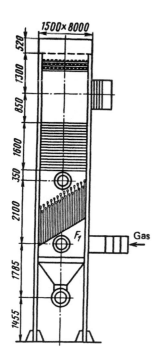

Wetting intensity $A \approx 1.4 \times 10^{-2}$ m³/m² s

$$\zeta \equiv \frac{\Delta p}{\rho w_1^2/2} = 960$$

$w_1 = \dfrac{Q}{F_1}$ (F_1 is the total cross-sectional area of the scrubber body).

"VTI" centrifugal scrubber[25]

Diagram
12-12

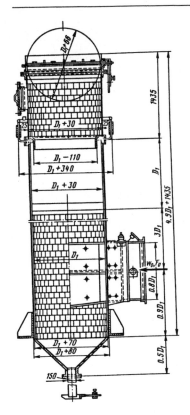

$$\zeta_0 \equiv \frac{\Delta p}{\rho w_0^2/2} = f(D_0)$$

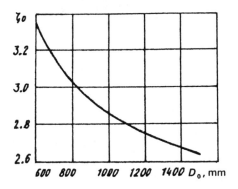

D_0, m		0.6	0.7	0.8	0.9	1.0
Water spray discharge, kg/s		0.22	0.28	0.33	0.39	0.45
ζ_0		3.38	3.17	3.04	2.94	2.87
D_0, m		1.1	1.2	1.3	1.4	1.5
Water spray discharge, kg/s		0.50	0.56	0.61	0.70	0.78
ζ_0		2.81	2.76	2.72	2.68	2.65

Modular unified filters of the "F_c type"[70,76]

Diagram
12-13

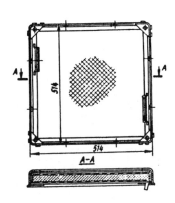

A–A

		Type of filter			
Characteristic		FcR	FcV	FcPF	FcEG
Working area F, m²		0.22	0.22	0.22	0.22
Throughput capacity Q (m³/s) at specific loading $q = 2$ m³/m² s		0.43	0.43	0.43	0.43
Resistance Δp of clean filter: Pa		39	49	59	29.5
Dust capacity z_d of FcR, FcPF, and FcV filters (with double increase in resistance) and of FcEG filter (with increase of resistance Δp from 30 to 40 Pa), kg/m²		1.5	2.0	0.2	0.3
Efficiency of cleaning (according to the "NIIST" technique) η_d (%), no more		80	80	80	80
Mass, kg		7.9	4.3	3.3	3.0

Modular unified filters of the "F_c type"[70,76]	Diagram 12-13

For the dependence of Δp on q and z_d of single filters, see graphs a and b. Curves 1 refer to filters of the FcR type with five screens filled with cells of size 2.5 mm, four screens filled with cells of size 1.2 mm, and the three screens filled with cells of size 0.63 mm; curves 2 refer to filters of the FcV type; curve 3, to the FcPF filter made of polyurethane foam (PF) (α, thickness of the layer is 10 mm, β – 20 mm, γ – 40 mm) and the FcEG filter, of elastic glass fiber (FSV, curve 3, α).

	$z_\alpha = 0$					
q, m³/m² h	4×10^3	6×10^3	8×10^3	10^4	1.2×10^4	1.4×10^4
m³/m² s	1.1	1.7	2.2	2.8	3.3	3.9
Δp, Pa (curves 1 and 3α)	14.7	29.4	49.0	68.7	88.3	108
Δp, Pa (curve 2)	14.7	29.4	58.8	88.3	137	187
Δp, Pa (curve 3β)	24.5	49.0	73.5	98.1	132	162
Δp, Pa (curve 3β)	58.8	98.1	147	196	255	314

	$q = 6 \times 10^3$ m³/(m² h)						
z_d, kg/m²	0.2	0.4	0.8	1.2	1.6	2.0	2.2
Δp, Pa (curve 1)	34.3	39.2	49.0	63.7	83.3	118	137
η_d (%)	82	82	83	83	84	85	85
Δp, Pa (curve 2)	58.8	63.7	68.7	78.5	88.3	–	–
η_d (%)	76	76	76	76	76	–	–

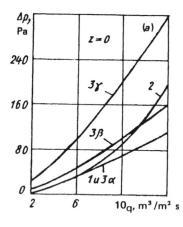

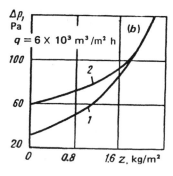

Bag filter of the "FVK type"[70,76]	Diagram 12-14

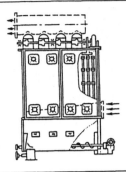

	Type of filter		
Characteristic	FVK-30	FVK-60	FVK-90
Surface area of filtering cloth, m²	30	60	90
Throughput capacity Q, m³/s:			
For pure air	1.38	2.78	4.12
For gas containing up to 20 g/m³ dust	0.35–0.418	0.70–0.835	1.05–1.28
Resistance Δp of the filter:			
Pa	800–900	800–900	800–900
Quantity, pieces of:			
Sections	2	4	6
Bags in a section	18	18	18
Bags in a filter	36	72	108
Bag material: filtering cloth			
Power of electric motor: of the shaking mechanism drive and of the screw drive, kW	0.6	0.6	0.6
Mass of filter (without inlet and exit collectors), kg	1053	1682	2300

Roll filters of the "FRU type"[70,76]	Diagram 12-15

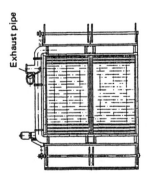

	Type of filter				
Characteristic	F2RU7	F4RU4	F16RU6	F8RU2	F12RU1
Throughput capacity Q, m³/s	5.56	11.1	16.7	22.2	33.3
Resistance Δp^* of the filter (at specific air loading q = 2.78 m³/m² s):					
Pa	40–50	40–50	40–50	40–50	40–50

Roll filters of the "FRU type"[70,76]				Diagram 12-15	

	Type of filter				
Characteristic	F2RU7	F4RU4	F16RU6	F8RU2	F12RU1
Area F of the working section, m^2	2	4	6	7.9	12
Filtering material	FSVU	FSVU	FSVU	FSVU	FSVU
Efficiency of cleaning (by the "NIIST" technique) η_d %	80	80	80	80	80
Dust content (with increase in resistance Δp from 40 to 140 Pa), kg/m^2	L_0 0.3	L_0 0.3	L_0 0.3	L_0 0.3	L_0 0.3
Power of electric motor, W	270	270	270	270	270
Quantity of sections of the filter front, pieces:					
Of width 0.8m	2	–	2	–	–
Of width 1.05 m	–	2	1	3	3
Width of filtering material in a roll, m	0.77	1.02	0.77, 1.02	1.02	1.02
Length of filtering material in a roll, m	25	25	25	25	25
Number of rolls, pieces	4	4	6	6	6
Mass, kg	353	408	623	717	970

*For FRP $\Delta p = f(q)$, see curve 2 of graph a, $\Delta p = f(z_d)$, see graph b; for FRU $\Delta p = f(q)$ see curve 1 of graph a.

	Type of filter				
Characteristic	F2RP7	F4RP4	F6RP6	FVRP2	F12RP1
Throughput capacity Q, m^3/s	5.56	11.1	16.7	22.2	33.3
Resistance Δp (at specific loading $q = 2.78$ m^3/m^2 s):					
Pa	98–118	98–118	98–118	98–118	98–118
Area of the working section F, m^2	2	4	6	7.9	12
Filtering material	FVN	FVN	FVN	FVN	FVN
Dust content (with double increase in resistance) z, kg/m^2	to 0.13	to 0.13	to 0.13	to 0.13	to 0.13
Power of electric motor, W	270	270	270	270	270
Number of sections over the filter front, pieces:					
With width 0.8 m	2	–	2	–	–
With width 1.05 m	–	2	1	3	3
Width of filtering material in a roll, m	0.77	1.02	0.77, 1.02	1.02	1.02
Length of filtering material in a roll, m	100	100	100	100	100
Number of rolls, pieces	4	4	6	6	6
Mass of filter, kg	406	–	597	–	–
Required discharge of air through a suction orifice, m^3/s	0.194	0.255	0.320	0.384	0.384
Efficiency η_d in trapping of fibrous dust, %	95–96	95–96	95–96	95–96	95–96

For curve 1						
$q \times 10^{-4}$, $m^3/m^2 h$	0.4	0.6	0.8	1.0	1.2	1.4	1.6
q, m^3/m^2 s	1.11	1.67	2.22	2.78	3.33	3.88	4.44
Δp Pa	24.5	49	78.5	108	137	177	226

Roll filters of the "FRU type"[70,76]

Diagram
12-15

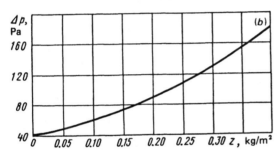

For curve 2		0.4	0.6	0.8	1.0	1.2
	$q \times 10^{-4}$, m³/m² h	0.4	0.6	0.8	1.0	1.2
	q, m³/m² s		1.11	1.67	2.22	2.78	3.33
	Δp Pa		15	22	29	39	59

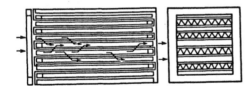

For graph b		0	0.1	0.2	0.3	0.4
	z_d kg/m²	0	0.1	0.2	0.3	0.4
	η_d (%)	–	81	81	81	81
	Δp Pa	39	59	88	127	176

Frame filter of the "LAIK type"[68]

Diagram
12-16

Material PUF-15 at (admissible temperature 60°C)
$$\Delta p = \Delta p_0 w \quad (w \text{ is the filtration rate, m/s})$$

Make of filter	Area of filtering surface (m²)	Dimensions (mm)		Flow rate, normal conditions (m³/s)	at loading 0.0417 m³/m²s (150 m³/m²h)	
		Inlet section	Length		Resistance Δp_0, Pa	Δp_0, Pa
LAIK SP-3/15	15.1	565 × 735	780	0.625	177	4248
LAIK SP-6/15					245	5880
LAIK SP-3/17	17.5	615 × 995	355	0.710	147	3528
LAIK SP-6/17					206	4944
LAIK SP-3/21	21.0	650 × 690	625	0.875	285	6840
LAIK SP-6/21					334	8016
LAIK SP-3/25	26	660 × 665	750	1.10	392	9408
LAIK SP-6/26					352	10848
LAIK-SYa (FcL1)	16	550 × 680	310	0.667	157	3768

Laboratory filters (analytical aerosol) of the "AFA type"[10]

Diagram 12-17

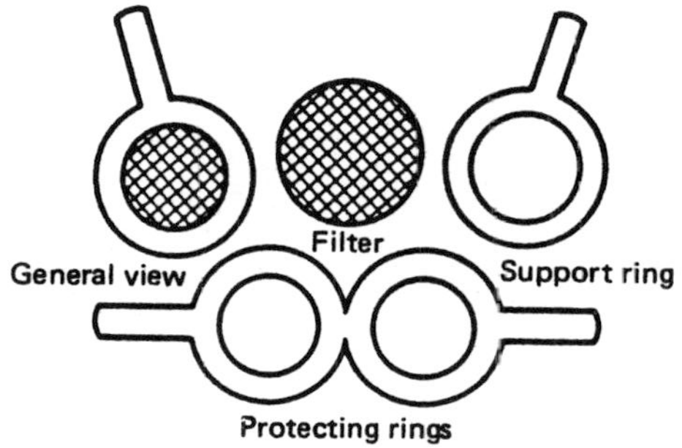

General view — Filter — Support ring — Protecting rings

Δp increases linearly with $\bar{w}$

$$\Delta p = \Delta p_0 w$$

Type of filter	η_d (%) at filtration rate $w = 0.01$ m/s	Δp, Pa at $w = 0.01$ m/s	Maximum loading Q, liter/min	Working surface area $S_0 \times 10^{-2}$ (m²)	Temperature of tested gas (not exceeding) (°C)
AFA-V-18	0.995	14.7	100	18	60
AFA-V-10	0.995	14.7	55	10	60
AFA-XA-18	0.970	19.6	100	18	150
AFA-XM-18	0.990–0.995	19.6	100	18	50
AFA XP-18	0.995	14.7	100	18	60
AFA XS-18	0.990–0.995	19.6	100	18	70
AFA RMP-3	0.995	39–98	20	3.0	60
AFA RMP-10	0.995	39–98	50	10	60
AFA RMP-20	0.995	39–98	100–120	20	60
AFA RMA-20	0.970	39–98	100–120	20	150
AFA RG-3	0.950	790–1470	0.3	3.0	60
AFA-D-3	0.995	30–50	10	3.0	60
AFA-B-3	0.970–0.990	19.6	20	3.0	150

Inlet sections of electrostatic filters and other apparatus with a perforated plate, screen (grid), packing, or other type of resistance placed in the working chamber[27,28]	Diagram 12-18

Conditions of flow incidence on the grid	Scheme	Resistance coefficient $\zeta \equiv \dfrac{\Delta p}{\rho w_0^2/2}$

Central

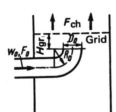

$$\zeta = \zeta'_{0or} + N_0 + 0.7\zeta_{gr}\left(\frac{F_0}{F_{ch}}\right)^2$$

$$+ \frac{0.013}{(H_{gr}/D_0)^2}\ \sqrt[3]{\zeta_{gr}} - 3\sqrt{\zeta_{gr}}$$

where ζ'_{0or} is determined as 0.5ζ of this bend from diagrams of Chapter 6; N_0 is determined from Tables 12-1 through 12-7; ζ_{gr} is determined as ζ of the grid, packing, or other type of resistance from the data of diagrams of Chapter 8; the last term in the above equation applies only within $0 < H_{gr}/D_0 < 1.2$

Peripheral

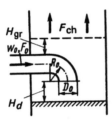

$$\zeta = \zeta'_{0oz} + 0.9\left[N_0 + 0.7\zeta_{gr}\left(\frac{F_0}{F_{ch}}\right)^2\right] + \frac{0.05}{(H_d/D_0)^2}$$

the quantity $0.05/(H_d/D_0)^2$ applies only at $H_d/D_0 < 1.2$

Lateral

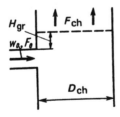

$$\zeta = N_0 + 0.7\zeta_{gr}\left(\frac{F_0}{F_{ch}}\right)^2 + 0.1 + \left(2 - 20\frac{H_{gr}}{D_{ch}}\right)$$

the quantity $\Delta\zeta = 2 - 20\,(H_{gr}/D_{ch})$ applies only at $H_{gr}/D_{ch} < 0.1$.

For a system of grids arranged in series ζ_{gr} is replaced by

$$\sum_{i=1}^{m_{gr}} \zeta_{ch,gr,i} = \zeta_{ch,gr,1} + \zeta_{ch,gr,2} + \ldots + \zeta_{ch,gr,i} + \ldots + \zeta_{ch,gr,m}$$

$$= \zeta_{gr,1}\left(\frac{F_{ch}}{F_1}\right)^2 + \zeta_{gr,2}\left(\frac{F_{ch}}{F_2}\right)^2 + \ldots + \zeta_{gr,i}\left(\frac{F_{ch}}{F_1}\right)^2 + \ldots + \zeta_{gr,m}$$

where m_{gr} is the number of grids in a series; $\zeta_{ch,gr,i} \equiv \dfrac{\Delta p}{\rho w_{ch}^2/2}$

Industrial electrostatic filters[27,28]	Diagram 12-19

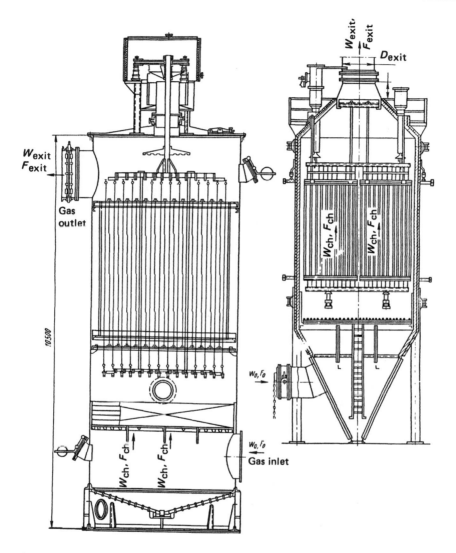

$$\zeta \equiv \frac{\Delta p}{\rho w_0^2/2} = \zeta_{in} + \zeta_{ex} + \zeta_{ch(annel)}$$

where ζ_{in} is determined as ζ from Diagram 12-18;

$$\zeta_{ex} = \zeta'\left(1 - \frac{F_{ex}}{F_{ch}}\right)\left(\frac{F_0}{F_{ex}}\right)^2$$

ζ' is determined as ζ from Diagram 3-6 as a function of α (degrees) and l/D_{ex}; at $l/D_{ex} = 0$, $\zeta' = 0.5$;

$$\zeta_{ch} = \zeta'_{in} + \zeta''_{ex} + \zeta''_{ch} \qquad \zeta''_{ex} = 0.5\left(1 - \frac{F_e}{F_{ch}}\right)\left(\frac{F_0}{F_e}\right)^2 \qquad \zeta''_{ex} = \left(1 - \frac{F_e}{F_{ch}}\right)^2\left(\frac{F_0}{F_e}\right)^2 \qquad \zeta''_{fr} = \lambda \frac{l_e}{D_d}\left(\frac{F_0}{F_e}\right)^2$$

depending on Re and $\bar{\Delta}$, see Diagrams 2-1 through 2-6; $D_e = 4F_e/\Pi_e$; F_e, Π_e are the cross-sectional area and perimeter of spaces between settling plates–electrodes or settling pipes.

Electrostatic air filter of the "EF-2 types"[71,77]	Diagram 12-20

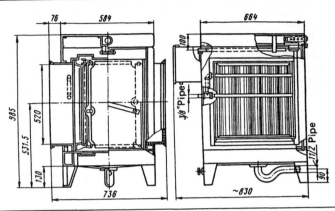

Throughput capacity Q, m^3/s, not more than	0.56 m^3/s
Initial resistance with an anticarrying filter, Δp	39 Pa
Cleaning efficiency (according to the NIIST technique), η_d	95%
Dust content with doubled resistance	0.3 kg/m^2
Power consumed by the power-supply unit	80 w
Current used	1 mA
Total surface area of settling electrodes, S_0	13.8 m^2
Water discharge per single cleaning, not less than	50 l
Time of one cleaning	3 h
Time between two cleaning cycles	4–6 weeks
Number of nozzles	15
Mass without power-supply unit	90 kg

Electrostatic air filter of the "FE type"[71,77]	Diagram 12-21

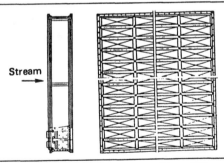

Stream →

	Type of filter						
Indices	F1E1	F3E2	F5E3	F8E4	F10E5	F14E6	F18E7
Working section area F, m^2	1.5	2.9	4.9	8.2	9.8	14	18.5
Throughput capacity at flow velocity 2 m/s and specific air loading 7200 m^3/m^2 h Q, m^3/s	2.78	5.30	9.20	15.3	18.0	27.8	36.0
Cleaning efficiency (according to NIIST technique) η_d, %	90–95	90–95	90–95	90–95	90–95	90–95	90–95
Initial resistance Δp^*:							
With anticarrying filter	39*/4	39/4	39/4	39/4	39/4	39/4	39/4
Without anticarrying filter	4.9/0.5	4.9/0.5	4.9/0.5	4.9/0.5	4.9/0.5	4.9/0.5	4.9/0.5

Electrostatic air filter of the "FE type"[71,77]

Diagram
12-21

Indices	Type of filter						
	F1E1	F3E2	F5E3	F8E4	F10E5	F14E6	F18E7
Dust content z_d (kg/m²) of the filter working section (with doubled resistance with anticarrying filter)	1.5	1.5	1.5	1.5	1.5	1.5	1.5
Voltage on corona electrodes, W	13,000	13,000	13,000	13,000	13,000	13,000	13,000
Voltage on settling electrodes, W	6,500	6,500	6,500	6,500	6,500	6,500	6,500
Current consumed, mA	7	14	24	42	54	81	110
Power consumed, mA	100	200	380	600	800	1,100	1,500
Water discharge for cleaning filter (at pressure 0.3 MPa), m³/h	0.5	1.5	2.5	4.0	5.0	7.0	9.0
Number of sections of width:							
765 mm, pieces	7	14	–	24	–	–	–
1015 mm, pieces	–	–	18	12	36	54	72
Mass of filter, kg	205	367	583	963	1,120	1,640	2,150

*In numerator, Δp is in Pa, in denominator it is in kg$_f$/m².

Honeycomb radiator with hexagonal or circular pipes[60]

Diagram
12-22

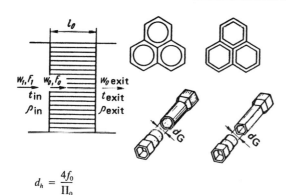

$d_h = \dfrac{4f_0}{\Pi_0}$

f_0 is the cross-sectional area of one pipe;
F_0 is the free-flow area of the radiator

$$\zeta_1 \equiv \frac{\Delta p}{\rho_{in} w_1^2/2} = \lambda\left(3 + \frac{l_0}{d_h}\right)\left(\frac{F_1}{F_0}\right)^2 + \zeta_{sp} + \Delta\zeta_t$$

where (1) at $35 \leq \mathrm{Re}^* = w_{0in}\Delta/\nu \leq 275$
$\lambda = 0.375\mathrm{Re}^{*-0.1}\overline{\Delta}^{0.4}$, see graph a;
(2) at $275 \leq \mathrm{Re}^* \leq 500$
$\lambda = 0.214\overline{\Delta}^{0.4}$, see graph a;

$\zeta_{sp} = \left(\dfrac{F_1}{F_0} - 1\right)^2$, see graph b;

$\Delta\zeta_t = \left(1.7 + \lambda\dfrac{l_0}{d_h}\right)\left(\dfrac{F_1}{F_0}\right)^2 \overline{T}$

$\overline{T} = \dfrac{T_{ex} - t_{in}}{T_{in}};$ $\overline{\Delta} = \dfrac{\Delta}{d_h}$

for Δ, see Table 2-3

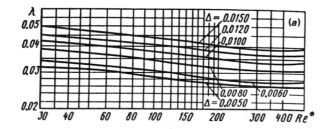

Honeycomb radiator with hexagonal or circular pipes[60]	Diagram 12-22

Values of λ

	$\bar{\Delta}$					
Re*	0.0050	0.0060	0.0080	0.0100	0.0120	0.0150
30	0.032	0.034	0.039	0.043	0.046	0.050
40	0.031	0.035	0.038	0.042	0.045	0.049
60	0.030	0.032	0.036	0.040	0.043	0.047
80	0.029	0.032	0.035	0.039	0.042	0.046
100	0.028	0.031	0.034	0.038	0.041	0.045
150	0.028	0.030	0.034	0.036	0.039	0.042
200	0.027	0.029	0.033	0.035	0.038	0.041
300	0.026	0.028	0.031	0.034	0.037	0.039
500	0.026	0.028	0.031	0.034	0.037	0.039

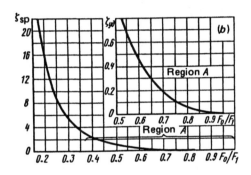

F_0/F_1	$(F_1/F_0)^2$	ζ_{sp}
0	∞	∞
0.1	100	81.0
0.2	25.0	16.0
0.3	11.1	5.43
0.4	6.25	2.25
0.5	4.00	1.00
0.6	2.78	0.45
0.7	2.04	0.18
0.8	1.56	0.06
0.9	1.23	0.01
1.0	1.00	0

Finned tubular radiator[6]	Diagram 12-23

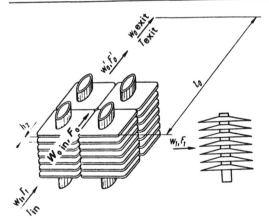

$$\zeta \equiv \frac{\Delta p}{\rho_{in} w_1^2/2} = \left(z_r \zeta_c + \lambda \frac{l_0}{d_h} \right) \left(\frac{F_1}{F_0} \right)^2 + \Delta \zeta_t$$

where $\lambda = 0.77/3\sqrt{Re}$, see graph a as a function of $Re = w_{0in} d_h/\nu$ taken within $3{,}000 \leq Re \leq 25{,}000$;

$$\zeta_c = 1.5 \left(1 - \frac{F_0}{F_0'} \right)^2, \quad \text{see graph b}$$

$$d_h = \frac{2 h_2 b_0}{h_2 + b_0}$$

Re $\times 10^{-4}$	0.2	0.3	0.4	0.5	0.6	0.8	1.0	1.2	1.6	2.0	2.5	3.0
λ		0.057	0.540	0.049	0.045	0.043	0.039	0.036	0.034	0.030	0.029	0.027	0.025

Finned tubular radiator[6]   Diagram
                                                              12-23

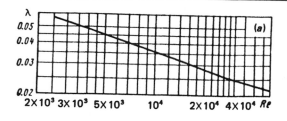

$$\Delta\zeta_t = \left(1.7 + \lambda\frac{l_0}{d_h}\right)\left(\frac{F_1}{F_0}\right)^2 \overline{T}$$

$$\overline{T} = \frac{T_{ex} - T_{in}}{T_{in}}$$

z_r is the number of rows of tubes

$\frac{F_0}{F_0'}$	0	0.1	0.2	0.3	0.4	0.5	0.6	0.7	0.8	0.9	1.0
ζ_{sys}	1.50	1.22	0.96	0.74	0.54	0.38	0.24	0.14	0.06	0.02	0

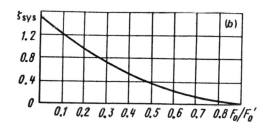

Tube and plate radiator[61]   Diagram
                                                              12-24

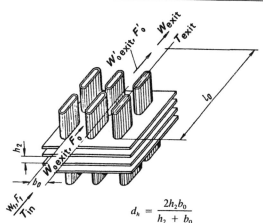

$$d_h = \frac{2h_2 b_0}{h_2 + b_0}$$

$$\zeta = \frac{\Delta p}{\rho_{in} w_1^2/2} = \left(z_r \zeta_c + \lambda\frac{l_0}{d_h}\right)\left(\frac{F_1}{F_0}\right)^2 + \Delta\zeta_t$$

where (1) within $4{,}000 < \mathrm{Re} = w_{0in}d_h/\nu \le 10{,}000$

$$\lambda = \frac{0.98}{3\sqrt{\mathrm{Re}}} = f(\mathrm{Re})$$

(2) at $\mathrm{Re} > 10{,}000$

$$\lambda = \frac{0.21}{6\sqrt{\mathrm{Re}}} = f(\mathrm{Re})$$

for ζ_c see graph b of Diagram 12-23;
$\Delta\zeta_t = [1.7 + \lambda(l_0/d_h)(F_1/F_0)^2 \overline{T}; \overline{T} = T_{ex} - T_{in}/T_{in};$
z_r is the number of rows of tubes.

Re × 10⁻⁴	0.3	0.4	0.5	0.6	0.8	1.0	1.4	2.0	2.5	3.0
λ	0.068	0.062	0.057	0.054	0.050	0.046	0.043	0.040	0.039	0.038

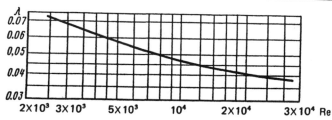

Air heaters[77]

Diagram
12-25

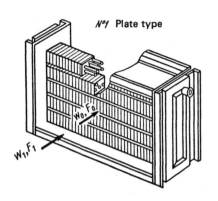

№1 Plate type

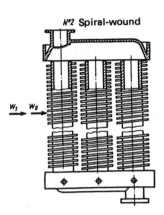

№2 Spiral-wound

Type and characteristics of air heaters	Resistance with respect to air Δp^a of one row of heaters at mass flow rates in the free area ρw_0, kg/m² s ($w_0 = Q/F_0$; F_0 is free area)												Resistance formula Δp, Pa
	3	4	5	6	7	8	9	10	11	12	13	14	
KVB–plate-type, one-channel, of moderate-size model; has three zigzag rows of tubes in the direction of air flow	–	15.6/1.6	–	31.0/3.2	–	50.4/5.1	–	73.5/7.5	–	100/10.2	–	133/13.6	$1.5 \times (\rho w_0)^{1.69}$
KFC–one-channel; KMC–multichannel, plate-type of moderate-size model; has three rows of in-line tubes in the direction of air flow	8.9/0.9	13.7/1.4	20.6/2.1	28.5/2.9	37.3/3.8	47.0/4.8	57.0/5.8	68.7/7.0	81.5/8.3	95.1/9.7	109/11.1	126/12.8	$1.2 \times (\rho w_0)^{1.76}$
KFB–one-channel; KMB–multichannel, plate-type, of large model; four in-line rows of tubes in the direction of air flow	11.8/1.2	18.7/1.9	27.5/2.8	37.3/3.8	49.0/5.0	60.8/6.2	75.5/7.7	90.5/9.2	106/10.8	125/12.7	143/14.6	160/16.3	$1.73 \times (\rho w_0)^{1.72}$
KFCO–spiral wound, one-channel, of moderate-size model; three rows of staggered tubes in the direction of air flow	30.4/3.1	53.0/5.4	83.5/8.5	116/11.8	165/16.8	215/21.9	270/27.5	336/34.2	405/41.2	486/49.5	572/58.2	656/66.8	$33.3 \times (\rho w_0)^{2.01}$

Type and characteristics of air heaters	Resistance with respect to air Δp^a of one row of heaters at mass flow rates in the free area ρw_0, kg/m² s ($w_0 = Q/F_0$; F_0 is free area)												Resistance formula Δp, Pa
	3	4	5	6	7	8	9	10	11	12	13	14	
KFBO–spiral wound, one-channel, of large model; four rows of staggered tubes in the direction of air flow	$\dfrac{36.3}{3.7}$	$\dfrac{64.7}{6.6}$	$\dfrac{99.0}{10.1}$	$\dfrac{141}{14.3}$	$\dfrac{191}{19.4}$	$\dfrac{245}{24.9}$	$\dfrac{308}{31.4}$	$\dfrac{381}{38.8}$	$\dfrac{458}{46.7}$	$\dfrac{543}{55.2}$	$\dfrac{628}{64.0}$	$\dfrac{721}{73.5}$	$4.2 \times (\rho w_0)_1^{1.94}$
STD 3009B–one-channel, STD 3010B–multichannel, plate-type, of moderate-size model; plane tubes parallel to air flow	$\dfrac{9.8}{1.0}$	$\dfrac{16.7}{1.7}$	$\dfrac{24.5}{2.5}$	$\dfrac{34.4}{3.5}$	$\dfrac{44.2}{4.5}$	$\dfrac{56.0}{5.7}$	$\dfrac{68.6}{7.0}$	$\dfrac{82.5}{8.4}$	$\dfrac{97.2}{9.9}$	$\dfrac{115}{11.7}$	$\dfrac{133}{13.5}$	$\dfrac{151}{15.4}$	$1.54 \times (\rho w_0)^{1.54}$

Air heaters[77] Diagram 12-25

a In numerator Δp is in Pa, in denominator it is in kgf/m².

The resistance (with respect to water) of all types of air heaters is determined from the curve $\Delta p_w = f(L, d)$ with the correction factor $k_1 = f(m_x)$; $\Delta p_{wm_x} = k_1 \Delta p_w$.

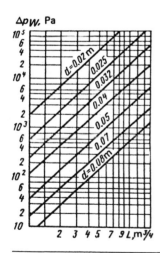

Δp_W, Pa

Number of channels in air heater m_x	1	2	3	4	5	6
k_1	1.0	1.5	2.0	2.7	3.4	4.1
Number of channels in air heater m_x	7	8	9	10	11	12
k_1	4.7	5.4	6.1	6.8	7.5	8.2

Smooth-tube air heater Diagram 12-26

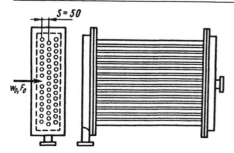

Two-row heaters $\Delta p = 0.613(\rho_{av} w_0)^{1.81}$ Pa, see curve 1; three-row heaters $\Delta p = 0.86(\rho_{av} w_0)^{1.81}$, see curve 2; four-row heaters $\Delta p = 1.11 (\rho_{av} w_0)^{1.81}$, see curve 3

$w_0 = \dfrac{Q}{F_0}$; F_0 is clear area

Smooth-tube air heater	Diagram 12-26

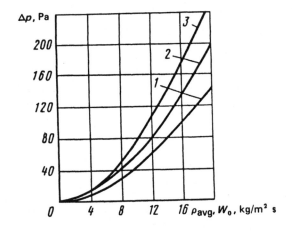

Values of Δp

	$\rho_{av}w_0$ (kg/m² s)										
Curve	1	2	4	6	8	10	12	14	16	18	20
1	0.59	2.16	7.55	15.7	26.5	39.2	58.7	76.5	96.3	115	140
2	0.79	3.04	10.8	21.6	37.3	55.8	77.5	102	129	160	197
3	1.08	3.92	13.7	28.5	48.1	71.5	100	132	168	206	255

	kg$_f$/m²										
1	0.06	0.22	0.77	1.60	2.70	4.00	6.00	7.80	9.80	11.7	14.3
2	0.08	0.31	1.10	2.20	3.80	5.70	7.90	10.4	13.2	16.3	20.1
3	0.11	0.40	1.40	2.90	4.90	7.30	10.2	13.4	17.1	21.0	26.0

Electric air heaters[77]	Diagram 12-27

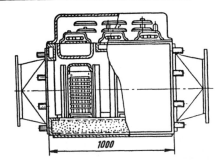

	Type of air heater					
Characteristics	SFO-25/1-T	SFO-40/1-T	SFO-60/1-T	SFO-100/1-T	SFO-160/2-T	SFO-250/1-T
Power, kW	25	40	60	100	160	250
Power of one section, kW	6.25	10	15	25	40	62.5
Clear area for air passage F, m²	0.076	0.133	0.255	0.318	0.555	0.800
Temperature drop t, °C	48	43	42	46	46	47
Throughput capacity with respect to air G, kg/s	0.592	0.94	1.43	2.50	3.33	5.20

Electric air heaters[77]						Diagram 12-27

Characteristics	Type of air heater					
	SFO-25/1-T	SFO-40/1-T	SFO-60/1-T	SFO-100/1-T	SFO-160/2-T	SFO-250/1-T
Resistance to air flow Δp^a	24.7/2.52	21.4/2.18	18.0/1.83	20.0/2.10	15.2/1.56	17.7/1.80
Mass, kg	67	100	134	197	312	421
Dimensions, m						
Length	0.48	0.48	0.48	0.48	0.48	0.48
Width	0.63	0.75	0.87	0.99	1.23	1.35
Height	0.657	0.807	0.957	1.107	1.407	1.707

a In numerator Δp is in Pa, in denominator it is in kg_f/m^2.

Bundle of smooth-wall staggered tubes (in cross-flow)[6.58] $3 \times 10^3 < Re_{av} = w_{0av}d_{in}/\nu < 10^5$	Diagram 12-28

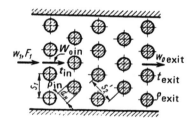

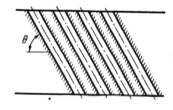

$$S_2' = \sqrt{0.25S_1^2 + S_2^2}$$

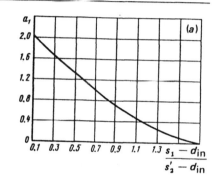

$$\zeta \equiv \frac{\Delta p}{\rho_{av}w_{0av}^2/2} = \psi A Re_{av}^{-0.27}(z_r + 1) + \Delta\zeta_t$$

$$\zeta_1 \equiv \frac{\Delta p}{\rho_1 w_1^2/2} = \zeta \left(\frac{\rho_1}{\rho_{av}}\right)^2 \left(\frac{F_1}{F_0}\right)^2$$

(1) $\dfrac{S_1}{d_{in}} < 1.44$ and $0.1 < \bar{s} < 1.7$

$$A = 3.2 + 0.66a_1 + (13.1 - 9.1\,S_1/d_{in}) \times (0.8 + 0.2a_1)$$

where $a_1 = (1.7 - \bar{s})^{1.5}$, see graph a; for $Re_{av}^{-0.27}$, see graph b; for ψ, see below

$$\bar{S} = (S_1 - d_{in})/(S_2' - d_{in})$$

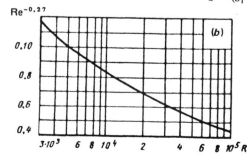

θ, deg	30	45	60	90
ψ	0.34	0.57	0.80	1.0

Bundle of smooth-wall staggered tubes (in cross-flow)[6,58] $3 \times 10^3 < \mathrm{Re}_{av} = w_{0av}d_{in}/\nu < 10^5$	Diagram 12-28

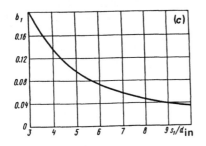

(2) $S_1/d_{in} \geq 1.44$ and $0.1 < \bar{s} < 1.7$
$\qquad A = 3.2 + 0.66a_1$
(3) $S_1/d_{in} < 1.44$ and $1.7 \leq \bar{s} < 6.5$
$\qquad A = (1.88 - S_1/d_{in})(\bar{s} + 1)^2$
(4) $1.44 \leq S_1/d_{in} \leq 3.0$ and $1.7 \leq \bar{s} \leq 6.5$
$\qquad A = 0.44(\bar{s} + 1)^2$
(5) $3 < S_1/d_{in} \leq 10$ and $\bar{s} > 1.7$
$\qquad A = 1.83b_1$, where $b_1 = (S_1/d_h)^{-1.46}$; see graph c.

$\bar{s}$	0.1	0.2	0.4	0.6	0.8	1.0	1.3	1.7
a_1	2.02	1.84	1.48	1.15	0.86	0.59	0.25	0

Re_{av}	3×10^3	4×10^3	6×10^3	8×10^3	10^4	2×10^4	4×10^4	6×10^4	8×10^4	10^5
$\mathrm{Re}_{av}^{-0.27}$	0.117	0.106	0.095	0.089	0.083	0.069	0.057	0.051	0.047	0.045

$\dfrac{S_1}{d_{in}}$	3	4	5	6	7	8	9	10
b_1	0.204	0.131	0.098	0.074	0.058	0.048	0.040	0.035

$$\Delta\zeta_t = 2\frac{T_{ex} - T_{in}}{T_{av}}; \quad T_{av} = \frac{T_{in} + T_{ex}}{2}; \quad \rho_{av} = \rho_0\frac{273}{T_{av}}; \quad w_{0av} = w_{0in}\frac{T_{av}}{T_{in}}$$

z_r is the number of transverse rows of tubes in a bundle; ν is determined as a function of T_{av}, see Section 1-2. For contaminated bundles $\zeta_{con} \approx 1.3\zeta$

Bundle of smooth-wall in-line tubes (in cross-flow)[6,58] $3 \times 10^3 < \mathrm{Re}_{av} = w_{0av}d_{in}/\nu < 10^5$	Diagram 12-29

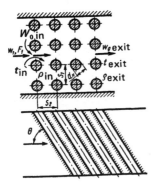

$$\zeta \equiv \frac{\Delta p}{\rho_{av}w_{0av}^2/2} = \psi A \mathrm{Re}_{av}^m z_r + \Delta\zeta_t$$

$$\zeta_1 \equiv \frac{\Delta p}{\rho_1 w_1^2/2} = \zeta\left(\frac{\rho_1}{\rho_{av}}\right)^2\left(\frac{F_1}{F_0}\right)^2$$

(1) $S_1/d_{in} \leq S_2/d_{in}$ and $0.06 \leq \bar{s}_1 \leq 1.0$

$$A = 1.8\left(\frac{S_1}{d_{in}} - 1\right)^{-0.5}; \quad m = -0.2; \quad \bar{s}_1 = (S_1 - d_{in})/(S_2 - d_{in})$$

for Re_{av}^m see graph a at $\bar{s}_1 = 1.0$

θ, deg	30	45	60	90
ψ		0.30	0.54	0.82	1.0

Bundle of smooth-wall in-line tubes (in cross-flow)[6.58] $3 \times 10^3 < \mathrm{Re_{av}} = w_{0av}d_{in}/\nu < 10^5$	Diagram 12-29

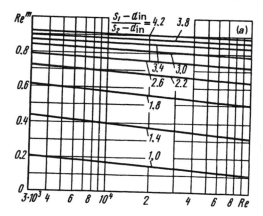

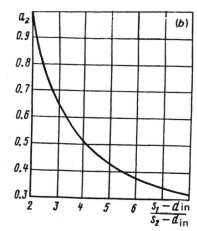

$$m = \frac{0.2}{\bar{s}_1^2}$$

for $\mathrm{Re_{av}^m}$, see graph a.

(2) $\dfrac{S_1}{d_{in}} > \dfrac{S_2}{d_{in}}$:

(a) $1.0 < \bar{s}_1 \le 8.0$;

$$A = 0.34\, a_2 \left(\frac{S_1}{d_{in}} - 1\right)^{-0.5}$$

where $a_2 = (\bar{s}_1 - 0.94)^{-0.59}$, see graph b;

Values of Re^m

$\bar{s}_1$	$\mathrm{Re} \times 10^{-3}$								
	3	4	6	8	10	20	40	60	90
1.0	0.20	0.19	0.18	0.17	0.16	0.14	0.12	0.11	0.10
1.4	0.44	0.43	0.41	0.40	0.39	0.36	0.34	0.32	0.31
1.8	0.61	0.60	0.59	0.57	0.56	0.54	0.52	0.51	0.50
2.2	0.72	0.71	0.70	0.69	0.68	0.66	0.65	0.64	0.63
2.6	0.79	0.78	0.78	0.77	0.76	0.75	0.73	0.72	0.71
3.0	0.84	0.83	0.83	0.82	0.81	0.80	0.80	0.79	0.78
3.4	0.87	0.87	0.86	0.86	0.85	0.84	0.83	0.83	0.82
3.8	0.90	0.89	0.89	0.88	0.88	0.87	0.87	0.86	0.86
4.2	0.92	0.91	0.91	0.90	0.90	0.89	0.89	0.88	0.88

$\bar{s}_1$	1.0	2	3	4	5	6	7	8
a_2	5.26	0.97	0.65	0.52	0.43	0.38	0.34	0.32

For $\Delta\zeta_t$, T_{av}, ρ_{av}, w_{0av}, z_r, ν, and ζ_{con}, see Diagram 12-28.

Transverse bundle of finned tubes[6]

Diagram
12-30

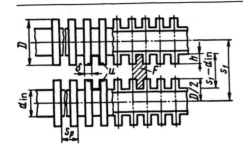

1. Staggered arrangement of tubes at $l/d_h = 0.16$–6.55
    (a) $2.2 \times 10^3 < \mathrm{Re}_l < 1.8 \times 10^5$

$$\zeta \equiv \frac{\Delta p}{\rho_{av} w_{0av}^2/2} = c_z c_s \mathrm{Re}^{-0.25} (z_r + 1) + \Delta\zeta_t$$

$$\zeta_1 \equiv \frac{\Delta p}{\rho_1 w_1^2/2} = \zeta \left(\frac{\rho_1}{\rho_{av}}\right)^2 \left(\frac{F_1}{F_0}\right)^2$$

where for c_z, see below

z_r	3	4	5	6
c_z	1.11	1.05	1.01	1.0
c_z	1.30	1.14	1.05	1.0

$c_s = 5.4(l/d_h)^{0.3}$

(b) $\mathrm{Re} > 1.8 \times 10^5$:

$$\zeta = 0.26 \left(\frac{l}{d_h}\right)^{0.3} c_z(z_r + 1) + \Delta\zeta_t$$

where for $(l/d_h)^{0.3}$, see graph a; $\mathrm{Re}_l = w_{0av} l / \nu$ [for l of tubes with circular fins, see Eq. (12-17) and for tubes with square fins, see Eqs. (12-19) and (12-20); for d_h, see Eq. (12-18)]

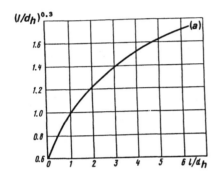

2. In-line arrangement of tubes at $l/d_h = 0.9$–11.0: $\bar{s}_1 = (S_1 - d_{in})/(s_2 - d_{in})$; $\bar{s}_1 = 0.5$–2.0 and $4.3 \times 10^3 < \mathrm{Re}_1 < 1.6 \times 10^5$: $\zeta = c_z' c_s' \mathrm{Re}_l^{-0.08} z_r + \Delta\zeta_t$, for c_z, see the table; $c_s' = 0.52(l/d_h)^{0.3} a_3$, where $a_3 = \bar{s}_1^{-0.68}$ see graph b; for $\Delta\zeta_t$, T_{av}, ρ_{av}, w_{0av}, z, ν, and ζ_{con}, see Diagram 12-28.

$\dfrac{l}{d_h}$	0.16	0.20	0.40	0.8	1.2	1.6	2.0	2.5	3.0	4.0	5.0	6.0	6.5
$\left(\dfrac{l}{d_h}\right)^{0.3}$	0.58	0.62	0.76	0.92	1.06	1.15	1.23	1.32	1.39	1.52	1.62	1.71	1.76

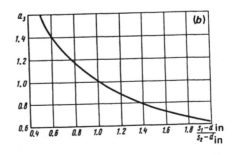

$\bar{s}_1$	0.50	0.75	1.00	1.25	1.50	1.75	2.0
a_3	1.60	1.22	1.00	0.85	0.76	0.68	0.62

Transverse tube bundles with different cross-sectional shapes[5]	Diagram 12-31

Tube arrangement and scheme	Resistance coefficient $\zeta \equiv \dfrac{\Delta p}{\rho_{av} w_{0av}^2 / 2}$

$$\zeta_1 \equiv \frac{\Delta p}{\rho_1 w_1^2 / 2} = \zeta \left(\frac{\rho_1}{\rho_{av}}\right)^2 \left(\frac{F_1}{F_0}\right)^2$$

Finned, staggered

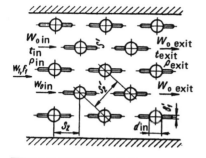

$\zeta = 1.2\zeta'$

where ζ' is determined as ζ from Diagram 12-28. If the fins enter the gaps between tubes, w_{0av} is replaced by

$$w'_{0av} = w_{0av} \frac{S_1 - d_{in}}{S_1 - d_{in} - \delta'_1}$$

Oval, in-line

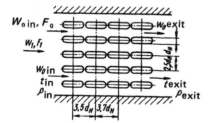

$10^4 < \text{Re} = \dfrac{w_{0av} d_{in}}{\nu} < 3 \times 10^4$

$\zeta = 0.059 z_r + 0.31 + \Delta \zeta_t$

Oval, staggered

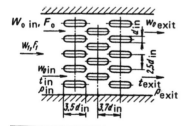

$10^4 < \text{Re} = \dfrac{w_{0av} d_{in}}{\nu} < 3 \times 10^4$

$\zeta = 0.20 z_r + 0.14 + \Delta \zeta_t$

Drop-like, staggered

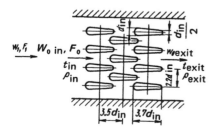

$10^4 < \text{Re} = \dfrac{w_{0av} d_{in}}{\nu} < 3 \times 10^4$

$\zeta = 0.12 z_r - 0.016 + \Delta \zeta_t$

Transverse tube bundles with different cross-sectional shapes[5]	Diagram 12-31

"Elesko"-type, staggered

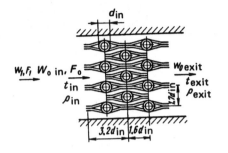

$$10^4 < \mathrm{Re} = \frac{W_{0\mathrm{av}}d_{\mathrm{in}}}{\nu} < 4 \times 10^4$$

$$\zeta = 0.46z_r + \Delta\zeta_t$$

With wire-finning

$$\frac{S_1}{d_{\mathrm{in}}} = 2.1\text{--}3.0; \quad \frac{S_2}{d_{\mathrm{in}}} = 1.5\text{--}2.5;$$

$$\frac{l_0}{h_2} = 0.1\text{--}0.3; \quad \frac{h_1}{h_2} = 0.8\text{--}2.5;$$

$$\frac{d_{\mathrm{in}}}{h_2} = 1.4\text{--}2.2$$

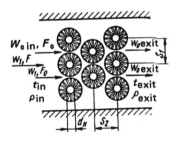

(a) $\mathrm{Re} = \dfrac{w_{0\mathrm{av}}h_2}{\nu} = 650\text{--}6000$

$$\zeta = 3.2z_r \mathrm{Re}^{-0.24}\left(\frac{l_0}{h_2}\right)^{-0.365}\left(\frac{h_1}{h_2}\right)^{0.15}\left(\frac{d_{\mathrm{in}}}{h_2}\right)^{0.1} + \Delta\zeta_t$$

(b) $\mathrm{Re} > 6000$

$$\zeta = 0.28z_r\left(\frac{l_0}{h_2}\right)^{-0.365}\left(\frac{h_1}{h_2}\right)^{0.15}\left(\frac{d_{\mathrm{in}}}{h_2}\right)^{0.1} + \Delta\zeta_t$$

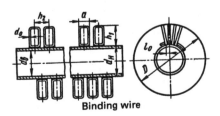

Binding wire

For $\Delta\zeta_t$, T_{av}, ρ_{av}, $w_{0\mathrm{av}}$, z, ν, and ζ_{con}, see Diagram 12-28.

Various heat exchangers	Diagram 12-32

Heat exchanger type and scheme	Resistance coefficient $\zeta \equiv \dfrac{\Delta p}{\rho_{av} w_{0av}^2/2}$

Shell-tube exchanger with longitudinal flow around tubes

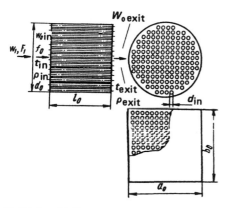

$$\zeta = \frac{\lambda_{out}}{d_h} + \Delta\zeta_t$$

where for λ, see Diagram 2-9.

Shell-tube with flow passage in tubes

$$\zeta = 0.5\left(1 - \frac{F_0}{F_1}\right) + \left(1 - \frac{F_0}{F_1}\right)^2 + \lambda\frac{l_0}{d_0} + \Delta\zeta_t$$

for λ, see Diagrams 2-1 through 2-6

Two-pass with transverse flow around the tube bundle (180° turn)

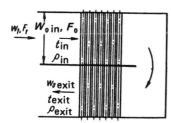

$$\zeta = \zeta_{180} + \zeta_{bun} + \zeta_t$$

where ζ_{180} is determined as ζ of a Π-shaped elbow at $l_0/b_0 = 0$ from Diagram 6-13; ζ_{bun} is determined as ζ of a corresponding tube bundle from Diagrams 12-28 through 12-31.

With mixed flow around the tube bundle (alternating sections of transverse and longitudinal flows)

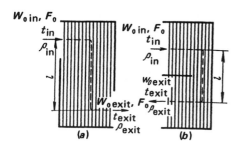

$$\zeta = \zeta_{bun} + \zeta_{fr} + \Delta\zeta_t$$

where for scheme a ζ_{bun} is determined as ζ of a corresponding bundle from Diagrams 12-28 through 12-31, taken only for half the rows of tubes in each zone of transverse flow; for scheme b ζ_{bun} is determined as ζ from the same diagrams, but for all the rows or tubes enclosed by the partition and for half the tubes protruding beyond it; $\zeta_{fr} = \lambda l/d_h$, where for λ see Diagram 2-9 (for longitudinal bundles); for $\Delta\zeta_t$, T_{av}, ρ_{av}, w_{0av}, and ν, see Diagram 12-28.

Recuperators[54,101]	Diagram 12-33

Characteristics	Resistance coefficient $\zeta \equiv \dfrac{\Delta p}{\rho_{av} w_{0av}^2/2}$

Ribbed, iron (d_h = 0.0425 m)

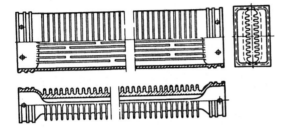

1. The air side (flow inside tubes):

$$\zeta = 1.06 + 0.040 \frac{l_0}{d_h} + \Delta\zeta_t$$

2. The gas side (external flow around tubes):
   (a) Re = $w_{0av}d_h/\nu < 10^4$

$$\zeta = (1.2 + 1.16z_r)Re^{-0.12} + \Delta\zeta_t$$

   (b) Re ≥ 10^4

$$\zeta = 0.4 + 0.334z_r + \Delta\zeta_t$$

   for contaminated tubes ζ_{con} = 1.2–1.3

Ribbed-notched

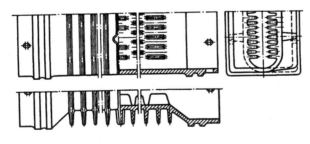

1. The air side (flow inside tubes):

   (1) Re = $w_{0av}d_h/\nu < 10^4$

$$\zeta = 1.06 + 0.77 \frac{l_0}{d_h} Re^{0.22} + \Delta\zeta_t$$

   (b) Re ≥ 10^4

$$\zeta = 1.06 + 0.10 \frac{l_0}{d_h} + \Delta\zeta_t$$

2. The gas side (external flow around tubes):
   (a) Re < 10^4

$$\zeta = (1.2 + 1.116z_r)Re^{-0.12} + \Delta\zeta_t$$

   (b) Re ≥ 10^4

$$\zeta = 0.4 + 0.334z_r + \Delta\zeta_t$$

   For contaminated tubes ζ_{con} = 1.2–1.3ζ

   For $\Delta\zeta_t$, T_{av}, ρ_{av}, w_{0av}, z_r, and ν, see Diagram 12-28.

Heating furnace with 180° flow turn[94] $Re = w_0 a_0/\nu \geqslant 8 \times 10^5$	Diagram 12-34

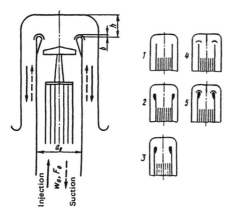

Suction

$$\zeta \equiv \frac{\Delta p}{\rho w_0^2/2}\,, \quad \text{see graph a}$$

injection

$$\zeta \equiv \frac{\Delta p}{\rho w_0^2/2}\,, \quad \text{see graph b}$$

Values of ζ with suction

Version	\multicolumn{11}{c}{h/a_0}
	0.2	0.25	0.30	0.35	0.40	0.45	0.50	0.55	0.60	0.65	0.70
1	–	12.0	9.0	7.5	0.65	6.0	5.7	5.5	5.4	5.5	5.6
2	11.5	9.5	7.6	6.3	0.55	5.2	4.9	4.8	4.8	5.0	5.3
3	11.0	8.5	7.0	6.2	0.57	5.4	5.2	5.1	5.2	5.5	5.6
4	–	5.4	4.1	3.6	0.33	3.2	3.2	3.3	3.4	3.5	4.6
5	5.8	4.2	3.5	3.2	0.31	3.1	3.1	3.2	3.4	3.5	3.7

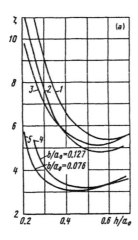

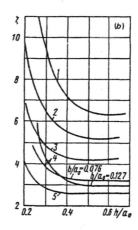

Values of ζ with injection

Version	\multicolumn{11}{c}{h/a_0}
	0.2	0.25	0.30	0.35	0.40	0.45	0.50	0.55	0.60	0.65	0.70
1	–	11.5	9.3	8.0	7.2	6.7	6.5	6.4	6.3	6.4	6.4
2	9.8	7.2	6.5	5.8	5.5	5.3	5.2	5.2	5.2	5.3	5.4
3	7.0	5.5	4.9	4.5	4.3	4.2	4.2	4.2	4.2	4.3	4.4
4	–	4.7	3.9	3.5	3.4	3.3	3.3	3.3	3.3	3.3	3.3
5	4.0	3.3	2.8	2.7	2.6	2.6	2.6	2.6	2.6	2.6	2.6

Deflectors[95,96]	Diagram 12-35

Deflector type and scheme	Resistance coefficient $\zeta \equiv \dfrac{\Delta p}{\rho w_0^2/2}$

TsAGI type,[a] circular

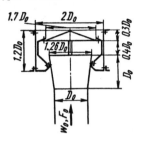

0.64

TsAGI type,[a] square, acute-angled with a cylindrical casing

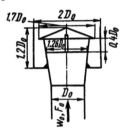

0.7
0.65

Chanard-Etoile[a] type

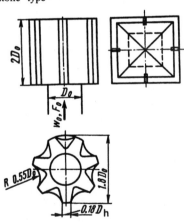

1.0

Grigorovich[a] type

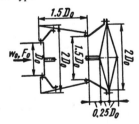

1.04

[a] Russian designations.

Deflectors[95,96]	Diagram 12-35

Deflector type and scheme	Resistance coefficient $\zeta \equiv \dfrac{\Delta p}{\rho w_0^2/2}$

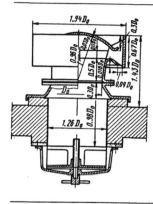

TsAGI type,[a] standardized, without reducing piece for railway cars

1.4 (without lid)
3.0 (with lid)

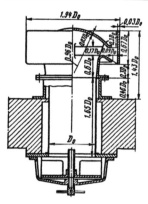

TsAGI type,[a] standardized, with reducing piece for railway cars

2.6 (with lid)

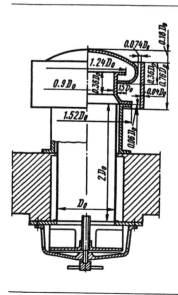

Chesnokov type[a]

10.6 (without lid)
11.6 (with lid)

[a] Russian designations.

Various types of roof ventilators[80]			Diagram 12-36
Type and scheme	α, degrees	l/h	$\zeta \equiv \Delta p/(\rho w_0^2/2)$

Baturin-Brandt,[a] with grid

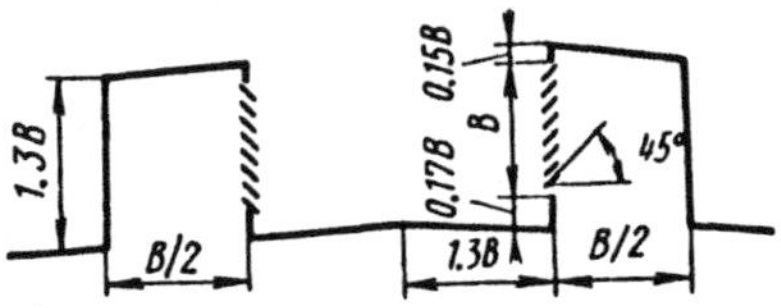

| | 45 | 1.3 | 6.5 |

The same, with flaps

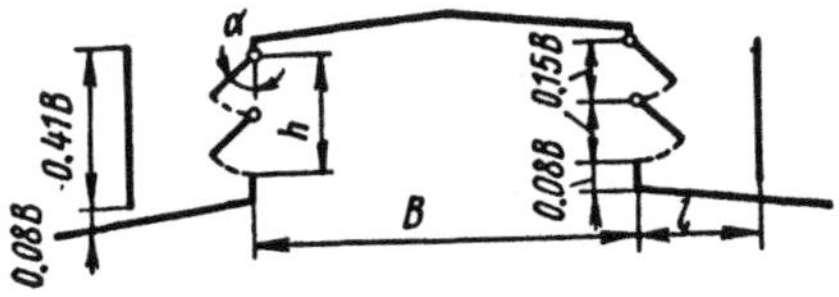

| | 80 | 1.3 | 6.8 |

LD-4[a]

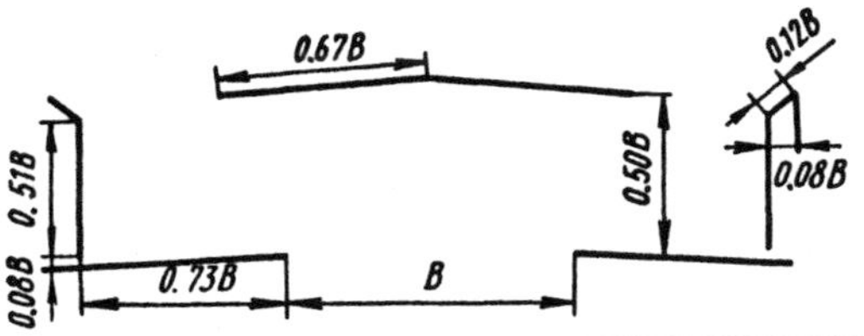

| | 0 | 1.46 | 8.3 |

LEN PSP[a] ventilator with two flaps
The same with three flaps

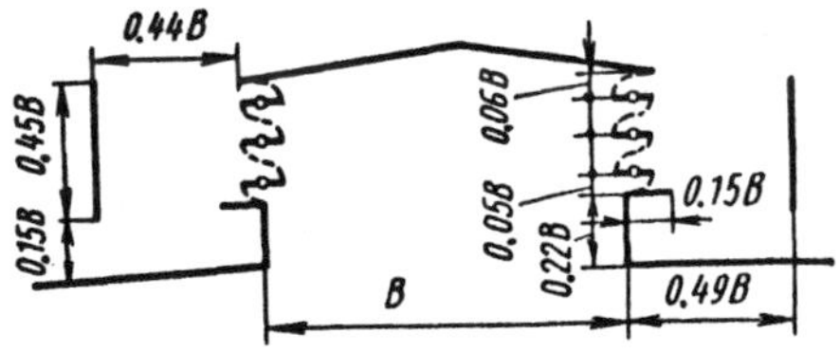

| | 80 | 1.49 | 3.9 |
| | 80 | 1.49 | 3.9 |

KTIS[a]

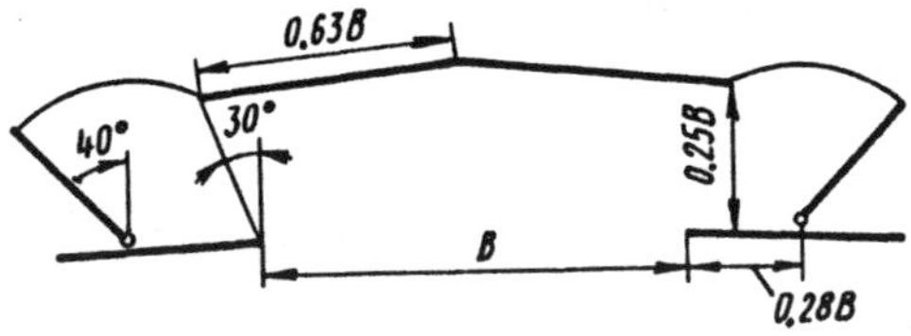

| | 40 | 1.12 | 4.3 |

MIOT-2[a]
MIOT-2a[a]

| | 0 | 0.69 | 9.0 |
| 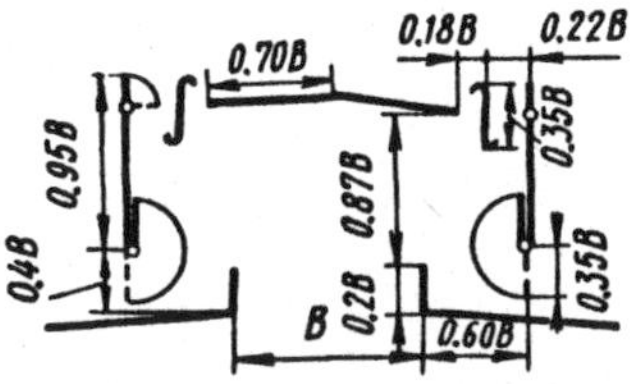 | 0 | 0.86 | 5.8 |

[a] Russian designations.

			Diagram 12-36
Type and scheme	α, degrees	l/h	$\zeta \equiv \Delta p/(\rho w_0^2/2)$

PSK-1[a]

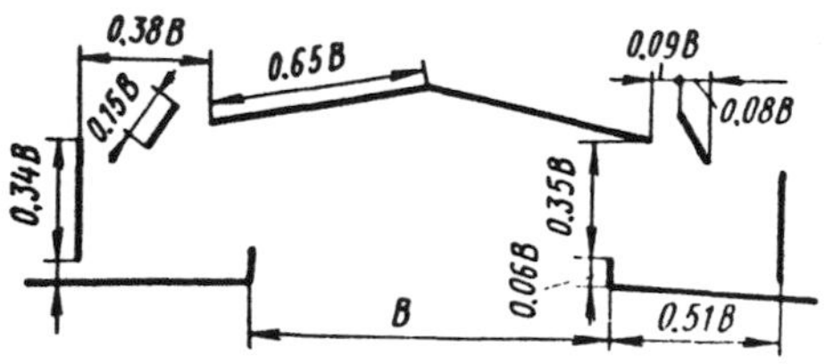

| | 0 | 1.45 | 5.3 |

PSK-2,[a] summer conditions
PSK-2,[a] winter conditions

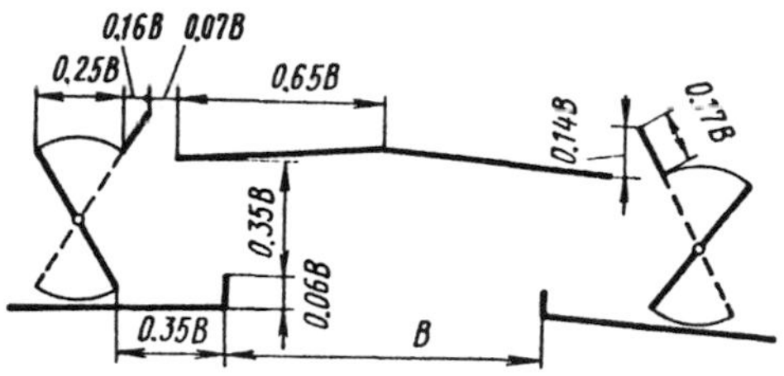

| | – | 1.0 | 5.1 |
| | | 1.0 | 8.6 |

Two-level

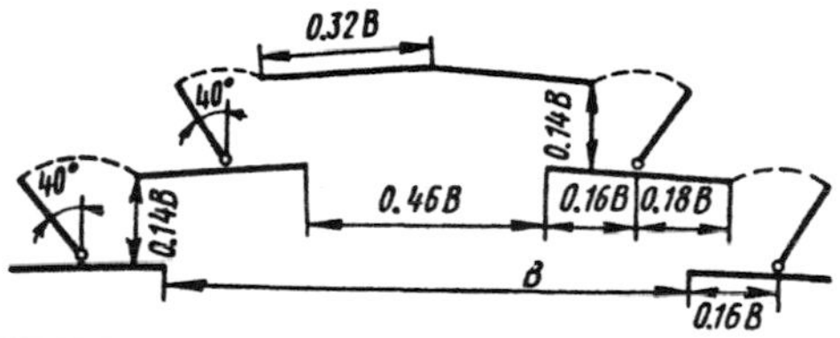

| | 40 | 1.12 | 4.2 |

Giprotis[a]

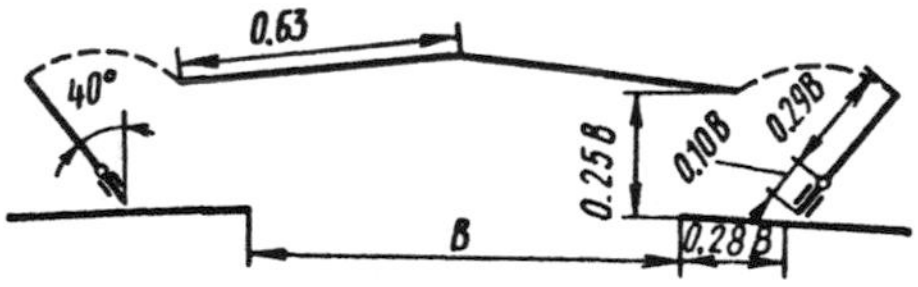

| | 40 | 1.12 | 4.6 |

Ryukin-Ilinsky[a]

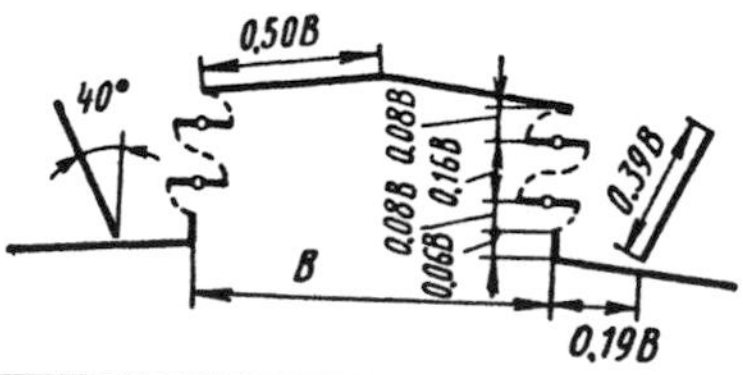

| | 40 | 0.58 | 4.3 |

Ventilating house

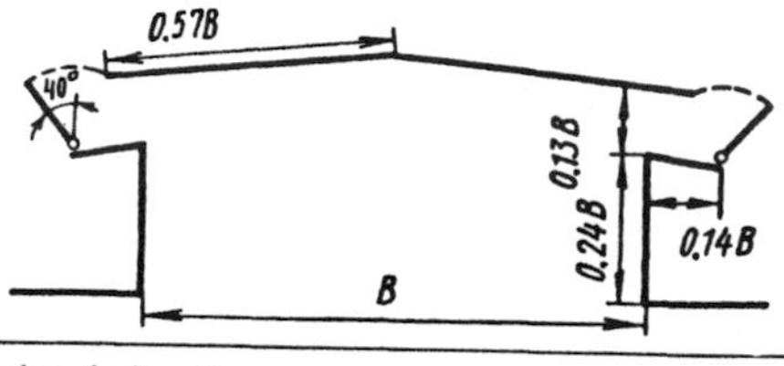

| | 40 | 1.12 | 3.3 |

[a]   Russian designations.

Rectangular roof ventilators with panels[92]	Diagram 12-37

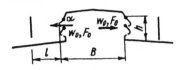

$$\zeta \equiv \frac{\Delta p}{\rho w_0^2/2} = a + \Delta\zeta$$

where $a = f(\alpha)$:

$$\Delta\zeta = \frac{3}{(l/h)_2} + \frac{0.2}{l/h} = f\left(\frac{l}{h}\right)$$

$\dfrac{l}{h}$	0.5	1.0	1.5	2.0	2.5	∞
$\Delta\zeta$	16	5.0	2.6	1.8	1.3	0.7

α, degrees	35	45	45
a	8.25	5.25	3.15

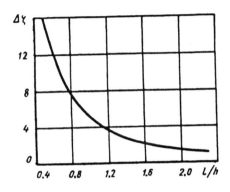

Separators, dryers[91]	Diagram 12-38

$$\zeta \equiv \frac{\Delta p}{\rho w_0^2/2}$$

where $w_0 = Q/F_0$; F_0 is the clear area

Type	Position	ζ
a	Behind the chamber	17.7
b	Behind the chamber	9.40
	Before the chamber	7.30
c	Behind the chamber	8.40
d	Before the chamber	3.40
e	Behind the chamber	13.9
	Before the chamber	8.90
f	Behind the chamber	10.7
g	Behind the chamber	8.00
	Before the chamber	5.50
h	Behind the chamber	8.80
i	The same	9.60
k	The same	16.9

Mutual effect of the "bend-bend" combination;[14,18,19,29,48,49,90] Re > 10^4 Diagram 12-39

$$\zeta_\Sigma \equiv \frac{\Delta p}{\rho w_0^2/2} = \psi \Sigma \zeta = \zeta(\zeta'_{loc} + \zeta''_{loc}),$$ where ζ_Σ is the overall resistance coefficient of the bends in the given system (assembly)

operating simultaneously; $\zeta'_{loc} \equiv \dfrac{\Delta p}{\rho w_0^2/2}$ and $\zeta''_{loc} \equiv \dfrac{\Delta p}{\rho w_0^2/2}$ are the resistance coefficients of the first and second bends, respectively,

reduced to the same velocity w_0 and determined from the corresponding diagrams of Chapter 6 for isolated bends; $\psi = \dfrac{\zeta_\Sigma}{\zeta_1 + \zeta_2}$ is the degree of the mutual effect; see the table.

Values of ψ

Relative radius of rounding R_0/D_0	Bend 1st δ_1	Bend 2nd δ_2	Angle of mutual orientation	Relative distance l/D_0 between the bends 0–1	>1 up to 2	>2 up to 6	>6 up to 10
1.0	90	90	180	0.80	0.80	0.75	0.80
	90	90	90	0.90	0.85	0.80	0.90
	90	90	0	0.60	0.65	0.70	0.80
	90	45	90	0.75	0.75	0.65	0.70
	45	90	90	0.95	0.95	0.80	0.70
	45	45	90	0.55	0.55	0.60	0.65
2.5	90	90	180	0.85	0.80	0.75	0.85
	90	90	90	0.85	0.80	0.75	0.85
	90	90	0	0.60	0.60	0.70	0.80
	60	60	180	0.85	0.85	0.85	0.90
	45	45	180	0.80	0.80	0.75	0.80
	45	45	90	0.95	0.95	0.90	0.85
	90	45	90	0.85	0.80	0.80	0.85

Mutual effect of the "bend-wye" combination (the bend with $\delta = 90°$; $R_0/D_0 = 2.3$; the wye with $\alpha = 90°$);[14,18,19,26,40,50,90] Re $> 10^4$	Diagram 12-40

$$\zeta_\Sigma \equiv \frac{\Delta p}{\rho w_0^2/2} = \psi(\zeta_{loc} + \zeta_2')$$

where $\zeta_{loc} \equiv \dfrac{\Delta p}{\rho w_0^2/2}$ is the resistance coefficient of the bend determined from the corresponding diagram of Chapter 6 for an isolated bend; $\zeta_2' \equiv \dfrac{\Delta p}{\rho w_0^2/2} = \zeta_{2c}\left(\dfrac{w_c}{w_0}\right)^2$ is the resistance coefficient of the corresponding branch of the wye (passage or side branch) reduced to the velocity w_0; ζ_{2c} is the resistance coefficient of the corresponding branch of the wye determined from the corresponding diagram of Chapter 7 for an isolated wye ($\zeta_{2c} = \zeta_{c.s}$ or $\zeta_{2c} = \zeta_{s.st}$); for ψ see the table; β is the angle of the mutual orientation of the elements.

Values of ψ

			l/D_0		
$\beta°$	Type of cross section and mutual orientation	0–2	>2 up to 4	>4 up to 10	>10 up to 20
		0.74	0.80	0.82	0.95
0	1-2s	0.87	0.88	0.90	0.95
	1-2p	0.20	0.40	0.70	0.95
90		0.92	0.93	0.97	1.0
		0.97	0.97	0.98	1.0
	1-2s	0.93	0.93	0.93	0.97
180	1-2p	0.90	0.90	0.90	1.0

For 2s; 2p; 1-2s; 1-2p, see Diagram 12-42.

Mutual effect of the "wye-bend" combination (the bend with $\delta = 90°$, $R_0/D_0 = 2.3$; the wye with $\alpha = 90°$);[14,18,19,26,48,49,90] $Re > 10^4$	Diagram 12-41

$$\zeta_\Sigma \equiv \frac{\Delta p}{\rho w_c^2/2} \psi(\zeta_{1.c} + \zeta'_{loc})$$

where $\zeta_{1.c} \equiv \dfrac{\Delta p}{\rho w_c^2/2}$ is the resistance coefficient of the passage or of the side branching of the wye reduced to the

velocity w_c and determined from the corresponding diagrams of Chapter 7 for an isolated wye; $\zeta'_{loc} \equiv \dfrac{\Delta p}{\rho w_c^2/2}$ is the

resistance coefficient of the bend reduced to the velocity $w_c \zeta'_{loc} = \zeta_{loc}\left(\dfrac{w_0}{w_c}\right)^2$ where $\zeta_{loc} \equiv \dfrac{\Delta p}{\rho w_0^2/2}$ is the resistance

coefficient of the bend determined from the corresponding diagram of Chapter 6 for an isolated bend; β is the
angle of the mutual orientation of the elements; for ψ see the table.

Values of ψ

$\beta°$	Type of combinations and mutual orientation	l/D_0			
		0–2	>2 up to 4	>4 up to 10	>10 up to 20
0		0.90 1.40	0.93 1.25	0.95 1.10	0.97 1.0
90		0.95 0.97	0.95 1.00	0.95 1.00	0.97 1.00
180		1.05 0.60	1.03 0.80	0.97 0.90	1.00 1.00

Mutual effect of the "wye-wye" combination[14,18,19,26,48,49,90] (wyes with $\alpha = 90°$) at $l_0/D_c > 6$; Re $> 10^4$	Diagram 12-42

$$\zeta_\Sigma \equiv \frac{\Delta p}{\rho w_c^2/2} = \psi(\zeta_{c.p} + \zeta'_{2.c})$$

where $\zeta_{c.p} \equiv \dfrac{\Delta p}{\rho w_c'^2}$ is the resistance coefficient of the wye passage (the length between the first and second side branches) determined from the corresponding diagram of Chapter 7 for an isolated wye; $\zeta'_{2.c} \equiv \dfrac{\Delta p}{\rho w_c'^2} = \zeta_{2.c}\left(\dfrac{w_c}{w_c'}\right)^2$ is the resistance coefficient of the second wye reduced to the velocity w_c'; $\zeta_{2.c} \equiv \dfrac{\Delta p}{\rho w_c^2/2}$ is the resistance coefficient of the corresponding branch (passage or side branch) of the wye determined from the corresponding diagrams of Chapter 7 for an isolated wye ($\zeta_{2.c} = \zeta_{c.s}$ or $\zeta_2 = \zeta_{c.p}$); β is the angle of the mutual orientation of the neighboring elements; for ψ see the table.

Values of ψ

			l/D_0			
$\beta°$	Type of combination and mutual orientation of side branches	0–2	>2 up to 4	>4 up to 6	>6 up to 10	>10 up to 20
	Outer collector					
0		1.45	1.3	1.2	1.10	0.95
90		1.15	1.0	0.97	0.95	0.95
180		0.70	0.67	0.75	0.85	0.95
	Mixed collector					
		0.80	0.87	0.95	1.0	1.0
0	1-2s	1.07	1.03	1.0	1.0	1.0
	1-2p	0.50	0.70	0.90	1.0	1.0
90		1.15	1.07	1.03	1.0	1.0
180		1.30	1.17	1.05	1.0	1.0
	1-2s	1.30	1.17	1.07	1.03	1.0
	1-2p	1.45	1.25	1.05	1.0	1.0

2s is the side branch of the second wye; 2p is the passage of the second wye; 1-2s is the length from the first element to the second wye; 1-2p is the length from the first element to the passage in the second wye.

Mutual effect of the "sectional wye-collector" and "bend-collector" combinations[14,18,19,26,48,49,90] ($\alpha = 90°$); Re $> 10^4$	Diagram 12-43

$$\zeta_\Sigma \equiv \frac{\Delta p}{\rho w_0^2/2} = \psi(\zeta_1 + \zeta_{2p} + \zeta'_{3.s}),$$

where $\zeta_1 \equiv \dfrac{\Delta p}{\rho w_0^2/2}$ is the resistance coefficient of the first element reduced to the velocity w_0 and determined from

the corresponding diagram of the corresponding chapter for an isolated element; $\zeta_{2.p} \equiv \dfrac{\Delta p}{\rho w_0^2/2}$ is the resistance

coefficient of the second section of the passage reduced to the velocity $w_0[\zeta_{2.p} = \zeta_{c.p}\left(\dfrac{w_c}{w_0}\right)^2$ where $\zeta_{c.p} \equiv \dfrac{\Delta p}{\rho w_c^2/2}$ is

the resistance coefficient of the wye passage determined from the corresponding diagram of Chapter 7 for an

isolated wye]; $\zeta'_{3.s} \equiv \dfrac{\Delta p}{\rho w_0^2/2}$ is the resistance coefficient of the second side branch of the wye (collector) reduced

to the velocity $w_0[\zeta'_{3.s} = \zeta_{c.s}(w_c/w_0)^2$ where $\zeta_{c.s} \equiv \dfrac{\Delta p}{\rho w_c^2/2}$ is the resistance coefficient determined from the corre-

sponding diagram of Chapter 7 for an isolated wye]; β is the angle of the mutual orientation of the elements; for ψ see the table.

Values of ψ

$\beta_1°$	Scheme	$\beta_2°$	l_1/D_0					
			0–2	>2 up to 4	>4 up to 6	>6 up to 8	>8 up to 10	>10 up to 12
0	l_1 l_2	0	0.50	0.70	1.0	1.15	–	–
0	l_1 l_2	0	0.50	0.70	0.95	1.20	1.40	1.55
90	l_1 l_2	0	0.72	0.80	1.0	1.25	1.45	1.60
180	l_1 l_2	0	1.05	1.15	1.25	1.40	1.60	1.70
0	l_1 l_2	180	0.60	0.85	0.93	0.95	1.00	1.07
90	l_1 l_2	180	0.90	0.95	0.95	1.05	1.10	1.15
180	l_1 l_2	180	1.05	0.95	1.00	1.03	1.10	1.20
0	l_1 l_2	90	0.65	0.87	1.07	1.20	1.35	1.45
90	l_1 l_2	90	0.75	0.80	0.90	1.05	1.20	1.30
90	l_1 l_2	90	0.80	0.85	1.00	1.12	1.25	1.35
180	l_1 l_2	90	1.0	0.98	1.11	1.25	1.40	1.5

Variation of the distance l_2/D_0 between the side branches of the outlet collector within (1-10) D_c does not virtually influence the coefficient ψ.

Mutual effect of the "shaped part-fittings" combination;[14,18,19,26,48,49,90] Re > 10^4	Diagram 12-44

$$\zeta_\Sigma \equiv \frac{\Delta p}{\rho w_0^2/2} = \psi(\zeta'_{loc} + \zeta''_{loc})$$

where $\zeta'_{loc} \equiv \frac{p}{\rho w_0^2/2}$ is the resistance coefficient of the shaped part (wye, bend) determined from corresponding

diagrams of corresponding chapters for isolated shaped parts; $\zeta''_{loc} \equiv \frac{\Delta p}{\rho w_0^2/2}$ is the same for fittings determined from

the corresponding diagrams of Chapter 9 for isolated fittings and reduced to the velocity w_0; ψ is the degree of the mutual effect, see the tables.

1. The combination "bend-fittings" for all possible orientations

Values of ψ

Combination	Relative distance between bends and fittings l/D_0		
	0–2	>2 up to 6	>6 up to 10
Bend-pass valve	0.90	0.93	0.96
Bend-angle valve	1.06	1.04	1.02
Bend-clinket gate	1.20	1.10	1.05

2. Combination "fittings-bend" for all possible orientations

Values of ψ

Combination	Relative distance between fittings and bend l/D_0			
	0–1	>1 up to 2	>2 up to 6	>6 up to 10
Pass valve-bend	0.97	0.97	0.98	0.98
Angle valve-bend	0.95	0.96	0.97	0.98
Clinket valve-bend	1.10	1.08	1.05	1.02

3. Combination "wye-fittings"
Values of ψ

Type of combination	Relative distance between the intersection of the wye axes and fittings l/D_0		
	0–2	>2 up to 6	>6 up to 10
	0.94	0.96	0.98

4. Combination "valve-wye"
Values of ψ

Mutual orientation of elements	Relative distance between fittings and intersection of the wye axes l/D_0		
	0–2	>2 up to 6	>6 up to 7
	0.98	0.99	1.0

REFERENCES

1. Abramovich, G. N., *Theory of Turbulent Jets*, Fizmatgiz, Moscow, 1960, 715 p.
2. Aleksandrov, A. Ye., Kostikov, D. Ye., and Lozovetskiy, V. V., Generalization of the relation for calculating the hydraulic characteristics of grid packing bundles, in *Current Problems of Hydrodynamics and Heat Transfer in the Elements of Power Plants and Refrigeration Engineering*, pp. 61–66, Moscow, 1982.
3. Altshul, A. D., *Local Hydraulic Resistances in Motion of Viscous Fluids*, Moscow, 1962, 250 p.
4. Antufiev, V. M. and Kazachenko, L. S., *Heat Transfer and Resistance of Convective Heating Surfaces*, Gosenergoizdat, Moscow, 1938, 290 p.
5. Antufiev, V. M. and Beletsky, G. S., *Heat Transfer and Aerodynamic Resistance of Tubular Surfaces in a Transverse Flow*, Mashgiz, Moscow, 1948, 310 p.
6. Mochan, S. I., Ed., *Aerodynamic Calculation of Boiler Equipment*, Energiya Press, Moscow, 1977, 255 p.
7. Lokshin, V. A., Fomina, V. N., Ushakov, Ye. A., and Agress, B. A., Aerodynamic resistance of tube bundles spaced nonuniformly in a cross-flow, *Teploenergetika*, no. 12, 30–33, 1976.
8. Ushakov, V. A., Fomina, V. N., Titova, Ye. Ya., and Samarin, V. A., Aerodynamic resistance of tube bundles of new profiles in a cross-flow, *Teploenergetika*, no. 4, 53–56, 1980.
9. Barakhtenko, G. M. and Idelchik, I. E., Effect of the swirler shape on the hydraulic resistance of a direct-current cyclone, *Prom. Sanit. Ochistka Gazov.* no. 6, 4–7, Moscow, 1974.
10. Basmanov, P. I. and Poplavskaya, V. A., *Analytical Aerosol Filters* (catalogue), Atomizdat, Moscow, 1968, 25 p.
11. *Battery Cyclones*, Goskhimizdat, Moscow, 1956, 104 p.
12. Bruk, A. D., *Smoke Exhausters of Gas-Purifying Works*, Moscow, 1984, p. 145.
13. Valdberg, A. Yu., Dubinskaya, F. E., and Isyanov, L. M., *Cleaning of Industrial Gases in Venturi Scrubbers*, TsNIITEnefteprom, Moscow, 1972, 45 p.
14. Goldenberg, I. Z., Aslaniyan, O. I., Dymov, A. S., and Rokhi, B. D., The problems of the design of catching vessels. Part 2. *Vessel Systems (Tr. Kaliningr. Tekh. Inst. Rybn. Prom. Phoz.)*, vyp. 55, 1974, p. 20.
15. Popov, Yu. A., Yankovskiy, S. S., Mazus, M. G. et al., *Dry and Wet Gas Cleaners* (catalogue), Ts-INTIChimneftemash, Moscow, 1984, p. 92.
16. Gervasiev, A. M., *SIOT Dust Trappers*, Profizdat, Sverdlovsk, 1954, 95 p.
17. Lokshin, V. A., Peterson, F. F., and Shvartz, A. A., Eds., *Hydraulic Calculation of Boiler Units (Standard Method)*, Moscow, 1978, p. 255.
18. Goldenberg, I. Z., Investigation of the Mutual Effect of Flow Turnings in Forced Flow Channels of Vessel Systems, thesis (Cand. Sc., Engng), Kaliningrad, 1967, p. 146.
19. Goldenberg, I. Z., Allowance for the mutual effects of tube branches when selecting "short", forced-flow channels, *Sudostroyeniye*, no. 4, 24–26, 1964.
20. Grabovskiy, A. M., Investigation of the mutual effect of local resistances, *Nauchn. Zap. Odess. Politekh. Inst.*, no. 3, 75–86, 1955.
21. Dzhapelidze, M. M. and Liseykin, I. D., Investigation of heat transfer and aerodynamic resistance of membrane staggered bundles in a cross-flow, *Teploenergetika*, no. 9, 63–67, 1982.
22. Dubinskaya, F. E., Calculation of the hydraulic resistance coefficient of sprayer tubes, *Prom. Sanit. Ochistka Gazov*, no. 3/4, 57, 1971.
23. Dubinskaya, F. E., Low-pressure head venturi pipes, *Obespylev. Ustroista Prom. Ventilyats.*, MDNTI im Dzerzhinsk, pp. 78–81, 1970.
24. Zhukauskas, A. A., *Convective Heat Transfer in Heat Exchangers*, Moscow, 1982, p. 472.
25. Zaloguin, N. G. and Shukher, S. M., *Cleaning of Flue Gases*, Gosenergoizdat, Moscow, 1954, 220 p.
26. Zyuban, V. A., Allowance for the Characteristics of the Elements of Pipeline Branching When Arranging the Vessel Cooling Systems, thesis (Cand. Sc., Engng), Moscow, 19.
27. Idelchik, I. E., *Aerodynamics of Technological Apparatus*, Moscow, 1983, p. 360.
28. Idelchik, I. E., *Aerodynamics of Industrial Apparatus*, Energiya Press, Moscow, 1964, 287 p.
29. Idelchik, I. E., Hydraulic resistance of cyclones (determination, magnitude and means of reduction), *Mekh. Ochistka Prom. Gazov*, 135–159, NIIOGAZ, Mashinostroenic Press, 1974.
30. Idelchik, I. E., Towards the problem of hydraulic resistance of cyclones, *J. Eng. Phys.*, Vol. 16, no. 5, 899–901, 1969.
31. Idelchik, I. E., Towards calculation and design of grouped cyclones, *Tr. NIIPIOTSTROM*, vyp. 1, 44–66, Novorossiisk, 1969.
32. Idelchik, I. E., On the procedure of experimental determination of the hydraulic resistance of cyclones, *Vodosnabzh. Sanit. Tekh.*, no. 8, 21–25, 1969.
33. Idelchik, I. E. and Malguin, A. D., Hydraulic resistance of the NIIOGAZ cyclones, *Prom. Energ.*, no. 8, 45–48, 1969.
34. Idelchi, I. E. and Aleksandrov, V. P., Choice of components arrangement of electrostatic filters in powerful energy units and their modelling, *Teploenergetika*, no.1, 28–30, 1971.

35. Idelchik, I. E. and Aleksandrov, V. P., On arrangement of electrostatic filters and their aerodynamic modelling, *Sb. Dokl. Mezhobl. Seminara Ochistke Gazov*, 31–45, Yaroslavl', 1972.

36. Idelchik, I. E., Aleksandrov, V. P., and Kogan, E. I., Investigation of direct-flow cyclones of the system of ash-trapping in electric power stations, *Teploenergetika*, no. 8, 45–48, 1968.

37. Idelchik, I. E. and Kogan, E. I., Towards investigation of direct-flow cyclones, *Probl. Ventilyats. Konditsionir, Vozdukha*, 318–326, Vysshaya Shkola Press, Minsk, 1969.

38. Idelchik, I. E. and Shteinberg, M. E., Some results of investigation of the TsN-15 cyclones operating in the system, *Khim. Prom.*, no. 2, 154–155, 1970.

39. Aslaniyan, O. I., Goldenberg, I. Z., Zyuban, V. A., and Pechyonkin, N. I., Investigation of axial velocity fields in intake wyes, *Izv. VUZov, Energ.*, no. 11, 110–116, 1987.

40. Liseykin, I. D., Koneliovich, A. M., Kravets, M. Z., and Didura, V. A., Investigation of heat transfer and aerodynamic resistance in membrane staggered transversely finned bundles, *Teploenergetika*, no. 2, 38–41, 1984.

41. Ishakov, N. N., Hydraulic resistance of tubular bundles in the region of low Reynolds numbers, *Tr. Leningr. Korablestroit. Inst.*, no. 45, 130–139, 1964.

42. Kazakevich, F. P., Effect of the angle of attack of a gas flow on aerodynamic resistance of tube bundles, *Izv. VTI*, no. 8, 55–60, 1952.

43. Kazakevich, F. P., Effect of roughness on the aerodynamic resistance of tube bundles in a transverse gas flow, *Teploenergetika*, no. 1, 23–27, 1961.

44. Kalmykov, A. V., *Aerodynamics, Heat and Mass Transfer in Dispersed Flows*, Nauka Press, Moscow, 1967, 185 p.

45. Karpukhovich, D. T., High-Efficient Cyclone STsN-40, *Information About Scientific-Technical Achievements*, Yaroslavl, 1985, 6 p.

46. Kirpichyov, E. F., *Cleaning of Flue Gases of Ash at Electric Power Stations*, BTI, TsKTI, Moscow, 1962, 270 p.

47. Klyachko, L. S., Method of theoretical determination of the throughput capacity of apparatus with a rotating axisymmetric liquid flow, *Teor. Prakt. Obespyliv. Ventilyats*, 195, Profizdat, LIOT, Leningrad, 1952.

48. Kovalyov-Krivonisov, P. A., Increase of the Service Life of Intake Water Cooling Pipelines by Improving Their Construction Under Repair, thesis (Cand. Sc., Engng), Sevastopol, 1982, p. 142.

49. Kovalyov-Krivonosov, P. A. and Goldenberg, I. Z., Experimental investigation of hydraulic losses on the interaction of fittings and bends in vessel pipelines, in *Hydraulics, Hydraulic Transport of Fish and Its Technical Means*, vyp. 69, pp. 48–53, Kaliningrad, 1977.

50. Korotayev, O. I., Puchkov, P. I., and Fedorovich, Ye. D., Hydraulic resistance of the pipe-coupling spacing elements for fuel rod bundles, *Teploenergetika*, no. 12, 36–40, 1979.

51. Kouzov, P. A., *The LIOT Cyclones with Water Film*, Prefizdat, Leningrad, 1953, 95 p.

52. Kouzov, P. A., Comparative estimation of different types of cyclones, *Obespyliv. Metal.*, 185–196, Metallurgiya Press, Moscow, 1971.

53. Kuznetsov, N. V. and Shcherbakov, A. Z., Experimental determination of heat transfer and aerodynamic resistances of an iron finned air preheater, *Izv. VTI*, no. 2, 51–55, 1951.

54. Kuznetsov, N. V., Shcherbakov, A. Z., and Titova, E. Ya., New formulas to calculate aerodynamic resistance of tube bundles in a transverse flow, *Teploenergetika*, no. 9, 27–32, 1954.

55. Liseykin, I. D., Heat transfer and aerodynamic resistance of the membrane convective heating surfaces, *Teploenergetika*, no. 12, 66–69, 1984.

56. Lokshin, V. A. and Liseykin, I. D., Investigation and calculation of the aerodynamics of membrane convective heating surfaces, *Teploenergetika*, no. 9, 35–37, 1971.

57. Lokshin, V. A., Liseykin, I. D., and Aronov, D. I., Investigation and calculation of heat transfer and aerodynamic resistance of inline tube bundles, *Teploenergetika*, no.1, 75–77, 1975.

58. Lokshin, V. A., Mochan, S. I., and Fomina, V. N., Generalization of information on the aerodynamic resistance of staggered tube bundles in a cross-flow, *Teploenergetika*, no. 10, 41–48, 1971.

59. Lugovsky, S. I. and Andrianov, I. S., *Cleaning of Gases from Cupola and Steel Electric Melting Furnaces*, Mashinostroenic Press, 1972, 175 p.

60. Mariyamov, N. B., Calculation of tubular-plate and tubular-finned radiators, *Tr. LII*, no. 18, 215, 1946.

61. Mariyamov, N. B., Experimental investigation and calculation of aircraft radiators, *Tr. TsAGI*, no. 367, 230, 1938.

62. Minsky, E. M. and Korchazhkin, M. P., Towards calculation of the throughput capacity of cyclonic separators, *Gazov. Prom.*, no. 11, 21–25, 1956.

63. Mikheleyev, M. A. and Mikheyeva, I. M., *Fundamentals of Heat Transfer*, 2nd ed., Moscow, 1977, p. 344.

64. Murashkevich, F. I., Efficiency of dust trapping by a turbulent washer, *J. Eng. Phys.*, vol 11, no. 11, 825–829, 1959.

65. Mochan, I. S., Fomina, V. N., Mikushkina, P. I., and Titova, Ye. Ya., Generalization of information on the aerodynamic resistance of smooth-tube bundles in a cross-flow, *Teploenergetika*, no. 11, 14–20, 1985.

66. Uzhov, V. N., Valdberg, A. Yu., Myagkov, B. I., and Reshidov, I. K., *Cleaning of Industrial Gases of Dust*, Moscow, 1981, p. 390.

67. Pavlov, G. G., *the Aerodynamics of Technological Processes and Equipment of Textile Industry*, Moscow, 1975, p. 152.

68. Petryanov, I. V., Kozlov, V. I., Basmanov, P. I., and Ogorodnikov, B. I., *Fibrous Filtering Materials*, Znanie Press, Moscow, 1968, 78 p.

69. Pirumov, A. I., *Aerodynamic Foundations of Inertia Separation*, Gosstroiisdat, Moscow, 1961, 170 p.

70. Pirumov, A. I., *Dust Removal from Air*, 2nd ed., Moscow, 1981, p. 296.

71. Pirumov, A. I., *Recommendations as to Designing Air Cleaning Apparatus in the Systems of Intake Ventilation and Air Conditioning*, Izd. TsNII Promzdanii Gosstroya SSSR, Moscow, 1972.

72. Rabinovich, B. V., *Introduction to Foundry Hydraulics*, Mashinostroenie Press, 1966, 320 p.

73. Rychagov, V. V. and Sholtz, M. Ye., Mutual Effect of Local Resistances in Forced-Flow Lines of Pumping Stations: Express-Information (TsBNTI Minvodkhoz, SSSR), ser. 6, vyp. 2, 1970, p. 20.

74. Skobeltsyn, Yu. A. and Khomutov, P. V., Mutual effect of differently shaped inner passages of sealing devices at low Reynolds numbers, *Transp. Khranenie Nefti Nefteprod.*, no. 7, 22–23, 1972.

75. Kotelevskiy, Yu. M., Ed., *Modern Constructions of Pipeline Fittings: Handbook*, Moscow, 1970, p. 250.

76. Birger, M. I., Valdberg, A. Yu., Myagkov, B. I., Padva, V. Yu., Rusanov, A. A., and Urbakh, I. I., *Handbook of Dust and Ash Trapping*, 2nd ed., Moscow, 1983, p. 312.

77. Staroverov, I. G., Ed., *Handbook of a Designer Ventilation and Air Conditioning*, Part 2, Moscow, 1978, p. 510.

78. Stasyulyavichyus, Yu. L. and Samoshko, P. S., Heat transfer and aerodynamics of staggered tube bundles in an air cross-flow, *J. Eng. Phys.*, vol. 8, no. 11, 10–15, 1964.

79. Tager, S. A., Calculation of the aerodynamic resistance of cyclone combustion chambers, *Teploenergetika*, No. 7, 18–23, 1971.

80. Taliev, V. N., *Aerodynamic Characteristics of New Constructions of Ventilators*, Gosstroiizdat, Moscow, 1955, 60 p.

81. Tarat, E. Ya. and Valdberg, A. Yu., On the hydraulic resistance of throughput trays in a foam regime, *Zh. Prikl. Khim.*, vol. 13, no. 8, 315–320, 1970.

82. Tebenkov, B. P., *Recuperators for Industrial Furnaces*, Metallurgiya Press, 1967, 358 p.

83. Teverovsky, E. N., Experience in service and in industrial testing of various ash-catchers and recommendations as to their selection, *Tr. Konf. Vopr. Zoloulavliv., Shlakoulavl, Shlakozoloispol'zov.*, 135–150, Gosenergoizdat, Moscow, 1955.

84. Teverovsky, E. N. and Zaitsev, M. M., Dust-trapping, absorptional and heat-exchanging apparatus "TP" with a high-velocity gas flow, *Tr. NIIOGAZ*, no. 1, 105–133, Goskhimisdat, Moscow, 1957.

85. Gurvits, A. A., Lyamin, Yu. A., Levin, L. S., et al., Retarding effect of the corona discharge in gas flow in an electrostatic filter, *Industrial and Sanitary Cleaning of Gases: Express-Information*, Ser. KhM-14, Moscow, 1985, p. 5.

86. Tulin, S. N., Heat transfer and resistance in bundles of wire-finned tubes, *Teploenergetika*, no. 3, 70–75, 1958.

87. Uzhov, V. N., *Cleaning of Industrial Gases by Electrostatic Filters*, Khimiya Press, Moscow, 1967, 344 p.

88. Uzhov, V. N. and Valdberg, A. Yu., *Cleaning of Industrial Gases by Wet Filters*, Khimiya Press, Moscow, 1972, 247 p.

89. Uzhov, V. N. and Myagkov, B. L., *Cleaning of Industrial Gases by Electrostatic Filters*, Khimiya Press, Moscow, 1970, 319 p.

90. Umbrasas, M.-R. A., Evaluation of the Failure-Free Operation of Vessel Bend-Involving Pipelines when Designing Sea-Water Systems, thesis (Cand. Sc., Engng), Sevastopol, 1984.

91. Uchastkin, P. V., Investigation of the efficiency and hydraulic resistance of eliminators, *Otoplenie Vent.*, no. 6, 33–39, 1940.

92. Frukht, I. A., Hydraulic resistance of ventilators equipped with wind-resisting panels, *Stroit. Prom.*, no. 1, 41–45, 1958.

93. Frukht, I. A., Effect of geometrical relationships on operation of wind-resisting intake ventilators, *Izv. VUZov Stroit. Arkhitek*, no. 31–37, 1959.

94. Khanzhonkov, V. I., Aerodynamic resistance of plane channels with the reverse symmetrical turn, *Prom. Aerodin.*, vyp. 21, 151–156, Oberongiz, 1962.

95. Khanzhonkov, V. I., Aerodynamic characteristics of a standardized TsAGI deflector for train cars, *Prom. Aerodin.*, no. 10 Oberongiz, 1958.

96. Khanzhonkov, V. I., *Ventilating Deflectors*, Stroiizdat, Moscow, 1947, 105 p.

97. *NIIOGAZ Cyclones*, Verlkhnevelzhak Press, Yaroslavl', 1971, 94 p.

98. Sholts, M. Ye., Concerning the mutual effect of local resistances, in *Problems of Hydraulics*, pp. 131–135, Moscow, 1969.

99. Shtromberg, Ya. A. and Kannunikov, V. F., Constructions of dust trappers of the Laboratory of Industrial Ventilation and Aerodynamics VNIIOT VTsSPS (Tbilisi), *Obespylivaniev Metallurgii*, 156–162, Metallurg Press, 1971.

100. Shcherbakov, A. E. and Zhirnov, N. I., Heat transfer and aerodynamic resistance of an iron-finned-notched air heater, *Teploenergetika*, no. 8, 25–30, 1954.

101. Popov, Yu. A., Yankovskiy, S. S., Mazus, M. G., et al., *Electrostatic Filters: Catalogue*, Ts-INTIChimneftemash, Moscow, 1986, p. 30.

102. Elperin, I. I., Turning of gases in a tube bundle, *Izv. Akad. Nauk USSR*, no. e, 70–78, 1950.

103. Yudin, Ye. Ya. and Yelin, I. S., The choice of the optimal parameters of axial fans, *Trudy TsAGI*, no. 591, 1–20, Moscow, 1946.

104. Brauer, H., Untersuchungen über den Strömungswiderstand und den Wärmeubergang bei flüchtend angeordneten Rippenrohren, *Tech. Mitt.*, vol. 55, no. 5, 214–226, 1962.

105. Robinson, K. K. and Briggs, D. E., Pressure drop of air flowing across triangular pitch banks of finned tubes, *Chem. Eng. Prog. Symp.*, vol. 62, no. 64, 177–184, 1966.

106. Zumann, R., Druckverlust bei quer angeströmten Glattrohrbündeln, *Chem. Ztg. Chem. Appar.*, vo. 86, no. 8, 275–281, 1962.

Page numbers in italics denote figures, numbers followed by the letter t denote tables; and numbers followed by *n* denote footnotes.